DATE DUE

			PRINTED IN U.S.A.

Literature Criticism from 1400 to 1800

Guide to Gale Literary Criticism Series

For criticism on	Consult these Gale series
Authors now living or who died after December 31, 1959	*CONTEMPORARY LITERARY CRITICISM (CLC)*
Authors who died between 1900 and 1959	*TWENTIETH-CENTURY LITERARY CRITICISM (TCLC)*
Authors who died between 1800 and 1899	*NINETEENTH-CENTURY LITERATURE CRITICISM (NCLC)*
Authors who died between 1400 and 1799	*LITERATURE CRITICISM FROM 1400 TO 1800 (LC)* *SHAKESPEAREAN CRITICISM (SC)*
Authors who died before 1400	*CLASSICAL AND MEDIEVAL LITERATURE CRITICISM (CMLC)*
Black writers of the past two hundred years	*BLACK LITERATURE CRITICISM (BLC)*
Authors of books for children and young adults	*CHILDREN'S LITERATURE REVIEW (CLR)*
Dramatists	*DRAMA CRITICISM (DC)*
Hispanic writers of the late nineteenth and twentieth centuries	*HISPANIC LITERATURE CRITICISM (HLC)*
Native North American writers and orators of the eighteenth, nineteenth, and twentieth centuries	*NATIVE NORTH AMERICAN LITERATURE (NNAL)*
Poets	*POETRY CRITICISM (PC)*
Short story writers	*SHORT STORY CRITICISM (SSC)*
Major authors from the Renaissance to the present	*WORLD LITERATURE CRITICISM, 1500 TO THE PRESENT (WLC)*

Volume 34

Literature Criticism from 1400 to 1800

Critical Discussion of the Works
of Fifteenth-, Sixteenth-, Seventeenth-, and
Eighteenth-Century Novelists, Poets, Playwrights,
Philosophers, and Other Creative Writers

Jennifer Allison Brostrom, Editor

GALE

DETROIT • NEW YORK • TORONTO • LONDON

∞™ This book is printed on acid-free paper that meets the minimum requirements of American National Standard for Information Sciences—Permanence Paper for Printed Library Materials, ANSI Z39.48-1984.

Library of Congress Catalog Card Number 94-29718
ISBN 0-8103-9976-8
ISSN 0740-2880
Printed in the United States of America

10 9 8 7 6 5 4 3 2 1

Contents

Preface   vii

Acknowledgments   xi

Preface

*L*iterature Criticism from 1400 to 1800 (LC) presents critical discussion of world authors of the fifteenth through eighteenth centuries. The literature of this period reflects a turbulent time of radical change that saw the rise of modern European drama, the birth of the novel and personal essay forms, the emergence of newspapers and periodicals, and major achievements in poetry and philosophy. Many of these historical forces continue to influence modern art and society. *LC,* therefore, provides valuable insight into the art, life, thought, and cultural transformations that took place during these centuries.

Scope of the Series

LC provides an introduction to the great poets, dramatists, novelists, essayists, and philosophers of the fifteenth through eighteenth centuries, and to the most significant interpretations of these authors' works. Because criticism of this literature spans nearly six hundred years, an overwhelming amount of scholarship confronts the student. *LC* organizes this material into volumes addressing specific historical and cultural topics, for example, "Literature of the Spanish Golden Age," or "Literature and the New World." Every attempt is made to reprint the most noteworthy, relevant, and educationally valuable essays available.

Readers should note that there is a separate Gale reference series devoted exclusively to Shakespearean studies. Although belonging properly to the period covered in *LC,* William Shakespeare has inspired such a tremendous and ever-growing corpus of secondary material that the editors have deemed it best to give his works extensive coverage in a separate series, *Shakespearean Criticism.*

Each author entry in *LC* presents a survey of critical response to a topic or an author's oeuvre. Early criticism is offered to indicate initial responses, later selections document any rise or decline in literary reputations, and retrospective analyses provide students with modern views. The size of each author entry is a relative reflection of the scope of criticism available in English. Every attempt has been made to identify and include the seminal essays on each author's work and to include recent commentary providing modern perspectives.

The need for *LC* among students and teachers of literature and history was suggested by the proven usefulness of Gale's *Contemporary Literary Criticism (CLC), Twentieth-Century Literary Criticism (TCLC),* and *Nineteenth-Century Literature Criticism (NCLC),* which excerpt criticism of works by nineteenth- and twentieth-century authors. There is no duplication of critical material in any of these literary criticism series. Major authors may appear more than once in one or more of the series because of the great quantity of critical material available and because of their relevance to a variety of thematic topics.

Thematic Approach

Beginning with Volume 12, the authors in each volume of *LC* are organized around such themes as specific literary or philosophical movements, writings surrounding important political and historical events, the philosophy and art associated with eras of cultural transformation, and the literature of specific social or ethnic groups. Each volume contains a topic entry providing a historical and literary overview, and several author entries which examine major representatives of the featured period.

Organization of the Book

Each entry consists of the following elements: author or thematic heading, introduction, list of principal works, annotated works of criticism (each preceded by a bibliographical citation), and a bibliography of further reading. Also, most author entries contain author portraits and other illustrations.

- The **Author Heading** consists of the author's name (the most commonly used form), followed by birth and death dates. (If an author wrote consistently under a pseudonym, the pseudonym is used in the author heading, with the real name given in parentheses on the first line of the biographical and critical introduction.) Also located here are any name variations under which an author wrote, including transliterated forms for authors whose native languages use nonroman alphabets. Uncertain birth or death dates are indicated by question marks. Topic entries are preceded by a **Thematic Heading,** which simply states the subject of the entry.

- The **Biographical and Critical Introduction** contains background information that concisely introduces the reader to the author or topic.

- Most *LC* author entries include **Portraits** of the author. Many entries also contain illustrations of materials pertinent to an author's career, including author holographs, title pages, letters, or representations of important people, places, and events in an author's life.

- The **List of Principal Works** is ordered chronologically, by date of first book publication, identifying the genre of each work. In the case of foreign authors whose works have been translated into English, the title and date (if available) of the first English-language edition are given in brackets following the foreign-language listing. Unless otherwise indicated, dramas are dated by first performance, not first publication.

- **Criticism** is arranged chronologically in each author entry to provide a useful perspective on changes in critical evaluation over time. For the purpose of easy identification, the critic's name and the date of first composition or publication of the critical work are given at the beginning of each piece of criticism. Unsigned criticism is preceded by the title of the source in which it appeared. All titles by the author featured in the critical entry are printed in boldface type. Publication information (such as publisher names and book prices) and some parenthetical numerical references (such as footnotes or page and line references to specific editions of works) have been occasionally deleted to provide smoother reading of the text.

- Critical essays are prefaced by **Annotations** as an additional aid to students using *LC*. These explanatory notes provide information on the importance of a work of criticism, the commentator's individual approach to literary criticism, and a brief summary of the reprinted essay. In some cases, these notes cross-reference the work of critics within the entry who agree or disagree with each other.

- A complete **Bibliographical Citation** of the original essay or book precedes each piece of criticism.

- An annotated bibliography of **Further Reading** appears at the end of each entry and suggests resources for additional study. In some cases, significant essays for which the editors could not obtain reprint rights are included here.

Cumulative Indexes

Each volume of *LC* includes a cumulative **Author Index** listing all the authors that have appeared in the following sources published by Gale: *Contemporary Literary Criticism, Twentieth-Century Literary Criticism, Nineteenth-Century Literature Criticism, Literature Criticism from 1400 to 1800,* and *Classical and Medieval Literature Criticism,* along with cross-references to the Gale series *Short Story Criticism, Poetry Criticism, Children's Literature Review, Authors in the News, Contemporary Authors, Contemporary Authors Autobiography Series, Contemporary Authors Bibliographical Series, Dictionary of Literary Biography, Concise Dictionary of Literary Biography, Something about the Author, Something about the Author Autobiography Series,* and *Yesterday's Authors of Books for Children.* Readers will welcome this cumulative author index as a useful tool for locating an author within the various series. The index, which includes authors' birth and death dates, is particularly valuable for those authors who are identified with a certain period but whose death dates cause them to be placed in another, or for those authors whose careers span two periods. For example, F. Scott Fitzgerald is found in *TCLC,* yet a writer often associated with him, Ernest Hemingway, is found in *CLC.*

Beginning with Volume 12, *LC* includes a cumulative **Topic Index** that lists all literary themes and topics treated in *LC, NCLC, TCLC,* and the *CLC* Yearbook. Each volume of *LC* also includes a cumulative **Nationality Index** in which authors' names are arranged alphabetically under their respective nationalities and followed by the numbers of the volumes in which they appear.

Each volume of *LC* also includes a cumulative **Title Index,** an alphabetical listing of all literary works discussed in the series. Each title listing includes the corresponding volume and page numbers where criticism may be located. Foreign-language titles that have been translated followed by the tiles of the translation—for example, *El ingenioso hidalgo Don Quixote de la Mancha (Don Quixote).* Page numbers following these translated titles refer to all pages on which any form of the titles, either foreign-language or translated, appear. Titles of novels, dramas, nonfiction books, and poetry, short story, or essays collections are printed in italics, while individual poems, short stories, and essays are printed in roman type within quotation marks.

A Note to the Reader

When writing papers, students who quote directly from any volume in the Literary Criticism Series may use the following general format to footnote reprinted criticism. The first example pertains to material drawn from periodicals, the second to material reprinted from books.

T. S. Eliot, "John Donne," *The Nation and the Athenaeum,* 33 (9 June 1923), 321-32; excerpted and reprinted in *Literature Criticism from 1400 to 1800,* Vol. 10, ed. James E. Person, Jr. (Detroit: Gale Research, 1989), pp. 28-9.

Clara G. Stillman, *Samuel Butler: A Mid-Victorian Modern* (Viking Press, 1932); excerpted and reprinted in *Twentieth-Century Literary Criticism,* Vol. 33, ed. Paula Kepos (Detroit: Gale Research, 1989), pp. 43-5.

Suggestions Are Welcome

Since the series began, features have been added to *LC* in response to various suggestions, including a nationality index, a Literary Criticism Series topic index, and thematic organization of entries.

Readers who wish to suggest new features, themes or authors to appear in future volumes, or who have other suggestions or comments are cordially invited to write to the editor (fax: 313 961-6599).

Acknowledgments

The editors wish to thank the copyright holders of the excerpted criticism included in this volume and the permissions managers of many book and magazine publishing companies for assisting us in securing reprint rights. We are also grateful to the staffs of the Detroit Public Library, the Library of Congress, the University of Detroit Mercy Library, Wayne State University Purdy/Kresge Library Complex, and the University of Michigan Libraries for making their resources available to us. Following is a list of the copyright holders who have granted us permission to reprint material in this volume of **LC**. Every effort has been made to trace copyright, but if omissions have been made, please let us know.

COPYRIGHTED EXCERPTS IN *LC,* VOLUME 34, WERE REPRINTED FROM THE FOLLOWING PERIODICALS:

The American Benedictine Review, v. 20, December, 1969. Copyright 1969 by The American Benedictine Academy. Reprinted by permission of the publisher.—*Annuale Mediaevale*, v. 22, 1982. Reprinted by permission of the author.—*The Chaucer Review*, v. 10, Summer, 1975. Copyright © 1975 by The Pennsylvania State University, University Park, PA. Reprinted by permission of the publisher.—*Comparative Drama*, v. 11, Spring, 1977; v. 12, Fall, 1978; v. 27, Winter, 1993-94. © copyright by the Editors of *Comparative Drama*. All reprinted by permission of the publisher.—*English Studies*, Netherlands, v. 73, August, 1992. © 1992 by Swets & Zeitlinger B.V. Reprinted by permission of the publisher.—*Journal of English and Germanic Philology*, v. 86, April, 1987 for "Equality and Hierarchy in the Chester Cycle Play of Man's Fall" by Norma Kroll. © 1987 by the Board of Trustees of the University of Illinois. Reprinted by permission of the publisher and the author. —*Journal of the History of Ideas*, v. 39, July-September, 1978. Reprinted by permission of the editors of the *Journal of the History of Ideas.*—*Neuphilologische Mittelilugen*, v. lxxxv, 1984. *Research Opportunities in Drama*, v. X, 1967. Copyright © 1967 by Northwestern University Press. Reprinted by permission of the publisher.—*Speculum,* v. CVI, January, 1981. Copyright 1981 by The Medieval Academy of America. Reprinted by permission of the publisher.—*Theatre Notebook*, v. XXI, Spring and Summer, 1967. Reprinted by permission of the publisher.

COPYRIGHTED EXCERPTS IN *LC,* VOLUME 34, WERE REPRINTED FROM THE FOLLOWING BOOKS:

Beadle, Richard. From "The York Cycle," in *The Cambridge Companion to Medieval English Theatre*. Edited by Richard Beadle. Cambridge University Press 1994. © Cambridge University Press 1994. Reprinted by permission of the publisher.—Beadle, Richard. From *York Mystery Plays: A Selection in Modern Spelling*. Edited by Richard Beadle and Pamela M. King. Oxford at the Clarendon Press, 1984. © Richard Beadle and Pamela M. King 1984. All rights reserved. Reprinted by permission of Oxford University Press.—Cawley, A. C. From an introduction to *The Wakefield Pageants in the Towneley Cycle*. Edited by A. C. Cawley. Manchester University Press, 1958. © 1958. Reprinted by permission of the author.—Chambers, E. K. From *English Literature at the Close of the Middle Ages*. Oxford at the Clarendon Press, 1945. Reprinted by permission of Oxford University Press.—Clarke, Sidney W. From *The Miracle Play in England: An Account of the Early Religious Drama*. Haskell House, 1964. Renewed © 1992. Reprinted by permission of the publisher.—Collier, Richard J. From *Poetry and Drama in the York Corpus Christi Play*. Archon Books, 1978. © Richard J. Collier 1977. All rights reserved. Reprinted by permission of Archon Books, an imprint of The Shoe String Press, Inc.—Craig, Hardin. From *English Religious Drama of the Middle Ages*. Oxford at the Clarendon Press, 1955. Reprinted by permission of Oxford University Press.—Davidson, Clifford. From *From Creation to Doom: The York Cycle of Mystery Plays*. AMS Press, 1994. Copyright © 1984 by AMS Press, Inc. Reprinted by permission of the publisher.—Ferster, Judith. From "Writing on the Ground: Interpretation in Chester Play XII," in *Sign, Sentence, Discourse: Language in Medieval Thought and Literature*. Edited by Julian N. Wasserman and Lois Roney. Syracuse University Press, 1989. Copyright © 1989 by Syracuse University Press,

PHOTOGRAPHS AND ILLUSTRATIONS APPEARING IN *LC*, VOLUME 34, WERE RECEIVED FROM THE FOLLOWING SOURCES:

English Mystery Cycle Dramas

INTRODUCTION

The English mystery cycles, also known as Corpus Christi plays or miracle cycles, dominated the English stage throughout the fourteenth and fifteenth centuries and are regarded by many critics as the most genuinely popular theater in English history. Reflecting the central role of the Church in medieval society, the plays dramatize the biblical stories and apocryphal legends that form the foundation of Christian faith, from the Creation story through the Last Judgement. Critics have observed that performances of the dramatic sequences may have served a combination of social purposes in medieval society, helping to promote local guilds while also educating the public in the Christian tradition. Community participation was a fundamental characteristic of the performances: the plays were written by local clergy, supported and staged by local crafts guilds, and acted by townspeople. Their accessibility to unlettered citizens was also a key feature of the plays, which were written in the vernacular rather than Latin.

Four cycles of plays survive—the York Plays, Chester Plays, Towneley Plays (also known as the Wakefield Cycle), and N-Town Plays (also known as the Ludus Coventriae, or Hegge Cycle). Each of these four cycles dramatizes important scenes from the Old and New Testaments of the Bible and incorporates elements of apocryphal religious legends in order to illustrate the expansive Christian theme of man's fall and redemption. Most scholars maintain that the English mystery cycles were often performed in conjunction with the feast of Corpus Christi, although there is disagreement concerning the specific nature of the relationship between this religious holiday and the plays. Some believe that the cycle dramas evolved as an extension of dumb-show pageants associated with the feast day, while others believe that the plays evolved prior to the establishment of Corpus Christi, as a result of the combining of elements of vernacular folk drama with liturgical dramas connected with the Catholic mass. As with many medieval texts, our knowledge of the original performance methods and authorship of the plays is often speculative due to the many alterations that may have been incurred during the copying of the manuscripts by scribes.

Although the plays were popular and successful dur

ing the fourteenth and fifteenth centuries, performances declined during the early sixteenth century as a result of suppression associated with the Protestant Reformation. Scholars prior to the twentieth century have generally regarded the plays as anthropologically interesting, but aesthetically inferior works. The nineteenth-century critics William Hone and Thomas Sharp, for example, contributed extensive historical research toward an understanding of the English mystery cycles, but said little about the nature of the plays themselves as works of literature. Considered among the first important critics of medieval drama, E. K. Chambers in 1903 examined the plays from an evolutionary perspective, viewing them as forerunners of what he believed to be the more highly developed plays of Shakespeare. During the twentieth century, critics such as G. R. Owst, H.C. Gardiner, A. P. Rossiter, Glynne Wickham, O.B. Hardison Jr., V.A. Kolve, and Rosemary Woolf have helped to elevate the reputation of the English mystery cycles by emphasizing, for example, the skillful and complex quality of performances, and the interplay between social recreation and worship in the dramas. Since the 1970s, the English mystery cycles have experienced a resurgence of popularity in performance, as well as critical acclaim for their value as literary works in their own right.

OVERVIEWS
E. K. Chambers (essay date 1945)

SOURCE: "Medieval Drama," in *English Literature at the Close of the Middle Ages*, 1945. Reprint by Oxford at the Clarendon Press, 1947, pp. 1-65.

[In the following excerpt, Chambers summarizes the background of the miracle plays, discussing performance season and location; the literary, ecclesiastical, and cultural sources used; the use of humor in the plays; the history of written records of the dramas; and their literary merit.]

Miracle plays are traceable during the fourteenth and fifteenth centuries in some forty English localities, predominantly perhaps in the northern and eastern parts of the country. Others can be added from sixteenth-century documents. They were known also in Scotland, and at Dublin in Ireland, which was much under the influence of English customs. The fact that most of the surviving texts represent performances of a particular type has perhaps rather obscured the variety of organization which the records disclose. It is probable that, when the plays were detached from the liturgy, the financial responsibility was often taken over from the established clergy by some of those religious and social gilds which contributed so largely to the development of medieval public life. In London this arrangement seems to have prevailed to the end. Here a gild of St. Nicholas, composed of parish clerks, gave performances, possibly with the assistance of boys from the cathedral school of St. Paul's, in the open at Skinners Well, near Clerkenwell in the suburbs. The plays are first noticed in 1300, when the Abbess of Clerkenwell complained to the king of the damage done to her fields and crops by the crowds who attended the 'miracles', as well as the wrestling bouts which the citizens were accustomed to hold in the same locality. The plays, however, continued. Stow says that they were given annually. The chroniclers record elaborate performances in various years from 1384 to 1508, lasting from four to seven days, and covering the whole span from the Creation to the day of Judgement. In 1508, however, they seem to have been given near St. Paul's. They took place in summer, twice at least on a day dedicated to St. John Baptist. London, however, had also, as in the days of William Fitzstephen, saints' plays. There was one on St. Catherine in 1393, and others at St. Margaret's Church, Southwark, on the feasts of St. Margaret and St. Lucy, in the fifteenth century. Outside London, SS. George, Thomas of Canterbury, Laurence, Dionysius, Susanna, Clara, and no doubt many others, were similarly commemorated. Some of these plays seem still to have been given in churches, and others are recorded in churchwardens' accounts well into the sixteenth century. Presumably, however, they were now detached from the liturgy, and the sacred edifice merely served to shelter them. At Hedon, in Yorkshire, in 1391, we find the town chamberlain making a payment to Master William Reef and his companions for playing on Epiphany morning in the Chapel of St. Augustine. Probably these companions were a gild. There are occasional notices also of plays in a gild hall, or by schoolboys at the manor-house of some person of local importance. But in the main miracle plays were an out-of-doors affair. Many of the small religious and social gilds disappeared during the Black Death, and by the fifteenth century the control of the plays, in the larger towns outside London, seems generally to have passed to the local governing body, itself often in some aspects by origin a gild of the merchant gild type. At Norwich, however, the gild of St. Luke remained responsible for the plays at least to 1527. Many of the performances seem to have been occasional only, given in the market-place or in some convenient 'croft' or 'stead'. At Aberdeen they were on Windmill Hill; at Lincoln in the cathedral close. More interesting, from the literary point of view, is the emergence of a type of play which was not

stationary but ambulatory, taking the form of a procession up and down the streets, with pauses here and there for the repetition of scene after scene at traditional spots. So used, the plays seem to have become, like the simpler processions of the Rogation days, popularly called Gang Week, a sanctification of the old perambulations of the pagan cults which took place at critical seasons of the agricultural year, in winter when the ploughing began, and again in the heats of summer when the crops were growing. At Hull, on Plough Day, a play of Noah was given on a stage in the form of a ship, which was also carried about the town in a ceremony which clearly represents a maritime version of the agricultural rite. Normally, however, the processional miracle plays took place in summer. At Chester and Norwich, where an early practice seems to have been preserved, they were at Whitsuntide. It is not clear whether Whitsun plays at Leicester and New Romney were processional or stationary. But elsewhere a new date was provided by the papal confirmation in 1311 of the feast of Corpus Christi, tentatively contemplated in 1264. This fell in May or June and was essentially a processional observance, in which the Host itself was carried around and displayed with ceremony at appointed stations. And to it in various ways the miracle plays often became attached. Many gilds of Corpus Christi were founded. One at Bury St. Edmunds, which claimed in 1389 to have existed from time beyond memory, was bound by its constitution to honour the occasion with an interlude. Corpus Christi plays now become traceable all over the country, but perhaps predominantly in the north and east, during a period of more than two centuries. They are found also in Scotland. At Aberdeen they were Haliblude plays. The Reformation hit them hard, but a last survival is recorded at Kendal, about 1612. Some of the performances were stationary and perhaps occasional only. But in many large towns, including most of those from which the surviving texts come, the processional type prevailed. It was so at York, Wakefield, Beverley, Doncaster, Newcastle, Ipswich, Coventry, and Worcester. The organization seems to have been much the same in all these places so far as the records enable us to judge. It was adopted also at Chester during the period which our information covers, although here the Whitsun date was retained. A general control was exercised by the council of the town. Subject to its approval, which would naturally be withheld in times of pestilence or public disturbance, the plays were given annually. The actual performance of them was still in the hands of gilds. These, however, were not of the old type, but were trade or craft gilds which, while still often retaining a religious and social side, were primarily organizations for the promotion and regulation of local industries. A cyclical theme, which usually extended from the Creation to the Last Judgement, was divided into a series of scenes, for the production of each of which a particular gild took responsibility. The performance was given on large wagons, which fol-

The Last Judgment

lowed each other in regular sequence to station after station about the town, at which scene after scene was repeated. These wagons were known as pageants. The origin of this term, which was also often used as an alternative to 'play' for the scenes themselves, is not quite clear. It may be derived from a Latin *pagina,* either in the sense of the page of a book or in that of a framework. There was some super-structure representing a *domus* or *sedes* for the actors, with a hell and the like, but it must have been rather sketchy, to allow of a view from all sides, and we know little about it, beyond a late Chester description which says that the performers had 'a highe place made like a howse with ij rowmes, beinge open on ye tope: in the lower rowme they apparelled & dressed them selues; and in the higher rowme they played; and they stoode vpon 6 wheeles'. The cost of maintaining and housing the pageants and of paying the actors fell upon the crafts, each member of which was bound to make an annual contribution for the purpose. This involved a good deal of work for the governors, as industries rose or fell and claimed to have or be relieved from a share in the performances. Such changes are often recorded in town documents or have left their marks on the structure of the surviving texts. These are mainly of late date and preserved in registers kept by the corporations, themselves compiled from 'originals' in the hands of the crafts. The plays flourished. *Vexillatores,* or banner-bearers, rode about in advance, reading banns which announced the subject-matter of the scenes. Spectators thronged in from neighbouring villages. Corpus Christi day became a great public holiday, which brought much profit to a town, although perhaps more to its hostelers and victuallers than to the productive trades on which the main financial burden fell. As a result, the religious procession tended to become overshadowed. This was sometimes met by shifting the plays, or even the procession itself, to a neighbouring day. But elsewhere, for example at Dublin, we find no more than a symbolical riding with the Host of personages taken from biblical or legendary narratives, perhaps formerly the themes of plays given in full. At Lincoln, on St. Anne's day, at Beverley on that of the Purification, and at Aberdeen on Candlemas, there were similar ridings which seem to have ended with plays, possibly still liturgical, in the churches. The enduring human instinct for *mimesis* is capable of many manifestations. It must be added that in course of time the term 'Corpus Christi play' seems to have been applied to any representation of the Passion and Resurrection, at whatever date it was given. It was so at Chester, where the civic plays seem to have been always at Whitsun, although in the middle of the sixteenth century the colleges and priests had an independent one of their own on Corpus Christi day. At Lincoln in the fifteenth century there were occasional plays, apparently distinct from the procession on St. Anne's day, among which a *ludus de Corpore Christi* took its turn with others. When the governors of a town, in the fourteenth century, wanted to establish a dramatic

cycle, they would naturally turn for a text to some local ecclesiastic, able to compose in English metre and free from theological prejudices against miracle plays. He might be a gild priest, or more probably, in a large place, a brother from some monastery, such as St. Werburgh's at Chester. The tradition of the liturgical drama would be behind him. And for its expansion he would have a considerable library at his disposal. He could gloss the narrative of the Bible itself with much legendary material that had grown up around it throughout the ages. Perhaps he would not have read the earlier works from which this took its start, such as the *Vita Adae et Evae,* the *Evangelium Nicodemi,* which comprised the *Acta Pilati* and the *Descensus Christi ad Inferos,* the *Evangelium Matthaei,* with its *De Nativitate Mariae,* the *Transitus Mariae.* But he would certainly be familiar with some of the great medieval compilations, such as the *Allegoriae in Vetus Testamentum* of Hugo de St. Victor, the *Historia Scholastica* of Peter Comestor, the *Legenda Aurea* of Jacobus de Voragine, the *Estoire de la Bible* of Hermann de Valenciennes. He might know the *Meditationes* on the life of Christ ascribed to St. Bernard of Clairvaux and St. Bonaventura of Padua, as well as the pseudo-Augustinian *Sermo de Symbolo* and the *De Antichristo* of Adso of Toul. There were vernacular poems, too, on which some of these sources had already had their influence, the Middle English *Harrowing of Hell,* the *Genesis and Exodus,* the *Cursor Mundi,* the *Northern Passion,* based on the *Passion des Jongleurs,* a similar *Southern Passion,* the *Life of Saint Anne,* the so-called *Stanzaic Life of Christ,* an English *Gospel of St. Nicodemus,* versions of the Holy Rood legend, and many lyrical poems, some of them of the *planctus* type. There was abundance of material, instructive and entertaining, to draw upon. Some of it, however, might not be available until well into the fourteenth century. The probability that some cycles of late origin may have borrowed or adapted plays from others already in existence must also be kept in mind. No doubt the earliest writers aimed primarily at edification. But the folk, on a holiday, had also to be entertained. They could be moved by the tragedy of the divine sacrifice, and perhaps exalted by the scheme of creation and redemption. But they found their relief in episodes which involved an element of humour, in the unwillingness of Noah's wife to enter the Ark, in the homely banter of the shepherds before the angel came, in the ranting of the potentates, Octavian, Herod, Pilate, in the 'bobbing' of the Redeemer by the torturers, in the dice-play of the soldiers over his garments, in the downfall of the tax-gatherers and other unpopular elements of society at the Last Day. Sometimes a play became so farcical in action, if not in language, that it had to be pruned or abandoned. At York the midwives were cut out of the Nativity, and the antics of Fergus at the bier of the Virgin provoked such unholy mirth that the responsible craft became unwilling to repeat them. It must be added that the texts of such plays as survive have come down to us in a very corrupt state. The earliest are of the middle of the fifteenth century; others are as late as the end of the sixteenth. Some have been completely rewritten. The older ones have often been patched in metres incongruous with those in which they were originally written. Much corruption has also been introduced by the characteristic unreliability in transcription of medieval scribes, often increased by blundering attempts to reproduce old linguistic forms which had become unintelligible. Many single lines and even longer passages have evidently been omitted, to the detriment both of sense and once more of metre. Whoso would read the plays to-day must often go darkling.

Of the many craft-plays, whose existence we can infer from records, edacious time has left us comparatively few examples. We have cycles, practically complete, from Chester, York, and Wakefield, two very long plays from Coventry, one from Newcastle, one from Norwich, and one other, the origin of which is unknown. The loss of the Beverley plays, which existed in 1377 and were already an ancient custom in 1390, and about which we have many details, is particularly regrettable, since they might link with the churchyard representation of a Resurrection about 1220.

Probably the earliest surviving cycle, at least by origin, is that from Chester. On this we have abundant material, but unfortunately it is nearly all of very late date, and has in part come to us through the hands of writers who blended an antiquarian interest in the history of their town with a Puritan dislike of the ecclesiastical tradition to which the plays belong. Performances, probably becoming no longer annual, had continued during the sixteenth century. The latest upon record were in 1572 and 1575, and both of these brought the mayors under whom they were given into trouble with the diocesan authorities and the Privy Council. An alleged revival in 1600 is likely to rest upon a misunderstanding. We have five texts of the cycle, dated from 1591 to 1607. According to Dr. W. W. Greg, who has carefully studied their interrelation, they are all ultimately derived, through one or more intermediate transcripts, from an official register, perhaps of the later half of the fifteenth century. One, however, in the Harleian collection, although the latest in date, seems to rest upon an earlier version of the register than the others. They include all the plays of which we have any record, except an Assumption, which existed in 1500 and 1540, but may never have been registered. We have also a separate text of the Antichrist, apparently from a prompter's copy, written about 1500, and late ones of the Trial and Flagellation from an original, and of a fragment of the Resurrection. We have two sets of banns, which record the crafts and the subjects of their plays. One is from an official document of 1540, but the dislocation of its metre by the incorporation of changes shows that it must have been by origin of much earlier date. The other probably represents a performance which may be as late as 1572. But in its

fullest form it has been much glossed with side-notes of Protestant comment, which may be due to one Robert Rogers, an archdeacon and prebend of Chester, who died in 1595. A final passage has been thought to suggest that an indoor representation was at one time contemplated. But this must remain very doubtful. Finally there are several copies of a late list of plays, showing them as twenty-five in all, but not including the Assumption, and indicating their distribution over the three days of performance. It is certain that during the course of over two centuries, through which the plays lasted, they had grown in number. There were only twenty or twenty-one about 1475, and twenty-four about 1500. Professor F. M. Salter has attempted to trace an earlier development by exploring craft records for indications of changes of responsibility, which can be correlated with the metrical irregularities of the early banns. As a result he infers that those banns were originally composed about 1467, and that the cycle then consisted of only eighteen plays. A discussion of his argument in detail would be inappropriate here, but some such development is likely enough.

One change, of which there is a fairly full record, may be cited, both for the light which it throws upon the handling of contentious citizens and because it involves something of a puzzle. In 1422 a dispute arose between the Ironmongers and the Carpenters or Wrights, both of whom claimed to have the assistance of a group of small crafts, headed by the Coopers, in the production of their plays. It came before the portmoot, who referred it for arbitration to a jury. As a result it was decided that neither contention should be accepted, but that the Coopers and their fellows should have an independent play of the Flagellation of Christ, while the Ironmongers should take the Crucifixion, which immediately followed it, and the Wrights should similarly have their own play, which, at any rate later, was the Nativity. It seems to have been long before this arrangement was recorded in the register, and then the method adopted was a very rough one. In the Harleian MS the Trial and Flagellation and the Crucifixion still form one play of the Passion, which is ascribed to the Ironmongers. In the other cyclical manuscripts they are also written as one play, but inserted stage-directions and additional lines show that in fact they were meant to be played as two. They are two also in all the late lists. The puzzle arises from the fact that the late banns once more treat them as one. This has led to a theory, espoused by Dr. Greg, that the change of 1422 was not a division but an amalgamation. It seems to me inconsistent with the terms of the arbitration, and also with the existence of a separate copy of the Trial and Flagellation alone, preserved by the Coopers Gild and dated in 1599. I take it that the writer of the late banns was misled by the Harleian MS or some other transcript of the unrevised register.

The twenty-five plays of the Chester cycle, as we have

them, cover the whole range of the divine scheme for humanity. Pre-Christian history is represented by a Fall of Lucifer, a Creation and Fall, a Noah, a Cain and Abel, an Abraham and Melchisedek, an Abraham and Isaac, a *Prophetae,* with Moses, Balaam and Balak, and Balaam's Ass. A Nativity group includes an Annunciation, a Visit to Elizabeth, Joseph's Trouble, further prophecies of Sibylla to Octavian, a Nativity with midwives, a *Pastores,* a *Magi* and Herod, with yet more prophecies, an Oblation of the *Magi,* a Slaughter of the Innocents, a Death of Herod, a Purification. To the missionary life of Christ belong a Disputation with the Doctors, apparently a late addition and borrowed from York, a Temptation, an Adulteress, a Healing of the Blind, a Raising of Lazarus. The Entry into Jerusalem, the Cleansing of the Temple, the Visit to Simon the Leper, and the Conspiracy of the Jews with Judas are dealt with, rather briefly, in a single play. The Last Supper and Betrayal at Gethsemane occupy another. Then come the Passion proper, a Harrowing of Hell, the Resurrection with the *Quem Quaeritis,* a *Peregrini,* the Ascension, the Pentecost. The legends of the end of the Virgin are untouched. But eschatology contributes the Prophets of the Day of Doom, an Antichrist, and the Day of Doom or *Judicium* itself. The sixteenth-century tradition, in its earliest form, assigned the origin of the plays to the time of John Arneway, who was mayor during 1268 to 1277, and apparently the actual writing of them to Henry Francis, a monk of St. Werburgh's Abbey in Chester, who was said to have obtained an indulgence from the Pope for all who beheld them in peace and devotion. Later notices substitute Randulph Higden, also of St. Werburgh's, as the author. These statements do not hold together. Higden, best known by his *Polychronicon,* took the vows in 1299 and died in 1364. Francis was senior monk of the abbey in 1377 and 1388. I have suggested elsewhere that Arneway may have been confused with Richard Erneis or Herneys, who was mayor from 1327 to 1329. This is not an impossible date for the initiation of a processional cycle. The ascription to Higden, however, is not very plausible. His was, no doubt, a famous name in the annals of the abbey. But all his known or suggested writings are in Latin, and in the *Polychronicon* he tells us that in his day English *in paucis adhuc agrestibus vix remansit.* He may have exaggerated, but probably his own vernacular was Norman French. The metre of the Chester plays differs from that of the other dramatic cycles preserved to us by its uniformity. It is a Romance metre of the type known as *rime couée* or tail-rhyme, written normally in eight-lined stanzas, in which two *pedes* of three four-stressed lines rhyming together are each followed by a three-stressed *cauda.* The *caudae* rhyme with each other. The *pedes* may have a common rhyme, but more often do not. The rhythm is normally iambic. There is little alliteration, except in occasional passages, which may have undergone revision. The technical formula for the metre is $aaa_4b_3ccc_4b_3$ or $aaa_4b_3aaa_4b_3$. Obviously it is

of a rather lyrical character, better adapted to romantic narrative than to drama, since it does not lend itself well to the quick exchange of speech and reply which dialogue often requires. But it is capable of some modification to suit changes of theme or tone or speaker, by reducing the number of lines in the *pedes,* or the number of stresses throughout. The intervention of a supernatural speaker, for example, is sometimes so marked. The early banns appear to have been originally written in the same stanza as the plays. It has been suggested that this metrical uniformity points to a wholesale rewriting of the plays at some stage in their history. I do not see any reason for this. What really wants explanation is the variety of form found elsewhere. Certainly the Chester stanza would have been available for a playwright as early as 1327; it had already been used for narrative romances in the north. It must be added that, in some of the plays, the original metre has certainly been patched with others by later hands. There are bits in couplets, in quatrains and octaves of cross-rhyme, variously stressed, even in rhyme-royal and its probably earlier four-stress equivalent. These signs of revision are particularly noticeable in the Fall of Lucifer and the *Pastores.* The episode between Christ and the Doctors, which was apparently borrowed from York and attached rather inappropriately to the Purification, is in cross-rhyme. A speech of Christ at the Resurrection, in a rather unusual form of cross-rhyme, with alternate four-stressed and three-stressed lines, may possibly be taken from some contemporary lyric poem.

I have an impression that behind the Chester cycle, as it has come down to us, lies a play of a more primitive type, the themes of which have been rather clumsily incorporated, with the result that discrepancies have been left in the action, which the late transcribers of the text have variously attempted to remove. The influence of the old play is clearest in those scenes in which an *Expositor,* also called *Preco, Doctor, Nuntius* or Messenger, comments to the 'Lordinges' of the audience on the significance of the topics represented. He calls himself Gobet on the Grene, and his demands for 'room' to be made, with the fact that both he and later the character *Antichristus* come in riding, suggest a stationary performance on a green or other open space, rather than one on moving pageants. The appearances and speeches of the *Expositor* indicate that the primitive play contained at least a Noah, an Abraham, a *Prophetae,* with Moses, Balaam and Balak, and Balaam's Ass, a Nativity, which was given on a second day and brought in the *Magi* as well as Octavian and Sibylla, and a Prophets of Doomsday. Probably it had also both a Doomsday itself and an Antichrist. The *Expositor* does not appear in the extant texts of these, but he foretells them. There is nothing to suggest any treatment in the primitive play of the missionary life of Christ or of the Passion and its sequels up to Pentecost. It is true that the *Expositor* is also in the Temptation and Adulteress episodes, but here I think he may have been borrowed by a later writer. The whole emphasis of the primitive play seems to have been on prophecies of the coming of Christ and of the Last Judgement. And here it fell into line with such earlier work as the Tegernsee *Ludus de Antichristo* and the Anglo-Norman *Adam* of the twelfth century, the Benediktbeuern and Riga *Prophetae* of the thirteenth, and the Rouen *Prophetae* of the fourteenth. Its *Expositor* looks very much like the Riga *interpres*. It might have been written as late as the fourteenth century, either in Latin or in French or in English, and if in Latin or French, it is conceivable, I suppose, that it might have been the work of Higden, although I attach little importance to the traditional ascription of the Chester plays to him. As to other possible sources available for a Chester playwright, little can be said. There was plenty of Latin material to be drawn upon. A phrase or two of French for a potentate is an insufficient basis on which to establish a connexion with any continental *mystère* known to us. Nor has any use of the fourteenth-century English *Cursor Mundi* been clearly demonstrated, although that encyclopaedic work was itself of northern origin. The so-called *Stanzaic Life of Christ,* apparently written at Chester in the first half of the same century, and in part at least based upon Higden's *Polychronicon,* may have contributed something.

It is difficult to arrive at any very clear estimate of the literary value of plays which were never intended to be read, and cannot be given life by the gestures and intonation of the actors. The Chester plays retain some attractiveness through their lyrical form, where that has not been blurred by the activities of revisers and scribes. Broadly speaking, they preserve more than the other vernacular cycles of the devotional impulse, which brought medieval drama as a whole into existence. Their preoccupation with prophecies, whether read into Old Testament narratives or derived from legendary sources, of the Redemption and the Day of Doom has already been made clear. They are also much concerned with the exposition of religious formularies, such as the Ten Commandments, and of Jewish and Christian ritual observances, such as the Sabbath, Circumcision, or the feast of First Fruits. The dramatic action is generally simple and straightforward, without much attempt to exploit the psychological possibilities of the themes dealt with. The human element, for example, in the relations between Joseph and Mary, which gives so much interest to the later cycles, is here little elaborated. There is some pathos, however, in the Abraham and Isaac play. The fundamental inhumanity of that story was, of course, not apparent to our medieval ancestors. The element of farce has as yet hardly obtruded itself. Lucifer takes his downfall with comparative submission. Cain is restrained in his attitude towards his brother. Balaam's Ass is not unduly exploited. The midwives in the Nativity remain decent. Noah's wife is already a little recalcitrant when she is asked to enter the Ark. She must have her gossips with her. But

the point is not overelaborated, and a change of metre for 'The Good Gossippe's Song' suggests a late addition. There is some realism about the construction of the Ark in this play, and more in the *Pastores,* with its humorous Tudd, and Trowle the *Garcius,* and the rustic banquet. But certainly the *Pastores* has been largely rewritten. The Pilate of the Trial is a more dignified figure than in the later cycles. But the accusers revile the Redeemer as a 'jangellinge ['talking idly'] Jesu', a 'dosyberde' ['simpleton'], a 'babelavaunte' ['babbler'], and a 'shrewe'. And the buffeters and scourgers do their work with a vigour which is accompanied by a characteristic shortening of the metre.

The York plays are probably of later origin than those at Chester, but how much later we do not know. There are many records of them in the civic Memorandum Book, which begins in 1376. The plays are first mentioned in 1387, but appear then to be well established. In 1394 they were given at stations *antiquitus assignatis*. Their fame invited a visit by Richard II in 1397. Two valuable lists of them compiled by a town clerk, one Roger Burton, are of 1415 and perhaps 1420-2. They come to us in a register written about 1475, and occasionally added to later. Here they are forty-eight in number, but blanks left in the manuscript and various annotations in a late-sixteenth-century hand show that a Marriage at Cana and a Visit to Simon the Leper have been omitted, and that some revised versions, together with *loquela magna et diversa* elsewhere, had never been registered. One of the annotations is addressed to a Doctor, and it may be inferred that they date from 1579 when a revival, the first since 1569, was contemplated, and the council directed that the book should be submitted to the Archbishop and Dean of York for approval. Probably this performance never took place. The council may well have taken alarm at the trouble brought upon Chester mayors by their revivals of 1572 and 1575. Records show that, at one time or another, there were independent plays on the Washing of Feet, the Casting of Lots, the Hanging of Judas, and the Burial of the Virgin, which no longer exist, although fragments of some of them may be incorporated in what we have. Evidently, therefore, the total number of pageants was much greater than at Chester, although individually the York plays are shorter. The second play on the Creation, in fact, consists of no more than a single long speech of eighty-six lines by the Almighty. A good deal of splitting up must have taken place. Moreover, the plays were given on a single day, against the three days of Chester. It was certainly a crowded one. The performances began at 4:30 in the morning. The *Peregrini,* which came late, had to be shortened because of the number of plays still to follow ('for prossesse of plaies that precis [presses] in plight, ['due order'])', and the Burial of the Virgin was suppressed in 1432, not only on account of the ribaldry which it evoked, but because it could not be given during daylight. It is not surprising that in 1426 the Minorite William Melton, while commending the plays, pointed out that they threw the religious Corpus Christi procession into the background, and suggested that they should be transferred to the following day. It was, however, the procession itself which got so displaced.

Evidently the York texts of the cycle as we have them are not all of one date. Dr. Greg accepts a grouping which involves three periods of literary activity. The first, which he would put about 1350, produced 'a simple didactic cycle, carefully composed in elaborate stanzas and withal rather dull'. This he supposes the work of a single author or a single small school. In a second period it was elaborated by more than one hand. An element of humour was introduced with Noah and the Shepherds, and to this period also belongs 'the work of a writer who is distinguished as being the only great metrist who devoted his talents to the English religious drama as we know it'. The third stage he would also ascribe to a single author, who worked largely on the Passion, and whom he would put not earlier than 1400.

> He is a very remarkable though uneven writer. A metrist he certainly is not: he writes in powerful but loose and rugged alliterative verse. He also writes at great length and with much rhetoric and rant. But he is a real dramatist, and his portrait of Pilate is masterly.

I agree largely with this analysis. Certainly the cycle is sharply differentiated from that of Chester by its variety of metrical form. A nucleus of early work is, however, to be found in twelve plays, which are all written in the same stanza of cross-rhyme. It is bipartite, with a four-stressed octave for *frons,* and for *cauda* a three-stressed quatrain on different rhymes. The technical notation is $abababab_4cdcd_3$. This stanza has sometimes been called the 'Northern Septenar', under a misapprehension, since it is not derived from the Latin *septenarius*. It is found in the earliest version of the narrative English *Gospel of Nicodemus,* which was a source for the northern playwrights, and may have been written as early as the first quarter of the fourteenth century. If to the plays composed in this metre we add six in simple quatrains or octaves of cross-rhyme, which are at least as early, we seem to get the outlines of the greater part of an original cycle. It was, as Dr. Greg says, didactic, herein resembling that of Chester, although it had no *Expositor,* and laid less stress upon the element of prophecy. From it survive its Adam and Eve in Eden, Building of the Ark, Abraham and Isaac, *Exodus,* Annunciation, *Pastores, Tres Reges, Doctores,* Transfiguration, Adulteress and Lazarus, Last Supper, Crucifixion, Harrowing of Hell, Apparition to the Magdalen, Ascension, Pentecost, Assumption, and *Judicium.* I do not know why Dr. Greg ascribes the octaves of the *Judicium* to his metrist. The original

Creation has been split up into short plays, and most of it rewritten. If there was a Cain and Abel, it is buried under a late farce. An addition has been made to the *Pastores.* Parts of a Purification survive in a metrical chaos. Most of the Passion has also been rewritten, although a few early fragments remain embedded. There must always have been a Resurrection, but the existing one is of later type than the plays of the nucleus.

For literary quality in the York plays we must look mainly to Dr. Greg's metrist and his dramatist, whom we may also call a realist. As to the latter I have little to add, except that, while he is chiefly to be traced in his revision of the Passion, he also prefixed a new opening to the *Tres Reges,* apparently with the purpose of turning one play into two, and that, while his conspiracy, Agony, and Betrayal and Condemnation are written in a stanza which may be a development from that employed in the early nucleus, the rest of his work is completely incoherent as regards metrical form. He seems to have picked up and dropped one type of stanza after another, as it suited him at the moment. No doubt the resulting scribal confusion has added to the chaos. Apart from the survival of certain fragments of earlier versions, which he left standing, there is no difficulty in determining the extent of his contributions. They are sharply differentiated from the plays of the nucleus by the combination in them of rhyme with alliterative stress. Herein they fall into line with the alliterative revival in narrative poetry, which developed during the later medieval period, and, although its origin may have been elsewhere, acquired great popularity in the north. The affinity with the narrative writers is very clear in the Condemnation, where the *cauda* is separated from the *frons* of the stanza by the introduction of a one-stress line, known technically as a 'bob'. There is, indeed, a varying amount of alliteration even in the earlier York plays, far more than in those of the Chester cycle. But here it is merely sporadic and ornamental, and the rhythmic movement of the verse remains iambic, with a normal sequence of an unstressed syllable followed by a stressed one. Certainly there are variations. Often the first unstressed syllable is omitted, or an unstressed syllable follows the last stressed one, in what is called a feminine ending. Some lines, as a result, are more naturally read with a trochaic than with an iambic rhythm. Or, again, a stressed syllable may carry two unstressed syllables before it. In alliterative verse this is normal and the number of unstressed syllables may even be greater than two. As a result, the rhythm becomes an anapaestic rather than an iambic one. Alliteration is now used to emphasize the stressed syllables, although it may also occur elsewhere. It often fails, and is sometimes noticeably stronger in the *frons* than in the *cauda* of a stanza.

The determination of the exact extent of the work to be ascribed to the York metrist is a much more difficult problem. Dr. Greg finds him in the Fall of Lucifer and the Death of Christ. Possibly he has also touched that part of the Condemnation which deals with the Remorse of Judas. In these plays he is doubtless a reviser. But I think that we must also give him the *Peregrini,* the Death of the Virgin, and the Assumption, which may not have been handled in the original cycle. These five plays, in different stanza-forms, one of which has a 'bob', are all alliterative. But the alliteration is far less tumultuous than that of the realist, and often falls off in the *caudae* of the stanzas. The unstressed syllables, moreover, rarely exceed the limits of an anapaestic rhythm. I am inclined to suggest that a clue to the presence of the metrist may often be traced in a marked tendency to concatenation, the linking up of the beginning of one stanza with the end of that which preceded it by the repetition or slight variation of verbal phrasing. This also is a feature of the non-dramatic poems of the alliterative revival. An outstanding example is the fourteenth-century *Pearl.* Isolated concatenations may of course merely arise from the natural give and take of dialogue and carry no significance as evidence of authorship. But it is otherwise when whole poems or continuous groups of stanzas are similarly connected. Concatenation has there become a deliberate literary device. It is so used in the York Condemnation, *Peregrini* and Assumption, but not in the Death of Mary. Our metrist was clearly a versatile writer, and did not tie himself to a single form. Possibly we can go further and find him again in plays which, although in metres other than that of the nucleus, are not, like the five already considered, alliterative. There are four in a stanza-form derived from *rime couée* by dropping two lines of the second *pes.* The technical description is $aaa_4b_2a_4b_2$. The result is markedly lyrical in character, with a dying fall. Often the first four lines are by one speaker, whom another answers in the last two, with something of the effect of the liturgical *versus* and *responsio.* Of these four plays, the Expulsion of Adam and Eve and the Resurrection have a good deal of concatenation, the Incredulity of Thomas a little, and the Temptation none. I think we must ascribe them to the metrist. It is conceivable that he is also responsible for the rather lyrical Adam and Eve in Eden and for the Way to Calvary, both of which are in forms also derived, although differently, from *rime couée.* But there is no clue of concatenation to help us here. And as to the authorship of six remaining plays, I can offer no decided opinion. The Flight to Egypt has an elaborate stanza not paralleled elsewhere in the cycle. Its technical description is $ababcc_4dd_2e_2ff_3$. That of the Fall of Adam and Eve is $abab_4c_2bc_4dcdc_3$, and that of Joseph's Trouble, the Nativity, the Baptism and the Entry into Jerusalem $abab_4c_2b_4c_2$, with a dying fall, and in Joseph's Trouble and the Entry a tendency to antiphonal speech and reply, which may perhaps again suggest the metrist. The Nativity alone has a little concatenation. Whatever its authorship, there is a good deal of literary merit in this last group. The Entry,

with its healing of the blind and lame and its final Hails, is an effective dramatic pageant. And Joseph's Trouble, the Nativity, and the Flight are humane plays, in which the relations between Joseph and the Virgin are touched with a delicate psychology.

From Roger Burton's two lists of the plays and of the companies responsible for them, when compared with some annotations in later hands, with various records in the civic Memorandum Book, and with the state of the register as it has come down to us, it is possible to infer that a good deal of redistribution and probably incidental revision took place between the years 1415 and 1432. We know that in the latter year the Burial of the Virgin was laid aside, and that at the same time the Goldsmiths asked for relief from one of two *Magi* plays which they had hitherto given, on the plea that *mundus alteratus est super ipsos.* This seems to give a likely date for the alliterative opening to the *Magi* written by the realist. His Condemnation may be ascribed to 1423, when an order was made for the combination in a single play of an older version of the theme, together with plays on the Hanging of Judas, the Scourging, and the Casting of Lots, which had apparently been detached from it later than 1415. But there is no Hanging of Judas in the register. Perhaps this episode, in which *Judas se suspendebat et crepuit medius,* had proved too realistic to be witnessed with due sobriety. If then the realist was active between 1415 and 1432, we may perhaps put the metrist in the earlier part of the fifteenth century.

It must be added that, besides the Corpus Christi play, York had another, known as the Creed play. This *ludus incomparabilis* was in the hands of a gild of Corpus Christi, founded in 1408. It had been given by one of its wardens, William Revetor, by a will of 1446, and in 1455 the original manuscript was so worn that it had to be transcribed. It dealt with the articles of the Catholic faith, as set forth in the Apostles' Creed, to which, according to tradition, each apostle had contributed a clause. It was given, instead of the Corpus Christi play, in every tenth year, not on Corpus Christi day, but at the feast of St. Peter ad Vincula on 1 August, which coincided with the harvest festival of Lammas tide. Possibly it consisted of a group of saints' plays. Several performances are recorded during the sixteenth century. But one contemplated in 1568 was abandoned, because Dean Matthew Hutton, to whom the book had been submitted, found things in it which did not agree with the sincerity of the gospel. To it may have belonged the interlude of St. Thomas, the papistical language of which had led to a prohibition by Henry VIII. Of a play on St. Denis of York, bequeathed in 1455 to the church which bore his name, no details are preserved. A *Paternoster* play will be considered later. Evidently the dramatic instinct of the northern city was strong.

The Wakefield cycle, like that of York, has come down to us in a register, written in a hand which may be as late as 1485. There are some gaps, one of which may have contained a Pentecost, or a play on the end of the Virgin. There is no Nativity, which is unusual, but there is no gap at this point. There are thirty-two plays in all, some of which are very long. Two at the end are misplaced additions. A few annotations have been made up to the end of the sixteenth century. In 1814 the manuscript was owned by the Towneley family, of Towneley Hall near Burnley in Lancashire, and the collection was long known as the *Towneley Plays*. It was supposed, according to varying traditions, to have come either from Whalley Abbey near Burnley, or from Wydkirk or Woodkirk Abbey near Wakefield, and it was conjectured that the plays might have been given at a fair held at Widkirk from an early date. There is of course no evidence that a cycle was ever given either in an abbey or at a fair, and none that one existed at Burnley. In the manuscript itself there is much to point to Wakefield as its origin. At the head of it is written in large red letters

> In dei nomine amen
> Assit Principio, Sancta Maria, Meo. Wakefeld.

This, on the face of it, looks like a title to the whole collection, but there is no separate title for the first play, as there is, again in red, for those which follow. That to the third play runs 'Processus Noe *cum* filiis, Wakefeld'. The others name no locality. Against four of the plays sixteenth-century hands have added 'Barkers', 'Glover Pag', 'Litsters' [(listers), 'dyers'], Pagonn', 'lyster play', 'fysher pagent', which at least affords evidence that those plays belonged to a craft cycle. In the *Secunda Pastorum* are two topographical allusions, which might fit either Woodkirk or Wakefield. One is to 'Horbery shrogys', ['bushes'] and Horbury is a village two or three miles from Wakefield. The other is to 'the crokyd thorne', which might indeed be anywhere, but might be a 'Shepherd's Thorn' at Mapplewell, near Horbury. So the matter stood when the E.E.T.S. edition of the plays was published in 1897. Since then, further evidence has accumulated, which leaves little doubt that the plays must be credited to Wakefield itself. The *Mactacio Abel* has the phrase, 'bery me in gudeboure at the quarell hede', and Wakefield had, as early as the fourteenth century, a lane called Godiboure, near which was a quarry. I do not accept the inference that Godiboure is a corruption of 'God i' the bower', and was so named because the plays were performed there. Other records have accumulated which show that, in the sixteenth century, Wakefield had in fact a Corpus Christi play. They begin in 1533 and end in 1566, when the Ecclesiastical Commission laid down such strict limitations as to what might be shown that the plays were probably not given. In 1556 they were to be on Corpus Christi day, but in 1566 at Whitsun. I think we may now safely regard the plays in the Towneley MS as a Wakefield cycle. It must, however, have come into existence at a much later date than either the Chester or the York cycle. During the fourteenth century Wakefield was a place of no importance. A poll-tax return of 1377 shows only one franklin and forty-seven tradesmen, spread over seventeen occupations, who were rich enough to be contributory. They cannot have formed gilds able to maintain plays. There was not much increase by 1395. But during the fifteenth century the town prospered and became a head-quarters of the wool trade. A church built in 1329 remained without its tower to about 1409. By 1458 it had been taken down and rebuilt. One can hardly put the initiation of a cycle earlier than about 1425. If so, it may have been fairly complete, on the model of existing cycles elsewhere, from the beginning. I doubt whether it is worth while trying to analyse its development into three stages, as at York, although here too, as at York, there was certainly a comparatively late period of revision. It is clear that five of the plays have been borrowed, more or less wholesale, from York itself. They are the *Exodus*, here called *Pharao*, the *Doctores*, the Harrowing of Hell, the Resurrection, and the *Judicium*. But they have been differently treated. The *Exodus* is not much altered. In the other plays passages have been paraphrased, sometimes in different metres, and others have been added. The Resurrection has a long speech for the risen Christ, of which parts are also found in the Chester Resurrection and in an independent lyric. The *Judicium* has been worked over by a late hand at Wakefield itself. In the borrowings from York there is much textual corruption. Dr. Greg does not think that it amounts to more than might be expected from the normal habits of medieval scribes. Others have suggested that it points to oral transmission, perhaps through the subornation of York actors. But there is nothing to show that certain 'parts' are better represented than others. A reward given at York in 1446 to a *ludens* from Wakefield, which is sometimes cited in this connexion, can of course have no significance. He was probably only a wandering minstrel. The Wakefield debt to York may not have been wholly confined to the five plays already named. A large part of its *Conspiratio* is, like three of those, in the characteristic York stanza of twelve lines, with a four-stress *frons* and a three-stress *cauda*. This may also have been the original form of the York *Conspiratio,* which has been rewritten in an alliterative variant of it by the realist. But I reject altogether a much discussed theory which supposes the York and Wakefield cycles, as we have them, to have gradually developed, through revisions, many of which can now only be conjectured, from a common 'parent cycle'. Apart from the amount of guess-work involved, it is clearly put out of court by a recognition of the fact that the origin of the Wakefield cycle must have been anything from a quarter to half a century later than that of its York predecessor. It is true that parallels of phrasing may often be traced in plays, other than those which Wakefield has admittedly borrowed. They are particularly noticeable in the two plays on Joseph's Trouble. Often they may be due to a common use of narrative sources, such as the *Northern Passion,* the *Gospel of Nicodemus,* or, in the case of Joseph's Trouble, some poem on St. Anne and the Virgin, other than those which have reached us. But occasionally they amount to two or three consecutive lines and, as the Wakefield writers were evidently familiar with the plays at York, they may easily have retained in their memories some noteworthy passages. Whether there was also borrowing from other towns, such as Beverley, we cannot say. The *Prophetae,* with a Sybilla, and scriptural passages annotating the text, is not unlike the manner of Chester.

From the literary point of view, the Wakefield cycle is the best which is preserved to us. The simpler plays use a considerable number of stanza forms, with a predominantly iambic rhythm, and less sporadic alliteration than those of York. And there is a greater tendency to vary the form for different episodes or different speakers within a play. Some of those in couplets and octaves are rather stiff and dull. On the whole the *rime couée* and its derivatives predominate. There is not much use of the cross-rhymed quatrain, either alone or with a *cauda,* except in the Flight to Egypt, which combines cross rhyme and *rime couée* in an elaborate stanza with a bob line, of which the technical description is $ababaabaab_3c_1b_3c_2$. There is some good poetry in the *rime couée* group, which shows itself particularly, as at York, in those plays which deal with a human theme in the varying relations between Joseph and the Virgin. The Annunciation, in particular, as Dr. Pollard has pointed out, is 'full of tenderness', and I will quote, after him, the beautiful verse which describes the occupation of Mary in the service of the Temple.

> When I all thus had wed hir thare,
> We and my madyns home can [began to] fare,
>   That kyngys doghters were;
> All wroght thay sylk to fynd them on [get
>   their living],
> Marie wroght purpyll, the oder none
>   Bot othere colers sere [various].

This touch comes from the *Evangelium Pseudo-Matthaei,* probably through one of the St. Anne poems. But the outstanding achievement of the Wakefield plays is to be found in the contributions of a single writer, who is generally known as the Wakefield Master. There is no tenderness about him, and no impulse to devotion. He is a realist, even more than his contemporary of York, a satirist with a hard outlook upon a hard age, in which wrong triumphs over right, but he is saved by an abundant sense of humour. His contribution consists in the main of five plays, all written in a characteristic metre of his own. This too has a 'bob' in it. Its technical description is $ababab_2c_1dddc_2$. The two-stressed lines give it an exceptional rapidity of movement. There is a good deal of alliteration, but this does not fall with such regularity on the stressed syllables as to constitute an alliterative metre, comparable to that of the York realist. The rhythm, however, is markedly anapaestic, and may even be called *plus-quam* anapaestic, since a stressed syllable often carries with it more than two unstressed ones. The five plays are the Noah, the *Pastores,* a second *Pastores,* the *Magnus Herodes* or Innocents, and the Buffeting. In the Noah the biblical theme of the salvation of mankind through the preservation of a single family, who are ultimately to produce the Redeemer, is transformed by this writer into what can only be called a *fabliau* of the recriminations and bouts of fisticuffs which take place between Noah and his wife, from the first building of the Ark to the ultimate return of the dove. The first *Pastores* is much dominated by what may be called a democratic outlook upon the disturbed conditions of the fifteenth century as they affected the rustic working classes. Gyb complains of the 'mekyll vncyl' [much unhappiness] of the world. His sheep are rotted; his rent is not ready. John Horne joins him, with laments against boasters and braggers, who do 'mekyll wo' to poor men with their 'long dagers'. Slaw-pace, bringing corn from the mill, enters and chaffs them. Jack *garcio* chaffs them all. They club their poor food together for a meal. Our writer has taken hints from the York play and given them life. Good wine of Ely brings some comfort and the shepherds sleep, after a rustic prayer. An Angel wakes them with news of the Nativity, and bids them go to Bethlehem. They comment, see the star, recall prophecies, and try to sing. The star leads them. And at Bethlehem the tone changes, and the simple gifts of the shepherds, a little spruce coffer, a ball for play, a bottle to drink from, are rather touching. Not content with this effort, our poet essayed another, which is even more audacious. The opening theme is much the same, with complaint of the weather, of the 'gentlery men' who tax the poor, and of the behaviour of wives, especially their own. The world is 'brekyll [brittle] as glas', and floods drown the fields. Daw's master and the dame bully him, but he will repay them with bad work. The sheep are left in the corn, but the shepherds will sing a part-song. Now enters Mak, a king's yeoman, with a southern tongue. There is mistrust of his honesty. He is a sheep-stealer. His wife drinks and has too many children. And now follows what can only be described as an astonishing parody of the Nativity itself. While the others slumber, Mak steals a sheep and carries it to his wife Gill, who hides it in a cradle, to look like a new-born child. Mak returns to the shepherds, and, when they wake, says that he has dreamed that his wife has had a child, and must go home. The others arrange to count their sheep and to meet at 'the crokyd thorne'. One is missing and they pursue Mak. There is nothing in his house but empty platters and a cradled child. After a vain search, they go, and return to give the child sixpence. But it proves to have the long snout of a sheep. They can only laugh at the joke, and content themselves with tossing Mak in a canvas. Then comes the angelic message and the visit to Bethlehem, with its gifts. Again the tone has changed.

Primus Pastor

Hayll, comly and clene!
Hayll, yong child!
Hayll, maker, as I meyne [mean],
Of a madyn so mylde!
Thou has waryd ['brought calamity to'] I
    weyne [think]
The warlo [wizard] so wylde;
The fals gyler of teyn [malice]
Now goys he begylde.
    Lo, he merys [is merry];
Lo, he laghys, my swetyng.
A welfare metyng.
I have holden my hetyng [scorn];
    Haue a bob [bunch] of cherys.

Secundus Pastor

Hayll, sufferan sauyoure!
Ffor thou has vs soght:
Hayll, frely foyde [noble creature] and floure
That all thyng has wroght!
Hayll, full of fauoure
That made all of noght!
Hayll! I kneyll and I cowre.
A byrd haue I broght
    To my barne, [child].
Hayll, lytyll tyné mop [baby]!
Of oure crede thou art crop [completion]:
I wold drynk on thy cop [cup],
    Lytyll day starne.

Tertius Pastor

Hayll, derling dere
Full of godhede!
I pray the be nere
When that I haue nede.
Hayll! swete is thy chere!
My hart wold blede
To se the sytt here
In so poore wede [clothing],
    With no pennys.
Hayll! put furth thy dall [hand]!
I bryng the bott a ball:
Haue and play the with all,
    And go to the tenys.

Our poet can lyricize, as well as satirize, when he chooses. But one wonders why Wakefield wanted two *Pastores* plays, and what was actually performed there.

In the *Magnus Herodes* the Master finds himself in his element with the vaunts of Herod and his knights, and in the battle of the mothers to defend their children. And so too in the Buffeting, where the *Tortores* lay on with many insults, as well as blows, and Caiaphas is as violent as Herod and as free-spoken as any Shepherd.

In these five plays the writer is unaided, and there is nothing to suggest that he was a reviser, except of himself. But he also inserted forty-two stanzas of his characteristic metre into the York *Judicium*, to be spoken by Tutivillus and a group of fellow-demons, in scarification of the unjust souls, whose records they bring. Herein is much social criticism, of fraudulent taxgatherers, perjurers, extortioners, simoners, lechers, and adulterers, and of the extravagance in dress of men and women. But it is Tutivillus who is a 'mastar lollar' [lollard]. The Wakefield writer was no heretic. An attempt has been made to date his work as not earlier than about 1426, from the references to costume. I do not find the evidence very convincing. Sartorial fashions rise and fall and rise again. One feature, in particular, which is relied upon, that of the woman's head-dress 'hornyd like a kowe', was already the subject of unkindly comment by John de Bromyard, as far back as 1360. Some traces of east Midland influence on the Master's northern dialect also seem to point to about 1426. But we have seen that the inception of the Wakefield cycle as a whole may not have been much earlier than this. The Master may therefore have been one of its original writers. I doubt whether he was influenced by the York realist, who writes, not merely with an anapaestic rhythm, but with the full alliterative stress. They may have been contemporaries, and perhaps rivals. Both, no doubt, use bob-lines, but the Master's two-stressed *frons* does not appear at York. Several of the Wakefield plays, the Conspiracy, the Scourging, the Crucifixion, the *Processus Talentorum,* which should be *Talorum* (dice), the *Peregrini,* the Ascension, the Lazarus, are again medleys, and have probably been revised. A few of the Master's stanzas are in the Conspiracy, the Scourging, and the *Processus Talentorum.* There are bob-line stanzas elsewhere, but they lack his two-stressed *frons.* Nor do I think that he has any responsibility for the *Mactacio Abel,* into which a farce, more elaborate than that of York, has been inserted.

From the Coventry cycle only two plays have come down to us, and those in very late and degraded forms. Local annals, of which the earliest are themselves only in a manuscript of about 1587, put the initiation of the cycle in 1416. There were certainly pageants earlier. The Drapers had one by 1393 and the Pinners by 1414. It is possible that these were only dumb-shows. A gild of Corpus Christi was founded in 1348, and was later merged in the corporation. In the ridings, *ex antiquo tempore,* from seventeen to twenty-two crafts took part about the middle of the fifteenth century. But for dramatic purposes these were combined into ten groups, of which the most important members took financial responsibility for the production of the plays, while the others were contributory. The ten plays appear to have been given at ten stations, one in each of the ten wards of the city. They were long, and crowded with characters, and some of the action apparently took place on supplementary scaffolds and even in the street. The two extant plays are those of the Shearmen and Tailors, and the Weavers. In the first a prophetic prologue by Isaiah is followed by a series of distinct episodes, covering the Annunciation, Joseph's Trouble, the Journey to Bethlehem, and the *Pastores*. A dialogue by two unnamed Prophets separates these from a second series, which has Herod and the *Magi,* the *Magi* at Bethlehem, a brief Flight to Egypt, and an Innocents. It has been suggested that two original plays are here combined, but there is no evidence that the Shearmen and Tailors ever formed separate gilds. The Weavers' play is similarly constructed, with a long prophetic dialogue for opening, followed by a Presentation in the Temple, a Visit of Joseph and Mary to Jerusalem, and a *Doctores*. The *Doctores* seems to be a late addition, with a text derived, as at Chester, from one like that of York, through some intermediate form. It may have been borrowed in 1520, when the annals record that there were 'new playes at Corpus Christi tide'. Of the other eight plays we can trace, mainly from gild accounts, a Trial and Crucifixion, a Burial, a Harrowing of Hell, with a Resurrection and *Peregrini,* and a *Judicium.* The rest must remain uncertain. There is some slight evidence for an Assumption. A Baptism, Entry into Jerusalem, Last Supper, Ascension, and Pentecost are all possible. It seems clear that there were no Old Testament plays at Coventry. The Prophets, of course, had long been attached to the Nativity theme. During the latter part of the fifteenth and the sixteenth centuries the Coventry plays seem to have had a more than local reputation. The Midland town was more accessible from London than those of the north. Several royal visits are upon record. A preacher on the Creed in 1526 bids his audience go to Coventry and see what he has told them represented there. John Heywood, in his *Foure P.P.* of about 1545, refers to one who had 'playd the deuyll at Coventry'. Certainly the revision of 1520 was not the last. According to the annals, the plays were given in 1568, after which they were 'laid down' for eight years, then revived in 1576, and last played in 1580. The texts which we have were 'correcte' or 'translate' by one Robert Croo in 1535, and to them are appended some rather pretty Elizabethan songs by Thomas Mawdycke, dated as late as 1591. This double recension has unfortunately left the plays completely unreadable. Much is a mere jumble of incongruous metres. One can at most discern in the chaos an original basis, as elsewhere, of quatrains, octaves, and *rime couée,* and a probably later addition of rhyme royal and its four-stressed equivalent. But all has been turned, by the clumsy insertion of superfluous unstressed syllables, which destroy the iambic rhythm without substituting an anapaestic one, into what can only be described as doggerel. It has sometimes been called 'tumbling verse', a term for which James VI of Scotland seems to be responsible. But I do not know that that is any more polite. There is also much aureate language, and in particular a constant use of latinized words ending in *-acion,* with a stress falling on the antepenultimate syllable. Apart from the cycle, the annals record saints' plays on St. Katharine in 1490, and apparently St. Christina in 1504, which were given in the Little Park and may have been stationary performances.

Outside the four craft-cycles already described, a few other plays of the same type are preserved. Two of these are certainly also craft-plays. From Newcastle-on-Tyne comes a Noah. Here the plays appear to have been stationary, in a 'stead', after the Corpus Christi procession was over. They are first recorded in 1427, and the extant text may be of much the same date. It only deals with the Making of the Ark, and probably a Deluge followed. The dialogue is mainly in quatrains, with occasional variants in other metres. It is fairly lively. A *Diabolus* gives Noah's wife a drink for her husband, presumably to check his enterprise, but so far the farcical element is not as strong as in the York and Wakefield versions of the theme. Of a Norwich Creation of Eve and Expulsion from Eden there are two late texts, one of a fragment of about 1533, the other, complete, of 1565. Both are in the seven line four-stressed stanza, with much doggerel and some aureate language. Among the characters are two allegorical figures, Dolor and Myserye. The records of the cycle go back to 1527, when the gild of St. Luke handed it over to the crafts. Possibly it existed as early as 1478, when a letter to Sir John Paston, written from Norwich on May 20, compared the behaviour of the Earl of Suffolk to one playing Herod in Corpus Christi play. The sixteenth-century performances at Norwich, however, were not on Corpus Christi day but in Whitsun week. An Abraham and Isaac, found in a manuscript at Trinity College, Dublin, probably only got there by accident. There is a record in 1498 of a dumb-show procession on Corpus Christi day at Dublin, but none of plays. The same manuscript contains a list of Northampton mayors up to 1458, and possibly the play came from that town, although there is no evidence that it ever had a cycle, beyond a rather vague reference to the storing of pageants in a hall there during the half-century before 1581. The dialect, however, seems to belong to the border between the east and west Midlands. The play, written mainly in *rime couée,* is not a bad one. The introduction of Sara as a character helps to humanize its theme. It has been conjectured that the writer knew some version of the French *Viel Testament.* A second Abraham and Isaac comes from a manuscript of 1470-80 preserved at Brome Manor in

Norfolk. It is dull, and mainly in doggerel. There is nothing to show whether it formed part of a cycle. Opinions have differed as to its relation to other dramatic versions of the story. Dr. Greg, who has made a minute study of their variants, thinks that the Chester one is the earliest extant, and that the Brome one may be derived either from that or from a common original. A play on the Innocents and the Purification is found in Bodleian Digby MS 133, which is a composite manuscript in more than one hand, and apparently contains pieces from different sources. This one has been glossed by a later hand with the date 1512 and the statement 'Iohn Parfre ded wryte thys booke'. Yet another hand, that of the chronicler John Stow, has added 'the vij booke'. An opening speech by a Poet shows that the play belonged to a cycle, but one spread over a series of successive years, and performed, like the Lincoln plays, on St. Anne's day. A *Pastores* and a *Reges* had come in the year before. There is nothing to suggest that the cycle was undertaken by craft gilds. Again we have unfortunately little but doggerel. The dialect points to a Midland author and a southern scribe. Finally, a very curious *Burial and Resurrection,* in a mid-fifteenth-century hand, is in Bodleian MS E. Museo, 160. I do not know why Furnivall thought that it was once part of the Digby MS. It was originally written as a 'treyte or meditatione' and then converted into a play to be given in part on Good Friday afternoon, and in part on Easter Day, thus becoming an isolated vernacular example of a liturgical play, extending to 1,631 lines. The Latin dialogue *Dic nobis, Maria* is incorporated, and there are directions for the use of the sequences *Victimae Paschali* and *Scimus Christum.* There is no evidence and little probability that the piece was ever performed. The dialect is northern, with some Midland forms. The metre is mostly *rime couée,* with some element of doggerel. There is aureate language. An elaborate lament of the Virgin is in octaves, and makes frequent repetition of the line 'Who cannot wepe, com lerne at me', which is also found as the burden of two fifteenth-century lyrics.

The Digby MS also contains two saints' plays. In view of the number of such representations disclosed by records, it is surprising that so few have survived. A *Conversion of St. Paul,* in four-stressed seven-line stanzas, is doggerel with aureate touches. The dialect is east Midland. A second hand has inserted a scene between two devils, Belial and Mercury. And against a prologue, headed *Poeta,* another has written 'Myles Blomefylde'. An alchemist of that name was born at Bury St. Edmunds in 1525. The performance was given at three 'stations', apparently spots in an open space, to which the audience moved successively. More interesting is a *St. Mary Magdalen,* in the second hand of the *St. Paul,* with the initials M. B. at the beginning. This too is in Midland dialect. The versification is much the same as that of the companion play, but even more metrically incompetent, although not without some

rough vigour. The whole life of the saint, as related in the *Legenda Aurea,* is covered, with action at a number of spots, for which elaborate stage-directions are given. Between them, a practicable ship comes and goes. 'I desyer the redars to be my frynd', says the writer at the end, and perhaps he hardly expected the play to be performed. To one of its episodes it will be necessary to return later. Yet another isolated text requires consideration. It is not hagiological, but it is a *miraculum* in the strictest sense, being based upon an actual miracle, which according to an appended note, signed, presumably by the author, R. C., took place at Eraclea, in the forest of Aragon, during 1461. The text, entitled *The Conversyon of Ser Jonathas the Jewe by Myracle of the Blyssed Sacrament,* may be not much later. But in fact the theme is traceable in continental legend, and even on the stage, as far back as the fourteenth century. From a literary point of view this is perhaps the most interesting dramatic relic, outside the craft cycles, which has come down to us. A Banns is prefixed, in which two *vexillatores* announce a performance at Croxton. There are several places so named, but as the dialect is east Midland, either one in Norfolk or one in Cambridgeshire seems most likely. A character is said to live near Babwelle Mill, and at Babwell, two miles from Bury St. Edmunds in Suffolk, was a Franciscan priory. Possibly the play originated at Bury, and was taken on tour, as we know that a Chelmsford play was in the sixteenth century. The action of the *Sacrament* opens with a long speech by a merchant Aristorius, who vaunts the range of his traffic, and sends his clerk to learn if any ships have come in

> Of Surrey [Syria] or of Sabe [either Sheba, or
> Saba, an island in the Dutch West Indies.]
> or of Shelys-down.

There may be a topical reference here. A Shelley is near the estuary of the Stour in Suffolk, but I do not know whether it ever had a harbour. The passage recalls one in the Wakefield *Magnus Herodes,* where the Nuncius similarly vaunts his lord's renown in many lands,

> Form Egyp to Mantua
> Unto Kemp towne.

Another character in the *Sacrament* is a Jewish Jonathan, who wants to test the truth of the Christian story of a cake, which a priest can turn into the flesh and blood of him 'that deyed upon the rode'. He approaches Aristorius, who is friendly with the priest Ser Ysodyr, and bribes him to dope the priest with wine, and steal a Host from the church, while he sleeps it off. The plot succeeds. Jonathan summons four other Jews. They prick the Host with their daggers, and it bleeds. They bring a cauldron of oil to boil it in, but it clings to Jonathan's hand, and he runs mad. The others nail him to a post, and pull the Host away, but his hand comes with it. The aid of a leech, Master Brundyche of Braban, is suggested, and an elaborate proclamation advertises his skill. He recalls the quack doctor of the folk-plays, who may also have influenced the *unguentarius* of some versions of the *Visitatio Sepulchri.* But he is sent away as useless. The Host is then thrown into the cauldron, the oil in which turns into blood. Finally it is baked in an oven, which is riven asunder, and Christ appears, as an image with wounds bleeding, and makes an appeal to the Jews. They repent, and at the prayer of a bishop the image becomes bread again. Aristorius in his turn repents. The rather odd moral is drawn, among others, that curates ought to keep their pyxes locked. It was an audacious piece to put before our forefathers in an age of devotion. But the author has a vigour of expression, unmatched in medieval drama, except by the Wakefield Master. He uses various stanza-forms, and can hold either an iambic or an anapaestic rhythm at will. In some passages only he alliterates his stressed syllables. Occasionally he uses an aureate phrase, such as 'mansuete [gentle] myrth' or 'largyfluent [copious] Lord'.

The evidence of these scattered plays suggests that a considerable variety in the manner of dramatic representation prevailed in the east Midland area. And this is perhaps confirmed by one other important text from that area, which has still to be discussed. This is the so-called *Ludus Coventriae,* about which almost the only certain thing is that it has nothing to do with Coventry. The misapprehension may have started with Robert Hegge, the first known owner of the manuscript, who was a Fellow of Corpus Christi College, Oxford, and died in 1629. It was taken up by his fellow-collegian, Richard James, librarian to Sir Robert Cotton, who wrote *Ludus Coventriae sive Ludus Corporis Christi* on a fly-leaf of the manuscript, and by Sir William Dugdale in his *Antiquities of Warwickshire* (1656), who alleged that the plays were given by the Grey Friars of Coventry. This probably rests on a statement in a late version of the Coventry *Annals,* which records that in 1492-3 Henry VII saw the plays 'by the Gray Friers'. These were doubtless the craftplays, which the king presumably watched from a station at the gate of the Grey Friars convent, and the existence of a second cycle in Coventry is as unlikely as the performance of any cycle by a religious house. The dialect of the *Ludus* seems to be an East Anglian variety of east Midland. To the text of the plays is prefixed a Banns by three *vexillatores,* who enumerate the 'pagents' and their subjects, refer to 'oure pleyn place', and announce a performance to begin on a following Sunday at 6 a.m. 'in N. towne'. It was evidently to be a stationary performance, and there is no mention of crafts. 'N. towne' might of course fit either Norwich, which, however, had craft-plays, or Northampton, where we have no clear record of plays. But I suspect that N. merely stands, as it does in the

Marriage Service, for *Nomen,* and that the *Ludus,* like the *Sacrament,* was a touring play. The text, which in many respects does not agree with the Banns, has forty-two. But both documents have undergone revision. The metre of the Banns is a thirteen-line stanza, with a *frons* and *cauda,* of which the technical description is $ababab ab_4 c_3 ddd_4 c_3$. This is also the metre of some of the plays, but others are in *rime couée,* or in octaves, and occasionally quatrains or couplets. Dr. Greg, who has made a valuable study of the manuscript, thinks that some of these have been introduced by successive revisers from other cycles, but for this I do not see any very strong reason, in view of the variety of metrical form shown in the York and Wakefield plays. What seems clearest is that the whole of the cycle, and with it to some extent the Banns, has been worked over by a late writer, who has added much material of his own composition, again in octaves, which can, however, be easily distinguished from those of the original by their long doggerel and aureate lines. According to Dr. Greg, he handed instalments of his revision to a scribe, who contributed further corruption to the text as we have it. The date 1468, which is found on one page of the manuscript, may well be that of his work. The activity of this writer is, I think, the main factor in the state of confusion to which the cycle has been reduced. The text, as it stands, does not agree with the Banns, or with the method of performance which they imply. The reviser, who also uses the East Anglian dialect, was a theologian, with a desire to expound at length the significance of moral and liturgical formulas, such as the Ten Commandments, the Psalter, or the Steps to the Temple. He had a special devotion to the 'clene mayd', the Virgin Mary, and he has added three plays on her Conception, her Presentation in the Temple, and her Visit to Elizabeth, of which there is no trace whatever in the Banns, and for which he seems to have borrowed some material from one of the extant poems on St. Anne. Moreover, he has arranged them in a way which is quite inconsistent with the Banns. Together with the Betrothal and Marriage, the Annunciation, and the Trouble and Return of Joseph, they make a self-contained group, which is introduced by a presenter *Contemplatio,* who informs the 'congregacion' that the matter of the 'processe' is of 'the modyr of mercy', makes further comment at intervals, and at the end thanks the audience for their patience, and adds,

> With Avé we begunne and Avé is our
> conclusyon.

Clearly the reviser has departed from the scheme of the Banns, and has arranged these six plays as a self-contained performance. Later comes a Purification, for which also the Banns, as we have them, do not provide, but which is not, I think, the work of the main reviser. He has, however, wholly recast and largely overwritten the Passion plays, inserting, rather oddly before the Entry into Jerusalem, a long prefatory speech by a Demon, a prophecy by John the Baptist, and a Conspiracy of his own. And here again, he contemplates a method of representation which is quite other than that of the Banns, for between the *Captio* and the Trial before Herod appears an *Expositor*, who is again *Contemplatio*, and announces to the audience,

> We intendyn to procede the matere that we
> lefte the last yere.

And here, I think, his main work ended. The later plays are mostly in their original metres, and he can only have lightly touched them. An exception is the Assumption, written in octaves and thirteen-line stanzas, curiously linked by intercalary lines. It is on an interpolated quire, in a hand other than that of the usual scribe. Of this also the Banns know nothing. Dr. Greg would, however, ascribe it to a writer distinct from the main reviser. I should add that at some time the main reviser appears to have made an attempt to alter the Banns themselves, in order to bring them into conformity with his expanded cycle. But this enterprise he must have dropped half-way. Obviously the revised *Ludus* can never have been performed as a whole. Dr. Greg points out that the text, ornamented with elaborate genealogical tables and notes on the dimensions of the Ark, was evidently intended for readers. Probably the reviser was a member of some religious house, which had a library. One thinks of Lincoln, where there was a special cult of St. Anne, and where a *Ludus Corporis Christi* was occasionally played in the latter part of the fifteenth century, or of Bury St. Edmunds. But the main reviser was not Lydgate, as has been suggested. When he ends a line, as he so often does, with a word terminating in *-acion,* he puts his last stress on the antepenultimate, but Lydgate, in a like case, on the ultimate syllable. As literature, of course, much of the *Ludus Coventriae* in its present state makes difficult reading. But some of the unaltered plays are not without lyrical merit, notably the *Pastores,* the *Magi,* and the Resurrection. Some passages of short-lined *rime couée,* apparently regarded as appropriate to *Milites,* are particularly attractive.

William Tydeman (essay date 1994)

SOURCE: An introduction to *The Cambridge Companion to Medieval English Theatre*, edited by Richard Beadle, Cambridge University Press, 1994, pp. 1-36.

[In the following essay, Tydeman discusses the surge of critical and popular interest in medieval theater, the geographical origins of plays and their respective staging patterns, and the critical controversy surrounding the extent of the influence of church ceremonies on the development of the dramas.]

> You that love England, who have an ear for
> her music. . .
> Listen. Can you not hear the entry of a new
> theme?

During the last few decades, the 'new theme' of medieval English theatre may be said to have swelled beyond all expectation. In the place of the modest harmonious arias of a few soloists we now confront a mighty but not totally co-ordinated anthem issuing from a many-throated chorus. In the past thirty years the status of medieval plays has been transformed, not merely through the advocacy of academics, but by the enthusiastic response of students and, even more remarkably, spectators. Much of the main repertory is accessible on the shelves of libraries and bookshops; civic and county archives are being scrutinised for practical details of local organisation and presentation. Periodicals and volumes replete with competing theories are announced frequently; live performances of medieval plays now seem as predictable a feature of the British summer as rain-threatened stagings of *A Midsummer Night's Dream.* Today there is probably greater awareness of the existence, nature and appeal of fourteenth- and fifteenth-century English drama than at any time since its creation.

The haphazard survival of early dramatic texts and documents makes it difficult to offer anything like a complete picture of what must once have existed. Medieval plays were not designed as reading matter, and the physical form in which they were recorded was manuscript, so it is not surprising that very few of them have come down to us from the time in which they were performed. It is as if we have inherited a small number of pieces, some few of which connect with one another, from a huge but lost jig-saw puzzle. The chronological table occupying the preceding pages gives a fractional idea of its temporal, and to some extent its spatial, dimensions, in terms of these surviving texts. The documentary evidence, which is rather more abundant, but altogether shadowier and more difficult of interpretation, is still in the process of being gathered. It is therefore largely the texts of the major English vernacular plays which form the focus of what follows, and, though shards of earlier dramatic traditions have survived, the chronological table discloses the obvious starting-point with the hazy origins of the mystery cycles and morality plays during the latter half of the fourteenth century. In the broadest sense, these powerful didactic genres took their rise as one element in a systematic campaign on the part of the Church to instruct the laity, in their own language rather than the Latin of the clergy or the Anglo-Norman French of the nobility, as to the essential features of their faith. These included the submerged narrative of the spiritual relationship between God and mankind, revealed by patristic exegetes in the articulation of the

New to the Old Testament, which found compelling expression in the Fall-Redemption-Doomsday structure of the mystery cycles. Equally arresting was the perpetual struggle between the forces of good and evil for possession of the individual soul, naturally coupled with the urgent imperatives implied in the facts of death and an imminent eternal afterlife in heaven or hell, which give shape to the morality plays. Plays associated with these subjects, and on the exemplary lives of saints, seem first to have become common in the later years of the fourteenth century, but it is generally not until the mid-fifteenth century or later that the texts as we now have them appear as manuscripts, whilst at the same time documentary evidence about how they were staged and financed becomes reasonably abundant in a few places. The extraordinary longevity of the plays is attested in records of performance stretching forwards until the last quarter of the sixteenth century, by which time the ideological shifts begun at the Reformation, combined with changes in literary taste and new theatrical possibilities, finally put paid to the old genres.

The chronological table is also important in suggesting geographical and other dimensions to the study of the medieval English theatre, such as patterns of staging across time and place. For example, it implies an interesting map of dramatic activity expressed in terms of the surviving texts, though it has to be said that another map drawn on the basis of the documentary evidence would look rather different. Traditionally, the main geographical emphasis has been placed on the great civic enterprises of the craft guilds in the north of England, where the surviving cycles from York and Chester, and the plays associated with Wakefield in the Towneley manuscript, can confidently be located. But urban drama, and the intricate social and economic infrastructure that supported it, though documented in sometimes remarkable detail, is not the whole story. More recently, attention has also been focused on the steadfastly rural region of East Anglia, which bibliographical and linguistic research has shown to be the home of a significant group of texts: the N-Town plays, the morality plays of the Macro manuscript, the saints' plays of the Digby manuscript, and other 'non-cycle plays and fragments'. Nothing in this repertoire can be connected with urban craft guilds, and it is probable that religious guilds and other rural parish organisations supported productions of at least some of the East Anglian plays. The central midlands, by contrast, are sparsely represented by parts of the Coventry cycle and a single play from Northampton, whilst great areas of the west midlands and the south (including, rather surprisingly, London), yield no surviving texts at all. This is true until we reach the Celtic-speaking areas of the extreme south west, which boasts the extensive body of Cornish drama, still not well known, and as interesting for its differences from as its similarities to that of the remainder of England. Staging patterns to some extent reflect the geographical distribution of the plays

that have survived. Processional performances using pageant wagons paid for by craft guilds were certainly a conspicuous feature in some northern towns, though not exclusive to that region, whilst 'place-and-scaffold' (or, more loosely, 'in the round') productions, sometimes in purpose-built earthenwork 'amphitheatres', are clearly detectable in Cornwall and East Anglia, but were not the only way that plays were presented in either region. A good many of the surviving scripts evidently reflect outdoor performances, and it is interesting to note that texts of plays designed for the typical type of indoor production ('great hall'), such as the interludes, do not come down to us in any quantity until around the turn of the fifteenth century, when they appear as printed books, rather than manuscripts. Finally, one may note that almost nothing from the repertoire of popular itinerant entertainers or the nascent professional acting troupes has survived in written form from any period before the end of the fifteenth century. Though broad generalisations of this kind, for what they are worth, are reasonably safe, closer acquaintance with the material soon acts to replace them with a more precise impression of an underlying complexity—generic, chronological and regional—which it is not the business of this book to simplify or shirk.

Because of the relative paucity of play texts, our knowledge of English medieval drama must rely in larger measure than in other eras on information gleaned from ecclesiastical injunctions, parish registers, legal depositions, civic accounts, family papers and so forth. The task of collecting and interpreting such documents is now being systematically undertaken, yet such are the limitations of terminology employed in the Middle Ages to designate the several branches of entertainment offering themselves, that too often we can never be certain as to what extent drama is the principal feature of what documents refer to, nor indeed whether at times we are dealing with drama at all. Were, for example, those popular 'ludi' objected to by outraged prelates 'plays' in our sense of the term, since the Latin word 'ludus' can be used to denote a sport or a pastime as well as a drama? Does a reference to a 'game' in Middle English parlance indicate a dramatic performance or a communal activity of another kind? How far should certain parts of the Roman Catholic church's schedule of divine worship—the church services known collectively as the liturgy—be accorded the title of 'drama', given that their originators probably saw them as no such thing? What should the familiar term 'pageant' convey to us, granted its several meanings for a medieval spectator? Which term—'mystery', 'miracle', 'craft cycle', 'Corpus Christi play'—most appropriately describes the great sequences of biblical episodes presented annually in medieval cities, since all these labels can mislead, and some 'Corpus Christi plays' were manifestly not presented as part of the Church's feast of Corpus Christi at all? These and similar semantic niceties have a more prominent role in today's discussions of medieval English drama than yesterday's innocent explorer would readily credit.

Recent increases in knowledge have rarely produced greater certitude: the new emphases not only challenge old assertions, but complicate the current picture, so that it is not merely novices in the field who are bewildered by the implications of newly-available data or the contentious claims of rival experts. Scholarly discoveries and critical heterodoxy are here to stay, and the present *Companion* is not designed to reduce the study of this dynamic phase in Britain's theatrical history to an undesirable state of drab conformity and limp consensus. Rather it seeks to guide readers, spectators, performers and directors through the profusion and diversity of accumulated evidence and interpretative opinion, in the hope of making it a little less formidable to grasp.

The Drama of Devotion

Almost all medieval drama inevitably has to be scrutinised through the lens supplied by the Church. Much of what survives is religious in character, but even our knowledge of secular dramatics is chiefly obtained from admonishments and embargoes emanating from a clerical establishment horrorstruck by the unrestrained vigour of the common people's pleasures. Much of what we glean of the nature of popular diversions must be treated as reflecting the viewpoint of prejudiced censors rather than detached observers, yet the Church did not disapprove of all forms of playmaking, and its eventual acceptance of drama as a means of instructing the laity may well represent an attempt to compete with less decorous amusements, by harnessing the methods of profane presentation to lure the worldly away from what was deemed to be imperilling their immortal souls.

At what point in its long history the Christian faith began to assimilate acts of apparent theatre into its modes of worship has not been universally agreed, but though some do not accept that the most commonly cited ceremony (found in a Latin manual of English provenance) offers valid evidence for the presence of acted drama in the liturgy by *c.* 970 AD, its nature and appearance warrant serious consideration. For many scholars the so-called *Visitatio Sepulchri* (Visit to the Sepulchre) testifies to a 'second birth' for Western dramatic art, following the dispersal of the heritage of Greece and Rome occasioned by the barbarian invasions of the occidental empire. Whether Christianity manifested theatrical tendencies at some earlier date is fiercely debated; several pseudo-dramatic passages, one from the seventh Advent lyric of the Old English *Exeter Book* and another in Latin from the so-called *Book of Cerne,* have been canvassed as constituting evidence of 'drama in the service of religion' as early as the

ninth century, but while these pieces superficially resemble play texts, there is not the slightest hint that they were ever presented before an audience, and their claim on our attention must be marginal.

Indeed, the whole question of whether material closely associated with the Roman Catholic liturgy (like the Easter practice already cited) can legitimately be annexed for the theatre involves the whole issue of medieval dramatic perception. Much hinges on the significance attached to any religious activity that consists of or incorporates imitative action, for many observers a key feature in drama. Clearly the priest celebrating Mass is not play-acting when he repeats certain of Christ's reported words at the Last Supper or utilises gesture in blessing the bread and pouring the wine, but advocates argue that if participation in a religious ceremony calls for one to display the presumed behaviour or to repeat the imagined actions of another without acknowledging the fact, then one may be said to be engaging in a form of impersonation, and this activity may be reckoned dramatic.

Others, notably O. B. Hardison Jr [in *Christian Rite and Christian Drama in the Middle Ages,* 1965], claim that to insist on imitation or impersonation as essential to medieval drama (whether staged inside or outside a church) is to invoke an outdated principle of naturalistic theatre where a play is expected to present spectators with an experience intended to convey the illusion of actuality passing before their eyes. Such a concept of theatre has in recent years been complemented by a revival of the notion that the essence of drama is not to imitate life, but rather to present a heightened sensation whose aesthetic premise lies in *transcending* strict verisimilitude, 'piercing the veil' of actuality so that what is done intensifies what we see or feel. It is said that no early performer would have been conscious of the need to identify with another human being, although late antique or medieval mime artists (such as Vitalis, whose epitaph alludes to his powers of mimicry) specialised in a form of illusionism. Some feel, however, that just as the priest at the altar does not 'play the part' of Christ when celebrating Mass, so a medieval player would not be required to impersonate the figure he was called on to represent or stand in for, and that elementary histrionics involved a different process. Others maintain that while medieval performance may have involved a more limited form of self-camouflage, when a participant in church ceremony is instructed to change his customary vestments or to conduct himself in an unwonted manner, we encounter what most of us would recognise as true drama.

Another objection to the standard account of the genesis of medieval church-theatre is that it is invidious to single out a single ceremony as being dramatic, since to the contemporary mind all worship could be deemed dramatic in character, not least the rite of the Mass, which was written of in terms of a divine drama by Amalarius of Metz prior to 850. Furthermore, it is clear that the *Visitatio* has been made to appear more like an embryonic play than it truly is by such editors as Karl Young [in *The Drama of the Medieval Church,* 1933], through the use of typographical devices which misrepresent the original context, and therefore preempt our response to it. Moreover, can a combination of a sung text and a series of ritual actions be truly regarded as forming a play, when it is nowhere alluded to us as constituting one and we possess no evidence to suggest that at its inception it was perceived as something separable from the remainder of the liturgy? Perhaps not, yet the dominant belief among scholars still remains that by bringing together within the framework of Christian worship a pre-created literary and musical text and the adaptation of pre-existing ceremonial actions, clerics created the first piece of medieval religious theatre.

That the earliest surviving example of a so-called liturgical drama is British in origin is no more than accidental, since the Easter routine was almost certainly developed originally on the continent, and imported to England. Its first appearance in an English document results from the initiative of the saintly Bishop of Winchester, Æthelwold, in attempting to bring a degree of conformity to the practices and conduct of members of the Benedictine order in about 965-75. A group of senior ecclesiastics, by drawing up a consuetudinary, a manual of customs and usages to be observed in monastic houses, entitled the *Regularis Concordia* or, more fully, *The Monastic Agreement of the Monks and Nuns of the English Nation,* laid down a code of observances and regulations in order to standardise such matters. The ceremony to which so much attention has been devoted was one of many projected, but because of its theatrical significance the *Visitatio Sepulchri* has too often been discussed out of context, arguably weakening its position as a proto-drama.

Among its many instructions the *Regularis Concordia* recommends that the proposed ritual, no doubt already in use in many churches, could be presented if so desired in the course of the Nocturn or Matins service held on Easter morning immediately after the first Mass of Easter Day. Its chanted text, adopted from a common liturgical embellishment or decoration known as a trope, was conceived in this instance as a short exchange of dialogue between a monk representing the angel at the empty tomb on Easter Day and three other monastic brethren standing in for the three Maries arriving at dawn to anoint Christ's dead body. The brothers enacting the roles of the women were instructed to wear copes (not customarily worn at this service) and to carry incense thuribles to represent the precious ointments. They were also advised to advance down the nave of the church 'in a hesitant manner as if seeking something'; as they neared the altar, the angel was to accost them and enquire what it was they sought, by chanting the Latin words 'Quem quaeritis in sepulchro, o Christicolae?' (Who are you seeking in the tomb, o dwellers in Christ?). The ensuing sung dialogue between angels and Maries taken from the trope revealed the fact that Christ had risen from the dead, and that the news should be shared with his followers. General rejoicing among the brethren was to culminate in the ringing of the abbey bells and the resumption of the regular office of Easter Matins.

Admittedly, the 'dramatic' portion of this service is not differentiated from the residue, and there is nothing in the *Regularis Concordia* to indicate that those sanctioning the celebration of the *Visitatio* were aware that they were consciously pioneering a new mode of stimulating devotional piety, apart from a rubric that speaks of the ceremony being introduced for the purpose of 'strengthening the faith of the neophytes' [novices to the order]. Yet sufficient indications of a limited concept of performance appear for many to feel that the *Visitatio* must be seen as a prototype religious play, albeit concealed in a document primarily addressed to issues other than the encouragement of dramatics in the monastic churches of the Benedictine order.

Whatever label we attach to the *Visitatio,* its blend of sung words and ceremonial actions initiated a period of artistic inventiveness in the eleventh and twelfth centuries which saw the creation of a vast repertoire of liturgical pieces, the majority of which are reproduced in Young. Ceremonies linked with Christmas and Epiphany came to join the Easter play, whose action was often extended backwards to form a Passion sequence; this involved the introduction of fresh characters and the elaboration of its dialogue. Gospel material was supplemented with the treatment of Old Testament matter: one of the finest of the liturgical plays is the *Ludus Danielis* (The Play of Daniel), composed and performed at the cathedral choir school in Beauvais in about 1180.

Although the best of such Latin plays with music are now mainly associated with continental centres, they range from Sicily to Dublin to Poland, and Britain once possessed a store of such pieces intended for church performance on feast days. Records confirm that Durham, York, Beverley, Lincoln, Lichfield, Norwich, Salisbury and Wells all had their liturgical repertoires: in 1150 Laurentius, Prior of Durham, composed a *Peregrinus,* now lost, commemorating, like many kindred pieces, Christ's post-Resurrection encounter with two disciples on the road to Emmaus. The most important texts from England to survive are the so-called 'Shrewsbury Fragments', actually originating in the Lichfield diocese and consisting of extracts from three scriptural plays. The 'fragments' are in fact copies of the lines assigned to the Third Shepherd, the Third Mary and the disciple Cleophas, in a Nativity, a Resurrection and a *Peregrinus* respectively, with appropriate cues and some music. The language is sometimes Latin, sometimes English, and the Shepherds' Play or *Pastores* bears some relationship to the comparable English play in the vernacular York cycle. Though these texts are of late date, during the episcopate of Hugh of Nonant (1188-98) Lichfield was (perhaps coincidentally) the venue for presentations on the three themes covered by the 'fragments'.

Such dramas of devotion were conceived of as aids to worship, not as vehicles of evangelism. A preface to one of the liturgical ceremonies devised by Lady Katherine of Sutton for use in the Essex nunnery of Barking in the mid-fourteenth century confirms that the aim was to strengthen and stimulate faith among those already initiated into the mysteries, Lady Katherine being spoken of as wishing to eradicate spiritual torpor and 'to excite the ardour of the faithful more intensely' towards the Easter celebrations. Her invention was clearly slanted towards the dramatic: of one ceremony we learn that she and her nuns had themselves shut into their chapel to assume the role of the Old Testament patriarchs confined to hell while awaiting delivery from Satan's bondage by Christ; a priest striking the doors with the words 'Lift up your heads, o ye gates!' represented the figure of the Messiah releasing the captive souls and leading them forth in triumph bearing palms and candles. It is hard to deny such graphic symbolism the status of theatre.

These and other rituals suggest that the Church frequently found the drama latent in the faith it professed so compelling as to require its realisation in action, but it must be emphasised that this was a form of theatre designed to confirm the devout in their beliefs and intended as an occasional augmentation of the functions of the divine offices, rather than as carrying the Church's doctrinal message to the people. Earlier in their history scholars were happy to accept that the liturgical music-dramas served as the precursors and progenitors of those religious plays in the European vernaculars that emerged in the twelfth century, and that they shared with them a common aesthetic and didactic purpose. In the last few decades many (though not all) commentators have come to believe that the spirit and conventions of the two styles of drama differed so profoundly that the genesis and development of the vernacular plays owed little debt to the Church's presentations. The Latin performances that surfaced from the divine offices were governed by the conventions of their place of origin; the vernacular plays were broader and more populist in their appeal, more daring in their assumptions and techniques for attracting attention from those more easily distracted by worldly concerns than monks and nuns. Indeed, the 'new wave' of religious playmaking was probably more dependent on the prevailing forms and traditions of secular drama than on the stiffer, more restrained and esoteric conventions of the Latin church dramas it came to complement. At the same time Rosemary Woolf [in *The English Mystery Plays,* 1972] may be correct in saying that the liturgical plays remained 'an abiding authoritative model' for the authors of the great sequences of scriptural dramas which are such a dominating feature of the theatrical literature of late medieval France, Germany and Britain.

. . . . .

The Drama of Salvaton

By far the great majority of plays in the existing medieval repertoire are devoted to religious purposes and primarily brought into being to render the salient truths of the Christian faith graphic and compelling for those unable to read the scriptures for themselves, even if the better-educated were not excluded from attending. It has become traditional to characterise the principal types of plays as Corpus Christi or craft cycles, moralities and moral interludes, saint plays, miracle plays and so on, but recent studies stress that such classifications are in many respects arbitrary, and can obscure interrelations of theme and character, or the wide range of elements within a single piece, and similarities of staging that cut across generic boundaries. For example, both *The Castle of Perseverance* and *Everyman* are styled moralities, yet one is built on an epic scale, the other almost frugally. Techniques employed in the so-called 'saint play' of *Mary Magdalen* have much in common with those employed in the cycles, yet the strong infusion of allegorical types aligns it with the morality form. Like many labels attached to literary genres for convenience's sake, those applied to the main forms of medieval play constitute no more than a set of rough-and-ready divisions. The plays' shared evangelising purposes should never be ignored: their authors' primary business was to instruct the populace in those truths essential for their salvation by rendering them accessible, and to alert men and women to the cosmic battles being waged over the fate of their own immortal and individual souls.

No single explanation can account for the rise and development of drama in the chief European vernaculars from the middle of the twelfth century onwards. The earliest text to use a popular tongue systematically is the *Sponsus* (c. 1150), a mainly Latin liturgical drama treating of the five wise and five foolish virgins of Matthew's Gospel, which employs the Provencal *langue d'oc* for certain portions of its sung dialogue. The inclusion of the demotic strand doubtless stems from an aesthetic desire for stylistic variation rather than to a wish to enlighten the laity, since it is only the foolish virgins who sing lines in the vernacular. Similarly, the Latin Passion play from Benediktbeuern (c. 1250) has a striking sequence in German in which Mary Magdalene leads a dancing chorus of girls on a shopping expedition to buy rouge and other allurements, a sequence which may owe something to secular convention.

However, the existence of French versions of certain stanzas in an Easter play from Origny-Saint-Benoîte (*c.* 1284) may reflect a different spirit, and an evangelising motive may well have underlain the composition of what appears to be the first religious drama entirely in a vernacular tongue, a unique but probably incomplete Old Castilian text entitled the *Auto de los Reyes Magos* (The Play of the Magi Kings), dating from *c.* 1155. Apparently standing independent of the liturgy, this *auto* was probably written for presentation in Toledo Cathedral during Epiphany. Almost contemporary with it is an astonishingly accomplished play in Norman French, the Ordo *representationis Ade* or *Le jeu d'Adam,* made up of a sequence of several Old Testament episodes, consisting of the creation and fall, the murder of Abel and the Messianic prophecies, an integrated vernacular sequence interspersed with liturgical chants taken from the office of Matins for Septuagesima and from other sacred texts including the Vulgate. Much interest has been generated by this most sophisticated piece, and its sequential development has led to speculation as to the origins of the accretive tendencies in medieval religious playmaking. Its inventive characterisations, and its psychological and theatrical deftness are undeniable, and suggest an established tradition of vernacular composition in existence by *c.* 1170. The fact that *Adam* is couched in Norman French postulates the presence of a lay rather than a clerical audience, for whose benefit the French scenes were devised to gloss the chanted readings and responses from the Latin. Its exact venue is keenly disputed, but performance for the benefit of the laity would suggest an open space outside a place of worship, though indoor presentation also has its strong advocates. Certainly *Adam* anticipates much of the energetic demotic appeal of the later cyclic drama, and its techniques are assured; associated with it is an unfinished and less remarkable Anglo-Norman piece of roughly comparable date, *La Seinte Resureccion,* which focuses on Christ's burial and restoration from the dead, and contains an interesting prologue on the suggested manner of staging the action, possibly at set locations established inside a church building, although its liturgical links are few.

The emergence of such pieces in the main European tongues precedes a great upsurge in the composition of religious drama in French, German, Italian, English, Dutch and Spanish during succeeding centuries, a phenomenon which has sent theatre historians in pursuit of a common explanation for it, but without complete success. Undoubtedly, the rise of vernacular drama could scarcely have taken place without that vital shift in spiritual sensibility that gave prominence to Christ's assumption of human form, an emphasis found as early as St Anselm's treatise on the Incarnation, *Cur Deus Homo?* (Why did God become Man?) of *c.* 1097. It seems unquestionable that the theological and devotional implications of this fresh assertion of Christ's significance as the type of vulnerable and suffering humanity acted as a powerful stimulant to religious thought and artistic creativity during the twelfth century. But it has also become customary in recent years to place equal emphasis on the emergence, from the conflicts besetting the twelfth-century Church, of the fraternal Orders of St Francis and St Dominic, in 1210 and 1215 respectively, and the missionary zeal of their members in expounding the message of personal salvation to the lay individual may well hold the key to the production of religious plays written in tongues accessible to the illiterate. By going out into the community and preaching the gospel of salvation though Christ to ordinary men and women, the Dominicans and Franciscans were perhaps establishing unawares a potential audience for popular Christian dramas in the vernacular.

Most scholars accept that these plays were inspired by different factors from those governing the growth of drama created from the ceremonies and discourse of church worship. Intended to divert as well as edify and instruct the laity, vernacular religious drama adopted many techniques associated with profane theatre in order to win acceptance for its doctrinal content. Characterisation had to be broad and arresting, dialogue racy, earthy and often declamatory, comedy prominent and often scabrous, though its didactic potential was also recognised, and frequently exploited. Such plays were not conceived as regulated aids to devotion or as serving the ulterior aims of formal worship, but rather as vehicles designed to bring home to the people their spiritual potentialities and responsibilities, and there is general agreement that the vernacular plays display a separate and distinct mode of aesthetic perception from that enshrined in the Latin music-dramas. There now seems little justification for the long-promoted view that the Church's dramas were expelled into the street and the market-place because of their disreputable populist tendencies. The impulse and spirit behind the two forms of medieval scriptural play seem too dissimilar to sustain the notion that the sacred material became 'secularised' and hence downgraded to become a popular form of entertainment of which the Church disapproved. Indeed, it is possible that the plays came into being in England to combat those unauthorised *miracula* to which the ecclesiastical hierarchy objected: rather than have sacred truths set forth by junior clerics in masks, the Church may have agreed to encourage worthier representations, and so have inspired the cycle plays for which it may have shared responsibility with the trade guilds.

It has been common to attach a good deal of importance to the institution of the feast of Corpus Christi during the fourteenth century as stimulating the growth of popular religious theatre. This festival, inaugurated as a thanksgiving for Christ's gift of his body on the cross and in the Eucharist for the benefit of humankind, was introduced into the Church calendar in 1311; its observance rapidly became a highpoint in the religious year, being celebrated in early summer with a street procession of clergy and lay dignitaries behind the Communion Host. At some centres, particularly in Spain, it became the custom for the townsfolk to dress in biblical costume as they accompanied the parade through the city, and then to organise a series of static tableaux on floats to form an integral part of the procession. It is at least plausible that these tableaux or pageants formed the excuse for the development of short dialogues which suitably expanded became the cycle, mystery or miracle plays associated in many countries with the Feast of Corpus Christi.

However, this explanation of the evolution of the genre must be treated cautiously, since it cannot account for the genesis of every scriptural sequence known to us. *Le jeu d'Adam* clearly pre-dates the establishment of Corpus Christi and was a winter play; the lengthy series of Creation and Passion performances by the clerks of London, recorded between 1390 and 1411, do not appear to be associated with the feast day either. At some centres Corpus Christi was not celebrated with a *sequence* of plays but with merely a single episode, nor was every sequence presented a scriptural one: Alexandra Johnston has recently argued that the plays performed at Coventry (of which two now remain) probably formed a work based on the Apostolic Creed rather than on the Old and New Testaments; even at York, where we know a Corpus Christi cycle took place, a Creed play was substituted every tenth year. Nor can we be certain, even where records state that a 'play' was presented, that it implies more than a series of tableaux touring the town streets with no human involvement by way of actors and dialogue. Not every acted sequence was performed at Corpus Christi either: the Chester cycle, for example, was played on the three days following Whitsunday. However, its origins doubtless lie in a Corpus Christi presentation, though at first this may have been set forth at a single site, rather than in processional form.

It is also interesting that none of the extant English cycles places conspicuous emphasis on the inauguration of the Mass at the Last Supper, as one might have expected if the Corpus Christi celebrations alone had stimulated the creation of dramatic pageants associated with the feast. Of course we do not need to seek one exclusive explanation for the cyclic impulse, but since in many European centres the form is closely akin to the British type, the method of serial accretion of episodes must be felt to transcend any pattern developed solely in association with the Corpus Christi parades. Moreover, the progress from Creation to Doomsday peculiarly characteristic of the English cycles is not reproduced abroad. Some continental offerings consist of a multiplicity of scenes with a staggering overall impact, but they nevertheless fail to embrace the whole of humanity's spiritual history as the English plays do.

In France and Germany the harvest is particularly rich: in Spain vernacular religious drama developed late, and even in the fifteenth and sixteenth centuries Easter and Christmas plays relied heavily on liturgical tradition. The earliest dramatic text dates from Mallorca in 1442, and a codex of forty-nine plays is associated with staging in Palma Cathedral. However, the largest group of biblical plays derives from pageants associated with Corpus Christi and involving the trade guilds of various cities including Valencia, Madrid, Salamanca, Seville and Toledo, though whether they presented stage plays or merely mounted tableaux and dumbshows is often unclear. In Italy the roots of vernacular drama can be traced to the *laudi* first created by the flagellants of Umbria in the latter half of the thirteenth century, such hymns of adoration often assuming a semi-dramatic form. Costumed impersonation led on to drama proper, and by 1400 spoken plays were common, paving the way to the splendidly spectacular *sacre rappresentazioni* of the fifteenth century, some hundred texts of which survive, all originating in Florence, home of the most elaborate performances. In 1454 a cycle of Old and New Testament plays required the erection of twenty-two *edifizi,* each representing a separate location; processional dramas on floats featured in the annual Feast of St John the Baptist. Passion plays were also popular, one being staged annually in Rome's Coliseum from 1460 to 1539, another at Revello in the Italian Alps in 1494.

The Passion play was also a favourite form in German-speaking countries, along with the Corpus Christi plays or *Fronleichnamspiele,* the earliest of which dates from 1391 and comes from Innsbruk. Another from Künzelsau in Württemberg was presented at least between 1479 and 1522, and other examples occur at Freiburg and Ingolstadt. These plays, like the Chester and York cycles, were presented processionally along a defined route, although tableaux probably alternated with staged scenes. By contrast, Passion plays seem to have been mounted within a confined area, as at Alsfeld in 1501, at Frankfurt and Villingen later in the century, and, above all, at Lucerne as late as 1583 and 1597, where detailed stage plans of the local Weinmarkt given over to the performances have proved an invaluable source of information on the principles of late medieval place-and-scaffold staging.

But pride of place must go to France, where Jean

Bodel's early thirteenth-century *Jeu de St Nicolas* and Rutebeuf's *Miracle de Théophile* (*c.* 1260) anticipate the creation of forty miracle plays presented by the Parisian guild of Goldsmiths in the mid-fourteenth century and known as the *Miracles de Nostre Dame par personnages,* in which sensational incidents and effects serve the ends of salvationist doctrine. Equally lurid in many cases are the *mystères* drawn from the lives of eminent saints, which in many instances involve the depiction of grisly tortures inflicted on martyrs and offer a gloss on William Fitzstephen's commendation of London's religious drama in around 1170. The vogue in France for hagiographic plays endured into the sixteenth century, one of the best-known being the *Mystère des trois doms,* a large-scale production of which was staged at Romans in 1509 as a civic thank-offering for delivery from the plague.

Some of France's scriptural dramas are monumental in their scope, and although their ostensible subject matter is Christ's Passion, they in fact incorporate not only scenes from Christ's earlier life but incidents from the Old Testament, too. The earliest specimens of the form are the *Passion du Palatinus* and the Ste Geneviève *Passion de Nostre Seigneur,* relatively modest texts of 2,000 and 4,500 lines respectively, but in 1420-30 appears Eustache Marcadé's somewhat sombre and prolix *Passion d'Angers,* some 25,000 lines long, and around 1450 appears its more inventive and versatile successor, Arnoul Gréban's *Mystère de la Passion,* containing roughly 35,000 lines. Indebted in large measure to Gréban is Jean Michel's *Passion* played at Angers around 1486, and on later occasions compilations were assembled which combined the best of Gréban and Michel with material from *Le Mystère du Viel Testament,* one particularly well-documented production being recorded at Mons in 1501. Other mammoth sequences included *Les Actes des Apôtres,* an immense epic by Simon Gréban of almost 62,000 lines, which interweaves apostolic activity with a vast tapestry of world events; mounted in a former Roman amphitheatre at Bourges in 1536, its presentation lasted a marathon forty days. By comparison, even the forty-eight pageants of the York cycle or the three-day spectacle presented at Chester seem modest ventures; if Britain saw similar stagings of the martyrdoms of the saints or the acts of the apostles, no traces survive.

Fragments of prologues to two lost plays form the prelude to religious drama in the English language. One, the so-called 'Cambridge Prologue' (*c.* 1300) portrays the messenger of a pagan emperor calling for silence so that the action can begin; the passage appears first in Anglo-Norman and then in English couplets. In the slightly later 'Rickinghall Fragment' from the Bury St Edmunds area, a pagan king summons his barons and vassals to his presence, also in two languages. The bilingual versions of both prologues have suggested a mixed audience of *hoi polloi* and governing class, but Lynette Muir has recently argued that they are a writer's trial-runs for alternative renderings of the speeches, the Frenchified version intended to characterise an exotic court, much as the Chester cycle creates an alien environment for Herod and the Emperor of Rome. The prologues may form part therefore of early religious plays, possibly ones blessed by the Church, but perhaps the unauthorised *miracula* generally deplored (85; 33, pp. 59-60).

Similar circumstances may have attended performances of the earliest English Christian drama to survive in more than fragmentary form; although *The Pride of Life* (*c.* 1350) is incomplete, its prologue and text characterise the action fully enough for us to perceive that its main strength lies in the vividness with which its doctrinal impact is realised. The boastful King Life (Rex Vivus) challenging Death in single combat is a powerful personification, and the play has some claim to be the forerunner of those notable fifteenth-century morality pieces that emphasise the effects of yielding to sinful temptation in a context of graphically delineated allegorical creations. *The Pride of Life* appears to have clear affinities with the later French *moralités,* of which some seventy survive, but the intervention of the Virgin to intercede for Rex Vivus recalls rather the *Miracles de Nostre Dame.* Relevant in this context are the plays of the Dutch Rhetoricians or *Rederijkers,* the *Spele van sinnen,* whose didactic function is also complemented by lively theatricality, and of which *Elckerlijc,* from which the English *Everyman* derives, is only one (albeit the best) example. In Rex Vivus too we find yet another instance of the arrogant stage tyrant, a figure whose discomfiture anticipates the fate of countless subsequent dramatic monarchs, not excluding the Herods, Pharaohs and Pilates of the cycle dramas.

. . .The first of the great panoramic surveys of biblical and eschatological events appears in Britain in about 1375, and is cast in the Cornish tongue. We cannot be certain at what point during the fourteenth century episodes ultimately to be incorporated into the cycle sequences began to be dramatised at other centres, but the Cornish *Ordinalia* probably includes the most ancient scripts to survive from a British source, although some would argue that the *Lieu d'Adam* should be regarded as a proto-sequence, and that its birthplace may well be somewhere in the south of England rather than in Northern France. However, it is irrefutable that documentary evidence for the preparation of biblical 'pageants' (whatever these involved, and their existence does not imply that they featured human elements) appears from about 1375 onwards in many English and Scottish cities and towns. For example, a 'pagine' is alluded to at York in 1376, and another at Beverley in the following year, though in neither case dare we deduce that the presence of 'pageants' means that acted dramas or mimed or static tableaux were being mounted on or within them, or that they were necessarily paraded through the streets, though this is the obvious inference. Certainly far fewer texts of plays survive than records of their performance, and many of our deductions concerning the cycles in general have to rely on scripts which may unfortunately be atypical of the genre as a whole. The greater part of the cyclic repertoire that survives in written form consists therefore of virtually complete works from the cities of York and Chester, a full sequence from the town of Wakefield (though not every scholar is happy with the ascription) and a composite text, somewhat imperfectly coordinated, associated with Bury St Edmunds or perhaps some other East Anglian locale (Thetford is suggested by Alan Fletcher below) and generally known by most scholars as the N-Town plays. This curious title stems from a reference in its trailer or 'banns' attached to the text, which indicates that a peripatetic company presented the play or more probably parts of it at sites of their choice within a finite region. Although it is the four major sequences which, along with the Cornish cycle, have received the lion's share of recent critical attention, the existence of isolated plays and fragments of pieces from Coventry, Norwich, Newcastle-on-Tyne, Northampton, and Brome in Suffolk indicates the widespread distribution of a popular type of dramatic offering.

At what point in their development the cycle texts came to take the form that they manifest today is difficult to establish, given the lack of sufficient intermediary versions, but there seems to have been a general increase in situational and verbal elaboration. Composition was of course continuous and spread over perhaps decades, involving constant revisions from radical rewriting to a process of minor modifications. Although major alterations were carried out on specific occasions—the distinctive contributions of the so-called 'Wakefield Master' must have considerably transmuted the flavour of that particular sequence—in general change was less drastic, and individual authors did not stamp their literary personalities too indelibly on the dramatic totality. It is impossible to gauge exactly what factors loomed largest in the minds of the revisers when changes were executed, but with increasing popularity and more regular presentation, those responsible for the plays' contents would have needed to adapt and develop their artistry in order to set forth the truths of Sacred Writ in pleasing, worthy and illuminating ways. Shifts in religious tastes and doctrinal preoccupations, organisational changes within the administrative structure of a particular community, public demand, the desire for novelty, even competition with other centres, may all have played a role in determining textual extensions or excisions. Sadly, the extant texts offer the scholar little assistance in determining the processes by which they came to read as they do today.

The plays' authorship has recently come under renewed scrutiny. That the anonymous dramatists were clerks in at least minor orders and more probably fully-fledged ecclesiastics has for a long time been regarded as virtually axiomatic. It is certainly clear that within broad limits the religious authorities of the late Middle Ages bestowed their blessing on the artistic aspirations of the various guilds and craft associations sponsoring the performance of Christian drama. Indeed, if the Church endorsed the cycle presentations in order to combat the less reputable *miracula,* its cooperation in providing scripts which contained nothing inimical to the transmission of God's message of salvation would seem a natural corollary. But Lawrence Clopper has pointed out [in "Lay and Clerical Impact on Civic Religious Drama and Ceremony," in *Contexts for Early English Drama,* 1989] that documentary support for clerical involvement in the cycles, as either authors or participants, has so far not been forthcoming, and that in our present state of knowledge the most likely creators of the sequences appear to be the laity. Nevertheless, it is reasonable to ask whether the needful literary skills and exegetical know-how were to be readily discovered within the secular community. The question will remain profoundly significant for future investigators.

Whatever the circumstances of their composition, whoever ultimately prove to be their creators, what must come as something of a shock initially is the nature of the cycle texts. Despite their subject matter and their scriptural and liturgical heritage, the plays in general demonstrate few of those qualities we might anticipate would be the hallmarks of reverential authorship. Whoever wrote the cycles (and we must be discussing the work of scores of writers) certainly appear to have been subject to few restraints when it came to devising methods of appealing to a broad spectrum of the medieval public. While the didactic task is not shirked and the implantation of doctrinal enlightenment not resisted, these texts should be regarded as essentially exercises in popularising what the medieval mind perceived as constituting the truths necessary for human survival in this world and the next, and no literary or theatrical strategies are deemed too downmarket in their associations to be rejected. Even where the faint patterns of liturgical discourse are still detectable, there is a demotic orientation which overrides the routines of organised worship. Elsewhere characterisation is forceful and immediate in its effect, even the virtuous being endowed with a welcome robustness of utterance, which though occasionally strident in its own defence, has the effect of rendering goodness palatable. The vicious may lack subtlety, but their overt defiance of God's will renders them comic as well as sinister, and they stand out as graphic emblems of the human perversions of which evil is capable. There is little hesitation shown in deriding those authoritarian figures—emperors, kings, prelates, governors—who set themselves up in opposition to the

Supreme Being or who seek to resist its mandate: the period's predisposition towards civic and social dissension is latent in the merciless satirisation of those whose conduct fails to match their status.

Similarly the dialogue, almost exclusively cast in rhymed stanzaic verse, is frequently concrete, pithy and colloquial, with no concessions made to a fallacious concept of decorum. These were plays for the public forum; they had to declare both openly and tacitly their affinities with the life of the market-place, the backstreet, the farmyard, and the language, both verbal and visual, had to convince onlookers that the men and women of the Bible looked, and, even more importantly, spoke as they did themselves. The admixture of popular saws and common images, of oaths and obscenities, of references to bodily functions, was not introduced as a colourful insertion of realism: they were part of the deliberate tactics employed to command not merely attention, but assent.

The manner in which the plays of the period exploit and transcend their conditions of presentation must never be taken for granted. What many recent analyses confirm is that their staging techniques, like their literary tactics, are consciously geared to the problems of attracting a mass audience and retaining its interest. Their authors' understanding of what popular taste will accept is usually, though not invariably, impeccable, and the unsentimental and unhectoring presentation of the Christian account of history can still command respect, even from those who do not endorse its doctrines.

At the same time we must be aware of treating the whole of this rich yet diverse material as if it constituted a homogeneous mass. Despite the clear affinities of purpose, method and impact of all the cyclic dramas, each has its own individual nature, and recent scholarship and criticism have combined to demonstrate beyond all question that each sequence has its own individualising traits which stand out by contrast with what is current elsewhere. Whether this tendency results from editorial activity late in the cycles' evolution (as would seem to be the case with the Chester plays), or whether the idiosyncrasies are inherent in the materials of which the sequences are made or in the approach adopted (which may be the case with N-Town), it is vital to remember that local differences are essential to the understanding of each individual series and must be respected in any future research into its textual and theatrical character.

. . . . .

The State of Play

On one level at least it is hard to fathom the appeal that the English medieval theatre appears to have for today's readers and spectators. Religious if not devotional in essence, most of what survives was written to serve the doctrinal and propagandist aims of a faith which ceased to be that of the majority of the British people over four centuries ago. Even among practising Christians now, the theological premises on which most medieval dramas rest are unlikely to command total assent. Yet all the evidence suggests that the repertoire can still stimulate a measure of interest and response that transcends the dutiful reactions of classroom and lecture hall, and meets some contemporary need which other stimuli fail to reach.

Several explanations for this phenomenon deserve consideration. Despite the heterodoxy and even the unbelief of the public at large, a vaguely Christian heritage is still something the majority of us share, if reluctantly, even if it amounts to no more than observing Christmas and Easter and being conscious of the rich legacy of churches and cathedrals which impinges on us at salient moments in our national and domestic existences. As we contemplate medieval plays on stage it may be that 'an age more spiritual than ours' is fleetingly restored to us, and a sense of shared confidence in a caring God and mutual values is briefly ours once again. Moreover, since the Second World War and the blurring of cultural distinctions not only between countries but between continents as the concept of the 'global village' takes hold, the British have become fiercely possessive of their national past as successive phases of the Coca-Cola culture have threatened to overwhelm them. Despite their close links with analogous continental dramas, ironically it is frequently the 'Englishness' of the cycle plays in particular which has been extolled as part of our legendary historical distinction, and which has in turn contributed to the effort to recover some awareness of a lost national identity.

In addition, one cannot fail to be aware of the role played in all this by a lost sense of *local* identity. It becomes clearer year by year that the regional affinities of the major medieval dramas are a central aspect of their success, both in their terms as well as in our own. If there has been one contemporary contribution to a fuller appreciation of medieval drama which deserves special commendation, it is the increasing realisation that for a true understanding of the texts and staging of the cycles and moralities, consideration of all those factors peculiar to a particular dramatic locality is paramount. Here the *REED* project is of major significance, providing as it will all the evidence available to modern systematic researchers, in order to assist our efforts to perceive how local conditions, resources, influences, preferences and prejudices helped to shape the dramatic experiences of which the extant scripts can provide us with only pallid reflections.

In this context a number of recent publications possess

considerable importance, not least the recent crop of freshly-edited texts of the main items in the medieval repertoire, which have increased awareness of the physical nature of the various manuscripts and their contents. For example, the Chester play manuscripts, once felt to preserve the earliest forms of the cycle sequences, have now been shown to contain a very late version of the cycle, because of, rather than in spite of, its direct diction, the regularity and simplicity of its metrical patterns, its placid, even inhibited register. Its most recent editors have demonstrated that Chester's tightly-organised unity probably results from the editorial labours of a single redactor. A similar figure appears to have been responsible for the textual complexities of the N-Town pageants, in that he was attempting to create a composite group of plays from a number of disparate texts. Into a sequence of a traditional scriptural type he wove episodes from a play on the life of the Virgin and an independent two-part Passion sequence. Here again local conditions may have been a factor in initiating this attempt to create a new whole from pre-existing parts. The latest edition of the York plays has also added considerably to our appreciation of medieval methods of dramatic composition and selection; unlike the Chester cycle, the York plays cannot be discussed as examples of cohesive wholes created according to conscious artistic principles, nor yet have they been assembled from heterogeneous sources as is the case with N-Town. What their modern editor suggests is that, while a whole series of episodes may have been transcribed into the master-copy (the Register), not every single piece was necessarily presented on each annual occasion on which performances were called for. Moreover, the plays' texts could clearly undergo considerable modification from one year's presentation to the next: the script should not be regarded as a static, unvariable specimen pinned to the page for all time, a point reinforced by recent textual scholarship in the Shakespearean field. The fluidity of early dramatic texts is something that the late twentieth century is only now starting to take into account.

Some of the major work on the genesis and evolution of texts has been devoted to the Wakefield or Towneley plays (Towneley being the name of the family in whose possession the manuscript resided for many years). Part of the reason for this is that the most distinguished dramatic achievements among all the cycle plays are arguably those of the so-called 'Wakefield Master', though here John Gardner has probably erred in his helpful book on the construction of the sequence [*The Construction of the Wakefield Cycle,* 1974] by trying to demonstrate that this charismatic figure sought to impose unity on the cycle as a totality. The quality of the Master's acknowledged work has made it the subject of frequent critical scrutiny, and the praise now bestowed on the general level of artistry and sophistication exhibited by medieval playwrights is in large

measure an extension of the admiration rarely withheld from the author of *The Second Shepherds' Play.*

A welcome feature of modern scholarship in this area is that staging is no longer viewed as an irrelevant or distracting aspect of the serious study of medieval dramatic literature. Regarding both Chester and York, much attention has been devoted to processional staging, which may have developed at the former centre with the transfer of the annual performances from Corpus Christi to Whitsun week. Here discussion has focused in part on Archdeacon Rogers's early seventeenth-century accounts of the plays, and the degree of reliance that can be placed on them. The York records too have generated a long and sadly inconclusive controversy relating to the feasibility of staging the lengthy series of civic pageants at a number of fixed stations along a processional route within the compass of even the longest summer's day. Various solutions have been propounded, but despite the exercise of much ingenuity and the discovery and dissemination of much valuable data, an agreed picture has so far not emerged, though most would now accept that the York performances were processional, that plays were acted at all twelve stations. Whether every play available for presentation was seen at every station on every occasion is another matter. Even here regional diversity must be stressed: the Wakefield plays may well have been staged at a single location using place-and-scaffold methods, and the same mode may well have been the norm for the N-Town sequence, even in its peripatetic form.

Certainly in stage terms techniques employed by medieval playwrights no longer seem as alien to us as would have been the case when the naturalistic methods perfected in the late nineteenth century governed assumptions concerning the proper social milieux, narrative content, scenic backgrounds, character psychology and linguistic register appropriate to drama. Successive waves of revolutionary change in the modern theatre, ranging from poetic symbolism and expressionism to concepts of 'the epic' and 'the absurd', have eroded the bulwarks of illusionism, and pre-Renaissance theatre with its unconscious but manifest rejection of naturalistic stage practices has in recent decades seemed so often to be at the forefront of the *avant garde* that we feel more at home with bare stages and token or makeshift scenery than in the ballrooms and sitting-rooms and waiting-rooms of Ibsen or Wilde or Shaw. The apparent processes of democratisation in British society over the last fifty years have also played a part by making us feel obliged to identify more readily with workmen and peasants than with duchesses or mill owners, though the empathetic procedures may in reality be equally spurious.

Finally, we live in an age increasingly attuned to the visual and preferably the pictorial. One of the most

Pageant vehicle.

significant advances in medieval theatre research since the 1950s has been the exploration of the multiple relationships to be traced between Gothic iconography of every kind and the *mise-en-scène* of dramatic entertainments. While being careful to treat questions of chronological priority with caution, thus avoiding the notion that artists merely copied what they saw mounted on pageant wagons or that devisers of pageants could only imitate existing art works, the leading investigators have alerted us to the undeniable fact that drama and the graphic and plastic arts were constantly drawing on a common cultural and iconographical pool while sharing countless basic assumptions about the function, interpretation and value of the visual image. To be reminded that in stained-glass window and misericord, in roof boss and richly-embroidered vestments medieval playwrights had ready access to a remarkable source of pictorial analogies to what they were seeking to bring to life on stage, is to recall once more that the drama they created was an integral part of the vibrant life of its times.

THE NATURE OF DRAMATIC PERFORMANCES

Katharine Lee Bates (essay date 1893)

SOURCE: "Miracle Plays—Description," in *The English Religious Drama*, The Macmillan Company, 1913, pp. 35-87.

[*In the following essay—originally a lecture delivered in July, 1893—Bates describes the nature of dramatic performance in the medieval community, noting the role of the guilds in the production of the miracle plays and interpretive variations in French, English, and German performances of the plays.*]

The Miracle Play was the training-school of the romantic drama. In England, during the slow lapse of some five centuries, the Miracle, with its tremendous theme and mighty religious passion, was preparing the day of the Elizabethan stage, for despite all crudities, prolixities, and absurdities of detail, these English Miracle Cycles are nobly dramatic both in range and spirit. In verbal expression they are almost invariably weak and bald, but on the mediæval scaffold-stage the actor counted for more than the author, and the religious faith and feeling of the audience filled in the homely lines with an unwritten poetry. Within the vast extent of these cyclic dramas, as within the length and breadth of the great cathedrals, there was room, however, for human life in all its various aspects. As the grotesque found place among the beautiful carvings of chapter-house and choir, so under the ample canopy of the old Miracle Play comedy grew up by the very side of tragedy, bringing the theatre at once into collision with the Church.

As long as the religious plays, although they had departed from the sacred edifice, remained under the exclusive control of the clergy, there was but little loss in solemn and tragic effect. Even in France, whose light and restless genius was the first to introduce a farcical element into the Mysteries, the Passion was acted with such intensity that, in one instance at least, the young priest personating Christ fainted on the cross. As for Germany, it is recorded that the play of the Foolish Virgins, presented at Eisenach, Easter, 1322, in the royal park, undermined with its horror the reason of the most distinguished beholder, the Landgrave Frederic of the Scarred Cheek. But it is not long before we find the Church regarding these out-of-door plays, whose language was fast slipping from Latin into the vernacular, with a doubtful countenance. By the middle of the thirteenth century, many of the bishops were inclined to prohibit the clergy from taking part in Mysteries set forth in "churchyards, streets, or green places," permitting them to act only in the liturgical dramas still played beneath the consecrated roofs at Christmas and at Easter. The way thus opened, a new class of actors came speedily to the front.

The conditions of feudal life, and the exactions of the pleasure-loving Keltic temperament, had early brought into existence, on the Continent, a class of *joculatores,* men skilled in any or all of the several arts of minstrelsy, story-telling, dancing, jugglery, mimicry, and it was natural,—indeed, inevitable that the Miracle Plays, decorously and piously performed in the first instance by clergy within their ecclesiastical domains, should, as soon as they had ventured out from the "dim religious light" of choir and nave into the merry sunshine, be seized upon by these profane imitators, who soon became rivals and supplanters, too often turning what had been illustrated Scripture into scandal and buffoonery. The Norman conquest naturally scattered these Gallic *joculatores* or *histriones* over England, where they soon fell under ecclesiastical condemnation. But here the clergy, aided by the fact that these gay Frenchmen could not readily gain the ear of the humiliated, angry Saxon peasantry, held their own fairly well, and maintained the lead in the establishment of the national theatre. The priests, nevertheless, did not preserve their laurels as playwrights and actors without condescending to some of the tricks in trade of their opponents.

But by the time we find the English Miracle Cycles in full career, the clergy have ceased to be the customary actors. Yet the lower orders of the priesthood, however often forbidden by their ecclesiastical superiors, continued even down to the sixteenth century to bear some share in the representation of the Miracles, of which they remained, almost without exception, the authors and compilers. Regularly at London, and undoubtedly often elsewhere, the Miracles were performed by inferior personages attached to the Church, especially the parish clerks, like Chaucer's "Joly Absolon" of whom the poet says:—

> "Sometime to show his lightness and maistrie,
>   He plaieth Herod on a scaffold hie."

These parish clerks of London, of whom "Joly Absolon" is the immortal type, obtained in 1233 their charter as an harmonic guild and became a company of high repute, playing before Richard II, in 1390, and before Henry IV, in 1409, the performance on this latter occasion covering a period of eight days. But in many of the leading English towns, as York, Chester, Coventry, the trading guilds, by the close of the thirteenth century, had taken the task of setting forth the Miracles upon themselves. The conduct of these festivals was a matter of concern to the city corporations, too. At York, for instance, the council decreed in 1476: "That yerely in the tyme of lentyn there shall be called afore the maire for the tyme beying iiij of the moste connyng discrete and able players within this Citie, to serche, here, and examen all the plaiers and plaies and pagentes thrughoute all artificers belonging to Corpus Xt^i Plaie. And all suche as they shall fynde sufficant in persone and connyng, to the honour of the Citie and worship of the saide Craftes, for to admitte and able; and all other insufficant personnes, either in connyng, voice, or personne to discharge, ammove and avoide."

The best players being thus selected from among the followers of each craft, preparations began at once. Every guild became responsible for the presentation of a single pageant, or scene, furnishing its own movable stage, and meeting all the expenses of the pageant from its own treasury. The guilds acted as hosts to the entire neighbourhood, who rewarded by childlike interest and responsiveness the generosity of their entertainers. Each company appointed two pageant-masters, who controlled the pageant-silver, a fund made up by contributions from the members. The pageant-masters also superintended all the arrangements of the play, and trained the performers. One cannot think of these histrionic tradesmen without an amused remembrance of Shakespeare's irresistible burlesque, though Bully Bottom and his fellows represent a later stage of citizen actorship. When the arrangements for the play were perfected, a special "bayn," or crier, was sent around the city, usually twice, to announce it. The form of proclamation for the Corpus Christi plays, at York, ran as follows:—

"Proclamacio ludi corporis cristi facienda in virgilia corporis christi.

Oiez, &c. We comand of ye kynges behalve and ye Mair and ye shirefs of yis Citee yat no mann go armed in yis Citee with swerdes ne with Carlill-axes, ne none other defences in distorbaunce of ye kynges pees and ye play, or hynderying of ye processioun of Corpore Christi, and yat yai leve yare hernas in yare Ines, saufand knyghtes and sqwyres of wirship yat awe have swerdes borne eftir yame, of payne of forfaiture of yaire wapen and imprisonment of yaire bodys. And yat men yat brynges furth pacentes yat yai play at the places yat is assigned yerfore and nowere elles, of ye payne of forfaiture to be raysed yat is ordayned yerfore, yat is to say xls. And yat menn of craftes and all othir menn yat fyndes torches, yat yai come furth in array and in ye manere as it has been used and customed before yis time, noght haveyng wapen, careynge tapers of ye pagentz. And officers yat ar keepers of the pees of payne of forfaiture of yaire fraunchis and yaire bodyes to prison: And all maner of craftmen yat bringeth furthe ther pageantez in order and course by good players, well arayed and openly

spekyng, upon payn of lesyng of C.s to be paide to the chambre without any pardon. And that every player that shall play be redy in his pagiaunt at convenyant tyme, that is to say, at the mydhowre betwix iiijth and Vth of the cloke in the mornynge, and then all oyer pageantz fast followyng ilk one after oyer as yer course is, without tarieng. Sub pena facienda camere VI s. VIII d."

The division of scenes among the guilds is a curious and interesting matter. In the York pageants, for instance, one can hardly think it is all by accident that the plasterers were chosen for the representation of the creation of the earth, the shipwrights for the building of the ark, the fishmongers and mariners for the voyage of the ark, the "goldbeters" and "monemakers" for the adoration of the gift-bringing Magi, the vintners for the turning of the water into wine at Cana, and the bakers for the last supper. Nor are these all the examples that might be adduced, while, on the other hand, in many cases, there seems to be no such correspondence between the guild and the pageant.

This term *pageant* was originally applied, in England, to the movable platform which served as stage, the name soon passing over from the framework to the play exhibited upon it. The pageant scaffold was a wooden erection, set on wheels and divided into two stories, the lower serving as dressing-room, while the upper was the stage proper. The following words of Archdeacon Rogers, a sixteenth-century witness of the Whitsun Plays at Chester, describes clearly enough both the scaffold itself and the method of procedure:—

"The maner of these playes were, every company had his pagiant, wch pagiante weare a high scafold with 2 rowmes, a higher and a lower, upon 4 wheeles. In the lower they apparelled themselves, and in the higher rowme they played, beinge all open on the tope, that all behoulders might heare and see them. The places where they played them was in every streete. They began first at the Abay gates, and when the first pagiante was played, it was wheeled to the highe crosse before the Mayor, and so to every streete, and soe every streete had a pagiante playing before them at one time, till all the pagiantes for the daye appointed weare played, and when one pagiant was neere ended, worde was broughte from streete to streete, that soe they might come in place thereof, exceedinge orderly, and all the streetes have their pagiants afore them all at one time playeinge togeather; to se w'ch playes was great resorte, and also scafolds and stages made in the streetes in those places where they determined to play theire pagiantes."

The French scaffold was more elaborate, presenting three platforms, one above another, with a black pit yawing beside the lowest. The highest platform was reserved for God the Father, God the Son, the Virgin

Picture of "hell's mouth".

Mary, and the angels. This was richly tapestried and furnished with trees and an organ. The second platform sufficed for saints, and the third represented earth, the pit beside it standing for "Hellmouthe," beheld as the gaping jaws, sometimes worked so as to open and shut, of a hideous monster, fondly supposed to resemble a whale. In Germany, comparatively little care was bestowed upon accessories. There heaven was located at one end of the platform, raised by a few steps above the level which represented earth, while, in some cases, at least, a huge cask had to do duty as hell, the Devil leaping in and out of this with as much agility as he could command. Another cask, set upside down, served as the Mount of Temptation or Transfiguration.

The difference between France and England in the arrangement of the pageant-house, the English scaffold presenting but one open stage, with the story below curtained off as a green-room, and the French scaffold exposing three stages, the respective abodes of Deity and angels, of saints, and of men, was instrumental in differentiating the rôle of devils in the two countries. These personages, to be sure, had their proper abode in hellmouth; but whereas, in England, the dragon-jaws emitted the devils only when they had some dismal task to perform, in France, while the scene of action was, for the time being, on one of the upper stages, the devils were accustomed to pop out of their prison, run across the human stage, and even leap down among the audience, playing tricks and executing gambols. So the French devils degenerated into drolls, while the English and German, though equally grotesque in appearance, aimed at producing impressions of terror, rather than of mirth. Into hellmouth, from which smoke and flame continually arose, these English demons, bristling with horsehair, and wearing beast heads, the ugliest possible—always a prominent item in the bill of costs,—dragged with much mockery and show of cruelty those souls whose black, red, and yellow coats, suggestive of the fire that awaited them, indicated their fitness for such habitation. Souls destined for heaven wore white coats and white hose, and the angels, duly plumed, were resplendent in gold. The high priests, Annas and Caiaphas, wore ecclesiastical robes, often borrowed from the church. The Virgin and the other Marys wore crowns. Herod was gay in blue satin gown, and gilt and silvered helmet, with various Saracenic accoutrements, as the crooked falchion. Pilate wore a green robe, and carried a leather club stuffed with wool. The tormentors of Christ wore jackets of black buckram, painted over with nails and dice. Our Lord was represented in a coat of white sheepskin, variously painted, with red sandals, the sandals of one who had trodden the winepress, and gilt peruke and beard. Gilt perukes and beards were worn by all the apostles, also, and by other saints whom the people were accustomed to see emblazoned on church walls, or windows, with a halo about the head. Judas was distinguished by his red beard and yellow robe. The most striking costume was that of the devil, who was as shaggy and beast-like as possible, black, horned, clawed, with cloven feet and a forked tail, and, sometimes, with pipes of burning gunpowder in his ears.

The bills of expense, which have been discovered at Coventry and elsewhere, throw much light on the stage accessories and wardrobes. In the lists of garments provided for the principal characters, we come upon some names among the *dramatis personæ* that the gospel reader would hardly expect, such as Pilate's Son, Herod's Son, Bishops, Beadle, Mother of Death, and Worms of Conscience. Records like the following, too, though penned in all devout simplicity, fall strangely on the modern ear.

Paid for a pair of gloves for God	2d.
Paid for four pair of angels' wings	2s. 8d.
Paid for nine and a half yards of buckram for the souls' coats	7s.
Paid for ale when the players dress them	4d.
Paid for painting and making new hell head	12d.
Paid for mending of hell head	6d.
Paid for keeping hell head	8d.
Paid for a pair of new hose and mending of the old for the white souls	18d.
Paid for mending the garment of Jesus, and the cross painting	1s. 3d.
Paid for a pound of hemp to mend the angels' heads	4d.
Paid for linen cloth for the angels' heads and Jesus' hose, making in all	9d.
Paid for washing the lawn bands for the Saints in the church	2d.
To Fawston for hanging Judas	4d.
To Fawston for cockcrowing	10d.

Item: Painting of the world.
Item: Link for setting the world on fire.
Item: Girdle for God.
Item: For mending the demon's head.
Item: Chevrel (apparently peruke) for God.
Item: Two chevrels gilt for Jesus and Peter.
Item: A cloak for Pilate.
Item: Pollaxe for Pilate's son.
Item: To reward Mistress Grimsby for lending of her gear to Pilate's wife.
Item: Divers necessaries for the trimming of the Father of Heaven.

Among the stage effects we find:—

A gilded cross with a rope to draw it up and a curtain to hang before it.
Scourges and a gilded pillar.
Trumpets and bagpipes.
A cord for Judas to hang himself.
Rock. Tomb. Spade. Rushes. Censers. Stars. Diadems.
Standard made of red buckram.
Starch to make a storm.

The barrel for the earthquake.
Pulpits for the angels.

But, however grotesque all this may seem to-day, there is good reason for believing that the English throngs drawn by these Pageants to the market-towns on high church festivals looked and listened to their æsthetic and spiritual edification. In France, where the performance of a series of Mysteries was undertaken by the town, irrespective of the guilds, all the people were eager to bear part in the representation, regarding such acting as a religious service, to be counted unto the actor for righteousness. A solemn trumpet-call, *le cri du jeu,* would summon all who might desire, for the glory of Christ, or the weal of their own souls, to assist in the representation. The volunteers placed in the hands of the magistrate a signed paper, wherein they made oath, on pain of death, or forfeiture of property, to study carefully the rôle assigned, and to be promptly on hand on the day of representation. Those of the ignorant rabble, who, eager to show some grace to Christ, and win His grace in return, flocked after the trumpet, were massed as Israelites in the wilderness, or the mob about the cross. Sometimes, half the town acted, while the other half looked on, together with the rustics of the outlying villages. But, even so, there was no entrance fee, although gifts to aid in defraying expenses were acceptable, not only on earth, but in heaven, such gifts partaking of the nature of a religious offering.

Yet, notwithstanding this truly devotional spirit, the rude, laughter-loving tastes of the populace so wrought upon the playwrights as to bring about the introduction of certain distinctly comic episodes into the sacred history. In the English cycles, the fun is chiefly furnished, in the Old Testament plays, by the buffoonery between Cain and his ploughboy, and by the shrill insubordination of Noah's wife, when the patriarch would persuade her to enter the ark; while to the story of the Saviour's life and death, evidently regarded then, as by the peasants of Oberammergau to-day, in the light of solemn and heart-moving tragedy, a foil was afforded by the clownish talk and actions of the shepherds. That this food for mirth was sometimes of the coarsest should not be taken as proving intentional irreverence on the part of players or of hearers. It points to social rather than moral causes. The conditions of family life for the lower classes of the English, in the years when Chaucer and Langland wrote, and Miracle Plays were in full tide of popularity, precluded delicacy of manners or of speech.

As a representative Miracle Cycle I would select the Towneley Mysteries, sometimes styled the Widkirk or Woodkirk Plays. The first of these two names, for Widkirk and Woodkirk are essentially the same word, is taken from Towneley Hall in Lancashire, where the manuscript was preserved. The second is derived from a vague tradition that this old parchment volume before coming, at an unknown date and under long-for-

gotten circumstances, into possession of the Towneley family, belonged to the "Abbey of Widkirk, near Wakefield, in the county of York." No modern research has succeeded in tracing any such abbey, or any place of that name in York, or, indeed, anywhere in England; but it appears that about four miles from the old town once known as "Merry Wakefield," where plays would naturally have been acted, there did exist a place called Woodkirk, which harboured, before the dissolution of the monasteries, a small religious brotherhood, a cell of Augustinian or Black Canons, subject to the flourishing house of St. Oswald, at Nostel. The dialect of all these Mysteries save four ("Processus Prophetarum," "Pharao," "Cæsar Augustus," "Annunciatio") reveals a Yorkshire origin, one or two local allusions occur, and the words "Wakefelde Barkers" (tanners), "Glover Pageant," "Fysher Pageant," written over three of the plays, would seem to warrant the conclusion that these Mysteries were composed, or adapted from a lost original, by the Woodkirk monks and acted by the tradeguilds of Wakefield at the fairs which, as old charters show, were sometimes held on occasion of high church festivals, in that town. Each guild had a particular pageant assigned it for representation, and probably, no less than three days were required to complete the series, which numbers thirty plays in order, from the "Creation" to the "Judgment Day," with two later additions, "Lazarus" and the "Hanging of Judas." These Mysteries, whose conjectural date is the fourteenth century, or even earlier, are rude but often forceful and vivacious in composition, familiar in style, dialectical in diction, and enlivened at intervals by the broadest kind of humour.

We must imagine an open market-place, in the centre of a mediæval English town,—rows of quaint, narrow, gabled houses, whose windows are alive with faces, closing in the square, which is thronged by a motley multitude,—Yorkshire rustics, green-clad yeomen, young clerks and squires in many-coloured, picturesque costumes, gowned and hooded friars, kerchiefed women, here and there a knight in glistening mail, everywhere beggars, children, dogs, all pressing toward the lofty stage adorned with crosses and streamers, which rises in the centre of the scene. On the upper platform, from whose edges rich draperies, wrought with Christian emblems, fall to conceal the dressing-room below, appears the white-vested, golden-haired figure of the Creator, seated upon a throne, and surrounded by His cherubim. He speaks:—

> "Ego sum Alpha et O,
> I am the first and last also,
>   Oone God in mageste;
> Marvelose, of myght most,
> Fader, and Sone, and Holy Ghost,
>   One God in Trinyte."

In this same abrupt, prentice-like measure the Deity

continues with assurances of His eternity, omniscience and omnipotence, His firm determination to maintain all these, and, finally, with an exceedingly succinct account of the creation, as He performs it on the stage by aid of lanterns, hawthorn branches, and wooden images of birds and beasts. The conception of the creative process is no less crude and childish than these illustrations themselves; the narrative is of the baldest, and the grammatical construction absolutely ragged. But as the cherubim break forth in a choral address to God, we are aware of a lighter movement, a freer fancy, and a distinct dramatic intent in the introduction, somewhat precipitate though it seems, of the praises of Lucifer.

> "Oure Lord God in trynyte,
>   Myrth and lovyng be to the [thee]
>   Myrth and lovyng over al thyng;
>   For thou has made, with thi bidyng,
>   Heven, and erth, and alle that is,
>   And giffen us joy that never shalle mys.
>   Lord, thou art fulle mych [much] of myght,
>   That has maide Lucifer so bright.
>   We love the, Lord, bright are we,
>   But none of us so bright as he.
>   He may well hight [be called] Lucifer,
>   For luffy light that he doth bere."

This anthem has an intoxicating effect upon the archangel's pride, and no sooner has God arisen from His throne and begun to walk toward the rear of the stage, than Lucifer usurps the vacant seat, appealing to his fellows to know if it does not become him as well as the Creator.

> "Say, fellows, how semys now me
>   To sit in seyte of trynyte?
>   I am so bright of ich a lym [every
>   lineament],
>   I trow me seme as welle as hym."

But the angels divide upon this question, and Lucifer, proposing to display his powers still further, attempts to fly off the stage and disastrously falls into hell-mouth, his adherents tumbling after. These bad angels, who are henceforth designated as demons, and who, perhaps, have torn off their outer robes of white on alighting in the pit and revealed inner garments black and ragged, raise cries of dismay and reproach.

> "Alas, alas, and wele-wo!
>   Lucifer, why felle thou so?
>   We, that were angels so fare,
>   And sat so hie above the ayere,
>   Now ar we waxen blak as any coylle."

The scene is presently transferred to the upper stage. God re-enters, or advances from the background, and without offering the slightest comment on past events, resumes His throne and tranquilly proceeds with His interrupted task of creation. Adam is moulded out of clay, and into him is breathed the divine life. A rib is taken from his side and transformed into a helpmate for him. The keeping of the garden is entrusted to the pair, with strict injunction as to the forbidden tree.

> *Deus.* Erthly bestes, that may crepe and go,
>   Bryng ye furth and wax ye mo,
>   I see that it is good;
>   Now make we man to our liknes,
>   That shalle be keper of more and les,
>   Of fowles, and fysh in flood.
>   *(Et tanget eum.)*
>   Spreyte of life I in the blaw,
>   Good and ille both shalle thou knaw;
>   Rise up, and stand bi me.
>   Alle that is in water or land,
>   It shalle bow unto thi hand,
>   And sufferan shalle thou be;
>   I gif the witt, I gif the strength,
>   Of alle thou sees, of brede and lengthe;
>   Thou shalle be wonder wise.
>   Myrth and joy to have at wille,
>   Alle thi likyng to fulfille,
>   And dwelle in paradise.
>   This I make thi wonnyng playce
>   [dwelling-place]
>   Fulle of myrth and of solace,
>   And I seasse [establish] the therin.
>   It is not good to be alone,
>   To walk here in this worthely wone
>   [dwelling]
>   In alle this welthly wyn [joy in
>   possession.];
>   Therfor, a rib I from the take,
>   Therof shalle be thi make,
>   And be to thi helpyng.
>   Ye both to governe that here is,
>   And ever more to be in blis,
>   Ye wax in my blissyng.
>   Ye shalle have joye and blis therin,
>   While ye wille kepe you out of syn,
>   I say without lese [lies].
>   Ryse up, myn angelle cherubyn,
>   Take and leyd theym both in,
>   And leyf them there in peasse.
> *(Tunc capit Cherubyn Adam per manum, et dicet eis Dominus.)*
>   Here thou Adam, and Eve thi wife,
>   I forbede you the tre of life,
>   And I commaund, that it begat,
>   Take which ye wille, bot negh
>   [approach] not that.
>   Adam, if thou breke my rede,
>   Thou shalle dye a dulfulle [doleful]
>   dede.
> *Cherubyn.*
>   Oure Lord, our God, thi wille be done;
>   I shalle go with theym fulle sone.

For soth, my Lord, I shalle not sted
Tille I have theym theder led.
We thank the Lord, with fulle good
  chere,
That has maide man to be oure peere
              [companion],
Com furth, Adam, I shalle the leyd,
Take tent to me, I shalle the reyd.
I rede the thynk how thou art wroght,
And luf my Lord in alle thi thoght,
That has maide the thrugh his wille,
Angels ordir to fulfille,
Many thynges he has the giffen,
And made the master of alle that lyffen,
He has forbed the bot a tre;
Look that thou let it be,
For if thou breke his commaundment,
Thou skapys not bot thou be shent [
  punished].
Weynd [wend] here in to paradise,
And luke now that ye be wyse,
And kepe you welle, for I must go
Unto my Lord, there I cam fro.
Adam. Almyghte Lord, I thank it the
That is, and was, and shalle be,
Of thy luf and of thi grace,
For now is here a mery place;
Eve, my felow, how thynk the this?
Eve. A stede me thynk of joye and blis,
  That God has giffen to the and me,
  Withoutten ende; blissyd be he.
Adam. Eve, felow, abide me thore,
  For I wille go to viset more,
   To se what trees that here been;
  Here are welle moo then we have seen,
  Greses, and othere smalle floures,
  That smelle fulle swete, of seyre
    [several] colours.

Adam, thus overcome by his masculine curiosity, leaves Eve unprotected, while he starts off on a tour of exploration about his new domain. Even as he departs, the menacing voice of the ruined archangel rises from the fiery cavern, and although four leaves of the manuscript are here torn away, we can easily imagine the temptation and the fall as enacted by the Wakefield tanners in the listening market-place.

The Eden scaffold is now drawn onward to the head of the first street, where, although still so early in the morning, an impatient concourse has been waiting for an hour past. Before the recent spectators have turned their eyes from the disappearing platform, a second pageant-carriage, upon which is to be enacted one of the liveliest miracles of the series, rolls into the square. The audience greets this platform, furnished and decorated by the glovers of Wakefield, with vociferous applause, which is promptly rebuked by the first character who steps out upon the stage, a mirth-provoking

personage, unknown to the writer of Genesis, but familiar to mediæval playgoers under the title of Garcio, or Cain's ploughboy. His saucy speech forms a rough prologue to the pageant, which actually opens with the appearance of Cain. The first murderer presents himself, not upon the scaffold, but in a reserved space of ground at its foot, where he is ploughing with a contrary team of mingled horses and oxen, and cursing the boy for the waywardness of the beasts. The boy, glorying in his mischief, acknowledges that he has filled the cattle's feeding-racks with stones, whereupon the ill-tempered Yorkshire rustic deals him a fisticuff in the face, straightway receiving as good as he sent. They are in the midst of a tussle, when Abel enters, with gentle words of greeting.

> "God as he bothe may and can
> Spede the, brothere, and thi man."

Cain's response is of the rudest insolence, but Abel, deprecating his wrath, urges the surly ploughman to go with him to sacrifice. Cain doggedly maintains that he owes God nothing.

> "When alle mens corne was fayre in feld
> Then was myne not worthe an eld;
> When I should saw [sow] and wantyd seyde,
> And of corne had fulle grete neyde,
> Then gaf he me none of his,
> No more wille I gif hym of this."

But Abel's entreaty finally prevails, and Cain, grumbling at every step, reluctantly follows his brother out of the half-ploughed field, and up a hill, which the scaffold represents. Here Abel offers his sacrifice with reverent prayer, upon which breaks in the harsh voice of Cain, his own address to God being as blunt and gruff as his speech to his fellow-men. The audience derives great delight from these defiant orisons, and from the grudging fashion in which Cain slowly selects the worst of his sheaves for the altar.

> "But now begyn wille I then,
> Syn I must nede my tend to bren [tithe to
>   burn].
> Oone shefe, oone, and this makes two,
> Bot nawder of thise may I forgo;
> Two, two, now this is thre,
> Yei, this also shalle leif withe me;
> For I wille chose and best have,
> This hold I thrift of alle this thrafe [twenty-
>   four sheaves];
> Wemo, wemo, foure, lo, here!
> Better groved [grew] me no this yere.
> At yere tyme I sew fare corn,
> Yit was it siche when it was shorne,
> Thystyls and breyrs yei grete plente,
> And alle kyn wedes that myght be.
> Foure shefes, foure; lo, this makes fyfe,

Deylle I fast thus long or I thrife,
Fyfe and sex, now this is seven,—
But this gettes never God of heven,
Nor none of thise foure, at my myghte,
Shalle never com in Godes sight.
Seven, seven, now this is aght."

But here Abel, piously shocked, interposes.

Abelle. Cain, brother, thou art not God betaght
        [submissive].
Cayn. We therfor, is it that I say?
        For I wille not deyle my good away;
        Bot had I gyffen him this to teynd
        Then wold thou say he were my
            freynd,
        But I thynk not, bi my hode,
        To departe so lightly fro my goode.
        We, acht, acht, and neyn, and ten is this,
        We, that may we best mys.
        Gif Him that that lighes thore;
        It goyse agans myn hart fulle sore.

        . . . . .

Abelle. Caine, of God me thynke thou has no
            drede.
Cayn. Now and He get more, the deville me
            spede,
        As mych as oone reepe,
        For that cam hym fulle light cheap;

        . . . . .

        For that, and this that lyys here,
        Have cost me fulle dere;
        Or it was shorne, and broght in stak,
        Had I many a wery bak;
        Therfor aske me no more of this,
        For I have giffen that my wille is.
Abelle. Cain, I rede thou tend right
        For drede of hym that sittes on
            hight.

And now Cain's fatal wrath begins to burn against his brother.

Cayn.   How that I tend, rek the never a
            deille,
        Bot tend thi skabbid shepe wele;
        For if thou to my teynd tent take
        It bese the wars for thi sake.
        Thou wold I gaf hym this shefe, or
            this sheyfe,
        Na nawder of thise two will I leife;
        Bot take this now, has he two,
        And for my saulle now mot it go,
        Bot it gos sore agans my wille,
        And shal he like fulle ille.

Abelle. Cain, I reyde thou so teynd
        That God of heven be thi freynd.
Cayn. My freynd? na, not bot if he wille!
        I did hym neveryit bot skille [reason].
        If he be never so my fo
        I am avised gif hym no mo;
        Bot channge thi conscience, as I do
            myn,
        Yit teynd thou not thy mesel [measly]
            swyne?
Abelle. If thou teynd right thou mon it fynde.

At this suggestion, with all that it implies, the rage of Cain blazes hotter than before.

Cayn. The deville hang the bi the nek;
        How that I teynd never thou rek.
        Wille thou not yit hold thi peasse?
        Of this janglyng I reyde thou seasse.
        And teynd I welle, or tend I ille,
        Bere the even and speke bot skille.
        Bot now syn thou has teyndid thyne,
        Now wille I set fyr on myne.
        We, out, haro, help to blaw!
        It wille not bren for me, I traw;
        Puf, this smoke dos me myche shame,
        Now bren, in the devillys name.
        A, what deville of helle is it?
        Almost had myne brethe beyn dit
            [stopped].
        Had I blawen oone blast more
        I had beyn choked right thore.

And while Cain, coughing and cursing, staggers back from the altar, Abel, who, in disregard of his brother's angry warnings, has lingered near the scene, cries with sorrowful foreboding:—

Abelle. Cain, this is not worthe oone leke;
        Thy tend should bren with outten
            smeke.

The answer vouchsafed to his fraternal solicitude is a furious snarl from the still choking and gasping husbandman.

Cayn. For the it brens but the wars.
        I wold that it were in thi throte,
        Fyre, and shefe, and iche a sprote
            [every sprout].

Then upon the ears of the reckless blasphemer falls a still, small voice,—never before or since, we may well believe, more irreverently greeted.

Deus. Cain, why art thou so rebelle
        Agans thi brother Abelle?
Caym. Whi, who is that Hob over the walle?
        We, who was that that piped so

smalle?
Com, go we hens, for perels alle;
God is out of hys wit.
Com furth, Abelle, and let us weynd,
Me thynk that God is not my freynd,
On land then wille I flyt [flee].

Abelle. O, Caym, brother, that is ille done.

Caym. No, bot go we hens sone;
And if I may, I shalle be
Ther as God shalle not me see.

Poor Abel, not daring to openly oppose the wild will of the outcast, in a feeble and *mal apropos* fashion proposes to go and feed the cattle.

Abelle. Dere brother, I wille fayre
On feld ther oure bestes ar,
To looke if thay be holgh [hollow] or
fulle.

Over Cain's tumult of passions his wrath, waxed dark and murderous, now obtains the mastery.

Cayn. Na, na abide, we have a craw to
pulle;
Hark, speke with me or thou go,
What wenys thou to skape so?
We, na, I aght the a fowlle dispyte,
And now is tyme that I hit qwite.

Abel. Brother, whi art thou so to me in ire?

Caym. We, theyf, whi brend thi tend so shyre
[sheer]?
Ther myne did bot smoked
Right as it wold us bothe have choked.

Abel. Godes wille I trow it were
That myn brened so clere;
If thyne smoked am I to wite [blame]?

With this Cain leaps upon his brother, apparently anticipating, as implement for the slaughter, the famous weapon of Samson.

Cayn. We, yei, that shal thou sore abite;
Withe cheke bon, or that I blyn
[cease],
Shal I the and thi life twyn [separate].
So lig down ther and take thi rest,
Thus shalle shrewes be chastysed
best.

Abel. Venjance, venjance, Lord, I cry;
For I am slayne, and not gilty.

The fratricide accomplished, Cain taunts his silent victim yet again, turns glowering upon the audience, and then, suddenly overcome by the terrors of conscience, creeps quakingly into a convenient hole provided on the stage. But the voice of God pursues him there.

Deus. Caym! Caym!

Caym. Who is that that callis me?
I am yonder, may thou not se?

Deus. Caym, where is thi brother Abelle?

Caym. What askes thou me? I trow at helle;
At helle I trow he be,
Who so were ther then myght he se,
Or som where fallen on slepyng;
When was he in my kepyng?

Deus. Caym, Caym, thou was wode [mad];
The voyce of thi brotheres blode
That thou has slayn, on fals wise,
From erthe to heven vengeance cryse.
And, for thou has brought thi brother
down,
Here I gif the my malison.

With this the play reaches its true dramatic conclusion, and up to this point, for all the naivete, the rudeness and grossness of language and action, there has been spirit, vigour, and even a just dramatic progression. The continual mounting of Cain's passionate temper, under Abel's well-intended but somewhat priggish admonitions, is well depicted, and the boy, with his ready sauce, his monkey play, and frank flavour of democracy, furnishes a needed foil to the tragic elements in the drama. The peculiar value of Cain, as a character, lies in his reality. We feel that this Cain is true, not indeed to oriental legend, but to human nature, as exhibited among Yorkshire boors in Chaucer's century. This fierce and niggardly ploughman, who might as well be called Dick or Robin, would be at home in the procession of Canterbury pilgrims, where he would find bullies, blusterers, and rascals, quite of his own crow-feather, and among these another ploughman of that Christ-type, which redeems even the type of Cain.

But the play fails utterly here at the dramatic climax. It is unable to rise to the tragic opportunity. It falls back foolishly, instead, on an iteration of Cain's sulky temper and the boy's buffoonery, until the scene degenerates into open farce. Then the pageant-carriage is wheeled away, not without having impressed its moral lesson. More than one foul-mouthed, violent-handed rustic in that holiday throng will remember for a few weeks or so to pay his farthings to the priest with fewer curses and use his heavy fist more sparingly.

These two opening pageants are fairly representative both of Miracles in general and of the Towneley collection in particular. The first illustrates the more conventional treatment of Biblical story—or what was supposed to be Biblical story,—the second the freer and more humorous. Of the remaining pageants we can let ourselves catch but glimpses, as the thirty glittering scaffolds roll in and out of Wakefield market-square.

There is the popular Noah pageant, with its white-haired patriarch lamenting over the sins of the world,

God descending from heaven and bidding him build the ark of refuge, the taunts of Noah's shrewish wife, the lively scuffle that ensues between these venerable worthies, heads of the only virtuous household left on earth, and the laborious building of the ark by the rheumatic old shipwright. But even then his stubborn dame refuses to leave her spinning on the hilltop, until the waves swash over her feet, and she comes bounding into the ark in terror of her life. Here, one regrets to record, Noah welcomes her with a severe flogging, because of her previous contumacy. She retaliates by calling him names, Wat Wynd and Nicholle Nedy, stoutly refusing to sue for mercy, although she is "bet so blo" that she wishes her husband dead and the husbands, likewise, of all the women in the audience. Noah, too, turns to the assembly with the sententious counsel:—

> "Ye men that has wifes, whyles they are
>   yong,
>   If ye luff your lives, chastice thare tong."

The following pageant sets forth the story of Abraham and Isaac, and, although the treatment is discursive and the text nowhere markedly poetical, the simple drama is not without a homely English beauty of its own. The childish docility of the boy, and the unavailing efforts of the submissive, bewildered father to strike the fatal blow are clearly realised.

> *Isaac.* What have I done, fader, what
>   have I saide?
> *Abraham.* Truly, no kyns ille to me.
> *Isaac.*   And thus gyltles shalle be arayde?
> *Abraham.* Now, good son, let siche wordes
>   be.
> *Isaac.* I luf you ay.
> *Abraham.* So do I thee.
> *Isaac.* Fader!
> *Abraham.* What, son?
> *Isaac.* Let now be seyn
>   For my moder luf.
> *Abraham.* Let be, let be!
>   It wille not help that thou wold
>   meyn;
>   Bot ly stylle tille I com to the,
>   I mys a lytylle thyng, I weyn.
>   He spekes so rufully to me
>   That water shotes in both myn
>   eeyn,
>   I were lever than alle warldly wyn,
>   That I had fon him onys unkynde,
>   But no defawt I faund hym in;
>   I wold be dede for hym or pynde.
>   To slo hym thus I thynk grete syn,
>   So rufulle wordes I with hym fynd;
>   I am fulle wo that we shuld twyn
>   [part],
>   For he wille never oute of my mynd.

What shal I to hys moder say?

The fifth pageant shows Jacob stealing the blessing and fleeing from the wrath of Esau. The sixth pageant sets forth in manner decorous and dull, without much action or effort at characterisation, Jacob's dream, his wrestling with the Angel and his reconciliation with Esau. The seventh pageant is rather a pomp than a play. Moses, rehearsing the ten commandments, David, quoting from the psalms, the Roman Sibyl,—a prophetic figure not unfamiliar to the Mysteries,—and the prophet Daniel all foretell, one after another, the coming of the Christ.

> "Of a madyn shalle he be borne,
> To save alle that ar forlorne,
> Ever more withoutten end."

The Old Testament pageants close with the story of Moses, who first appears in shepherd garb, informing the audience that he is now

> "set to kepe
> Under thys montayn syde,
> Byschope Jettyr shepe,"

but presently confounds Pharaoh and his magicians, calls down the ten plagues, and leads the Israelites in safety through the Red Sea.

The first of the New Testament platforms is occupied by Cæsar Augustus, a vainglorious bully, who ingratiates himself with the audience by offering to behead any one of them who dares utter a word during the pageant. His rage and dismay, on learning from his two councillors that a child is to be born in Judea who shall excel him in glory, are absurdly extravagant. He sends his messenger "Lyghtfote" to bid his cousin, Sir Siranus, attend him, and to this sage knight confides his anxiety. Sir Siranus suggests that a general poll-tax, or "heede penny," be decreed, and Cæsar prays the messenger, as he "luffes Mahowne," to speed that mandate on. The Annuciation Pageant follows, God avowing that He will visit the long affliction of Adam His handiwork with "oylle of mercy."

> "For he has boght his syn fulle sore,
> Thise V thousand yeris and more,
> Fyrst in erth, and sythen in helle."

Gabriel is despatched to bear to Mary the mystic salutation.

> "Angelle must to Mary go,
> For the feynd was Eve fo;
> He was foule and layth to syght,
> And thou art angelle fayr and bright."

The pageant dwells less upon the visit of Gabriel to

Mary, however, than upon the perturbations of simple old Joseph, who lends to these earlier Gospel scenes a touch of mingled pathos and comedy. The *Salutation* consists of a brief dialogue between Mary and Elizabeth, pleasing for the unwonted ease of the verse and for the loving courtesy of woman to woman.

> *Maria.* My lord of heven, that syttys he,
> And alle thyng seys withe eee,
> The safe, Elezabethe.
> *Elezabethe.* Welcom, Mary, blyssed blome,
> Joyfulle am I of thi com,
> To me, from Nazarethe.
> *Maria.* How standes it with you, dame,
> of quart [spirits]?
> *Elezabethe.* Welle, my doghter and dere hart,
> As can for myn elde. . . .
> Fulle lang shalle I the better be,
> That I may speke my fylle with
> the,
> My dere kyns woman;
> To wytt how thi freyndes fare,
> In thi countre where thay ar,
> Therof telle me thou can,
> And how thou farys, my dere
> derlyng.
> *Maria.* Welle, dame, gramercy youre
> askyng,
> For good I wote ye spyr
> [question].
> *Elezabethe.* And Joachym, thy fader, at hame,
> And Anna, my nese, and thi
> dame,
> How standes it with hym and hir?
> *Maria.* Dame, yit ar thay bothe on lyfe,
> Bothe Joachym and Anna his
> wyfe.
> *Elezabethe.* Else were my hart fulle sare.

The next two pageants, both dealing with the night-watch and adoration of the shepherds, serve as a farcical interlude between the tender gravity of the plays immediately preceding, and the solemnity, deepening into tragedy, of the plays to come. These two comedies are not in sequence, but independent versions of the shepherd story. The leading characters of the former are a group of Yorkshire boors, Gyb, John Horne, and Slow-Pace, preposterous simpletons all three, and Jak Garcio, a rough fellow of a shrewder cast. After much grumbling and quarrelling, and after a supper of such coarse scraps as each has begged during the day, they say their extraordinary prayers and go to sleep. Startled awake by the angel's song, they fall to naïve discussion of the *Gloria,* and ludicrous attempts to imitate it. At last, they are guided by the star in the east to the manger of Bethlehem, where, like the very clowns they are, they linger bashfully about the door, each pushing his fellow forward. But, once in presence of the Child, they fall on their knees, and eagerly tender their simple gifts,—a little spruce coffer, a ball, and a bottle. The other *Pagina Pastorum* is an equally remarkable instance of historical incongruity, being another rude, realistic sketch of Northumbrian shepherd life in the days of the early Edwards. This rollicking farce was undoubtedly the favourite pageant of the series, greeted with clamorous applause as it moved from street to street. Here, too, the introductory characters are three shepherds, the weatherbeaten Colle, the hen-pecked Gyb, and the boy Daw, who is something of a rogue. But the prime rogue of the comedy is Mak, a lazy, lawless vagabond, ready to shift sail with every wind that blows, and well mated in his wife Gylle, a scold and a slut, who sharpens her tongue on her husband early and late, letting the larder shelves, which his thriftlessness keeps bare, be overrun by spiders. But it is impossible not to delight in this scampish, hungry, fun-loving Mak, whose character is cleverly and consistently sketched from his first appearance on the moor, by mischance, before the shepherds whom he has it in heart to rob, and whose recognition he tries to escape by muffling himself in his cloak and disguising his voice, to the final detection in his cottage, where, the stolen sheep being tucked away as a new-born baby in the cradle, he brazens out the situation with one lie clapped upon another, and, when nothing else will suffice, with a promise of amendment,—the greatest lie of all.

The shepherds, who, on discovering the loss of the sheep, instantly turn their suspicions upon Mak and his wife, are about to leave the cottage after a fruitless quest:—

> *Tercius Pastor.* Alle wyrk we in vayn! as
> welle may we go.
> But hatters [except spiders],
> I can fynde no flesh
> Hard nor nesh [tender],
> Salt nor fresh,
> Bot two tome [empty]
> platters.
>
> . . . . .
>
> *Uxor.* No, so God me blys, and gyf
> me joy of my chylde.
> *Primus Pastor.* We have marked amys; I hold
> us begyld.
> *Secundus Pastor.* Syr, don.
> Syr, oure lady hym save.
> Is youre chyld a knave
> [boy]?
> *Mak.* Any lord myght hym have
> This chyld to his son.

At the door the shepherds pause, struck by a kindly thought.

> *Primus Pastor.* Gaf ye the chyld any

	thyng?
Secundus Pastor.	I trow not oone farthyng.
Tercius Pastor.	Fast agayne wille I flyng,
	Abyde ye me there.
	Mak, take it to no grefe,
	if I com to thi barne.
Mak.	Nay, thou does me greatt reprefe, and fowlle has thou farne.
Tercius Pastor.	The child wille it not grefe, that lytylle day starne.
	Mak, with youre lefe, let me gyf youre barne,
	Bot vj pence.
Mak.	Nay, do away; he slepys.
Tercius Pastor.	Me thynk he pepys.
Mak.	When he wakyns he wepys.
	I pray you go hence.
Tercius Pastor.	Gyf me lefe hym to kys, and lyft up the clowtt.
	What the deville is this? he has a long snowte.
Primus Pastor.	He is markyd amys. We wate ille abowte.
Secundus Pastor.	Ille spon [spun] weft, iwis, ay commys foulle owte.
	Ay, so?
	He is lyke to oure shepe.
Tercius Pastor.	How, Gyb! may I pepe?
Primus Pastor.	I trow, kynde wille crepe
	Where it may not go.
Secundus Pastor.	This was a quantte gawde [quaint trick] and a far cast.
	It was a hee frawde.
Tercius Pastor.	Yee, syrs, wast.
	Lett bren this bawde and bind hir fast.
	A fals skawde [All false scolds] hang at the last;
	So shalle thou.
	Wylle ye se how thay swedylle
	His foure feytt in the medylle?
	Sagh I never in a credylle
	A hornyd lad or now.
Mak.	Peasse byd I: what! lett be youre fare;
	I am he that hym gatt, and yond woman hym bare.
Primus Pastor.	What deville shall he hatt?
	Mak, lo God, Mak's ayre.
Secundus Pastor.	Let be alle that. Now God gyf hym care, I sagh.
Uxor.	A pratty child is he
	As syttes on a woman's

	kne;
	A dylle doune, parde,
	To gar a man laghe.
Tercius Pastor.	I know hym by the eere marke; that is a good tokyn.
Mak.	I telle you, syrs, hark: hys noys was broken.
	Sythen told me a clerk, that he was forspoken [enchanted].
Primus Pastor.	This is a false wark. I wold fayne be wrokyn: Gett wepyn.
Uxor.	He was takyn with an elfe: I saw it myself.
	When the clok stroke twelf Was he forshapyn.
Secundus Pastor.	Ye two ar welle feft, sam in a stede.
Tercius Pastor.	Syn thay manteyn thare theft, let do thaym to dede [death],
Mak.	If I trespas eft, [again] gyrd [cut] of my heede.
	With you wille I be left.
Primus Pastor.	Syrs, do my reede.
	For this trespas,
	We wille nawther ban ne flyte,
	Fyght nor chyte,
	Bot have done as tyte,
	And cast hym in canvas.

The supernatural incidents added to this frank drama of common life have only the slightest thread of connection with the main plot. There is no further burlesque, after Mak has been exposed and tossed in a blanket, except in the persistent attempts of the shepherds to try their cracked voices at the angel song. When they are in the presence of the Holy Child, there is not a trace of intentional irreverence. The stable scene is one of great naiveté, but the shepherds' homely terms of endearment, their simple gifts,—a bird, a ball, a "bob of cherys," and their pleasure when the "swetyng" "merys," and "laghys," are not without tender suggestion of the sanctities of hearth and home.

The next play in order has for theme the coming of the Magi. The central character is Herod, swaggering about fiercely in his blue satin gown and gilded helmet. He is the prince of blusterers, and a devout worshipper of Mahomet. This noisy pageant is succeeded by a quiet night-scene at Bethlehem. Joseph is called from his sleep by an angel

"As blossom bright on bogh,"

and bidden rise and flee. The countrified old carpenter appears, as usual, bewildered and reluctant. It is some time before the angel can make him understand what is wanted of him, and then he protests that he is sick and sore, and his bones ache, and that he doesn't know the way to Egypt. But toward Mary, whose alarm is all for her child, Joseph assumes an air of dignified rebuke, bids her give over her "dyn" and dress the baby and pack up the "gere" at once. What Joseph does is not apparent. Perhaps he saddles the ass. At all events, he finds time to bemoan his lot at length, and warn all young men against matrimony. Then comes a stormy pageant presenting, somewhat absurdly, the slaughter of the Innocents. Three soldiers, at the instigation of the furious Herod, engage in hand to hand combat with three distracted mothers, and, having slain each a child, ride back in triumph to their master, claiming to have killed "many thowsandes." The delighted tyrant, for reward, offers each a fair bride, but they delicately suggest that gold and silver would be more acceptable, and so he promises them a hundred thousand pounds apiece, with castles and towers. Herod then returns thanks to "Mahoune," exults over the thought of the multitude of innocents bloodily murdered, and closes his long address with the unexpected recommendation:—

> "Sirs, this is my counselle,
> Bese not to cruelle,
> Bot adew to the devylle;
> I can no more Franche."

From this it is a natural inference that Herod, as a socially exalted personage, originally was accustomed, in some or all of his discourses, to use the Norman tongue.

The conclusion of the next Mystery in order, *Purificatio Mariæ,* and the commencement of the following, *Pagina Doctorum,* are lost. Simeon, describing with homely vividness his manifold infirmities of age, prays for a sight, before he dies, of the long-promised Immanuel. Two angels assure him that his prayer is heard in Heaven, and bid him seek the newborn Christ in the Temple. He turns his slow steps thitherward, wondering at the ringing of the bells, and encounters Joseph and Mary on their way to make the offering of turtledoves. Angel voices call to him to behold the child in Mary's arms,—and here the leaf is torn away.

Pagina Doctorum, suffering from the same mutilation, opens abruptly in the midst of a discussion of the Rabbis, concerning Messianic prophecy. One of them, as he pores over the ancient roll, not unpoetically expands the Hebrew reference to "a root out of Jesse."

> *Tercius Magister.* Masters, youre resons ar
> right good,
> And wonderfulle to neven,
> Yit fynde I more by
> Abacuk;

> Syrs, lysten a whyle unto
> my steven [voice].
> Our baylle, he says, shalle
> turn to boytt,
> Her afterward som day;
> A wande shalle spryng fro
> Jessy roytt,
> The certan sothe thus can he
> say.
> And of that wande shalle
> spryng a floure,
> That shalle spryng up fulle
> hight,
> Ther of shalle com fulle swete
> odowre,
> And therupon shalle rest and
> lyght
> The Holy Gost, fulle mych of
> myght,
> The Goost of wysdom and of
> wyt
> Shalle beyld his nest, with
> mekylle right,
> And in it brede and sytt.

The child Jesus steps in among the Rabbis with gentle greeting, and is bidden by two of them run away, as they are too busy to be troubled by "barnes"; but the third, the sweeter spirit who had so lovingly dwelt on the old text, calls Jesus to his knee and offers to teach him. The boy quietly protests that he knows as much as they, and when they would test him with questions, excites their wonder and admiration by reciting the ten commandments. At this point Joseph and Mary enter some remote door of the Temple (the mediæval playwright evidently conceiving of the building as a Gothic cathedral), distressfully seeking the lost child, but the sight, afar off, of Jesus among the Rabbis restores their peace. Mary strives in vain to persuade Joseph to go forward and call the boy away, while Joseph, as always, hangs back, abashed by the costly clothes of the Pharisees.

> *Maria.* Now, dere Joseph, as have ye
> seylle [happiness],
> Go furthe and fetche youre son
> and myne;
> This day is goyn nere ilka deylle,
> And we have nede for to go hien.
> *Josephus.* With men of myght can I not melle
> [mingle], Then alle my travelle
> mon I tyne [lose];
> I can not with thaym, that wote
> ye welle,
> Thay are so gay in furrys fyne.
> *Maria.* To thaym youre erand forto say
> Surely that thar ye dred no deylle,
> Thay wille take hede to you alway
> Be cause of eld, this wote I weylle.

Josephus. When I com ther what shalle I say?
　　　For I wote not, as have I ceylle,
　　　Bot thou wille have me shamyd for
　　　　　ay,
　　　For I can nawthere crowke ne knele.
Maria.　Go we togeder, I hold it best,
　　　Unto yond worthy wyghtes in
　　　　　wede,
　　　And if I se, as have I rest,
　　　That ye wille not then must I nede.
Josephus. Go thou and telle thi taylle fyrst,
　　　Thi son to se [thee] wille take
　　　　　good hede;
　　　Weynd furthe, Mary, and do thi
　　　　　best,
　　　I com behynd, as God me spede.

Mary addresses herself to her son, who reminds her that he must be about his "fader warkys," but, nevertheless, says a courteous farewell to the Rabbis, of whom the first two give him praise and good wishes, while the third would have him take up his abode with them, and accompanies Mary and Joseph from the Temple. The Madonna's heart brims with gladness.

　Maria. Fulle welle is me this tyde,
　　　Now may we make good chere.

But the uncourtly carpenter is only anxious to be off.

　Josephus. No longer wylle we byde.
　　　Fare welle alle folk in fere [company].

The nineteenth pageant, Johannes Baptista, is distinguished among the others by its dull and prosaic character, and by its jogging metre. John, who introduces himself and his errand to the audience in the initial speech, is instructed by two angels to baptise Jesus there in the "flume Jordan." He objects, both as feeling himself unworthy to touch the Lord's body, and as considering it more reverential that he should go and meet the Saviour, rather than await by the riverside Christ's coming. But when the angels insist that it is better that the Lord should come to him, John deduces a moral.

　"By this I may welle understand
　That chylder shuld be broght to kyrk,
　For to be baptysyd in every land."

Later on, too, in the very act of the baptism,

　"In the name of thi Fader fre,
　In nomine Patris et Filii
　Sen he wille that it so be,
　Et Spiritûs altissimi,
　And of the Holy Goost on he,"

John inserts a priestly discourse on the seven sacra-

ments.

　"Here I the anoynt also
　With oyle and creme in this intent,
　That men may wit, where so thay go,
　This is a worthy sacrament.
　Ther ar Vj othere and no mo,
　The whiche thi self to erth has sent,
　And in true tokyn, oone of tho
　The fyrst on the now is it spent."

It is of interest to notice that these lines have been crossed out in the manuscript, the figure Vj altogether erased, and against the passage the words written: "Correctyd and not played." The inference is that the pageant was acted at least once or twice after the Reformation. The rite of baptism concluded, Jesus gives a lamb to John, who remains preaching in the wilderness.

Now comes the third and last group of the Towneley Mysteries, where, however rude the expression, the intent throughout, with the exception of a single scene, is tragic. The representation of the Saviour's Passion, physically realistic as these primitive playwrights strove to make it, was doubtless beheld in all devoutness by a hushed, heart-smitten audience. Pilate is the blusterer now, and it is he who takes the lead in the conspiracy against Jesus. The Last Supper is presented, the dialogue adhering closely to the Gospel text. The rhyming is often imperfect, and the diction bald, but here and there occurs a touch of poetry, and the feeling is always reverent and tender.

　"Now loke youre hartes be grefyd noght,
　Nawther in drede nor in wo,
　But trow in God, that you has wroght,
　And in me trow ye also;
　In my fader house, for sothe,
　Is many a wonnyng stede [dwelling-place],
　That men shalle have aftyr thare trowthe,
　Soyn after thay be dede.
　And here may I no longer leynd [tarry],
　Bot I shalle go before,
　And yit if I before you weynd,
　For you to ordan thore,
　I shalle com to you agane,
　And take you to me,
　That where so ever I am
　Ye shalle be with me.
　And I am way and sothe-fastnes,
　And lyfe that ever shalbe,
　And to my fader comys none, iwys,
　Bot oonly thorow me.
　I wille not leyf you all helples,
　As men withoutten freynd;
　As faderles and moderles,
　Thof alle I fro you weynd;
　I shalle com eft to you agayne,

This warld shalle me not se,
But ye shalle se me welle certan,
And lyfand shalle I be.
And ye shalle lyf in heven,
Then shalle ye knaw iwys,
That I am in my fader even
And my fader in me is."

Later comes the prayer of Gethsemane:—

"Fader, let this great payn be stylle,
And pas away fro me;
Bot not, fader, at my wylle,
Bot thyn fulfylled be."

After the betrayal come the scenes of the buffeting and scourging, with all the brutality emphasised and elaborated. These painful effects are continued throughout the trial scene and the scene in the Via Dolorosa, while the crucifixion pageant is wellnigh intolerable. Every detail of the physical torture is forced into prominence, and the spiritual glory that, in the Gospel narrative, makes the anguish of Calvary a "sorrow more beautiful than beauty's self" is almost utterly wanting. As a relief from the tragic tension, the casting of lots for the seamless vesture is farcically handled, and is followed by the popular pageant known as the Harrowing of Hell, which gives the actors who take the devil-rôles their opportunity. The spirit of Jesus, while the body still slumbers in the sepulchre, treads the steep path to hell. As the gleam of light shed before the steps of the coming deliverer grows brighter and brighter, the imprisoned souls wax eager in anticipation, Isaiah, Simeon, John the Baptist, and Moses confirming the new hope. The demon warders grow restless, and listen fearfully for the awful voice that soon thunders at their gates: "Lift up your heads, O ye gates! And be ye lifted up, ye everlasting doors! And the King of Glory shall come in." After vain parley with the threatening stranger, Beelzebub calls up Satan, the Lord of Hell, who ascends in all his terrors, but is smitten down by the resistless arm of Christ. For Judas, Cain, and the Roman Cato—poor Cato, who must need all his philosophy to reconcile him to such a classification—there is no rescue, but the other spirits, hand in hand, led by Adam, who is led by Christ, troop up from the black jaws of hellmouth, singing the Te Deum.

The Resurrection pageant follows with comparative fidelity the Gospel narrative, although the Saviour, on emerging from the tomb, utters a long and touching appeal to the audience, beginning,—

"Erthly man that I have wroght
Wightly wake, and slepe thou noght,
With bytter baylle I have the boght,
    To make the fre;
Into this dongeon depe I soght
    And alle for luf of the."

He displays his wounds, rehearses his agonies.

"Sen I for luf, man, boght the dere,
As thou thi self the sothe sees here,
I pray the hartely, with good chere,
    Luf me agane;
That it lyked me that I for the
    Tholyd [suffered] alle this payn.
If thou this lyfe in syn have led,
Mercy to ask be not adred,
The leste drope I for the bled
    Myght clens the soyn,
Alle the syn the warld with in
    If thou had done."

With outspread arms the white-robed figure yearns toward the tearful listeners.

"Lo how I hold myn armes on brade,
The to save ay redy mayde,
That I great luf to the had,
    Welle may thou know!
Som luf agane I would fulle fayn
    Thou wold me show.
Bot luf noghte els aske I of the,
And that thou fownde [try] fast syn to fle,
Pyne the to lyf in charyte
    Bothe night and day;
Then in my blys that never shalle mys
    Thou shalle dwelle ay."

The fishers of Wakefield set forth the walk to Emmaus, and the evening meal, the episode of doubting Thomas follows, and then the ascension pageant. Doomsday completes the series. The dead have just arisen from their graves, sworded angels drive the greedy demons away from the righteous, while the cloud-enthroned Christ, with the sound of trump, descends from heaven for judgment. The devils quake before Him, but claim their legitimate prey, gleefully reading from their books long lists of evildoers. Their harsh tones and harsher laughter are hushed by the voice of Christ, Who, displaying His pierced hands and wounded side, tells over once again the story of His sufferings.

"Thus was I dight thi sorow to slake,
Man, thus behovid the borud [ransomed] to
    be,
In alle my wo tooke I no wrake [vengeance],
My wille it was for luf of the:
Man, for sorow aght the to quake,
This dredful day this sight to se,
Alle this suffred I for thi sake,
Say, man, what suffred thou for me?"

To the souls on the right and to the souls on the left their dooms are meted out, and while the demons seize upon their victims, with scoff and threat, the saints sing the Te Deum, and the last pageant-carriage, leaving behind it pale faces and quivering nerves, rolls out of Wakefield market-square and on from street to street until the evening falls.

THE MEDIEVAL WORLDVIEW AND THE MYSTERY CYCLES

Katharine Lee Bates (essay date 1893)

SOURCE: "Miracle Plays—Dramatic Values," in *The English Religious Drama*, The Macmillan Company, 1913, pp. 168-200.

[*In the following essay—originally a lecture delivered in July, 1893—Bates discusses the role of the apocryphal gospels in certain sections of the mystery cycles, emphasizing what she perceives as the restraint evidenced by the plays' authors in light of the pervasive influence of these legends on the popular interpretation of scripture. Bates views the plays as sincere depictions of what the medieval mind perceived as the true history of the world, free of literary "consciousness."*]

There are two ways of regarding our old Miracle Plays. Many students of English literature think of them confusedly, contemptuously, as the primal dramatic chaos out of which the Elizabethan stage rose, not by process of evolution, but by divine fiat,—"Let there be Shakespeare," and there was Shakespeare. Others see in this five-centuried growth not merely the dramatic elements, but those displayed on a grand scale and already shapen into a huge, roughhewn, majestic Gothic drama. They see in the Miracle Play not merely collision, but tremendous clash of conflict; not merely scheme, but inevitable development of event from event, and these events colossal; not merely life-like characterisation, but realised humanity, deviltry, and Divinity; not merely passion, but all the passion that surged through the great, child-like, mediæval heart. The upholders of this second view must to a large degree ignore detail, often uncouth, often unseemly, often ridiculous, and persistently fix attention upon the mass of the Miracle structure, the sweep of outline, and dignity of design. They must have limitless forbearance for the halting, tedious, undeveloped speech,—that most beggarly attire with which the vast idea is clothed upon. No poet ear listened for the cadences that should form a fitting music for the splendid spectacle. No poet brain brooded the mighty thought until mighty language was born to compass it. Feeble linguists, uncertain melodists, dull versifiers, toiled over those tattered play-books, whose inherent drama was no one man's invention, no one nation's achievement, but the life-pulse of mediæval Christendom.

The composite authorship of the cycles is, indeed, a critical problem of delightful difficulty, which has already claimed much attention from scholars, Ten Brink's analysis being the most thorough up to date, and will undoubtedly claim more. The relation of group to group, with all the concomitant study of interpolations, adaptations, and possible foreign originals, is a subject that will not fail of patient and persevering investigation. Meanwhile it is, we trust, permissible to note with the naked eye, over the click of all these crowding German microscopes, the general aspects of the dramatic conglomerate.

What is the stuff of these old Miracle Plays? From what quarries was their varied material taken? These bright-hued pageants, where the silent story of rich-stained glass and fresco came to life in breathing, moving figures, have indeed been designated a living *Biblia Pauperum,* but many of the *dramatis personæ* are unknown to Hebrew annalist or evangelist. It is in the Cornwall Plays, however, that we meet with the largest admixture of legend, and the statement may be admitted that the Keltic peoples, as a rule, gave in their Mysteries more place to fable, while the Teutonic held more closely to the Biblical text. Our English Miracles sprang from a Saxon-Norman stock, in some cases, notably in that of the Coventry Plays, under strong French influence, and so present a blending of record and of legend, the record predominating. Without going into the minutiæ of the subject, the chief sources of Miracle material in England may be ranked as the Vulgate, the Apocryphal Gospels, and the manners of the time; especially among the poorer classes.

The handling of Old Testament subjects was, as has been seen, marked by extraordinary freedom. To the vision of the Creation, received as literal history, was persistently added the wild, feudal legend of the Fall of Lucifer,—a legend which twice in English literature has attained epic grandeur: once with the inspired dreamer, Cædmon, and once with the Puritan protagonist, Milton. The story of Cain and Abel was embellished by the transformation of Cain into a Northumbrian boor. The story of the Ark was saturated with fun arising from the vixenish characteristics which, in an astonishing outburst of posthumous slander, the Miracle dramatists have well-nigh universally agreed in bestowing upon Noah's wife. Upon the story of Abraham and Isaac was lavished all the wealth of tenderness and pathos and homely piety which lie deep at the roots of English domestic life. These are the main themes taken from the Old Testament by the Miracle writers, and the additions are, on the whole, less of the nature of legend than of bold and spirited elaboration,—an elaboration carried out on purely mediæval and English lines, without the faintest attempt at reproducing either the life of the patriarchal ages or the customs of the East.

When we come to the New Testament history, we

recognise at once the false strands in the web,—the incidents and characterisations drawn from the Apocryphal Gospels. These gospels had their *raison d'être* in a natural curiosity to know more of the personal life of Jesus Christ than is recorded in the canonical books. Such fragments of tradition as were abroad relating to Joseph and Mary and their kindred, to the birth and childhood of the Redeemer, to His trial and crucifixion, the fate of His persecutors, the future of His friends, found their way into written narrative, sometimes introductory, sometimes appendical, but always supplementary to the Evangelical accounts. The works of the early Christian Fathers, Justin, Irenæus, Clement of Alexandria, and others, contain a few passages apparently confirmatory of some of these traditions, as in the query of Athanasius, occurring in his treatise on the "Incarnation of the Word,"—a query which would demonstrate the Godhood of Christ by the method of comparison: "Who, among righteous men or kings, went down into Egypt and the idols of Egypt fell?" With such evidence in their favour, it is in no way remarkable that the mother-church attached great importance to the Apocryphal Gospels, incorporating certain stories from them into the Roman breviary and service-books. That famous compilation of mediæval myths, the *Legenda Aurea,* drew largely from these spurious narrations. The Apocryphal Gospels were, indeed, extremely popular throughout the Middle Ages, being read, translated, paraphrased, and reproduced in many literary forms, as well as in painting, and, above all, in the sculpture, wood-carving, and glass-staining of the cathedrals. But, confining attention to the field of literature, it is said that versions of these Apocryphal stories have been discovered not only in Britain, France, Spain, Germany, Italy, but in Greece, Egypt, Syria, Persia, India, and as far north as Iceland. In English literature, they found expression not only in the religious drama, but in homilies, histories, and carols.

The longer one dwells on the Apocryphal Gospels, the more one comes to appreciate the omissions of the Mystery writers,—their comparative reticence in regard to the many legends of Christ's infancy and boyhood, and in regard to much else that closely concerned His person. In general, the old playwrights contented themselves with borrowing from the spurious accounts more or less matter relating to the marriage of Joseph and Mary, and to Joseph of Arimathea, the Harrowing of Hell, the fate of Pilate, with his vain efforts to shelter himself within the seamless vesture, the ascension and coronation of the Virgin, and the legends of Veronica, who was believed to have stood among the weeping women by the Via Dolorosa, and have received upon her handkerchief, still exhibited as a holy relic at Rome, the impress of the Saviour's face,—a woman identified in the Apocrypha with her who had an issue of blood twelve years and was healed by Jesus. The Gospels of Nicodemus, which are of the nature of appendices to the canonical books, are the most celebrated of the New Testament Apocrypha. From these Gospels of Nicodemus is taken, amongst much other matter, the *Harrowing of Hell,* with many of its familiar accessories, such as the meeting of the rescued souls, on their entrance into Paradise, with Enoch and Elijah, soon joined by the thief from Calvary, bearing his cross upon his shoulder.

Tribute should be paid to the taste of the early English dramatists in so largely ignoring another class of legends besides those relating to the personal life of Jesus. It has been noted already that the list of English religious dramas, apart from the Latin compositions of Hilarius, comprises little in the way of Saint Plays. Probably some such plays have been lost. Protestantism, which barely tolerated the Mysteries, would hardly have suffered anything so unmistakably Romish as a Saint Play to show itself by daylight. Yet much which was more alien than these to the spirit of the Reformation lived on in the dark, and if there had ever existed any considerable number of Saint Plays, assuredly records and allusions relating to them, if not the very manuscripts, would have been preserved. When, therefore, one remembers the multitude of such miraculous legends afloat through the Middle Ages, how they invaded almost every department of literature,—chronicles, homilies, even Chaucer's *Canterbury Tales,*—the Mystery writers are again to be commended for what they have left unsaid.

After all, in the depths of the English heart there is, and ever has been, a sense of the Divine,—the saving salt of any literature and of any nation. It was this sense which, working obscurely and often dubiously, guided these rude old playwrights in their selection of dramatic subjects and in their handling of the subjects chosen. Badly as they bungled the Christian story, the person of Christ was always sacred to them. With the minor characters, as Joseph and the Christmas shepherds, they did not hesitate to take enormous liberties; but no touch of burlesque mars the majesty of that central figure. It is true that the speeches assigned to Christ are sometimes stiff and dull,—at their best, a weak dilution of the Gospel text; but this was due to inadequacy of literary art, not to irreverence of spirit.

As sources of the Miracle Plays, it should be added, the Vulgate and the New Testament Apocrypha served as remote springs, original fountainheads, rather than the immediate feeding streams. The incidents of the Apocryphal Gospels, in particular, were commonly taken not from the text itself, but from the legends of the text as caught up into current speech and art and story.

The Miracle Cycle, then, has for its fundamental material the Christian faith, crudely comprehended, given, with startling realism, personal embodiment and physical environment, sprinkled over with legend and anachronistic touches of rural English life, yet still in essential features the Christian history.

There is intrinsic dramatic quality in the theme, how-ever conceived. No greater theme is possible to art than this. But as conceived by the Middle Ages, the Christian story is frankly and forcibly dramatic. For the power of these cycles lies in their mighty range. It is the complete history of God's creation that they depict,—a history dramatically treated. The Mystery playwright knew no philosophy of evil as the mere negation of good. To his vision the earth was the arena where two tremendous Spirits, the Eternal God and the Arch-fiend of Rebellion, wrestled in strong contention over the soul of man. We see these two towering fig-ures in their first encounter; we witness Satan's over-throw, followed so soon by his fateful triumph in the garden; we pursue the bitter consequences of that tri-umph through scenes of strife and disaster,—the mur-derous blow of Cain and Lamech's fatal archery, God's hand appearing here and there to snatch His righteous servant from the flood, or His chosen people from the bondage of Egypt. Then are heard the chanting voices of the procession of prophets, foretelling the advent of a glorious champion for humanity, even the Son of God. Hereat the Powers of Evil wax more furious and malignant. Herod rages, the Pharisees plot, Judas be-trays, the soldiers seize, the disciples fall away, the judges exult, the tormentors scourge and mock, the mob denies, Pilate condemns, the cross uplifts its bur-den, and the victory of Satan would seem to be com-plete. But the heart of the spectator is enwrapt by a strange hope and confidence. From the first silver shin-ing of the Bethlehem star upon that peaceful group, the fair young mother with the child clasped to her breast, shepherds kneeling at her feet, and kings has-tening to offer gifts, all through that life of ineffable sacrifice and suffering, grace and majesty, to the dark-ening of the heavens above Mount Calvary, from whose central cross gleams the motionless white figure, there has been ripening in men's minds an apprehension of a new force born into the world, the all-conquering force of love, before which even the bolts and bars of hell shall yet give way. Thus in crudely dramatic fash-ion that wan and tortured form rises from the sepul-chre in kingly might, descends the black and sheer approach to Satan's fortress, bursts the gates of brass, is locked in terrible wrestle with the arch-enemy soon overthrown, and leads out of those deep dungeons up to the light of Paradise the victims of the gray deceiv-er's craft. Then are beheld the ascension of Christ the Son and Mary Mother, the gratulation of the angel hosts, a last struggle of Satan in the shape of Anti-christ, renewed victory of the Son of Man, and the final awful spectacle of Doom, with the bliss of Par-adise on Christ's right hand and the torments of Pur-gatory on his left.

So for a long summer's day, or for three days, or for nine, scene after scene the great tragedy flashed by,

and the eyes of the attendant multitude read it literally as the creed of their own belief, the book of their own life, and their hearts swelled or fainted, melted or were enraptured within them.

It was all so very real in those centuries of faith and art and passion. The French Miracle scaffold, with the heaven-stage above and the hell-stage below, both in-tent on the earth-stage between, graphically confesses the mediæval conception of the universe. No Coperni-cus had yet arisen to daunt men's minds by the disclo-sure that this marvelous world of theirs was but one of an innumerable host of stars, weaving "the web of the mystic measure" through the wilderness of space. The personal being and eventful history of Lucifer were not in question. That smoke-blackened monster, with crooked horns and snout, peering with menacing as-pect out of hellmouth, wore the veritable likeness of the fallen archangel, ever on the scent for prey. There was no old school and no new school of Old Testa-ment criticism, with wordy debate of myth and scribe and epoch. Noah's Ark was as genuine a craft to the fourteenth century as the *Pinta* is to us, and Eve's apple far more certain than Wilhelm Tell's. Most sig-nificant of all, no Strauss, no Renan, even no Chan-ning, had troubled the ear of those primitive play-go-ers. It was the semblance of their very God they saw in the child clinging to Mary's neck, in the boy ques-tioning the white-bearded Rabbis, in the youth baptised by John in Jordan, in the patient sufferer wounded for their transgressions and bruised for their iniquities. With what white lips the men looked upon, how the women turned their faces from the crucifixion! It was no mere spectacle. It was no mere historic execution. It was truth itself,—the truth by which they lived. And Doomsday! In the other pageants it was the past revived in change-ful picture, but this is future for each appalled beholder. Have not the clergy taught how the mighty contest be-tween God and Satan is waged not only for humanity in mass, but for every human soul? The Devil has lost the larger stake. Hell has been emptied once, but there is Purgatory still, and there is the consciousness of un-shriven sin and the dread of the demons' grip.

Allowing for all crudities of comprehension, still the conception is colossal. So long as light strives against darkness and good against evil, so long will the theme retain its power. And not only this, but so long as spirit is housed in flesh and fact made manifest through form, the theme will lend itself to art and compel that art either to some vague correspondence, as in Cima-bue's Virgin,

> "planned
> Sublimely in the thought's simplicity,"

or to clear correspondence, as in the masterpieces of Raphael, with its own magnitude. The soulless must make men and women soulless, the abstract must make men and women abstract, before these can eradicate from humanity the spiritual craving for spiritual life, or the concrete need of concrete revelation of that life.

> "For Wisdom dealt with mortal powers,
> Where truth in closest words shall fail,
> When truth embodied in a tale
> Shall enter in at lowly doors."

What license of poetic imagery we allow to Milton, we may better allow to the Miracle playwrights. For Milton is hardly sincere with his Ptolemaic universe, his crystal "orbs involving and involved," his classic hell, circumscribed by the river of oblivion, his seraphic gunners waving their fire-tipt reeds above the triple row of cannon. But our mediæval dramatists are supremely sincere. If they used imagery, they did not know it. If they personified, they did not mean it. If the truth was not the symbol, and the symbol not the truth, they did not distinguish. Nevertheless, they had the theme, and the theme shaped their dramatic art, as it shaped their plastic art, rudely indeed, but greatly. That most appreciative of the Miracle critics, the late Mr. Symonds, has recognised this power in several of the sub-themes handled in the cycles:—

> "Language in the Miracles barely clothes the ideas which were meant to be conveyed by figured forms; meagrely supplies the motives necessary for the proper presentation of an action. Clumsy phrases, quaint literalism, tedious homilies clog the dramatic evolution. As in the case of mediæval sculpture, so here the most spontaneous and natural effects are grotesque. In the treatment of sublime and solemn themes we may also trace a certain ponderous force, a dignity analogous to that of fresco and mosaic. Subjects which in themselves are vast, imaginative, and capable of only a suggestive handling, such as the Parliaments of Heaven and Hell, Creation, Judgment, and the Resurrection from the dead, when conceived with positive belief and represented with the crudest realism, acquire a simple grandeur."

It is that very effect of "simple grandeur" which I would claim for the Miracle Cycles as a whole, viewed from a sufficient distance, where details are lost in the general outline and relief. "The cycle is the drama, of which the pageants are but shifting scenes." A grand dramatic framework is discernible through the awkward language and the naïve ideas. In all the groups, York, Towneley, Chester, Coventry, the cyclic features are the same. Lucifer puts himself in defiant antagonism to God, Who smites him and his adherents down to hell, creating Adam and Eve that they and their descendants may fill the vacant seats of heaven. The motives for the fierce Satanic warfare against God and man are thus made plain,—revenge and jealousy. Strife is henceforth an assured element. We have the dramatic opposition and the dramatic anticipation of a clash. Although the Titan combatants do not meet face to face, we see evil warring against good in the Cain pageant, the Pharaoh pageant, the Balaam pageant, while the chorus of the prophets leads expectation forward to the second act. Here God, in the person of Christ, openly takes the field against Satan, but in the Coventry cycle alone is the Devil brought much upon the stage to oppose Him. The temptation in the wilderness, which Milton sets, as crucial point, against the fall of man, the old dramatists pass hastily over, reserving their climax for the Harrowing of Hell. They like to represent the wily adversary as prescient of this storming of his feudal hold and as striving by the instrumentality of Pilate's wife to avert the crucifixion. None the less is Calvary the apparent victory of Satan. The two great battle-chiefs have closed at last, and God is overthrown. But there is a third act to come, the triumph-act of Christ, opening with the Harrowing of Hell and closing with the Judgment.

Even such, in outline, is the structure of that Elizabethan drama which the ruder Miracle drama fathered. Still the theme is rebellion against the divine law, as Macbeth rebelled, as Antony rebelled, as Faustus rebelled, each to be dashed to death against the right he had defied. Still, although technically the first and last acts are each sub-divided into two, the action progresses through three main movements, from cause to climax, from climax to consequence. Still there is the subtle effect of gain through loss, fainter lights cast from Calvary being shed on such sights as "the tragic loading" of that couch where the Desdemona-heart of love, the Othello-heart of faith have triumphed even in defeat over the Iago-heart of malice. Still there is the mighty range of the old drama, "rough, unswayable, and free." Elizabethan tragedy, with the careless strength of a young giant, shook off the troublesome conventions of the stage, unity of time, unity of place. Was not England reared upon dramas that embraced heaven, earth, and hell within their limits, that encompassed all of time that had been and yet should be? What did it matter, after that, if Perdita and Marina grew from babyhood to womanhood in a single afternoon, or the scene in the Globe playhouse was shifted back and forth between pre-Christian Britain and Renascence Italy? May not Shakespeare be forgiven even for providing Bohemia with that unhappy sea-coast and letting Julio Romano be contemporary with the Delphic oracle, when we remember how his antecedent playwrights made Noah swear by St. John, and Pharaoh by Mahound, the shepherds of Bethlehem drink Ely ale, and Joseph and Mary be arraigned before the Bishop and his ecclesiastical court? Shall heedlessness of detail call out a sharper criticism than falseness or feebleness of conception? The Gothic drama abounded in robust vitality. Its nerves were not worn by overmuch civilisation. It was not easily shocked. A strain of heathen ferocity showed in it even to the end,—to Hamlet, to the Duchess of Malfi. Greek authority might enjoin the relation, rather than the portrayal, of deeds of bloodshed, violence, and horror, but Kyd and Webster were scions of a race that had looked for generations upon the Bethlehem massacre, the Harrowing of Hell, Calvary, and Doomsday.

But if the Miracle Cycle is to be held responsible for the Elizabethan disregard of the more artificial dramatic canons, the Elizabethan carelessness in minutiæ, and even the lingering brutalities of the Elizabethan stage, it must not be forgotten that these same rude Mysteries set examples not only of sweeping scope and massive structure, but of truth to human life. Unity of action is as binding on the old York playwright as on Shakespeare himself. But this sovereign law of the drama was observed by the mediæval playwrights, as by the Elizabethan, less because they consciously proposed to observe it than because it was inherent in the material they had chosen. Their plots were woven not in fallible human brains, but in the loom of Life, unerring artist. Here and there an Elizabethan strove to be original. Tourneur spun his own plots and spoiled his tragedies. But Shakespeare was content to take a tragedy that had been lived and make it live again. These stories on which he flashed the prismatic light of his genius had their strands already deep dyed with actual blood and tears. He could not greatly offend against the prime dramatic law, while he walked with Plutarch and with Holinshed, who had walked with men. In like manner the Miracle playwrights have the Biblical record chiefly to thank for the unity of action that marks the Miracle Cycle.

Yet granting this, the selective quality, which is the dramatist's distinctive gift, has an indispensable part to play. Any student of Shakespeare who has compared *Lear, King John, Henry the Fifth,* with the so-called "old plays," though but a few years earlier, on the same themes, needs no more impressive revelation of the function of the artist. As the architect compels the weight of stone and marble to the soaring arch and airy tower that in perfected beauty haunt his vision, so the dramatist selects and disposes his no less stubborn material in strict conformity with that one controlling action, that one organic human deed,—seed and flower and fruit,—which he recognises and reveals by prerogative of genius.

The Mystery playwrights possessed in rudimentary form this dramatic sense. The Miracle Cycle had grown up about the three liturgical dramas of Christmas, Good Friday, and Easter, and to these it shaped itself throughout, concentrating attention on Christ the champion, and keeping steadily in view the great collision toward which the forces of good and evil were converging. Guided by this principle of unity, the early dramatists resolutely denied themselves many an effective pageant from the Old Testament. The story of Abraham and Isaac, it is true, appealed to their sense of pathos too strongly to be excluded, but even Balaam and

Pharaoh, pageants not altogether out of connection with the trend of the divine event, were individual experiments that did not win the general consent of the cyclists. The Cornwall dramatist, freer of fancy than his Saxon neighbours, ventured on the story of David, but found himself forced to bind it to the rest by the legend of the three miraculous rods: Likewise in dealing with the Gospel narrative, there is a tendency to subordinate not only the temptation scene, which might anticipate the triumph of Christ over Satan, reserved for the Harrowing of Hell, but also the Lazarus scene, lest this should forestall the continued victory of Christ in His breaking the bonds of death, reserved for the Resurrection pageant.

In addition to the sense of dramatic unity, these simple playwrights clearly had the sense of dramatic situation. This we continually encounter from the initial *Creatio,* where Satan, usurping his Maker's throne and receiving the homage of one-tenth the host of heaven, is cut short in his blasphemous boasts by the approach of God, and by the mere aspect of that dread figure is smitten down to hell, to the final *Damnatio,* where each song of thanksgiving from the throng of the saved is answered by a wail of agony from the throng of the lost, the white Christ standing calm above the tumult, with blessing in His outstretched right hand and cursing in His left.

One important feature of the Miracle Cycle, a feature which the Elizabethan drama duly inherited and fearlessly appropriated, remains to be noted,—the blending of comedy with tragedy. It can easily be conceived that to the devout spectator the heartstrain of the Passion pageants was almost intolerable. Very clear, it is true, was the shining background of divine love, with its promise of divine victory. As any master tragedy, from Æschylus to Browning, gives strange delight, in place of overwhelming pain, because the dark shadow-tracery throws into brighter relief the firm beauty of righteousness behind, so the assured faith of the mediæval audience made Whitsuntide and Corpus Christi, with their solemn spectacles, soul-refreshing holidays. The Christian tragedy met the basal requirement of Aristotle in that the minds of the beholders were purified by pity and by terror. But still the foreground effect was one of suffering, and the responsive sympathy was exhaustingly intense. In the drama, as in life, there was need of comedy to relieve the tension of emotion. The early playwrights, as the early carvers, were pupils of nature, and did not dream that anything which pertained to life could be alien to art. The grotesque seems to have been spontaneous with both classes of workmen, and, to a degree, unconscious. Reference here is had rather to the significantly intrusive figures and the studied comic rôles. It is life that gives warrant for the imp in the angel choir of Lincoln. It is life that gives warrant for Noah's thorny-tempered wife and sheepish old Joseph. And art, in holding close to life, finds herself the gainer. As the humours of the grave-digger throw into deeper shadow the waiting churchyard, with its open grave, and Hamlet's brooding heart, as King Lear's elemental agony of wrath shows more pitiful beside the whimsies of his sweet and bitter fool, so have the Miracle Cycles artistic need of their scolding dame and blundering old carpenter.

Shakespeare gave his august sanction to this fidelity of the Gothic drama to life. The musicians pass their idle jests while, to all appearance and belief, death lies on Juliet

> "like an untimely frost
> Upon the sweetest flower of all the field."

The black passion of Shylock is encircled by mirthful romance. And more and more, with Shakespeare's ever deepening comprehension of humanity, the comedy presses nearer and nearer to the very seat of tragedy. The helplessness of king and husband before the unbridled tongue of Paulina provokes the smile of the bystanding lords, even in their painful apprehension for Hermione. Out of his cloud of gloom Hamlet will still make sombre sport of "tedious old fools," and Timon's angry eyes must bear to be confronted by a burlesque of his own life-wasting misery in Apemantus.

The earliest of the great English realists, Chaucer, a secular dramatist born before the secular drama, holds the mirror up to life as frankly as does Shakespeare. But the star-bright idealists, Marlowe, Spenser, Shelley, are hopelessly at a loss before the comic. Lovers of Marlowe trust that most of his comic scenes, gross and pointless as they too often are, were written for him. The audience knew, and Marlowe knew, that comedy, though not such comedy, should relieve the terror of *Faustus,* but it was not in him to find and furnish it, for the idealist is a runaway from the school of life to the far-horizoned uplands of dreamland. Such truants are enviable in their escape from the coarse and the degrading. It is with the realistic comedy of Chaucer and Shakespeare that there come in the vulgar jokes and all that offensive indecency of expression which Chaucer so cheerily and ingeniously maintains is required by the laws of realistic art.

Turning from the structural principles of the Miracle Cycle to its characterisation, we meet again the realistic method. The third main source of Miracle material is to be looked for in the rural life of mediæval England, especially among the shepherds of Yorkshire and Lancashire, merry of mood, even in their poverty, and especially by the humble domestic hearth, where, no less than in Wordsworth's day, the baby boy lay busied with his mimic games,

> "Fretted by sallies of his mother's kisses,

> With light upon him from his father's eyes."

There is no one feature of these rude old dramas more winning than the warmth of sympathy they evince with all the pure and tender, wholesome and generous brood of household affections. It was this kindly touch of nature which so endeared the Abraham pageant to these simple audiences, which stirred them to such vehement wrath against Herod, murderer of the innocents, which gave its beauty to the group about the manger, its pathos to the group about the cross, which made the women wail and sway in unison with the long lament of the Mater Dolorosa, as the lacerated body of her son was laid across her knees.

It is palpably absurd that these oriental scenes, dating from the dawn of the Christian era or from dim patriarchal times, should be given a fourteenth-century Northumbrian or Midland setting. The immediate cause was ignorance. The insular monks and tradesmen who composed and presented these plays were without information as to the customs of the East and of antiquity. Possibly there was also a remote cause. If the populace of Rome so late as the seventeenth century implicitly believed that the Divine Tragedy had been enacted within their own city at the very spots where they were accustomed to see it represented by the erection of a manger, or a cross, the scattering of palms, or the strewing of cypress boughs, it is not strange that mediæval simplicity made the Christian story so inherent a part of English life as to feel no incongruity in framing the Holy Family in a Yorkshire environment. At the heart of this folly lay, perhaps, a sleeping wisdom, in that the drama of Palestine is indeed not bound to locality or date, but belongs to all peoples and to all time.

The characterisation in the Mysteries is purely realistic, with the vividness of actual portraiture, where it concerns the rank and file of society. Noah's wife—for the Noah of the Mysteries is a yeoman—might have joined, with her distaff, any gossiping group of "spinsters in the sun" from Lancashire to Devon, and held her own in racy monologue against the Wife of Bath herself. The Coventry sompnour would have outroared in jovial fellowship his boisterous brother of the "fyr-reed cherubynnes face," and one can readily picture the Bethlehem shepherds, chafed as they were by their social discontents, listening on the village green with confirmatory nods and frowns, while some gaunt clerk of Oxenford read aloud from well-thumbed manuscript a canto of *Piers Plowman.* Democratic satire of a burly, good-natured sort painted the ranting tyrants, Pharaoh and Cæsar, Herod and Pilate, but whatever secular criticism might have manifested itself in the delineation of the ecclesiastics was kept down by the clerical authorship or revision.

The Mystery treatment of the devils is amusing in its

childish egotism. They are viewed simply as the enemies of the human race. After the first plunge of Lucifer and his faction into hellmouth, their deviltry is taken for granted, and their doom accepted as irreversibly sealed. Their rôle in the universe is settled, their costume determined, and nobody wonders about the look behind the mask. Later centuries may wax inquisitive. Milton may trace the deterioration of Lucifer, the fading of the bright archangelhood. Mrs. Browning may seek to comprehend the fire of his torment:—

> "that fire-hate
>
> . . . . .
>
> Wherein I, angel, in antagonism
> To God and His reflex beatitudes,
> Moan ever in the central universe
> With the great woe of striving against Love."

But our Mystery poets are supremely unconcerned as to the secrets of demon consciousness. Their presentation is distinctly objective. The devils are shown at their work, and busy enough about their mischievous labours, and pleased enough with their numerous successes these agents of evil seem to be. In their loss of spiritual susceptibility, they appear rather of the Mephistopheles type, but among their victims is no Faustus to wreak his restless curiosity upon them and force their frightful confidence. The human personages of the Miracle Cycles evidently regard the devils much as pioneers regard wild beasts, scientific inquiry being suspended for terror of claws and teeth. The very simplicity of the characterisation makes these grotesque fiends graphic and, in crude fashion, dramatically effective. Yet, although they sometimes gave an impressible man the nightmare, the average spectator had a lurking affection for the lesser devils. They were all he had left of the goblins, kobolds, and pixies of his ancestral heathenism. As for Satan himself, there was a delicious excitement in viewing the shaggy monster on the pageant scaffold, with God or Christ at hand to hurl him down presently into hellmouth. Seeing Satan off the stage might be quite another matter.

The characterisation of the third class of *dramatis persona*, divine and angelic beings, was attended by graver dangers, which the Miracle Cycles did not escape. The first authority in English drama, Mr. Ward, says in regard to this:—

> "These Mysteries teach, in their way, the lesson which the strange oaths of the Middle Ages teach in another, that a constant familiarity with the bodily presentment of sacred persons and things bred a material grossness in the whole Æsthetical atmosphere of the people."

This is a serious charge, and one which cannot be gainsaid. As the gilt peruke grew familiar, the dream of the halo faded away. As the attire and demeanour of the celestial beings became conventionalised and hackneyed, the commonplaces of the pageant scaffold, the uplift and the glory of conception melted and were gone. The stage properties hung like clogs on the wings of heavenly imagination.

But if this be true of the æsthetic influence of the Miracles, what must have been their religious effect? That they were originally charged with devout passion who can doubt? Christendom was more than any nation. The Church enfolded all. Within the vast embrace of her beautiful walls there was room for all of human life, its mirth and sin and sorrow, its household charities and altar mysteries, its broken human loves and baffled Godward longings. Perhaps no one of the essential dramatic elements is stronger in the Miracles than the element of passion. Playwrights, actors, audience, all combined in flooding these unkempt plays with irresistible fervours and ardours. These were religious, but not as later centuries understand the term. Not exclusive, but inclusive, was that consecrated passion which carved waggish designs on the misereres of Chester cathedral, and called forth peal on peal of laughter from the throngs who flocked to see the Chester pageants. But this passion, to maintain itself pure and rich, needed to be fed from a more ethereal height than the scaffold platform. The angels, who waved their gilt wings century after century on those trundling stages, made no advance in individuality or symbolic beauty. That is not so strange. Angels are not easily persuaded to stoop to human acquaintance. Since the days of Ezekiel, or, at latest, of the seer of Patmos, no poet save Dante has looked upon the angels. But the Miracle conception of the Creator need not, one would think, be quite so bad. It is, with few exceptions, either puerile and preposterous, or remote and colourless. It was on Christ and Mary Mother that the ardent devotion of mediævalism lavished itself. It was those gracious Presences that made the pageant scaffold holy. The rude, warm heart of England still throbbed in love and adoration for these, long after the snow-white vesture and crimson shoes had lost significance in familiarity. But none the less the material presentment was slowly chilling that great religious heart. An ascending Christ, whom the angels had to draw up by ropes, could not hold fealty forever. The modern world refused allegiance, and the pageant scaffold fell. For, while the Middle Ages were the ages of art, as they were the ages of faith, it was a romantic art, in certain features a barbaric art, unguided, untaught; and it was a blind faith, bowed in ignorant obedience before the authority of Rome. The Renascence drew back the curtain which had so long hidden the classic world, and, as the severely ordered beauty of its noble art became revealed, the wild, joyous, youthful riot of the mediæval blood was awed and tamed. But it is not enough to say that the refined taste of the Renascence period laughed down the crude old dramas. The Reformation frowned them down. They had rendered religious service. Who can doubt it? They had impressed one aspect of the Christian revelation, but it was time that another aspect should claim attention. In the main the Mysteries were faithful to the watchword: "God is love." That patient figure of the buffeted, taunted, crucified Christ, to curse and insult answering not again, turning His cheek to the smiter, uttering with dying lips a prayer for His tormentors,—how it tutored, mastered, transformed, exalted the fierce Northmen, who, for five centuries and more, gazed upon the enacted tragedy! The lesson, even yet, is far from learned. The victories of force, the flash of animal courage, still appeal to English instinct more promptly than the victories of gentleness, the glow of moral heroism. Yet the Gothic blood was under schooling for this very fault all through the Middle Ages. The Griseldas, the Nut-brown Maids, the Fair Annies united with saint-lore and martyr-lore, and with the constant spectacle of sad-robed monks, grasping missal and rosary instead of sword and bridle-rein, of barefoot friars, of nuns and penitents, to stamp the fundamental tenet of Christianity deep upon the rugged Teutonic heart. Central in that mediæval object-teaching stood the white, golden-haloed figure, about whom all the pageants of the Miracle Cycle sprang up, but the occasional false note, as the pageant of the Harrowing of Hell, with the overthrow of the Fiend by Christ in furious wrestle, shows too clearly that the native paganism in the beholders was not completely melted, that the old war-song of *Beowulf* still echoed in the air.

Nevertheless, the prevailing tendency of the New Testament pageants was to show the beauty of meekness, the grace of forgiveness, the redemptive power of love. But the text "God is love" is not the only key-word of the Christian religion. It was said again: "God is a Sprit, and they that worship Him must worship Him in Spirit." Because this word had been wellnigh forgotten by mediæval Catholicism, Protestantism swept over northern Europe like a fresh, strong, purifying wave. And none of the products of the Middle Ages had sinned more grievously against spirituality than the Miracle Plays, with their God in a gilt peruke and their Christ in red slippers, their insistence upon the physical agonies of Gethsemane and Calvary, their palpable Immaculate Conceptions and Resurrections. The Reformation, hungering and thirsting after the Divine, could not brook the triviality, the grossness, the falseness, of the old religious stage. It swept the land clear of it. It destroyed records and manuscripts,—all with the same headstrong vehemence, the same impetuosity of indignation with which it tore down the long-worshipped images of the Virgin, rifled the shrines of the saints, scraped away frescoes, and multilated carvings, and crushed into myriad fragments the enchanted windows, which not all the wizardry of modern art and science can replace. The Miracle Plays but went the way of all

who have served their time, who have done with much of evil more of good, and whose mission is ended. Their opportunity was a large one. Jusserand exclaims:—

> "Cinq à six cents ans de popularité! Quelle pièce de théâtre occupa si longtemps la scéne! Est-il une seule œuvre littéraire qui soit restée tant de siècles vivante, au grand soliel, avant d'aller tristement jouir de l'immortalité, a l'ombre des bibliothèques des savants? Au premier abord, nous avons peine à comprendre aujourd'hui cette admiration universelle, car enfin ce n'etait pas seulement la foule des marchands et des laboureurs qui allait voir Pilate et Noé; c'etait toute la ville et même toute la nation, les gens du peuple, les bourgeois, les nobles, les clercs, et le roi."

And with all other service rendered by the Miracle Cycles, they served the Elizabethan drama well. They not only bequeathed to it scope and freedom, great constructive principles, reality of characterisation, and intensity of passion, but they paved the way for its reception. They made England a nation of actors, a nation of theatre-lovers, a nation of deep dramatic cravings, who would be content with no such learned and elegant trifling as amused the court and university, but cried out for range, for earnestness, for life. To follow the history of feudal England through a series of plays was little for those whose grandsires had followed the history of mankind. Londoners had looked already on a more heart-moving tragedy than *Hamlet*.

Charles Mills Gayley (essay date 1904)

SOURCE: "The Dramatic Development of the English Cycles," in *Plays of Our Forefathers*, Duffield and Company, 1907, pp. 144-52.

[*In the following essay, originally published in 1904, Gayley discusses the development of the English mystery cycles, noting the role of the guilds in the secularization of drama, and the affirmation of community bonds as a social function of performances. The critic emphasizes the plays' affinity with comedy rather than tragedy, the latter of which, he comments, derives from secular histories "of the individual in opposition to the social, political, and divine."*]

When, after the reinstitution of the festival of *Corpus Christi* in 1311, the miracle plays began in England to be a function of the guilds, their secularisation, even though the clerks still participated in the acting, was but a question of time; and the injection of crude comedy was a natural response to the civic demand. Indeed, if we consider comedy in its higher meaning as the play of the individual achieving his ends, not by revolt, but by adjustment to circumstance and convention, the miracle play. . .was in its essence a preparation for comedy rather than tragedy. For the theme of these dramas is, in a word, Christian: the career of the individual as an integral part of the social organism, of the religious whole. So, also, their aim: the welfare of the social individual. They do not exist for the purpose of portraying immoderate self-assertion and the vengeance that rides after, but the beauty of holiness or the comfort of contrition. Herod, Judas, and Antichrist are foils, not heroes. The hero of the miracle seals his salvation by accepting the spiritual ideal of the community. These plays, accordingly, contribute in a positive manner to the maintenance of the social organism. The tragedies of life and literature, on the other hand, proceed from secular histories, histories of personages liable to disaster because of excessive peculiarity,—of person or position. Tragedy is the drama of Cain, of the individual in opposition to the social, political, divine; its occasion is an upheaval of the social organism. The dramatic tone of the miracle cycle is, therefore, determined by the conservative character of Christianity in general; the nature of the several plays is, however, modified by the relation of each to one or other of the supreme crises in the biblical history of God's ways toward man. The Massacre of the Innocents emphasises not the weeping of a Rachel, but the joyous escape of the Virgin and the Child. In all such stories the horrible is kept in the background or used by way of suspense before the happy outcome, or frequently as material for mirth. The murder of Abel gradually passes into a comedy of the grotesque. Upon the sweet and joyous character of the pageants of Joseph and Mary and the Child we shall in due course dwell. They are of the very essence of comedy. Indeed, it must be said that in the old cycles the plays surrounding even the Crucifixion are not tragedy; they are specimens of the serious drama, of tragedy averted. The drama of the cross is a triumph. In no cycle does the *consummatum est* close the pageant of the Crucifixion; the actors announce, and the spectators believe, that this is "Goddis Sone," whom within three days they shall again behold, though he has been "nayled on a tree unworthilye to die."

But though the dramatic edifice constructed by our mediæval forbears is generally comedy, it is also divine. And not for a moment did these builders lose their reverence for the House Spiritual that was sacred, nor once forget that the stones which they ignorantly and often mirthfully swung into strange juxtaposition were themselves hewn by Other Hands. The comic scenes of the English Miracle should, therefore, be regarded not as interruptions to the sacred drama, nor as independent episodes, but as counterpoint or dramatic relief. Regarding the plays as units, we may discover in one, like the beautiful Brome play of *Abraham and Isaac,* or its allied pageants of Chester, York, and Wakefield, a preponderance of the pathetic; in another, like the York or the Wakefield *Scourging of Christ,* a preponderance of the horrible; in the Joseph and Mary plays of the *Ludus Coventriæ* a preponderance of the romantic, and

so on. But when we regard them as interdependent scenes of the cycles to which they might, or do, belong, the varied emotional colours blend: indigo, gamboge, vermilion producing an effect, gorgeous—sometimes disquieting, but always definite. Not only definite, but homogeneous and reposeful, when, in moments of historic vision, the tints grow misty, subliminal, and all is moss-green, lavender, or grey,—as when with self-obliteration one contemplates the stained glass window of a mediæval church, King's College Chapel, St. Mark's of Venice, or Nôtre Dame.

The best comedies of the cycles—the York and Wakefield pageants of the *Flood,* the N-Town *Trial of Joseph and Mary*—pass from jest to earnest as imperceptibly as autumn through an Indian summer. In the Second Shepherds' Play, one cannot but remark the propriety of the charm, as well as the dramatic effect, with which the foreground of the sheep-stealing fades into the radiant picture of the Nativity. The pastoral atmosphere is already shot with a prophetic gleam; the fulfilment is, therefore, no shock or contrast, but a transfiguration—an epiphany. It is, moreover, to be remembered that such characters and episodes as are comically treated are of secular derivation, or, if scriptural, of no sacred significance. Thus the comic and the realistic in the poet were set free; and it is just when he is embroidering the material of mystery with the stammel-red or russet of his homespun that he is of most interest to us. When the plays have passed into the hands of the guilds, the playwright puts himself most readily into sympathy with the literary consciousness as well as the untutored æsthetic taste of the public if he colours the spectacle, old or new, with what is pre-eminently popular and distinctively national. In the minster and out of it, all through the Christian year, the townsfolk of York or Chester had as much of ritual, scriptural narrative, and tragic mystery as they desired, and probably more. When the pageants were acted, they listened with simple credulity, no doubt, to the sacred history, and with a reverence that our age of illumination can neither emulate nor understand; but we may be sure that they awaited with keenest expectation those invented episodes where tradition conformed itself to familiar life—the impromptu sallies, the clothyard shafts of civic and domestic satire sped by well-known wags of town or guild. Of the appropriateness of these insertions the spectators made no question, and the dramatists themselves do not seem to have thought it necessary to apologise for their æsthetic creed or practice.

It is as a propædeutic to comedy, then, rather than tragedy that I prefer to treat the miracle plays. And I find it easier to trace some order of dramatic development by approaching them from this point of view.

I have elsewhere attempted to show [in *Representative English Comedies*] that the later dramatists did not invent their art; they worked with what they found, and they found a dramatic medium of expression to which centuries and countless influences had contributed. An extended study of the history of English drama should therefore determine, so far as possible, the relative priority, not only of cycles, but of dramatic stages within the cycles; what each has contributed to the enfranchisement of the artistic spirit and the development of the technical factors of the art,—to what extent each has expressed or modified the realistic, satirical, pathetic, romantic, or humorous view of life, and in what ways each has reflected the temper of its time, the manners and the mind of the people that wrote, acted, and witnessed these early dramas. If I arrange the plays that bear upon the development of popular drama according to my conclusions regarding priority of composition, the order, broadly stated for our present rapid survey, would seem to be: First, the Cornish and the Old Testament portions of the Chester and N-Town, then the productions of the second and third periods of the York, and closely following these the crowning efforts of the Wakefield or Towneley, then the New Testament plays of the Chester and N-Town, and finally the surviving portions of the collections of Digby and Newcastle. This order, which is roughly historical, has the advantage, as I perceive after testing it, of presenting a not unnatural sequence of the æsthetic values or interests essential to a kind of drama which is rather comic than tragic:—first the humour of the incidental, then of the essential or real, and gradually of the satirical; afterwards the accession of the romantic, pathetic, and sublime; the wonderful, the allegorical, and the mock-ideal; and finally of the scenic and sensational. Of course beneath this woof of cumulative art and colour there is the warp of the original intention: the mystery, the sacrifice, the lesson. The presence of the serious and supernal goes without saying; but it is in the increment of other qualities that the transmutation of the spectacle from liturgy to popular drama is most readily to be observed.

Of the Old Testament, that is, the earlier Chester and N-town plays, the most useful for our present purpose are *The Death of Abel* and *Noah's Flood*. With them may be considered the Cornish version. The Cornish miracles present us with dramatic situations in the liturgical-epical germ, and characters in the undifferentiated "rough." The *Cain,* for instance, is but boor and niggard; his possibilities for comedy are undeveloped, but it is impossible that they should long be repressed. The devils, indeed, who come forward like a chorus at the end of each important scene, were probably pressed into the service of merriment; but the dramatic motive for which they exist is serious, and the part assigned to them is more consistent than in any of the other cycles. The Chester play of *Cain,* a conglomerate running from the Creation to the death of Abel, is not only one of the crudest of the cycle (much more so, for instance, than the sacrifice of Isaac based upon the Brome Play), but one of the most naïve on the subject. The character

of the potential fratricide, with his canny offering of the earless corn that grew next the way, and his defiant "God, thou gotteste noe better of me, Be thou never so gryme," is manifestly nearer the primitive conception than the Cayme of York or Wakefield. He is not yet wit, wag, and dare-devil. The episode in the Chester is didactic, but still realistic; less imaginative than in the York or Wakefield, but creative. Evidently more modern than the Chester play, which it somewhat resembles, is the *Cain and Abel* of the *Ludus Coventriæ* or N-Town. The villain is well-conceived, and elaborated with pith and humour. He discusses the Almighty with a worldly wisdom that remotely approaches that of the Wakefield, and he expresses his opinion of Abel—

> Among all fools that go on ground
>   I hold that thou be one of the most:
> To tithe [give away in tithes] the best that is
>   most sound,
>   And keep the worst that is near lost—

with somewhat the same vivid and natural use of the vernacular. The action between the brothers is more elaborate than in Chester, but the dramatic quality depends rather upon dialogue than development of the situation. Its versification is certainly not that of the earliest stage of the cycle to which it belongs, and its lyrical quality might even indicate a later period of composition than the corresponding plays in the York and Wakefield; but it is not derived from either of them.

The development of a situation from the serious to the humorous is admirably illustrated by still another play of this earlier group. In the dramatisation of the Flood, the Cornish cycle presents the serious aspect of the naïve conception. Noah and his wife are on affectionate terms; she is obedient and helpful. It has not occurred to the writer to introduce an extraneous interest, as, for instance, that of conjugal strife. The play is interesting, however, because it displays some slight ability to discriminate characters. Likewise unconscious of comic possibilities is the N-Town play of the Flood. Though probably of later composition than the corresponding plays in other cycles, it is, in its greater part, one of the earlier, though not of the earliest plays of its own cycle. The characters (the sons' wives now begin to play a part), pious, prosaic, and uninteresting, are perfunctorily portrayed, but the construction of the play is ingenious, especially in its manipulation of the episode of Lamech, not as an extraneous action, but as a factor in the organic development of the motive; a hint of a sub-plot. In the Chester play, on the other hand, the characters are distinct and consistently developed. The comic episodes are natural and justifiable, for they serve to display, not to distort, character, and they grow out of the dramatic action. They are, moreover, varied, and, to some extent, cumulative. This play is indeed a vast dramatic advance upon the N-Town. It is approximately on the same plane of dramatic development as the York play of *The Flood,* and should be considered with reference to it, although in spite of one or two unique resemblances in language and conception, neither pageant can be regarded as dependent upon the other.

It is noteworthy that the York play on the building of the Ark, one of the earliest of that cycle, is serious. The play on the Flood, however, which is in a somewhat later stanza, indulges in an altercation between Noah and his wife. The humour of this in turn is surpassed by that of the Chester, so also the technique. While in the York the amusing episode is sudden and of one sequence, in the Chester the clouds upon the domestic horizon gather with artistic reluctance, and, when they burst, refresh the soil in more than one spot. Noah is not yet the henpecked husband of later comedy, though prophetic thereof. Peaceably inclined, but capable of a temper, he serves God and apostrophises the perversity of women. The possibilities of his wife's character are cunningly unfolded. At first apparently amenable to reason, her progress toward "curstness" is a study in the development of character. Few situations in our early drama are better conceived than her refusal at the critical moment to enter the Ark unless her gossips are also taken aboard. Cam's "Shall we *all* feche her in?" the drinking song,—a rollicking song, too, with the lilt, "Back and side, go bare, go bare,"—Noah's collapse of temper and the *alapam auri,* all these are good fooling, and must have left our ancestors thirsty for more. The "business" is of course enhanced by the multiplication of participants, by the solicitude of the children, and the apathy of the gossips. The song, I am afraid, is a later addition; but even without that the appropriateness of diction to the naïve (not vague or poetic) statement of details marks an essential advance in realism.

Hardin Craig (essay date 1955)

SOURCE: An introduction to *English Religious Drama of the Middle Ages*, Oxford at the Clarendon Press, 1955, pp. 1-18.

[*In the following essay, Craig discusses how the Corpus Christi plays reflected the "symbolic" and "naïve" dramatic conventions of medieval drama, and explains how these conventions themselves arose from the highly effective organization of the church and the innate conservatism of the medieval worldview.*]

When one considers the origin of the mystery plays within the medieval church, an origin without thought of dramatic or histrionic effect, and when one considers also how these plays passed into the hands of very simple medieval people—authors, players, managers, and all—one can see that their technique was inevita-

bly naïve and firmly conventional. Their distances were symbolic distances, and their time was symbolic time. Noah had to build the ark in the midst of his taunting neighbours, had to get his live-stock and his recalcitrant wife on board, had to endure forty days and forty nights of rain, had to make a landing on Mount Ararat, and had to rear his famous sons all in a matter of minutes. The drama of the medieval people was anachronistic because it was symbolic and not realistic and because, like most Elizabethans also, its portrayers had not in the modern meaning an historical sense. This drama had no theory and aimed consciously at no dramatic effects, and, when it succeeded, its success came from the import of its message or from the moving quality of some particular story it had to tell.

The mystery plays were not much more backward in this matter than was the contemporary secular drama of the sixteenth century. Many conventions lived on into the age of Queen Elizabeth, for the technique of the mystery and miracle plays and of the main current of English popular drama consisted merely in telling a story on a stage by means of dialogue, impersonation, and action. Early Tudor plays have no definable technique unless they have imitated it from Latin comedy and tragedy. They have, even some of Shakespeare's, rotation speeches such as the mystery plays had, and, as for monologues, regular procedures in drama, they had no fixed function, and were, as in the mystery plays, frankly addressed to the audience. Prologues also come through in the same vague and untutored way. Perhaps the most striking of these inherited conventions was the unlocated scene. In mystery plays events relatively unconnected with place were played in the *platea,* and in the Tudor drama such events still continue to have and, in spite of the diligence of editors, still continue to need no particular place in which to happen. In the religious plays there also appeared from the beginning hymns and antiphons as service pieces, and they no doubt prepared the way for the free use of songs in Elizabethan drama. Actors on the pageants often pretended to be making long journeys over short distances, and the process did not make them ridiculous to the spectators. They lay down and pretended to sleep when the story demanded it. They neither had nor needed regular provision for entrances and exits, since usually all actors were, whether acting and speaking or not, on the stage all the time, and in the matter of visions, of which many were called for, substantial figures merely appeared and, since they were only symbols, were accepted without question as insubstantial. For some of these visions or assumptions the players employed windlasses, pretty crude affairs no doubt, and for the Assumption of the Blessed Virgin Mary the clouds used were made of white linen. An idea of the *mise en scène* of the mystery plays may be gained from selected records many of which are cited in this book.

As for Corpus Christi plays and other large dramatic

pieces, they are not the result of the inspiration of an individual author who sat down and wrote a Corpus Christi play as the spirit moved him. They originated in the early fourteenth century mainly by the joining together in an all-inclusive cycle of a number of smaller pre-existent cycles and perhaps single plays. They were communal in the sense that they were instituted, performed, and managed by communities, and they grew by a sort of incremental amplification by anonymous writers from time to time. By the middle of the fifteenth century, when three of the greater English cycles were written down, this process had been going on for more than a century. The Corpus Christi plays were, moreover, no small or incidental things. To bring one into full form such as that of the cycles we possess required the support of a substantial municipality, and the learning and religious culture that went into the making of such cycles as the York and the Hegge plays were not present in more than a dozen places, if that many, in all England. Let us get rid of the idea that the Corpus Christi cycles were written, managed, and acted by ignorant peasants and townspeople of low class. Into them went the finest things that the English Middle Ages knew and felt.

The basis of a quiet and continued acceptance of a philosophy of life is hope and not comfort or gain. It may be the hope of an earthly paradise, but a heavenly paradise has certain advantages since it is not liable to be discredited by evil events and tendencies. It was the hope of an eternity of bliss for the faithful that supported and kept satisfied the people of the long and varied period we describe so summarily as the Middle Ages. But there was something else necessary to secure this lasting peace, and that too the people of the Middle Ages possessed. They were allowed to cling to and exploit actual present human life, although they were not allowed to put a premium on it. Human life must be considered as dross and dregs compared to life after death and must be renounced in favour of immortality. To renounce the present and all that goes with it is really to renounce self, and there is an instinct very strong in human nature to renounce self and escape its responsibilities. There was, no doubt, enough poverty, hardship, monotony, and danger to make it relatively easy for medieval people to lift their eyes to the hills and ignore the squalor of the valleys, but the men of the Middle Ages had a hope that pacified their impatience and reconciled them to the lot that it had pleased Almighty God to award to them. With this it must be remembered that the people of the Middle Ages, particularly rural and provincial people, had no patterns for an individual life. They did not dread it more than we do, for they did not know about it. That knowledge was of course not altogether absent, but it was not to come in a compelling flood until the dawn of the Renaissance. Meantime, the very thought of an aspiring individual life was submerged in a common union, and in union there is strength. No doubt medieval people found com-

fort in the absence of the worries and frustrations of a self-propelled individuality, and they did not know the sources of their peace and were not so anxious as are modern men to take refuge in a newly invented dominant ideology, because they had not been taught to strive as individuals. They did not seek to save the world, because they knew the world had already been saved.

There was also an essential liberty within their grand system of law. Men were allowed to satisfy their creative impulses, not in the building of cathedrals only, but also in the tasks of ordinary workmanship, and, since there was little repression of the creative instincts of the individual, there was little frustration. People must not be bored, and the church by providing almost endless ceremony, and the community by the activity of its guilds and orders, provided fields of action that compensated for the loss of an unwanted self. Communal action made the situation of the non-participant unendurable, and not to belong meant impotence. Within limits medieval men might pursue material gain and seek prosperity for themselves and their families, and they were not deprived of the honour that comes from skill in handicraft and leadership in the classes to which they belonged.

The social organization for the realization of a life of subordinated self was unsurpassed. The collective body was all-important, and man's eternity was provided for by the doctrines of the church. Men did not despise their lives as such. Indeed, they were eager to live, although they must believe that the life they were living was a mere propaedeutic of life as a whole. Possessions and comforts were minimized in their importance, for men are always ready to give them up in return for hope. In such a situation dreams and visions become potent instruments. It is treason to be practical in the presence of holiness and heavenly glory. It was not necessary to understand; it was necessary to believe, and uncertainties lost their power to disrupt. Combative and defensive instincts were not forgotten. Satan was never more important than in medieval life and religion, and there were Turks, pagans, and heretics to share his wicked eminence. Medieval life and religion were not without the stimulus that comes from unified and directed hate. So complete had uniformity become in the great community of the Middle Ages and so liberally on the whole did the system provide for the happiness of man on earth that many thinkers since have regarded the Middle Ages as the greatest social achievement of the world.

Medieval Christianity had great ability in organization, and our most enduring social institutions come from the time when it was dominant. In the study of the medieval religious drama in England one has to do, to be sure, with the 'waning' of the Middle Ages, a period of somewhat less than two centuries when the medieval church passed from the height of its power in the age of Abelard and St. Thomas Aquinas to a less effective and more corrupt state in the later fifteenth century. It follows that the farther back one goes toward the thirteenth century the purer and nobler in purpose is the medieval drama, but it is also true that in provincial England disruptive influences, whether theological or secular, were slow in their operation. From the point of view of religious discipline as it affected ordinary lives, fifteenth-century England, although possibly more ignorant and certainly less gifted than were thirteenth-century Europe and fourteenth-century England, adhered for the most part closely to the medieval system and lived contentedly within its bounds.

The struggles of the Christian religion were in a long-forgotten past. The Christian church was no longer a martyrs' church. The persecuting emperors—Nero, Domitian, Trajan, Maximian, Decius, Valerian, and Diocletian—were merely painted devils, and the compulsions of Constantine, Justinian, and their successors were needed mainly against Wyclifites and Hussites. The heresies of the patristic age, although for want of something better still devoutly preached against, were relatively without significance. Nobody's salvation was threatened by Arianism, Nestorianism, Monophysitism, and Monothelitism. The teachings of the Fathers, eastern and western, had been digested into proper places. The fruits of Origen, Athanasius, Basil, the Gregories, and Chrysostom, as well as Ambrose, Jerome, and Augustine, had been gathered, selected, sorted, and put into manuals, and the works themselves were shelved away where they would cause neither harm nor good. The selections, it may be said, were well and judiciously chosen. The religious world was wound up like a clock, and one is forced to conclude that, if it had had more competent and attentive winders, it would not have run down when it did.

The organization of medieval religious life was so magnificent in its completeness that it has been an article of faith of innumerable men that the immediate power of God manifested itself in the church, its growth, and its institutions. We have to do with the church before the Council of Trent and are not concerned with the clarifications, adaptations, and regulations that have been carried into effect since the sixteenth century. The older church was undoubtedly more loosely organized than is the modern church, but it was nevertheless effective in its very variety and adaptability. It was a growth of the ages as well as an intelligent system. Like the Oxford of fifty years ago it operated with astonishingly few apparent rules and regulations. Oxford was an organized body that knew its own ways of doing things, although the statutes according to which it operated were deeply buried in the Registry. The medieval church had the necessary administrative features of an efficient corporate body, with division of functions among its hierarchy and deputation of pow-

er. We are not so much concerned with the directive—the Holy Father, the College of Cardinals, and the councils of the church—as with the all-important diocese, which seems to have had considerable independence. Parish priests and minor clergy were face to face with the popular dramatic activities we are about to consider. Monks and friars permeated the religious life of the Middle Ages and blended their functions with those of the secular clergy. They also lived in contact with ordinary people, and the complex presented is difficult to unravel. They had to do with charities, schooling, and the higher and more learned kinds of worship. Especially in their scholastic activities, monks and friars must have been an indispensable factor in the development of the medieval drama. Indeed, one does not know any other source from which the learned culture that went into the plays could have come. Since monastic orders continued to be proponents of learning, it must be that they supplied much of the knowledge and talent of the vast amplification that the Latin drama of the church underwent in the hands of the laity. We must not think because monks and friars were the targets of satirists that they failed as a whole to discharge their religious and social duties.

Obedience, as we shall see, was no doubt the characteristic feature of religious life in the Middle Ages, and the disorders of Holy Innocents' Day and rowdyism at plays and religious services were committed by ordinarily obedient people. Credulity and obedience go hand in hand, and the people of the Middle Ages were credulous to a degree we can hardly understand, and their masters were often as credulous as they; but their leaders enjoyed and had enjoyed for ages almost a monopoly of learning. There is no known way of securing enduring power equal to an alliance between government and learning, since from men of learning come the ideas on which both change and continuance are based. The dominance of the church had brought about an established order of uniformity that went so far indeed as to bring about a situation that has been puzzling to modern critics, namely, a state and practice of anonymity. There is nothing more unintelligible to the modernistic thinker than is anonymity, and anonymity was one of the first medieval practices discarded by the Renaissance. As we have seen, anonymity was mainly due to the supremacy of class and community. It may in part have arisen because medieval artists sometimes preferred having their names written in the book of life to the enjoyment of personal renown.

The medieval mind seems to have been controlled by hierarchical authority and maintained by faith and ceremony. To enlighten it, it had the Hebrew Bible, the New Testament, and their accretions and commentaries, and the story presented was so lifelike, so plausible, that, when it was selected and digested, it not only carried conviction but presented a form and order of man's life on earth greater in themselves than any others ever achieved. In the fourteenth and fifteenth centuries, in which the vernacular religious drama flourished in England, men confronted a Christianity that was the result of a gradual and perfect growth. Is it any wonder then that the ordinary man did not desire freedom from his bonds, did not know anything about individual liberty, and would not have known what to do with it if it had been thrust upon him?

The medieval religious drama existed primarily to give religious instruction, establish faith, and encourage piety. It did not exist as a free artistic enterprise as did the Elizabethan drama, the French classical drama, or drama in the modern world. Medieval religious drama has a right to be judged on its own intentions and its success in carrying them out. The best preparation for understanding and appreciating this drama is a knowledge of the Middle Ages. This in turn will bring with it an appreciation of the greatness resident in simple humanity and a respect for medieval Christianity. Let us not confine our interests to the decay of a noble form, whether that comes from the intrusion of farce and worldliness or from the verbose tendencies of a slowly awakening, although still ignorant, Renaissance.

To adopt or to inherit a doctrine of human life as a mere inconsiderable preliminary to endless living, however mitigated such a doctrine was, was to adopt a conservative philosophy with an appropriate conception of time. Time to the men of the Middle Ages was not irrecoverably dissipated here on earth. Its elapse was relatively futile, and there was slight reason to measure it in segments further than those provided by day and night. Time, so to speak, did not travel horizontally from one secular event to another. [In a footnote, the critic cites: George Poulet in *The Hopkins Review,* Spring-Summer, 1953, pp. 7-25. For suggestions with reference to the medieval conception of time the author is indebted to an unpublished paper by Mr. Alan Stephens of the University of Missouri.] Time developed here on earth and rose vertically into eternity, and the more completely merged with eternity mundane time became, the closer it came to permanence. It follows that earthly time was permanence incomplete and good as far as it went, being, as it was, in process of achievement and guided toward permanence by the forms inherent in being. Time with its brood of events was thus the ally of permanence, for its achievements, to some degree in man's control, furnished the materials out of which eternity was built. So far as ideas, methods, merits, forms, and styles existed, they were good, and the task of man on earth was to complete them and carry them to perfection. They were never exhausted and to be thrown away. Men did not start over again with something new, and that which the Middle Ages possessed they conserved with a view to its fulfilment. Thus life on earth was not to be condemned utterly, but used, for this life was but heavenly life defective and unfinished. To have rejected earthly things *per se* would have been an invitation to priva-

tion and evil. Indeed, the idea of evil as privation is indirectly the motive force of the age-long building operations, both material and institutional, of the people of the Middle Ages. This principle is illustrated in their architecture, their literature, and their social and religious systems, all of which are hierarchical in their conservatism and incremental in their procedure.

Moreover, in medieval philosophy heaven had its order of precedence, and so did earth. There was a shape or coherent scheme outlined in degrees of being, and each degree had its function and its virtue. In the proper discharge of its function each degree had its superiority. A stone, although inferior hierarchically to a flower, was superior to a flower in hardness, durability, and structural utility. Each order of being had its right to be judged generically, a peasant as a peasant and a king as a king. Each by divine plan operated in its own sphere. Hence men, as well as material objects, ideas, and angels, were defined in terms of the class to which they belonged. Men did not possess individuality so much as an identity that carried with it that strange equality that we so often mistake for democracy. We cannot imagine inferiority without disgrace, but in the Middle Ages each man had a soul to be saved and had the possibility of an angelic immortality. The men of the Middle Ages were truly a field full of folk. The criterion for recognition was sameness, each man's class being the essence of his existence. His name was in the logical sense an accident, often derived from his class or occupation, but he was free to operate within his class; whereas in the modern world men are recognized as individuals, may belong to any class, and difference is the criterion.

In this conservatism, resting as it did on a fixed ideal with a constant effort toward perfection, lies the story of the growth and development of the medieval religious drama. When and as often as the medieval drama lost this formative idea, it ceased to exist as such. The religious drama was thus in its relatively unimportant way a medieval institution like the church, the state, and the university. The institution and many similar medieval institutions came about through an adherence to a genuine conservatism sustained by obedience and the willing acceptance of subordination, qualities as natural to the medieval man as are independence, equality, and personal ambition to the modern man.

The habitual medieval procedure suggested above characterized the growth of all the cycles of mystery plays. They were built in the same fashion as buildings were built. Their changes were in some respects like new styles in architecture and, like them, seem more extraneous than they were. Outside influence was the exceptional and merely suggestive thing. We are able to understand the development and the meaning of the religious plays from their simple beginnings within the church by means of an absolute doctrine that provided a complete account of the religious universe. Consequently the drama might begin with a tiny incident and grow by the addition of other tiny related incidents, but its beginning was a real beginning and its additions were real fulfilments of a grand and predetermined plan. The Latin *officia* were like the strong threads at the centre of a great tapestry by which the whole fabric might be picked up and moved. Extremely old elements might lie securely at the heart of the medieval drama, for additions were fulfilments and, even when they were secular, the liturgical centre maintained its power and its significance.

This incremental method appears throughout. It is seen, for example, in a subject of some importance to us in this study, namely, in poetic style. English poetry inherited from French and from Medieval Latin the tetrametric rhymed couplet and quatrain, and the *rime couée;* also the Burns stanza, which W. P. Ker says in [in *Mediaeval English Literature*, 1912] was invented by William of Poitiers about the year 1100. These simple forms contain or suggest most of the stanzaic effects achieved in Middle English poetry. One may often see these primitive forms still intact in the oldest parts of the fully developed cycles, and one may also see that later and more complicated stanza forms were built up out of these ancient elements. By preserving and using what they had the poets invented the complicated stanzas of the later plays. This merely illustrates a general practice. There were no doubt extraneous forms and new inventions, but in general poets did not reject older forms in favour of something new and different. They let these older forms remain in the total fabric of their newer structures. One need not suppose that in this matter poets were ignorantly following a medieval tendency. On the contrary, they did what they did because they knew their poetics so well, nor need one suppose that the later poets were indifferent to or unappreciative of the simple symbolic parts of very old plays that they chose to leave standing. These older parts were perhaps their inspiration and served for their enlightenment, as they still do for us. We must bear in mind that in this study we have to do with the conservatism and the slow perfectionism of the Middle Ages. It need not disturb us too much if we find that these efforts towards perfection were often extremely ill-judged.

V. A. Kolve (essay date 1966)

SOURCE: "The Corpus Christi Drama as Play and Game," in *The Play Called Corpus Christi*, Stanford University Press, 1966, pp. 8-32.

[*In the following essay, Kolve explores the medieval view of drama, arguing that "the English Middle Ages described their religious drama as play and game. . .there was little fundamental distinction made between drama and other forms of men's playing." Kolve explores the medieval "uneasiness" concerning dramatic representation of both sacred and evil figures and views the Passion of Christ as the central subject of the Corpus Christi.*]

Medieval drama owes nothing to the tragedy and comedy of either Greece or Rome; it was a fresh beginning, unrooted in any formal tradition of theater. The notion was common among learned men that Roman dramatic performances consisted of a poet or reciter reading from a pulpit while others mimed in silence the action he described. A few scholars, among them John the Scot, Peter Abelard, and Gilbert de la Porrée, seem to have realized that the persons who recited were also the persons who mimed, that actors represented in speech as well as by gesture the substances of other individuals. The contribution of Boëthius to the Trinitarian controversy of the early sixth century, *De Duabus naturis et una persona Jesu Christi, contra Eutychen et Nestorium,* which used a conception of personae and masks drawn from the classical stage, may have helped spread such a realization, for it was a work of theological importance. Yet this was, in sum, a small legacy. Despite fragmentary survivals of the entertainer's craft after the fall of Rome, and despite the nun Hrothswitha's literary imitations of Terence, there was no continuing tradition of the dramatist's art. Indeed, it is precisely because the Middle Ages were not inhibited by any real knowledge of earlier theater that they were free to invent their mimetic modes in direct response to the Christian story that had once again called formal drama into being. The story existed *before* the genre was reconceived and reformulated, and we may be sure the exigencies of that story were of the first importance in redefining the nature of the medium. The story turns on supernatural and miraculous actions; it involves a sequence of events spread out across all historical time; and it employs a very diverse and complex group of characters. Certain characters, in fact, posed problems so great that they might have prevented the development of a religious drama altogether.

If the Corpus Christi plays had been concerned merely with human beings—Adam and Eve, knights and Jews, midwives and thieves—the range of dramatis personae would have presented no real difficulty. But medieval men believed that human history could not be explained in purely human terms, and therefore in their drama, a mimesis and interpretation of that history, they could not restrict themselves to the representation of human characters. God the Father must appear, God the Son in his human form; there must be angels and devils, there must be the Mother of God. Here a crucial difficulty arises, which Etienne Gilson, in another context, has stated concisely: "Images so obviously participate in the nature of their objects that to religious images, for instance, is often attributed a sort of inherent sacredness that really belongs to that which they represent, that is, to their meaning." Thus a player for the Waterleaders' Guild in Chester could take the role of Noah without jeopardy: since Noah was a man and is to be acted by a man, the image and its referent are of the same nature. But a player for the Drapers' Guild chosen to enact God ran a certain risk, as when he opens the play of *The Creation* with these words:

> I God, most in maiestye,
> in whom beginning none may be,
> endles alsoe, most of postye,
> I am and haue bene ever.

Here the image and its referent are so different in kind that blasphemy or sacrilege may be involved. The actor's human nature risks defiling the most awesome of Christian images; man is not God, and God will not be mocked. Lucifer, they believed, fell because he imitated God. By sitting on God's throne and demanding the forms of adoration due to God alone, he sinned in pride and was condemned to hell. (The Chester cycle stages this very action.) Might it not be analogous to the Corpus Christi dramatic endeavor?

Authors writing in genres less imitative than the drama were certainly conscious of the risk involved. For instance, though the *Cursor Mundi* poet cannot resist describing what the historical Christ looked like, he prepares the way with an elaborate apology:

> Of his visage þat es sa bright
> Me for to mele it es vn-right,
> For angels es na sun sa light,
> þair mast ioi es on his sight,
> To se him þar he sittes nu,
> In heuen als we aght to tru,
> Bot of his licknes þat he bar
> Quils he went prechand here and þare.

Plays as decorous and reverent as The Creation and those of the ministry of Christ pose this problem acutely enough, but the mature Corpus Christi drama went much further. Its central subject is the Passion of Christ, which entails not merely the representation by a human actor of God the Son, but also the playing of His humiliation, torture, and death. It involves the mimetic maltreatment of a sacred figure. The question was put: if men taunt and scorn and put on a cross him who plays Christ, are they not guilty of the very crimes they represent? There were those who thought so. Gerhoh of Reichersberg (1093-1169), writing about monastic performances, said that those who represent Antichrist or the rage of Herod are guilty of the very vices they portray. A Wycliffite preacher, whose attack on the vernacular drama is our most important contemporary notice of it, believed all social assemblies to be occasions of sin, and when he says that he would prefer the playing of "pure vaniteis" and "rebaudye," he is not advocating a secular drama. He

means only that this would be less sinful than a sacred drama, the playing of the miracles and Passion of Christ, the history of Antichrist, the Doom.

The problem was not new; there is evidence of occasional uneasiness throughout the medieval drama, even in the Latin drama of the Church. It may lie behind the fact that the Rouen *Pastores,* probably dating from the eleventh century, uses men and a boy to impersonate the shepherds, the midwives, and the angel who makes the Announcement, while at the center of the action, the Virgin Mary is represented by a constructed image. Much Latin drama was equally cautious, though not all; but always it relied on its liturgical setting, the use of sung dialogue, and an extreme liturgical decorum to grant it safety.

The mature vernacular drama could not limit itself in these ways. The cycles had more complex ends in view, and they resolved these problems instead in terms of a specific conception of the dramatic genre. For neither a single author nor a group of authors could produce a dramatic cycle of such length without some coherent notion of what they were attempting, what means were available to them, and what advantages and difficulties these means entailed. In response to new problems, a new idea of theater was born. Fundamental to any idea of theater is a notion of precisely how the theater is to relate to reality. To reconstruct that conception—to investigate the generic "self-awareness" of the Corpus Christi drama—is the purpose of this chapter. Hardin Craig—and here he speaks for many others—can provide us with both a caution and a challenge:

> Indeed, the religious drama had no dramatic technique or dramatic purpose, and no artistic self-consciousness. Its life-blood was religion, and its success depended on its awakening and releasing a pent-up body of religious knowledge and religious feeling. Therefore to carry to the study of the medieval religious drama a body of criteria derived from Aristotle, Horace and their Renaissance followers, or of specialists in the technique of the modern drama or of drama in general is to bring the wrong equipment.... Few studies of the techniques of playwrights and actors of the medieval religious drama have been made, except by persons who have not understood this aspect of the task, and perhaps for lack of definite materials none can be made.
>
> This drama had no theory and aimed consciously at no dramatic effects, and, when it succeeded, its success came from the import of its message or from the moving quality of some particular story it had to tell.

I think this underestimates the evidence available, and, perhaps as a result, underestimates the importance of the question as well.

I shall begin by asking a very simple question: What words were used to describe theater? For a time, the answers I get may seem as simple as the question, but this semantic evidence will make it possible to harmonize facts about the drama text, the personae, and contemporary production techniques, deducing from them a conception of theater at once coherent, sophisticated, and significantly different from those other ideas of theater that in time succeed it.

The Latin liturgical drama of the Church was almost entirely sung or chanted, and the performers themselves (the priests and the choir) were often the only audience of the piece. The first episode to be dramatized by the Church was the visit of the Marys to the tomb on Easter morning; of the four hundred-odd texts extant of this dramatic episode, that of the *Concordia regularis,* a tenth-century manual directing Winchester usage, has particular interest: *Aguntur enim haec ad imitationem angeli sedentis in monumento atque mulierum cum aromatibus venientium ut ungerent corpus Ihesu.* Even at this early date, the Church conceived of dramatic action as something performed *ad imitationem,* although most of the generically descriptive words that came to be used did little more than emphasize the formal, liturgical element: titles such as *ordo* or *officium,* and plays designated only by their subject, such as *De Peregrino,* are common and have no specifically dramatic connotation. More suggestive of genre are *similitudo, exemplum, miraculum,* and most common of all, *repraesentatio.* (The records can be studied in Karl Young's *Drama of the Medieval Church.*) Though these plays continued to be performed until the Reformation, the most elaborate texts had all been composed by the end of the thirteenth century; and it is a striking fact that the vernacular cycle-drama, which came into existence in the last quarter of the fourteenth century, in naming itself rarely used an English translation of any of these words. Instead, it employed English equivalents of a much rarer term, *ludus,* which seems to have been used only in late Latin plays—in the *Ludus breviter de Passione,* the piece entitled *Incipit ludus, immo exemplum, Dominicae Resurrectionis* (both from the *Carmina Burana* manuscript of the thirteenth century), the superb Beauvais play of Daniel (*Incipit Danielis ludus*), and a play of the twelfth century by Hilarius, the *Ludus super iconia Sancti Nicolai.* As a generic term, its lack of precision has tried the patience of distinguished scholars. Thus Chambers has written that *ludus* is "a generic term for 'amusement,' and the special sense of dramatic play is only a secondary one," and Young has called it "a designation rendered generally ambiguous through its common association with popular revelling." Yet this very ambiguity may prove an entrance into the medieval idea of theater, for it is this word *ludus,* in its English equivalents "play" and "game," that becomes the ubiquitous generic term for the vernacular drama.

Certain vernacular words not deriving from *ludus* are used on occasion. "Processe" and "processyon" occur in the (non-cycle) Digby Plays, implying in the first instance little more than a formal arrangement of speech and action, and in the second, the act of playing the *Conversion of St. Paul* at three different stations with the audience following it to each, in procession. A more common word is "pagent," used to describe both the wagons on which some cycles were played and the episodes staged on them. Manuscripts of the Chester cycle preface each new play with the Latin form, *pagina;* its English equivalent is sometimes used in the Digby plays and it occurs frequently in the Proclamation to the *Ludus Coventriae.* It had a secondary sense of trick, deceit, or merry game. The word "shewe" was also in use, both as substantive and as verb, and involved conceptions such as revealing, displaying, demonstrating. The term "miracles," very common in contemporary notices of the drama, clearly should indicate subject rather than medium, but it was applied so loosely that the protesting Wycliffite preacher uses miracles as a blanket term for plays of the Passion, the Antichrist, and the Doom, as well as for plays of miracles performed by Christ and the saints. Each of these terms is important, but none rivals the Englished *ludus* in frequency or suggestiveness. The Corpus Christi drama was spoken of as "play" or "game" ["Game" as a substantive could also mean simply "pleasure." "Play" and "game" were both used to mean amorous sport, and heaven and hell could both be described (with differing connotations) as places of "play" or "game." The only usages of interest here are those that are demonstrably generic in force].

The gathering of evidence that the English Middle Ages used the word "play" for a dramatic performance might seem tedious and unprofitable. Yet evidence of medieval usage does have value, for the word has gone dead; its specialized dramatic sense is now largely divorced from its root. Some of its original force can be restored by quoting several contexts in which it is used (it is the commonest generic term of all) and I shall then bring forward "game" usages to confirm the richer meaning of "play" evident in passages such as these. From the Chester Banns:

> you bakers, see that the same wordes you
>   utter,
> as Christ hym selfe spake them, to be A
>   memoriall
> of that death and passion which in play ensue
>   after shall.

And from the Chester *Prophets:*

> Moe prophetis, lordinges, we might play,
> but yt wold tary much the daye;
> therfore six, sothe to say,
> are played in this place.

From York, when Herod lays a trap for the three Kings, and is content to await their return thus:

> Go we nowe, till þei come agayne,
> To playe vs in som othir place.

From the Proclamation to the *Ludus Coventriae:*

> In þe xxiij^ti pagent palme sunday
> in pley we purpose ffor to shewe.

And from the same Proclamation:

> the mawnde of god þer xal they play.

Of Mary, from a prologue by *Doctor* later in that cycle:

> how sche was assumpte · here men schul be
>   pleyand.

And as a final example, stage directions from that cycle's *Passion* play:

> here enteryth Satan in to þe place in þe most orryble
> wyse · and qwyl þat he pleyth þei xal don on jhesus
> clothis · and ouerest A whyte clothe and ledyn hym
> A-bowth þe place and þan to pylat be þe tyme þat
> hese wyf hath pleyd.

Many other instances could be cited, but these few will serve to alert us to a slight resonance of meaning no longer present in modern speech. The frequent description of action as being performed "in play" is suggestive, and it is important, too, that the verb is always "to play," where we might use "to act," "to produce," "to perform." This was so because drama was conceived *as a game,* and was frequently identified by that word as well. In England in the Middle Ages, one could say "We will play a game of the Passion" and mean what we mean when we say "We will stage the Passion." The transition from one to the other is more than a semantic change; it is a change in the history of theater.

"Game" usages are crucial to an understanding of the medieval conception of drama. Because even the twelve-volume *Oxford English Dictionary* takes no clear notice of this usage, evidence for it must be presented in some detail. From the Proclamation to the *Ludus Coventriae* comes this description of the play of *The Fall:*

> and þan almythy god ffor þat gret dyspite
> Assygned hem grevous peyn · as ye xal se in
>   game
> In dede.

In a concluding passage, the whole cycle is designated so:

> whan þat ye come þer xal ye sene
> this game wel pleyd in good a-ray
> Of holy wrytte þis game xal bene
> and of no fablys be no way.

The word is twice used to describe the earliest extant morality play, *The Pride of Life,* as here by the play's prolocutor:

> Nou beit in pes & beit hende,
>   & distourbit noyt oure place
> ffor þis oure game schal gin & ende
>   Throgh Jhesu Cristis swete grace.

And the long and beautiful morality play called *The Castell of Perseverance* concludes with this speech by God:

> all men example here-at may take,
>   to mayntein þe goode, & mendyn here mys:
>   þus endyth oure gamys!

There survives a short play from the early sixteenth century entitled a "Cristemasse game, made by Maister Benet Howe. God Almyghty seyde to his apostelys, and echon off them were baptiste, and none knewe of othir." Similarly, John Skelton's morality play, *Magnyfycence,* probably to be dated 1516, closes with an address to "ye that haue harde this dysporte and game." Sixteenth-century records from Bungay, Suffolk, dealing with the Corpus Christi drama in that town, speak of the "game gear," the "game booke," the "game pleyers," and of "ye game on corp's xxi day." In Harling, Norfolk, payments were recorded in 1457 for the "Lopham game" and the "Garblesham game," in 1463 for the "Kenningale game," and in 1467 (clearly a variation on the same) for the "Kenyngale players" (Lopham, Garboldisham, and Kenninghall all being towns near Harling). In 1493, the churchwardens of St. Nicholas' Church, Great Yarmouth, were paid for a "game" played on Christmas Day. Bishop Bonner in 1542 enjoined that no "common plays, games, or interludes" be permitted in holy places. And as late as 1605, in Ben Jonson's *Volpone,* Nano the dwarf announces an entertainment to be performed by himself, the eunuch, and the hermaphrodite, with the words, "Now, room for fresh gamesters" (I, ii). Finally, to establish the currency of the term throughout the centuries that saw the birth and the full maturity of the vernacular religious cycles, there are two drama fragments, the first of them dated by Robbins as not later than 1300 and possibly written twenty-five years earlier. It is a prologue, and includes these lines:

> nu sittet stille and herknit alle
> zat hur no mis ting ev bifalle
> and sittet firme and wel a-twe
> zat men moyt among ev go

þey zat beut igadert fale
ne maknet nayt to lude tale
hit uer ev bot muchel scame
for to lette hure game.

The second, from the sixteenth century, is an epilogue that concludes with an appeal for money:

Souereyns alle in same ye that arn come to
  sen oure game

. . . . .

Vnto holy chirche to ben in-cressement
alle that excedith þe costes of oure play.

"Play" and "game" are here used interchangeably, in exact apposition, just as in these lines from *Magnyfycence:*

For though we shewe you this in game and
  play,
Yet it proueth eyrnest, ye may se, euery day.

It is clear that the "play" usages cited earlier also carry with them this reinforcing sense of "game."

Some of the formulas in which these words customarily occurred, and some of the ideas associated with them, provide further and especially important clues to the medieval idea of theater. Then, as now, play or game could describe children's pastimes, adult sports, and elaborate jokes alike: elements of pleasure, diversion, or gratuitous action are always involved. Both words were used as antonyms of "serious," as in the *Cursor Mundi* description of Lot's terrible warnings to the citizens of Sodom:

Bot al þat loth to þaim can sai
þam thoght it was not bot in plai.

Another example is the *Gawain* poet's description of his hero as he rides out to keep his promise in a Christmas "game" which may cost him his life:

Now ridey þis renk þury þe ryalme of Logres,
Sir Gauan, on Godey halue, þay hym no
  gomen þoyt.

Lydgate wrote, in his *Troy Book,* "It is an ernest and no game," and in the *Assembly of Gods* he used the phrase, "Chaunge from ernest in to mery play." Two kinds of human action and motive, fundamentally different, were distinguished by these words, and from a conception of drama as play and game—as something therefore not "in ernest"—a drama involving sacred personages and miraculous events could be born.

In *Magnyfycence* we can find the antithesis used in both its general and its generic senses. Counterfet Countenance explains his duplicity in these terms:

Counterfet eyrnest by way of playes.
Thus am I occupied at all assayes.

And later the dramatic world is itself offered as a game and play analogue to a world in which actions *are* "eyrnest," that is, to the world of everyday reality:

Beholde howe Fortune on hym hath frounde.
For though we shewe you this in game and
  play,
Yet it proueth eyrnest, ye may se, euery day.

We are thus shown truth "vnder pretence of play." This polarity, "play" and "ernest," also explains the Wycliffite preacher's antagonism toward the drama. His attitude is somber: "al holynesse is in ful ernest men," and play, by nature not in earnest, is therefore both foolish and false, and can offer nothing to men who wish to be holy. He mentions a defense that men make for the drama: "And sythen as ther ben men that only by ernestful doynge wylen be convertid to God, so ther been othere men that wylen be convertid to God but by gamen and pley. . .now it is tyme and skilful to assayen to convertyn the puple by pley and gamen." But he denies it out of hand: only things done in earnest are relevant to truth and Christian life. We shall examine his other arguments later; here it is enough to note that he defines the nature of the drama just as the banns, proclamations, and drama texts themselves do, as "play" and "game," opposed to "ernest." He sees, too, its kinship with the game amusements of children and men; the drama is only one kind among others:

Dere frend, beholdith how kynde tellith that the
more eldere a man waxith the more it is ayen kynde
hym for to pleyn, and therfore seith the booc,
"Cursid be the childe of han hundred yeer!" And
certis the world, as seith the apostil, is now at his
endyng, as in his laste age; therfore, for the grete
neyyng of the day of dome, alle creaturis of God
nowe weryen and wrathen of mennus pleyieng,
namely of myraclis pleyinge.

Cursed be any man who has not put away childish things. The only scholar ever to pay close attention to this Wycliffite sermon was the late George Raleigh Coffman; he noted that in the course of it the preacher uses six specific examples of play: Sara's abstention from play and the company of players; Ishmael's playing with Isaac, which caused him to be driven into the desert; the playing of the followers of Abner and Joab, in which they destroy one another; the playing of the children of Israel before the Golden Calf; the playful mocking of Elisha by the children of Bethel, who were torn to pieces by bears in punishment; and David's playing before the ark of the Lord. That this variety of event was all designated by the same word seemed to Coffman incomprehensible, and he considered it an adequate reason for disregarding the whole treatise: "A man who shows such a confused state of mind with regard to the use of important terms can certainly not be expected to give us a logical idea of what the dramatic type, Miracle Play, includes." But he is fighting the facts. The Latin drama of the Church had avoided the Crucifixion and had little connection with game. The church and the liturgy were its natural milieu. It was simple, dignified, ritualistic, limited in its means; it was called *ordo, processio, repraesentatio.* When the drama moved into the streets and the market place, into a milieu already the home of men's playing and games, it was redefined *as* game and allowed to exploit fully its nonearnest, gratuitous nature at the same time as its range of subject and its cast of sacred personae grew. It was a special kind of game, of course, its unique character clearly defined in a Latin-German dictionary, the *Variloquus* of Johannes Melber (*c.* 1479), where play itself is given as one of the meanings of *scena:* "Etiam pro ludo capitur in huiusmodi loco facto ubi rusticus efficitur rex vel miles, et ludo peracto quolibet est sicut prius rusticus fuit." It is the kind of game in which a peasant is made a king or knight, and after it is over becomes once again a peasant.

My preliminary exposition is at an end. I have put forward evidence that the English Middle Ages described their religious drama as play and game; that this conception of genre involves the common medieval antithesis, "game" and "ernest"; that there was little fundamental distinction made between drama and other forms of men's playing. And I have argued that this conception of theater developed in response to difficulties intrinsic to the Corpus Christi story.

To go deeper into this matter, we must leave philology. The nature of drama conceived as a game needs also to be explored within a larger and more theoretical framework, and Johan Huizinga's admirable analysis of the nature of play, in *Homo ludens,* can serve us as a new point of departure. Once its implications have been examined, it will be possible to attempt a full-scale generic description of the Corpus Christi drama, to relate what we know about medieval staging to the dramatic theory I have been seeking to reconstruct in these pages. Huizinga wrote:

> Summing up the formal characteristics of play we might call it a free activity standing quite consciously outside "ordinary" life as being "not serious," but at the same time absorbing the player intensely and utterly. It is an activity connected with no material interest, and no profit can be gained by it. It proceeds within its own proper boundaries of time and space according to fixed rules and in an orderly manner. It promotes the formation of social groupings which tend to surround themselves with

secrecy and to stress their difference from the common world by disguise or other means.

> It is. . .a stepping out of "real" life into a temporary sphere of activity with a disposition all of its own. Every child knows perfectly well that he is "only pretending," or that it was "only for fun.". . . The consciousness of play being "only a pretend" does not by any means prevent it from proceeding with the utmost seriousness. . . . . The inferiority of play is continually being offset by the corresponding superiority of its seriousness.

These generalizations deserve to be read carefully. They are broad enough to cover all forms of drama, as well as children's games, athletic contests, dance marathons, or what you will. But the seriousness of "ye game on corp's xxi day," as the Bungay records term it, goes beyond the absorption intrinsic to any form of play. In ways we have already examined, it "imaged" sacred personae of the highest importance to man, and it sought to instruct in matters central to the salvation of souls: it was considered profitable game. Formal and repetitive in nature, it played year after year within a specifically limited time and place. Within those limits special conventions applied, creating a temporary world within the world of real life, and dedicating this created world to the performance of an act in some sense gratuitous to urgent daily concerns. Once this conventional world had been established, it was easily recreated until it became traditional. Like all play, this drama depended on formal order, without which progress within a game and pleasure from a game are alike impossible: anyone who breaks the rules spoils the game, makes it a poor and foolish thing. The formal order of the Corpus Christi game, its sequence of action, was determined by the playbook; failure to observe this order, an arbitrary limitation on the possibilities of action, was considered an offense punishable by civic authority. Records exist of fines paid by guilds and individuals for playing badly or incorrectly, to the shame and displeasure of the community. The particular order that this game sought to create was not only aesthetic, but historically true: it sought to pattern human experience, to give to the history of men an order that would reveal its meaning.

Play and game thus creates a world within the real world, and the dramatist's art relates the two worlds meaningfully to each other. But the two need never be mistaken or confused. When the *Ludus Coventriae* promises us "the mawnde of god þer xal they play," we may be sure that this is to be serious, all-engrossing play, but play nevertheless, which is to say of an order of seriousness different from the historical Maundy Thursday which is its referent. Similarly, when the Chester Banns alert the city at Whitsuntide that the days from Monday through Wednesday are to be devoted to the playing of the cycle, and when the location of stations has been determined, a formal world has been delimited within which the dramatic game can be played. One may see how important was this sense of a world apart by juxtaposing two late anecdotes concerning the devil. The fourth tale of *A Hundred Mery Talys,* published in 1526, is entitled "Of hym that playd the deuyll and came thorow the waren & mayd theym that stale the connys to ronne away," and concerns a player from a pageant who wears his devil's costume while going home, frightening everyone grievously. A very different reaction can be found in the reminiscences of Mrs. Tattle in Ben Jonson's play, *The Staple of News:* "My husband Timothy Tattle, God rest his poor soul! was wont to say there was no play without a fool and a devil in't; he was for the devil still, God bless him! The devil for his money would he say, I would fain see the devil." Although Timothy Tattle enjoys seeing a devil within the carefully circumscribed world of play, the villagers are terrified when a refugee from that world suddenly enters the world of real life.

Though the Wycliffite preacher shares with the dramatists an exact sense of the drama as play, he understands differently how this play world relates to the world of actual experience. He is unable to see the dramatic artifact as something analogous, but in a root-sense "unrelated," to real life: "And therfore many men wenen that ther is no helle of everlastynge peyne, but that God doth not but thretith us and is not to do it in dede, as ben pleyinge of miraclis in sygne and not in dede." He believes the drama teaches men that hell is only a *locus* on a pageant stage, and that the wrath of God is merely a dramatic attitude, for it is obvious to any spectator that the damned souls are not really punished in any Judgment Day pageant. This view grows out of his belief that only real action should occupy men, and that all else is falsehood, feigning, and a work of the devil (three terms constantly equated in his mind): "Not he that pleyith the wille of God worschipith hym, but onely he that doith his wille in deede worschipith hym." Here his argument is intrinsically more convincing, but it remains irrelevant. The duration of play is a momentary interval in, and abstention from, the real concerns of life; when the audience disperses they resume these concerns, the most significant of which for the Christian Middle Ages was the doing of the will of God. For a religious drama to have existed with the full approval of the Church, such a consciousness of the dramatic medium was necessary. The Wycliffite critic is interesting, not so much because he opposed the drama—a hyperzealous, Lollard fear of images and idolatry could lead to that very naturally, and the practical consequences of his opposition probably amounted to little—but because he often summarizes the arguments of those who valued the plays, and because his own objections furnish an explicit contemporary statement of some of the difficulties that seem from the very beginning to have shaped the medieval conception of theater. His final answers are confused, because he thought action that was unreal was therefore untrue, clinging rigidly to two polarities: real and unreal, true and false. Whatever was false he considered to be an abomination to God and a peril to men's souls. In this he may have been right, but his categories are muddled: the world of play (and its mode of meaningfulness) lies outside the antithesis, truth or falsehood. This fact is common to children's games, knightly tournaments, champion wrestling, and all drama that has ever been.

Although any drama can be reduced to a game analysis, the medieval cycles furnish for the English theater the first major example of that genre, influencing in ways that have not yet been fully understood the great drama of the Elizabethan and Jacobean periods. And what is more, they furnish the purest, most explicit, and most comprehensively detailed example of a theater of game that has existed until our own time. After the Restoration, theater in England and elsewhere took a very different turn, reaching its climax in the heavily naturalistic theater of the early years of this century. Dryden, as early as 1672, had signaled this new direction, in claiming deception as the dramatist's aim; in his *Of Heroic Plays, An Essay,* he argued that trumpets, drums, cannons and sound effects offstage are essential "to raise the imagination of the audience, and to persuade them, for the time, that what they behold in the theatre is really performed. The poet is then to endeavour an absolute dominion over the minds of the spectators; for though our fancy will contribute to its own deceit, yet a writer ought to help its operation." Until recently, we were heirs chiefly of this "theater of illusion"—a very different kind of dramatic game. Though we never actually confuse dramatic action with real life, we are asked to grant it our maximum credence within the structure of the theatrical experience. Everything about the texts, the acting, and the staging is carefully contrived to make the fact of "theater" as unobtrusive as possible. The medieval drama required different habits of its spectators, and gave them a different kind of artistic experience in return. Today, playwrights like Brecht, Ionesco, and Beckett have gone back to this older idea of theater or have worked in terms consonant with it. But the cycle can give us the thing itself in its first flowering, and if we would read them, stage them, and understand them properly, we must learn first of all to respond to the game nature of their action. In the pages that follow, I shall examine the relationship between this theory and the procedures and practices of the medieval stage.

The Corpus Christi drama took place in broad daylight, in the streets and open places of the town. The audience surrounded the playing area, as clearly visible to one another as the players were to them; occasional exits, entrances, and even dramatic action took place on street level in their midst. Richard Southern's researches into the meaning of "place" and *platea* in medieval dramaturgy have led him to an important conclusion: the "place" was simply the area in front of the stage or scaffold, to which the actors might descend if necessary. It was never geographically localized, and there was no pretense that what went on there went on in an imagined locality relevant to the action. Action itself told the story, and it happened *there* in England, in front of and amid the spectators. In Southern's words, "It was not until the Italian Renaissance that the place of a performance could become attired in costume like an actor and take a part in the drama—and scenery was born." The pageant wagon or scaffold would indicate the *locus* or *loci* of the action, but in terms of the "place" itself these reference points were only conventions in a game: when Mary and Joseph traveled from Bethlehem into Egypt, the meaning of the action was clear, though the actual distance between the *loci* may have been only several yards.

Furthermore, this drama used actors from the community who were known to the audience in real life. From Coventry records we learn of "Ryngold's man Thomas thatt playtt Pylatts wyff"; of wages "payd to Robert Cro for pleayng God iij s iiij d"; and of fines levied by the Weavers' Guild in 1450 against Hary Bowater, who played Simeon's clerk, Crystover Dale who played Jesus, and Hew Heyns who played Anne. A few records in York suggest that occasional performances were graced by actors imported from outside: the visits of three players from Donnington, one from Wakefield, and four from London are noted in the mid-fifteenth century. But this was the exception, not the rule; local, familiar faces in biblical roles would have made any fully developed kind of theatrical illusion impossible. Moreover, because each pageant wagon had its own complete cast to play its episode at each assigned station on the route, no single actor (except perhaps in the *Ludus Coventriae* Passion plays) performed the entire role of any major character. The York cycle, for example, employed in any given year no fewer than twenty-four different Christs in the adult episodes alone; the Chester and Towneley cycles both used eleven. This does not necessarily imply incoherent characterization, for there were undoubtedly traditional approaches to the major roles; but it did serve as a powerful check against illusion. These townsmen would have been astonished by Stanislavsky. They were ordinary men engaged in a certain kind of game, distinguished from their fellows only by a more generous mimetic gift. To take an extreme case, those who played God would not have sought (even for the duration of the pageant) to *be* God, nor to get inside His personality: such a notion would have seemed to them blasphemous and absurd. They presented not the character of God but certain of His actions. This approach encouraged a formal stylization in both writing and acting wholly foreign to the chaotic world of real life.

Such a conception of theater also made possible the presentation of large, complex actions in swift and simple terms. In every cycle Noah builds the ark in front of the audience, either using prefabricated parts or wheeling a finished model onto the pageant stage; but always he claims it is taking him a hundred years, and the audience enjoys the speed with which the ark is actually readied as a kind of merry joke unique to the drama. The Chester stage direction makes the game nature of the action clear: "Then noy with all his familie shall make a signe as though they wrought vpon the shipe with diuers instrumentis." When the ark is ready to be filled, painted boards representing the birds and the beasts are brought on; there are instructions that the verses and pictures should strictly accord in sequence. The escape of Moses and the Israelites from Pharaoh and his forces was played with the same game literalness. In the *Exodus* I saw produced on a pageant wagon in front of York Minister in 1957, the Red Sea was a long linen cloth, painted with waves, and held facing the audience while Moses and the Israelites walked behind it; when Pharaoh and his men came in pursuit, it was thrown up and over them, and they lay "drowned" beneath. The Israelites rejoiced in song as the wagon was pulled away. The action, strong, clear, and delightful, probably represented something very close to medieval practice; records from Coventry specify, with no sense of incongruity, "it. p'd for halfe a yard of rede sea vj d."

There was need for a kind of theater that could stage mythic actions as well, which could make phenomena never experienced in the normal course of things visible and dramatically "real." Because these plays were intended as "quike bookis" for the unlearned, they sought to make the whole of doctrinal meaning tangible in this way. Greban's *Le Mystère de la Passion*, written before 1452, begins by staging the creation of the world, a difficult but unavoidable subject, with a Prologue to explain that so far as possible it will be shown literally—shown, that is, in a way the spectators can apprehend through their *senses*:

> Mes la creacion du monde
> est ung mistere en quoy se fonde
> tout ce qui deppend en apprès:
> si la monstrons par mos exprès;
> car *la maniere du produyre*
> *ne se peust monstrer* ne deduire
> par effect, *si non seulement*
> *grossement et figuraulment;*
> *et selonc qu'il nous est possible,*
> *en verrez la chose sensible.*
> [my italics]

Just as the halo around a saint's head in a picture imparts abstract meaning and gives the saint a kind of appearance familiar only in pictures, so the medieval drama stages actions which, though unlike anything we encounter in ordinary human life, are nevertheless as "real" as anything else in the play world. Thus the whole drama becomes charged with a mythic quality, where inner meaning is made as external as any other kind of outward appearance. Mary rides on an ass into Egypt, and she is physically "assumpt" into heaven: in this drama, both actions *happen,* and they happen in equally literal ways. God was played by a man, but He was distinguished from the order of men by a gilt face. And, as in the visual arts, the profound mystery of the Trinity was established very simply: in the Chester play of the *Pentecost* the actors playing God the Father and Christ sit together to hear the prayer of the disciples that they be sent some comforter, and when God the Father speaks He refers to *His* incarnation, even though the incarnation was performed by the Son at his side. It is *Deus Pater* who says:

> But while I was in that degree,
> in earth abyding as man should be,
> chosen I haue a good menye,
> on which I must haue mynd.

When His long speech of recapitulation is finished, the stage direction reads, "Tunc Deus emittit Spiritum sanctum in spetie ignis." The doctrine of the Trinity has been made visible as three-in-one, the most mysterious of its membership—the Holy Ghost—being shown as fire, probably in the form of a hank of burning hemp lowered from above.

In all the cycle plays there is much mechanical to-an-fro-ing between earth and heaven. When the York Jesus is about to ascend into heaven he says, "Sende doune a clowde, fadir" and a cloud comes down; He gets into it and is hoisted aloft out of sight. The action was not designed to resemble reality, but rather to translate it into a game mode, a play equivalent. It is possible that the guilds staged the seven days of the Creation with movable charts, decoratively painted, as we might illustrate a lecture, for part of the compact implicit between the medieval audience and dramatist was the acceptance of such devices as signifying reality. Even music in these plays was symbolic, and was never used simply for atmosphere or emotive effect. In the words of its best student:

> It is there, like God's beard of gold, or the horned animal heads of the devils, because it signifies something. It is easy to be misled by the directions which require music to be played, or sung, at some of the great dramatic moments. The point was not to increase dramatic tension or to "soften up" the audience, but *representation.* "Heaven is music," so at the crises in the drama when heaven actively intervenes, music too intervenes.

The need to instruct in doctrinal truth, to clarify and make visual certain important meanings that were spiritual and mysterious in nature, undoubtedly played its part in shaping the medieval conception of theater: it had to be a medium in which these things could "happen." This necessity liberated it, and greatly increased its expressive potential.

Never was a suspension of disbelief invited; instead, the game episodes were played in their turn, and in the Chester cycle and the *Ludus Coventriae,* characters like *Nuntius, Expositor, Contemplacio,* and *Poeta* served to direct them, introducing new actions and making doctrinal comments. Their function is to enclose the action, whether natural or mythic, in a frame of commentary which puts the playing unmistakably at a distance from reality. The Chester *Expositor,* for example, really does control the game—hurrying here, moralizing there, now briefly narrating a story that cannot, because of time, be played, and occasionally stepping forth to address the audience directly on what they have been watching together. The French medieval drama often used a *meneur* (or *maître*) *du jeu,* and we know from a miniature by Jean Fouquet that he could be in the very middle of the action, holding the playbook in one hand and a baton in the other, conducting the game. We know also that the *meneur du jeu* often spoke the moralizations and sermons of the play. It is possible that the Chester *Expositor* or the *Poeta* of *Ludus Coventriae* moved among the actors in this same fashion, although no evidence exists one way or the other. What matters is that a similar conception of genre is involved, one far removed from that later kind of theater in which the happenings on stage, once under way, have the air of being autonomous, inevitable, and independent of author or director.

Classical conceptions of the "three voices" of poetry were available to the Middle Ages, one tradition deriving from Suetonius through Isidore of Seville, the other more important one deriving from the fourth-century grammarian Diomedes, through Rabanus Maurus; though they were not greatly different, the Diomedes version was more widespread and its definitions more extensive. To distinguish the dramatic from the lyric and the epic voices, Diomedes had offered this definition: "Dramaticon est vel activum in quo personae agunt solae sine ullius poetae interlocutione, ut se habent tragicae et comicae fabulae." [The "dramatic" or the "acted" is that in which characters perform alone without any interruption from the poet speaking in his own person, as is the case with tragedy and comedy.] But such a distinction, *sine ullius poetae interlocutione,* is superbly ignored by the Chester and *Ludus Coventriae* cycles, where the *Expositor* figure (by whatever name) exists solely in order to speak for the dramatist—responsible for the design of the episode—and for God—responsible for the total historical and ethical design that the cycle imitates. (In York and Towneley it is not uncommon for a character actually involved in the story to address the audience to the same end.) This convention fundamentally affects the kind of drama we see;

characters conceived in this way demonstrate biblical history, but no attempt is made to sustain an illusion of being men caught up in that history. The technique may be fairly represented in this speech by the Chester *Expositor,* which bridges the plays of the *Temptation* and the *Woman Taken in Adultery:*

> Thus overcome Christe in this case
> the Devill, as played was in this place,
> with those three synnes that Adam was
> of wayle into woe wayued.

He has not himself "acted" in the play of the *Temptation,* but he is there to underline a doctrinal meaning (the Second Adam has withstood the temptations by which the first Adam fell), to acknowledge genre ("as played was in this place"), and to introduce the episode that follows. He creates in his own person a drama of play and game, an experience, as it were, in quotation marks. As Alan Nelson has noted, a spectator "cannot think of himself both as Noah and as the object of Noah's exhortation."

The Passion episodes, of course, created the greatest difficulties and provided the greatest challenge for the Corpus Christi drama. I shall take up the artistic challenge and achievement in a later chapter, but the solution to those problems that were generic—that concern the propriety of playing God the Son and His torture and death—may properly bring this present inquiry to a close. The Wycliffite preacher argued "by figure" from the Old Testament to prove that men should play neither Old Testament patriarchs and prophets, nor most especially the Passion of Christ. The terms of his argument should now have a special resonance for us:

> Frend, peraventure yee seyen that no man schal make you to byleuen but that it is good to pleyen the passion of Crist, and othere dedis of hym. But here ayenus herith, how, whanne Helyse steyede up into Bethel, chyldre pleyingly comyng ayenus hym, seiden, *"Steye up, ballard, steye up, ballard;"* and therfore hee cursid hem, and two bores of the wylde wode al totoren of hem two and fourty childre; and as alle seyntis seyen the ballednesse of Helisee betokeneth the passion of Crist, thanne synthen by his storye is opynly schewid that men schulden not bourden with the figure of the passion of Crist, ne with an holy prophete of Crist. . . . Men shulden not pleyn the passion of Crist, upon peyne myche grettere than was the venjaunce of the childre that scornyden Helisee. For siker pleyinge of the passion of Crist is but verre scornyng of Crist.

Whereas the Latin drama of the Church had rarely played the Passion, and then only in a grave and stylized way, the vernacular plays emphasized the scorn, the jesting, and the violence, and thus the problem was correspondingly acute. An anonymous poet who satirized the friars and the plays they presented offers an interesting description:

> First þai gabben on god þat all men may se,
> When þai hangen him on hegh on a grene tre,
> With leues & with blossemes þat bright are of
>   ble,
> Þat was neuer goddes son by my leute.
>
> . . . . .
>
> Þai haue done him on a croys fer vp in þe
>   skye,
> And festned in hym wyenges, as he shuld flie.
> Þis fals feyned byleue shal þai soure bye,
> On þat louelych lord, so forto lye.

He attacks what seems to him the ludicrous unconvincingness of this drama: characters who are so clearly "only" friars playing, stage conventions that are unrealistic, "mythic" costumes and properties.

But the poem is primarily an attack on the friars themselves; their plays are only a secondary target. It is, throughout, an expression of hatred and contempt, and had we seen the performance, it is possible we might have judged it differently. We may enjoy the poem's sardonic description of a friar,

> Þer comes one out of þe skye in a grey goun,
> As it were an hog-hyerd hyand to toun,

yet if we would estimate accurately the mood and look of the medieval drama on stage, we might well set against this description that moment in the York *Resurrection* when the first Mary says to the others as they make their way to the tomb:

> Sisteris! a yonge child as we goo
>   Makand mornyng,
> I see it sitte wher we wende to,
>   In white clothyng.

This derives from Mark 16:5, "And, entering into the sepulchre, they saw a young man [*iuuenem*] sitting on the right side," but its translation is affected by dramatic tradition: the angel is being played by a child in white clothing. It is unlikely that the audience would join in the scorn of the anti-friar poet, because they know that the actors are engaged in a mimetic game, and that the purpose of the game is to reveal, not to deceive (even temporarily or in part) through illusion. As we have seen, it was important to the medieval Church that men should be able to imagine in their hearts and minds the Fall, the Passion, and the Judgment; and though *all* images are inadequate, yet they have their use and suitability. In a remarkable passage from *Diues et Pauper,* an early fifteenth-century work now too little known, Diues asks, "Why ben aungelles peynted in liknes of yong men sith they be spirites &

haf no bodies," and Pauper replies:

> Ther may noo peyntoure peynte a spirit in his kynde
> And therfore to the bettre representacion they be
> peyntyd · in the lyknesse of a man / Which in soule
> is mooste accordyng to aungellys kynde And
> thoughe the aungel be nat suche bodily · as he is
> peyntyd · he is nathelesse suche gostly / & hath
> suche doing & beyng spirituel.

Men and angels and God are different in kind, and the image that unites them is to that degree discordant, yet men are next to angels in the order of creation and are made in the likeness of God. No more suitable *material* for the image may be found.

A post-Reformation copy of the Banns to the Chester plays, included in Roger's Breviary of 1609, advertises a performance very different from those of the Middle Ages. God will not be acted, it says; only a voice will be heard speaking His lines, for no man can "proportion" to the Godhead. The medieval vernacular drama was more confident of its modes. To conceive of theater as a special game world furnishes a generally satisfactory solution, and other devices were employed as well. In the twelfth-century Anglo-Norman *Mystère d'Adam,* God is named (in the Latin stage directions) first as *Salvator,* and immediately afterwards as *Figura;* all His speeches in the text bear the latter designation. It is not God, but a "figure" of God who plays. More characteristic of later medieval drama is a sudden abandonment of the dramatic role within the play itself. In the Chester cycle, when Christ has shown Himself resurrected to several apostles, including Thomas, He concludes the play with this speech:

> Who so to this will consent,
> that I am god omnipotent,
> as well as they that be present,
> my Darlinges shalbe aye.
>
>   . . . . .
>
> Whosoeuer of my father hath any mynd,
> or of my mother in any kynde,
> in heaven Bliss they shall it fynd,
> with out any woe.
>
> Christ geue you grace to take the way
> vnto that ioy that lasteth aye!
> for thers no night but ever day;
> for all you thither shall goe.

Until the last quatrain the actor speaks as Christ. To sustain this role, he need only have blessed the spectators in the words Christ might have used, "I geue you grace to take the way." But instead, he steps out of character and invokes *Christ's* blessing upon them. The *Ludus Coventriae* episode of the *Woman Taken in*

Adultery likewise ends with a speech technically outside Christ's role:

> Now god þat dyed ffor all mankende
> saue all þese pepyl both nyght and day
> and of oure synnys he us vnbynde
> hyye lorde of hevyn þat best may.

The conclusion of the Towneley *Crucifixion* is of the same sort; Joseph and Nichodemus are taking Christ's body away for burial, but Nichodemus' final speech is not focused on the actor's body in their arms:

> It shall be so with outten nay.
> he that dyed on gud fryday
>   And crownyd was with thorne,
> Saue you all that now here be!
> That lord that thus wold dee
>   And rose on pasche morne.

The Castell of Perseverance closes with the character of God leading the singing of *Te Deum laudamus;* the actor playing the resurrected Christ in the French *Passion de Semur* does the same thing. Such moments are not frequent, but they should not be regarded as indications of naïve simplicity or careless writing; a sophisticated game conception of theater leads to them quite naturally.

On the strength of this evidence, I think we must dissent from the judgment of Hardin Craig that this drama had no "theory," no self-awareness as genre. The aim of the Corpus Christi drama was to celebrate and elucidate, never, not even temporarily, to deceive. It played action in "game"—not in "ernest"—within a world set apart, established by convention and obeying rules of its own. A lie designed to tell the truth about reality, the drama was understood as significant play.

We, for the most part, have to reconstruct this idea of theater as a historical phenomenon. It was the only kind of theater the Middle Ages knew.

THE DOCTRINE OF REPENTANCE AND THE MYSTERY CYCLES

Eleanor Prosser (essay date 1961)

SOURCE: "The Doctrine," in *Drama and Religion in the English Mystery Plays: A Re-Evaluation,* Stanford University Press, 1961, pp. 19-42.

[*In the following essay, Prosser discusses the importance of the doctrine of repentance to the medieval worldview and, hence, to understanding the mystery cycles. Prosser argues for the educational role of the performances in relation to liturgical doctrine.*]

In light of the history of both the Church and the theater, it is appropriate to begin a study of the mystery cycles with the doctrine of repentance. Knowledge of this doctrine is essential for an understanding of all medieval literature. Repentance was the key to salvation in a world that still believed man culpable for sin, not the pitiable pawn of social and physical necessity. Even more, then, is the doctrine important for the medieval drama, which was frankly written to show Christians the way to Redemption.

Repentance had been a key doctrine since the days of the early Church, although the doctrine did not become refined and codified until the middle of the twelfth century, when Peter Lombard recognized penance as a sacrament in the strict sense. Growing emphasis on the doctrine is reflected in an edict of the Fourth Lateran Council, the "Great Council" convened by Pope Innocent III in 1215. Canon XXI, the famous *Omnis utriusque sexus,* required annual confession and communion. Suddenly, all the faithful, on pain of minor excommunication, were required to confess at least once a year, each to his own parish priest. At the same time, the Church recognized that neither priesthood nor laity were adequately prepared to fulfill the injunction. Equally suddenly, then, the Church instituted an intensive campaign of education in essential repentance doctrine.

The thirteenth century thus became the century of emphasis on penitence and preaching. The two were closely interrelated. Most historians attribute the new emphasis on preaching to the advent of the friars (the Dominicans reached England in 1221, the Franciscans in 1224). There is general agreement that the preaching friars swiftly gained power among the people and that the diocesan clergy soon realized they must enter into direct competition. Therefore, historians believe, bishops called for increased instruction of the parish priest specifically to combat the new threat. This causal argument may, however, be *post hoc, ergo propter hoc.* It seems probable that the intensive program of education was instituted not to meet the new competition but to prepare both parish priests and their parishioners to fulfill the requirements of the *Utriusque sexus.* That the reform of the clergy and emphasis on preaching grew directly out of the emphasis on the requisite doctrine of repentance is attested by many documents, among them the decree by Walter of Cantilupe, Bishop of Worcester, in 1240. Parish priests were to preach the Ten Commandments, the Seven Deadly Sins, the Creed, and the Seven Sacraments for a specific purpose: to teach the penitent the correct way to examine his conscience and to present his confession.

Throughout the century, the campaign to reform clerical discipline and combat ignorance grew rapidly. In 1222 (before the influence of the friars, it should be noted), the Bishop of Salisbury was appalled to learn that many of his parish priests could not pass a simple test on the first prayer in the Canon of the Mass. Some even refused to answer. In the same year the Council of Oxford, convened by Stephen Langton, branded some of the clergy as "dumb dogs." The Council reaffirmed the decrees of the Fourth Lateran Council, and the reform movement gained impetus. Shortly thereafter, Robert Grosseteste issued a set of Constitutions requiring priests to know and teach the Ten Commandments, the Seven Deadly Sins, the Seven Sacraments, and the Creed. Others followed with like instructions: the Bishop of Worcester in 1240, the Bishop of Chichester in 1246. In 1281 John Pecham, immediately upon becoming Archbishop of Canterbury, called a general council at Lambeth. The resulting Constitutions of Lambeth, appropriately known as *Ignorantia sacerdotum,* begin, "The Ignorance of priests casteth the people into the ditch of error." Each priest was commanded to instruct his parishioners on basic doctrine four times a year in their own tongue. Recognizing the priests' lack of preparation, the Constitutions appended a summary of the vast body of codified material.

The result of this concern was a flood of instruction and sermon manuals for the priesthood and, shortly thereafter, countless books for private devotion. Throughout the thirteenth century, most of the manuals were in Latin, as were the Constitutions, but around the turn of the century works expressly designed for the "lewd" began to appear in the vernacular: for example, the *Lay Folks Mass Book* and *Cursor Mundi,* with its "Boke of Penance," written in the late thirteenth century; and *Handlyng Synne,* begun in 1303. By the second half of the fourteenth century, we have evidence of a fully developed campaign in the *Lay Folks Catechism* (1357) and the widely distributed *Pricke of Conscience,* and the movement kept expanding into the early fifteenth century with works such as John Mirk's *Festial* and *Instructions for Parish Priests.* We are thus justified in approaching the drama of the fourteenth and fifteenth centuries with the working hypothesis that the writers may have used a coherent body of repentance doctrine with which they knew their audiences would be familiar.

The choice of the doctrine of repentance as a starting point is again indicated when we consider the development of vernacular drama. To my knowledge, it has never been noted that the development of the mysteries closely parallels the campaign of education discussed above. In the early fourteenth century, the Church began stressing vernacular instruction in that doctrine which led to repentance; in 1311 the Council of Vienne confirmed the Feast of Corpus Christi; in 1318 we find the first recorded Corpus Christi procession in England (at Canterbury); by 1328, according to an old tradition, a mystery cycle had been instituted at Chester. Although this tradition has been challenged, it is clear that by the last decade of the century, cycles were firmly established in several cities throughout England. A connection between the campaign of education and the Feast of Corpus Christi, and thus between the campaign and the development of vernacular mystery cycles, seems probable.

It will be remembered that the *Utriusque sexus* required confession at least once a year in preparation for receiving the Eucharist. The Feast of Corpus Christi is, of course, in honor of the Holy Eucharist, of the Real Presence. The service is a commemoration of the Sacrifice offered for man's Redemption. Thus the attendant doctrine emphasized by the medieval Church was preparation for receiving the Sacrament: "Repent now; partake not of Christ's Body in sin." St. Thomas Aquinas wrote a new office for the Feast, appropriately selecting the lesson from the First Epistle of Paul to the Corinthians:

27 Therefore, whosoever shall eat this bread or drink the chalice of the Lord unworthily, shall be guilty of the body and of the blood of the Lord.

28 But let a man prove himself: and so let him eat of that bread and drink of the chalice.

29 For he that eateth and drinketh unworthily eateth and drinketh judgment to himself, not discerning the body of the Lord.

The canticle, *Lauda Sion,* generally considered one of the most beautiful in the liturgy, echoes the text:

> Sumunt boni, sumunt mali:
> Sorte tamen inaequá i,
> 　Vitae, vel intéritus.
> Mors est malis, vita bonis:
> Vide paris sumptiónis,
> 　Quam sit dispar éxitus.

> [The good, the guilty share therein, / With sure increase of grace or sin, / The ghostly life, or ghostly death: / Death to the guilty; to the good / Immortal life. See how one food / Man's joy or woe accomplisheth.]

Thus the homiletic exhortation found in Lenten and Easter sermons also marked the Feast of Corpus Christi. Canon XXI did not limit the period of shriving to Easter, as one preacher found necessary to explain: "that lawe 'Omnis vtriusque sexus,' et cetera, forbedeth the not to be oft shryven and thou haue nede, but rathur counceyls the that thou shuldest be oft shryven like as nede askes." In his sermon for Corpus Christi, Mirk announces a papal indulgence of a hundred days to all who have been shriven and attend the day's services. Thus it is clear that the faithful have gone through a second period of shriving in preparation for receiving the Sacrament on Corpus Christi.

At first glance, the connection between the doctrine concerning repentance and the mystery cycles may seem minor. Indeed, Hardin Craig finds in the liturgy for the Feast "nothing. . .that would suggest an ocular and corporeal representation of the whole story of man's fall and redemption." But in fact, there would seem to be an intimate relation between the cycles and the text of the office for Corpus Christi: "Repent now. Partake not of Christ's Body unworthily." Recognizing this relationship is, I believe, essential if we are to approach the plays with an accurate understanding of their purpose. The cycles were not compiled by a loose following of chronology, from Creation to Judgment. Episodes have been carefully selected to fulfill a strictly theological theme: man's fallen nature and the way of his Salvation. For this reason Cain is included: the first inheritor of Adam's fall, the first murderer, the first impenitent, the first man to be damned eternally (for Adam, all knew, was released by Christ's Harrowing of Hell). For this reason those who prophesied Christ are included, as are Abraham and Isaac, who prefigure the blood sacrifice of the Crucifixion. The rest of the Old Testament is omitted (except in the unique Cornish plays).

Episodes from the New Testament have been carefully selected to further the theme of repentance and Salvation. As a result, Christ's ministry is passed over almost entirely. Only four events are portrayed, all of which include teaching on repentance: Jesus heals the blind and the lame, to show His suprahuman power over natural law (His power to erase sin); the release of the woman taken in adultery and the conversion of Magdalene are shaped to become straight repentance plays; and Lazarus, who prefigures the Resurrection and therefore Salvation, is explicitly related to the doctrine in the Towneley cycle, in which he gives a sermon on repentance. The relevance of the Passion plays is self-evident. Indeed, the torture scenes become more understandable when we remember that meditation on the wounds and agonies of Christ was a dominant appeal to awaken repentance. The Last Supper in the Hegge cycle is carefully adapted to fit the text of the Corpus Christi office ("Do not presume to receive the Host unworthily as did Judas"). In the Resurrection plays of both the Chester and the Towneley cycles, at the climax of the Christian mystery, *Christus Resurgens* is given an interpolated Corpus Christi sermon of exhortation. The cycles close with the Last Judgment and its graphic warning: "Repent now!"

The causal relationship suggested above is not intended to imply that vernacular drama sprang full-blown from the first Festival of Corpus Christi. There is evidence that a Resurrection play was produced between the buttresses on the north side of St. John's Church in Beverley as early as 1220, and possibly it was in the vernacular. There is ample evidence of earlier plays, and Hardin Craig's conjecture that the cycles were compiled from pre-existent plays still seems probable. The significance suggested here is that relevant plays were compiled, expanded, cut, and adapted to fit a specific theme. An earlier Resurrection play, for example, probably presented an object of devotion to behold. In contrast, the cycles present an argument: the necessity of Redemption.

Thus we may conceive of a typical Corpus Christi cycle as one vast sermon on repentance: a sermon complete with *exempla,* meditations, and exhortations; a sermon utilizing all the techniques in which the medieval preacher was trained—from comic castigation of folly to impassioned prophecy of doom.

In any attempt to evaluate the effectiveness of these dramatized "sermons," the modern critic is at a serious disadvantage. If he is to respond to the plays as did a member of the medieval audience, he must be able to respond to the many doctrinal signs that the mystery playwright knew his audience would recognize. Today, despite the continuity of Roman Catholic tradition, even a Catholic would not be able to catch many of the subtle references that had meaning for medieval man. It would be relatively simple to apply the fully expanded repentance doctrine of the *Summa Theologica,* but such a method might lead us into reading unintended subtleties or even doctrinal errors into the plays. What actions, ideas, signs would the contemporary audience clearly recognize? The Wakefield fisherman, the York ironmonger, the Chester blacksmith—the common folk who produced and attended the mysteries—knew scholastic or patristic doctrine only as it was filtered through the parish priest or, more rarely, through vernacular literature.

In order to see the plays through the eyes of these common folk, we must therefore become familiar with the doctrine as it was presented to them. Many medieval sources are relevant: both instruction manuals for the typical parish priest and various manuscripts specifically written for the "illiterate" laity—that is, for those who could not read Latin. Eleven sources have been found especially useful for both this and future studies in medieval drama.

In an attempt to determine exactly what points of doctrine had wide currency, we perhaps find our surest guides in manuals of instruction for the clergy and in collections of sermons. Two manuals, *The Lay Folks Catechism* and *Instructions for Parish Priests,* provide interesting evidence of exactly what the average parishioner was taught both from the pulpit and in the confessional. The *Lay Folks Catechism,* commissioned by Archbishop Thoresby in 1357, was not a text for the laity but an aid for the priest; it was to be used as a basis for oral instruction by the question-and-answer method. Although the book is not specifically stated to be a manual for the confessional, it is a compact summary of the material by which the priest helped the penitent to examine his conscience. John Mirk's *Instructions for Parish Priests* (written after 1400) is specific in purpose. Mirk instructs his reader that preaching is primarily a call to confession, and exactly one-half of the book is devoted to repentance doctrine. His manual is especially significant for the present study in that it was written for the most ignorant and ill-equipped priests. (The confessor is warned not to cough or spit in confessional, not to fidget lest a woman think she is being laughed at.) Mirk expands the material given in the *Lay Folks Catechism,* adding thorough explanations, and instructing priests to use the Paternoster, Ave, Creed, Articles of the Faith, Ten Commandments, Seven Deadly Sins, and venial sins, as well as miscellaneous questions, as the basis for examination of the confessing penitent.

In its campaign of education, the hierarchy realized that the parish priest would need more than an intensive theological textbook. Thus volumes of sermons became increasingly available. Typical is Mirk's *Festial,* a companion piece to the *Instructions for Parish Priests,* which offers a series of sermons as appropriate models for the uneducated parson who had no books of his own. Most of the sermons are for saints' days, expansions of legendary material rather than lessons in doctrine. Nonetheless, Mirk provides some of the most succinct statements of repentance doctrine in his recurring exhortations to meditate on the saintly life. Two other collections, *Middle English Sermons* and *Jacob's Well* (both compiled by about 1425), provide sermons that were actually preached to lay audiences. Together with the manuals of instruction, such compilations are valuable not only in determining the specific points of doctrine known by even the illiterate folk, but also in learning to recognize repeated words and ideas that had become familiar symbols.

In addition to these five aids for the clergy, six sources represent material that was actually in the hands of the laity. From among the many didactic treatises of the late Middle Ages, *Handlyng Synne, The Book of Vices and Virtues,* and *The Pricke of Conscience* have proven particularly illuminating. All three seem to have arisen in the tradition of the penitential manual. *Handlyng Synne,* a free translation of the *Manuel de Pechiez* undertaken by Robert Mannyng in 1303, presents a series of exemplified lessons on how to "handle sin" at confession. The first part (*exempla* organized under the Ten Commandments, the Seven Sins, and the Seven Sacraments) merely provides the necessary background for the final extended section on shrift. With no direct ties to liturgy, *Handlyng Synne* is particularly significant for determining the degree to which scholastic tenets filtered down to the people, though, in this case, fairly well educated people. The *Book of Vices and Virtues,* one of many translations of the influential *Somme des Vices et des Vertues,* also presents in lay terms a vast body of codified material such as that enjoined in the Lambeth Constitutions. The *Pricke of Conscience,* though strikingly different in method, was written for the same purpose: to make men know themselves.

> And for to stir tham til right drede,
> When thae this tretisce here or rede,
> That sal prikke thair conscience with-yn,
> And of that drede may a lofe bygyn.

Through seven dismal and redundant books, the reader is called to meditate on the wretchedness of man's state, the unstableness of the world, death, purgatory, doomsday, the pains of hell, and, finally, the joys of heaven—and thus is led to repentance. The importance of the doctrine as well as its emotional appeal seems reflected in the fact that over one hundred manuscripts have survived. Apparently this thoroughly tedious poem was the most popular work of the fourteenth century.

Supplementing these didactic treatises for the laity are many devotional works. The *Lay Folks Mass Book,* originally written in the mid-twelfth century (probably in French), was translated into English and remained in use until the fifteenth century. Despite the title assigned by its editor, the *Mass Book* is not a translation of the missal but a layman's guide on how to hear mass, a series of suitable meditations and prayers to be read privately as the priest reads the Latin office. Similar evidence of private devotions is found in *The Prymer,* an early-fifteenth-century version of the common medieval prayer book. Primers were mainly shortened offices of the Church intended for private devotions: prayers, psalms, hymns, and adorations arranged according to the seven canonical hours. Translations into the vernacular were common by the latter half of the fourteenth century as the primers became increasingly popular. Less formal but perhaps more indicative evidence of the common man's devotions is found in his favorite prayers, many of which were scribbled on various manuscripts and have thus been preserved. In two useful papers, Rossell Hope Robbins has gathered many of the simple verse prayers which were current among the literate laity as well as the illiterate folk. The majority are simple petitions for forgiveness through Christ's Passion and general confessions, again reflecting the emphasis on repentance.

Vernacular sources such as the eleven which have been noted, ranging from intensive instructional manuals for the parish priest to the simple prayers of the farmer, enable us to understand the faith of the medieval audience. What, then, were the points of doctrine understood by the simplest mind, by the typical spectator of the mystery cycles? Minor points of doctrine will be discussed as they arise in the individual plays; here it is enough to summarize the general, familiar outlines.

First, as we have noted, sacramental penance was a dominant emphasis of the Church. Confession, writes a fifteenth-century homilist, "shuld be done afore all othur good werkes." Even more than the privation of grace that results from sin, preachers emphasized the debt of punishment incurred: "for all thyng that ys not clansed here by schryft and penance, schall be clansed yn purgatory." Men were called to contrition and confession to efface the stain of sin, and to penance in order to mitigate the debt of punishment that necessarily must follow either in this world or in purgatory. A vast body of procedural doctrine was familiar to the laity, each point giving signs by which true repentance could be recognized—signs especially important for the dramatist. A series of steps in time, all involving acts of the will, could be traced from the first inception of fear to the final infusion of divine grace.

How is man motivated to repent? First, repentance begins, as it ends, in God's grace.

> [Christ] graunteth hym grace, hys shryfte
>   bygynne,
> Any yn hys shryfte, to sorowe hys synne.

The first desire to repent, no matter how weak, in itself marks a gift of grace. Man is warned to "receive not the grace of God in vain." "But thogh ye felen hym gracyous, be neuer the boldyr to lye yn synne; but hyth you forto clanse you therof." He who denies this first stirring of the spirit will be doubly damnable for denying God. Moreover, he may not be blessed with the gift again, for

> "he that wyl nat whan he may,
> he shall nat, when he wyl."

The most succinct statement of the motivation to repent is by Mirk:

> I rede of a woman that was defowled with the synne of lechere, and almost fell yn dyspayre. For when scho thoght on Crystys dome, scho knewe hur gylty; when scho thoght on the paynes of hell, scho knew well that thylke paynes wer ordeynet for such as scho was; when scho thoght on paradyse, scho wyst well scho myght not come ther, for scho was vnworthy; when scho thoght on the passyon of Cryst scho wyst well that scho was vnkynde to hym that suffred so moche for hur. At the last, scho bethoght hur how that chyldern don no vengeans, but lyghtly ben saht, thogh thay ben wrothe. Wherfor scho cryet to Cryst prayng hym for his chyldhede that he wold haue mercy on hor.

The most servile movement of fear may be the first step up the ladder of repentance. Dread is the first gift of the Holy Ghost, for it destroys pride (the "parent" sin), awakens the sinner, and puts humility in his heart.

The stated purpose of the *Pricke of Conscience* reflects Mirk's statement of progressive motives: contemplation of death and the horrors of damnation leads to humility, thus to love of God and yearning for Heaven, and thus to amendment.

But fear alone is only the beginning. "Dreed of helle, more principally for dreed of peyne than for dreed of wretthyng of god" may help a sinner amend, but it will not lead to salvation. To the fear of Hell must be added love of God, *caritas,* before true contrition can begin. In all of the literature we find the recurring phrase: man must be moved to sorrow "not only for the peyne that he hath deseruyd but for he hath greuyd god so vnkendely." This addition of charity—displeasure at the sin because it pains God—marks repentance as an act of the will, a point so important that Mannyng makes it the first point of shrift.

> 'with thy gode wyl and hertë fre,
> whan thou art yn thy lyfë best,
> Awey thou shalt thy synnë kest;'
>
> . . . . .
>
> Abyde nat tyl thou most nedly,
> For than hyt ys with fors and maystry;
> Thou shryuest the than for drede,
> Nat for loue, but more for nede.

How does the sinner move from fear of Hell to love of God? Recall Mirk's story of the sinning woman: "when scho thoght on the passyon of Cryst scho wyst well that scho was vnkynde to hym that suffred so moche for hur." Medieval literature abounds with meditations on the Passion, meditations that vividly portray the agonies of the Cross to this end. As has often been noted, the excruciatingly realistic details of the mystery Crucifixion plays arose in this tradition. Paradoxically to us, perhaps, it was meditation on the wounds that could lead medieval man to refer to the "Blissful Passion," a concept which, as Gardiner has noted, we must understand.

> Ihesu, late me fele whate ioy it be
> To suffren wo for loue of the;
> Hou mery it is for [the] to weep,
> Hou softe it is in harde clothes to slepe.

The more man can visualize Christ's pain, the greater he senses Christ's love to be and the greater his own love for his Saviour; and the greater he senses Christ's love, the more unworthy man must deem himself. Thus the sinner's contrition is marked by joy in pain.

The final motivating step that Mirk suggests is an act of faith, faith in the mercy of God through the merit of Christ's Passion. The doctrine of the superabundant satisfaction was perhaps too complex to present to the untutored laity: the doctrine that man, because of his sinful nature, could never render satisfaction to God equal to his offense, but that Christ offered Himself as a sacrifice sufficient to balance the scale (that is, man's penance plus Christ's sacrifice equals equivalent satisfaction). The doctrine is never stated explicitly to the common people. Instead, the one essential is emphasized: man is made worthy through faith—faith in the mercy of God through Christ's Passion. "His pitee is more thenne al oure wrecchidnesse; and ther-fore do we that is in vs. and in triste of hym with reuerente drede goo we to hym, For whi his worthinesse schal maken vs worthi to do hym seruise." Recurrent is the imagery that Christ ransomed us, that shrift "purchacest to vs grete pru." Again, one cannot be sure that the theological intricacies were understood, but the insistence that Christ's Passion is essential to Salvation was dominant. One of the private prayers provides an interesting note:

> Iesu, for Thy Holy Name,
> And for Thy bytter Passioun,
> Saue me frome synne and schame
> And endeles dampnacion.
>
>   . V . Pater Nosters, . V . Aue
> Marias and a Credo
>   . V . thowsand days of pardon.

An indulgence of five thousand days was phenomenal.

Catholicism was not consistent on the question of when a penitent should make an act of faith. In the plays, therefore, a statement of faith may be before contrition (that is, part of the motive, in accordance with St. Thomas), before or after confession, or—in later and careless moralities—merely assumed. Nonetheless, contrition must be coupled at some time with faith or man is led into despair, "the moste ewill that may fall to anny man."

> For wanhope [despair] wenyth that the foly
> Be more than Goddës mercy.

Understanding the orthodox concept of despair is of great importance for both medieval and Renaissance drama. The term is, of course, used so loosely today that critics often miss the full implications. We tend to forget that within the Christian tradition despair was (and is) the most heinous of sins, a sin against the Holy Ghost. Despair, and not the betrayal, was the sin for which Judas was eternally damned. Many medieval sources stressed this point. When Jesus was condemned, Judas went to the Jews, cast down the thirty pence, and then hanged himself. Why did he not ask for mercy? He confessed his wrong to the Jews; he was sorry; he gave back the money. Confession, contrition, amendment—these three suffice. His sin was that he believed his guilt greater than God's mercy: he despaired. That displeased Christ more than the betrayal. This explanation was often given from the pulpit to emphasize that no sin is too great to be forgiven if the sinner has faith.

Now, properly motivated, man is ready to undertake the three formal steps of repentance.

> Ane is sorrow of our hert that we have
>   synned;
> Anothir is open shrift of our mouth how we
>   haf synned,
> And the third is rightwise amendes makyng
>   for that we haf synned.
> This thre, with gode will to forsake our syn,
> Clenses us and wasshes us of alkyn synnes.

This is the ladder of repentance—contrition, confession, satisfaction (amendment, penance)—especially useful for the dramatist, marking, as it did, three specific actions in time.

The first step, contrition, is not mere sorrow; it is a deliberate act of the will. True contrition is marked by choice, the choice to loathe the past sin and amend.

> Sykyr thou be, thou shalt be a-teynt,
> whan [that] thou art nat yn wyl
> The to wythdrawë fro thyn yl.

True contrition is also marked by *caritas,* as noted. Man must sorrow for his sin through love, because he has offended God. This emphasis by medieval preachers explains the importance of Magdalene.

> I rede of no fastynge that she fasted be-forn that
> tyme, ne of no barfote goynge, ne wulward. I rede
> of non suche penaunce that she dud. How myght it
> than be that she was made so clene?

The answer is clear: because she loved so much. The homilist also might have added that we also read of no contrition, no act of the will, no stated purpose to amend. The significant point for medieval preaching and drama was that she wept in adoration. The external manifestation, tears, became the accepted sign not only of contrition but often of full repentance.

> I trauelide in my weilyng; y schal wasche my
>   bed
> bi ech night, y schal moiste my bedstre
>   with my teeris.

The second step, confession, is an acknowledgment that one has sinned against God and deserves punishment.

> For y knouleche my wickidnes; & my synne
>   is euere agenes me.

I haue synned to thee aloon; & y haue don
    yuel
bifore thee, that thou be justified in thi
wordis, & ouercome whan thou art demed.

A large body of material on the method of confession developed. From the thirteenth century on, the Gregorian analysis was standard: all sinful conduct was classified under one of the seven vices. The method became much more complex, however. In addition to the Seven Deadly Sins, examination was based on the Seven Petitions of the Paternoster (each petition of which came to be considered antithetic to one of the sins), the Creed, and so forth. With the refinement of the doctrine in the thirteenth century, penitentials (manuals listing sins and their appropriate penances) began to go out of use. In place of the voluminous listing of penances for given sins, general principles were developed by which the confessor could estimate the gravity of the offense. By official decree of the Lateran Council, the principle of "circumstances" became dominant in the thirteenth century: a method of analyzing the sin by the circumstances under which it was committed. Mirk introduced the section on confession with one of the mnemonic devices the priest used for remembering the many questions he was to ask the penitent: "Quis, quid, vbi, per quos, quociens, quomodo, quando." The sinner's acknowledgment that he deserves punishment often seems to be lost under a plethora of details in the literature of the confessional.

The third step, penance, is again an act of the will: the choice to make full satisfaction, insofar as man is able, to God. It has two functions, punishment and cure: the priest is both judge and doctor. Despite the fact that manuals, sermons, and Protestant histories might lead us to believe that penance was largely negative punishment, the dramas stress its healing power. That is, as a cure, penance roots out the cause of the sin (cures the past) and also turns the will so that it will be guided by right reason (preserves for the future). Medical imagery recurs continuously in all penitential literature, and it was from a medical principle that the concept of equivalent penances developed. Since "contraries are cured by their contraries," the priest would enjoin a penance corresponding to the sin.

> Fastyng hit clansythe a mannys flesch of evyll
> steryng and lyst to syn of gloteny and of lechery;
> for thes byn synnys of the flesch. Devout prayer hit
> mekythe a man sowle, and pyttythe away slowthe
> and envy. Almes-dede hit qwenchyth the fure of
> couetyse, and pyttythe away dedly wrath out of a
> mannys hert, and makythe hym mercyabull.

Although the penance is to be carried out after receiving the Sacrament, it suffices for absolution that the penitent's will be resolved to fulfill this satisfaction.

The penitent is now ready to be absolved, and, kneeling before the priest, he makes an act of contrition as the priest pronounces the absolution. It is interesting to compare the act of contrition included in Mirk's *Instructions for Parish Priests* (A) with the general confession in the *Lay Folks Mass Book* (B) and a modern version (C).

> A. God, I crye the mercy,
>   And thy moder seynt mary,
>   And alle the seyntus of heuen bryght,
>   I crye mercy wyth alle my myght,
>   Of alle the synnus I haue wroght,
>   In werke and worde, & sory thoght,
>   Wyth euery lyme of my body,
>   Wyth sore herte I aske god mercy,
>   And the, fader, in goddes place,
>   A-soyle me thow of my trespace,
>   Geue me penaunce also to,
>   For goddes loue that thow so do.
>
>   (ll. 1789-1800)

> B. I know to god ful myght,
>   And to hys modur, mary mayd bryght,
>   And to all halows here,
>   And to the fadur gostely,
>   I haue synnud largely,
>   In mony synnus sere,
>   In thowthg, in speche, and in delyte,
>   In word, in werke, I am to wyte,
>   And worthy for to blame.
>   Therfor I pray sent Mari
>   And all the halows holly,
>   here in goddus name,
>   And the prest to pray for me,
>   That god haue mercy and pete,
>   ffor his mon-hedde,
>   Of my wrecched synfulnes,
>   And gyf me grace of for-gyfnes
>   Of all my mysdede.
>
>   (ll. 65-82)

> C. O my God, I am heartily sorry for having offended Thee, and I detest all my sins because I dread the loss of heaven and the pains of hell, but most of all because they offend Thee, my God, who art all good and deserving of all my love. I firmly resolve, with the help of Thy grace, to confess my sins, to do penance, and to amend my life.

Neither of the medieval versions specifically mentions supernatural sorrow ("for having offended Thee"); neither includes specific intent to amend; neither even states sorrow clearly (other than "wyth sore herte"). The emphasis is on the acknowledgment of sin, on the intercession of the Virgin and the saints, and on the petition for mercy. In both medieval versions, note too the familiar formula: the penitent has sinned "in werke and worde, & sory thoght." The phrase appears again and again. Such familiar words and phrases became useful dramatic signs, for playwrights could rely on audience recognition.

Finally, then, with absolution comes the infusion of God's grace and a restoration to friendship with Him. The imagery is consistent: man is relieved of his burden; he is washed clean of his wickedness. More, grace provides a bulwark, the strength to persevere in amendment.

> And gyf grace to laste and lende
> In thi seruise to here ende.

Just as the grace of God alone cannot effect repentance without the cooperation of man's free will, even so free will cannot persevere without continuing grace.

Two other points should be noted before turning to an analysis of the plays themselves. In emphasizing God's boundless mercy, priests were continually preaching that it is never too late to repent. The point was essential and needed to be stated often; but a danger was inherent, for the sinner might feel encouraged to rest easy in sin until old age or illness made repentance an urgent necessity. Thus one of the most insistent themes of the Church was "repent *now*," a theme discussed at length in isolation and almost always appended to any discussion of mercy. The urgency—"for now is the time of mercy"—was adapted to the seasons throughout the liturgical year: the approaching "time of mercy" was thus heralded on Septuagesima Sunday, Ash Wednesday, the first and succeeding Sundays in Lent, Easter, Corpus Christi, the first Sunday in Advent, and so on. Many reasons for immediate penance were given: sins will be forgotten; all life lost in a graceless state is wasted and must be accounted for after death; all life lost in a graceless state marks so much loss of bliss; death may come unexpectedly and then the sinner would be irrevocably damned; one should heed the call of grace when it is given for it may not come again; old age is often too weak to do the necessary penance. One final reason is given by a fifteenth-century preacher, a refreshingly sensible observation which brings a welcome smile to the tired investigator who is wandering down the labyrinth of theoretical doctrine: "And what mede is [an old man] worthy to haue to do penaunce, that is vnmyghty to do good othur evell?"

A doctrinal problem of great significance for both Corpus Christi and medieval drama requires special attention. In its insistence that all sins can be forgiven, the Christian Church has been faced throughout its history with an ambiguous warning of Christ: "Every sin and blasphemy shall be forgiven men, but the blasphemy of the Spirit shall not be forgiven." The Bible does not define "blasphemy," and for centuries the passage has been variously interpreted. In some way, all agree, it is a turning from, a turning against, the

Holy Ghost; however, most agree (including all medieval sources consulted) that the sin could be forgiven. The point emphasized was that such a sin was seldom repented and therefore seldom forgiven. As Latimer was to put it some years later, tenderly assuring a fearful penitent, "it was a vehement manner of speaking in scripture."

The most typical medieval definition is the one found in the *Book of Vices and Virtues.* The sin against the Holy Ghost is classed under envy. In general, it is to "werreye," to make war upon, the Holy Ghost. In general, a man "synneth proprely bi malice of hymself." Five of the specific sins listed are extremely important in the following discussion of the plays: presumption, despair, hardness of heart, hatred of penance, and the harassing of the grace of the Holy Ghost in others (for example, deriding another man's repentance). The key words are of such significance that the entire passage bears quoting:

> [The first is] presumpcion, that is ouerboldnesse, that is to make the mercy of God to large, and to lite take hede or recche of his rightfulnesse; and therfore many men synneth in hope to come to amendement a-nothur tyme when they mowe tende to. The secunde is wanhope, th[al]t bynemeth God his mercy right as presumpcion is rightfulnesse. The thridde is obduracion, that is hardenesse of herte, whan a man is so harded and beten in his euele that ther may no man make hym bowe ne come to amendment. The ferthe is despit of penaunce, that is whan a man thenketh and sitteth in his herte that he nele nought leue his synne ne repente hym and do penaunce for no man. The fifthe is to werreye the grace of the Holy Gost in othere men or wommen.

Presumption, "overboldness," is of special interest for the Corpus Christi cycles. As noted, the text for the Feast warned against partaking of the Eucharist unworthily. Every man and woman must ponder

> what perill it is to resceyve it, considerynge well thise to, euery man and womman, that thei presvme not hem-selfe to resceve that worthy Lord but thei be worthy.

Feigning at the Sacrament was technically classified as presumption, the ultimate sin against the Holy Ghost, for it arose in malice, in scorn of Christ's mercy. When a medieval audience heard the words "presumption," "boldness," or "malice," when they saw a man receive the Eucharist hypocritically, when they saw him scorn a penitent, when they heard him claim his sin to be greater than God's mercy, we may be sure that the implications were immediately clear.

In brief summary, then, this is the doctrine of repentance which, if we too are to recognize the many signs

and grasp the implications, we must bear in mind as we approach the mystery cycles. Understanding the abstracted doctrine, however, is still only a beginning. In addition we must be thoroughly familiar with the vast body of tradition about the scriptural stories that were dramatized by the mystery playwrights. In their search for the sources of the religious plays, scholars have usually turned to the major patristic and scholastic works familiar to the Middle Ages: gospel harmonies such as Augustine's *De Consensu Evangelistarum,* historical treatises such as Peter Comestor's mammoth textbook, *Historia Scholastica,* and the many Latin commentaries. The last fifty years, however, have seen a growing awareness that vernacular sources may be much more significant for an analysis of the mystery plays. We must remember that the medieval citizen was not familiar with the Bible in translation. He knew the stories of Cain and Abel, of Joseph and Mary, only as they were retold and interpreted for him in sermons or vernacular narratives. If we are to see the Cain plays through medieval eyes, we must know what the audience expected, what it was prepared to recognize. Hence to locate the biblical traditions as well as sources of repentance doctrine, I have turned to vernacular works, in order not only to compare how different playwrights adapted familiar materials, but also to understand how the audience may have reacted.

Many narratives of biblical materials were available to the laity either in manuscript or through the preaching of friars or the parish priest. Five such sources have been found invaluable in analyzing the dramatic effectiveness of the mystery plays.

Although most biblical harmonies are concerned solely with the life of Christ, the *Cursor Mundi* moves from the Creation to the Last Judgment. Scholars of the York cycle are especially familiar with this vast epic of 24,000 lines, which "runs over the whole world" in an earnest attempt to draw lessons from all history. Of added interest for the present study is its appended "Boke of Penance," a homely "sermoning" for the lewd who have not been taught.

More limited in scope and more detailed are four gospel harmonies, narratives of the life of Christ that were based on the first four books of the New Testament. The *Southern Passion,* a verse narrative limited to the Passion sequence, is characteristic in purpose and method. It is thoroughly homiletic, directed to the unlearned laity and to the priest, who is clearly intended to use it for oral instruction. Even when there are contradictions in the Gospels, it carefully harmonizes details, constantly explaining, constantly defining terms. Its counterpart, the popular *Northern Passion,* is a much more vivid narrative, which its editor believes to be a verse homily actually written for the pulpit. The addition of much lively legendary material and the use of direct discourse made it particularly useful for a playwright, and it has been clearly identified as a source for the York, Towneley, and Hegge cycles.

Even more illuminating are *A Stanzaic Life of Christ* and *The Mirrour of the Blessed Lyf of Jesu Christ.* The *Stanzaic Life* is useful not only because it is from Chester and was probably a source for the Chester cycle, but also because of its extended commentaries, written specifically for the laity. Every gospel account is handled in "seven points," "five reasons," and the like. Thus we have valuable discussions of Magdalene, Judas, and others, in terms of their familiar homiletic significance. *The Mirrour of the Blessed Lyf,* Nicholas Love's translation of the pseudo-Bonaventuran *Meditationes Vitae Christi,* is of great importance. The work is actually not a series of meditations but a narrative with comment on the events of Holy Week, thus serving as a gospel harmony. Although this translation dates from the early fifteenth century, Mannyng had translated part of it probably as early as 1315, and the *Meditationes* had filtered down to the people for over a century through many homiletic works such as the *Southern Passion* and through the drama. Vigorously anti-Lollard, Love periodically pauses in his translation to give meticulous answer to Lollard teachings. Thus his *Mirrour,* like the *Stanzaic Life,* is especially valuable for the twentieth-century novice in medieval religious tradition.

In the following chapters, we shall be only secondarily concerned with the above works as identifiable sources of the plays. Primarily we shall be concerned with the different traditions that they contain. In the diligent search for sources of the mystery plays that has occupied scholars for over a century, often the mere location of a source has been seen as the end of research. This study has found careful comparison of the traditions contained in the sources to be absolutely essential. We cannot fully react to Magdalene as a character in a medieval play if we know only the contradictory gospel accounts about her. The medieval Magdalene was someone quite different. By the fourteenth century, stories that are skeletal in the Bible had been expanded by legend; gospel contradictions had been modified, explained, made to harmonize; biblical figures had become homiletic symbols. Just as we must be alert to doctrinal echoes, we must also be as familiar with the aura of tradition surrounding a given play as was the audience of the Middle Ages.

THE FALL FROM GRACE IN THE MYSTERY CYCLES
Rosemary Woolf (essay date 1972)

SOURCE: "Plays of the Fall," in *The English Mystery Plays,* University of California Press, 1972, pp. 105-31.

[*In the following essay, Woolf discusses the treatment of the subject of the fall from grace in the mystery cycle dramas, contrasting the plays' dramatic interpretation of supernatural events with the description of those episodes in the Bible and in the commentary of theologians.*]

The mystery cycles begin and end in the heavens, the opening play of the Fall of the Angels being on a subject never dramatised before and rarely since. The story was reconstructed by the Fathers by the piecing together of a number of biblical texts: of these the most important were the apostrophes addressed to the Prince of Babylon (Isaiah xiv. 12-15) and to the King of Tyre (Ezekiel xxviii. 2-19), which were understood in the light of Christ's words in Luke x. 18, 'I beheld Satan as lightning fall from heaven', and applied figuratively to the devil; to these was sometimes added the account of the war in heaven (Revelation xii. 3-9). The account of Satan's Fall, first amply and consistently expounded in *The City of God,* is now best known from the elaborate narrative in *Paradise Lost,* and present-day criticism of Milton has made everyone highly conscious of the pitfalls that await those who venture to treat this theme in literary rather than theological form. Medieval authors largely evade these pitfalls by a concise and symbolic treatment of the subject, the most symbolic of the plays, that in the York cycle, being also the most successful.

The characters, God with the good and bad angels, are all supernatural, and might therefore seem to present the dramatist with even more perilous and intractable material than the narrative poet. Iconography, however, provided a straightforward solution to the appearance of angels, for, though they were held to be immaterial and therefore invisible, the Bible recorded many scenes in which they had adopted a visible, human form, and some of these such as the Annunciation were represented in art over and over again. However, even with the help of traditional iconography, the portrayal of God presented difficulties, for in the heavens He is not any one person of the Trinity but the Trinity itself. Pictorial representations dealt with the mystery in a variety of ways, ranging from the depiction of three identical human figures to the more abstract and intellectual symbol of geometrical patterns, interlaced triangles or circles of different colours such as Dante imagined at the end of the *Paradiso.* But such representations were disturbing in narrative art though theologically exact when the subject was the work of Creation, since it had been accepted from the time of Augustine that the plural forms in Genesis i. 26, 'And God said, Let us make man in our image, after our likeness', indicated the work of the Trinity. Artists occasionally showed the world or Adam being created by three identical figures or by a somewhat Janus-like figure with three faces, but more often at the cost of theological precision, scenes of the Creation depicted the creator as though He were God the Father alone, a reverend, white-bearded figure. The authors of the plays adopted the latter tradition; within the greater realism of the plays the adoption of the former seems inconceivable and would certainly have passed the boundary which divides the strange or mysterious from the grotesque.

The authors of the plays therefore had a twofold problem: the one, earlier described, that though God appeared in human form, He was incorporeal and uncircumscribed; the other, that though He appeared as God the Father, He was yet the three persons of the Trinity. In all the plays this problem is solved by an opening speech in which God defines Himself, His eternal and unique self-understanding being deftly implied by the fact that He speaks without directly addressing the angels within the play or the audience without. He is alpha and omega, the first and the last, God without beginning or end, maker unmade, the true Trinity, Father, Son and Holy Ghost. In the York play, in particular, the splendour of the thought is sustained by the measured stanza form made weighty by alliteration:

> I am gracyus and grete, god withoutyn
>   begynnyng,
> I am maker unmade, all mighte es in me,
> I am lyfe and way unto welth wynnyng,
> I am formaste and fyrste, als I byd sall it be.

The York author does not quite succeed in sustaining this opening dignity throughout, and the other writers are perhaps altogether less successful; the aureate diction of the later Chester play nowadays sounds mannered rather than magnificent. Nevertheless it is clear that all aim at and largely achieve the same effect. In particular all are careful not to give God any words that would suggest that His corporeal appearance was other than symbolic: with one tiny exception in the *Ludus Coventriae,* God never speaks of Himself as having a body, and in the York play He does not even move, but stands throughout with symbolic stillness.

The second and yet more difficult problem consists of how to depict the Fall itself. To this problem the authors adopted different solutions reflecting divergent theological traditions about the nature of Satan's sin and the moment of its commission. In his commentary on Genesis, St Augustine in a sentence that was to be much quoted later said that the devil had sinned 'ab initio temporis'. This theory, while excellent in cutting the Gordian knot in regard to the question of how an angel, created perfect, could have sinned, laid itself open to a Manichaean interpretation, and therefore proved unacceptable to the orthodox. In the Middle Ages the question, 'An aliqua mora fuerit inter [angelorum] creationem et lapsum' was asked by Peter Lombard in the *Sentences,* and all subsequent theolo-

gians therefore commented upon it, amplifying Peter Lombard's own answer that 'fuit ibi aliqua morula, licet brevissima'. St Thomas gives as the more probable view 'quod statim post primum instans suae creationis diabolus peccaverit', the point being that the good angels in the first instant after their creation in their free will 'by one meritorious act came to beatitude', and the devil, conversely exercising his free will, fell. From the dramatists' point of view the theory that Satan sinned after the first moment of his creation was as convenient as the belief that he had sinned instantly, for it enabled them to show Satan as fallen from the moment that he spoke. The author of the Chester cycle who alone does not follow the scholastic theologians on this issue is much the least convincing, since he inevitably raises in his diffuse play a moral and psychological problem that it was well beyond his capacity and intention to answer: he therefore has to show an abrupt and unmotivated change of heart in Satan, and his treatment seems mechanical, even crude.

A related question was that of the precise form that Satan's pride took, in other words what was meant by his ambition to be like to the most high (Isaiah xiv. 14). Some eleventh-century theologians, Rupert of Deutz in his *De Victoria verbi Dei* and Honorius of Autun in his *Elucidarium* (a work which continued to be well known throughout the Middle Ages) understood this in its fullest sense: according to them Satan wished to rule as a tyrant over the other angels, desiring to be adored and worshipped by the angelic hosts 'tanquam Deus et Dominus ipsorum'. The scholastic theologians, however, expounded a more subtle view. According to St Thomas Satan did not wish to be as God 'per aequiparantiam. . .quia scivit hoc esse impossibile naturali cognitione' (for nothing can desire to belong to a higher order of being, since one could not achieve this without losing one's identity); rather he wished to be as God *per similitudinem,* that is he wished to have what he would anyway have attained had he remained unfallen, but 'quasi propria virtute, et non ex virtute Dei': to put it simply he wanted to be the source of his own happiness, to derive his beatitude, not from God, but from himself. In the mystery cycles the York author follows the latter tradition, the other three the earlier.

The best of these three is the play of the Fall in the *Ludus Coventriae,* in that it is the most lively and economic, and the weakest is the Chester play in that it is the most ample in narrative content and the most unsmiling (the Chester cycle is alone in not putting wit to the service of theology). After God's opening monologue in the *Ludus Coventriae,* the angels sing the three verses from the *Te Deum* describing how the angels unceasingly cry 'Sanctus, Sanctus, Sanctus, Dominus Deus sabaoth'. Whereupon Lucifer, speaking for the first time, asks with impudent bravado: 'To whos wurchipe synge ye þis songe, / To wurchip god or reverens me?' But of course what is impudence in

Lucifer is inventive audacity on the part of the poet. After his rejection by the good angels, Lucifer then completes his blasphemy visually by sitting upon God's throne (God having presumably withdrawn during the singing of the *Sanctus*). At the corresponding point in the Towneley cycle the author catches well a tone of coarse and blustering self-assertiveness:

> Say, felows, how semys now me
> To sit in seyte of trynyte?
> I am so bright of ich a lym,
> I trow me seme as well as hym.

In these two plays the authors do not attempt to imagine the quality of angelic pride: instead they show an already fallen angel who is a boastful and crude impostor, and the jingly brashness of his speech in context reflects the monstrous indecorum of his action.

The theological doctrine here followed has led naturally to a fairly flamboyant treatment, whereas the theory that Satan rejected his status as creature leads in the York play to a more subdued and subtler style. In this play after the good angels have again sung the *Sanctus,* the first good angel begins his speech in praise of God and in gratitude for his creation:

> A! mercyfull maker, full mekill es þi mighte,
> Þat all this warke at a worde worthely has
>   wroghte,
> Ay loved be þat lufly lorde of his lighte,
> That us thus mighty has made, þat nowe was
>   righte noghte.

And Lucifer, joining in as it were antiphonally, replies with praise of himself:

> All the myrth þat es made es markide in me,
> Þe bemes of my brighthode ar byrnande so
>   bryghte,
> And I so semely in syghte my selfe now I se,
> For lyke a lorde am I lefte to lende in þis
>   lighte,
> More fayrear be far þan my feres,
> In me is no poynte þat may payre,
> I fele me fetys and fayre,
> My powar es passande my peres.

There follow four further stanzas in which the good angels adore God as the source of their being, while Satan with increasing confidence and rapture praises his own beauty and excellence and rashly asserts his immutability. Then as Lucifer works himself up to the epitomisation of his rebellion, 'I sall be lyke unto hym þat es hyeste on heghte', he falls within the space of one extended metrical line, 'Owe! what I am derworthe and defte.—Owe! dewes! all goes downe!' In the other plays Satan falls at God's command, but here he is shown to fall not as a penalty or judgment imposed by

God, but as the inevitable consequence of what he himself says: God is present but silent. Up to this point the York author has deliberately excluded all action and all dramatic dialogue (Satan and the good angels do not address each other). Whereas the other authors used a theological tradition that provided them with a plot (Satan usurps God's throne, demands adoration from the angels, which is granted by some, refused by others), the York author follows a tradition which deliberately excluded a narrative of the Fall, yet contrary to normal assumptions he is for this very reason the more successful. What is so acutely presented in logical argument by St Thomas is here most deftly and imaginatively translated into literature.

All the plays end with the lament of the devils in hell. There was a long tradition, going back to the sermons of the eastern Fathers, of the plaints of the devil (the first part of the Old English *Christ and Satan* is founded upon it). This tradition confers upon the devil the human dignity of one who grieves for intolerable loss. The effect of this within the framework of drama can be seen in German plays, and particularly in the *Egerer Fronleichnamsspiel,* where Lucifer in a moving lyric lament calls upon all created things to intercede for him, the beauty of the natural world thus invoked contrasting poignantly with his own dark dungeon:

> Ich klag dirs paide windt und lüfft,
> Ich klag dirs regen, tau und tüfft,
> Ich klag dirs hiz, kelt und auch schne,
> Ich lkag den plümen und grünen klce, . . .
> Ich klag dirs suess vogelgeschall,
> Ich klag dirs perg und tieffe tall,
> Ich klag dirs fells und allen stain,
> Ich klags auch aller welt gemain:
> Das got ie von seinnen gnaden schüeff,
> Zu den thu ich heut meinen rueff,
> Das si fur mich mit guttem sitten
> Den almechtigen noch wolten pitten.

This approach, however, is not compatible with the degradation of the devil in the English plays into a brutish and contemptible figure, a conception which seems to have its origins in iconography rather than patristic tradition.

Milton's conception of Satan as 'not less than archangel ruined' had its origins in the Fathers and particularly in the writings of Gregory the Great, which stressed that Satan was a fallen angel with the stress as it were as much upon the second word as upon the first. However, while devils like angels were thought to be immaterial and invisible, hagiographic narratives required that the tempter should take visible form, sometimes that of an animal in order to terrify or of an angel of light in order to deceive. Most commonly, however, he appears as a black man—he is sometimes called an Ethiopian—and this form is obviously a symbol of his character through the primitive association of darkness with evil. When from the twelfth century onwards wall-paintings of hell with the Last Judgment became frequent in churches, it became customary to represent the devil by a far more striking moral symbol, the evil of his nature being indicated by the repulsive ugliness of his appearance. In giving shape to this ugliness artists seem to have been influenced by the deformed creatures found in antique art. In medieval iconography, therefore, the devil may be shown half man, half beast, erect like a man, but with claws, horns, bat's wings, tail and perhaps with an animal face. He is often hairy like an animal, and may have more than one head, the others being placed in grotesque or obscene positions. Some of these details will have been actually represented on the stage: the inventory for the Drapers' Pageant of the Last Judgment at Coventry includes masks for the devils and coats of canvas covered with hair.

The important point at the moment, however, is not the relevance of iconography to stage presentation but to the dramatists' imaginative understanding of the fallen angels, for they evidently seek to arouse in their audience the contempt and disgust which were the normal responses to the devil in art. The very brief eight-line lament of Lucifer in the *Ludus Coventriae*, of which the following is the second verse, illustrates this point:

Now to helle þe way I take,
In endeles peyn þer to be pyht.
Ffor fere of fyre a fart I crake
In helle donjoon myn dene is dyth.

The satirising of evil in terms of lavatorial humour is especially characteristic of the morality plays, *Mankind* in particular, and anal emphases in the depiction of hell are found in works as disparate as the poems of Dunbar and the paintings of Bosch. The force of this passage, however, is that the devil is shown to acquire a body by falling, for words here grossly indicate a real body as opposed to a corporeal symbol, and a body which, like human bodies after the Fall, alarmingly no longer obeys the will.

The same effect is achieved by the York playwright but more delicately. Here the debasement and deformity of the devils is indicated by the shattering of the hitherto shapely stanza into little scraps of raucous ejaculation, screamed by the devils as they attack each other in the turmoil of hell:

Lucifer   Walaway! wa! es me now, nowe es
             it war thane it was.
              Unthryvandly threpe yhe, I sayde
             but a thoghte.
2nd devil   We! lurdane, þu lost us.
Lucifer   Yhe ly, owte! allas!

I wyste noghte þis wo sculde be
             wroghte.
              Owte on yhow! lurdans, yhe smore
             me in smoke.
2nd devil   This wo has þu wroghte us.
Lucifer   Yhe ly, yhe ly!
2nd devil   Thou lyes, and þat sall þu by,
             We lurdans have at yowe, lat loke.

It is only on the page that this passage can be recognised as metrical. Similar effects of stridency are found in the other cycles but less ingeniously contrived.

In the plays of the Fall of the Angels patterns are begun which are to recur throughout the cycles. God and the good angels are necessarily characterless, but Satan's hollow displays of power and his delight in his own existence and beauty are later echoed in the speeches of Herod and Pilate. Similarly the contrast between the dignity and tranquillity of heaven and the noise and agitation of hell, all visually, verbally, and metrically emphasised, begin one of the most important recurring themes in the cycles, which again will receive its climax at the Crucifixion. Whilst of course none of the plays should be judged solely as a self-sufficient unit without relation to its position within the larger pattern, this is particularly true of the Fall of the Angels, of which the reverberations will not be exhausted until the play of the Last Judgment. It is the fact that the authors are dispensed from the need to provide narrative self-sufficiency that enables them to treat the subject so symbolically and therefore so effectively. For there seems to be no successful middle path between an ambitious and thoroughly anthropomorphic presentation such as Milton's and the impressionistic brevity of the English mystery plays. Comparison of the English plays with their French and German analogues draws attention to their authors' sense of timing and contrast and their economy of design. There is an attempt in the *Mystère du viel testament* to make the action more naturalistically ample by a long episode in which Lucifer appeals to his followers and they promise obedience and worship; but this makes the play neither more dramatically nor more theologically impressive. The Chester play, which was probably influenced by Continental models, equally illustrates the futility of employing normal dramatic methods in the treatment of this subject and, despite some skill in Satan's speeches, is the weakest of the English plays. The York play which is at the opposite pole from it is the best.

The plays of the Fall of the Angels, in keeping with the traditional exegesis of Genesis i. I, had presented the creation of the angels as God's work on the first day: the work of the next five days succeeds the Fall. This is the construction of all the cycles save Towneley which, contrary to normal tradition but with considerable gain in convenience, extends God's initial creation speech to the creation of the animals on the fifth day, and can therefore begin the scene of the Fall of Man with the creation of Adam. The subject of the Creation is one of the few that the techniques of medieval drama were inadequate to mould into effective form, for in this reliance upon iconographic parallels would not solve aesthetic difficulties. Medieval art, though it does not rival the grandeur of Michelangelo's scenes of creation, is often able to suggest something of creative energy and of the beauty of the newly created world. The opening folios of the *Holkham Bible Picture Book* are a good example of what art could achieve and may also indicate what the stage attempted. When in the plays the creating Trinity spoke the monologues of Creation, He may well have held such a pair of gigantic compasses and behind Him there may well have been a backdrop with birds and animals painted upon it (alternatively painted cloths or boards may have been held up in turn to show the work of each day, as the stage directions require in the *Mystère du viel testament*). But this can only have been a crude imitation of art, and the splendour of poetry could alone have compensated for the missing beauty of painting or sculpture. Imaginative intensity, however, or sublimity of style are not within the compass of the authors of the mystery cycles.

These monologues, however, should not be dismissed as a running commentary ineptly attributed to God: for God created by His word, and His speeches therefore do not simply describe the act of creation but represent that act itself. Furthermore, whilst one may regret the absence of a noble style to correspond to the majesty of the idea, the dramatic relaxation that results comes usefully between the more compelling scenes of the successive falls. Throughout the cycles the authors deliberately allow some poetically humdrum scenes to provide links between scenes of heightened comedy or horror. It might, however, be thought that it was still too early in the cycles for relaxation to be needed, and if so, the author of the *Ludus Coventriae,* who despatches the five days of creation in twelve lines, may seem the most successful.

None of the plays of the Fall of Man is as elegant and well contrived as the York Play of the Fall of the Angels: the multifarious problems of representing the subject upon the stage are met with varying degrees of skill; now one cycle shows an especially felicitous touch, now another. The opening difficulty of showing the garden, in which Adam and Eve are set, as a place of abundance and delight is tackled only by the author of the *Ludus Coventriae.* The initial rubric of the *Mystère d'Adam* had specified that the scaffold for paradise should contain trees of various kinds with fruit hanging from them 'ut amoenissimus locus videatur'. The authors of the York and Chester cycles presumably also assumed stage properties of this kind, but they cannot have been sufficient to convince the imagination that Eden was a place of supreme pleas-

antness and charm. Within the *Adam* Eden is described in the kind of negative statements that had already been applied to it by Augustine: it is a place where man will feel neither hunger nor thirst, cold nor heat, but its physical abundance is only once alluded to when the Figura says to Adam, 'De nul delit n'i troverez falture'. In contrast to this brevity, God speaks as follows in the *Ludus Coventriae:*

> Now come Fforth Adam to paradys,
> ther xalt þou have all maner thynge,
> bothe flesch and ffysch and frute of prys,
> all xal be buxum at þi byddyng.
> Here is pepyr, pyan, and swete lycorys,
> take hem all at þi lykyng,
> both appel and pere and gentyl rys.

In this passage the dramatist has evocatively drawn upon the alliterative catalogues of spices and fruits from other literary gardens, that of Mirth in the *Romance of the Rose* of the earthly paradise visited by King Alexander. By poetically recalling the exotic and sensuous delights of the idealised medieval garden the poet is able to establish that Eden is truly *Locus amoenissimus.*

In the *Ludus Coventriae* the dramatist neatly returns to the theme of the delightful abundance of the garden in order to motivate the separation of Adam and Eve which, in accordance with the impressionistic narrative style of the Bible, is left unaccounted for Adam praises the fruits as *woundyr dowcet,* adding:

> In þis gardeyn I wyl go se
> all þe fflourys of fayr bewte
> and tastyn þe frutys of gret plente
>   þat be in paradyse.

Whilst neither art nor any authoritative source could have helped with this transition, earlier vernacular narratives such as the *Cursor mundi* had made a functional link, however brief, 'Adam yode walkand in þat welth', and the author of the Towneley cycle uses the same explanation: the skill of the author of the *Ludus Coventriae* therefore lies not in invention but in relating this necessary transition to a larger pattern. In the York cycle the Temptation forms a separate play, and there is thus no need to motivate Adam's departure: he is simply not on stage when the play begins. But the Chester author, who is the least talented in dramatic craftsmanship, seems unaware of the problem: presumably the producer directed Adam to leave the stage inconspicuously, unless (and more awkwardly) Adam, as in the mosaics of San Marco, stood with his back turned as though not a part of the scene.

At this point with the appearance of the devil, the central episode of the Temptation begins, and problems of theology, psychology and stage-craft come thick and fast. According to the usual theological tradition the tempter was the devil who had entered into the serpent of Genesis: a legend of rabbinic origin, however, told that the species of serpent used by the devil had a woman's head, and this bizarre variation was included in the *Historia scholastica* of Peter Comestor, thus acquiring authority and becoming thereafter almost invariable in art and literature. The construction of the York and Chester plays requires that the devil first appear in his own form, in which he explains his fall and his envy of mankind, and then change into a snake, a double appearance also found sometimes in English art. In the Chester play it is untheologically, but for obvious stage convenience, a matter of disguise rather than transformation, and the devil announces that he will put on his 'adders coate', words no doubt accompanied by action. In the York play, however, it is conceived as a genuine change (Satan says, 'In a worme liknes wille y wende'), and how this was contrived is indicated neither by text nor stage direction. The adoption of serpent form also posed a problem in plausibility, which theologians had recognised and thereby emphasised. Scholastic commentators, following Augustine, had argued that God had restricted the devil's choice of form: Peter Lombard suggested that he might have preferred the form of a dove, Bonaventura said that he might have preferred human forms as being *affabilior,* and St Thomas that he would have preferred 'formam boni persuasoris scilicet angeli' but this was prohibited by God. In some artistic traditions, however, such as the illustrations of the *Speculum humanae salvationis,* the tempter appears in a strange but magnificent shape—a winged dragon, rather than a snake, and the reference in the Chester plays to an 'adder' which has 'wynges like a byrd' indicates that it was this tradition that the author had chosen to follow (in the York cycle the presentation of the animal must have been at the producer's discretion).

In all the plays save that of the *Ludus Coventriae,* which is eccentric, the tempter explains himself in an opening speech. In Towneley this appears to be spoken in hell (it is addressed to other devils): unfortunately the rest of the play is lost so that the author's further disposition of the action is not known. In Chester the tempter arrives in paradise, and in a place apart laments his fall, that pride had cast him down, and now moved by envy he grieves and grudges that Adam 'a Caytife, made of claye' should take his place in heaven. The same situation occurs in the York, except that Satan gives a new and extraordinary motive for his rebellion in heaven, namely that God had purposed to take upon him man's nature:

> And we were faire and bright,
>   Þerfore me thoght þat he
> The kynde of us tane myght,

And þer-at dedeyned me.

In an apocryphal tradition, repeated by some of the early Fathers, it had been held that Satan had resented God's decision to create men in His own image, but Satan's base fancies of favouritism towards man here take what must be a late shape in that they depend upon the theory of Duns Scotus and other Franciscan theologians that the Incarnation would have taken place irrespective of the Fall. This motive reappears in the seventeenth-century play of the Fall, Vondel's *Lucifer,* where the wicked angel's determination to fight against God is aroused by Gabriel's announcement: 'Ye shall behold the everlasting Word, / Clothed in the flesh and blood of human kind.' In the York play, however, this motive is introduced with an unusual disregard for consistency, and whether the relic of an older version, or introduced by the injudicious vagary of a later redactor, it remains a startling blemish, in which one may suspect the hand of a polemical Franciscan.

The temptation of Eve and her consequent persuasion of Adam is managed rather formally in the York and Chester cycles: where they can the authors keep close to their source in Genesis, though the Chester author is a little more daring in allowing the tempter's malice to be blatantly revealed, when he says to Eve, 'yow may well wyt he [God] was your foe'; where they have no source, as for the nature of Eve's persuasions of Adam, they are brief. Dramatists could have found sanctions for invention even in so momentous an episode in Augustine's comment that Eve gave the apple to Adam, 'fortassis cum verbo suasorio, quod Scriptura tacens intelligendum relinquit', but little guidance from theologians on Eve's motives, whether amiable or base. There had, however, been detailed analysis of the nature of Adam's sin: theologians, following I Timothy ii. I4, held that Adam, unlike Eve, had not been deceived by the serpent's promise that they would be as gods, and following Augustine, that Adam had consented out of 'amicabili quadam benevolentia', the good will of one creature towards another. The York playwright, however, entirely ignores this interpretation and adopts the mechanical course of showing Adam deceived by the serpent's promise which Eve repeats. The author of the Chester plays is more subtle and more theologically correct. In this work Adam appears overtly to be merely pleased by the fruit (he says, 'the fruite is sweete and fayre in feere'), but, though gluttony was considered an element in the Fall, dramatically it seems insufficient in this context, and we are therefore more aware of Adam responding to the affection in Eve's speech:

> Adam, husband, life and deere,
>   eate some of this apple here;
>   it is fayre, my leeif fere,
>   it may thou not forsake.

These loving endearments suggest that it is Eve rather

than the apple that Adam cannot bring himself to reject. This interpretation of the episode, which Milton later was so movingly and magnificently to adopt, is found also in the Cornish plays, where Eve threatens, 'Since thou wilt not believe / Thou shalt lose my love.' But whereas the Cornish author depicts crude blackmail, the Chester dramatist in his treatment is gentle and elusive: at what point, if any, innocent affection merges with feminine wiles, it is impossible to detect.

Whilst the Chester author by this slight touch succeeds in suggesting the mood in which Adam slipped to sin, the author of the *Ludus Coventriae* is more adept in indicating the insidiousness of the tempter's speech to Eve. He, like the authors of the late Norwich plays of the Fall, follows an apocryphal tradition, which had earlier appeared in the *Mystère d'Adam* and *Genesis B,* and which ultimately derived from the apocryphal Book of Enoch, namely that the devil when tempting took the form, not of a serpent but of an angel of light. That in later times the devil tempted in this form (his appearance being thus as deceptive as his words) was established by tradition based on 2 Corinthians xi. I4, but to suppose that he thus tempted Eve goes bluntly against the text of Genesis, and, as we saw above, had been obliquely but specifically denied by St Thomas. From the dramatic point of view the value of this apocryphal fantasy is that it allows the tempter to proceed in a more elevated and therefore deceptive manner; he does not have to approach the issue by cunning questioning, but, knowing already the best point of attack, he greets Eve as though she were a noble lady from the world of romance:

Tu es fieblette e tendre chose,
E es plus fresche que n'est rose;
Tu es plus blanche que cristal,
Que neif que chiet sor glace en val;
Mal cuple em fist li criator:
Tu es trop tendre e il trop dur;
Mais neporquant tu es plus sage,
En grant sens as mis tun corrage.

The opening words of the tempter in the *Ludus Coventriae,* 'Heyl Ffayr Wyff and comely dame', are not so poetically beautiful (and of course do not so subtlely attempt to awaken in Eve a desire to be superior to Adam), but they show the same stratagem of winning Eve's interest through flattery. Similarly in the earlier of the two Norwich plays the tempter's first words are 'O gemme of felicyté and femynyne love', and in the later, 'Oh lady of felicité'. In contrast in the York play the serpent simply addresses Eve by her name and in the Chester play yet more bluntly as 'woman'. St Thomas, again following Augustine, had said that Eve at the tempter's earliest promptings had felt an *elation* that laid her open to his subsequent and more concrete proposal of evil: in these plays it is skilfully demonstrated that Eve's initial responsiveness springs from

an awakening of feminine self-esteem, an interpretation that is more closely defined than was perhaps theologically orthodox but is dramatically very convincing.

So advantageous is this approach in terms of at least momentary psychological realism that it probably accounts for the English dramatists' adoption of this apocryphal theme; for, unlike the Cornish playwright, who shows a constant preference for apocryphal legends with their weird narrative solidity, they normally proceed in paths central to theological and literary traditions. However, while in narrative the serpent could splendidly flatter Eve as he does in poems which stretch in time from Avitus's *Poematum de Mosaicae historiae gestis* to *Paradise Lost,* on the stage high-flown compliments from an actor in some snake-like costume would have seemed incongruous: in drama dignified words to be convincing have to be spoken by a dignified figure. It could only be a serious dramatic reason of this kind that could have led the author of the *Ludus Coventriae,* who is the most theologically alert of the English dramatists, to choose or tolerate in his source a highly eccentric and unorthodox motif.

In their handling of Adam and Eve's remorse and their expulsion from the garden, the plays again vary in style and quality. The dialogue outlines for this episode in Genesis iii. 9-19 are unusually complete and consistent, and provided a firm structure for the plays. The dramatists in their amplifications, however, provide two imaginative insights into the condition of the fallen world and fallen man that are rewarding. On the question of unfallen man's knowledge of God, theologians held that they did not behold God face to face as do those who in heaven enjoy the beatific vision but they beheld Him more clearly than fallen man: Adam and Eve saw in a glass but not darkly. This is reflected in the York play, where Adam replies to God's question, 'Where art thou?', not with a paraphrase of Genesis iii. 10, 'I heard thy voice in the garden, and I was afraid, because I was naked; and I hid myself', but with a statement far more movingly evocative of his changed condition, 'I here þe lorde and seys the noyt'; and this change is expressed yet more poignantly in the *Ludus Coventriae:* 'A lord for synne oure flourys do ffade / I here þi voys but I se þe nought.' The conjoining of the idea of man's diminished apprehension of God with the beautiful and perennial symbol of transience is especially effective: the poetry conveys a nostalgic sense of loss rare in medieval literature, the withered flowers seeming rather to anticipate Herbert's posy and Herrick's daffodils, or, to take a more relevant example, the garland of roses in *Paradise Lost* which, after Eve's first base speech of persuasion, drops already faded from Adam's hands.

In their treatment of Adam and Eve's relationship after the Fall—their recriminations and repentance—the authors of the York cycle and the *Ludus Coventriae* again illuminate our understanding of the scene. The Chester author is alone in simply paraphrasing the Genesis text, and thus shows Adam willing only to shift the blame to Eve and Eve to shift the blame to the serpent: neither gives a dignified impression by acceptance of responsibility and neither expresses contrition whether towards God or each other. The author of the *Ludus Coventriae,* however, has taken pains to minimise the unpleasant impression left by the Genesis accusations by enclosing them in two pairs of less self-exculpatory speeches. Instantly upon eating the apple Adam blames Eve, 'Alas, Alas ffor þis fals dede / my flesly frend my fo I fynde', but continues by making an equal confession of guilt, 'oure lordys wurd wold we not drede / þerfore we be now caytyvys unkynde'; and Eve similarly, whilst first lamenting the speech of the 'fals Aungel' continues, 'Alas oure makers byddyng is brokyn / Ffor I have towchyd his owyn dere tre'. Whilst at this point Adam and Eve fittingly think of their relationship towards God, after the biblical accusations, Eve thinks of the harm she has done Adam, 'my husbond is lost because of me', and invites him therefore to kill her; and, whilst Adam rejects this invitation to murder with some colloquial anger, his tone suggests shared responsibility for sinning, 'our wytt was nesch', and of shared companionship in the hardships to follow.

In the York cycle the recriminations of Adam and Eve are amplified at length, an expansion to some extent necessitated by the division here, as elsewhere, of single subjects into distinct scenes acted by different gilds: the expulsion from Eden thus has to be full enough to stand on its own, and this is achieved by making the angel of the banishment repeat God's condemnations, which are interspersed with further excuses and reproaches from Adam and Eve. Eve here enlarges upon her self-exculpatory accusations by hitting back at Adam's anti-feminist reproach, 'Allas! what womans witte was light!', with the rebuke that he should therefore have ruled her, 'Mans maistrie shulde have bene more', the traditional moral allegorisation of Adam and Eve as reason and senses or soul and body thus providing the material for what in human terms is spirited but profitless wrangling. Nevertheless in this final episode there occur some beautiful lines of lyric lament in which Adam and Eve cease recriminating and think only of the nature of their loss and their sin. Adam is given an exceptionally long complaint, of which the following stanza is a part:

> Gone ar my games with-owten glee,
> Allas! in blisse kouthe we noyt bee,
> For putte we were to grete plente
> > at prime of þe day;
> Be tyme of none alle lost had wee,
> > sa welawaye.

The idea of the short space of time from prime to noon (from early morning until midday) which elapsed between Creation and Fall was in accordance with theological speculation, but it has been transformed in this stanza into a nostalgic sense of the brevity of happiness, awareness of responsibility for its loss intensifying regret. And whilst Adam follows this with further reproaches of Eve (which will be later considered from another point of view), Eve at last meets and checks them with a counsel of resignation and a grieving confession of fault:

> Be stille Adam, and nemen it na mare,
> > it may not mende.
> For wele I wate I have done wrange,
> And therfore evere I morne emange,
> Allas! the whille I leve so lange,
> > ded wolde I be!

This speech Adam matches with an expression of resignation to God's will and a prayer for His help: on this muted note the play ends.

Up to this point we have considered the plays as though they were independent works, the authors' problem being to present a theological understanding of the Genesis text with sufficient narrative consistency and psychological plausibility to make it alive upon the stage. But in traditional thought the Fall of Man was only half the story, it was an event to be reversed and repaired at the Redemption, and the plays must therefore be considered in relation to the later parts of the cycles. It was not of course necessary to state the Redemption at length or explicitly in cyclic plays of the Fall: it is only in the second Norwich play, which could be acted apart from the parent cycle, that the hope of salvation is strongly emphasised, and the work can thus fittingly end with a song of praise. But in all plays some brief allusion or some symbolic adumbration was needed.

It is possible that intimations of future redemption were sometimes supplied visually in the plays, as they were also in art. In the *Holkham Bible Picture Book,* for instance, there is a nest at the top of the tree in which a pelican feeds her young from her wounded breast (a common bestiary type of the Redemption). In the Caedmon manuscript there had already been a little cross at the top of the tree in the scene of the Creation, and in later Continental manuscripts one even finds a crucifix set within the branches. This type of iconography was not, however, so common that we should assume that it was regularly imitated in the mystery plays: it is in fact only in the *Ludus Coventriae* that such a visual foreshadowing would correspond admirably with the text, since it is in this cycle alone that the Crucifixion is specifically mentioned—in the seraph's dismissal of Adam and Eve to misery,

> Tyl a chylde of a mayd be born

And upon þe rode rent and torn
To save all þat ye have forlorn
Your welth for to restore.

Whilst Adam's disobedience to God's command by taking the fruit of the forbidden tree was only fully reversed when Christ in obedience hung upon the tree of the Cross, the reversals that were equally stressed were Mary's obedience at the Annunciation in contrast to Eve's disobedience, and Christ's rejection in the wilderness of Satan's temptations to pride, avarice and gluttony, which reversed the Fall in which, according to Gregory the Great and many subsequent writers, Adam and Eve had manifested these very sins. The authors of the cycles seem in general to have been uninterested in the latter parallelism. In their plays of the Temptation in the Wilderness the authors of the York cycle and the *Ludus Coventriae* make no mention of Adam, whilst the Towneley cycle as preserved does not even include a play on this subject. The Chester author, who is particularly interested in typological correspondences, is therefore alone in making Christ expressly draw a parallel between his own temptation and that of Adam. There is, however, nothing in the play of the Fall to indicate that at this point he already had the parallelism in mind and was laying the foundations for subsequent recapitulation.

By far the most important parallel, and the one that most interested the authors of the plays, was that between Eve and Mary: it was a comparison expounded from the time of the early Fathers, and the potentialities of this symmetrical antithesis were gradually explored with astonishing ingenuity. During the Middle Ages the conjunction of the Fall and the Annunciation is frequently demonstrated in art: in the *Bible moralisée,* the *Biblia pauperum* and the *Speculum humanae salvationis,* type and antitype, the Annunciation and Eve tempted by the serpent, invariably accompany one another. Even in non-typological art, the banishment from the garden is often found in some subordinate position in representations of the Annunciation: over and over again on the closed panels of triptychs, as the subject of medallions or other decorative carvings in the Virgins' chamber, or as distant figures in a landscape, Adam and Eve are shown leaving the gates of paradise, whilst inside the shutters or in the forefront of the painting the Blessed Virgin receives in obedience and humility the angel's message.

In literature the parallelism between Eve and the Blessed Virgin was worked out in a different way, the two figures corresponding to two literary styles, the satiric literature in denigration of women and the formal, ornate poetry in praise of women. In satiric attacks upon women they are possessed of every vice, they are faithless, avaricious, lecherous, vain, obstinate and disobedient, and a source of disaster to their husbands: a list of wicked women from the Bible became a commonplace

in the literary form of the dissuasion from marriage and in other more serious treatises, and this catalogue was headed by Eve. In the complementary poems written in praise of women (such pairs might be written by the same author), women were seen as the source of every virtue, they were gentle, loving, gracious and faithful, and Mary was their prototype. In the Middle English debate between the Thrush and the Nightingale on the subject of women, their defender, the nightingale, at last triumphs in argument by quoting the example of the Blessed Virgin.

In the plays of the Fall an attack upon women grows naturally out of Adam's biblically based accusation of Eve, but becomes far more heavily accentuated than the narrative and psychological context could warrant. In Chester Satan in his opening monologue explains his decision to approach Eve in a flagrantly anachronistic generalisation, 'That woman is forbyd to doe, / for any thinge therto will shooe': Eve's sin is thus reduced to the level of sheer obstinate perversity, a common theme, as we shall see, of anti-feminist satire. The theme in one of its many variations is resumed by Adam in a direct address to the audience later in the same play:

> Now all my kinde by me is kent,
> to flee womans intisement;
> whoe trustes them in anye intent,
> truly he is decayved.
>
> My licorous wife hath bene my foe,
> the devilles envye shent me also,
> they twayne together well may goe,
> the sister and the brother!

A similar warning is given in the York play, where Adam, after reproaching Eve for her disobedience and evil counsel, adds, 'Nowe god late never man aftir me / triste woman tale'.

This theme is repeated on a large scale in the play of Noah, where the authors are free to depict a woman who by her speech and conduct exemplifies these vices. Eve, however, could not be characterised with mocking derision: contempt is displayed in what is said about her but not in the presentation of her as a debased and comic figure. There is therefore a discrepancy between Eve herself and the comments made upon her by the devil and Adam, a discrepancy that would jar if understood in terms of psychological realism. But anachronism and discrepancy are used ostentatiously to draw attention to the beginnings of a pattern: the unexpected satiric tone heard in Adam's speeches serves obliquely as a promise of Redemption, not of course within the play, but to the audience. The heavy emphasis upon Eve as the prototype of foolish, obstinate, disobedient women, very obviously begins a pattern which is incomplete, and thus signals that only half the story has been told: Eve thus derided can only be the *first* Eve and the *second* Eve is yet to come.

When parallelisms between the Fall and the Redemption were worked out, they might be extended to Cain and Abel. Tertullian makes a comparison between Eve the mother of the first murderer and Mary the mother of the Redeemer. This extension of the Fall to include the murder of Abel is sometimes reflected in iconographic schemes, as, for instance, on the eleventh-century bronze doors of Hildesheim, where eight scenes of the Fall are adjoined to eight scenes of the Redemption, the last two scenes of the Fall being taken from the story of Cain and Abel. Reasons for this extension are easily understandable. Whilst the sin of Adam and Eve was pride, an inordinate wish to be as God, and thus the greatest of the seven deadly sins, the actual form that it took was obviously not an example of monstrous depravity. The prohibition upon eating the apple was understood as a minute obligation imposed by God as a reminder of His sovereignty; the tree was not supposed to have any special properties in itself, being called the tree of the knowledge of good and evil only because of its effect. Medieval literature often stresses the triviality of the action itself: the famous lyric, 'Adam lay I-bowndyn' does so by a touch of rollicking style, 'And al was for an appil, an appil þat he tok', and Langland by a characteristically laconic expression 'Tho Adam and Eve eten apples unrosted'. Origen in a passage later cited by St Thomas had stated that someone placed in the highest state of perfection could not suddenly drop to the lowest grade of wickedness, 'sed paulatim et per partes defluere eum necesse est'. The distinction is made clearly in the *Ludus Coventriae,* where Adam recoils from Eve's suggestion that he should kill her in retribution, 'Ffor yf I xulde sle my wyff / I sclow my self with-owten knyff'. In terms of ordinary reckoning man has obviously still a long way to fall, and the Fall is therefore in a sense not complete until Cain has slain his brother Abel.

The dramatists' interest in showing a continuation of the Fall can be seen by omission in their treatment of Abel. Abel had a double typological significance: his offering of the lamb was a type of the eucharistic sacrifice, his death a type of the Crucifixion. That the evil consequences of the Fall are arrested in Abel is of course made clear: his obedience, to God, to his father, and to his brother are everywhere stressed; and his virtuous offering of the best of his flock is made important, though it is only in the *Ludus Coventriae* that the parallelism between Abel's lamb and Christ who will suffer on the Cross 'in a lombys lyknes' is made explicit. There is, however, no dramatic concentration upon Abel at his death, the attention is solely upon Cain. Abel never speaks before his death; though in the Towneley cycle he makes one powerful cry as he lies slain (the author has given a daring twist to Genesis iv. 10): 'Veniance, veniance, lord, I cry! / for I am slayn,

and not gilty.' But, though the second line here undoubtedly anticipates the Crucifixion it is from the point of view of man's wickedness rather than God's love. How the authors might have presented the murder of Abel, had they wished to stress its typological significance, can be seen from the *Mystère d'Adam,* where Cain's statement of murder, 'Jo t'occirai', is followed by a substantial dialogue: during the course of this Abel expresses his obedience to God's will, 'Del tut me met a son plaisir', and dies, as is fitting, with a prayer, 'Deu pri qu'il ait de mei merci'; at this point the stage directions instruct that Abel shall fall upon his knees, facing to the east. Abel, like Christ, therefore dies a willing sacrifice. This treatment of the victim the authors of the mystery plays reserve until the Sacrifice of Isaac.

A more positive method of showing the pattern of descent into evil was by overtly relating the story of Cain and Abel to that of Adam and Eve, so that in the one episode the fallen but soberly virtuous Adam is contrasted with the fallen and unequivocally evil Cain. There is an element of this in the *Ludus Coventriae,* in which Adam, now a dignified patriarch, gives grave advice to his sons on the duty of sacrifice (an incident deriving from the *Historia scholastica*) and sends them forth with a prayer for God's blessing. It is, however, in the Chester plays that the management of the episodes is self-evidently organised to display this pattern. The Chester author firmly embeds the murder of Abel in the life-history of Adam and Eve, the Fall and the murder in fact forming one play. There comes, however, a large jump in time after the expulsion for, when Adam speaks next, his sons are grown men; one misses here the journey of each succeeding pageant-wagon which must have served well to indicate the passage of time, progress in space being a common symbol for progress in time. The play, unusually, begins with a long monologue in which Adam relates the vision granted to him during the creation of Eve, in which, according to common exegesis, the Redemption and Last Judgment were revealed to him. After he has given the instructions on sacrifice, Eve echoes him with a shorter speech, describing the penalties of the Fall and the importance of doing God's will. Against this background Cain and Abel depart to the sacrifice and the murder, and to this background Cain returns to relate his crime, and the play ends with the laments of Adam and Eve. The incident of Cain's return is implausible, but may have been imposed upon the author by his decision to excise from his play the apocryphal character of Cain's sister, Delbora, who in the *Mystère du viel testament* is the bearer of the news. But Eve's lament for Abel is essential to the pattern, since it begins a series that will be resumed when the mothers of the Holy Innocents mourn their children and will reach its climax in the *planctus* of the Blessed Virgin at the foot of the Cross. When in the sixteenth and seventeenth centuries this scene was illustrated in art, the disposition of the figures was modelled upon that of a *Pietà,* Eve contrary to any tradition holding the body of Abel in her lap. In his treatment of the murder of Abel the Chester author showed evil in its most monstrously human forms, and related this to Adam and Eve, who are both its begetters and partially its victims (a point more didactically emphasised in the Cornish *Origo mundi*). This position of Eve, however, has been partially redressed, for, whilst she is the mother of the first murderer, she is also the mother of Abel, the first type of Christ; in this concluding episode the dignity thus obliquely conferred upon her is revealed through her *planctus,* which, though poetically more subdued than that later spoken by the Virgin, unmistakably anticipates it.

It is, however, in the character of Cain himself that the full abysses of the Fall are horrifyingly shown, superbly of course in the work of the Wakefield Master in the Towneley plays, but pointedly and skilfully in all of them. Though the Chester dramatist is more interested in revealing religious significance through the patterning of episodes, his Cain is far less woodenly and perfunctorily treated than in most Continental versions of the story. Even in his very first speech there is a hint of base self-interest in his declaration that he will offer a sacrifice of corn to God and then 'will make to looke if he [God] will send me any more'. Churlish avariciousness is even plainer when he comes to select the corn for the sacrifice: here he explains in realistic detail how he will keep the 'eared corne' for himself, and offer only sheaves of the corn from which animals have nibbled away the grain, a decision accompanied by the significant oath 'the divill hang me'. The same type of Cain is presented in the *Ludus Coventriae* but intensified. Whilst Adam is less important here, Abel's speeches of grave virtue throw into relief Cain's avariciousness and lack of natural feeling. Cain not only hates Abel, resenting his virtue, as Ambrose had early described, but also feels contemptuous indifference towards his father, replying to Abel's insistence that they should visit him with the words, 'thow my fadyr I nevyr se / I yyf not þer of An hawe', and he agrees to Adam's counsel to do sacrifice grudgingly and insolently, 'and yitt I say now to yow both too / I had levyr gon hom well ffor to dyne'. Cain's contempt and antagonism extend also to God. His resolve to 'tythe þe werst' is shown not to spring from simple miserliness but from a furious contempt for God:

> What were god þe bettyr, þou sey me tyll,
> to yevyn hym awey my best sheff
> and kepe my self þe wers:
> he wyll neyther ete nor drynke
> Ffor he doth neyther swete nor swynke;
> þou shewyst a ffebyl reson me thynke,
> what, þou fonnyst as a best I gesse.

In Cain's base thought the fact that God is incorporeal and uncircumscribed evokes not awe but jeering.

This lively sketch of Cain as a grotesque, half comic, half ugly, is overshadowed by the characterisation of Cain in the Towneley plays, in which this style is developed with extraordinary freedom and lack of reserve. In this play Cain's role of the surly, avaricious farmer, fiercely grudging of the tithes that he must pay, is given unaccustomed solidity. Other dramatists seem to use the concept of tithes for the practical purpose of making the unfamiliar notion of a burnt offering recognisable in contemporary terms, thus removing a possible barrier between play and audience. But the Wakefield Master with his ostentatious reference to a priest who has Cain's farthing, and his adaptation of traditional excuses—Cain maintains that he is too poor, his last crops were bad, it is better to be thrifty than to be driven to beggary, etc.—excuses similar to those cited in sermons against false tithers, gives to the figure a sharply contemporary ring. Whilst no doubt some satirisation of contemporary false tithers was intended, this conception of Cain forms part of a more complex pattern. Cain's laborious counting of his sheaves with his miserly reluctance to part with any is built up into a focus of sheer farce, but this theme, as in the *Ludus Coventriae,* is subordinated to the larger one of Cain's alienation from God.

As elsewhere this is expressed in Cain's abusive speech, his swearing by the devil, and the contemptuous replies which he gives to any suggestion that is against his narrowly conceived self-interest. But this style is greatly heightened in the Towneley play. Cain here is extraordinarily foul-mouthed: his opening dialogue with Abel consists of little but scatalogical abuse. He begins with a coarse but no doubt current greeting, 'Com kis myne ars!', and responds to Abel's injunctions to sacrifice with an obscener variant: 'Hold thi tong, yit I say / Even ther the good wife strokid the hay.' These verbal violations of decency reach a blasphemous climax in Cain's determination to offer no more than two mean sheaves to God, 'Not as mekill, grete ne small / As he myght wipe his ars with all'. Earlier Cain had twice told Abel to kiss the devil's arse, and one can therefore see how violently Cain has obliterated the distinction that for stage purposes dramatists had skilfully and decorously drawn between the apparent corporality of God and the devil. When God has entered and reproached Cain, he answers with further extravagant blasphemy, reducing God to the level of the hobgoblin of folklore:

> Whi, who is that hob-over-the-wall?
> We! who was that that piped so small?
> Com, go we hens, for perels all;
> God is out of hys wit.

But in its very exuberance and verbal jocularity (God has presumably spoken in a deep and solemn voice), this passage seems less sinisterly evil than Cain's earlier abuse. In sum, however, Cain in the Towneley plays comes close to being a serious study in damnation, not a state of damnation that is magnificent in its anguish and apprehension of loss, but one that is mean, ugly and churlish. Such a study, however, might have upset the balance of the cycle by giving excessive imaginative weight to one play, and for this reason the author seems to have contrived an ending which is formal and comic, thus distancing Cain and exploding the scene in farce.

This ending depends upon the presence of a third character, Cain's servant, who had opened the play with lively and obscene abuse of the audience. The provision of a servant at a point in historical time when there could not have been one is in itself striking, and strongly suggests the adaptation of established convention: indeed the *garcio* here oddly anticipates the many comic servants of sixteenth-century biblical plays, both English and foreign, who were regularly invented upon the model of Plautus. Cain's *garcio* appears in fact to be a diminished descendant of the stock figure of the witty, intriguing slave of Roman comedy, who in turn was adopted in the twelfth-century Latin *comoediae,* such as the *Amphitryo,* and who re-appeared in French farces including the earliest of them, *Le gargon et l'aveugle.* This farce, as Gustave Cohen has pointed out, was imitated by the authors of the *Passions* who often provided the man born blind and Longinus with a rascally boy to lead them about.

The grumbling abusive servant is a familiar figure in French farces and farces also provide some striking stylistic analogues to the concluding set piece of the Wakefield Cain and Abel, in which Cain proclaims for himself and Garcio a king's pardon, using the appropriate legal formulas. This mock pardon is only tenuously related to the substance of the play, being immediately provoked by Garcio, who, like his forbear, Byrria, is an amusing coward. One can of course see it as a comic transformation of the mark which God set upon Cain to protect him from human vengeance (Genesis iv. 15) or, more fancifully, as recalling the legal pardon which elsewhere Christ conferred upon man at the Crucifixion (it would then imply Cain's exclusion from the Redemption since the only pardon that he can have is one delivered by himself). But the elaborate contrivance of the episode, including Garcio's comic asides, suggests that it should primarily be taken at its face value of stylised farce. The pardon proceeds in alternate lines of dialogue (being the first example of stichomythia in an English play):

Caym	I commaund you in the kyngis nayme,
Garcio	And in my masteres, fals Cayme,
Caym	That no man at thame fynd fawt ne blame.
Garcio	Yey, cold rost is at my masteres hame.

Caym	Nowther with hym nor with his knafe,
Garcio	What, I hope my master rafe.
Caym	For thay ar trew, full many fold;
Garcio	My master suppys no coyle bot cold.
Caym	The kyng wrytis you untill.
Garcio	Yit ete I never half my fill.
Caym	The kyng will that thay be safe,
Garcio	Yey, a draght of drynke fayne wold I hayfe.
Caym	At thare awne will let tham wafe;
Garcio	My stomak is redy to receyfe.

The joke of this passage is obviously that whilst Cain announces the pardon in a stylistically serious proclamation, Garcio consistently undercuts this, either with colloquial asides about food and drink or with a line which completes Cain's sentence in a way manifestly unintended by the speaker. The process of deflation is in general reminiscent of much medieval parody, in which, for instance, lines of famous hymns were used to lead into the praise of drink, money or love. A typical example is: 'Jam lucis orto sidere / statim oportet bibere.' More interestingly perhaps the dramatic outline is reminiscent of the opening of the *Miles gloriosus* of Plautus, in which the parasite undercuts the high-flown boastings of the braggart soldier with asides to the audience about the quality of his food, '. . .his cook makes a marvellous olive salad' or 'Oh dear, what I have to suffer for my stomach's sake'. It would be imprudent, however, to assume that the Wakefield Master could have known the plays of Plautus, and in fact one can more safely find yet closer parallels in French farces of the fifteenth century. On one of these Petit de Julleville commented: 'Ce procédé par lequel un personnage bouffon se fait l'écho d'un personnage sérieux, est fréquent dans nos farces et traditionnel au Moyen Age.' The farce of which he speaks is *La Présentation des joyaux,* in which a messenger brings to a lady various gifts from her prospective bridegroom and offers them to her in a complimentary and courtly monologue. This monologue is constantly interrupted by the base or bawdy comments of the *sot* who observes the scene. The following is a typical passage:

Dame, d'honneur le parement,
Dieu vous doint honneur et liesse
Et maintienne cette noblesse,
En vivant très joyeusement. . .
Tenez ce chappeau gracieux
Qui est honneste, riche et gent.

Il a bien cousté de l'argent;
Pleust a Dieu qu'il fust en ma bource!

Another example is the *Cris de Paris,* in which the dialogue of the two young gallants about the evils of marriage is punctuated by the street-cries of the fool, such as mustard, pickled herring, old iron, etc., cries which metrically complete the couplet and also often complete the speaker's sentence with unexpected aptness. In yet another farce, that of the *Gaudisseur et le sot,* the *gaudisseur* boasts in high-flown terms of his military or amatory achievements, whilst the fool interrupts sardonically with the base truth: the *gaudisseur,* for instance, vaunts of his prowess in a certain battle, whilst the fool comments that he in fact spent the time hidden in a ditch, and came out only when the fighting was over in order to go pillaging. The joke of these farces is invariably that of serious or bombastic speech continuously undercut by fool or servant, and it is very probable that some farce of this kind was known to the Wakefield Master. His adaptation, however, is unique in its ingenuity, far surpassing in its complex subtleties any extant analogue in French secular drama.

As in all the plays of the Wakefield Master, the *Mactacio Abel* partly keeps close to convention, is partly entirely distinctive. Its comedy is grimmer, its moral understanding darker, its literary manners more self-consciously artful. The underlying religious pattern, however, is never forgotten, and often intensified. In the *Ludus Coventriae* the theme of the continuing fall reaches its conclusion in Cain's banishment: as Adam and Eve became exiles from paradise, so Cain becomes an exile from all the dwellings of men; but Adam and Eve still awaited 'sum comforth', whereas Cain will 'nevyr make merthis mo'. But in the Towneley cycle Cain takes his leave of the audience as follows:

> Now fayre well, felows all, ffor I must nedis
>   weynd,
> And to the dwill be thrall, warld withoutten
>   end:
> Ordand ther is my stall, with Sathanas the
>   feynd.

In this cycle therefore the Fall reaches its final end in the eternal damnation of hell.

FURTHER READING

Bibliography

Berger, Sidney E. *Medieval English Drama: An Annotated Bibliography of Recent Criticism.* New York: Garland Publishing, 1990, 500 p.

> Offers "annotated entries for editions, collections, and scholarship of various kinds [concerning medieval drama]."

Criticism

Beadle, Richard, ed. *The Cambridge Companion to Medieval English Theatre.* Cambridge: Cambridge University Press, 1994, 400 p.

> Presents selected essays on medieval English theater, including discussion of the Chester, N-Town, Towneley, and York cycles.

Bethurum, Dorothy, ed. *Critical Approaches to Medieval Literature: Selected Papers from the English Institute, 1958-1959.* New York: Columbia University Press, 1960, 171 p.

> Presents selected essays representing the reappraisal and "present vitality" of medieval literature criticism.

Dutka, JoAnna. *Music in the English Mystery Plays.* Early Drama, Art, and Music Reference Series, 2, edited by Clifford Davidson. Kalamazoo, Mich.: Medieval Institute Publications, 1980, 171 p.

> Argues that music is essential to the production of the English mystery plays and examines the function of music within the plays through contemporary records of performance details.

Gayley, Charles Mills. "The Dramatic Development of the English Cycles." In *Plays of Our Forefathers,* pp. 144-52. Duffield and Company, 1907.

> Discusses the role of the guilds in the secular-ization of drama and the social function of performances.

Nelson, Alan H. *The Medieval English Stage: Corpus Christi Pageants and Plays.* Chicago: The University of Chicago Press, 1974, 288 p.

> Aims "to discover how, when, where, and for whom the Corpus Christi plays were performed" and "to discover something about their origins."

Ruggiers, Paul G., ed. *Versions of Medieval Comedy.* Norman: University of Oklahoma Press, 1977, 252 p.

> Presents selected essays on comedy in medieval literature, including discussion of the English mystery cycles.

Sheingorn, Pamela, and Bevington, David. "'Alle This Was Token Domysday to Drede': Visual Signs of Last Judgment in the Corpus Christi Cycles and in Late Gothic Art." In *Hono, Memento Mor Finis: The Iconography of Just Judgment in Medieval Art and Drama,* by David Bevington and others. Medieval Institute Publications, 1985, pp. 121-45.

> Examine the religious and dramatic function of the final judgment scene in the mystery cycle dramas.

Wickham, Glynne. *Early English Stages,* 1300-1660. 3 vols. London: Routledge and Kegan Paul, 1959-81.

> Examines a variety of issues associated with medieval English theater, emphasizing the Church's adaptation of secular stagecraft to serve its own purposes.

———. *The Medieval Theatre.* London: Weidenfeld and Nicolson, 1974, 245 p.

> Examines the development of drama in Europe between the tenth and sixteenth centuries.

Young, Karl. *The Drama of the Medieval Church,* Vol. II. London: Oxford at the Clarendon Press, 1933, 611 p.

> Divides discussion into two sections: "Plays Associated with the Nativity," and "Plays Upon Other Subjects from the Bible and from Legends."

The Chester Plays

INTRODUCTION

Scholars once regarded the Chester Mystery Cycle as the crudest, least developed of the four surviving cycles of medieval English religious drama. The cycle itself is comprised of twenty-five plays that chronicle biblical history from the Creation to the Last Judgement. Little is known about the plays' authorship and performance history, though one theory attributes them to a member of a local monastery. The plays were originally staged in Chester sometime during the fifteenth century by different trade/craft guilds, but they were eventually banned during the Reformation in the latter half of the sixteenth century. Although twentieth-century scholars concur that Chester Cycle is the least attentive to matters of the ordinary human condition, they agree that its dramatic sequences are the most fideistic, and regard its author as more knowledgeable of the Bible than any of the cycle masters.

Textual History

Before 1474, the Chester cycle was probably little more than a short pageant dramatizing Christ's Passion that was staged by various trade or craft guilds on the feast of Corpus Christi. After years of revision and expansion, the pageant eventually evolved into an extended series of individual plays, becoming an elaborate theatrical event performed by and for the secular community. Early in the sixteenth century the performances had developed into a longer cycle which, by the mid-sixteenth century, was performed over a three-day period on several stages in the city of Whitsuntide. As the cycle became a popular annual civic event, it also came under strong scrutiny by Protestant religious officials. By 1561 revisions had been made to placate Protestant objections regarding certain subject matter, but Civic leaders in Chester still faced pressure from the Protestant authorities to cease the production of the plays on the grounds that they were theologically unsound. As a result, many plays, such as "The Assumption," were suppressed altogether. The last performance of the Chester cycle probably occurred in 1575, the year that the Archbishop of York banned its performance altogether.

The plays within the Chester Mystery Cycle are generally categorized either by their sequence, their subject matter, or the name of the guild that performed them. The Cycle itself survives in eight manuscripts—five of which contain cyclic versions of the Chester plays, and three which contain fragments—that date from the fifteenth to the early seventeenth century. The Manchester Fragment (a portion of the "Resurrection" play) and Peniarth 399 (which contains the entire "Antichrist" play) are the earliest known manuscripts of the cycle as they both date prior to 1500. The Chester Coopers' Guild manuscript contains the entire "Trial and Flagellation" play and dates from 1599, nearly twenty-five years after the cycle's the last performance. The later date of this manuscript suggests it was probably written as a preservation copy for the archives of the guild.

Major Themes

The Chester Mystery Cycle dramatizes the Old and New Testament episodes that illustrate the general theme of mankind's salvation. In the first two plays of the cycle, for example, the Fall of Man is presented as a thematic parallel to the Fall of Lucifer. Throughout the course of the cycle, the eventual reconciliation of God and man is represented through the stories of characters like Abraham, Isaac, and Noah, and culminates in plays like the "Passion," "Crucifixion," and "Resurrection." While the God/man theme persists at one level, the cosmic struggle between good and evil—illustrated by dramatic representations of Lucifer and God battling for the souls of men—operates at another.

The Chester Cycle distinguishes itself from the other English medieval cycles in various other ways. Whereas other cycles tend to emphasize Christ's humanity so much so that scholars can easily identify a Franciscan influence, the Chester cycle emphasizes Christ's divinity. Also, Chester's representations of Mary and Eve—and of women in general—differ from the other cycles in that they occupy either a less-significant or less-developed role in the dramatization of good triumphing over evil, or of the reconciliation of man to God.

Critical Reception

The Chester Plays have been the focus of increased critical attention since they were acclaimed in the mid-twentieth century as being more than crude medieval representations. Scholars once regarded the Chester cycle as the earliest and least structurally complex of the four surviving cycles, probably due to its brevity. In the 1950s, however, F.M. Salter challenged the general supposition that the plays were written in the early fourteenth century by deducing Sir Henry Francis composed the plays in 1375. Though Salter's suggestions were much disputed, his work helped stimulate new critical discussion of the plays. Critical study has shifted in the past two decades from discussing the dates and authorship of the plays to examining the cycle's thematic and dramatic structures. Kathleen Ashley, for example, discusses in her 1978 article "Divine Power in *Chester Cycle*", the medieval, theological representation of God and his struggle with Satan and the Antichrist. Similarly Norma Kroll, in her 1987 article "Equality and Hierarchy in the Chester Cycle Play of Man's Fall", examines as part of the dramatic conflict in the "Fall of Man", the themes of power and authority in the relationships between the human characters and between man and God. Critics have also become more interested in the use of comic devices in the plays as part of the overall structure of the cycle. R. M. Lumiansky, Sidney W. Clarke, and Albert Tricomi, for example, have studied the thematic relevance of comic episodes in the cycle. Critics have also considered possible sources of the Chester cycle. In 1913 Hardin Craig suggested the cycle may have developed from medieval Christmas plays, and in 1931 Robert Wilson speculated that *The Stanzaic Life of Christ* influenced several plays within the cycle. More recently, critics such as Kevin J. Harty have studied the influences of monasticism and nominalism on the cycle. Modern critical approaches to the Chester Mystery Cycle have been as diverse in methodology as in academic focus. As a result, the plays have once again gained stature and influence within the English dramatic tradition.

THE PLAYS†

I. Fall of Lucifer—the Tanners

II. Adam and Eve; Cain and Abel—the Drapers
III. Noah's Flood—the Waterleaders and Drawers of Dee
IV. Abraham, Lot, and Melchysedeck; Abraham and Isaac—the Barbers
V. Moses and the Law; Balaak and Balaam—the Cappers
VI. The Annunciation and the Nativity—the Wrights
VII. The Shepherds—the Painters
VIII. The Three Kings—the Vintners
IX. The Offerings of the Three Kings—the Mercers
X. The Slaughter of the Innocents—the Goldsmiths
XI. The Purification; Christ and the Doctors—the Blacksmiths
XII. The Tempation; the Woman Taken in Adultery—the Butchers
XIII. The Blind Chelidonian; the Raising of Lazarus—the Glovers
XIV. Christ at the House of Simon the Leper; Christ and the money-lenders; Judas' Plot—the Covisors

XV. The Last Supper; the Betrayal of Christ—the Bakers
XVI. The Trial and Flagellation—the Fletchers, Bowyers, Coopers, and Stringers
XVIa. The Passion—the Ironmongers
XVII. The Harrowing of Hell—the Cooks
XVIII. The Resurrection—the Skinners
XIX. Christ on the Road to Emmaus; Doubting Thomas—the Saddlers
XX. The Ascension—the Tailors
XXI. Pentecost—the Fishmongers
XXII. The Prophets of Antichrist—the Clothworkers
XXIII. Antichrist—the Dyers
XXIV. The Last Judgement—the Websters

†Accompanying each title is the name of the guild that staged the play's performance.

PRINCIPAL EDITIONS

Chester Mysteries: De Deluvio Noe. De Occisione Innocentium, edited by J. H. Markland, 1818

The Chester Plays, edited by Thomas Wright, 1843-1847, reprinted in 1853

The Chester Mystery Plays: Seventeen Pageant Plays from the Chester Craft Cycle, edited by Maurice Hussey, 1957

The Chester Myster Cycle: A Facsimile of MS. Bodley 175, edited by R. M. Lumiansky and David Mills, 1973

The Chester Mystery Cycle, edited by R. M. Lumiansky and David Mills, 1974

The Chester Mystery: A Reduced Facsimile of Huntington Library MS 2, edited by R. M. Lumiansky and David Mills, 1980

The Chester Mystery Cycle: A Facsimile of British Library MS Harley 2124, edited by David Mills, 1984

Hardin Craig (essay date 1913)

SOURCE: "The Origin of the Old Testament Plays," in *Modern Philology,* Vol. 10, April, 1913, pp. 473-87.

[*In the following excerpt, Craig argues that the Old Testament plays in the Chester Cycle originated within the church itself "from the* lectiones *and* responsoria *of the period of Septuagesima and Lent. . .some weeks before Easter," and later joined with the Easter and Christmas plays to form the cycles.*]

The current theory of the origin of the Old Testament plays in the religious drama is derived from M. Sepet's [1867] dissertation, "Les Prophètes du Christ." He there propounds the theory followed by subsequent writers [e.g. E.K. Chambers, in *The Medieval Stage*, 1911] that the plays on Old Testament subjects made their appearance in connection with the various prophets of

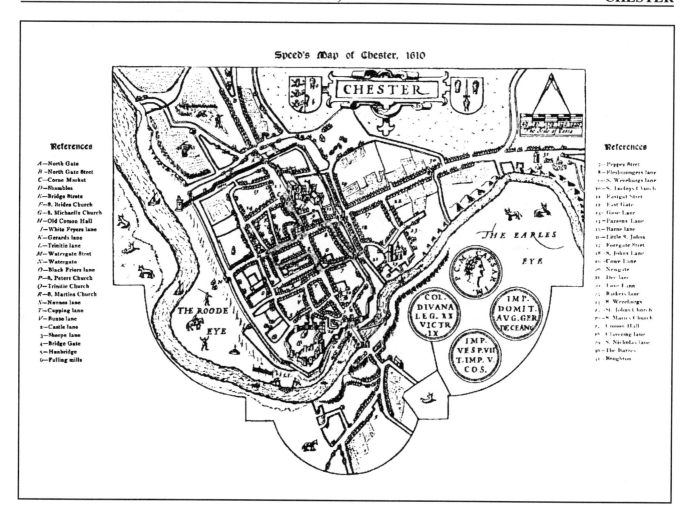

Map of Chester, 1610.

the *Processus Prophetarum* until there arose the whole series of Old Testament plays from the Fall of Lucifer to the Nativity of Christ.

The theory that the Old Testament plays, to use Mr. Chambers' expression, "budded off from the stem of the *Prophetae*," has not seemed to me to be adequate, and I venture to offer the following materials in support of another theory; namely, that the Old Testament plays, particularly those derived from the Book of Genesis and those relating to the Fall of Lucifer and the angels, in other words, the stock plays of the English cycles and of the popularly developed Continental cycles, did not originate from the *Processus Prophetarum*, but from the addition to the Passion play of a body of epical and homiletic material derived, in the first instance, from the *lectiones* and accompanying ritual of the church. Such additions must have been in the nature of deliberate amplification in the direction of a cyclical completeness long familiar in mediaeval literature and theology, as witnessed, for example, in the Old English poem of *Genesis* together with the

other poems of that manuscript, in the sermons of Ælfric, and in the *Cursor mundi*. Such an amplification was, moreover, a natural development of the Passion and Resurrection and was required to bring out the full significance of those plays. This would connect the Old Testament plays with those that grew up at Easter, and not with those that grew up at Christmas. It presupposes the borrowing in certain cases, but by no means all, of the *Prophetae* into the Easter play, and there is no disposition to deny that for the Balaam play, the Nebuchadnezzar play, and probably others, Sepet's theory may be entirely correct.

M. Sepet's chief documents are the Rouen *Prophetae*, preserved in a fourteenth-century *ordinarium*, and the *Ordo representationis Adae*, a late twelfth- or early thirteenth-century play of Norman-French origin. With regard to the former, M. Sepet points out that, following a tendency which he calls "assimilation," the number of prophets in the procession has been increased. To the original list appearing in the eleventh-century Limoges *Prophetae*, which is a dramatized version of the famous pseudo-Augustinian *Sermo contra Iudaeos, Paganos et Arianos de Symbolo,* has been added a considerable number of prophets. Such a tendency no doubt operated widely, and there were probably other local amplifications similar to those at Rouen; but in examining the plays in their later forms no evidence can be found for any basal list of prophets more extended than that of the original sermon. The prophets common to the various English, German, and French plays are apparently the original set; namely, Isaiah, Jeremiah, Daniel, Moses, David, Habakkuk, Simeon, Zacharias and Elizabeth, and John the Baptist, together with Virgil, Nebuchadnezzar, and the Sibyl. This does not bear on the question except negatively, as tending to show that a simple form of the *Processus Prophetarum* was disseminated over a wide territory, and that its variations were of a local character.

In the Rouen play there are two cases of what M. Sepet calls the tendency to "amplify certain prophecies." The second one of these and the one of less importance is the Nebuchadnezzar episode. When the time comes for Nebuchadnezzar to utter his messianic prophecy, there is introduced a little play of Shadrach, Meshach, and Abednego with a fiery furnace "in medio navis ecclesiae." This play does not appear anywhere as a regular Old Testament play, and may be regarded as sporadic. The other is the Balaam play. When Balaam appears in the procession, he is seated "super asinam," and there is enacted the little play of the speaking ass. Only the first words of the speeches are given, but it is possible to follow the plays by reference to the sources.

The Balaam play is of fairly wide currency. It occurs as an appendage to the *Ordo Prophetarum* of Laon, a *processus* of primitive structure, where the Balaam episode is apparently a borrowing, and if so, an illustration of the mediaeval tendency to borrow widely rather than to originate from mere opportune suggestion. A Balaam episode occurs also in a somewhat imperfect form in the Benedictbeuern Christmas play, in the **Chester Whitsun Plays,** and in the French *Mystère du Viel Testament.* In the **Chester cycle** the Balaam scene is merely an episode, though the principal one, in the *Processus Prophetarum,* as it is in the Benedictbeuern play, and had been from the time of its origin. The *Mystère du Viel Testament* is a compilation and as a whole probably not of popular growth; but it is to be noted that we have to do with the same Balaam play. In spite of considerable literary development, it shows traces of its origin. At the end of the play Balaam utters his familiar prophecy, "Une estoille istra de Jacob, etc." The play is out of its historical sequence and appears as an episode in the life of Moses. In the **Chester cycle,** also, Balaam follows Moses and the Tables of the Law.

Sepet's theory may hold also for the Beauvais *Daniel,* but neither the *Balaam* nor the *Daniel* ever became, as did, for example, the **Noah** and the **Abraham and Isaac,**

a regular member of the cycles, found wherever Old Testament plays were played. The *Ordo Joseph,* recently discovered by Professor Karl Young, shows the liturgical origin of the widely current play of Joseph and his Brethren. The material of the play would indicate that, although it seems to have had an existence independent of the cycles, it belongs to the group to be treated later. There is, however, in several liturgical plays of the Slaughter of the Innocents, a confusion of the Rachel who utters the *planctus* with Rachel, the wife of Jacob and the mother of Joseph, which may have suggested the composition of the play. It at any rate shows no connection with the *Prophetae.* The fragmentary *Isaac* and *Rebecca* of the Kloster Vorau is treated below. Nothing can be told of the *Elisaeus* mentioned by Gerhoh of Reichersberg or of the elaborate battle plays of the Riga performance except that they seem to be outside of the current of the popular development of Old Testament plays.

The *Ordo representationis Adae* is made up of a long and elaborate Adam play with full stage directions, a shorter Cain and Abel play in the same style, and a prophet play ending with the part of Nebuchadnezzar. There is also in the manuscript a version of the Fifteen Signs of Judgment, material connected with the Sibylline prophecy. The *Adam* and the *Cain and Abel* show deliberate literary composition, and the play as a whole is evidently an early attempt at cycle making. The plays are based upon the Scriptures, or rather, as I believe, upon the pericopes from Genesis read in the week of Septuagesima Sunday, and show little, if any, legendary or apocryphal influence. Because of the presence of the prophets, the *Adam* is usually regarded as a Christmas play; but there is some reason to think that the play belongs rather to Easter and is in fact the fragment of a Passion play. The play looks strongly forward to the Redemption. Adam bewails his fate and relies upon the promise of salvation through Christ; Adam and Eve, Cain and Abel, and each successive prophet are dragged off to Hell. I do not know of any other cases where the prophets are so disposed of, though they sometimes appear as patriarchs in Hell awaiting redemption. There are several other cases where the *Prophetae* was borrowed into the Easter series, and Adam and Eve are in like manner dragged off to Hell in the Vienna Passion play and in several other plays of the same structure. This use of a prophet play is exceptional, for the normal and original function of the prophets is to foretell the Nativity. Then, as against Sepet's idea of the origin of the *Adam* and the *Cain and Abel* from the *Prophetae,* it is to be pointed out that the traditional machinery of the prophet play, the introductory speech, does not precede the Adam play, but occurs at the beginning of the *Prophetae* in its usual place, as if the prophet play had been appended as a unit.

The *Adam* is also singular in the fact that Adam and Eve are carried off to Hell before the murder of Abel, a feature which does not elsewhere appear. If the play is in the line of popular development at all, it is the forerunner of such a cycle as *La Nativité, la Passion et la Résurrection* of the Sainte-Geneviéve manuscript, to which in general structure it seems to bear some resemblance. The mass of popularly developed cycles had a restricted number of subjects, and usually practically the same subjects; namely, the Fall of Lucifer, Adam, Cain and Abel, Noah, Abraham and Isaac, and usually Moses and the Exodus. Round about these themes were sporadic episodes from the same field, such as the Death of Adam, the Death of Cain, Abraham and Lot. The French *Mystère du Viel Testament* has been written in solidly with most of the Old Testament stories as far as Solomon and the Queen of Sheba. There seems to be a tendency, the cause of which is not very clear, to regard the simpler French cycles as abridgments of the longer, more highly developed ones; but, in the face of so many plays in France and in other countries showing a like lower stage of development, it seems unnecessary to do so. *Le Mystère du Viel Testament* is a composite work based upon popularly developed cycles. It contains, for example, the complaint of Adam, as do all Old Testament cycles, and the debate of the Four Daughters of God, and these scenes look forward to the redemption, as if a passion were to follow. *La Création, Passion et Résurrection* of MS Bibl. nat. fr. 904, *La Création, et la Chute de l'Homme,* etc., of the Douai-Valenciennes MS, and possibly also the *Texte de Troyes* and the prologue to Gréban's *Passion,* show only the traditional subjects. Other plays with the longer more amplified list of subjects are the Eger Passion play the Künzelsau Corpus Christi play, and the Cornish *Origo mundi.* The last-mentioned has been amplified by the embodiment of the Seth legend. The English cycles which have been preserved, and the lists of subjects in lost cycles, show a general use of the conventional subjects in England.

In Germany the Passion plays developed into complete dramas of the Fall of man, the Passion of Christ, and the Resurrection, with or without Old Testament plays, and, as I think, independent of the *Prophetae.* The stages of this development can be seen by an examination of the various plays preserved, though of course it is necessary to take into consideration the forms of the plays and their degrees of development as well as the dates of their preservation. In Germany, and certainly in France also, we have developed, from the simple Latin plays of Passion and Resurrection, logically complete cycles with no regularly present Old Testament plays and frequently no prophets. The plays show an amplification of the rôle of the Devil. At first he is merely the scriptural Satan; later he becomes Lucifer, and the story of his fall and his betrayal of man is introduced. The most primitive plays introduce Satan only in connection with the Harrowing of Hell, and in other places demanded by the sources. In the Benedictbeuern Passion play Satan appears as a mute character in connection

with the part of Judas. The play is fragmentary and breaks off before the Harrowing of Hell scene, though that was doubtless part of the original, as it certainly was of the fragmentary Anglo-Norman Resurrection. The Kloster Muri fragments contain a simple Harrowing of Hell scene in which Satan appears. There is also a somewhat primitive conception of Satan in the Innsbruck play of the Resurrection and the plays of its type, the Frankfort *Dirigierrolle,* the St. Gall play, and others. In the Donaueschingen Passion play Satan appears in the Temptation, the Remorse of Judas, Pilate's Wife's Dream, and the Harrowing of Hell. Disregarding certain developments of the part in the direction of *diablerie,* we may regard this play as presenting the normal appearances of Satan in the more primitive plays. In another large number of plays, in which the part of the devil is greatly amplified, there is the introduction of the story of Lucifer and his betrayal of man. Such plays are the Redentin Passion play, the Frankfurt play, and the plays of that group, the Alsfeld play, and the Tyrol plays. In this series of plays the stories of the fall of Lucifer and of man are frequently introduced in connection with the prayers of Adam and the patriarchs for redemption from bondage, a characteristic also seen in the French plays. There are, however, German Passion plays which show an arrangement according to chronological sequence. The Vienna Passion play, which is one of the oldest preserved, dating, as it does, from early in the fourteenth century, begins with the presentation of the fall of Lucifer and the fall of man. This is also seen with the fullest development of Old Testament subjects in the Eger Passion play and in the Künzelsau *Frohnleichnamsspiel,* both of which, however, treat Nativity subjects, as does the similarly constructed Middle-Frankish play from Mastricht. *Der Sündenfall* seems to be the fragment of a cycle chronologically arranged; the introductory speech of the Proloculator seems to indicate this, as also the contents of the play. It has a full list of Old Testament subjects, a complaint of Adam and the patriarchs in limbo, a debate of the Four Daughters of God, and, at the end, the presentation of Mary in the Temple. The Innsbruck *Frohnleichnamsspiel* of the end of the fourteenth century, a procession of prophets, apostles, and Magi, begins with the thanking of the Savior by Adam and Eve for their release from Hell, as if the scene had been borrowed directly from a Harrowing of Hell play. In some of the Passion plays the prophets appear; but, when they do, they are usually in the rôle of patriarchs awaiting redemption, which is manifestly not their original or their commonest function in the religious drama. They are primarily prophets of the Nativity, and there are a large number of plays and many indications within the great composite cycles which tend to show that the play of the prophets was closely bound up with the plays of the Nativity, a thing which would be very natural, since they all unquestionably grew up at Christmas time. Sepet devotes a section of his article to proving that the *Processus Prophetarum* is the regular prologue to the

Nativity. He cites the Benedictbeuern Christmas play, the St. Gall Nativity play, *Laus pro Nativitate Domini* from a manuscript in Bibl. Vallicelliana in Rome, and the Rouen Incarnation and Nativity. Several other French plays show the same thing, and in the English plays there is also the closest connection between the *Prophetae* and the Nativity. The prologue to the Annunciation in York is a summary of a prophet play. In the play of the Shearmen and Taylors of Coventry, Isaiah acts as a prologue to the Nativity, and in it and in the Weavers' play, there is evidence that the *Prophetae* has been split up into parts and distributed among the plays of the Nativity. At **Chester** the prophet play has been divided, and one portion of it incorporated with the Annunciation.

It is evident then that there are two types of cyclic plays—the one, familiar to us in the English Corpus Christi plays, is chronologically arranged and complete; the other, familiar to us in the German and French plays, is usually not chronologically arranged and not complete, since it has no Old Testament plays, and frequently has no Nativity plays, and no *Prophetae*. The latter, however, sometimes approximate the former both in content and in arrangement and are logically complete, since they embrace the fall and redemption of man. Since it is possible to trace the growth of the second type, even when entirely independent of *Prophetae* and Nativity plays, to a stage approximately parallel to the first, it has seemed to me reasonable to believe that the first type is only a variety of the second; namely, a Passion play to which has been added a number of scenes derived from the Old Testament. I am inclined to think that this amplification occurred before the Easter and Christmas plays were united into a single cycle, and the form of the original Easter play at such a city as Chester could then be arrived at by withdrawing from the cycle the *Processus Prophetarum* and all the plays of the Nativity group. It would be absurd to think that the Lucifer and Adam scenes of the German passion plays originated from the *Prophetae*, because their development bears every mark of being entirely within the Passion plays themselves. They were demanded by the subject, and we have a natural point of growth provided for them in the Harrowing of Hell and other scenes of the Passion and Resurrection.

Neither the documents cited by M. Sepet, nor the evidences of the manner of development of the larger plays, so far as they are ascertainable, seem to establish his theory; let us, therefore, inquire more directly into the origin of the Old Testament plays.

The series of Old Testament plays, referred to above, stand as a single conventional group with practically the same subjects and in the same order, as if they had been introduced as a unit from one principal source, or at least introduced to conform to one definite pattern. It is evident that a parallel exists between the cycles of

plays and the great religious epics of the Middle Ages. The conception of an epic of redemption had long been in existence. The contents of Junian MS XI show just the features needed to make of the drama as developed within the church a complete cyclical presentation of man's fall and redemption. Besides the *Genesis, Exodus,* and *Daniel,* it contains a poem known as *Christ and Satan,* which is made up of, first, the Fall of Lucifer, secondly, the Harrowing of Hell, the Resurrection, the Ascension, and the return to final judgment, and, thirdly, the Temptation. I have no disposition to regard this or Avitus as a source for the plays; but they both offer examples of the epical treatment of the earlier Old Testament themes with manifest consciousness of their theological significance. The *Cursor mundi* represents a very much more amplified form of religious epic than the one which seems to be paralleled in the more primitive cycles of plays. The *Historia Scholastica* of Petrus Comestor is a summary of Old Testament events, and contains most of the legendary materials involved; but it goes very much farther in its account than the mystery plays do. It gives only a brief form of the Lucifer story, as compared to the Old English *Genesis* and the thirteenth-century *Genesis and Exodus.* The *Genesis and Exodus* and the Vienna *Genesis* follow the scriptural accounts with a fair degree of closeness. The *Canticum de Creatione* refers to most of the events of the Book of Genesis and gives special prominence to the Seth legend. Grosseteste's *Castle of Love* presents, from the Old Testament, only the Fall. *Die Erlösung* shows a selection of material somewhat similar to the *Castle of Love* and offers a parallel to the amplified Passion plays of the German type, a thing which may also be said of *Das Passional,* though it confines itself to the life of Christ.

Such epical accounts may have had influence on the later forms of the plays, or suggested the cyclical idea; but I think it is not necessary to go so far afield for the sources of the earliest Old Testament plays. In fact the Adam and the Cain and Abel plays of the *Ordo representationis Adae* seem to bear upon their faces the evidences of their source. The stage direction at the beginning of the play contains these words: "Tune incipiat lectio: *In principio creavit Deus celum et terram,*" to which the Chorus sing the response, "Formavit igitur Dominus." After Adam has been placed in Paradise, they sing this response, "Tulit ergo Dóminus hominem." When God forbids Adam to eat of the forbidden fruit, they sing the response, "Dicit Dominus ad Adam"; after the Fall, the response, "Dum ambularet"; after Adam and Eve are expelled from Paradise, the response, "In sudore vultus tui." When Adam and Eve are outside of Paradise, "quasi tristes et confusi," the Chorus sing the response, "Ecce Adam quasi unus." After the murder of Abel, they sing the response, "Ubi est Abel, frater tuus." These are regular responses which accompanied the *lectiones* from Genesis for the week of Septuagesima Sunday. The subjects for the week, as indicated by the *responsoria,* were the Creation, the Temptation and Fall, and the story of Cain and Abel. The actual selections read in the service varied to a certain extent, but the subjects were always the same, and it will be noticed that the responses themselves carry the story. The *Adam* is practically a dramatization of the *lectiones* and *responsoria* of the week of Septuagesima Sunday. In like manner the *lectiones* and *responsoria* of the Sunday and ferial services of the week of Sexagesima were devoted to the story of Noah and the Flood; those of Quinquagesima, to the story of Abraham; those of the second Sunday in Quadrigesima, to Isaac, Jacob, and Esau; those of the third Sunday in Quadrigesima, to the story of Joseph and his Brethren; those of the fourth Quadrigesimal Sunday, to Moses and the Exodus. I have followed the order of the Sarum Breviary; but the use of these subjects for readings for the period of Septuagesima and Lent, as shown by the *responsoria* and by the *lectiones* from sermons which accompany them in various service books, was general. We have here the entire list of Old Testament subjects appearing in the more primitive cycles except for the play of the Fall of Lucifer. The play of *Isaac and Rebecca* of the late twelfth century Latin fragment from Kloster Vorau in Styria seems to bear some traces of origin from *lectiones* of the week of the second Sunday in Quadrigesima; there is at least a chorus which accompanies the action with the narrative of that time. The Fall of Lucifer could have been derived from sermons on the Creation; there is a full account in Ælfric's *De initio creaturae.*

In view of the obviousness and availability of the lessons of the service and of their adequacy, I should be disposed to believe that the Old Testament plays originated from the *lectiones* and *responsoria* of the period of Septuagesima and Lent. It was a time of preparation and penance, and the devotions constantly looked forward toward Easter. The subjects of the lessons had the closest bearing upon the events commemorated at Easter. Christ was the second Adam and head of the spiritual family, as Adam was the father in the flesh. Abel was a type of Christ, and his sacrifice is mentioned in connection with those of Abraham and Melchisedech in the canon of the mass. Isaac was also regarded as a type of Christ, and is so called in a *lectio* drawn from a sermon of St. John Chrysostom and read on Sexagesima Sunday. Ælfric in a sermon for the second Sunday after Epiphany says that the slaying of Abel betokened God's Passion; that the ark betokened the church and that Noah betokened Christ; and that by Abraham we are to understand the Almighty Father, and by Isaac, his beloved Son, the Savior Christ. In a sermon for Midlent Sunday he gives an elaborate explanation of the typical significance of the subject of Moses and the Exodus; it shows how that subject was related to the season. Almost any series of sermons of the period will illustrate the points given; and the subjects in question have so close a connection both theological and liturgical with the Pas-

sion, that it is impossible to escape the belief that the plays dealing with them must have grown up as parts of, or as preliminary scenes to, the plays of the Passion and Resurrection. If the Old Testament plays originated within the church itself, which in some cases at least they probably did, and at a season some weeks before Easter, then they must have been united later with the plays of Easter itself; and the whole group of Easter plays later joined with the whole group of Christmas plays to form the cycles.

The Cathedral Statutes of Bishop Hugh de Nonant (1188-98) show that at Lichfield the *Pastores* was acted at Christmas and the *Quem quaeritis* and *Peregrini,* at Easter. At York the traditional Statutes of York Cathedral provide for *Pastores* and *Stella* at Christmas time as late as about 1255. At Aberdeen the Christmas and Easter groups seem never to have been united. The most striking case is that of the Cornish cycle. It is made up of an *Origo mundi,* which presents the Fall of Lucifer, and a series of Old Testament plays, a *Passio Domini,* which begins with the Temptation, and a *Resurrectio Domini,* which ends with the Ascension. There are no *Prophetae* and no Nativity plays and no evidence of there ever having been. If the Christmas series was acted by the same people, it must have been acted separately, and is now lost. It is difficult to see how such a cycle could have come into existence except upon the supposition that Old Testament plays are originally and organically part of the Easter series of plays rather than of the Christmas series. Professor Manly points out that the plays of the Kentish town of New Romney were also of the Continental type, and probably had no Nativity plays.

If the theory which I have advanced is true, the English cycles ought to show some evidence of having been made up by the union of the two groups. In all of the cycles there are wide gaps before and after the plays of the Nativity, and all of them, I think, show evidence of such a composition. One case in particular is very striking. I should like to present it here briefly and give a fuller study of the subject in a later paper. It is the case of the component parts of the **Chester cycle**.

The Benedictbeuern Christmas play is made up of a combination of dramatic themes of the season of Christmas. Augustine appears as Expositor, and the play opens with a *Prophetae,* in which, however, only a limited number of prophets appear. Among these prophets is Balaam, "sedens super asinam," and although the ass does not speak, the angel with the sword appears, and it may be said that it is a Balaam play in miniature. After an extended dispute between Augustine and the prophets on the one side and Archisynagogus and the Jews on the other, there is the Annunciation and immediately after it the Visit to Elizabeth; then, in a somewhat confused form, a *Pastores* and a *Stella.* At this point a stage direction gives the statement, "Herodes corrodatur a verminibus," and provides for the crowning of his son Archelaus. Then comes the Slaughter of the Innocents and the Flight into Egypt, which is followed by some purely secular matters, and then comes the Falling of the Egyptian idols. The play ends with fragments of an Antichristus play. The play is not only confused but corrupt, and yet it is possible to see in its general content a remarkable parallel to the **Chester plays,** particularly in those themes in which the **Chester plays** are exceptional. In the **Chester *Processus Prophetarum,*** a *Princeps Synagogae* appears, and it has a Balaam play growing out of it. It places a Salutation immediately after the **Annunciation.** The Sibyl plays an important rôle in the **Nativity.** In the **Slaughter of the Innocents** the legend of the falling of the idols and of the **Death of Herod** appear. In a later play, ***Ezechiel,*** we have further materials from the *Prophetae,* and, lastly, we have the altogether exceptional play of ***Antichrist.*** My inference from this parallel is that one of the component elements of the **Chester cycle** was a Christmas play of somewhat the same general content and form as the Benedictbeuern play. If so, the original Christmas play, back of the **Chester cycle,** must have been divided into parts, and these parts given appropriate places in the cycle.

A justification for the introduction of the **death of Herod** and the theme of the **Antichrist** into the Christmas plays can be drawn from a sermon by Bishop Haymo of Halberstadt (d. 853), *De Sanctis Innocentibus,* a portion of which, containing a comparison of Archelaus to Antichrist, was used as a *lectio* at matins, according to the Sarum Breviary, on the Vigil of Epiphany. The paragraphs of the sermon which precede the *lectio* give an elaborate account of the death of Herod.

F. M. Salter (essay date 1955)

SOURCE: "A Great Reckoning," in *Medieval Drama in Chester,* University of Toronto Press, 1955, pp. 81-130.

[*In the following excerpt, Salter describes the meager cultural background of the Chester Plays, lauding their "significant contribution to drama" achieved "within the limits of the possible."*]

It is customary to look upon the mystery plays of the late Middle Ages as the crude and childish productions of a childish and crude people. Bernhard Ten Brink [in *History of English Literature, II*] long ago said, "Only a few details made any aesthetic effect—such as character, situation, scenes; the whole was rarely or never dramatic." Katherine Lee Bates [in *The English Religious Drama,* 1917] admits that "A grand dramatic framework is discernible," but only "through the awkward language and the naive ideas." C. F. Tucker Brooke [in *The Tudor Drama,* 1911] refers to "the artless and

provincial makeshifts of guild performances and the yet ruder devices of the incipient morality." More recently, Harold C. Gardiner in his *Mysteries' End* speaks of "their more sober and moving devotional aspects, which undoubtedly impressed the simple minds of the English craftsman and laborer and, indeed, of king and noble, too." And in 1950 A. P. Rossiter [in *English Drama from Early Times to the Elizabethans,* 1950] sums up a half-century's scholarship with the statement, "From the literary point of view the workmanship is never far from crude and, in the older strata, insipid to a degree." By the "older strata" he seems to mean the **Chester Plays** which, as I have tried to show in earlier lectures, do not really deserve to be called older. Rossiter says also, "Probably most 'effects' were nearer children's improvisations than 'production.'"

With this view I find it hard to sympathize; but I might be more disturbed by the solid unanimity of modern criticism of the mystery plays if I had not had the annual experience of reading the essays of Freshmen who patronize Chaucer. It is admittedly difficult for us who have reached the pinnacle of culture not to look with contempt upon our ancestors who had neither Hollywood, soap opera, nor the atomic bomb. These are great achievements which set our minds free for productive labours. Besides, we have running water in our homes, upholstered furniture, and all those time-saving mechanisms which have eaten up our leisure. Still further, all of us can read and write, after a fashion. But comforts and machinery are not an absolute necessity of the higher life—unless the Greeks were less civilized than we have been led to believe. A man may be well educated though unlettered; learning by book is not the only way to learn. Students in our classrooms seem content to sit hard, provided there is some challenge in what they hear; and many of them have actually been known to learn more by ear from men than by eye from books. As a matter of fact, we tend to overestimate the illiteracy of the Middle Ages; every monastery had its school, and bailiffs and merchants kept records. I should be very glad to debate—in the affirmative—that there was more real and genuine beauty surrounding the whole life and being of the ordinary man of the Middle Ages than is to be found in a street-car and assembly-line society. The men who dreamed cathedrals and built them to centre every town; who made, for the wage of a pound a year, less than a penny a day, stained-glass windows such as have never been equalled and of such great beauty that in modern times of war we have taken them out and catalogued the thousands of pieces before burying them for safe-keeping; who created the magnificent ceremonial and music of the Mass; who could fill their churches with such carving and statuary as the world would not lose; who could preserve for us the work of Chaucer, Erasmus, and Holbein: such men were not necessarily childish or crude.

Moreover, we have seen that business men were under

heavy expense to keep the plays going. Business men in all ages have prided themselves on knowing the value of money; yet we have seen the Chester gildsmen, or their representatives who formed the civic council, fight bitterly against the opposition of the new Church to retain the privilege of heavy expenditure on mystery plays. Still further, these plays had universal appeal and universal approval for more than two hundred years. If our ancestors were childish, why did they not tire sooner of their provincial makeshifts and childish improvisations? Let us not seek escape in the naive notion that two hundred years then was somehow shorter than two hundred years now. Set it out in panorama: we must travel almost from the Spanish Armada back through the reign of Philip and Mary and the restoration of the Church of Rome, back through Henry VIII and the Disestablishment, back through the dawn of the English Renaissance and the introduction of printing, back through the long Wars of the Roses, past Agincourt, past the boy king whose cousin in civil war drove him from the throne, past the Peasants' Revolt, past Wycliffe and his preaching friars, and well into the long reign of Edward III. During that immense period of swift and violent change, the mystery plays held their own. For dramatic longevity their only rival is Shakespeare; and I take it that the real duty of criticism is not to brush them aside as crude and childish, but to ask what there was in them that could appeal to sane and sensible men in a civilized country for more than two hundred years.

When the scales have fallen from our eyes, we shall see at once that the mystery plays had the advantage over all other drama and over all literature except the Bible, Dante, Milton, and a few minor authors, of the grandest, most sublime, and most powerfully moving of all themes. When a theme is greater than its handling, the effect is inevitably comic—like a clown parading in clothes too large; but nobody has ever found the mysteries unintentionally comic. They were saved from that fate, I should say, by simple sincerity and good taste. And when we call them crude, naive, and undramatic, we are only expressing our own inability, or refusal, to see them as they actually were. What we need is a faith that our ancestors were not silly; we need also the auditory and visual imagination that will enable us to attend a performance, sitting cheek by jowl with dignitaries of the Church or officials of the city, or rubbing shoulders in the streets with men and women who had the same appreciation of art in all its forms that we have—or perhaps an appreciation not quite so dulled as ours has been by the clanking machinery of modern life, or left so uncultivated as ours by the absence of artistic objects around us.

One thing must be admitted: blank verse not yet having been invented, and prose not yet having found her Dryden, the mystery plays had to struggle with the Procrustean requirements of an unsuitable medium. Nor had

Shakespeare yet enunciated his great doctrine that "The play's the thing," or demonstrated that poetry should be the handmaiden of drama, and not its mistress. These were things that Shakespeare had to learn for himself; and if even he could in his early days be confused on this issue, we can hardly blame the common people for writing their plays in verse—and sometimes, be it admitted, in verse at all costs. We only continue their error, however, when we look for "literary" qualities in the mystery plays. What we should look for in drama is drama; and seeking it in the mysteries, we shall find.

We should look for the same things that we always look for in the theatre: entertainment, beauty, representations of human life, the power to grip and hold an audience, and—above all—meaning or significance or, if I may say so, moral value.

And, in all fairness, there are certain things we should remember. One is that we may not have true witness to the mysteries in the manuscripts which survive. All of the copies of the **Chester Plays** were made by late scribes who, often enough, did not understand their exemplars, and who tried to make them intelligible—with sad results. We should therefore keep in mind an apt remark of Sir E. K. Chambers [in *English Literature of the Close of the Middle Ages,* 1947]: "Whoso would read the plays to-day must often go darkling."

Perhaps we should bear in mind the mere possible itself. If the greatest dramatic genius of all time had had the task of working up the Biblical story into drama at the end of the fourteenth century, what could he have done? As I have said, there was no Shakespearean example for him to follow; so far as he knew, the theatre of the ancient world did not exist; the theatre of modern times did not exist; neither blank verse nor prose had yet been created as a vehicle of expression. What is to be expected? On the other hand, after the stage and the vehicle and the Elizabethans have been created and done their work, what is to be expected? Considering our possible, have we so much to glory in after 1623? Nobody has yet surpassed Shakespeare, our inheritance. Did the mystery plays—even on the basis of what I have already pointed out about them—fail to surpass their heritage? It is a nonsense question. On the ground of that relativity alone, without even considering what the intrinsic merits of the plays may be, we can say at once that the unanimous modern opinion that the mysteries are crude and childish is the teaching of false prophets.

Again, to take one element which is constant in the plays, let us think of the singing. We cannot suppose that the potentials of the human voice have improved a great deal in the last five hundred years, or that the happy mother singing about her housework in the Middle Ages did so in a voice much worse than those that now bleat at the modern housewife from the morning radio. Indeed, since there was no radio then, and since people had to create their own amusements, it is likely that the ordinary person had better skill of this sort then than the ordinary person has today; and along with that universality of skill, there was perhaps taste and appreciation in judging the accomplishments of others. The term "Merrie England" has no modern relevance: it is a phrase that fitted an England that was "a nest of singing birds" long ago. When the Angel sang "Gloria in excelsis," or Old Simeon, "Nunc dimittis," or Noah and his family within the Ark sang, "Save me, O God," when the angels at the Last Judgment choired, "Rejoice in the Lord" or "The Lord and Saviour of the World," we may be perfectly sure that the singing was as well worth hearing as most of that which we now pay dollars per seat to hear. Indeed, we may spend a wry moment in the thought that with all our modern superiority, the great hymns of the Church are still those of the Middle Ages.

Neither the musical heart nor the merry one need be unrealistic; and the people of the Middle Ages came to close grips with life in a way in which we, on the whole, do not. Among the people of the Western world there has never been in modern times anything like the Black Death. Seeking for comparison one must go to the dreadful scourges of the Far East or think of that Christian gift which our own superior civilization and culture dropped upon the Japanese at Hiroshima. It is said that in the great plague of 1348 only one house in Chester remained unvisited by the Angel of Death; and the owner of that house inscribed in great letters across the front, "The House of God's Providence." There were whole villages in England in which every man, woman, and child died of the plague. Time after time in their flourishing period, the **Plays of Chester** could not "go" because of the pestilence, and the bodies of the dead were carried in dump carts to great community graves beyond the walls. What would the people of those times think of the "modern realism" of sophomoric writers lapped in security and comfort and uncompromisingly facing life in the raw at second, third, or fourth hand? A peasant woman once said to such a sophisticate, "Ach, what do you know of life? Haf you effer been hungry?" For a great deal of modern literature our ancestors would have had the contempt that we have for drugstore cowboys and beardless men of the world.

It would, indeed, be easy to pull out of the **Chester Mysteries** passages that would shock any modern audience out of their seats—even an audience brought up on the suggestiveness of Hollywood, the "raw meat" that offends Boston, and, perhaps, such unrelieved filth as *Tobacco Road*. What would a modern author do with such a subject as the Slaughter of the Innocents? The writers of the **Chester Plays** had no desire to shock for the sake of shocking, but simply wished to tell the truth. The difference is that they were much closer to the basic truths of life than we are. They knew that, who-

ever gave the command to slaughter all male children under two years of age, the soldiers who carried out the order were hardly likely to be gentlemen and scholars, but such as Hitler found to man the concentration camps. And they knew that women will not quietly allow their babies to be murdered. How does one find out or prove that a child under two years of age is male or female? The simple naturalism of the mediaeval dramatist has both more freedom and more honesty than much of our modern realism.

Let me turn away from that subject and remark that in the **Chester Slaughter of the Innocents** there is one touch of the grimmest dramatic irony. It was Herod who commanded the slaughter of the children and, among the rest, Herod's own son is slain. The Nurse has genuine touches of characterization. When the child is slain, she cries out:

> Out! Out! Out! Out!
> You shall be hanged, all the rowt!
> Theues, be you neuer so stout,
>   Full fowle you haue done.
>
> This Child was taken to me
> To looke to: Theues, wo be ye!
> He was not myne, as you shall see,
>   He was the kinges sonne.
>
> I shall tell whyle I may drye,
> His child was slayne before myne eye.
> Theues, ye shall be hanged hye,
>   May I come to his hall.
>
> But, or I go, haue thou one!
> And thou another, Sir John!
> For to the kinge I will anone,
>   To playn uppon you all.

Thus, after laying about her with a will, this raging tigress ramps off to the King.

He rages also, but there is a final touch of irony in that the **Slaughter of the Innocents** was commanded in order to kill the child who threatened to become King of Judaea; and broken-hearted Herod has to admit that of all the children in the land his own was least likely to be spared:

> He was right sicker in silk aray,
> In gould, and pyrrye that was so gay,
> They might well know by his aray,
>   He was a kinges sonne.

While this play is before us, a few further remarks may not be amiss. After hearing of the death of his son, Herod goes on:

> Alas! What the devill is this to mone [mean]

Designs for angel costumes.

Alas! My days be now done;
I wott I must dye soone,
  For damned I must be.

My legges rotten and my armes;
I haue done so many harmes,
That now I see of feendes swarmes
  From Hell cominge for me.

Presently he dies. The line, "My legges rotten and my armes" may recall to our minds that in what Sir Winston Churchill has called "the quaint account," he perished eaten by worms. It was not quaint to our ancestors: they had seen flesh turn black and rot time and again in the terrible visitations of the Black Death.

Herod dies, and a very lively and engaging Demon enters to drag him off; for, like the Elizabethans, the mediaeval dramatist had to get rid of "dead bodies":

Warr, warr! for now unwarly wakes you woe!
For I am swifter than is the doe.
I am commen to fetch this lord you froe
  In woe ever to dwell.

And with this croked cambrock your backs
  shall I cloe,
And all falce beleuers I burne in a low,
That from the crowne of the head to the right
  toe,

I leave no wholl fell.

From Lucifer, that lord, hither I am sent
To fetch this kinges sowle here present,
And to Hell bring him ther to be lent
  Euer to lyve in woe.

Ther fyre burnes bloe and brent;
He shall be ther, this lord, verament;
His place euermore therin is hent,
  His body neuer to goe froe!

Like Shakespeare, the mediaeval dramatist could convert a handicap into an asset. The handicap, the difficulty, is the dead body of Herod. In disposing of it, he creates this lively Demon and drives home the lesson that the wages of sin is death.

As if the spectacle of a magnificent King, with a pageboy to hold up the train of his robes, being dragged off to Hell, were insufficient to emphasize the equality of all men under God, the Demon now turns to the audience with a warning to another class of sinners:

No more shall you Tapstars, by my lewtye,
That fills your measures falcly,
Shall bear this lord Company,
  They gett none other grace.

I will bring this into woe,

And come agayne and fetch moe,
As fast as ever I may go.
    Farewell and haue good day!

No doubt the Innkeepers once had a connection with this play. However that may be, this lusty Demon has no sooner dragged Herod off the stage than an angel appears to the Holy Family and tells Joseph and Mary to return with the child Jesus into Judaea. But it took Shakespeare years to learn the value of contrast in drama.

Time is telescoped in this play—as, indeed, it has to be in all drama. But the material is there for a good production with the grimmest reality, terrifying irony, demonic gusto, and, for contrast, the Angel who, before the Slaughter began, warned the Holy Family to go forth into Egypt.

Let us turn back for a moment to that earlier scene. Leading forth Mary, Joseph, and the child Jesus, the Angel says:

Come now furth in God's name!
I shall you sheild from all shame,
And you shall see, my leefe dame,
    A thing to your lykinge.

For Mahometis, both one and all,
That men of Egipt gods can call,
At your coming downe shall fall,
    When I begin to singe.

True enough, the stage direction reads: "Then they will go forth, and the Angel will sing, 'Behold, the Lord will rise above the clouds, and will enter into Egypt, and the images of Egypt will fall down before the face of the Lord of Hosts,' and if it can be done, let some statue or image fall." Certainly it could be done! We cannot escape the conviction that our ancestors knew the value of stage effects.

Though I began with the question of truth or reality in drama, let us review what is to be found in the **Slaughter of the Innocents** so as to visualize one complete unit from the **Chester Plays**. First of all, Herod appears, raging that the Magi have eluded him. He calls for "petty Prat" his messenger, and sends him after his "doughty and comely knightes." With this preparation, we can easily imagine just how loathsome and foul his comely knights will be. Having waked these slumbering beasts, petty Prat brings Sir Grimbalde, Sir Launcherdepe, and Sir Waradrake to the King. They at first object to the commission: the killing of infants is no fit task for such doughty men of war; in the end, however, off they go. While they approach Bethlehem, the Angel warns the Holy Family and leads them away; and as he approaches Egypt with them, we see the images fall at the sound of his song. Immediately we turn to the

sharp, grim horror of the Slaughter itself, at the end of which the Nurse rushes to scream at Herod that his son has been slain. Herod dies, and the boisterous Demon fetches him off to Hell, with a promise to return in the twinkling of an eye to carry away other sinners. The Angel appears again to Joseph and Mary, saying:

Now you be ready for to goe,
Joseph and Mary also,
Forsooth I will not depart you froe,
    But help you from your foe.

And I will make a melody,
And singe here in your company,
A word was sayd in prophesye
    A thousand yeare agoe.

And the play ends with the Angel's song.

If that isn't drama, then in the name of all that's mysterious, what is? Is it possible that Shakespeare is only drama because we have *seen* him on the stage? Have we no imagination to present to the inward eye and ear that which we have not actually beheld and heard? There have been in modern times some enchantingly beautiful motion pictures, and some with grim elemental significance: I shudder to think what our imperceptive mediaeval scholars would make of them if they were limited to the written scenarios as, in a sense, we are limited when we read mystery plays. Here, at any rate, in this many-faceted gem, in this little play of the **Slaughter of the Innocents,** surely there is God's plenty of contrast, of beauty and ugliness, of effective staging, of vivid and memorable teaching of the word of God. The scenes shift with the rapidity which we find elsewhere only in ballads, but they build up into an impressive wholeness and unity—and that in a bare 496 short lines. The play could be produced today, or any day, with grim and beautiful and powerful effect, but not by producers who think our ancestors crude, simple, and naïve, and not by actors who, like some I have heard on the air, suspend their animation when they approach a mediaeval Christmas play.

If, out of deference to modern proprieties, I have spared you the naturalness of the lines spoken during the *mêlée* of women and soldiers in the **Slaughter of the Innocents,** neither can I quote from the **Crucifixion** lines which terribly impress upon the mind the ugliness and horror of that spectacle. Our forefathers, as I have said, lived at grips with nature and close to earth. Every man, woman, and child in Chester had seen animals slaughtered for food; they knew the details that express in beasts the last extremes of pain and torment. Nay, they had seen human animals hanged at the High Cross or burnt at the stake; and our Lord, the Son of God, was also a human animal. When they exhibited Him "tugged, lugged, all to-torn," they could do so with such reality as makes the lines excessively painful reading, shattering to the soul, so that the play, when produced, must have been one of the most terrible things ever seen on a stage. I shall spare you details natural to our ancestors, and quote some of the grisly joy of the soldiers as they bind the Lamb of God to the Cross:

Fourth Soldier:

>   Fellows, will ye se
>   How sleight I will be,
>   This fyst or I flye,
>   Here to make fast?

First Soldier:

>   Yea, but as mott I thee,
>   Short-armed is he:
>   To bring to this tree,
>   it will not long last.

Second Soldier:

>   Ha! therefore care thou nought!
>   A sleight I haue sought:
>   Ropes must be brought
>   To strean him with strength.

Third Soldier:

>   A rope, as behight,
>   You shall haue, vnbought.
>   Take here one well wrought,
>   And draw him on length.

>   *Tunc ligabunt Cordam ad sinistram*
>   *manum quia dextra erat prius fixa.*

Fourth Soldier:

>   Draws, for your father kynne!
>   Whyle that I dryve in
>   This ilke iron pynne
>   That, I dare lay, will last.

First Soldier:

>   As ever haue I wynne,
>   His arm is but a fynne!
>   Now dryves on, but dyn,
>   And we shall draw fast.

>   *Tunc tres trahent et quartus transfiget*
>   *clavem.*

Lest the lines seem unintelligible to hearing, let me paraphrase them. The soldiers are binding our Lord to the Cross. The Fourth Soldier says, "Look, you fellows—see what a good job I can make of nailing down this fist!" The First replies, "Yeah, but he's short-armed. How kin we nail his other arm to the other side?" The Second puts in, "That's no trouble! We'll stretch him." The Third produces a rope which they fasten to the left hand of our Lord since the right is already nailed down. The Fourth Soldier cries, "Haul, you fellows, while I drive in the nail!" The First exclaims, "By cracky, his arm's only a fin! Go ahead, drive in your nail while we

haul on the rope." Then the three go at it with a yo-heave-ho, stretching the arm while the Fourth Soldier hammers in the nail. A similar grisly touch of ghoulish inhuman glee comes when the Fourth Soldier cries,

>   Fellows, will ye see
>   How I haue stretcht His knee?
>   Why prayse you not me
>   That haue so well done?

Is it possible that our forefathers who lived close not only to life but to the Church knew nothing whatever about the basic principles of art? Is it possible that they did not know that the poignancy and holiness of that cry, "Father, forgive them, for they know not what they do," would stand out in tragic and terrible loveliness against such a revolting scene as this? Or did they think an audience could, without being powerfully moved, turn directly from these gleeful brutes and their ghoulish humour to Mary the Mother of Jesus as she weeps:

>   Alas, my love, my lyfe, my lee,
>   Alas, mowrning now madds me.
>   Alas, my bootë looke thou be,
>   Thy mother that thee bare!

>   Thinke on my freut! I fosterd thee
>   And gaue thee sucke vpon my knee;
>   Vpon my payne haue thou pitty!
>   Thee faylës no power.

>   Alas, why ne were my lyfe forlorne?
>   To fynd my foodë me beforne
>   Tugged, lugged, all to-torne
>   With traytors now this tyde?

>   With neilës thrust, and crown of thorne,
>   Therfore I madd, both even and morne,
>   To see my birth that I haue borne
>   This bitter bale to byde.

But the way of modern criticism is to label such a piece a *planctus Mariae,* and having exhausted itself in that effort, to pay—blunted with community—no more attention to it. Well then, it is *not* a *planctus Mariae,* or not that merely—it has a powerful, and deeply moving dramatic effect.

The comic element in the **Chester Plays,** I have been trying to say, is always defensible on artistic grounds. Would that the same statement could be made of all our drama! It may be that this phenomenon is due to the Church under whose jurisdiction, as I have tried to show, the plays remained until 1531; and to the new Church whose gaze was stern. But elsewhere, we are told, similar plays are not primarily didactic and decorous, but violate their fundamental purpose. And here I can hardly do better than quote from Gayley [*Representative English Comedies,* 1926]:

The French mystery poets, while they develop, like the English, the comic quality of the shepherd scenes, introduce the drinking and dicing element *ad lib.,*—and sometimes the drabbing; they make, moreover, a specialty of the humour of deformity, a char-acteristic which appears nowhere in the English plays. The Germans, in their turn, elaborate a humour peculiar to themselves,—elephantine, primitive, and personal. They seem to get most fun out of reviling the idiosyncrasies of Jews, whose dress, appearance, manners, and speech they caricature—even intro-ducing Jewish *dramatis personae* to sing gibberish, exploit cunning, and perform obscenities under the names of contemporary citizens of the hated race. In general a freer rein seems to have been given to the sacrilegious, grotesque, and obscene on the Continent than in England.

The English plays, in short, and especially those of Chester, never got out of hand, never forgot their sacred mission.

If there is in these plays grim realism and tragic beauty, they are not without minor qualities of humour and local chit-chat of a sort always popular with audiences. For example, Octavian in the Nativity play, sending his messenger with orders to have the Jews numbered, of-fers him for reward the "highe horse besides Bough-ton." Boughton is a district outside one of the gates of Chester, and the "highe horse" is the gallows. The impudent messenger answers in kind that such a horse should be ridden by great lords "of your degree," and continues:

> They bene high in dignitie,
> And also high and swifte is he;
> Therefore that reverance takes yee,
> My deare Lord, I you praye.

Similarly, when Cain is banished and condemned to be a "lurrell" (rogue or blackguard), he turns to the audi-ence as the play closes and says:

> Now I goe, to all that I see
> I graunt the same gifte.

In the highest art there is a kind of simplicity, an ele-ment of the obvious to which we say, "Of course!" But before that element arrived, it was as distant from our thoughts as Aldebaran or Orion's sword. It is at this point that art and science meet, for the great discoveries of the scientific world have been things which seemed utterly obvious once they were pointed out. That quality of the simple, yet unexpected, undreamed-of inevitable I find in an unobtrusive stage direction of the **Nativity** play of **Chester.**

But first let me ask a question: The ox and ass of the sacred manger, where did they come from? Most of us will have supposed that they were always there! And why were they not cows or horses?

When Octavius Caesar issued his mandate that all the people of his dominions should be numbered and pay tribute, Joseph and Mary went from Nazareth to Beth-lehem for this purpose, and Mary rode upon the ass. To provide tribute money, Joseph took the ox along. He says:

> An oxe I will take with me
> That there shall be sould.
>
> The silver of him, so mot I thee,
> Shall finde us in that city,
> And pay tribute for thee and me.

There follows the stage direction: "Then Joseph will bind the ox to the tail of the ass, and place Mary upon the ass." They are now ready to set out on their journey. But what a picture this is: Joseph, an old man on foot, leading the ass on which the young and lovely Mary rides, and the ox following behind tied to the tail of the ass! And that humble procession adds one more surpris-ing, yet obvious touch to the most appealing story our ears have ever heard.

Similarly in the **Shepherds Play,** the four boys who serve the Shepherds approach the child Jesus in the manger:

The First Boye:
> Now to you, my fellowes, this doe I say:
> For in this place, before I wende away,
> Vnto yonder Child lett us goe pray,
> As our masters haue done vs before.

The Second Boye:
> And of such goodis, as we haue here,
> Lett us offer to this prince so dere
> And to his Mother, that mayden clere,
> That of her boddy hasse him borne.

The First Boye:
> Abyde, Sirres, I will go first to yonder
> king.

The Second Boye:
> And I will goe next to that lording.

The Third Boye:
> Then will I be the last of this offryng,
> This can I say, no more.

The First Boye:
> Now, lord, for to geue thie have I no
> thing,
> Nother gould, siluer, broch, nor ring,
> Nor no rich robes meate for a king,
> That I haue here in store.

But tho it lack a stoppell,
    Take thie here my well fayer botell,
    For it will hold a good pottell.
      In faith, I can geue thie no more.

The Second Boye:
    Lord, I know that thou arte of this virgine
      borne,
    In full poore araye sitting on her arme.
    For to offer to thie I haue no skorne
      All though thou be but a child.

    For jewells haue I non to geue thie,
    To mainteyne thie royall dignitie;
    But my hudd thou take it thie,
      As thou art god and man.

The Third Boye:
    O, noble child of thee!
    Alas, what haue I for thee
     Saue onely my pipe?
     Ellis trulie no thing.

    Were I in the rockis or in,
    I could make this pipe
    That all the wood should ringe
      And quiver, as it were.

The Fourth Boye:
    Now, child, all though thou be comon
      from God,
    And be God, thie self, in thie manhood,
    Yett I know that in thie childhood
      Thou wilt for sweete meat looke.

    To pull downe peares, appells, and
      plomes,
    Old Joseph shall not neede to hurt his
      thombes,
    Because thou hast not plentie of cromes,
      I geue thie here my nvthocke.

Could anything be more obvious, more simple, more inescapable, or more beautifully appealing? *Of course* the Shepherds have boys, apprentices! Only, we had never thought of them and never would have thought of them. And of course the boys would worship the Child with the Shepherds; and of course they would offer gifts. But what have they to offer? *They* carry no gold, frankincense, and myrrh in their pockets. They give what they are likely to have and to treasure: a bottle without a cork, in which, no doubt, the lad carries a refreshing drink to the fields; the prized hood which protects from the bitter wind; a willow whistle; and a nut-hook for pulling down apples, pears, and plums. The virtue of a gift is that it should mean something to the giver, include the element of sacrifice and the element of love. No modern writer could possibly have imagined that most obvious and simple scene: it has the true medi-aeval touch.

Nor could it have been written by Geoffrey Chaucer, our greatest mediaeval English writer. He, it is true, does show us the Widow's cottage, and he shows us a few other humble characters; but he sees them, as we see them with him, from the outside. The mystery author saw those shepherd boys from the inside, and felt their reverence. Further, as J.E. Tiddy [in *The Mummers' Play,* 1923] has pointed out, "in all the abundant realism of these plays [the mysteries] there is certainly no realistic portrayal of a gentleman"—but to have failed to notice Chaucer's interest in gentility is not to have read Chaucer. The world of the mystery plays is a world utterly foreign to the courtly and learned poets. In the mysteries you will find no tortured allegory, no three-ply dream visions, no fragrant gardens of love and the rose, no women set on the sham pedestals—or whited sepulchres—of courtly love, no Dresden china maidens whose every feature from grey eyes to dainty feet is catalogued in unrealistic detail. But you will find men and women, coarse, robust, and real, like as we all are or ought to be, with our grumbling and humour, our normal confusions, tempers, and sins. The Virgin Mary herself is a sainted version of the nursing mother next door; she is neither Criseyde nor Queen Guenevere, but as simple and real and true and natural as the girl of eighteen across the way with her first baby. In the mysteries you will find no debates on love and courtly manners, on points of courtesy and gentility; their authors have no such sophistication; and the audience for whom they were written would take no delight in fine points of argument upon subjects to them trivial. The mystery plays, in short, are folk drama.

Further, no matter how we may sweat our Freshmen through the Prologue to *The Canterbury Tales* and proclaim that here is a cross-section of English life in the Middle Ages, in reality the life of the Middle Ages hardly appears in Chaucer at all. What does appear is London and the courtly circle, their prepossessions and interests, with an occasional glimpse of the passing procession of life seen from the sidewalk and brought back to amuse the Court. Among those glimpses there is one of Absolon playing Herod "upon a scaffold hie"— in itself evidence that Chaucer had not seen processional plays. Why, if Chaucer was so great a part of all that he had met in England, is there no single scrap of a mystery play from his gifted pen?

Indeed, why is it that up until this moment nobody has ever been able to give a name that would stick to any single author of a mystery play? True, Ritson long ago suggested that Lydgate may have written such plays, but we look in vain for evidence that he did. What he may well have written is a royal entry or two, but that is a horse of a very different colour—if it is a horse at all. The name of Sir Gilbert Pilkington has been proposed as author of the Towneley Plays, but it has not stuck. Chambers formerly believed that Randall Higden wrote the **Chester Mysteries,** but has recanted. I have myself advanced as the originator of the Chester Plays not a court poet, but a Carmelite monk, Sir Henry Francis. Not a single other name can be associated with any of the mystery plays of England, plays which at one time were the bloom of life itself in a hundred towns.

The truth is that the plays had no authors—or, to say the same thing otherwise, they had the same authors as the ballads; and they require for their appreciation much the same taste as the ballads require. Crude the ballads are, if you will, and often enough their language breaks down; but they reach felicities which no sophisticated writer could achieve. One such bit is the line in the ballad of the Wife of Usher's Well: "The channering worm doth chide." Not even Shakespeare could have written that line. So it is with the mysteries: they are the product of folk artistry—and the folk *are* artists. Professional drama has its achievements and its glory; and so has that of the folk: "There is one glory of the sun, and another glory of the moon, and another of the stars: for one star differeth from another star in glory."

No doubt in the first instance some member of a church or monastery, some Henry Francis of this period or that, was requested to provide a play for this or the other gild of craftsmen. Then the gildsmen took it over, altering here, adding or deleting there, simplifying, intensifying, humourizing, bringing the artistic expression closer and closer to life as they knew it until in a play like that of the Towneley Shepherds there is a work of art such as no single author, labouring upon any single bank and shoal of time, could possibly have created. Even though official revisers from time to time trimmed up the plays, they still come to us encrusted with the living and thinking of real people, dwelling in real towns, experiencing plague and pestilence, rain and sunshine, revelry and tragedy, life, birth, marriage, child-bearing, and decrepitude through generation after generation of brief lives. So brief were those lives, with a life expectancy at birth of twenty-five years in the fourteenth century—as against sixty odd years now—that the promise of an Hereafter was immediate and important to them, and religion was their daily bread. Chaucer we are obliged by his artistry to know, Chaucer and Gower and Lydgate and the courtly romancers; but they are not all England, but one small corner only. There is another England that looms large and comparatively neglected in the ballads and mystery plays.

This is an England clustered closely around the hospitable and all-inclusive Church. In it, every craft gild had its special altar. In it, the craftsmen maintained their sick in the only hospitals there were, their poor and destitute in the only homes for such persons the Middle Ages provided. In it, in the carvings of pillar and altar could be seen that sense of the homogeneity of all life from which we have now escaped. The birds of the air are no longer fellow creatures of ours in this twentieth century; the animals of the field are no longer our brothers. To us St. Valentine and St. Francis of Assisi are names out of fairy tales. It seems merely naïve to us to bring on the stage Balaam's Ass and let him speak in human words; and no man today would ever dream, as did the builders of Laon Cathedral, of placing high in the nave representations of the oxen that hauled the stone for that inspiring House of God. No modern artist would dream of depicting the whole human race rising from the penis of Adam as it may be seen in the crypt of Glasgow Cathedral. I have refrained from reading to you passages from the **Chester Plays** which would only seem to a modern audience coarse and shocking. But to our forefathers, close to earth and reality as they lived, these things came quite properly within the circle of life as they knew it—and, do not forget, down to 1538, and even thereafter, the **Chester Plays** were first performed before Church officials at St. Werburgh's. Between our mediaeval ancestors and ourselves many things have intervened—among others, an age when the word "leg" became vulgar and unmentionable; but if we wish really to understand mediaeval times, we shall do well to leave courtly circles occasionally behind and see life whole in the mystery plays. And the first thing we shall learn is that the religion of those times was a living thing which included all life.

There was room in religion even for fun, as for every other element of life. One of the merriest households whereof this world holds record was that of St. Thomas More who, nevertheless, wore a hair shirt next his skin. And Dante was never a truer mediaevalist than when he reserved a special corner in Hell for those who do not smile in the sunshine and the sweet air of Heaven. The nonsense of the Boy Bishop and the mock sermon in no way profaned the Holy of Holies, but could be enacted before the High Altar itself. In the play of the Towneley Shepherds, the very cradle which is used for riotous comedy and in which the stolen sheep is hidden, is used a few seconds later for the infant Jesus. In the same way, the raw, rude Shepherds at Chester doing their best to make out the words of the angelic song, "Gloria in excelsis Deo et in terra pax hominibus bonae voluntatis," represent something we cannot appreciate as our fathers did. To one Shepherd the first word was "glere," to another it was "glori," to a third, "glarum"; and they go on disputing about the word though none of them understands its meaning. I have often thought of them while listening to grand opera, and even to church choirs. Stop a moment: satire on the enunciation of singers is commonplace enough, but these Shepherds were not poking fun at the singing of a prima donna: they were making hash of the song of an *angel!* And that song, "Glory to God in the highest, and on earth peace," was the most beautiful, the most enchanting, the most inspiring song ever heard by the ears of man. That song alone, the first Christmas morning, announced the end of five thousand years of slavery to sin and the beginning of a new era when salvation of our souls became possible. The greatest tidings man has ever heard, that this erring dust might really take on the image of God and inherit eternal bliss, came to us in that angelic song. And that was what the mediaeval dramatist with his rude shepherds was burlesquing. For breath-taking, colossal impudence the scene is without rival in drama. But in the Middle Ages God himself had a sense of humour and fully appreciated the absurd and ridiculous. Between that God and us, Puritanism has intervened and dissolved the merriment of Merrie England.

Merrie England it was, in spite of daily hardship and privation and terrible scourges such as modern man may imagine, but cannot know. And this is the England you will find in the mystery plays. It is an England with the gift of naturalness which has rarely appeared in our literature since the Reformation; it is an England with artistic instincts of a high order; an England with a deep sense of the homogeneity of man and beast and fowl, of all living things; an England deeply devout, into every moment of whose life religion entered as a living force; an England merry in the sunshine, in the springtime, in the summer festivals; an England whose sanity and wholesomeness and balance ought to be an inspiration to all who come after.

Specifically, as I have said, the **Chester Plays,** as compared with other cycles, never lose sight of their primary purpose. Perhaps a comparison can best be presented in the words of Tiddy as he compares the York, **Chester,** and Brome plays of Abraham and Isaac:

> In the **Chester Play,** where Isaac is represented as a child, his boyish fright and his simple affectionate prattle are almost unbearably moving and pathetic. In the York Play, where Isaac is a type of Christ and is represented as a man thirty years old, the pathos and dramatic value of the episode are swept away. In the Brome Play, on the other hand, this ecclesiastical bias is neglected and the scene is even finer than in the Chester cycle.

All of the cycles have, in the whole and in individual plays, their special excellences. With fewer plays than York or Towneley, the **Chester cycle** seems to have a greater unity; and it is guided, throughout the whole cycle from **the Fall of Lucifer** and **the Creation of the World** up to **the Coming of Antichrist** and **Judgment Day,** by a restraining logic. The result is that the multiplicity of individual plays does not confuse, but conveys a single overpowering impression of God's might and majesty, His justice, and His mercy.

I would not be taken to say that there are no crudenesses or gaucheries in the mystery plays, any more than I would make the same claim for Jonson or Shakespeare. One instance in the Betrayal of Christ is a sort of *Post hoc ergo propter hoc* in reverse. Peter threatens Malchus:

> Thy ear shall of, by Godes grace,
> Or thou passe from this place.

That is, we know that Peter clipped off the ear of Malchus; therefore we have him threaten to do so—and transform him, in the process, from a crude, flailing, angry man into the very butcher of a silk button, calling his shots in advance. And it is certainly unskilled workmanship that lets the characters of the plays step before us and say, "I am God," "I am Herod," etc. Yet Shakespeare's Richard III steps out alone on the stage to say, "I am a villain," and even Iago is not far from exemplifying the same device. But drama, like politics, is largely the art of the possible, and largely convention. Shakespeare could have managed *Othello* without the crudeness or the conventionality of permitting Iago to announce himself, but would the audience wait for him to do so? The possible is two hours' traffic of the stage. And Shakespeare himself, confronted with the task of a dozen Biblical plays to be staged on wagons during one day, might have done no better with them than Masefield has done with his modern adaptations of the mysteries.

If, then, we may believe that the mystery plays are genuinely dramatic in that they present conflict in abundance, as well as beauty and entertainment, in that they reveal life, and convey the deepest significance, we may now ask what they contributed to drama in general, and especially to the Elizabethans who remain the chief glory of our stage.

They contributed, first of all as I have tried to show, the physical stage itself, a stage on wheels which could readily convert an inn-yard into a theatre, box office and all. And with that stage, they contributed the whole repertoire of stage apparatus and effects. As we have seen, Ophelia's grave is no new device; it is centuries old, the necessary hole or trap in the floor for the Devil's ascent into the world or for the sinners' descent into Hell. The curtained inner stage and the "discovery" so frequent in Elizabethan drama are equally ancient, as we learn from payments made for curtains and cords. On this point a stage direction in the Last Supper of *Ludus Coventriae* is quite explicit:

> Crist enteryth in-to þe hous with his discipilis and ete þe paschal lomb and in þe mene tyme þe cownsel hous beforn-seyd xal sodeynly onclose schewying þe buschopys prestys and jewgys syttyng in her Astat lyche as it were A convocacyone.

Many other examples could be given. Most of the Elizabethan stage effects have their ancestors in the mysteries; and as I have said, Ariel flying about in *The Tempest* is only a vagrant angel from older days.

No doubt the mysteries also established some characters which became part of the Elizabethan stock. The Vice of the moralities has often been pointed out as such a figure: he connects the mummers' plays, through mystery, morality, and interlude, and even classical adaptation, with the Elizabethan stage. But swaggering Pistol must surely inherit some of the blood and characteristics of Herod, and the impertinent Fool must go back to the Garcio or Messenger of many mysteries. Such identifications might be questioned, for there are, after all, ancestors in classical drama and in the *Commedia dell' Arte,* and even in folklore, for many of the stock characters of the Elizabethans; but such matters as these, I leave, like Chaucer, to "divines"—or experts.

Only, there is one thing which definitely did not come to Elizabethan drama from the theatres of Greece and Rome, and that is the inextricable mixture of tragedy and comedy which Shelley called "an extension of the dramatic circle." It is because of this very extension that Shelley calls *King Lear* the greatest play ever written—and that tradition of mixed comedy and tragedy, as we have seen, is the mingled yarn of the mysteries, the very stuff of which they are woven.

Another mediaeval tradition so strong that it need only be mentioned is the tradition of music and song brought in at every possible moment to set the stage, create the scene, or inspire a mood. And still another element which did not derive from classical drama is the capricious freedom with which time and place are handled. Sir Harley Granville-Barker [in *Prefaces to Shakespeare,* 1927] has said that the actors of Shakespeare "carry time and place with them as they move." They do so because their predecessors had done so for hundreds of years. The mysteries also contributed to the tradition, sometimes unfortunate, of poetical drama. But their greatest gift to the glory of the stage under the Virgin Queen is twofold: they fostered a tradition of acting which put the professional actor through his apprenticeship; and they prepared an audience capable of rising to Shakespeare.

At some undetermined time between 1580 and 1595 there were in the town of Chester 410 householders assessed to provide armour in time of war. This little town which could never, before 1600, have contained within its walls more than 5000 people, made, as I have tried to show, a genuinely significant contribution to drama, a contribution as yet unequalled by cities on this continent twenty and forty and a hundred times as large and prosperous. Considered as an achievement within the limits of the possible, the **Chester Plays** are great indeed.

Sidney W. Clarke (essay date 1964)

SOURCE: "The Chester Plays," in *The Miracle Play in England: An Account of the Early Religious Drama,* Haskell House, 1964, pp. 34-42.

[*In the following excerpt, Clarke discusses the comical and tragic apects of the Chester Plays, contending that Chester "is the only series that shows any real effort to serve the religious object to which Miracle Plays were supposed to be directed."*]

The **Chester plays** are more serious in tone than those we have already considered; the humour, though present, is not so boisterous as in the Towneley series, and a didactic tendency is shown in the introduction of an Expositor, who at the end of each play explains its significance and lesson. This is the only series that shows any real effort to serve the religious object to which Miracle Plays were supposed to be directed. The plays are twenty-five in number, and they were acted by the twenty-five trade companies of the city on the Monday, Tuesday, and Wednesday in Whitsun week, from 1268 to 1577, and again in 1600. In the year 1328 the plays received a great impetus by the act of Pope Clement, who decreed a 1000 days of pardon, to which the Bishop of Chester added another month, to everyone who should resort "in peaceable manner with good devotion to hear and see the said plays from time to time as oft as they shall be played within the city." The series commences with the **Fall of Lucifer,** performed by the Tanners; next the **Creation and Fall,** by the Drapers; the effect of the representation of the Creation was heightened by sending among the crowd as many strange animals as could be brought together, the creation of birds being imitated by sending up a flight of pigeons. **The Deluge** was done by the Water-Carriers of the Dee, and was one of the humorous plays, being almost entirely taken up by an altercation between Noah and his wife. The play begins with God's announcement to the patriarch of the coming deluge, and the command to him to build the Ark. Noah replies—

> O Lorde, I thanke thee, lowde and still,
> That to me arte in suche will,
> And spares me and my howse to spill,
> As I nowe southly [Truly] fynde.
> Thy byddinge, Lorde, I shall fulfill,
> And never more thee greve nor grill [Provoke],
> That such grace hath sent me till,
> Amonght all mankinde.

[Turning to his sons and their wives]

> Have done, you men and wemen all,
> Hye you, leste this watter fall,
> To worche this shippe, chamber and hall,
> As God hath bedden us doe.

After this the wife and sons of Noah say a few words relating to their respective duties during the construction. Noah commences the building of the "shippe," and the play proceeds as follows:—

NOAH

"Now in the name of God I will begyne
To make the shippe that we shall in,
That we maye be ready for to swyme
At the cominge of the fludde:
Thes bordes heare I pynne togeither,
To beare us saffe from the weither,
That we maye rowe both heither and theither,
And saffe be from the fludde.
Of this treey will I make the maste;
Tied with cabbelles that will laste,
With a saile yarde for iche blaste,
And iche thinge in their kinde:
With toppe-castill, and boe-spritte,
With cords and roppes, I hold all mete
To sayle fourth at the nexte weete;
This shippe is att an ende.
Wyffe, in this vessel we shall be kepte:
My children and thou, I woulde in ye lepte.

NOAH'S WIFE

In fayth, Noye, I hade as liffe thou slepte!
For all thy frynish [Nice] fare,
I will not doe after thy rede [Advice].

NOAH

Good wyffe, doe nowe as I thee bydde.

NOAH'S WIFE

Be Christe! not or I see more neede
Though thou stande all the daye and stare.

Noah laments the "crabbed" nature of womankind. The ark, however, is at length finished, and after enumerating the animals that are to take refuge therein, Noah enters the ark with all his family, excepting his wife. Here considerable liberty is taken with the Biblical version, and a strange scene is witnessed. Noah's wife, a person of exceedingly whimsical temper, in reply to her husband's appeal to her to enter the ark, gives vent to a volley of strong language, saying that unless her "gossips" are allowed to go in with her she "will not oute of this towne," and she tells him to row where he lists, and to get a new wife. At last the dutiful Japhet compels his mother to enter by main force, and immediately upon her entrance she vigorously boxes Noah's ears. He remarks—

Ha, ha, marye, this is hotte!
It is good for to be still.

Ha, children, methinkes my botte remeves,
Our tarryinge heare hyghlye me greves,
Over the lande the wather spreades;
God doe as he will.
Ah, greate God, that arte so good,
That worckes not thy will is wood,
Nowe all this worlde is one a fludde,
As I see well in sighte.
This wyndowe I will shutte anon,
And into my chamber I will gone,
Tell this watter, so greate one,
Be slacked through Thy mighte.

The window of the ark is now closed for a short time, supposed to be during the period of the flood, after which it is opened, and Noah thanks God for granting him such grace. The Almighty replies, and blesses the patriarch, and the play finishes with the following speech by God:—

My bowe betweyne you and me
In the firmament shal be,
By verey tocken that you shall see,
That suche vengance shall cease.
That man ne woman shall never more
Be wasted with watter, as hath before;
But for synne that greveth me sore.
Therefore this vengance was.

. . . . .

My blessinge Noye, I give thee heare,
To thee, Noye, my servante deare;
For vengance shall noe more appeare,
And nowe farewell, my darlinge deare.

The examples already given of the literature of the miracle plays have been of a humorous nature. I now want to draw attention to these old playwrights' power of building up a tragic and pathetic play, and for this purpose I take the play of the **"Sacrifice of Isaac,"** the fourth play in the **Chester** series:—God calls to Abraham, and bids him offer his son as a sacrifice. Abraham replies—

My Lorde, to thee is myne intente
Ever to be obediente;
That sonne that thou to me hast sente,
    Offer I will to thee;
And fulfill thy commanndemente,
With heartie will, as I am kente [Taught],
Highe God, Lorde omnipotente,
    Thy byddinge done shal be.
My meanye [Company] and my children eich
    [Each] one
Lenges [Remain] at home, both alle and one
Save Isaake, my sonne, with me shall gone
    To a hill heare besyde.

Abraham then says to Isaac:—

> Make thee readye, my deare darlinge,
> For we must doe a littill thinge.
> This woode upon thy backe it bringe,
>   We maye no longer abyde.
> A sworde and fier that I will take;
> For sacrefice me behoves to make;
> Gode's byddinge will I not forsake,
>   But ever obediente be.

> ISAAC.—Father, I am all readye
>   To doe your byddinge moste mekelye,
>   To beare this woode full beane [Obedient]
>   am I,
>   As you commaunded me.

> ABRAHAM.—O Isaake, my darlinge deare,
>   My blessinge nowe I give thee heare,
>   Take up this faggote with good cheare,
>   And on thy backe it bring;
>   And fier with us I will take.

> ISAAC.—Your byddinge I will not forsake;
>   Father, I will never slake
>   To fulfill your byddinge.

They go to the place of sacrifice, where Isaac, being frightened, says:—

> Father, I am full sore affeared
> To see you beare that drawne sworde:
> I hope for all myddel earde [The world]
>   You will not slaye your childe.

> ABRAHAM.—Dreede thee not, my childe, I
>   reade;
>   Our Lorde will sende of his godheade
>   Some manner of beaste unto this steade,
>   Either tame or wild.

Soon after, Abraham tells Isaac that he must kill him.

> ISAAC.—Alas! father, is that your will,
>   Your owine child for to spill
>   Upon this hille's brinke?
>   If I have treasspasede in anye degree,
>   With a yarde you may beat me;
>   Put up your sorde, if your will be,
>   For I am but a childe.

> ABRAHAM.—O, my deare sonne, I am sorye
>   To doe to thee this great anoye:
>   Gode's commaundmente doe must I,
>   His workes are ever full mylde.

> ISAAC.—Woulde God my mother were here
>   with me!
>   Shee woulde kneele downe upon her

> knee,
>   Prainge you, father, if it may be,
>   For to save my life.

Abraham replies that he must obey the divine command, and Isaac then asks his father's blessing.

> Father, seinge you muste nedes doe soe,
> Let it passe lightlie, and over goe;
> Kneelinge on my kneeyes towe,
>   You blessinge on me spreade.

> ABRAHAM.—My blessinge, deere son, give I
>   thee
>   And thy mother's with hart free
>   The blessing of the Trinitie
>   My deare sone, on thee lighte.

> ISAAC.—Father, I praye you, hyde my eyne
>   That I see not the sorde so keyne,
>   Your strocke, father, woulde I not seene,
>   Leste I againste it grylle [Rebel].

Isaac is then bound and laid on the altar.

> ISSAC.—A! mercye, father, why tarye you soe?
>   Smyte of my head, and let me goe;
>   I pray you rydd me of my woe,
>   For nowe I take my leve.

> ABRAHAM.—Ah, sonne! my harte will breake in
>   three,
>   To heare thee speake such words to me.
>   Jesu! on me thou have pittye,
>   That I have moste in mynde.

> ISAAC.—Nowe, father, I see that I shall dye:
>   Almightie God in magestie!
>   My soule I offer unto thee;
>   Lorde, to it be kinde.

Abraham takes the sword, and is about to cut off his son's head, when an angel appears and stays his hand. He points out a lamb entangled in some briars, which Abraham offers in sacrifice. God appears and utters his blessing upon Abraham and his seed, and the play is concluded by the Expositor explaining the moral.

> This deed you see done here in this place,
> In example of Jesu done it was,
> That for to win mankind to grace
>   Was sacrificed on the roode.
> By Abraham, I maie understande
> The father of heaven that can fand [Find],
> With his sonne's bloode to breake that bande
>   [Curse],
>   That the devill had broughte us to.
> By Isaake understande I maie,
> Jesu, that was obediente aye,

His father's will to work alwaie,
   And death for to confounde.

At this point a messenger riding through the crowd of spectators arrives at the pageant to announce the coming of the next play in the series, and the Barbers and Wax Chandlers who acted the **Sacrifice of Isaac,** go off in their pageant to re-enact the play in another part of the city. The next play, which is on the subject of Balaam and his Ass, and is not to be found in any other English collection, concludes the representation of the Old Testament history, and in the next pageant the **Salutation** and the **Nativity** are played. Then comes the **Shepherds' play,** which, as in other cycles, is an elaborate picture of country life. In succeeding plays the main incidents of the life of Christ are set out; then we come again, in the nineteenth of the series, to the ever popular **Harrowing of Hell,** which, like the play of the **Judgment Day,** was made the medium of much topical allusion. Thus, we find that one of the dwellers in the infernal regions is a woman who tells the audience that—

Some tyme I was a tavernere,
A gentill gossipe and a taptere,
Of wyne and ale a trustie brewer,
   Which wo hath me wroughte;
Of cannes I kepte no trewe measuer,
My cuppes I soulde at my pleasuer.
Deceaving manye a creature,
   Tho my ale were naughte.

She had adulterated her ale, and brewed thin beer, offences of too grave a nature to permit any pardon, and in consequence she is left to the tender mercies of the devil, who exclaims—

Welckome dere ladye, I shall thee wedd,
For many a heavye and droncken head,
Cause of thy ale were broughte to bed
   Farre worse than anye beaste.

The following proclamation contains the earliest authentic mention we have of the **Chester plays,** and gives an interesting account of the origin of the plays and the manner of their performance:—

The proclamation for Whitsone plays, made by Wm. Newall, clarke of the Pendice, 24 Hen. 8., Wm. Snead, 2nd yere maior.

For as much as of old time, not only for the augmentation and increase of the holy and catholick faith of our Saviour Jesus Christ, and to exort the mindes of comon people to good devotion and holsome doctrine thereof, but also for the comenwelth and prosperity of this city, a play and declaration of divers storyes of the Bible, beginning with the creation and fall of Lucifer, and ending with the generall Judgment of the World, to be declared and played in the Whitsonne weeke, was devised and made by

one Sr Henry Frances, sometyme monck of this monastery disolved, who obtayning and got of Clement, then bishop of Rome, a thousand dayes of pardon, and of the bishop of Chester at that time forty days of pardon, graunted from thensforth to every person resorting in peaceble manner with good devotion to heare and see the sayd plays from tyme to tyme, as oft as they shall be played within the sayd citty (and that every person or persons disturbing the sayd playes in any manner wise to be accused by the authority of the said pope Clement's bulls untill such tyme as he or they be absolved thereof), which playes were devised to the honor of God by John Arnway, then Maior of this citty of Chester, his brethren and whole community thereof, to be brought forth, declared, and played at the cost and charges of the craftsmen and occupations of the said citty, which hitherunto have from tyme to tyme used and performed the same accordingly.

Wherfore Mr. Maior, in the King's name, stratly chargeth and comandeth that every person or persons, of what estate, degree, or condition so ever he or they be, resorting to the said playes, do use themselves peacibli, without making any assault, affray, or other disturbance whereby the same plays shall be disturbed, and that no manner of person or persons, whosoever he or they be, do use or weare any unlawfull weapons within the precinct of the sayd citty during the time of the sayd playes (not only upon payn of cursing by authority of the sayd pope Clement's bulls) but also upon payne of enprisonment of their bodyes and making fine to the King at Mr. Maior's pleasure.

Kathleen M. Ashley (essay date 1978)

SOURCE: "Divine Power in *Chester Cycle* and Late Medieval Thought," in *The Chester Mystery Cycle: A Casebook,* edited by Kevin J. Harty, Garland Publishing, Inc., 1993, pp. 48-68.

[*In the following excerpt, first published in* Journal of the History of Ideas *in 1978, Ashley contends that the dominant theme of the Chester cycle—the idea of divine power—is a reflection of "the philosophical and theological preoccupations of its day."*]

Scholars have often noted the enlightened portrayal of human emotion and detail in late medieval religious art, a phenomemon which appears to grow out of Anselmian theology, Bernardian devotion, and Franciscan interest in Christ's humanity. Among the English Mystery cycles, York and Towneley are most influenced by the trend. **Chester cycle** accommodates less easily to generalizations about late medieval devotionalism or realism; on the whole, most readers of **Chester** are struck by its solemnity, its spareness, and its austere uniformity of style and meter. Arnold Williams [in *The Drama of Medieval England,* 1961] has commented on the cycle's "calmness, an evenness, a narrative and lyrical rather than a theatrical technique," with the observation that "some unexplained conservatism has kept out of **Chester** the spectacle, the fervor, and the naturalism which fifteenth century revisers introduced into the other cycles."

Although some critics have offered the aesthetic verdict that **Chester** is the "least imaginatively exciting" of the four cycles, I would prefer to follow Salter in his judgment [in *Medieval Drama in Chester*, 1968]:

> With fewer plays than York or Towneley, the **Chester cycle** seems to have a greater unity; and it is guided, throughout the whole cycle, from the Fall of Lucifer and the Creation of the World up to the Coming of Antichrist and the Judgment Day, by a restraining logic. The result is that the multiplicity of individual plays does not confuse, but conveys a single overpowering impression of God's might and majesty, His justice and His mercy.

Salter does not elaborate on the "restraining logic" which guides the cycle. What I will do here is explore one major way in which the effect of overpowering divinity noted by Salter has been achieved. I propose that the dramatic choices made in assembling and writing the cycle were guided by a concern to demonstrate both the reality and the quality of God's omnipotence. The idea of divine power—a, if not *the*, chief theme of the **Chester cycle**—is also a major theme in philosophical discussions of the fourteenth and fifteenth centuries especially the discussions of the nominalist philosophers. **Chester** with its emphasis on the divinity of God rather than the humanity of Christ, seems to reflect this doctrinal focus of nominalist argument.

Nominalism was dominant in the universities throughout the fourteenth and fifteenth centuries, and, even more important for the religious drama, nominalist theology was preached widely. Heiko Oberman, [in *The Pursuit of Holiness in Late Medieval and Renaissance Religion,* 1974] arguing for the term "nominalism" or *via moderna* (rather than Scotism in the fourteenth century or Ockhamism in the fifteenth), says:

> In the first place, "Scotism" and "Ockhamism" suggest too strongly a merely academic setting, whereas the ideas of the *via moderna* are on a wide scale absorbed by non-Franciscans, infiltrating even the doctrinally well-disciplined Dominican order and shaping the piety of thousands of sermons preached all over Europe—a source still largely untapped by scholarship. In the second place, nominalism proves to be the more comprehensive category, as the movement that not only survived, but even flourished long after Ockham and Ockhamism were condemned by the University of Paris in September, 1339, and again in December, 1340.

I shall suggest that the "conservatism" of **Chester** can

best be explained not as a result of its folk origin or its roots in the liturgical drama, but as a trait to be expected in the cycle which is closest to the philosophical and theological preoccupations of its day.

In the **Chester cycle,** the words "might," "majesty," "power," "mastery," and "potesty" constitute a cluster present in every play. The word "potesy" or "postie"—that is, "power"—dominates the image cluster of **Chester**. The word occurs at least once and usually many times in all but five of the twenty-four plays which make up the cycle, with the greatest concentration at the theological high points: the Nativity, the Passion, the Antichrist plays, and the Last Judgment.

Beyond frequency of reference, the selection and interpretation of events throughout the cycle are governed by a need to prove God's power. According to the cycle's repeated pun, the "preving" of God's "posty" simultaneously "preves" the devil of his "posty." It is possible to conclude that virtually every important episode and character in the **Chester cycle** is thematically controlled by the idea of power.

As might be expected, the rulers who oppose God's will are especially sensitive in this cycle to their own power; they continually usurp the divine titles, such as "prince most of posty" and "omnipotent," and claim powers only God can legitimately boast. The **Chester** Herod provides a good example. The *Slaying of the Innocents* scene in **Chester cycle** emphasizes not the vanity of Herod (as in the Towneley characterization of the king) but the power he represents. It does so by dwelling at length on the behavior of Herod's knights, who are repeatedly described in terms referring to strength: they are "doughty" men, "hardy" men, "stout" men, "men of strength," the equals of Sampson. The extended murder therefore becomes a dramatic portrayal of what the world's ill-directed power leads to—the ruthless slaying of innocent children. The essential quality of unchecked earthly power is its destructiveness. The play ends, however, on a satisfying note with the death of Herod, moralized by the angels as "the marring of might and mayne", showing that earthly power ultimately fails when opposed to the divine.

The preeminent quality of power as depicted in **Chester** is mercy. God's power is demonstrated over and over in the cycle by His miracles, especially those involving healing, which might be one rationale for the inclusion of more scenes from Christ's ministry in **Chester** than in any other cycle. The motif of a healing Christ is introduced in the *Adoration of the Shepherds* with the distinctive complaint of the **Chester** shepherds that their animals are diseased, ridden with scab and rot. Just as in the Towneley *Second Shepherds' Play* complaints of foul weather and avaricious landlords transcend topical allusion to become symbolic of the state of the world on the eve of the Savior's birth, so the diseased sheep in

Chester anticipate the dominant image of Christ in this cycle: the Good Shepherd who heals His flock, demonstrating His divine power through His grace.

Jesus makes this point explicitly in the first ministry play, *Christ, the Adulteress, Chelidonius,* where He declares Himself to be the Good Shepherd, empowered to do His father's work of healing the sick and restoring the blind to sight. The miracles He will perform only show God's power. Christ's ministry to the blind man Chelidonius, the raising of Lazarus, the healing of Simon the Leper, the cleansing of the temple, all follow and in each instance the recipient of the grace, observers, and Christ reiterate that they have been witnesses to the divine power. The increased presence and power of an adult Jesus in the New Testament plays of the **Chester cycle** parallel the numerous appearances of God the Father in the Old Testament plays of the cycle. The God figure appears on stage and interacts with the other characters more directly in **Chester** than in any other English cycle, a fact particularly noticeable in the Cain and Abel episode, the *Deluge,* and the *Sacrifice of Issac.*

The first half of the **Chester cycle** is characterized by the presence of God in the dramatic foreground, followed by the image of an effective and powerful Christ, both portraying the reality and the quality of God's power in the world. How then does the cycle handle the seeming impotence of Christ as He undergoes the Passion? As critics [such as Peter Travis in "The Dramatic Strateging of Chester's Passion Pagina," *Comparative Drama* 8, 1974] have noticed, the tortures and sufferings of Christ are less evident in **Chester** than in York and Towneley, as if the **Chester** dramatist had little inclination to portray Jesus' human vulnerability. Excruciating action is held to a minimum in the **Chester** *Passion play.* Interest is instead focussed on the repeated taunts by Annas, Cayphas, Pilate, and Herod as well as some Jews, that Jesus now show them His power and thus prove his divinity. As He hangs on the cross both followers and tormenters remind Him of all the people He has healed, begging or challenging Jesus to heal Himself. Jesus cures instead the blind knight Longeus (Longinus) who vows his belief that "in days three / thou wilt ryse through thy posty". Joseph of Arimathea and Nichodemus conclude the play with their testimony, based on the miracles they have witnessed, that Christ is "god Almight" who will be resurrected "of his posty".

The **Chester cycle** concludes uniquely with two lengthy Antichrist plays just before the *Last Judgment.* The Chester dramatist incorporated them, I would contend, in order to form the necessary structural counterthrust to the divine power so evident throughout the cycle; the Antichrist provided the appropriate apocalyptic challenger to God. In York and Towneley cycles the human types of good and evil carry most of the interest, but in **Chester** the focus is on ultimate forces: God and the Devil, Christ and Antichrist. The menace of a powerful anti-divinity effectively underscores the ultimate power of the deity.

As the final pageant opens, all rivals to divine power have been vanquished. God declares again "that I am Peerles [Peerless] of Posty / Apertly [Openly] shall be proved". The angels and the souls who have been saved testify that it was through His might that all was created and saved, while Jesus appears to remind the audience that His death had "prived the Devyll of his posty". The very last line of the play is "laus maxima omnipotenti" which sums up the major theme of the whole cycle—God's omnipotence—and perhaps also harks back to the opening lines of the cycle where God in Latin announces His power ("potentia") and freedom to act ("licentia").

The theme of God's omnipotence, the deliberate inclusion of references to divine power, and the shaping of scenes to illustrate that power, do not appear in the French passion plays which have been suggested as contemporary vernacular sources for the **Chester cycle**. Indeed, in passages where the wording is very close, the mention of God's power—almost without exception—does not occur outside of the **Chester play;** in those places where it does the reference can be traced to a common source in the Biblical account. The *Stanzaic Life of Christ* would also make an attractive source for this motif of power in **Chester cycle,** since it was assembled in Chester from Latin sources; but, again, if **Chester** has used the *Stanzaic Life* for the management of certain episodes, the theme of God's power is not among the features which was adopted.

If we cannot offer a specific vernacular source for the theme of divine power in **Chester** we can at least show that the cycle reflects a larger philosophical emphasis of its time, that **Chester** responds thematically to the late medieval obsession with God's omnipotence. This obsession—and I think the use of the term is justified—has been noted by every historian of philosophy and theology of the period. Although this is not the place to undertake a detailed analysis of the theme in various late medieval works, I shall briefly sketch its general development through the fifteenth century before returning to further discussion of the **Chester cycle.** I shall rely primarily on the interpolations of historians of philosophy and theology, although it should be noted that the study of late medieval nominalism is now in a state of considerable ferment, with resulting modification of previously held views and a general consensus that much more work needs to be done in the field, including publication of much primary materials, before the definitive history can be written.

The emphasis on God's power arose in response to the new works of Aristotle which entered the western medieval world in the twelfth and thirteenth centuries. The chief Islamic interpreters of Aristotle known to the Latin

West were Avicenna (Ibn Sina) and Averroes (Ibn Rusd). As Van Steenberghen [in *Aristotle in the West,* 1955] points out, "Aristotle" for much of the thirteenth century in the West means Aristotle expounded through these commentators. Avicenna's exposition of God's nature suggests a number of theses contrary to orthodox Christian belief: first that there was no initial act of creation by which God made the world; rather creation is an eternal process flowing from God's nature. Second, that God necessarily produces an effect, which flows down through the hierarchy of intelligences to the world; God therefore only works indirectly in the world. Averroes discards Avicenna's emanation doctrine in his commentaries on Aristotle, but in his discussion of the Unmoved Mover reaffirms the concept of a necessitated universe.

The possibility that God had not created the world *ex nihilo,* in time, and of His own free will was anathema to the western recipients of the works of Aristotle. Consequently, the reaction to Aristotle's *Physics* and *Metaphysics*—at least those portions interpreted to deal with creation—was generally unfriendly and resulted in a series of condemnations throughout the thirteenth century. The most significant condemnation for medieval history of ideas was that of 1277, promulgated by Stephen Tempier, Bishop of Paris. It denied as heretical 219 somewhat ambiguous and repetitious propositions which modern scholars have attributed to Aristotle, his Arabic commentators, Averroes and Avicenna, and his Christian interpreters, Siger of Brabant and Aquinas (who had been dead three years). An important theme of these propositions was, as in all previous condemnations of the century, the idea of determinism. That God, ignorant of individual things, was not the providential intervener in history, and that the world had existed from eternity, are ideas that recur on the list of heresies. The developments in Paris affected all of intellectual Europe. Eleven days after the Tempier condemnation, the Archbishop of Canterbury, Robert Kilwardly, condemned 30 similar propositions at Oxford. Similarly, as D. E. Sharp [in *Franciscan Philosophy at Oxford in the Thirteenth Century,* 1964] has shown, the Franciscan philosophers at Oxford in the thirteenth century (these include Robert Grosseteste, Thomas of York, Roger Bacon, John Pecham, Richard of Middleton, and Duns Scotus) deny to a man the eternity of the world and see creation as a product of the divine will, even as they are busy incorporating other aspects of Aristotelianism into their vocabularies and their systems.

This articulated horror of determinism which characterizes the thirteenth-century reaction to Aristotle had far-reaching effects on the fourteenth and fifteenth centuries. In particular, attention came to be focussed on God's omnipotence, since the most effective way to combat the notion of God's lack of freedom seemed to be to argue that as an all-powerful Being God could do anything He willed. The fourteenth century sees a new

emphasis on God's will, which is now elevated above His reason. In contradistinction to the thirteenth-century synthesis in which God was known chiefly through the laws and operations of His creation, there is a growing dichotomy in the fourteenth century between the omnipotent creator and His works. Anything that suggested a limitation on God's freedom to act as He willed, that made God the servant of His laws, was now downplayed, and most divine characteristics—including infinity, justice, goodness, omniscience—receded into the background as omnipotence came to dominate all discussions. We can see that in fourteenth-century commentaries on the *Sentences* of Peter Lombard, the theological textbook of the Middle Ages, many of the proofs of God's existence, His nature, and His attributes are missing, or greatly reduced and subsumed under the attribute of will.

A most significant distinction is now made between God's ordained power (*potentia ordinata*), that is, the power by which he created and sustains the world, and His absolute power (*potentia absoluta*), His omnipotence, which is outside of time and space and "uncommitted to upholding any set order in the universe." This distinction had been used earlier, notably by Peter Damian in the eleventh century [in *De Divina Omnipotentia*], to preserve God's freedom of action, but now in the fourteenth century it was taken up with new vigor. Where in the past philosophers had considered the workings of God in human affairs to be their major subject of study, leaving His absolute powers outside their ken, now the positions are reversed and absolute power becomes the principal concern.

The focus on God's omnipotence is especially noticeable in nominalist thought. While Duns Scotus used the idea of omnipotence to assert the contingency of all things upon God's will, Ockham goes a step further with the concept of divine power to show that God has no need to follow any preordained order; He can will and do anything, even things contrary to the laws of the universe as we know it. Ockham, for example, postulates an experience of seeing a star in the sky although that star does not actually exist. Its effect on us has been produced by God (miraculously) since He can produce and conserve immediately whatever He produces by means of secondary (i.e., created) causes. In Ockham's words, "intuitive cognition of a non-existent object is possible by divine power. I prove this first by the article of faith 'I believe in God the Father almighty' which I understand in the following sense: Anything is to be attributed to the divine power when it does not contain a manifest contradiction." As Boehner has pointed out, the star is present to our vision through God's absolute power, not through His ordained power.

The fascinating idea of God's omnipotence as expounded by Ockham gave rise to numerous paradoxes in the works of his English followers. God could cause men

The Abbey Gate; Chester.

to hate Him; He could overrule a state of beatitude or save the damned; God could deceive and lie, and could cause Christ to deceive His own disciples, because what He reveals in the Word of God may never come to pass. Robert Holcot, Adam of Woodham, and Thomas Buckingham were the three fourteenth-century Ockhamists who perhaps took these paradoxes to their extreme. To make the claims that Ockham's followers made was to stray far from orthodoxy, even though, as we have seen, the initial impulse was that of protecting the faith. The result was that the rational foundations of faith were undermined; as God became increasingly unknowable except by faith, philosophical inquiry into His nature ceased to command the attention it had in the twelfth and thirteenth centuries, and attention was refocused on the human sphere which was still open to proof and demonstration. One of the charges levelled against the nominalists, in fact, was that they paid too much attention to purely human capabilities and endeavors in achieving salvation and forgot the priority of God's grace.

Thus the orthodox reaction to Aristotle spawned a new unorthodoxy, some aspects of which were in turn condemned by Church authorities, notably Thomas Bradwardine, the Archbishop of Canterbury. Bradwardine's *De Causa Dei contra Pelagianos* attacks nominalist views on grace and future contingents, but what I find most signifcant is that although Bradwardine is Ockham's opponent in many areas, he operates in the same philosophical arena as all the other fourteenth-century thinkers: he addresses himself to the question of God's will and its relation to the world and, by quite a different route than the Ockhamists, ends up buttressing the idea of God's absolute sovereignty and His transcendence over the rationally knowable universe. In the end, all fourteenth-century philosophers whether Realists or Nominalists, Augustinians or Thomists (which is not to suggest that there were not very real differences between these schools, philosophically and theologically) feel the need to defend the idea of God's absolute power against the threat of determinism. In doing so, they all assert God's essential freedom and ultimate inscrutability.

The **Chester plays** stop short of the extreme nominalism which argued that God's incarnation as a man was not necessary: by means of His absolute power He could have been incarnated as an ass or even a stone. Similarly, **Chester's *Last Judgment*** play is far too traditional theologically to hint that God could love the damned or hate the righteous. Rather, the divine ability to penetrate all excuses and lies to see the truth about each human life becomes the supreme example of God's power, as "Justicarius Damnatus" ruefully admits. Recalling his lifelong practice of advocating false causes, he realizes, "before the Judge of such posty / that me will not avayle".

Nevertheless, the formulation that God is, above all things, omnipotent, the blending of other characteristics into that of divine power, the stress on the divine freedom of action, which are typical of nominalist thought, are to be found in the **Chester cycle**. The other cycles offer various descriptions of God—His wisdom, love, beauty, justice, truth, righteousness. **Chester** is almost exclusively concerned with the one concept of omnipotence. **Chester's** simplicity, its singlemindedness, are not, I suspect, clues to its folk origins, as some have suggested; **Chester** is, instead, closer than the other cycles to the philosophical preoccupations of the fourteenth and fifteenth centuries, and thus more influenced by the nominalist inhibition about discussing God in terms other than power.

At the specific level of dialogue we find in **Chester** statements typical of the nominalist exposition of God's omnipotence. It should be noted that similar statements may occasionally appear in the other English cycles; what differentiates **Chester** from them, and nominalism from its predecessors, is not any one claim or any one idea but the emphasis that claim receives within the total dramatic work or philosophical system. Philosophers and theologians before Ockham certainly believed in and used the concept of the two powers of God (*potentia ordinata, absoluta*), but it was only in the nominalist system that divine omnipotence came to play such a central role. For all the cycles, too, God is automatically "God omnipotent, that made heaven and earth and firmament"; but only in **Chester** is that idea transformed into a motif which is echoed in nearly every reference to God within the cycle, which shapes both the portrayal of Christ and the response of His followers and His antagonists. It is perhaps not accidental that the words cited above from the Apostles Creed—words which are offered by nominalists as the basis for their belief in God's *potentia absoluta*—are to be found in **Chester** (*Sending of the Holy Ghost*, ll. 311-58), alone among all the cycles.

The cycle and nominalist theology emphasize, above all, that God could potentially do anything He wants.

The *potentia Dei absoluta* means that "nothing to Gods myght and mayne / Impossible is" (*Nativity*). An interesting version of this statement, theologically as well as artistically instructive, is made by Jesus in the garden just prior to the betrayal. The vivid and well-known Biblical model for Christ's prayer is, "Father, *if it is possible, let this cup pass away from me, yet not as I will but as thou willest*" (Matt. 26:39). The Towneley Christ stays very close to the Biblical wording, with His submission of human to divine will (*Conspiracy*); the York Christ is more lyrical in expressing His agony, but when He makes the request to be spared the Passion, He also echoes the Bible, "if it possible be" (***The Agony and the Betrayal***). The N-town version is so free and far removed from the Bible that it is, for our purposes here, not relevant.

The **Chester** Christ, however, addresses his request to God in words that are significantly different because they are so recognizably close to the Bible. It is clear that the dramatist still has the original speech in mind, but chooses to change it slightly. He transforms a request based on a conditional *if* into a strong statement about God's absolute power: "All thing to thee possible is; / nevertheless, now in this, / at your will I am, iwys; / as thou wilt let it be" (***Christ's Betrayal***). To use the "if" of the original would be to suggest that God was not omnipotent, that He was in some way bound to carry through the Passion—that he was necessitated, the very specter that nominalist theology was most concerned to exorcise. The writer thus clears God's absolute power by affirming it first; God could, if He willed it, change the course of redemption history, even at the last hour. Yet the ordained events will take place: Christ will die on the cross. The change in the line shows that the Passion represents God's freely wielded *potentia ordinata*. The demands of the dramatist's theology are satisfied by the revision, with the result that one more line of dialogue has been shaped toward the cycle's overall theme of divine omnipotence. We cannot do justice to the uniqueness of this cycle if we do not appreciate the way even such small details contribute to the dramatization of the major theme.

The statement analyzed above carries with it the implicit message that although God did create the world, He might just as plausibly have created another order, or none at all. The thoroughly contingent nature of the created universe is emphasized in **Chester** by God's repetition of "through my might" and "all at myne owne will," as well as by the recognition on the part of many characters that they hold their power and authority only through God's might. For the most part, the events in the cycle that are attributed to God's power belong to the realm of His *potentia ordinata*, to the order of creation and history. However, God can also reveal His power and His nature by contravening the laws of nature and doing what seems impossible. It is as a logical extension of the idea of divine freedom that nominalism shows renewed interest in God's potential for immediate intervention in the world, bypassing ordained laws and structures. The possibility of miracles is an index of God's *potentia absoluta*; a miracle pulls back the curtain to reveal both the contingency of His creation and the omnipotennce of God. In **Chester,** the miracles are always proofs for their witnesses of the divine omnipotence. For Nichodemus at the crucifixion, the mourning of the elements—the eclipse of the sun, the earthquake—and the dead rising from their graves are events that show Jesus' power over the natural universe and its laws: "I may say he is god Almight / such Signes that can show" (***Passion***).

Within the cycle, as for nominalism, "miracles are probable reasons which engender the act of faith." As we have noticed, each witness to a miracle testifies that it functioned to make him believe in the divine power, even if he could not rationally comprehend it. The observation that man cannot fully understand the workings of God's power, which are infinitely above human reason, is a favorite theme in the sermons of three fifteenth-century nominalists: Geller, Gerson, and Biel. The nominalists as a group seem to have regarded themselves as superior to other philosophers in this respect; Pierre D'Ailly says that the nominalists "unlike others, go to adore the poor infant in the manger, recognizing the impotence of profane science to reveal the divine secret." We hear this idea in the **Chester** *Ascension* where Jesus, in response to a query from Phillip, refuses to reveal the future: "Brother, that is not to thee / to know my fathers privity; / that towcheth his owne posty, / wyt that thou never may."

An inscrutable God of free will and absolute power who rules over an essentially contingent creation might seem to elicit only terror and humility from His creatures but, paradoxically, nominalist theology pictured man as a creature of free will as well as substantial natural capability for right behavior. Holcot and Biel, for example, reject Bradwardine's image of man as God's instrument in favor of the idea that man is God's partner through a covenant into which man freely enters. In the **Chester cycle** also, the individual is never so subservient that His freedom of will is ignored. It is typical of this cycle that Noah and Abraham are God's "servants free" while Mary is His "maiden free" and Peter, Phillip, and other apostles are "my Brethren free." This repeated adjective may be a small point to bring up, but the epithet does not occur in the other cycles and in **Chester** it does contribute to a certain dignity which all the characters possess. They recognize God's sovereignty, but they never grovel in obeisance or succumb to displays of emotion as York or Towneley characters are apt to do. This dignity is all the more impressive since, as we have seen, the **Chester** character usually speaks directly with God Himself.

The peculiar combination of divine omnipotence and human efficacy that characterizes both the theology of nominalism and the **Chester cycle** becomes more intelligible when we see that its focus is on deeds, the active life rather than the passive death of Christ. Oberman, in his discussion of Gabriel Biel, a mainstream nominalist of the fifteenth century, notes that this aspect of nominalist thought seems almost a return to pre-Anselmian interpretations of Christ. The image of a suffering Christ, dying on the cross to expiate the sins of mankind, is largely replaced by the image of a victorious Christ, whose fulfillment of God's work on earth culminates in the Harrowing of Hell and the Resurrection. The Devil, who had been considerably demoted by Anselm, was again the great enemy of mankind, holding men in bondage until Christ proved His superior power through His perfect deeds. *Christus Victor* functions not as focus for man's loving sympathy but as the model for man's imitation in life. Man is asked to demonstrate his freedom from the Devil's power by actively following the lead of Christ.

The congruence between this outline of nominalist Christology and the outstanding features of **Chester's** portrayal of Christ cannot, I think, be denied; it provides the strongest support for the argument that what we have in **Chester cycle** is not the earnest and most conservative cycle, but the one closest to the prevailing trends in theology in the late Middle Ages. The **Chester** Christ is a figure distinguished for His persuasive deeds, His active fulfillment of God's will during His life. In death His aim is not so much the merciful replacement of mankind on the cross but victory over the Devil. Thus the unique scene in the ***Chester Ascension*** in which Jesus shows his bloody wounds and clothing. Entering heaven, He astonishes the angels with His display of power: "Comely he is in his clothinge, / and with full power goeinge; / a number of sayntes with him leading; / he semes great of posty". On the basis of His victory, Christ is able to rescue men from the power of Hell. When the angels ask about His bloody appearance Jesus answers: "for the Devill and his power, / that mankynd brought in great Dangere, / through death on Crosse and bloud so clear, / I have made them all myne". The drops of blood are, he continues, symbols of his victory, to be presented to God the Father in earnest of Jesus' promise to good men: "for good workes that they wrought, / everlasting blisse that they sought, / to prove the good worthy".

The same interpretation of the Passion is offered in the **Chester** *Last Judgment,* where Jesus displays the instruments of the Passion and again discusses the significance of His blood. The purpose of the scene is to prove God's omnipotence over the Devil and inspire man to righteous deeds. The comparable scene in the York and Towneley *Judgments* (which are substantially identical) highlights the pain Christ suffered in the scourging, the crowning with thorns, the torments of the crucifixion itself. Over and over Christ stresses that it was done out of love for man, and in return asks love; the effect of the scene is pathetic and its purpose is to elicit loving sympathy: "All this I suffered for thi sake, / Say man, what suffered thou for me?" (York, *Judgment,* II). For the **Chester** Christ, however, the enemy is not seen as man's sin or his indifference but the Devil. The blood is shed, Christ says, "to prive the Devyll of his posty, / and winne that was away". The blood was then presented to the "father Almighty / at my Ascention" with the plea that God show mercy to man. Far from symbolizing Christ's humanity and vulnerability, the blood proves His divinity: "behould on me, and you may leere / whether I be god in full power, / or ells man onely". Furthermore, because the blood signifies the divine omnipotence and efficacy, it should teach those who perform good deeds that they will earn bliss and those who "dyd amys" that they will be damned. The divine victory is designed to call forth man's own fullest powers for it promises that those who do their best will be rewarded. Christ's omnipotence is the guarantee for the fulfillment of the promise.

It is thus—in ways ranging from the variation on a single line of dialogue to the portrayal of character and the structuring of entire episodes—that **Chester** becomes a paean to an all-powerful God. Our appreciation of the artistic achievement of the **Chester cycle** is surely impaired if we do not perceive God's omnipotence to be the theme that shapes the entire cycle. But the impetus toward this theme is more than purely aesthetic; it is theological. Where some of the philosophical speculation of the late Middle Ages may seem capricious in its exposition of God's omnipotence, the drama does not, for it is concerned with putting the divine power to use. The efficacy of God's power to achieve salvation for those who have faith in it motivates the appearance of the theme in the Chester cycle—as Jesus says to His disciples and to the audience of this Christian drama: "Who so to this will consent, / that I am god omnipotent, / as well they that be present, / my Darlinges shal be aye" (*Appearance to Two Disciples*).

The focus of this paper has been **Chester cycle** itself, but the importance of the idea of divine omnipotence in the cycle raises a number of questions for which our present knowledge of the theological background of the late Middle Ages gives no ready answers. What were the routes of transmission between the universities, where the philosophers and theologians discussed the two powers of God, and the religious vernacular drama? Sermons were presumably the chief route, as Oberman suggests, yet few of the sermons of the period have been edited and studied in relation to nominalist theology. How, specifically, did the Chester dramatist gain access to these ideas, in particular to a Christology which differs radically from that commonly accepted as the late medieval norm? The theologians who have been most thoroughly studied so far are continental. The presence of "nominalist" Christology in an English drama

cycle calls out for more research into English theology of the fourteenth and fifteenth centuries. In light of the need for such research the **Chester cycle** becomes a cultural artifact of great significance in the current re-evaluation of the intellectual history of the late Middle Ages.

Peter W. Travis (essay date 1982)

SOURCE: "The Development of the Chester Cycle: A Historical Analysis," in *Dramatic Design in the Chester Cycle,* University of Chicago Press, 1982, pp. 30-69.

[*In the excerpt below, Travis traces the dramatic history of the Chester Cycle pageants, and investigates issues regarding its authorship, sources, development, and cohesiveness.*]

The great Corpus Christi plays, one would like to think, are in many ways similar to the great English cathedrals. The cathedrals, like the cycles, are each the work of more than one master draftsman. The construction of each, we may assume, was originally undertaken in accordance with a fully developed plan of the whole; but because they were built up over several generations (at the least), each finished work is in fact a composite of various artistic precepts and techniques. Although as a consequence all are stylistically "impure," some or many of them may nevertheless have realized a final, unique, and "organic" perfection—a blend of styles and elements which no single draftsman (save the last) could ever have fully imagined. We admire a cathedral's achieved unity of form in part because we recognize that writ large in the work itself is the history of its construction. Presumably our admiration of a cycle's finished form would be similarly enhanced if we could discover its several layers of composition. But precisely how to identify those strata is a scholarly problem of no mean proportions. We know that certain laws apply quite strictly to a cathedral's building sequence: one is structural (the supporting piers of the nave, for example, must antedate the clerestory above); another is stylistic (because a certain cathedral's Lady chapel is Gothic, it must postdate the Romanesque chapel adjacent to it). But similar laws do not generally apply to a cycle's order of composition. Structurally, it does not appear imperative that a pageant on one subject be written earlier than a pageant on another. Stylistically, we can no longer assume that a cycle's so-called "Gothic" elements (realistic, humorous, sensational) are all later additions to a core of early "Romanesque" plays (sober, hieratic, didactic). Indeed, the texts of the cycles as they stand before us now are as much akin to well-worn palimpsests as to cathedrals: one or two hands beneath the surface script may at times be visible—but in many cases one suspects that only very sophisticated techniques, comparable in their power and objectivity to ultraviolet light, could successfully discriminate all the underlayerings of a cycle's composition.

I
The Documents and Studies
Related to Chester's Development

Of the four English cycles, **Chester** is in fact the one which appears least receptive to any sort of "palimpsest" scrutiny. The text of the N-Town cycle, it has been shown, underwent at least five revisions in the course of its history. Although critics still argue about the number of layers apparent in the texts of the York cycle and the Wakefield cycle, agreement is nearly unanimous in identifying the respective pageants which were the work of those two dramatic geniuses, the York Realist and the Wakefield Master. But in **Chester** no Master has left his distinctive stylistic signature, nor does the cycle as a whole contain any very obtrusive patches or seams indicative of piecemeal revision. **Chester**'s apparent stylistic and thematic homogeneity could signify that the early cycle, once completed, was revised little, or that perhaps it was later revised once and completely; if either inference is true, there would be little profit now in looking internally for layers of compositional accretion. However, two matters militate against both of these suppositions. The first is that **Chester,** despite its impressive interior consistencies, is clearly a composite of pageants constructed in quite different ways: some have an Expositor figure, for example; some juxtapose two "plays" to form one pageant; some are written predominantly in cross-rhyme, rather than tail-rhyme, stanzas; some are obviously influenced by *A Stanzaic Life of Christ;* others are influenced by Peter Comestor's *Historia Scholastica;* some are highly indebted to the Gospel of Saint John; some include French; others use live animals; one is influenced by a York pageant; another is influenced by a noncyclical play; and so on. It is possible that one playwright or one reviser was responsible for all of these variant dramatic constructions. But considering how much the three other cycles were fitfully revised over the course of their two-hundred-year histories, it would not appear very likely that **Chester**'s twenty-four extant pageants were all the creation of one playwright or all the recreation of one reviser. The second matter is that because there are a number of surviving dramatic records, we need not restrict ourselves entirely to an "interior" study of the literary texts themselves. Among the surviving cycles, **Chester** is in fact second only to York in its wealth of civic and guild records relating to the production of the plays. To learn if and how the **Chester cycle** changed over time, therefore, it will be useful first simply to gather for perusal all the records and documents that could assist in such a venture.

The **Chester cycle** survives in not one but five manuscripts (with a sixth manuscript for two of its pageants and a part of a third). Attached to three of the full-cycle manuscripts are the Chester Late Banns: composed and revised between 1548 and 1572, these post-Reformation banns describe in some detail the cycle's twenty-four pageants and ascribe them to their proper guild or guilds. Copies of the Late Banns are also included in two versions of Archdeacon Robert Rogers' Breviary: this Breviary, a personal collection of antiquarian documents, includes a number of unique references to the **Chester plays,** among them a possible eyewitness account of how the pageants were performed processionally through the city streets over Whitsuntide. The cycle's Early Banns also have survived, although in only one copy: revised at least once between 1521 and 1532 (and later partially excised), these banns may perhaps still contain evidence of the cycle's earlier, fifteenth-century, configurations. Revised at about the same time as the Early Banns (and later partially excised) is William Newhall's Proclamation—an announcement of the plays which claims to identify, as do the Late Banns, the cycle's original playwright and time of first performance. The earliest unretouched document to indicate the number, order, and identity of the cycle's pageants, however, is a single-leaf list of dramatic guilds (Harley 2104) dated by calligraphic tests to circa 1500. Finally, there is the Harley 2150 List of Companies, composed after 1548, and the invaluable "dramatic" civic and guild records of the city of Chester, recently edited by Lawrence Clopper for *Records of Early English Drama.*

One striking characteristic of these documents is that they are almost all very late. The earliest version of the Rogers' Breviary is dated 1609/10—that is, about thirty-five years after the cycle's final performance. The five cycle manuscripts, transcribed between 1591 and 1607, postdate the plays' last production—and thus their last acting texts—by about a generation. The three individual pageant manuscripts, the Early and the Late Banns, the Newhall Proclamation, the Harley Guild List and the Harley List of Companies are all sixteenth-century documents. And of the hundreds of civic and guild records that pertain directly to the production of the **Chester cycle,** no more than twenty can confidently be dated prior to 1500. Thus it would seem, at least at first glance, that only the last seventy-five years of the cycle's history could be described with any amount of accuracy. A second significant characteristic of the extant Chester documents is that few have survived unchanged. The Proclamation and the Early Banns were both revised and excised—apparently because the cycle was changed and because the Reformation effected a change in the official attitude toward the plays. The Late, post-Reformation, Banns were amended at least twice, and were perhaps revised somewhat to accord with later revisions in the cycle. The revisions most easily documented are those of the Rogers' Breviary, which was composed and then three times recomposed (by Rogers' son David) over a span of fourteen years. The result is that four different and somewhat contradictory versions survive: for example, we are given four different dates for the cycle's first performance—1329, 1332, 1339, and 1328. Thus these dramatic documents are sometimes like palimpsests themselves: their own layers of composition demand scrutiny before the evidence they contain may be used to assist in discovering the cycle's layers of compositional growth. Finally, matters are made even slightly more complicated by the emotional allegiances evident in some of these late documents—namely, a civic pride which may have exaggerated the antiquity of "these anchante playes," and a post-Reformation prejudice against the plays' so-called "Clowde of Ignorance" which may have clouded commentary on more empirical matters as well. Although late, Chester's "empirical" documents are plentiful and useful; but they often are as rife with "textual" problems as are the dramatic texts themselves.

Among the scholars who have attempted to discover evidence of **Chester's** dramatic development, only a few have relied exclusively on internal data. These studies, each concentrating on a single pageant, have employed metrical, linguistic, and stylistic criteria for the bases of analysis (supported then by "literary" evaluation) to prize apart strata of composition. Oscar Brownstein [in "Revision in the 'Deluge' of the Chester Cycle," *Speech Monographs* 36, 1969], for example, has determined that eight or ten stanzas near the center of the **"Noah"** pageant constitute a late addition to an earlier and more unified play; Bernice Coffee [in "The Chester Play of *Balaam* and *Balak*," *Wisconsin Studies in Literature* 4, 1967], after examining the two different but closely related **Chester Balaam pageants,** concludes that the H MS play is the earlier and "better" version; and Hans-Jürgen Diller [in "The Composition of the Chester *Adoration of the Shepherds*," *Anglia* 89, 1971] has managed to descry three layers of composition in the Shepherds pageant, the earliest constituting a "nuclear core" which contains a mixture of both comic and sacred elements. Neither these nor any other similar study, however, attempts to date the original composition or the time of its revision; none claims that the selected pageant's recomposition is in any way paradigmatic of the entire cycle's; nor does any such study even ask why the pageant, or the cycle, was ever revised. Perhaps the resolution of such problems requires first a complete textual, stylistic, linguistic, and metrical analysis of the entire cycle. But this sort of major "palimpsest" study of **Chester** is probably more than a single scholar could or should undertake, and would require among other things the full resources of a computer as well as an unusually rich and sensitive computer program.

The majority of critical inquiries concerning the development of the **Chester cycle** have been based upon external documents and upon the question of their proper interpretation. Among the many significant contributions in this area, the most reliable work has been that of Lawrence Clopper, whose recently published "The

History and Development of the Chester Cycle" [1978] will certainly remain definitive for decades to come. What neither Clopper nor any other recent critic has attempted, however, is an alignment of **Chester's** external and internal evidences to see whether they complement each other in ways whereby the overall pattern of **Chester's** compositions may be discerned. Such a venture was undertaken once, by F.M. Salter in his 1939-40 monograph "The Banns of the Chester Plays." Salter's study, concluding with a chart of the probable entry date of **Chester's** twenty-five pageants into the cycle and the probable development of each thereafter, is an important work of critical synthesis and conjecture; unfortunately, as Salter himself later admits [in *Mediaeval Drama in Chester*, 1955], he manipulated some of his material in order to sustain his supposition of the cycle's great antiquity. When one considers the range of editorial, historical, and critical contributions to the field of Chester studies since the time of Salter's article, it would seem appropriate to attempt again in an unbiased way the kind of integration Salter had sought to achieve.

For several reasons, such an undertaking is in my judgment an appropriate beginning to the study of the **Chester cycle** itself. The question of **Chester's** dramatic development incorporates a number of important related problems—its authorship, the mode of its inception, its subsequent sources and influences, its manner of production, its means of support, and the relationships among its manuscripts. For the past generation (at least) these problems and scholars' attempts to resolve them have never been considered in one place. To review these issues here should be a service in itself, and will grant me the opportunity to offer my own judgments concerning several of them. . . . This survey (and it is meant in part to be just that) will acquaint the general reader not only with **Chester's** dramatic history but also with several of the more important studies of the cycle made during the "classical" period of medieval drama scholarship (that period, covering approximately the first half of this century, when anything but the cycle's dramatic excellence was normally considered fit material for examination). My attempt to uncover the cycle's earlier form will raise questions concerning the principles by which the cycle has been variously unified over time. That is, one may ask whether the designs employed by an early playwright were the same as those used by a later reviser, and whether the last reviser of the cycle must necessarily be accepted as the best. Indeed, it logically follows from these questions to ask whether those "deep structures" an ingenious critic is wont to discover within a cycle's final form could in fact ever have been intended by any one of its revisers. My primary intent here is to review **Chester's** dramatic history and to offer a new thesis concerning its development. In addition, however, this chapter is meant as a specific historical foundation and a theoretical corrective to all the formal arguments which follow.

Because of the several purposes of this chapter, I have chosen to focus upon three critical phases in **Chester's** dramatic history, each raising a different set of interpretive problems. The cycle's beginnings are the major concerns of part II; since no contemporary documentation of the cycle's origin has survived, what this means is a cautious review of the Chester "legends." These "legends" (which need by no means be all untrue) are of two sorts: those propounded in the sixteenth century by Chester citizens and those propounded in the twentieth century by critical conjecture. To balance my own rather tentative suggestions concerning the cycle's early design, I will offer in part III a fairly bold hypothesis concerning the expansion of that design circa 1519, as the cycle was shifted from its one-day performance on Corpus Christi to its three-day performance during Whitsuntide. Here I will argue that the careful alignment of internal and external evidence may reveal in considerable detail the elements of the earlier, fifteenth-century Corpus Christi play, as well as some of the principles which were employed to give unity to the newly expanded Whitsun cycle. In part IV, finally, as I trace the last years of the cycle's production history, I will attempt to determine from among the five surviving cycle manuscripts those variants which belong, and those which clearly do not belong, to the cycle's finished form. In doing so, I will once again raise the question of dramatic unity. . . .

II
The Inception and Early Form
of the Chester Cycle

Newhall's Proclamation, the Early Banns, the Late Banns, and two of the five versions of the Rogers' Breviary agree that "Sur Iohn Aneway was maire of this Citie/ when these playes were begon truly." However, there is little agreement among these documents concerning the play's authorship. The Proclamation asserts that it was Sir Henry Francis, "monk of this. . .monesty" (Saint Werburg's Abbey), who wrote the plays and gained from Pope Clement and the bishop of Chester numerous days' pardon for those who resorted peaceably to the plays. The Late Banns, however, state that the **Chester plays** were "the deuise of one Rondoll Moncke of Chester Abbaye," as do in fact all versions of the Breviary except the Lysons copy, which contends: "These playes weare the worke of one Rondoll higden a monke in Chester Abaye." All versions of the Breviary agree, however, that the plays were first performed circa 1330: either 1329, 1332, 1339, or 1328. If any sense is to be made out of these various statements of putative fact, it appears that four matters must be settled in conjunction: whether or not the plays were first performed during the mayoralty of John Aneway (Arneway), Chester's most famous mayor; whether or not they were first performed circa 1330; whether or not the play's author was Henry Francis, monk Rondoll, or Chester's most famous man of letters, Randle (Ran-

ulph) Higden; and whether or not at the time of the play's composition there was a Pope Clement in Rome. There are several problems here. John Arneway (who was erroneously believed to have been Chester's first mayor) died in 1278, and thus could not have been the plays' champion circa 1330. There were three Pope Clements in the fourteenth century: Pope Clement V (1305-14), Pope Clement VI (1342-52), and Antipope Clement VII (1378-94). Obviously none could have granted pardons to Chester playgoers circa 1330, although Clement VI could have a decade or two later. Ranulph Higden, author of the *Polychronicon,* died in 1364 and thus could have composed the plays in the 1340s; however, it is quite likely that Higden knew no English. Finally, Henry Francis, who was abbot of Saint Werburg's in the 1370s and 1380s, could have been the plays' author; but it is unthinkable that he would have sought indulgences from an antipope at Avignon.

Several scholars have tried to make sense out of this welter of contradictory materials. In *The Mediaeval Stage* (1903), E.K. Chambers suggests that Higden was the plays' author, and that the appropriate mayor was Richard Herneys—a man "bearing a name very similar to Arneway's"—who held office from 1327 to 1329; "About 1328 is just the sort of date to which one would look for the formation of a craft-cycle. However, in 1945 Chambers concedes that the notion of Higden's authorship is "not very plausible." In *Mediaeval Drama in Chester* (1955), F.M. Salter opts for Henry Francis as the plays' begetter, suggesting that the pope in question may have been Urban VI, and dismissing the Arneway and Higden attributions as propaganda for the plays' antiquity and excellence. In *English Religious Drama* (1955), Hardin Craig restores Higden to authority as the man who translated the plays (from the French) around 1328; he suggests that it was probably Henry Francis who later went to Rome (apparently to Clement VI) to seek papal indulgence. In his recent study of the Rogers' Breviary, Lawrence Clopper dismisses—as did Salter—the Arneway and Higden material as local fiction; he passes no judgment on the Proclamation's assertions concerning Henry Francis and Pope Clement; and he concludes that we are unlikely ever to discover the plays' authorship, although "it is conceivable that a man named Rondoll did write most of them and that, as time passed, this monk was identified with Chester's well-known historian.

My own position is that in these documents no assertion concerning the cycle's inception is likely to be trustworthy, and that scholarly attempts to identify **Chester's** authorship and birth date have often in the past been unduly influenced by prior assumptions about when it should have been conceived. **Chester** has traditionally been held up as the oldest of the English cycles, but in plain fact the first firm evidence of the cycle's existence is a guild record dating from 1422. If one were to accept the only assertion in these documents about which there is no disagreement—that Arneway was mayor when the plays began—then the **Chester cycle,** established before 1278, would antedate by at least fifty years the introduction of the Corpus Christi feast and by at least a hundred years the first solid evidence of the existence of any other English cycle. This is highly unlikely. I would prefer to appreciate the Arneway, Higden, Francis, and Pope Clement stories as all similar phenomena: late legendary constructions answering the need to have the plays' origins explained in ways which made them central to the city's cultural history. Quite a different phenomenon, however, is the David Rogers 1329/-32/-39/-28 syndrome: here we see an antiquarian's vexed attempts to make historical sense out of a host of unreliable records. All that is left, then, is monk Rondoll: it is possible that he is the cycle's original author, and his belonging to a cloistered order (rather than a secular or mendicant one) could shed some light on the plays' original "spirit." However, I think it best to leave the **Chester plays** anonymous, to suggest in passing that the **Chester cycle** may very well not be the oldest English cycle, and then to turn to related matters where conjecture is perhaps more likely to shed some light on the plays' original form and purpose.

Scholars in the past have not been reluctant to describe in some detail the manner of the cycles' creation, their original elements, and the place and day of their first performance. In the case of the **Chester cycle,** Glynne Wickham's scenario has been the fullest and most imaginative. Wickham suggests in volume 1 of *Early English Stages* (1959) that **Chester** existed first as a Latin play similar in shape to the 1303 Italian Montecassino Passion: opening with the fall of man and closing with Antichrist and the Last Judgment, the rest of the play consisted of Christ's ministry, Passion, and Resurrection. Acted by clerics in the large area before the gates of Saint Werburg's Abbey, the plays were performed on Midsummer (the birthday of Saint John), known locally in Chester as Saint Werburg's Day. During Arneway's mayoralty, Wickham fancies, the play shifted from Midsummer to Whitsun; some time later (apparently after 1350) the play was changed from Latin into English—"closely modelled on the liturgical Latin drama but not a literal translation of it, and written by ubiquitous friars rather than by officiating priests." Wickham's full-blown vision of Chester's early years at least has the advantage of covering almost every major problem one would like to see resolved. Like a number of other critics, Wickham is convinced that, since the cycles apparently could not have been created ex nihilo, they must have been fashioned out of older plays. But there is absolutely no evidence that there existed in medieval England a Latin play of the length or the shape Wickham has imagined; in addition, most critics now agree that there can be recognized within the extant cycles very little evidence of the direct influence of liturgical drama. A corollary theory espoused by several

scholars is that the original **Chester cycle** was a translation of a long French play. Despite the existence of certain similarities between some episodes in Chester and some episodes in certain medieval French plays, this theory I believe, is equally untenable. What is more nearly possible, however, is that **Chester** was somewhat influenced by the long (now lost) London history-of-the-world play, which in turn may have been influenced by French sources. It is better, at any rate, to consider **Chester** not as a translation of any sort but as an original dramatic construction which drew upon a variety of sources the majority of which probably were nondramatic.

Wickham's hypothesis that the **Chester plays** were first produced for the Midsummer festivities is equally suspect, for all the empirical evidence we have indicates that the **Chester Corpus Christi play** was performed first on Corpus Christi day, and that it became known as the Whitsun plays when it was moved circa 1519 to the first three days of Whitweek. Nevertheless, Wickham's curiosities concerning the nearness in time (and spirit?) of the Whitsun, Corpus Christi, and Midsummer festivities deserve further rumination. We know that **Chester's** last performance (in 1575) was held on Midsummer rather than during Whitweek, and we know that at least toward the end of its history some of the cycle's most popular characters processed (and performed?) in the Midsummer Watch. The dishonest alewife shaking her "cuppes & cannes," for example, who appears in the records of the Watch as well as in four of the five manuscripts of the **"Harrowing of Hell"** pageant, may possibly have been first fashioned not for the cycle but for the secular festivities of Midsummer. Reputed to have been established in Chester in the eleventh century, containing festivities which some sixteenth-century reformers felt were "vnlawfull and not meete," the Midsummer holiday may have included as early as the thirteenth century (as it did elsewhere in England) dramatic productions of a popular nature. It is therefore worth wondering whether any dramatic or other activity from this secular holiday could have influenced the construction of the early **Chester cycle.**

To entertain the possibility of the initial influence of such secular activities may be at odds with the traditional assumption that the early cycles were perforce more somber, didactic, and spiritual than their later "Gothic" accretions. But it is worth noting that two scholars, Chambers and Salter, both apparently having started with this as one of their assumptions, conclude their search for the earliest form of the **Chester cycle** with a play that contains a full mixture of the popular and the pious, the "Gothic" and the "Romanesque." What is additionally striking about their attempts at rediscovering the early play is that they have envisaged a continuous drama performed stationarily (like popular folkplays) rather than individual pageants produced in ambulatory processions. Here is Chambers' scholarly intuition [from his *English Literature at the Close of The Middle Ages*, 1945]:

> I have an impression that behind the **Chester cycle,** as it has come down to us, lies a play of a more primitive type, the themes of which have been rather clumsily incorporated, with the result that discrepancies have been left in the action, which the late transcribers of the text have variously attempted to remove. The influence of the old play is clearest in those scenes in which an *Expositor,* also called *Preco, Doctor, Nuntius,* or Messenger, comments to the 'Lordinges' of the audience on the significance of the topics represented. He calls himself Gobet on the Grene, and his demands for "room" to be made, with the fact that both he and later the character *Antichristus* come in riding, suggest a stationary performance on a green or other open space, rather than one on moving pageants.

If Chambers is at all accurate in his reconstruction of a "primitive" play performed stationarily and dominated by the Expositor (Salter's reconstruction is in substantial agreement), a few elements in that play as well as the work of a few more recent scholars suggest that at its inception it could have been influenced by the nearly contiguous activities, dramatic and nondramatic, of Midsummer. Not only has Diller found in his "palimpsest" study of the "Shepherds" pageant that the pageant's earliest layer includes the popular entertainment-form of the wrestling match, but Richard Axton has reconfirmed the surprisingly high incidence in **Chester** of theatrical techniques typical of secular drama. Axton concludes:

> If the **Chester plays** were originally thought of (as they undoubtedly were in the sixteenth century) as in some sense a rival or alternative attraction to the Midsummer show, taking advantage of an established summer occasion of outdoor revels and folk-plays, then the festive style of much of the playing is placed in a new perspective. The use of formulae of presentation, the "game" with the audience, the repeated cries of "room!" are explicable as the inherited social framework of a popular drama, old secular bottles for new ecclesiastical wine.

The creative genius responsible for this new dramatic vintage, for this unusual integration of didactics and theatrical fun, may be—in theory at least—not hard to identify. The yoking together of high and low, of sacred and secular, is a technique—as several recent studies have shown—distinctive of the popularizing aesthetics of the Franciscans and by no means at odds with the sacramental themes of Corpus Christi. Where we are rapidly led, then, is back toward a reconsideration of Wickham's vision, parts of which are quite plausible. Perhaps in fact the **Chester cycle** in its original form was a stationary play rather than a processional production; perhaps it was a single long drama of a shape similar to the Montecassino Passion's; and perhaps its

original authors (or at least a major influence at its inception) were, in Wickham's words, those "ubiquitous friars." All of the conjectures in the preceding sentence I confess I am quite partial to; but in arriving at these conjectural conclusions, I am obviously reasoning in a fairly subjective way from circumstantial evidence.

As an antidote to these conjectures, we should remind ourselves that the first evidence even of the existence of the **Chester cycle** is a 1422 record of a dispute between two parties, the Fletchers, Bowyers, Coopers, Stringers, and Turners on the one side and the Ironmongers on the other, concerning their respective obligations *in luso Corporis christi* for producing the **"Flagellation"** pageant and the **"Crucifixion"** pageant. This single record itself indicates that the **Chester** play at this time was apparently a "cycle" of some sort; that it was apparently divided into individual pageants; and that each of these pageants was apparently the responsibility of a guild or group of guilds. Since these pageants were given on wagons, it would seem to appear a safe inference that they were performed—as in York and several other English cities—several times for different audiences along the Corpus Christi procession route. And, if we limit ourselves to those very few dramatic guild records which have survived from the fifteenth century, it would also appear a fairly safe inference that the early **Chester play** contained at least these scenes—if, that is, the guilds mentioned in these records were associated with the same plays then that they were in the sixteenth century: **Creation** (Drapers), **Nativity** (Wrights), **Magi** (Mercers), **Last Supper** (Bakers), **Flagellation** (Fletchers, etc.), **Crucifixion** (Ironmongers), **Emmaus** (Saddlers), **Ascension** (Tailors), **Pentecost** (Fishmongers), **Prophets of Doomsday** (Shermen), and **Last Judgment** (Weavers, Walkers, and Chaloners).

But because the empirical evidence surviving from between 1422 to 1500 is so sparse and so often cryptic, it would appear that even the most cautious inferences must border on conjecture and that conjectures concocted with little regard for (or knowledge of) this meagre evidence could possibly at times be quite correct. In this chapter, however, I would not have given such attention to the hypothetical reconstructions of **Chester's** beginnings did I not believe there was some truth in some of them. Nor would I have done so were I not confident that the validity of some could be substantiated by using more reliable evidence and more objective methods of reasoning. The pertinent pieces of evidence come surprisingly late: there are certain dramatic documents surviving from the early sixteenth century which, when examined together, may possibly suggest a good deal about the cycle's earlier career. Working with these records, Lawrence Clopper has given his support to the recently unpopular notion of the original Corpus Christi play's having been stationarily produced: the play was

Design for devil costume.

of the Chester Cycle

With the possible exception of its last performance in 1575, the **Chester cycle's** configurations in all likelihood changed most dramatically in the years between 1505 and 1532. It was during this time that the Corpus Christi play came to be called first (in 1521) the Whitsun play and then (by 1532 and thereafter) the Whitsun plays. And it was during this time that it shifted from its one-day Corpus Christi (and presumably stationary) performance to a processional and three-day performance during Whitsuntide. Although the play's gradually increasing size may well have been one cause for the shift in time and venue, the technical modifications which accompanied this change probably also required that the cycle be further revised and amplified as it gradually adjusted to its new environment. If these dramatic renovations can be determined with any certitude, we should be able to assess with considerably greater precision than before those elements which belonged to the cycle when it was a fifteenth-century Corpus Christi play. In addition, we may be able to discover from these renovations certain underlying principles—stylistic and structural—which unified the earlier Corpus Christi play and which were then revised at least somewhat to make the longer Whitsun cycle an equally coherent drama. To reach a point where these internal modifications may be scanned, however, one must begin with the pertinent external documents, most notably the Harley Guild List, the guild records, and the Early Banns. The first and foremost problem—as one comes to expect—is that the various sets of information supplied or suggested by these documents often appear to be mutually contradictory.

One of the most significant of Chester's guild records is the agreement made in August of 1531 or 1532 between the Goldsmiths and the Masons to share the pageant-wagon owned by the Vintners and the Dyers. As Salter first pointed out, this arrangement was eminently feasible (if the cycle's pageants fell into their normal Whitsuntide divisions): the Vintners' **"Magi"** was the penultimate play performed on Monday, the Goldsmiths' **"Herod"** opened the Tuesday sequence, and the Dyers' **"Antichrist"** was the penultimate play for Wednesday. As Clopper sensibly argues, this arrangement was agreed upon only at this time (rather than much earlier in Chester's history) because the cycle had just recently shifted to a three-day and processional performance—making it necessary that each play performed on a single day have its own wagon. It is likely that previous to this time, as both Salter and Clopper suggest, the Vintners shared with the Mercers a single **"Magi"** play, which may in fact also have been combined with the Goldsmiths' **"Herod"**; then, some time between 1521 and 1532, this dramatic material was divided and amplified to make up Paginae VIII, IX, and X. Our primary concern here is that the Early Banns, revised at least once between 1521 and 1532 in order to keep abreast

given, he reasons, not processionally but at the end of the Corpus Christi procession (probably before Saint John's Church) on pageant-wagons forming place-and-scaffold stages. Working with the same documents but also with the play texts themselves, I plan to identify most of the dramatic episodes which I believe have survived from the "old" play of Corpus Christi. I plan, in addition, to identify certain structural principles and stylistic features, first of the "old" Corpus Christi play and then of the "new" Whitsun cycle. And although I do not pretend to have rediscovered the **Chester play** at the moment of its conception, I claim that the configurations of the **Chester cycle** early in its career can now be seen with greater clarity than they have ever been seen before. To arrive at those configurations, and to evaluate with greater confidence all earlier conjectures, it is best therefore to turn to the cycle during those years, from 1505 to 1532, when it was revised, amplified, and shifted to a new time and a new mode of production.

III
The Whitsun Amplifications

of changes in the cycle, apparently retained in the varying number of lines describing the pageants indications of some of these changes. That is, all but six of the pageants are described in four-line half-stanzas; described by full stanzas or longer (and thus stanzas apparently revised) are the three pageants mentioned above (VIII, IX, and X), and also the Tanners' pageant (I), the Wrights' (VI), and the Shermen's (XXII). It has therefore appeared to follow that the pageants accorded anomalous stanza descriptions underwent revision, or were added to the cycle, after the original composition of the Early Banns but before their revision. This one quirky indicator is not likely to have registered all changes, but it should serve as an important criterion as we attempt to reconstruct the cycle's transformations during these years.

Another important document for the reconstruction of **Chester**'s shift to Whitsuntide is the Harley 2104 Guild List: this, in Clopper's judgment, was a list of those guilds which marched in the Corpus Christi procession before the Corpus Christi play. What is perhaps most notable about the list is the absence of three guilds that by the time of the Early Banns were responsible for three pageants in the cycle: the Tanners (**"Fall of Lucifer"**), the Cappers (**"Balaam and Balaak"),** and the Painters (**"Shepherds"**). Because the Early Banns describe the Tanners' play in an eight-line stanza, we may assume that it entered the cycle after the Early Banns' composition but before their revision; because the Cappers' and Painters' pageants are each accorded four-line half-stanzas, we may assume they entered the cycle before (perhaps only shortly before) the Early Banns' composition. We know that the play of the Shepherds was in existence in 1515/16, for it was then performed together with the **"Assumption of the Virgin"** in Saint John's churchyard. From another record we know that the Cappers had been granted special privileges by mayor Thomas Smyth so that they might "brynge forthe A playe concernynge the store of kynge balak & Balam the proffet"; Thomas Smyth was mayor of Chester in 1504-5, 1511-12, 1515-16, 1520-21, and 1521-22. From these bits of information we can conclude: that the Cappers' play entered the cycle no earlier than 1505 but no later than 1522, that the Early Banns were composed within this same period of time but after the Cappers' play entered the cycle; and that the Painters' pageant in all likelihood was brought into the cycle at approximately the same time. Since the Early Banns appeared to have been originally composed for the play performed on Corpus Christi, and since the play came to be called the Whitsun play in 1521, the probability is high that the Whitsuntide shift occurred near the end of the second decade. Perhaps Alan Nelson's suggestion that 1519 was the crucial year is correct: because the Corpus Christi feast coincided with the Midsummer Watch in 1519, the imminent conflict of activities may have been anticipated and resolved by advancing the plays to the previous, Whitsun, week. Between this time and 1531/32, when the Newhall Proclamation announced a three-day performance, a number of further and important changes were made in the cycle, and the Early Banns were consequently revised.

Since they entered the cycle within such a short time of each other, it is natural to wonder whether the Tanners', the Cappers', and the Painters' pageants could have been composed by the same playwright—and if so, whether this playwright's dramatic "signature" may then be discovered elsewhere in the cycle. But the only obvious stylistic idiosyncrasy (shared by just two of the three pageants) is a distinctive rhyme scheme: whereas the dominant rhyme scheme of the **Chester cycle** is tail rhyme (rime couée), the Tanners' play and a significant proportion of the Painters' play are written in cross rhyme. It is possible that the Tanners' playwright wrote or revised the Painters' pageant, and was responsible also for the occasional cross-rhyme passages that appear in the rest of the cycle—specifically, in Paginae III, V, VIII, X, XI, XVII, XVIII, and XXIII. This at least is the position taken by Salter, who talks confidently of the work of **Chester**'s "cross-rhyme redactor." But the dangers of assuming that any variation in stanzaic form is immediate evidence of a different authorial hand are self-evident. There is no prima facie evidence that a single dramatist could not have employed two or more rhyme schemes, nor is there any reason why two or more dramatists could not have employed the same rhyme scheme. If the "cross-rhyme redactor" added his pieces to the cycle for the Whitsun shift, it would seem to follow that the rest of the cycle, written primarily in tail-rhyme stanzas, constitutes the Corpus Christi play in its original form (the only major exception would have to be the two rather long rhyme-royal passages, in Paginae VIII and XIII, which presumably were added to the cycle very late in its history): this, in a general way, has been the assumption of a number of critics in the past. Salter's position, however, diverges from this assumption (as well as from the logic of his other contentions) in one regard: "The fact that the bulk of the **Chester Plays** come to us in a single stanza form," he writes, "is presumptive evidence of a very thorough revision *in toto* at some period." It would therefore seem best in such matters to proceed with considerable caution. We have determined that the two pageants with the highest proportion of cross rhyme in the cycle entered the cycle at approximately the same time; but the significance of this fact can be measured only after it has been integrated with the other forms of evidence we have been given.

Another possible indicator of the stages of **Chester's** development is the figure of the Expositor. Chambers and Salter, as we have seen, both work from the assumption that this didactic explicator must have been part of the original play; therefore elements of the pageants in which he now appears (Paginae IV, V, VI,

XII, and XXII) constituted a major portion of the cycle's first level of composition. But one of these pageants, the Cappers' play (V), we now know is a late addition, having entered the cycle early in the sixteenth century. If the Expositor is likely to have been the creation of only one playwright, or if he is the kind of paradramatic didactic figure which—as Chambers and Salter assume—would have been created at only one time in the cycle's history, it must follow that the five pageants listed above were devised or revised around the time of the Whitsun shift. This would of course effectively reverse certain standard assumptions about how the aesthetics of the cycles developed: rather than progressing from the "stolid" and "didactic" to the "playful" and "realistic," **Chester** may have developed a "naive" and "presentational" dramatic form in its early years, which in later years became more "self-conscious" and "self-interpretive." But surely the Expositor's appearing in a single late pageant does not preclude his having been invented or used by earlier Chester dramatists. It is possible, of course, that the Expositor and the episodes in which he appears are all the work of one sixteenth-century playwright; but, as with the matter of the cycle's variant rhyme schemes, the validity of the Expositor figure as a register of the cycle's development must be determined in conjunction with the other kinds of information supplied.

A final important register is one that, in all likelihood, had to be the work of a single playwright: the incorporation into the cycle of passages adapted from *A Stanzaic Life of Christ*. Written in Chester itself, the *Stanzaic Life* is a verse narrative (intercalated with numerous glosses) compiled from two famous Latin works, Ranulph Higden's *Polychronicon* and Jacobus de Voragine's *Legenda Aurea*. In the judgment of Frances Foster, editor of the EETS (1926) edition, the *Stanzaic Life* had to have been composed in the fourteenth century, although the manuscripts are all from the fifteenth century. This judgment she bases upon the fact that all the passages in the **Chester cycle** influenced by the *Stanzaic Life* are written in tail rhyme: and tail rhyme, she assumes, was the stanza from used exclusively by the cycle's original, fourteenth-century, playwright. But, as Robert Wilson has shown in his 1931 study ["*The Stanzaic Life of Christ* and the Chester plays," *North Carolina Studies in Philology* 28], if the passages obviously influenced by the *Stanzaic Life* are removed, there remains in most cases a fairly complete play; presumably, this play is the pageant in an earlier, if not its earliest, form. Thus it would seem apparent that the *Stanzaic Life* indeed was composed in the fifteenth century, as the manuscripts attest; and it would appear that the *Stanzaic Life* material was incorporated into the cycle not at its beginning but by a later reviser. However, it has never been determined when these amplifications were made.

In my judgment it is absolutely certain that the *Stan-*

zaic Life episodes were added to the cycle for the cycle's shift to Whitsuntide, and that the nature of these amplifications can in most cases determine or confirm the reliability of the criteria mentioned earlier (Expositor, rhyme schemes, etc.) as further registers of the Corpus Christi play's transformation into the Whitsun plays. . . .

The influence of the *Stanzaic Life* is quite easily measured in the case of six of **Chester's** pageants; in the case of a seventh, however, it is difficult to determine what, if anything, happened. As Utesch recognized in 1909 [in *Die Quellen der Chester-Plays*], the Cooks' **"Harrowing of Hell"** pageant in the **Chester cycle** conforms in its details and their sequence much more closely to the *Legenda Aurea* than to the traditional *Gospel of Nicodemus* account. But since the *Stanzaic Life's* source for its Harrowing of Hell account is also the *Legenda Aurea*, it appears impossible to determine which work served as the source for the Cooks' pageant (or if both did). My suspicion is that the **Chester "Harrowing of Hell"** was untouched by the *Stanzaic Life* reviser, and that its single source was the *Legenda*. This judgment I arrived at, however, only after examining the principles of expansion evident in those six pageants which obviously have been influenced by the *Stanzaic Life*. While examining these expansions, I will also consider the most distinctive dramatic techniques employed within them.

The most complicated expansion was probably that of Pagina VI., the Wrights' **"Nativity."** The "old play" appears to have contained the following episodes: the Annunciation, Mary's visit to Elizabeth, Joseph's troubles, and Octavian's ordering the poll tax; the meeting between Joseph and Octavian's messenger; the journey to Bethlehem, and finally the Nativity itself. Intercalated into this nearly perfect "old play" (presumably very little has been discarded) are four dramatic sequences adapted from the *Stanzaic Life*: the senators' advising the emperor's self-deification, and Octavian's consultation with the Sybil concerning the promised birth of a child-king; Mary's vision of the mournful and the happy men, which is then explained by an angel; Salome's doubting Mary's virginity, her punishment, and her restoration of faith; and a rather long concluding narrative given by the Expositor, concerning the prodigies which occurred at Rome at Christ's birth—into which is inserted the dramatic episode of Octavian's conversion.

Most of the other dramatic adaptations of the *Stanzaic Life* material were less complicated than the **"Nativity"**'s. To create Paginae VIII and IX as they now exist, a single early **"Herod and Magi" play** was evidently divided, and each part then was amplified by the addition of an episode taken from the *Stanzaic Life*. The first 112 lines of the Vintner's **"Magi"** (VIII) constitute an episode on Mount Victorial, as the kings await the star and then set out to Bethlehem on their dromedaries: all the details from this unusual dramatic scene—including our being informed that a dromedary "will goe lightly on his way/ an hundreth myles upon a daye"—are derived from the *Stanzaic Life*. Near the beginning of the Mercers' **"Offerings"** (IX), a passage has been inserted where the kings offer an extended, three-level exposition of the meaning of their gifts: these allegorical glosses are taken, almost line for line, from the *Stanzaic Life*. Two of the other pageants were no more complicated in their revisions. The Tailors' **"Ascension"** was simply split apart at the moment that Christ begins to ascend: added here is a powerful episode of ninety-nine lines adapted from the *Stanzaic Life*, dramatizing Christ's ascension as a prolonged rite of passage, with antiphons sung by Christ, by a chorus, and by angels who query his identity. The dramatic episode of Christ's temptation in the Butchers' pageant (XII) was apparently part of the early play of Corpus Christu; then, for the Whitsun shift, there was appended to that episode the Expositor's gloss—an interpretation of the significance of Christ's triumph over Satan taken from the *Stanzaic Life*. However, when it was that the pageant's second dramatic episode (the woman taken in adultery) and its gloss (given by the Expositor) were added to the cycle is not at all clear: it is certain, though, that neither this episode nor its exposition was influenced by the *Stanzaic Life*.

The final pageant influenced by the *Stanzaic Life* is Pagina XI. Known throughout its history simply as the **"Purification,"** the Blacksmiths' pageant comprises two major parts each of which reveals the influence of another work. The first part opens with Simeon's twice "correcting" the scriptural text prophesying the Virgin Birth, and an angel's twice restoring the original reading; this scene, climaxing with Simeon's acceptance of the miracle, is derived from the *Stanzaic Life* (ll. 2737-816). Then follows all that apparently remains of the earlier "Purification" play—Simeon's reception of the Holy Family in the temple. The pageant's second half is a cross-rhyme adaptation of York's "Christ among the Doctors." About half as long as the York play, **Chester's** version has translated about half its stanzas from the York pageant, successfully creating a new dramatic interpretation of Christ's youthful triumph in the temple. Because the relevant stanzas are scattered throughout both York and Chester, it is highly likely that no version of "Christ among the Doctors" existed in Chester before this adaptation.

Setting aside the problematic **"Harrowing of Hell"** pageant, I think a number of remarks can be made concerning these dramatic amplifications. First, in most cases it is quite easy to rediscover the major outlines of the old play and to see how it was opened up to receive its new *Stanzaic Life* material. The **"Nativity"** was divided at four places; the **"Magi"** and the **"Offerings"** were each given a new episode near the beginning; the **"Ascension"** was cleanly opened at its center; and the **"Temptation"** drama, presumably unchanged from its earlier form, simply had added to it the Expositor's theological gloss. Only the reconstruction of the **"Purification"** seems complicated—and these complications may be the result of Protestant attempts in the late sixteenth century to alter and amend this "Marian" play. In the case of the other pageants, it appears that little, or nothing, was discarded from the earlier Corpus Christi play: new episodes were simply added. Second, it is quite evident that the dramatic interests and aesthetic principles of the *Stanzaic Life* reviser differed considerably from those of the earlier, Corpus Christi playwrights. Each addition from the *Stanzaic Life* offers an increased emphasis upon the marvelous—whether upon sensational dramatic spectacle, upon the wondrousness of an explicated theological system, or upon the magic of divinely wrought miracles. Thus in the **"Nativity"** we find added Mary's prophetic vision (interpreted by an angel), the midwife's sensational expression of doubt ("corrected" by an angel) and numerous Roman prodigies (reported by the Expositor). In the **"Magi"** we are awed by the exotic sight of three live "dromedaries"; in the **"Offerings"** we are impressed by the theological neatness of the kings' threefold explication of their gifts. In the **"Purification"** the miraculous restoration of scriptural prophecy (itself auguring a miracle) is performed by an angel before our eyes; and in the **"Temptation"** the typological perfections of Christ's triumphs over the devil are fully explained by the attentive Expositor. Finally, and most impressively, we are offered in the **"Ascension"** an extended rite of passage as Christ processes in graduated stages through the clouds toward heaven. It is obvious that the earlier versions of these plays were less theatrically ambitious: closer to Scripture and to orthodox tradition, the early Corpus Christi pageants were more conservatively concerned with presenting biblical events for their own sake, rather than for their "higher" meanings or histrionic brilliance. The aesthetic principles of these two layers are therefore quite distinct: a powerfully naive drama which interpreted little and relied heavily on the numinous significance of faithfully reenacted sacred events; and a layer of later accretion often spectacularly theatrical and sometimes hyperactively committed to sensational effects and "high sentence." As we shall see in the forthcoming chapters, however, one of the most impressive characteristics of the pageants influenced by the *Stanzaic Life* is how intelligently and carefully the two aesthetics have been combined: the result in each case is a quite new, and newly unified, play having been fashioned out of the old.

That the *Stanzaic Life* reviser did not redesign all six of these pageants at once is indicated by the Early Banns: whereas Paginae VI (**"Nativity"**), VIII (**"Magi"**) and IX (**"Offerings"**) are accorded full stanza descriptions, Paginae XI (**"Purification"**), XII (**"Temptation"**), and XX (**"Ascension"**) are described in quatrains. Evidently, then, three were revised for (or before) the shift to Whitsuntide, whereas the other three (all performed on Whitmonday) were amplified for the three-day production. One reason for these amplifications may have been practical: in order to maintain a nearly continuous performance of the cycle at each station, it was necessary (as several time-studies have shown) to control quite carefully the lengths of individual pageants.

Thus to this point we have determined that three pageants (I, V, and VII) were added to the cycle early in the sixteenth century and that six others were revised at the same time (VI, VIII, IX, XI, XII, and XX). Is it possible to discover any further additions or amplifications made during this shift to Whitsuntide? I think it is, although the reasoning from this point on will be based on less solid evidence. First to be determined is whether or not the Expositor's appearances throughout the cycle are a consistent register of the cycle's expansion. In the case of three pageants, **"Balaam"** (V), **"Nativity"** (VI), and **"Temptation"** (XII), we have determined that the Expositor and his glosses were added early in the sixteenth century. Does this hold as well for the two other pageants in which he appears, IV and XXII? Pagina IV, the Barbers' **"Abraham, Lot, Melchysedeck and Isaac,"** clearly existed in some form in the fifteenth-century Corpus Christi play, because the Barbers appear in their proper place in the Harley 2104 Guild List. But one distinctive characteristic of this pageant is that its last part constitutes an adaptation and distillation of the Brome **"Abraham and Isaac"** play. Because only one other pageant in **Chester**, Pagina XI, clearly contains an adaptation of a dramatic source ("Christ among the Doctors" from York); because Pagina XI was undoubtedly expanded during the Whitsun shift; and because in both of these dramatic adaptations (**"Abraham and Issaac"** and **"Christ among the Doctors"**) the principles of compression are extremely similar, it is quite likely that both Paginae IV and XI are in their present form the work of the same redactor. In addition, it is worth noting that Pagina IV is constructed very similarly to Pagina V (which was added to the cycle between 1505 and 1522): each pageant is divided into three, discrete, "analogically related" units, and each is fully explicated by an Expositor. Finally (as we shall see fully in the next chapter) the design of salvation history these six dramatic units and their expositions support is so carefully patterned that it is extremely unlikely that the two pageants (IV and MS H of V) as they now exist were not the construction of a single craftsman.

There remains, therefore, only one other pageant in the cycle where the Expositor appears: the Shermen's **"Prophets of Antichrist"** (XXII), in which, as in Pagina V (H MS), the Expositor enters to interpret the augurings of each prophet. The similarity of construction between these prophecy/exposition episodes is itself suggestive; in addition, since we know (from the Harley 2104 Guild List) that Pagina XXII existed in the fifteenth century, whatever amplifications, if any, it may have been given would in all likelihood have involved not the prophecies themselves but expositions. This inference is well-nigh confirmed when we turn again to the Early Banns: the one remaining pageant accorded an "abnormal" (full-stanza) description is, in fact, the Shermen's **"Prophets of Antichrist."** Thus these two registers are mutually supportive: the Expositor's appearances and the Early Banns' variant-stanza descriptions prove to be consistently valid signs of a pageant's having been constructed or revised for the Whitsun shift. Chambers and Salter were therefore correct in assuming that the Expositor is an accurate indication of one layer of composition, but this layer I have determined was not the cycle's earliest; rather, in the early sixteenth century it constituted part of what was a major transformation of a kind of Passion play into a full-scale history-of-the-world cycle.

Of the remaining possible registers of the Whitsun shift, I think one is invalid and the other only sporadically meaningful. Salter assumed that the cycle's longest pageants were among the earliest, and that many of the shortest entered the cycle late. But no correlation can now be seen to exist between a pageant's length and age: its length was surely determined in large part by the events it presented (and how they were dramatized), also quite possibly by a guild's forceful contention that it merited a "sizeable" play and, in some cases, by the pageant's place in the processional "queue." Rhyme scheme, on the other hand, appears occasionally to be a valid sign of authorship, or layer of composition. For instance, it is quite likely that one playwright (the "cross-rhyme redactor," if you will) was responsible for Pagina I (**"Fall of Lucifer"**), Pagina VII (**"Shepherds"**), and (in Pagina XI) **"Christ among the Doctors."** But I can discover no shared significance among the few remaining patches of cross rhyme. According to W.W. Greg [in *Bibliographical and Textual Problems of the English Miracle Cycles*, 1914] "wherever a change of stanza occurs without discoverable reason we are justified in supposing that we have not got the play in its original form." But this rule of thumb simply does not work in **Chester**. We know that with the six *Stanzaic Life* pageants, although each is written throughout in tail rhyme, "we have not got the play in its original form"; conversely, in most of **Chester's pageants** where the rhyme scheme shifts "without discoverable reason," those shifts seem only an expression of poetic caprice. Thus, by itself, a pageant's changing rhyme schemes are usually too crude a register to serve as a measure of authorial signature. The two long rhyme-royal passages appear, nevertheless, to be an exception to the rule, and have universally been accepted as late sixteenth-century additions to Paginae VIII and XIII. However, because these two episodes have been so carefully integrated into their respective pageants, I suspect that they, too, were added to the cycle for the Whitsun shift.

It would seem useful now to summarize what this chapter's explorations have, and have not, ascertained so far. **Chester's** original configuration, authorship, and time and manner of inception—despite all conjecture—appear to be permanently beyond our ken. Almost equally as obscure is the development of the play during the fifteenth century, although some sparse evidence has survived. In the section above, I have succeeded in clarifying certain particulars concerning the play's development in the early sixteenth century; but even here there have been numerous issues not raised, let alone resolved—such as how many playwrights were involved in the Whitsun shift, the sequence of their additions, their variant dramatic styles, and so forth. Even as a "palimpsest" study, this chapter has managed so far to descry only two layers—one of these a rough conglomerate of all earlier compositions, the other comprising the Whitsun additions (all of which we probably have not found). Nevertheless, I think we can now see the old Corpus Christi play, circa 1500, more clearly than it has ever been seen before. Centered in its Passion/Resurrection sequence (which was changed little, if at all, during the Whitsun shift), completed by a Doomsday epilogue (also changed only slightly), the play of Corpus Christi differed from the Whitsun cycle's configurations most strikingly in its Old Testament/Nativity prologue. The only elements I am certain were contained in the Old Testament part of this prologue were the **"Fall of Man"** (first half of II), most of **"Noah"** (III), and some part of **"Abraham"** (IV); the Nativity Group was also abbreviated, lacking the **"Shepherds"** (VII), all the *Stanzaic Life* additions, and other episodes (such as the rhyme-royal sequence) as well. Even the Ministry offerings were more limited, and before the **"Last Supper"** (XV) they may have included only the **"Temptation"** (first part of XII), the **"Lazarus"** (last part of XIII), and selected episodes from XIV.

Thus if the English Corpus Christi play as a dramatic genre is to be defined, typically, as a history-of-the-world cycle which reaches into eternity at both ends, the **Chester play of Corpus Christi** (circa 1500) clearly belonged to another order: Chester's special triptych design in 1500 would seem to have been a slightly modified version (as was the 1303 Montecassino Passion's) of what Rosemary Woolf [In *The English Mystery Plays*, 1972] has called the "Septuagesima cycle-form." The implications of the structural and aesthetic differences which now can be discerned between the "old" **Chester play** and the "new" are therefore, I believe, extremely significant. First, any theory is quite suspect that would still maintain a direct and causal relationship between the Corpus Christi feast and a definitive, "proto-cyclic," and universally shared design for all the English Corpus Christi plays. In **Chester's** case, as we have seen, the play in fact did not realize its "definitive" cyclic form until, ironically, it was moved to Whitsuntide. Second, the play's unique transformation during these years should help in this present study to define more clearly those structural principles which give the cycle its theological unity and historical shape. . . .

One cannot assume, however, that the **Chester cycle** as it has survived to be printed in twentieth-century editions is in fact the play that was designed for that Whitsun shift; thus it is important to trace at least briefly the cycle's fate in its last years of production.

IV
The Cycle's Last Years;
Its Manuscript Difficulties;
Its Dramatic Unity

The Chester Whitsun plays were apparently produced in the same "stop-to-stop" processional fashion from the time that the revised Newhall Proclamation announced (in 1531/32) their three-day schedule, through what proved to be their penultimate performance in 1572: that is, each play, mounted upon its pageant-wagon, was wheeled through the streets to be performed first before the clergy at the abbey gates, next before the mayor and the city council at the Pentice at High Cross, and then two or three more times at other places in the city. As the Rogers' Breviary remarks, an uninterrupted performance of the cycle at each station was brought off with remarkable skill: "the[y] came from one streete to another. kepinge a directe order in euerye streete/for before thei firste Carige was gone from one place the seconde came. and so before the seconde was gone the thirde came. and so tell the laste was donne all in order withoute anye stayeinge in anye place." But the Whitsun plays as a unified cycle did not proceed through the last decades of their career with comparable ease and fluidity. The cycle apparently was never mounted annually (perhaps because of its great expense), but rather was given at two- or three-year intervals. In response to Reformation pressures, the play was reduced in size and deprived of some of its more "papist" elements; the Wives' **"Assumption,"** for example, was allowed to disappear completely, the Bakers' **"Last Supper"** was left out of the cycle for at least a decade, and other pageants were examined and sometimes amended. These pressures became so concentrated that the plays almost did not "go" in 1572: a contemporary record mentions that "an Inhibition was sent from the Archbishop [of York] to stay them but it Came too late. Not all the criticism of the plays (or of parts of them) was external, however, for another 1572 entry remarks, "In this yeare the whole Playes were playde thoughe manye of the Cittie were sore against the settinge forthe therof." Even with the increasing criticism, however, there was in Chester such strong feeling not to discontinue this great dramatic tradition that it was decided to mount the plays again in 1575, when almost all other performances of the

Corpus Christi cycles in England had been permanently halted.

Everything we know about the 1575 production of the Whitsun plays proves that it was unique. The City Assembly was cautious from the outset, determining that the plays "shalbe sett furth. . .with such correction and amendement as shalbe thaught Convenient by the said Maior." Even after these amendments were apparently made, some of the pageants, "for the superstition that was in them," were not performed at all. Those that were performed were mounted on the secular holiday of Midsummer and performed over a four-day sequence, rather than the normal three. And (as it had been done more than a half-century earlier) the cycle was produced stationarily and "in on part of the Citty"—this "on" part perhaps being the first "civic" station, at the Pentice at High Cross. Not only is this last performance of the cycle an interesting aberration in Chester's traditional production patterns of the sixteenth century, but its peculiarities raise a number of questions important to a formal analysis of the play. To what extent, in other words, do the five manuscripts, collectively or individually, represent the cycle—either as it was produced in 1575 (in partial and "corrected" form), or as it was produced in 1572 (as "the whole Playes"), or as it was produced earlier but under Protestant censorship, or as it was produced before any attempts were made to alter its shape and contents? This question surely will never be answered fully, but a brief inquiry into the cycle's reformation in its last years and into the relationship of its manuscripts at least should lead to a less than random—or editorially foreordained—definition of what the cycle is that we are to study.

In fact, little more than has already been mentioned about the cycle's changing configuration from mid-century onward appears to be forthcoming from the civic and guild records, despite their notable increase in number during this time. Earlier, in the latter part of the reign of Henry VIII (1508-47), the cycle appears to have thrived: having achieved its fullest size, remaining Catholic and "medieval" even though many of its parts were written for the **Whitsun** shift, the cycle's security and great popularity during these early Reformation years were by no means paradoxical. Because the English Reformation, as Harold Gardiner [in *Mysteries' End; An Investigation of the Last Days of the Medieval Religious Stage*, 1946] has written, did not enter a phase of "doctrinal change" until after Henry VIII's death. "The beliefs and feelings of the people at large remained, until well beyond the middle of the sixteenth century, Catholic in all essential matters. But immediately upon the accession of Edward VI (1547-53), Chester felt the doctrinal displeasures of London and York. The procession and the (lost) clergy's play of Corpus Christi were both suppressed in 1548. In 1550 the Bakers' **"Last Supper"** dropped away from the cycle, the vacuum

left by it being partially filled by a slightly amplified Shoemakers' play; and at about the same time the cycle was deprived forever of its **"Assumption."** These cleansings of **Chester,** all obviously doctrinal, were similar to those expurgations of other Corpus Christi plays elsewhere in England: York, for instance, lost its "Assumption of the Virgin" play in 1548, and the Wakefield cycle at about the same time was excised of certain passages concerning the seven sacraments and transubstantiation. During Mary's reign (1553-58), certain older religious activities, such as the Corpus Christi procession, were briefly reinstituted; but it apparently was not until early in the reign of Elizabeth that **Chester** recouped one of its losses (the **"Last Supper,"** presumably in its original form), and that the Shoemakers' play consequently returned pretty much to its earlier design. Only in the case of the Shoemakers' pageant, known as **"Jerusalem Carriage,"** do the documents suggest something about internal modifications: whereas the pre-1550 pageant placed Christ's anointing by the Magdalene in her and Martha's house, the post-1561 pageant places the episode in Simon the Leper's house.

The Late Banns, composed between 1548-61 and revised between 1561-72, should be expected to offer further information about the cycle's internal modifications during its last quarter-century. Like the Early Banns, the Late Banns are written in two stanza-lengths: the pageant descriptions written in quatrains would appear the original layer of composition, while those written in rhyme royal would appear to have been revised. The seven pageants described in rhyme-royal stanzas are the **"Fall of Luficer," "Nativity," "Shepherds," "Last Supper," "Passion," "Resurrection," "Antichrist,"** and **"Last Judgment."** But there is not much evidence in these pageants, insofar as I can determine, which might indicate late revision. The Late Banns may be more helpful in the pageant descriptions themselves, for they mention (as does the 1548 List of Companies) certain characters and episodes not mentioned in the Early Banns: but none of these citations should, in my judgment, be accepted alone as proof of a pageant's revision or amplification. Where the Late Banns are perhaps most helpful is in revealing the local, "orthodox" attitude taken toward the plays—an attitude which is at once apologetic, "jollified," and critical. The Banns scorn the stupidity of the plays' original audiences: "the fine witte at this daye aboundinge / At yat daye & yat age, had uerye smale beinge." However, the Banns see the plays' composition as having been proto-Protestant in spirit, for the monk who authored them, "nothinge affrayde / With feare of burninge hangeinge or cuttinge of heade," heroically chose to make the Scriptures known to the people "In a common englishe tonge. Disturbed nevertheless by the high incidence of nonscriptural events in the plays, the Late Banns advise that those "thinges not warranted by anye wrytte" were included in the plays "onely to make sporte."

Most obviously troublesome were those moments most closely identified with Catholic belief. The **"Last Supper,"** rather than a sacramental celebration, was thus to be treated in performance as a happy "memorall," after which the Bakers from their wagon should "caste godes loues [loaves] abroade with accustomed cherefull harte. Whether any aspects of this Protestant attitude seen in the Late Banns penetrated the surviving texts of the cycle itself, however, has yet to be determined.

Also as yet to be determined is the precise interrelationship of the four cycle-manuscripts known as the Group (HmARB), and the nature of their relationship—individually and collectively—to H, the last of the manuscripts transcribed, written out apparently as a presentation copy. . . . Why I raise the problem of manuscript relations here is that the Chester manuscripts (it has always been assumed) all derive from an archetype known throughout the cycle's history as the "Regenall." Recopied, and presumably somewhat changed, several times in the cycle's last years, the "Regenall" was a master-text containing all the plays: kept by the city, it was used when guilds wanted fresh copies of their plays, and may have served after mid-century as a way of controlling the doctrinal contents of the pageants performed. A fundamental question editors therefore must ask is, what pageant-versions in which manuscripts are closest to the "Regenall" when the "Regenall" existed in its least adulterate, most nearly pure, state? Or, since the "Regenall" itself has not survived, let the question be more hypothetical: what should an editor do if he were ever to discover five variant versions of the "Regenall"—say, from 1540 to 1575—and had to publish only the best, or the best synthesis of the five? Certain decisions he made would have to be based upon a sense of the cycle as a unified work of religious art, rather than upon his statistical tables of manuscript variants. Similarly, I think it is incumbent upon any scholar studying the entire **Chester cycle** to make several preliminary judgments about the surviving texts. . . .

Had only one manuscript of the **Chester cycle** survived and had we known nothing about Chester's dramatic history, it would perhaps have been advisable from the outset to share that common critical bias recently restated by Phillip McCaffrey [in *Historical Structure in the Chester Old Testament Pageants: The Literary and Religious Components of the Medieval Aesthetic*, 1972].

> A modern student's only reasonable course seems to be to recognize the surviving form of the cycle as one of its many historical forms, and to analyze it as a single art work, judging its effectiveness as a unit in spite of its multiple authorship and irretrievably complicated history. Whatever virtue and whatever flaw is found in the work must simply be ascribed to the total, without hope of identifying individual contributors or nonliterary factors.

But in Chester's case, "to recognize the surviving form of the cycle" is itself an act of creative scholarship. For all their objectivity, for example, the editors of the recent EETS volume chose to amend Hm, their base-text, by adding to it a pageant it lacked entirely, the Tanners' **"Fall of Lucifer."** The common sense evidenced in that decision I think we can apply elsewhere to resolve most of the major differences among the manuscripts' offerings. The raven-and-dove episode is found only in the **"Noah"** of the H MS, but its exclusion from the play we wish to study would seem rather pointless. The H **"Shepherds"** lacks the Group's closing scene, where the shepherds' boys appear and offer their gifts: although this epilogue is not essential, to include it would seem only in keeping with the pageant's own generosity of spirit. The H **"Passion"** lacks Peter's denial of Christ, an episode not essential to the pageant itself; but it is quite acceptable as part of the cycle, for it anticipates Peter's remorse, dramatized later. The H and Group **"Passions"** also differ slightly in their closing episode; however, since the same characters say nearly the same things in the same order, only an editor might wish to quibble over the "better" choice. Nor would most wish to argue about the appropriate closure to the **"Resurrection"**: HmAB stop abruptly as Magdalene approaches the angel, whereas HR finish this episode and conclude with Christ's forgiving Peter. For an editor these may all present major problems. But since there appear to be no reasons to exclude any of these passages—reasons arising either from historical evidence or from concerns about artistic integrity—these issues appear not to be matters demanding scholarly concern.

However, there are three places (at least) where I think common sense and a generous spirit need critical assistance. The first is an old problem in Chester studies: of the H version and the Group version of the Cappers' play, which (if either) is older or is to be preferred? Of those scholars who have compared these two quite different **"Balaam"** plays, all but one have said either that the issue has yet to be resolved, or that the Group version is older (and, for some, better). Bernice Coffee's is the one dissenting voice and it is her arguments I find convincing: the language in H is more often older, the meaning of its lines is more often more intelligent. But why two versions, and why not now accept both—as we do with the two Wakefield "Shepherds" plays? There are two versions, I would argue, for the same reason that the Smiths in 1575 had to present two versions of their play "before the Aldermen to take the best." In the case of the **Cappers' play,** we know which version was determined the best in 1575 because it is clear from its last stanza that the HmARB **"Balaam"** closed the first day's sequence of plays: "tomorrowe nexte yee shall have more." The reason the H version was rejected in 1575 I find equally apparent: the prophecies uttered in its *processus prophetarum* (which is not included at all in HmARB) are "Marian," and thus papist, in cast.

And the reason I reject the Group play and accept the H version is that the latter is Roman Catholic, medieval, and absolutely essential to the cycle's historical scheme of Old Testament time.

My second and third pieces of editorial revising both involve some minor textual surgery. All manuscript versions of the **"Noah"** include those stanzas Brownstein has proved were an addition to an early, more unified, pageant: linguistically late and poetically crude, these stanzas break with the character consistencies of what Brownstein called the "Old Play." But—after accepting without pause all the Whitsun additions—it would seem indefensible here were I to excise one episode, full (as it is) of delightful anachronisms (such as Mrs. Noah's swearing by "Sancte John") and thematically justifiable as a comic scene typologically mediating between Eve's disobedience and Mary's humility. But the "Old Play" version of **"Noah"** is the one I insist on in the cycle. . . . those added verbal anachronisms were (unwittingly) in violation of a carefully controlled dramatic tense, and of a historical vision of "pre-Christian" time, both central to the design of Chester's Old Testament Group. I suggest that this farcical patch was added late, and. . .that it is "possible that Mrs. Noah's *maistrie* is a state of topsy-turvy licensed by traditional practice on St. John's Day, Midsummer Day." The other episode I intend to excise is one that we know was licensed by the topsy-turvy practices of Midsummer: the alewife epilogue, added (in the Group manuscripts) to the **"Harrowing of Hell"** pageant. Salter has hypothesized that this episode is a fragment surviving from an old "Tapsters' Play" (the existence of which has yet to be documented), equally unconvincing is Lumiansky's attempt to prove that this satiric farce offers an appropriate artistic and thematic closure to the **"Harrowing."** From the Late Banns we can see that the Catholic version of what Christ did while in hell was not approved; but since there was no official Protestant version, the alewife scene was apparently tacked on to leaven the seriousness and the importance of the entire pageant. This pageant's only proper version is that retained in H: it concludes with the "Te Deum laudamus," as Michael leads the saved toward heaven.

What remains after these minor operations, then, is the "preferred" cycle. . .although the exact text of this cycle is not to be found in any edition of the plays. All that I have done, however, has been to restore to the body of the text most of the episodes that the recent EETS edition relegates to the Appendices section, and to remove from that body an appendix or two it never in fact needed. These few editings may be self-serving, but they are in line with certain historical implications as well as with my own aesthetic judgments. Alan H. Nelson [in *The Medieval English Stage*] has surmised that "characters from the Whitsun plays were introduced

into the Midsummer Show in 1554." Relying upon the same "doubtful evidence" as he did, I would surmise that a mutual interchange of characters and playlets between these two festivities was begun soon after 1548, and as a consequence of this exchange as well as of Reformation emendations the cycle as we have it now is somewhat corrupt. That none of the English cycles died a natural death has been well documented, but we should remind ourselves that in their later years most were in partial decline: not only were parts excised and patches added on, but certain sacred scenes were not treated seriously, and others may have been mocked. Because this mockery of the plays themselves is so foreign to the comic joy of the pre-Reformation dramatic productions, I think it appropriate (when possible) to recover the plays' designs before their decline: in Chester's case this means before the influence of the Midsummer frolics and of Protestant reprobation. My "preferred" text does not represent the **Chester cycle** quite at its height (that is, during the second quarter of the sixteenth century), but with the exception of the lost **"Assumption"** it would seem reasonably close enough so that we may consider it a full and unified cycle. . . .

In conclusion, then, it would seem appropriate to return to the analogy with which I opened this discussion of **Chester**'s construction. Since I have been considering a single cycle, let me counterpose a single work of religious architecture. Romsey Abbey, admired as one of the finest English examples of the Romanesque, is in fact—like Chester—a composite of various styles and stages of construction. The choir, transepts, and four bays of the nave are late Romanesque; the three other bays of the nave and the west front are Early Gothic; added later, in the Decorated style, are the two east windows; and the style of the north aisle, because it was widened in the fifteenth century, is Perpendicular. Yet the achieved effect of these different stages of construction and of these various styles is one of nearly perfect harmony. The Abbey is handsome, balanced, strong and (perhaps surprisingly) "Romanesque"; so, too, is the **Chester cycle**. But neither work is perfect. In Romsey's south transept there is a fifteenth-century ogee canopy: cutting off sight of the window behind it, crudely plastered onto the wall, this canopy is a grotesque mistake—to accept it as part of the whole is to embrace all taste and to exercise none. In **Chester**, as well, we have found that a few of the cycle's accretions had to be removed, not as a desecration of any of its integral parts but as an act of reverence for the unity of the whole. And although I have hardly managed to discover in **Chester** as many layers of composition as can easily be seen in Romsey Abbey, I hope that our imperfect education in the cycle's plans of construction will lead in the direction of a deeper understanding of its finished form. . . .

Karl Tamburr (essay date 1984)

SOURCE: "The Dethroning of Satan in the Chester Cycle," in *Neuphilologische Mitteilungen,* Vol. LXXXV, No. 3, 1984, pp. 316-28.

[*In the following excerpt, originally given as a paper at Villanova University on September 26, 1981, Tamburr describes the uniqueness of the Chester Cycle's dramatization of the* Fall of Satan.]

Some recent studies of the English cycle drama have shown how the medieval playwright would often go beyond the confines of his sources to emphasize particular stage actions. If repeated, these actions could become dramatic motifs that would, in turn, stress some larger theological point. For example, Thomas Rendall [in "Liberation Bondage in the Corpus Christi plays," *Neuphilologische Mitteilunge* 71, 1970] shows that the continual binding and loosing of Jesus during the Corpus Christi Passion sequences become a metaphor for the redemption of mankind from the bondage of sin. Another such motif, the dethroning of the devil in Chester, also has a larger significance in the cycle, for it appears in two episodes, *The Fall of Lucifer* and *Christ's Descent into Hell,* while an echo of it takes place in *The Coming of Antichrist*. Nevertheless, it has received practically no critical attention even in its unique occurrence in a representation of the Harrowing of Hell. While this action lends a kind of unity-through-repetition to the cycle, it also reinforces typological connections between these three plays. In both ways, it helps to reveal the victory of God, Father and Son, over Satan in their power struggle throughout and even beyond history.

This use of a motif suggests a kind of artistic license, but paradoxically **Chester** is for the most part stricter than the other cycles in following its sources, whether orthodox or apocryphal. There seem to be fewer allusions to contemporary medieval life and less of what one critic [Arnold Williams, in *The Drama of Medieval England,* 1961] calls "the spectacle, the fervor, and the naturalism which fifteenth century revisers introduced into the other cycles." There also seems to be less of the Franciscan emphasis on Christ's humanity that characterizes so much late-medieval drama and lyric poetry in England. Some scholars have felt that this relative conservatism makes **Chester** the "least imaginatively exciting" of all the cycles, but such criticisms seem based on modern notions of originality and forget the overwhelming concern of a medieval writer with literary authority. Fortunately, other critics have recognized in **Chester's** distinctive, though admittedly less flamboyant, style a conscious effort to stress the majesty of God and Christ's divine power rather than His human suffering. In an important, recent article ["Divine Power in Chester Cycle and Late Medieval Thought," *Journal of the History of Ideas* 39, 1978], Kathleen M. Ashley

has traced this focus in Chester to contemporary nominalist thought and concludes that "virtually every important episode and character in the **Chester cycle** is thematically controlled by the idea of power." Although she does not deal with the motif of dethroning, this stage action captures the essential struggle between God and devil and is clearly an integral part of the larger theme of power.

Lucifer's assuming God's throne on the first day of Creation became the traditional image for his pride, while his fall signaled the reestablishment of divine order. Based on Isaiah 14:12-15 and Luke 10:18, these actions are the crucial events, both structurally and thematically, in the plays representing the Fall of the Angels. All four cycles stage them, but do so differently. In York Lucifer's boasts of his own beauty and glory form a counterpoint to the loyal angels' homage to God. When he is so swollen with pride as to assume the Lord's throne, he immediately falls to hell. While this is the pattern in the *Ludus Coventriae,* God is present when the angel enthrones himself. He condemns Lucifer to hell for his "mekyl pryde," and the devil submits to the divine will and leaves heaven, "crak[ing] a fart" as he goes. Towneley breaks with the traditional placement of this event on the first day of Creation and stages it on the fifth when God made the "bestys crepand, / That fly or go may." Appropriately, Lucifer declares he will fly to reveal his new glory right after he assumes God's throne. His attempt ends in failure as he immediately falls.

In **Chester** after God has created the angels, He establishes Lucifer as their "Governour" and charges each one of them to "touche not [His] trone," but "kepe well his place". At first Lucifer shows the obedience of the other angels, but upon God's leaving the scene, begins to glorify himself as he becomes obsessed with sitting on the divine throne. Although repeatedly chided by the other angels to avoid pride, he eventually succumbs to it and enthrones himself with his cohort-*alter ego,* Lightbourne, at his side in a parody of the Trinity. When the loyal dominations order them back to their original seats, Lucifer maintains he would sit where he is even if the Lord were before him. God immediately returns and condemns those "that sate so nighe the majestye" to the pit of hell forever.

While Rosemary Woolf [in *The English Mystery Plays,* 1972] views the **Chester** version of this episode as the weakest artistically, others—including myself—contend that it shows a consciously crafted and imaginative handling of the Fall of the Angels. Here God makes a specific prohibition, in effect a "Covenant", against sitting on His throne. This begins a series of pacts made, broken, and renewed between God and mankind in the Old Testament plays—in *The Creation* with Adam and Eve, Cain and Abel, in *The Deluge* with Noah, in *The Sacrifice of Isaac* with Abraham. All these serve to demonstrate the struggle in men between their own wilfulness and their obedience to God. The Chester playwright wisely makes the initial covenant of the cycle the pattern against which the subsequent ones can be measured just as medieval theologians invariably point to Lucifer's pride as the source and pattern of all sin. True, **Chester** sacrifices the immediacy, the "shock," of his fall through the good angels' repeated warnings against pride. However, the "suspense" created underscores not the impulsiveness of Lucifer's act but its deliberate wilfulness because it is the prototype of disobedience that will be repeated in the plays that follow.

Another point important to our later discussion is the association, made in several places in this play, between God's throne and wisdom. This connection may be explained by St. Augustine in his commentary on the Fall of the Angels in *De Civitate Dei*. There he equates God's wisdom with His approval of Creation, especially the light but not the darkness, which the Bishop of Hippo interprets as God's blessing the good angels and casting out the rebellious ones on the first day. In **Chester** God explains to Lucifer and Lightbourne that they will act "righte wislye" if they maintain the place He ordained for them. Obedience then constitutes true wisdom. Yet for Lucifer, seizing the throne will, he thinks, make him omniscient as well as all-powerful: "All in this trone if that I were, / then sholde I be as wise as he". Overweening pride leads him to self-deception. This irony also happens to be theologically sound, for as St. Augustine explains, ". . . suo recusans esse subditus creatori et sua per superbiam uelut priuata potestate laetatus, ac per hoc falsus et fallax. . . ." Moreover, the deception of the devil is a concept central to patristic explanations of God's plan of redemption and figures prominently in the *Descent into Hell,* the next play to use the motif of Satan's dethronement.

Although essentially over, *The Fall of Lucifer* goes on for another seventy lines. The playwright seems consciously striving for an ending that is both artistically and theologically sound. He provides motivation for the Fall of Man in the next play when Primus Demon swears revenge against mankind for assuming the place of the fallen angels in God's favor. The dramatist also looks ahead to Judgment and suggests the plan of divine providence as well as the scope of the drama that represents it. Finally, he reestablishes the tone of harmony, the sense of divine order, by ending the play with the creation of the light and its separation from the darkness. Here he seems to affirm the traditional position that the Fall of the Angels occurred before the Creation, though he may be following St. Augustine who sees their rebellion and punishment subsumed in the separation of the light and the darkness. Interestingly, this initial act of creation is repeated at the beginning of the next play. The unnecessary repetition signals the dramatist's re-

turn to his scriptural source and for a medieval audience provides a sense of the harmonious, uninterrupted, and complete Creation found in Genesis.

While Satan is next dethroned in *Christ's Descent into Hell, The Temptation* is, properly speaking, the next episode to show the devil defeated by God, in accordance with Matthew 4:1-11. The playwright follows St. Gregory's interpretation of this event. As the Expositor clarifies, Christ defeats Satan by resisting the temptations to gluttony, vainglory and covetousness, the three particular ones that brought about the downfall of Adam. Throughout the play the dramatist takes pains to make clear the figural connection between Adam and Christ, the Second Adam. Through his choice of terms he emphasizes even beyond scriptural authority that this confrontation is one of power, of rival kingship: Satan swears by his "soverayntie" and "principalitie" to test Jesus because He always abases the devil's majesty. After Christ resists the first temptation to turn stone into bread, He proclaims that Satan's "posty" must fail when it confronts the divine sustenance of "gods will omnipotent". The devil laments Jesus' "victory", His gaining "Mastry" over him, and tempts Him a second time so that He may do "a fayre mastry" and "show [His] power". Seen in the context of power, the second and third temptations recall **Chester's** motif of enthronement. Christ's standing on the pinnacle of the Temple or viewing the kingdoms of the world before Him is the image of dominion. Yet by not revealing His divine kingship or showing any human weakness in doing homage to Satan, not only is Christ victorious over His antagonist but He also maintains the mystery surrounding His identity that ensures His future triumph during the Descent.

In this way, the Temptation is only a part of Christ's victory, the one He performs in His life on earth: this is later completed when He appears as divine spirit during the Harrowing. The Chester *Temptation* makes this point clear: Satan tempts Christ specifically to establish His identity because as he states, ". . . if he be god in mans kinde, / my craft then fully fayles". While he knows who Jesus' mother is and later concludes He is human because He hungers, he is still ignorant about His father and worried because this prophet is honored by men as God. Thus, the theme of deception reappears at the moment when Christ begins to reverse the Fall. By maintaining His anonymity, Jesus deceives the devil and ensures that the plan of redemption can continue. Even though Satan is thwarted by being kept in ignorance, he senses the release of Adam and his own punishment which are to come: "Nowe sone out of sorrow he [Adam] must be shut, / and I pyned in hell pitt. . ." Thus, the medieval audience would have been well prepared for Satan's deception and second dethronement in the *Descent into Hell*.

The Harrowing of Hell had been a tenet of faith long

before the creeds of the fourth century asserted that Christ "descendit ad inferos." Its importance was unquestioned in the Middle Ages. It was a focal point in human history, the moment when grace was extended to the generations that had lived before the coming of Christ. No longer would the souls of the righteous automatically be subject to the power of Satan because of the sin of Adam. After Christ broke down the infernal gates and defeated the devil, He drew Adam by the hand out of hell, typologically completing his role as the Second Adam.

In general, the Corpus Christi plays follow the account of the Descent popularized in the apocryphal *Gospel of Nicodemus* and later transmitted to the drama through such works as the Caxton translation of *The Golden Legend* and *The Stanzaic Life of Christ*. While the drama represents the Harrowing as a power struggle between Christ and Satan, the terms of this conflict are different in at least three of the cycles. All stage the breaking of the gates, which for some critics is the decisive action of the play. This is certainly true for the *Ludus Coventriae*. The York-Towneley version extends the military metaphor usually associated with the Descent by having the devils set the watch against Christ only to find (in Towneley) that hell is besieged. Satan arms himself to fight the intruder, but the actual confrontation takes the form of a debate in which the devil, quoting passage from the Old Testament, tries to establish his rights over the souls in hell. Christ's successful refutation of his argument completes His victory.

Chester eliminates this debate as well as some of the military imagery of the other cycles, but in other respects follows *The Gospel of Nicodemus* more closely. It is distinctive because it depicts the conflict between Christ and Satan as a clash of rival kingships. The episode abounds with terms, phrases, and actions suggesting power: Christ has come "maisterly" to "pryve [Satan] of [his] posty" and to "Degrade [him] of [his] Degree". The devil realizes that, unless he fights for his position ("degree"), Christ will overthrow his "maisterdome", "Soveraity", and "posty". When the righteous souls see the Light of Christ shining in the darkness of hell, they kneel in homage ("Omnes genu flectantes"); David, the anointed warrior-king whose descendants culminate in Christ the Messiah, hails Him as the "king of blisse". In all the manuscripts of the **Chester play,** Satan is presented as a rival monarch sitting on a throne ("sedens in Cathedra"). In four versions he leaves his seat when Tertius Daemon urges him to fight against Christ ("Tunc surgens sathanas de sede . . ."). But even before the destruction of the gates, the devil realizes he is powerless against Him and offers no resistance, not even to argue the justice of his cause as he does in York and Towneley. His leaving the throne is then a dramatic image for his essential defeat.

One manuscript of this play, Harley MS. 2124, offers an even more striking presentation of Christ's victory. Here Tertius Daemon orders his lord to fight even though he recognizes that Satan's "Soveraity / fayl[e]s cleane", here echoing the devil's previous lament in **The Temptation**; no longer does his master deserve to sit on the throne of power. As the manuscript rubric explains, he and the other demons then literally throw Satan down from his seat ("Iaceant tunc Sathanam de sede sua"). The Prince of Darkness acknowledges that he is repaid for his temptation of Adam and the punishment it brought on mankind. The devil's cohorts too recognize Christ's dominion over them, showing that they are in reality His servants, not Satan's henchmen.

The forcible dethronement of the devil by his own minions appears to be unique and original to this version of the Harrowing. It is found neither in Greek nor in Latin texts of *The Gospel of Nicodemus* nor in Middle English translations of it either in poetry or prose; nor in *The Golden Legend* nor in *The Stanzaic Life of Christ,* which some critics argue is the direct source for the **Chester play;** nor in Latin liturgical, Cornish, or contemporary French drama, which other scholars suggest had an influence on this cycle; nor in any patristic exegesis I have read on the Descent; nor in any representation of the Harrowing I have seen in the visual arts. Apparently, the author of Harley MS. 2124 was following a version of Nicodemus known as the Latin A recension. There the character Inferus orders Satan to fight against the King of Glory and casts him outside, or as the text reads, "Et eiecit Inferus Satan foris sedibus suis." What the Chester playwright appears to have done is to change the idiomatic expression "foris sedibus suis," meaning "outside," to the more literal "de sede sua," meaning "from his seat." He also eliminates the character, Inferus, that as Satan's superior personifies hell and substitutes three demons as his subordinates. What is in *Nicodemus* a comic but minor action becomes in **Chester** the central one depicting the devil's defeat. As such, it provides an original variation to the *Christus Victor* motif.

Moreover, this change in the text seems to be a conscious one by the playwright, not merely a misreading of his sources. He links this dethronement to the earlier defeat in **The Fall of Lucifer** by having the devil lament, "never sith god made the first day, / were we so fowle of right". Satan's words recall his loss of place and favor on the day traditionally assigned to his rebellion and fall. As part of his punishment in both plays, he is bound in the pit of hell. In connecting the two victories over the devil, the dramatist may be voicing an idea, evidenced in a homily ascribed to Eusebius of Alexandria, that during the Harrowing Christ came "to bind him who for rebellion was condemned." Finally, the dramatist once more shows the devil deceived over Christ's true identity. Following *The Gospel of Nico-*

demus, he has Satan believe that Jesus is only a man, subject to death and therefore rightfully his because of the sin of Adam. But by accepting one of greater power, the devil is overthrown and repaid for his deception of Adam a second time. While *The Fall of Lucifer* and *Christ's Descent into Hell* are connected figurally, the Chester playwright reinforces traditional typology through dramaturgy that goes beyond his literary authority: both plays show the reestablishment of divine power, and both do so through the same action, dethronement. Both plays focus on a moment crucial in mankind's relationship with God: *The Fall* marks the end of Lucifer's covenant and the beginning of Adam's; the *Descent* shows a renewal of this second one under the law of grace instituted by Christ, for now the gates of heaven are open once more to the souls of the righteous.

The authors of the Descent plays signal the change from the time of law to the time of grace by a procession of patriarchs and prophets—in Chester, Adam, Isaiah, Simeon, John the Baptist, Seth, and David—most of whom have appeared earlier in the cycle. In this way the episode provides an abbreviated recapitulation of the cycle's major events up to the Passion. But if the Chester *Descent* looks back in time, it also looks ahead. The Harrowing of Hell prefigures **Judgment**: just as Christ led the souls from the bondage of Satan into heaven, so at the end of time He will lead them from this world to the next. Of the four cycles, **Chester** alone preserves from *The Gospel of Nicodemus* the episode in which the rescued souls encounter Enoch and Elias as they enter Paradise. The prophets foretell their struggle with Antichrist which precedes Doomsday, and **Chester** is the only cycle to stage these apocalyptic events. *The Prophets and Antichrist* enumerates the Fifteen Signs of Doom, while *The Coming of Antichrist* depicts his rise to power, his victory over the two prophets, and his defeat by the archangel Michael. As in the *Descent,* the dramatist employs a pattern or "rhythm" of prophecy and fulfillment in these two later plays.

While not actually Satan, Antichrist is called a demon by some exegetes. More often though, he is viewed as the devil's tool or the ape of Christ. Thus, in **Chester** Elias refers to him as "the Deuyll" as well as the "Devills lymme" and "the Devills owne nurry". Antichrist's opening speech is then both a parody of God's at the start of the Creation play and a reminiscence of Lucifer's bombast. The tone recalls the rants of other tyrants in the cycle which invert the idea of the humble being exalted.

Like Satan, Antichrist uses deception to establish his dominion over the world. One trick is his power to raise the dead, which is instrumental in his being acclaimed the Messiah. In the *Descent* the mention of Christ's raising Lazarus has a similar significance, for it establishes His identity as the Son of God as well as His power over death, which along with Satan and Hell was traditionally one of the infernal trinity ruling over the damned. In addition, the raising of Lazarus is a *figura* for the general resurrection that precedes Judgment. Antichrist further reveals his power over death by rising from the grave in a deceitful parody of Christ's own Resurrection. This act is crucial to the play, for it leads directly to his enthronement ("Tunc Ascendet Antichristus ad Cathedram)," the dramatic image of power, which **Chester** derives from the most influential source of this legend in the Middle Ages, the *Libellus de Antichristo* by Adso of Montier-en-Der. At the same time the action demonstrates to the audience the necessity of faith to oppose the deceptive evidence of the senses, a point explicitly made throughout the play.

When Enoch and Elias challenge Antichrist's power, his blasphemy against the Trinity recalls Lucifer's and Lightbourne's at the beginning of the cycle. Through the power of the Eucharist though, the two prophets reveal his triumph over death to be a sham. Antichrist then arms himself, descends from his throne, and slays Enoch, Elias, and the four kings who have now been shown the error of their earlier submission to him. The tyrant reascends the throne (". . . postea vero redibit ad Cathedram") where apparently he remains until he is slain by Michael. As this summary suggests, his throne is the central *locus* of the play; it symbolizes spiritual and political dominion over this world, the third major place of action in the cycle. Antichrist's descent from it to fight for his power recalls Satan's in the Harrowing play and likewise serves as a prelude to his eventual defeat.

Michael's reappearance here after the *Descent* confirms his role as Christ's champion whose special charge is to lead resurrected souls to heaven in both plays. This stage action helps again to reinforce the typological connection between the Harrowing and the Judgment, the subject of the final play which follows immediately. Just as Satan is punished at the end of the *Descent* by being more narrowly confined in the abyss, Antichrist will descend into the pit where he will be seated next to Satan. A clear parody of Christ's sitting at the right hand of the Father after His Ascension, Antichrist's enthronement is the final, eschatological fulfillment of Lucifer's in the first play.

In **Chester** dethronement is used to depict God's victory over Satan or his representative in heaven, in hell, or on earth because of the cycle's special focus on the concept of power. However, one need not assume that one writer was responsible for this motif. In fact it is highly unlikely that one person wrote the whole cycle even though my argument may have suggested that at times, and it is possible that three different dramatists composed the three plays considered. Moreover, the throne's inevitable appearance in the tradition of Lucifer's fall and in the legend of Antichrist is almost a commonplace so that no degree of originality can be ascribed to the author or authors using it in the plays showing those events. But its use in the *Descent,* especially in the Harley MS. 2124 version, shows that particular playwright recognized and exploited its potential for drama. By envisioning the Harrowing of Hell as a dethronement of Satan, he creates a tripartite unity based on a dramatic image that reinforces traditional typological connections. In so doing, he follows a pattern that would have been well known to a medieval audience from sermons and homilies, the pattern of prefiguration and fulfillment found in Christian allegory. *The Fall of Lucifer* provides the *figura* of the devil's dethronement (i.e., the "literal" level), which is completed during Christ's life during the Descent (i.e., the allegorical or christological level). The action is fulfilled eschatologically (i.e., the anagogical level) with the defeat of Antichrist. The course of this motif then coincides with an established pattern of medieval thought. The beginning, middle, and end of the cycle, corresponding to its three major segments before, during, and after the life of Christ, are thus drawn together. The recurrent triumph of divine power outlines the cyclical time-structure that one associates with God's providence, which like the circle, the medieval symbol of perfection, has neither beginning nor end. This framework exists in a kind of tension with historical time, the succession of epiphanies in man's relationship with his Lord, represented dramaturgically by the procession of pageant wagons through the streets of Chester. The circular overview of history formed by *The Fall of Lucifer, Christ's Descent into Hell,* and *The Coming of Antichrist* would reassure a medieval audience of the inevitable triumph of justice and mercy even though the human characters in that history—the patriarchs, prophets, apostles, and common people—may be blind to it. Thus, it is in dramatic actions like the dethroning of Satan that the medieval playwright could demonstrate originality both in his sense and ours—following his sources closely and yet sometimes going beyond them to create drama that was, inextricably, both theologically sound and artistically satisfying.

David Mills (essay date 1985)

SOURCE: "'None Had the Like nor the Life Darste Set Out': the City of Chester and its Mystery cycle," in *Staging the Chester Cycle,* edited by David Mills, The University of Leeds School of English, 1985, pp. 1-16.

[*In the following excerpt, Mills gives a comprehensive overview of the history and staging of the Chester Cycle.*]

Few manuscripts of English mystery cycles have survived. In many towns—such as Beverley,—where the craft guilds once enacted the major interventions of God

in human history from the creation of the angels to the Last Judgement, only the cryptic references in guild and civic records and accounts remain. In some places—such as Newcastle, Norwich or Coventry (which had perhaps the most famous cycle-play)—we are fortunate to have one or two plays from the cycle still. Exceptionally—as at York, Wakefield and one other unidentified location—unique manuscripts preserve virtually complete cycles. In contrast to this general dearth of textual evidence, Chester's play-cycle is attested by three manuscripts containing all or part of individual plays and five manuscripts containing versions of the full cycle.

Yet no civic "master-copy" survives from Chester, as it does from Wakefield and York. All the cycle-texts and at least one single-play manuscript were copied long after the last performance of the cycle, at Midsummer in 1575. The scribes who undertook the difficult and laborious task of deciphering the "Regynall", a much-altered and dog-eared master-text, did so either for their own antiquarian interest or for that of a patron, for Chester's cycle seems to have been regarded with interest, nostalgia and pride by many Cestrians. What we know about the scribes who signed their copies suggests that they were conforming guildsmen or churchmen, not recusants. George Bellin, who copied the complete cycle twice—in 1592 and in 1600—was a member of the Ironmongers' company, serving them as clerk, as well as the Cappers' and Pinners' company, and also the Coopers' for whose records in 1599 he made the copy of their play of the **Trail and Flagellation of Christ** which they still possess. He was parish clerk to Holy Trinity church, Chester, and was known to Randle Holme, the Chester antiquarian who later came to possess his 1600 manuscript. The latest manuscript, of 1607, is a scholarly edition of the cycle written by three scribes, one of whom was James Miller, prebend of Chester cathedral and rector of St. Michael's church, Chester. As yet we know rather less of the other scribes, but William Bedford, copyist of the 1604 manuscript, was in 1606 clerk to the Brewers' guild at Chester and, judging from the appearance of the manuscript, was making a copy out of personal interest (as indeed Bellin may have been doing in 1592). And, though the 1591 scribe, Edward Gregorie, came from a recusant centre, the Cheshire village of Bunbury, he was churchwarden there in 1607-8 and the fact that he calls himself *scholler* in his colophon suggests a self-consciously scholarly motive behind his enterprise.

Further circumstantial evidence of local affection for the cycle is provided by the *Breviary of Chester History,* a compilation (or perhaps better, series of compilations) of the antiquarian notes of Archdeacon Robert Rogers of Chester Cathedral, who died c.1595. His son, David, made a number of copies of these notes, of which five manuscripts in his hand still survive—the earliest from 1609. Evidently there was local demand for material about the city's history. The *Breviary* includes an important account of "the playes of Chester called the Whitson Playes" which is set within chapter 4, a chapter headed "Now for the lawdable exersises yearelye vsed within the Cittie of Chester". The account betrays an interesting ambivalence on the part of this Anglican divine. He could not commend the content of a cycle whose origins lay within the teaching and ceremonial of the Roman Church—he calls it an "abomination of desolation". But the length and detail of the account suggests that he was fascinated by the scale of preparation, the organisation and co-ordination of the production, and the popularity of a major civic event.

Without such affection for the cycle, it would be difficult to explain the dangerous decisions of 1572 and 1575 to stage the cycle again, for no-one in Chester could have been unaware of the opposition to such events by Queen Elizabeth and her ministers. Indeed, when the Archbishop of York had sent a prohibition against the 1572 production, which allegedly reached Chester too late, it was both dangerous and unnecessary to risk a further performance in 1575. It seems that there was strong local support for the venture, a sense of pride in an event unique to Chester, and a belief that the production could be plausibly defended.

The History of the Cycle

Factually, it is impossible to establish any firm continuity of practice for the **Chester cycle;** what was played and copied in Chester in the later sixteenth century had been much modified or reconstructed. The first reference to the cycle is in the record of a dispute between the Ironmongers and the Carpenters about help with their responsibilities in its production in 1422. By then the cycle was already established. But it was performed on Corpus Christi Day (varying in date between 23 May and 24 June), in conjunction with the procession of lights which accompanied the Blessed Sacrament in its progress from St. Mary's-on-the-Hill near Chester Castle to the collegiate church of St. John near the River Dee. The performance was evidently completed within the single day. For half a century from 1475 the records contain no allusion to the play, but an indenture of 1521 between the guilds of the Smiths and the Pewterers, the next record, refers to responsibilities for "Whitson Playe and Corpus Christi Light", indicating a separation of play and feast which involved a change in the date of the play's performance. The Early Banns and Roger's *Breviary* indicate that the clergy became responsible for the production of a play at St. John's at the conclusion of the Corpus Christi procession. Banns and Breviary, and other documents, subsequently indicate that the guild-cycle was divided into three sections (Creation-Magi's Gifts; Innocents-Harrowing of Hell; Resurrection-Doomsday) which were played serially on the Monday, Tuesday and Wednesday of Whit week. The

tendency to call the cycle the "Whitson playes", with plural reference, which is first found in the Proclamation of 1531-2 by the town-clerk, William Newhall, may reflect this arrangement.

We do not know why the date of performance was changed, or why a one-day production became a three-day production. Elsewhere, civic celebrations such as the mystery plays often became indicators of civic dignity and prosperity. Chester seems to have flourished economically, and certainly politically, during the "period of silence", for in 1506 it was granted palatinate status by its "Great Charter" from Henry VII, gaining a degree of political independence which was to be eroded under the later Tudors. Whatever the reasons for the changes, the cycle came later to be regarded as typifying the city's independent spirit and established traditions.

The potential for changes of a different kind was built into the administration of the productions, for assent of the mayor and council was required for any performance. There is no evidence to suggest that such assent was given at any regular intervals, and nothing to support Rogers' claim that the productions were annual. Moreover, the mayor and council had to approve the text for each performance, and we know that changes were made. There are discrepancies in the descriptions given of the cycle in the Early and the Late Banns, and between them and the extant texts—the most notable perhaps being the presence in the Early Banns of a play of the **Assumption of Our Lady** by the "worshipful wives" of the town, omitted from the Late Banns and not in the extant texts. . . . In particular, there are two versions of the Cappers' play of **Moses** and **Balaam and Balak**—one designed to end a day's performance, and the other lacking such a closure but containing a series of prophets who provide a link with the following **Nativity**. The Smiths' accounts of 1575 include the item:

> Spent at Tyes, to heare 2 plays before the Aldermen to take the best
>
>   xviiid

The text was not stable.

The preamble to Newhall's *Proclamation* makes explicit the congruent interest of the Church and City in Chester in their cycle:

> Not only for the augmentation and increase of the holy and catholick faith of our saviour Jesu Christe and to exort the mindes of comon people to good devotion and holsome doctrine therof, but also for the comon welth and prosperity of this citty.

In contrast to the route of the Corpus Christi procession, the cycle's performance began at the ecclesiastical centre of Chester, the gate of St. Werburgh's Abbey (later the Cathedral), where the clergy saw the play. From there the waggons moved down the hill to the Pentice, the civic annex against St. Peter's church at the High Cross, where the mayor, aldermen and council saw the play. The route thus linked the two official interests. Other stations—notably in the Bridge Street—may have been regarded as being for the citizens, for the play traditionally went out into the city and its people and the 1575 production was disliked "because the playe was in on part of the citty". Possibly the separation of the guilds' Whitsun plays from the clergy's Corpus Christi play resulted from or encouraged a stronger civic influence in the cycle. Characters from the cycle rode in Chester's great secular occasion, the Midsummer Show:

> The Painters rode with their angels on stilts, the Smiths with Simeon, the Shoemakers with Mary Magdalene and occasionally Judas, the Innkeepers with the alewife and her devils.

The choice of Midsummer rather than Whitsun for the final performance in 1575 was not, therefore, completely without reason. It is possible to argue that the cycle originated as a religious celebration which was progressively and consciously assimilated into the secular cycle of civic celebrations.

The Defence of the Cycle in the Late Banns

As the century progressed, play-cycles came under severe attack. Their origins in the Feast of Corpus Christi which celebrated the now controversial doctrine of transubstantiation, and other aspects of doctrine which they might contain, made them theologically and politically subversive. Moreover, particularly to a Puritan mind, they could seem a blasphemous mimesis of sacred subjects which blurred the important distinctions between worship and entertainment, between divine miracle and dramatic illusion. And economically they were expensive and their cost was statutorily imposed upon all guild-members. In Chester in 1575 Andrew Taylor went to prison rather than pay his share to the production of **Antichrist** by his guild, the Dyers. Whatever the specific causes of complaint an entry in the 1572 Mayor's List; "The whole Playes were playde, thoughe manye of the cittie were sore against the setting forthe thereof" indicates serious discontent. To defend their activities to the Privy Council, the ecclesiastical authorities, and their fellow-citizens, the promoters of the cycle relied primarily upon the Banns and the text itself.

The primary defence of the cycle after the Reformation was brilliantly ingenious. The Late Banns claim that Chester anticipated the Reformation by being the first city in England to dare publicly to present the Scriptures to the people in the vernacular. The claim elaborates a tradition about the cycle's origins:. . .sometymes there was mayor of this cittie

> Sir John Arnewaye, knighte, whoe moste worthelye
> contented himselfe to sett out in playe
> the devise of one Rondall, moncke of Chester Abbaye
>
> (4-7)

Arneway was historically mayor of Chester in 1268-76, but antiquarians of the time mistakenly believed him to have been Chester's first mayor and to have been in office in 1328. *Rondall* was Ranulf Higden, a monk at Chester from 1299-1364, particularly famous as the author of a history of the world, the *Polychronicon*. The cycle was thus seen as the product of the endeavours of the two most famous representatives of City and Church, an ancient custom. And the traditional congruence of dates would mean that it began in 1327-8, which would make it the oldest play-cycle in the land if it were true.

Two arguments follow from this thesis. First, the cycle was an unprecedented and hazardous experiment in generic creation. It was done in haste; it attempted to give only a flavour of the biblical original; and it tried to entertain, using some unscriptural matter. Though it has shortcomings, it was nevertheless the product of Higden's revolutionary vision, un-monk-like in his Protestant vision and courage:

> This moncke—not moncke-lyke in Scriptures, well seene,
>
> (8)
>
> This moncke—and noe moncke—was nothinge affrayde
> with feare of burninge, hangeinge, or cutting of heade
> to sett out that all may deserne and see,
> and parte of good belefe, beleve ye mee.
>
> (24-7)

The Banns imply that a Protestant Church will be sympathetic to such an endeavour.

Second, the antiquity of the cycle is also its defence. The Banns stress that some of language is so old that it is no longer intelligible:

> Condemne not oure matter where groosse wordes you heare
> which importe at this daye smale sence or understandinge—
> as sometymes "postie", "bewtye", "in good manner" or "in fearee"—
> . . .At this tyme those speches caried good lykinge.
>
> (49-51, 53)

They claim that Arneway ordered the guilds to perform the plays and was responsible for the demand "for everye pagiante a cariage provided whitall", as if processional production is another curious mark of antiquity. Finally, the cycle was not intended for the sophisticated sixteenth century with its fine actors, dramatic devices and discerning audiences. Dramatic crudities, such as presenting God on stage in human form, are indicators of the age of the cycle, and hearers are urged to remember that the plays were written to be performed by craftsmen before "commons and contry men". Though without historical foundation, tradition becomes its own justification and defence.

In defending Higden as a proto-Protestant disseminating scriptural material, however, the Banns also offer some assurance that the material in the cycle was approved and accepted. Indeed, they sometimes draw attention to "nonscriptural" sections in order to explain and reassure. The presence of two midwives at Christ's birth, which ultimately derives from apocryphal Nativity narratives, is explained as comic relief, to be taken "in sporte". The "contemporary" business of the **Shepherds' Play,** with its feasting, wrestling, singing and gifts, is explained as necessary elaboration of a sketchy biblical account:

> Fewe wordes in the pagiante make merthe
>   trulye,
> for all that the author had to stande uppon
> was "glorye to God on highe and peace on
>   earthe to man."
>
> (100-2)

The **Fall of the Angels,** though not scriptural, is affirmed by recognised authorities. The **Harrowing of Hell** is an event attested by the Apostles' Creed, and although there is less firm authority for the actual details of that visit (they derive ultimately from the apocryphal *Gospel of Nicodemus*), nevertheless the author is following "the beste lerned" in his account.

The Concern with Authority in the Cycle

The cycle similarly seeks to authenticate the events which it dramatises by referring the audience repeatedly away from the drama to the accepted texts, critiques and beliefs of Christianity. The historical action of the cycle, stretching from the creation of the angels to the removal of the last of the damned at Doomsday, is "framed" by two moments out of time—God's self-characterising speech at the start and the speeches of the four evangelists at the end. This frame incorporates the dual perspective of the **Chester cycle,** that the events reveal God's ongoing plan through history as it unfolds; and that, for contemporary Man, most of the plan is complete and authoritatively accessible to them in the Bible.

An awareness of that pre-existent authority pervades the cycle. It opens with God's affirmation that all things are subordinated to his will:

> Ego sum alpha et omega,
> Primus et novissimus.
> It is my will it shoulde be soe;
> hit is, yt was, it shalbe thus.
>
> (1/1-4)

But it therefore opens with a biblical quotation, from the—as yet unwritten—Book of Apocalypse. And hence it begins in Latin, the language of scholarship, liturgy, of the Vulgate. There are 57 quotations from the Vulgate Bible in the 1591 text of the cycle, quite apart from the use of Latin more extensively in the liturgical music of the plays. At the moment of Judgement, a devil reminds God that He promised to separate the wicked and send them into everlasting torment. But on this legal occasion it is important to have the exact words of the promise:

> which wordes to clearkes here present
> I wyll rehearse.
>
> "Sic erit in consummatione seculi: exibunt angeli et seperabunt malos de medio justorum, et mittent eos in caminum ignis, ubi erit fletus et stridor dentium."
>
> (24/579-80+Latin)

The Latin will be understood by the *clearkes*. The audience here as elsewhere is not required to understand it, and is given a translation or paraphrase; but they recognise it as authoritatively underpinning the action.

The Doomsday devil is also reminding God that His deeds must match His earlier words, for those words constitute a promise and hence a prophecy. Divinely inspired words generated the historical events which are seen to generate the dramatic action of the cycle. Adam's divine ecstasy in which he foresaw the whole course of history before his fall raises expectations of the dramatisation of the Flood, Incarnation and Judgement, as Balaam's Messianic prophecy guarantees the Star of Bethlehem, the coming of the Magi and the revelation to the Gentiles. Herod's Doctor reads the Jewish prophets to prove that present events are the fulfilment of a pre-ordained plan (play 8). The 1607 manuscript presents the Jewish prophets of Christ in sequence after Balaam and Antichrist has his prophets (play 22) and reminds us that his coming was foretold.

Chester, nevertheless, indicates the interdependence of the two confirmatory elements in belief emphasised by St. Paul in his Epistle to the Romans. Those who had read the Scriptures could recognise the fulfilment of their words in Christ. But, even lacking the Scriptures, men can read the will of God in his creation:

> For the invisible things of him from the creation of the world are clearly seen, being understood by the things that are made, even his eternal power and Godhead; so that they are without excuse.
>
> (Romans 1/20)

Actions in the cycle exist not in their own right but as demonstrations of divine truth. The Nativity star is God's communication to the Shepherds, who know something of the Scriptures; to the Magi, who have only Balaam's prophecy; and to the pagan Roman emperor Octavian, who has only his innate awareness of the distinction between mortal and divine and the aid of the inspired Sibyl but who, unlike King Herod with Scriptures and exposition to hand, is convinced. Christ can concretise the movement from spiritual darkness to enlightenment by healing a blind man and, with a startling change of image, the movement from spiritual death to life by raising Lazarus. Wonders and signs herald Christ's birth and also Doomsday, and God descends with the instruments of his Passion as signs of His authority to judge.

Simeon's "Book Miracle" in play 10 characterises these various concerns with authority. Finding the prophecy "Behold, a virgin shall conceive. . ." (Isaiah 7/14), he disbelieves it on logical grounds and emends the mis-translation to "a good woman". In his absence, an angel restores "virgin". Anna assures him that God is not bound by natural laws. And when a second attempt to change the reading produces the same result, Simeon accepts the sign that the text is indeed the unalterable word of God. The action defends the biblical text, making effective dramatic use of sign. Beneath it, as elsewhere in the cycle, is an informed and scholarly mind that knew that the Judaic word meant "a young woman of marriageable age" and that its function as a Messianic prophecy was disputed between Jewish and Christian commentators.

The same play also illustrates the cycle's joyous affirmation of the truth of Christian belief, as Simeon affirms his faith by singing the "Nunc Dimittis" and then translating it. Such transitions to the language and music of the Church at culminative moments again direct the audience towards an external, nondramatic authority. For the cycle as a whole, such joyous affirmation culminates in play 21 when the twelve Apostles, under the direct influence of the Holy Spirit at Pentecost, compose the Apostles' Creed, the authoritative statement of the fundamental tenets of the Christian faith, which the audience would recognise from catechism and liturgy. The Creed refers, and gives new point, to major events previously or subsequently dramatised in the cycle. And the re-enactment of its composition in the Whitsun plays coincides with the liturgical commemoration of the historical Pentecost. The Late Banns suggest that this was the true climax of the cycle:

> This of the oulde and newe testamente to ende all
> the storye which oure author meaneth at this tyme
> to have in playe
>
> (165-6)

Such pervasive allusions to the authorised body of Christian belief must have gained added point when the plays were performed outside the gate of the Abbey, the guardian and transmitter of that faith in the city.

The Cycle as Religious Drama

. . .**Chester's** use of prophecy and sign gives the cycle an exceptional structural and thematic tightness which offsets the inevitable disruption of unity caused by splitting the cycle into three sections to be performed on waggons on successive days. The cycle presents itself simultaneously as ongoing historical action and as completed recorded history. Man learns by reading experience rationally, like Octavian or the doubting midwife, and by reading God's word believingly, like Noah or Simeon. *The* **Chester** sin is to resist truth revealed through sign, as do the Pharisees, or through the word, as does Herod. This exemplary pattern of belief/disbelief is cumulatively repeated within the unfolding historical action and its prophetic and significant cross-references.

The audience's response to this action is narrowly directed by a series of "figures of authority". Some,—Herod's Doctor, Octavian's Sibyl or Simeon's Anna—are historical figures with special knowledge. Others may move out of their historical role on occasion. Balaam responds to Balak's requests, but baffles the king when he is suddenly inspired to deliver his Messianic prophecy out of character and time; and Christ explains the Last Supper to His disciples, but expounds the Eucharist directly to the audience as He leaves the tomb. Or a contemporary "Expositor" may interpose himself between audience and action to explain Abraham's deeds, the prophecies of Balaam and his Jewish counterparts, the three temptations of Christ and the fears of the Pharisees, or the prophecies of Antichrist.

Such figures are the most obvious manifestation of the contemplative distance which the cycle establishes between audience and action, well illustrated by the sacrifice of Isaac in play 4. Its source, the Brome play of **Abraham and Isaac,** ends naturalistically with the released Isaac bewildered and scarred by his experience, unable to understand God or to trust his father again—an effect not dispelled by the Doctor's concluding, and obscenely inadequate, insistence upon the virtues of obedience. In **Chester** the audience is led slowly but firmly away from the ritual and pathos through a series of "frames". First, God announces the historical reward, his covenant with Abraham. Then the contemporary Expositor explains the figural meaning of the action to his less learned audience. Next he becomes a contemporary Everyman, kneeling with them to pray for the gift of Abraham's exemplary obedience. Finally, the Messenger whirls in to announce the approach of the next waggon. The audience has been taken to a meditational distance from the play and then returned to the reality of Chester's Bridge Street. The action is carefully controlled, circumscribed, and functionally redirected; and the audience must view it with a quiet mind, emotionally disengaged.

In fact, beneath the **Chester cycle** there seems to lie a suspicion of the functional neutrality of pure drama. Its unique **Antichrist play** can be read as a warning of how readily illusion can become delusion when it is divorced from moral function. Historically, Antichrist is admitted into God's scheme under licence; his power is circumscribed, as the Doctor in the preceding play reminds the audience, but for a time evil is able to reveal its true potential. The Geneva Bible explains the significance of the episode:

> [God] advertiseth the godlie (which are but a smale portion) to avoide this harlots flateries and bragges, whose ruine without mercie they shal se, and with the heavenlie companies sing continual praises.

But in the dramatic context, for a moment the moral function of the cycle seems set aside and a spirit of shameless parody and duplicity enters. What Antichrist offers is, in the words of the Geneva Bible, "Faire speache and plesant doctrine", the suggestion that spiritual salvation is compatible with the love of all the women in the world, with the possession of all power and wealth, and with the ability to transform the environment unnaturally—pleasurable fantasies which the kings joyfully but facilely accept. Antichrist is an actor who replicates for his own ends the wonders which we have seen Christ perform as signs of His godhead—or, more accurately, which we have seen other actors replicate for us. Antichrist speaks the language of authority; he introduces himself in "fair speech", a specially composed Latin verse which sounds just as impressive to the un-Latinate as the Vulgate texts which he quotes later. He offers disruptions of the natural order as signs; he can perform the conjuring trick of turning trees upside down and bringing fruit from their roots, which seems just as marvellous as raising the dead or dying and rising himself. He blurs the distinction between literal and spiritual significance in words and deed, and kings and audience are happy to accept the interpretation which he offers.

Above all others, this play emphasises the need for a proper scepticism in the face of ostensible miracles, and for the help of an authoritative guide. As 1 John 4/1 puts it:

> Beloved, believe not every spirit, but try the spirits whether they are of God: because many false prophets are gone out into the world.

Hence in play 10 Simeon is right both to listen to Anna's advice and also to test the wonder again. Here the kings are initially sceptical but are too easily de-ceived through their lack of spiritual understanding. Their conversion is achieved through the intervention of Enoch and Elias, two figures of authority, who remind us that there is an absolute point of reference beyond the self-validating world of illusion, that marvellous things are not necessarily miracles. The illusions created by Antichrist cannot stand against the miracle of the consecrated bread. Antichrist is then stripped of his role. In contrast to his opening triumphal descent in Latinate glory, he is now ignominiously killed and borne off to hell in a mode of diabolical low comedy. God's actors are resurrected and process to Heaven singing a Latin hymn. Two different kinds of drama, and their associated values, separate.

Antichrist, the longest play of the cycle, exposes the corrupting potential of religious mimesis upon the spiritually unattuned and scripturally ignorant mind. The danger that a playwright or actor might use religious material for his own ends had been recognised before the end of the fourteenth century: as *A Tretise of Miracles Pleyinge* puts it:

> These miracle playeris and the fautours [patrons] of hem, as they maken the miraclis of God onely a mene [means] to ther pley, and the play the ende of the miraclis of God, han at more pris [value] ther pley than the miraclis of God.

Such tendencies lead to the "Antichrist" promoters of the popish mystery plays from which the Late Banns so carefully distinguish **Chester's cycle** as Protestant in its scriptural material and didactic ends. The tendency for drama to acquire a life of its own is held in check by constant reference to external authority. But the same tendencies are present in contemporary secular theatre where the players, like Antichrist, gain financial rewards and wordly renown. This drama of "good players and fine wittes" is contrasted in the Late Banns with the theatrical crudities of **Chester's cycle.** But "oure playeinge is not to gett fame or treasure" and its transparent shortcomings emphasise that its concerns are with meaning rather than production. The Late Banns seek to dissociate the cycle both from other cycles and also from other kinds of drama and to present it as *sui generis,* something unique:

> And then dare I compare that, this lande
>   throughout,
> none had the like nor the like darste set out.
> (40-1)

And its appeal is not that of emotional engagement but of rational detachment, to

> All that with quiett mynde
> can be contented to tarye.
>
> (210-11)

Coda

We would give much to have a tape or a video of the debate in Chester's Common Hall on 30th May 1575. The proposition was:

> Whether the accostomed plaies called the Whiston Plaies shalbe sett furth and plaied at Midsummer next or not

and the voting was: "Yes"-33, "No"-12, a resounding majority, which suggests that the arguments were convincing. Later in the year, after the new mayor had been installed, the retiring mayor, Sir John Savage, was leaving the Common Hall when he was served with a summons to go to London to explain to the Privy Council why he had allowed the cycle to be performed in defiance of the prohibition of the Archbishop of York and the Earl of Huntingdon.

We still have a copy of the letter Sir John wrote to his fellow aldermen from London, asking that they send a sealed certificate to confirm that he was only carrying out their collective will. This was done. The council justified their production as:

> Acordinge to an order concluded and agreed upon for dyvers good and great consideracons redoundinge to the comen wealthe, benefite, and profitte of the saide citie in assemblie there holden, according to the auncyente and lawdable usages and customes there hadd and used fur above remembraunce. . .

i.e. that it was for civic advantage and within the city's customary jurisdiction. This was a defence already prepared and, since no proceedings were taken against Sir John, we must assume that it was allowed, though hardly accepted. The council did not take such a risk again.

Norma Kroll (essay date 1987)

SOURCE: "Equality and Hierarchy in the Chester Cycle Play of Man's Fall," in *Journal of English and Germanic Philology,* Vol. 86, No. 2, April, 1987, pp. 175-98.

[*In the excerpt below, Kroll describes how the Chester author's deviating from traditional scriptural hierarchies when depicting the fall of man presents "not the stark moral oppositions of the other cycle plays but complex earthly problems that make the dramatic interactions in his play reflective of the human dilemmas in the world of his audience."*]

Scholars of medieval drama agree that the **Chester play of man's fall** differs notably from the York, Towneley, and N-town versions in its simple faithfulness to Scripture. Yet, the dramatist does not merely emulate the original text: he also, as Rosemary Woolf [in *The English Mystery Plays,* 1972] puts it, "firmly embeds the murder of Abel in the life-history of Adam and Eve, [with] the Fall and the murder in fact forming one play." This reworking of Scripture suggests that the **Chester play** might be more unusual than has yet been recognized. As we shall see, it is a rereading of Scripture that, paradoxically, is both closer to and further from the original text than the other cycle versions. The other playwrights build their plots on the action recounted in Scripture but derive the form and meaning of the action from doctrine, not from the original text. Very differently, the Chester dramatist exploits the language of the prior text in ways that transform the traditional God/man, man/woman, and human/earth hierarchies into mutual relationships. Adam and Eve's bodily ties to each other and their sons, rather than the debt to God underscored in Scripture and doctrine, provide the moral center of the action. The Chester playwright portrays the disintegration of family relationships as an even greater evil than the loss of Eden.

I

The complex representation of a human-centered world in the **Chester play** can be better understood if we first look briefly at the ways the York, Towneley, and N-town versions portray the God-focused world in Genesis. In Scripture, God both makes Adam in His image and emphasizes that the first man is preeminently a bodily creature. Accordingly, the original text implies that in some sense God might also have a bodily nature. Medieval doctrine nullifies any such possibility by interpreting the original in ways that prove God is pure intelligence and that the divine part of man is his mind, not his body. The cycle dramatists, then, could choose whether to build on the Old Testament imagery of the body, risking the suggestion that God gives value to man's corporeal desires, or to follow doctrine, highlighting man's intellectual desires. The three dramatists differ from the Chester author primarily because they take the latter approach, representing the scriptural God/man hierarchy as a dramatic Mind/mind opposition.

The York God creates Adam in the shape of His mind to satisfy His desire for creatures intelligent enough to revere Him: a "skylfull [rational] beeste þan will y make, / Aftir my shappe and my liknesse, / The whilke shalle wirshippe to me take." The play's second use of the term, in the phrase "shappe of man" (III.36), establishes a clear distinction between Adam's bodily form, which makes him like the lower animals, and his intelligence, which makes him like God. Similarly, the Towneley God makes "man to oure liknes," investing Adam with intellectual power: "I gif the witt, I gif the strenght, / of all thou sees, of brede & lengthe; thou shall be wonder wyse.' Although the N-town God creates Adam not in His image but "be name," He authorizes the first man to name his wife and every other creature (I.108), a task implying intellectual resources that somehow correspond to God's.

In emphasizing the doctrinal Mind/mind hierarchy, the York, Towneley, and N-town playwrights skillfully omit all but the few bodily images essential to a portrayal of the creation of man. The York God refers to Adam's bodily substance—"Of þe sympylest parte of erthe þat is here / I shalle make man" (III.25-26)—but only for the sake of its spiritual purpose—to remind Adam "to a-bate his hautand cheere, / Both his grete pride and other ille; / And also for to haue in mynde / Howe symple he is at his makynge" (III.27-30). The N-town play, like the **Chester,** includes the vivid scriptural "Fflesch of þi fflesch" and "bon of þi bon" (I.100) but assigns a solely negative role to the human body. This play's Eve prefaces her postlapsarian desire that Adam "wrythe on to my necke bon" with the telling lament, "my wyt a-wey is fro me gon" (I.388-89). Adam responds accordingly, using bodily imagery to highlight the failure of their intelligence: "Wyff þi wytt is not wurth a rosch / leve woman turne þi thought / I wyl not sle fflescly of my fflesch / Ffor of my fflesch þi fflesch was wrought / Oure hap was hard [for] oure wytt was nesch" (I.391-95). The N-town play, like the York, presents only an apparent mind/body polarity since the body is given no value or force of its own.

The characters' motives for opposition to God in the three plays also reflect a prevailing doctrinal principle, succinctly expressed in St. Thomas' notion that the Genesis Adam and Eve rebelliously sought divine wisdom in order to become His equals (*Summa* I-II, Q.84). The York Adam and Eve disobey God out of their irrational desire to obtain reverence and power akin to His—the more-than-human "wirshipee" and "maistrie" (V.56-59) to be had by becoming "als wise / als god" (V.96-97). The Towneley temptation of Adam and Eve is missing, but its Satan, in a council in hell, makes wisdom, albeit the perverted wisdom of the fallen angels, the crux of his temptation of Eve: "bot thens [from Eden and from God's approval] thay [Adam and Eve] shall, if we be wise" (I.267). The N-town play represents a first couple who sin out of desire for the practical knowledge—to be "wys of Connyng. . .lyke on to god in al degre" (I.184-85)—that would allow them godlike control over the farthest reaches of the created universe. Throughout, this play stresses Adam's desire to be "goddys pere" (I.190, 196, 203, 213, 215, 244). Although the dramatic conflicts in the three plays are caused by Adam and Eve's folly, which overrides their God-given wisdom, the two humans keep God, not each other or some other earthly good, as the focus of their desires. Even their rebellions are testimony to the supereminence of God.

If we examine the dramatic conflicts in these plays

carefully, we see that the Mind/mind hierarchies develop as dialectical Other/self polarities. In each, Adam and Eve's minds are, as doctrine has it, both like and radically different from God's. They seek absolute likeness to God, but in so doing achieve absolute difference. In other words, the first couple's attempt to transform their human natures and become literally equivalent to, if not a substitute for, God is clearly a struggle to become an entirely other order of being, for to be God's peer is to be nonhuman. Ironically, the fallen Adam and Eve in each play do become entirely other than they were originally, albeit not in the way they had expected. Thus, the emphasis on the human mind shown by the York, Towneley, and N-town dramatists enables them to create coherent readings of the fall that make its meaning and morality unequivocal in Christian terms.

In contrast, the **Chester play** emphasizes the indeterminacies of meaning and morality when seen from the perspective of the human characters' bodily existence. This play's focus on the corporeal is an expansion of the figurative representation of God in Genesis: metaphorically, the Old Testament God has human form and acts as a bodily being would. The **Chester play** capitalizes on the original imagery to establish a Body/body hierarchy. The rubrics describe a God whose acts are literally corporeal: "Then goinge from the place where he was, commeth to the place where he createth Adam"; "Then the creatour bringeth Adam into paradice, before the tree of knowledge"; "Then God taketh Adam by the hande and causeth him to lye downe, and taketh a ribbe out of his syde." The physicality of God's acts—both in building and in managing His creation—make the values at issue altogether different from those indicated in the N-town God's twice-announced journey—"my wey to hefne is redy sowth" (I.130) and "ffor to hefne I sped my way" (I.140). The Chester God's corporeal involvement places greater importance on the earthly and the physical than on the spiritual, in effect validating earthly over heavenly existence. He advises Adam to "be wise" and "bringe not thyselfe in streife" (II.111-12), lest he lose his earthly paradise, not the other-worldly rewards valued in the other three plays.

The key conflicts in the Chester version derive, as we shall see, from the God-given *sine qua non* of human continuance: the male/female and parent/child interactions which set up an earthly system of values and ironically compete against allegiance to God. The dramatist skillfully uses Genesis to portray a God who highlights Adam and Eve's ties to the earth and each other:

"Faciamus hominem ad imaginem et similitudinem nostram, et praesit piscibus maris, et volatilibus caeli, et bestiis, universaeque terrae, onmique reptili, quod movetur in terra" (Gen. 1:26). "Et creavit Deus hominem ad imaginem suam: ad imaginem Dei creavit illum, masculum et feminam creavit eos" (Gen. 1:27). "Benedixitque illis Deus, et ait: Crescite et multiplicamini, et replete terram, et subiicite eam" (Gen. 1:28).

> Now heaven and earth is made expresse,
> make wee man to our likenesse.
> Fishe, fowle, beast—more and lesse—
> to mayster he shall have might.
> To our shape now make I thee;
> man and woman I will there bee.
> Growe and multyplye shall yee,
> and fulfill the earth on hight.
>
> (II.81-88)

The scriptural words, "likenesse" and "shape," also used in the York and Towneley versions of the Genesis 2 creation of Adam, establish a correspondence between man and God that seems conventional. But in the Chester, the only cycle play to incorporate the Genesis 1 creation of the first man and woman, the words take on exceptional significance. Since God's "shape" provides the pattern for Eve's as well as for Adam's body, the two humans are like each other as well as like God. In essence, they are not only equivalent but are also equal, an equality that is confirmed even as it is finally destroyed when the fallen Eve is newly subjected to Adam (II.318). Before the fall, Eve is to "Growe and multyplye" with Adam, a command which emphasizes their mutual physical activity, rather than the divine grace underscored in the York God's promise—"Thy kind shall multeply" (IV.65).

The Chester relationship is further complicated by the playwright's inclusion of the earth as a partner. Only this play omits the scriptural phrase, "subiicite eam," so that Adam and Eve are given lordship over the earth's produce—"all that in yearth bine livinge" (II.93)—but not, as in the other three plays, over the earth itself. Instead, the Chester Adam and Eve are to reproduce for the earth's sake—to "fulfill the earth" (II.88)—as well as for their own. In return, the earth is, as God commands, "To helpe" them in kind (II.89), actively repaying them for their progeny with its produce.

This human/earth relationship has no parallels in the other cycle plays of man's fall. The York God's "Rise vppe, þou erthe in bloode and bone" (III.35), for example, stresses Adam's inferiority to God. In the **Chester** version, however, the fact that Adam's body was "of yearth made" (II.428) is emphasized as a special act of creation which distinguishes him from all other creatures who were made of "nought." In fact, the earth is not a stage for, but a participant in, a complex set of physical interactions after as well as before the fall. The postlapsarian earth and Adam are to suffer together: in man's arduous earthly labor, "warryed [cursed] the earthe shalbe" (II.326).

The suffering is motivated by the interaction between the two humans, an interaction built on the playwright's revision of the Genesis 2 version of Eve's creation:

> "Dixit quoque Dominus Deus: Non est bonum esse hominem solum: faciamus ei adiutorium simile sibi" (Gen. 2:18). "Immisit ergo Dominus Deus soporem in Adam: cumque obdormisset, tulit unam de costis eius, et replevit carnem pro ea" (Gen. 2:21). "Et aedificavit Dominus Deus costam, quam tulerat de Adam, in mulierem: et adduxit eam ad Adam" (Gen. 2:22). "Dixitque Adam: Hoc nunc, os ex ossibus meis, et caro de carne mea" (Gen. 2:23).

> Hit is not good man only to bee;
> helpe to him now make wee.
> But excice sleepe behoves mee
> anon in this man heare.
> One sleepe thou arte, well I see.
> Heare a bone I take of thee,
> and fleshe alsoe with harte free
> to make thee a feere.
>
> (II.129-36)

As in Scripture, the dramatist represents a God who takes a rib and flesh from Adam, but, omitting the Genesis God's use of the flesh to close the gap in the first man's side, he has the Creator explicitly add it to Eve's body. The play thus emphasizes that Adam and Eve share a double corporeal bond: they are close because they have the same bodily form—bone—and the same earthly substance—flesh. This doubling gives primary importance to Eve's role as Adam's equal complement and "feere," not to the adoration of God required of their counterparts in the York, Towneley, and N-town plays. The York God makes the two corporeally unequal, creating Adam first, and spiritually equal, giving them their souls simultaneously (III.42). This Eve satisfies Adam's need for a "feere" who is a "faithfull freende and sibbe" (III.37, 40) so that, together, they may love God (III.67). But He gives only Adam, made "of nought," the position of "Lordshippe in erthe" (III.70-71). The N-town God similarly gives Adam a "wyf and make" (I.101) in order "þat þer may be pres [of descendents] / me [God] worchipe for to do" (I.111-12). The Towneley God sets both Adam and Eve "to gouerne that here is" (I.189) but specifies that Adam is created to be not Eve's but the angels' "feere" (I.209). Thus, Adam's value lies not in his earthly but in his heavenly role—the "angels ordir to fulfill" (I.213-15)—and in his mind rather than his body, for angels have only intellectual forms and subtances (*Summa* I. Q.93, A.3 and Q.63, A.1, A.2).

In the context of the Chester playwright's reading of Genesis, however, the doubling of the characters' bodily ties also makes them emotionally interdependent, a connection approved by God as well as by Adam:

"Dixitque Adam: Hoc nunc, os ex ossibus meis, et caro de carne mea: haec vocabitur Virago, quoniam de viro sumpta est" (Gen. 2:23). "Quamobrem relinquet homo patrem suum, et matrem, et adhaerebit uxori suae: et erunt duo in carne una" (Gen. 2:24). "Erat autem uterque nudus, Adam scilicet et uxor eius: et non erubescebant" (Gen. 2:25).

> I see well, lord, through thy grace
> bonne of my bones thou hir mase;
> and fleshe of my fleshe shee hase,
> and my shape through thy sawe.
> Therfore shee shalbe called, iwisse,
> 'viragoo', nothinge amisse;
> for out of man taken shee is,
> and to man shee shall drawe.
> Of earth thou madest first mee,
> both bone and fleshe; now I see
> thou hast her given through thy postee
> of that I in me had.
> Therfore man kyndely shall forsake
> father and mother, and to wife take;
> too in one fleshe, as thou can make,
> eyther other for to glad.

Then Adam and Eve shall stand naked and shall not bee ashamed.

(II.145-60 and rubric)

The Chester Adam's intense thankfulness not only affirms God's traditional role as the source of all good but also supplements the original text by celebrating his and Eve's original corporeal closeness. The physical substance and form linking Adam and Eve are again underscored by the repetition of the images, "bonne of my bones" and "fleshe of my fleshe" (Gen. 2:24), and by the allusion to Adam's "shape." As Adam emphasizes, the biological correspondence between this first man and woman virtually erases the difference between self and other. Eve is indeed "viragoo" (a woman taken from man's body [*OED*]), a Genesis term used in no other cycle play. The non-scriptural disclaimer, "nothinge amisse," evokes the conventional meaning of a manlike woman, ironically marking the critical sexual difference within corporeal likeness that makes procreation possible.

In Eden, likeness takes precedence over difference, with likeness signifying not identity but mutuality. The dramatist supplements the Old Testament's one-directional statement—"man shall forsake his father and mother for his wife"—with Adam's assertion that, in return, woman "shall drawe" to man. Lest the audience miss the corporeal basis for prelapsarian mutuality, the playwright represents an Adam who again repeats the scriptural "bone and fleshe," ending with the explicit "that I in me had." This context transforms the Old Testament metaphor, "too in one fleshe," into a literal ref-

erence to physical kinship, a God-given closeness that underlies the human characters' proper emotional ties to each other. These ties, too, are mutual: Adam and Eve are intended "eyther other for to glad," a phrase highlighting the latent possibility of reciprocal pleasure and desire in the Genesis text.

The expanded value the **Chester play** gives to desire makes morality ambiguous. Adam and Eve do not have either their scriptural archetypes' or their cycle counterparts' clear-cut choices between good and evil courses of action. Instead the Chester couple choose between two goods, opting for a deeper accord with each other at the expense of their ties to God. Ironically, it is Adam and Eve's desire to strengthen their interaction which drives them apart, turning reciprocity and equality into hierarchy and inequality.

II

The corporeal and emotional reciprocity enjoyed by the Chester Adam and Eve shapes both the temptation and the fall. Since the characters' relationships are defined by their bodies, any bodily changes necessarily alter the form and quality of their subsequent earthly interactions. This medieval version of an existential correspondence between the characters' natures and deeds provides an appropriate underpinning for drama, in which character is revealed through action. The action in the **Chester play** elaborates on the bodily interactions implied in Genesis in ways that reverse the traditional Other/self hierarchy and make the human self rather than the divine Other the focus of earthly existence.

In this one cycle play, the fall proceeds as a sequence of changing attitudes toward the human body. The Chester Satan's malevolence toward Adam and Eve is primarily a reaction to their corporeal substance: "Should such a caytiffe made of claye / have such blisse? Nay, by my laye!" (II.177-78). This fallen angel's explicit desire—to destroy Adam and Eve because they are made of and enjoy the earth—differs significantly from his counterparts' envy of the first humans' intellectual nature and links to God. The York Satan turns against man because he knows that God intends to scorn the "kynde of vs [angels]" and to assume the "kynde of man" (V. 10-13), making the human divine. The Towneley Satan plans to prevent man from taking the lost angels' places in heaven. The N-town Satan is similarly envious, not of man's earthly nature or existence, but of his heavenly potential: "That man xulde leve above þe sky / where as sum tyme dwellyd I" (I.321-22). Each of the three tempters moves against Adam and Eve because he is threatened not by their human otherness but by their potential for extrahuman sameness.

The Chester Satan, however, is paradoxically both like and unlike Adam and Eve in bodily terms. As Lucifer, he had called attention to his own bodily form, accepting Lightborne's adulation of his "bodie cleare" (I.164) and commanding the lesser angels to worship his "bodye, handes and head" (I.188). This Satan, both before and after his fall, has a bodily form that could well correspond to the first humans', even though his is superphysical and theirs is physical. The angel and the humans also have a similar need for others in order to attain their goals. If Adam and Eve must have each other to grow and multiply, the first angel must have the support of the angels to rebel. As Lucifer, he asks "all" the other angels for "comforte" (I.130-33) before he takes God's seat. As Satan, his address to the fallen second angel—"Ruffyn, my frende fayer and free, / loke that thou keepe mankinde from blesse" (I.260-61)—suggests the intensity of his need for friendship and support even in hell.

The fallen angel's scheme to take advantage of Eve's desire for Adam highlights the symmetry of the angelic and human need for mutual relationships. The good angels had warned Lucifer and Lightborne not to attempt their rebellious "parlous pleye" and "daunce" (I.207-209). Satan, in turn, decides to "teach his [Adam's] wiffe a playe" because "her to disceave I hoppe I may, / and through her brynge them both awaye" (II.180-82). This repetition of the term, "playe," in a different but parallel context gives new meaning to its preceding use, highlighting the latent corporeal tension in Lucifer's rebellion. In the angels' case, the rebellion is a bodily, if not a physical interaction: Lucifer and Lightborne command the good angels to bow to them instead of to God (I.178-201), and, in response, the good angels charge the two to "Goe (back) to your seates and wynde you hense" (I.206). In Adam and Eve's situation, "playe" takes on physical and sexual implications: "And of the tree of paradice / shee shall eate through my contyse; / for wemen they be full licourouse, / that will shee not forsake" (II.197-200). Thus, otherworldly and earthly interactions alike involve bodily interdependency, with the struggle for primacy and power or for sex and love shaped by the same inherent need for others.

This correspondence implicitly accounts for the Chester Satan's astute reading of human nature. He deliberately assumes a bodily form that complements Eve's in order to intervene in her and Adam's bodily reciprocity. Instead of the brief scriptural reference to the serpent's singular subtlety—"serpens erat callidior cunctis animantibus terrae" (Gen. 3:1)—we have a corporeal manifestation of his cunning. Satan chooses the body of a "maner of an edder [that] is in this place / that wynges like a bryde shee hase—/ feete as an edder, a maydens face—/ hir kynde I will take" (II.193-96). To earn Eve's trust, he becomes like her, female and young. But the reformed Serpent also has wings, an enticing critical difference between his earthly nature and Eve's. The addition subtly suggests superiority to creatures confined to the earth. Yet, by choosing birdlike rather than angelic wings, the Serpent avoids any sense of reaching toward the heavens. The Chester Satan well knows that Eve's primary attachments are to Adam and to the earth.

No such human or earthly chords are struck in the other two cycle descriptions of the Serpent. The York playwright depicts the fallen angel in the conventional form of a "worme" (V.23, 91), whereas the N-town playwright makes the Serpent a combination of animal and angelic forms, a "ffayr Aungell," "þe fals Aungel," and, finally, a "werm with an Aungelys face" (I.238, 261, 302). These tempters take on bodily forms which emphasize their radical otherness, thereby appealing to the first humans' desire to become other than they are.

In the Chester temptation, however, the characters choose the self over the Other. Accordingly, the Serpent appeals to Eve's sensual and sexual desires in ways that make her aware of herself not as a potentially superhuman but as a human female. He addresses her twice as "Woman" (II.209, 221), focuses on her attraction to earthly things, and, finally, invokes her closeness to Adam. This Serpent offers wisdom as a sensory experience, echoing Genesis 3:5 in promising that her "eyne shalbe unkynt." He also offers earthly pleasure, assuring her that "yt [the apple] is good meate" (II.227, 234). Even the guarantee, "Like godes yee shalbe" (II.228), promises no more than enhancement of their human natures, for no mention is made of becoming God's peer, the key lure in the York and N-town plays. In fact, the Chester Serpent shrewdly emphasizes the otherness of God as a way of enabling Eve to pre-absolve herself of responsibility for any ensuing strife: "Yee may well wotte hee [God] was your foe" (II.231). These assurances prepare for Satan's closing argument, the promise that Adam and Eve can benefit mutually—"both too, / thou and thy husband alsoe"—from doing as he advises (II.237-39). The Chester Eve sins because she desires not to be other than herself but to become a greater self, which, for her, involves even closer ties to Adam.

The force of Eve's human desires makes transgression far easier for her than for her cycle counterparts. The York and N-town Eves show no concern with the fruit *qua* fruit, despite the Genesis reference to gluttony. They seek only the godlike rewards promised by the Serpent. Differently, the Chester Eve emphasizes the earthly: "this tree is fayre and bryght, / greene and seemely to my sight, / the fruite sweete and much of myght" and, almost as an afterthought, notes that "godes it may us make" (II.241-44). In fact, she sees eating the fruit as a primarily sensory test of its material nature, "to assaye which is the meate" (II.246), as the Serpent had suggested, rather than a means to acquire divine wisdom, as in Scripture (Gen. 3:6).

Eve's temptation of Adam is shaped by her instinctive bodily intelligence, emphasized in the play's elaborate departure from the flat statement in Scripture—"deditque viro suo, qui comedit" (Gen. 3:6). Unlike the York Eve who offers Adam divine status and the N-town Eve who promises divine wisdom, the Chester Eve shows her mastery of the subtle "playe." In a scene that is no less charming for its profound irony, she tempts her husband not with promises of transcendent power or knowledge but with the winsomeness of her appeal: "Adam, husbande liffe and deare, / eate some of this apple here. / Yt is fayre, my leeffe feare; / hit may thou not forsake" (II.249-52). In effect, persuasion becomes seduction.

Similarly, the Chester Adam's quick response to temptation, more like the brief scriptural "and he ate" than his counterparts', is shaped by his physical and emotional instincts. Like Eve, Adam finds the apple tempting because it appeals to his senses—"That is soothe, Eve, withouten were; / the fruit is sweete and passinge feare" (II.253-54). Nevertheless, he is beguiled by Eve's demeanor rather than by the fruit as he obeys her "prayer" that he eat (II.291) instead of God's command to abstain. Unlike his counterparts in the other cycle versions, the Chester Adam offers no resistance, making his and Eve's disobedience curiously tensionless. The point is that the two are more caught up in desire for each other than for the forbidden apple. Accordingly, they experience no sense of strife until their sin alters their perception of their bodies.

The Chester dramatist makes the fall an ironic reversal of Adam and Eve's original sense of a shared self, exploiting the implications of the scriptural narrator's unelaborated "cognovissent se esse nudos" (Gen. 3:7). The dramatic expansion—Adam's emotional "I am naked, well I see. / Woman, cursed mote thou bee," for "Now have I brooken, through reade of thee, / my lordes commandemente" (II.258-59, 263-64)—reopens the opposition between self and other. This Adam is far angrier than his counterparts in the other plays, understandably so since he and Eve were far more interdependent and loving. Adam, in fact, explicitly pinpoints the cause of the fall as his and Eve's physical connection: "yea, sooth sayde I [Adam] in prophecye / when thou [Eve] was taken of my bodye—/ mans woe thou would bee witterlye! / therfore thou was soe named [virago]" (II.269-72). Ironically, Eve's sexuality—given by God to strengthen the first humans' ties to each other and to the earth—divides rather than joins them: "My licourouse wyfe hath bynne my foe" (II.353). Adam's words echo Satan's claim, "for wemen they be full licourouse," and confirms the latter's insight into the laws of human nature. Even more notably, Adam's curse marks his alienation from Eve, an emotional withdrawal that transforms her into an other, an opposed as well as a separated self.

Very differently, the York and N-town dramatists use the characters' sense of nakedness to emphasize their loss of intellectual potency. The York Adam manages only a rather feeble, "For I am naked as me thynke" (V.111), followed by an intellectually and emotionally weak attempt at blaming Eve: "þis werke, Eve, hast þou wrought, / and made þis bad bargayne" (V.118-19). Despite the N-town Adam's references to their bodies—"my flesly frend," "pore preuytes" (I.248, 253), and "fflesscly eyn [which] byn al vnlokyn" (I.264)—he is principally concerned with the effects of sin on their minds—"vn-hede" they are also "vn-kynde," unnatural rather than natural and intellectually rather than physically other. In all, however, Adam's tone is accepting and rational rather than angry or bitter: "Ryth grevous is oure synne / of mekyl shame now do we knowe" (I.268-69). His reactions, like the York Adam's, provide an unambiguous resolution for conflicts set in motion by Lucifer's rebellion in heaven (presented as one play in the Towneley and N-town cycles and as a series of brief playlets or scenes linked to Lucifer's treason by superterrestrial expositors in the York).

The more equivocal **Chester** emphasis on the human body underlies an exceptional revision of the Genesis verses on Adam and Eve's postlapsarian need for clothing:

> "Fecit quoque Dominus Deus Adae et uxori eius tunicas pelliceas"
>
> (Gen. 3:21).

> Hilled behoveth you to bee.
> Dead beastes skynes, as thinketh mee,
> ys best you one you beare.
> For deadly nowe both bine yee
> And death noe way may you flee.
> Such clothes are best for your degree
> and such shall yee weare.
>
> (II.362-68)

The **Chester** reading virtually contradicts the original text, transforming a protective gesture into its opposite, a sign of the loss of the protection implied when God made Adam and Eve in his image. With the extrascriptural phrases, "Dead beastes" and "death noe way may you flee," the playwright depicts an Adam and Eve who are physically debased to suit their vitiated humanity. Henceforth, the characters must endure a fatal internal opposition: although still alive, still themselves, they are "deadly" and destined for death, for irreversible otherness. Adam and Eve have become corporeally other, different from their original natures and from each other. Ironically, the characters' natural strengths, founded on their attachment to each other and the earth, were sufficient for them to fulfill their human potential and yet impelled them to undo their humanity. However simple the Chester fall might seem, its playwright crafts a highly complex set of interactions based on the human desire for sensual pleasures and earthly rewards.

III

The **Chester** portrayal of Adam and Eve and of Cain and Abel is indeed a descent into evil but, unconventionally, the evil stems from increasingly distorted attempts to rethink and reaffirm the idea of the self in relation to others. The initial self/self interaction between Adam and Eve in Eden becomes a self/other hierarchy that shapes family interactions in the postlapsarian world. Each member of the first family finds his sense of self contingent on his position vis-à-vis those who are other: Cain and Abel act to merit their parents' approval, and Adam and Eve act to enhance their children's well-being. The medium of interaction has changed, however, for they are no longer alike enough to rely solely on bodily complementarity. Although the links between the generations are built on the characters' bodily relationships, their ties are advanced and destroyed by their readings of each other's words. The danger is that language allows for the possibility of serious misreading, particularly when a character's sense of self is dislocated by his sense of another.

Ironically, the Chester Adam's belief in the postlapsarian restoration of his own value is a misinterpretation predicated on his attachment to his children:

> Hight God and highest kynge,
> that of nought made all thinge—
> beast, fowle, and grasse growinge—
> and me of yearth made,
> thou gave me grace to doe thy wyllinge.
> For after greate sorrowe and sikinge
> thou hast mee lent greate likinge,
> too sonnes my hearte to glade:
>
> (II.425-32)

The root of the problem is again the human body: Adam mistakenly assumes that his special bodily nature, substantially different from every other kind of creature's, and the birth of his children, extensions of his bodily substance and form, are signs of God's forgiveness. He has, after all, fulfilled what God had designated as his and Eve's central interaction, to grow and multiply. But Adam misreads the cosmic and human significance of having children. If Abel is Adam-like, virtually Adam's much desired second self, Cain proves to be the opposite of both, not another but *the* other.

Adam's words to his sons, an extended revision of the brief scriptural designation of Abel as a shepherd and of Cain as a farmer—"Fuit autem Abel pastor ovium, et Cain agricola" (Gen. 4:2)—are an attempt to help them become like him. In this one play, the division of labor between Cain and Abel is deemphasized for the sake of stressing Adam's fatherly love and the first

family's common ties to the earth. Adam makes his affection explicit: "Cayne and Abell, my childrenn deare" (II.433) and "my leefe children fayre and free" (II.493). But relationships are now unequal, so that affection alone is no longer sufficient. Accordingly Adam makes the morality of his children's and his own practical duties equally clear: "Nowe for to gett you sustenance," "For sythen I feele that myschaunce / of that fruite for to eate, . . . with this spade. . . / I have dolven. Learne yee this at mee, / howe yee shall wynne your meate" (II.489-96). Since Cain is the only son actually to work the earth, the Chester Adam invokes the spade and the act of digging as symbolic of all human activity, as it is in *Piers Plowman*. He thereby stresses that every man is earth-dependent, for God's approval and human survival depend on their ability to use the earth.

In contrast, the N-town Adam, the only other cycle play father-teacher, is wholly impersonal, demonstrating neither parental love nor practical concern for his sons' earthly "sustenance." Despite his references to his "ryth gret labour" and his "delvyng and dyggyng" (I.405-406), he values the earth's produce solely as an offering which might make Cain and Abel deserving of heaven: "suche good as god hath yow sent / the fyrst frute offyr to hym in sacryfice brent / hym evyr be-sechyng with meke entent" (II.41-43). Lest the point of the lesson be missed, the N-town Adam highlights their proper goal: "þat ye may come to þat blysse þat hym self is inne / With gostly grace / þat all your here levyng / may be to his plesyng" (II.56-59).

The Chester Adam's lesson is far more ambiguous, opening possibilities for its own misreading, much as Scripture, by virtue of what it omits, suggests the terms of its own dramatization. Adam gives value to the need for proper interactions between his children and the earth but ignores the rules required for interaction with each other, rules that are vital for negotiating unequal postlapsarian relationships. In other words, Adam transmits a set of explicit and implicit values which, taken together, could suggest that interactions with the earth are more vital than interactions with a brother or with God. Ironically, he teaches about constructive behavior but his lesson implicitly contributes to Cain's destructive acts.

In this one play, Eve also speaks. Her address to her children is an elaborate transformation of the brief Genesis comment—"Possedi hominem per Deum" (Gen. 4:1)—which underscores the importance of human relationships in shaping human destiny:

> My sweete children, darlinges deare,
> yee shall see how I live heare
> because enbuxone so wee weare
> and did as God would not wee shoulde.
> This payne, theras had bine no neede,

I suffer on yearth for my misdeede;

(II.497-502)

Another sorrowe I suffer alsoe:
my children must I beare with woo,
as I have donne both you too;
and soe shall wemen all.
This was the divell, our bytter foe,
that made us out of joy to goe.
To please, therfore, sonnes bee throwe,
in sinne that yee ne fall.

(II.505-12)

Where Adam had offered practical advice about his sons' and the earth's reciprocity, Eve tells only of her feelings about her children, her fallen state, and her enemy. In fact, the omission of the Genesis "per Deum" implies that Eve, unlike Adam, sees the birth of her children as her own doing, unmediated by God. Her salutation is also far more emotional than Adam's, suggesting that her ties to Cain and Abel might be more intense than her husband's and might override her marital concerns. In any case, the shift of her primary concern from her husband to her children provides a way to satisfy a central constraint of drama, the need to motivate action and interaction, even between parents and children, by passion.

As in Eden, where the Chester Eve was more concerned with the problem of covering her own and Adam's nakedness than with God's anger, her moral sense remains limited by her sense of personal devotion to her family. Although she acknowledges her disobedience to God, she regrets not her betrayal of Him but the "payne" she "suffer[s] on yearth." Indeed, Eve shifts the blame for the fall to "the divell, our bytter foe, / that made us out of joy to goe." In this context, her use of "enbuxone" is tellingly ironic, for it meant unyielding or disobedient in the courtly sense of ungracious or unsubmissive ("buxom to" meant "yield to"; "buxomness" meant "obedience," "submissiveness," "graciousness," and "blitheness" [*MED*]). Although the courtly code was essentially ethical and complemented medieval religious traditions, Eve's implicit denial of personal responsibility indicates that her courtly sensibility is as superficial as her religious and moral sense. By implication, her warning to her sons "To please" God lest they fall further into sin stems from fear not of losing some unspecified spiritual reward but of destroying what earthly joy they still have.
Given the Chester characters' concern with the earth and with each other, its Cain responds as affectionately and sensibly as his parents might wish:

Mother, for sooth I tell yt thee,
a tyllman I am and soe wilbe,
As my father hath taught yt me,
I will fulfill his lore.
    Hear he bringe in the plough.

Of corne I have great plentee;
sacrifice to God sonne shall yee see.
I will make too looke if hee
will sende mee any more.

(II.513-21)

This speech is radically different from the N-town Cain's unwillingness even to hear his father, for he stupidly thinks it "but vanyte / to go to hym [Adam] ffor Any spekyng / to lere of his lawe" (II.16-18). Only the Chester Cain offers to sacrifice without any of the recalcitrance displayed by his cycle counterparts. Yet his words and gestures are shaped by his misreading of his responsibilities. He takes into account his father's lessons on the way to deal with the earth but not those on God's promise of the earthly redemption of the human body and of His future corporeal ties to men: "light into my kynde; / and my blood that hee will wyne / that I soe lost for my synne" (II.452-54). Cain, like Eve, is willing to be good but cannot comprehend that man's relationship to God is as crucial as his interactions with those who are physically and emotionally close to him. Thus, he does not trust God who is Other as he trust his parents who are like him, although he is eager to please his parents and willing to take a calculated risk, on the chance that sacrificing might increase his earthly good.

In essence, the Chester playwright recasts the conventional significance of Cain's acts. He characterizes the elder brother as one who thinks he is responding properly to his parents' advice, not, as in the other plays, one who thinks he knows better than his teachers. The York Cain, whose crude rusticity underscores his lack of intelligence, proclaims that the angel's advice is stupid: he "thynkeþ þat werke were waste, / That he [God] vs gaffe geffe hym agayne" because "if he be moste in myghte and mayne, / what nede has he?" (VII.60-66). The Towneley Cain, a still more elaborately characterized rustic, unthinkingly and self-righteously spouts platitudes: "ffor had I giffen away my goode, / then myght I go with a ryffen hood, / And it is better hold that I haue / then go from doore to doore & craue" (II.140-43). The N-town Cain, although less broadly comic than the York and Towneley, believes as they do that tithing reveals the weakness of man's intelligence—a "febyll skyll" and a "ffebyl reson" (II.109, 116). Thus, he decides that "I more wysly xal werke þis stownde / to tythe þe werst" (II.96-97) because "it wolde me hyndyr and do me greff," while God "wyll neyther ete nor drynke / Ffor he doth neyther swete nor swynke" (II.109-15). The N-town Cain, like the York, foolishly measures God by physical standards, clearly failing to distinguish between the self and the Other. In each of these plays the motivating principle is not a desire for importance in relation to others, but an unambiguous solipsism which nullifies all personal and moral values.

In contrast, the Chester Cain skimps on his offering

because he, like Adam and Eve, responds to the human/earth interaction more strongly and naturally than to the God/man hierarchy. He cannot bear to sacrifice the earth's produce for an extra-earthly purpose: "Hit weare pittye, by my panne, / those fayre eares for to brenne," preferring instead to offer "This earles corne [which] grewe nexte the waye" (II.537-41). Yet, even the undeveloped corn is not entirely valueless to him, for he believes it to be sufficient not only to pay his debt to God but also to obligate God in return: "I hope thou [God] wilte white mee this / and sende me more of worldly blisse; / ells forsooth thou doest amisse / and thou bee in my debt" (II.549-52). Clearly, Cain has a sense of his acts as part of an ongoing interaction, but, because his happiness in the postlapsarian world depends on his position in an asymmetrical hierarchy instead of in an equal interaction, his hope of having God in his "debt" is tantamount to an attempt both to control the interaction and to gain a measure of power over Him.

For Cain, earthly happiness is not just a matter of material goods, as it is for his cycle counterparts. Hierarchy proves still more important. His eagerness to make the first offering is a matter of position and opposition: "I am the elder of us too, / therefore firste I will goe" (II.529-30), adding for emphasis, "anone withouten lett" (II.548). Cain is moved by pride in his seniority over Abel, not by his sense of obligation to God. Yet Cain's desire to get something from God in return is not simply, as Bennett Brockman sees it [in "Cain and Abel in the Chester Creation: Narrative Tradition and Dramatic Potential," *Medievalia et Humanistica* 5, 1974] the conventional hypocrisy displayed in the other cycle versions, but rather an expression of a distorted sense of the critical difference between himself and the Other.

This Cain is all too conscious of the regard of others, both of his family and of God, as we can see in the **Chester** revision of the scriptural narrator's objective comment: "iratusque est Cain vehementer, et concidit vultus eius" (Gen. 4:5). The dramatist personalizes the image by giving it to Cain and by substituting "shame" and "envy," evocative of courtly responses and thus of hierarchical relationships, for the Genesis and the other cycle plays' "angry": "My semblant for shame shakes / for envy of this thinge" (II.575-76). His immediate feelings depend on a sense of his own failure within a situation involving others; his "worth" is secondary, a result of his shame and envy, not of his original rejection.

The extent of the change in Cain's emotional nature is marked by a corresponding change in his bodily nature:

"Dixitque Dominus ad eum: Quare iratus es? et cur concidit facies tua" (Gen. 4:6). "Nonne si bene egeris, recipies: sin autem male, statim in foribus peccatum aderid? sed sub te erit appetibus eius, et

tu dominaberis illius" (Gen. 4:7).
Cayne, why arte thou wroth? Why?
Thy semblant changes wonderously.
If thou doe well and truely,
thou may have meede of mee.
Wottys thou not well that for thy deede
yf thou doe well thou may have meede;
if thou doe fowle, fowle for to speede
and syccere therafter to bee?

(II.577-84)

Cain's body, like Adam and Eve's, is the vehicle of the self, and, as the change reveals, the self has its own potential for otherness. Very differently, the briefer Towneley version of the same Genesis verses omits any reference to Cain's face (II.291-96). Correspondingly, his character and feelings do not change. The tension in this play is built on the low comedy of Cain's anger—"Com kys the dwill right in the ars" (II.286)—not on the idea of a fall from at least partial virtue into evil.

As we might expect, the Chester dramatist's idea of morality does not correspond to the Towneley's. The Towneley God simply requires pious behavior—Cain must "tend right" (II.294). The Chester God asks for a mutual exchange—a good sacrifice for a good position within the family:

But, Cayne, thou shalt have all thy will,
thy talent yf thou wilt fulfill.
Synne of hit will thee spill
and make thee evell to speede.
Thy brother buxone aye shalbe
and fully under thy postee;
the luste therof pertaynes to thee.
Advyse thee of thy deede.

(II.585-92)

These lines transform the meaning of the scriptural "sin is waiting at the opening; unto thee it will have its desire" in two ways. First, the **Chester** reworking subverts the implications of the original by personalizing desire, negating the scriptural association of desire with sin and instead makes desire morally neutral, an inner potentiality that is neither good nor evil in itself. This play's God promises Cain the satisfaction of his "will" and "luste" if he fulfills his own "talent" or natural ability to grow corn, an earthly occupation which provides the material for both food and sacrifice and thus serves both physical and spiritual purposes. Second, the play expands the scriptural promise by God to accept Cain's subsequent offerings, if they prove sufficient, into a promise of "postee" over Abel. The Chester God thus validates medieval concepts of hierarchy, affirming that dominance, like desire, is morally neutral. Ironically, the Chester God's words echo the language in earlier speeches by Eve and Adam. In a hierarchical world, to be "buxone"—yielding or submissive—is vital. Yet God's kindness intensifies rather than dispels the destructive tendencies in Cain's nature, perhaps because his sense of "shame" has distorted his reading of God's words.

Cain's misinterpretation is exacerbated by his sense of a devalued self:

> Say, thou caytiffe, thou congeon,
> weneste thou to passe mee of renowne?
> Thou shalt fayle, by my crowne,
> of masterye yf I may.
> God hath challenged mee nowe heare
> for thee, and that in fowle manere;
> and that shalt thou abye full deare
> or that thou wende away.
> Thy offeringe God accept hase,
> I see by fyer that one yt was.
> Shalt thou never efte have such grace,
> for dye thou shalt this night.
> Though God stoode in this place
> for to helpe thee in this case,
> thou should dye before his face.
> Have this, and gett thee right!
>
> (II.601-16)

This violent speech, a pre-Freudian projection of Cain's ungratified desire for status onto his perceived enemies, is an expression of personal frustration caused by his external situation. He kills his brother not only because he wants Abel to "fayle . . . of masterye" but also because he wants to repay God for giving the mastery to Abel. Cain's reading of the situation is shot through with irony. First, he fails of self-mastery, causing his own destruction; second, he misinterprets Abel's intention, taking simple obedience as a power play; and third, he misconstrues God's advice, taking encouragement as a threat. Cain's promise to confront God "before his face" echoes Lucifer's previous challenge "before his [God's] face" (I.213). But the parallel highlights the differences between the heavenly and earthly declarations of enmity. Lucifer attempted to establish a new set of relationships with God and the angels—"Above greate God I will me guyde" and then "All angells, torne to me I read, / and to your soveraigne kneele one your knee' (I.182, 190-91). Cain attempts to destroy all relationships, since he feels he cannot maintain his original position within the family and the world. Thus, his doubly focused anger, against God and Abel, makes the climactic blow in the **Chester play** a far more intense and complex act than it is in the other cycle versions.

IV

The Chester playwright resolves the indeterminacies of the characters' motives and deeds not in Cain's killing of Abel, the play's climax, but in his return to his parents, an extraordinary scene of moral and dramatic closure. Cain's interaction with Adam and Eve is far more unusual than his N-town counterpart's final ap-

pearance. The latter is a solitary self-pitying figure who is primarily concerned with saving his own life and who, thinking only of himself, almost welcomes the relative safety of a life apart from other men. The Chester Cain, however, moves from self-pity (II.633-48, 665-76) to a strong but ironic sense of his and his parents' mutual responsibility. The final bitter exchange between parents and son suggests that Cain can no longer repress his own guilt—"there maleson both too / I wott well I must have" (II.678-79). Yet he also wishes them to face theirs. Adam and Eve are indeed partially responsible, for every act is both singular and part of an interaction. Thus, Cain's grim mix of resignation and resentment reflects his sense of shame and loss not just for himself but for all involved.

The **Chester** conclusion also emphasizes the irony of the human need for language as a vehicle of interaction: Cain, like Adam and Eve, uses language to teach but his words are a weapon that instructs far better than his parents's loving advice. His use of "dam," the female parent of animals or, contemptuously, a human mother *(OED),* and "syre," a father or male parent of domestic animals *(OED),* strikingly marks his withdrawal of the affection so highly valued by Adam and Eve. In addition, Cain's words ironically evoke the "Dead beaste skynes" his parents once wore, suggesting a further reduction in their humanity and his own. Also ironically, his avowal "I have slayne my brother Abell / as we fell in a stryffe" (II.683-84) echoes and nullifies God's initial warning to Adam against bringing himself "in striefe" (II.112).

Adam and Eve do finally grasp the lesson they should have understood when they fell, but only because Cain's words destroy all possibility of self-deception. They recognize their guilt as Cain sees his, in the destruction of their family unit: "Alas, alas, is Abell deade? / Alas, rufull is my reade! / Noe more joye to me is leade, / save only Eve my wyfe" (II.685-88). Adam realizes that he had not earned God's forgiveness and affection simply by behaving well. Rightly or wrongly, he looks no more to God for support. Yet, Adam's position on earth need not be wholly insupportable, as he recognizes, for he still can consider the possibility of finding joy in his relationship with his wife.

Eve, however, sees no such comfort. Apparently because her bodily ties to Cain and Abel are more direct than Adam's, her desire for Adam, unlike his for her, is irrevocably displaced by her love for her children. Her grief at their loss (an ironic inversion of the *Planctus Mariae*) is immeasureably greater than it was at the loss of her Edenic equality with Adam. In fact, this second loss is greater, for Eve and Adam were at least allowed to stay together, which was all she then cared about, while Cain is exiled and Abel is dead:

> Alas, nowe is my sonne slayne!

Alas, marred is all my mayne!
Alas, muste I never be fayne,
but in woe and morninge?
Well I wott and knowe iwysse
that verye vengeance it is.
For I to God soe did amysse,
mone I never have lykinge.

(II.689-96)

Only now does Eve feel the consequences of her dis-obedience to God, seeing her own guilt in the physical destruction of one child and the moral destruction of the other.

The Chester dramatist deals with the aesthetic problem of closure in a play that is both complete in itself and part of a larger cycle by crafting a work which is closed in one sense and open in another. To evoke the sense of completion vital to dramatic form, he portrays a Cain who brings all familial interactions to an end. But he also embeds in the play the possibility of further human interactions by supplementing the original myth. Genesis recounts the banishing of Cain, lists his off-spring, tells of Lamech, and circles back to tell of Adam, Eve, and their second set of children, both completing the circle and suggesting a new beginning. The **Chester play** is linear, presenting two episodes within the cycle of Christian history, but it includes an Adam who has a prophetic dream that links the fall of man to the incarnation of Christ. Thus, the bodily images that form the play's central motif also contain the seeds of the interactions in subsequent plays that lead to Christ's birth. This dramatist concurrently high-lights both the dramatic or personal and the theologi-cal or universal significance of the human body. What he substitutes for closure, for harmony restored and reconciliation achieved, is not resolution of the charac-ters' desires but the displacement of desire by despair. Eve's final lament reveals the hopelessness stemming from the loss not just of loved ones but even of desire for love—"mone I never have lykinge" (II.696).

The Chester playwright shapes situations that anticipate the tragic reversals of the characters in Renaissance plays. The Cains in the other cycle plays do not fall, since they are never wise or good and thus cannot change. The Chester Cain does, moving from his position as a virtuous son, if not a virtuous servant of God, to a position outside all family relationships. He simulta-neously transforms his parent's joy to pain, inflicting a punishment on them that surpasses anything suggested in Scripture or in the other cycle versions. No other cycle dramatist portrays Adam, Eve, and Cain as char-acters whose acts are shaped primarily by earthly situ-ations and needs which necessitate choosing between opposing goods. Thus the Chester dramatist presents not the stark moral oppositions of the other cycle plays but complex earthly problems that make the dramatic interactions in his play reflective of the human dilem-mas in the world of his audience.

Judith Ferster (essay date 1989)

SOURCE: "Writing on the Ground: Interpretation in Chester Play XII," in *Sign, Sentence, Discourse: Lan-guage in Medieval Thought and Literature,* edited by Julian N. Wasserman and Lois Roney, Syracuse Uni-versity Press, 1989, pp. 179-93.
seaton
[*In the following excerpt, Ferster regards the Chester Cycle's* Woman Taken in Adultery *from a Jewish per-spective, relating it to other plays within the cycle, and also examines the play's significance for late medieval ideas about interpretation.*]

In Play XI of the **Chester Mystery Cycle,** the righ-teous old priest Simeon, who expects the coming of a savior but does not know that he has already been born, is startled to read that Isaiah predicts the birth of "Eman-uell" to a virgin. He not only refuses to believe that a virgin could bear a child, but also insists that the book is "wronge written." After he speaks briefly with a woman named Anna, he takes up the Bible again and is amazed to see that the words he has substituted for those of Isaiah are gone and that in their place stands "a virgin" in red letters. He reveals this "miracle" (61) to Anna and decides to test it by erasing the text again and substituting his own version, "that soother ys" (69). Indeed, the miracle is repeated: when he opens the book again, his words are now replaced with golden letters that reaffirm Isaiah's prophecy. He at last declares his willingness to believe the prediction (94-95), and the angel who has been miraculously restoring the text appears to him and tells him that he will live long enough to meet his savior, the miraculous child.

This story of the contest between manipulative misin-terpreter and the guardian angel of the text must have had great resonance for late medieval writers because of the increases in literacy and resulting increased inter-est in the use and misuse of texts. Simeon is a blatant misuser, for whom the Bible is a book to be corrected and appropriated to reflect his own opinion of what is true. He demonstrates that not only may texts fail to win acceptance for the beliefs they advocate but they may prompt revisionary interpretation as well. The an-gel who guards the integrity of the Bible in Play XI is one solution to the problem of the vulnerability of texts.

Another supernatural solution appears in the very next play of the **Chester Cycle,** which includes the episode of the woman taken in adultery. The story, which comes from the Gospel according to John (8:1-11), is the only account we have of Jesus writing. It solves the prob-lem of the text's vulnerability to interpretation not by preventing misreading but by describing a special cor-respondence between the intentions of author and audience. I want to focus on the extraordinary story of Jesus' writing on the ground and the Jews' interpretation of his text. Why does he write when he could speak to them? Why does he write on the ground? What is the significance of the Jews' responses to his text? I believe that the work of Paul Ricoeur can help to illuminate this episode, its relation to some of the other plays in the cycle, and its significance for late medieval ideas about interpretation.

The Semantic Autonomy of the Written Text

The Chester version of the story seems to try to explain some of what is left obscure in the Gospel. John does not explain the content or the function of the writing. An undisclosed number of scribes and Pharisees bring an adulteress to Jesus, citing the Old Testament law about stoning adulterers and asking him for his judgment. They hope "that they might be able to accuse him" (8:6). He writes on the ground with his finger, but they are not deterred from their questioning. He speaks— "Let him who is without sin among you be the first to cast a stone at her" (8:7)—and writes again. The scribes and Pharisees depart "one by one, beginning with the eldest" (8:9), leaving Jesus and the woman alone. He asks her who accuses and condemns her. When she replies, "No one," he says, "Neither will I condemn thee. Go thy way, and from now on sin no more" (8:11). In this story, the first writing seems to have no effect. When the questioning persists, his speech supplements the writing, and either the speech alone or the speech and the second writing together cause the Jews to abandon the scene. The medieval plays specify the number of Jews at two (**Chester**), three (N-Town), and four (York). The number of Jews was surely influenced by the exigencies of production—how many actors were available, how many could fit on the set, etc. But a result of the small number of Jews is that they can all *see* the writing, as they could not in a large crowd. The speech comes first and has no impact: in the **Chester play,** Primus Pharaseus repeats the case to Jesus—"shall shee be stoned or elles naye. . . ?" (246)—as though he had not heard Jesus' moral principle. Only after the Jews read the writing do they flee, each one chastened by what he has read, each one claiming that he does not dare to stay and accuse the woman. The first fears worldly shame, and. . .says he must leave because "I see my synnes so clearly" (after 255). In the Gospel, the writing is ineffective (the Jews may not even read it) and must be bolstered or explained by the speech. In the play, by contrast, the speech is insufficient and the writing chases the Jews away by showing them not merely a moral principle about the fitness of judges and executioners, but their own sins.

The importance of the writing in the **Chester play** is clear if we compare the Chester version to the two other cycles. In the N-Town, the woman enters asking for mercy; in the York, Jesus asks her to repent, and she

does. Although penitence is not the focus of the story in John, these two plays make the story into an *exemplum* of repentance. In the **Chester play,** however, there is no mention of repentance. The woman converts when she recognizes Jesus as God because his writing displayed a supra-human knowledge of her accusers:

> For godhead full in thee I see
> that knowes worke that doe wee.
>
> (277-78)

The writing is what frees Jesus from the trap set by the Jews and what makes the woman abandon sin for his sake.

Thus, the writing, undisclosed and almost nonfunctional in John, is turned in the Chester play into a magic text that discloses to each man his own sin. This is an extremely interesting kind of text in the late Middle Ages. Medieval narratives are full of stories of people seeing themselves in a text as if in a mirror. The most famous example is perhaps Augustine, who converted when he read a portion of the Bible "as if addressed to himself." The insomniac narrator of Chaucer's *Book of the Duchess* finds Ovid's story of Ceyx and Alcyone memorable chiefly for its reference to a god of sleep, of whom he was previously unaware. The narrator focuses on the part of the story that addresses his self-interest. In Chester Play XI, Simeon interprets according to his preconceived notions of what is possible in nature.

This is the fate of any written text—to be appropriated by its readers, who interpret it according to their own needs. They can interpret it as they like, just as they can control the experience of it by reading it in the wrong order, skipping, or skimming at will. Even the freedom not to read is a part of the license a reader has that a listener does not, and this license must have been growing clearer in the late Middle Ages as more and more people could read and could afford books. Conditions of reception in the late Middle Ages highlighted the reader's role as a shaper and interpreter of the text, and the reader's role often became part of the subject matter of the work. This is to say that the late Middle Ages was paying more and more attention—was being forced by the changing conditions of reception to pay attention— to what Paul Ricoeur [in *Interpretation Theory: Discourse and the Surplus of Meaning,* 1976] would call the semantic autonomy of the text. With writing, says Ricoeur,

> the author's intention and the meaning of the text cease to coincide. . . . Inscription becomes synonymous with the semantic autonomy of the text, which results from the disconnection of the mental intention of the author from the verbal meaning of the text, of what the author meant and what the text means. The text's career escapes the finite horizon lived by its author. What the text means now matters

more than what the author meant when he wrote it.

The increasing reading audience, and the increasing likelihood that readers would have access to a text they could read alone, meant that writers were becoming especially conscious of the likelihood that their works might be subjectively interpreted by private readers. I do not mean to suggest that works read aloud in groups or for that matter conversation cannot be misinterpreted. I do mean that the situation of texts was changing enough to bring the question of interpretation to consciousness as subject matter for late medieval writers. For example, the Church's anxieties about access to the Bible by readers untrained in authorized exegetical methods indicates ecclesiastical awareness of the power of those who could read for themselves.

Active Readers

In the **Chester cycle,** the Expositor is an example of an active reader. In Play XII, he applies the commentary of St. Gregory to the first episode, the story of the temptation of Christ, interpreting the three sins to which he was tempted as gluttony, avarice, and vainglory (calling the opportunity to eat after forty days of fasting "gluttony" is very medieval). After the episode of the adulterous woman, he interprets in several ways. For instance, he decides a point not perfectly clear from the play by saying of the Jews that

> . . . non of them wiser was,
> but his synnes eych man knewe.
>
> (307-8)

In Play V, the Expositor is an even more obtrusive reader in that he acknowledges that the story he takes from the Bible is cut:

> But all that storye for to fonge
> to play this moneth yt were to longe.
> Therfore moste fruitefull ever amonge
> shortly wee shall myn.
>
> (45-48)

The story that is too long to tell is the central one of the giving of the Law to Moses. At the end of the play the Expositor acknowledges that the Balaam and Balak episode from Numbers has been shortened:

> Lordings, mych more mattere
> is in this storye then yee have hard here.
>
> (440-41)

He claims that the cuts destroy none of the meaning:

> But the substans, withowten were,
> was played you beforen.
>
> (442-43)

His claim that God's book can be condensed without loss is striking, especially in light of his great busyness in this play. He not only notes cuts in the story; he narrates an important event (the rewriting of the tablets of the Ten Commandments) instead of letting it be dramatized, and he intrudes (in the Harley manuscript) after every prophet in the prophets' procession to interpret the prophet's speech (usually typologically, with reference to Christian history). He interrupts even where he asserts that no interpretation is necessary:

> Lordinges, these wordes are so veray
> that exposition, in good faye,
> none needes; but you know may
> this word "Emanuell."
> "Emanuell" is as much to saye
> as "God with us night and day."
>
> (H305-10)

Despite his claim here of the transparency of the prophet's meaning, the claim undermines itself: transparency that needs labelling isn't transparent, and besides, the word "Emanuell" needs translating. At the end of the procession, during which, with his help, Old Testament prophets predict the events of the New Testament, he himself predicts (444-55) the events of two of the next plays, Play VI (**the Nativity**) and Play VIII (**the Magi**). Several of the Expositor's comments explicitly address the shaping power of interpretation—both his own as a reader and that of his audience of playgoers. He labels his role as reader ("as reede I," 53) and acknowledges the importance of the interpreter's will when he interprets Ezekiel's gate as a reference to the conception of Jesus:

> By this gate, lords, verament
> *I understand in my intent*
> that way the Holy Ghost in went
> when God tooke flesh and bloode
> in that sweet mayden Mary.
>
> (H321-25; emphasis mine)

Although this is certainly a traditional reading of the gate, it is important that he mentions neither the tradition nor the writer's intention, but instead his own, the *reader's* intention. He may be meant as a guide to interpretation of the material the plays present. But his activities as reader call attention to the ways in which readers are independent.

The Expositor explicitly refers to his audience when he predicts what will be played next ("played as yee shall see," 57; "as yee shall played see," 445), and acknowledges his hearers' power to decide for themselves when he exhorts, "leeve yee mee" (444, H81). This emphasis on the audience's interpretation is consonant with the theme of belief in the Christian story. In a number of places in the Gospels, Jesus' miracles depend on the belief of the person they affect. For instance, in Mark, a woman's belief allows her to be cured when she touches Jesus, even though Jesus does not notice her or intend her to be cured (Mark 5:25-34; this episode also occurs in Luke 8:43-48 and Matthew 9:20-22). The **Chester cycle** registers the importance of belief in Play XIII, which contains two miracles, the curing of the blind man and the raising of Lazarus from the dead. When the Jews curse the blind man and ask Jesus if he is the Christ, Jesus tells them that he has already answered the question:

> That I spake to you openlye
> and workes that I doe verelye
> in my Fathers name almightie
> beareth wytnes of mee.
>
> But you beleeve not as you seene,
> for of my sheepe yee ne beene. . .
>
> (239-44)

The discussion of belief becomes more intense in the second half of the play because it becomes more specific. Now the issue is kinds of belief among members of the fold. When Jesus arrives at the home of Mary and Martha, who are grieving for their brother, Martha speaks first:

> And this I leeve and hope aright:
> what thinge thou askest of God almight,
> hee will grant yt thee in height
> and grant thee thy prayer.
>
> (377-80)

Martha affirms her belief *before* Jesus promises to help her, but her belief is limited to trust that Jesus could have prevented the death of Lazarus had he been present at the time:

> A, lord Jesu, haddest thou binne here leade,
> Lazar my brother had not binne deade. . .
>
> (373-74)

All she wants from Jesus now is advice ("but well I wott thou wilt us reade," 375), and when he promises that Lazarus will rise, she assumes that he refers to the resurrection of the dead on Judgment Day:

> That leeve I, lord, in good faye,
> that hee shall ryse the last daye;
> then hope I him to see.
>
> (382-84)

When she shows Jesus the body and its advanced state of corruption (435-37), he must reemphasize the importance of her belief:

> Martha, sayd I not to thee
> if that thou fullye leeved in mee

> Godes grace soone shalt thou see?
> Therfore doe as I thee saye.
>
> (438-41)

Ironically, Martha's profession of faith reveals the limit of her faith.

Jesus reiterates the importance of faith in his lyric in Play XVIII, **"De Resurrectione"**:

> And that bread that I you give,
> your wicked life to amend,
> becomes my fleshe through youre beleeffe
> and doth release your synfull band.
>
> (174-77)

In the raising of Lazarus, Martha's belief did not have to be total or precise. Here in the resurrection lyric, however, Jesus speaks as if transubstantiation depended absolutely on the faith of the communicants. The intentions of the "audience" are necessary to the meaning of the event. The "author's" intentions do not suffice. Interpretation is crucial.

Many Meanings from One Text

We are now more prepared for questions about why Jesus wrote at all and why he wrote on the ground. To answer the first question, we may look at the two other cycles' versions of the episode of the woman taken in adultery because they highlight the important issue of privacy even more than the Chester, and the issue of privacy highlights the oddity of Jesus' writing. To communicate to the Jews, Jesus need only have spoken. As we saw, in the Gospel according to John the number of Jews was unspecified: possibly not all the Jews could have heard him. In the plays, however, there are only a few, and speaking is easier and faster and requires no bending. However, when one speaks, all who are present hear, and the peculiar effect of Jesus' writing is to prevent that. In all the plays, each Jew seems not to have learned the sin(s) of the other(s) from reading the writing. For instance, the Pharisee in the N-Town Cycle is afraid because

> If that my fellowes that did espy
> They will tell it both far and wide.
>
> (219)

Others voice similar fears. In the N-Town play, the woman herself has special horror of *public* humiliation:

> I pray you kill me here in this place
> And let not the people upon me cry.
> If I be slandered openly
> To all my friendes it shall be shame.
> I pray you kill me privily!
> Let not the people know my defame.
>
> (216-17)

Ironically, writing, the instrument that bridges distance, mediates absence, and publishes, is here an instrument of privacy. This means not only that the Jews read silently to themselves and not out loud (reading out loud was common in the Middle Ages), but also (unless each Jew did the same foul deed) that the same text (Jesus does not write again after the first Jew reads) means different things to the different men.

One text with many meanings can sometimes be a formula for chaos. In Chaucer's *Squire's Tale,* the people of Cambyuskan's court are puzzled by the brass horse brought by the "strange knight." They speculate about it, and

> Diverse folk diversely they demed;
> As many heddes, as manye wittes [opinions,
>   minds] ther been.
> They murmureden as dooth a swarm of been,
> And maden skiles aftir hir fantasies,
> Rehersynge of thise olde poetries,
> And seyden it was lyk the Pegasee,
> The hors that hadde wynges for to flee;
> Or elles it was the Grekes hors Synon,
> That broghte Troie to destruccion,
> As men in thise olde geestes rede.

This passage is interesting both for its identification of the source of ideas as fantasies shaped by "olde poetries" and for its reduction of a crowd of individual speakers into an inarticulate swarm of bees. Furthermore, nothing is settled about the horse until the king asks the knight who arrived on it to explain it. The knight explains how to work it, but not how it works, but this seems to satisfy the king. Judgment is deferred until authority steps in with instruction and evasion. The moment is emblematic of the structure of the *Canterbury Tales* as a whole, a chorus of voices each presenting a world view in a contest never finished and never judged, but closed by the instructions and evasions of the *Retraction,* and by its deference to God.

The particular interest of the late Middle Ages in the multiplicity of interpretations is reflected in the scene of Jesus' writing but in a problematic way. The chaos is part of Jesus' tactic of divide and conquer. Because the Jews fear each other, they flee each other as well as Jesus. Their plot to force Jesus to violate either Moses' teaching or his own, fails. Their reading is self-interested; that is, each seems to read his own sins into the text, and yet the interpretive anarchy that results seems to be exactly Jesus' purpose, a way not of solving but of dissolving the double bind into which the Jews have placed him. Jesus' magic polysemous writing, which mirrors each man's sin, disperses the conspiracy.

The best analogue for this positive version of interpretive anarchy is Scripture as Augustine speaks of it in the *Confessions.* Augustine insists that Scripture is polysemous and that no one interpretation is exclusive. He praises Moses' style specifically for its openness to interpretation from many points of view, by hypothesizing that if he, Augustine, had been "commissioned" by God to write Genesis, he would have prayed for "such skill in writing and such power in framing words, that. . .those who can should find expressed in the few words of your servant whatever true conclusions they had reached by their own reasoning; and if, in the light of truth, another man saw a different meaning in those words, it should not be impossible to understand this meaning too in those same words." Interpretive anarchy is not a disaster; it is a divine miracle, testimony to the plenitude of God's meaning. Scripture is a spring with many channels, an orchard with hidden fruit. However, it is also true that Augustine's system has some safeguards. Scripture cannot mean just anything; it can only mean something that is elsewhere revealed "in the light of truth," that is, by other passages or Church doctrine. What each interpreter sees in Scripture can correspond to his own personality and preoccupations; that is, it can be self-interested. But it must also be true.

The story of the woman taken in adultery does not provide such theoretical statements about interpretation, but in the light of Augustine it is perhaps possible to see Jesus' writing on the ground as an analogue to the safeguards in Augustine's system. Of course, the commonsense explanation is that Jesus writes on the ground because it is handy; it eliminates the need for tools—writing surface, writing implement, a means of support. If the purpose of the writing is to make the audience go away, the text can be temporary, erasable by a foot or a breeze. And what better place than earth to write about human sin? But to write on the ground is also to keep the audience from physically controlling the text. If one writes on the ground a message designed to disperse the audience, one is separating audience and text, keeping them from gaining mastery over it. They cannot, like Chaucer's reading audience for the *Canterbury Tales,* "Turne over the leef and chese another tale. . ." (I, 3177). They cannot fold, spindle, or multilate; they cannot reread. Jesus' choice of writing surface enforces a kind of control over the audience's use of the text.

Writing on the ground is a way to control—even if only symbolically—what is usually uncontrollable, an audience's uses of texts. The only way to achieve absolute control over a text is to refuse to publish it, and the cycle plays usually include the story of Moses' temporary censorship of the Ten Commandments. When God chooses a human agent to transmit the Commandments, he risks having the message interpreted, transformed in some way. There is no hint that when Moses wrote the tablets himself, he did not write them exactly as God had first written them (Exodus 34:4), but Moses' action upon God's first version, written by his own finger, is radical; and it assures that the audience will never see it, never interpret it, and never use it for their own purposes. Of course he does finally give the Commandments to the people, but the moment of refusal to give the text away is an interesting analogue to the later episode.

The fact that Jesus both speaks and writes reinforces the idea that the episode—especially in the medieval versions—is about control of a reader's interpretation by an author's intention. In the Chester version, Jesus' oral statement of the impropriety of sinners' judging other sinners has no impact until the Jews read the writing about their own sins. General principle means nothing until it can be applied to the individual, until each one, in Augustine's formulation, takes it as a counsel "addressed to himself." Jesus provides both aphorism and application, both (oral) text and (written) gloss.

In his retelling of the story, the Expositor implies that the Jews' interpretation of the writing is correct, that is, accords with Jesus' intention. He says

> [t]hat wyst Jesu full well their thought,
> and all theire wyttes hee sett at nought—
> but bade which synne had not wrought
> cast first at her a stonne;
> and wrote in claye—leeve yee mee—
> their owne synnes that they might see,
> that ichone fayne was to flee,
> and they lefte hir alonne.
>
> For eychon of them had grace
> to see theire sinnes in that place . . .
>
> (297-306)

Thus the miraculous nature of this text: each reader sees himself in it, yet this idiosyncratic, even selfish reading occurs through grace and is in an important way "authorized." According to Ricoeur, what I have called idiosyncratic interpretation is not necessarily self-enclosed, because reading can be the occasion for learning about the self:

> Far from saying that a subject already mastering his own way of being in the world projects the *a priori* of his self-understanding on the text and reads it into the text, I say that interpretation is the process by which disclosure of new modes of being—or if you prefer Wittgenstein to Heidegger, of new forms of life—gives to the subject a new capacity for knowing himself. . . . The reader . . . is enlarged in his capacity of self-projection by receiving a new mode of being from the text itself.

Jesus' writing is an ideal case. The readers' self-recognition (not particularly pleasant or welcome, but true) coincides precisely with the author's intentions.

The issues of interpretation I have discussed here show

how Play XII fits into the **Chester cycle**. They also show how the play, along with the story of Simeon's book in Play XI, addresses late medieval concerns about the dangers of interpretation. In the Middle Ages, Jesus as writer has the power many writers, medieval and modern, must have wished for: the power to touch readers individually and with force, but without being misunderstood.

Jean Q. Seaton (essay date 1992)

SOURCE: "'What Have I Offended Unto Thee?': God as Three-in-one in the Chester Mystery Cycle," in *English Studies,* Netherlands, Vol. 73, No. 4, August, 1992, pp. 300-10.

[*In the following excerpt, Seaton discusses the unorthodox dramatization of the Holy Trinity in the Chester plays, stressing the necessity of the Chester author's using "trinitarian attributes both to characterize God and to show how unable Lucifer is to take God's place."*]

In the opening pageant of the **Chester cycle,** God is presented as reacting to Lucifer's attempted usurpation of the throne with lines that, from the realistic standpoint, simply express hurt feelings. Upon discovering Lucifer seated on his throne, God asks:

> Lucifer, who set thee here when I was goe?
> What have I offended unto thee?
> I made thee my frende; thou art my foe.
> Why haste thou tresspassed thus to me?
>
> (222-25)

Later, commenting on Lucifer's fall, he again shows emotion and hurt:

> A, wicked pride! A, woo worth thee, woo!
> My meirth thou hast made amisse.
> I may well suffer: my will is not soe
> that they shoulde parte this from my blesse.
>
> (274-77)

A few lines later, he continues,

> And though they have broken my
> commaundement,
> me ruse it sore full suffrently.
>
> (282-83)

Coming from a playwright as knowledgeable in theology as the author of these plays appears to be, all this expression of emotion by the deity is surprising. It flies in the face of the traditional view, expressed, for example, by St. Augustine, [in *The City of God*] that God is impassible, 'unchangeable, and wholly proof against injury', and that to him, 'no evils are hurtful'.

It would be easy to explain the Chester author's method by saying that he is simply following biblical precedent, as shown, for example, in Genesis 6:6, where 'It repented him [God] that he had made man on earth, and [he was] touched inwardly with sorrow of heart'. This verse underlies lines 13-16 of the **Chester Noah** play, where again God shows he can be hurt by creatures' evildoing.

Yet it does not seem to me that biblical parallels explain the extent of God's reaction in Chester I. This reaction is not necessary for the dramatization of Lucifer's fall, as it might be thought to be in the *Noah* lines with their explicit biblical basis. It is not present in the first plays of the other three extant cycles, where God's response to Lucifer's overreaching follows the tradition of divine impassibility. In the York play, *Deus* does not immediately react at all: Lucifer simply falls by his own folly, and later God remarks calmly, 'Those foles for þaire fayrehede in fantasyes fell. . . .' (129). Again, in the Wakefield first pageant, God gives no response as Lucifer attempts to 'fly too high' and falls. In N-Town, God orders Lucifer and those who hold with him to 'ffalle from hefne to helle', but shows no personal reaction. Why, then, is the Chester God so apparently unorthodox?

Several critics have given answers to this question in terms of the effect such 'humanization' of God may have on the audience. [Robert W.] Hanning [in "You Have Begun a Parlous Pleye'" *Comparative Drama* 7, 1973], for example, sees God's 'injured tone' as humanizing in order to involve the audience's moral perceptions, as 'suggesting that Lucifer's sin is recreated each time we behave selfishly toward another who deserves better of us'. [Peter] Travis, in his book on the Chester cycle [*Dramatic Design in the Chester Cycle,* 1982], concludes that the Chester God's 'quite human sense of hurt and disappointment' helps to 'dramatize [his] just and loving character, and underscore the freedom of choice all the angels shared equally before the fall of Lucifer'—a freedom of choice 'by which humankind in time can accomplish good or evil'. [Norma] Kroll [in *Medieval and Renaissance Drama in England* II, 1985] takes the deity's humanizing speeches as designed to narrow the distance between God and the angels, so that dramatic interaction between them is possible. The result of this interaction, for the audience, is to 'intensify [its] sense of the horror of all evil'. All three of these critics thus see the value of giving God human emotions in order to involve the audience in personal moral choices, as its members see God's generous love and concern rejected by Lucifer's egotism. Kroll adds to this the value, for dramatic conflict itself, of a God with whom the angels can interact.

These answers in terms of audience reaction are valuable, but they explain the Chester author's unusual portrayal of God in moral terms only, whereas it seems to me that God's emotional reaction in the play serves more strictly theological or doctrinal purposes also. Of course the moral and the theological purposes are interrelated. For example, one probable reason for including God's statements of disappointment in his 'A, wicked pride!' speech (274f.), is implicit in Travis's emphasis on Lucifer's freedom of choice. In Chester I, the interaction of God and Lucifer is presented by means of an analogy to the human relationship between a 'good lord', who 'schewiþ himself free of yiftes', and an upstart, ungrateful courtier. This analogy works in the play on the human level, but once remember that the 'good lord' in this case is the timeless, omniscient God, and the perennial question of his foreknowledge arises: if God knew that Lucifer would rebel, why make him vicegerent and thus contribute to his downfall? In order to make clear that God is not responsible for Lucifer's free choice, the Chester playwright has him point out the angel's ingratitude, in such lines as 'I made thee my frend; thou art my foe' (224). He also, and especially, makes God show how strongly he does not will Lucifer's fall, by vehement expression of hurt in 'My meirth thou hast made amisse' (225) and 'me ruse it sore full suffrently' (283). That these expressions are meant to absolve God from responsibility for Lucifer's choice is suggested in lines 276-77 of the same speech, where God says, 'I maye well suffer: my will is not soe / that they shoulde part this from my blesse'. Here 'suffer' in conjunction with 'my will' suggests the meaning, 'I may put up with this, but I do not will it'. Thus the lines present the traditional idea, found for example in relation to Lucifer's fall in St. Anselm's *De casu diaboli,* that God permits, but does not will, evil. One justification for Chester's emotional God, then, which partly explains his vehement reaction to Lucifer's treachery, is that the hurt expressed helps provide a theodicy that supports the play's emphasis on the angel's free choice. God's reaction makes this freedom obvious to the audience, at the same time as it suggests a theological or doctrinal point.

I believe, however, that there is a more strictly doctrinal justification for God's questions in lines 222-5, one which not only pertains to this play itself but helps prepare for the orientation of the whole cycle. This is the fact that throughout the play God is presented as the Trinity. . . . [A]s 'good lord' in the play he expresses the traditional trinitarian attributes of power (the Father), wisdom (the Son), and love or goddness (the Holy Spirit). I see this presentation of the Trinity as central to the play; it affects even the role of Lucifer, who, while trying to take God's place, enacts a poor 'trinity' of his own. He sees himself as sovereign, having God's power (e.g., line 91); as being potentially as wise as God (lines 130-1); and as being the 'comforte' of the angels (192) as God is (123), though he wishes comfort himself from them (133). Given this orientation, it is even more necessary for the Chester author than for the authors of the corresponding plays in the other three extant cycles to solve the problem of how to present the three-in-one. His treatment demands that he does not simply state that God is the Trinity, but uses the trinitarian attributes both to characterize God and to show how unable Lucifer is to take God's place.

The author of the corresponding York play has a different orientation. He is showing in his pageant the distance between God as Creator and Lucifer as created, so his emphasis is on God's uniqueness. For this reason, his solution to the problem of presenting the Trinity on stage is to stress the unity. His God speaks always as the Creator, as 'I'. This author does not omit all reference to the Trinity: the 'vita, via, veritas' (John 14, 6) of the opening Latin line suggests the Son, and the two liturgical texts sung by the angels, the *Te Deum* and the *Sanctus,* are trinitarian. However, since God's triune nature is not significant for the central action of his play, he includes in the actual lines no explicit reference to the Trinity nor to the Persons.

The N-Town playwright, in contrast, uses God's opening speech to present him explicitly as three-in-one. This God refers to himself as the Trinity, names his Son and 'Gost', and explains that he possesses the trinitarian attributes, here given as power, justice, and spiritual illumination with goodness:

> O god thre. I calle
> I am fader of myth
> my sone kepyth ryth
> my gost hath lyth
> and grace with-alle.
>
> (22-26)

His trinitarian nature is emphasized following this speech, when the angels sing the *Sanctus,* as they do in the York play. There is also a possible reference to God's wisdom, the attribute of the Second Person, in lines five and six, 'And all þat evyr xal haue beynge / it is closyd in my mende'. One might expect in this play an emphasis on the Trinity, and especially on wisdom, since such an emphasis would help prepare for the rest of the cycle, in which Christ is presented as the Second Person, Wisdom, incarnate. . . . But although Lucifer's self-admiration is shown as folly in the York play, here the emphasis is on God's will and 'wurth', the inherent superiority of the Creator to the creature. It is this superiority that Lucifer challenges, seeing himself as 'wyrthyer' than God (53). This is a challenge to God's power (line 59); as Hanning points out, Lucifer's action 'only serves to show how all must bow to the creator'. Since the trinitarian attributes of wisdom and goodness are not at issue in the play, the playwright presents God as Trinity by means of statement in the opening speech, but does not make use of these other trinitarian attributes, nor of the Persons, in the rest of the pageant.

As in N-Town and the other creation plays, the stress in the first Towneley play is on God's power to create, but here Lucifer's delusion is that, in effect, he has created himself: '[O]f me commys all this light'. In this play, God presents himself as 'On god in trinyte' (6) in the first two stanzas of his introductory speech, and then goes on to complete the work of creation through the fifth day. The playwright includes in this speech no explicit reference to the Persons, but, like the author of the N-Town pageant, he does suggest, along with power, the attribute of wisdom: 'All maner thynge is in my thoght' (14). Since he brings part of God's work of creation into this opening speech, he is able to use a method of presenting the Trinity not available to the other three playwrights. The result is that his God can show, rather than simply state, his trinitarian nature, using 'I' and 'my' interchangeably with 'we' and 'our' during his work, as in lines 25 to 28:

> Darknes we call the night,
> and lith also the bright,
> It shall be as I say;
> after my will this is furth broght. . . .

This author thus solves his problem of how to present the Trinity in drama by following the tradition which interprets God's plural pronoun in Genesis 1, 26 as trinitarian. He does not use liturgical acclamation, as the York and N-Town playwrights do, to suggest that God is the Trinity, but his shifting pronouns permit his God-figure to 'act' the Trinity, showing by a more dramatic method than these other playwrights that God is both one and three. Such presentation is consonant with Lucifer's attempt in the play to make himself God. After having repeatedly emphasized his power—even though it cannot, in the nature of things, be creative power—Lucifer asks, 'Say, felows, how semys now me / To sit in seyte of trynyte?' (104-105). Thus the play shows that Lucifer aspires to be, and to have the power of, the Trinity. Hence the author indicates, by God's statement of his nature and by the interchangeable singular and plural pronouns, that only God can be the three-in-one.

As has been suggested, the Chester author, given his treatment of Lucifer's rebellion, has even more need than the Towneley playwright to establish for his audience that God is both one and three. Like the N-Town and Towneley authors, he has God present his own nature in the opening speech, where the fact that God is the Trinity is stated three times, in lines 9-10, 24-25, and 28-31. Although this playwright does not mention the Persons explicitly, he includes, like the N-Town author, the trinitarian attributes, having God emphasize his power in such lines as 'all is in mea licencill' (18), mention his wisdom in, for example, his statement that he is 'set in substanciall southnes / within celestial sapience' (26-27), and imply his goodness in his reference to 'mansuetude, / cum Dei potentia' in lines fifteen and sixteen, as I interpret them. The Chester author also, like those of York and N-Town, uses sung liturgical texts to suggest God's trinitarian nature, notably the first antiphon for both Vespers of the Feast of the Trinity:

Gloria tibi trinitas equalis una
deitas: et ante omnia secula et nunc et im-
perpetuum.

The position of this antiphon in the play gives it added emphasis. It is sung just as God 'returns' and discovers Lucifer's usurpation, giving the implication that, as in the Towneley play, the Trinity is to be glorified, not Lucifer. The fact that the author places the antiphon where it is, and the fact that it comes from the liturgy for the Feast of the Trinity, suggest just how consciously planned the Chester playwright's presentation of the Trinity is.

The methods of presenting God's nature just mentioned—by his opening speech and through liturgical song—the Chester author shares with the other playwrights, but to establish the 'character' of God as Trinity he uses less static methods as well. He includes in God's lines in the play not only further expressions of the trinitarian attributes, especially those of wisdom and goodness, but also lines which are appropriate to each of the Persons. We can see the first of these methods being used in God's exhortations to Lucifer and Lightborne. In the speech that begins at line 64, after having reminded the angels of his power in 'Here have I you wrought with heavenly mighte' (64), he says,

Nowe, Luciffer and Lightborne, loke lowely
   you bee.
The blessinge of my begyninge I geve to my
   first operacion.
For crafte nor for cuninge, cast never
   comprehension;
exsalte you not to exelente into high
   exaltation.

                                                    (68-71)

In this context, to be 'lowely' includes, for these angels, recongnizing that they cannot understand, and will never be able to understand, the divine wisdom. The lines following God's admonition here support this interpretation, as he goes on to create the world, traditionally seen as the work of the divine Wisdom who speaks in Proverbs 8, 'I was with him forming all things. . .'. Later in the play, when making Lucifer his lieutenant, he mentions the third trinitarian attribute, love, explicitly: '[A]nd here I set you nexte my cheare, / my love to you is soe fervente' (88-89). In none of the other opening pageants, not even that of N-Town, does God bring up his wisdom and love or goodness in dialogue, as he does in Chester. Thus the Chester author has

God not only state his attributes, but show them in his relationship with creatures.

This playwright also, as has been suggested, gives God lines which could appropriately be spoken by each of the trinitarian Persons. It is in consideration of these lines that we return, finally, to God's question to Lucifer in lines 222 to 225. The lines appropriate to God the Father are called to the audience's attention when God says, in the closing speech of the play, that 'I and two persons be at one assente' (286) to create man. . . . Since God's opening speech and other indications within the text have suggested that the 'I' of the play has been the Trinity, this change to the Father alone is surprising. 'I and two persons' does, of course, correspond to the plural pronoun of Genesis 1, 26, and call attention to the traditional teaching that man is made in the image of the Trinity. But it also, I believe, provides lines whose function is to dramatize God the Father. Earlier in the play, lines have been provided which suggest the Holy Spirit, when God tells the angels, 'Here will I bide now in this place / to be angells comforture' (122-23). 'Comforture' implies that God is here speaking as the Third Person, as the references to 'comfortour' in the MED show. The word had been used to translate 'consolator' and 'paraclitus' since at least the time of Wycliffe.

I believe that, as in these examples, one function of God's emotional reaction in lines 223 to 225 is to suggest his trinitarian nature, in this case through lines associated with the Son. Line 223, 'What have I offended unto thee?' translates the 'Quid molestus fui tibi?' of Micah 6, 3, where God is represented as asking the people of Israel what he has done to them, that they should be so ungrateful for his benefits. This biblical verse and the one following form the basis for the first of the 'Improperia' or Reproaches, in the Good Friday liturgy, in which Jesus is seen as asking the people,

Popule meus, quid feci tibi, aut in
quo contristavi te? Responde mihi; quia eduxi
te de terra Egypti, parasti crucem Salvatori
   tuo.

Thus through the liturgy the question God asks Lucifer is associated with Christ, the incarnate Son. This question is appropriate to the action of the play, where Lucifer's ingratitude after God's generosity to him is dramatized and made repulsive, but it also implies the voice of the Son in the Chester author's presentation of the Trinity. The same may be true of 'I made thee my frend', in the following line, which possibly echoes Jesus' 'I have called you friends', in John 15, 15. In any case, the question asked in the Improperia, like the designation 'Comfortour' for the Holy Spirit, could have been known to an English-speaking audience even though the liturgy was in Latin. There is, for example, a fourteenth-century lyric by Friar William Herebert, based on the Reproaches, and another anonymous poem from later in the century in R.T. Davies' [1964] collection of medieval English lyrics. Thus the Chester author's 'What have I offended unto thee?' would likely be associated with Christ by a wider audience than the learned alone.

In giving God lines which suggest each of the Persons as well as showing his attributes in the course of the play, this playwright is going beyond any of the other authors in his presentation of the Trinity. He is, I believe, attempting the near-impossible feat of dramatizing the three and the one at the same time. York, as we have seen, emphasizes the one; N-Town mentions the three-in-one and the Persons, but dramatizes the one; Towneley dramatizes both unity and plurality, but not the Persons. In Chester, however, God not only states that he is the Trinity, but in his lines dramatizes both the one and the three, keeping the unity by speaking as 'I' throughout, and showing the three by lines associated with each of the Persons, and with their trinitarian attributes of power, wisdom and love. God's first emotional reaction in the play, then, can be seen as contributing to a doctrinally exact presentation of the Trinity, in which 'alia est-. . .persona patris: alia filii: alia spiritussancti. Sed patris et filii et spiritussancti una est divinitas'. The Chester author does not, I believe, give his God untraditional expressions of emotion simply in order to humanize him, nor simply to show that he is not responsible for Lucifer's choice, but to establish his nature as the Trinity who, in the play, is the divine king with the attributes of power, wisdom and love.

As Stevens [in *Four Middle English Mystery Cycles,* 1987] has pointed out, the emphasis on the Trinity in this cycle affects the presentation of Christ in the New Testament episodes. By focussing attention on the Trinity in the opening play, the Chester playwright prepares for the emphasis in the cycle on the kingship and divinity of Christ, the Son made man, who, in the unity of the Trinity, is the divine king, like God in Chester I. Apparently the Chester author would agree with St. Bernard, for whom, as Jaroslav Pelikan [in *The Christian Tradition: A History of the Development of Doctrine* 3, 1978] writes, 'Only an impeccably orthodox doctrine of the Trinity could guarantee that the Saviour was God in a complete and unequivocal way. This orthodox doctrine insists that God is three and one, neither simply the one nor the other, and it is this doctrine that underlies the **Chester cycle's** concept of the actions of God in time.

Evidence for the trinitarian basis of salvation history, as enacted in the **Chester cycle** can be seen in the way Christ's coming is adumbrated in the Old Testament plays. In the N-Town plays. . . Christ is seen as the Son, the Second Person of the Trinity, under the attribute of wisdom. In Chester, too, Christ is the divine Son, the Second Person, as Jesus's reiterated 'my Father' makes clear. In N-Town, the most frequently

mentioned 'figures' (7, 41) foreshadowing the Son's coming are those associated with the virgin birth, such as the rod from the root of Jesse. To further emphasize the importance of Christ's birth from a virgin, there are in the cycle three episodes from the life of Mary, and in the Parliament of Heaven play the Father explains in advance that, to accomplish the incarnation of the Son, he will send the angel Gabriel to 'Mary þat xal Al Restore' (11, 196). In Chester, however, the emphasis on the three-in-one means that passages and episodes foreshadowing the incarnation and suffering of the Son most often imply the relation of the Son to the Father within the Trinity, rather than the virgin birth. For example, when Adam recounts his dream in Play II, he says he has seen

> that God will come from heaven on hie,
> to overcome the devill so slee
> and light into my kynde. . . .

(449-51)

'God will come', Adam says, not 'God will send his Son'. The Chester account of the Annunciation in Play VI makes clear that it is God the Son who is to 'come from heaven on hie', but because in the Athanasian formula each of the Persons is God, 'and yet there are not three Gods, but one God', the distinction between Father and Son is simply omitted. Similarly, God's promise of the rainbow at the end of the **Chester Noah play** requires the trinitarian unity for its interpretation. God says of the bow that 'The stringe is torned towards you / and towardes me is bente the bowe' (III, 321-22). This image of the bow with which man can shoot an arrow at God implies, I think, the human capacity to impose suffering on the incarnate Son at the Crucifixion. God, however, refers simply to 'me', not 'my Son', so that the attack on Christ is seen as an attack on God, as, for the three-in-one, it is. Both Adam's dream and the rainbow covenant look forward to the coming of Christ, but imply the equal divinity of the Persons within the Trinity rather than the special mission of the Second Person.

Not all adumbrations of Christ's coming in the Chester Old Testament plays emphasize the divine unity as strongly as the examples just given. Play IV, for example, is composed of two episodes containing types of the Father and the Son: Abraham and Melchizidek, and Abraham and Issac. The Expositor sees Abraham as representing 'the Father of Heaven' in both episodes (138 and 469), and Isaac as Jesus (473). Melchizidek he describes as 'a pryest. . .to minister that sacramente / that Christe ordayned' (139-41). The context provided by the rest of the Expositor's speech at the end of the Melchizidek episode, with its contrast between 'the newe testament' (118) and 'the owld lawe' (121) shows that the author is here thinking of Melchizidek in terms of Hebrews 7-9, where he is a type of Christ, 'likened to the Son of God. . .' (Hebr, 7,3). Both episodes, then, suggest the relation between the Father and the Son, and each requires two actors, rather than the one actor needed for God in the **Noah** play. Thus Lynette Muir's statement ['The Trinity in Medieval Drama,' *Comparative Drama,* 1976] that 'In Chester no distinction of Persons is made' is not wholly true. At the same time, however, Preco's announcement in the opening speech that Abraham will begin the play 'in worshippe of the Trynitie' (10) provides a context that maintains the author's focus on the Tri-unity that underlies the Father-Son relationship here as it does the other adumbrations of Christ's earthly life. It foreshadows the saving work of the Trinity in time, rather than the virgin birth.

Since Stevens has already brought to our attention the trinitarian basis of Jesus' portrayal in the Chester New Testament plays, I shall not comment on these plays here. But the **Antichrist** play, XXIII, can provide a final brief example of how important trinitarian orthodoxy is to the Chester playwright. Like Lucifer in the opening play, Antichrist attempts to imitate the Trinity. He calls himself 'verey God of might' (221), using the attribute of the Father; he exclaims, 'I high justice' (89), an attribute of the Son; and he tells the representative kings, 'I will nowe send my holye ghooste' (193). He repeatedly claims to be God and Christ. Yet when Enock affirms faith in 'God in Trynitie. . .that sent his Sonne from heaven-see' (484, 486), Antichrist attacks the doctrine, with

> Owt on you, theeves: What sayen yee?
> Wyll you have on God and three?
> Howe darre you so saye?
> Madmen, madmen! Therefore leeve on mee
> that am on god—so ys not hee!
>
> (498-502)

His attempt to imitate the Trinity and his insistence that he is not three but one, only, obviously contradict; yet he does not appear to understand that in denying the doctrine of the Trinity he is denying the godhead he himself has claimed. Like Lucifer in the opening play, he shows in this way how incapable he is of understanding God: if there is no Trinity, Christ is not God, so Antichrist as 'I Christ that made the dead to ryse!' (190) is not divine either. His question 'What ys the Trinitye for to saye?' (491) is not, I believe, 'ridiculous', as Emmerson suggests, [in *Antichrist in the Middle Ages: A study of Medieval Apocalypticism,* 1981] but is caused by his meeting the crucial test of his pretence. Hence Helias shows up his false resurrection of the dead by offering to those 'risen' bread blessed not only in the name of Jesus, but in the name of the Trinity, 'on God and persons three' (576). The author of the play is here using the tradition of invoking the Trinity to drive out demons, who cannot stand the test of true faith. Thus he demonstrates that the real power is not the false king, Antichrist, but the Trinity, three and one, on which is based the kingship and divinity

of Christ, the true Son made man. His ironic portrayal of Antichrist depends upon his basis in the orthodox, paradoxical doctrine of the Trinity.

The **Antichrist play,** along with the **Judgment play** which follows it, brings full circle the treatment of disruption in the creation which begins with Lucifer's fall in the first play of the cycle. God in that play is the divine king, the three-in-one, who can be hurt if Jesus, the divine king incarnate, is hurt. Hence he asks, 'What have I offended unto thee?' with all the implication of God's generosity and undeserved suffering the question has in the context of the Crucifixion. To remedy Lucifer's deception of man, he comes to earth in the person of Christ, the Son, foreshadowing his coming by signs indicative of trinitarian actions. Christ as divine is 'come owte of the Trynitie' (IX, 117), and the final triumph against the disruptive forces, as represented by Antichrist, is that of the Trinity, God as three-in-one (XXIV, 5-6), who at the same time refers to 'my crosse' (17), and later in the play is Jesus, is the judge at the Last Judgment. Thus the careful portrayal of the Trinity in the opening play of the **Chester cycle** prepares for a drama concerned not simply with the coming of a Saviour, but with the actions of the Trinity in time, both in heaven and on earth.

FURTHER READING

Baird, Lorrayne Y. "'Cockes face' and the Problem of *Poydrace* in the Chester *Passion.*" *Comparative Drama* 16, No. 3 (Fall 1982): 227-37.

> Examines several possible interpretations of the medieval insults used in the *Chester* play depicting Christ's Passion.

Cardullo, Bert. "The Chester Sacrifice of Isaac." *The Explicator* 43, No. 3 (Spring 1985): 3-4.

> Explains how the speeches of the Expositor in the Chester *Sacrifice of Isaac* play is necessary for a Medieval audience's complete comprehension.

Clopper, Lawrence M. "The Principle of Selection of the Chester Old Testament Plays." In *The Chester Mystery Cycle: A Casebook,* edited by Kevin J. Harty, pp. 89-102. Garland Publishing, Inc., 1993.

> Examines the authorial selection of Old Testament subject matter in the Chester cycle.

Emmerson, Richard Kenneth. "'Nowe ys Common This Daye': Enoch and Elias, Antichrist, and the Structure of the Chester Cycle." In *Homo, Memento Finis: The Iconography of Just Judgement in Medieval Art and Drama,* edited by David Bevington, pp. 89-120. Kalamazoo: Medieval Institute Publications, 1985.

> Examines the impact of the *Coming of Antichrist* play on the structure of the Chester Cycle by focusing on the serious—rather than farcical—aspects of the play.

Greg, W. W. "Bibliographical and Textual Problems of the English Miracle Cycles." *The Library* 5, No. 17 (January 1914): 1-30, 168-205.

Essays transcribed from a series of four lectures given at Cambridge University in 1913 that describe the bibliographic and textual disparities among the extant manuscripts of the Chester Mystery Cycle.

Harty, Kevin J. "Adam's Dream and the First Three Chester Plays." *Cahiers Elisabethains*, No. 21 (April 1982): 1-11.

Discusses how interrelationships between the first three Chester plays demonstrate the playwright's dramatic skills, and also explains how "the inclusion of Adam's dream in Chester Play II is consistent with the principles of medieval historiography.

————. "The Unity and Structure of the Chester Mystery Cycle." *Mediaevalia: A Journal of Mediaeval Studies* 2 (1976): 137-50.

Examines how the influence of monasticism contributed to the unity and structure of the Chester Mystery Cycle.

Kroll, Norma. "Cosmic Characters and Human Form: Dramatic Interaction and Conflict in the Chester Cycle 'Fall of Lucifer'." In *Medieval and Renaissance Drama in England: An Annual Gathering of Research, Criticism, and Reviews,* edited by J. Leeds Barroll, III, pp. 33-50. New York: AMS Press, 1985.

Discusses how the Chester author's use of bodily images in depicting Lucifer's rebellion serves as an integral part of the dramatic action, and distinguishes the play from other medieval Cycle portrayals.

Lumiansky, R. M. "Comedy and Theme in the Chester *Harrowing of Hell.*" In *The Chester Mystery Cycle,* edited by Kevin J. Harty, pp. 162-70. New York: Garland Publishing, Inc., 1993.

In this 1960 essay, Lumiansky maintains that the comic scene in the Chester *Harrowing of Hell* "is a functional and effectively unified portion" of the play.

Lumiansky, R. M. and David Mills. In an introduction to *The Chester Mystery Cycle,* edited by R. M. Lumiansky and David Mills, pp. ix-xl. London: Oxford University Press, 1974.

A thorough discussion of the extant manuscripts of the Chester Mystery Cycle.

McGavin, John. J. "Sign and Transition: The *Purification* Play in Chester." *Leeds Studies in English* XI (1980): 90-104.

Considers the issue of individual authorship and its effects on the structure of the *Chester Purification* play.'

Mills, David. "'In This Storye Consistethe our Chefe Faithe': The Problems of the Chester's Play(s) of the Passion." *Leeds Studies in English* XVI (1985): 326-36.

Examines the description of the Chester plays in the medieval Banns—the public announcement of the play's performance— and its possible influence on the development of the cycle.

Moore, E. Hamilton. *English Miracle Plays and Moralities.* London: AMS Press, 1907. Reprinted in New York, 1969, 199 p.

Examination of the history and influence of the English Mystery Plays on the modern theater.

Nelson, Alan H. "Chester." In *The Medieval English Stage: Corpus Christi Pageants and Plays,* pp. 154-69. The University of Chicago Press, 1974.

Describes the Chester Cycle's evolution from the Various Corpus Christi pageants and processions that took place in the city of Chester throughout the fifteenth and sixteenth centuries.

Ovitt, George. "Christian Eschatology and the *Chester* 'Judgement'." In *Essays in Literature* X, No. 1 (Spring 1983): 3-16.

Analyses the Chester Cycle's version of the Final Judgement, arguing that it "succeeds in uniting, and transcending, all of the elements, dramatic and didactic, contained in the other versions.

Salter, F. M. "The Banns of the Chester Plays." In *The Review of English Studies* XVI, No. 61 (January 1940): 1-17, 137-48.

Relates the performances and the textual revisions of the Chester plays to the Early Banns.

Stock, Lorraine Kochanske. "Comedy in the English Mystery Cycles: Three Comic Scenes in the Chester *Shepherds' Play.*" In *Versions of Medieval Comedy,* edited by Paul G. Ruggiers, pp. 211-26. Norman: University of Oklahoma Press, 1977.

Closely examines the Chester *Shepherds' Play.*

Tricomi, Albert H. "Reenvisioning England's Medieval Cycle Comedy." In *Medieval and Renaissance Drama in England: An Annual Gathering of Research, Criticism, and Reviews* V, edited by Leeds Barroll, pp. 11-26. New York: AMS Press, 1991.

Examines the diversity and purpose of comic elements within the Chester cycle.

Wilson, Robert H. "The *Stanzaic Life of Christ* and the Chester Plays." *Studies in Philology* XXVIII, No. 3 (July 1931): 413-32.

Considers the extent to which the Middle English poem, the *Stanzaic Life of Christ,* is a non-dramatic source of the Chester plays.

N-Town Cycle

INTRODUCTION

Of the four complete mystery cycles in the extant body of Middle English biblical drama, the N-Town plays are the most enigmatic. The single manuscript in which the cycle is preserved contains an amalgamation of scribal and authorial efforts. The institutional and geographical origins of the plays have been the subject of extensive research and debate, as has the means by which they were staged. Even the name of the cycle has been unstable: designated variously as the *Ludus Coventriae,* the Hegge cycle (after the first known owner of the manuscript), and the Lincoln plays, the plays are now commonly referred to as the N-Town cycle because the Proclamation that opens the collection refers to their performance in "N-town."

Like other biblical cycles, the N-Town plays contain stories from the Old and New Testaments and apocrypha. The opening Proclamation, spoken by three vexillators, describes a numbered series of pageants that does not correspond exactly to the dramatic episodes and plays contained in the manuscript that has come down to us. The divisions between plays are often unclear, with relatively few announced in the manuscript with specific titles or rubrication. The cycle includes a number of scenes unique to this collection, including the cherry tree incident involving Mary and Joseph, and the killing of Herod. Even more noteworthy, the N-Town cycle incorporates two smaller cycles that can be performed separately: a series of plays on the life of Mary, and a two-part Passion play. The N-Town cycle is also distinguished by what numerous scholars have identifed as an unusual concern with themes of redemptive promise, grace, and mercy.

Textual History

A central issue in the study of medieval texts is their instability and indeterminancy. Medieval manuscripts are seldom complete and were typically revised, separated, compiled, or erased in the process of copying. The N-Town manuscript is a case in point. It was originally attributed to the city of Coventry, in the West Midlands, because of the label ("Ludus Coventriae") placed on the manuscript's flyleaf by a seventeenth-century librarian. Its dialect and calligraphy, however, indicate the involvement of at least four scribes from four different locales in East Anglia (modern-day Norfolk and Suffolk). The manuscript also contains evidence of additions and revisions at various points in its history. Early in the twentieth century, Esther L. Swenson suggested that the cycle's various meters indicated different scribes or authors. Although this idea has since been dismissed, more recent scholars, such as Stephen Spector (1991), have observed that sections that share metrical forms also have thematic and verbal affinities. A character named Contemplacio frames the series of Mary plays, probably indicating the sequence's prior independent existence; the manuscript's revisions of his speech may represent changes made to fit the self-contained sequence into the larger cycle.

The manuscript's eclectic character has given rise to debates over its provenance. While the early attribution of the cycle to the Grey Friars in Coventry has been discredited, most scholars agree that the cycle was associated with a religious institution of some sort. It is generally agreed that the manuscript was probably generated in the rich social and cultural environment of East Anglia in the late fifteenth century. Many scholars have accepted Gail McMurray Gibson's argument (1981) that the cycle originated in the abbey of Bury St. Edmunds, home of poet John Lydgate, but others insist that other sites nearby are just as likely.

The manuscript also contains unusually detailed stage directions, leading to a great deal of speculation as to how the play was staged. Like Continental drama of the time, many of the N-Town plays seem to require a fixed stage, or *plataea,* with various *loci,* or stations, rather than the movable pageant wagons more typical of English drama in that period. Most scholars agree that the cycle may never have been staged wholly in the manner in which it survives. Still, its plays allow for some of the most spectacular stage effects in medieval drama. In the Passion sequence the stage directions are particularly detailed, calling for rapid juxtapositions of scene and simultaneity of action.

Major Themes

Scholars have noted the cycle's unusual concern with Mary, more typical of Continental dramas than of English cycles. The Mary of N-Town is only intermittently the pious and humble Madonna; more consistently, she figures as the glorious virgin queen whose purity the cycle dramatizes to the fullest. Critics also find in the cycle an unusually strong emphasis on theological concepts. Unlike other cycles, N-Town focuses on Christ's dual nature as God and Man and on Christ's Incarnation as the central act of mediation between God and humankind. N-

Town is heavily peopled with ecclesiastical characters—bishops, priests, etc.—who mediate the action and underline its connections to the liturgy. The sacraments, especially Communion, and prayer are brought to the fore as practical, quotidian methods of communication between God and humanity.

Critical Reception

Most of the critical discussion of the N-Town cycle has centered on the origins of the manuscript and the staging of the plays. After Hardin Craig (1914) proposed Lincoln as the origin of the cycle, his idea was not seriously contested until Gibson put forward her argument in favor of Bury St. Edmunds. Current critical consensus is that the plays originated in East Anglia, but that the exact location is yet to be convincingly determined. With regard to staging, Swenson suggested that the Mary cycle and the Passion plays were produced on a fixed stage, while the others were acted on movable stages. Kenneth Cameron and Stanley J. Kahrl (1967) maintained that the older plays in the cycle were acted on movable stages and the newer ones on fixed plataeas. Anne C. Gay, on the other hand (1961), argued for a continuous place-and-scaffold staging and found no evidence of movable stages at all. Alan H. Nelson (1972) and Martial Rose (1973) similarly found no evidence of movable staging. Spector remarks only that the staging of the plays is open to conjecture, suggesting that the construction of the manuscript "seems to suggest a tendency toward the isolation of plays rather than continuous acting, or indifference to such issues during compilation."

The eclectic nature of the N-Town plays has led to arguments for and against the cycle's thematic unity. While critics such as Peter Meredith (1991) observe that the process of compiling the manuscript appears to have been haphazard, many would agree with Spector that "the eclecticism of the text does not preclude the possibility of thematic and artistic unity." Timothy Fry (1951) saw in the cycle a unified theological message, while Patrick J. Collins (1979) identified fruit and growth imagery and other motifs that perform a unifying function. Kathleen M. Ashley (1979) argued that the limited nature of human wisdom is a dominant theme throughout much of the cycle.

THE PLAYS

Banns
1. *The Creation, and Fall of Lucifer*
2. *The Creation, and Fall of Man*
3. *Cain and Abel*
4. *Noah, and Lamech*
5. *Abraham and Isaac*
6. *The Ten Commandments*
7. *The Tree of Jesse*
*8. *The Conception of Mary*
*9. *Mary in the Temple*
*10. *The Betrothal of Mary*
*11. *The Parliament of Heaven and the Annunciation*
*12. *Joseph's Trouble about Mary*
*13. *The Visitation*
14. *The Purgation of Mary and Joseph*
15. *The Birth of Christ*
16. *The Shepherds*
17. *The Magi*
18. *The Purification*
19. *The Slaughter of the Innocents*
20. *Christ and the Doctors in the Temple*
21. *The Baptism*
22. *The Temptation*
23. *The Woman Taken in Adultery*
24. *The Raising of Lazarus*
†25. *The Conspiracy, and the Entry into Jerusalem*
†26. *The Last Supper*
†27. *The Betrayal*
　　　Doctors' prologue
‡28. *The Preliminary Examination: Annas and Caiaphas*
‡29. *The Examination: before Pilate, and before Herod*
‡30. *Pilate's Wife's Dream, and the Trial before Pilate*
‡31. *The Crucifixion*
‡32. *The Harrowing of Hell (i)*
‡33. *The Burial*
‡34. *The Harrowing of Hell (ii), and the Resurrection*
35. *The Maries at the Sepulchre*
36. *The Appearance to Mary Magdalene*
37. *The Appearance to Cleophas and Luke, and to Thomas*
38. *The Ascension*
39. *Pentecost*
40. *The Assumption of the Virgin*
41. *The Last Judgement*

*constituent of the "Contemplacio" group of plays (plays 8-13)
†constituent of "Passion Play I" (plays 25-7)
‡constituent of "Passion Play II" (plays 28-34)

PRINCIPAL EDITIONS

Ludus Coventriae: A Collection of Mysteries Formerly Represented at Coventry on the Feast of Corpus Christi (edited by James Orchard Haliwell) 1841
Ludus Coventriae: or The Plaie called Corpus Christi (edited by K. S. Block) 1922
The Corpus Christi Play of the English Middle Ages (modern English translation, R. T. Davies) 1972
The "Mary Play" from the N.Town Manuscript (ed. Peter Meredith) 1987

The "Passion Play" from the N.Town Manuscript (ed. Peter Meredith) 1990
The N-Town Play: Cotton MS Vespasian D. 8 (ed. Stephen Spector) 1991

CRITICISM

Hardin Craig (essay date 1914)

SOURCE: A note to the University of Wisconsin Studies in Language and Literature, Vol. 1, October, 1914, pp. 72-83.

[In the following excerpt, Craig surveys nineteenth- and early- twentieth-century scholarship on the N-Town plays and suggests Lincoln as the home of the cycle.]

It has never been known where the cycle of mystery plays published by the Shakespeare Society in 1841 as "Ludus Coventriae: a Collection of Mysteries formerly represented at Coventry on the Feast of Corpus Christi," were acted, although it has long been known that they are not the Coventry plays. The editor of the cycle, J. O. Halliwell(-Phillips), follows a tradition to the effect that this cycle was formerly acted by the Grey Friars of Coventry. The first connection of the manuscript with Coventry is an entry on folio 1*r, said by Halliwell to be in the handwriting of Dr. Richard James, librarian to Sir Robert Cotton to the following effect: "Contenta Novi Testamenti scenice expressa et actitata olim per monachos sive fratres mendicantes; vulgo dicitur hic liber Ludus Coventriae, sive Ludus Corporis Christi; scribitur metris Anglicanis." The manuscript had formerly belonged to Robert Hegge of Durham, a fellow of Corpus Christi College, Oxford; he has written his name on it in several places. At his death in 1630 the manuscript passed into the hands of Sir Robert Cotton. Halliwell states on the basis of a letter in the Cottonian collection that James was about that time engaged at Oxford in collecting manuscripts for Sir Robert Cotton. The only other descriptive entry on the manuscript is at the top of folio 1r: "The plaie called Corpus Christi." This is in a seventeenth-century hand, I should think, but not the hand of Robert Hegge, as stated by Mr. S. B. Hemingway [in English Nativity Plays], or that of James in the preceding entry. Sharp attributes the former entry to Dr. Smith, a later Cottonian librarian, who enters it in a catalogue of the Cottonian MSS. in 1696, as "A collection of plays, in old English meter: h. e. Dramata sacra, in quibus exhibentur historiae veteris et N. Testamenti, introductis quasi in scenam personis illic memoratis, quas secum invicem colloquentes pro ingenio finget Poeta. Videntur olim coram populo, sive ad instruendum sive ad placendum, a Fratribus mendicantibus representata." It should be noted with regard to the former entry that James

does not say that the cycle is "Ludus Coventriae," but merely that "vulgo dicitur Ludus Coventriae." It is obvious that James had not read the plays, since he speaks of "Contenta novi testamenti," whereas there are Old as well as New Testament subjects treated. It may or may not be significant that Dr. Smith says nothing about Coventry.

The connection of this cycle with Coventry was perpetuated by the following passage from Dugdale's History of Warwickshire, edition of 1656, page 116: "Before the suppression of the monasteries, this city [Coventry] was very famous for the pageants that were played therein, upon Corpus-Christi day; which occasioning very great confluence of people thither from far and near, was of no small benefit thereto; which pageants being acted with mighty state and reverence by the friars of this house [the Gray Friars of Coventry], had theaters for the several scenes, very large and high, placed upon wheels, and drawn to all the eminent parts of the city, for the better advantage of spectators: and contained the story of the New-Testament, composed into old English Rithme, as appeareth by an ancient MS. (in bibl. Cotton. sub effigie Vesp. D. 9 [8]) intituled Ludus Corporis Christi, or Ludus Coventriae. I have been told by some old people, who in their younger years were eyewitnesses of these pageants so acted, that the yearly confluence of people to see that shew was extraordinary great, and yielded no small advantage to this city."

Thomas Sharp, writing in 1825, perceived that Ludus Coventriae "were no part of the Plays or Pageants exhibited by the Trading Companies of the City," but he did not reject Dugdale's tradition as to plays by the Grey Friars, and this he thought might be the cycle they had acted. In this opinion he is followed by Halliwell. Sharp cites an entry in the Coventry Annals, "solitary mention in one MS. (not older than the beginning of Chas. I.'s reign) of Henry VIIth's visit to the City in 1492, 'to see Plays acted by the Grey Friars.'" In this I think we may find the source of Dugdale's error. Dugdale was born in 1605, and the Coventry Corpus Christi plays were discontinued in 1580. He pretends to give only a somewhat general tradition as to the plays and the crowds that they attracted. This vague tradition is rendered definite for him by two things; the first is the note on the MS. by James. James died in 1638, and Dugdale, according to Sharp, page 6, was introduced to Sir Thomas Cotton and the Cottonian MSS. that year. Sir William Dugdale was working on his History of Warwickshire as early as 1642, and, according to the Dictionary of National Biography, was using Sir Thomas Cotton's library in 1652, and no doubt used it a great deal during the years he was at work on the book. The second document that misled him was the MSS. Annals. There are at least four of these books of annals still to be found in manuscript. Two, A. 26 and A. 43, are among the Corporation manuscripts at Coventry; neither is of very great age, and both contain pretty much the same materials: lists of mayors, notable or miraculous events, and a number of mentions of plays. There are also two at the British Museum, Harl. 6388 and 11346 Plut. CXLII. A.; the latter is of no great value as regards pageants. Harl. 6388 was written by Humphrey Wanley, and is dated Dec. 17, 1690. Wanley says: "This book was taken out of manuscripts, the one written by Mr. Cristofer Owen Mayor of this citty which contains the charter of Walter de Coventre concerning the commons *etc.* to Godfrey Leg Mayor 1637, the other beginning at the 36 mayor of this citty and continued by several hands and lately by Edmund Palmer late of this city. . . , and another written by Mr. Bedford and collected out of divers others and continued to Mr. Septimius Bott. And two other collected by Tho. Potter and continued to Mr. Robert Blake, and another written by Mr. Francis Barnett, to the first year of Mr. Jelliffs Majoralty, and another written by Mr. Abraham Astley, and continued to Mr. Sept. Bott, and another written by Mr. Abraham Boune to Humfrey Wrightwick, 1607." In Dugdale's *Warwickshire* there is also a list of mayors of Coventry with annals. Sharp quotes *MS. Annals* and *Codex Hales,* and there was at least one copy of Coventry annals in the Birmingham Free Reference Library at the time of the fire in 1879, so that Sharp may represent an original.

The entry with which we have to do is given as follows: "Corp. MSS. A. 26 and A. 43: Thomas Churchman, bucklemaker, Mayor, 1492. This year the King and Queen came to Kenilworth; from thence they came to Coventry to see our plays at Corpus Christitide and gave them great commendation. Dugdale and 11346 Plut. CXLII. A: In his Mayoralty K. H. 7. came to see the playes acted by the Grey Friars and much commended them. Harl. 6388: The King and Queen came to see the playes at the greyfriers and much commended them." The entry as given in Dugdale gave rise to the impression in his mind, I think, as it certainly did in the mind of Thomas Sharp, that there were plays in Coventry acted by the brotherhood of the Grey Friars. James's note had suggested monks or mendicant friars; here was this entry in the Coventry annals which he prints. It is easy to see that we have to do with a misunderstanding. "Acted by the Grey Friars" need not mean that grey friars were the actors; but may mean "at the Gray-friars church." The grey-friars was a common way of indicating the church. Wanley so understands the entry, for he says in Harl. 6388, "to see the playes at the greyfriers." He worked from a large number of manuscripts, and there is no doubt but that the entry means simply that the King and Queen watched the Corpus Christi play as it was presented by the craft guilds in front of the Grey Friars church, where there would certainly have been a station; just as Queen Margaret had seen them at a station in Earl Street in 1456.

The only mention of a place of performance in the cycle itself is at the end of the general Prologue:

A Sunday next, yf that we may,
At vj. of the belle we ginne oure play,
In N. towne, wherfore we pray,
    That God now be Youre Spede.

This was understood by somebody, Sharp does not say whom, to indicate a series of plays for exhibition at Corpus Christi festival generally, rather than expressly for Coventry, since N. (nomen) is the usual mode of distinguishing a person or place under such circumstances, "as N. stands in the marriage ceremony unto this day." Halliwell says, "If the opinion I have formed of their locality be correct, I can account for this by supposing that the prologues of the vexillators belong to another series of plays, or that these mysteries were occasionally performed at other places. . . . it must be confessed that the conclusion would suit a company of strolling players much better than the venerable order of the Grey Friars." The idea that **Ludus Coventriae** is the play-book of a strolling company has been very generally entertained since that time. Ten Brink [in *English Literature*] follows that idea and assigns their dialect to the North-East Midlands; so also Pollard [in *English Miracle Plays*]. Ten Brink's conclusion as to dialect is in part confirmed by a study of the dialect by M. Kramer, *Sprache und Heimat des sogen. Ludus Coventriae,* who, however, thinks that the plays are of southern origin but rewritten in the North-East Midlands. Chambers does not consider the strolling company hypothesis as proved. He perceives that they are stationary plays in their present form, but does not take the trouble to ascertain that the manuscript is divided into separate plays, although the numbers are large and in red. Another mistake he makes is that, although he sees that the Prologue must have been written for the plays, he thinks that it is later in date than they are. It represents, as Miss Swenson's dissertation [*An Inquiry into the Composition and Structure of Ludus Coventriae*] clearly shows, an earlier, purely cyclic stage of the same plays. Still Chambers does not rule out the idea that we have to do in the Hegge cycle with a series of craft-plays. He suggests Norwich and says that the elaborate treatment of the legends of the Virgin suggests a performance, like that of the Lincoln plays, and of the Massacre of the Innocents in the Digby MS., on St. Anne's day (July 26).

I wish to make the last suggestion much more definitely, having arrived at considerable certainty with regard to it from other points of view. There are, I think, good reasons for fixing upon Lincoln as the home of these plays. The somewhat scanty records of the Lincoln plays seem to point to a Corpus Christi play which was transferred to St. Anne's day, and acted regularly as a St. Anne's play until near the middle of the sixteenth century. It was apparently an ordinary cyclic play with certain features appropriate to St. Anne's day. The so-called **Coventry cycle,** or to use the name of a former owner of the manuscript, the **Hegge cycle,** is unique in the possession of a group of plays dealing with the nativity and childhood of the Virgin Mary, a subject of unmistakable connection with St. Anne's day. The Corporation records show that each Lincoln alderman was required to furnish a silk gown for one of the "kings" in the procession of St. Anne. This has been supposed to refer to the Three Kings of Cologne in the Magi play; but there were only three of the magi, and there must have been more than three aldermen. The Hegge prophet play calls for no less than thirteen kings, and is, moreover, unique among prophet plays. The prophets foretell the birth of Mary and not of Jesus. The play might be described as a dramatic form of the mediaeval theme of the "Root of Jesse." They had, as we shall see presently, some special kind of prophet play known particularly as *visus,* or "sights," though the name was applied to the whole St. Anne's play too, and this Jesse, it is so called in the manuscript, with the accompanying Virgin plays would be most appropriate.

The available information about the Lincoln plays is contained in the 14th Report of the Historical Manuscripts Commission, and in an article entitled *Some English Plays and Players* by Mr. A. F. Leach in the Furnivall Miscellany. Canon Wordsworth has also published a few bits of information in his *Lincoln Statutes* and his *Notes on Mediaeval Services in England.* One can not be sure whether or not the principal manuscripts have been read carefully for the purpose of getting all possible information about the plays, or whether a study of completer forms of the references already found might not yield a good deal more information than they do in their imperfect versions. The Chapter Act Books and the Chapter Computi seem particularly promising. The Historical MSS. Report on the Manuscripts of the Dean and the Chapter of Lincoln gives no information, and that which we have comes from Mr. Leach's article.

We know of unusual dramatic activities on the part of vicars of the choir and clerks of the Cathedral in the thirteenth century from the hostile writings of Bishop Grosseteste [in his *Letters*]. He denounces *ludos* and *miracula* together with the Feast of Fools. In 1390 the vicars and clerks are still liable to censure because they dressed like laymen, laughed, shouted, and acted plays, which they commonly and fitly called the Feast of Fools. There was apparently much dramatic activity in the minster. Chapter Computi for 1406, 1452, 1531, have entries of payments, "In serothecis emptis pro Maria et Angelo et Prophetis ex consuetudine in Aurora Natalis Dñi hoc anno." There is one very puzzling entry given by Canon Wordsworth in these terms: "In 1420 tithes to the amount of 8*s* 8*d* were assigned to Thomas Chamberleyn for getting up a spectacle or pageant ('cujusdam excellentis visus') called *Rubum quem viderat* at Christmas." This is possibly to be connected with the prophet play mentioned above, since Moses was in most versions of the *processus* the first prophet—hence the allusion to the burning bush—and with him possibly the

play of the Tables of the Law.

Further references point to an identification of the Corpus Christi play with the play acted on St. Anne's day. Leach gives entries from a list of mayors and bailiffs of the reign of Henry VIII with annals of the city. Amongst the entries are references to plays, two being to the Corpus Christi play, namely, in 12 of Edw. IV, 1471-2, and 14 of Edw. IV, 1473-4. One of the Chapter Act books, according to Leach, has a reference in 1469 to the Show or Play of St. Anne. And if we trace this St. Anne's play by means of the Corporation Minute Book covering the early fifteenth century, we find that it was probably the Corpus Christi play under a new name. There were no doubt extensive changes in the play to make it more appropriate to St. Anne's day; but it is evidently, to all intents and purposes, a Corpus Christi play transferred to another date, a thing familiar in the Chester and Norwich Whitsun plays. The following entries will indicate the circumstances of the St. Anne's play so far as they can be determined from the materials at hand:

> 1515, 27 July. It is agreed that whereas divers garments and other "heriorments" are yearly borrowed in the country for the arraying of the pageants of St. Anne's guild, but now the knights and gentlemen are afraid with the plague so that the "graceman" (chief officer of the Guild of St. Anne) cannot borrow such garments, every alderman shall prepare and set forth in the said array two good gowns, and every sheriff and every chamberlain a gown, and the persons with them shall wear the same. And the constables are ordered to wait upon the array in procession, both to keep the people from the array, and also to take heed of such as wear garments in the same.

> 1517, 10 June, 22 Sept. Sir Robert Denyas appointed St. Anne's priest. . .having yearly 5*l.,* he promising yearly to help to the bringing forth and preparing of the pageants in St. Anne's guild.

> 1518, 16 June. Ordered that every alderman shall send forth a servant with a torch to be lighted in the procession with a rochet (1521, "an onest gowne") upon him about the Sacrament, under pain of forfeiture of 6*s.* 8*d.,* and also under like penalty, send forth one person with a good gown upon his back to go in the procession. That every constable shall wait on the procession on St. Anne's day by 7 of the clock. . . . In 1525 the alderman are each to provide a gown of silk for the kings. . . . It is ordered that every occupation shall prepare and apparel in all preparation except plate and cups ("copes"). List of defaulters in 1526. In 1527 the parishioners of St. John Evang. in Wykford refuse to lend "honroments."

> 1519, 18 June. Agreed that every man and woman in the city, being able, shall be brother and sister in

St. Anne's guild, and pay yearly 4*d.,* man and wife, at the least.

Every occupation belonging to St. Anne's guild to bring forth their pageants sufficiently, upon pain of forfeiting 10*l.*

1521, 16 July. George Browne, alderman, elected in the place of the graceman of St. Anne's gild, complains that as the plague is reigning in the city he can not get such garments and "honourments" as should be in the pageants of the procession; wherefore it is agreed to borrow a gown of my lady "Powes" for one of the Maries, and the other Mary to be arrayed in the crimson gown of velvet that belongeth to the gild; and the prior of St. Katharine's to be spoken with to have such "honourments" as we have had aforetime.

30 Oct. The foundation of a priest to sing in the church of St. Michael upon the hill. . .with a proviso that the said chaplain shall yearly be ready to help to the preparing and bringing forth of the procession of St. Anne's day, and after Mr. Dighton's decease to be called for ever St. Anne's priest.

31 Dec. (?) Every alderman to make a gown for the kings in the pageant on St. Anne's day, and the Pater Noster play to be played this year.

1539, 18 July. Agreed that St. Anne's gild shall go up on the Sunday next after St. Anne's day in manner and form as it hath been had in time past.

12 Nov. The stuff belonging to St. Anne's gild to be laid in the chapel of the bridge, and the house in which it lieth to be let.

1540, 2 June. Agreed that St. Anne's gild shall go forward as it hath done in times past; that every alderman shall have a gown and a torch, and every sheriff to find a gown, and every occupation to bring forth their pageants according to the old custom, and every occupation that hath their pageants broken to make them ready against that day, on pain of forfeiting 20*s.*

1542, 10 June. St. Anne's gild to be brought forth the Sunday after St. James' day (St. Anne's day in 1539 and 1547).

On Nov. 14, 1545, the Great Gild made over its lands, tenements, and hereditaments for the relief of the city and its plate on the 5th of February, 1546. On Nov. 5, 1547, jewels, plate, and ornaments belonging to St. Anne's Gild are ordered sold for the use of the common chamber; but that year, 13 June, the procession and sight upon the Sunday next after St. Anne's day shall be brought forth as hath been in times past, and every occupation shall pay to the same as hath been accustomed.

1554, 6 July. Agreed at a Secret Council that St. Anne's gild with Corpus Christi play shall be brought forth and played this year, and that every craft shall bring forth their pageants as hath been accustomed, and all occupations to be contributories as shall be assessed.

1555, 3 June. St. Anne's gild to be brought forth as hath been heretofore accustomed.

To these entries add the following one summarized by Leach, page 224, "Again, on Nov. 12, 31 Henry VII, it was agreed by the Common Council that a large door should be made at the late schoolhouse that the pageants may be sent in, and rent was to be charged for warehousing of 4*d.* for each pageant, 'and Noy schippe 12*d.*'"

There were, therefore, a Corpus Christi play and a procession on St. Anne's day, directed by the mayor and the graceman; the guild priest helped in the preparation of the pageants; the host was carried in the procession; the content, so far as it can be determined, is normal; Noah, a play containing kings, an Ascension and an Assumption and Coronation of the Virgin. In 1555 the order is for "St. Anne's guild and Corpus Christi play." It is altogether probable that the entries in the annals for 1471-2, 1473-4, refer to the same play. The **Hegge cycle** has the striking quality of possessing elaborate St. Anne's day characteristics and of having been at the same time, it is stated in the Prologue, a Corpus Christi play. Both these plays and the Lincoln plays were apparently regularly acted on Sunday.

The Lincoln plays seem to have been processional, and yet to have been acted, at least in part, upon a fixed stage. We have, on the one hand, the records of the procession, and, on the other, a record which proves that the Assumption of the Virgin was acted in the nave of the cathedral. We possess, moreover, a list of stage properties which may reasonably be believed to have been employed in the Corpus Christi play, and were certainly the properties of a stationary stage. Leach, page 223, gives an entry in this form: "For example, in 1469, one of the Chapter Act Books (A. 2. 36, fol. 32) has a reference to the Show or Play of St. Anne. The Chapter provided for the expenses of J. Hanson, chaplain, about the show (*visum*) of the Assumption of the Virgin on St. Anne's day last past, given in the nave of the church, with a reward to him out of the money coming from the next opening of the high altar, i. e., of the collection box there." And again to quote the same authority, this time following more closely a passage in one of the "act-books or minute-books of the Chapter A. 31, f. 18:" "On Saturday, the Chapter Day, June, 1483, in the high choir of the Cathedral Church of the Blessed Mary of Lincoln, after compline, Sir Dean with his brethren, the Precentor, Chancellor, Treasurer, and Alford standing according to custom before the west door of the choir, and discussing the procession of St. Anne to be made by the citizens of Lincoln on St. Anne's day next, determined that they would have the play or speech (*sermonium*) of the Assumption or Coronation of the Blessed Mary repaired and got ready, and played and shown in the procession aforesaid, as usual in the nave of the said church. The question being raised at whose expense this was to be done: they said at the expense of those who were willing to contribute and give anything to it, and the rest to be met by the common fund and the fabric fund in equal shares, and Sir Treasurer and T. Alford were made surveyors of the work."

This state of things is exactly reflected in the **Hegge cycle**. The Prologue of the cycle is divided into pageants and the word is freely used in the Prologue. "Pageant" frequently meant the vehicle on which plays were acted and was usually associated with that idea. This Prologue contemplates a regular processional play; but what do we find? We find that the mass of the plays were acted on a fixed stage; so far as we find indications at all. Those which are unmodified and agree with the Prologue may possibly at any time, however late, have been acted on pageants. In two plays pageants were actually employed, namely, in the Noah play, where Noah goes out and brings in the ark, and then when the play is over, withdraws with it; and in the Trial of Joseph and Mary where the play begins with the stage-direction: "Hic intrabit pagentum de purgatione Mariae et Joseph." Pageants may have been used in many other parts of the cycle for all you can tell from the manuscript. The cycle is, moreover, divided in the manuscript into separate plays, even when there is no break in the action. Now, why should this have been done? It seems to me that it was done to preserve the identity of these different plays, although they were no longer separate pageants; and that would have been necessary in order to preserve the responsibility of the different trading companies. This responsibility was preserved at Lincoln and thus fulfills the special conditions of the manuscript. The manuscript of the Hegge plays (Brit. Mus. Cotton MS. Vesp. D. viii.) shows the play of the **Assumption of the Virgin** written in a different hand from the rest of the manuscript, but evidently of about the same date as the other plays; it was incorporated in the manuscript at the time that it was made up. It is numbered and rubricated and even corrected in the hand of the scribe. It was evidently a separate play-book; another case of that is certainly the Passion play in two parts, the first pages of which look as if they had been exposed as outside covers. We evidently have to do with an "original" which has been made up of old and new parts. It is probably an official document analogous to the Corporation Register at York.

There is preserved at the back of a Lincoln Corporation minute-book the following entry of stage properties: 1564, July.—"A note of the perti. . .the properties of

the staige. . .played in the moneth of July anno sexto regni, reginae Elizabethae, etc., in the tyme of the mayoralty of Richard Carter, whiche play was then played in Brodgaite in the seid citye, and it was of the storye of Tobias in the Old Testament. First, hell mouth with a neither chap; item, a prison with a coveryng; item, Sara ('s) chamber: lying at Mr. Norton's house in the tenure of William Smart. Item a greate idoll with a clubb; item, a tombe with a coveryng; item, the citie of Jerusalem with towers and pynacles; item, the citie of Raiges with towers and pynacles; item, the citie of Nynyve; item, the King's palace of Nynyve; item, olde Tobyes house; item, the Isralytes house and the neighbures house; item, the Kyngs palace at Laches; remanyng in Saynt Swythunes churche. Item, a fyrmament with a fierye clowde and a duble clowde, in the custodye of Thomas Fulbeck, alderman." It has been suggested that some of these properties, if not all, are those of the defunct Corpus Christi play; but be that as it may, it is evident that a number of these properties could have been employed in presenting plays in the Hegge cycle. "Hell mouth with a neither chap," "Jerusalem with towers and pynacles," a "tombe with a coveryng," and a "fyrmament with a fierye clowde and a duble clowde," could have been used in presenting the play of the Assumption of the Virgin. In the case of the first three it is not a matter of much significance; but with regard to the last-mentioned strange piece of mechanism it is certainly most significant to find evidence of its use. Before the death of the Virgin Mary she desires to see the Apostles, who are abroad in distant lands; suddenly St. John appears and says:

> In Pheso I was prechyng a fer contre ryth,
> And by a whyte clowde I was rapt to these
>   hyllys.

Later all the Apostles suddenly appear; only Peter and Paul speak; Peter says:

> In dyveris contreys we prechid of youre sone
>   and his blis,
> In dyveris clowdys eche of us was suddenly
>   curyng;
> And in on were brouth before youre yate here
>   i-wys
> The cause why no man cowde telle of oure
>   comyng.

One further slight point of some value is that the Hegge play of the **Assumption of the Virgin** makes use of a choir and an organ, as if it were acted in a church.

The suggestion that the plays belonged to Lincoln has been made before, and there are apparent agreements in the matter of dialect and content with what we should expect to find there. The hypothesis explains at a glance many of the perplexities and problems which have involved the cycle. In fact it would be so rare to find in any other place such a set of conditions as those of Lincoln that the identification must gain in credibility the more it is considered. Lincoln was a great ecclesiastical center, and at that place we have a close and intimate connection between the cathedral clergy and the town plays, a set of circumstances which exactly accounts for the remarkable homiletic and apochryphal interest of the **Hegge cycle**.

In her recent paper, entitled "The Problem of the *Ludus Coventriae*" [*Modern Language Review* 9] Miss M. H. Dodds has also reached the same general conclusion as Miss Swenson's study; namely, that the Prologue represents an earlier cycle which was the foundation of the present *Ludus Coventriae*; but disagrees widely with Miss Swenson's paper when she concludes that we have in *Ludus Coventriae* a composite made up of five cycles from five different places. Miss Swenson's conclusion is that we have to do with one cycle and the changes it has undergone in one place.

Arguing from the last stanza of the general Prologue, she makes two statements with regard to the original **N. Town plays**: (1) That the plays must have been accurately described by the Prologue; (2) that they must have been founded upon stories from the Bible. With the first of these propositions I agree perfectly, and, in general, I agree that the earlier plays were simple and scriptural in their nature; but I find many disagreements with her application of the principles stated.

In the first place, Miss Dodds' study of the relations between Prologue and plays has taken no account of meters, nor of minor differences in incident, and an insufficient account of stage-directions. This leads her to conclude that the play dealing with the girlhood of the Virgin and the Easter play have been incorporated as wholes and not simply combined with old plays on the same subjects, and she makes no attempt to discriminate between old and new elements in these plays. She says that the first seven plays, including the **Prophets**, belong to the original cycle, but she fails to note the emphasis upon the Virgin both in the Prologue and the play of the **Prophets** and consequently concludes that all the plays treating the subject of the girlhood of the Virgin (**Barrenness of Anna** to the **Visit to Elizabeth**), as well as the stanzas in the Prologue which correspond to them, have been incorporated about 1468 by some compiler who was eager to glorify the Virgin.

The theory that the Prologue has been left intact except in the case of the quatrains numbered fourteen and fifteen, as noted by Miss Swenson above, and that the Girlhood plays are made up of old and new elements can not, I think, be refuted simply by the statement in the Prologue that

> Of holy wryth this game xal bene
> And of no fablys be no way.

The people of England in 1468 did not draw a very sharp distinction between those stories which were definitely in the Bible and those generally accepted as "gospel truth" by the Church at large. Such stories as the **Betrothal of Mary** might be included and accepted as very truth and "no fablys." Miss Dodds also fails to notice the strange mixture of elements in the Easter cycle; although in this case she concludes somewhat inconsistently that the Prologue has been allowed to stand as it was. The play thus incorporated, or, as I think, the play thus rewritten, she would end with the Three Maries. It seemed to Miss Swenson more probable, from a study of meter, stage-directions, and minute differences in incident, and also because the prologue spoken by Contemplacio promises only a Passion play (not a Resurrection play) that the influence ends with the scene of the Burial.

There is, I think, no reason for considering the plays from the **Adoration of the Shepherds** to the **Death of Herod** as a separate cycle, as Miss Dodds does. They are not self-consistent in style or independent of the rest of the cycle in style or meter, but seem to be a normal Nativity group. The **Purification** is evidently from a different source altogether. It is not mentioned in the Prologue and is in a meter rarely used in the cycle; but otherwise the Nativity group has seemed to me to belong with the rest of the cycle. And so I should not agree that any of Miss Dodds' five groups are independent of the cycle or imported from the outside.

There are other significant omissions in Miss Dodds' paper; such as her failure to make note of such excrescences as the Lamech episode, the Cherry-tree episode, and in general the passages written in tumbling meter; also the way in which stage-directions are employed and plays introduced and concluded and many points of disagreement between Prologue and cycle; but these will be sufficiently plain by a comparison of her paper with the. . .one by Miss Swenson.

G. K. Chesterton (essay date 1920)

SOURCE: "The Humor of King Herod," in *The Uses of Diversity: A Book of Essays*, Methuen & Co. Ltd., 1920, pp. 96-100.

[*In the following essay, Chesterton relates the so-called Coventry Nativity play to more familiar Renaissance dramatic conventions and asserts that the proximity of comedy and tragedy began with medieval miracle plays.*]

If I say that I have just been very much amused with a Nativity play of the fourteenth century it is still possible that I may be misunderstood. What is more important, some thousand years of very heroic history will be misunderstood too. It was one of the Coventry cycle of mediæval plays, loosely called the **Coventry Myster-ies**, similar to the Chester Mysteries and the Towneley Mysteries.

And I was not amused at the blasphemy of something badly done, but at a buffoonery uncommonly well done. But, as I said at the time, the educated seem to be very ignorant of this fine mediæval fun. When I mentioned the **Coventry Mystery** many ladies and gentlemen thought it was a murder in the police news. At the best, they supposed it to be the title of a detective story. Even upon a hint of history they could only recall the story of Godiva; which might be called rather a revelation than a mystery.

Now I always read police news and I sometimes write detective stories; nor am I at all ashamed of doing either. But I think the popular art of the past was perhaps a little more cheerful than that of the present. And in seeing this Bethlehem drama I felt that good news might perhaps be as dramatic as bad news; and that it was possibly as thrilling to hear that a child is born as to hear that a man is murdered.

Doubtless there are some sentimental people who like these old plays merely because they are old. My own sentiment could be more truly stated by saying that I like them because they are new. They are new in the imaginative sense, making us feel as if the first star were leading us to the first child.

But they are also new in the historical sense, to most people, owing to that break in our history which makes the Elizabethans seem not merely to have discovered the new world but invented the old one. Nobody could see this mediæval play without realizing that the Elizabethan was rather the end than the beginning of a tradition; the crown and not the cradle of the drama.

Many things that modern critics call peculiarly Elizabethan are in fact peculiarly mediæval. For instance, that the same stage could be the place where meet the extremes of tragedy and comedy, or rather farce. That daring mixture is always made a point of contrast between the Shakespearean play and the Greek play or the French classical play. But it is a point of similarity, or rather identity, between the Shakespearean play and the miracle play.

Nothing could be more bitterly tragic than the scene in this Nativity drama, in which the mothers sing a lullaby to the children they think they have brought into safety the moment before the soldiers of Herod rush in and butcher them screaming on the stage. Nothing could be more broadly farcical than the scene in which King Herod himself pretends that he has manufactured the thunderstorm.

In one sense, indeed, the old religious play was far

bolder in its burlesque than the more modern play. Shakespeare did not express the unrest of King Claudius by making him fall over his own cloak. He did not convey his disdain for tyranny by letting Macbeth appear with his crown on one side. This was partly no doubt an improvement in dramatic art; but it was partly also, I think, a weakening of democratic satire.

Shakespeare's clowns are philosophers, geniuses, demigods; but Shakespeare's clowns are clowns. Shakespeare's kings may be usurpers, murderers, monsters; but Shakespeare's kings are kings. But in this old devotional drama the king is the clown. He is treated not so much with disdain as with derision; not so much with a bitter smile as with a broad grin. A cat may not only look at a king but laugh at a king; like the mythical Cheshire cat, an ancient cat as terrible as a tiger and grinning like a gargoyle. But that Cheshire cat has presumably vanished with the Chester Mysteries, the counterpart of these **Coventry Mysteries;** it has vanished with the age and art of gargoyles.

In other words, that popular simplicity that could see wrongful power as something pantomimically absurd, a thing for practical jokes, has since been sophisticated by a process none the less sad because it is slow and subtle. It begins in the Elizabethans in an innocent and indefinable form. It is merely the sense that, though Macbeth may get his crown crookedly, he must not actually wear it crooked. It is the sense that, though Claudius may fall from his throne, he must not actually fall over his footstool.

It ended in the nineteenth century in many refined and ingenuous forms; in a tendency to find all fun in the ignorant or criminal classes; in dialect or the dropping of aitches. It was a sort of satirical slumming. There was a new shade in the comparison of the coster with the cat; a coster could look at a king and might conceivably laugh at a king; but most contemporary art and literature was occupied in laughing at the coster.

Even in the long lifetime of a good comic paper like *Punch* we can trace the change from jokes against the palace to jokes against the public-house. The difference is perhaps more delicate; it is rather that the refined classes are a subject for refined comedy; and only the common people a subject for common farce. It is correct to call this refinement modern; yet it is not quite correct to call it contemporary. All through the Victorian time the joke was pointed more against the poor and less against the powerful; but the revolution which ended the long Victorian peace has shaken this Victorian patronage. The great war which has brought so many ancient realities to the surface has re-enacted before our eyes the **Miracle Play of Coventry**.

We have seen a real King Herod claiming the thunders of the throne of God, and answered by the thunder not merely of human wrath but of primitive human laughter. He has done murder by proclamations, and he has been answered by caricatures. He has made a massacre of children, and been made a figure of fun in a Christmas pantomime for the pleasure of other children. Precisely because his crime is tragic, his punishment is comic; the old popular paradox has returned.

K. S. Block (essay date 1922)

SOURCE: An introduction to *Ludus Coventriae or the Plaie Called Corpus Christi*, edited by K. S. Block, Early English Text Society, 1922, pp. xi-lvii.

[*In introducing her edition of the cycle, Block describes the details of the manuscript. This excerpt includes her assertions that the manuscript is a compilation and that the cycle differs from other cycles in its ritual and dramatic complexity.*]

The general evidence of the various features of the MS . . .shows that the collection contains parts or the whole of four separate groups: (1) the composite *Contemplacio* group (viii to xiii); (2) the first *Passion* group (xxvi to xxviii); (3) the second *Passion* group (xxix to xxxii), dovetailed on by means of the *Descent into Hell* (xxxiii), of different style, to a *Burial* play (xxxiv) of similar style, which in its turn is joined (p. 314, beginning of U quire) to a (4) *Resurrection and Harrowing* play connected in style with xxxiii and forming a group with the *Three Maries* and, as it stands in the compilation, with the *Mary Magdalen* play. An examination of the text gives two more groups showing that (5) the first three plays (*Creation, Fall,* and *Cain and Abel*) and (6) the *Visit of the Magi* and *Massacre of the Innocents* and *Death of Herod* (xviii and xx) form respectively continuous sets, diction and metre connecting also the *Shepherds* play with the latter suite. There are also two interpolated separate plays: *The Purification* and *The Assumption.*

The evidence as to the composition of the series to be drawn from the characteristics of the MS. is complicated and often ambiguous, but the following points emerge:

  1. MS. Vesp. D. viii is the compiler's book, not a transcript of another MS.

  2. It contains a collection of plays made according to a plan which was subject to alteration as it proceeded.

  3. Some of the plays and groups of plays had had a separate existence, having been acted as separate plays or groups.

  4. One portion of the MS. certainly, and probably

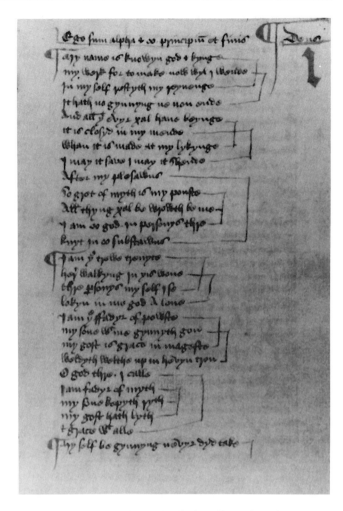

Page from The Creation, and Fall of Lucifer *in the only extant manuscript for the N-Town plays.*

two, quires N, P, Q, R, and quires S, T, have also had a separate existence.

In support of 3, besides the evidence already adduced, may be noted the preservation of their distinctive character by the groups in the series, by the *Contemplacio* group, and especially by the two *Passion* groups the stage directions of which are conspicuously different from any others in the collection; the variety of the headings of the single plays—*introitus* (ff. 20^v, 25^v, 31), *modo de.* . .(ff. 106, 212), *hic incipit.* . .(ff. 127^v, 201, 210, 223^v), *hic intrabit pagetum de.* . .(fo. 75); the conclusion of the *Disputation* play addressed to *All þat hath herd þis consummacion of / þis pagent* as to the audience of a separate performance, and to a less extent the sermon-like conclusions of the *Temptation* and the *Woman taken in Adultery* plays; and the fact that—as the modernizing revision of certain plays, the added stage directions (e. g. p. 327), and the worn condition of the *Magi* portion of the MS. show—certain plays continued to be so acted.

5. The compiler had command of other versions of plays or groups of plays from which he drew.

The evidence for this is mainly to be deduced from the variation of the plays from the description of them in the Proclamation, chiefly in the first *Contemplacio* group and in the two *Passion* groups, but it is supported by the fact that the later users of the MS. obviously had access to such other versions (cf. the references in the later hand in the *Harrowing* play to *anima latronis,* fo. 185ᵛ, to extra speeches of the devil and of *anima caym*), and by the presence in the MS. of the detached *Doctors' Prologue* written on a blank folio at the end of quire R. This introduces characters not found together in any play or group of plays in this collection—the eleven apostles, John the Baptist, and St. Paul, who only appears in the *Assumption* play. It would seem to be part of another group in the possession of the performers of the *Passion* groups, copied for convenience on a blank sheet of the MS. of the latter. So the allusion to the 1st and 2nd prophets in notes (pp. 240-1) appears to refer to some other combination of plays than that of the text.

The evidence of the MS. supports the view that a compiler is putting together parts to make a whole rather than the view suggested by Dr. Foster (*Northern Passion,* E.E.T.S. 147, p. 99) that a reviser has separated a whole into groups, though he drew apparently on a cycle—or the remains of a cycle—of plays in thirteen-lined stanzas as well as on single plays and on groups of plays. To unravel the tissue of compilation and revision in these plays demands a full study of literary and linguistic characteristics. The examination of the MS. affords no conclusive evidence on such questions, but it gives much to support the theory that the MS. represents a selection from the repertory of a body of ecclesiastical actors. As Dr. Smith says: 'Videntur olim coram populo sive ad instruendum sive ad placendum *a Fratribus mendicantibus* repraesentata.' Nor does the evidence from the MS. throw clear light on the question of the identity of the compiler with any of the writers or revisers of the plays, but some inferences can be drawn.

The relation of the plays to the Proclamation shows, as has been said, that the Proclamation was composed in its present form in close connexion with the compiling of this series. The relation is particularly interesting at the point of divergence in the second *Passion* group. Here the interpolated portion (ff. 184, 185, 186) in the text corresponds with the Proclamation, from which the rest of the text diverges, and that with regard to a feature—the division into two scenes of the Harrowing—that is peculiar to this treatment of the theme. The inference suggests itself that the compiler was himself the writer of this link passage, which again is connected with the latter part of the *Resurrection* play and through that, by the evidence of metre and more elusive evidence of diction, with the *Magi* plays. The conclusion

to be drawn from this agrees with that of Mr. Greg (*Problems of English Miracle Cycles*) in that it associates the composition of the *rime couée* portions of the cycle with the process of compilation. Dr. Greg postulates a further overworking by the writer of the *Contemplacio* prologues and possibly of the long octave plays and passages, who would therefore be the actual compiler of the Vesp. D. viii MS. But there is evidence that the long octave *Contemplacio* plays underwent a further revision by a writer drawing on Bonaventura's *Meditationes Vitæ Christi,* to whom, as well as the *Salutation and Conception,* the *Purification* play must be attributed. Now it would appear unlikely, had this reviser been the compiler, that the *Purification* play should not be mentioned in the Proclamation, and that the description of the *Salutation and Conception* in the Proclamation should not have been made to refer to the compiler's own work. The theory that the writer of the *rime couée,* parts, with which the corresponding passages in the Proclamation agree closely, is the compiler seems to present the stronger case. This writer draws also on Bonaventura, and both revisions are probably connected with the compilation.

This MS. has known the turn of fortune described by Robert Hegge, its first recorded owner, when after the invention of printing 'old MSS. were stright bequeath'd to the Moths: and pigeons and Jack daws became the only students in church libraries'; and many of its blank pages have been used for idle scribbling—attempts at copying the MS. writing, signatures, stray phrases, mostly in sixteenth-century hands. It would appear that it fell early into irreverent schoolboy hands, for some of the scribbled copying of lines of the text seems to be rather rough contemporary work than later imitation of an older script. The first or last line of a folio is often imitated, and in one instance a passage of some length has been carelessly and roughly copied on the blank page opposite (fo. 201). A jumble of ill-formed Greek and fancy letters on fo. 119ᵛ with what appear to be notes on a fraction sum on the opposite folio suggests the hand of a schoolboy. The names that occur among these scribblings are Wyll*i*am Dere (91ᵛ, 136), Polerd (91ᵛ), Hollond, Joh*a*n & Hary (151ᵛ, 152ᵛ, 153ᵛ, 155ᵛ), H Kinge the yownger (111ᵛ), John Hasycham (91ᵛ), and on the same page (91ᵛ) 'John Taylphott of parish Bedonson' with the motto 'wee that will not when we paie [*sic*] when we would we shall find (? or saie) nay'. The oddness of the personal name throws doubt on that of the parish, and no record of a parish of Bedonson has been found.

By a coincidence that is possibly nothing more the names William Kinge the younger his booke 1656, John King his brother and John Holland of Brabant occur among the scribblings in the Chester plays (MS. Add. 10305, ff. 55 and 111); the motto quoted above is also found (of. 124) in a four-lined form, of which, however, unfortunately the first line is missing.

Of a different character are the two signatures of R. Hegge, Dunelmensis, the title of the plays, and some annotations of the original scribe. The first signature comes on of. 10 above the opening of the first play. It consisted of the full name Robert Hegge, Dunelmensis, written in large Roman hand, but, having been cut away with the margin, the Christian name is now indecipherable. The second, on of. 164, the outside sheet of the S and T quires, is more elaborate. At the top of the page in Roman type is written: 'In no*mj*ne Dei. Amen'; in the middle of the page, in a slender cursive hand, 'ego R. H. Dunelmensis possideo'; . . .

The title 'The plaie called Corpus Christi' in a small Elizabethan hand stands at the top of fo. 1 above the speech of the first vexillator. Mr. Hemingway in his *English Nativity Plays* speaks of this title as being in Hegge's handwriting, but this is not so. It is writing of an earlier and altogether different type.

The notes forming part of the original MS. consist of three genealogies, of Adam to Noah (ff. 16ᵛet seq.), of Noah to Abraham (ff. 21 et seq.), of the Virgin Mary (fo. 37); the measurements of Noah's ark (fo. 24); a list of the five Annas of scriptural importance (fo. 37ᵛ) and three dates of the ecclesiastical calendar (fo. 74ᵛ). The genealogies are in liturgical script, the note on the dates and on the Annas in smaller bookhand, and the genealogies are handsomely rubricated, one part of that of Mary being entirely in red. These marginal additions give support to the conclusion to be drawn from the general characteristics of the compilation, that it is of ecclesiastical and not of civic origin. . . .

This cycle is later in its compilation than the civic cycles, but it seems to have borrowed little from them beyond the general choice and treatment of material, and even in these respects there are noticeable divergencies. There are more plays peculiar to this cycle than to any other, and the absence of farcical passages in the *Cain, Noah,* and *Shepherds* plays distinguishes it from all the others.

The opening of the speech of God the Father in the first play, *Ego sum á et ù* is found in all cases, and the further likeness of a few phrases in the Towneley play (cf. 'All maner thyng is in my thoght' and 'all þat evyr xal haue beynge / it is closyd in my mende') would seem due to the same natural coincidence. An interpolated passage in the *Shepherds* play—the solitary attempt at humour—p. 148, ll. 78-89, may be a reminiscence of a similar farcical discussion of the angels' song in the Chester *Shepherds* play; a line in the scourging scene recalls a line in the same context in the Towneley play (cf. p. 277, ll. 168-71, and 'we shall teche hym I wote a new play of yoyll') and there are coincidences in the Towneley and *L. C. Passion* plays due to the use in both of the *Northern Passion,* but otherwise there is nothing that may not be accounted for as due to sim-

ilarity of theme and form.

Besides the plays which have no counterpart in the other cycles (*The Conception of Mary, Mary in the Temple, The Betrothal of Mary, The Trial of Joseph and Mary*) the following episodes are found only in the *L[udus] C[oventriæ]*—the death of Cain at the hands of Lamech (play 4), the testifying of the kings (Matthew i. 6-10) with the prophets (play 7), the 'parliament of heaven' (play 11), the miracle of the cherry-tree (play 15); Veronica appears only in this series, but her action is performed by one of the Maries in the York plays; in no other cycle is the crucifying of our Lord assigned to the highborn Jews ('No man xal towche your kyng / but yf he be knyght · or gentylman born; cf. also fo. 181, stage direction); characteristic of this collection again are the pithy short sermons put into the mouth of different characters: two from John the Baptist, one at the close of play 22 (p. 192) on repentance, and one as prologue to the *Passion* play (p. 229) on the dangers of overconfidence and of despair; one from Peter in the *Entry into Jerusalem,* scene (p.238) on the spiritually blind, lame, and dumb; one from Christ expounding the Eucharist (p. 254). To these may be added the ironic discourse of Lucifer, a 'bountevous lord' to 'reward synners', at the opening of the *Passion* play (p. 225), and the exposition of the Commandments in the sixth play, which there is nothing to match in the Chester play in which the Commandments are recited.

In this exposition of the Commandments the writer is drawing on the usual homiletic interpretation of the time. A treatise of the Commandments in a MS. at St. John's Coll.. Oxford, ed. by J. F. Royster (University of N. Carolina, Studies in Philology, vol. 6, 1910), who dates it between 1420 and 1434, contains much the same material (cf. *L[udus] C[oventriæ].,* p. 55, ll. 134-7, and 'Bot agaynes þis commaundement doos he þat slaes with hond or with word or will'; and p. 57, ll. 179-82, and 'In the siyste commaundement is forboden þe dede of lechere. . .and in þis commaundement þe wille of þe syn is forboden'; cf. also *Court of Sapience*).

The discourse of Lucifer is specially interesting as helping to date the compilation. Attacks on extravagant fashions are common in the fifteenth century; the one in the text seems to be dealing with the same objectionable features in costume as the poem in MS. Harl. 372, printed by J. Payne Collier for the Percy Society, vol. xv, p. 55, and assigned to the mid-century—'not later than 1467' (cf. *L[udus] C[oventriæ]*, p. 227, ll. 69 et seq., and 'Ye prowd galonttys hertlesse / With your high cappis witlesse / And youre schort gownys thriftlesse / Haue brought this lond in gret heuynesse / With your long peked schone. . .And your long here in to your eyen. . .With your wyde furryd hodes. . .leue your short stuffide doublettys and your playtid gownys'). Similar fashions, however, seem to be attacked later in the century in the morality *Nature* (the 'side hair', the 'short gown', and 'wide sleeves' that 'would make a doublet and coat for some lad in this town').

The mingling of the kings of Jesse's race with the prophets in the seventh play is not found in any other play of this type that has come down to us, but Sepet in *Les prophètes du Christ* takes it as the surviving example of a class: 'L'idée de faire paraître à côté des prophètes proprement dits la ligne de Jesse, les rois de Juda, fils de David et ancêtres du Messie, n'est pas particulière au Ludus Coventriæ. La scène a certainement eu ce caractère dans les mystères français.' He quotes in support of this view a description of a similar combination in a Corpus Christi procession still held at Mayenne in the seventeenth century.

The Lamech episode is found in *Le Mystère du Vieil Testament,* but here the boy who guides Lamech and whom he slays is his own son, Tubal-cain. The writer of the *L[udus] C[oventriæ]* interpolation seems to have drawn straight from P. Comestor. . . .

The independence of this cycle is perhaps most clearly illustrated in the treatment of a theme common to all the cycles—Christ and the Doctors. Five plays on the subject have come down to us, and, of these, four—those in the York, Towneley, Chester, and Coventry civic cycles—go back to one original; the fifth, that in the *Ludus Coventriæ,* stands alone; and the play with the learned brag of the opening speeches and the theological problems and paradoxes introduced into the discussion is characteristic of the more ecclesiastical and perhaps also of the more sophisticated and 'stagy' cast of this compilation. The questions raised—(*a*) the unity of the Trinity, (*b*) the distinction of the three persons, (*c*) the manner of the incarnation, (*d*) the reason for the choice of the second person, (*e*) the 'double birth' of Jesus, (*f*) the reasons for the marriage of Mary—were all theological commonplaces, but the writer deserves some credit for original ingenuity in collecting them.

A connexion has been often suggested between this cycle and other religious plays of the fifteenth century. There are obvious similarities in the stage directions of the *L[udus] C[oventriæ] Passion* plays and those of such plays as *Mind, Will and Understanding,* the *Candlemas* play, *Mary Magdalene, The Croxton Play of the Sacrament,* which suggest similar methods of staging and perhaps similar business on the part of the actors. There are also similarities in diction and in metre and in the handling of metrical form—the varying of the metre to suit the speaker or the situation—and in other characteristics of treatment which deserve further investigation but which lie outside the scope of this introduction. *The Castle of Perseverance* offers one or two special points of contact. It has, like the *L[udus] C[oventriæ],* a prologue in thirteen-lined stanzas for vexillatores in which the name of the town at which the play is to be performed is left to be filled up. It

introduces the debate of the Four Daughters of God (*The Parliament of Heaven*) over the fate of the soul of *Humanum Genus,* though in this case it is the salvation of the individual and not the redemption of the race that is in question, and the debate does not lead up to the Incarnation. It introduces also the figure of Death; the entry of this character has not the quality of dramatic irony that makes the entry in the **Death of Herod** play so impressive (*Humanum Genus,* an old man, has just remarked 'on Coveytyse is al my lay / And schal; tyl deth me ouer-throw'—Herod: 'I was nevyr meryer her*e* beforn / Sythe þat I was fyrst born / Than I am now ryght in þis morn')—but the general effect is similar as are (naturally) the two speeches of Death. In *The Castle of Perseverance* is found also one of the geographical lists of which there are examples in the Towneley play *Herod the Great* (considered by Mr. Pollard to be one of the group of later plays), in the L[udus] C[oventriæ] **Temptation** play, and in *The Croxton Play of the Sacrament.* The arrangement of names of countries and towns in lists, often alphabetical, in the geographical treatises of the time afforded convenient material for the alliterative artist (cf. *Rel. Ant.,* vol. i, p. 271, and MS. Arundel 123). Though some of the names are common, the lists seem to be independent, but they testify doubtless to some kinship, as do perhaps the attacks in all the *Macro Moralities* and the **Ludus Coventriæ** on the extravagant fashions in clothing of the time.

The **Ludus Coventriæ** has generally been considered inferior in literary merit to the other cycles. It lacks the genuine feeling that dignifies the York cycle (cf. *Birth* and *Flight into Egypt* plays); it has nothing to compare with the pathos of the Chester *Isaac* play or the humour of the Towneley second *Shepherds* play. Though Mary plays such an important part, no speech of hers in the **L[udus] C[oventriæ]** has the poetic quality of the Lament, in the Towneley *Crucifixion* play, of the Mother at the foot of the Cross. Apart from the greetings of the Shepherds, the speech of Death, the lament of Adam and Eve, and a few *rime couée* passages there is very little poetry in the pages of Vesp. D. viii. But the plays of this collection offered their audience compensations for deficiencies—more singing, more 'devices', more processions, more harangues, and, above all, in some cases, more acting. The passages of couplet dialogue in the Trial scenes (ff. 168ᵛ, 169, 171ᵛ, 177, 178, 178ᵛ, 179) mark an important advance from recitation and declamation to acting, and in several of the plays the writer of writers show command of stage effect, and understanding of the impressiveness of significant gesture and movement. A comparison of the **Woman taken in Adultery** in this series and in the York and Chester cycles illustrates the superior skill of at least one of the **Ludus Coventriæ** writers in developing a dramatic situation. The preliminary sermon of Christ on forgiveness, the angry comments of the Jews, the arrival of Accusator with his welcome scandal ' a ryght good

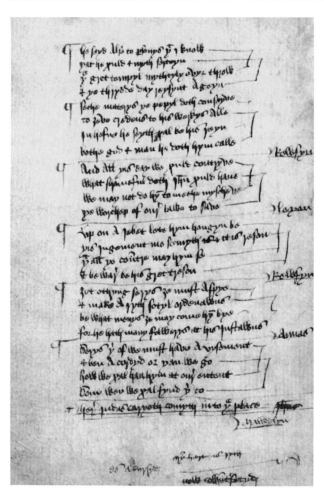

Manuscript page of The Conspiracy *and* The Last Supper, *from*
Passion I.

sporte I kan yow telle', the breaking open of the door
of the house, the escape of the man 'If any man my
wey doth stoppe. . .I xal þis dagge *e* putt in his croppe'
the pleading of the woman 'I pray yow kylle me prevely. . .lete not þe pepyl up on me crye'—all these dramatic features are found only in the *Ludus Coventriæ*
example. The most dramatic passage in the series is,
perhaps, the unnoted entrance of Death in the midst of
the revelry of Herod and his knights, where, as has
been said, the style rises above the usual level. The
effect of silent stealthy movement followed by sudden
outcry on the imagination of an audience is again recognized in the stage direction for Pilate's wife's dream:
'her xal þe devyl gon to Pilatys wyf · þe corteyn drawyn as she lyth in bedde *and* he xal no dene make but
she xal sone after þat he is come in · makyn a rewly
noyse · comyng and rennyng of þe schaffald. . .leke a
mad woman'; and this direction 'he xal no dene make'
is the more significant as Pilate's wife afterwards describes the 'sounds unheard': 'As wylde fyre *and*
thondyr blast / he cam cryeng on to me'. Very effective, too, must have been Judas's secret passings to

and from the scaffolds in the *Last Supper and Conspiracy* play: 'here Judas rysyth prevely' and 'here
Judas goth in sotylly'. The excitement of escape is
suggested in the vivid stage direction *et curret* which
follows Pilate's dismissal of Barabbas, and again in
the description of the flight of the young man in the
Woman taken in Adultery—'hic iuuenis quidam extra
currit in deploydo calligis no*n* ligatis et braccas in manu
tenens'. And we can still feel the thrill that stirred the
'gentyllys and yemanry' of *N*. town in the fifteenth
century when we read the stage direction which opens
the first Trial scene: 'here xal a massang*er* com i*n* to
þe place ren*nyng and* cri*yng* Tydyng*ys* tydyng*ys* · *and*
so round abowth þe place · Jh*es*us of nazareth is take
þ Jh*es*us of nazareth is take'. Such an appeal may be,
in the words of the mediaeval preacher, more to 'þe
siyt wiþoute forþ' than to 'þe feiþ wiþinne forþ', but
there is no doubt of its potency, and in this effective
stage representation the *Death of Herod,* the *Woman
taken in Adultery,* and the *Passion* plays of the *Ludus
Coventriæ* are outstanding.

Timothy Fry (essay date 1951)

SOURCE: "The Unity of the Ludus Coventriae," in
Studies in Philology, Vol. XLVIII, No. 3, July, 1951,
pp. 527-70.

[*By relating the doctrinal content of Ludus Coventriae
to the writings of patristic authorities, Fry argues that
the theory of the Redemption as a response to the
devil's abuse of power unifies the cycle.*]

Scholars have been pretty well agreed that the *Ludus
Coventriae,* as the compilation of plays now stands, is
[as E. K. Chambers puts it in his *English Literature at
the Close of the Middle Ages,* 1945] "in a state of
confusion." Studies devoted to the cycle as a cycle have
been chiefly concerned with the stages in the development of the compilation of plays that comprise the *Ludus
Coventriae.* As necessary as these studies were to clear
the ground, they did not give a full understanding of the
cycle, principally because the most important aspect was
overlooked, or disregarded, namely, the doctrinal content of the plays. Within recent years the cycle has been
re-examined from this more cogent aspect with the result that earlier opinions must be revised.

It is the purpose of this short study to show that a
particular Patristic theory of the Redemption unifies this
cycle, the plays being related to this theme as integral
elements of the theory, and that the plays which find no
direct bearing on the theory are brought into its circuit
by constant references to the Redemption, and other
devices utilized by the dramatist. *The Prologue of
Demon,* far from "forcing" the plays into a unit, is
rather one of the integral parts of this specific theory
of the Redemption. It is the contention of the present

writer that critics have too long been satisfied to rest content with the mere statement that the cycle plays in general are based upon the theme of the Redemption of man. This generally safe assumption seems to have been responsible for the neglect of scholars to consider the role that some of the theological theories of the Redemption may have in plays of a religious nature.

Our procedure in this study will be as follows: 1) to present a short summary of the development of the particular theory of the Redemption which unites the plays of this cycle; 2) to give a brief conspectus of the dominant patterns of that theory as worked out by the dramatist in the *Ludus Coventriae;* and 3) to analyze the plays in some detail to show how the dramatist has utilized a theory of the Redemption to mold the cycle into a compact unit.

PATRISTIC ABUSE-OF-POWER THEORY OF REDEMPTION

The theory of the Redemption on which the *Ludus Coventriae* is built is known as the abuse-of-power theory in theological parlance, and was developed during the Patristic era. Briefly, the theory supposes that when Adam and Eve fell into original sin, Satan was permitted to inflict death on them and all mankind and hold them captive in hell. Christ born of the Immaculate Virgin Mary, was not subject to that law of death. Satan, however, was deceived by the human nature of Christ, and, in bringing about His death, abused his power, and lost the souls in hell.

The idea of the abuse-of-power is found first among the Greek Fathers. St. John Chrysostom (344?-407) is usually the first writer to whom historians of the dogma of the Redemption point, but his statement of the theory is elementary. Several important items of the theory in his works are that the divine subterfuge by which Satan was overcome manifested divine wisdom and that Judas was inspired by the devil. The formulation of the same elementary theory is found in the commentaries of St. Cyril of Alexandria (376-444), known as the doctor of the Incarnation, and the staunch opposer of the Nestorian heresy at the Council of Ephesus (431). His writings constitute a final synthesis of the teaching of the Greek Fathers. Relative to the abuse-of-power theory, he stressed the fact that Christ did not overcome the devil by the power of His divinity nor with an army of angels, but by becoming incarnate and allowing the devil to apply to Him the sentence of death. But in killing an innocent and just Person, the devil committed an act of injustice and perforce lost his power over men.

The theory received full development among the Latin Fathers of the fourth century. The Ambrosiaster [a Commentary on the Epistles of St. Paul, which was during the Middle Ages attributed to St. Ambrose] affords perhaps the greatest array of texts. The idea repeated throughout the commentary is that the devil overstepped his rights in bringing about the death of the innocent Christ. It was St. Augustine [in *De Trinitate*] who drew out the implications of the foregoing principles. He insisted on the justice by which God gave man over to the dominion of the devil, and with equal insistence he defended the justice by which the devil was despoiled of his rights over man. His point of emphasis is that God overcame the devil by justice and not by power. After St. Augustine there is not much development of the theory, except for the addition of details. Pope St. Leo the Great (390?-461) follows St. Augustine and must be mentioned because of the great popularity of his sermons, many of which were incorporated into the Divine Office of the Church. Mention must also be made of Pope St. Gregory the Great (540-604) because as a popularizer his works were influential in the spread of the theory.

The abuse-of-power theory is not the only phase of the doctrine of the Redemption to be found in the *Ludus Coventriae*. A great deal of the Scholastic tradition—from St. Anselm of Canterbury (1033?-1109) to Duns Scotus (1266 or 1274-1308) and others—on the doctrine is present, but it is woven into the structure of the abuse-of-power theory. That theory remains basic to the cycle and binds the plays together into a dramatic whole.

It should be pointed out that many of the Scholastics questioned the idea of the "rights" of the devil, and that by the time of these plays the theory of the abuse-of-power had practically disappeared from treatises on the Redemption. St. Anselm [in *Cur Deus Homo*] was probably the first to deny the "rights" of the devil. He is followed notably by Peter Abailard (1074-1142). But the idea persisted in one of the most influential books of the Middle Ages, the famous *Sentences* of Peter Lombard (1100?-1160 or 1164), which was one of the texts for theological students until well into Renaissance times.

The essential divisions of the theory and other aspects of the doctrine of the Redemption as found in the *Ludus Coventriae* may be outlined as follows: a) Setting the stage for the dominion of Satan; b) Preparatory stages of the divine plan of Redemption; c) Entry of the Protagonist and limited recognition of His divinity; d) The conflict and final defeat of the antagonist. With these essentials of the theory in mind, we are now ready to analyze very briefly the dominant patterns in this cycle.

DOMINANT PATTERNS OF THE THEORY IN
"LUDUS COVENTRIAE"

Setting the Stage for the Dominion of Satan

We must assume in the first place the fall of the angel Lucifer from a state of happiness in heaven to eternal pain in hell. This event against which all the actions of the drama have meaning is provided in the first play, *The Creation of Heaven and the Angels and the Fall of Lucifer.* God then created man, who was destined to fill the vacancies left in heaven by Lucifer and the fallen angels. However, man was to achieve his destiny on the provision that he remain obedient to the commands of God. Satan or Lucifer, envious in his evil nature of the ultimate destiny of man, brought about the fall of man by the temptation in paradise. Satan tempted Eve to the sin of desiring to be like God in knowledge, the sin of "cunnyng," as is so often repeated in these plays.

The entry of sin into the world marks the beginning of the dominion of Satan over man. Because man failed to live up to the commands of God, he was given over to the power of the devil. The Fathers looked upon this as the justice of God in operation, but they were careful to point out that God did not command or do this, but merely permitted it. The power given the devil was that of inflicting death on men, and holding their souls captive in hell, in which was the section for the just souls called the *limbus patrum.* These are the souls Christ will rescue in the Harrowing of Hell. The dominion of Satan over mankind is set forth in the cycle chiefly in the Old Testament plays of **Cain and Abel,** play 3, and **Noe,** play 4. These plays show the terrible effects of the sin of Adam on the human race, vividly portraying the depths of the degradation to which it had plunged in the hold of Satan. By implication the stress on the degradation of man shows the need of a Redeemer. As we shall see in more detail in the analysis of the plays, this concept is not explicitly stated, but the cumulative effect of emphasis on this point together with the presence of the Redemptive theme logically leads to that conclusion or inference. It is also the practice of the dramatist to keep the theme of the Redemption before his audience in these Old Testament plays by repeating the promise of a Redeemer from time to time.

With the play of **Moses** we have the introduction of the frequent cries for mercy during the Old Testament period of awaiting the coming of the Redeemer, which reach their culmination in the play of **The Prophets,** play 7. Throughout these Old Testament plays there is a constant looking forward or anticipation and yearning for the Redeemer. The Old Testament plays cannot be considered as a series of detached plays without any connection with the cycle or the theme of the cycle. The dramatist has been careful to bind up these plays into the theme of the entire cycle, so that they find their place in it not only because of the Biblical chronology, but also, and chiefly, because they provide the essential background to the abuse-of-power theory of the Redemption.

Preparatory Stages of the Divine Plan of Redemption

In the accomplishment of the divine plan of Redemption, the conflict between God and Satan emerges to reach its termination in the play of **The Harrowing of**

Hell and the Resurrection. Christ is the protagonist and Satan the antagonist. In the **Ludus Coventriae** that conflict appears in the first play in which Lucifer revolts against God. He refuses to offer the worship due to God, his creator. However, from this first play until the appearance of the devil in the play of **The Massacre of the Innocents** and **the Death of Herod,** that is, throughout the Old Testament plays and the Mary plays the devil does not appear as the active antagonist. Rather, in these plays he works against God by bringing about the fall of many men into sin. This is particularly obvious in the play of **Noe.** But in the play of **The Massacre of the Innocents** and *the* **Death of Herod,** the devil is aligned with those opposed to Christ, and in the play of **The Temptation,** Satan as the active antagonist confronts Christ, and from this point on he appears at frequent intervals. The dramatist uses the devices of prologues and soliloquies to remind us constantly of the conflict. In fact, the devil has more appearances in the **Ludus Coventriae** than in the other three English cycles. This, indeed, appears significant from the dramatic point of view, for it demonstrates in another way the dramatist's skill in developing the conflict inherent in the abuse-of-power theory of the Redemption, and thereby making the more interesting drama.

The actual execution of the divine plan of man's Redemption begins with a series of preparatory plays on the life of the Blessed Virgin Mary, the so-called Mary plays. Many of these plays are unique to the **Ludus Coventriae,** and the dramatist's handling of the materials of these plays shows an awareness of his structural theme of the abuse-of-power theory of the Redemption. We shall have occasion to point out some of these details in the analysis of the plays that is to follow. Suffice it here to note that the theme of the Mary plays is the preparation of the young maiden Mary to be the Mother of the Redeemer. To this end the dramatist provides the immaculate conception of Mary in a unique manner in the play of **The Conception of Mary.**

It is in **The Parlement of hefne,** play 11, that the dramatist sums up the pleas of mankind for the Redeemer and uses the device of the parliament to show the necessity of a God-man for the redemption of man. A basic hypothesis of the abuse-of-power theory is that man could not redeem himself, since he was under the dominion of Satan, and that the Redemption could be accomplished only by a person over whom Satan had no power. Any descendant of Adam would be incapable of redeeming man, because every person born into this world was stained by original sin and consequently susceptible to death and Satan's dominion. Therefore, a God-Man was necessary for the Redemption. The idea of the necessity of the Redemption is found among the Patristic writers, but usually it is no more than an expression of the convenience or fitness of the Redemption by a God-Man. St. Anselm's treatise on the necessity of the Redemption, *Cur Deus homo,* probably exerted a great influence on the traditional *Parlement,* which may be reflected in the **Ludus Coventriae** play. The gravity of the offense of man in disobeying the commands of God figures as an important aspect of the necessity of the Redemption. The early Fathers did not enter into this problem. It is only with St. Anselm that a study was made of the nature of the sin of man. The gravity of sin, according to St. Anselm [in *Cur Deus Homo*] is measured by the greatness of the one offended, and God demands satisfaction according to the quantity of the sin—"secundum quantitatem exigit Deus satisfactionem." God is an infinite Person; therefore, the sin of man is infinite. Because satisfaction is measured by the dignity of the person satisfying, it is far beyond the power of finite man to make adequate satisfaction. Thus, a God-Man must make the necessary satisfaction.

Directly connected with the idea of the gravity of the sin of man is the divinity of the Redeemer. It is not possible for a human being to reach the Infinite and make adequate satisfaction for the offense against an Infinite Being. In that even the task of Redemption reverts of necessity to a Divine Person. This idea is found in **The Parlement of Hefne,** and from this play on through the cycle the divinity of Christ receives increasing emphasis—an emphasis achieved through the use of miracles from apocryphal sources on the infancy of Christ, the miracles of His public life, and by the constant repetition of the idea by word and phrase.

Entry of the Protagonist and Limited Recognition of His Divinity

From the unsullied flesh of the Virgin Mary, Christ takes His human nature. The incarnation of Christ is accomplished by the Holy Ghost, and Christ is born of the Virgin, events which are dramatized in the plays of **The Parlement of hefne and the Salutation and Conception,** and **The Birth of Christ.** These events had been prophesized throughout the Old Testament plays, particularly in the play of **The Prophets,** which chronicled in detail the life of the Redeemer, Christ. It is important to keep this binding up of the Old Testament plays with the New Testament plays in mind as far as the unity of the cycle is concerned. For it is hardly accidental that the dramatist emphasizes the Redemption in the Old Testament plays more than the dramatists of the other three major English cycles. But what is of more significance in this same regard is the fact that he uses devices peculiar to this cycle to make that bond between the Old Testament and New Testament plays more apparent.

The design of the dramatist for the Mary plays becomes apparent in the play of **Christ and the Doctors,** for it is here that the boy-Jesus explains the reason for the marriage of the Blessed Virgin to St. Joseph, an expla-

nation which forms an integral part of the abuse-of-power theory of the Redemption. The Virgin was married so that the devil would not suspect anything out of the ordinary in the birth of the Divine Person, Christ, from a virgin. This holy "deceit" was looked upon by the Fathers as showing the supreme wisdom of God in effecting the downfall of the devil and thus the Redemption of man. It is also an essential element in the abuse-of-power theory. Christ's human nature, or the "wede" of man as it is called in **The Parlement of hefne,** shielded His divine nature from the devil. In popular nontheological terms, that was the purpose of the Incarnation—to hide the divinity of Christ. It was likewise the humanity of Christ which led the devil to tempt Him in the desert, for Christ appeared as an ordinary man in showing the effects of fasting.

The Conflict and Final Defeat of the Antagonist

The temptation in the desert is also the first stage in the actual conflict between Christ and the devil. The words of Jesus to the devil, "Vade retro, Satana," were interpreted by the Fathers as the first blow against the power of the devil, for they reminded Satan of his apostasy. Before taking up the next stage of the conflict the dramatist introduces a **Prologue of Demon** at the beginning of what Miss Block calls Passion Play I. In itself the **Prologue** is not a part of the abuse-of-power theory, but it is of first importance from a dramatic viewpoint for it gives the dramatist an opportunity to make known the stratagems of Satan, and increases the interest in the conflict. Demon tells at this point of his unsuccessful attempt to tempt Christ to sin, and smarting under this defeat, he lays plans for the capture of Christ. The human nature of Christ deceived him, and now the same human nature entices Satan to attempt to kill Christ and bring Him to hell as his captive. It is in this attempt to kill Christ that Satan oversteps the bounds of the power allowed to him by God. That power was a so-called right of inflicting death on all mankind stained with the original sin of Adam. In killing Christ, Satan went beyond his rights because Christ was an innocent and just Person born of the unsullied flesh of the Blessed Virgin. From this we have the term "abuse-of-power." From this same **Prologue of Demon** we learn that the devil is making ready the Passion for Christ—"In-novmberabyl xal his woundys be . of woful grevauns (54). He will "Arere new Engynes . of malycious conspiracy" (50). This probably refers to his incitation of the Scribes and Pharisees against his Victim. St. Leo the Great calls them servants of the devil. Judas Iscariot will be the special agent of Satan—"A tretowre xal countyrfe . his deth" (50). After Judas has received the Body of his Lord in the play of **The Last Supper,** Demon has a soliloquy in which he calls Judas "Derlyng myn" and tells him to "Sped up þi matere þat þou hast begonne." Another effective soliloquy of the devil opens the play of **Pilate's Wife's Dream and the Trial before Pilate.** Satan reviews what he has done to capture Christ, but now begins to have doubts concerning His divinity. He realizes that if he kills Christ, He will come to hell, and he fears the meeting. Satan goes to hell to prepare the chains for the attack on Christ, but the demons reject the whole plan of Satan. They will not hear of his bringing Christ to hell. Satan then realizes that he has gone too far, and that if hell is to be saved, Christ must not die. To that end he plots to save Christ through the influence of Pilate's wife upon her husband at the trial of Christ. The execution of this plan begins with the dream of "Vxor pilaty." The Fathers also held that the cries of the Jews to Christ to come down from the Cross represent the last attempt of Satan to prevent the death of Christ.

With the death of Christ on the Cross the work of the Redemption is accomplished. From a dramatic point of view, however, that culmination is exhibited in visible actions in the **Harrowing of Hell.** As Anima Christi comes to the gates of hell, Belyall admits that Christ is God and that he must do His bidding. Christ binds Satan with His Blood, takes the souls of the just from hell, and the conflict is at an end. God and man are now reconciled, or made at one. This point likewise marks the end of the various elements of the abuse-of-power theory of the Redemption.

Confirmation of the Apostles for the Redemptive Mission And the Final Accounting

The remaining plays of the cycle are concerned with the certification of the Resurrection and the confirming of the Apostles in the Faith for the redemptive mission to all nations of the world. But remaining true to his practice, the dramatist constantly reverts to the theme of the Redemption. In a final tribute to the Virgin Mary, he shows her as the Mediatrix of the redemptive graces, and in the final play of **Doomsday** demonstrates vividly that the "salvati" were saved because they cooperated with the redemptive graces of Christ, and that the "damnati" were damned to hell because they refused the graces of the Redemption.

ANALYSIS OF PLAYS IN THE *LUDUS COVENTRIAE*

Setting the Stage for the Dominion of Satan

The preceding brief résumé of the cycle has shown the dominant patterns of the doctrine of the Redemption in this cycle, and in turning to the analysis of the plays we find in the Old Testament group, the predominant theme of the dominion of Satan over mankind, but throughout there is also the recurrent promise of the Redeemer, frequent prayers for His early coming, and prophecies of the events of His life. The ideas appear concurrently, or sometimes stressed more in one play than another. Basically, as far as the theory of "rights" is concerned, these plays provide the setting for the events narrated in later plays of the cycle.

Shortly after the creation of the angels by God, Lucifer rises in open rebellion against his Creator, and as a punishment he is cast into hell. Here, at once, the dramatist sets in the first play the conflict that remains basic to the whole cycle. The emphasis on the omnipotence of God in a unique manner balances with the force of evil to make the conflict the more interesting.

Adam and Eve, created by God in a paradise of bliss and conditionally destined to take the place of the fallen angels in heaven, arouse the envy of Satan. In the second play, **The Creation and Fall of Man,** Satan is the active antagonist directly against man, and indirectly against God. The basic element of the temptation by which Satan brings about the fall of man is the desire of knowledge. Satan says to Eve:

> Of þis Apply yf ye wyl byte
> Evyn as god is so xal ye be
> Wys of Connyng as I yow plyte
> lyke on to god in al degre
>
> (2.182-185)

This idea recurs in two later plays, **The Parlement of hefne** and **Christ and the Doctors,** and is thus an important subsidiary means of unifying the cycle.

With the fall of man the dominion of Satan is established, *i. e.,* the right of inflicting death on man. This is indicated in the speeches of Adam and Eve after the eating of the apple. Eve says:

> I dyd his byddyng Alas Alas
> now we be bowndyn in dethis las
> I suppose it was sathanas
> to peyne he gan vs pete
>
> (2.305-308)

Adam and Eve, depressed and quarrelling in their misery, are expelled from paradise, but they are given the hope that their sad lot will be changed by a Redeemer, a doctrine stressed in this play:

> Deus to Diabolus:
> Vpon þi gutt þou xalt glyde
> As werm wyckyd in kende
> tyl a mayden in medyl-erth be born
> þou ffende I warn þe be-forn
> thorwe here þi hed xal be to-torn
> On wombe a-wey þou wende
>
> (2.343-348)

> Seraphim to Adam and Eve:
> here-in come ye no more
> Tyl a chylde of a mayd be born
> *and* vpon þe rode rent *and* torn
> to saue all þat ye haue forlorn
> your welth for to restore
>
> (2.373-377)

This significant promise of a Redeemer foreshadows the victory of Christ in the impending open conflict with Satan.

The plays of *Cain and Abel,* play 3, and *Abraham and Isaac,* play 5, and *Moses,* play 6, contain notàble references to the Redemption, whereas, *Noe,* play 4, shows the dominion of Satan over mankind by sin. Through the doctrinal theme of the worship of God through tithing, the dramatist has incorporated a reference to the Redemption. Abel sees in the lamb which he tithes or offers a prefiguration of the great Lamb of God to be offered for the sins of man:

> This lombe xal I offre it up to the
> accept it blyssyd lord I þe pray
>
> . . . . .
>
> and þer to þi grace grawnt þou me
> thorwh þi gret mercy
> which in a lombys lyknes
> þou xalt for mannys wyckydnes
> Onys ben offeryd in peynfulnes
> *and* deyn ful dolfoly.
>
> (3.68-78)

The heinous effects of sin, particularly the sin of lechery, are chronicled in the play of *Noe,* play 4, thus providing a meaningful background for the promise of the Redeemer given to Abraham in the next play. In the play of *Abraham and Isaac,* Abraham is given the promise of a Redeemer, Who shall be of his own progeny, as a reward for his willing obedience to sacrifice his son, Isaac.

> and all men on erthe as I þe seye
> thei xal be blyssed in thi sede
>
> (5.227-228)

The period from the time of the promise of a Redeemer to Adam and Abraham until His coming was one of many pleas from the prophets and patriarchs for God to show His mercy and to send the Promised One. The many cries for mercy in the play of Moses are then particularly in place for this period of waiting. The fact that Moses asks for "mercye sone" indicates that he has reference to the future Redeemer—mercy is the Redeemer:

> I pray þe lord god with all my mende
> to us incline þi mercy sone
> þi gracyous lordchep lete us fynde
>
> (6.6-8)

When this cry for mercy is placed alongside the supplications in the introductory part of *The Parlement of hefne:*

> haue mende of þe prayour seyd of Ysaie

> lete mercy meke þin hyest mageste
>
> (11.7-8)
>
> . . . . .
>
> let þi mercy make hym with Aungelys dwelle
> of locyfere to restore þe place
>
> (11.47-48)

the pleas for mercy of Moses become important in linking this Old Testment play to the theme of the Redemption in the cycle.

The utterances of the prophets of the Old Testament concerning the birth of the Redeemer are grouped together to form the play of *The Prophets,* uniquely built on the device of the Tree of Jesse. The best expression of that prophecy is in the words of Ysaias:

> I Am þe prophete callyd Isaye
> Replett with godys grett influens
> *and* sey pleynly be spyryte of prophecie
> þat a clene mayde thourgh meke obedyens
> Shall bere a childe which xal do resystens
> Ageyn foule Zabulon þe devyl of helle
> mannys soule ageyn hym to defens
> Opyn in þe felde þe fende he xal felle
>
> (7.1-8)

This play contains many elements of Biblical and theological tradition, such as the virginity of the Blessed Virgin Mary, her divine Maternity, the royal priesthood of Christ, and His position as Judge, but there is thoughout a definite shaping of all this material to give prominence to the doctrine of the Redemption.

Preparatory Stages of the Divine Plan of Redemption

The series of plays on topics from the New Testament begins with the group of so-called Mary plays which portray the preparation of the Blessed Virgin to be the Mother of the Redeemer. The theme of the *Conception of Mary* is the barrenness of Anna, and that she shall bear a maid-child, yet the whole point about the maid-child is that she will in turn bear Christ, Who is to save mankind. Angelus tells Joachim of Anna:

> So of here xal be bore . with-out nature Jhesus
> That xal be savyour . vnto al man-kende
>
> (8.170-171)

In other words, the doctrine of the Redemption is the focal point. Mary is immaculately conceived by Joachim and Anna, so that her flesh is not contaminated with the stain of original sin. She is thus prepared to be the Mother of the Redeemer. The same slanting of doctrine is found in *Mary in the Temple,* play 9, and *The Betrothal of Mary,* play 10; everything is directed towards the Redemption. Several items in these plays must be singled out for comment, because they give evidence of a binding together which most commentators will not grant. In *Mary in the Temple,* the virginity of the Blessed Virgin is placed in juxtaposition to her divine Maternity, or as expressed here, she is to be "goddys wyff." This idea is significantly carried over to *The Parlement of hefne,* for Spiritus Sanctus tells Filius:

> I love to your lover xal yow lede
> þis is þe Assent of oure vnyte
>
> (11.183-184)

The "Parlement" is also forecast by Angelus, when he says to Mary:

> Ffor ye xal here aftere haue A salutacion
> þat xal þis excede it is seyd Amonge vs
> The deyte þat dede xal determyn *and* dyscus
> ye xal nevyr lady be lefte here A-lone
>
> (9.254-257)

The Betrothal of Mary, play 10, is also linked in several ways with the pivotal play, **The Parlement of hefne.** Contemplacio in the prologue to the present play, holds out to his audience the play of **The Parlement of hefne** as worth all their patience and waiting, which implies that the play was the focal point of interest for all concerned:

> hath pacyens with vs we be-sech yow her
> And in short spas
> The parlement of hefne sone xal ye se
>
> (Prol., 12-14)

Another important connection of this play with **The Parlement of hefne** has been overlooked by commentators on this cycle. After the marriage of Joseph and Mary, Joseph goes to find a house, while Mary remains in the temple praying the "sawtre." When she stops praying, she says:

> I haue seyd sum of my sawtere *and* here I am
> at þis holy psalme in dede
> Benedixisti domine terram tuam
> In this holy labore . lord me spede
>
> (10.453-456)

Why does Mary stop at this psalm? "Benedixisti Domine terram tuam" is the introductory part of the first verse of psalm eighty-four. This psalm contains the verse which is the basis of the play of **The Parlement of hefne:**

> Misericordia et veritas obviaverunt sibi:
> justitia et pax osculatae sunt.

In this light, Mary's stopping as she reaches this psalm eighty-four has great importance. Chronologically, peace and justice had not yet kissed. That was to take

place at the Incarnation, which is present in the next play. From the viewpoint of the structure of the cycle, this fact serves as a salient link between the plays of **The Betrothal** and **The Parlement of hefne.** Against this background, the one reference to the Redemption in this play has more meaning.

The predominant and thematic doctrine of **The Parlement of hefne** is the Redemption, emphasized strikingly in the episode of the "Parlement," which is unique to the **Ludus Coventriae,** and serves to introduce the Annunciation to the Blessed Virgin that she is to be the Mother of God. The presentation of the Redemption in this play reflects an extremely interesting and rich theological heritage. The completeness of the scope of doctrines related to the Redemption is also a remarkable characteristic of this play.

Perhaps the richest and most complete statement of the Redemption and the issues involved occurs in the final summary of the controversy of the Four Daughters of God by Filius:

> I thynke þe thoughtys of pes . *and* nowth of wykkydnes
> this I deme to ses your contraversy
> If Adam had not deyd . peryschyd had ryghtwysnes
> And Also trewth had be lost þer-by
> Terrewth *and* ryght wolde chastyse ffoly
> yiff a-nother deth come not . mercy xulde perysch
> þan pes were exyled ffynyaly
> So tweyn dethis must be yow fowre to cherysch
>
> But he þat xal deye ye must knawe
> þat in hym may ben non iniquyte
> þat helle may holde hym be no lawe
> But þat he may pas at hese lyberte
> Qwere swyche on his prevyde *and* se
> And hese deth . for mannys deth xal be redempcion
> All hefne *and* erthe seke now ye
> Plesyth it yow þis conclusyon
>
> (11.137-152)

The core of the doctrine of the Redemption is explicitly stated—Christ's death will be the Redemption of man (150). The particular idea of the Redemption presented in the quoted passage is that of a penal satisfaction necessary for the reconciliation of the Four Daughters of God. This satisfaction requires the death of Christ— "yiff a-nother deth come not . mercy xulde perysch" (142). The emphasis on the necessity of a satisfaction is evidently a reflection of the teaching generally attributed to St. Anselm. The idea of the necessity of a satisfaction for the reconciliation of the Daughters occurs frequently. The fact that "trewth had be lost" (140) and that "mercy xulde perysch" (142) is quite similar to St. Anselm's teaching that unless a Redeemer is sent the creation of man has been in vain, and the divine plan should come to naught. The same idea is the basis for the conclusion of Pax—"þat mannys sowle it xulde perysche it wore sweme" (127). The summing up of the argument by Pax leads to the conclusion that man must be redeemed (113-122).

Other phases of the doctrine of the Redemption in this play are: (1) the conflict between Christ and Satan alluded to by Veritas in speaking of man—"He dyspysyd þe *and* plesyd þi ffo" (69)—an idea which is a popularization of the doctrine and is inherent to the theory of the abuse-of-power; (2) the place of the love of God in the Redemption of man, a phase of the doctrine particularly emphasized by St. Bernard (1090-1157) and Abailard:

I mercy haue ronne . þe hevynly Regyon
    rownde
and þer is non of þat charyte
þat ffor man wole suffre A deddly wounde
                                    (158-160);

(3) that God had mercy for man from all eternity, which may reflect the Thomistic theory *ex suppositione, i. e.,* that the Redemption was in the eternal decrees of God, Who foresaw the fall, and in that event the Redemption was necessary—"*and* þou seyst endlesly . þat mercy þou hast kept ffor man" (83); (4) that man should have an eternal punishment for offending the Eternal God, an idea of first importance in the theology of St. Anselm and St. Thomas:

man offendyd hym þat is endles
Therfore his endles punchement may nevyr
    sees
                                    (92-93);

and (5) that man was in the hands of the devil, which is one of the basic concepts of the theory of the abuse-of-power:

Also he forsoke his makere þat made hym of
    clay
And the devyl to his mayster he ches
                                    (94-95)

The clearest expression of another aspect of the theory is in the words of Filius, namely, that the Redeemer must be free from sin that hell may not hold Him. Directly connected with this idea is the doctrine of the divinity of the Redeemer, a point upon which St. Anselm and St. Thomas insisted. The necessity of a divine Person for the Redemption of man is stated by Filius:

Ffadyr he þat xal do þis must be both god
    and man

lete me se how I may were þat wede
                                    (177-178)

The sanctity or holiness of the Redeemer is implied in the fact that He must be free from iniquity (146). But to all outward appearances Christ is only man—He wears the "wede" of man. The idea will appear in greater detail in the play of *Christ and the Doctors,* and is basic to the play of *The Temptacion,* and *The Prologue of Demon* in the first Passion Play.

Another important element in the solution of the difficulties of the Four Daughters of God is the reason for the choice of the Second Person of the Trinity for the Redemption of man. Pater says:

In your wysdam son . man was mad thore
And in wysdam was his temptacion
þerfore some sapyens ye must ordeyn here-fore
and se how of man may be salvacion
                                    (173-176)

As we shall see, the same explanation occurs in the play of *Christ and the Doctors,* and the emphasis on "cunnyng" in the temptation of Eve has been noted above. This idea becomes an important feature in the unification of the cycle. Clearly, we have in this play, then, a blending of St. Anselm's views and the view that is best represented by St. Augustine that the devil abused his power in killing the Innocent One. Through the use of *The Parlement of hefne* the author or compiler has broadened the scope of the presentation of the doctrine of the Redemption. He was thus able to include various phases of the doctrine which the ordinary limitations of the usual Annunciation play precluded. *The Parlement of hefne* emphasizes the profundity of the greatest mystery of Christianity, adds immeasurably to the significance of *The Prophets,* and thus brings the Old and New Testament plays into a very definite coherence.

In the plays of *Joseph's Return,* play 12, and *The Visit to Elizabeth,* play 13, all doctrinal references point to the Redemption as the *terminus ad quem. The Trial of Joseph and Mary,* play 14, is connected with *The Salutation and Conception* by Mary's reference to Gabriel's message.

Entry of the Protagonist and Gradual Recognition of His Divinity

A dominant theme developed along with the Redemption in this group of plays is the divinity of Jesus Christ. As we noted earlier, the divinity of the Redeemer is an important assumption in the theory of the abuse-of-power. Christ in human flesh now shows His divinity more and more, but the devil is not convinced, for he tries to tempt Him to sin in the play of *The Temptation.* An outstanding characteristic of most of the plays in this group is the pointing of the doctrinal theme of the play to the Redemption or the establishment of the Redemption as the main theme.

The means which the dramatist uses to connect most of these days with the theory of the abuse-of-power and to the cycle as a whole provides an interesting part of this study. *The Birth of Christ* is manifestly connected with the earlier play of *The Prophets* by Joseph's reference to the promised Redeemer as One to be born of "þe kynde of jesse." The announcement of the angel to the shepherds at the opening of the play of *The Adoration of the Shepherds* offers a most significant instance of concern with the doctrine of the Redemption. The announcement reads:

> Joye to god þat sytt in hevyn
> And pes to man on erthe grownde
> A chylde is born be-nethe þe levyn
> thurwe hym many ffolke xul be vn-bownde
> Sacramentys þer xul be vij
> Wonnyn þurowe þat childys wounde
> Therefore I synge A joyful stevene
> þe flowre of frenchep now is founde
> God þat wonyght on hyy
> he is gloryed mannys gost to wynne
> he hath sent salue to mannys synne
> Pes is comyn to mannys kynne
> thorwe goddys sleytys slyy
>
> (16.1-13)

In this entire announcement of Angelus there is but one reference to the birth of Christ (3). The remaining twelve lines show how man is to be saved. Indeed, these lines set the tone and fix the theme of the entire play, for the main doctrine is the Redemption. A reference to the seven sacraments (5-6) may at first sight seem to be entirely out of place in a play dealing with the adoration of the Shepherds, particularly in the greeting of the angel. But the important point is that the relationship of the sacraments to the Passion of Christ is indicated— "Wonnyn þurowe þat childys wounde" (16)—a theological idea unique to this cycle. The theology basic to this concept is that the sacraments receive their efficacy from the Passion of Christ, *i. e.,* the culmination of Christ's redemptive work. Consequently, the reference to the sacraments is not out of place in the angel's announcement. On the contrary, it is an important element which contributes to the broad scope of the doctrine of the Redemption in this cycle. The prophecy of Radix Jesse in the play of *The Prophets* (7.17-22) is recalled in the line of Angelus: "þe flowre of frenchep now is founde" (8), and constitutes a distinct link of the New Testament plays with those of the Old Testament. *The Parlement of hefne* also is recalled (12-13). It is evident that the reference to "pes" in these lines connotes more than the general reference contained in the opening lines "pes to man on erthe grownde" (2), chiefly because of the words "goddys sleytys slyy," which

express the Patristic notion of the deceit of the devil matched by the deceit, often called wisdom, of God. Moreover, this idea is basic to the abuse-of-power theory. From the standpoint of the structure of the cycle, this mention of an essential element of the abuse-of-power theory is definitely another link of this play to the permeating and motivating concept of the cycle. In lines four and ten two popular concepts of the Redemption of man are present: that mankind was bound in the chains of the devil until the time of the Redemption, and that the actual Redemption was a conflict in which Christ was "to wynne mannys gost."

The idea of the hidden divinity of Christ is basic to the theory of the abuse-of-power, as we saw above, and the dramatist uses the idea in one of the early plays on the Infancy of Christ, *The Adoration of the Magi.* The use of the concept in this play is in keeping with the Biblical concept that Christ gradually manifested His divinity. It is important to note too the definite allegiance of Herod with the devil as another means of sharpening the conflict between the forces of good and evil, and thus increasing the dramatic interest. The actual appearance of the devil in the play of *The Massacre of the Innocents* to claim the dead body of Herod as his victim further emphasizes the alignment of the powers as well as the conflict.

Besides presenting the Christ-Child as the boy prodigy—a feature we noted as parallel to the Blessed Virgin as the girl prodigy in the play of *Mary in the Temple*— the dramatist uses the play of *Christ and the Doctors* to give further details of the abuse-of-power theory. The problem of the reason for the Second Person's becoming incarnate rather than the First or Third Persons enters into the very heart of the doctrine, and connects this play with *The Fall of Man* and *The Parlement of hefne.* The answer to the problem is given by Jhesus:

> this is þe cawse why sertys *and* non other
> Ageyn þe secunde þe trespas was wrought
> Whan þe serpent adam to synne browth
>
> He temptyd him nowght be þe faderys myght
> Of þe gostys goodnes spak he ryght nowght
> but in connynge he temptyd hym ryght
>
> (21.115-120)
>
>   . . . . .
>
> To þe sone connynge doth longe expres
> ther with þe serpent dyd Adam A-say
> Ete of þis Appyl he seyd no lesse
> *and* þou xalt haue connynge as god verray.
>
> þus þe secunde person Attrybute
> Was only towchyd be temptacion
> Wherfore hym self wyl hold þe sewte
> And kepe his propyrte fro maculacion
>
> (21.125-132)

In the analysis of *The Fall of Man,* we noted that the basis of the temptation was "cunnyng" and in *The Parlement of hefne* the same reason for the Incarnation of the Second Person was given (11.173-176). In explaining the virginal conception of Christ, Jhesus recalls the prophecy of Isaias (179-184), which links this play with the Old Testament play of *The Prophets,* and in demonstrating the reason for the marriage of the Virgin Mary, Jhesus shows the part of "deceit" in our Redemption, which is an integral part of the abuse-of-power theory, as we have noted above:

> To blynde þe devyl of his knowlache
> *and* my byrth from hym to hyde
> þat holy wedlock was grett stopage
> þe devyl in dowte to do A-byde
>
> (21.245-248).

Since this play is unique in that it does not use the Ten Commandments as the device to show the knowledge of the boy prodigy Jhesus, as the other cycles do, the emphasis on the doctrine of the Redemption is then of foremost importance.

The Conflict and Defeat of the Antagonist

The actual conflict begins in the play of *The Temptation,* play 23, and the episode is introduced by a "parlement" of the devils, a feature unique to this cycle which the commentators have overlooked. It likewise forms a balance with the "parlement" in the play of *The Parlement of hefne.* The purpose of the "parlement" is to decide upon the best method of ascertaining whether Christ is God. Belyall suggests the method finally adopted (40-48), *i. e.,* the temptation in the desert. Basic to the devil's fear of Christ is the doctrine of the Redemption. He fears that Christ will take the souls of the just out of hell:

> he wyll don us all tene
> he wyll be lorde ouer hevyn *and* helle
> *and* ffeche awey all oure catelle
>
> (23.35-37)

In the last temptation is the notion that the entire physical universe was in the hold of Satan until the Redemption, a doctrine resting ultimately on the Patristic idea of the power of the devil. Despite Satan's unsuccessful attempt to bring Christ into sin, he is still not certain of His divinity, although that was the very purpose of the temptation. After the last temptation, Sathan says:

> I woundyr sore what is he this
> I can not brynge hym to no trespas
> nere be no synne to don a-mys
> he byddyth me gon a-bakke
> What þat he is I kan not se
> Whethyr god or man what þat he be
> I kan not telle in no degre
>
> (23.188-194)

This seems to be inconsistent with the purpose of the temptation outlined by Belyall (40-48), for he stated that should Christ succumb to the temptation He could not be the "kynge of blyss." From this it seems that Satan should have known that Christ was God. Actually, it appears that he did not. If he had known that fact at this point, all the future stratagems of Satan in this cycle would be pointless. However, what Satan learned from this temptation of Christ is told us by St. Augustine. Satan knew only that Christ was the Promised One, but the fact that Christ had a human nature and in His fast in the desert underwent the pangs of thirst and hunger, etc., shielded His divinity from the devil, and troubled him—"torquebatur," as St. Augustine says.

The Prologue of Demon introduces the Passion plays and forms a recapitulation of Satan's plans to thwart the redemptive work of Christ. The doctrinal contents of the *Prologue* agree with the various elements of the abuse-of-power theory of the Redemption evidenced thus far in the cycle, and serve to motivate the actions in the following plays. The fact that this *Prologue* follows the plan indicated in the play of *The Temptation,* namely, that Satan still does not know whether Christ is divine despite his failure, which according to his plan should have been proof of Christ's divinity, is further evidence of the architectonic plan of the cycle. Demon now reveals that he still does not know that Christ is divine (Prol., 27-32). In his ignorance of the divinity of Christ, Demon believes that he holds securely all in hell, because of the text: "Quia in inferno nulla est redempcio" (41-48). He expects to destroy Christ by killing Him— "When þe soule fro þe body . xal make separacion" (44), an idea we shall meet again in *The Descent of Anima Christi into Hell.* He also reveals his plans to inspire the Jews to kill Christ: "I xal Arere new Engynes . of malycious conspiracy" (50), and to inspire Judas to betray his Master—"A tretowre xal countyrfe. his deth . to fortyfye" (55), both of which ideas are elements of the abuse-of-power theory.

In *The Council of the Jews,* play 26, the Jews decide on the means of taking Christ. We have seen that Demon stated in his *Prologue* that he would "Arere new Engynes . of malycious conspiracy" (Prol., 50). Evidently this refers to the present *Council of the Jews,* although there is no indication of that fact within the body of the play itself. But in the light of Patristic tradition, best represented by Pope St. Leo the Great, that the Pharisees and Jews were inspired by the devil as his servants in this last attempt to destroy Christ, and Demon's own statement, it becomes apparent that this play is a definite part of the structure of the abuse-of-power theory. As Jhesus approaches the city in the episode of the Entry into Jerusalem, He announces to His disciples the redemptive purpose of His mission (179-182). In fact, throughout the plays of this group there is constant reference to Christ's fulfilling His purpose and the prophecies. This is one means besides the actual conflict by which the dramatist enriches and keeps his theme before his audience.

There are several appearances of the devil in this group of plays which add immeasurably to the interest in the conflict between the forces of good and evil. The soliloquy after Judas' unworthy reception of the Body of the Lord in the play of *The Last Supper* is unique to this cycle. At this point the devil seems to be wavering in his determination to capture Christ and perhaps is beginning to realize that Christ is divine, for he fears the meeting with Christ if Judas should bring Him to hell:

> But yet I fere he xuld do þer sum sorwe *and*
> wo
> þat all helle xal crye out on me þat sel
>
> (27.793-794)

Hell does, in fact, cry out later, in the play of *Pilate's Wife's Dream and the Trial before Pilate*. There is also in this present soliloquy definite evidence that Judas was inspired by the devil, for Demon says: "Sped up þi matere þat þou hast be-gonne" (795). A soliloquy of Satan opens the play of *Pilate's Wife's Dream and the Trial before Pilate,* play 31, and here we see a complete change in the devil's procedure against Christ, a change foreshadowed in the previous soliloquy. He is still plotting the death of Christ and preparing the instruments of the Passion, but recalling his previous unsuccessful attempts to snare Christ in the temptation, Satan is filled with doubts. He knows that if he kills Christ, He must come to hell, and he fears the issue:

> And sythyn he xal come to helle . be he nevyr
> so stowte
> *And* yet I am Aferd *and* he come . he wole do
> som wrake
>
> (494-495)

Satan then goes to hell to prepare the chains for the attack, but Hell cries out:

> Out upon þe . we conjure þe
> þat nevyr in helle we may hym se
> ffor And he onys in helle be
> he xal oure power brest
>
> (503-506)

Hell's refusal to allow Christ to enter makes Satan realize that he has gone too far and that, if hell is to be saved, Christ must not die. Therefore, he plots to save Christ through the influence of Pilate's wife upon her husband at the trial of Christ. This he accomplishes through the dream of "Vxor pilaty."

The words of Christ as He dies on the Cross in the play of *The Crucifixion,* play 32, are unique for the idea that He now goes to "harrow helle":

> In manus tuas domine
> holy fadyr in hefly se
> I comende my spyryte to þe
> for here now hendyth my fest
> I xal go sle þe fende þat freke
> ffor now myn hert be-gynnyth to breke
> wurdys mo xal I non speke
> Nunc consummatus est
>
> (891-898)

This statement demonstrates in an explicit manner the continuity of the action of this play with the following *Descent of Anima Christi.* The work of Satan in bringing about the Passion is now completed. He has brought about Christ's death, the consequences of which he realized too late.

After the short laments of Mary and John at the close of the play of *The Crucifixion,* Anima Christi enters the scene of action, continuing the action with which the last play closed. The continuity of action is set forth in the declaration of Anima Christi:

> I am þe sowle of cryst jhesu
> þe which is kynge of all vertu
> my body is ded þe jewys it slew
> þat hangyth yitt on þe rode
>
> (979-982)

Christ's soul is on the way to harrow hell, while His Body remains hanging on the Cross. The action in this short play of forty-eight lines closes with Anima Christi at the gates of hell and in the next play, *The Burial and the Guarding of the Sepulchre,* shifts back to the scene at the foot of the Cross on Calvary. This scene demonstrates clearly a continuity of action not present in the other cycles. The position of this episode of the descent of the soul of Christ into hell immediately after His death on the Cross is unique in all extant English drama. At this point of the drama there is not the least doubt in the minds of the devils concerning the divinity of Christ. Heretofore, we have seen the devil trying to find out whether Christ was divine, as in the play of *The Temptation, The Prologue of Demon* to *Passion Play* I, and in the soliloquy of Demon after Judas' unworthy reception of the Holy Eucharist. In the incident of Pilate's wife's dream, the devil realizes the error of his course against Christ, and attempts to stop the Passion and death he has prepared. Now Belyall voices the conviction of the devils that Christ is divine:

> Alas Alas out *and* harrow
> Onto þi byddynge must we bow
> þat þou art god now do we know
> Of þe had we grett dowte
>
> (1002-1005)

From a dramatic point of view, the abrupt close of this play as Christ is at the doors of hell is highly effective.

The conflict that had been building up throughout the cycle is about to be resolved. But just as that moment arrives, the dramatist takes us back to Calvary and holds in suspense the final meeting of Christ and the devil.

As the scene shifts to the foot of Calvary again in *The Burial and the Guarding of the Sepulchre,* play 34, we find the Centurion giving testimony to the divinity of Christ and His redemptive mission. And with the next play, *The Harrowing of Hell and the Resurrection,* play 35, the scene of action changes to hell, and Anima Christi leads the just souls to paradise. Dramatically, the binding of Satan marks the end of the drama, for now the long conflict has been resolved in the victory of Christ over Satan. However, from a theological point of view the culmination of the Redemption was in the crucifixion and death of Christ. The Harrowing of Hell is but a minor part of the Redemption, but as far as the visualization of the victory of Christ is concerned, the Harrowing with the binding of Satan makes the more impressive drama. In the Resurrection, Christ as the victor over death comes forth triumphantly from the tomb in all His glory to seal the defeat of His adversary, Satan.

Epilogue: Confirmation of the Apostles for the Redemptive Mission to All Nations, and the Final Accounting

In the final plays of the cycle, which actually form an epilogue to the main action of the drama, the dramatist portrays briefly the last events of our Lord's earthly life, pays a final tribute to the Mother of the Redeemer, and in the last play gives a graphic description of the final day of reckoning at which time all souls will be judged according to the way in which they participated in the redemptive graces of Christ. Along with the theme of the confirmation of the Apostles for their mission by strengthening their faith in their Redeemer, the dramatist still holds the idea of the Redemption before us, even though the climax has been reached. The epilogical character of these last plays of the cycle is further indicated by the fact that the plays are very short, with the exception of the play of *The Assumption.* The brevity of most of these concluding plays is in keeping with the design of the cycle, for once the climax was presented, there was no point to dwelling at length on the last events of our Lord's life on earth. To do so would have destroyed the effectiveness of the climax. Accordingly the dramatist presents the last events as graphically as possible to make ready for the plays of *The Assumption* and *Doomsday,* yet retaining enough of the materials to compose a complete dramatic unit for each play.

The plays of *The Assumption* and *Doomsday* may be said to form an anticlimax to the cycle, for *The Assumption* is the final rounding out of the part of the Blessed Virgin Mary in the application of the Redemption to man. The cycle is unique in English drama for the number of so-called Mary plays. In the first group of plays the Blessed Virgin was presented as preparing to be the Mother of God, *i. e.,* for her part in the Incarnation of Christ, and in this last play of *The Assumption,* we see the signal honor bestowed on her for her part in the Redemptive work of Christ and in the application of the redemptive graces to man. Consequently it seems but natural that the dramatist would devote a play to these two latter ideas as a final tribute to her. What is perhaps of greater importance is that there are references in this play to several aspects of the abuse-of-power theory, which becomes important in linking this play to the theme of the cycle. The conflict and triumph of Christ over the devil are recalled by Angelus in assuring Maria that she need not fear the devil at her death:

> What nedith it to fere you empres so hende
> syn be the fruth of youre body . was convycte
>   his vyolens
> that horible serpent . dar not nyhyn youre
>   kende
> and youre blosme . schal make hym recistens
> that he schal not pretende
>
> (131-135)

Two devils do in fact appear in this play, but true to the facts presented in *The Harrowing of Hell* and the theory of the abuse-of-power, "Sathan, Belsabub and Belyal," the principal devils, are spoken of as remaining in hell. Only the demons, *i. e.,* the lesser devils, leave hell. This indeed constitutes a final demonstration of the victory of Christ over Satan and also the intercessory power of the Blessed Virgin Mary over the "convycte vyolens" of the foe of mankind.

In the last play of the cycle, *Doomsday,* play 42, the dramatist places in bold relief the termination of mercy, which has been a recurrent and persistent theme throughout the cycle, and the application of strict justice at the general judgment of all souls. The Book of Life will reveal how men avail themselves of the redemptive graces of Christ. Despite the great love of the Son of Man and His sufferings for man, the damned souls would not perform His will:

> ffor youre love was I rent on rode
> and for youre sake I shed my blode
> Whan I was so mercyfull *and* so gode
> Why haue ye wrought ayens my wylle
>
> (88.91)

The saved souls realize that it is only through the Redemption that they have reached the bliss of heaven (57-61). The play is incomplete in the MS., but in comparison with the other cycles, it is surprisingly complete doctrinally. The several references to the Redemption are significant as far as the cycle is concerned, and suggest that the play probably contained a restatement of the dramatist's theme, emphasizing for the last time the importance of the Redemption to the audience and to the cycle.

The most important conclusion this analysis leads to is that the **Ludus Coventriae** is a closely unified cycle of plays worked out according to a definite pattern. Most critics have looked upon it as a "patchwork" of plays. But in the light of the present analysis such a view is no longer tenable. The **Ludus Coventriae** is a unified cycle constructed on the Patristic abuse-of-power theory of the Redemption. The unique features of **The Parlement of hefne,** the "parlement" of the devils, **The Prologue of Demon,** and the explicit statements of the various elements of that theory in different plays are conclusive evidence that the dramatist was interested in the Redemption not only in a general way, but also in a very specific explanation handed down through the ages.

None of these features alone "forces" the plays into a unity or explains the cycle as Miss Benkovitz claims for **The Prologue of Demon,** but each feature takes its place as a definite part of the theory of the abuse-of-power, and in the architectonic structure of the cycle. In that theory, the following plays are structurally important:

a) Setting the stage for the long-range conflict: **The Creation and Fall of the Angels** and **The Creation and Fall of Man.** Taking up the promise of a Redeemer in **The Fall of Man,** the dramatist throughout the plays from **Cain and Abel** to **The Prophets** keeps before us an anticipation and expectance of the Redeemer in the many prayers and pleas of the patriarchs and prophets, which are culminated in the play of **The Prophets.**

b) Preparatory stages of the divine plan of the Redemption: **The Conception of Mary** (her Immaculate Conception), **Mary in the Temple** (anticipating **The Parlement of hefne**), **The Betrothal of Mary** (reason for her marriage), and **The Parlement of hefne,** show the Virgin Mary prepared to be the Mother of the Redeemer and her part in the divine plan. In **Joseph's Return, The Visit to Elizabeth** and **The Trial of Joseph and Mary,** the virginal conception of Christ is further attested.

c) Entry of the Protagonist and limited recognition of His Divinity: **The Birth of Christ, The Adoration of the Shepherds** (because of the announcement of Angelus), **Christ and the Doctors** (explanation of theory). The divinity of the Redeemer and His mission of mercy are exemplified in **The Adoration of the Magi, The Purification** and **The Baptism.**

d) The conflict and final defeat of the Antagonist: **The Temptation, The Prologue of Demon** and **Council of Jews, The Last Supper and Conspiracy of the Jews**

and Judas, Pilate's Wife's Dream and Trial before Pilate, The Crucifixion, The Descent into Hell of Anima Christi, and **The Harrowing of Hell and Resurrection,** portray the details of Satan's stratagems, and his falling into the "trap" of the divine plan. The other plays of this group add details of the Passion and keep before us the purpose of the mission of Jesus.

Epilogue: **The Assumption and Doomsday**

This Patristic theory was employed by the great homilists in impressing upon their audiences the importance of man's Redemption, and the great cost of the redemptive act of the God-Man, Jesus Christ. Our dramatist has used this theory, which by its very nature is dramatic, in preference to any strict theological interpretation found in the whole of tradition. It gives the drama an interesting conflict, which is apparent from the first play with the fall of Lucifer to the last play of **Doomsday** with the devils claiming the souls of the damned. The dramatist has employed to advantage every opportunity of intensifying that conflict, especially by the frequent appearances of the devil as the active antagonist in plays which normally do not call for this specific device, the definite alliance of the Jews and the Pharisees with the devil, and the inspiration of Judas by the devil to betray his Master.

However, at many places it is evident that the dramatist has also drawn on elements of the tradition of the doctrine of the Redemption contributed by the Scholastic theologians. There are many echoes of the teaching of St. Anselm in **The Parlement of hefne,** and throughout the cycle there is a close affinity with the Thomistic emphasis on the infinite value of the death of Christ to balance the infinite gravity of sin. This, the cycle has in common with most fifteenth century religious literature. But the Scholastic elements are not prominent. Rather they are blended with the Patristic theory of the abuse-of-power.

Plays outside those basic to the structure of the theory are united to the pattern (1) by constant references to specific aspects of the Redemption; (2) by the recurrence of certain doctrinal ideas, some of which have been indicated in the course of this survey, which is additional evidence that the cycle as we have it is the result of the compiler's efforts to unify the plays by more than the unity provided by the chronology of Biblical events, as is the case with the other cycle; (3) by reference, backwards and forwards, to actions in other plays, especially the fact that **The Parlement of hefne** is anticipated in Mary's particular way of praying psalm eighty-five in the play of **Mary in the Temple,** which indicates the observance of a unifying process seldom admitted by the critics of this cycles; (4), by the general use of certain phrases repeated from play to play indicating continuous sets of plays, as Miss Block has shown, and adding to the cogency of the argument for a designing hand in the cycle. The forecasting and recalling of specific plays is also most important to this consideration.

Another feature of this cycle which most critics do not observe is its architectonic structure, both from a doctrinal point of view and dramatic. The part of the Blessed Virgin Mary is not unduly emphasized to overshadow Christ if the doctrines are taken as presented. Thus, in the play of *The Prophets* it is not the birth of the Virgin Mary that is emphasized, but the fact that she will bear the Redeemer. The most outstanding example of the balance maintained with regard to the Virgin Mary is the play of *The Assumption* with its special emphasis on the Christological basis for honoring the Mother of God.

Structurally, the balance of *The Parlement of hefne* with the the "parlement" of the devils in *The Temptation* ranks first in importance. Next in order we may rank the girl prodigy Mary in the play of *Mary in the Temple* and the boy prodigy Jesus in *Christ and the Doctors,* and *The Prologue of Demon* and *The Prologue of Johannes Baptista*.

From this analysis the *Ludus Coventriae* emerges as a well unified cycle of plays constructed on the Patristic theory of the Redemption called the abuse-of-power, which the dramatist used to impress on his fifteenth century audience the message of the great cost of their Redemption.

Kenneth Cameron and Stanley J. Kahrl (essay date 1967)

SOURCE: "Staging the N-Town Cycle," in *Theatre Notebook*, Vol. XXI, Nos. 3 and 4, Spring and Summer, 1967, pp. 122-38, 152-65.

[*In the following excerpt, Cameron and Kahrl explore the staging of plays in Lincoln, as well as internal evidence from the N-Town cycle, in order to argue for the use of both movable and stationary staging methods in the cycle.*]

Much attention has been given to problems of doctrine, of supposed unity, and of geographical ascription in the **N-Town Plays**. Known also as the *Ludus Coventriae* or the Hegge MS. plays, this lengthy cycle has been frequently examined because of its great complexity and the many problems it poses. Its staging, however, has seldom been analyzed in any great detail, and except for two unpublished dissertations [by Anne C. Gay and Izola Curley Harrison], little attempt has been made to solve the cycle's intricate and often contradictory production problems. Among recent work, probably Margaret Birkett's production of a large part of the cycle as "The Lincoln Plays" in Martial Rose's mod-

Fifteenth-century stained glass depicting Christ among the Doctors, *located in East Harling Church in Norfolk, near the N-Town plays' cultural origins.*

ern text at Grantham in June, 1966, came closest to a serious analysis, and one that seemed flawed only when it ignored the rich multiplicity of scaffolds in the Passion sequence.

Any approach to the **N-Town Plays'** staging must take into account a good deal more than the extant MS. of the plays themselves. Despite the fact that parts of the cycle, particularly the Passion sequence, are uniquely rich in stage directions, other sections are so lacking in them as to seem enigmatic. Staging indications within the text are numerous, but not always clear, and often intriguing more for the questions they ask than for the answers they supply (the launching and recovery of Noah's dove may be cited as an easy example). Many points of staging, then, must be solved by using other materials. Of these, we may note particularly iconographic materials, such as stained glass and sculpture of the Plays' period; other medieval dramas whose staging seems to be similar, notably those in the Macro MS. and the Digby MS.; and evidence in the city of Lincoln, the probable site of the Plays' staging, including geographical details of the city itself, the iconography of the cathedral, and Lincoln documents. Of special interest are the Cordwainers' accounts found by Hardin Craig and the minutes of Lincoln Common Council.

Using such evidence, it is possible to reconstruct much of the original staging. Before such reconstruction can be done, however, it must be made clear that the cycle as we have it represents a compilation of at least two separate stageable cycles and a third block of plays (the Old Testament dramas) that are different in doctrinal emphasis, in period of composition, and in staging method. In brief, we must note that the Passion sequence, as has often been noted, is an outstanding example of simultaneous, in-the-round staging of the type described by Richard Southern in *Medieval Theatre in the Round,* while the plays of the cycle having to do with the life of the Virgin (the so-called Marian Cycle) show some characteristics of staging in the round and some of processional staging. The OT plays, on the other hand, are basically processional. In addition, one play of the entire cycle must be set apart—the *Assumption of the Virgin*—as a unique play staged inside Lincoln Cathedral under very special conditions that necessitate its being discussed separately. These summary remarks must be made because of an unfortunate tendency on the part of many scholars to think of the **N-Town Plays** as a unified whole, one whose staging methods could be defined for the entire body of plays; thus, if a kind of staging could be found in the Passion sequence, in this view it could then be extended over the whole cycle. Such is simply not the case.

Mrs. Gay's discussion ["A Study of the Staging of the N-Town Cycle," 1961] is a signal example of the results of basing a study of the staging on a belief in consistent staging practices maintained throughout the cycle. Arguing backward from the Passion plays, Mrs. Gay breaks the cycle into seven groups, each group of roughly the same length of printed pages in Miss Block's [1922 EETS] edition, and each group running in the rubricated MS order. Assuming that "we may allow roughly two hours for the performance of each group," Mrs. Gay sees this kind of neat breakdown as allowing for presentation of the entire cycle over subsequent days or years. Her final conclusion, then, uses the idea of unity far too simply: "Such compelling evidence for the plays having been acted in groups rather than individually removes the plausibility of believing that the plays of the **N-Town Cycle** were ever intended to be mounted on individual pageant-carts and moved about the streets of a city." The trouble with this generalization is that it is simply not true for the entire cycle.

Nevertheless, some relatively late attempt was made to bring the plays together into a loose whole. The MS. itself is evidence of just such compilation, although the effects of compilation on the staging are inconsistent through the entire work. As Mrs. Gay herself points out, "The fact that Adam reappears in the third play; the fact that Cain remains within the general playing-area for the episode of Lamech in the fourth play; and that the 'place of the play' is cleared by an 'exit' at the end of the fourth play (**Noah**) seems sufficient evi-

dence for believing that continuous playing was intended for this group of plays." Such details may point, at least, to a late attempt to adapt processional plays to a fixed playing area, and they tend to reaffirm our belief that the **N-Town plays** as we have them are in a state of development from one kind of staging to another. The very idea of a sense of "development" of course is fallacious, since we tend to look upon staging in the round as a mode that was developed *toward* during the fifteenth century, while the processional mode of York, for example, is certainly older. All that we can properly say is that the **N-Town Plays** represent the theatre in a state of flux, as it always must be if it is vigorous and ambitious. Such flux may defeat our attempts at unification or over-simplified clarity, but it does not absolutely defy analysis. To begin that analysis, we must look further at the evidence of the **N-Town Plays** themselves. . . .

Production Organization in Lincoln after c. 1470

If we turn now from the staging levels of the cycle to its most probable site, the city of Lincoln, we find an explanation of how these developments came about and how the cycles were produced. To recapitulate well-known material: the Cathedral Chapter Accounts of Lincoln Cathedral show the development of trope dramas, generally staged in the choir, during the fourteenth century, some of which persisted through the middle of the sixteenth century; Episcopal records show evidence of Corpus Christi celebrations, with plays, over two days by 1419, while the Registers of the Common Council mention Corpus Christi celebrations as late as the sixteenth century; the Guild Returns of 1393 and the Common Council Registers show the existence of two city-wide religious guilds of considerable importance, the Corpus Christi Guild and the Guild of St. Anne; finally, the Cathedral records mention the joining of a nave Assumption Play to the St. Anne's Day sights in 1483. The conclusion that in Lincoln the two city-wide guilds were producing two cycles, one (St. Anne's) having to do with the life of the Virgin, the other (that of Corpus Christi) including both Old Testament plays and plays of the life of Christ, seems tenable.

The Corpus Christi cycle of 1419, played over two days, is probably the thirty-nine play proto-cycle discussed earlier. If so, it would seem that its production was under the control of the Corpus Christi Guild, which in turn parcelled out production details to individual trade and craft guilds. Perhaps "parcelled out" is poor terminology in this context, for almost certainly the development toward a complete cycle was the natural outgrowth of the earlier processional customs of many of the Lincoln guilds. It must be remembered, therefore, that cycle production was a religious custom in both its origin and its practice; the Corpus Christi Guild, founded in 1350, antedated all but a few trope dramas, just as related craft guilds antedated even the most primitive of the plays actually in the N-Town MS. Despite a lack of evidence about the Corpus Christi Guild, we may extrapolate back from a wealth of material about the St. Anne's Guild, whose relation to the craft guilds in the presentation of the Marian cycle is very clear.

Thanks to the sixteenth-century Registers of the Common Council, we are able to say that the powerful Marian concern of Lincoln became a civic as well as a religious attitude, and that, in fact, the two were indistinguishable by the sixteenth century. When, for example, the Corporation completed the building of the new Stonebow (a gate in the city wall across the High Street that is still in existence) in 1519-20, two statues were placed in niches on each side of the central arch, one of the Virgin Mary and one of the Angel Gabriel. This iconographic reminder of the Annunciation is a fitting introduction to pre-Reformation Lincoln. It explains why, as well, the Council Registers from 1511 to 1569 showed a continuing deep concern for the management of St. Anne's Guild, to the point where former mayors became gracemen of the guild. The many mentions of "pageants," of "sights," and of "processions" in these records cited in the Historical Manuscript Commission Report have been noted extensively before; they are mentioned here as further proof of the vitality of the Marian cycle production in the sixteenth century and of the Lincoln Corporation's interest in it.

In examining the St. Anne's production more closely, we find again that civic and guild involvement cannot always be separated, but that a pattern becomes clear: in actual production, the plays run by St. Anne's Guild and staged on or about the day of St. Anne's Feast were encouraged and supported by the Common Council, artistically controlled by the Guild, and staged by craft guilds, of which two—the Tilers and the Cordwainers—have left clear indications of the part they took. As well, costumes for one play (significantly the **"Prophets"** or **"jesse tree play,"** the first in the Marian cycle) were supplied by the aldermen and the sheriffpeers, while properties for unspecified plays were supplied by parish churches (presumably religious objects for processions such as those of the Nativity Magi).

The function of the aldermen in the presentation of the **"Prophets"** play has already been discussed by Hardin Craig (*ERD*, p. 278); Craig's assumption that the "kings" for whom the aldermen were to provide gowns were indeed the kings of the "Prophets" and not the Magi is certainly accurate, and he notes further mention in the same entries of "a man in an honest gowne to go as profytte" to be provided by each sheriffpeer; however, we must also notice the responsibility of the Tilers Guild to provide actors to play the kings. Now, there were twelve aldermen, who, with the mayor, could have supplied thirteen gowns; the N-Town "Prophets" is a lengthy procession of thirteen kings and fourteen prophets (including "Radix Jesse"). Production of this

play, then shows a clear, if rather intricate, cooperation among civic officials, a craft guild, and the St. Anne's Guild: expensive costumes like silk gowns were here provided by supposedly wealthy aldermen; cotton gowns *and* actors to wear them were to be provided by the lesser dignitaries, the sheriffpeers; actors alone seem to have been required of the Tilers.

In the case of the Cordwainers Guild of the B.V.M., on the other hand, much more was required of the craft. Craig's published records of the Guild give us a picture of the Guild's theatrical function. First, we know of five principal properties: a pageant of Bethlehem; "a gret hed gilded, set with vii beames and vii glasses for the same, and one long beame for the mouth of the said hed"; three stars with a cord; two angels with censers; and a cage with doves. The "gret hed," as we have indicated elsewhere, is probably a godhead to rise over the Nativity stable. The three stars with a cord are, similarly, a Nativity property, a simple machine for pulling three stars over the stable for each of the three sightings of the Nativity sequence. The first is for the shepherds:

> [1ᵘˢ pastor]   The prophecye of boosdras is
> spedly sped
> now leyke we hens as that lyght
> us lede.
>
> (fo. 89v)

And, shortly following, there is a marginal stage direction, *"stella celi extirpauit."*

A second appearance of the star is necessary in the "Adoration of the Magi":

> [1ᵘˢ rex]   . . .Ffro Saba haue I folwyd
> fferre
> the glemynge of yon gay sterre.
>
> (fo. 92r)

Then, after the *Herodes,* the Magi move on to the manger:

> [primus Rex] Go we to sek owr lord and our
> lech
> yon stere will us tech the
> weyis full sone.
>
> (fo. 95r)

At first glance, it would seem that a single star on a cord and pulley would have sufficed for all three appearances; however, unless a very complicated rigging would have allowed it to make a complete circle around the place of the Nativity, it would have been necessary to pull it back and forth for each appearance. Such a reversal of direction is theatrically wrong; the star is supposed to *lead* in a single direction. The simple solution, then, was indeed to use three stars, each of which could be pulled from a masked entrance, over the Nativity site, and out by a masked exit. Such a solution, too, is quite in line with the practices of the in-church *Stella* plays of an earlier period, where the moving of the star was accomplished with a cord and pulleys.

The final Cordwainers' property, the cage of doves, is not required by any of the Christmas sequences, but it is a very necessary object in the N-Town **"Purification"** play. The climax of this final Marian play is the offering of birds upon the alter:

> *And ther mary offeryth ffowlys on to the Autere and seyth*

(Maria)   All-myghty-fful fadyr. mercyful kynge

Receyvyth now this lytyl offerynge

Ffor it is the fyrst in degree

that your lytyl childe so yynge

presentyth to-day be my shewying

to your hyy mageste.

(fo. 100V)

Finally, a Cordwainers' entry of 1539 mentions the "angels of the hersse" in the St. Anne's procession. In the light of the other properties used by the Cordwainers, it is likely that the "hersse" is the "hous of haras" in which Mary and Joseph shelter for the birth of Christ (f. 83r), the stable. A more detailed discussion of this property will be found later (see I. "Principal loca, pageants and properties"); here, it is enough to point out that the Cordwainers Guild of the B.V.M. appears to have been responsible for the major properties and the setting (scaffold or wagon) of Bethlehem, the Nativity, the major properties (godhead and stars) of the *Pastores, Stella,* and *Magi,* and the most important small property of the "Purification."

Historically, the Cordwainers may always have been responsible for the Nativity pageant. The 1393 Guild Returns mention their processing with "Mary, St. Blaise [the patron saint] and two angels," probably a tableau of statues that included censing angels of the kind seen over the stable in Nativity iconography. If this is true, then the Cordwainers, as well as the Tilers, represent craft guilds whose plays moved from the proto-cycle to the Marian cycle at the time of its creation as a separate drama. In that it is unlikely that plays would have continued to appear in both cycles, the Cordwainers' Accounts help us to see which plays in the Nativity sequence were probably removed from the Corpus Christi proto-cycle: the Birth of Christ, the Miracle of Salome, the *Pastores, Stella,* and *Magi.* We can only guess that the popular Herod plays, including the brilliant N-Town **"Death of Herod,"** may have remained with the Corpus Christi cycle to hold the primary emphasis of the Marian cycle on the Virgin.

Continued production of other plays in the Corpus Christi cycle, particularly those from the Old Testament, is debatable. It is tempting to think that only the Passion sequence was staged as the Corpus Christi cycle after the 1470's, but a reference from the Common Council Registers makes this highly unlikely. On 12 November 1539, it was ordered that the old schoolhouse was to be made into a pageant storeroom, with Noah's ship to be charged 12d, three times the rental of the other pageants. Preservation of this important property indicates that the play was still being given, and we must conclude that Old Testament materials remained in the Corpus Christi repertoire long after the revisions of the late fifteenth century.

The exact functions of St. Anne's Guild and the Corpus Christi guild in relation to the sub-cycles and to each other is not yet entirely clear. The Common Council accounts of 12 November 1539 also indicate a separation of properties—the "stuff" of St. Anne's guild in one place, Noah's ship and other pageants in another. Two sets of theatrical properties are probably indicated here; however, by 1554, an order in Secret Council that "Seynt Anne Guyld w corpus xpi play" will be brought forth suggests that the impact of the Reformation had greatly diminished the city's theatrical activity, and had, in fact, reduced its production to a single cycle.

In brief, then, the production responsibilities were as follows:

St. Anne's Guild (supported by the Common Council):

"The Prophets" with Tilers Guild, Aldermen and Sheriffpeers

"The Conception of Mary"

"Mary in the Temple"

"The Betrothal of Mary"

"The Parliament of Heaven"

"The Salutation and Conception"

"Joseph's Return"

"The Visit to Elizabeth"

"The Trial of Joseph and Mary"

"The Nativity"

"Adoration of the Shepherds"

"Adoration of the Magi"

"The Purification"

The Corpus Christi Guild (probably supported by the Common Council)

Old Testament plays, **"Creation"** through **"Moses"**

"The Massacre of the Innocents"

"The Death of Herod"

The early life of Christ, from **"Christ and the Doctors"** through **"Lazarus"**

The Passion Sequence, from **"The Entry into Jerusalem"** through **"The Ascension"**

"Doomsday"

The Cathedral Clergy, independently of the guilds,
but as a finale to the St. Anne's plays
"The Assumption of the Virgin."

A Note on the Actors

Although we have noticed the provision of actors by the Tilers and the sheriffpeers for the "Prophets" play, we need not take this case as typical. The "Prophets" is a static series of declamations, requiring little interplay and probably little rehearsal. More typical is the Cordwainers' Nativity sequence, and here again the Cordwainers' Accounts are very helpful. Evidently, the guild supplied three men as shepherds, but paid "the plaiers" for other roles. (In 1532, for example, the expenses include "It paid in expenses for the plaiers ijd. It. paid to the plaiers above all that was gathered vijd.") Two payments to actors seems strange, but it is possible that "expenses" of the players were for their own costumes or hand props (the kind of thing a modern theatre takes out of petty cash), while a payment "above all that was gathered" indicates that a set fee had been agreed upon, for which a collection was taken, and that the guild made up the difference. These actors, then, were well paid by late medieval standards; a glance at the plays suggest that they played Mary and Joseph, and possibly the Magi. The reason why Mary and Joseph particularly would not be supplied by the guild (as the shepherds evidently were) is that they are the only continuing characters of the Marian cycle, and the same professional actors would have played them in all the St. Anne's plays. To support this, we cite again the reference to two Marys for the entire production, whereas a sequential presentation of the Marian plays, with each play using different actors, would have required eight Marys. The Magi are an enigma; it is possible that they were provided by another guild (since they were not continuing characters throughout the cycle) just as the Tilers provided actors for the Kings of the "Prophets." One conclusion, nevertheless, is inescapable: that in the sixteenth century the major continuing roles of the Marian cycle were taken by paid actors.

One further detail concerning actors may be mentioned. Only one proper name appears against a character in the entire cycle, that of "Worlych" (f. 207r) in "The Castle at Emmaus." "Vade Worlych" is written in the margin (apparently a stage-manager's note) one speech before the entrance of Peter and Thomas, with "*nota Worlych*" immediately after, while a crossed-out "*nota Worlych*" is written under the name of Peter next to his first speech. It is not important here to determine whether the actor played Peter or Thomas, although Peter seems the more likely character; what is important is that this rare Lincolnshire name can be identified with William Worleyge of Weston (Holland), whose lengthy will included a bequest to "oure mother churche of Lincoln." The name, spelled variously as Worlich or Worlegge, is that of a well-to-do Weston family; it

indicates that either the cycle, or part of it, was presented in places other than in Lincoln (and the "N-Town" of the Banns suggests this) or that citizens of towns a day's journey from Lincoln could involve themselves in the plays. In neither case does Worleyge's involvement suggest that the use of a professional actor in an important role was invariably the case in the late fifteenth and the sixteenth centuries.

Staging the plays at Lincoln

In a sense, the political-social entity that was the medieval city of Lincoln does not gibe well with the geographical Lincoln of the fifteenth and sixteenth centuries. Beguiling as the Chapter Acts and the Common Council Registers may be, it must be remembered that the early sixteenth-century city was rather small, linear in shape because of its terrain, "a sleepy little city, struggling along its great street, aroused into life. . .by the markets. . ." More vigorous in the fifteenth century than in the sixteenth, it suffered gravely from the removal of the wool staple and from the plagues, its population declining to about two thousand people by the early fifteen-hundreds' as Sir Francis Hill notes, following Leland, its craft gilds shrank and its medieval political structure began to crumble after about 1500.

Yet it was geographically the same city as in its medieval prime: a walled enclave, bounded on the south by the River Witham, dominated by its hilltop cathedral, whose spires can still be seen from miles away. The city was strung along the street that still climbs a crooked route from the Stonebow up a very steep incline (now known as Steep Hill) to debouch into an open area between the Castle and Exchequer Gate, the primary opening in the Minster Close Wall facing the cathedral's west front. Beyond the Stonebow at the bottom of the hill the street continued as the High Street, where an important part of the medieval city lay; the structure known incorrectly as John of Gaunt's House and several early churches were there.

Two other ways up the hill were possible: the stairs known as Greestone steps, good for the pedestrian but impossible for vehicles, and another route that traced an old Roman road and wound finally to the North side of the Cathedral, probably in the vicinity of Eastgate and the recently-uncovered Roman double gate.

Hardin Craig (*ERD*, p. 271) has mentioned the difficulty of processing with pageants over Lincoln's hilly terrain, for example up Steep Hill from the Stonebow to the Cathedral. Yet we must accept the fact that the procession of St. Anne's Guild began at the bottom of the hill, for the properties and pageants (whether that word connotes wheeled vehicles or portable objects does not matter here) were stored in the lower town: in 1539 in a chapel on the bridge over the river, while Noah's ship and other objects were stored in the old school house, also located in the lower town, and the Cordwainers' pageant was stored at the White Friars, farther out the High Street. Although it is possible to climb today from the Stonebow to Exchequer Gate in twenty minutes at a very easy pace, the slope of the principal street would demand much more time of any heavy or wheeled object being transported by men, or horses, or both. Still, the climb is possible (the street, built originally by the Romans, was evidently used by farm carts every day) and even with the loss of time necessary for the beginning of any parade, a procession that gathered at seven o'clock could have been at Exchequer Gate within two hours.

We must consider the possibility that a different route could have been taken, of course; Greestone Stairs are unlikely, but the longer route to Eastgate, although taking more time, would probably have been no easier.

A large question remains: why climb the hill at all? The obvious answer is that Lincoln *was* the hill, and any procession that sought to show itself to the citizens, as the Common Council Registers make very clear the St. Anne's procession did, would have wanted to take the principal streets, hill or no hill. As well, the Guild returns of St. Anne's Guild and several of the craft guilds include procession to the cathedral as part of the yearly custom; thus, processions up the hill were usual even in the fourteenth century. The continuing emphasis on procession and display in the Council Registers—the use of torches, of silk gowns, of men for "going in the procession"—and the fines for non-participation show that, whatever the theatrical element may have been, display of the city's pomp for the citizens was an important part of the St. Anne's and Corpus Christi feasts.

Still, the question of where the cycles were played remains unanswered. If the proto-cycle was processional, with its thirty-nine plays presented in sequence on movable wagons or stages (and it seems to have been), Lincoln's geography suggests that the city was not very hospitable to such staging. Unlike York, medieval Lincoln presented few open street spaces; on the other hand, the presence of at least two large spaces—one within the Minster Close, between the west front and Exchequer Gate; the other between Exchequer Gate and the Castle—made central staging ideal. Therefore, while a few stations can be suggested (at the two turns in the central hill street and at the Stonebow, for example) the topographical possibilities for central staging may explain the revision evident in the N-Town Plays' staging. It can even be questioned that more than one location was ever used for the proto-cycle; rather, a single station may have been used for the entire audience, with the plays presented sequentially at first, simultaneously later (after about 1470). The slight overlapping between plays in the Old Testament series noted by Anne C. Gay may be explained by a single-station staging of sequential pageants.

Three facts tend to influence our thinking in favour of the Minster Close for this single station. The first is the custom of procession to the Cathedral that was common to several guilds; another is the addition of the Cathedral Assumption play to the St. Anne's Day plays. As well, Cathedral records of canonical dinners noted first by Hardin Craig, and recently found to exist in greater detail, contain a number of references between 1473 and 1500 to the canons' seeing "Corpus Xpi play," "the play of Corpus Xpi" or merely "the play." The suggestion that this took place within the Close (as the dinners certainly did, one (1477-78) having been given in the chamber of John Sharp within the Close) is almost inescapable. Finally, the specific mention of payments by the Cordwainers for "costs and charges to the mynster with the pageant of Saint Anne day" in 1539 indicates that the Cathedral and its surrounding Close were, indeed, the place to which the Guild processed. While the Close, as we shall see, was not "the only place in the old city of Lincoln where there could be such a concourse of people," much of the available evidence does point to its use as the primary location.

The Minster Close was (and still is) a splendidly large area. Although irregular, it had ample room for crowd and plays. While no dependable maps or drawings from the period still exist, Speed's map of 1610 from *The Theatre of the Empire of Great Britain* presents at least the negative evidence of no permanent structures in the Close. The seventeenth century engravings of Wenzel Hollar are disappointing, since they fail to show the only area of interest in this context (that before the west front). Later paintings and drawings present merely negative evidence, and one can conclude that the medieval Close before the west front was substantially the same as it is today, except that the raised curbstone, the paving, and the low iron railing now forming a rough semicircle of about thirty yards diameter around the facade are modern additions; they do not appear in a view as late as that of W. & H. Burgess in 1812. The buildings surrounding this part of the Close on the south, the Deanery and Sub-Deanery, antedate the plays, as does the Exchequer Gate on the west. The long curving line of eighteenth-century houses that at present cuts off the very large northwest corner of the otherwise rectangular area is, of course, more recent than the plays, but it probably follows an older line of structures. Entrances into this area could have been made through the Exchequer Gate's three arches, through a much smaller gate (no longer in existence) in the line of the present eighteenth-century houses, along the north side of the Cathedral (from the vicinity of Eastgate) or from the south side of the Cathedral (from the vicinity of Potter's Gate).

The west front of the Cathedral is one hundred and forty-four feet wide, while the entire area is about two hundred and five feet wide; it is about one hundred and ten feet deep, from Exchequer Gate to the Cathedral front. Of the approximately twenty-two thousand five hundred square feet in this area, about six thousand are taken up by the line of houses, leaving about sixteen thousand five hundred square feet of usable space.

An audience, of course, would have had to be contained within this space; entrance could easily have been controlled through the Minster Close gates, forming the kind of enclosed theatre prescribed by Richard Southern in *Medieval Theatre in the Round*.

The principal processional entrance would have been through the central arch of the Exchequer Gate, which is nine and one-half feet wide and slightly over fifteen high at the peak of its ogival arch. The only other constriction in a route from the lower town that might have limited the size of objects in the procession would have been the Stonebow, whose central arch is larger than that of Exchequer Gate (and will, for example, easily accommodate a double-decker omnibus). Exchequer Gate itself would have offered a few prime viewing points for the enclosed playing space, in six windows on the Minster side and on its flat top, stairs to which still exist. Windows in the Deanery and Sub-Deanery could have been used, of course, and a fifteenth-century bow window in the Sub-Deanery that looks along the west front of the Cathedral would have provided an excellent "box" for selected spectators.

It is clear that a practicable theatre site existed in the Minster Close for centrally or sequentially staged plays, with sufficient audience and playing space, excellent viewpoints for privileged members of the audience, both civic and clerical, and limited access. Taking the actual references to performances in the Close together with the practicability of the site, we are inclined to believe that here was the location of the St. Anne's Day plays.

A sixteenth century reference in the Common Council Registers proves that the Minster was not the only possibility, however. When, after the suppression of the cycles at the beginning of Elizabeth's reign, a play was wanted, the Council voted to present "a standyng play of some storye, of ye bibell" for two days. On 26 January, 1566 the play of "Toby," evidently the 1564 play, was selected to be presented, as it was again on 24 November, 1567 (apparently for Whitsunday of 1568). At the end of the same volume of entries is a property list for this Tobit play, with the note that it "was then played in Broadgate in the said city (Lincoln)." From these references we can see that the old pattern of at least the Corpus Christi cycle was being imitated: presentation, over two days, of a "standing" (centrally staged) play. The specific mention of Broadgate must focus our attention on that part of the city. This is a Tudor name for the much older "Wardyke" or ditch that lay just outside the city wall on the east. Although the vagueness of the term "Broadgate" before the modern

street was laid down makes identification difficult, Speed's map of 1610 clearly shows an open rectangle where the Warkdyke had been, with Clasketgate at its north-west corner and two squares of houses forming its eastern boundary, while the western boundary was the city wall. By Speed's "Scale of Pases" measured against a modern map, we can estimate this space as about three hundred feet long by about ninety feet wide. Neither dimension prohibits theatrical use, and the shape, although far from the Macro MS. circle, is comparable to that for the settings of the sixteenth-century Lucerne Passion Play. In that the Tobit play would have needed at least ten stations for each day, it can be seen that a departure from the small, five-stations circle of "The Castle of Perseverance" would have been necessary. As in the case of the St. Anne's plays and the Minster Close, then, we must admit that historical evidence, however scanty, can be joined with our knowledge of the city's topography to give another theatre location in medieval Lincoln's Broadgate.

Whether Broadgate was used for the post-Reformation Tobit play because Broadgate had always been a theatre location, or because a wholly new location (separate from the Cathedral) was needed, is not known. The most important point is that Broadgate was used for a play that directly imitated the centrally-staged Corpus Christi cycle in its theatricality. Further analysis of the **N-Town Plays** themselves will show that the proto-cycle and its sub-cycles were created for theatres very much like those of the Minster Close and Broadgate. . . .

Principal Loca, pageants and properties

Although certain pageants and scaffolds have been discussed above, a detailed description of important structures would still seem to be necessary. The list below, although far from complete, is not intended to be merely representative; it includes those structures that are of primary theatrical importance in the cycle, and for which both textual and external evidence (iconographic or literary) exists:

1. *Hell*. Necessary for at least the Passion sequence and the post-Resurrection plays, the N-Town Hell was undoubtedly the familiar animal Hell-mouth of medieval iconography. The two excellent hell-mouths on Lincoln Cathedral (one in the row of Romanesque carvings on the West front, the other inside the porch on the South side) are good examples of the type. The 1564 Tobit play mentioned in the Lincoln Common Council Registers had among its properties "Hell-mouth with a nether chap" and "A person [*sic*] with a covering," evidently a Hell with adjoining prison like that of the Valenciennes illustration. In that the Tobit properties may be the remainder of the Lincoln cycle properties, this hell may be the stationary set-piece from the Passion sequence. The prison was essential to the N-Town Harrowing of Hell: "The sowle [of Christ] goth to helle

gatys and seyth" (fo. 185v); ". . . *ueniet Anima Christi de inferno cum Adam et Eua. Abraham johan baptista et Alijs.*" (fo. 191r)

2. *Noah's ship.* One of the most spectacular movable properties in the cycle, the ship was apparently large and probably realistically detailed. The Council order for enlarging the door of the school house and charging the ship triple rent has already been cited; one may note also the votive ship used by the Mariners' Gild of nearby Grimsby, so large that the town's bridges had to be reconstructed for its passage. Wheeled, it had to have repairs made to its "axietrees."

3. The Cordwainers' *Bethlehem.* Although already discussed in some detail, this movable pageant warrants further study. As described above (p. 130) it was probably a stable with two mechanical censing angels on its roof, a godhead rising above these, and a machine in front for pulling the three Nativity stars over the stable. The building was apparently open: "In An hous that is desolat with-owty Any wall / Ffyer nor wood non here is." (fo. 83v). It was probably equipped with a bed for Mary and the child: "Heyle perle peerles prime rose of prise / heyl blome on bedde. . ." (fo. 90r). That the structure was made to resemble a stable is clear from the Third Shepherd's "Heyl in a bestys bynne / Be-stad in a stalle" (fo. 90v), and the reference to it as a "hous of haras" (fo. 83r).

4. *Graves and sepulchres.* Three plays—"Lazarus," the Burial and Resurrection section, and "Doomsday" use burial properties. There would, at first, seem to be a difference in these plays between graves dug in the ground and monuments raised above the ground. The tomb of Lazarus, for example, is described as a dug grave: he is "buryed in a cley pitt," "in caue," "this pytte," (fo. 130r). This tomb was apparently covered with a stone: "A grett [stone] stoppyth the pyttys gate," (fo. 132r) and "Sett to your handys take of the ston," (fo. 134v).

The Doomsday graves are also treated as underground: *"Omnes resurgentes subtus terram clamauit"* (fo. 224r), although this stage direction probably applies to part of a movable pageant. Much clearer, and much more detailed, are the burial places of Christ in the Passion and Resurrection sequences. The manuscript as we have it uses two different kinds of tombs, probably resolved in actual production into one: the revised "Burial" play seems to suggest underground burial: "to pylat now wole I goon / and aske the body of my lord jhesu / to bery that now wold I soon / in my grave that is so new" and "to bery jhesu is body I wole the pray." (fo. 186v); "here thei xal leyn cryst in his grave." (fo. 188v).

Clearly, the grave has a cover, as the sealing indicates. In post-Resurrection plays, however, *"sepulcrum"* and *"monumentum"* are the Latin terms used, and the tomb

is evidently large enough to be entered: *"Petrus intrat monumentum"* and *"hic intrat Johannes monumentum."* (fo. 198r and 198v); Magdalene enters it to find Christ's body gone (fo. 196v). Because of the theatrical use of *Anima Christi* to revive the dead Christ, no elaborate opening of the tomb by angels seems to have been required in this cycle; however, use of the single actor severely limits the size and weight of the grave's cover. If a grave, rather than a monument, was intended, then the actor playing *Anima Christi* would have had to stay in it for the remainder of the day's playing (not long if the marginal note on fo. 196r is a true indicator). If a constructed tomb was used, the actor could probably have escaped through a masked exit.

The 1564 Tobit play lists "A tomb with a covering" among its properties. This weighs the evidence slightly in favour of a raised structure, while the Lincoln iconographic evidence is too slight to be of help: the Cathedral Easter sepulchre, while handsome and massive, has no relevant theatrical characteristics, and the Resurrection misericord in the Cathedral choir shows Christ stepping from what appears to be a coffin.

5. *The Council House.* Although there is considerable information given us about this set-piece, at least one important detail—its height from the ground—remains unclear. We know from the stage directions that it was curtained and could "close" and "unclose" (fo. 147v), that it would hold at least six people (in fact, ten, if the attendants of Annas and Caiaphas accompanied them), and that it was shaped like a chapel or shrine. The curtaining is possible only in a structure that is roofed or at least provided with overhead supports, in which case it obviously must have had a pillar at each corner, and, if set in "myd place" it must have been open on all sides so that its interior would be visible to the entire audience. However, when such a structure's curtains were closed, at least some of the audience would have had its view of the following scene (the Last Supper, for example) blocked. Evidently, from the special mention of its location in "myd place," the oratory was the only structure there; Symon's house was apparently then on the periphery of the place, possibly raised to clear sightlines over the council house. Only negative evidence exists to bear out any theory that the peripheral scaffolds were not raised: there is little covering dialogue for movements from one scaffold to another, whether by such occupants as Annas and Caiaphas or by the various messengers. Production of the cycle at Lincoln, whether in Broadgate or the Minster Close, would have taken place in an already enclosed space lacking the raised dyke upon which Southern postulated the erection of the scaffolds of the *Castle of Perseverance.* Thus, despite the reminiscences of the *Castle* in the **N-Town plays,** we need not assume that the central staging of the Passion sequence was precisely the same as that of the *Castle.* If we look to Continental analogues, we must reject, at least in part, the Fouquet miniatures,

"The Martyrdom of St. Appolonia," and "The Rape of the Sabine Women," whose high scaffolds are possible because the centre of the place is free of blocking structures. Staging similar to that shown in the Lucerne drawings, with a variety of structures of varying heights located around the place, with stands for spectators between and behind them, is the likely conclusion to be drawn for the **N-Town plays** at Lincoln.

Conclusion

We have postulated for the **N-Town plays** two rather different systems of staging, both familiar from English and Continental experience. That the two systems are the result of change in theatrical theory is hardly surprising, nor is it surprising that the manuscript is a composite example of that change in the making. What may be surprising, however, is that two such different systems could have been used before the same audience on successive days; one is at first hard put to accept the idea of a theatre audience adapting readily to two theatrical systems which seem to us to be so opposed; such adaptation, on the other hand, is exactly what goes on in members of a modern audience who may sit through three hours of a proscenium-stage play on one night and watch a play staged in the round or on a thrust stage the next. We are demanding a degree of sophistication of the medieval audience, then—demanding, in fact, that they have been able to accept, even to admire and appreciate, two staging methods that used vastly different focal systems.

For it is in their essential focus that the systems differ. It is not merely a matter of movable, as opposed to fixed *loca;* far more importantly, it is a question of central, as opposed to peripheral focus, and it is in the "lytil oratory. . .clenly be-seyn lych as it were a cownsel hous" that this question of focus becomes clearest. In the "last yere" plays, this structure is in "the myd place": at the centre of the place, just where the castle of the *Castle of Perseverance* is located, and where Galilee was placed in the much older Anglo-Norman Resurrection Play. It is "clenly be-seyn," suggesting that the author was fully aware of the potentials of the focal centre as they are outlined in the Macro MS. sketch for the *Castle of Perseverance*. Much of the "last yere" action takes place in this council house, and it is both metaphorically and literally central to the action; similarly, the "mothalle-council house" of the second Passion group is an active centre throughout the trials, the burial and the resurrection. If it is indeed the same structure, the parallelism of the two Passion sections is obvious. However, in the transition to the post-Resurrection plays, this structure was lost; it had no further function. With it went central focus, unless we conjecture that the most important new locus of the post-Resurrection plays—Heaven—was centrally sited. Such conjecture contradicts the use of the movable pageants for the final plays, unless we conjecture further that

these pageants were merely sited as if they were fixed scaffolds, denying both their function and the episodic, disconnected quality of their sequence. Furthermore, fixed, peripheral siting of pageants would deny them a forward playing area, unless a forward platform was provided for every pageant, a seemingly wasteful and difficult piece of construction. It is sounder, both because it accepts the tradition of sequential staging and because it is simpler, to think of the pageant staging as having had no central focus and using, instead, the same type of large platform described for the Marian plays.

In this transitional form—that is, in the state suggested by the N-Town MS., where clearly processional plays are mixed with clearly central sequences—the use of a platform would also have provided the pattern for the scaffolds that surrounded the place in the Marian and Passion sections: localized interiors with a forward playing-area. These obviously varied greatly in size, but they had two common qualities: they were curtained to open and close (Caiaphas "shewyth him-self in his skaf-hald," fo. 140r; Symon's house "xal sodeynly un-close around Abowtyn," fo. 153v); and they had room for playing within them or in an area immediately adjacent, as the Last Supper and the first trial of Christ were played within Symon's house and the Annas-Cayphas scaffold. In this respect, then, the N-Town scaffolds seem to differ from those of the Fouquet miniatures, which, although curtained, lack any playing area. Despite the many actions played in the place, therefore, we must think of the **N-Town Passion plays** as having been staged in large part on and within scaffolds whose historical precedent was the pageant wagon drawn alongside another wagon or platform, while that original platform was itself the precedent for the unlocalized place.

Anne Cooper Gay (essay date 1967)

SOURCE: "The 'Stage' and the Staging of the N-Town Plays," in *Research Opportunities in Drama*, Vol. X, 1967, pp. 135-40.

[*In the following except, Gay revises previous notions of medieval stage structures, arguing that the N-Town plays differ from other cycles not in the stage structures themselves but in dramatic techniques.*]

The term "stationary ("fixed" or "standing") stage" has long been applied to the **N-Town Plays** because the term stands for the opposite of "movable ("perambulatory") stage." Certainly, the stage directions of the N-Town **"Passion,"** combined with the evidence for continuous playing within sequences of plays in other parts of the cycle, preclude perambulatory wagon staging as we have understood it from David Rogers' description of pageant carts and their use.

Since the publication, however, of Richard Southern's

The Medieval Theatre in the Round (London, 1957), and Glynne Wickham's *Early English Stages,* Vol. I (London, 1959), it is no longer logical to divide medieval stages into the two mutually exclusive categories, "movable" and "stationary," for such a division originated in the mistaken belief that perambulatory wagon staging (as described by Rogers) was the rule for the performance of the English religious cycles, and that "stages" which did not move about upon wheels were exceptions. However semantically reasonable such a division may once have seemed, it is no longer compatible with the results of present research, and to continue to use such classification is to perpetuate the invalid assumption that the crucial differentiating feature among medieval stages was the wheel.

The success of any descriptive term in its particular application to medieval stages depends upon our having a clear idea of what it is we are talking about when we use the word "stage," but the very problem lies partly in our present confusion about the exact architectural restrictions which reside in the word itself. For example, "movable stage" always refers to wagons, but "stationary stage" may refer to anything (from a soapbox to an amphitheatre) as long as it appears to stand still. To compound the problem, there has been a notable failure to distinguish clearly between the physical entity called a "stage," on the one hand, and the various uses made of that "stage," on the other. Hence, the substitution of "perambulatory" for "movable" always assumes, not only wagons, but also the particular method of using them which Rogers described. This substitution renders the reference of "stationary" less specific than ever: there is very little essential difference, after all, between a wagon and a scaffold, if both are standing still. Thus, the adjectives we have been using to describe medieval "stages" have come to refer more and more to method, and less and less to the stage itself.

The application of the adjective "stationary," then, to the otherwise undefined stage of the **N-Town Plays** tells us only (by negative implication) how these plays were *not* performed, and on the basis of such implication we have assumed that wagons were not anticipated by the compiler of the present manuscript. However, the word "pagent" appears in both the N-Town **"Banns"** and the play of the **Purgation** (14), and has led many to conclude that at some point in its history the **N-Town cycle** utilized perambulatory staging. (The reasoning behind this assumes that the word "pagent" necessarily implies a wagon, and that wagons necessarily imply perambulatory staging—an interpretation which hardly agrees with the obvious continuity of long sequences of plays in the cycle.)

For these reasons the attempts to classify the staging of the **N-Town Plays** in terms of the traditional either-or alternative have never allowed anything but a stalemate of contradictory opinions on the complexities of

the text which bear on the staging of the plays (and on the relationship of the staging to the structure of the plays themselves).

Southern and Wickham have, in general, forced us to reexamine our assumptions, but Southern, in particular, has presented a reconstruction of a theatre plan which has special relevance to the N-Town **"Passion."** An appraisal of the **"Passion,"** with particular reference to Southern's study, both substantiates the essential features of his "place-and-scaffold" theatre and illuminates the most probable method of staging which may be applied to the **N-Town Plays** as a whole cycle.

The **"Passion,"** despite the manuscript numbering which arbitrarily divides the **"Passion"** sequence into separate "plays," was written as a single long play, divided into two parts. The stage directions are predominantly in English. (Line references and quotations are taken from K. S. Block's edition of the Hegge manuscript, ***Ludus Conventriae, or the plaie called Corpus Christi,*** EETS, Extra Ser., CXX [London, 1922].) There are six separate stations required for the performance of the **"Passion."** In Part I these are: "Heaven," "scaffold," "stage," "council house," "Simon's house," and "þe mount of olyvet. . .a lytyl þer be-syde. . .a place lych to A park" (after line 908). That five of these stations are real structures is clearly indicated in the stage directions, for players must go into them, come out of them, or go down from them. At least three of these structures are apparently elevated: Heaven, the scaffold, and the stage. In the case of Heaven, there is the suggestion of some sort of hoisting device, for the angel (after line 956) "Ascendyth A-yen sodeynly." At least four of these structures probably use curtains, for the council house and Simon's house ("**Passion I**") must "vnclose sodeynly"; the "cortayn" is "drawyn" on Pilate's wife's scaffold ("**Passion II**"); and Herod's scaffold must also "vnclose" ("**Passion II**").

The use of the word "stage" in the opening stage direction of the "**Passion I**" is of basic significance to this discussion. If the word is not taken out of the whole context of the subsequent movement of the players, its reference is clearly to a scaffold and to nothing else. In connection with this point, it is of equal importance to note that the "place" is considered here to be an area separate and distinct from the structures representing the six different stations, for to gain access to the "place," players must go into it (from the council house, from Simon's house, and from the "place lych to A park"), or they must go down to it (from the scaffold and from the stage). To get from one station to another, players must first go into the "place," where they usually meet with someone else and play a scene before completing the move to the next station. (A direct cross is rare.) Twice, however, players must go around or about (or both) before they reach the next station.

The opening direction of the **"Passion II"** suggests that players who make their initial appearances in scaffolds must enter such structures from the "place" before the play begins. All entrances made after the play begins are made directly into the "place" from an unspecified area *outside* the "place." (The only exception to this is Pilate's wife [**"Passion II"**] who first appears late in the play, but in a curtained scaffold.) To make a final exit from the play, characters are taken out of the "place." Properties (such as the cushions in the council house) are evidently set before the play begins, or they are brought on by the players themselves during the action (as Simon with his "Kan of watyr"). From this, we may infer that what we now call "backstage" was here the area outside the "place."

Once these features have been established, a clear picture of the "place" begins to emerge. Christ's exit, riding on the ass (**"Passion I,"** after line 221), indicates that the "place" was, in fact, the ground. And if, as it appears we may, we equate the words "stage" and "scaffold," the "place" then becomes, as Southern defines it, "the ground before the stage" (*Theatre in the Round,* p. 235). More specifically, it is the ground before, between, and below three separate stages and something representing a mountain and a park. The only structures which appear to be surrounded by the "place" are the council house and Simon's house (neither one of which appears to be raised), and we know that the council house, at least, was situated in "þe myd place." We may state with certainty, then, that in the N-Town **"Passion,"** the "place" is clearly differentiated from that kind of structure which was called, indifferently, a "stage" or a "scaffold."

Once the "place" becomes clear, and the uses made of it, we find that the audience apparently surrounded the "place" (as in Southern's reconstruction), for I can think of no other reason for having Simon's house "sodeynly vnclose rownd Abowtyn" (**"Passion I"**), or for having the messenger (**"Passion II"**) run "rownd Abowth þe place" shouting of Christ's capture, or for leading Christ so elaborately "Abowth þe place" during the devil's scene with Pilate's wife (**"Passion II"**), unless the spectators were also "round about"—and being given full benefit of what was going on.

The stage direction which opens the **"Passion II"** deserves further comment here, for it requires a procession to "enter into þe place," whereupon Herod, Annas and Cayphas, and Pilate "take" their scaffolds. It seems clear that the scaffolds were already in position in the "place" before the procession entered, that the actors were part of the procession, and that they had to enter into the "place" before they could "take" their respective scaffolds.

Turning now to the rest of the cycle, we find, again despite manuscript numbering (which implies separate

plays), that there are whole sequences of plays which were evidently intended for continuous playing. The combination, addition, and rewriting of material, combined with the presence of connective stage directions and the duplication of the same stations and speaking roles in one "play" after another, indicate that, at the very least, plays 1-4 (**"The Creation"** through **"Noah"**) and plays 8-20 (**"The Barrenness of Anna"** through **"The Death of Herod"**) must be regarded as continuous sequences. It is of particular interest here to note that in order to perform a continuous Marian-Nativity sequence (plays 8-20), it would be necessary (again) to have six separate stations: a "Heaven," a "temple," a "Mary domus," a "hous of haras," a "Herod" station, and another *domus* for Anna and Joachim, Elizabeth and Zachary, and possibly Simon.

Of the remaining plays in the manuscript (outside the obviously continuous sequences), plays 22 and 23 (**"The Baptism"** and **"The Temptation"**) and plays 36 and 37 (**"The Appearance to the Three Maries"** and **"The Appearance to Mary Magdalen"**) are connected by stage directions. Of the ten remaining and textually unattached plays, the **"Assumption"** (41) in its present form is clearly an interpolation unabsorbed into the surrounding material of this manuscript, but it requires many of the same speaking roles (notably the Disciples and Mary) as the plays which immediately precede it. Furthermore, although the stage directions are in Latin, the requirements for staging are generally similar to those of the **"Passion"** and **"Marian"** sequences. The **"Assumption"** also requires the same spectacular use of Heaven and of flying devices which are necessary as well to the **"Ascension"** (39) and to **"The Day of Pentecost"** (40). Even if this **"Assumption"** is the same play which was acted in the nave of Lincoln Cathedral, there is nothing about the staging to have prevented it from also being performed in combination with the plays immediately preceding (and following) it.

There are no direct references to scaffolds or to stages outside the **"Passion,"** but Satan falling to his "stynkynge stalle" (1), and Herod in his "kage ful hye" (18) are suggestive. There is, however, further real evidence for the use of a "place" as Southern defines it. Throughout the cycle there is an overwhelming abundance of scenes played in undesignated areas: while characters are moving from one station to another, after they have entered the general playing area but before they have entered a specifically designated station, or after they have left a station but before they have left the play. It is clear, in almost every case, that these scenes are *outside* the specific stations but within the view and hearing of the audience. There are scenes such as these in forty of the forty-one "plays" in the cycle; notable examples are Herod's entrance on horseback in **"The Adoration of the Magi"** (18), The Cherry Tree Episode in **"Joseph and the Midwives"** (15), the lengthy journey of Cleophas and Luke (38), and the procession of the disciples with Mary's body in the **"Assumption"** (41). (The one exception is the play of the **"Prophets,"** 7.) Scenes such as there must have necessitated using a "place," and in connection with this, many of these scenes indicate that spectators occupied such a "place" as well as the players. Den, clearing a path for the Bishop in the **"Purgation"** (14), evokes an immediate connection with Southern's definition (pp. 81-87) of the function of "stytelers," and Mary, in **"Christ and the Doctors"** (21), appears to be talking to the audience as she wanders through the crowd looking for Jesus.

There are only two stage directions outside the **"Passion"** sequence which directly mention "place," but these two are important. One, in the play of the **"Visit to Elizabeth"** (13), has been noted by Southern in his definition of "place" (p. 222), for it is clear in its implications: *"et sic transient circa placeam."* Joseph and Mary must go across around the "place" to get from their house to Elizabeth's. (The verb *transire* is used frequently in the Latin stage directions of the cycle.)

The second direction of relevance here occurs in the play of **"Noah"** (4): *"Hic transit noe cum familia sua pro naui quo exeunte locum interludij sub intret statim lameth conductus ab adolescente et dicit."* Southern contends that the word *locus* (when it is used at all in medieval plays) "probably has a meaning different from what we understand by Place in our present study" (p. 41). It seems here, however, from the action preceding and following this direction, that the *locum interludij* must, in fact, be a "place." When we realize that Cain (from the preceding play of **"Cain and Abel"**) does not, apparently, exit at the end of that play, but hides instead in order to be killed "behind yon grett busch" in the Lamech episode; that Noah and his family vacate the *locum interludij* to accommodate the action of the Lamech episode; and that Lamech in turn vacates (*"recedat statim"*) the same area when Noah and his family return to the play with their famous boat, we also realize that one playing area is accomodating four scenes in succession and must also accommodate a boat of sizable proportions. For all practical purposes, then, the function here of the *locum interludij* is the same as that of a "place."

It has been my intention in this discussion to point out certain basic discrepancies in the reasoning which has previously been applied to the **N-Town Plays,** and to suggest what I feel to be the only theory of staging which is supported by the evidence available in the Hegge manuscript. The invalid classification of medieval stages into the two mutually exclusive categories, "movable" and "stationary" has, in turn, led to inconsistent interpretation when attempts were made to force specific dramatic texts to conform to one or the other alternative. Combined with this, the assumption that the word "pagent" is necessarily synonymous with the word "wagon" has created an apparent necessity to reconcile the assumed existence of wagons (and therefore perambulatory staging) with a "stationary" set of plays. Once these assumptions are cleared away, however, we can see that there is nothing in the Hegge manuscript which suggests that perambulatory staging was ever considered in connection with these plays. Wagons may well have been used in the **N-Town Plays,** but it is Noah's boat which suggests this, not the use of the word "pagent" in the Banns or the ambiguous reference of the word "pagetum" [*sic*] in the **"Purgation."** The important point here is that once we are aware of the distinction which must be made between method (staging) and structure (stage), we realize that the use of wagons is not inconsistent with "place-and-scaffold" staging and does not, therefore, have to be rationalized at all.

It is impossible, in so short a space as this, to consider in detail all the problems connected with the **N-Town Plays** and their staging, or the relationship of these problems to questions concerning the compilation of the Hegge manuscript, but it seems generally clear, although the compilation as we have it is neither consistent nor thorough with regard to the stage directions and the action they imply, that the kinds of alterations which have been made in this manuscript would not, in most cases, have been considered unless a theatre and method of staging like that of the **"Passion"** sequence had been, quite simply, taken for granted.

It is my conclusion that the N-Town **"Passion"** firmly supports both Southern's definition of "place" and his arrangement of the audience and the stations; that the entire cycle bears evidence of "place-and-scaffold" staging; and, finally, that the use of the word "stage" must, in connection with this cycle, be limited to refer to a scaffold. The real difference, then, between the N-Town and other cycles (Chester, for example) lies not so much in its "stage," but in its "staging."

Theresa Coletti (essay date 1977)

SOURCE: "Devotional Iconography in the N-Town Marian Plays," in *Comparative Drama*, Vol. 11, No. 1, Spring, 1977, pp. 22-44.

[*By exploring the Marian plays' connection to devotional art, Coletti reveals how the cycle embodies its audience's spiritual concerns.*]

The Middle English **N-Town cycle** evinces an extraordinary consciousness of the motifs and interpretations that characterized late medieval devotion to the Virgin. Of the four Middle English Corpus Christi plays, only the **N-Town cycle** includes a group of plays, extending from *The Conception of Mary* to *The Trial of Joseph and Mary,* specifically concerned with the life of the Virgin before the birth of Christ. The scope of Marian attention in the cycle also embraces plays such as the *Nativity* and *The Adoration of the Magi,* and the N-Town manuscript shares a *Death and Assumption* play only with the York cycle. Many scholars have noted the unique Marian preoccupation of the cycle, but the iconographic and devotional richness of this group of plays remains largely unexamined. The cycle's manifest awareness of Marian concerns thus invites an exploration of the relationship of devotional iconography to dramatic import. This study explores the **N-Town Marian plays** as a form of devotional art. It proposes ways in which stage iconography could have embodied the spiritual concerns of the dramatic audience.

Since the publication of Émile Mâle's *L'art religieux de la fin du moyen âge,* few students of the medieval religious drama have disputed the significant relationship of late medieval art forms to the affective spirituality that characterized Christian devotion in the fourteenth and fifteenth centuries. Among the dominant forms of pictorial art in the late Middle Ages, the illuminated Book of Hours is particularly relevant to a consideration of devotional iconography in the **N-Town Marian plays.** For like that cycle, this most popular of late medieval prayer-books emphasized the Virgin; the Book of Hours always contained the Little Office of the Virgin, which was frequently illustrated by a pictorial narrative sequence of scenes from her life. The typological meanings of the Virgin, her role in the miraculous nativity of Christ, and her capacity as intercessor are only some of the subjects of the **N-Town Marian plays** represented in the illuminated Book of Hours. Because the miniatures of Books of Hours suggestively illustrate how the late Middle Ages visualized the relationship of the Virgin to redemptive history, they offer persuasive evidence for an imaginative reconstruction of devotional iconography in the Marian plays.

I

Recent students of the **N-Town cycle** agree that the entire play is amenable to *platea* and *loca* staging, with a variety of stations situated around or inside a rather large playing space. The Marian plays call for an elevated Heaven, a Temple, several *loca* (variously designated as the homes of Anna and Joachim, Mary and Joseph, and Elizabeth and Zechariah) and a playing area for numerous journeys. We can suppose Heaven to be a raised scaffold centrally located toward the edge of the *platea.* The repeated requirement for a Temple in the early Marian plays and the frequent juxtaposition of activities in the Temple with God's presence in Heaven suggest that the Temple would have been placed near Heaven. The proliferation of divine messengers in these plays (angels visit Anna, Joachim, Mary, Joseph, the shepherds, and the Magi) suggests that other principal *loca,* and especially the place of the Annunciation,

would have been arranged relatively close to the Heaven scaffold. Such a stage plan would confer a visual as well as a dramatic unity upon the events in the life of the Virgin and the early life of Christ.

The Conception of Mary, the first of the Marian plays, presents a microcosm of universal history after the Fall. The play dramatizes the movement from *tristitia* to *gaudium* [from grief to joy] by showing the transformation of Anna's barrenness to blessedness through the birth of Mary. The *Conception* thus provides a spiritually resonant opening for the series of plays elaborating the Virgin's crucial role in God's redemption of mankind. The text of the **N-Town cycle** shows an awareness of the interpretive tradition which found Christological meanings in the activities of the Virgin before the birth of Christ, meanings which are also apparent in Marian iconography of Books of Hours.

In the play ***Mary in the Temple*** the Virgin receives these instructions from Episcopus as she enters the Temple:

> ye must serve · and wurchep god here dayly
> Ffor with prayyer · with grace and mercy
> Se the haue · A resonable tyme to fede
> Thanne to haue a labour bodyly
> Þat þer in be gostly and bodely mede.
>
> (78.171-75)

Though Episcopus does not designate the nature of Mary's "labour bodyly," the ultimate source for his directive is the apocryphal *Protevangelium* 10.2, which states that the Virgin and the women in the Temple engaged in cloth-making. The motif of the Virgin's spinning and weaving in the Temple was a popular one in the later Middle Ages. For example, *The Golden Legend* notes that work and prayer were Mary's principal activities in the Temple. The *Meditations on the Life of Christ* specifically observes that the Virgin worked daily at her spinning from the third to the ninth canonical hour; after that she prayed until an angel brought her food. Also the presence of the cloth-making motif in the Middle English *Evangelie* and in the Towneley cycle assures that it would have been well known to the English dramatic audience.

The "Presentation" miniature in the *Hours of Catherine of Cleves* shows two women spinning at the Bishop's feet as the Virgin enters the Temple. This pictorial motif also occurs in a number of miniatures executed by the Boucicaut Master and his shop. One "Annunciation" miniature from the Boucicaut workshop shows in the marginal illustration an imposing portrait of the Virgin weaving as an angel brings food to her. The Boucicaut Master frequently juxtaposed images of the cloth-making Virgin with representations of the Annunciation, thereby suggesting a theological and historical relationship through the spatial proximity of the two themes.

In the **N-Town play** of *Mary in the Temple* we find a clear analogue to the Boucicaut miniature. Shortly after the Virgin enters the Temple, the bishop, his ministers, and Anna and Joachim depart, and Mary remains alone with her maidens (79.208ff). She kneels before "þis holy awtere" and prays until an angel "bryn-gyth manna in A cowpe of gold" (80). The angel prais-es Mary, alluding to her role in the coming redemption (80.244-51) and to the Annuciation: "Ffor ye xal here aftere haue A salutacion / þat xal þis excede" (254-55). The stage directions then call for a lengthy spec-tacle: "here xal comyn Allwey An Aungel with dyvers presentys goynge and comyng and þe tyme þei xal synge in hefne is hympne · Jhesu corona virginum · And After þer comyth A minister" (81). The most like-ly activity for the Virgin during her discourse with the angel, the presentation of the heavenly gifts, and the singing of the hymn is surely spinning or weaving. The Bishop's advice about the necessity of a "labour bodyly" and the presence of the cloth-making motif in late medieval miniatures and spiritual texts support the iconographic presence of the Virgin's handiwork. Moreover, the mean-ing of this activity in its pre-Annunciation context further corroborates its dramatic presence on stage. The Annunciate Virgin is important because she is the agent through whom Christ assumes His human nature. St. Anthony of Padua, a principal Franciscan exegete, in fact describes the Incarnation in terms of a cloth-making metaphor: "Out of the sack-cloth of our nature Jesus Christ made a tunic for Him-self which He made with the needle of the subtle work of the Holy Spirit and the thread of the Blessed Vir-gin's faith. . . ."

The Virgin's cloth-making could thus serve as a visual allusion to the approaching Incarnation; furthermore, it evokes the Passion because it suggests the *tunica in-consutilis* which appears regularly in Passion narratives as a garment that the Virgin made for Christ. The *Stan-zaic Life of Christ* describes Christ's seamless robe as "that wede. . .that wrought our lady swete Mary" and as that "wiche Mary hys moder hym made." Rosemary Woolf observes that in the popular medieval allegorical tradition of Christ as the Knight of the Crucifixion, his *aketoun* was understood as "the human flesh which the Virgin gave him in her womb" (*English Mystery Plays*, p. 267). Significant too is a speech by Filius in the N-Town *Parliament of Heaven* play in which He refers to the Incarnation as the taking on of a garment: "lete me se how I may were þat wede" (103.178). The Towne-ley cycle devotes an entire play, *The Play of the Tal-ents*, to Christ's seamless garment; and in the Towneley *Crucifixion* the Virgin conflates the idea of the woven garment and the garment of flesh in her speech at the Cross:

> To deth my dere is dryffen,
> his robe is all to-ryffen
> That of me was hym gyffen

And shapen with my sydys.

(270.386-89)

Showing the Virgin involved in her cloth-making activ-ity in the Temple scene would thus provide an unusually resonant piece of stage iconography, suggesting both the birth and death of Christ.

The apocryphal tradition that named spinning as the Virgin's activity in the Temple is even richer in asso-ciations. Though Scripture provided no specific warrant for it (Gen. 3.16-19), spinning was also designated as Eve's immediate occupation after the Fall. In the **N-Town cycle** Eve laments her punishment to Adam: "ye must delve and I xal spynne / in care to ledyn oure lyff" (29.415-16). A curious miniature in the *Rohan Hours* (fig. 18) shows Adam and Eve at work; it also conflates this image with what the legend calls "la nativité de Caym et d'Abel," and thus the picture combines three different Eves in a single image. Dressed in blue, Eve, the mother of Abel (himself a type of Christ), holds a child. The image is virtually indistinguishable from countless representations of the Virgin and child, and it assaults visual expectation because it depicts a Virgin-like Eve in a scene that illustrates the punishment of man's first parents. What the Rohan miniature calls to mind, however, is the common medieval juxtaposition of Eve, the mother of sin, and Mary, the mother of grace. If Eve spins as a labor of restitution for her sin, then the Virgin's handiwork, because it is associated with the Incarnation, subtly alludes to the event which brings ultimate restitution to Adam, Eve, and all man-kind. In view of the **N-Town cycle's** deliberate refer-ence to Eve's post-lapsarian labor, the likelihood of its presenting the Virgin's spinning in a pre-Annunciation context appears all the more strong.

In the **N-Town cycle** the Annunciation occurs in the play that begins with the **Parliament of Heaven** (No. 11). Following the **Betrothal** play, the **Parliament of Heaven** takes place after Joseph finds Mary "a lytyl praty hous" and then departs, leaving her in her "con-claue." The modulation of scenes is extremely dramatic at this point, for the action moves from earth to heaven, then back to earth again as Gabriel descends to the Virgin. In this rapid change of dramatic focus the audi-ence would see a strikingly unified stage image, for the action requires that the Virgin remain in view while the Trinity holds the Parliament in Heaven. Gabriel in fact moves from Heaven to earth and makes his Salutation in only two lines: "I take my fflyth and byde nowth / Ave Maria gratia plena Dominus tecum" (104.216-17). The scenic juxtaposition of Heaven and earth would furnish opportunities for meaningful stage action; e.g., God the Father might gesture toward the Virgin when he says: "The name of þe mayd ffre / Is Mary þat xal Al Restore" (103.195-96). Furthermore this juxtaposi-tion would assert the solution of the heavenly Parlia-ment—the Incarnation—even while the dispute in Heaven takes place and thus confirm the redemptive promise.

Given the visible theological significance inherent in the cycle's placement of the **Salutation and Conception** immediately after the **Parliament of Heaven,** we might consider how stage iconography for the Annunciation could have expressed devotional concerns. Each of the "Annunciation" miniatures in the Books of Hours under consideration shows the Virgin either seated or kneeling, a consummate symbol of her humility. Medieval emphasis on this virtue derived from interpretations of the Virgin's reply to Gabriel in Luke 1.38: "Ecce ancilla domini." A twelfth century treatise on the virtues attributed to Hugh of St. Victor, *De fructibus carnis et spiritus,* defined humility as the *radix virtutum* [the root of virtue]; because of her humility the Virgin became the mother of Christ. **The N-Town Marian plays** repeatedly evince an awareness of the Virgin's humility. When angels visit Mary in the Temple, she expresses her unworthiness: "Mercy my makere · how may þis be ment / I am þe sympelest creature · þat is levynge here" (80.242-43). Similarly, at the Annunciation she speaks of her "grett shamfastness" (105.236) and humbly receives Gabriel's message:

> With All mekenes I clyne to þis A-corde
> Bowynge down my face with All benyngnyte
> Se here þe hand-mayden of oure lorde
> Aftyr þi worde · be it don to me.
>
> (106-07.285-88)

The angel responds with praise for her "grett humylyte" (107.291). In the N-Town **Annunciation,** then, the audience would surely see a seated or kneeling Virgin.

The presentation of individual scriptural events in relation to the teleological design of Christian history was, of course, a fundamental structural and dramatic principle of the Corpus Christi play. Late medieval pictorial art also reveals this consciousness of redemptive history, as the Boucicaut workshop's "Annunciation" with the marginal illustration of the Virgin weaving has shown. In several instances the N-Town **Annunciation** calls attention to the meaning of the Incarnation in the plan of universal history; and we can, I believe, assume that this awareness undoubtedly informed and vitalized stage iconography.

When Gabriel addresses the Virgin, he urges her to assent to the Incarnation in order to win "All mankende savacion" (106.282). Two Annuciation miniatures supply iconographic details which illustrate the import of Gabriel's words. Both the Boucicaut and Chevalier "Annunciation" miniatures show altars on which burning candles rest. Millard Meiss [in *The Boucicaut Master*] notes that miniatures of the Boucicaut workshop frequently place the Annunciate Virgin at an altar instead of the usual *prie-dieu,* though the two motifs

often exist side by side. The *Speculum humanae salvationis* glosses the candle as Christ, the candlestick as the Virgin: "Ipsa enim est candelabrum et ipsa est lucerna. . .Christus, Mariae filius, est candela accensa." The altar is still more evocative, for by its very lack of any detail except the candle, it alludes to both the coming of the Savior and His sacrifice, which is reenacted at the altar in the Eucharist. Though the text provides no specific warrent for it, the transposition of a motif such as this into the dramatic setting would serve as a visible referent to Gabriel's words to Mary. It would also confirm through stage iconography the promise of salvation which Gabriel announces in his final speech:

> qwen of hefne · lady of erth: and empres of
>   helle be ye
> socour to All synful · þat wole to yow sew
> Thour your body berythe þe babe · oure blysse
>   xal renew.
>
> (108.335-37)

At the moment of the Incarnation in the **N-Town Marian plays,** there occurs an interesting and detailed stage direction: "here þe holy gost discendit with iij bemys to our lady · the sone of the þe godhed nest with iij bemys · to þe holy gost · the fadyr godly with iij bemys to þe sone · And so entre All thre to here bosom. . ." (107). The direction undoubtedly describes stage iconography at this highly dramatic moment. Though the significance of the action is not immediately apparent, it seems to refer to an explicit theological meaning which would not have been lost on the dramatic audience. Most intriguing in the stage direction for the Incarnation is the emphasis on light, the "iij bemys" that descend from the Father to the Son to the Holy Ghost, to rest finally in Mary's bosom.

From the beginnings of Christian theology light had supplied a metaphor for religious mysteries, and the Incarnation was frequently compared to sunlight passing through glass: "Just as the brilliance of the sun fills and penetrates a glass window without damaging it. . .neither hurting it when entering nor destroying it when emerging: thus the word of God, the Splendor of the Father, entered the Virgin chamber and then came forth from the closed womb. . . ." The metaphor became extremely popular among late medieval painters, who frequently employed it to illustrate the Incarnation. The Chevalier "Annunciation" shows a golden light focusing on the Virgin from a great Gothic window; the Rohan and Boucicaut miniatures draw deliberate attention to beams of light which suggest the *splendor Patris,* for their source is an image of God the Father. In each miniature the Holy Ghost appears as a dove.

The presence of this motif in many late medieval paintings of the Annunciation, Meiss notes, is explained by its wide diffusion in theological treatises, hymns, and Latin and vernacular poems ("Light as Form and Symbol," pp. 176-77). Undoubtedly instrumental in spreading its popularity was *The Revelations of St. Bridget,* in which Christ likens his Incarnation to the passage of sunlight through glass. Possibly Bridget's *Revelations* provided the source for the metaphor in the **N-Town cycle,** where it occurs in the play of **Christ with the Doctors** (181.97-100) and in **The Resurrection** (328.18).

The N-Town stage direction for the Incarnation suggests an awareness of the popular metaphor that compared the event to sunlight passing through glass; the explicit reference to this metaphor in other parts of the **N-Town cycle** supports this reading. At the moment of the Incarnation the stage requirement for "iij bemys" calls to mind the Incarnational light which pierced the Virgin while still preserving her purity; the Holy Ghost probably appears in the form of a dove, just as in the miniatures described above. The expressive power of this stage image is suggested by its counterpart in the *Rohan Hours,* where an imposing God the Father, displaying the symbol of His power, points to the Incarnational light directed toward the Virgin's breast. His Word becomes flesh at that moment through the Holy Ghost, and Mary confirms the Trinitarian participation in the event when she states: "Now blyssyd be þe hyy trynyte" (107.312).

II

Like the early Marian plays, The N-Town *Nativity* employs theological motifs appearing in late medieval spiritual texts and miniature illustrations. The play seems to have been influenced by *The Revelations of St. Bridget.* We have already noted the presence of one Brigittine motif in three places in the cycle, a motif which also occurred in the iconography of Books of Hours. Bridget's text was in fact a major source for Nativity iconography in the late Middle Ages, and thus it may prove useful in proposing devotional stage iconography for the N-Town *Nativity* play.

Henrik Cornell [in his *The Iconography of the Nativity of Christ,* 1924] attributes the appearance of a new iconographic type of the Nativity in the late Middle Ages to *The Revelations of St. Bridget.* While earlier representations show the Virgin lying in bed and the Christ child nearby in the manger, later Nativity scenes present her kneeling, as she adores the child on the ground before her. A reverent Joseph is often present as well. According to St. Bridget, the Virgin, Joseph, the ox, and the ass enter the place of the Nativity; Joseph brings Mary a burning candle and goes outside so that he will not witness the birth. The Virgin makes herself ready for the birth, removing her shoes, mantle, and veil and turning her back to the manger. She kneels in prayer and the Christ child is miraculously born. Bridget tells how she saw radiating from Christ "such an ineffable light and splendour, that the sun was not compa-

rable to it, nor did the candle, that Joseph put there, give any light at all." After the birth Mary worships the child; and when Joseph returns, he joins in the adoration.

The important characteristics of the Brigittine Nativity are all present in the "Nativity" miniature in the *Hours of Catherine of Cleves* (Pl. 2), which shows the Virgin with her back to the manger. Mary and Joseph kneel on the ground, the naked Christ child before them. Joseph holds his useless burning candle in a scene bathed in light. The N-Town *Nativity* play also contains evidence of a Brigittine version of this event, thereby suggesting its iconographic resemblance with the Cleves miniature.

In the **N-Town play** Joseph and the Virgin seek their lodging in a poor "chawmere." The place is probably dark and barren, for Joseph mentions "An hous þat is desolat with-owty Any wall / Ffyer nor wood non here is" (138.101-02). Perhaps at this moment Joseph lights a candle. Further evidence for a Brigittine version of the play, however, is supplied by the Virgin's speech immediately before the birth of Christ:

> Therfore husbond of your honeste
> A-voyd yow hens out of þis place
> And I a-lone with humylite
> here xal abyde goddys hyy grace.
>
> (139.113-16)

The Virgin describes a stage image that accords with two of the primary features of the Brigittine Nativity: Mary asks Joseph to go out of the place, and she calls attention to her "humylite," a detail which iconographically could only mean that she is sitting or kneeling. Joseph then departs, seeking "sum mydwyuys yow for to ese" (139.119), and the stage direction indicates: "hic dum joseph est Absens parit Maria filium unigenitum."

The influence of Bridget's *Revelations* on the N-Town *Nativity* also appears in the response of the midwives who return with Joseph. Though Bridget does not include the midwives in her *Revelations,* in the **N-Town play** they call attention to an important iconographic motif of her version of the Nativity. They marvel at the "gret bryghtness" which illuminates the scene: "mone be nyght nor sunne be day / Shone nevyr so clere in þer lyghtness" (140.163-64). Their comment on the "woundyrfful lyght" in fact strengthens the possibility of Joseph's earlier appearance with a candle, for Bridget contrasts the divine light emanating from Christ with Joseph's mundane attempt to brighten the darkness. When Mary cheerfully reproves his doubt, Joseph asks forgiveness: "I Aske yow grace for I dyde raue / O gracyous childe I aske mercy" (141.193-94). At the moment of his plea, Joseph might kneel alongside the Virgin in worship of the child before them.

Still other iconographic motifs can be suggested for

the cycle's *Nativity* play. From early Christian times the Incarnation had been given Eucharistic interpretations, and patristic writers such as Ambrose, John Chrysostom, and Gregory the Great developed and expanded the sacramental associations of the Nativity. The Eucharistic meanings of the Nativity were strengthened by the etymological interpretation of Bethlehem as the *domus panis*—house of bread—and hence by the analogy between the birth of Christ and the Bread of Life. By the late Middle Ages this analogy was extremely widespread, appearing in a variety of spiritual texts. The Middle English *Meditations on the Supper of Our Lord,* for example, equates the Christ child with the Eucharist: "Þat sacrament þat þou seest þe before / Wundyrfully of a mayden was bore."

The N-Town *Nativity* and the scenes that follow it surely were intended to evoke sacramental meanings, and undoubtedly these meanings would have been translated into stage iconography. The speeches of the shepherds point to the salvific promise inherent in the Nativity, for they allude to the benefits that will be won from the sacrifice on the Cross (147.34-37, 42-43; 149.93). The angel who proclaims the Nativity to the shepherds also says that "Sacramentys þer xul be vij / Wonnyn þurowe þat childys wounde" (146.5-6). Perhaps the best evidence, however, for the appropriateness of Eucharistic iconography in the N-Town *Nativity* play is supplied by the Towneley cycle, which includes two entire plays elaborating the meanings of food and the Eucharist, Christ and the lamb—the *First* and *Second Shepherds' Plays.* That the Wakefield Master saw fit to give extensive play to Eucharistic meanings at the dramatic moment of the Nativity certainly indicates that the dramatic audience would have been familiar with these meanings and further that they would have expected them.

Eucharistic interpretations are also apparent in pictorial representations of the Nativity, which supply suggestive possibilities for stage iconography. An "Adoration" miniature in the *Boucicaut Hours* (fig. 31) shows the Christ child lying on a white cloth that is spread on an elaborately decorated bed. To the left of Christ, the Virgin kneels before an open book that also rests on the bed. The miniature displays a ritualistic quality which glosses the scene it presents. The white cloth suggests that the bed, which here replaces the manger, is a symbol of the altar, where the Eucharist becomes the body of Christ. The association of the manger and the altar was well known, appearing in various places in the writings of the Church Fathers. The iconographically rich Cleves "Nativity" also may allude to Eucharistic meanings. It too shows the Christ child resting on a white cloth and displays a curious basket hanging on the wall above the Virgin's head. Ursula Nilgen [in "The Epiphany and the Eucharist," *Art Bulletin* 49, 1967] mentions an Epiphany panel painting that shows a bread basket hanging by a hook from the roof directly over the Christ child. Given the clear sacramental

references in the N-Town *Nativity,* we can imagine that iconographic details such as these easily could have been translated into stage iconography. Indeed the absence of visible reference to the Eucharist at this dramatic moment would be the more surprising eventuality.

In the N-Town *Magi* play the first king to address the Christ child states: "Heyle be þou kyng Cold clade / heyll with maydynnys mylk fade" (159.235-36). The king's speech calls attention to a motif extremely popular in the late Middle Ages—the *Maria lactans,* or the Virgin nursing the Christ child. The precedent for linking the Magi's visit with the *Maria lactans* image may be in St. Bernard's Epiphany sermons: "Adorant Magi, et offrunt munera adhuc sugenti matris ubera."

The abundance of pictorial representations of the Virgin nursing in medieval painting suggests that the image had a marked spiritual significance. Millard Meiss states that the image of *Maria lactans* "set forth that character and power which arose from her motherhood, i.e. her role as *Maria mediatrix,* compassionate intercessor for humanity before the impartial justice of Christ or God the Father. . . . In the Middle Ages the Virgin was believed to be the mother and nurse not only of Christ but of all mankind" (*Painting in Florence and Siena,* pp. 151-52). One popular fifteenth century version of the *Maria lactans* image shows the Virgin exposing her breast to her son. Speaking of this type, Yrjö Hirn [in *The Sacred Shrine,* 1912] points out that Christ "could not. . .refuse His assent to any of her prayers, if only she reminded Him of the time when He lay as a child at her bosom." The conjunction of the Virgin's functions as *nutrix* and *mediatrix* is well illustrated by a fourteenth century sequence which associates Christ's nursing at the Virgin's breast with the nourishment mankind derives from the blood of his wounds. The Virgin's milk serves as an analogue to the salvific nourishment of Christ's blood, and consequently images of *Maria lactans* inevitably evoke associations with the redemptive promise.

Pictorial representations of *Maria lactans* in the Louvre fragment of the *Belles Heures de Notre Dame,* known as the *Turin Hours,* and in a psalter illuminated for Henry VI of England show the Virgin exposing her breast to her Son, while Christ shows His wounds to the Father. A comparable configuration occurs in the *Hours of Catherine of Cleves,* where a saint and Duchess Catherine pray before a crucifix. The Virgin kneels, exposing a breast that spurts milk, and she looks up to her Son on the Cross, who in turn casts an appealing glance to God the Father. The miniature illustrates a passage from St. Bernard quoted in the *Stanzaic Life of Christ*: "Securum accessum habes, o homo, ad Deum vbi mater ante filium, filius ante patrem, mater ostendit filio pectus & vbera, filius ostendit patri latus & vulnera: Nulla ergo poterit esse repulsa, vbi tot concurrent caritatis insignia" (p. 318). The *Turin Hours,* the illuminated psalter, the *Stanzaic Life,* and the *Cleves Hours* all present a chain of intercession. In the Cleves miniature Catherine appeals to the Virgin, the Virgin to Christ, and Christ to the Father. The image, "caritatis insignia," is a visual assurance of the capacity of the Virgin and Christ to intercede for sinful man. The Virgin makes her plea to Christ in terms of her capacity as *nutrix.* In the Cleves miniature Catherine's banderole reads: "Ora pro me sancta dei genetrix"; the Virgin in turn appeals "propter ubera."

The rich spiritual content of the Cleves miniature helps to explain how fitting an image of *Maria lactans,* signalled by the first king's speech, would be at the dramatic moment of the N-Town Epiphany. When the Magi depart, one of the kings asserts: "we haue fownde our lord and lech" (160.270). The *Maria lactans* image would lend visual corroboration to the play's primary theological action. Christ became the sinner's "lech" when he became man to die for man's sins. And the promise that Christ the physician extends to mankind finds an echo in the iconography of the Virgin nursing, for the milk that nourished the redeemer is at the same time the milk of salvation.

III

If the N-Town *Magi* play provides the opportunity for the dramatic representation of the Virgin's capacity as intercessor, the *Death and Assumption* play celebrates that capacity with lavish grandeur. The Assumption is the honor bestowed on the Virgin for her role in man's redemption and for her potential to participate continuously in the redemptive action through her prayers. The liturgy for the Vigil of the Assumption emphasizes this attribute of the Virgin, and the **N-Town play** asserts it as well. Paul praises the Virgin with "heyl incomparabil quen · goddis holy tron / of you spreng salvacyon · and all oure glorye / heyl mene for mankynde · and mendere of mys" (364.250-52). At the moment of her death, the Virgin assumes her role as intercessor: "A swete sone Jhesu now mercy I cry / ouer alle synful thy mercy let sprede" (365.282-83). Textual evidence suggests that the *Death and Assumption* play presented an elaborate spetcacle, with the mysterious apparition of the Apostles, the solemn procession, the comings and goings of *Dominus* and angels, and the actual ascent of Mary. The play also evinces an awareness of its sources and a consciousness of both theological and iconographic tradition.

The N-Town *Death and Assumption* closely follows the account of the event presented in *The Golden Legend,* from which it adopts its description of the Virgin's funeral procession. In the *Golden Legend* the apostle John asks Peter to lead the procession. Peter declines, insisting on John's greater worthiness, and says that instead he will bear the body. Then Paul

offers to assist Peter in carrying the bier (IV.239). The same dialogue occurs in the **N-Town play** (367.328-40). *The Golden Legend* also seems to have been the source for Fouquet's miniature of the "Funeral of the Virgin" (Pl. 4). Fouquet meticulously maintains his manner of representing the apostles throughout the Chevalier miniatures, and there can be no doubt that here he shows John leading the funeral procession as Peter and Paul take up the bier. The display of tall lit candles corresponds to the N-Town stage direction: "hic portabunt corpus versus sepulturam cum eorum luminibus" (367).

The *Cleves Hours* also suggests possible stage iconography for the N-Town *Assumption*. One of its miniatures shows a Trinity after the Crucifixion. Christ appears as conqueror, His feet on the globe of the earth, and He displays His wounds. Such a dramatic image at the Virgin's Assumption would add an historical dimension to the event and visually reinforce the means by which the Virgin became the intercessor for mankind—she is the mother of the One who was crucified. The N-Town *Assumption* text does not describe the *Dominus* who comes to take the Virgin to Heaven; but a regal-looking Christ, still bearing the mark of His wounds, could descend to the *platea*, while the Father and Holy Ghost remain on the Heaven scaffold. Peter remarks that *Dominus* appears in his "manhed clere" (372.470); because Christ suffered His wounds as man, stage iconography along these lines seems all the more appropriate.

Iconographic motifs and interpretive tradition may also help us to imagine stage iconography for the actual ascent of the Virgin into Heaven. The Virgin at her Assumption was frequently associated with the Woman of the Apocalypse of Rev. 12.1. The biblical passage furnished the Introit for the Feast of the Assumption, and the image of the Woman of the Apocalypse was extremely popular in Assumption iconography, occurring in works such as the *Speculum humanae salvationis*. The Assumption miniature in the *Cleves Hours* shows the Virgin as the Woman of the Apocalypse, clothed in the Sun, the moon at her feet. It is wholly credible that the N-Town Assumption could have been managed on a platform appropriately adorned after the manner depicted in the Cleves miniature. The ability of late medieval dramatic craftsmen to execute vertical spatial movement with remarkable ingenuity has been noted by Orville Larson [in "Ascension images in Art and Theatre," *Gazette des Beaux-Arts* 54, 1959].

A stronger justification for such an iconographic presentation, however, arises from the forms of late medieval spirituality. The image of *Maria in Sole* was very popular in the late Middle Ages; indulgences were granted for saying a prayer before an image of the Virgin in the Sun. A miniature in the *Boucicaut Hours,* which shows the Maréchal and his wife kneeling in prayer before an image of the Virgin as the Woman of the Apocalypse, provides a particularly good illustration of the devotional efficacy that the late Middle Ages attributed to such images. Depicting the Virgin as both mother and queen, the miniature illustrates the tribute that *Dominus* gives to her in the N-Town ***Assumption*** play: "thus schul ye clepyd be / qwen of hefne and moder of mercy" (373.497-98). To conclude the play with an iconographic motif sanctioned by pictorial tradition and informed by the late medieval understanding of the Virgin's role as merciful mother and intercessory queen would be a profound visual testimony to the devotional meanings inherent in the treatment of the Virgin throughout the cycle.

Sarah Appleton Weber notes [in *Theology and Poetry in the Middle English Lyric,* 1969] that through her Assumption Mary becomes the means for reuniting man and God: "As Queen of Heaven she becomes intercessor for man. Her role is the full fruit of the pain she suffered at the crucifixion which made her the mother of man, and it provides the basis of the title. . .Mother of Mercy." Moreover, the Virgin's Assumption is "both the pledge and type of man's own future resurrection and glory." In the iconography of the Virgin's Assumption and in the words with which *Dominus* receives her—"ye schal have the blysse wyth me moder · that hath non ende" (372.484)—the dramatic audience would see and hear the fulfillment of the salvific promise which was in fact the central theme of the Middle English cycle play. Stage iconography thus embodies the play's deepest religious meaning. Drama and devotion are one.

Lynn Squires (essay date 1978)

SOURCE: "Law and Disorder in Ludus Coventriae," in *Comparative Drama*, Vol. 12, No. 3, Fall, 1978, pp. 200-13.

[*By exploring fifteenth-century law, Squires suggests that many of the plays of the N-Town cycle contain severe criticism of the contemporary legal establishment.*]

My purpose is to provide a new context for the late medieval cycle of plays traditionally referred to as ***Ludus Coventriae*** by investigating the fifteenth-century legal conditions reflected in these plays. Critics of medieval drama have not recognized the importance of laws as a religious ideal and so have not noticed its significance in late medieval and early Renaissance religious drama. Because we no longer link law with religion, we must remind ourselves that law, for the medieval Englishman, was the formal expression of divine will; it was the common belief that the common as well as the ecclesiastical law originated in the mind of God. This did not prevent Englishmen from criticizing their legal institutions, however; law was, in fact, an extremely

controversial topic in the fifteenth century, no less so than in the sixteenth.

Law stood for the principle of virtue itself; it stood for the ordering forces in society and, more importantly for our purposes, in drama. When fifteenth-century lawyers, politicians and dramatists argued for legal reform, like John Wyclif before them, they were arguing for reform of their entire society. Although it was an age of reverence for law, in theory, and an age of prosperity and relatively good repute for the legal profession, it was also an age critical of its degenerate common law system and of its litigious citizens who overtaxed that system. The plays in ***Ludus Coventriae*** speak out against the people responsible for vexatious prosecutions in court and against the many legal abuses practiced in and out of court as well as against the inadequacy of the old legal system to curb lawlessness. In the words of the legal historian William Holdsworth [in *A History of English Law,* 1923] the law itself had become a "sword for the unscrupulous": "The forms of law and physical violence had come to be merely alternative instruments to be used as seemed most expedient." The forms of law are used, for example, in the ***Ludus Coventriae*** passion sequence as a means of destroying Jesus. The plays in that sequence show how the crucifixion of Christ, far from being a travesty of justice, accurately reflects justice as Englishmen then knew it; in that sequence, the trial and punishment of Christ is carried out specifically within the jurisdiction and following the procedures of the fifteenth-century court of common law. In other words, Englishmen watched themselves try, condemn, and crucify Christ, and in this way they took responsibility *themselves* for his death. Not only did Christ die *for* them but also *because* of them—as a victim of their own courts of law. Thus the passion sequence—which I will discuss in some detail—leads its audience to a re-evaluation of the existing court system and of their own principles of justice.

It can be argued that parallels between English and Judaic legal matters are due simply to the habit of anachronism or that, for example, contemporary clothing had to be used for costuming because no one knew how a Jewish bishop or judge would have dressed during Jesus' lifetime. The plays go so far beyond scriptural requirements, however, that it becomes necessary to attribute special meaning to contemporary characters, costumes, and incidents which serve non-scriptural purposes. For example, the ***Ludus Coventriae*** playwright uses the capture of Jesus to demonstrate the most familiar evil of the age: maintenance, and its attendant evils perjury, champerty, and conspiracy to defraud. The retrogression to feudal disorder in the fifteenth century is a historical commonplace; the cause of disorder is said most usually to be the indentured retinue or band of retainers serving the often violent purposes of their sworn lords. In ***The Taking of Jesus,*** the adherents of the Old Law have gathered a fellowship and armed themselves with "Cressetys lanternys and torchys lyth / And þis nyth to be þer redy / With exys gleyvis and swerdys bryth" (27.663-65) in order to capture Christ. This represents a considerable embellishment and particularization of the capture as set forth in the Gospels: "Therfor whanne Judas hadde takun a cumpany of knyytis, and mynystris of the bischopis and of the Fariseis, he cam thidur with lanternys, and brondis, and armeris" (*John* 18.3-4), and *Luke* 22.66-67 tells us only that the "eldre men of the puple, and the princis of prestis, and the scribis camen togidir, and ledden hym in to her councel" [Wycliffe, *New Testament*]. Taking scripture as a point of departure for critizing the practice of retaining, the *Ludus Coventriae* playwright shows each of the judges going to stand with his "meny" (company). The stage directions for the taking of Jesus indicate ten persons *"weyl be-seen in white Arneys and breganderys and some dysgysed in odyr garmentys with swerdys gleyvys and other straunge wepone as cressettys with feyr and lanternys and torchis lyth"* (28.972*sd*). This must have evoked a common enough scene, the liveried band with torches and weapons at the ready. This is just one example of the way in which the *Ludus Coventriae* playwright embellishes the biblical story to make political and legal commentary.

The parallels that I draw between the plays and the problems of law and order in the period in which they were written are necessarily conjectural. Still, there is strong evidence, in the stage directions and elsewhere, to support a direct connection. For example, the striped robes of the doctors described in the stage directions for *The Council of the Jews I* correspond exactly to the dress for sergeants-at-law as described by Sir John Fortescue [in *De Laudibus Legum Anglie,* 1942]. And Herod, in *Herod and the Three Kings,* oversteps the biblical requirements of his role and sends out spies to gather evidence (18.94-110), an offense commonly complained of during this time. Whatever the playwright's intentions were, the audience could hardly have been blind to the persistent and accurate paralleling of the old Judaic law to their present-day law, and of the practices of Jewish rulers to those of their present-day kings. Nor could they have failed to notice that the New Law of Christ—which the plays promote—bears resemblance to the new wave of equitable law practiced in Chancery and in mercantile courts during their own day. The contrast between mercy and the old law which Stanley Kahrl notices in the council scenes and *Maundy III* operates throughout these plays to create dramatic tension and to emphasize the need for legal reform.

Since it is not possible here to discuss the entire cycle of 43 plays, I will focus on the **Passion I** segment and broadly outline the plays which lead up to it. In so doing, I necessarily leave out much that is interesting from a legal and political point of view, especially in the trial of Jesus in **Passion II** where the English courts

and their exact procedures are satirized.

The cycle begins with four plays which teach obedience to the law: *Creation and Fall, Cain and Abel, Noah,* and *Abraham and Isaac.* They each (1) state a law, (2) show someone breaking or keeping it, and (3) show the immediate punishments or rewards. By demonstrating the perils of breaking and the profits of keeping the law, these four plays set the tone and introduce a major theme of the cycle. In case the audience misses the point, the fifth play, *Moses,* restates it in the form of a lengthy sermon intended to teach God's law to man: "your soulys may þei [laws] saue at þe last Asyse" (6.58). The threats and promises of the first plays prepare the audience for the more detailed explanation in *Moses* of what these laws in fact are. With the sense of urgency established, the lesson follows. The lesson is actually a descriptive sermon on the ten commandments. God gives Moses the stone tables, saying, "with my ffynger in hem is wrete / all my lawys þou vndyrstonde" (6.39-40) and then commands Moses to teach them to the people. Moses interprets the commandments in terms of the commonplace sins of his fifteenth-century audience: he interprets "non habebis deos alienos" (6.67) as a prohibition against the worship of worldly riches—a problem especially acute in this prosperous age; "memento vt sabbatum sanctificets" (6.99) as a prohibition against wearing showy garments on Holy days (there were fifteenth-century laws to control over-elegant or extravagant dress); and "non occides" (6.131) as a prohibition against wicked language, for "wyckyd spech many on doth spyll" (6.137)—a contemporary problem to be taken up below with *The Trial of Joseph and Mary.* In a significant variation from his treatment of other laws, Moses delivers the eighth commandment strictly as it stands, without any homely embellishment:

> The viij^{te} precept þus doth þe bydde
> Ffals wyttnes loke non þou bere
> þe trowth nevyr more loke þat þou hyde
> with ffals wyttnes no man þou dere
> Nowther ffor love ne dred ne fere
> Sey non other than trowth is
> Ffals wytnes yf þat þou rere
> Ayens god þou dost grettly amys.
>
> (6.155-62)

False witness was, in fact, one of the chief sources of injustice at the time that these plays were performed.

Strictly speaking, *Moses* is not a play at all; it is a lecture illustrating the ten commandments in light of contemporary problems. It is easy to understand why a playwright might deviate from dramatic action to include a lecture on obeying the law if we keep in mind that the law was so seldom obeyed at this time: royal orders were regularly ignored and writ-bearers are known to have been forced to eat their writs by disgruntled citizens.

After the five plays which teach obedience to the law, the next group, designated by R. T. Davies as the *Mother of Mercy* sequence, takes up a more theoretical legal subject. The plays contain a crucial debate between the advocates of the Old and of the New Law—the Old Testament law of an eye for an eye and the New Testament law of mercy. The debate takes the form of a trial, wherein Jesus is "sentenced" to atone for man's sins. Jesus is to be reminded of this "supreme court" decision later in **Agony at Olivet** before he is taken by the Jews for his earthly trial, and he admits "It is nowth to say A-yens þe case" (28.958). The Old Law (defended by Righteousness and Truth) and the New Law (defended by Mercy and Peace) are formally tried in conjunction with Jesus in **Parliament of Heaven**. The arguments put forth by Truth, the rebuttals of Mercy, the counter-arguments of Righteousness, and finally the concluding statements by Peace together constitute an able and informed theological review of man's position as suppliant vis-á-vis God as his divine judge. In both format and subject matter, this debate is strikingly similar to the *Somnium Vigilantis,* a 1459 tract dealing with the defeat of the Yorkists, in which several orators debate the wisdom of giving clemency to the exiled lords who had opposed the king. In this pamphlet, perhaps the oldest political pamphlet in English prose, the king's orator argues for punishment according to the letter of the law and the orator for the exiled lords argues, like Peace and Mercy in the **Parliament of Heaven,** for clemency. Political necessity was no doubt responsible for the summing up in *Somnium Vigilantis* in the king's favor; the opposite conclusion is arrived at in the **Parliament of Heaven** where the ideal view, rather than the politically realistic one, could prevail. The four advocates in **Parliament of Heaven** accept the suggestion of Peace: "putt bothe your sentens in oure lorde / And in his hyy wysdam lete hym deme" (11.123-24). The arguments made, they turn to the judge for a verdict. Righteousness attributes "very equyte" to God's judgment, thereby indicating the nature of the divine court. It is a court of "conscience," according to the nomenclature of the fifteenth century ("equity" was the rarer synonym). The Son as Judge pursues a complex reasoning to arrive at his decision: "þat helle may holde hym [man] be no lawe" (11.147). The "sentence" is determined out of court, as it were, by a "counsel of þe trinite." The three voices of God briefly decide "Whiche of vs xal man restore" (11.172), and Mercy joyfully announces the "loveday" to follow (11.185), that is, the occasion of settling a legal dispute out of court. The device of the Parliament of Heaven is used here, as in the *Castle of Perseverence,* to justify man's salvation and to describe the nature of God's mercy. Although the Old Law/New Law conflict was as old as Christianity itself, here it is used as a formal rationalization for the triumph of the New Law over the Old

Law which is a major theme of the cycle—and a major issue at the time: the New Testament was in circulation for the first time in English; several hundred copies are known to have circulated among the increasingly literate population and the transition from a stern view of justice to a gentle one was proving understandably difficult.

The superiority of the New Law over the Old is actually demonstrated in the eleventh play, **The Trial of Joseph and Mary**. In this play the ecclesiastical court, which is clearly an English rather than an ancient Judaic institution, is shown to adhere to the Old Law which prescribes revenge against moral offenders. Mary and Joseph, on the other hand, adhere to the New Law of mercy which prohibits taking earthly revenge against wrong-doers. The play, like others in the cycle, warns against taking personal vengeance, particularly in the form of an unnecessary law suit. The law suit in this case is between Mary and the so-called "detractors" (and the bishop's court which supports them); it arises from some gossip about Mary's "unseemly" pregnancy which is overheard by the bishop. In fact, numerous fifteenth-century lawsuits were based on rumor, gossip, and imagined wrongs, often severely damaging an innocent defendant. This occurred in the fifteenth century (and before) because remedies were readily available under English law to each citizen, male or female, free or villain, lettered or unlearned. Naturally in a society where for centuries each man has been responsible for apprehending criminals (once the hue and cry is raised), where each legal division of the population is responsible to some degree for crimes committed within its boundaries, and where each person is empowered to bring suit against a neighbor in the king's name, there will be the problem of overuse or of too-ready application to legal process. Sir William Plumpton, for example, who figures in an important set of private correspondence of the fifteenth-century, was said to be so fond of litigation that he was suing "every true man in the Forest of Knaresborough, where he lived".

The Trial of Joseph and Mary provides an example of a too-hasty condemnation. The Bishop overhears the two detractors, Raise-Slander and Back-Biter, slandering Mary; as was common with moral offences, the Bishop, after hearing the detractors' charges, then conducts the suit himself. As early as Edward I's time, the common law had provided for the punishment of defamation of magnates (though not of commoners) primarily to safeguard the peace of the kingdom: "This was no vain fear at a time when the offended great one was only too ready to resort to arms to redress a fancied injury" (Holdworth, III, 409). The audience knows that there indeed are offended great ones, that God himself could destroy their enemies, but lacking this insight, the detractors and judges act with the assurance that Joseph and Mary would have no legal recourse for the slandering of their names. Local courts freely entertained cases of defamation as did ecclesiastical courts, but the worst that would happen in real life to the detractors would be the fine of a few pence. Thus the second detractor in the **Trial of Joseph and Mary** can taunt the bishop and his lawyers by saying of Mary: "a fayr wench / And feetly with help sche can consent / to set A cokewolde on þe hye benche" (14.94-96). As might be expected under such conditions, the plays argue for forgiveness and argue against bringing suit against one's neighbor. At the end of the cycle, in the Doomsday play, the devils point accusingly at the dammed souls whose sins are written on their foreheads:

> In wratth þi neybore to bakbyte
> them for to hangere was þi delyte
> þou were evyr redy them to endyte. . . .
>
> (42.101-03)

Looking ahead to the first Passion sequence, we find the focus narrowing from a general concern with obedience to God's laws and the advent of the New Law to a more precise concern for reforming English law of the fifteenth century. I am arguing here that the audience was meant to respond to the law of Jesus' day as if it were present-day English law, as well as ancient Judaic law. Jesus opposes Judaic law with his own law of mercy. This conflict, between the existing law identified in the stage directions as the Old Law and Jesus' New Law, presents an interesting question: which aspects of English law as the audience knew it would be criticized by association with the old or corrupt law and which would be help up for emulation as the new or merciful law?

Passion I begins with a prologue in which Lucifer, or Sir Satan as he also calls himself, sets forth the most common criminal abuses of the fifteenth century and takes credit for their proliferation. He uses legal terms and lists the abuses for which he claims responsibility: conspiracy (in order to arrange a conviction); false "reprevys" or evidence; and false witness, "þus xal I false þe wordys þat his pepyl doth testefy" (26, Prologue, 1. 52). He recommends to the audience what was probably the single greatest threat to social order in the fifteenth century: "And yf þe lawe repreve þe[,] say þou wylt ffyth / And gadere þe A felaschep after þin entent" (11. 91-92). Many of the lords and those who swore homage and fealty to them were guilty of carrying out the devil's further advice: "Loke þou sett not be precept nor be comawndement / Both sevyle and Canone [law] sett þou at nowth" (11. 93-94) and "Seyse nere sessyon lete perjery be chef" (1. 114). Perjury was of particular importance since it was the means by which sworn retainers could protect their lords in court. As a crime it was punishable only by common law if committed by jurors; otherwise the notoriously lax ecclesiastical courts had jurisdiction, so, as Holdsworth explains [in *A History of English Law*] perjurors were relatively safe.

After this introduction to contemporary perversions of law and order, the audience can identify the work of the judges and lawyers who conduct the trial of Jesus in **Passion I** and **II** as the work of the devil. After describing his motives and his methods, Lucifer retires and allows the more familiar legal figures to act out his words.

This exposé of contemporary legal abuses begins in the next play, **The Council of Jews**. The **Ludus Coventriae** playwright elaborates on the brief biblical description of the council ("alle the prestis and scribis and eldere men") in order to describe contemporary figures of authority. He dresses Annas like a fifteenth-century ecclesiastical judge: "*in a skarlet gowne and ouer þat a blew tabbard furryd with whyte and a mytere on his hed after þe hoold lawe*" (26.40sd). R. T. Davies explains that Annas is described as a bishop of the Old Law as contrasted with the New Law of Christ and that Jewish High Priests were commonly represented as mitred bishops. Obviously, the association was a damaging one for contemporary English bishops. To the common people, Annas and Caiaphas presented a realistic picture of English bishops—who were hardly known, even to their clergy, except in their judicial capacity—as well as an imaginary picture of Jewish judges. Their entourage is also realistic in fifteenth-century terms. The two doctors accompanying Annas wear furred hoods and furred caps, the traditional dress of fifteenth-century lay and ecclesiastical judges. Caiaphas, also accompanied by two lawyers, is arrayed like Annas. Rewfyn and Lyon, two more furred judges, represent the common law; more specifically, their striped robes identify them as sergeants-at-law. This makes six realistically costumed lawyers. The council scene as a whole is carefully constructed so as to impress the audience with a show of contemporary power: the costumes and characters represent the range of authority in a late medieval town.

These lawyers and judges meet in a council strikingly similar to the so-called king's "Council Learned in the Law," a part of Henry VII's council especially concerned with judiciary matters. This body was composed of two bishops and ten other justices and lawyers. Since the council appears to have functioned mainly as a debt-collecting agency for the king, it seems unlikely that it served as a model for the council of the Jews. However, the king's council at large, whether under Henry VII or any of his predecessors, might well have served as such a model. As a court of law, the king's council acted like a presenting jury, that is, it investigated charges, examined witnesses, and drew up indictments. Its jurisdiction did not extend to treason, so it would have referred a case like that of Jesus to a common law court, which is precisely what happens in **Ludus Coventriae**. The fifteenth-century council's indictment procedure was supposedly an unbiased attempt to find the facts before arresting a subject. In reality, the council rarely went to the trouble to indict unless its objective was to get an offender before the courts. In this respect, the Council of the Jews is realistic; it is biased from the start. It sends out for evidence which will support its views. The judges follow due process, as they must—"We may not do hym to meche myscheve / Þe worschep of oure lawe to save" (27.448-49)—but they have already decided to prosecute Jesus.

In the fifteenth century such an injustice could only be carried out by careful attention to procedural details. At the beginning of the *Passion I* sequence, in *Council of Jews I,* the second doctor of laws reminds Annas:

> Sere remembre þe gret charge þat on yow is
>   leyd
> Þe lawe to ke[ep] which may not ffayle
> Yf any defawth prevyd of yow be seyd
> Þe jewys with trewth wyl yow a-sayl
> Tak hed whath cownsayl may best provayl.
>   (26.25-29)

He goes on to suggest that Annas call two "temperal jewgys, þat knowyth þe parayl," a procedure unique to this cycle. When Caiaphas appears, he agrees that they must "seke A mene on to hym reprevable" (26.55) which I understand to mean "seek a means of proving something against him" or, in practical terms, find an accusation which will ensure a conviction. He admits that they nothing with which to convict him at the moment: "for yf he procede be prossesse oure lawys he wyl felle" (26.60), and again, "I cannot dem hym with-outh trespace" (26.140). The members of the council make their feelings clear to the audience, even while they mouth the appropriate legal formulas. Rewfin calls him "An eretyk and a tretour bolde. . .worthy to dey with mekyl peyn" (26.145-48), and the first lawyer with Annas informs the "rewelerys of þe lawe" that they must give judgment that "Let hym fyrst ben hangyn and drawe / and þanne his body in fyre be brent" (26.153-56). Annas reasserts the "rule of law" with which they all agree, saying:

> These ix days let us A-byde
> We may not gyf so hasty jugement
> but eche man inqwere on his syde
> Send spyes A-bouth þe countre wyde
> to se and recorde and testymonye
> And þan hese werkys he xal not hyde
> nor haue no power hem to denye.
>   (26.170-76)

In the next play in *Passion I, Jesus' Entry into Jerusalem,* Jesus' free and simple mercy contrasts markedly with the intricate manipulations of the law in the council play. His four-line refrain beginning, "Ffrendys beholde þe tyme of mercy / þe wich is come now withowtyn dowth" is repeated again at the end of the play. In contrast to the complexity of the Old Law, or of the common law which is analogous to it, are Jesus' simple laws, to love God above all else and to love thy neighbor as thyself.

The second Council of the Jews play follows Jesus' entry into Jerusalem; while he is preaching mercy, the judges and lawyers are plotting. The dialogue in the second council play—like that of the first—alternates between conscientious legalities and brutality until finally the identification of one with the other is inescapable.

This play, in its turn, is followed by two plays about mercy: *Maundy II* in which Maria Magdalen appeals to Jesus for mercy and is forgiven and *Maundy III* which, as Stanley Kahrl suggests (p. 64), contrasts even more skillfully with the council scenes. Jesus eats his paschal lamb "in the same form as the old law does specify," and "as in the old law it was commanded." Here as elsewhere he is careful to abide by the old precepts. As he does so, the Jews in their council plot to kill him for supposedly disobeying those strictures. the irony works effectively to stress the inhumanity of the Mosaic law and to promote the New Law of mercy.

What can we say, in summary, are the legal abuses complained of in the *Passion I* sequence and the legal reforms promoted by these nine plays? The crimes described by Lucifer—conspiracy, use of false evidence, and false witness—are committed by the bishops, Annas and Caiaphas, who are costumed so as to implicate present-day bishops in their actions, and by the council as a whole, whose costumes, as Eleanor Prosser explains [in *Drama and Religion in the English Mystery Plays,* 1961] were basically contemporary. The councilmen conspire to convict Jesus, they send out spies to gather evidence against him, and they pay Judas to be their false witness. These pretrial proceedings against Jesus are described in extra-scriptural detail (the council scenes in *Ludus Coventriae* number a total of 242 lines as compared to the biblical 2) because these formed the weakest link in common law procedure at that time (Bellamy, pp. 213-14). Those in power, particularly the king, tampered with legal process only where no proper rules existed, that is, most especially with the machinery for indictment. Thus, in the fifteenth century, we find the king's legal advisers increasingly framing indictments and conducting extensive interrogations in order to get a confession before putting a defendant on trial (Bellamy, p. 213) which is precisely the situation presented in *Passion I.* This covert form of pressure is protested most strongly in the council scenes. These scenes, reflecting as they do the range of authority in a late medieval town, contain severe criticism of the fifteenth-century legal establishment as a whole—an establishment which is shown to be prone to bias, to perversion of procedures, to hypocrisy, and to brutality. Annas and Caiaphas clearly state their rejection of the supremacy of law—that is, of the rule of law—and they state this twice for emphasis. The plays, using Jesus as an exemplar, promote instead acceptance of the rule of law (Jesus is shown carefully obeying the law in both spirit and letter) and reformation of the Old Law into the New Law. Jesus stands as a living symbol of the New Law: he is the sacrifice which will redeem all men. He enters Jerusalem, holding open his arms, saying "Ffrendys be-holde þe tyme of mercy," offering the audience his simple all-embracing law. Coming as it does after the backroom scheming and conscientious but hypocritical legalities of the council scenes, Jesus' entrance dramatizes the desired legal reform: the audience is invited to turn away from the complexity and corruption of the common law and accept instead Jesus' two simple laws: to love God above all else and to love thy neighbor as thyself.

Gail McMurray Gibson (essay date 1981)

SOURCE: "Bury St. Edmunds, Lydgate, and the N-Town Cycle," in *Speculum*, Vol. CVI, No. 1, January, 1981, pp. 56-90.

[*In this seminal essay, Gibson asserts that the* N-Town *plays originated not in Lincoln but in the abbey of Bury St. Edmunds.*]

No scholar of medieval English drama needs to be reminded of the old and unsolved puzzle of the provenance of the fifteenth-century cycle of mystery plays preserved in MS B. L. Cotton Vespasian D.viii. The so-called *N-Town Cycle* has been plagued by a series of misnomers, erroneous catalogue descriptions, and confusions of place attribution ever since about 1629, when Sir William Cotton's librarian wrote on the flyleaf of the manuscript, "vulgo dicitur hic liber Ludus Coventriae." Three hundred and fifty years and many errors later, all that can be said with complete confidence about the Cotton manuscript is that [according to Mark Eccles in "*Ludus Coventriae:* Lincoln or Norfolk?" *Medium Ævum* 40, 1971] it "has absolutely nothing to do with Coventry," and that it badly needs a standardized title of reference. Having neither local habitation nor a name, the *N-Town* plays remain the most mysterious of mystery plays. All efforts to reconstruct text, images, and staging are grievously hampered by our ignorance about the local historical circumstances which shaped them.

Thomas Sharp in his *Dissertation on the Pageants or Dramatic Mysteries, Anciently Performed at Coventry* pointed out as early as 1825 that the plays in the Cotton Vespasian manuscript are entirely different from the two extant plays in the *Coventry Cycle* and inconsistent with everything that was recorded about the subjects, costumes, and staging at Coventry. In 1893 Bernhard ten Brink noted [in his *Geschichte der Englischen Litteratur* 2, 1893] that the dialect and scribal characteristics

of the so-called *Ludus Coventriae* pointed to the East Midlands rather than to the western region of Coventry, and a few early scholars like Pollard and Dodds expressed the opinion that [according to Pollard in his *English Miracle Plays, Moralities, and Interludes,* 1922] "further investigation will lead to the decisive connection of this cycle, not with Coventry but with the Eastern Counties." But in the ensuing years there have been a host of other candidates for N-Town, including towns as far removed from East Anglia as Durham (because the manuscript's earliest known owner, Robert Hegge, was from Durham) and Northampton (simply because it was a large and prosperous medieval town whose name started with *N*), and there have been scholars who argued that the N-Town of the banns stood simply for the "Nomen" to be supplied by a touring company, and that therefore the *N-Town Cycle* had no name in the strict sense. E. K. Chambers [in *The Mediaeval Stage,* 1903] suggested that the *N* stood for Norwich, and several recent studies have supported the Norwich theory on the basis of the dialect of the plays, even though the contradictions between what was recorded of the lost Norwich plays and the *N-Town* manuscript are every bit as great as the contradictions which 150 years ago eliminated Coventry from consideration.

The hypothesis of Hardin Craig [in his *English Religious Drama of the Middle Ages,* 1955] that the cathedral city of Lincoln was the home of the *N-Town Cycle* was published in what became the classic (if nowadays sometimes maligned) survey of medieval English drama; since Craig's *English Religious Drama* has been read and cited so often, sheer repetition as well as the weight of Hardin Craig's authority has made the theory of the Lincoln provenance of the *N-Town Cycle* more widely known than any other. Despite the manifest differences between the East Anglian dialect of the Cotton Vespasian manuscript and the dialect of medieval Lincolnshire, Craig's attribution of the *N-Town* plays to Lincoln remained an attractive and viable hypothesis to many scholars, largely because they viewed the learned Latin notes in the *N-Town* manuscript as evidence that the text was a collector's literary compilation and not an official register or local acting version of the plays. The Lincoln theory of origin was reaffirmed by Kenneth Cameron and Stanley Kahrl in an article entitled "The N-Town Plays at Lincoln," [*Theatre Notebook* 20, 1965] but Kahrl's exhaustive search through the Lincoln records [as recorded in his *Records of Plays and Papers in Lincolnshire 1300-1585*] uncovered "no new documents bearing directly on the location of the N-Town cycle." Moreover, Kahrl and Peter Meredith have recently acknowledged [in *N-Town Plays*] that the inscriptions and marginal notations in the manuscript prove that the text was not merely an antiquarian's collection, but had been revised as a prompt book, "clearly for theatrical production."

I intend to show that it is possible to counter Craig's

oft-repeated proofs for a Lincoln provenance of the *N-Town Cycle* with arguments for Bury St. Edmunds, a town which not only passes all Craig's tests for likelihood of origin, but also offers the right dialect. The setting at Bury St. Edmunds is appropriate to the unique nodal construction of the cycle and its apparent use for touring performances. And Bury St. Edmunds provides the necessary link with John Lydgate, an extremely likely influence, direct or indirect, upon the composition of the plays.

I

As far as I have been able to determine, a rather off-hand paragraph by Madeline Dodds in 1914 ["The Problem of the *Ludus Coventriae*," *Modern Language Review* 9] was the first (and nearly the last) time in modern drama scholarship that Bury St. Edmunds was nominated as the home of the *N-Town* plays. Since that paragraph appeared as an afterthought at the end of an article whose attempts to reconstruct the original play groups of the *N-Town* manuscript were subsequently roundly refuted, it is understandable why her suggestion was not taken more seriously. It has now been more than fifty years, in fact, since Bury St. Edmunds has been considered a serious contender for the place of origin of the *N-Town Cycle*.

One reason for this neglect is the fact that the public records of Bury St. Edmunds offer few suggestions about the town's significance as a dramatic center. Bury St. Edmunds, unlike York or Chester or Wakefield or Coventry, was a monastic borough; the ancient, great Benedictine abbey of St. Edmund served as administrator of the town without its walls as well as of the community of monks within. Since the borough was under the jurisdiction of monastic lords, it was forbidden a merchant guild and was largely exempt from royal taxation and control by the crown, so that it lacks many of the usual historical records which medieval towns left for posterity. Whatever municipal records did exist were kept by the abbey, and most perished with it during the dissolution in the sixteenth century. Even the register of the abbey's history, which had been carefully kept in the early Middle Ages, was allowed to lapse in the fifteenth century. As more than one historian has lamented, [including Walter F. Schirmer *John Lydgate: A Study in the Culture of the XVth Century,* 1961] "we know little about the last ninety years of the monastery's existence."

From the sparse documents that do survive from Bury St. Edmunds in the fifteenth century, historians have pieced together the picture of a vigorous and thriving town, grown enormously prosperous in the Suffolk cloth trade and reconciled to administrative control by the abbey after failed attempts in the fourteenth century to secure self-government by riot and rebellion. And, unlike most English monastic houses in their final years,

St. Edmunds Abbey seems to have been blessed with prosperity and achievement as great as that of the burgesses it ruled. Especially under the great abbot William Curteys, personal friend and advisor to Henry VI, the fifteenth century brought a golden age for the abbey. As A. Goodwin commented [in *St. Edmundsbury*],

> As far as any interpretation can be placed on the activities of the monks in the fifteenth century, it must be concluded that the decay of the monastic spirit, which was typical of most English abbeys at the time, had no place at St. Edmunds. The reorganization of the finances, the reform of discipline, the erection of the monastic library, the complete rebuilding of the abbey church after 1465, and the vindication of the abbey's jurisdiction over the town make the period one of solid achievement.

Even John ap Rice, one of Cromwell's most notorious scandalmongers, could find little more to report from his visitation to St. Edmunds Abbey in 1535 than that the abbot "lay much forth in his granges," liked to play at dice and cards, and "seemeth to be addict to the maintaining of such superstitious ceremonies as hath been used heretofore." "As touching the convent," his letter to Cromwell continues, "we could get little or no reports among them, although we did use much diligence in our examination. . . ."

It is certain that there were religious dramatic observances in late medieval Bury (ap Rice's "superstitious ceremonies"?), although the records tell us little more than the fact that they existed. The guild certificate returns of 1389 list eighteen religious guilds and confraternities at Bury St. Edmunds; one of them, the Corpus Christi guild of St. James Church, included as one of its official functions that of providing an "interludium" of Corpus Christi. Nothing is recorded of the subject of the play, but Karl Young, [in "An Interludium for a Gild of Corpus Christi," *Modern Language Notes* 48, 1933] hypothesized that the seriousness with which the Corpus Christi guild's responsibilities for the "interlude" are detailed suggests "that in its subject the play at Bury St. Edmund's was related to the central theme of Corpus Christi day." The sole surviving craft guild records from Bury, the Weaver's Craft Ordinances of 1477, specify that one half of fines paid for craft rule violations was to be paid to the sacristan of the abbey (who had titular control over all town markets and trade) and that one half was to go for

> the sustentacione and mayntenaunce of the payent of the Assencione of oure Lord God and of the yiftys of the Holy Gost, as yt hath be customed of olde tyme owte of mynde yeerly to be had to the wurschepe of God, amongge other payenttes in the procession in the feste of Corpus Xri.

Since we know nothing about other craft guilds in late

medieval Bury, there are no clues about what the subjects of those "other payenttes" might have been, or even, as E. K. Chambers observed [in *Mediaeval Stage*], whether the Weaver's Guild document refers to a dumb show procession or a mystery play. A second brief reference to the Bury "pageants," hitherto unnoticed by drama historians, appears at the foot of a note of rents, dated 1558, from the Bury Guildhall. At the bottom of this paper roll is the heading for an inventory (apparently not completed) of all movable goods possessed by the Guildhall "except for certain pageants," presumably by this time merely old carts or timbers stored among the Guildhall possessions. That there were elaborate liturgical processions in fifteenth-century Bury can be inferred from a will of 1463 which leaves money to build a new door in St. Mary's Church so that when "the parysh lyke to go p[ro]cessyon through the north ele, and so forth before the hy[g]h awter. . .the dore may be of a resonnable heyghte that they may passe with the cros in goodly wyse"; what cannot be inferred is whether such processions were also part of liturgical dramas.

But if these records of dramatic performance and procession in Bury St. Edmunds do little more than attest to the fact that religious drama and ceremonial was observed there, the cumulative evidence of surviving East Anglian play texts presents remarkably suggestive evidence for the importance of Bury as a dramatic center in the late Middle Ages. One of the very earliest English dramatic texts is the so-called *Rickinghall Fragment,* an early fourteenth-century parchment scrap containing fragments from a speech by a tyrant king and a single Latin rubric directing, "Tunc dicet nuncio." This fragmentary speech, rendered in Anglo-Norman with English paraphrase, appears on the back of accounts of the year 1370 relating to Rickinghall Manor, a Suffolk estate which belonged to the abbots of Bury St. Edmunds until the seizure of abbey lands in the sixteenth century. Dialect argues for also assigning a fifteenth-century fragmentary drama text, the *Dux Moraud Fragment,* to Bury St. Edmunds; as Norman Davis has observed [in *Non-Cycle Plays and Fragments,* 1970] the closest analogues to the dialect of the *Dux Moraud* text are found in B. L. Sloane 2593, a manuscript which "is clearly from Bury St. Edmunds, probably as Greene says, from the monastery." The *Croxton Play of the Sacrament,* apparently performed at Croxton, Norfolk (about fourteen miles north of Bury), contains a reference to Babwell Mill, a mill just outside the north gate of Bury which appears in the possessions list of the abbey in the royal appropriation accounts of 1538/39. Most significantly, the two most important English medieval morality play manuscripts, the *Digby Plays* and the *Macro Plays,* are known to have been in Bury St. Edmunds in the sixteenth century; indeed all the evidence seems to suggest that the texts were once owned by the abbey itself.

As Howard Patch first noted, and D. C. Baker and J.

L. Murphy have recently verified [in "The *Ludus Coventriae* and the Digby Massacre," *PMLA* 35, 1920; "The Late Medieval Plays of Ms. Digby 133: Scribes, Dates and Early History," *Research Opportunities in Renaissance Drama* 10, 1967], the East Anglian *Digby Plays* can be linked with Bury St. Edmunds through Myles Blomefylde, whose name appears several times in the margins of the manuscript. Blomefylde, an alchemist, physician, and book collector who was born in Bury St. Edmunds in 1525, may have been related, suggest Baker and Murphy, to the William Blomefylde who a century earlier was a monk of Bury monastery. Beyond the relationship suggested by the name is the fact that Miles Blomefylde owned a copy of a philosophical treatise written by the monk Blomefylde in which he inscribed a lengthy note indicating considerable personal knowledge of the earlier Blomefylde's life, scholarship, and command of languages.

The *Macro Plays* texts are also in an East Anglian dialect. They mention a "tapster of Bury" (in the play of *Mankind*) and allude to several other local Suffolk, Norfolk, and Cambridgeshire towns circumscribing the Bury St. Edmunds area. Latin inscriptions in the margins of the manuscript reveal that a "Monk Hyngham" was the owner of the plays, almost certainly, as D. C. Baker and J. L. Murphy have recently argued, the Richard Hyngham who was abbot of Bury St. Edmunds from 1474 to 1479. The *Macro Plays* manuscript first surfaced in the eighteenth century in the collection of an antiquary and book collector named Cox Macro. Not only was Cox Macro a native of Bury St. Edmunds, but his father, Thomas, had served five terms as mayor of the town and for several years as one of the elected governors of Bury School, a free grammar school which until the dissolution of the monastery had been administered by the monks of Bury St. Edmunds. Many of the manuscripts in Cox Macro's collection, including the *Great Register of Bury Abbey* from the time of the abbacy of William Curteys, had come from the library of the monastery, and there is reason to think that the *Macro Plays* manuscript was one of them.

D. C. Baker and J. L. Murphy conclude from their researches into the owners of the *Macro* and *Digby* manuscripts that "the monastery at Bury St. Edmunds was the center of some interest in drama in the fifteenth and early sixteenth centuries; some monks, or at least one, apparently prized religious plays in their libraries; there is at least the possibility that some of those plays were performed there." When we consider the fact that Bury St. Edmunds can be associated with a Corpus Christi "interludium" and pageant, with play texts and fragments including morality plays (*The Castle of Perseverance* and *Mankind* from the *Macro* manuscript), saints' plays (the Digby *Mary Magdalen* and *Conversion of St. Paul*), and a mystery play (the Digby *Killing of the Children*), we must assume that Bury St. Edmunds was not only the center of "some interest in drama" but the center of important and diverse dramatic activity at which the surviving texts can only hint. When Bury St. Edmunds first emerged as a center of dramatic activity, we have, of course, no way of knowing. But it may be significant that by 1150 the monastery at Bury St. Edmunds owned a manuscript containing not only the complete comedies of Terence, but eight plays of Plautus which seem to have been otherwise unknown in England until the very end of the Middle Ages. In the twelfth century, St. Albans, East Anglia's other great Benedictine monastery, also owned a rare manuscript of the plays of Terence, and although St. Edmunds Abbey has left us no visual record of dramatic performances like that which Otto Pächt has argued [in *The Rise of Pictorial Narrative in Twelfth-Century England*, 1962] survives in the famous *St. Albans Psalter,* it may be that both of these monasteries, like the great Benedictine houses of France, developed an early and sustained interest in drama. Certainly it is true, as R. M. Thomson has observed [in "The Library of Bury St. Edmunds Abbey in the Eleventh and Twelfth Centuries," *Speculam* 47, 1972] that the Bury library resembled "Northern French libraries such as those of. . .Fleury rather than other large English collections, particularly in its possession of unusual classics. . . ," and, as Rosemary Woolf has warned [in her *The English Mystery Plays,* 1972] that medieval ignorance of the classical dramatic tradition has been overemphasized. Many other old and confidently held assumptions about medieval drama are now undergoing revision, and we may come to see that classical dramatic texts exerted far more influence upon the emerging Christian drama than we have realized.

It would be very interesting to know what exactly was in the "play boks" which were bequeathed by a Sir Robert Cooke, vicar of Haughley, in a Bury will dated 1537, just two years before the dissolution of the monastery. But whatever plays, classical or medieval, may have been in those play books or on the backs of now-lost manor accounts and school-boy scribblings, I think it very possible that one of Bury St. Edmund's dramatic texts was the *N-Town Cycle*.

One important argument for associating the *N-Town Cycle* with Bury is its similarity to the other two East Anglian drama manuscripts, the *Macro Plays* and the *Digby Plays,* which seem to have come from the monastery library. The Macro play of the *Castle of Perseverance* is introduced by a bann which is very like that which proclaims the *N-Town Cycle*; in the case of the *Castle of Perseverance,* a blank instead of the phrase "N-Town" signals where the appropriate town name is to be inserted. Rubrics also suggest that the staging of the *Castle of Perseverance*—scaffolds grouped around a central platea—closely resembled the staging of the once-independent Passion plays which were incorporated into the *N-Town Cycle*. Relationships between the *N-Town Cycle* and the *Digby Plays* are even more

clear. The *N-Town Cycle* and the Digby play of *Mary Magdalene* employ similar staging conventions (the moving pageant wagon ships, for example, used in conjunction with a place-and-scaffold stage in the *N-Town* **Noah** play and in *Mary Magdalene*) and use a similar dramatic technique of rapid shifts back and forth from one scaffold to another to establish the effect of simultaneous action or an irony of juxtaposition. The poignancy achieved in the *N-Town* "Conception of the Virgin" by the rapid shift from Joachim's prayer in the wilderness to Anna's "simultaneous" prayer at home (as each asks that God spare the other spouse the pain and humiliation of their barrenness) is one notable example of a technique of dramatic simultaneity that is characteristic of both of these texts. The sudden shift in the Digby *Mary Magdalene* from the banquet of Cyrus to the courts of Herod and Pilate, and then back again to Cyrus's banquet as sickness and death inexplicably seize him, creates a dramatic irony remarkably like the sudden entrance of Death in the *N-Town* "Death of Herod." And in the Resurrection episodes in *N-Town* and the Digby *Mary Magdalene*, the family resemblance between the dramaturgy of the two texts extends to some unusually close verbal correspondences, even for a dramatic episode as conservative in its development as the *Visitatio*:

(N-Town) "*Sey to my bretheryn* þat I *intende*
　　　　　to *stey to my fadyr* and to yowre
　　　　　to oure lord both god and frende
　　　　　I wyl Ascende to *hevyn towre.*"
　　　　　　　　　　　　　(*LC* 46-9)

(Digby) "Butt go, *sey to my brotheryn* I will *pretend*
　　　　　to *stey to my Fadyr* in *hev[n]ly towers.*"
　　　　　　　　　　　　(emphasis mine)
　　　　　　　　　　　　(Digby 1076-7)

The closest relationships of all exist between the *N-Town Cycle* and the Digby *Killing of the Children*. These include not only the same dialect and scribal characteristics but similar stanza forms (an "unusual combination of tumbling metre with double quatrains" [according to the *Manual of the Writings in Middle English*]), the same kind of expository prologue and unusually full English stage directions, and even the same unusual placement of the Purification play before instead of after the play of the **Massacre of the Innocents**. The stylistic relationship between the Digby *Killing of the Children* and the *N-Town Cycle* is so close that Howard Patch even suggested that the Digby *Killing of the Children* might once have been a part of the *N-Town Cycle*. It may also be significant that the *poeta* to the Digby *Killing of the Children* makes it clear that the play was performed on St. Anne's Day, just when, many scholars have argued, the Marian plays from the *N-Town Cycle*, with their unusual emphasis upon the figure of St. Anne, must have been performed. The exposition on the importance of the Candlemas feast (celebrating the Purification of the Virgin) in the prologue of the Digby *Killing of the Children* and the reverent treatment of the Purification in the *N-Town Cycle* (in which Mary is hailed as "Salver of Seknes" and "lanterne of lyght") suggest not only another shared feast day emphasis, but a special appropriateness to the town of Bury St. Edmunds. M. D. Lobel in a study of medieval Bury St. Edmunds has observed that the Candlemas Guild was the most prominent religious guild in Bury in the fifteenth century. It performed those administrative duties which a central merchant guild performed in non-monastic boroughs and acted as guardian of the town's common funds and trustee for lands left to the town. After the dissolution of chantries and religious guilds in the sixteenth century, the Bury Candlemas Guild seems to have simply changed its name and quietly become in fact what it had long been in essence, the governing corporate body of the town. It should give us pause that the only play singled out by a specific date in the *N-Town* manuscript is the **"Play of the Purification"** (dated 1468), a play which would have been of particular civic importance to Bury.

Nearly all we know about the Candlemas Guild at Bury comes from brief statements in will bequests and from the 1389 guild certificates which indicate that the guild, there listed as the Gild of St. Mary of St. James church, assembled for mass at the feast of the Purification and held a colloquium or court called "Morwespeche" the following day. Since February 2, the feast day of the Purification, would have been an obviously inauspicious time for outdoor dramatic performances, it is possible that the guild transfered part of the celebration of the feast to St. Anne's Day and summer. But the absence of records make this pure speculation; if we had better fifteenth-century records from Bury St. Edmunds we might know not only much more about the functions of the prestigious and powerful Candlemas Guild, but perhaps also more about dramatic activity at Bury. We might also know whether it is merely coincidence, or the missing documentary proof of the origin of the *N-Town Cycle*, that an early sixteenth-century bequest in the Bury probate office mentions a Robert Hegge in connection with the Candlemas Guild, the very name borne by the Durham antiquary who a hundred years later will be the first recorded owner of the *N-Town Cycle* manuscript.

Even without this kind of "happy historic find" which Elbert Thompson [in "The Ludus Coventriae," *Modern Language Notes* 21, 1906] yearned for in 1960 to solve the mystery of the provenance of the *N-Town Cycle*—documentary evidence which could establish a connection between the Hegge family of Bury and the Durham family of that name—enough evidence exists, I think, to show us Bury St. Edmunds as a likely place of origin, not only for the Digby *Killing of the Children*,

but for the *N-Town Cycle* to which it is related.

If we turn from the evidence for drama texts at Bury to the manuscript of the *N-Town Cycle* itself, the likelihood of Bury as a place of origin becomes still clearer. First of all, as we have already seen, Craig's assertion that "the dialect of the manuscript points straight to Lincoln" has been shown to be patently untrue. Scribal peculiarities and dialectal features, especially the appearance of x for s in words like *xal* and *xulde,* at once rule out a Lincolnshire scribe, and both Mark Eccles [in "*Ludus Coventriae*"] and Jacob Bennett [in "Language and Home," *Orbis*, 1973] have presented detailed linguistic analyses of the East Anglian features of the text. Both studies were written with the intention of proving the Norwich provenance of the *N-Town* plays, and were largely motivated by the extensive records of dramatic performances which survive from late medieval Norwich. But although Jacob Bennett declares that "the language of the cycle as it has come down to us can be shown to conform to that of Norfolk in the fifteenth century," it is important to realize that all the dialect features he discusses are equally characteristic of fifteenth-century Suffolk. In fact, both Bennett and Eccles acknowledge throughout their analyses that the "Norfolk" dialectal features of the *N-Town* manuscript appear in works by John Lydgate from Bury St. Edmunds and by Osbern Bokenham from the nearby Suffolk town of Clare. This should hardly be surprising; in matter of dialect as well as of government, Suffolk and Norfolk formed a single unit in the fifteenth century, a vestige of the time when both counties had been joined as the ancient kingdom of the East Angles. As Samuel Moore observed in his study of fifteenth-century literary patronage in East Anglia ["Patrons of Letters in Norfolk and Suffolk, c. 1450," *PMLA* 27, 1912] "Norfolk and Suffolk, though nominally two counties, were practically but one. They were (for many purposes, at least) an administrative unit, and were presided over by a single sheriff." Very recent and as yet unpublished researches of Angus McIntosh and Michael Samuels have assigned the main scribe of the *N-Town* manuscript to the neighborhood of Harling, in south-central Norfolk (less than twenty miles from Bury St. Edmunds), and Stephen Spector ["The Provenance of the N-Town Codex," *The Library*, 1979] reports that "Professor Samuels ascribes one play, the interpolated **'Assumption of Mary,'** to a Bury exemplar and suggests that the scribe who copied this play may have been a Bury man himself." The fact that all the scribal hands in the *N-Town* manuscript show distinct East Anglian dialectal features makes the possibility of East Anglian scribes writing in Lincoln highly unlikely; as Stephen Spector concludes, "the fact that the constituents were added by several East Anglian scribes, each of whom evidently wrote at a different time, would appear to prove the case for compilation and transcription in East Anglia."

Hardin Craig's second major argument for the Lincoln

provenance of the *N-Town* plays was that the theological complexity of the cycle, most clearly demonstrated by the learned problems and paradoxes put to the child Jesus in the **"Christ and the Doctor's Play"** and the elaborate and Latinate verse of the play of **"The Assumption of the Virgin,"** were proof of origin in a learned, ecclesiastical center:

> The learning, the theological culture, and the religious sincerity that appear in the Hegge plays could have been supplied by relatively few places in England in the fifteenth century and in none of them so characteristically as at Lincoln.

It is accurate to characterize the *N-Town Cycle* as learned, Latinate and theologically sophisticated, but whatever "ecclesiastical culture" Lincoln could have offered as a major cathedral town would have been dwarfed by comparison with Bury St. Edmunds. The ancient Benedictine abbey of St. Edmunds was one of the greatest centers of ecclesiastical learning in England in the Middle Ages, the home of many Oxford-trained monks and of a library that contained the then-enormous number of 2,000 manuscripts, which in the fifteenth century was probably second only to Oxford itself. Indeed Derek Pearsall [in his *John Lydgate,* 1970] has characterized the Bury monastery in the time of Lydgate as "something like Oxford or Cambridge colleges in the eighteenth century—wealthy, privileged, celibate, rich in books and heavy with tradition, learned and scholarly. . . ." Lydgate's abbot, William Curteys, undertook the construction of a special building to house the library in about 1430 and the collection was carefully recatalogued. An allotment of four hours or more for reading and study was part of the daily Benedictine routine; at St. Edmunds the monks had available to them patristic commentators and scholastic theologians, classical texts (both standard and rare), chronicles, encyclopedias, books of medicine, mathematics and astronomy. The Bury scriptorium, especially renowned for its twelfth-century *Bury Bible,* continued to produce books throughout the fifteenth century, and many texts were composed as well as transcribed and illuminated there. There was a rich literary as well as scholarly tradition at Bury, especially of vernacular saints' lives; between Denis Pyramus's Anglo-Norman verse life of St. Edmund in the twelfth century and Lydgate's famous *Legend of St. Edmund* written for presentation to Henry VI, Bury monks wrote such works as an Anglo-Norman *Life of St. Faith* and a *Miracles of the Virgin,* a narrative poem of the "Fifteen Joys of Mary" in tail-rhyme stanzas, and the only preserved English carols in honor of St. Nicholas and St. Edmund.

The third, perhaps the major, argument made by Hardin Craig in favor of Lincoln's "theological culture" as the source of the *N-Town Cycle* was the connection he saw between the marked Marian emphasis of the *N-Town* plays and the evidence at Lincoln for a cathedral play of the Assumption of the Virgin and of special veneration of Mary and St. Anne. Although it is true that the *N-Town* "Assumption" play shows evidence of a once-independent existence and perhaps of staging in a church (if we assume that the organ referred to in the rubrics was not a portable instrument), Assumption plays seem to have been common in East Anglia. Alan Nelson has published the record of an Assumption play from the Corpus Christi cycle at Ipswich [in *Medieval English Stage,* 1974] and after searching unpublished drama records in Suffolk and Norfolk, John Wasson has reported [in "Drama Approached through Historical Documents," a paper delivered at the Research Approaches to Medieval Drama Seminar at the 1978 MLA convention] that "there were several Assumption plays in towns whose churches were dedicated to the Virgin." If the interpolated **"Assumption of the Virgin"** in the *N-Town Cycle* is connected to a specific church and to church performance, there is a likely candidate at Bury St. Edmunds in the parish church of St. Mary. Built by the abbey within its own grounds to serve as one of the two parish churches for the Bury townspeople, St. Mary's seems to have been specifically dedicated in the fifteenth century to the "Assumption of the Blessed Mary"; that, at least, is the title given to it by the medieval historian William Worcestre who visited the church and carefully recorded the structure's measurements in his *Itineraries* of 1478-80. It may also be significant that there is documented evidence of "pleyers at ye orgenys" in St. Mary's Church by 1463.

Craig's claim for Lincoln as "a place especially dedicated to the worship and honour of the Blessed Virgin Mary" is a nearly meaningless assertion about a town in fifteenth-century England, a land so famed for its Marian piety that it was popularly known as "Dos Mariae," or the Dower of Mary. Everywhere in England in the late Middle Ages devotion to the Virgin and to her miracles and intercessions threatened to overshadow the worship of her son, and Bury St. Edmunds was no exception. It is certain that Bury St. Edmunds can offer just as much, if not more, evidence of veneration of the Virgin Mary as Lincoln. The first monastic establishment at Bury was founded about 637 to the honor of the Virgin; it was in the Church of St. Mary at Bury, then called Bedericsworth, that Edmund, last of the East Anglian kings, was invested in 856. After Edmund's martyrdom by the Danes and subsequent canonization, his remains were brought to Bedericsworth, where a new church was specially built to receive his shrine. Although Bedericsworth became St. Edmund's Bury, its earlier patroness was not forgotten; the new abbey church was known as "the Basilica of St. Mary and St. Edmund," and the original church of St. Mary continued to be used as a parish church by the townspeople. When expansion of the abbey church in the time of Abbot Baldwin (abbot from 1065 to 1097) necessitated the destruction of the old St. Mary's

Church, the first of the parish churches of St. Mary built on the present site of the southwest corner of the monk's cemetery was begun.

During the abbacy of Simon de Luton (1256-1279) the abbey's chapel of St. Edmund was pulled down and a larger and more splendid Lady Chapel built in its place at the northeast end of the choir. This chapel, fully 70 or 80 feet long and 42 feet wide, was named the "Chapel of the Salutation of the Conception of the Blessed Virgin," an appropriate dedication since it was the feast that Anselm, abbot of Bury from 1121 to 1148, had been instrumental in introducing to England. Although only sparse ruins remain of the abbey church, some idea of the Lady Chapel's iconographic scheme and its splendor can be reconstructed from surviving early fourteenth-century transcriptions which record the inscriptions on paintings and stained glass in the Lady Chapel; of special interest is an inscription which makes it clear that the decoration of the Lady Chapel included a scene of that same allegorical meeting of Pax and Justicia that inaugurates the *N-Town* "**Annunciation Play.**" It was about the time of the construction of the abbey Chapel of the Conception of the Virgin that a Bury monk named Simon of Walsingham wrote his Anglo-Norman *Miracles of St. Mary* and that a monk named Martin wrote "The Fifteen Joys of Mary." Literary praise of the Virgin was also undertaken by a Bury monk named Galfrid Waterton (or Bedericius) who about 1350 wrote both a commentary on the Annunciation and a *Mariale* in praise of Mary.

By the fifteenth century, evidence of veneration of the Virgin at Bury St. Edmunds is omnipresent. Between about 1409 and 1411, John Lydgate, Bury's most famous poet-monk, wrote his *Lyf of Our Lady,* the most ambitious, certainly the longest (5,932 lines), *vita* and hymn of praise to the Virgin in the English language. At about the same time, the present Perpendicular Gothic church of St. Mary was begun, the last and greatest of the parish churches of St. Mary built by the abbey. Like the earlier church, it stood within the gates of the monastery and was financed by the sacristan of the abbey. It is thus clear that although the monastery and town bore the name of St. Edmund, in the fifteenth century as in most of the preceding centuries much of the religious devotion, the energies, the literary and architectural arts, and financial resources of Bury were being directed toward worship of the Virgin. It is a fitting sign of the degree of veneration accorded Mary at Bury St. Edmunds that when Abbot Curteys commissioned a new silver pastoral staff in 1430, he specified that it should have a figure of St. Edmund under a tabernacle in its crook, but on its head the Assumption of the Virgin on one side and the Salutation of the Virgin on the other.

Evidence of individual devotion to the Virgin Mary recorded in Bury wills could be listed indefinitely, but a single important example, the 1463 will of John Baret of Bury, a wealthy clothier and lay treasurer of the abbey, may suffice to demonstrate the extent of the veneration accorded the Virgin by one of Bury's prominent townspeople: John Baret's will specifies that at his funeral, along with five men clad in black in token of the five wounds of Christ that there be "v. wommen clad in white in wurshippe of oure ladyes fyve joyes, eche of them holdyng a torche of clene vexe. . . ." John Baret leaves in his will precise directions for converting the former Lady Chapel of St. Mary's Church into his chantry (a new and larger Lady Chapel was subsequently built for the church by the alderman of Candlemas Guild, Jankyn [John] Smyth). Baret directs that chimes and "the ymage of our lady that Robert Pygot peynted" be set up at the Mary altar, that a new crown be made for the statue of the Virgin at that altar, and that a door to his chantry be constructed near the image of "our lady with the virgenys afore hire." John Baret leaves ten marks "to the peyntyng of rerdoos and table at Seynt Marie awter of the story of the Magnificat," and even directs that within the panels of the Magnificat altarpiece "there be wreten the balladys I made therefore." Finally he leaves funds and characteristically detailed instructions for the repair of the city gate called Rysbygate (the abbey's master mason, Simon Clerk, was to be called in for advice on the soundness of the foundations), specifying that "a twyn the batilment and the arche in the myddys I wil haue an ymage of oure lady, sittyng or stondyng, in an howsyng of free stone, and rememberaunce of me besyde. . . ."

Hardin Craig's argument for Lincoln as home of the *N-Town Cycle* on the basis of the importance of its St. Anne cult is a slightly more useful criterion than that of the ubiquitous cult of the Virgin Mary, although the cult of the Mother of the Virgin, too, as Rosemary Woolf has observed, was firmly fixed in the liturgy by the fifteenth century and influenced several Continental plays. Indeed, Woolf suggests, "one could go as far as to say that the absence of plays on this subject in the other English cycles is an indication that their structure was fixed before the fifteenth-century flourishing of the cult of St. Anne." What may be a more significant consideration in the assessment of likely locations for the *N-Town Cycle* is evidence not of a fifteenth-century cult of St. Anne, but of devotion to Anne in the preceding century when her cult was still relatively unknown in England. St. Anne's Day was not made a feast of obligation until 1382, and even as late as 1389 the guild certificates ordered by Richard II listed only four St. Anne guilds among the 471 religious guilds and confraternities which filed reports. One of these guilds was the St. Anne guild from Lincoln, to which Hardin Craig referred, but another, founded in 1309 (and nearly 40 years before the Lincoln guild) was the Guild of St. Anne from the parish church of St. James in Bury. Since St. James, like St. Mary's, was built within the grounds of the monastery, we must infer that there was by an early date a notable cult of Anne in the abbey church as well. We do know that by the early fifteenth century there was a St. Anne's Chapel in the abbey church and that hymns for the celebration of St. Anne's Day were being given prominent place in monastery service books. The Bury monk John Lydgate wrote two of the four extant Middle English hymns to St. Anne for his patroness, Anne, countess of Stafford, and Lydgate's contemporary Osbern Bokenham, from the nearby Suffolk priory of Clare, included a versified life of St. Anne in his *Legendys of Holy Wommen* (c. 1445). Roscoe Parker has even suggested [in *The Middle English Stanzaic Versions of the Life of Saint Anne*, 1928] that the late fifteenth-century "Invocation to St. Anne" which survives in an East Anglian manuscript in Trinity College, Cambridge, is the text for a quasidramatic St. Anne's Day celebration "written, or at least copied, for the celebration of the annual festival of the St. Anne's Guild of Bury St. Edmunds."

Thus it can be seen, I think, that Hardin Craig's arguments for Lincoln's unique qualifications to be considered as the home of the *N-Town Cycle*'s plays of St. Anne and the Virgin can be discredited along with his arguments based on the dialect of the plays. I do not suggest that the evidence at Bury St. Edmunds of a large monastic library, a widespread veneration of the Virgin Mary and St. Anne, and a church dedicated to the Assumption of the Virgin is proof that Bury is the place of origin of the *N-Town Cycle;* such facts simply provide evidence that the ecclesiastical climate at Bury St. Edmunds would have been a possible place of origin, a place of origin which changes from possible to likely only when we add to these facts the appropriateness of the *N-Town* manuscript's dialect to Bury and the large number of other East Anglian play manuscripts with Bury St. Edmunds connections. The physical and textual evidence of the *N-Town Cycle* manuscript itself—its apparent compilation from an earlier cycle, an independent Mary group, two independent Passion plays, and several other individual plays—argues that its home must have been such a major dramatic center. "At the least," concludes Stephen Spector after a careful analysis of the layers of dramatic material in the manuscript, "it was a place where copies of plays and even small cycles could be obtained and incorporated into a larger cycle, and where revisers and compilers were available over a period of time."

We could also add to these facts the argument that the Bury St. Edmunds provenance of the *N-Town Cycle* might explain what has often been seen as the great contradiction inherent in the *N-Town Cycle* text; that is, it would resolve the apparent contradiction between the "theological sophistication and the dramatic sumptuousness" [Woolf] of the *N-Town* plays and its banns implying a company of itinerant players. If we accept the hypothesis that the monastery at Bury St. Edmunds was the source of the *N-Town Cycle,* this seeming contradiction disappears, for what we have in the *N-Town Cycle* is precisely what we would expect from a large cycle of religious plays which were compiled by a rich and learned monastery for production not only in the borough of Bury itself but also in other parishes, both neighboring and distant, that lay within the administrative and pastoral responsibility of the abbey.

The "First Minister's Account" of the abbey's possessions, compiled at the time of the appropriation of the monastery in 1538-1540, reveals the farflung nature of the monastery's jurisdiction and influence in a staggering list of manors, rectories, tenant and dominical tithes, and leases from lands, tenements, and windmills in dozens of parishes in the western third of Suffolk, in Thetford and several other towns in Norfolk (including two parishes in Norwich), in towns as far removed as Beccles in the far northeast corner of Suffolk, and even in distant Hertfordshire. Direct involvement of the abbey in the affairs of these parishes ranged from the abbey's responsibility to provide peasestraw (*stramen pisarum*) for the church floor at Mildenhall, Suffolk, to the abbey's rights to exact tolls from all strangers passing through the town of Beccles, as well as rights to fair tolls there, percentages of profits "of stalls or shops. . .occupied by divers persons at fair-time," and "tolls of oxen and cows at fair-time." Beccles, along with the towns of Mildenhall, Woolpit, Long Melford, and of course Bury, for which there is also documented evidence of the abbey's control of fairs, would have been likely locations for performances of mystery plays, since such performances would not only have instructed the parishioners whose souls were the responsibility of the abbey, but by attracting visitors and trade to the fairs would have added to the abbey coffers as well. This last fact would have been of no little importance even to a monastery as wealthy as St. Edmunds, especially in the years following 1430 when the collapse of the great West Tower of the abbey church brought huge reconstruction costs to the monastery; in 1432 Abbot Curteys had the remaining walls of the West Tower pulled down and obtained from Rome a free pardon for all those who contributed to the cost of their reconstruction.

That the abbey church was still under construction as late as 1457 can be inferred from the Bury will of Lady Ela Shardelowe who in that year left 100 shillings "ad fabicam noui campanilis mon. de Bury." That new steeple was short-lived. On January 20, 1465, there was a disastrous fire in the abbey church, started by a brazier left burning by builders working on the church tower. An eyewitness account of the fire which survives in British Library MS Cotton Claudius A.xii tells how the church spire and tower collapsed into the choir of the church in flames, burning fiercely all around the shrine of St. Edmund (whose wooden canopy was consumed although the gold shrine itself, says the writer, miraculously remained unscathed), and then how fire raged through the Lady Chapel until it was totally destroyed ("nec prius assistit quam ipsam, licet vino et aqua copiose respersam, scuissimis flammis humi prostrauit"). The account of the Bury fire ends with verses imploring the faithful to replace the lost ornaments of the church. The date 1468 which appears following the *N-Town* play of the Purification and has usually been taken to be the date of the main compilation of the manuscript may well relate to this fire of only three years before. There is ample evidence in East Anglia of the performance of village and community plays to raise money for a local parish church; perhaps the ambitious compilation of plays in the *N-Town* manuscript was made for the purpose of rebuilding the great monastery church of Bury St. Edmunds. What more fitting way could there have been to raise money to restore the abbey's ruined Lady Chapel than performances of a mystery play cycle which set the life of the Virgin at its heart.

It seems to me a very attractive hypothesis that the abbey of Bury St. Edmunds, a monastery of wealth and influence greater in the fifteenth century than most English cities, commissioned and sponsored the cycle of religious plays in the Cotton Vespasian D.viii manuscript and supervised the performance of the cycle, or of play groups from it, at Bury and at various other parishes within the boundaries of the Liberty of St. Edmund. What gives considerable credence to this hypothesis is the quite remarkable fact that at least eleven Suffolk towns and villages with documented evidence for plays or play manuscripts before the Reformation were either under the rectorship of the Bury St. Edmunds monastery, or were towns where the abbey owned property or fair rights. If the *N-Town Cycle* was composed for presentation at some of these towns, it is easier to understand why the cycle was constructed as a collection of self-sufficient play groups, of which the Old Testament plays with their concluding sermon by Moses, the **Contemplatio** group which comprises most of the Mary section, the two **Passion** play groups, and the independent play of **"The Assumption of the Virgin"** are the most conspicuous examples. Perhaps the cycle was performed in its entirety in Bury itself, and then play groups from it presented at other Suffolk parishes as logistics, the number of actors available, and the particular occasion required. Marginal notations which have been added to folios 189 through 196 of the Cotton Vespasian manuscript suggest that the complex scene changes of place and scaffold staging in several of the Resurrection plays were revised for a simplified performance of what must have been a two-day play at Easter, changes which may indicate that the cycle was adaptable to staging limitations as well as to the requirements of an individual location and occasion.

If it was indeed the monastery of Bury St. Edmunds which sponsored the *N-Town Cycle,* it is reasonable to suppose that the plays would have been performed with the aid of religious guilds from Bury, which, as we have already seen, fulfilled much the same function in

Bury St. Edmunds as the trade guilds of non-monastic boroughs, and which had close ties to the monastery. There is evidence from inscriptions on St. Nicholas tokens which have been found on the abbey grounds at Bury that one such guild, a confraternity of St. Nicholas known popularly as the "Dusse Gild" (from "Douze," the twelve), at least collaborated with the Bury monks on local dramatic festivities associated with the ceremony of the Boy Bishop. Although there is no specific evidence linking the Bury Candlemas Guild to abbey-sponsored religious plays, the sheer civic importance and influence of that guild, as well as the documented fact that "pageants" were stored in the guildhall where the Candlemas Guild had held its meetings, single it out as the most likely group to have supervised such dramatic activities. Certainly one of the most striking facts to emerge from the recent REED edition of the dramatic records from York is the crucial role of religious guilds in the production of plays even in a city like York which had strong and well-organized civic trade guilds.

As for the hypothesis that abbey and guild-sponsored plays would have been performed at Bury during fair times, there is some substantiation in the fact that one of the abbey's Bury fairs was a three-day fair held on the feast of Saint James (from 24 to 26 July). The culminating day of the St. James fair would thus have been July 26 or St. Anne's Day, the very day which Hardin Craig argued must have been the date of performance of the *N-Town Cycle.* After the dissolution of the Bury monastery, control of the Bury fairs passed to the crown and then, after the incorporation of the borough of Bury St. Edmunds in 1606, to the town corporation. By the eighteenth century, Bury Fair meant a single three-week fair held around the feast of St. Matthew in September, a fair which drew tradesmen and the likes of Defoe's Moll Flanders from all over England. It also drew actors. Although no earlier evidence survives about dramatic activity at Bury Fair, there is abundant evidence in the eighteenth century that plays were customarily performed then. The Bury Guildhall was rented to "the players during Bury fair" in 1722, and in 1734 the Bury market cross was converted into a playhouse, a purpose for which it was used until 1819.

Elsewhere in the Bury area, one of the most likely fairs for the performances of the plays now comprising the Cotton Vespasian manuscript would have been the annual nine-day fair held at Long Melford at the feast of Whitsunday. The abbots of Bury St. Edmunds owned not only tolls and rights to the Long Melford fair, which was held on the village green adjacent to Holy Trinity Church, but also the advowson of the church, Melford Hall and manor, and numerous other lands and tenements in the village. Despite its small population, Long Melford, about fifteen miles from Bury St. Edmunds, was one of the most prosperous woolen cloth-producing towns in Suffolk. In the fifteenth century, Long

Melford Church was rebuilt to near-cathedral proportions by the wealthy cloth merchants who helped make Long Melford the abbey's single greatest source of revenue. We know from an inventory of 1529 that Long Melford Church had an altar of St. Anne as well as of St. Edmund, and its spectacular late fifteenth-century Lady Chapel built to the east of the church is ample witness of the town's devotion to the Virigin Mary.

Although no records survive of medieval mystery play performances at Long Melford, it is at least certain from an early sixteenth-century reminiscence that liturgical dramas were observed there, and certain that during the brief restoration of Catholicism under Queen Mary, what the churchwardens' accounts call "games" were presented on the same village green on which the Bury monastery had held its Long Melford fair. The Long Melford churchwardens' accounts for 1555 list a variety of expenses connected with these "games," including the costs of malt and rented pots, of proclaiming the "games" at Ipswich and Braintree, of ringing when the bishop came to town, and of "setting xiii settes in the Churcheyerde." Richard Parker in his *History of Long Melford* glossed these "games" as a church ale, but since the word "Ale" is used in the account records elsewhere to refer to church ales, and especially since "settes" (which can mean *sedes* or scaffolds) were required, since the "games" were proclaimed as far away as Braintree and Ipswich, and since the bishop himself attended, it seems likely that the word "game" refers here, as indeed it does in the banns to the *N-Town Cycle,* to a play. The evidence for the advertisement of the "games" at Ipswich and Braintree is entirely consistent with the evidence which Richard Wright has uncovered about the multi-community involvement in play performances in rural East Anglia before the Reformation. The *N-Town* banns themselves seem to invite people in neighboring towns to a dramatic center (*N-Town,* the name to be filled in as appropriate), rather than to imply that the play will be performed in each village where it is proclaimed:

> whan þat ye come þer xal ye sene
> this game wel pleyd in good a-ray. . . .
>   (518-19)

The possibility that the Long Melford "games" of 1555 were revived mystery plays is an intriguing one (as is the comment in the churchwardens' accounts of the same year, long after the dissolution of Suffolk's religious houses, that viii d. had been "layd oute to the nunnes for the mendyng of the vestiments"). The possibility of a dramatic tradition at Long Melford originally linked to the Bury St. Edmunds monastery is made even more intriguing by a stained-glass window in the north aisle of Long Melford Church in which still may be seen an image of St. Edmund with a donor portrait of a kneeling abbot with mitre and crozier. An inscription visible

in 1688, when it was recorded by a Long Melford rector, implored the viewer to pray for the soul of "Hengham, nuper Abbatis de Bury," the very fifteenth-century abbot of Bury St. Edmunds who Baker and Murphy have concluded was the "Monk Hyngham" whose name appears on the margins of the *Macro Plays* manuscript.

II

Abbot Hengham's portrait may not be the only clue in Holy Trinity Church to Long Melford's link with a dramatic tradition at Bury St. Edmunds. Painted in late fifteenth-century script along the top of the walls of the Clopton Chantry which adjoins the north side of the Holy Trinity chancel are stanzas from John Lydgate's "Testament" and from his English rendering of the famous Marian lament, "Quis dabit meo capiti fontem lacrimarum?" The presence of Lydgate's poems here at Long Melford, painted within forty or fifty years after his death, is, as J. B. Trapp [in "Verses by Lydgate at Long Melford," *Review of English Studies,* 1955] has observed, visual testimony to the important contemporary reputation of the Bury monk and poet, and the way in which his poems are arranged on the chantry walls to be used as aids to meditation can offer interesting testimony about the way Lydgate's contemporaries read and responded to his devotional poems. The stanzas, for example, which were painted directly above the chantry altar, and so above what must have been a crucifix or *imago pietatis* on view there, are the stanzas from Lydgate's "Testament" in which the poet implores in Jesus' voice that man "lefte up thyn eye, & see" the bloody wounds which he has suffered on mankind's behalf, in order that man

> empyrnte theese thyng in your inward thought
> and grave him depe i your remembraunce
> thynke on theym well & forgete theym nought
> al this I suffered to don you allegeaunce. . . .

We may also see in this fifteenth-century handwriting on the wall a reminder useful for our search for the provenance of the *N-Town Cycle,* a reminder that Lydgate the monk and writer of devotional lyrics was also the author of the most ambitious life of Mary in the English language and the most famous writer of pageants, royal entries, and mummings in fifteenth-century England. Lydgate was the author of verses for several London and court mummings (some of which he also directed) in his role as unofficial poet laureate for the Lancastrian kings, and of the "Procession of Corpus Christi," an exposition on the Corpus Christi feast written for a London Corpus Christi procession. Schirmer quite rightly observes [in *John Lydgate*] that the exposition of Old and New Testament mysteries in the "procession of Corpus Christi" must have been written to accompany "a succession of pageants bearing enactments of dramatic scenes, as in the mystery plays."

Whether this procession was a series of *tableaux vivants* or of actual plays, Lydgate's verses are important as one of our very few sources of information about what the lost London plays called Corpus Christi were like. The "Procession of Corpus Christi" is also significant confirmation of the strong Marian emphasis in Lydgate's religious poetry; three of the stanzas from the "Procession of Corpus Christi" are not an explication of the mystery of the sacrament at all but rather of the miraculous virginity of she who "bare þe fruyt, þe celestial bred."

Lydgate was so famed as a writer of dramatic pageants that in 1445, in his old age, he was called out of apparent retirement at Bury St. Edmunds to return to the London court to write verses for the royal entry of Margaret of Anjou. This was an immensely important state occasion; as the young Henry VI wrote to his friend Abbot Curteys (to whom he was appealing for a loan from the Bury monastery), hopes for a final peace with France lay heavily upon this union with Margaret. Money was urgently needed, wrote the king, so that Margaret could be brought in all haste to England and "in suche wise as it shal be according to the state and worship of us, of hir, and of this oure reaume, and, that doone, to purveye for the solemnite of hir coronation in maner and fourme accustumed." It was John Lydgate who was charged with creating the proper "solemnite" for Margaret's arrival in London. Since Lydgate's verses for the Margaret of Anjou entry were long presumed lost and do not appear in the Early English Text Society edition of Lydgate's other processions and mummings, they are not as well known as they deserve to be. The pageants for the entry of Queen Margaret are, in fact, extremely valuable evidence, not only of the concerns of Lydgate in the final years of his poetic career, but of Lydgate's interests in the mystery play cycle form.

In the first pageant, Margaret was greeted at the Southwark side of London Bridge by two welcoming figures representing Peace and Plenty and by the divine commandment of Genesis 1.28: "Ingredimini et replete terram." On the middle of the bridge was a pageant of "Noes Shippe" in which Margaret was compared both to Noah and to the dove with the olive branch of peace. As Margaret's white carriage passed over to the London side of the bridge, the welcoming pageants turned from Old Testament themes to New Testament history and exegesis. The first episode to herald the new covenant was, as it is in both Lydgate's *Life of Our Lady* and in the *N-Town Cycle,* a pageant of the meeting of the Four Daughters of God—Truth, Mercy, Justice, and Peace. But here instead of heralding the coming conception of Christ, God's allegorical daughters of Truth, Mercy, Justice, and Peace met to promise the future progeny and peace which would be the fruits of the (in fact, ill-fated) royal marriage. Structural analogy with the mystery play cycles was continued at the next stop, at Cornhill before the prison known as "The Tun,"

where a pageant depicting the legend of St. Margaret was presented. The holy life of Margaret's own patron saint, "shewed here pleynly in this storie / Our Queene Margarete to signifie," also, of course, signified Christ, on whose paradigmatic life and Passion the lives and martyrdoms of all the saints were patterned.

After the Passion pageant, the theme of the royal entry turned, as it does in the mystery play cycles, to the preparation of mankind for the final moments of sacred history. There was a pageant of the Wise and Foolish Virgins, and then, as Margaret's carriage approached the gates of St. Paul's Cathedral, the blessing of the Virgin Mary, "Assumpt above the hevenly Ierarchie," was asked for the new queen, not only in her coming reign, but afterward "in blisse eterne." The allegorized, temporal flattery of Margaret now gave way to a pageant of the Last Judgment and general Resurrection, in which Lydgate warns that even kings will have to make their final reckoning:

> This storie to youre highnes wolde expresse
> The grete Resurecioun generall
> Where of oure feith bereth pleyn witnesse
> The ferefull sowne of Trumpe Iudiciall
> Vppon the poeple yt sodeynly shall calle.
> Eche man to make a compte and rekenynge
> Right as hys consciencie be wreien shalle
> All be it Pope Emperour or Kynge. . . .
>
> (155-62)

Unlike the Doomsday of the Coventry Cycle of 1457 which Queen Margaret would fail to see "for lak of day," Lydgate's concluding pageant before St. Paul's was duly witnessed by England's queen. The close relationship between Lydgate's "pageants of divers histories" and the mystery play cycles is evident. What is also evident is that just as Bury St. Edmunds fulfills the requirements of a likely place of origin for the *N-Town Cycle,* John Lydgate amply possesses the prerequisites to have been one of its originators. He was a prominent writer of mummings, dumb show processions, and dramatic pageants, at least two of them, the "Verses for a Procession of Corpus Christi" and the "Verses for the Entry of Margaret of Anjou," demonstrating close relationships to the mystery play cycles. He was a learned poet whose religious poetry was much influenced by the cult of the Virgin and of St. Anne. And he was a monk whose final years at the monastery of Bury St. Edmunds, except for the royal entry of Margaret and an unfinished philosophical tract, are almost totally unaccounted for. The possibility that Lydgate was either directly or indirectly an important influence on the creation of the *N-Town Cycle* must, I think, be seriously considered.

Although Schirmer did not list the *N-Town Cycle* with the spurious works of Lydgate in his catalogue of the Lydgate canon and pseudo-canon, the *N-Town Cycle* was actually attributed to Lydgate in 1748 in Bishop Tanner's *Bibliotheca Britannica Hibernica,* and Joseph Ritson, apparently following Tanner, in his *Bibliographia Poetica* of 1802 ascribes to Lydgate both the "Procession of *Corpus Christi*" and "A procession of pageants from the creation." This attribution both Mac-Cracken and Chambers have characterized as a confusion joined with a wild guess, suggesting that Bishop Tanner mistook Lydgate's descriptive verses for the Corpus Christi procession at London for a complete cycle of mystery plays and simply deduced that the Cotton manuscript in the British Museum must be that cycle. The easiest explanation, in fact, is that Bishop Tanner's attribution of the plays in the Cotton Vespasian D.viii manuscript to Lydgate was just such a simple mistake. But it should at least be considered a possibility, especially in the face of evidence suggesting links between the Cotton Vespasian manuscript and Lydgate's monastery at Bury St. Edmunds, that there was still in the eighteenth century knowledge or rumor linking Lydgate to the *N-Town Cycle*. Lydgate is a far from unlikely candidate.

III

Despite the fact that *N-Town Cycle* is composed of separate, once-independent groups of plays, the imaginative coherence of the cycle has led Rosemary Woolf to postulate "a poet, writing in the middle of the fifteenth century, who for different occasions composed a Passion play and a Nativity play and a full cycle of which these independent plays formed a part." More recently, Stephen Spector [in "Provenance"] has argued on the basis of an exhaustive study of the Cotton Vespasian manuscript, its scribal characteristics, and its prosody that the actual compilation of plays in the form they take in the *N-Town Cycle* was accomplished only as the manuscript was being transcribed (apparently the bulk of it in 1468, the year which appears in the manuscript following the "Purification" play). If Spector is correct, the thematic unity which Woolf and others have sensed in the *N-Town Cycle* would thus be a result of the incorporation of amended and expanded material (much of it, like the Contemplatio group, with its own self-unity) into a more or less unified earlier version of a mystery play cycle. John Lydgate's name has already emerged many times in this essay in connection with the general devotional and iconographical characteristics of the *N-Town Cycle,* but there are also some quite specific relationships between Lydgate's religious poetry and the *N-Town Cycle,* connections striking enough to suggest that Lydgate may have been one of those poets who contributed to the *N-Town Cycle*. If Spector is correct about 1468 being the main date of the cycle's compilation, Lydgate (who died in 1449 or 1450) could not have supervised the final shape of the cycle, but he may well have been involved at an earlier stage. There are relationships which argue that the Mary plays from the *N-Town Cycle* can be traced to Lydgate's direct influence if not to his very hand.

The Mary plays from the *N-Town Cycle* share with Lydgate's Marian lyrics a stately yet simple style antithetical to the aureate *amplificatio* of much of Lydgate's secular poetry. Lydgate's emulation of Latin hymns in poems like "An Invocation of Seynte Anne," "Ave Jesse Virgula," and "Ballade at the Reverence of our Lady, Qwene of Mercy" leads not to rhetorical pretentiousness so much as to a splendid and deliberate verse which Schirmer aptly described as "heavy and stiff as rich brocade." It is verse very like the slow and graceful macaronic ritual of praise between Mary and Elizabeth in the *N-Town* "Visitation Play," or the near-liturgical celebration of the young Mary's ascent of the Temple steps in the *N-Town* "Presentation Play"; none of the other extant English mystery plays contain verse remotely like it. The Madonna of Franciscan simplicity who inhabits the York, Towneley, and Chester cycles is far removed from the mystical Virgin of Lydgate's lyrics and of the *N-Town* plays, the Mary who is paradoxically both handmaiden and exalted queen. "Gramercy ye lanterne off lyght" praises the Gabriel of the *N-Town* "Salutation and Conception" after Mary has given her consent to God's plan for redemption; Hayle luminary & benigne langerne," begins Lydgate's English rendering of the Latin hymn "Ave Regina Celorum," the hymn of praise sung at the conclusion of the *N-Town* "Visitation Play." It is, in fact, Latin hymnody which is constantly evoked in both Lydgate's Marian poetry and in the *N-Town* Mary plays. In both there is a deliberate attempt to replace the humanized Mary of the English vernacular religious lyric, even the noble lady of English court poetry to the Virgin, with a mystical queen who is celebrated in a high lyric style derived from the Latin sacred lyric. In Lydgate's Marian lyrics and in the *N-Town Cycle* Mary bears along with her titles Queen of Heaven and Lady of Earth, the still more awesome title, "empress of Hell"; she is that sovereign lady whom the prophets and the patriarchs worship from the very jaws of Hellmouth.

J. O. Halliwell as long ago as 1841 pointed out the close similarities between Lydgate's anagrams on the name of the Virgin and the anagram in the *N-Town* "Presentation of the Virgin," and there are numerous other such similarities of Marian epithet and formulaic praise which could be pointed out between the Marian plays in the *N-Town Cycle* and Lydgate's Marian lyrics and *Lyf of Our Lady*—the repeated use of the phrase "tabernakyl of þe hyy trinite," for example. This language, though rare in English vernacular texts and nonexistent in the York, Towneley, and Chester cycles, might well have been drawn from the common stock of Latin meditation and liturgical celebration of the Virgin Mary. What is not drawn from the Latin devotional tradition and what is a far more significant relationship between Lydgate and the *N-Town Cycle* is a shared theme like the apocryphal trial of Joseph and Mary by the Jews.

The Trial of Joseph and Mary appears in both the *N-Town Cycle* and in Lydgate's verse but not, to my knowledge, in any other English literary text, vernacular or Latin, except texts and paraphrases of the Gospel of Pseudo-Matthew itself, like the Minnesota manuscript of the Middle English Life of St. Anne. It is so rare a theme in the visual arts that a much-defaced sculpture in the Lady Chapel at Ely Cathedral (by whose bishop, incidentally, Lydgate was ordained) seems to be the only surviving representation of the theme in English medieval art. The curious apocryphal tale of the Trial of Joseph and Mary was even ignored by the *Meditationes vitae Christi* of the Pseudo-Bonaventura, which enthusiastically reported nearly every other apocryphal detail, both ancient and newly invented, that could be summoned forth to embroider the sparse gospel accounts of Mary's life. Yet Lydgate included a leisurely discussion of the Jews' magical trial of the Virgin in his *Lyf of Our Lady,* and, even more remarkably, in his poem "Fifteen Joys and Sorrows of the Virgin" he made the absolutely unprecedented designation of the Trial of Joseph and Mary as one of the Virgin's fifteen sorrows and her triumphant vindication as one of her fifteen joys. As Rosemary Woolf notes, with considerable understatement, "this subject seems particularly to have interested Lydgate." The presence of an entire play of the Trial of Mary and Joseph by the Jews (complete with an elaborate ecclesiastical court and the allegorical brothers Slander and "Bakbytere" who kiss in a perverse parody of the meeting of the Daughters of God) in an East Anglian manuscript of the mid-fifteenth century should be cause alone to suspect a link between Lydgate and the *N-Town* Mary plays.

But there is still more suggestive evidence of a relationship between Lydgate and the *N-Town Cycle* in a rubric in the *N-Town* "Adoration of the Shepherds" which directs that the shepherds are to leave the Bethlehem manger singing "Stella caeli extirpavit. Rosemary Woolf noticed that this hymn is the same Latin hymn for which Lydgate wrote two of the three existing English translations, but she does not comment on either how close a connection with Lydgate this suggests or how curious a choice this hymn is for the musical good news of the shepherds. Unlike the famous Marian hymn "Ave Regina Celorum," which also appears both in the *N-Town Cycle* and in translation by Lydgate, "Stella caeli extirpavit" is an obscure hymn rarely found in service books either in England or on the Continent. Even more remarkably, "Stella caeli extirpavit" is not a hymn of celebration, as its context in the *N-Town* shepherds play might suggest, but a plague hymn, a lyric invoking, in its Latin version and in Lydgate's Middle English, the protection of the Virgin Mary against the threat of pestilence:

> To the we pray, on vs cast doun thy siht,
> Oonly of mercy that thu nat disdeyne
> Off infect heyr the mystis to restreyne,

> That be thy gracious moost holsom influence
> We haue no cause on hasty deth to pleyne,
> Which sleeth the peeple by swerd of
>   pestilence.

Lydgate wrote several such poems on the plague, probably during the severe epidemic of 1434, when there was "A grete pestilence in London, both of men, women and children. . .and also thurgh England þe people dyed sore." Characteristically, Lydgate uses these plague hymns as opportunities to extoll the Virgin Mary as much as to implore her mercies against the plague. His second English version of "Stella caeli extirpavit," for example, goes beyond an appeal for protection against the infected airs and pestilential mists to extravagant praise of that Lady who counters the death which Adam brought into the world, and who "puttist away eternal pestilence." Lydgate's hymn closes by asking Mary's intercession on behalf of the poet's soul so that he "may come to the blisse where drad is no pestilence."

The presence of such a hymn in the *N-Town* "Adoration of the Shepherds" surely acknowledges the ever-present threat of the plague which visited and revisited medieval towns in the late Middle Ages with fearful regularity, and it probably even testifies to the terrors of a present epidemic in East Anglia at the time the *N-Town* "Adoration of the Shepherds" was written. (Margery Kempe tells how she was reluctant to go from Norfolk to the abbey at Denney in Cambridgeshire when her visit was requested by the abbess at some time in the first third of the fifteenth century, "for it was pestylenstyme"; and we know that in 1446 the Marquis of Suffolk presided in lieu of the king at the laying of the foundation stone of King's College, Cambridge [about thirty miles from Bury], "owing to the pestilence there"). Significantly, the plague hymn "Stella caeli extirpavit" functions to recast the theme of Christ as healer of his flock, developed in the shepherd plays of the other English cycles, in the uniquely Marian terms of Lydgate's devotional poems and of the *N-Town Cycle*. In the *N-Town* "Adoration of the Shepherds," it is the Virgin Mary who is revered as the healer of the flock of believers, Mary who is the soul's physician, the redemptress who saves men both from the plague and from the death which Adam's sin brought into the world.

At the very least what we must conclude, I think, is that John Lydgate was a literary influence on the composition of the *N-Town Cycle,* and that the nature of the relationships between Lydgate's verse and the *N-Town Cycle* increases the likelihood of a provenance for the plays in Bury St. Edmunds. Whoever composed the Marian plays in the *N-Town Cycle* knew Lydgate's devotional lyrics, *Lyf of Our Lady,* even a little-known hymn closely associated with Lydgate, and could appropriate Lydgate's style, phrasing, and favorite themes at will. But as Chambers long ago warned,

> The task of the playwright was one less of original composition than of adaptation, of rewriting and rearranging existing texts so as to meet the needs of the particular performances in which they were interested.

It is certain that the English mystery cycles, like the great medieval cathedrals to which their construction is often compared, were genuinely and not accidentally anonymous works. But it does not seem improbable that John Lydgate, the poet who wrote the *Lyf of Our Lady* and numerous hymns to the Virgin Mary and to St. Anne, who wrote lyrics explicating murals and mummings, who wrote and supervised the elaborate pageants for the royal entry of Margaret of Anjou as well as undertaking local commissions as humble as a translation of the 129th psalm to hang on the wall of his abbey church, would have lent his hand to the shaping of the mystery plays which were performed on festive Sundays in local N. towns. It does not seem improbable that the *N-Town Cycle* is the Bury St. Edmunds Cycle.

Peter Meredith (essay date 1990)

SOURCE: An introduction to *The Passion Play from the N. Town Manuscript*, edited by Peter Meredith, Longman, 1990, pp. 1-36.

[*In an excerpt to his introduction to this edition, Meredith discusses the staging and general themes of the* Passion Play.]

Play and pageants

It is sometimes implied or stated that the present *Passion Play* is a revision of earlier pageants (those described in the Proclamation) to make a continuous play. While it is impossible to disprove this it seems to me that in the case of *Passion I* and the first part of *Passion II* (up to I. 880) this is unlikely. The demonstrable overlaps between the episodes in the play and the Proclamation are not numerous. *Passion I* deals with the events from the beginning of the Conspiracy against Christ to his taking in the garden of Gethsemane. The scribe has numbered the play as a series of pageants, 25 to 27 (Proclamation 23 to 25). The descriptions in the Proclamation only very inadequately describe the play episodes. The first description (one of the 'half-stanza' ones) runs:

> In þe xxiijᵗⁱ pagent, Palme Sunday,
> In pley we purpose for to shewe,
> How chylderyn of Ebrew with flourys ful gay,
> Þe wey þat Cryst went þei gun to strewe.

The text to which this applies, numbered 26 in the

manuscript, contains two prologues, of the Demon (I. 1-124), and of John the Baptist (I. 125-64); the beginning of the conspiracy (I. 165-342); the fetching of the ass; the preaching of Peter and John (I. 343-98); and the entry into Jerusalem with the healing of the blind (I. 399-442). Moreover the incident to which the description refers is contained in a stage direction (or at most a stage direction and four lines of text).

The second description runs:

> In þe xxiiijᵗᵉ pagent, as þat we may,
> Cryst and his apostelys alle on rewe,
> The mawndé of God þer xal they play;
> And sone declare it with wordys fewe.
>   And than
> Judas þat fals traytour,
> For xxxᵗⁱ platys of werdly tresour,
> Xal betray oure Savyour
>   To þe Jewys, certan.

Here, the text, numbered 27, has Christ's lament over Jerusalem and his preparation for the Last Supper (I. 343-518); a continuation of the conspiracy (I. 519-82); the anointing of Christ by Mary Magdalene, and the foretelling of the betrayal; Judas's betrayal (I. 588-662); and an extended Last Supper—'declare it with wordys fewe'?—(I. 663-884). Not only is the emphasis wrong but the order is reversed.

The final section, numbered 28, is the shortest (under 200 lines) and the least complicated. Its only unusual feature is the visit of Magdalene to the Virgin Mary at the very end, and this is not contained in the Proclamation.

The same is broadly true of the first part of *Passion II*. In the second part a simple mixing of pageant and play material largely takes over.

More important than the lack of overlap between play and Proclamation however, is the fact that so much of the play is devoted to the very episodes which are most unlikely to occur in separate pageants—e.g. the linking/walking speeches like Peter's sermon (I. 343-74) or Christ's words to his disciples as he walks towards Simon's house (I. 495-502)—and the considerable sections of the play which make sense only in continuity—e.g. the interrelatedness of first Annas's and then Caiaphas's doubts about Christ, the necessity of a meeting, the involvement of the Pharisees (I. 165-342); all of which seems far too long for a pageant but is appropriate to the opening of a play (nearly 200 lines simply to decide to conspire).

Furthermore, when what appears to be pageant material is introduced into *Passion I,* the stanza form used (wholly in one case and partly in the other) is one which is common in the pageant part of the manuscript but does not appear at all in the *Passion Play,* the thirteener. It might be expected that if the *Passion Play* were a revision of existing pageant material this would show more in the type of stanza used.

Passion I

It is important to take the two parts of the *Passion Play* separately because their manuscript origins and the treatment given them by the scribe are quite different. As has already been said, *Passion I* is a separate booklet bound into the present manuscript but written in the same hand throughout, that of the main scribe, before the compilation was made. It is therefore in every sense a separate play. There is no evidence, even, to suggest that it had a second half, except that if it did not it was a rather odd series of episodes to choose. The only interference with the original play by the scribe occurs on f. 143 and ff. 149-51.

The first is the interpolation of the incident of the fetching of the ass, on a single leaf (f. 143), probably originating from old pageant material. The incident is not mentioned in the Proclamation description, but that description is a very short one. This addition was clearly written out by the scribe specially to be incorporated here, making use of a piece of scrap paper (it had several large ink blots on it before he wrote his text). The purpose of the addition seems to have been simply to supply an incident that was not present—and is not necessary.

The second interference is a somewhat longer interpolation. This occurs between ff. 148 and 152 and consists of two sections continuous in the manuscript: the repentance of Magdalene (f. 149) and the foretelling of the betrayal (ff. 150-1). These three leaves, now called quire O, have been interpolated between two original quires, now N and P. In both cases the additions have no necessary narrative or dramatic purpose and seem to be merely the result of the scribe's desire for all-inclusiveness.

In view of the distinct and separable nature of these interpolations, it is fair to say that the form that *Passion I* took is clear. I would not go so far as to say that we have the original or even the final form. The prologues are not perhaps as well integrated with the play as one might have expected, nor is their relationship to each other entirely clear. There are elaborate stage directions for much of the play but there are none for the prologues and some of those later in the play tend to be more narrative than practical—but what medieval English play does have consistently full stage directions? It looks like a play in the course of development, and we are lucky that it reached the relatively developed stage that it has and that it is so free from the scribe's adaptation.

Passion II

The second part of the *Passion Play* shows at first every sign of being a similar text to the first part. It looks like a separate play, with a prologue that links it in some detail with the events already played 'þe last yere' (II. 6). The two quires on which much of it is written show signs of having been a separate manuscript. Around f. 184, however, there is clearly some kind of disruption. Two leaves, ff. 184-5, have been interpolated into the middle of the quire, but the text that they contain is continuous with what precedes and follows it and is not detachable in the way that the interpolations into *Passion I* are. Moreover, at the place about a third of the way down f. 183v where the writing becomes somewhat cramped, no doubt signalling the introduction of ff. 184-5, a new stanza form appears, the romance stanza. It seems that this marks the end of *Passion II* as an entity and the beginning of the scribe's somewhat undigested mixing of play and pageant material. After II. 880 there are far more romance stanzas than any other, while before that line there are no romance stanzas and the quatrain is far and away the commonest form. It would be wrong to base conclusions simply on stanza forms, but when the evidence they provide is taken with the manuscript evidence, it overwhelmingly suggests the introduction of new material. The later material in the play is not in the same order as it is in the Proclamation but it is often close to it in content, and the conclusion seems inescapable that the scribe is blending *Passion Play* and pageant text in a rather unsubtle way. . . .

Metre, Language and Style

In *Passion I* the commonest stanza forms are the quatrain (122 examples) and the octave, or double-quatrain, rhyming *ababbcbc* (71). There are a very small number of subsidiary forms: five couplets, a couple of single lines and a single octave rhyming *abababab* which opens the play. The scribe is normally reliable in indicating stanzas, though he occasionally omits his stanza marker (the *capitulum*) and occasionally misplaces it. In one case he imposes his own idiosyncratic pattern, when he divides Demon's prologue into quatrains on the recto of the leaf and octaves on the verso (I. 1-124). He does not indicate any twelve-line stanzas in this part of the *Passion* though there is a good deal of stanza-linking of octaves and quatrains.

In *Passion I* the couplet appears only during the Last Supper (if we discount the two single lines at I. 341-2 which are unlikely to be intended, and do not deserve to be considered, as a couplet). The first example (I. 763-4) contains the repeated words of Christ as he gives the sacramental wafer to each of the disciples:

> This is my body, flesch and blode,
> Þat for þe xal dey upon þe rode.

> (I. 763-4)

The words echo those of gospel and mass 'Hoc est enim corpus meum' and the couplet form underlines their solemnity by isolating them, this isolation being emphasised by the repetition. The pattern of repetition is broken by Christ's question and Judas's reply in the form of another couplet. The next couplet again breaks a series of repetitions, this time of the single or half line 'Lord, it is not I', the denial by the disciples of Christ's betrayal, and again by a question, Judas's: 'Is it owth I, lord?', confirmed by Christ's reply: 'Judas, þu seyst þat word'. The change to question allows Judas verbally to isolate himself as previously Christ has isolated him by a question (I. 765). A further couplet emphasises Judas's guilt. The last couplet is, expectedly, Christ's words for the administering of the consecrated wine, which, Judas having departed, is repeated without interruption.

It is best to divide *Passion* II into two sections (a) and (b). Before 1. 880, *Passion* II(a), the dominant forms are the quatrain (139 examples) and the couplet (67); after that line, *Passion* II(b), the romance stanza predominates (an eight-line stanza, usually rhyming *aaabcccb* and with variation in number of stresses between the *b* lines and the others). There are octaves in both sections, 15 before 1. 880 and 31 after, but in *Passion* II(b) they mainly form an almost continuous series at the end of the play. There are no romance stanzas before 1. 880 and no couplets after it.

The formal and specific use of the couplet in *Passion* I is quite unlike its use in *Passion* II(a). From II. 177 until 879 the couplet is one of the commonest stanza forms and is used primarily for its flexibility in moving quickly from character to character and allowing the impression, within limits, of everyday speech. It is particularly associated with Pilate who has more lines in couplets than in any other stanza form, which perhaps helps to suggest the view of him as an ordinary, well-meaning official, characteristic of *Passion* II(a). The use of the couplet is particularly sustained in II. 182-209, 314-37, 390-9, 639-74 and 683-97. Something of the isolating effect of the single couplet appears in its first use in *Passion* II where it appears as the culmination of a speech by Caiaphas. In the first part of the speech, marked by broken lines, exclamation and question, he is shown blustering. A single line (II. 166) indicates a return to a more reasonable approach and the couplet, marked by a more regular rhythm, is used as a containing vehicle for the oath with which Caiaphas finally makes his demands of Christ. The breaking up of the speech between quatrain, single line and couplet partly echoes the broken nature of Caiaphas's attack—his pauses for the demanded reply—but it also echoes the changing nature of his attack, from anger to adjuration.

In a culture where verse is the normal literary form, it is not surprising to find some that is rhythmically little different from prose. The verse in these plays has neither the regularity of syllabic rhymed metre nor the sustained cohesiveness of good alliterative verse. But nor is it merely rhymed prose. It moves between regularity of rhythm and freedom with considerable skill and dramatic aptness. What any performer is struck by in the early part of *Passion* II is the freedom and naturalness of the language and rhythm. In *Passion* I, however, there is a greater sense of form and formality in, for example, the opening speeches of Annas and Caiaphas, Peter's sermon or, most particularly, Christ's exposition of the meaning of the Passover.

There is clearly a reluctance on the part of the playwright to break stanza forms and therefore where quick exchanges are required the couplet is useful. In only a small number of cases is a stanza divided between speakers. This leads to a certain appearance of formality on the page, but it is only occasionally noticeable in performance. Oddly, though the *Mary Play* is more formal in tone its playwright divides the stanzas between speakers far more freely, and not just by making, as it were, an octave into two quatrains, but by giving the first or last one or two lines to another speaker.

In both parts extra-metrical lines appear. In *Passion* I there are only two (I. 341-2) unless 'Lord, it is not I' (I. 775) is taken as a separate rather than a half line. In *Passion* II the single lines are mainly used to allow for a natural response by the crowd at Christ's trials (e.g. '3a, 3a, 3a!' at II. 179, 345sd, 646sd, 672sd), but there is also the repetition of 'Ho was þat?' in the game refrain (II. 188 and 193), Longeus's cry for mercy (II. 1155) reminiscent of the use of the extra-metrical lines in the *Mary Play,* and the line already referred to added to Caiaphas's emotional cross-questioning of Christ (II. 166).

There is some freedom of rhyme in the *Passion Play:* rhyming *-n* with *-m,* e.g. *cam/Satan* (I. 1/3), *on/lom* (II. 109/111), *com/everychon* (II. 135/137); other assonances, e.g. *everychon/wrong* (I. 809/811), *not/fop* (II. 162/ 163), *vnqwyt/skyp* (II. 507/509); variation of vowel, e.g. *God/good* (II. 5/7), *trespas/crosse* (II. 671/673). Rhymes of this kind make it just possible that I. 341-2 *(reson/ same)* is a couplet, though the diversity is a bit more extreme. Some rhymes depend upon stressed or unstressed forms of the same word: e.g. unstressed *sertayn* rhyming with *woman* (II. 1862/1864) and stressed *sertayn* with *peyn* (I. 310/312). There are also a few rhymes that depend upon the stressing of inflections: e.g. *awntys / grawnt us* (II. 1699/1701), and most notable, since it seems to be a deliberate playing with the device, *þis/Jewys* (II. 875/876) next to *þus/Jewus* (II. 877/878).

The *Passion Play* is not characterised by a rich literary language. Aureate diction is not a special feature of the play and alliteration is not used to an extent sufficient to produce a wide range of alliterative words. Two words *obeycon* (II. 306) and *perdure* (I. 368) are according to the *MED* unique to this play, and *sorwatorie* (II. 947), apparently a combination of *sorwe* and 'purgatory', is not recorded in OED. *Hoberd* (II. 897 and 905) appears only here and in the *N. town* **Herod** pageant (Block, p. 169). For *eternalyté* (3A5), *seryattly* (I. 754), and *ouerest* (II. 486sd) this is *MED*'s first recorded use; *brace* (2A44) and *batte* (II. 184) are recorded here first with this meaning, and *vnete* (I. 727) and *vnlosne* (1A9) are recorded here first with these forms.

Alliteration and learned language, rhetorical balance and repetition do play some part in the play, however, though in general the language tends towards the straightforward and plain. Alliteration is used scantily: Annas and Caiaphas both introduce themselves (I. 165ff. and 209ff) with an alliterative line (both alliterating on *pr-*, stemming from *prelat* and *primat*) but only Satan in **Passion** II (ll. 487ff.) appears with a heavy burst of alliteration. The use of a learned Latinate vocabulary depends upon the needs of character and circumstance. Caiaphas employs a learned vocabulary (I. 209-16) because he is a bishop and because he is pompous, as well as because he is making his first appearance. Appropriateness of language register is often true of the use of language generally; that it reflects the character, the state of mind or the situation from which the speech springs relatively naturally: e.g. the First Doctor's careful approach to Caiaphas (I. 225 ff.) allowing the Second a more open attack (I. 233ff.)— cf. Annas's two doctors (I. 185-96); the blustering incoherence of Annas's speech (II. 338-45) and Caiaphas's laborious emphasis upon the evident 'truth' of an irrelevant fact (II. 354-61); the politely veiled threat of the approach to Symon of Cyrene (II. 719-26); and the chanted game of the first mocking (II. 186-93). The language clearly remains more formal than ordinary speech, and characters often say too much about what they are doing or throw in too many conventional tags, but nevertheless it often embodies rather than simply conveying natural emotions and reactions.

The more elaborately-worked rhetorical speeches are also more integral and less decorative than for example those in the *Mary Play*. Christ's exposition of the meaning of the Passover feast is the clearest example. Repetition and balance are again the main devices used:

> And as we stodyn, so dede þei stond. . . (I. 671)
> And as we ete it, so dede þei, hastyly. . . (I. 674)

Sometimes this is linked with word-play or alliteration:

> Weche xal be of my body, þat am your hed. . .
> (I. 676)
> Of my flesch and blood in forme of bred.
> (I. 678);

or reversal of order:

> For mannys love I may do no mo,
> Þan for love of man to be ded.
> (I. 807-8).

Balanced phrases end Peter's first stanza of preaching:

> He xal cawse þe blynde þat þei xal se,
> Þe def to here, þe dome for to speke.
> (I. 349-50)

There is also a deliberate rounding-off of Christ's speech over Jerusalem by a return to the first line:

> O, Jherusalem, woful is þe ordenawnce. . .
> O, ceté, ful woful is þin ordenawns!
> (I. 443/458).

. . . . .

Staging

It is very seldom that we possess information both about how the staging of a play was envisaged and also about how it was actually performed. The wealth of textual and documentary evidence for the staging at Lucerne or Mons reveals just how lacking the English evidence is. In Lucerne not only do we have texts, plans, descriptions, but we also have an idea of when and why many of the documents were drawn up. The plans of the square in which the Easter Play was performed, for example, were made by Cysat, the director, at the time of the 1583 performance, and the description of the layout of the play was made by Hardmeyer, the city clerk of works, after the 1583 performance in readiness for the next. A stage plan of the *Castle of Perseverance* exists, but who drew it up and for what purpose? Is it the playwright's ideal of how the play should be staged? Or is it a plan, like Hardmeyer's, of the way in which it had already been staged—successfully enough to make it worth while recording? Even though its purpose and origin are not as clear as the Lucerne plans, however, it is plain that it is concerned with practical matters of staging, and that it is unlikely to have sprung out of a theatrical vacuum—staging of this kind must have existed. Much the same can be said of most stage directions; they are also concerned with practical matters of staging and should tell us something about contemporary methods, but, like the plan of the *Castle,* they should not automatically be treated as though they were descriptions of an actual performance.

Most important of all for staging is **Passion I,** since here we are dealing with what is known to be a self-contained play; but even here evidence for the overall layout is lacking. Two stage structures are specifically mentioned, a 'stage' for Annas (I. 164sd) and a 'scaffold' for Caiaphas (I. 208sd), and two others are described in such a way as to show that they are similar structures, *a lytil oratory* (I. 288sd) and the *hous* of Symon Leprows (referred to in I. 494sd, 510sd, 518sd and 662sd). Besides these there is frequent mention of the 'place' and also reference to what appears to be a part of the 'place' separated off, Mount Olivet and *a place lych to a park* (I. 900sd). The likelihood of a separate scaffold for Mary for the short scene right at the end of the play seems to me doubtful but not impossible. The *lytil oratory* has been vacant for some time and it may even be that its description as an oratory derives from its use as such by Mary.

Not only are the scaffolds mentioned but to a certain extent their appearances are described. The *lytil oratory* is neatly laid out with *stolys and cusshonys. . .lych as it were a cownsel hous* (I. 288sd). Later the appearance of the actors sitting in it *in astat* is said to be *lych as it were a convocacyon* (I. 518sd), underlining the legal solemnity of what the Jews are doing and contrasting with their frequently thuggish language and methods. Importantly there is also mention of curtaining. Both the *lytil oratory* and the *hous* of Symon *sodeynly onclose* (I. 518sd and 662sd); the latter unclosing *rownd abowtyn* and thus suggesting more than merely a front curtain. The garden of Gethsemane is not mentioned by name but is the *place lych to a park* (I. 900sd) and presumably therefore fenced off from the main 'place'. The *mount of Olyvet*, mentioned three times (I. 900sd, 908sd and 920sd), is not described but a raised area not a scaffold seems likely. The only other possible scaffold is a heaven. It is only the phrase *ascendyth ayeyn sodeynly* (I. 948sd) which really suggests any necessity for such a thing, since it could imply some form of raising mechanism; but given the total absence of any other action connected with heaven, and the apparent unimportance of this direction, it seems unnecessary to add this scaffold to the total layout. The problem is really part of a much larger one, namely that the physical context of the play is unknown. If this were being performed somewhere where access to the necessary mechanism was easy, it would be foolish not to use it. By itself, however, the stage direction is not sufficient to build a scaffold on.

What appears from the stage directions and from the text are four scaffolds, a 'place' and a part separated off perhaps with a raised area. The possibilities of layout for these scaffolds are numerous. The circle and the semi-circle are possibilities but by no means the only ones; their advantage is that they automatically define the area of the 'place'. Preference is often given to the circle because of the layout in the *Castle* plan, supported as it is by the Cornish *Ordinalia* and *Meriasek*. These are excellent evidence for the existence of such a layout but there are a very large number of plays recorded for which evidence of stage layout is lacking and it would be wrong just because of the existence of one plan to impose circularity on all non-processional

plays.

One of the most striking aspects of the staging of this play is the use of movement. Not simply processions, though they do exist, but of individuals. Annas and Caiaphas do not appear on the same scaffold to discuss the taking of Christ, as they well might, nor does one arrive at the other's scaffold. Instead a messenger is sent to arrange the meeting, and spends thirty-five lines getting from one place to the other. He is then sent back with a reply, and meets the two judges, Rewfyn and Leyon, who are already moving across the 'place'. The messenger goes ahead of them to report, at which Annas decides to go to meet Caiaphas, who in turn decides to go and meet Annas. All meet in the *myd place*. This kind of movement is partly an inevitable result of 'place and scaffold' staging, but that alone does not explain the deliberate exploitation of it. It has much to do with the defining of space. An audience is aware of the space between the scaffolds as dead ground, a gap which has no meaning. The movements of the messenger, and later other figures, give a sense of identity to the space, 'a local habitation', as a bounded area in which events will take place. Indeed it becomes Jerusalem, *þis ceté* (I. 392), *þis cyté* (I. 400), over which Christ will weep, and along the streets of which he will walk—*þis path is cald Syon* (I. 495)—and through which he will finally be dragged. Movement in, around, across the space therefore reduces the distancing effect that 'place and scaffold' staging can have by giving what appears to be merely a gap, an existence of its own.

Movement also is connected with one of the most important theatrical devices used in the ***Passion Play,*** overlapping action. As the messenger runs towards him, so Caiaphas's scaffold uncloses; as the conspiracy builds against Christ, the eating of the Passover is taking place; as Christ prays on Mount Olivet, his disciples sleep and the crowd approaches to seize him. The stage directions only occasionally emphasise this overlapping, yet it is inevitable when there is physical space to be covered by actor or actors. No entry is sudden in this kind of staging, unless through the sudden unclosing of the curtains of a scaffold.

One of the most important elements in the stage directions of ***Passion*** I is that relating to costume. They are not full descriptions of costumes but tantalising, though to a considerable extent informative, hints. When Annas is described as *beseyn after a busshop of þe hoold lawe* (I. 164sd), he was clearly not being visualised as wearing a contemporary bishop's regalia but rather that described in Exodus and Leviticus. That some at least in the fifteenth century were familiar with this idea is clear from the variety of attempts to reproduce it pictorially (see note to I. 164sd). In the sixteenth-century Lucerne Easter play Aaron is described as dressed like an Old Testament priest 'mitt der Alb, Leuiten Rock oder yberkleid vmbhenckt, vnden mitt Cimbalen; item das brusttaffel, yffeln vnd anderm', presumably the linen garment, the tunic with the bells at the hem, the rational and the mitre of the bible. Though the identification of the N. town Annas and Caiaphas costumes with the Old Testament vestments is certain, the embodying of this idea is left to the individual director in performance. Annas is said to be wearing a scarlet gown and over that a blue tabard edged with white fur; Caiaphas is like Annas except that his tabard is red with white fur—red on red? Their mitres (Annas's certainly, Caiaphas's presumably) are of the Old Testament—there is considerable room for variety in the interpretation of this (see note to I. 164sd). None of these descriptions exactly calls for the linen garment, the violet tunic (with bells and pomegranates at the hem), the ephod (with onyx stones on the shoulders) on which was fitted the breastplate or rational, or the mitre with the plate of gold attached to it. It seems to me that the two high priests are intended to be wearing costumes that will definitely not remind anyone of contemporary bishops but that will rather create an air of strangeness—in this case ecclesiastical strangeness—rather than that of a precise Jewish past. But clearly the final effect will depend on the knowledge and resources of the director and performers. This same sense of the exotic is called for in the Jewish caps *with a gret knop in þe crowne* of the doctors and the 'Saracen-ness' of the messenger (I. 164sd). The judges in their *ray tabardys* and *ray hodys abouth here neckys* (I. 244sd) are rather different; reminiscent of the real world but (apparently) intensifications of it. What is striking is the care that is taken to describe the costumes in *Passion I,* a concern nearer to Mons or Lucerne than to the other English plays.

Three other costume details help to bring the play visually alive. At the entry into Jerusalem a stage direction describes how the citizens, in a strangely penitential scene, stand barelegged in their shirts, with their gowns slung round their shoulders or tied round their waists, ready to be spread at Christ's feet as he dismounts from the ass. At I. 406sd the citizens *makyn hem redy,* presumably by taking off shoes and gowns, to meet Christ. It is difficult to imagine a more striking way of emphasising the contrast between this 'Royal Entry' and a worldly one. Moreover the penitential aspect of the scene is conveyed solely in the stage direction. In the taking of Christ there are also a number of costume details (I. 964sd), not only the expected armed guards with their combination of rigid and flexible armour (*white arneys and breganderys*) but also the implied strangeness of the others *dysgysyd in odyr garmentys*—why mention the fact that they are dressed in *odyr garmentys* unless they are in some way unusual? There is finally the reference in the text to the Jews' difficulty in distinguishing Christ from his disciples because of their similarity of dress (I. 637), which implies the still traditional costuming of the disciples and Christ in cloak and robe.

Moments of action are often realised visually in the stage directions. The entry with men and children welcoming Christ has already been mentioned. The silent departure of the conspirators (I. 662sd) and their silent approach to take Christ (I. 964sd) are strikingly conveyed. But most important of all is the Last Supper, where the stage directions not only convey an image of the scene but also in many cases suggest, if not actually indicate moves. There is first the tableau with the disciples seated in order (*in ere degré* I. 662sd) at the table with Christ in their midst. Then the blessing of the host and, after Christ's long explanatory sermon, the slow movements of the disciples taking the sacrament until the pause over Judas. Then the dismay at the announcement of the betrayal, the repeated denials, again the pause and Judas's hasty departure. Then the reestablishment of order with the slow taking of the wine echoing the taking of the host.

The stage layout of *Passion* II(a) was presumably envisaged as in general similar to that of *Passion* I. The first stage direction describes the opening procession with Herod, Pilate and Annas and Caiaphas taking up their positions on their scaffolds. Later Herod's scaffold *xal vnclose shewyng Herowdys in astat* (II. 377sd)—again the use of curtaining and of the set tableau. Pilate's wife runs off her scaffold to Pilate (II. 543sd)—the scaffold previously having been closed for the scene with Satan? Later stage directions, however, in *Passion* II(b), refer variously to scaffolds and to locations like *templum, sepulcrum, monumentum* as pageants and play material are merged, and it becomes impossible to recover the staging pattern in any satisfactory sense. This uncertainty and also in some cases the total absence of stage directions means that the staging of some of the most interesting effects of *Passion* II—the appearance of Anima Christi after Christ's death on the cross, the entry into the sepulchre and the Resurrection—are lost.

Altogether five scaffolds seem to be required: Pilate and his wife, Annas and Caiaphas, Herod, the Council House and Hell. There is no evidence for a heaven scaffold. Of these Herod's, Annas and Caiaphas's, the Council House and Hell have a considerable amount of action taking place on or around them. It is possible that for all but the Council House the action takes place off the scaffold. Herod's scourging of Christ, the first mockery and Peter's denial could all occur in the 'place'. Hell is rather more difficult to deal with since for its main action it falls outside the continuous play and is not described. It is however clear from the text that no action takes place inside Hell. With the Council House the case is different. It first enters the action when Pilate arrives at it and Christ is brought up to him. Annas and Caiaphas too almost certainly go up to him and the crowd is left below in the 'place'. Pilate remains there until the return of Christ from Herod (there is no reason for him to move) and it is there that his wife finds him to tell him of her dream. During the next examination of Christ, Pilate *ledyth hym into þe cowncel hous*. Since this conversation is intended to be heard there must be an inner area where this action is clearly visible and from which the dialogue is clearly audible to the audience. As Pilate moves backwards and forwards between the Jews and Christ at this point, it seems almost certain that this was a scaffold with a forestage as well as a curtained inner stage. At the judgement, Pilate formally sits and again perhaps the inner area is used. Annas and Caiaphas go in with him (II. 656sd) and the prisoners are brought to the bar. This is no large structure. It may already be in position on the forestage or it may be set up at this moment. With the departure of Annas and Caiaphas after the judgement, it would be possible for the action to move up onto the scaffold—brutality taking over from law—for the carefully described second mocking and scourging of Christ, especially since Christ is seated for much of this. If this is a reasonably accurate reconstruction of the action then it is clear that the Council House needs to be a largish structure.

Calvary is fully described except for its relationship with the scaffolds and its position in the 'place'. It should be remembered that once the judgement is over the identity of the Council House need no longer be maintained. With the departure of Christ on the road to Calvary the Council House scaffold could very well become the mount to which they are journeying—and later too perhaps the sepulchre. Comparison with Lucerne is useful here. The Cysat plans seem to suggest a whole series of chronologically disparate scenes in position at the same time. In fact it is clear from his notes that the stage staff are constantly on call to move one stage prop off, turn it round, alter its position, as scene gave way to scene. The movement around the place gives the opportunity for the transformation of the Council House or simply for a stripping of its identity.

Movement and overlapping action are as important here as in *Passion* I. The only additional kind of movement is the opening procession, which raises the question of who was in it. All the characters? If Lucerne is anything to go by it would not include the Anima Christi since those who were concealed in the 'place' took up their positions in advance. The idea of overlapping action also raises a number of questions. Does the 'game' of the mocking go on behind Peter's denials? Does the hanged Judas remain visible, and for how long? Do the women, Simon of Cyrene and Veronica only appear when they are needed? The only overlap to which attention is drawn is the episode of Pilate's wife's dream and the processional return of Christ from Herod (II. 486sd), which could be quite a difficult piece of timing.

Costume description centres on Christ but goes little further than the biblical accounts: the white cloth at Herod's scaffold—unmentioned in the text—(II. 486sd), the purple cloth of silk at the second mocking (II. 698sd), and the putting on and off of Christ's clothes (II. 461sd, 486sd, 696sd, 698sd, 746sd). Satan is merely described as appearing in *most orryble wyse* (II. 486sd). Only the description of Pilate's wife in her shirt and carrying her *kyrtyl* (II. 543sd), and the thieves, bare-legged and in their shirts, provide a kind of theatrical reality (II. 656sd).

Properties too are largely those which are a necessary part of the story or of the tradition. The sitting of Christ at both the mockings is a part of the tradition, as is the forcing on of the crown of thorns with *forkys* (II. 698sd) and the ropes used to make Christ's body fit the nail holes on the cross. The one simple device which is described is the board with the inscription already on it which Pilate pretends to write (II. 874sd).

Despite the later difficulties and the gaps, the stage directions in *Passion* II(a) are especially important for the picturing of the action which takes place without dialogue: the entry of the messenger—a master-stroke of 'place and scaffold' staging—(II. 89sd), the first mocking (II. 181sd), the hanging of Judas (II. 257sd), Pilate's wife's dream (II. 543sd), the second mocking (II. 696sd and 698sd) and the elaborate scenes which take place around the cross (II. 774sd, 786sd, 790sd, 798sd, 854sd).

Teaching and Meaning

Passion I is about law and judgment, love and mercy, but many other elements of Christian teaching are touched on in the course of the play. Many are direct teaching. John the Baptist in his Prologue preaches the importance of balancing dread of God's judgment with hope in his mercy. When Peter preaches to Jerusalem (and to the audience) he teaches the importance of the two New Testament commandments of 'love God' and 'love þi neybore' (I. 363-4) He also encourages contrition and confession (I. 369) and keeping the commandments (I. 357). Christ himself teaches directly as well: those who receive the sacrament will be saved, but those who do not will die (I. 817-22). It is likely that some at least of the direct teaching is a response to Lollard criticisms of matters such as eucharistic belief and oral confession. This is particularly noticeable in the stress laid on the transubstantiation of the bread and wine into Christ's body and blood (I. 696-8), on Peter's demonstration of the reverence due to the host (I. 755-8), and perhaps too on the assurance that those who do not fully understand the mystery should simply put their faith in God and believe (I. 729-30). In general, however, it seems to me that the complexity of the presentation of the eucharist here must have got in the way of such specific teaching.

The power of direct teaching, coming from a figure of biblical distance and authority, must not be under-estimated, but it is not the only kind of teaching. Christ's life has always been seen as a source of exemplary teaching and there is an element of that here, particularly in his submission to the will of God. Peter, too, is an exemplary figure in his honest ordinariness. His goodness, as seen in his attitude to the sacrament (I. 755-62), his human limitations, as seen in his precipitate responses: his refusal at first to allow Christ to wash his feet (I. 829-32), his instant denial that he will run away (I. 869-72), his eagerness to defend Christ (I. 989-90sd). Opposed to him is Judas: receiving the sacrament in deadly sin, lying, cheating, deliberately selling his master.

There is, however, more to the play than this. Central to its story is the Last Supper. In no other English play is this episode so dominant. It is used, as has already been said, for direct teaching about the eucharist but it is also being used to give a sense of human reality to what to many people must have been simply an esoteric mystery. As the **Mary Play** might be called 'How the *Ave* was made', in as much as one of its purposes is to give a human solidity and clarity to a muttered prayer, so **Passion I** might be called 'How the mass was made', and in the same way anchors something distant down in a local time and place, a historic narrative of recognisable human emotion.

The Last Supper is, however, even more central than this. As I have said, the play is about law and judgment, love and mercy. The Demon's opening speech establishes the law for mankind: 'Sin, and go to hell, where there is no getting out'. Humanity cannot escape the fall of Adam. John the Baptist modifies this, but obliquely: 'Tread the path between over-hope in God's mercy and over-dread of his judgment and you will be saved'. But is John talking within the time-scheme of the play or outside it? If he is inside, then this is still a pious hope rather than a fact. *Quia in inferno nulla est redempcio* (I. 48) still reigns. The insistence on the law returns Annas and Caiaphas, Rewfyn and Leyon, the judges spiritual and temporal, and their hangers-on. The law is embodied in them as they make clear (I. 165-72 and 209-16) and consequently a threat to the law is a threat to them. Christ is seen as overthrowing that law and so must be done away with—not according to the law, but anyhow. If nothing can be found against him, fabricate it, and if that does not work, kill him anyway.

Christ, however, comes not to overthrow but to fulfil the law. He is the embodiment of numerous prophecies, his mission, the salvation of man, is clearly seen and stated. It is at this point that the extended Last Supper is absorbed into the theme. Christ's exposition of the Passover in spiritual terms is an exposition of how the Old Law is fulfilled and brought to fruition in the New (I. 675-8). It is interesting to note that there is here no

suggestion of the wrongness of the Old Law. It is the practitioners of it who are corrupt. Instead there is a sense of solemnity at the passing of a great and ancient wonder. As Christ shows, they have all fulfilled to the letter the law of the Passover (I. 663-74), and he goes on to explain how that is to give way to the new law of the eucharist (I. 683-6). The trappings of the old Passover become spiritual instruction for the living of the new (I. 707-50). But the sacrament has no meaning without the final fulfilling of the law: *Man for man an hende must make* (I. 502).

In the play more is made of Christ's manhood than is usually the case. He prays to his Father for the power to consecrate the bread (I. 687-94), for

> . . .be my manhood I am of lesse degré.
> (I. 690)

It seems to involve a different power from that of giving sight to the blind or overthrowing those who come to take him. It is God the Father who has the power to create the mystery of the sacrament. Emphasis upon Christ's manhood here gives a greater reality to his human reactions to events, his grief at his betrayal, for example:

> Me þu ast solde þat was þi frende
> Þat þu hast begonne brenge to an ende.
> (I. 777-8)

And underlines his affection for his disciples, previously expressed in the words of the gospel:

> And with fervent desyre of hertys affeccyon
> I have enterly desyryd to kepe my mawndé
> Among yow er þan I suffre my passyon.
> (I. 679-81)

The emphasis upon his manhood also gives additional meaning to Christ's promises for the future; his body 'þat for þe xal dey' (I. 764), his blood 'wheche xal be xad for mannys love' (I. 798), 'outh of myn herte it xal renne' (I. 804). The power to create the mystery of the sacrament resided outside him in his Father, the power to give meaning to the sacrament, i.e. the salvation of man, in one way also lies outside him, in the future. But in another way it is inside him: until he has died, nothing of what he is saying has any meaning.

> For mannys love I may do no mo
> Þan for love of man to be ded.
> (I. 807-8)

Without that death, however, he will have done nothing. This becomes more apparent when instead of the confident assurance of the Entry into Jerusalem,

> Frendys, beholde þe tyme of mercy,

Þe wich is come now withowtyn dowth;
Mannys sowle in blysse now xal edyfy,
And þe prynce of þe werd is cast owth.

(I. 415-18)

we come to the repeated threats of his coming death, the
pressure of prophecy:

Þe day is come I must procede
For to fulfylle þe prophecy.

(I. 853-4; and cf. I. 881-2, 887-8)

The statement of his rising again at I. 865-8, set in this
context, does not sound so certain, especially when a
few lines further on:

My flesch for fere is qwakyng fast.

(I. 884)

Remarkably in the agony in the garden, the play revers-
es the direction of the three prayers of Matthew's gospel (xxvi, 39-44). Instead of fear giving way to acceptance and then twice-repeated fearful acceptance of his
passion, we have fear giving way to acceptance and
then changing back to a twice-repeated fear (I. 909-16,
921-18, 929-36). It is only the sight of the meaningless
chalice and wafer (I. 936sd), meaningless, that is, without his death, that brings Christ back to an acceptance
of his destiny (I. 949-52).

As with the **Mary Play,** when Mary hesitates before
agreeing to the initiating act of salvation and there is a
real sense that it is possible for it not to happen (1323sd),
so here the playwright seems to emphasise Christ's
manhood to give a real sense that it might also be possible for the completion of the act of salvation not to
happen. Every celebration of the mass then becomes for
the receiver an understanding of Christ's tortured acceptance of the burden of his death for the salvation of
mankind.

The theme of the law is also present. Fulfilling the law
needs more than simply performing the rites of the
Passover and moralising its trappings to transform it
into the sacrament of the Eucharist. It needs death on
the cross—it *xal be sacryd be me* (I. 685) does not
merely mean 'I will bless it'. The final fulfilment of the
law is satisfaction for the sin of Adam, man for man,
Christ's death for his death *as þe parlement of hefne
hath ment* (I. 941).

Because of what has gone before, Mary's lament for
Christ's suffering humanity at the end of the play has a
far greater pathos. How could God allow his *owyn dere
son* to *sofre al þis,* who *evyr was obedyent*? (I. 1065-
6). One does not often feel the strain of that obedience
so strongly. Mary also finally draws attention to the
absolute necessity of Christ's suffering; *May man not
ellys be savyd be non other kende?* The answer is, of
course, no. His blamelessness, which Mary sees as the

reason why he should not suffer, is the very reason
that he must. Mercy thereby has triumphed, the law
has been fulfilled, but we have been made humanly
aware of the cost.

The tight organisation of **Passion** I may once have
existed in **Passion** II, but it is now only possible to
judge it by its first part, **Passion** II(a). This appears to
be dwelling on narrative story-telling and human characterisation. Its teaching of the story of Christ's sufferings is consequently direct and theatrically effective,
but it does not seem to be trying to go beyond that. As
with **Passion** I, there is a measure of direct teaching; for
example, Christ's prophecy of the power of Veronica's
kerchief (II. 745-6), Mary's emphasising of Christ's great
mercy (II. 835-8); and also exemplary teaching in, for
example, Peter's repentance (II. 214-25), but what is
primarily striking is the power of the story. That this is
a result of a carefully controlled simple language in an
easy metre is clear when one turns to **Passion** II(b).
This is not without some effective passages, e.g. the
rising of Anima Christi (II. 1005-8), the setting of the
watch (II. 1304-67), the characterising of the easy confidence of Annas (II. 1628-31), though many of the
most effective episodes are almost certainly the remnants of the old **Passion Play,** such as the restoring of
Longeus's sight (II. 1123-55). Too often the thinness of
the language is revealed by the demands of the metre.
There is a pleasure, it is true, in the greater regularity of
the metre but it often cannot make up for the commonplace nature of the thought, the tags and the empty repetitions. It is at its most bathetic in one of Mary Salome's
speeches on the way to the sepulchre:

My name is Mary Salomé,
His modyr and I, systerys we be,
Annys dowterys we be all thre;
    Jhesu, we be þin awntys.

Teaching and meaning come together in **Passion** I. It
may still have been in the process of development as a
play—something which could be said of most medieval
English plays—but it has already become a very powerful medium for a striking Christian and human message.

Gail McMurray Gibson (essay date 1993-94)

SOURCE: "Writing Before the Eye: The N-Town
Woman Taken in Adultery and the Medieval Ministry
Play," in *Comparative Drama,* Vol. 27, No. 4, Winter,
1993-94, pp. 399-407.

[*Here, Gibson argues that the* Woman Taken in Adultery *play enacts the Christian mystery of the connection between the flesh and the divine.*]

Richard Beadle has recently observed [in a review in

Medium Aevum 60, 1991] that "If any area of medieval English studies can be said to have changed out of all recognition over the past twenty years or so, it must be that of the drama." Certainly, twenty years ago I could have asserted the perversity of teaching a field of scholarly inquiry—the medieval English mystery play—whose very name ("mystery" play) was a modern scholarly invention perpetuating a linguistic confusion. As E. K. Chambers had nagged [in *The Medieval Stage*] in 1903, the word 'mystery' "is not English at all, in a dramatic sense, and in France first appears as *misterie* in the charter given by Charles VI in 1402 to the Parisian *confrérie de la Passion*." In a note he adds: "The first English use of the term 'mystery' is in the preface to Dodsley's *Select Collection of Old Plays* (1744)." The medieval "mystery" plays, as I have more than a few times nagged to my own students, were in fact, *ministerium* plays, that is, plays performed by medieval craft or parish guilds. The Latin word *ministerium* and its vernacular Middle English forms 'myster' or 'mysterie' meant occupation, craft, or ministry. The biblical plays thus came to be called 'mysteries' in the sense of the post-Reformation Chester Banns: "by xxiiii^tie occupationes—artes, craftes, or misterye—these pagiantes should be played."

But all medievalists must eventually learn to accept linguistic confusion as evidence of divine providence—which, as medieval theologians and exegetes knew, loves nothing so much as a good Latin pun. So it is that after twenty years I have come to realize that though, linguistically speaking, the field of my scholarship should be "the ministry play," the biblical drama of the streets of England was indeed a mystery—that is, a *mysterium*—and have come to see that it was an art form of signs and actions curiously antithetical to *ministry*. I have even come to see that E. K. Chambers was wrong in saying that there is no medieval English use of the word *mysterium* for this drama; John Lydgate's banns for a London Corpus Christi procession quite explicitly call those pageants "mysteries grounded in scripture":

> This hye feste nowe for to magnefye,
> Feste of festes moost hevenly and devyne,
> In goostly gladnesse to governe vs and guye,
> By which al grace doothe vppon vs shyne;
> For now this day al derkenesse tenlumyne;
> In youre presence fette out of fygure,
> Shal beo declared by many unknouthe signe
> Gracyous misteryes grounded in scripture.

Nor was Chambers correct in insisting that even the French use of "mystery" in a dramatic sense was an afterthought; as early as 1372 the French soldier, diplomat, and scholar Phillipe de Mézières wrote a play of the *Presentation of the Virgin Mary in the Temple*—written in Latin, though to be played, as he explains, either in Latin or in the vernacular as one wills—and in his lengthy, self-conscious prologue explained

that since the play is to be in honor of Mary whose human life "reveals what is deep and hidden," its actions in fleshly acts and signs are means by which the mind, released from the weight of the flesh, may be enabled to arrive at knowledge of the invisible and visible elements of God's mysteries [misteriorum Dei] as it were through visible things, signs, and works, in accord with apostolic teaching.

The Latin word *mysterium,* from Greek *mysterion,* originally signaled the secret initiations into epiphanies showing the riddles of life and of death in the cult religions of the Graeco-Roman world. According to Hippolytus, the climax of the famous Eleusinian mystery cult observed near Athens was a single harvested head of grain revered in profound simplicity and silence. But the esoteric Greek word *mysterion* and then the Latin vulgate's *mysterium* (and finally 'mystery') entered the mainstream of Western tradition because of its surprising use, especially by the apostle Paul, in the New Testament. In Pauline paradox the guarded secret of the sacred *mysterion* has now become the good news, the good ministry. The fertile victory over death imaged by the cycle of the grain is transfigured by God becoming incarnate human flesh and offering resurrection to his followers: "Behold, I tell you a mystery [mysterium]," St. Paul writes in *I Corinthians:* "We shall all indeed rise again. . . . In a moment, in the twinkling of an eye, at the last trumpet: for the trumpet shall sound, and the dead shall rise again incorruptable: and we shall be changed" (15.51-52; Douay-Rheims Version).

The Incarnation as vehicle of transcendence was for Paul the central Christian mystery; medieval biblical drama was likewise incarnate *mysterium.* The Word made flesh was both dramatic theory and theological justification of these biblical plays—plays by which, as Phillipe de Mézières explained, the mind stirred by visible signs and actions "may be enabled to arrive at knowledge of the invisible and visible elements of God's mysteries."

The medieval biblical drama does in fact insistently identify the highest truth with "visible signs and actions," with sacramental image rather than human speech—with mystery rather than ministry. For medieval religious sensibilities the sacraments of the church—baptism, eucharist, penance—were themselves, as St. Augustine had explained them [in *De Doctrina Christiana*] "a sort of visible word." In 1215 sermons had been officially ordered by legislation of the Fourth Lateran Council and a minimum number required of parish priests on the most solemn occasions of the church year, but the elevation of the Host remained the highest, most sufficient argument that the Word had been made flesh. Vernacular words in the texts of the medieval English biblical plays were likewise in a crucial way subordinate to the incarnate spectacle and even second to any words of Latin liturgy and Latin scripture, which, as in the East Anglian **N-Town cycle,** were often left conspicuously untranslated, to function as [what Roger Ellis calls in *Word, Picture, and Spectacle,* 1984] "intrusive sacred sign," a kind of visual icon of the revealed wisdom of God.

What bothers me most about the current scholarly quibbling over which archival documents record biblical "dramas" and which record visual pageants—"mere" silent tableaux processing in the streets—is that the distinction is not only unmedieval but misses the crucial point that it is, after all, the *imaging* of scripture in human flesh that is the generating force of the medieval religious drama. The highest purpose of medieval biblical drama, I would argue, was not explication of the word—not preaching or *ministry* at all—but the sacramental revelation of the *mysterium* of word made flesh. In this theater, ministry is almost always transfigured into mystery; the revelation of a harvested head of grain has become the revelation of the unspeaking word, the *infans* Christ humbled in a manger or in weighty silence facing the raucous taunts of his unknowing accusers or in wordless dying implicating the spectators in the horrors of the cross, finally to rise, to triumph, to reign again. Such iconic and laconic centers are, in fact, precisely what make performance so essential to the study of medieval drama and what make reading these terse registers of dialogue removed from their iconographic and cultural contexts rather like attempting to understand medieval religious art by scrutinizing only the painted words on banderoles unfurling from the mouths of the sacred characters. The profoundest meaning of the mystery plays often lies in speechless silence—in the astonishing rubric of waiting, for example, as the **N-Town** Virgin Mary pauses to consider the Annunciation angel's message and to agree to play her role in redemption; in the silence of Christ in his agonizing Passion—and, nearly as eloquent, that silence that passes human understanding as Jesus in the **N-Town** play of *The Woman Taken in Adultery* silently writes with his finger the mysteries of sin and salvation upon the ground.

The much admired **N-Town** play of *The Woman Taken in Adultery* is a play which strikes me as a kind of meta-mystery, a play revealing the very meaning and purpose of this medieval *mysterium* drama. Significantly, the York and Chester compilations also contain a play of the woman taken in adultery, and Eleanor Prosser even assumed [in *Drama and Religion in the Early Mystery Plays,* 1961] that "unfortunately the Towneley play is lost." The existence of three plays on this subject in the medieval English dramatic repertoire is remarkable, for, as several medieval drama scholars have observed, there is a paucity in the cycles of what is usually termed "Ministry plays," that is, of plays concerning Christ's adult life, his preaching and teaching. The only "obligatory" play, as V. A. Kolve noted, [in *The Play Called Corpus Christi*, 1966] seems to have

been *The Raising of Lazarus,* which is not a preaching play at all; it is less a play of the "Ministry" of Christ than a play of the central mystery of Christ's victory over death, a typological foreshadowing of Christ's own Resurrection. Both Kathleen Ashley [in "The Resurrection of Lazarus in the Late Medieval English and French Cycle Drama," *Papers in Language and Literature* 22, 1986] and Clifford Davidson [in *From Creation to Doom,* 1984] have noted the puzzling reservation of medieval dramatists about representing the events of the "acts and teachings of Christ's adult life" and have tried to explain why "the Ministry series may at first seem abbreviated and perhaps disappointing." Peter Travis went so far [in *Dramatic Design in the Chester Cycle,* 1982] as to characterize the reservation of the Chester playwright about dramatizing the Ministry as a "Neo-Romanesque" strategy of the Chester playwright who with deliberate restraint creates a stylized Christ and a small group of Ministry plays of "starkly Christocentric" focus.

But except for the ***Woman Taken in Adultery,*** all the extant cycles show this same restraint concerning the Ministry of Christ. A question I have long struggled to answer is why *did* medieval dramatists seize this quirky little passage in St. John's Gospel—a passage that the Revised Standard Version decreed a third-century uncanonical interpolation and relegated to the small print at the bottom of the page—and decide it should stand for the entire teaching and adult life of Christ? An important part of the answer, I think, is that this narrative is transparently a text about mystery. It is scripture much less about words said, less even about mercy and absolution than about some unspoken words, icons traced enigmatically in the dirt.

The Vulgate told the story in ten brief verses in Chapter 8 of St. John's Gospel. It is early in the morning, before the temple. The scribes and the Pharisees bring before Jesus a woman taken in adultery and attempt to entrap Jesus on the horns of a dilemma. The law of Moses says the punishment should be death by stoning, "But what sayest thou?"

> But Jesus bowing himself down, wrote with his finger on the ground.

> When therefore they continued asking him, he lifted up himself, and said to them: He that is without sin among you, let him cast a stone at her.

> And again stooping down, he wrote on the ground.

> But they hearing this, went out one by one, beginning at the eldest.

Jesus remains alone with the woman; he asks if there is anyone there to condemn her. She answers, "No man, Lord." (That simple, reverent "Lord" speaking all.)

"And Jesus said: Neither will I condemn thee. Go, and now sin no more." (*John* 8.5-11; Douay Rheims Version)

In the gospel text there is enormous tension between the heavy and loaded question—"But what sayest thou?"—and Christ's riddling response. But especially there is the enigma of the writing on the ground. Jesus writes how? Nervously? Peevishly? Distractedly? Or is this some apocalyptic handwriting on the wall? The gospel text is deliberately mysterious here, yet insistently emphasizes the action by using it to frame Jesus' response to the Scribes and Pharisees. Not once but twice, Jesus stoops down and writes upon the ground. Writes what? Ambrose and Augustine interpreted this writing as scriptural fulfillment of *Jeremiah* 17.13: "they that depart away from thee, shall be written in the earth: because they have forsaken the Lord, the vein of living waters." Jerome agreed and suggested further that what Jesus wrote in the earth were the hidden sins of the accusers; as Judith Ferster [in *Sign, Sentence, Discourse,* 1989] has written of the adultery play in the Chester cycle, "What better place than earth to write about human sin?"

In the remarkable **N-Town** *Woman Taken in Adultery,* the scene begins with outrageous slapstick comedy. A certain young man surprised *in flagrante* runs out of the adulterous woman's house with his untied boots flapping about his ankles and his breeches clutched in his hand. This staged, comic disorder of sin contains much cursing and crude threat; the young man, still apparently clutching his breeches, manages somehow both to threaten his accusers with a dagger and to run away from the melee. The accusing Scribe all the while yells out obscenities to the woman within the house: "Com forth, þu hore and stynkynge bych clowte!" (l. 147). Perhaps this taunt means stinking "rag of a whore," as Stephen Spector has glossed it [in *The N-town Play,* 1991] but, as I think more likely given the verbal emphasis in this and other East Anglian plays on the "ordure" of sin, probably means something more like, as David Mills memorably renders the line [in *The Macro Plays,* 1969] "Come forth thou whore and stinking dog-turd!"

The befouled earth of sin in *The Woman Taken in Adultery* is silently transfigured by Christ's mimed actions—actions given typically trinitarian emphasis in the **N-Town cycle** by the stage directions that specify three times that Christ "nichil respondit, sed semper scrybyt in terra." Jesus three times and in silence writes the words that are revealed before the eyes of his accusers as their own secret sins. Incredulously the Pharisee exclaims that "All myn synnys evyn propyrly namyd / yon prophyte dede wryte befor myn eye" (ll. 235-36).

It is such "writing before the eye" that is Paul's mys-

tery; Christ "was seen also by me," he put it simply in his first letter to the Corinthians (15.8). What is in this play as simply imaged and literally "grounded" in scripture is the mystery of Christ's grace. "Go, and now sin no more" is sufficient conclusion to whore and to accusors and to audience. Woman *is* humanity in medieval symbolic theological discourse; but though Adam in his fallen nature encompassed the full generous possibilities of human sin, a fallen woman in this same symbolic discourse sins, of course, in the only way that a fallen woman sins, by her sex. The whore is thus humanity—is Everyman—as the outward glancing speeches that frame the play's action make clear:

> What man of synne be repentaunt,
> Of God if he wyl mercy craue,
> God of mercy is so habundawnt,
> Þat, what man haske it, he xal it haue.
>
> (ll. 285-89)

Several commentators have been struck by the way this play in the **N-Town cycle** functions as effective climax to the themes of temptation, sin, and repentance traced in the preceding plays, but what I find most striking (and best witness to the complex unity in this eclectic text) is the way that Christ's writing of hidden sins in the earth foreshadows that final moment in the **N-Town** *Judgement Day* play when the damned souls call out to the "clowdys of clay" to break asunder to let them pass. At last, and alas too late for mercy, the Primus Diabolus chortles that "on here forehed wyttnes I take. / For þer is wretyn with letteris blake / Opynly all here synne." The sins written in earth are now written upon the foreheads of the earth creatures—kin of Adam and of clay—who find the time for Christ's tender mercies past. The final extant lines of the **N-Town** *Judgement Day* ominously replay the *Woman Taken in Adultery* as "Sybile Sclutte," whose life was "leccherous lay" and who refused to clothe the naked when they implored in God's name, is condemned to the torments of Hell. The sin of refusing naked need thus fulfills in divine comedy what had been the very human comedy of those naked sinners in the earlier *Woman Taken in Adultery,* and the final, all-seeing eye of judgment is the fulfillment of Christ's mysterious reading of the sins of the accusors.

But before time is played out, sin is written in the earth and then the mystery of divine grace is written before the eye. The **N-Town** play of *The Woman Taken in Adultery* ends with hopeful blessing, by Jesus—although emended to "Doctor" in the manuscript by a medieval editor, mindful perhaps of the straining anachronism in Christ's final words: "Now God þat dyed for all mankende / Saue all these pepyl both nyght and day. . ." (ll. 293-94).

It is the vulnerability of this incarnate God, his very dying, that will, as both St. Paul and the **N-Town** plot testify, bring salvation. The *mysterion* of the medieval religious drama is this inscrutable mystery. It is un-flinching enactment of the fact that, to say it most sim-ply [as does Caroline Walker Bynum in her *Fragmen-tation and Redemption*] "Body is what we've got." Flesh is human vulnerability, flesh is human sin, even death. But as the medieval religious drama existed to affirm, flesh is also what joins human actor to that enfleshed God and to his saving, amazing grace.

Alan J. Fletcher (essay date 1994)

SOURCE: "The N-Town Plays," in *The Cambridge Companion to Medieval English Theatre*, edited by Richard Beadle, Cambridge University Press, 1994, pp. 163-88.

[*In the following excerpt, Beadle describes the prove-nance of the N-Town manuscript, arguing against Gibson's suggestion of Bury St. Edmunds as its origin. He also asserts that the manuscript is a composite, and offers a general overview of the plays.*]

INTRODUCTION

'Corpus Christi plays', 'cycle plays': these are just two of the more familiar boxes in which modern critics have tried to contain the resisting diversity of much late medieval English drama. Indeed, such pigeon-holing has a long pedigree. Whoever wrote 'The plaie called Cor-pus Christi' on the first page of the play manuscript that concerns this chapter, British Library MS Cotton Ves-pasian D. viii, is the earliest known member of this critical family tree. He would hardly have foreseen that his sixteenth-century attempt to sum up the plays in front of him would have provided the title for one of the most successful studies of medieval drama in recent years, [V.A. Kolve's *The Play Called Corpus Christi*, 1966] a study whose equally unforeseen consequence has been the encouragement of some homogenised ways of thinking about what a 'Corpus Christi cycle' might be. The fact is, however, that the plays of Cotton Ves-pasian D. viii are not tidily compliant, and resist the totalising project that the idea of a 'Corpus Christi cycle' has sometimes risked becoming. There is no evidence that these plays ever had anything to do with Corpus Christi, at least not in the most basic sense of their having been performed then; on the contrary, some were originally intended for performance on a Sunday. Nor has the Creation-to-Doom scope of the manuscript's content, which superficially invites comparison with the other three major mystery play collections of Ches-ter, Wakefield and York, come about for comparable reasons. The former independence of some of its prin-cipal component parts has been suppressed: originally, these parts were never arranged according to any grand Creation-to-Doom design whatsoever. So in sum, it is juster to recognise the fascinating *difference* of this manuscript, and this sense of difference will, I hope,

be an undertow to my introduction of it and of the plays of which it is no neutral transmitter.

A MANUSCRIPT IN SEARCH OF A CONTEXT

If the scribe-compiler of Cotton Vespasian D. viii (for so I shall refer to him) ever made a note of where and when he was working, the place in which he might well have recorded it, in some *explicit* at the end of his manuscript, no longer exists, for what was likely the final play in his collection, **Judgment Day,** lacks its concluding folios, finishing imperfectly with the prom-ise of a speech from God that we never get to hear. When and where, then, was Cotton Vespasian D. viii compiled? Answers to these questions, far from being merely incidental, would help to contextualise the manuscript and so illuminate it as a material product of a specific cultural and historical matrix. The first question seems the less problematic: the scribe-com-piler probably worked sometime after 1468, the date written on fol. 100v at the end of the Purification play, perhaps *c.* 1500, the period to which his handwriting seems best to correspond. But the question of where he worked is more difficult and has set scholars hunt-ing widely afield, even though their excursions have mainly taken them through the same general part of England. The earliest critics, misled by a description written on the flyleaf of the manuscript by Sir Robert Cotton's librarian, Richard James, believed the plays were from Coventry. Indeed, James's note that *vulgo dicitur hic liber Ludus Coventriae* ('this book is com-monly called the Play of Coventry') gave rise to one of the most popular names for the plays, the **Ludus Coventriae,** a name which stuck even when critics had come to doubt their Coventry connection. It was the late-nineteenth-century investigation of the dialectal affinities of the manuscript's Middle English that start-ed to shift attention away from Coventry to the east of England. As late as the 1960s, Lincoln was often cham-pioned as the home of the plays, even though any Lincoln affilation of their written dialect had already by then been seriously undermined, and East Anglia looked increasingly like the area in which the main scribe had been trained to write. Of course, a scribe raised on the spellings of his region might move to a part of England where others prevailed yet continue to spell as before, but, this granted, the extant records of dramatic activity in medieval Lincoln were hard pressed to correspond to the sort of drama Cotton Vespasian D. viii actually contains. Although Lincoln rightly fell from favour as the city in which the plays were writ-ten, the tendency to foster them on a centre of cultural importance persists, and there are persuasive reasons why it should: the scribe-compiler was working some-where where he had access to at least four different exemplars of dramatic texts (one of these, the Assump-tion play, he incorporated bodily into his compilation), and possibly to even more; and secondly, he seems also to have been somewhere where he could consult theological material, about which more later. So although in theory he could have been working anywhere, what little is known of his circumstances suggests at least that it was not in some utterly out-of-the-way place, nor, probably, very far from East Harling in south-central Norfolk, where the latest study on Middle English scribal dialects would seek to place him.

Assuming he did not stray too far from home, the question then arises, where in East Anglia would have provided the right kind of cultural context for the manufacture of a play manuscript such as his? Norwich once seemed attractive until it was observed that whatever its provenance, the manuscript probably had no relation to the Norwich civic play cycle, for the content of this, as far as it can be determined, differed from that of the manuscript in several important respects. Moreover, the famous lines at the end of the banns of the plays: 'At vj of þe belle we gynne oure play / In N-town' (**Proclamation,** lines 526-7), from which the plays derive their most appropriate modern name, the **N-Town** plays, are now generally thought to mean that the name of whatever town the plays were to be performed in should be substituted for the 'N' just as, for example, the letter N. (for *nomen*) in many a medieval liturgical manuscript was a cue to its reader to insert whatever name he required. In short, the **N-Town** plays (or more precisely, the plays that the banns referred to, for they apply only to a portion of the manuscript's contents) were probably intended for touring, not for performing in one specific city. It is worth bearing in mind, though, that since there is no evidence that the plays in Cotton Vespasian D. viii ever came from any civic cycle, lack of correspondence between them and the civic cycle of Norwich is not the best reason for rejecting Norwich as the manuscript's home. Even so, Norwich has lost ground and has been eclipsed in some of the most recent criticism by a case argued powerfully [e.g. by Gail Gibson in "Bury St. Edmunds, Lydgate, and the *N-Town Cycle,*" *Speculum* 56, 1981] in favour of a home in Bury St Edmunds. This argument requires scrutiny.

Bury St Edmunds was undeniably an important dramatic centre throughout the fifteenth century, and even before then there are signs of an interest in drama there. It was in its prosperous abbey of St Edmund that the Benedictine monk and poet John Lydgate spent much of his life, and his concern with drama is well attested in the mummings and pageants that formed part of his copious output. Possibly the style of some **N-Town** plays betrays Lydgatean influence. Possibly, too, certain of the morality plays in the Macro and Digby manuscripts were at one time in the abbey's possession, and there is a little evidence that players or minstrels were hosted there.

But does all this therefore mean that Bury was the town in which the **N-Town** plays were compiled? There are difficulties in believing so that should not be minimised. One is theoretical. Once an important dramatic centre is established, and undoubtedly Bury was, there may be a temptation to foster on it any play text that can be shown to come from the same general area of England in which the centre is located but whose exact provenance is otherwise unknown, as in **N-Town's** case. Records prove, however, that late medieval East Anglian drama might sometimes get written down in places that were not conspicuous cultural or dramatic centres. For example, Robert Reynes, a late-fifteenth-century churchwarden of the village of Acle in Norfolk, copied play extracts into his commonplace book. Had all evidence of his whereabouts been removed from his manuscript, a comparatively out-of-the-way Norfolk village would surely not have struck critics as its likely provenance. Notwithstanding the undisputed existence of dramatic centres, cases like this should encourage respect for the diffusion of dramatic activity throughout East Anglia in the fifteenth century. Yet as noted earlier, the scribe-compiler's access to several source texts suggests that the compilation of **N-Town** probably did somehow depend upon a centre of relative cultural significance. Are we back, therefore, to Bury St Edmunds? A glance at a map of East Anglia in the fifteenth century suggests another possibility with as good a claim, and this is the town of Thetford in south-central Norfolk, about twelve miles north of Bury.

Apart from the fact that it is the nearest big cultural centre to the area indicated by the spelling of the scribe-compiler, Thetford too is linked with drama. Its Cluniac Priory of St Mary, one of East Anglia's greatest monastic houses, is known to have made payments towards plays in Thetford and its surrounding villages. These payments might also fit a context of touring, inter-village drama such as is known to have existed in the region, and some kind of touring drama, as we saw, seems implied by the **N-Town** banns. Another contemporary East Anglian play with banns, the Croxton *Play of the Sacrament,* has also been thought to have a Thetford connection. **N-Town's** unique series of plays on the early life of the Virgin Mary were conceivably organised by some lay religious guild, as were also its plays on the Passion. (These groups of plays will be discussed later.) If they were, Thetford too had social infrastructures suited to producing them. A well-endowed guild of St Mary was active there, and as early as 1422 Thetford had a guild of Corpus Christi. One small hint at provenance may be contained in one of the marginal glosses that the scribe-compiler appears to have added to his manuscript. On fol. 74v is a note of the date of the feast of the translation of St Mary Magdalene. This feast, though rare in English liturgical use, was commoner in continental, especially French, uses of the sort that might be expected in a place like a Cluniac priory. All this does not establish Thetford as a home of N-Town, of course, but it makes Thetford as persuasive a cultural epicentre as Bury St Edmunds.

Wherever exactly the scribe-compiler worked, some of the plays he collected, those to which the banns refer, were evidently once intended for touring, and in the present state of our knowledge, it seems safest to say that this was to villages around the Norfolk and Suffolk border in the late fifteenth and early sixteenth centuries.

THE ARCHAEOLOGY OF THE MANUSCRIPT

Precisely because the plays of **N-Town** cannot be convincingly linked to any known external records of performance, as can plays from places like Chester or York, their manuscript assumes a singular importance. As the sole source of information on everything to do with them it needs careful searching for clues to the nature of the East Anglian dramatic milieu of which it is in some sense a reflex and which in turn it once helped to sustain; various revisions made in it by someone who had acquired it shortly after completion by the scribe-compiler show that it was eventually being used in actual play production. Whether that was the scribe-compiler's original intention for it is, however, much less clear. Basically, it looks as if he wanted to compile a play repertiore, organised within a Creation-to-Doom framework, which would be more comprehensive than anything available in any one of his sundry individual exemplars, even if doing so meant replacing some plays in whole or in part with others. This repertoire he gradually pieced together, sometimes taking the trouble to co-ordinate coherently its originally disparate materials, sometimes not bothering, or sometimes beginning and then simply abandoning the attempt part way through. Probably a cleric, he was also someone with access to certain nondramatic, theological writings which it seemed worth his while to draw upon for providing his manuscript with a set of marginal glosses. These argue for a rather learned or readerly interest in the material he worked with. Perhaps his manuscript was destined for actors—without question it soon fell into their hands—yet its glosses betray a desire to give it a certain literary 'finish' indifferent to practical dramatic use. Whoever the scribe-compiler was, he seems to have been acquainted with the ethos of glossed and annotated texts, for in its own small way his manuscript reveals, too, the sort of concern for respectable textual presentation, for *ordinatio,* that might be expected in someone clerically trained.

So distinctive an artefact is his manuscript that it stands apart from those of all other early English plays. However difficult now to pinpoint the purposes for which it was intended, they were evidently quite different from those served, for example, by the antiquarian compilers of the Chester manuscripts, by the medieval York scribes employed to copy their city's official play register, or by the scribe of the plush Wakefield manuscript. It is much humbler than any of these. But an-

other important aspect of its distinctiveness, its manufacture from texts many of which once had utterly independent dramatic existence before being compiled, highlights a radical critical question: how is a critic to speak about a composite entity like **N-Town**?

There is no doubt that it is composite. From about the beginning of this century an appreciation has slowly grown of its textual complexity. The scribe-compiler had access to a major play collection which seems to have formed the basis for his work, and for which the banns at the beginning of the manuscript were written. These banns were composed to describe a sequence of forty different episodes (each is called a 'pagent') from the Creation, through events of the Old and New Testaments, to the Judgement Day. The banns refer to plays that had already been subject to revision and editing before the scribe-compiler started copying them. I will refer to the banns and their pageants as the **Proclamation Play,** reserving the word 'pageant' for episodes that derive from it (though critics have sometimes referred to it as the 'banns' or the 'pageant' play). The **Proclamation Play** was the one intended for touring and whose performance someone had imagined as happening on Sunday at N-Town 'at vj of þe belle'. Possibly the scribe-compiler, in being content to copy this, envisaged similar production circumstances for his own collection. But as we have seen and will see again later, he reveals himself less as being interested in the practical dramatic aspects of what he copies than as being a literary editor who, while not zealous to remove every narrative discrepancy to which his magpie collection is prone, is still concerned enough to make a few gestures in the direction of logical narrative continuity. In view of his apparent disposition in this respect, it is not at all clear that the staging envisaged by the banns should be regarded as applicable to the contents of the entire manuscript in any really meaningful way. If he had intended this, he would have removed the mention at the beginning of **Passion Play II** that **Passion Play I** had been performed 'last yere' (Play 29, line 7). In fact, when the manuscript eventually does fall into the hands of a practical dramatist, Reviser B as he has been called, he quarries and adapts some of its contents for a two-day performance, and does not struggle to do what the banns seem to prescribe.

The scribe-compiler worked very roughly as follows. First he copied the **Proclamation Play** until the end of the seventh pageant, a procession of prophets foretelling the Virgin and her son. After this occurs the first major break in his copying process. Here he laid aside his Proclamation Play exemplar and took up another having in it a self-contained play on the early life of the Virgin. This **Mary Play,** in five episodes, presented her conception, presentation in the temple, marriage to Joseph, Annunciation (preceded by a Parliament of Heaven, a deliberation among the three Persons in Trinity as to which of them should set in motion the machinery of man's salvation) and finally her Visitation to Elizabeth. Like the **Proclamation Play,** the **Mary Play** too had already undergone some revision in its exemplar before the scribe-compiler acquired it. Its first two plays, those of her conception and presentation, he copied more or less as they stood, but when he came to her marriage to Joseph, he decided to amalgamate it with another two pageants of similar topic that were also to be found in the exemplar of his **Proclamation Play.** The result was a blended text. Yet curiously, rather than hide the seams between **Mary** and **Proclamation Play** material, he chose rather to reveal most of them, and this he did by dotting in red the lobes of the paragraph marks before speeches lifted from the **Mary Play,** but leaving blank those before speeches from the **Proclamation Play.**

After finishing this composite marriage episode, he put aside his **Proclamation Play** exemplar and resumed exclusively that of the **Mary Play** for the **Parliament of Heaven** and **Annunciation,** ignoring another **Annunciation** in the **Proclamation Play.** Then, taking up the **Proclamation Play** exemplar once again, and leaving that of the **Mary Play** (apart perhaps from lifting just a few lines from it, he copied the play of Joseph's doubts about Mary. Finally he returned to the **Mary Play** exemplar for the last time and copied its **Visitation to Elizabeth**.

From here on he worked steadily from the **Proclamation Play** exemplar until reaching the **Purification Play,** for this episode, not mentioned in the banns, had presumably therefore no pageant dealing with it. After the **Purification,** the **Proclamation Play** exemplar was followed for a long stint. He copied its **Slaughter of the Innocents,** its **Christ and the doctors** in the temple, its pageants on Christ's ministry and **Passion,** through at least as far as the setting of the guard on Christ's sepulchre, and perhaps even farther, before radically changing his mind. At some point late in his copying from the **Proclamation Play** exemplar, he now decided to incorporate what was once an independent **Passion Play.** This was in two parts. The first, **Passion Play I,** which he had already copied into a separate booklet on some previous occasion, was originally free of any **Proclamation Play** material. He physically incorporated this booklet, suppressing in the process much of the **Proclamation Play's Passion** pageants that he had copied earlier, but retaining and interpolating a little of their material. I will explain this in more detail shortly. He produced **Passion Play II,** on the other hand, quite differently, for this time he copied it from the outset with a view to its amalgamation with the **Proclamation Play** material which he had already copied earlier. This second part of the **Passion Play** is more substantially a blend of material than the first. It has no distinct ending, probably because the original ending of the play contained in the **Passion Play** exemplar was suppressed in the process of dovetailing it

with pageant material. The **Proclamation Play** exemplar was now resumed and followed exclusively until the **Assumption,** a play that some completely different scribe had copied into a once independent booklet. The scribe-compiler incorporated it wholesale and rubricated it to conform it to the layer of the rest of his compilation. Finally he returned to the **Proclamation Play** exemplar to copy its **Judgement Day** pageant.

So a modern critic, viewing all this complicated textual architecture, has options like those available to someone viewing the interior of some great medieval cathedral: one may be content simply to take in an overall impression that the place makes, or looking more narrowly one may prefer to discriminate and trace the shifts of style between, say, Decorated and Perpendicular, from which overall impressions are finally constituted. Since either way of observing tends to shade into the other, the most natural thing might be to do a bit of both. Similarly, **N-Town** has had its general surveyors, mainly in the form of those who have perceived in it overarching thematic unity, just as it has had its textual archaeologists—those who have preferred to focus narrowly on its bricks and mortar. Less effort, however, has been made to see how both views relate to each other, or to come to terms with the fundamental reason for their existence. In fact, the problem raised earlier of knowing how to speak about a manifestly composite text has created apparent critical alternatives. Alone, each has its limitations: finding **N-Town** to be inhabited by a presiding and coherent spirit, a sort of *genius loci* to whom thematic unity can be credited, even if in some sense true, is nevertheless a recipe for stifling its diversity and marginalising its undisputed textual disparateness; conversely, seeking to excavate earlier textual structures, though informative, is finally an unachievable task and one indifferent to the possibility that the compilation they have been built into might have a structure of its own, whether planned or fortuitous. To put it briefly, is it useful to dwell on textual continuities at the expense of discontinuities, or vice versa? **N-Town,** the result of an unforeseen collaboration between texts (unforeseen in the sense that several of them were once discrete and formally unrelated to each other) tends therefore perhaps more than any other early play collection to polarise the critical approach.

Where both approaches originate, however, is in the activity of the scribe-compiler, and here may be the place to look for guidance about how to understand his collection. We may expose and thereby perceive the modernity of these approaches if we once apprehend something of his medieval textual practice. What are the attitudes to his text and its function that are implicit in his ways of working? We need to look at some text closely, holding critical and bibliographical issues simultaneously in focus.

BUILDING A PASSION PLAY

Passion Play I is written on five quires of paper: the first (quire N) is of twelve folios, with a singleton (fol. 143), bringing it up to thirteen folios, added after leaf seven; the second (quire O), is of three folios, wanting one leaf after the third; the third (quire P) is a bifolium; the fourth (quire Q) is similar; and finally the fifth (quire R) is a regular quire of eight leaves. The paper watermarks of quires N, P, Q and R are of the bull's head type, but quire O is the odd man out, employing a bunch of grapes type. In itself a change of paper might not mean much, but other evidence confirms the suspicion that quire O (containing pageant material from the Proclamation Play) is, in fact, an addition made by the scribe-compiler to a set of quires he had already completed. If we therefore leave quire O aside for the moment and also the singleton added in quire N that probably belongs to this same phase of the scribe-compiler's revision, we can discern an earlier completed scribal stint in four quires (N, P, Q and R), and one of the interesting things to notice about it is the varied number of leaves that make this unit up: one quire is of twelve, two are of two and the fourth is of eight. We are evidently dealing with a scribe-compiler who is used to producing booklets, and he is happy to re-cycle one of them in the course of preparing his longer work.

Let us return to quire O and the singleton fol. 143 in quire N to see how and why the scribe-compiler has introduced them. To take the singleton first. Originally fol. 142v ended with a stage direction: 'Here enteryth þe apostyl Petyr, and John þe Euangelyst with hym, Petyr seyng', and then the first six lines of the opening eight-line stanza of Peter's speech, which begins 'O ye pepyl dyspeyryng, be glad'. The last two lines of this speech's opening stanza would then have followed at the top of the next folio. However, the stage direction and the six lines of speech on fol. 142v were subsequently crossed out, and bracketed against the word *vacat* ('leave it out') in the left-hand margin. This was done to allow the new material introduced on the singleton fol. 143 to flow on sequentially. The new material starts at the top of this folio with a speech of Jesus which begins: 'Frendys, beholde þe tyme of mercy, / The whiche is come now, withowt dowth. / Mannys sowle in blys now xal edyfy, / And þe Prynce of þe Werd is cast owth'. However, exactly the same four lines appear again a little later (on the top of fol. 145v), where they are addressed by Jesus to the citizens and children of the crowd at his triumphal entry into Jerusalem. Considering that nowhere else are plays given to such verbatim repetition, the lines at the top of the singleton fol. 143 begin to look suspicious. Moreover, the next thirteen lines, the rest of Jesus's speech in which his apostles are told to fetch the ass, plus the response of an apostle who says they are going off to get it, are written in the metre characteristic of the **Proclamation Play** (as indeed are the next two thirteen-line stanzas, which run over onto fol. 143v). It seems that what happened was this: the scribe-compil-

er, finding he had **Proclamation Play** material for the dispatch of the apostles for the ass, an episode probably not treated in the **Passion Play,** decided to incorporate it into his original **Passion Play** booklet when he was marrying the booklet into his larger compilation. In this respect his motives seem rather like those of some medieval gospel harmoniser who wants to produce the fullest possible account of the story; perhaps harmonies suggested to him a model. However, since the speech as it stood in the **Proclamation Play** exemplar would otherwise start much too bluntly ('Go to yon castel þat standyth yow ageyn. . .'), he needed a lead into it. It is worth noting that here he had an opportunity to solve his problem by writing a line or two of connecting dialogue, an opportunity he did *not* take. Instead, he lifted the four lines that were roughly suitable for his purposes, even though they would be heard again later on.

If there is an important clue in this that our scribe-compiler may be a reluctant verse writer, nevertheless when necessary he does not jib at rewriting stage directions. It will be recalled that the deleted stage direction towards the bottom of fol. 142v, 'Here enteryth þe apostyl Petyr, and Johan þe Euangelyst with hym, Petyr seyng', originally prefaced the speech of Peter, 'O ye pepyl dyspeyryng, be glad', which, like the stage direction, was also later marked for omission. After the scribe-compiler had incorporated the Proclamation Play's episode of fetching the ass, he was free to bring back the suppressed six lines of Peter's 'O ye pepyl' speech, and did so at the bottom of fol. 143v. But this time the stage direction prefacing the speech has changed, and it is almost certainly the scribe-compiler who changed it: 'Here Cryst rydyth out of þe place and he wyl, and Petyr and Johan abydyn stylle; and at þe last, whan þei haue don þer prechyng, þei mete with Jesu.' Realising that his interpolation had brought Jesus and the ass on early and that there was a lot of intervening text (the sermon-like speeches of Peter and John and the preparation of the citizens for the triumphal entry) before Jesus spoke again, he allowed him the option of riding off in readiness for his entry later. In his adjustment the scribe-compiler appears aware of the dramatic inappropriateness resulting from his compiling activity, although his desire to be inclusive can overwhelm his sensitivity in this respect—for example, the Virgin Mary exits twice from the cross. His drafting in of a singleton to accommodate a **Proclamation Play** episode, while managed fairly efficiently, nevertheless damages the integrity of his earlier **Passion Play** text, for with great dramatic tact this had originally delayed the appearance of Jesus until the very moment of his triumphal entry.

Quire O seems to have been intruded for similar reasons, and with similar consequences. It contains Jesus's expulsion of the seven devils from Mary Magdalene (a popular scene in medieval East Anglian drama, occurring also in *Wisdom* and *Mary Magdalen*) and her pouring of the precious ointment onto his feet (fol. 149r-v). After this, Jesus announces that he is to be betrayed by one of his disciples, and each, appalled, utters a four-line disclaimer, until finally Judas asks whether he is to be 'þat traytour' (this material occupies fols. I50-1). Judas then goes out with the stage direction: 'Here Judas rysyth prevely and goth in þe place and seyt "Now cownter. . ."'

The material contained in quire O again derives from the **Proclamation Play** exemplar, this time either from two different pageants or from an amalgamated one, and, judging by tell-tale alterations at the bottom of fol. 148v, it seems clear that the scribe-compiler added one lot of material, then changed his mind and added some more. Fol. 148v, the last before the insertion of quire O, originally ended with the stage direction 'Here Judas Caryoth comyth into þe place' and, in ink of similar dark colour at the very bottom of the folio, 'now cownter-fetyd'. Both the stage direction and 'now cownterfe-tyd', the catchword referring to a speech of Judas that begins at the top of fol. 152 (the start of quire P), were subsequently deleted to make way for the first batch of new material. It appears that the scribe-complier next copied the section where Jesus announces that he is to be betrayed (it begins at the top of fol. 150 with his speech 'Myn herte is ryght sory, and no wondyr is') up to the exit of Judas on fol. 151. He then noted the name of who was to have been the next speaker, Jesus, in the right-hand margin of fol. 148v, and wrote a new catchword, 'Myn hert is ryth', just above the old one, 'now cownterfetyd', that he had earlier deleted. However, now noticing even more material, a scene too good to miss about Mary Magdalene and her seven devils in another part of the **Proclamation Play** exemplar, he decided that he might also incorporate the scene here. So he copied this second batch of pageant material, probably on a second bifolium of similar paper (the bunch of grapes variety), which he then folded around what now became the inner bifolium of the quire, the one that began with the speech 'Myn herte is ryght sory, and no wondyr is'. The consequence of this was that the catchword he had earlier revised to 'Myn hert is ryth', and the name of its speaker, Jesus, were now thrown out again. He crossed them through, and wrote 'Mawdelyn' as the name of the next speaker and the new catchword 'as a cursyd', the opening words of her speech on fol. 149.

Unravelling all this, complicated though it may have seemed, is important not for its own sake, but precisely because it exposes the scribe-complier's working method, and implicit in this is an interesting attitude towards text. His procedure amounts to another critical approach, this time a medieval one offering an alternative that modern critics, often caught in the binary preoccupation with unity and its absence, can also usefully contemplate. There is no evidence in **Passion Play I** (or anywhere else in the manuscript for that matter)

that the scribe-compiler ever wrote verse, even when he had ideal opportunities for doing so. On the other hand, he rewrites a stage direction ('Here Cryst rydyth out of þe place and he wyll. . .') in a perfunctory attempt to salvage the narrative coherence lost as a result of compiling disparate material. Such activity is similar to his half-hearted renumbering of the pageants of the banns to try to correlate them with his finished compilation, as well as to his fussing over small details of manuscript layout that bring the compilation into line with his concept of *ordinatio*. He changes his mind about what he wants to copy, and sometimes rapidly, which suggests limited forward planning. In sum, his involvement with his manuscript corresponds fairly well to medieval notions of the *compilator,* the scribe who adds little or nothing of his own to what he copies, but substantially rearranges and combines his materials in the way he thinks best suits the general terms of his *compilatio.*

What those general terms seem to have been in his case—a Creation-to-Doom narrative—constitute a flexible framework, one with any amount of room for expansion or contraction between two nodal points. His inclination, as we saw, was towards expansion and inclusiveness, sometimes at the local cost of narrative coherence. Yet this inclusiveness implies no concomitant obligation for users of the *compilatio* to engage with all its compiled material; on the contrary, it facilitates their scope for *choice*. And this is once more exactly in the spirit of *compilatio*. A *compilator* often provided his work with an *accessus,* a means to open its contents for selective use as required. So too the *compilatio* of the scribe-compiler is not a closed text; it incorporates alternatives (as you wish, use of this or that ending, e.g. 'si placet' (if you wish) at the end of the **Mary Play,** options ('Here Cryst rydyth out of þe place and he wyll', and see also Play 27, s.d., lines 465+), even perhaps in the **Mary Play** a guide to disentangling what is compiled with what, which opens its text to determination by its users. The banns too could even be regarded as a sort of index or *tabula* by which a user can find his way around the collection as he wishes. In short, responsibility for the final form that the *compilatio* takes is turned over to those who use it. Such selective use of it by Reviser B is an early instance of exactly this. The scribe-compiler foresees and provides for the fact that the form of his *compilatio* will finally be determined out in the community where it is used. In a sense its ultimate authorship is communal, and as such, repeatedly negotiable.

The implications of this for the two modern approaches noted earlier are weighty. A search for general unifying themes in the *compilatio,* though in some measure valid, risks closing its structure, and can claim no priority over the 'archaeological' approach, since it is liable to refuse the implicit invitation of the *compilatio* that the user undo it. But equally the scrutiny of individual plays and their textual layers, though it might appear happily aligned with this self-undoing aspect of *compilatio,* is only partially so, because it in fact proceeds from quite a different motive, the modern desire to discern, as one modern authority [Fredson T. Bowers, in *Textual and Literary Criticism*] put it, 'the original purity of the most authoritative preserved forms of [an] author's words'. Searching for the 'original purity. . .of [an] author's words' would have been largely alien to the scribe-compiler. Text for him, of this sort at least, was common property; it had not quite the private status of the kind accorded to texts in such modern textual criticism. Even if he added no dialogue of his own, he did not fully privilege the text in his exemplars. Like many another medieval *compilator,* he felt free to dismantle their structure where necessary. His attitude recognises the fact that since most of an author's words exist before he is born, they are to that extent a public domain over which he has no absolute control.

To view **N-Town** as a *compilatio* is to expose the modernity of the ideologies underpinning both these modern approaches; it is also to remind us that the past is a country where people do things differently.

'SOMETHING RICH AND STRANGE'

A third modern approach to **N-Town,** one which side-steps the literary double bind described earlier, is the question of how its plays were staged. Interest in this was shown even as early as the seventeenth century, when William Dugdale [in *The Antiquities of Warwickshire Illustrated*, 1656] confidently described them as being presented in 'Theaters' which were 'very large and high, placed upon wheels and drawn to all the eminent parts of the City'. But the 'City' he was thinking of as their home was Coventry. Subsequent critics have been less sure about **N-Town's** scope for a processional, pageant wagon staging. The **Passion Play** was early recognised as being a stationary, place-and-scaffold production, although as late as the 1960s it was still thought that other plays in the manuscript were produced processionally. Since the 1970s, opinion has generally turned against theories of processional staging for any parts of **N-Town**. A good case can be made that the **Proclamation Play** intended stationary, place-and-scaffold staging, and the **Mary Play,** a play even conceivably performed indoors, was probably similar. This would mean that the principal play exemplars of **N-Town,** though themselves originally unrelated, all shared a similar production mode.

The debate over **N-Town's** staging has been fuelled by its stage directions, which, after Chester, are the next richest in English mystery drama. Understanding them is a difficult business. It is clear that to some extent they correspond to the particular source texts that the scribe-compiler worked from: stage directions in **Proclamation Play** material are normally in Latin and are relatively few; the **Mary Play** has proportionally more, in Latin and in English, and the **Passion Play** has a wealth of them, predominantly in English. Less clear is which stage directions are original and which added later, whether as a result of armchair revision or actual play production. Yet in spite of their difficulties, they still give invaluable insight into what the drama of **N-Town** was like.

It has often been said that medieval drama presents the biblical past in terms of the medieval present but the stage directions of **N-Town** lead one to wonder how useful this generalisation is. Take the first stage direction of **Passion Play I:**

> Here xal Annas shewyn hymself in his stage beseyn aftyr a busshop of þe hoold lawe in a skarlet gowne, and ouyr þat a blew tabbard furryd with whyte, and a mytere on his hed after þe hoold lawe; ij doctorys stondyng by hym in furryd hodys, and on beforn hem with his staff of astat, and eche of hem on here hedys a furryd cappe with a gret knop in þe crowne; and on stondyng beforn as a Sarazyn, þe wich xal be his masangere

(Play 26, s.d., line 164+)

The Jewish High Priest Annas is not dressed like a contemporary medieval bishop, but 'after þe hoold lawe.' (The next stage direction will require the doctors attending Caiaphas to be clad 'aftyr þe old gyse': Play 26, s.d., line 208+). Also, the messenger of Annas is a 'Sarazyn'. The thrust of the stage direction is clearly towards producing a sense of difference, of the exotic. Familiar things may be present, but are often combined in unfamiliar ways, or yet with things themselves unfamiliar, and noticeably when the divine or infernal are in view. In the same play, Christ is arrested by ten people 'with swerdys, gleyvys [halberds], and *other straunge wepoun*'—no average medieval militia this—and when in **Passion Play II** the Jews have crucified Christ, they dance around him:

> Here xule þei leve of, and dawncyn abowte þe cros shortly.

(Play 32, s.d., line 76 +)

For a while they are like carollers dancing in a ring. Dances in the centre of which some action took place were familiar pastimes, but when, as here, that central action is a crucifixion, the familiar is suddenly estranged. Collocations of this sort are like Ariel's sea-change: all turns rich and strange. **N-Town** repeatedly defamiliarises the medieval here-and-now in a polysemous play of signs. It self-consciously advertises its semiotic means in the process.

What its stage directions imply in this respect matches what is going on in its text. For example, **N-Town's** farting devil is not just scatalogically apt; he is presented for a moment doing something that medieval jesters often did. Eve, costumed, presumably in such a way as to suggest nakedness, was nevertheless made by God 'a gret lady in paradys for to pley', and thus verbally glossed paradise too is presented not only as the traditional *locus amoenus,* but as a *hortus conclusus,* an aristocratic walled garden of delights opened with a private key. Backbiter and Raise Slander, two common bedfellows in medieval theological literature, acquire a human habitation and name in the 'real' world of the bishop's court in the pageant of the **trial of Joseph and Mary;** and in the **Parliament of Heaven** in the **Mary Play,** familiar institutions are translated into unusual circumstances: petitioners (who represent mankind) make a plea (which angels transmit) to a deliberative council (of the Trinity) which determines in familiar judicial fashion a 'loveday' (the reconciliation of God's daughters Mercy, Truth, Justice and Peace). Instances could be multiplied (e.g. Play 20, lines 151-4, Herod's feast; Play 26, lines 442-9 + s.d., Jesus's 'royal' entry). The **Mary Play** in particular is remarkable for such transformations of the familiar. But as a final illustration let us turn to the pageant of the doctors disputing with Jesus in the temple. This is a fine example of how defamiliarisation releases possibilities of meaning not otherwise readily broached. The doctors are taught to recognise superior wisdom where ordinarily it ought not to be, in a child, and their recognition is embodied in significant action:

> Hic adducunt Jesum inter ipsos et in scanno altiori ipsum sedere faciunt, ipsis in inferioribus scannis sedentibus. . .
>
> (Play 21, s.d., line 144 +)

(Here they lead Jesus into their midst and make him sit on a higher seat, while they themselves sit on lower ones)

In semiotic terms, the diminutive Jesus (an icon of childhood) nevertheless utters divine wisdom (an icon of Godhead, of the second Person in Trinity), and both are foregrounded by elevation on the highest *scannum* (literally, a seat or bench). An interesting contemporary stained-glass depiction of this scene in East Harling church, a church geographically close to the play's cultural origins, makes the seat of a throne, and thus takes the further step of putting the child Jesus on a traditional symbol of kingly authority.

While we can talk in this way about what stage directions and text suggest concerning the nature of **N-Town**'s dramatic illusion, and even partially test our notions through practical production, there is a way of conceiving what is happening in more medieval terms: **N-Town** often engages a special sort of textual awareness, one prevalent in the culture of the time. Jesus in the temple alleges a Latin authority of scripture—*Omnis*

sciencia a domino deo est—before he ever speaks in English, as would a medieval preacher who announces his scriptural theme before discoursing on its substance. Indeed, **N-Town** is full of preachers and preaching method. Some are obvious, as when Moses turns preacher in his exposition of the Decalogue. Some are less so, as when Death intervenes in Herod's feast after the **Slaughter of the Innocents.** Herod invites his knights to banquet, imagining all is well after eliminating Christ:

[Herod]

          . . . . .

Þerfore, menstrell, rownd abowt,
Blowe up a mery fytt!   [*tune*]

Hic, dum buccinant, Mors interficiat Herodem et duos milites subito, et Diabolus recipiat eos.

[Devil]

All oure! All oure! þis catel is myn! [*property*]
I xall hem brynge onto my celle.   [*shall*]
I xall hem teche pleys fyn,   [*fine*]
And shewe such myrthe as is in helle!

          . . . . .

[Death]

Off kynge Herowde all men beware,
Þat hath rejoycyd in pompe and pryde.
For all his boste of blysse ful bare,
He lyth now ded here on his syde.
For whan I come I can not spare;
Fro me no whyht may hym hyde.   [*creature*]

          . . . . .

Thow I be nakyd and pore of array
And wurmys knawe me al abowte,   [*gnaw*]
Yit loke ye drede me nyth and day;   [*night*]
For whan Deth comyth ye stande in dowte!
                              [*are uncertain*]
Evyn lyke to me, as I yow say,
Shull all ye be here in þis rowte,   [*gathering*]
Whan I yow chalange at my day,
I xal yow make ryght lowe to lowth   [*bow*]
And nakyd for to be.
Amongys wormys, as I yow telle,
Vndyr þe erth xul ye dwelle,
And thei xul etyn both flesch and felle,
As þei haue don me.
          (Play 20, lines 231-6, 246-51, 272-84)

(s.d., line 232+: Here while they are trumpetting let Death kill Herod and his two soldiers suddenly, and let the Devil take them)

The way that Death explains the significance of his action is comparable to the method of a medieval preacher who, having delivered a dramatic exemplum, draws out for his congregation its moral significance. At the end of the play, Death takes his exemplifying procedure a step further. In making an exemplum of himself—the audience is invited to contemplate through him their own mortality—he introduces a new level of exemplary meaning. Such integumental layering of exempla is unusual in preaching, if exempla are common in themselves, and so, as here, reminiscence of preaching can be complex. But more importantly, **N-Town**'s preoccupation with preaching and preaching method seems a function of something deeper.

At the heart of **Passion Play I,** at the institution of the Eucharist itself, Jesus explains 'by gostly interpretacyon' the meaning of the paschal lamb (Exodus 12) eaten with unleavened bread and bitter herbs, and initiates another transformation, as the rites of the old law cede to the new: 'þis fygure xal sesse; anothyr xal folwe perby' (Play 27, line 361). The playwright may have derived the substance of Jesus's commentary, either directly or through an intermediary, from the *Glossa ordinaria,* the standard medieval Bible commentary that began in the great twelfth-century school of Laon. Medieval exegesis raised a many-layered edifice of interpretation over the literal sense (the *sensus litteralis*) of the text. At this point in **Passion Play I,** Jesus turns exegete. He glosses the *sensus litteralis* of Exodus 12 not only verbally (some of his terms are technical hermeneutic ones), but also gesturally, by the elevation of a Eucharistic wafer, the new paschal lamb:

> And as þe paschal lomb etyn haue we
> In þe eld lawe was vsyd for a sacryfyce,
> So þe newe lomb þat xal be sacryd be me
>   [*consecrated*]
> Xal be vsyd for a sacryfyce most of price. *of*
>   [*supreme value*]
>
> Here xal Jesus take an oblé in his hand
>   lokyng vpward *Mass wafer*
> into hefne, to þe Fadyr. . .
>   (Play 27, lines 369-72+ s.d.)

Moments like this when exegesis is thoroughly enmeshed in the very narrative of the drama, when it surfaces, as it were, to be dramatised in its own right, may be a clue to what the playwrights of **N-Town,** consciously or unconsciously, were doing: they were making exegesis into a game, and this not only where exegesis is explicitly enacted in the drama's narrative, as happens in **Passion Play I.** In a more general sense too, the polysemous play of signs mentioned earlier could be regarded as drama's counterpart to exegesis, as an extension into dramatic terms of exegetical awareness: the *sensus litteralis* of the narrative is glossed and re-glossed into multivalence by a drama which, like ex-

egesis itself, liberates audiences from the necessity of limiting apprehension of meaning to single possibilities. The excitement of **N-Town**'s drama is partly founded in surprise, as dramatic signs, ever likely to display themselves in the unconventionality of their referents, take spectators 'in aventure þer mervaylez meven', whether they intuited connections between their experience of what they saw and habits of thought characterising contemporary clerical culture or not; quite likely they just enjoyed all the heady exuberance in a spirit of play and game. Moreover, it is a surprise liable to spring from the smallest details of the drama: wherever gaps are to be perceived between the words uttered and the actions enacted (and medieval drama in general is likely to have accentuated any discrepancy because often its words and actions occur simultaneously) there exists pretence, an awareness that, even if disbelief be suspended, everything performed is illusion, whatever the high seriousness, or otherwise, of the illusion in its effect. In such a context, where words may, but as equally may not, be referential, language itself can be defamiliarised; when their traditional referents are prone to replacement by newer ones invented in the playful dramatic world, a curtain rises on the slipperiness of words themselves. Words too are actors, but this is a cause of delight rather than of any unsettling apprehension of how arbitrary words are, for the destabilisation of language in the dramatic context is only analogous, after all, to the established medieval pursuit of the higher levels of exegesis above the *sensus litteralis.* These levels, while holy games of invention, may nevertheless give access to salvation.

N-Town's spectators, whatever selection from the *compilatio* they were served with, could not have seen their world reflected as in a plane mirror, but playfully refracted into something rich and strange. For all that the possibilities of meaning may have been sumptuous, meaning's teleological end, the intimation of God's purposes for mankind, was nevertheless thought to be single. No doubt **N-Town**'s playwrights hoped that by means of a drama that glossed the audience's perception of the world in this way, the audience might come to know the place for the first time.

FURTHER READING

Ashley, Kathleen M. "'Wyt' and 'Wysdam' in N-Town Cycle." *Philological Quarterly* 58, No. 2 (1979): 121-35.
    Explores the elements that produce N-Town's learned tone as a basis for the unity of the cycle.

Benkovitz, Miriam J. "Some Notes on the 'Prologue of Demon' of *Ludus Coventriae.*" *Modern Language Notes* 60 (1945): 79-85.
    Argues that the "Prologue of the Demon" that introduces the Passion group ties the cycle together; also

contends that the author of the Prologue was a theologian.

Cameron, Kenneth, and Stanley J. Kahrl. "The N-Town Plays at Lincoln." *Theatre Notebook* 20, No. 2 (1965-6): 61-9.

Reviews scholarship and extends the argument that the N-Town cycle is based in Lincoln and that it represents a step in the development from movable to fixed stages.

Cawley, A. C., *et al.*, eds. *The Revels History of English Drama. Vol. I: Medieval Drama.* London: Methuen, 1983, 348 p.

Offers overviews on staging, religious ritual, and morality in medieval drama, as well as specific analyses of individual cycles and plays by several different authors.

Coletti, Theresa. "Sacrament and Sacrifice in the N-Town Passion." *Mediaevalia* 7 (1981): 239-64.

By exploring N-Town's connections to pictorial arts, suggests that the sacrament of Corpus Christi is the central theme of the Passion plays.

Dodds, Madeleine Hope. "The Problem of the 'Ludus Coventriae.'" *Modern Language Review* 9 (1914): 79-91.

Asserts that the *Ludus Coventriae* is the product of five earlier cycles from five different places, brought together for an occasion connected with the monastery of Bury St. Edmunds.

Eccles, Mark. "Ludus Coventriae: Lincoln or Norfolk?" *Medium Aevum* 40, No. 2 (1971): 135-41.

Basing his argument on the plays' dialect, the critic holds that they were most likely staged in Norwich or Lynn and copied in Norfolk.

El Itreby, Elizabeth J. "The *N-Town* Play of 'The Woman Taken in Adultery'—Central to a Recapitulative 'Redemption Trilogy.'" *Ball State University Forum* 26, No. 3 (1985): 3-13.

Argues that "The Woman Taken in Adultery," "The Temptation," and "The Raising of Lazarus" constitute a trilogy within the N-Town cycle that prefigures the redemptive process of the later Passion sequences.

Fletcher, Alan J. "The Design of the N-Town Play of Mary's Conception." *Modern Philology* 79, No. 2 (1981): 166-73.

By exploring the relation of the Marian Conception Play to its primary source, argues that the play's goals are specifically didactic.

——. "Layers of Revision in the N-Town Marian Cycle." *Neophilologus* 66, No. 3 (1982): 469-78.

Working from the principle that the Mary plays constitute a miniature cycle in their own right, the critic

seeks to identify the results of scribal revisions to the original cycle.

Forrest, Sister M. Patricia. "The Role of the Expositor Contemplacio in the St. Anne's Day Plays of the Hegge Cycle." *Medieval Studies* 28 (1966): 60-76.

Argues that the Expositor's central role is to underline the moral and doctrinal import of the cycle.

——. "Apocryphal Sources of the St. Anne's Day Plays in the Hegge Cycle." *Medievalia et Humanistica* 17 (1966): 38-50.

Argues that the St. Anne's Day plays originate from the apocryphal Gospels, which a scribe arranged from memory.

Gibson, Gail McMurray. "'Porta haec clausa erit': Comedy, Conception, and Ezekiel's Closed Door in the *Ludus Coventriae* Play of 'Joseph's Return.'" *Journal of Medieval and Renaissance Studies* 8, No. 1 (1978): 137-56.

In a close analysis of "Joseph's return," argues that the figure of Joseph links the secular and humorous world of the spectators with the sanctity of the play's subjects.

Hunt, Alison M. "Maculating Mary: The Detractors of the N-Town Cycle's *Trial of Joseph and Mary*." *Philological Quarterly* 73, No. 1 (Winter 1994): 11-29.

Explores the figure of the detractor in romance and anti-heretical writings in order to argue that the cycle's detractor figures reveal anxiety about the capacity of language to destroy human community.

Meredith, Peter. "'Nolo Mortem' and the *Ludus Coventriae* Play of the *Woman Taken in Adultery*." *Medium Aevum* 38, No. 1 (1969): 38-54.

Argues that the *Woman Taken in Adultery* takes the form of a sermon on the first line of the play, "nolo mortem peccatoris" (I do not wish to die for my sins).

——. "A Reconsideration of Some Textual Problems in the N-Town Manuscript." *Leeds Studies in English* 9 (1977): 35-50.

By close-reading several manuscript passages, argues that the N-Town scribe made changes based on meter rather than dramatic efficacy.

Merideth, Peter, and Stanley J. Kahrl. Introduction to *The N-Town Plays: A Facsimile of British Library MS Cotton Vespasian D VIII*, pp. vii-xxix. Leeds, England: University of Leeds, 1977.

Describes the physical features and history of the N-Town manuscript.

Nelson, Alan H. "The Temptation of Christ; or, the Temptation of Satan." In *Medieval English Drama*, ed. Jerome Taylor and Alan H. Nelson, pp. 219-29. Chicago:

University of Chicago Press, 1972.

> In a close reading of the three extant plays of the temptation of Christ, argues that all three exhibit Satan's persistent ignorance of Christ's nature.

Nichols, Ann Eljenholm. "The Hierosphthitic Topos, or the Fate of Fergus: Notes on the N-Town Assumption." *Comparative Drama* 25, No. 1 (1991): 29-41.

> Tracing the imagery of the holy touch in saints' legends and other religious texts, argues that the same imagery is implicit in the end of the N-Town Assumption play.

Patch, Howard R. "The *Ludus Coventriae* and the Digby *Massacre*." *PMLA* 35, No. 3 (1920): 324-43.

> Examining the meters of the plays, suggests that the Dublin *Abraham and Isaac* and the Digby *Massacre* might have formed part of the cycles or groups from which the compiler of *Ludus Coventriae* made his selections.

Plummer, John F. "The Logomachy of the N-Town Passion Play I." *Journal of English and Germanic Philology* 88, No. 3 (1989): 311-31.

> Analyzes the figures of Satan and Christ in order to argue that the cycle teaches that control of language is control over man's sense of reality.

Poteet, Daniel P. II. "Time, Eternity, and Dramatic Form in *Ludus Coventriae* 'Passion Play I.'" *Comparative Drama* 8, No. 4 (1974-5): 369-85.

> Arguing against common misconceptions about medieval religious and aesthetic values, analyzes "Passion Play I" in terms of its theologically based opposition between earthly time and divine timelessness.

Rose, Martial. "The Staging of the Hegge Plays." In *Medieval Drama,* edited by Neville Denny, pp. 197-222. London: Edward Arnold, 1973.

> Culls evidence from throughout the cycle to argue for a stationary and centralized production of the plays.

Spector, Stephen. "The Composition and Development of an Eclectic Manuscript: Cotton Vespasian D VIII."

Leeds Studies in English, n.s., 9 (1977): 62-83.

> Revising previous studies of N-Town's prosody, suggests a new pattern and chronology of the process of manuscript compilation and authorship.

————. "The Composition and Development of the N-Town Cycle" and "The Play." In *The N-Town Play: Cotton MS Vespasian D. 8,* edited by Stephen Spector, pp. 537-43, 550-54. The Early English Text Society, 1991, .

> Describes the eclectic manuscript of the N-Town plays and the history of critical theories about authorship and textual issues.

Sugano, Douglas. "'This game wel pleyd in good a-ray': The N-Town Playbooks and East Anglian Games." *Comparative Drama* 28, No. 2 (1994): 221-34.

> Argues that the N-town cycle is a compilation, not a single integrated drama, and suggests that the various plays that comprise it were lent out to be performed as part of regional "games" or fundraisers.

Swenson, Esther L. *An Inquiry into the Composition and Structure of the Ludus Coventriae.* Minneapolis: University of Minnesota Press, 1914, 88 p.

> Describes the manuscript of the N-Town Cycle and makes the argument (since called into question) that different metrical patterns show evidence of different scribes.

Taylor, George Coffin. "The *Christus Redivivus* of Nicholas Grimald and the Hegge Resurrection Plays." *PMLA* 41 (1926): 840-59.

> Argues that the Renaissance playwright Grimald was dependent on the plays of the Hegge cycle.

Thompson, Elbert S. "The *Ludus Coventriae.*" *Modern Language Notes* 21 (1906): 18-20.

> Argues that the *Ludus Coventriae* derived from pageant plays, suggests their connection to guilds, and makes tentative conclusions about staging.

Wright, Robert. "Community Theatre in Late Medieval East Anglia." *Theatre Notebook* 28, No. 1 (1974): 24-38.

> Using evidence obtained from churchwardens' books, demonstrates the prominence of the rural Corpus Christi event in the annual religious calendar.

> **Additional coverage of the N-Town plays is contained in the following source published by Gale research:** *Dictionary of Literary Biography, Vol 146: Old and Middle English Literature.*

Towneley Plays

INTRODUCTION

The Towneley plays, also referred to as the Wakefield plays, are a cycle of medieval English mystery dramas comprised of thirty-two religious pageants dramatizing biblical history from the Creation to Judgment Day. Although few details are known about their authorship or mode of presentation, a number of the Towneley plays have been attributed to the anonymous author commonly called the Wakefield Master. Praised for their skillful handling of language, adept use of humor, and successful blending of secular and sacred themes, the plays have received much critical attention in the latter half of the twentieth century; two Towneley dramas in particular, *Noah* and *The Second Shepherd's Play,* are among the best-known and most frequently anthologized of all mystery plays.

Textual History

The only extant manuscript of the Towneley plays was in the possession of the Towneley family of Burnley, Lancashire, until they sold it in 1814. The family, scholars believe, probably obtained it from the Abbey of Widkirk, near Wakefield, York. Historians have proposed that the plays began to be written down in the late thirteenth century and were completed around the early fifteenth century, with the only known manuscript dating from the sixteenth century. Textual evidence from the plays themselves links the pageants to the locality of Wakefield, but, although the manuscript identifies the plays as the "Wakefield Cycle," scholars have concluded that no such cycle actually existed. Rather, the manuscript seems to have been a collection from which to chose individual productions, and, judging from signs of heavy use, probably a transcription intended for acting purposes. There are few staging instructions in the manuscript, but many of the plays as written could not have mounted on the typical pageant wagon. Because of the specific, complex staging requirements of individual dramas, scholars believe that they may have been acted out on multi-level scaffoldings.

The group now consists of thirty-two plays; two additional plays are believed to have been lost, and two (numbers xxxi and xxxii) to be placed out of order in the manuscript. Considered the most pieced-together of all the mystery play groups, the Towneley plays were much revised and rewritten over time. Based on the metrical and stanzaic forms used in the texts, scholars have discerned three layers of influence in the plays: ordinary didactic-religious plays, plays derived from the earlier York group of plays, and plays that appear to have been written by a single author and that are characterized by a bold sense of humor. The five plays derived from York are *Pharao, Pagina Doctorum, Extraccio Animarum, Resureccio Domini*, and *Judicium*. Critics are in agreement in attributing the *Mactacio Abel, Processus Noe cum Filiis, Prima Pastorum, Secunda Pastorum, Magnus Herodes,* and *Coliphizacio* to the Wakefield Master. Written in a North Midland dialect, these plays display the Wakefield Master's trademark style—use of thirteen rhyme words in each nine-line stanza, humor, and word play.

Plot and Major Characters

The plot of the Towneley plays is the plot of biblical accounts of the creation, humankind's fall from grace, the life of Jesus, his crucifixion, and resurrection. The plays were intended to show, by example and illustration from various biblical and apocryphal stories, how humankind deviated from the path that God ordained for them, and how they may be saved. Major characters in the plays are personages from the Bible, with Noah, Jesus, Herod, and Pilate having some of the most prominent parts. Scholars have pointed out that, while characters are often similar in various plays and in various cycles, they can also vary from play to play. So, for example, Pilate can be a buffoon in one pageant, and a wise judge in another.

Major Themes

The Towneley plays blend liturgical and everyday themes, often with humor and satire, and sometimes, as in *Noah* and *The Second Shepherd's Play*, with humor that is downright boisterous. The bickering between the henpecked Noah and his wife, and the concerns of the petty thieves in *The Second Shepherd's Play* coexist in those plays with serious commentary regarding God's plan for humankind and with admonishment about the dangers of straying from the path of Christian behavior. In other plays, religious themes are placed alongside social criticism—for example, a critique of cock-fighting or exposition of corrupt churchmen. The range of situations depicted in the various pageants showcases humankind's suffering as a result of sinfulness as well as their seemingly endless capacity for hope and self-improvement. Therefore, the plays exhibit a mixture of realistic detail and biblical typology, humor and didacticism, along with a pronounced interest in rhetoric, linguistic playfulness, and the legal terminology of the day.

Critical Reception

Martial Rose has deemed the Towneley plays "the most dramatic series of [the medieval mystery] plays" because of their varied themes, colorful characters, and linguistic brilliance. Despite those characteristics, however, the plays were considered rather primitive popular entertainments up until the early twentieth century. When modern scholars turned their attention to the Towneley plays, one of the main critical debates that emerged regarding their artistic merit was the question of their unity. Some critics theorized that, while humor is one of the unifying elements in the cycle, it is also misplaced thematically because it subverts, especially in *Herod* and *The Second Shepherd's Play,* the sacred meaning of the plays. Acknowledging that the plays are a mixture of folk drama, mummers' plays, and liturgical drama, most critics now view the Christian themes in the plays as overriding and as that which structures as well as lends unity to the plays. Another point of discussion among critics has been deciding to what extent, if any, the Wakefield Master can be credited with the final shape of the Towneley plays. Some critics limit his role to the six plays closely identified with his style, others, like John Gardner, maintain that he may have been the final reviser and shaper of all the plays, and still others, like Martin Stevens, theorize that he may have been the author of the entire cycle, the "guiding intelligence" of all the Towneley plays. In the latter decades of the twentieth century, *The Second Shepherd's Play* has received the most critical attention of any of the Towneley plays, yet scholars continue to demonstrate an interest in exploring the plays, both individually and as a group. So, for example, E. Catherine Dunn has studied the several manifestations of the narrative voice in the plays, Jeffrey Helterman has focused on the interplay of typology and realism, and several critics have charted the interconnection between the use of humor, didacticism, and rhetorical style in the Towneley plays.

THE PLAYS

1. *The Creation* (incomplete)
2. *Mactacio Abel (The Killing of Abel)*
3. *Processus Noe cum Filius*
4. *Abraham* (incomplete)
5. *Abraham and Isaac* (incomplete)
6. *Jacob*
7. *Processus Prophetarum* (incomplete)
8. *Pharao*
9. *Cesar Augustus*
10. *Annunciatio*
11. *Salutacio Elezabeth (The Visitation)*
12. *Prima Pastorum (First Shepherds' Play)*
13. *Secunda Pastorum (Second Shepherds' Play)*
14. *Oblacio Magorum (The Gifts of the Magi)*
15. *Fugacio Joseph & Marie in Egiptum (The Flight to Egypt)*
16. *Magnus Herodes (Herod the Great)*
17. *Purificacio Marie (The Purification)* (incomplete)
18. *Pagina Doctorum (The Doctors)* (incomplete)
19. *Johannes Baptista (John the Baptist)*
20. *Conspiracio (The Conspiracy)*
21. *Coliphizacio (The Buffeting)*
22. *Flagellacio (The Scourging)*
23. *Processus Crucis (The Way of the Cross)*
24. *Processus Talentorum (The Talents)*
25. *Extraccio Animarum (The Harrowing)*
26. *Resurreccio Domini (The Resurrection)*
27. *Peregrini (The Pilgrims)*
28. *Thomas Indie (Thomas of India)*
29. *Ascencio Domini (The Ascension)* (incomplete)
30. *Judicium (The Last Judgment)* (incomplete)
31. *Lazarus*
32. *Suspencio Jude (The Hanging of Judas)* (incomplete)

PRINCIPAL EDITIONS

The Towneley Plays, edited by J. Raine, or J. Hunter, or J. S. Stevenson, 1836
The Tonweley Plays, edited by George England, 1897; reprinted 1973
The Wakefield Pageants in the Towneley Cycle, edited by A. C. Cawley, 1958
The Wakefield Mystery Plays, edited by Martial Rose, 1969

CRITICISM

Alfred W. Pollard (essay date 1897)

SOURCE: An introduction to *The Towneley Plays*, edited by George England, 1897. Reprint by Oxford University Press, 1925, pp. ix-xxxi.

[*In the following excerpt from his introduction to George England's highly respected edition of* The Towneley Plays, *Pollard discusses the relative merits of several of the plays and singles out* The Second Shepherd's Play *as "perfect as a work of art."*]

Long before the publication of the York Plays, the composite character of the Towneley was recognized by its first editor, though the reasons he assigned were less happy than his surmise itself [In a footnote, the critic adds: "He says that there are no Yorkshireisms in the **Pharao,** which we now know to be mainly borrowed from the York cycle, and remarks **Cæsar Augustus** is plainly by the same hand as **Pharao.** The heroes in both swear by "Mahowne"—a habit shared by most potentates in miracle plays."], and later writers have not failed to enlarge on the point. It thus becomes interesting to see how much of the cycle we can claim on sure evidence as composed especially for it. It is no bad beginning to be able to say at once, at least one-fourth, and this the fourth which contains the finest and most original work. The evidence for this is irresistible. We find the Wakefield or Woodkirk editor interpolating two broadly humorous scenes, the one containing 297 lines, the other 81, on the impressive York play of the Judgment. These scenes are written in a complex metre, a 9-line stanza riming *aaaa bcccb,* with central rimes in the first four lines (I should prefer to write it *aaaa bbbb cdddc*), and we find this same metre used with admirable regularity throughout five long plays, viz.—

III.	Processus Noe cum filiis	558 lines
XII.	Prima Pastorum	502 (2 lines lost)
XIII.	Secunda Pastorum	754 (2 lines lost)
XIV.	Magnus Herodes	513
XXI.	Coliphizacio	450

—or, including the two passages in the **Judicium,** in no less than 3155 lines, occupying in this edition almost exactly 100 pages out of 396. If any one will read these plays together, I think he cannot fail to feel that they are all the work of the same writer, and that this writer deserves to be ranked—if only we knew his name!—at least as high as Langland, and as an exponent of a rather boisterous kind of humour had no equal in his own day. We may also be sure that the two other plays, **Flagellacio** (No. XXII.) and **Processus Talentorum** (No. XXIV.), contain about the same proportion of his work as does the **Judicium.** They are closely akin to the **Coliphizacio,** and contain the one 24, the other 8 of his favourite stanzas.

For one other play which it is very tempting to assign to the same hand, the **Mactacio Abel** (No. II.), we lack the evidence of identity of metre; in fact, the frequent changes from one metrical form to another would make us suspect that we had here an instance of editing, if it were not quite impossible to isolate from the present text any underlying original. But the extraordinary boldness of the play, and the character of its humour, make it difficult to dissociate it from the work of the author of the Shepherds' Plays, and I cannot doubt that this also, at least in part, must be added to his credit.

When the work of this man of real genius has been eliminated, the search for another Wakefield, or Wood-

kirk, author becomes distinctly less interesting. . . .

As to the two fragments [**Isaac** and **Jacob**] the late Professor Ten-Brink wrote [in *History of English Literature*]—

> About a generation—but hardly much more—separates this oldest extant English drama [*i.e.* the *Harrowing of Hell,* 'composed shortly after the middle of the thirteenth century'] from the next. The play of **Jacob and Esau,** as we take the liberty of calling it, appears to have been composed not far from the mouth of the Humber, and probably to the north of the dialect line. The influence of the East Midlands is seen in the choice of subject, which was not popular on the earlier stage elsewhere, and the manner of treatment also reminds us of the districts and the century which produced the poems of **Genesis** and **Exodus.**
>
> In **Jacob and Esau** the dramatic art is still of a low standard; the situations are not made much use of; the characteristics show little depth or originality. The poet is full of reverence for his subject, and dramatizes faithfully what seems to him its most important traits, without putting to it much of his own originality, etc.

In his Appendix, Prof. Ten-Brink supported this view of the play with the following note—

> This play has been handed down in the Towneley Collection: unfortunately it is mutilated at the beginning, and also divided into two parts: **Isaac** and **Jacob.** However, it originally formed, and, in fact, still forms, one drama, which was produced independently without regard to any cycle of mysteries, and indeed earlier than most of the others, probably than all the other parts of the cycle in which it was subsequently incorporated. All this can easily be proved by means now at the disposal of philology, but this is not the place for entering into the subject. Less certain is the local origin of the piece. The assumption that few of the rhyming words have been altered in their transmission could, for instance, allow of the supposition that the drama might have been produced in the north of the East-Midland territory, rather than in the southern districts of Northumbria, a supposition which would coincide very well with many other peculiarities of the work.

I have quoted these passages from Prof. Ten-Brink in full, because the opinion of the writer who has produced the only really good history of our early literature, is a thousand times more important than my own. But my difficulties in accepting his theory in its entirety are both numerous and great. The *Harrowing of Hell* itself seems to me—as it has seemed to my betters before me—rather a dramatic poem than a Miracle Play properly so called, and I cannot conceive on what occasion, or by whom, an isolated play on **Jacob and**

Esau could come to be acted in the vernacular. In a cycle, the presence of a play on Abraham might easily suggest a continuation dealing with his immediate descendants, and its simpler and more archaic form might be partly accounted for by the nature of its subject. I should prefer, also, to attribute differences of dialect to the removal from one district to another of a play-writing monk, rather than to the acceptance in one district of a play which had been composed for another many years before. It is obvious, however, that these two fragments do belong to a period, whether prae-cyclic or cyclic, at which the narrative and didactic interest of the representation was uppermost, and before the constantly increasing importation of external attractions had produced a distaste for the simpler and more exclusively religious form of drama. We know from Chaucer's allusions, as well as from the evidence of the York plays, that by the last quarter of the fourteenth century Noah and his quarrelsome wife and the ranting Herods and Pilates were already stock characters, and we may thus well believe that the cycle 'of matter from the beginning of the world' in its simplest form, must have been in existence during the first half of that century. The fact that this play has only come to us in fragments, is probably good evidence that it was considered antiquated at the time our manuscript was written, and that only a few speeches from it were used.

I must confess, however, that I cannot find anything either in the style or the language of these fragments which need compel us to separate them from the couplets in the play of the *Creation* and the *Annunciation*; and I incline strongly to believe that in these plays, and the others which I have mentioned as written wholly or partly in the aa⁴b³cc⁴b³ stanza, we possess part of an original didactic cycle, of much the same tone as the Chester Plays, on to which other plays, mostly written in a more popular style, have been tacked from time to time. In any case I do not think it can be doubted that the four plays, VII., IX., X., and XI., are the work of the same writer, and the rest seem to me to go with them.

The plays of the *Magi* (XIV.) and of the *Flight into Egypt* (XV.) are marked off from this group by their much greater use of alliteration, and seem to me— though my opinion on questions of dialect is worth very little—to have been written by an author of somewhat different speech. The *Abraham* and *John the Baptist* again are in a totally different metre, and may belong to the period when the York plays were being incorporated into the cycle. As regards these York plays, . . .it is worth noting that the predominant metre of the *Conspiracio* (XXᵃ.) is the same as that of three out of the five plays connected with York (the *Pharaoh, Doctor,* and *Extraccio Animarum*), and may possibly be based on a lost alternative to the extant York play on this subject. A similar guess may be

Page from a Towneley manuscript.

hazarded as to the play of the *Peregrini* (XXVII.), the metre of which is the same as that of the *Resurrectio* (XXVI., York XXXVIII.), while the obvious corruptions and interpolations of the text may well lead us to doubt its being indigenous. The fragment of the *Suspencio Iude,* printed at the end of the cycle, but which would naturally come immediately before the *Resurrectio,* is in the same metre, and subject to the same hypothesis.

As regards the work of the one real genius of the Towneley cycle, the author of the two plays of the *Shepherds,* and of the others written in the same metre, the converse of the arguments of which we admitted the force as regards the *Isaac* and the *Jacob,* will naturally lead us to assign to them as late a date as possible.

As noted. . . , the allusion in the *Judicium* to the headgear which could make a woman look 'horned like a cow,' enables us to be sure that this play-wright was a younger contemporary of Chaucer. We must not, indeed, like the cataloguer of the auction-room, argue

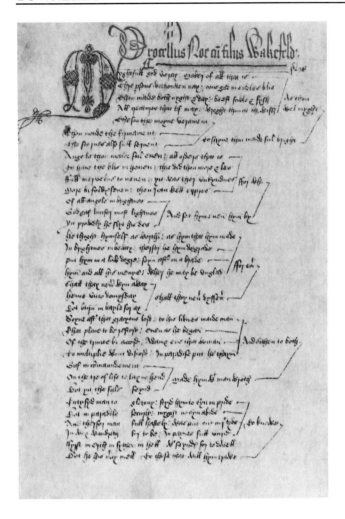

Page from a Towneley manuscript.

that because Stow writes that in the days of Anne of Bohemia 'noble women used high attire on their heads, piked like hornes,' therefore these plays may be assigned approximately to the date of her arrival in England. I imagine that in those days as in these the fashions in the Yorkshire countryside were apt to be a little behind those of London; the piked head-gear is found in manuscripts as late as about 1420. . . , and the other allusions of these plays, *e.g.,* the reference to tennis, the frequent and rather learned talk about music, and the general talk of Shepherds and Devils about the state of the country—all agree very well with the early years of the fifteenth century. In a writer so full of allusions, the absence of any reference to fighting tends, I think, to show that the plays were not written during the war with France, and thus everything seems to point to the reign of Henry IV as the most likely date of their composition. The date of our text is probably about half a century later, but the example of the York Plays shows us that in its own habitat the text of a play could be preserved in tolerable purity for a longer period than this. In the direction of popular treatment

it was impossible for any editor, however much disposed towards tinkering, to think he could improve on the play-wright of the 9-line stanzas, while it is reasonable to presume that the hold of these plays on the Yorkshire audience was sufficiently strong to resist the intrusion of didactics.

As regards the only plays not mentioned. . . , the *Capcio* (XX[b].), *Processus Talentorum* (XXIV.), *Ascension* (XXIX[b].) and *Lazarus,* there has been so much editing and interpolating, and the consequent mixture of metres is so great, that it is difficult to arrive at any clear conclusion about them. But, subject to such corrections as the survey of the dialect now being undertaken by Dr. Matthews may suggest, I think we may fairly regard this Towneley cycle as built up in at least three distinct stages. In the first of these we find the simple religious tone which we naturally assign to the beginning of the cyclical religious drama, the majority of them being written in one of the favourite metres of the fourteenth-century romances which were already going out of fashion in Chaucer's day. In the second stage we have the introduction by some playwright, who brought the knowledge of them from elsewhere, of at least five—possibly seven or eight—of the plays which were acted at York, and the composition of some others in the same style. In the third stage a writer of genuine dramatic power, whose humour was unchecked by any respect for conventionality, wrote, especially for this cycle, the plays in the 9-line stanza which form its backbone, and added here and there to others. Taken together, the three stages probably cover something like half a century, ending about 1410, though subsequent editors may have tinkered here and there, as editors will, and much allowance must be made for continual corruption by the actors.

It may be as well to note here that whatever weight we may be disposed to attach to the tradition that the cycle belonged to the Woodkirk monks and was acted at Woodkirk Fair, it is impossible to believe that the plays noted in the MS as connected with Wakefield form in any way a group by themselves. The Barkers' play of the Creation, however much edited, belongs in its origin to our first stage; the *Pharoh,* played by the Wakefield Litsters, but based on York XI., to our second, to which also I should assign the *Peregrini* played by the Fishers, written in the metre of the York *Resurrectio.* Lastly, the *Noah,* against which Wakefield is written, is in the 9-line stanza of the Shepherds' Plays, and the Glovers' play of *Abel,* whether re-written by the same author or not, is, in its present form, certainly late work. With the exception of the *Fishers,* we might say, without much exaggeration, that all the three crafts named, Dyers, Tanners, and Glovers, had some connection with the sheep, their hides and wool, which were probably the chief commodities sold at the Woodkirk fair, and so might have taken a special interest in any pageant likely to bring customers to it. But we are bound to remember that the connection with Woodkirk is a mere tradition, and that it is quite possible that the whole cycle belongs to Wakefield, which is the only place with which it is authoritatively connected.

To bring literary criticism to bear on a cycle built up, even approximately, in the manner which I have suggested, is no easy task. The plays were not written for our reading, but for the edification and amusement of the uncritical audience of their own day; and we can certainly say of them that, whatever effect the playwright aimed at, he almost always attained. Of the simply devotional plays the *Annunciation* seems to me the finest. The whole of this play, indeed, is full of tenderness; and there are touches in it in which Rossetti, if he knew it, must have delighted. The reconciliation between Joseph and the Blessed Virgin is delightful; and the passage in which Joseph describes his enforced marriage is really poetically written. One verse is especially quotable:

> Whan I all thus had wed hir thare,
> We and my madyns home can fare,
>   That kyngys daughters were;
> All wroght thay sylk to find them on,
> *Maric wroght purpyll, the oder none*
>   *bot othere colers scre.*

If this touch had been entirely of the dramatist's own invention he must, indeed, have been Rossetti's spiritual forbear; but it is needless to say that it comes from the apocryphal gospel of Mary, though he deserves all credit for bringing together two widely separated verses.

The plays which I have put into my second group are on the whole very dull. The dramatist of the *Abraham* could not fail to attain to some pathos in the treatment of the scene between Isaac and his father; but though he avoids the mistake of the York playwright who represented Isaac as a man of thirty, his handling of the scene is distinctly inferior to that of the Brome Play and the Chester cycle. The general characteristic, indeed, of the group is, that the playwright plods perseveringly through his subject, but never rises above the level of the honest journeyman.

Between the dull work and the abounding humour and constant allusiveness of the author of the plays in the 9-line stanza, the distance can only be measured by the two words respectability and genius. It is all the more pleasant to use the first to denote the dull level from which he keeps aloof, in that I have a strong suspicion that during his life the author of our 9-line stanza plays may have been censured for the lack of this very quality. His sympathy with poor folk, and his dislike of the "gentlery men" who oppressed them, seem something more than conventional; and his satire is sometimes as grim as it is free. From his frequent allusions to music, his scraps of Latin and allusions to Latin authors, his

dislike of Lollards, and the daring of some of his phrases, which seems to surpass what would have been permitted to a layman, it is probable that he was in orders; and the vision of the Friar Tuck of Peacock's *Maid Marian* rises up before me as I read his plays. As a dramatist it is difficult to praise him too highly, if we remember the limitations under which he worked, and the feeble efforts of his contemporaries and successors.

The *Secunda Pastorum*. . .is really perfect as a work of art; and if in the *Prima Pastorum* our author was only feelings his way, and in the *Noah, Herod,* etc., was cramped by the natural limitation of his subject, we have the more reason to regret that a writer of such real power had no other scope for his abilities than that offered by the cyclical miracle play. Even within these limits, however, he had room to display other gifts besides those of dramatic construction and humour. The three speeches of the Shepherds to the little Jesus are exquisite in their rustic tenderness, and even if we may not attribute to him the really terrific picture of corruption in the *Lazarus,* there is contrast enough between these and the denunciation of the usurers and extortioners in the *Judicium*. Without his aid, the Towneley cycle would have been interesting, but not more interesting than any of its three competitors. His additions entitle it to be ranked among the great works of our earlier literature.

Homer A. Watt (essay date 1940)

SOURCE: "The Dramatic Unity of the *Secunda Pastorum,*" in *Essays and Studies in Honor of Carleton Brown*, New York University Press, 1940, pp. 158-66.

[*In this influential early study of the literary value of* The Second Shepherd's Play, *Watt examines such aspects of the piece as structure, symbolism, parallelism, and use of music.*]

Considered as effective drama many of the English miracle plays are, it must be admitted, pretty sorry stuff. Indeed, they could hardly be otherwise. The essential story was dictated by biblical material that did not always offer a dramatic conflict. In transferring this material from Bible to play the anonymous authors were concerned primarily with the task of putting brief episodes into dialogue form and not with that of developing action, conflict, characters. Where they tried to season the playlet with contemporary elements, they found themselves cramped by the necessity of sticking essentially to the biblical episodes. As a result there is often a lack of unity and economy in the plays, and the added bits of contemporary realism are foreign to story and mood. The entire effect, in brief, is agglutinative, as though the authors were torn between a responsibility to reproduce the biblical originals and a desire to entertain the audience by odd items of bickering among characters, monologue acts, and occasional slapstick stuff wedged into the play to provide entertainment but totally unrelated to the main biblical action. So Cain's boy in the Towneley play of *The Killing of Abel* is an obvious intruder, as is also Iak Garcio of the first shepherds' play of the same cycle. When, therefore, one of the miracle plays appears on analysis to be an exception, it is a pleasure to demonstrate the extent to which it anticipates those dramatic techniques that emerge in the best work of the Tudor dramatists. Not all of the Tudor playwrights, as a matter of fact, in spite of their acquaintance with classical models, have displayed the technical ability of the 'Wakefield Master,' anonymous author of the justly praised *Secunda Pastorum* of the Towneley cycle.

Like his dramatic descendants, the Tudor playwrights, the Wakefield Master was under the pressure of tradition, but, like the best of them, he succeeded in subduing the tradition to his dramatic needs. What, in a nativity play, was his dramatic problem? He was committed, certainly, to a dramatic representation of the shepherd story from the second chapter of Luke, and this commitment he fulfilled as charmingly as has been done in any nativity play. But the Bible story occupies only a climax of one hundred and seventeen lines of a total of seven hundred and fifty-four, and the rest of the play seems to be, at first sight, an unrelated comic interlude. Actually, as will be shown, it is far from being only this. Another traditional pressure upon the Wakefield playwright was that of using not Palestinian shepherds but English contemporary types. But here too he succeeds in merging these diverse elements so as to secure essential dramatic unity. The *Secunda Pastorum,* indeed, will stand up under the strictest structural analysis.

The play has a traditional beginning in which each shepherd comes in grumbling. In these "complaints" there is little that is new. Coll, Gyb, and Daw all complain about the weather; Coll, the old shepherd, sighs about hard times and about the oppression of the poor by the rich; Gyb, the second shepherd, is henpecked, and advises the young men in the audience against marrying in haste lest they repent at leisure; Daw, the boy, has in him the seeds of youthful rebellion, and believes that apprentices are exploited by their masters. The grumblings of the three herdsmen are more effusive and detailed than are those of the shepherds in the *Prima Pastorum* but are not different in kind. In the first nativity play of the cycle the second shepherd complains that "poore men ar in the dyke' (l. 93) and that in the conflict between master and apprentice he wots not 'wheder is gretter, the lad or the master' (ll. 70-71); and the first shepherd, henpecked like Gyb in the second play, quotes with approval the proverb that

> A man may not wyfe
> And also thryfee,
>   And all in a yere.
>
> (ll. 97-99)

This differs little from Gyb's advice to young men in the *Secunda Pastorum:*

> These men that ar wed / haue not all thare
>   wyll;
> When they ar full hard sted, / thay sygh full
>   styll;
>
> (ll. 73-74)
>
>   . . . . .
>
> Bot, yong men, of wowyng, / for God that
>   you boght,
> Be well war of wedyng. . . .
>
> (ll. 91-92)

Such plaints, and especially those against social and economic conditions, are probably the expressions in drama of the same verbal rebellion of those who swink which may be found in other contemporary literary forms, such as the debates and the dream allegories. It is just possible, however, that the author of the *Secunda Pastorum* was aware of the foil which they provided for expressions of joy over the golden age that came with the birth of Jesus. His play, certainly, begins on a note of sorrow but ends on a contrasting note of joy.

> It is not as I wold, / for I am al lappyd
>   In sorow,
>
> (ll. 4-5)

mourns Primus Pastor when he first appears. And the exploited shepherd boy expresses at the end of the play the thought of all three that the nativity of Jesus brings better days,

> Lord, well were me / for ones and for ay,
> Myght I knele on my kne / som word for to
>   say
>   To that chylde.
>
> (ll. 685-687)

Such a formula has the flavor of the typical Elizabethan comedy—sad, unstable beginning and happy ending.

But the dramatic unity of the play is determined by elements even more marked. Of these the most striking appears in the skill with which the author has bound together in a single theme episodes that seem superficially to be unrelated. He does not show, of course, all of Shakespeare's genius in using the dream motif as the flux for diverse elements in *A Midsummer Night's Dream,* but he possessed very evidently some sense of the dramatic value of a single theme to give unity to a play. In the **Secunda Pastorum** his unifying theme is, of course, that of the birth of a child. When the play is so considered, it becomes at once apparent that the Mak-Gyll episode is no unrelated part but is very definitely connected in theme with the conventional nativity scene that follows it. Indeed, Mak's special complaint, upon his first appearance, is that he is like the old woman in the shoe:

> Now wold God I were in heuen, / for there
> > wepe no barnes
> > > So styll.
>
> > > > (ll. 193-194)

Moreover, his conversation with the shepherds in his first encounter with them contains frequent allusions to his wife's unhappy and inconvenient power of reproduction, which keeps him poor in body and in pocket:

> *I. Pastor.* How fayrs thi wyff? by my hoode, /
> > how farys sho?
> *Mak.* Lyys walteryng, by the roode, / by the
> > fyere, lo!
> And a howse full of brude / she drynkys well
> > to;
> Yll spede othere good / that she wyll do
> > > Bot so!
> Etys as fast as she can,
> And ilk yere that commys to man
> She bryngys furth a lakan,
> > And som yeres two.
>
> > > > (ll. 235-243)

The mind of Gyll, too, runs in the same direction. Indeed, in her plot for hiding the stolen sheep she makes capital of her known reputation for reproduction:

> *Vxor.* A good bowrde haue I spied, / syn thou
> > can none;
> Here shall we hym hyde / to thay be gone,—
> In my credyll abyde,— / lett me alone,
> And I shall lyg besyde / in chyldbed, and
> > grone.
>
> > > > (ll. 332-335)

Later the entire stage business of the pseudonativity shows on the part of both Mak and Gyll considerable practice in playing childbed and nursing roles. After Mak first enters, in short, the theme of a childbirth dominates the play to the very conclusion.

The unity of the play that arises out of the nativity theme is enhanced still further by a most remarkable foreshadowing of that contrast of burlesque and serious which is so frequent a device in Elizabethan comedies. It is not to be supposed, of course, that the Wakefield Master knew anything about that juxtaposition of masque and antimasque which created such unity and contrast in the English comedies of two centuries later. It would seem certain, however, that he would have understood and appreciated this device fully, for in the Mak interlude and the conventional nativity scene which follows, the contrast is as well marked as in many of the best of the Elizabethan comedies. In the Mak episode, in fact, it is not the sheep-stealing but the sheep-hiding details which are the more essential to the play, for in these latter appears a perfect burlesque of the charming Christ-child scene that concludes the play. Between the burlesque and the religious episodes the three shepherds provide the character links. Twice a birth is announced to them, and twice they go seeking—once to unearth a fraud, and a second time to worship the newborn Lord. The comparative details are so obvious, once the key is apparent, that pointing them out should hardly be necessary. However, such a comparison reveals the amazing extent to which the Wakefield Master kept in mind throughout his composition of the play the dual episodes of the burlesque and the conventional nativity.

It has been said already that Mak's complaint of his wife's perennial fertility prepares the minds of the three shepherds for his more specific announcement of her latest gift to him. This preparation is not entirely unlike their foreknowledge of the coming of the Christ child:

> *II. Pastor.* We fynde by the prophecy— / let
> > be youre dyn—
> Of Dauid and Isay / and mo then I myn,
> Thay prophecyed by clergy / that in a vyrgyn
> Shuld be lyght and ly, / to slokyn oure syn
> > And slake it,
> Oure kynde from wo;
> ffor Isay sayd so:
> *Ecce virgo*
> > *Concipiet* a chylde that is nakyd.
>
> > > > (ll. 674-682)

But no prophets foretell the coming of Mak's heir, and no angel announces his arrival. Mak had planned with his rascally wife to say that she

> . . .was lyght
> Of a knaue childe this nyght
>
> > > (ll. 337-338),

and he tell the shepherds that the news has come to him in a dream—or rather in a nightmare, for it makes him quite unhappy—:

> Now, by Sant Strevyn,
> I was flayd with a swevyn,
> > My hart out of-sloghe:

> I thoght Gyll began to crok / and trauell full sad,

Welner at the fyrst cok, / of a yong lad
ffor to mend oure flok. / Then be I neuer
    glad;

                                              (ll. 383-388)

In both the burlesque and the conventional nativity
scenes the news of the child's birth comes to the shepherds just after they have slept. In this respect the two
scenes are identical; but the arrival of the sheep-baby
is absurdly reported by his putative father, whereas the
announcement in the Bethlehem scene is in the simple
biblical tradition:

*Angelus cantat 'Gloria in exelsis'; postea
    dicat:*
Angelus. Ryse, hyrd-men heynd! / for now is
    he borne
That shall take fro the feynd / that Adam had
    lorne:

                                              (ll. 638-639)

In the two sleep episodes, incidentally, one is irresist-
ibly reminded of the burlesque dream of Bottom and
the romantic ones of the lovers in *A Midsummer Night's
Dream,* and of the similarly contrasting sleep scenes in
Lyly's *Endymion.* The sleeping shepherds of Bethlehem the Wakefield Master did not have to invent; his
cleverness is apparent in his creation for his Yorkshire
trio of a burlesque parallel nap.

The succeeding parallel detail comes with the journeying from the plain where the herdsmen slept to the
birthplace. The Yorkshire shepherds are not, to be sure,
drawn to Mak's hut by his announcement that his wife
has given birth to a man-child, although on their arrival they are at once plunged into a nativity situation. It
is to be supposed that the journey to the manager of
Jesus at the end of the play is a serious duplication of
the burlesque journey to the hut of Mak. Says Daw,
after the loss of the sheep has been discovered, and
Mak has been suspected of having stolen it:

Go we theder, I rede, / and ryn on oure feete.
Shall I neuer ete brede / the sothe to I wytt.
                                              (ll. 467-468)

And his master, after the angel's announcement, begs
for similar haste:

To Bedlem he bad / that we shuld gang;
I am full fard / that we tary to lang.
                                              (ll. 665-666)

Thus twice the three shepherds make a journey to the
crib of a newly-born child, probably measuring the
distance to their goal in both instances by parading
around the pageant-wagon.

There is no indication in the Towneley manuscript that

the Bethlehem shepherds were drawn to the stable
where the Christchild lay by a song of the Virgin to
her child. But since songs were often sung at a production but not subsequently written in the manuscripts,
there is, on the other hand, no certainty that, as the
herdsmen approached the holy site, the boy who played
Mary did not sing one of the lullabies of Our Lady of
the kind that Carleton Brown has put into his volumes
of medieval religious lyrics. The Wakefield Master was
evidently a trained musician, for not only in the *Secunda Pastorum* but in the *Prima Pastorum* as well
(ll. 656-659 and 413-414, respectively), he has put into
the mouths of the shepherds technical comments on
the singing of the angels. It is doubtful if he would
have overlooked an opportunity to include a sacred
lullaby, especially since it would have provided an
excellent foil for Mak's fearful cradle song in the sheep-
hiding scene. For in their Yorkshire phase, as it may
be called, the music-loving shepherds are almost re-
pelled from Mak's hut by a lullaby that no longer exists,
unfortunately, but that was very evidently a hideous
and unmelodious burlesque. The gloss of the Early
English Text Society edition of the play alludes to this
effusion as a 'noise,' but it was without doubt a song
by Mak with his wife groaning a stiff burden from her
childbed. For so they had planned it:

Vxor. Harken ay when thay call; / thay will
    com onone.
Com and make redy all / and syng by thyn
    oone;
Syng lullay thou shall, / for I must grone
And cry outt by the wall / on Mary and Iohn,
    ffor sore.

                                              (ll. 440-444)

But the shepherds are quick to recognize Mak's deficiencies as a singer:

III. Pastor. Will ye here how thay hak? / Oure
    syre lyst croyne.
I. Pastor. Hard I neuer none crak / so clere
    out of toyne;

                                              (ll. 476-477)

With so many contrasts in the play it is difficult to
think that the author would fail to use this harsh lullaby as a burlesque opposite a sweet song by the Virgin. Incidentally, Gyll's crying out on Mary and John
effects an excellent forward link with the conventional
nativity.

The Yorkshire shepherds, like the Bethlehem shepherds, find the babe in swaddling clothes (ll. 433,
598-599), but warned away by the 'parents' they
hesitate to approach the cradle. The scene in Mak's
hut is divided between the comic business of hunting
for the stolen sheep and the fencing with Mak and
Gyll over

. . .this chylde
That lygys in this credyll.

(ll. 537-538)

Failing to find their sheep the herdsmen actually leave the hut but return at the suggestion of the aged Coll:

I. Pastor. Gaf ye the chyld any-thyng?
II. Pastor. I trow, not oone farthyng.
III. Pastor. ffast agane will I flyng,
        Abyde ye me there.

(ll. 571-574)

It is the boy Daw's attempt to press 'bot sex pence' into the hand of the 'lytyll day-starne' that leads to the discovery of the fraud and the punishment of the rascally Mak. The link with the nativity episode here is, of course, the gift-giving, in the Mak scene burlesque, in the later episode simple and touching. Daw's term of endearment to Mak's swaddled 'infant'—'lytyll day-starne'—is applied, incidentally, by Gyb, the second shepherd, to the Christ-child (l. 727).

One final device employed by the Wakefield Master to give structural unity to the play and also to divide the little drama into definite scenes is the introduction of song. Reference has already been made to the possible contrast of Mak's lullaby and the song of the Virgin, and the biblical original forces the introduction of the *'Gloria in exelsis'* of the Angelus. The three other songs are sung by the shepherds. Of these the second is their attempt to imitate the angel's *'gloria'*—a device employed also in the **Prima Pastorum** (ll. 413 ff.). The first is a three-part song—'tenory,' 'tryble,' and 'meyne' (ll. 182-189)—used to mark the conclusion of the first scene and the coming of Mak. Finally, the play closes with a 'going-out' song by the shepherds, a device exactly similar to that used frequently by the Elizabethan playwrights to mark the ending of a comedy and to clear the stage. The song that the shepherds sang as they left the stable of the Christ-child and brought both burlesque and conventional nativity episodes to an end does not appear in the Towneley manuscript. But Mary's command to the shepherds—'Tell, furth as ye go' (l. 744)—and their own feeling—'To syng ar we bun' (l. 753)—indicate clearly that it was no jolly shepherd song that they sang but one of an angel, a star, three simple shepherds, and a babe in a manger. It may have been not unlike the song which the shepherds of the Coventry Corpus Christi nativity play sang as they left Joseph and Mary and the Christ-child:

Doune from heaven, from heaven so hie,
Of angeles ther came a great companie,
With mirthe and ioy and great solemnitye,
    They sange terly terlow,
So mereli the sheppards ther pipes can blow.

And thus *'Explicit pagina Pastorum.'*

A. C. Cawley (essay date 1958)

SOURCE: An introduction to *The Wakefield Pageants in the Towneley Cycle*, edited by A. C. Cawley, Manchester University Press, 1958, pp. xi-xxxiii.

[*In the following excerpt from his introduction to his much-admired translation, Cawley offers a general assessment of the style of the plays, focusing especially on the Wakefield playwright's adept and masterful use of language.*]

INFLUENCES ON THE WAKEFIELD PAGEANTS

Although the raw materials of the Wakefield pageants are as variegated as life itself, it is clear that the Christian tradition is the dominant influence on these pageants.

The Towneley cycle, like every other Corpus Christi cycle, is firmly based on the Vulgate and on the patristic interpretation of scriptural history; together these give unity of meaning to the whole cycle and admit it to full membership of the Christian arts in the Middle Ages. Further, in several pageants can be seen the influence of the Christian liturgy: for example, the liturgical Christmas plays in Latin have helped to determine certain features of the Shepherds' and Herod pageants in the Towneley cycle, just as in the other English cycles.

Sometimes, however, there are verbal similarities between the Towneley pageants and the corresponding pageants in other cycles which are striking enough to suggest not merely their descent from a remote liturgical play in Latin, but some kind of vernacular connexion between them. It is possible to account for these similarities by supposing that one English cycle has borrowed from another, or even that both are derived from the same parent cycle. But such similarities may also be due on occasion to the use by different playwrights of the same vernacular source. Thus the English *Northern Passion* has left its mark on both the **Coliphizacio** and the corresponding pageant (Play XXIX) in the York Cycle. Again, the English religious lyric is known to have influenced the Shepherds' Plays in all the cycles. Another general influence is that of the vernacular sermon, to which may be due 'similarities [between sermons and plays] in the actual handling of the matter, the details of certain characters and topics, the very texture and language'. The close connexion which evidently existed between the dramatic cycles and other kinds of religious literature in the vernacular reminds us that 'the plays are not isolated phenomena springing from a Latin Bible, Latin Apocrypha, etc., detached from English literature, but that the dramatists, like the lyric poets, drew from the common store of English tradition'.

The apocryphal writings and the legends which grew up round the biblical narrative are an integral part of the Christian tradition in the Middle Ages. The influence of the New Testament apocrypha on the Wakefield Group is slight, and seems to be confined to the **Magnus Herodes** and **Coliphizacio**. But the medieval legends concerning Cain and the ancient story of Uxor's truculence have an important part to play in the **Mactacio Abel** and **Processus Noe**.

Next in importance to the influence of the Christian tradition and the legends it attracted to itself is that of popular material such as proverbs, folk-tales and folk-drama. The pageants of the Wakefield Group are rich in proverbs. The rustic trots out a homely English proverb (I.436):

ill-spon weft ay comes foule out.

The 'man of astate' quotes a well-known Latin proverb (6.I43-4):

Et omnis qui tacet
Hic consentire videtur.

There are indeed so many proverbs used in these pageants that an attempt has actually been made to determine the extent of the Wakefield author's work on the basis of the proverbial content of any given pageant. A traditional tale of the men of Gotham and the story of Moll and her pitcher of milk contribute to the comedy of the **Prima Pastorum,** while a folk-tale of a sheep-stealer and the trick to conceal his theft is the main comic episode of the **Secunda Pastorum**.

The influence of folk-drama is harder to determine. But the Christian liturgy and liturgical drama, and so inevitably the Corpus Christi cycles derived from them, all seem to have absorbed the pre-Christian ritual pattern of conflict between good and evil, of the death and victorious resurrection of the royal hero-god, which is preserved in fragmentary form in folk-drama, and especially in the mummers' plays. Given this identity of basic pattern, it is reasonable to suppose that medieval folk-drama coalesced with and made an impression on the Corpus Christi cycles. In particular, it is likely that some of the comic elements in the Corpus Christi pageants show the influence of medieval folk-drama or festival. Thus the parody of the Nativity in the **Secunda Pastorum** is comparable with the burlesque ceremonies enacted on the Feast of Fools, when the folk spirit of revelry found untrammelled expression. There is an important difference between them, it is true, since in the Feast of Fools an irreverent comic use was made of sacred ritual, while in the **Secunda Pastorum** the comedy is subservient to the sacred theme it so closely parallels. Nevertheless, it is plain that the spirit of nonsense has infected the Wakefield playwright, who wrote his pageants for Corpus Christi day,

just as it did the subdeacons who played the fool on the feast of the Circumcision. Nor is there anything unique about the juxtaposition of religion and comedy in the Corpus Christi pageants; the comic scenes in the Wakefield pageants are of a piece with the marginal babewyns of the Gorleston Psalter, the mitred for preaching to a congregation of hens on a misericord at Boston, and the monkey's funeral (with a cock reading the service) in the nave windows of York Minster. In fact, the 'mixing of the story of the redemption with horse-play and farce. . .is seen to be the natural expression of medieval life and thought'.

In this summary review of the more important influences at work on the Wakefield Group it is unnecessary to mention more than a few of the details of contemporary life which have found their way into the pageants. Local topography and place-names, disputes over rights of common, economic grievances, aristocratic and plebeian dishes, digs at corrupt churchmen, tyrannophobia, music, spinning, night-spells, cock-fighting, skittles—these are some of the endless ramifications of medieval life and thought and superstition in the Wakefield pageants. The essential meaning of all these diverse elements, pagan, secular, and divine, is to be found in their author's fusion of them into a Christian pattern.

Finally, it should be remembered that the Wakefield plays are both guild pageants and Corpus Christi pageants. As guild pageants they were written for, and acted by, master craftsmen organized in societies which achieved a union of secular and religious activities no less remarkable than that to be found in the Wakefield Group. As Corpus Christi pageants they were written for, and acted on, the annual festival commemorating the Mass and celebrating the Real Presence of Christ in the Blessed Sacrament. The Corpus Christi play was, indeed, a grand occasional piece; and, in keeping with the occasion, it took the form of an elaborate dramatic presentation of 'every phase of the Christian story as a commentary on the daily ritual of the Mass'.

THE STAGING OF THE PAGEANTS

There are grounds for believing that the Wakefield Corpus Christi pageants, like those of York and Chester, were acted processionally. The evidence is provided by the Wakefield Burgess Court 'paynes' for 1556, some of which are strongly reminiscent of the Mayor's 'Proclamacio ludi corporis cristi' at York (1415). Thus at York every player must 'be redy in his pagiaunt at convenyant tyme, that is to say, at the mydhowre betwix iiij^th and v^th of the cloke in the mornynge', and likewise at Wakefield every player is enjoined to 'be redy in his pagyaunt at setled tyme before 5 of ye clocke in ye mornynge'. Again, the York injunction that 'men yat brynges furth pacentes yat yai play at the places yat is assigned yerfore and nowere elles' recalls the 'payne' imposed at Wakefield that the 'players playe where setled and no where els'. Although not as explicit as its York counterpart, the Wakefield 'payne' almost certainly refers to the different 'stations' at which the pageants were acted in turn.

Apart from this external evidence for processional presentation, the pageants themselves give some idea of the manner in which they were 'brought forth'. To begin with, there are no convincing indications that the Wakefield pageants were acted indoors. References to *flett* 'floor' (2.223), *dowore* 'door' (4.362), and *wonys* 'dwelling' (4.526, 5.169, etc.) must be taken very literally before they can be used as evidence of indoor presentation. There are more reliable indications that the pageants were acted on a stage which represented more than one locality, so that the action could go forward without the actors having to leave the stage. It will be noticed that much of the action in the Wakefield pageants is divided between two groups of people who are supposed to be in different localities. By grouping the actors at opposite ends of the stage it would be possible for an actor to go from one locality to another without doing more than cross the stage. In the **Processus Noe,** for example, there is constant coming and going between the Ark and the hill where Uxor does her spinning. Appropriately enough, it is Uxor who remains seated and Noah who does the running about, and the Latin stage direction before line 190 in the **Processus Noe** calls our attention to this: *Tunc perget ad vxorem.* Similarly, in the **Secunda Pastorum** a lot of the action alternates between the open fields, where the shepherds meet, and Mak's cottage. Here also the two localities were probably represented by different parts of the stage, so that movement from one to the other would simply mean crossing the stage. The grouping and movement of the actors make the same sort of pattern in the **Magnus Herodes** and **Coliphizacio.** Here the great men remain in one place, and their subordinates come and go as required.

The normal stage could be extended in at least two different ways—by the use of the street or ground-level and of a balcony or upper stage. Both of these devices seem to have been used in the **Mactacio Abel.** If Cain's plough horses and oxen were real animals, they must have made their entrance on an open space close by the stage. Again, there is reason to believe that God spoke to Cain from a balcony representing heaven.

Descriptive details in the text no doubt often took the place of scenery: Uxor sits *on this hill* (2.337), Gyb walks *ouer the corne* (3.83), Coll says he will *abyde on a balk, or sytt on a stone* (4.49), and the Angel's radiance lights up the wood (4.650). On the other hand, a large-scale model of a ship, or a pageant-wagon with the superstructure of a ship, would have provided a strong scenic attraction for the **Processus Noe.**

It appears that animals were sometimes used, as well as properties of various kinds. Eight animals pull Cain's plough, and Slawpase of the **Prima Pastorum** comes in leading a horse. In the **Prima Pastorum** the properties used probably included a *mayll* (224), a *skayll* (249), and a *panyere* (281). But it is not always certain whether the things referred to in the text were real or make-believe. It is difficult to tell what attempt, if any, was made to represent the embarkation of Noah's *cat-all* (2.326). Again, it seems likely that the shepherds' meal in the **Prima Pastorum** was mostly make-believe.

There are a few indications of costume. Thus Noah takes off his *gowne* and works in his *cote* (2.262). Mak makes his first appearance *in clamide se super togam vestitus,* and comic use is made of his 'chlamys'. It is known that care was taken over the costumes in the guild pageants: we learn from the records of the Coventry Smiths' Company that distinctive costumes were worn by the actors taking the parts of Herod, Annas and Caiaphas, and the torturers. We can imagine the Wakefield Annas and Caiaphas, like their counterparts at Coventry, wearing 'myttyrs' and 'a byschops taberd of scarlet', and the torturers dressed in 'jakketts of blake bokeram'.

No-one can read the Wakefield pageants without realizing that the spoken words are continually being reinforced by expressions, gestures, and movements. Thus in the **Processus Noe** the activities of Noah and his wife embrace carpentry, spinning, and brawling as well as the repeated sounding of the flood waters with a plumb-line and the release of the raven and doves. These are their main activities. But some of the minor details of their movements are no less effective, whether it is Noah removing his gown in preparation for his shipwrighting, or Uxor taking over the tiller from her husband (2.435). On occasion, however, the very absence of action can be striking and significant. In the **Coliphizacio** the contrast between Christ and his tormentors is heightened not only by Christ's silence but by his immobility in the presence of Caiaphas, with his violent words and movements, and of the torturers, who buffet Christ and drive him along like an animal. A playwright who knows when to set his characters in motion and when to immobilize them is an experienced man of the theatre. Such a playwright was the Wakefield Master, who had learned how to hold the attention of his audience, 'nunc silentes, nunc cachinnantes', through a long summer's day.

THE WAKEFIELD PLAYWRIGHT'S USE OF LANGUAGE

The Wakefield playwright draws on a varied vocabulary of English, Scandinavian, and Romance words. It must have taxed his ingenuity to the utmost to find thirteen rhyme-words for each of his nine-line stanzas.

But he has managed it by pressing into service all the different sounds, forms, and words of his North Midland dialect, in which Northern and Midland, English and Scandinavian, elements existed side by side.

He has a superb command of ludicrous diction and of the language of violence and abuse. He is equally at home in the verbal worlds of the foul-mouthed Cain and the smooth-tongued Annas. He finds the right words to express moods of anger and indignation, pathos and tenderness. Not once does his 'Middle English', or his handling of it, let him down.

He is especially fond of producing comic effects by using words figuratively, as when Noah yells *ram-skyt* (2.217) at his wife, or when Uxor longs for *a measse of wedows coyll* (2.389). His shepherds make comic-figurative play with the everyday words of a shepherd's life: *mangere* (3.201) in the sense of 'board, table', *cryb* (3.208) meaning 'eat', *purst* and *foder* (3.209). Again, the contemptuous use of *barke* by Caiaphas, when he curses the man who first made him a priest and taught him *On bookys for to barke* (6.308), tells us as much about Caiaphas and his attitude to his clerkly profession as a single word can be expected to do.

He is always exploiting the ambiguities of words for comic purposes. We find him punning on words, or juggling with the incongruous meanings of words like *croyne* and *knaue* (4.554). The word *knaue* can mean not only 'boy' but 'low-born person, rascal', so that when the Second Shepherd asks Mak, *Is youre chyld a knaue?*, his question has an edge to it. Mak assumes it to be maliciously meant, for he replies with dignity (4.555-6):

> Any lord mygt hym haue,
> This chyld, to his son.

We also find him making comic use of the Southern dialect. It is a welcome change to find a Northerner enjoying himself at the expense of the Southerner's linguistic habits, and so reversing the situation found in the *Reeve's Tale*.

His verbal humour is not always of an obvious kind. The humour of the First Shepherd's phrase *boyte of oure bayll* (3.247), to describe the *Good holsom ayll* he is about to drink, depends upon our realizing that this phrase is a dignified alliterative formula used elsewhere of God or Christ. When Herod's messenger pompously announces that his master's realms extend *From Egypt to Mantua, unto Kemptowne* (5.47), we may not be able to identify *Kemptowne* with any certainty, but we can safely guess that bathos is intended. Sometimes an idiomatic phrase is given a humorous twist which may escape the reader in a hurry. Thus when the Second Shepherd in the **Prima Pastorum**

wishes his oppressors *good mendyng With a short endyng* (3.78-9), he is playing a spiteful variation on the saying 'to mend or end'. He does not suggest the mending and ending as alternatives, but wants the *good mendyng* to be followed by a *short endyng*.

In contrast to this comic use of words, the language of violence and abuse leaps out of the verses of both the **Magnus Herodes** and the **Coliphizacio**. Herod's language is indeed the man himself: it is impossible to separate this wrathful, fear-ridden tyrant from his spluttering maledictions. The same is true of Caiaphas in the **Coliphizacio**. But this pageant is also distinguished by its use of legal language. Annas and Caiaphas have been refashioned by the Wakefield playwright as a pair of corrupt ecclesiastical lawyers of his own day. It is appropriate therefore that they should display an easy command of legal jargon.

The humorous and colloquial elements in the diction of the Wakefield author are so much in evidence that it is easy to over-stress them, and to lose sight of both his serious purpose and the serious language he often uses to express it. In the **Processus Noe,** for example, the speeches expressing God's anger and Noah's contrition, which are gravely worded in traditional poetic language, have an essential contribution to make to the meaning of the Noah legend. There is nothing commonplace about the spiritual meaning of this legend; and there is nothing plebeian about poetic phrases like *Beytter of bayll* (2.311) or words like *all-weldand* (2.494) and *anoynt*. Again, in the Shepherds' Plays the tenderness of the adoration scene is achieved by a blend of affectionate colloquial idiom and dignified figurative language (4.724-7):

> Hayll, lytyll tyne mop!
> Of oure crede thou art crop;
> I wold drynk on thy cop,
> Lytyll day-starne.

In the **Magnus Herodes** the Second Woman pleads for her baby in words which are universal in their simplicity and spontaneity (5.350-1)

> Mercy, lord, I cry!
> It is myn awne dere son.

In fact, the Wakefield dramatist may be a master of racy, colloquial idiom, but he is not trying to be racy and colloquial all the time. What he is doing is to juxtapose and harmonize the comic and serious elements that all together make up his Christian interpretation of life. He is a distinguished dramatist because he finds the right words and the right rhythms to express many different moods—tender, gloomy, and reflective as well as 'sharp, stinging, defiant'. So far from being a crude gag in his mouth, his language is an integral part of his vision and achievement.

THE AUTHOR

Although the pageants of the Wakefield Group may be confidently assigned to a single playwright of Wakefield, nothing is known about his identity. An attempt has been made to identify him with Gilbert Pilkington, the alleged author of the *Turnament of Totenham*. But while there is no good evidence for assigning the authorship of either the *Turnament* or the Wakefield pageants to Gilbert Pilkington, it can be shown that they have certain features in common, including a similar stanza-form. And even if it cannot be proved that the *Turnament* is by the author of the Wakefield Group, at least it is possible that one work has influenced the other.

The Wakefield playwright was no doubt a cleric or a man with clerical training, judging by his use of Latin and his biblical knowledge. We are at liberty to guess that he was a subdeacon or a chantry priest, but there is little or no evidence on which to base such guesses. All that we can be fairly sure of is that he was neither a friar nor a Lollard.

We may learn something of the man's personality from the pageants attributed to him. His sympathy for the underdog, his sharpness of eye and tongue, his sense of humour, broad, hilarious, and sometimes deliberately brutal—all these qualities force themselves on our attention. He is a man of many moods, amused and indignant, harsh and tender in turn. He has lived an uncloistered life in which people, books, and music have all played a part; his knowledge of men and their nature ranges from king to peasant; he is artist enough to make good use of the most unpromising materials—crabbed legal language, blanket-tossing, and Hot Cockles. Above all, he is an artist for whom life has meaning—a religious meaning. His drama is part and parcel of the great Christian drama which gives shape and purpose to human life, opposing harmony to conflict and love to hatred, but without minimizing the conflict or pretending that the hatred does not exist.

DATE

Date of the Wakefield Author's contributions to the Cycle

The available evidence favours a date during the first half of the fifteenth century for the Wakefield author's work. The use of the musical term 'crotchet' in the **Secunda Pastorum** and the reference to tennis in the same pageant suggest a period not earlier than *c.* 1400. Certain sound-changes, established by rhyme, support a date later than the fourteenth century for the Wakefield Group as a whole. There are grounds for believing that the Wakefield playwright was influenced by the 'York realist', whose work has been dated after 1415. Some of the allusions to costume in Plays 2, 5, and XXX

seem to point to a date not earlier than *c.* 1420. Again, the manuscript containing the Wakefield pageants may itself be not much later than *c.* 1450.

While the weight of the evidence is therefore in favour of the years 1400-50, there is no strong evidence for preferring one particular decade to another. The pageants of the Wakefield Group were possibly written at different times during several decades. But it is doubtful whether the chronological sequence of these pageants can be determined at all accurately on the strength of the metrical differences between them, and there is certainly no way of measuring metrical progress in terms of years and decades.

Martial Rose (essay date 1961)

SOURCE: An introduction to *The Wakefield Mystery Plays*, edited by Martial Rose, 1961. Reprint by W. W. Norton & Company, Inc., 1969, pp. 19-55.

[*Below, Rose discusses the staging of the Wakefield plays, elaborating on his theory of the use of a circular set and the combined staging of several of the plays.*]

THE STAGING OF THE WAKEFIELD PLAYS

The reference concerning the suppression of the Wakefield Plays in the records of the Diocesan Court of High Commission at York is one of the very few pieces of external evidence that Wakefield possessed a cycle of mystery plays. The document tells us that the plays were planned for 'Whitsonweke. . .or thereabouts', that the bailiff and burgesses of Wakefield were responsible for their organization, and that in the plays, . . .as, for instance, in **John the Baptist** and **The Resurrection,** certain references were made to the sacraments which were unacceptable to the reformed church.

The only other external evidence that Wakefield had its own cycle of *Corpus Christi* plays is the Wakefield Burgess Court Rolls which, in Queen Mary's reign (1553-1558), have the following entries:

> PAYNES LAYD BY THE BURGES QWEST AS
> FOLLOYT. IN ANNO 1554 Itm a payne is layd
> yt gyles Dolleffe shall brenge In or Causse to be
> broght ye regenall of *Corpus Xty* play before ys
> & wytsonday In pane. . . . Itm a payne layde yt
> ye mesters of ye *Corpus Xti* playe shall Come &
> mayke thayre a Count before ye gentyllmen
> burgessus of ye toun before this & may day next.
> In payne of everye one not so doynge 20s.
>
> PAYNES LAYDE BY THE BURGES ENQUESTS AT THE
> COURTE KEPTE AT WAKEFELDE NEXTE AFTER THE
> FEASTE OF SAYNTE MICHAELL THARCHAUNGELL IN
> THIRDE AND FOURTE YEARE OF THE REIGNES OF OUR

SOVERAIGNE LORDE AND LADYE KINGE PHILYPPE AND QUENE MARYE, 1556

Itm a payne is sett that everye crafte and occupation doo bringe furthe theire pagyaunts of *Corpus Christi* daye as hathe bene heretofore used and to give furthe the speches of the same in after holydayes in payne of everye one not so doynge to forfett xls.

Itm a payne is sett that everye player be redy in his pagyaunt at setled tyme before 5 of ye clocke in ye mornynge in payne of every one not so doynge to forfett vjs. viijd.

Itm a payne is sett yt ye players playe where setled and no where els in payne of no (sic) so doynge to forfett xxs.

Itm a payne is sett yt no man goe armed to disturb ye playe or hinder ye procession in payne of everye one so doynge vjs. viijd.

Itm a payne is sett yt everye man shall leave hys weapon att hys home or at hys ynne in payne of not so doynge vjs. viijd.

Ye summe of ye expens of ye Cherche mester for ye *Corpus Christi* playe xvijs. xd.

Item payd to ye preste	xijd.
Itm payd to ye mynstrells	xxd.
Itm payd to ye mynstrells of *Corpus Christi* playe	iijs. ivd.
Itm payde for ye *Corpus Christi* playe & wrytynge ye spechys for yt	iijs. viijd.
Itm payd for ye Baner for ye mynstrells	vjs. viijd.
Itm payd for ye ryngyng ye same day	vjd.
Itm payd for garlonds on *Corpus Christi* daye	xijd.

It is understandable that the return to the throne of Queen Mary, a Catholic monarch, should have provided the encouragement for the re-staging of the mystery plays which in the reigns of Henry VIII and Edward VI had been discredited through the anti-papal policies of the crown. The loss of the Wakefield plays dealing with the death, assumption, and coronation of the Blessed Virgin, which were probably contained in those twelve leaves, now missing, between *The Ascension* and *The Judgement,* may have coincided with the prohibition in 1548 of the corresponding York plays. H. C. Gardiner writes [in *Mysteries' End,* 1946] '. . .the excision of the plays on the Death, Assumption, and Coronation of the Blessed Virgin in York in 1548 shows that, apart from any official decree, the spirit of Protestantism was at work'.

The time of year in 1554 when the Burgess Banns (Paynes) were laid down is not clear, but from the records of Norwich and Coventry we gather that the citizens set about preparing for their *Corpus Christi* plays at Easter or soon after. In these Wakefield Banns the phrase 'before this and may day next' may indicate that their meeting took place on or just after May 1st. According to the records of the York Diocesan Court

the plays were performed during 'Whitsonweke. . .or thereaboutes'. The phrasing suggests that the plays were not presented on one day only but on two or more days. The Chester cycle, though called the *Corpus Christi* plays, was performed on Monday, Tuesday and Wednesday of Whit week; a procession was held on *Corpus Christi* day followed by a play presented by the clergy (Glynne Wickham, *Early English Stages,* 1959; E. K. Chambers, *The Mediaeval Stage,* 1903). The shifting of the plays from *Corpus Christi* day to Whit week took place at Chester as early as 1462; at York in 1569 they were performed on Whit Tuesday, and Norwich and New Romney also record performances of the *Corpus Christi* plays in Whit week.

The 1556 Banns were prepared at the first meeting of the Burgess Court following the feast of St. Michael (29th September, 1555). The frequency of the Burgess Court meetings is unknown, but by the contents of the Banns for 1556 this particular meeting could not have been too distant from the *Corpus Christi* festivities. It seems, from the hint given in the 1554 Banns, that the 1556 meeting was probably on May Day, and that this was the occasion of the Court recording the expense accounts of those responsible for the previous year's *Corpus Christi* play; that of the churchwarden's is one such account. The churchwarden's account must refer to the festivities of the previous year (1555) because all the 1556 Banns concern the preparations for the 1556 procession and play. Surely no accounts would be submitted until after performance, and we gather from the second item in the 1554 Banns that the wardens of the *Corpus Christi* play were allowed almost a year in which to make up their accounts and submit them 'before ye gentyllmen & burgessus' of Wakefield.

The very last item in the churchwarden's account, 'payd for garlonds on *Corpus Christi* day xijd.', seems to prove that the crafts brought forth their pageants 'of *Corpus Christi* daye' on *Corpus Christi* day. But there is more than a strong suggestion in the Banns that the procession and the plays took place on separate days. The crafts are asked to bring forth their pageants on *Corpus Christi* day—and it is for this day the garlands are required—but it is 'in after holydayes' that they are 'to give furthe the speches of the same'. Does this mean that the procession took place on *Corpus Christi* day, a Thursday, and that the following Friday and Saturday were treated as holidays on which the plays were performed? Does the bringing forth of pageants then mean the joining in the *Corpus Christi* day procession which moved from the parish church through the town returning again to the church? Was there singing on the way, and did the pageants at certain stations draw back their curtains to a dumb-show representation of the drama they were to perform 'in after holydayes'? Questions abound; answers supported by circumstantial evidence are scarce. But it is clear that the

Banns suggest a separation of the procession and the plays. No man may go armed lest he 'disturb ye playe or hinder ye procession'; there are two separate payments to the minstrels, one of which specifies 'ye mynstrells of *Corpus Christi* playe'; the garlands, the ringing of bells, the minstrels in procession with their very expensive banner, and the officiating priest are indications of the procession. The playbook (regenall), the rewriting of parts, the injunction to play 'where setled' and no where els' are obvious references distinguishing the plays from the procession. In York, where before 1426 the plays and the procession were undertaken on the same day, the Proclamation of 1394 introduces a difference of phrasing in its reference to the location of the plays which may be significant: 'And þat men þat brynges furth pagentes þat þai play *at the places* þat is assigned þerfore and nowere elles. . .' The Wakefield 'where setled' is ambiguous; obviously at York there were in 1394 many stations; at Wakefield in 1556 there may have been but one.

If the plays were not performed in Wakefield until after *Corpus Christi* day why should the Burgesses be asking for the master copy of the plays ('ye regenall' or original) to be returned to them before Whit Sunday? To whom did the churchwarden pay 3s. 8d. for the *Corpus Christi* play and for the writing of speeches for it? And who, anyway, was Giles Dolleffe that he should have the manuscript of the plays in his keeping? It may be that Whit Sunday marked the beginning of the preparations for the *Corpus Christi* festival when the master copy was called in to be, if necessary, 'corectyd', and to be the source for the copying out of parts and, possibly, of whole plays. The twelve days between Whit Sunday and *Corpus Christi* day might seem too inadequate a time in which to rehearse the whole cycle, but contemporary evidence points to very little time being spent on rehearsal: 'these pagente shulde be played after breeffe rehearsal' (*The Banns of the Chester Plays*, 6o). The Coventry Smiths held their first rehearsal in Easter week and their second in Whit week. In the Coventry records there are seldom more than two rehearsals before performance; the outstanding exception is the Cappers' record of five rehearsals in 1584 for the new play *The Destruction of Jerusalem* (Hardin Craig, *Two Coventry Corpus Christi Plays*, 1957). It is significant that this play was especially written for Coventry to replace the *Corpus Christi* cycle. If the craft-guilds who undertook the performance of this play, which from all accounts appears to have been of a similar length to the cycle it was displacing, required only five rehearsals, it is reasonable to assume that two would have sufficed for the mystery plays which had been in existence for well over a hundred years, and which by annual performance had ingrained their contents in the mind and memory of spectators and players. It was traditional for the players to perform the same parts year after year. Only the rare change of cast would have necessitated a part being copied out. The scribe who undertook to copy parts out from the original, since he was paid by the churchwarden, was most probably one of the parish clergy. At Coventry in 1495 payment is made 'for copyyng of ij knyghts parte and demons', and in 1540 one penny is paid 'for writyng a parte for Herre Person'. (Hardin Craig). Apparently 'Herre Person' had a very small part; on the other hand the Wakefield scribe, if he earned his 3s. 8d., must have had either many parts to copy out or a new play to write. The Coventry Smiths, Cappers, and Mercers, each paid John Green five shillings for copying from the manuscript of *The Destruction of Jerusalem* the particular plays that were the responsibility of their respective companies. The 3s. 8d. in the Wakefield accounts may conceivably have been due, not only to the copying of parts but also for the writing of *The Hanging of Judas,* the only play in the manuscript which is written in a sixteenth-century hand. The scribe, it will be noticed, is paid 'for ye *Corpus Christi* playe & wrytynge ye spechys for yt'. It is obvious from his payment that he was not employed to copy out the whole master copy; he may however have copied out one play which, according to Coventry rates of pay in the sixteenth century, would have earned him about five shillings. But the scribe may also have been paid for 'bearing' the book, which E. K. Chambers interprets as acting as prompter. The Coventry Smiths in 1494 record that they 'paid to John Harryes for berying of the orygynall that day vjd'.

If the Wakefield scribe then had possession of the 'original' soon after Whit Sunday, when it was handed to him through the agency first of the Burgess Court and then of the churchwarden, what was the 'original' doing in the possession of Gyles Dolleffe until Whit Sunday? The Coventry Cappers in 1584 pay one shilling 'for the kepynge the boke', but it is not clear whether payment is for prompting or for safe-keeping of the play after performance. It is more likely that Gyles Dolleffe had the plays in his safe-keeping and that he was himself one of the wardens or producers. His, too, may have been the task to prepare the text for the 1556 performance and to submit it for approval to both the Burgess Court and the ecclesiastical authorities before rehearsals commenced. We know he was a prominent citizen of Wakefield, a burgess himself, attending the Burgess Court meetings, living in Kirkgate and by trade a draper. [J. W. Walker, *Wakefield, Its History and People,* 1934.] His wife's death is recorded in the Archbishop's Registry at York under March 25th, 1604: 'Agnis doliffe late wife of Giles Doliffe buried XXVij^th daye' [J. W. Walker.] It would be interesting to know a good deal more about Gyles Dolleffe, for he may have been, as Thomas Colclow was for the Coventry Smiths' play (Hardin Craig, *TCCCP*), a highly paid producer whose contract extended over a number of years.

The 1556 Banns of the Wakefield Burgess Court order

every player to be ready in his pageant by 5 a.m. The 1394 York Proclamation decreed 4:30 a.m. as the time when all should assemble. A town-clerk of York, Roger Burton, made two lists of the York Plays, one undated containing fifty-seven plays, and the other dated 1415 containing fifty-one: the unique manuscript contains forty-eight (L. T. Smith). Assuming that only forty-eight plays are to be performed in the day, we have then a drama whose total length is 13,121 lines, the average length of each play being 273 lines. The plays, as tradition has it, were performed at a number of different stations in York, the whole cycle being presented at each successive station. The number of stations varied: in 1417 there were twelve, in 1519 there were fourteen, and in 1554 sixteen (L. T. Smith). The playing of 273 lines, including the music and movement, would take about fifteen minutes. At the first station, allowing five minutes for the time taken between the end of one pageant and the beginning of another, the whole cycle would last for about fifteen hours; if it started at 4:30 a.m. it would finish at 7:30 p.m. At the second station, allowing five minutes for the journey and five minutes for the combined preparation for the journey at the first station and for the playing at the second—and we have to bear in mind that these are horse-drawn pageants making their way in procession not at a gallop—performance would begin at 4:55 a.m. and the cycle would finish at 7:55 p.m. At this rate the first pageant would begin at 9:05 a.m. at the twelfth station and the last would finish just after midnight. It must be recognized that these estimates are almost impracticably conservative, and the pace at which such a schedule could be maintained would put an intolerable strain on both performers and spectators. Yet records indicate that fifty-seven plays were performed at sixteen different stations. The processional street-pageant staging of the York cycle has been too readily accepted without due consideration given to the practical problems. Why, for instance, were *all* the players asked to assemble at 4:30 a.m. if at the first station the cast of **The Judgement Day** had to wait until 7 p.m. until they performed? And were performances continued after nightfall? The records indicate provision for lanterns, cressets, torches, tapers, iron lamps for the pageants, but since an important part of both the York Proclamation and the Wakefield Banns is concerned with minimizing the possibility of rowdiness and rioting, would not the normal curfew be stringently enforced? If not, how can we account for the fact that when Queen Margaret visited Coventry in 1457 she saw at the first station a performance of the whole cycle 'save domes-day, which myght not pleyde for lak of day'? Even for the Queen of England playing could not be permitted after sun-down. If this were true also of York, what happened to the fifty-seven plays at sixteen different stations?

A study of the extant cycles reveals general similarities but individual differences, and this applies to the staging as well as to the text of the plays. In making a statement concerning the staging of the Wakefield Plays, because of the scarcity of local external evidence, recourse is had to analogy. Of those towns whose mystery cycles have survived, York is the nearest to Wakefield. Furthermore the York and Wakefield cycles have certain plays in common, and their Banns also show concern for similar problems: the necessity of an early start; the danger of armed men at the procession or the plays; the need for the players to play 'where setled'. Furthermore the Wakefield cycle is of a comparable length to the York. It contains 12,276 lines; including the lines from the missing twenty-eight leaves the total number would approach 15,000, which would make it longer than the existing York manuscript. Wakefield then shares with York the practical problem, indeed the practical impossibility, of performing the whole cycle at a number of stations in the compass of a day.

At York in 1426, for the first time, the procession and the plays were separated. The plays were performed on *Corpus Christi* day and the procession took place the day following (R. Davies, *Extracts from the Municipal Records of the City of York during the Reigns of Edward IV, Edward V, and Richard III*, 1843). At Chester the three-day performance of the plays took place in Whit week, and the *Corpus Christi* procession in the following week on the day of the festival. At Norwich the plays were performed on the Monday and Tuesday of Whit week, and, as at Chester, the procession followed on *Corpus Christi* day (O. Waterhouse, *Non Cycle Mystery Plays*). The separation of the plays from the procession arose in the first place from their divergent origins—the liturgical drama predates the *Corpus Christi* procession—and in the second from the extreme difficulty of finding time for both on the same day. In consequence the plays were generally put first and the procession followed later, either the next day, as at York, or the next week, as at Chester and Norwich. Since the York schedule shown earlier for the station-to-station playing is scarcely practicable, the stations at some stage may have been used not as acting areas for performance of the whole cycle, but rather as stopping places during the procession at which each pageant presented its scene in tableau. After 1426 the York procession took place on the day following *Corpus Christi*. If the plays performed on *Corpus Christi* day began at 4:30 a.m. they would have lasted at least until nightfall at just one station, and if the procession began the following day at 4:30 a.m. it would take the most part of the day, if combined with the religious services and the singing, to thread its way from station to through the town. This is purely conjectural, but all the pageants moving off together does at least make sense of that reference in the Proclamation to all players being ready at 4:30 a.m. It is difficult to believe that the actors in **The Judgement Day** waited from dawn to dusk before their first line was spoken.

A similar problem attends the presentation of the Wake-field cycle. A single performance at a single station is all that is possible in a day, and this makes no allow-ance for the procession. The procession had to be sep-arated from the performance, and the first item in the 1556 Banns suggests such a separation. The crafts are asked to prepare their pageants for the procession on one day and to perform the plays ('to give furthe the speches of the same in after holydayes') on the days that follow. If this interpretation is correct then Wake-field reversed the order at York, where the procession preceded the plays. From the 1576 record of the Dioc-esan High Court at York we may gather that under a Protestant monarch, with the prohibition of Catholic festivals, performance of the plays at Wakefield was planned for Whit week.

The thirty-two plays of the Wakefield cycle average 384 lines each. If they were performed processionally they would have taken over fourteen hours at each station. If however they were performed at one station only, and by such an arrangement reducing the time spent in procession and in preparation before and after each performance, then the total playing time would have stretched from dawn to dusk. This playing time may at a later stage have been spread over two or more days. One possible explanation of there being two Shepherds' plays in the cycle is that *The First Shep-herds' Play* was performed at the end of the first day's playing and *The Second Shepherds' Play* at the be-ginning of the second. It is certainly true that if the missing leaves of the manuscript are taken into ac-count the play would be divided into three equal parts if breaks were made after *The First Shepherds' Play* and after *The Crucifixion*. (The Chester Plays which were performed on three successive days broke at *The Adoration of the Magi* and at *Christ's Descent into Hell;* the Ancient Cornish Drama, lasting also three days, broke at *The Execution of Maximilla* and *The Crucifixion*.) But whether the plays were performed on one, two, or three days, there is sufficient evidence to suggest that they were performed in the mid-fifteenth century at least, when the Wakefield Master had writ-ten his plays and made so many other revisions in the cycle, in one fixed locality, on a multiple stage, and in the round.

THE ONE FIXED LOCALITY

One particular feature of the manuscript of the Wake-field Plays, which sets it apart from the York and Chester cycles, is the sparse reference to the guilds. The names of four guilds—Barkers (Tanners), Glov-ers, Litsters (Dyers), and Fishers—are written on the title pages of four of the plays, but in a sixteenth-century hand. The fifteenth-century manuscript would, in its original state, have contained no reference to any of the guilds. In this the Wakefield Plays resemble the *Ludus Coventriae*. The strong case made by Hardin

Craig (*E.R.D.*) to establish that the *Ludus Coventriae* and the Lincoln *Corpus Christi* plays are one and the same might lead us by analogy, through what we know were the conditions under which the Lincoln Plays were produced, to the organization and staging of the Wakefield cycle.

The *Corpus Christi* plays at Lincoln were the respon-sibility not of the trade-guilds but of a religious guild, either the *Corpus Christi* guild or that of St. Anne. Every man and woman of Lincoln was a member of the St. Anne guild, paying annually a minimum of four pence each towards the maintenance of their guild. The *Corpus Christi* procession after about 1470 took place not on *Corpus Christi* day but on St. Anne's day (26th July). Hardin Craig maintains that on this occa-sion the pageants passed in procession through the city but that there was no performance until they reached the Minster. 'All the pageants would be there. It should also be remembered that all the citizens of Lincoln were, failing good excuse, obliged to be there. It may be said also that the only place in the old city of Lin-coln where there could be such a concourse of people was the cathedral with its close and the vacant areas around it. It is surely no wild conjecture to suggest that the plays were acted there. One play we know was regularly performed on St. Anne's day in the nave of the cathedral church, that is, the Assumption and Cor-onation of the Blessed Virgin Mary. And we are not without another plausible piece of evidence that plays were to be seen at the cathedral.' (Hardin Craig, *E.R.D.*)

One established playing site in a large area, having scaffolds specially erected for the spectators, and with the pageants moving into the spaces left between the scaffolds to complete a circle, or a horse-shoe, tallies exactly with the staging arrangements which must have prevailed for the performance of the *Ludus Coventriae,* and if these were the Lincoln *Corpus Christi* plays performed outside the cathedral church, the upper win-dows of The Close houses would also have provided excellent viewing.

The *Ludus Coventriae* resembles the Wakefield cycle in that it is an apparent compilation of diverse materi-al, later than either the York or Chester cycles, but showing marked signs, particularly in the Passion se-quences, of continuity of action and actors. The forty-eight York plays, both in their brevity and in their insulation, tend to become fragments rather than dra-mas and this, perhaps, is due to their being broken down to the requirements of the numerous guilds. On the other hand the *Ludus Coventriae* and the Wake-field Plays show an overall design which might well indicate that both the editing—if not the writing—of the plays and their preparation for performance was directed by a single organization, whether religious guild or corporation, and that responsibility for the individual plays was not assumed by the trade-guilds.

In the late fourteenth and early fifteenth century the York guilds may well have numbered over sixty. The very fact that there were at one time fifty-seven plays in the York cycle points to the flourishing guild organizations in that city. On the other hand, Wakefield in 1377, when each person over sixteen had to pay a four-penny Poll Tax, could only muster £4. 15. 8d. 'The list for the town of Wakefield shows a population of 567 over the age of sixteen years, and among the traders are found 2 mercers, 4 walkers or fullers, 5 websters or weavers, 8 tailors, 3 barkers or tanners, 3 drapers, 2 cattle-dealers, 4 wool merchants, 1 franklin or gentleman, 2 butchers, 2 wheelwrights, 1 skinner, 2 ostlers (hotel-keepers), 4 smiths, 1 mason, 1 goldsmith, 1 glover. . . .' (J. W. Walker, *Wakefield, Its History and People,* 1934.) We can assume then that in 1377, apart from beggars, there were approximately two hundred and eighty men living in Wakefield. But there are two hundred and forty-three different parts in the plays, and even if the population of Wakefield had doubled by 1425 it is extremely doubtful whether the plays would have been the responsibility of the guilds. For instance the Barkers would require at least eleven actors to perform **The Creation,** quite apart from the team to prepare the pageant for performance and to assist with properties and general problems of stage management. It may well have been the case that it was not until the sixteenth century that the guilds were large enough in Wakefield to undertake full production responsibilities. How then were they organized in the fifteenth century?

Performed on the trade-guild system existing in York and Chester there is the likelihood that two hundred and forty-three different actors would have been required to fill all the roles, but if the plays were performed on the basis of the *Ludus Coventriae* production, where there was one organization only to cast and direct the plays, far fewer actors would be required for, as so strongly indicated in the *Ludus Coventriae* Passion sequence, the same actors would almost certainly play the parts of the main characters throughout. In the York cycle there are twenty-seven plays in which Jesus appears. We are given to understand that in performance twenty-seven different actors played the part. Wakefield, through sheer lack of manpower, quite apart from any artistic consideration, could not support such a principle of production, at least not until well into the sixteenth century.

Where a religious guild undertook production of the plays, as at Lincoln, it was stoutly supported by the trade-guilds, without whose co-operation no progress could have been made. But the direction of the plays by a religious guild would have followed more closely the traditions laid down by the liturgical drama. The religious guild's close association with the drama still acted in the church is evident in the Lincoln example of the clergy performing **The Assumption** in the nave

of the cathedral as the culmination of the St. Anne's day celebrations. Religious plays on the continent were less dependent on the trade-guilds than in England, and their staging derived more directly from liturgical drama.

> For most liturgical plays the so-called "simultaneous staging" was the rule. Thus in the Fleury *Conversion of St. Paul,* Jerusalem is on one side of the playing-space, Damascus on the other; in the Daniel plays, the *domus* of the hero to which he retires, the lions' den, and the throne occupied successively by Belshazzar and Darius, all are in view from the opening of the plays. Similarly the various St. Nicholas plays move the chief characters from one part of the playing-space to another, but always to stations visible to the audience from the beginning to the end of the performance. Only in such a highly organized spectacle as the *Presentation of the Virgin* do we find some provision for a distinct change of locale: in that *ordo* the two stages have a symbolical value, the second connoting Mary's reception into the church after her presentation. Processions were, of course, introduced at times to suggest journeys and therefore scene-shifts, but once the actors had arrived at the playing-space, the stage-setting, however farflung the action, remained fixed.' (Grace Frank, *Medieval French Drama,* 1954)

If at Wakefield the plays were produced by a religious guild, and if shortage of man-power brought about continuity of actors (that is one actor playing Jesus, or Pilate, or Caiaphas, and so on, throughout), it is more than likely that continuity of action took place in a stage-setting which 'remained fixed'.

The Norwich cycle of plays was also the responsibility of a religious guild, St. Luke's, and here, too, although they went forward in procession on *Corpus Christi* day, performance on Whit Monday and Tuesday is considered to have been stationary (O. Waterhouse). When in 1527 the strain of maintaining the plays became too burdensome for the St. Luke's guild, its members 'petitioned the corporation to divide the responsibility and expense among the various guilds'. A similar shedding of responsibility for certain of the plays might have taken place at Wakefield, and the appearance in the manuscript in a sixteenth-century hand of the four guilds (Tanners, Glovers, Dyers, and Fishers) tends to confirm this.

The evidence suggests that where the religious guilds assumed responsibility for the plays, although the procession remained a regular feature of the *Corpus Christi* festival, the performance was given in a fixed locality. The *Ludus Coventriae* and the *Digby Plays,* none of which was associated with trade-guilds, were also given in fixed localities. Indeed, performance by pageants in procession is the exception rather than the rule, as the stationary presentation of plays at Louth, Reading, Bassingbourne, Chelmsford, Shrewsbury, Cornwall,

Aberdeen, and Edinburgh prove. (E. K. Chambers) Furthermore, the staging of the Wakefield Plays calls for a fixed locality in which heaven, paradise, earth, limbo, and hell stand always in the same relationship to each other. Also the variety of levels, the repetition of the journey motif (**Abraham,** the **Shepherds,** the **Magi,** Mary and Joseph, the road to Emmaus), and the frequent use of a messenger, crossing from one acting area to another (**Pharaoh, Caesar Augustus, Herod**), argue a complexity and spaciousness of staging which would be quite beyond the range of the processional pageant play, performed in the congestion of a medieval street. Above all, the continuity of action which informs the Passion sequence could only be realized through continuity of acting in one fixed locality.

MULTIPLE STAGING

The repeated requirement in the Wakefield Plays for staging a journey with two distinct acting areas, at the beginning and at the end, suggests the use of more than one pageant and lays considerable stress upon the acting area between the pageants. The journey motif is best exemplified in **The Second Shepherds' Play** and **The Offering of the Magi,** In the former Mak's house is opposed to the manger; the shepherds pass from one to the other and even sleep on the green (634) between the two mansions. **The Offering of the Magi** is similarly staged with Herod's palace replacing Mak's house; similarly, too, the kings sleep, but this time in a litter (590), between the two mansions. To suggest that the Wakefield Plays, which contain references to two or more mansions, could nevertheless be staged on the same pageant is to turn a blind eye to the stage directions, whether implicit in the dialogue or explicit in the rubrics, which, for instance, indicate that the three kings make separate entries from different directions on horseback, that their dialogue is continued on horseback for one hundred and forty lines, and that when they set off together to follow the star they are still mounted. On reaching Herod's palace they dismount and remount on leaving (492), but when they discover that the star they have been following is obscured—and this they attribute to Herod's malignant influence—they dismount ['here lyghtys the kyngys of thare horses' (504)] and pray. The star then appears over the mansion of the Nativity, where they go to present their gifts. This riding of horses between mansions would seem to dispose of the possibility that the mansions were placed on the same pageant. The very frequent references to characters riding horses in medieval drama suggest the use of real and not make-believe animals (the York *Flight into Egypt,* Chester *Abraham and Isaac,* the Ancient Cornish Drama, the *Ludus Coventriae Adoration of the Magi,* Caro's horse in *The Castle of Perseverance, The Conversion of St. Paul*). But horses were not the only animals used. In the Wakefield **Slaying of Abel,** for example, we have to account for Cain's plough-team of four oxen and four horses (25-43) [A. C. Cawley,

The Wakefield Pageants in the Towneley Cycle]. There are also Abraham's ass (**Abraham** 117), Pharaoh's chariots (**Pharaoh** 404), the Third Shepherd's mare (**The First Shepherds' Play,** 164), the ass on which Mary rides (**The Flight,** 151), and the Centurion's horse (**The Resurrection,** 44). It is certainly indisputable from the Norwich and Coventry records that live animals were used, at least for the drawing of the pageant, and by the extraordinary detail that was lavished on their decoration they may well have been used in the performance of the actual plays. There is a Canterbury record that 'the steeds of the Magi were made of hoops and laths and painted canvas' (E. K. Chambers), but unfortunately the play is not extant. The probability is that where riding is indicated in the stage directions real horses were used. Given the acting area it would have been easier in the Middle Ages to have used a real horse rather than one made of hoops, laths, and canvas. It is interesting to note that when the animal is played by actors, as in the case of the ass in the Chester *Balaam and Balak,* it is specifically where the beast has a speaking part (Karl Young, *The Drama of the Medieval Church*].

The most weighty evidence, however, for the multiple staging of the Wakefield Plays lies in the Passion sequence, which sweeps on in continuous action from play to play and from stage to stage. For instance, **The Conspiracy,** the first play of this sequence, if divided into distinct acting areas would be represented as follows:

1. Pilate's hall (1-313)
2. Jesus and his disciples (314-333)
3. John and Peter on their way to Jerusalem, and
4. Their meeting with Paterfamilias outside his house (334-345)
5. The chamber of the Last Supper (strewn with rushes), the scene of the washing of feet (346-491)
6. The two levels of Olivet, one where Jesus prays and the other where the disciples sleep (492-599)
7. During which scene God appears in heaven's tower (528-555)
8. Pilate's hall (560-651)
9. From Olivet to the place of capture (652-707)
10. Pilate's hall (708-747)
11. Malcus and the soldiers lead Jesus to Caiaphas' hall (748-755).

This play is probably the combination of two plays, **The Conspiracy** and **The Capture,** and such a consideration underlines the unity of effect which the reviser of the Passion sequence, if not of the whole cycle, was striving to achieve. This unity could not be achieved by allowing one acting area to be used for a variety of scenes: Pilate's hall must be reserved exclusively for the scenes in which Pilate appears; God, as throughout the cycle, appears from heaven's tower; Mount Olivet is the hill on which Jesus prays, and below which his disciples sleep; the chamber strewn with rushes, set with table and benches to seat Jesus and the twelve disciples, is also most certainly a fixture throughout this play. The common area then appears to be the ground between this chamber and the other mansions, or stations; and there is every indication dramatically that the capture is staged on ground level midway between Mount Olivet and Pilate's hall.

In reconstructing the staging of *The Conspiracy* the picture that is formed is of four pageants set well apart representing heaven, Pilate's hall, Mount Olivet, and the chamber of The Last Supper, and whatever action does not take place on these pageants, such as the very first passage, in which Jesus dispatches John and Peter to find a room for the paschal feast, and the capture itself, takes place on the ground between the pageants. The pageants are placed at points on the circumference of circle so that the action between the pageants takes place in the centre of the circle. The spectators whether on raked scaffolds or thronging on the ground, fill the gaps on the circumference between the pageants.

E. Catherine Dunn (essay date 1969)

SOURCE: "The Literary Style of the Towneley Plays," in *The American Benedictine Review*, Vol. 20, No. 4, December, 1969, pp. 481-504.

[*Dunn examines the narrative voice in the various parts of the Towneley cycle, characterizing it as prophetic and lyrical. She also comments on the function of language and its role in the development of the plays.*]

A. POINT OF VIEW IN THE CYCLE

The nature of the meaning in the Towneley cycle, like that of other Corpus Christi plays, is historical in the sense that the Sacred Scriptures are historical, and by the same token, prophetic of a realization yet to be achieved by the dynamic historical process. The genre of the history play underlies all of the structural relationships involved in the cycle, and raises certain problems of compositional artistry that appear in this particular representative of the type, associated with the town of Wakefield in Yorkshire. Because it is so intimately involved in prophecy and prefiguration, it is controlled by a prophetic principle, a principle serving to limit the choice of incident, character, and expression to those elements that unfold God's plan for the salvation of His people and His wonderful works on their behalf. In modern critical theory this limitation of subject is often called "point of view," a term that has become popular since the vogue of Henry James' novels, with their technique of filtering the plot and the characterization through the intelligence or the attitudes of a personage centrally situated for interpretation of the narrative. Such a concept is valuable for

use in dramatic criticism, because it illuminates the unity of meaning in a complex cycle and provides a control for the interplay of the speeches in the total design.

The principle demands a technique of strategic disposition. Although we cannot properly speak of a person as narrating the cycle's events, nor even of an Expositor formally designated to comment and explain, the center is still point of view. The end accomplished is no less than the interpretation of the plot's unfolding design, and because of the cycle's vast scope and complexity, the device had to be a flexible one, rich in possibilities of adaptation to the variety as well as the unity of the whole.

Some assistance in understanding this technique in a dramatic context comes to us from the European critics who have worked with the Latin liturgical drama of the High Middle Ages (1200-1350). They designated the Latin cycles of this period as "synoptic," discerning a genre of Nativity drama composed of several scenes and prefaced by a prophetic prologue—a genre at once much more complex than the Christmas tropes had been, and yet much smaller in scope than the later vernacular cycles. It was the control of these Christmas dramas by a single point of view that allowed them to become genuine works of art. In the case of the famous Benediktbeuern *Nativity* (from a monastery in Munich) the material was synthesized by the person of the pseudo-Augustine, the interlocutor of the prophetic prologue. His task was not only to summon prophetic witnesses to the Messiah, but also to produce the scenes of the Christmas play as a dialectic over the truth of Christ's message with Archisynagogus, leader of the Jewish auditors present on stage. Augustine's was the synoptic view that deployed the materials into a drama with a beginning, middle, and end in the theatrical sense of these terms (the structuring and resolution of a conflict).

The unified prospect created by a single person with a prophetic viewpoint was thus a pattern available to the builders of the later cycles. Its use in more complex form by the vernacular writers of mystery plays was no accident. Nor can it be called an evolution of literary form. It was a literary experiment and as such the key to many imitations in the vernacular plays of Western Europe. Since our task is an analysis of the Towneley cycle, scope does not permit elaboration of the history back of the Latin experiments, but they can be designated briefly as experiments in voice structure.

This synoptic or unified viewpoint in the Latin cycles and their vernacular imitations achieved its technical instrument in the use of a basic voice recurring at crucial moments throughout the dramatic sequence of events. The voice is comparable not only to a narrator in a modern novel but also to a chorus in the classical drama of Greece and Rome. It is instructive and enlightening, and also mediative and ruminative, capable of clarifying an event or an action and of expressing wonder at the mystery of God's ways with men. Its modes of operation vary with the developing nature of the cycle's meaning and with the kind of address occurring from one speech to another. It therefore has a stylistic range of considerable scope, but nevertheless a large measure of homogeneity in its dignified and elevated language and rhythms.

THE BASIC VOICE

The basic voice in a mystery cycle, I propose, is the voice of the Church *(la voix de l'Église).* This denotes an authoritative commentator, recognized by medieval men for the interpretation of Scripture. It denotes also the wisdom of a collective entity existing through many ages and penetrating the great human problems of all times with a philosophical awareness. It implies also a detachment from the immediate dramatic event, that serves to distance the turmoil or conflict or even comic action and envelop these things in a luminous veil. (One might think of an analogy with the modern theatrical device of visual distancing with a "scrim" curtain dropped before the spectators.)

This basic voice is easily enough recognizable in the rather limited scope of the Anglo-Norman *Mystère d'Adam,* where Marius Sepet discovered it in the Latin choral speeches intruding upon the vernacular dialogue of Adam, Eve, and the serpent. It is not so easily detected in a cycle with many thousands of lines—in the vernacular—especially in Towneley, which contains no character designated as Expositor nor group marked as Chorus. We must often search for this voice in strange contexts, masked by a *persona* who is involved to some degree in the drama's conflict, and who is perhaps an unlikely vehicle for *la voix de l'Église.* Temporarily any character may serve as this voice, and it would be well to regard any of the numerous *dramatis personae* as potential "aspects" of the basic voice. Some of the most ingenious fictive constructions of character result from this dovetailing of functions in a character's role.

Since much of the commentary made by the basic voice is interpretative, its function is essentially expository. The interplay of dramatic dialogue with expository comment creates two major kinds of speech throughout the mystery cycle. The dialogue of the drama's characters is dynamic, in that it deals with events in a developing plot sequence. The basic voice, on the other hand, is static, concerned with the meaning of the action and thus with the ideas and concepts involved in it. The reference is static, for example, when the voice is ruminating, or pondering the significance of the reality framed in the dramatic cosmos.

The very large amount of static reference in the medieval drama, both in Latin and the vernaculars, is of crucial importance for comprehension of its stylistic patterns. The fundamental reason for this fact is the origin of the plays in the liturgical chanting of the Divine Office and the Mass. Although the narrative plots present in the plays are ultimately founded upon sacred history in the Bible, the intermediary between Scripture and drama was the liturgy, the Church's official prayer and worship. The matrix of speech patterns is to be discovered in the chanting of the liturgical passages, and these are cast into a generally static form. Even when they deal with biblical events, the latter are abstracted, so to speak, for contemplation and become the points of departure for reflection, wonder, aspiration, and all the possible varieties of prayerful expression. This interplay of the contemplative with the dynamic element is the *form* of medieval drama, seen in its totality, and hence the role of the basic voice is an extremely important one, whether the Expositor fills it or mimetic *personae* assume it from time to time.

The general tendency of the medieval drama toward language of static reference calls into consideration the subjects or themes talked about—perhaps we can say, the reality imitated by the speech. This reality is capable of distinction according to the speaker's relation to it. If he is discussing the plan of salvation or the *magnalia Dei,* his reference is to objective reality, external to his own psyche. If he is speaking of his personal response to the *magnalia Dei* or to the design of history, he is setting forth an interior or subjective reality. In the latter case, he is the vehicle of "lyricism," and it is in this sense that I employ the term "lyrical" throughout—for poetry that creates its speech patterns by reference to interior, subjective reality.

LYRICAL QUALITY

It is at precisely this point that the lyrical cast of the Towneley plays emerges into prominence—lyrical in the context of basic voice, expository comment, and static reference. All of these items are fundamental to an understanding of Towneley's literary art; for the chief characteristic of the cycle's structure is its lyrical beauty, residing in a pattern of recurrent motifs for shaping the static discourse into fine poetry of a subjective cast.

Because there are these two general kinds of thematic reference in the static passages of the cycle, the basic voice must be flexible enough to encompass both of them. That is why the use of a formal Expositor (like that of the Hegge cycle) would be a restrictive and sometimes awkward technical device. He is likely to interpret a doctrine or explain an action satisfactorily enough, but he may be too detached and rigid a *persona* to express an emotional response or subjective reaction: In other words, he may not be an apt vehicle for the lyric poetry. Towneley's distinction lies in the abandonment of a formal Expositor as a basic voice, and the distribution of his tasks among many of the characters, thus multiplying the "aspects" of that basic voice and creating many opportunities for objective, intellectual exposition and for the lyricism of personal expression.

A question may arise here about the validity of designating *la voix de l'Église* as an intermittently subjective voice technique. The difficulty is connected with the highly individualistic content of modern (nineteenth century) lyric poetry, to which we have become accustomed because it is a major part of the Anglo-American heritage. Romanticism as associated with the poetic activity of a Wordsworth or Coleridge connotes an idiosyncrasy and particularity that we would be slow to equate with the voice of a Church universal. I think the difficulty can be solved by regarding the lyrical expression of medieval dramatic characters as a subjectivity common to Christians in their collective nature as members of the Church. Perhaps the best way to think of this lyricism is to equate it with the affective response made by a monastic choir taking part in liturgical prayer, and *par excellence* in that kind of response that would be formally designated as hymnody. This is the collective (but deeply personal and subjective) answer to the *magnalia Dei,* having the highly emotional nature of affective prayer, but also the gravity and universal sentiment prevailing in the Roman liturgy.

The monastic choir chanting a Latin hymn or antiphon recalls the musical quality of medieval lyricism. This is not the place for elaborating a complete theory of the lyric, but the association of music and lyric is an historically important one. In classical antiquity the lyric (designated as melic poetry) was widely regarded as a subdivision of music, and was composed to be sung. This tradition became the medieval heritage and survived until the Renaissance, when Italian critics studying the *Poetics* of Aristotle developed from hints in his treatise a theory of the lyric not as music but as *mimesis* (imaginative imitation), and distinguished it from narrative and dramatic poetry by the subjective or interior reality it imitated. The study of troubadour poetry, to choose a medieval example, will reveal the close integration of these poems with musical accompaniment, instrumental and vocal; and the whole institution of liturgical prayer as a sung or chanted performance by a monastic or cathedral choir demonstrates the relationships of the musical and the verbal arts there involved. These relationships are important for a religious drama that owed its origin to liturgical prayer.

The Latin liturgical plays were thus quasi-operatic, sung in a manner that perpetuated the chanting of the monastic choir. Of this fact there cannot be the slightest doubt, for the manuscripts contain the musical notation along with the words of the plays. It has never been possible, however, to prove that the vernacular cycles were performed in the same way, although speculations have been offered that the dialogue was chanted. Unquestionably the cycles contained many formal hymns and songs, in Latin and in translation; these provided many opportunities for melic poetry in the classical sense, but we remain in doubt about the normal dialogue of the plays and even about passages of heightened intensity where verbal artistry itself was intricate enough to serve as a substitute for musical tone and tempo.

The perplexing historical and theoretical problems involved here need not prevent use of the term "lyrical" adjectivally to indicate a type of poetry in the Towneley cycle that has subjective reference and a high degree of patterned sound structure. The cycles are essentially drama, not lyric, and it is therefore not necessary to solve the problem of whether the vernacular plays were sung or chanted or spoken. The adjective "lyrical" nevertheless provides a method of dealing with the Towneley plays in their most distinctive feature—an implementation of the prophetic principle by *la voix de l'Église* in an aesthetic design of repeated lyrical motifs worthy of special contemplation and study.

B. THE PROPHET PLAY

From a stylistic standpoint, the basic voice of the Towneley cycle has established its norm in the ***Processus prophetarum,*** the seventh play in the series. It is here that the synoptic viewpoint, the static reference, and the expository comment (both objective and subjective) have found a motif capable of repetition and imitation in many parts of the cycle. Since the ***Processus*** belonged to the primitive layer of the cycle, it served as a point of departure for later construction. There are four prophets here who utter testimony to the Messiah—Moses, David, Daniel and the Sibyl. These represent a small procession in comparison with the many speakers making up the Latin prophet plays, but they produce a satisfying sense of completeness, progression and climax. Moreover, the language and the rhythms of their lines are varied enough to permit imitation and adaptation by other speakers in the cycle where the voice of the Church enters to interpret or foretell at some critical juncture.

The Towneley ***Processus*** is an English version of the Latin prophet play. The latter, continental in origin, dates back to at least the twelfth century as drama, is even older as a *lectio* of the Matins Office, and ultimately as a sermon of about the fifth century erroneously attributed to St. Augustine. Often referred to as the "Vos, inquam" from its opening words, it was a series of testimonies to the coming Messiah from the mouth of prophets who were summoned by an interlocutor (the pseudo-Augustine), and who delivered their Scriptural witness at his request, in an attempt to persuade an imagined audience of Jewish listeners. In the Divine Office of the Christmas season this *lectio* had been a suitable part of the Nativity festival, a kind of summary of the Advent liturgy that had preceded the festival for several weeks. The serial format and the style in the *sermo* and the *lectio* were gradually adapted to dramatic form and thus were transformed into the Latin prophet play.

The style of this Towneley vernacular version is set at a level of dignity and gravity by four Latin quotations from the "Vos, inquam" original. The first lines of the play, designated as "Prolog," are the words of Moses, repeating almost verbatim the speech of this prophet in the Latin versions:

> Prophetam excitabit deus de fratribus vestris;
> Omnis anima, que non audierit prophetam
>   illum,
> exterminabitur de populo suo;
> Nemo propheta sine honore nisi in patriâ suâ.

Moses translates these lines (including the fourth one, taken from Christ's own words in the Gospel) in the opening stanzas of his lengthy speech in the play and goes on to say much more, for he expounds the Ten Commandments before he withdraws to make way for David. The lines of Latin, together with their vernacular explication, are formal prophecy, expressed in the objective reference proper to a revelation of the Divine plan. The manner in the Latin is measured, ponderous, even awesome and would seem to preclude any kind of elaboration other than a homiletic one.

It is surprising, however, what the English poet here has made of the Latin quotation, and the passage becomes a simple illustration of a stylistic dualism that will characterize many imitations of the prophetic technique in the play and throughout the cycle. The warning contained in "omnis anima. . .exterminabitur" (ll. 2-3 of the Prolog) appears in an English stanza of six lines in which the Latin abstractions have been reduced to concrete images:

> when his tyme begynnys to day,   [dawn]
> I rede no man fro hym dray   [withdraw]
> In way, ne stand on strut;   [conflict]
> ffor he that will not here his sagh,   [word]
> he be shewed as an out-lagh,   [outlaw]
> And from his folkis be putt.
>   (ll. 13-18)

The images of the dawning, of a divergent roadway, of physical combat, and of outlawry all *realize* the implications of the grave Latin concept in "exterminabitur."

The Northern diphthongs in four of the rhyme words

create a sound pattern quite different from that of the richly assonant but unrhymed Latin lines. The palatalized a+y sound (day, dray) balances the guttural a+[gh] (sagh, lagh) to give identity in the dominant *a* phoneme and diversity in the off-glide sound. This difference in both visual image pattern and in phonemic structure results in a stylistic effect on a different level of elevation from that of the Latin. We are dealing with an interplay between two languages, one of which has a long tradition of heightened and sonorous rhetoric behind it, and the other of which is still in an experimental stage of the alliterative poetic revival (perhaps about 1375). It would be too much to say that the first is written in the "grand" style and the second in the "middle," for the precise stylistic categories of classical rhetoric were not preserved in medieval writing; but there is a difference in elevation that can be discerned in the interplay of the two passages. Moreover, it is highly probable that the Latin quotation would have been chanted, as it had been chanted for centuries in the liturgical Matins *lectio* and in the Latin prophet plays, while the English lines would have been read as alliterative verse. Such a difference in vocal pitch would have sharpened the difference in style levels.

Moses' vernacular lines show also an increase in subjective reference over the reserved and impersonal manner of the Latin speech. The use of the first person pronoun throughout the long passage is frequent—"I will you tell" (l. 2), "I rede no man fro hym dray" (l. 14), "I warne you well" (l. 19) etc. Moreover, in spite of the admonitory message about loss of membership in the people of God through unbelief, the dominant emotion of the passage is one of joy. The message is fundamentally a promise of redemption: "I will you tell / Tythyngis farly goode" (ll. 2-3), (*farly* here meaning "wonderfully"); "that same prophete / shall com hereafterward, full swete, / And many meruels shew. . . ." (ll. 19-21). Moses, in urging a joyful acceptance of his prophecy, has first assimilated the wonderful news himself, and his little flashes of lyricism are a personal response to it.

PROPHETIC VOICE IN DAVID

The prophecy of David is a finer revelation of the *stylistique* in the prophet play. Moses' lines rise above homiletic rhetoric only in a phrase or a short passage here and there, and much of his verse, especially in his exegesis of the Ten Commandments (not properly a theme of a *processus prophetarum*) is prosaic. David, musician as well as prophet, speaks a qualitatively different language from that of the patriarch who has just withdrawn from center stage. In his lines, better than any others, we can perceive the interrelationship of the prophetic speech (revealing fragments of a mysterious wisdom extraneous to his own) and the interior response to it. The Towneley David is thus the best example in the play of the prophetic voice with two aspects.

He enters (at l. 90) with a quotation from the "Vos, inquam" *sermo,* "Omnes reges adorabunt cum, omnes gentes seruient ei," a line that he probably chants. The oration had used this and two other Davidic statements, and the Latin prophet plays of St. Martial, of Laon and of Rouen had contained these brief extracts from the Psalms with virtually no expansion. It is really remarkable, then, that Towneley's David has seventy-two lines of verse, drawing more freely upon the Psalms and expressing great joy and "myrth." Lines 127-29, e.g., merely paraphrase the statement about Christ with which David had begun ("Omnes reges adorabunt cum. . . ."):

> he shall be lord and kyng of all,
> Tyll hys feete shall kyngis fall,   [to]
>   To offre to hym wytterly.   [surely]

But many lines are of a heightened intensity, suffused with joyful praise bordering on ecstasy—

> Therfor, both emperoure and kyng,
> Ryche and poore, both old and ying,
> temper well your gle,   [joy]
> Agans that kyng lyght downe,   [in preparation for
>   that king's coming]
> ffor to lowse vs of pryson,
> And make vs all free.
>
>   (ll. 145-50)

David *sings* his lines; we are not left to speculate or guess about it, for he tells the audience,

> As god of heuen has gyffen me wit,
> shall I now syng you a fytt,   [song]
>   With my mynstrelsy;
> loke ye do it well in wrytt,   [put it on record]
> And thereon a knot knytt,
>   ffor it is prophecy.
> Myrth I make till all men,   [to]
> with my harp and fyngers ten. . . .
>
>   (ll. 103-10)

David says that his playing of the musical instrument is for joy in the Incarnation that is to come ("ffor that I harp, and myrth make," l. 118); and he concludes his performance with a final reference to his manner of delivery: "Now haue I songen you a fytt."

There is a notable increase in sound patterning when he begins his references to music. The ornaments of alliteration, consonance, and echoic rhyme mark his song, tending to set off his whole prophecy in speech pleasant to contemplate and notably more elevated than the rather prosaic lines of Moses. Alliteration is sporadic. A single line in a stanza will suddenly emerge with the pounding of identical sounds ("Myrth I *make* till all *men*," l. 109). A single phrase will be *fore-*

grounded (to use a term of the Prague Formalists) by this alliteration, and may have clashing cadence of two primary stresses in immediate succession ("And théron a knótt knýtt,", l. 107). The effect here is intensified by the pronunciation of the initial consonant cluster "kn," which in the Northern dialect of the late fourteenth century would most probably still have its guttural component. One notes the occurrence of two or three alliterated words distributed into separate lines but echoing the repeated sound—

> ffor to be mans *s*aueyoure,
>   and *s*aue that is forlorne. . . .   (ll. 116-17)
> *M*en *m*ay know hym bi his *m*arke,
> *M*yrth and lovyng is his warke. . . .
>
>   (ll. 139-40)

Finally, a marked interest in the rhyme patterns is shown by the large number of aab/aab stanzas in this passage instead of the play's normal pattern of aab/ccb, so that the same sound (the "a" rhyme) occurs four times in the scheme. The twenty-seventh stanza has a peculiarly striking auditory effect, because its "b" lines almost duplicate the "a" rhymes, except that a medial "y" (palatal aspirate) is inserted. Thus the rhymes have virtually a six-line uniformity: fytt, it, *myght;* wytt, pytt, *lyght.*

The intensification of sound patterns here seems to signalize the musical accompaniment and to make his prophecy a hymn. Although David's lines have been misnamed an "isolable lyric" comparable to the poems of secular minstrelsy, they are simply the dramatist's extension of the Latin prophecies by embellished lyrical utterance, transforming the merely objective statement of prophecy to an interior yearning for the One thus expected and foretold. The author has given David a role as biblical harpist, not as troubadour:

> Myrth I make till all men,
> with my harp and fyngers ten,
>   And warn theym that thay glad:
>   [admonish]
> ffor god will that his son down send,
> That wroght adam with his hend,
>   And heuen and erth mayde.
>
>   (ll. 109-14)

The mood of the passage is joyful, only a touch of sadness being suggested as David recognizes that he will not see Christ's first coming:

> well were hym that that lordyng,
> and that dere derlyng,
>   myght bide on lyfe and se.
>
>   (ll. 136-38)

THE SIBYL AND DANIEL

The other two prophets in the play (the Sibyl and

Daniel) could be studied in the same manner as Moses and David have been. The Erythraean Sibyl's lines had already been extensive in the "Vos, inquam" oration, quoted as they were from St. Augustine's *De civitate Dei,* a passage of twenty-seven verses, and the only prophecy in the "Sermo" exceeding two or three sentences in length. Even here, however, the English dramatist expands, exactly doubling the extent. More important, the Sibyl in the English version goes beyond her traditional prediction of the Judgment Day with all its terrors; she startles the listener in her very first line by inviting the attention of all who would "here tythyngis *glad.*" Her stress is not on the dire warnings, but on the Second Coming of Christ, which she presents primarily as redemption rather than judgment. The justification of her place in a procession of prophets, of course, is her witness to Christ the Messiah.

Daniel's prophecy, which closes the play, gives some evidence of having been partially lost, for it is only seventeen lines in length, and as the [*Early English Text Society*] editor notes, folio 19 is left blank in the manuscript at the end of the passage, and is followed by another empty page. The prophecy, however, ends on a satisfactorily conclusive theme, a consolatory word that the Son of God will come "oure trespas to amend" (l. 228) and "to saue all that are forlorne" (l. 233). This final reiteration of mercy and salvation as the theme of the play contrasts strikingly with the single line of Daniel's prophecy from the "Sermo," quoted by him as he enters the stage: "Cum venerit sanctus sanctorum cessabit unctio vestra," a reference to the historical situation of the royal line at the time of Christ's birth.

In both quantitative and qualitative terms, then, these four prophetic speakers in the Towneley play illustrate a general tendency of this cycle to expand, elaborate and particularize the cryptic Latin style of the earlier medieval Latin drama. In this process the cycle is a participant in the great stylistic development of Gothic into Flamboyant that characterized literature and the graphic arts as the high Middle Ages became late medieval. Much has been written about this general phenomenon both by art historians and literary critics, among whom Professor Helmut Hatzfeld, J. Huizinga, Erich Auerbach, and Walter Schirmer have been leaders. Towneley's special distinction, however, in a general European movement, is not the expansion or elaboration of an austere Latin Idealism in literary manner—although this is the basis of the process—but rather the transformation of the objective prophetic revelation of the Latin *Processus* into a florid and richly emotional subjectivity. In this adaptation the English poet (or series of poets and editors) created a more complex motif in the prophet play and gave it an increased flexibility for continued stylistic modification in various parts of the cycle. If the English writer had

continental models for this particular kind of adaptation applied to the prophet play—and it is highly probable that he did—he lends support to the general theory of Marius Sepet that the Latin *Processus prophetarum* became the Old Testament vernacular cycles by literary adaptation.

Finally, the *Processus* was a successful device for structuring a large amount of Scriptural meaning in an imagined or fictive motif. After all, there is no such procession of prophets in the Bible itself. Its first appearance was a deliberate technique created by the author of the pseudo-Augustinian "Sermo." In its dramatized form, moreover, it was capable of transcending the rhetorical goal of persuasive teaching for which the "Sermo" had been composed; staged and set to music, it could become a framed reality visible and audible as a mimetic piece, which the spectators could contemplate without any necessary reaction to a didactic message. The voice and address were then subsumed within the dramatic cosmos, and even *la voix de l'Église,* expository and interpretative, was assumed by *dramatis personae* and not addressed immediately to an audience outside the framework.

In Towneley we can see this fictionalizing through an imagined speech situation. Moses, David and Daniel directly address auditors who are *on stage.* The **Processus prophetarum** is the seventh play in the cycle, but it actually should change places with Play No. VIII, **Pharao,** as Pollard observes in his Introduction. The "Pharao" is the dramatization of the Exodus, and ends with Moses and the Israelites on the far bank of the Red Sea, as he urges them to praise God for their deliverance. The very first line of the Prophet Play (after a four-line Latin prologue) is Moses' address to the Israelites, "ye folk of israell," and he continues to speak to them from the stance of an Old Testament prophet looking forward to the Incarnation. This is clearly the case also in the speech of David and Daniel. Moses predicts that

> Therfor will god styr and rayse
> A prophete, in som man dayes. . . .
> All that will in trowth ren   [walk in truth]
> shall he saue. . . .
>
> (ll. 7-8; 25-26)

David includes the Israelites with himself as he declares that all must be excluded from heaven until the Incarnation:

> Thou shew thi mercy, lord tyll vs,
> ffor to thou com, to hell we trus,   [until You come]
>   we may not go beside. . . .
>
> (ll. 151-53)

David, too, looks forward, with the Israelites whom he

is addressing, to the Redemption:

> Therfor wyll god apon vs rew,
>   And his son downe send
> Into erth, flesh to take. . . .

(ll. 224-26)

Although the medieval English audience present in the theater or around the pageant wagon were, by extension, God's people, they were not here being directly addressed. They were overhearing an address to a people gathered on stage. Each prophet has, of course, a message that is meant indirectly for the spectators and ultimately for all humanity, but he is speaking to the "folk of Israel" within a dramatized story that is essentially set off to be contemplated as any play is watched or any concert heard—for its success as an entertaining and beautiful composition.

The solution to the whole problem of art *versus* didacticism in the medieval religious drama lies in this fictionalizing of the framed reality, the shaping of it into an imagined story line (a structured narrative), and the containment of the voices within the little world of the stage. This is not to deny an indirect didacticism that meant much to the religious dramatists of the time, but it is to designate this indirect message as extraneous to the art work in its essential nature. An Expositor, such as the Chester plays have, destroys this very illusion of a contemplated design, and his approach to the spectators for explicit clarification and instruction must have turned the cyclic performance into a fundamentally prosaic and rhetorical composition, and a homiletic rather than an artistic experience for the audience.

The Towneley *Processus,* of course, was only one of many medieval attempts to solve the problems of religious theater, but it is valuable in its testimony. The motif is that of an imagined procession, such as never occurred in sacred history. Its repetitive format and its combination of prophecy and lyrical response are a beautiful fiction. They set a pattern for the cycle in its larger scope and are the foundation of the aesthetic form prevailing throughout it. The prophecies themselves are the stylistic norm for all of the revelatory aspects of the basic voice, and the lyrical embellishments of prophecy are the norm for all the subjective responses to the wonderful plan of God for man's salvation. Perhaps the *Second Shepherds' Play* in the cycle can best illustrate the way in which the Prophet Play serves as norm for imitation.

C. IMITATION OF THE PROPHET PLAY IN THE "HAIL LYRICS"

The Wakefield Master wrote two Christmas plays for the Towneley cycle. The *Second Shepherds' Play* is well known, with its amusing presentation of Mak the thief and his pretense that the stolen sheep is his newborn child. The *Prima pastorum* is less well known

but equally worthy of study. In these plays two types of shepherd speech occur, one comic and "low" in style, the other grave, dignified, and learned. This dualism of rhetorical style appears with striking effect especially in the "Hail lyrics" that accompany the presentation of gifts to the Christ Child. Here the voice structure in the Towneley cycle controls not only multiple aspects of fictive characterization, but also an Imitation of the Prophet Play in its lyricism. The "Hail Lyrics" in this way participate in the stylistic principle of the whole work.

These lyrics have elicited the admiration of literary critics for many years, and for several reasons. Often the Wakefield Master has been exalted above all other English medieval dramatists on the basis of his caustic satire and bitter humor, nowhere more evident than in these shepherd plays. When he draws the curtain back from the Bethlehem stable, however, and brings his rough, unruly shepherds to their knees before the crib, he demonstrates the flexibility of his famous stanza and of his Yorkshire vocabulary, for the "Hail lyrics" have muted the rugged accents of discontented poverty and coarse joke to allow an almost musical expression of love and joy. The suggestion of music as background is not fortuitous, because the shepherds really seem to be chanting the stanzas of a reverent Christmas hymn.

Here we are again concerned with a prophetic voice, but in its lyrical rather than its revelatory function. It is subjective rather than objective in reference. As a passage of formal prophecy has preceded the shepherds' arrival at Bethlehem in both Nativity plays, this series of lyrics serves to complement the prophetic motif. The stanzas of formal prophecy are a direct imitation of the *Processus prophetarum,* showing the majestic gravity of the revelatory speeches in the Prophet Play. The lyrics, on the other hand, are the subjective and personal response of these quasi-prophetic characters to the revelation they have just proclaimed and explicated, and to the actual fulfillment of the age-old promises in the Infant whom they now find. These passages resemble the subjective expression of the prophets in the seventh play of the cycle, the drama I have analyzed above and designated as the stylistic norm for the basic voice in the entire span. Since I have devoted a separate essay to the formal prophetic passages in these plays ["The Prophetic Principle in the Towneley *Prima Pastorum,*" in *Linguistic and Literary Studies in Honor of Helmut A. Hatzfeld,* ed. A. Crisafulli, 1964], it will perhaps be sufficient here to quote one of the shepherd speeches typical of their manner. It occurs after the angel's announcement of Christ's birth:

> *ijus pastor.* we fynde by prophecy—/ let be
> youre dyn—
> Of dauid and Isay / and mo then I myn,

They prophecyed by clergy / that in a vyrgyn
shuld he lyght and ly / to slokyn oure syn
    And slake it. . . .
                    (*Shepherds' Play,* **II**, ll. 674-78)

A special historical circumstance, however, has entered into the composition of the lyrical stanzas, helping to account for the solemnity of the shepherd speech, so much out of character with their peasant status. Their response to the mystery they have encountered is not simply naive but quite complex. The Wakefield Master had available for imitation here not only the lyrical parts of the Towneley *Processus,* but also the tradition of the shepherds as "ruling the choir" in the Latin liturgical Christmas plays. This tradition will need an explanation before its relevance to the "Hail lyrics" can be understood.

Karl Young found [in *The Drama of the Medieval Church,* 1933] that the rubrics for the Latin Christmas plays directed the clerics who had acted as shepherds in the dramas to "rule the choir" in the Mass following Matins, and even to engage in dramatic dialogue at other times on Christmas day in the chanting of the Divine Office. No other characters in the whole range of liturgical drama have so much ceremonial and dramatic activity outside their own play. "Ruling the choir" meant that they chanted the opening phrases of choral pieces. In various texts, moreover, they were assigned considerable parts of the chants in the Mass and at Matins or Lauds. At Padua, e.g., they were to intone the invitatory verse of Matins, "Christus natus est nobis, venite adoremus." In one of the Rouen plays the rubric for the Mass following the Christmas play reads: ". . .Pastores regant chorum et cantent *Gloria in excelsis Deo,* et epistolam, et tropa [sic]." At Rouen also the Archbishop at the beginning of Lauds interrogated the clerics who had played the shepherd roles, using the first antiphon of Lauds, which supplied both question and response: "Quem vidistis, pastores, dicite? Annuntiate nobis in terris quis apparuit? Natum vidimus in choro angelorum Salvatorem Dominum, alleluia, alleluia."

This extension of the shepherd activity beyond the limits of the Christmas Matins play created a dimension for the characters beyond that of their dramatic roles and gave them a type of liturgical speech fitted rather to the monastic chorus than to themselves. Although such a stylistic phenomenon occurs in other dramatic roles as well, the shepherds are the least likely subjects *suo jure,* to have a grave, dignified and really "grand" style imposed upon their speech. It is all the more remarkable, then, that they ruled the choir extensively and that they were the most active of all liturgical characters outside their own play. This strange development is a direct cause for the later stylistic complexity of the shepherds "Hail lyrics" that accompany their gifts to the Christ Child in the English plays.

The extra-dramatic activity and choral expression of the shepherds find a counterpart *within* some of the Latin Christmas plays as well, notably in their salutation lyrics. The "Salve, Virgo singularis" illustrates this shepherd speech in an address to the Mother of the Child; its speech is not that of shepherds suddenly called in from a countryside:

Salue, uirgo singularis,
uirgo manens Deum paris   [give birth to]
ante secla generatum
    corde Patris.
Adoremus nunc creatum
    carne matris.
Nos, Maria, tua prece
a peccati purga fece
nostri cursum incolatus;   [sic; semicolon should
    sic dispone   be in the line above.]
ut det sua frui natus
uisione.

This lyric (in a Rouen Christmas play) is actually a liturgical Sequence imported into the drama, and one that has been praised by a French historian as "un des fragments les plus précieux comme paroles, et surtout comme musique, de l'art du moyen âge." The sequences were, as a genre, a form of trope and, if strictly regarded, must be called extraliturgical; they were characterized by a high degree of affectivity, intended to arouse the fervor and enthusiasm of the faithful, especially in the expression of joy. The "Salve, Virgo," then, was not written for the drama but for a liturgical chorus at the Gradual of the Mass. It has here been made a greeting of the shepherds, an instance of their elevation to a form of expression not naturally their own. It is a metaphysical approach to the mystery of the Incarnation, and its rhetorical parallelism and paradox suggest the "metaphysical wit" that characterized medieval Latin religious lyric and later developments of Renaissance "Concettismo."

RELATIONSHIP TO MAGI PLAYS

The shepherd role, then, seems to have been a kind of magnet drawing alien elements into itself. The shepherd lyrics, finally, were influenced by relationship to the Magi plays. In the Scriptural accounts, gifts are not presented to the Christ Child by the shepherds, but only by the kings from the East. Both Hemingway and Cawley have noted that in the English cycles as a whole the shepherds, too, present gifts and both account for this new element as a borrowing from the Magi story. Their lyrics of presentation, therefore, may owe a debt to the speeches of the Wise Men in the Latin plays. The "Salve, Virgo," has already in the Rouen Christmas play something of the stylized and formal quality that characterizes the greetings of the three kings, and further imitation of the Magi is very probable. The prestige of the Epiphany plays was great, as the abundance of texts and their dramatic sophistication indicate; they outshone the Nativity plays and even, in a sense, absorbed them. A simple form of the triple offering by the Magi can be seen in a brief formula of reverence and obeisance pronounced in unison by them, "Salve, Princeps seculorum," followed by individual presentation of the gifts. A more carefully patterned rhetorical stylization occurs in the triple repetition of the "Hail" greeting:

> Primus dicat: "Salue, Deus Deorum."
> Secundus: "Salue, Princeps seculorum."
> Tercius: "Salue, uita mortuorum."

An even more elaborate set of salutations can be found in a Montpellier manuscript of the twelfth century, where the Magi oblations become a kind of "Hail Lyric" in prose.

The shepherd lyrics, we may say in summary, reveal the convergence of all the traditional elements I have been discussing: the shepherds as "ruling the choir," as imitating the ardor of the Latin sequences, and as taking over the formal greetings spoken more properly by the Magi. The poet-dramatist of Wakefield, writing in English, has adapted many of the features characterizing medieval Latin hymnody and has also expended the rich resources of sound and meaning available to him in the school of Northern alliterative verse. The highly affective language in these stanzas of oblation has the kind of subjectivity I have linked to the chanting of liturgical prayer by a monastic choir. It is a collective response of Christians as members of the Church; it is elevated and rather formal even in the very ardor of its emotion. The striking thing about these stanzas, however, is the falling off of formality in the second half of each one, and the replacement of collective expression by individual, as each shepherd offers a homely, but treasured gift. The subjectivity is sustained, but it passes from a prophetic to a personal phase. *La voix de l'Église* is assumed and then dropped for the voice of a peasant shepherd.

STANZAIC PATTERN

The division of the stanza occurs in such a way that a "grand" style appears in the first four or five lines and a colloquial speech in the final four. The use of the two idioms seems to me a juxtaposition or counterpointing. The first group contains longer lines, with four heavy stresses, the closing lines being much shorter and marked by only two stresses. The "Hail" ejaculation, repeated so often as to give an intensely emotional quality to the speech, is confined to the long lines, while the short and rapid verses contain the shy, affectionate gift-offering to the Child. This dualism is the stylistic crux of the matter. Here is one of the lyrics from the **Prima pastorum:**

> Hayll, kyng I the call! hayll, most of myght!
> hayll, the worthyst of all! hayll, duke! hayll,
>   knyght!
> Of greatt and small thou art lorde by right;
> hayll, perpetuall; hayll, faryst wyght!
>   here I offer!
> I pray the to take—
> If thou wold, for my sake,
> with this may thou lake,—   [play]
>   This lytyll spruse cofer.
>
>   (ll. 458-66)

The passage is marked by a sound pattern of rich vocalic and consonantal harmony. It is dominated by the vowel "a," which is followed by the liquid consonant "l" not only in the frequently repeated "Hayll" but also in the internal rhyme words—"call," "all," "small," and "perpetuall." In the Northern dialect of the fifteenth century, "y" following a vowel was normally a sign of that preceding vowel's length, and was not itself pronounced; by analogy even diphthongs containing the "y" sound were smoothed to a single "phone," and thus the word "Hayll" would in all probability form a perfect interior harmony with the four "a" rhymes of the passage (call, all etc.) The same phonological principle would give to other words throughout the passage an assonantal relationship to the "hayll," namely, "faryst," "pray," and "may," and, of course, to the rhymed words of the triplet ("take," "sake," and "lake").

The conscious effort to create an ornamental richness is noticeable also in the word patterns. Ejaculatory phrases of approximately equal length (*isocolon*) are found with similar grammatical structure (*parison*): "Hayll, most of myght," "Hayll, the worthyst of all." This feature is outlined in bold relief by the *anaphora* (repetition of first word of lines) which begins each line with the word "Hayll" itself. The Latin "Salve" greetings of the Magi plays mentioned above display these same patterns of repetition and parallelism that are the time-honored devices of classical rhetoric adapted to the Medieval Latin hymn and later to vernacular lyric.

Alliteration, too, plays a part in the repetitive patterns here delineated. Although identity of initial sounds does not form a prominent feature of the Wakefield Master's prosody in general, its presence serves to mark a grand and impressive language with stately cadence. Its prominence in the longer lines of the "Hail lyrics" is quite noticeable, and its absence in the shorter concluding lines cannot be overlooked. The above-quoted stanza is a good illustration, and the lyrics of the **Secunda pastorum** display this feature much more strikingly. Perhaps one may say that the alliterative pattern *dies off* in the second part of the stanza, thus emphasizing the shift from stately and elegant diction to the homely and intimate manner of the concluding lines. We can observe the florescence of this pattern in the following stanza from the **Second Shepherds' Play:**

> *ijus pastor*. Hayll, sufferan sauyoure! ffor thou
>   has vs soght:
> hayll, frely foyde and floure that all thyng has
>   wroght!
> hayll, full of fauoure that made all of noght!
> hayll, I kneyll and I cowre. A byrd haue I
>   broght
>   To my barne.
> hayll, lytyll tyné mop!
> of oure crede thou art crop:
> I wold drynk on thy cop,
>   Lytyll day starne.

(ll. 719-27)

It is well to use the terms *frons* and *cauda* for the two parts of the stanza, since the daul structure is a late [and] elaborate development of the simple *rime couée* or tailrhyme of Medieval Latin verse (ab/aab). The shepherds speak, then, with one voice in the *frons* and another in the *cauda,* i.e., they speak as would members of a liturgical chorus first, and then drop the formal and grave manner for one completely in character as peasants. In the latter role, they make intimate and colloquial presentation speeches for the gift of ball or coffer or bottle. It is proper that in this "caudal" section of the stanza they should drop the rhetorical parallelisms, the elevated diction, and the alliterative sound patterns that have adorned the long lines of the opening address. As each shepherd kneels and trembles, he makes his offering to the "barne," calling upon affective connotations in the diminutive "tyné mop" (little baby) and "lytyll day starne" (day star, i.e., sun).

This duality of style level is not present in the Latin Nativity plays. Only the formal, liturgical language appears in the "Salve, Virgo" and in the "Salve" greetings of the Magi examined above. The Wakefield Master, apparently recognizing the inappropriateness to homely shepherds of the grand style in the Latin prototypes, gave to his shepherds an opportunity to fall back into character after the temporary elevation of their formal greeting. This division of stanza is not without parallel in English drama, for very similar techniques have been found in the York cycle, where two levels of speech give at times the effect of antiphonal chanting. For a brief moment here in the Wakefield lyrics, the shepherds assume the voice of the Church in praising God made Man, then resume their function as dramatic characters drawn by a little Child to wish Him a "Happy Birthday."

To put the matter more technically, the shepherd voice has two aspects in the "Hail lyrics,"—first, that of a liturgical chorus chanting a formal lyrics of praise and secondly, that of homely rustics speaking the idiom of farm and village. The duality is striking, but it possesses the unity imposed by the Wakefield Master's

stanza, with its bipartite structure of *frons* and *cauda*. The stylistic feat here performed is the integration of an assumed manner, that of choral commentator, with the speech techniques of simple rustic characters. The composite could not have been intelligible without the tradition of the Prophet Play and without the long-familiar characterization of the shepherds in the Latin Christmas plays. "Pastores regant chorum." Let the shepherds rule the choir!

Walter E. Meyers (essay date 1969)

SOURCE: An introduction to *A Figure Given: Typology in the Wakefield Plays*, Duquesne University Press, 1969, pp. 7-20.

[*In the following excerpt, Meyers describes his approach toward studying the Wakefield plays and his particular focus on typology in order to demonstrate the plays' unity and sophistication as literary works.*]

The traditional view of the Middle English cycle plays has been unenthusiastic: it has claimed that the cycles cannot be judged as works of dramatic art since each cycle as a whole lacks an overall unifying structure, and that the individual plays are formless and hopelessly mixed in style. This is the traditional view, and probably the most common one even today. But a recent movement in criticism, focusing attention on particular plays of the Wakefield Cycle, has demonstrated that some of the plays are well-structured, in fact, intricately woven. This movement began with Homer A. Watt's study, "The Dramatic Unity of the 'Secunda Pastorum'," in 1940. Watt compared the action of the "burlesque" scenes of the **Second Shepherds' Play** with the action of the Biblically-based scenes of the Nativity. He found a surprising and daring correspondence of the two episodes, wherein each plot parallels the other. It was not until the last decade, however, that his lead was followed, and other plays of the Wakefield Cycle were examined in the same way. When his method was employed, it was found that parallel plots unify the serious and comic elements in several plays. This parallelism has been discovered in the **Noah** play, the play of the **Annunciation,** and the **First Shepherds' Play**. It has also been hinted that parallelism occurs in the **Slaying of Abel** and the **Crucifixion**. Here then are six plays suspected of having in common a major structural element, a fact which should at least arouse curiosity. This study attempts to show that parallelism of plot is to be expected in the cycle plays, and that the cause of the parallelism is a particular theory of time arising from the typological method of exegesis. Consequently, if we are to look for the unifying element of the whole cycle, the search should proceed along the lines indicated by typology and its attendant theory of time. Although critics have mentioned the importance of typology, no such study has been done for the

Wakefield Cycle. I believe that this investigation can overcome the point of view that regards the cycle plays as fragmented and primitive. Once unity has been demonstrated, it is hoped that the cycle will stand forth as the sophisticated work of art which commanded the attention of more than two centuries of all ranks of English society.

The Wakefield Cycle has been chosen, rather than those of York, Chester, or N-Town, because of two reasons: first, it has been praised for the excellence of certain individual plays, plays which by their very individuality would seem to resist attempts to see them as part of a larger whole. Secondly, the Wakefield Cycle has been the subject of numerous studies devoted to "levels" of authorship, but if the theory I propose is correct, possible composite authorship is not an insurmountable barrier to the consideration of a cycle as a work of art.

We must begin with typology. Typology, in brief, is the system of Scriptural exegesis that "has its name from the fact that it is based on the figurative or typical relation of Biblical persons, or objects, or events, to a new truth." A "type" is a "person, thing, or an action, having its own independent and absolute existence, but at the same time intended by God to prefigure a future person, thing, or action," which person, etc., is the antitype. This method of exegesis is to be distinguished from allegory, since both type and antitype have a genuine historical existence. For example, Abraham's near-sacrifice of his son Isaac is seen as a prefiguring of Christ's Passion, yet the action of Abraham and Isaac had a real, historical existence, wholly independent of the Passion. It was held that, when a type of Christ appeared in the pages of Scripture, "the Old Testament author himself foresaw this deeper meaning in his words through a certain vision, or *theoria,* granted him by God." Therefore, the typical sense should be considered along with the literal sense as "founded on the *words* of the inspired author *in the meaning intended by him.*" As Charles Donahue says [in "Patristic Exegesis in the Criticism of Medieval Literature: Summation," in *Critical Approaches to Medieval Literature,* ed. Dorothy Bethurum, 1960], "a clear distinction should be made between the 'existential' or typological method of Christian exegesis and the allegorical method of Greek exegesis. It is the first that is dominant in the exegetical tradition as expounded by the best minds. Typology is also basic to the Western liturgies."

One example of a "type" is Melchisedec, King of Salem, who, in Genesis 14 gave an offering of bread and wine in the presence of Abraham. Melchisedec as a priest foreshadowed Christ, the High Priest, and his offering of bread and wine was a type of the New Testament use of bread and wine in the sacrifice of the Mass. As St. Paul says, Melchisedec is "likened to the Son of God:"

If perfection was by the Levitical priesthood (for under it the people received the Law), what further need was there that another priest should rise, according to the order of Melchisedec, and said not to be according to the order of Aaron? For when the priesthood is changed, it is necessary that a change of law be made also. For he of whom these things are said is from another tribe, from which no one has ever done service at the altar. For it is evident that our Lord has sprung out of Juda, and Moses spoke nothing at all about priests when referring to this tribe. And it is yet far more evident if there arise another priest, according to the likeness of Melchisedec, who has become so not according to the Law of carnal commandment, but according to a life that cannot end. For it is testified of him, 'Thou art a priest forever, according to the order of Melchisedec.'

(Heb. 7:3, 11-17)

The tradition of interpreting Melchisedec as a type of Christ begins in the Epistle to the Hebrews and continues to the present day. In the Chester group, in the *Pagina Quarta de Abrahamo et Melchisedech et Loth,* "Melchisedec" comes on stage, "versus Abraham, offerens Calicem cum vino et panem super patinam." The Expositor follows with an explanation:

I will expound apertlie,
that lewed, standing hereby,
may knowe what this may be.
This offring, I saie verament,
signifieth the new Testament,
that now is vsed with good intent
throughout all Christianitye.

As an eighteenth-century example, we may turn to the entry for "Melchisedeck" in Samuel Mather's *Figures or Types of the Old Testament, by which Christ and the Heavenly Things of the Gospel were Preached and Shadowed to the People of God of Old,* and find "*Melchizedek* was also a type of Christ; and most especially in regard of the *Excellency* and *Eternity* of his Person, Priesthood and Kingdom."

The history of typology is contemporaneous with the history of Christianity, having been used by the earliest Christian writers. St. Justin Martyr, writing about 135 A.D., says, "The Holy Spirit sometimes caused something that was a type of the future to be done openly." Examples of typological interpretation could be multiplied, from every Church Father, from every century. It is to be found in St. Clement, St. Justin, St. Irenaeus, St. Jerome, St. Augustine, in short, in almost every Christian commentator of importance. Once the method had been established by the Fathers, it was preserved for the Middle Ages: "Toute l'interprétation de l'Écriture se caractérise avant tout par *le sens de la tradition,* et plus précisément par *une fidélité étroite, rigoureuse, et souvent servile à l'exégèse patristique,* à ses principes, à ses méthodes, et à ses conclusions" [P. C. Spicq, *Esquisse d'une histoire de l'exégèse latine au moyen age*, 1944]. Besides the obvious importance which typology has in the cycle plays, I would like to suggest that typology demands a certain theory of history in regard to events from the Bible, and that this theory of history carries over, consciously or unconsciously, to the writers of the cycle plays.

The fulfillment of the types was the central event of history, the life, sufferings, and death of Jesus Christ. Since the foreshadowings and types in the Old Testament point to the life of Christ in the New, this one-way direction in the movement of history leads to the representation of time as a straight line that "traces the course of humanity from initial Fall to final Redemption. . . . Indeed, as Chapter 9 of the Epistle to the Hebrews and I Peter 3:18 emphasize, Christ died for our sins once only, once for all. . . . The development of history is thus governed and oriented by a unique fact, a fact that stands entirely alone. Consequently, the destiny of all mankind, together with the individual destiny of each one of us, are both likewise played out once, once for all, in a concrete and irreplaceable time which is that of history and life" [Henri-Charles Peuch, "La Gnose et le temps," *Eranos-Jahrbuch,* XX, 1951].

Yet there are at least two parts of Christian theology that modify a purely "straight-line" depiction. The first factor, as T[om] F[aw] Driver points out [in *The Sense of History in Greek and Shakespearean Drama,* 1960], is the hypostatic nature of Jesus, at once the Christ, born into time and existing within time as man, and at the same time the Second Person of the Blessed Trinity, eternally existing outside of time as God. This means that despite its occurrence as an historical event, the Incarnation "was not an event which was totally new, but rather the complete revelation and fulfillment of that which had existed always."

The second modifying factor, more complex, is outlined by Mircea Eliade in his *Cosmos and History.* Eliade says that despite the basic teleological nature of Christianity, there "still survive certain traces of the ancient doctrine of the periodic regeneration of history." Foremost among these traces is the liturgical year of the Church, commemorating the life of Jesus: a "personal and cosmic regeneration through reactualization *in concreto* of the birth, death, and resurrection of the Savior."

What we have then is a straight-line view of history with certain modifications. The Christian cycle plays, like the Christian liturgical year, create not just a New Year, but re-enact and join together all of human time. The "Christian" time looks from two sides toward the central point of the Incarnation: from the Old Testament on the one hand and from the present moment on

the other. Typology had engendered the habit of seeing events as part of a unified whole, rather than as discrete incidents. It was possible for events in Scripture to foreshadow events occurring after New Testament times: "For of that Church of the Gentiles which was to come, the woman that had the issue of blood was a type: she touched and was not seen; she was not known and yet was healed." St. Augustine continues, saying that the question of the Lord—"Who touched me?"—was itself a figure: "As if not knowing, He healed her as unknown: so has He done also to the Gentiles. We did not get to know Him in the flesh, yet we have been made worthy to eat His flesh, and to be members in His flesh." Again, St. Augustine interprets the incident of the odor of the ointment filling the house in St. John 12:1-3 as a figure of the preaching of the gospel of Christ throughout the world: "let the name of Christ be proclaimed, with this excellent savor let the world be filled." When Jesus was born, the event gave meaning to future as well as past time. His birth was at once the fulfillment of the prophecies of the past and the promise of the future. The Resurrection was as relevant for the English medieval actor on Corpus Christi day as it had been for the apostles in Jerusalem and as it had been for the patriarchs and prophets of the Old Law confined in Limbo. In Eliade's phrasing, all modalities coincide at that moment. The audience sees the cycle plays from the same standpoint from which God sees history. St. Augustine had said that even the perception of normal time requires going beyond time, in a sense. In Book XI of the *Confessions,* he says that the past exists only as memory, the future only as expectation. Both past and future, therefore, have their existence in the present conception of them in the mind. If time is continuously transcended in the everyday perception of it, how much more is the history of humanity—the whole sequence of human time—transcended by the divine memory and expectation shown in the types. The viewer of the pageants sees the whole sequence; in case he should miss the interconnections of the drama, the various types and themes are constantly pointed out to him.

It is necessary at this point to distinguish two kinds of material in the cycle plays. Older studies usually divide a play into "dogmatic" and "realistic" parts. Without trying to define what the authors of these various articles meant by their use of the particularly difficult term "realism," it can readily be seen that the material they refer to is all non-Biblical, usually comic, usually folk material, as opposed to the received, serious elements. This assumption is borne out by the illustrations critics select to show "realism": the by-play of Cain and his boy; the burlesque of the shepherds in both Shepherds' Plays; the antics of the devils in the ***Last Judgment*** (all these from the Wakefield Cycle). If the distinction is along the lines of Biblical and non-Biblical, then let us call it that, and make the division between sacred and secular material. For our purposes, sacred material includes all characters and incidents received from tradition. By this definition, even apochryphal stories like the flowering of Joseph's staff would be sacred. Sacred material is universal throughout the Church and has some relation to salvation history. The secular material, on the other hand, is contemporary and particular. In one instance, it may have been part of another tradition—folk-tale, perhaps even a survival of a pagan rite, but in any case, was originally unconnected with salvation history as related in Scripture or in Church tradition.

The need for this division becomes clear when we examine the effect of typology and a "unified" time on the cycle drama. Critics are increasingly recognizing the importance of typology for what we have termed the sacred material of the drama. It has been seen that the subjects chosen by the writers from the wealth of available material were apparently selected on the basis of the suitability of their typology. The dramatists "did not attempt to cover the whole of the Old Testament, but only a few selected foreshadowings and prophecies of the central incident, the redemption of mankind on the cross" [Arnold Williams, *The Drama of Medieval England*, 1961]. Some may question, however, whether typology can profitably, or even legitimately, be used to interpret the secular material. We have seen how the typological habit of looking at Scriptural events produced a theory of history that tended to harmonize disparate events. If time is re-structured in the cycle plays to bring secular material in line with Biblical, showing a repetition of patterns in secular as well as sacred history, then typology can be used to interpret the secular material of the plays as well.

The most obvious re-structuring of time in the cycles is the so-called "anachronism." When Cain swears "bi hym that me dere boght," the line reveals not a childish naiveté on the part of the Wakefield author, but hints that this anachronism is being used purposefully. The best example of this purpose is the **Second Shepherds' Play,** the most familiar of the cycle plays to the modern reader. The beginning of the play immediately gives a clue that its setting may not be first-century Bethlehem: the First Shepherd enters and laments his oppression under purveyance and maintenance, two contemporary customs. The Third Shepherd swears, "Crystys crosse me spede / and sant nycholas!" (1. 118) The heavy use of proverbs in the play has been noted; for example:

> "had I wyst" is a thyng / it seruys of noght; (1.93).
>
> And men say "lyght chepe / letherly for-
>   yeldys." (1. 171)
>
> I were eten outt of howse / and of harbar;
>   (1.245)
>
> Bot so long goys the pott / to the water, men
>   says,
>   At last

Comys it home broken.

(11. 317-319)

In the unlikely instance that a man wholly unfamiliar with the cycle plays of medieval England or the gospel stories themselves had attended the play to this point, he would have seen nothing and heard nothing that would lead him to believe that the pageant was set elsewhere than the England he knew. The local allusions, well-known from their part in determining the connection of this cycle with the town of Wakefield, may be mentioned here. Searching for his lost sheep, the First Shepherd says, "I haue soght with my dogys / All horbery shrogys" (11. 454-455), where "horbery" is "Horbury, a town some three miles south-west of Wakefield." The Shepherds had earlier parted, agreeing to meet "At the crokyd thorne" (1. 403), again a reference to a place near Horbury. The familiar oaths, the familiar sayings, the familiar places, and their frequent repetition effectively produce the impression that the play is taking place in fifteenth-century England. This impression is not confined to the **Second Shepherds' Play,** but occurs more or less regularly in the various plays of the cycle. Yet in a few minutes after they are searching "horbery shrogys," the shepherds are worshipping the Christ Child. The bonds which channel human time in a straight line from the Fall to the Last Judgment are broken here, and the whole of history is compressed and particularized to a certain day in June in a small town south of York. It makes little difference whether we say that the Biblical material is fitted into the contemporary or that "the scenes which render everyday contemporary life. . .are. . .fitted into a Biblical and world-historical frame." What matters is that the two are seen as one, that there is a unity of Biblical and contemporary material, and that "the spirit of the frame which encompasses them is the spirit of the figural interpretation of history." (As we have been using the term, "typological" is synonymous with Auerbach's "figural" in the above quotation.)

Most modern critics agree that the anachronisms achieve relevance by negating a strict historical sequence. As Arnold Williams says [in *Drama*], "educated men in the Middle Ages were not so ill-informed as to think that Mohammed was born before the Exodus. Underneath the anachronism we see a pattern and a purpose. The whole attempt of the cycle plays is to dress the great mysteries and the great stories of religion in a garb familiar to their audience." Or, as J. D. Hurrell says, "the acceptance of the idea that behind apparent differences of time and place there is a pattern of God-given unity, or that the separate phenomena which we call historical events or geographical locations are in no real (i.e., spiritual) sense isolated from each other, makes it possible for the dramatist to mold an artistic form out of what is usually called his use of anachronism" ["The Figural Approach to Medieval Drama," *College English* XXVI, 1965]. Once given the typological way of looking at history, the usual barriers of time become meaningless, and from this view of history flows the idea that all ages are spiritually contemporary. There is no need then for a strict historical separation of the "accidents" of human existence: habits of speech, dress, etc. These are elements which are not essential and can be changed at the discretion of the playwright.

Now we have an answer to the question posed by H. H. Schless: "the **Processus Noe** and the **Secunda Pastorum** are constructed on surprisingly similar patterns. In both, Biblical material, beautifully transposed, furnishes the main plot and the main themes; in both, folkloric material, artfully integrated, provides the comic elements and a descant upon the main themes. . . . Why [the Wakefield Master] merged these two seemingly disparate levels is probably a question to which he himself could not have given any single answer— if he could have given any answer at all." We can attempt an answer by using the typological method to compare the two levels, remembering that the first "signifies not only itself but also the second, while the second encompasses or fulfills the first." Applying the method to the secular material, though perhaps new for the medieval drama, was not unheard of in other genres. As Erich Auerbach notes [in "Figura," in *Scenes from the Drama of European Literature,* trans. Ralph Manheim, 1959], "At a very early date profane and pagan material was also interpreted figurally; . . . In the high Middle Ages, the Sybils, Virgil, the characters of the *Aeneid,* and even those of the Breton legend cycle (e.g., Galahad in the quest for the Holy Grail) were drawn into the figural interpretation." The figural, or typological approach has the whole range of human existence from which to draw its exemplars. The method had its historical origins in the interpretation of Scripture, to be sure, but it implies the essential unity of every human action, good or bad. The unity is easily seen in the case of the individual: a man will be like Abel, or like Cain; he will dwell in the City of God, or the city of man. Whatever his actions, they will connect him, through the Scriptural types, to Christ or to Antichrist. The types are not confined to Hebrews and Christians, since even pagans can be prophets of the Messiah:

> Dies Irae, dies illa
> Solvet saeclum in favilla
> Teste David cum Sybilla.

Explaining the inclusion of a pagan as Dante's guide, Auerbach says, "Thus Virgil in the *Divine Comedy* is the historical Virgil himself, but then again he is not; for the historical Virgil is only a *figura* of the fulfilled truth that the poem reveals, and this fulfillment is more real, more significant than the *figura*. With Dante, unlike modern poets, the more fully the figure is interpreted and the more closely it is integrated with the

eternal plan of salvation, the more real it becomes." What, then, do we have if we apply this to our example of the **Second Shepherds' Play?** We can say that the shepherds, Coll, Gyb, and Daw, are medieval English shepherds, and then again they are not. They are types of the shepherds at the birth of Christ. It may seem paradoxical to say that they are their own fulfillment, but this is the case. We have already noted their successive existence at two points in time: one in medieval England, one in first-century Bethlehem. In their character as Englishmen of the Middle Ages, they are types which point backward in time to that event which gives their English existence its real significance. And if we can say this about their persons, why can we not say it about their actions? Using typological methods in this way approaches the often noted correspondence of sacred and secular material in this play (which we earlier called plot parallelism) from yet another direction, and confirms that connection between the plots. In this light, it is irrelevant whether, as John Speirs suggests [in "The Mystery Cycle: Some Towneley Plays," *Scrutiny,* XVIII: 2 (Autumn, 1951)], the sheep which they find in the cradle is a remnant of a pagan rite of a horned god or not—pagan material had been used before in other genres and may be the raw material of this artistic creation. What does matter is that this first "incarnation" is a foreshadowing of the second, real Incarnation which the three shepherds are to witness later. The "child" in the first scene is a lamb; in the latter scene, the child is the Lamb of God.

This "typological" time is a mode of looking at history in which discrete events are ordered, not by their sequential arrangement, but by congruities of pattern. Thus, it is enough that both the first worshippers of Christ and Coll, Gyb, and Daw are shepherds. The habit of perceiving history as an arrangement of patterns, as has been pointed out, was acquired from the interpretation of providential history in the Scriptures. This habit is carried over into secular history. The mystery plays, containing much of both sacred and secular material, are therefore a highly likely place to suspect that this method will be operating on a literary level, tying together a multitude of "historical" personages and incidents. In fact, it would be more remarkable if we did not see such a unification in the plays.

The science of typology is the root from which this mode of looking at history branches. The effect which typology produces in the plays has never been fully outlined, yet even if the types in the plays had been fully discussed, those types are not the same thing as the unification of time which we find there. Typology itself, the science as a whole, operating over hundreds of years, produces the habit of seeing events as part of a non-linear pattern. The types to be found in the plays are proof that the attitude was widespread and well known at the time when the drama was being composed, but are not themselves the cause of the "unified" time we find there. An analogy may help to illustrate the point: Latin grammars had been in existence for a millennium and a half before the first English grammars appeared. It is not at all surprising, when, in the late sixteenth and early seventeenth centuries, English grammars began to be written, that they were modeled on the familiar Latin works. The first English grammars were influenced by a way of looking at written language in general which had become habitual from looking at a particular language, Latin. If we call grammars of English based on this Latin organization "traditional," we shall find that tradition persisting until well into the nineteenth century. Yet it was not the publication of Latin grammars in the nineteenth century that caused English grammars to be organized in this way; it was the habit of centuries of Latin grammars.

Similarly, the individual types actually used in the cycle dramas did not produce the theory of unified time found there: rather, all of typology, the work of St. Augustine, St. Irenaeus, St. Justin Martyr, etc., produced both the theory of time found in the plays and the elements of typology in the plays. I believe the point is worth this elaboration because the unification of the plays is achieved through what may be called a typological outlook, rather than through the rigid application of the particular types. Types indeed have a major part in tying the plays together, but they extend primarily to the sacred material found there. The typological outlook, seeing history as the repetition of patterns, brings together the secular material and unites it with the sacred.

Supposing, then, that there is a "unified" view of time in the plays, how would it be shown? The first evidence of it ought to be a radical restructuring of time itself. In the definition of restructuring of time should be included all attempts to bring the past or future into the present, the first through a recounting of the actions of Providence, the second through prophecies of what is to come.

The second evidence of a different view of time is parallel structure, in any of several planes. Through the breakdown of what modern man would think of as the immutable sequence of time, all events, at whatever time they occur, become contemporaneous. Parallel structure, the most noticeable indicator of this contemporaneity, operates in several ways. There is, for example, a literary parallelism, expressed in echoes of the liturgy. When Cain ends his role with "warld withoutten end," and "ffor now and euer more," he is strictly translating the liturgical prayer ending *per omnia saecula saeculorum* (Wakefield, *Mactacio Abel,* 11. 465, 472). It is as if there were a correspondence between the sacred and secular elements in the society of medieval England. This correspondence has been more fully outlined in other arts—architecture or music: "the

custom of writing vernacular words to well-known liturgical pieces is widespread, its best known example in English being the lovely *Singe cucu.* . . . The Middle Ages saw nothing unseemly in borrowing church music for profane songs, even drinking and love songs." The parallelism exists here between two contemporaneous parts of the same culture. The situations celebrated in the medieval English love songs were seen as somehow "like" the situation described in their hymns.

Besides this literary parallelism, there can be a parallelism of action, as we have seen in connection with *Secunda Pastorum.* Consideration of this point leads us into the question of anachronism, since the way in which plot parallelism works is similar to one of the kinds of anachronism which is regularly used. Since anachronisms are easily spotted, their ease of discovery has been equated with artistic simplicity by some critics. But they are more complex in their arrangement than has been generally realized. The first kind of anachronism implies that the English audience is being taken into the time sequence of the play. The most common occurrence of this kind is the direct address to the audience, which, as J. W. Robinson notes [in "The Late Medieval Cult of Jesus and the Mystery Plays," *PMLA* LXXX, 1965], is "the supreme anachronism of a kind of drama that is regularly anachronistic." Again, when Moses speaks to the audience at the beginning of the *Prophets' Play* in the words, "All ye folk of israell, / herkyn to me" (Wakefield, *Processus Prophetarum,* 11. 1-2), the crowd watching the play is even more tightly drawn into the action. Being addressed as Israelites, the crowd is placed in the relation of antitype to the type of the original Israelites. The circles of correspondence are set up between the Hebrews of the Exodus, and the Englishmen of Wakefield, cutting across the bonds of time.

If we have had the audience brought into the world of the play by means of one kind of anachronism, the other brings the characters of the play into the world of the audience by means of homely native characterization, local allusions, proverbs, etc. Instead of making the attending farmer into an actor, this second kind of anachronism cloaks the actor in the farmer's garb. Thus, the "shepherds watching their flocks by night" become Coll, Gyb, and Daw.

These, then, are the signs we will be looking for in an examination of the Wakefield Cycle: connection of characters, places, and events by typology; drastic changes in the structure of time; parallelism in language or action; and finally, deliberate use of anachronism. Besides merely pointing out all these devices, an attempt will be made to assess their effect on the cycle as a whole.

Rosemary Woolf (essay date 1972)

SOURCE: "Navity Plays, II," in *The English Mystery Plays*, University of California Press, 1972, pp. 182-211.

[In the brief excerpt below, Woolf analyses the First *and* Second Shepherd's Play *in the light of their portrayal of shepherds and their role in other English mystery plays.]*

The dramatists in their treatment of the Nativity and of the events preceding it had a wealth of apocryphal or meditative amplifications to draw upon. The story of the shepherds, however, had gained no accretions of this kind. The basis therefore remained Luke ii, 8, 'And there were in the same country shepherds abiding in the field, keeping watch over their flock by night'. Though the idea of rustic innocence has acquired for us the many overtones of a pastoral convention unknown to the Middle Ages, there would seem to be some idyllic quality inherent in Luke's narrative, and patristic and medieval glosses, which explained that the Christ-Child was first revealed to the shepherds because they too were poor, humble and innocent, confirmed these implications. The mystery plays, however, drew surprisingly little upon this idealisation of simple virtue.

The only shepherds to conform to it entirely are, not those of the Nativity sequence, but the three who guard Joachim's sheep in the *Ludus Coventriae.* After his disgrace in the Temple, Joachim withdraws to his flocks in the country and to his shepherds of 'lytel pryde'. They greet him gravely and warmly, assuring him of the welfare of his sheep: 'A welcome hedyr blyssyd mayster: we pasture hem ful wyde, / they be lusty and fayr and grettly multyply.' When they realise Joachim's distress they are compassionate and devout, 'Sympyl as we kan, we xal for yow pray', and, after they have heard of the angel's message, they rejoice with Joachim in their simple way: 'We xal make us so mery now þis is be-stad / þat a myle on your wey ye xal her us synge.' This brief scene provides an illuminating background to the treatment of the later shepherds, for it shows that medieval writers were quite capable of combining simplicity with dignity and of not confounding innocence with rude ignorance. There are no other plays that preserve this balance.

The English shepherds' plays divide roughly into two groups: those that are brief and comparatively formal though sometimes with passages of feeling simplicity and those that are large, elaborate and grotesque containing long stretches of invented comic action. The most severe and reserved is the play in the *Ludus Coventriae,* which opens immediately with the angels singing the *Gloria in excelsis,* and continues with a series of speeches in which the shepherds explain their understanding of the revelation in terms of the Old Testament prophecies. The author is evidently influenced by allegorical expositions in which the shepherds (*pastores*) mystically signified the clergy who also watch over their flocks and can penetrate to a spiritual meaning beneath the letter of the text. In realistic terms the shepherds are thus incongruously learned, though there is a possibility that the eclogues of Virgil which were known throughout the Middle Ages provided for the poet at least a literary context in which the shepherd as a man of learning would not seem out of place. The shepherds on their way to Bethlehem then sing a well-known hymn to the Virgin, 'Stella caeli exstirpavit', and on arrival salute the Child in apostrophes which again show considerable theological understanding. The shepherds are thus entirely uncharacterised and the sole point of the play is to show the meeting point between prophecy and fulfilment.

The York play opens equally formally with the shepherds rehearsing Old Testament prophecies but progresses to a more imaginative and tender conclusion. Unlike those in the *Ludus Coventriae,* the prophecies here precede the angelic revelation, and this the shepherds greet, not with instant understanding, but with colloquial shouts of astonishment; moreover, while the author is too concerned with the dignity of simple virtue to use the favourite English joke of the shepherds being puzzled by the Latin of the *Gloria* and their grotesque attempts at imitation, there is a hint of this theme when the first shepherd boasts that he could sing as well as the angel. In the climax of the play, which corresponds to the *Shrewsbury Fragments,* the shepherds offer gifts that reflect their simplicity and poverty, a brooch with a tin bell, two cobnuts on a ribbon and a hornspoon. This theme, which is common to all western European drama and is particularly frequent in late French Nativity poems, is obviously modelled upon the offerings of the three Kings; but, whereas they offer gifts that reflect their riches and Christ's divinity, the shepherds offer presents that reflect their poverty and Christ's humanity. Three themes are interwined in the shepherds' speeches of adoration: regret for their poverty and simplicity, an affectionate delight in the Christ-Child as a baby, and a faith in His power: like the penitent thief on the Cross they can see through the humble circumstances and the suffering to God Himself:

> ii. *Pas.* þou sonne! þat shall save boþe see
> and sande,
>   Se to me sen I have þe soght,
>   I am ovir poure to make presande
>   Als myn harte wolde, and I had ought.
>   Two cobill notis uppon a bande,
>   Loo! litill babe, what I have broght,
>   And when ye shall be lorde in lande,
>   Dose good agayne, forgete me noght.

This conclusion to the York play is infused with the devotional understanding of the annunciation to the shepherds expressed in the *Mediatationes:*

> Wherefore cristes innocens and childhode conforteth
> not iangeleres and grete spekeres; cristes wepynges
> and teris conforteth noyt dissolute lawheres; his
> symple clothinge conforteth not hem that gone in
> proude clothynge; and his stable and cracche
> conforteth noyt hem that loven first seetes and
> worldes worschippes. And also the aungels in cristes
> Nativite apperynge to the wakynge scheephirdes
> conforten non othere but the povere travailloures;
> and to hem tellen they the ioye of newe liyt and
> noyt to the riche men that haven her conforte here.

The end of the York play therefore perfectly matches the tone of the preceding Nativity.

While the meditative tone of the conclusion of the York play resumes that of the Nativity, in the Coventry play a meditative interpretation of the Nativity is achieved largely through the treatment of the shepherds. The actual Nativity dialogue here consists of only fifteen lines sandwiched between two comparatively long shepherds' scenes: and, whilst these lines contain a brief adoration of the Child by Mary and Joseph, some emphasis upon the cold and a reference to the animals warming the Christ-Child with their breath, the episode is far too short to carry the necessary weight. But Mary's lament, 'Al Josoff, husebond, my chyld waxith cold, / And we have noo fyre to warme hym with', is given intensity of meaning by the shepherds' previous complaints (three times made) about the bitterly cold night. This theme of hardship is resumed in the nature of two of the gifts: one shepherd offers his hat, another his mittens. These gifts to clothe the naked are accompanied by speeches of naïve charm:

> Now, hayle be thow, chyld, and thy dame!
>   For in a pore loggyn here art thow leyde,
> Soo the angell seyde and tolde us thy name;
>   Holde, take thow here my hat on thy hedde!
>   And now off won thyng thow art well sped,
> For weddur thow hast noo nede to complayne,
> For wynd, ne sun, hayle, snoo and rayne.

Between the shepherds' first remarks about the coldness of the night and the offering of the gifts of covering for the child there occur some of the traditional elements of the shepherds' plays. Prophecies are quoted, though there is perhaps a faint suggestion that these prophecies are not so much learned information as the kind of traditional folk wisdom that is passed down from father to son. The shepherds are also ignorant of Latin and misrepeat the words of the *Gloria,* though the author refrains from introducing the embellishment of the ludicrous quarrelling born of self-assertive ignorance. Nevertheless, despite the predominantly meditative tone, elements of the allegorically learned and comically grotesque lurk in this play. The gift of the shepherd's hat, for instance, is obviously very differ-

ent in tone from the detail in the *Meditationes* of the Virgin removing her veil in order to provide a covering for the Child. Therefore, whilst the episodes of the shepherds are undoubtedly meditative in function, they teeter on the border between the sweetly comic and the grotesque.

The other three plays, Chester and the alternatives in Towneley, are entirely different in tone and design. In these the authors have given a large part of each play to establishing the shepherds before the story of the annunciation begins: the construction resembles that of some of the *Canterbury Tales,* such as the Merchant's or Pardoner's, in which the borrowed plot provides a sequence of rapid and important action in about the last third of the tale. The chronological position of the shepherds' plays is unusual in the cycles, for the action that takes place before the angelic annunciation belongs to the old world before Christ is born, and the cycle has therefore moved back in time (Coventry and French plays of course preserve correct chronological order by dividing the subject of the shepherds into two parts with the Nativity intervening). It is important to remember this regression in time, as it is clearly the intention of the dramatists to show something of the old world before Christ is born; but the methods by which this is done are unusual in the cycles.

The plays all begin with long explanatory monologues. In the Chester play the first shepherd begins with a self-congratulatory monologue in which he sets out his skills in curing sheep-diseases, and he is followed by the second shepherd who describes how he uses his wife's cooking utensils for brewing medicaments when her back is turned. In the *Prima pastorum* the first shepherd begins the play by lamenting that all his sheep have died of *rot* (a specific disease). It has already been well pointed out by Professor Kolve [in *The Play Called Corpus Christi*] that this theme has religious associations, those of Christ as physician and Christ as the good shepherd. The reference to *rot,* however, also has a realistic and topical appearance, since outbreaks of murrain throughout the Middle Ages had accompanied the successive outbreaks of plague. There could also be hints of a further meaning in this topicality. In a satirical approach, now more familiar to us from the *Shepherds' Calendar* and *Lycidas,* Petrarch in his sixth and seventh eclogues had drawn upon the details of the contemporary murrain to satirise the corruption of the Church. If this type of allegory were in the mind of the dramatists, the sheep dying of *rot* would be mankind before the Incarnation. It may seem more likely that there are hints of this in the *Prima pastorum,* in which the first shepherd has lost all his flock, than in Chester, where the shepherds are confident of their pharmaceutical skills. But the moral position of the Chester shepherds is also, as we shall see, ambivalent.

The shepherds talk about their excellence in this craft

but with suspiciously boastful exaggerations: the first shepherd, for instance, announces immediately that there is no better shepherd than he 'from comelic Conway unto Clyde' (i.e. anywhere). The only things that they actually do, however, are to eat and take part in the sport of wrestling. What Wilmotte [in *Le Wallon*, 1893] called an extraordinary gastronomic interest is displayed in the shepherds' plays and in the Nativity poetry of many places. Wilmotte suggested an association with the Roman Saturnalia, but Professor Kolve's theory of a connection with the Christmas feasting after the Advent fast is far more plausible. The use made of eating or of the gastronomic list varies from work to work in general it evidently serves to root the shepherds very firmly in realistic material enjoyments, corresponding perhaps to Jean Michel's shepherds' scene, in which the shepherds linger over, not the delights of food, but of nights spent with shepherdesses. Within the harsher, satirical tone of Towneley and Chester, however, the shepherds' feast has perhaps further overtones. For it becomes clear that the shepherds are more interested in feeding themselves than in feeding their flocks, a duty semantically indicated by the Latin word *pastor,* and within religious allegory by Christ's command to St Peter, 'Pasce oves meas'. The mood of the Towneley and Chester shepherds' scenes reminds one of Breughel's *Land of Cokayne,* in which the peasants are stretched out in lazy sleep around a table laden with food. Breughel has imposed an atmosphere of coarse repulsiveness upon the traditional never-never-land of abundant food.

If there is a similar atmosphere in the Chester play, it would follow that the dramatist intended a contrast between the three shepherds and Gartius, who alone is actively caring for the sheep. It is not quite clear whether the Chester author, like the Wakefield Master, has conceived the *pastores* as small farmers, who have in their joint employ a boy to guard their sheep, or whether they are all employees of a lord, the boy then being a groom who would work with them and under their supervision: the boy's hint that he has difficulty in getting his wages out of them (cf. l. 232) suggests the former. At any rate it is clear that it is not the *pastores* who are keeping watch by night, but the boy; and he, though impudent, is conscientious in his care for the sheep and satisfied with his lot. The boy's contempt for the shepherds and their dirty food ('the grubbs thereon do creepe') and his abusive dismissal of them, 'To the devill I all you betake', seems in the play to be dramatically well-founded in their lazy self-indulgence. This understanding of the relationship of Garcius to the shepherds would accord well with the interpretation of Professor Kolve, who sees in the wrestling-match, in which the boy overthrows each of the shepherds in turn, the allegorical pattern of Christ's victory, a victory which, one might add, had already been foreshadowed in the defeat of Goliath by David, 'that Shephard with his Sling', as Herod calls him in

the next play.

The moral distinctiveness of the shepherds' boy is further indicated in the second half of the play which deals with the angels' message and the visit to the Christ-Child: here the symmetrical arrangement makes the boy the leader, a privilege more often given, as in Coventry, to the third shepherd. In Chester each step forward in religious understanding is taken first by the boy. When the star first appears, the shepherds speaking in turn express fear and surprise: it is Gartius who instantly dedicates his life to it and recognises 'Gods might' (ll. 329-38); then, when after the angelic singing, the shepherds embark upon their comic misunderstandings of the Latin, Gartius does not at first join in, but speaks only of the feeling of delight that the words gave him. Admittedly after that Gartius joins equally in the stupid misunderstandings, but it is again Gartius who first speaks the words that biblically belong to the shepherds, 'Now wend we forth to Bethlem' (cf. Luke ii. 15), and again after the angel's reassurance, 'To Bedlem take we the waye'. By the end of the play the shepherds and Gartius are of course all equal in proclaiming their devotion to the Christ-Child and in their resolution to lead the life of secular priests and religious, though it may not be chance that it is the boy, who in resolving to adopt the life of an anchorite, chooses the most contemplative form of life.

It would of course be a mistake to read the Chester shepherds' play as though it were similar in design to the plays of Flood where the surface realism is founded on solid religious allegory. It is immediately clear that there is no typological characterisation in the shepherds' play: the shepherds are not Cain nor the boy Isaac. Whilst there are hints at religious allegory that cannot be ignored, the dramatist's main purpose is obviously to depart from the previous stylisation of character, which might seem to show the Christ-Child born into a world aesthetically removed from the contemporary and familiar. Sin and virtue are reduced to size; Gartius is a dutiful shepherd, but his attitude to life, which resembles Autolycus's 'I care for nobody no, not I', is as indicative of an unredeemed world as is the lazy shepherds' preoccupation with food and stupid self-esteem. All therefore equally need the unrealistic conversion to priestly orders that is brought about by their recognition of the Christ-Child.

Insofar as there is any plot in the Chester shepherds' play before the biblical story begins it lies in the wrestling-match: in other words the author has invented action by drawing upon the common sports of the peasant community. The Wakefield Master proceeds differently in that briefly in the **Prima pastorum** and lengthily in the **Secunda pastorum** he dramatises the type of plot that in France was the subject of independent farces. The secular plot of the **Prima pastorum** is that of the Three Wise Men of Gotham, which now survives only as a story in jestbooks. Within it, however, as a short inset, is the story of Moll and her pitcher, which is the subject of a lost French farce, and which a little later Gil Vicente, the Portuguese dramatist, incorporated in a Nativity play composed for performance on Christmas Day. The plot of the *Secunda pastorum* now has only a close parallel in a late eighteenth-century ballad, but in type it resembles the plot-type involving ingenious trickery which is used in many French farces, including the most famous of them all, *Maître Pathelin*. Plots of this kind were evidently floating ones, appearing in exempla, novellae, jest and farces. There is thus no way of telling precisely from what source or genre the Wakefield Master borrowed his plots, but. . .he in all likelihood knew the genre of the French farces, and must therefore have been conscious that he was adapting the material of farce to a religious context.

The interesting point is of course the manner in which these plots are adapted to their new context. The theme of the Wise Men of Gotham as also of Moll and her pitcher is foolishness and make-believe. These elements the Wakefield Master heavily underlines, using the second of the plots to illuminate the first. According to the jest, two shepherds quarrel over the issue of whether one of them may bring back the flock of sheep that he is about to buy over a certain bridge, part of the foolishness consisting in the fact that these sheep are as yet unbought. In the *Prima pastorum* this is elaborated: the first shepherd who has lost his sheep through *rot,* has scarcely any money to buy more sheep at the fair to replace them, yet in the quarrel he asserts that he will bring back a hundred sheep—a provocatively large number—and, further to enrage the other, acts the part of driving them on, 'Go now, bell weder'. The entire illusoriness of the situation is emphasised by the third shepherd, who sets himself up as a wise man and tells the story of Moll and her pitcher to illustrate their folly: the shepherd's hundred sheep are thus as much in the imagination as Moll's dreams of wealth, all lost when she dropped the pitcher. The third shepherd, however, is just as foolish, for to make a more telling illustration, as in the jest, he empties his sack of meal, which he then demonstrates to be as empty of meal as the heads of the other shepherds are empty of wits. At this point the author of *A Hundred Merry Tales* draws a moral: 'This tale showeth you that some man taketh upon him to show other men wisdom when he is but a fool himself.' The Wakefield Master at the same point introduces the character of Garcio to draw the same moral:

> Now god gyf you care, foles all sam;
> Sagh I never none so fare, bot the foles of
>   gotham.
> Wo is hir that yow bare, youre syre and youre
>   dam,
> had she broght furth an hare, a shepe, or a

> lam,
> had bene well.
> Of all the foles I can tell,
> ffrom heven unto hell,
> ye thre bere the bell;
>   God gyf you unceyll.

Like the Chester Gartius, Garcio is in the employ of the shepherds, and his attitude to them is yet more pointedly contemptuous. It is again he who is looking after the sheep, and when he invites the shepherds to come and see for themselves how flourishing they are, the shepherds prefer to sit down and eat the grotesque abundance of provisions that they have brought with them. After that they are weary, and when the angel appears, far from watching their sheep they are fast asleep. The turning point in the *Prima pastorum,* however, comes much sooner than in Chester, for, once the angel has announced the Nativity, the shepherds become learned men, as they are in the *Ludus Coventriae,* and they interpret the angel's message in the light of the prophecies. The third shepherd is even able to quote the prophecy of Virgil's shepherd in the fourth eclogue in Latin. Their salutations of the Christ-Child and their offering of simple gifts mark the climax of their devotion. As in Chester, there is no psychological continuity between the foolish, lazy, grumbling shepherds of the first part and the devout worshippers of Christ in the second.

More than half of the long *Secunda pastorum* is taken up by the plot of the sheep-stealing, which is contrived as a burlesque of the Nativity and antecedent themes. It is as though the world before the Incarnation contained not types of the Redemption but deformed adumbrations, or, to put the matter with less seriousness, the whole episode could be considered a witty pretence at typology. There are, to begin with, clear equivalences between the plot and characters of the sheep-stealing episode and the sequence of the annunciation to the shepherds and the visit to the Christ-Child which follows. Mak (the sheep-stealer) tells the shepherds when they wake up of the supposed birth of his child; in the cottage when the shepherds arrive are Mak, the hen-pecked husband and ostensible father, his wife who has been feigning the pains of childbirth, and a lamb in the cradle. Then in the unmasking episode (which the dramatist must have invented since it is the nature of the plot that the trickster should be successful), the fraud is discovered through the third shepherd's kindly wish to give the child a present: the affectionate term, 'Lytyll day starne' by which he refers to him, is of course later used of the Christ-Child and is a title proper only to Him.

The Mak episode has been compared to the sub-plot of Elizabethan drama or the anti-masque. The parallel with *The Midsummer Night's Dream,* for instance, is interesting but there is the important difference that, whereas the antics of Bottom and his companions follow upon the serious love story, the sheep-stealing in the *Secunda pastorum* precedes the religious matter that it buffoons. The placing of the Mak episode is in fact important, for, whilst in one way it provides a type or rather, like the Fall of Man, an antitype of part of the Redemption, it also pretends to be in itself a fulfilment of earlier typological patterns. This is particularly clear in the relationship of Mak and his wife. Mak in his cottage is obviously a debased version of St Joseph, and like St Joseph he sees himself in the role of the unhappily married man. But his wife, who is the leading partner in the fraud, to some extent casts herself as the second Eve. Thus whilst Mak complains about the sufferings in an evil marriage, his wife is given to *sententiae* about the virtues of women: 'Yit a woman avyse helpys at the last' (her comment upon the good advice that she has given about the trick) or 'Ffull wofull is the householde / That wantys a woman.' Other figures should similarly be seen in a twofold relationship: for instance, the sheep purporting to be a baby anticipates the baby who was symbolically a lamb, but it is also a grotesque fulfilment of the lamb offered by Abel and the sheep offered in place of Isaac.

The Wakefield Master has set the story of Mak within a fairly straightforward treatment of the three shepherds. In contrast to the other plays these shepherds are genuinely suffering from oppression, truly poor and actually looking after their sheep: they are not feasting, wrestling or quarrelling. It is not that their complaints are to be taken entirely straight. The second shepherd who has a monstrously ugly wife ('She is browyd lyke a brystyll, with a sowre loten chere') and who warns the young men in the audience against marriage, is the undignified husband of anti-matrimonial satire; whilst the first shepherd who complains that taxes and the oppression of the *gentlery-men* have made him too poor to cultivate his land is speaking no more than a half-truth. But, while the shepherds' explanations of their predicament are slightly comic and rebound upon themselves, that they live a life of hardship is plain, and their sufferings cast light upon the sufferings of the Christ-Child. At the end of the play the second shepherd says compassionately of the Christ-Child, 'he lygys full cold'; but earlier in the play the effects of cold had been described in realistic detail: the shepherds complain that their feet are numb in their boots, their eyes water, and their hands are chapped. To emphasise the Christ-Child's sufferings through cold was, as we have seen, part of the meditative tradition, but it is only in this play that the actual sensations of cold are made alive to the imagination by describing them with such unelevated precision. Since the shepherds in this play deserve through their sufferings the comfort of the revelation of the Nativity, it is fitting that their speeches of adoration should be the most moving; and, whilst this is partly through their poetic quality, it is also partly because they are rooted in the earlier presentation of the shepherds: they do not have to become

entirely new and different men before they worship the Christ-Child.

Whilst the shepherds in the *Secunda pastorum* are treated with more evident devotional purpose than in the *Prima pastorum* or Chester, the play is undoubtedly dominated by the Mak episode, and it is therefore not surprising that the author only supplied it as an alternative. For, though the episode has a religious orientation lacking in the comic sequences of, for instance, the Rouen *Nativité*, it could easily be missed by the unsophisticated, who would then understand it only as simple farce. To understand it this way would of course be great impoverishment: though quite well done, the dramatisation of the fraud is much inferior to the urbane *Maître Pathelin*, and of course crude beside Chaucer's narrative comedies. But, when understood within a religious framework its subtlety and literary self-awareness are reminiscent of Chaucer's manner and one wonders whether it may have been written for performance on some special occasion when it would have a fitting audience.

The dramatist's tone in his treatment of the shepherds in the *Secunda pastorum* is less ambiguous than in the *Prima pastorum* or in Chester, though at the point at which the third shepherd appears to accuse the others of being niggardly employers, it is less certain, and, as in the *Prima pastorum*, the shepherds are not guarding their sheep but asleep when the angel appears. In general it can be said that the authors of these three plays have put the shepherds into a morally intolerable position. In historical terms they are small farmers rather than shepherds, and their employment of a boy or groom to look after the sheep on their behalf is a practical arrangement since it leaves them with the necessary time to cultivate the arable land which they would own or hold on lease. But within the play this customary and sensible arrangement becomes morally odd, for it is necessary that the men should be called shepherds and that they should be abroad at night. But since their night wanderings serve no practical purpose, it gives them a vagabondish air and leaves them with time for senseless quarrels and feastings. It is now very difficult to recapture how this would have seemed or exactly what the authors' intentions were. In Wakefield, which had grown prosperous on the cloth industry, many of the audience must also have been small farmers, and the fact that the shepherds are unnamed (or have *ad hoc* names), in contrast to Cain, who is the historical Cain first and a farmer second, must have increased their appearance of contemporaneity. Furthermore, whilst some of their grumblings about the oppression of the rich must be taken with a certain reserve (they have a slightly archaic air in that they would fit the social conditions of the late fourteenth century more appositely than those of the mid-fifteenth) and they perhaps reflect equally upon the grumbler and the rich, the complaints about maintained men are evidently genuine satire of contemporary abuse. It is clear, however, that there is no idealisation of poverty as the meditative tradition would have required: the dramatists had as sharp an eye as Langland for the portrayal of the grumbling and lazy poor. All the elements of social satire, fantasy and farce yield in every play to the idealised picture of the adoration of the Christ-Child, and this contrast is evidently the primary purpose of the design of the plays. But nowadays it is impossible to recapture the precise mood of the first part of the contrast, for whereas in other plays the key to their understanding lies in other forms of literature, in these it fairly certainly lies in life.

The **Adoration of the Shepherds** is followed in all the cycles by a long interwoven sequence which begins with the meeting between the Three Kings and ends with the **Massacre of the Innocents**. The figure of Herod dominates this sequence. . . .

John Gardner (essay date 1974)

SOURCE: A prologue to *The Construction of the Wakefield Cycle*, Southern Illinois University Press, 1974, pp. 1-12.

[*In the following prologue to his study of the structure and unity of the Wakefield plays, Gardner argues that, although the dramas may have been written by different hands, "at a late stage of cycle evolution, one poet took the whole hodgepodge in hand and, by ingenious revision and some rewriting, shaped the collection into an artistic unity."*]

If we concentrate principally on the more obvious features of the techniques found in the Wakefield pageants—the characteristic stanza, the randy language, the social criticism—we find the pageants unusual. But if we look at other, less obvious features of the technique found here, such as the thematic use of verbal repetition, the ironic use of scriptural typology, the consistent manipulation of patterns of imagery (especially satanic imagery), and the oddly modern cutting of transitional devices, we find distinct similarities between such superficially dissimilar works as the *Mactacio Abel* and the *Abraham,* or the *Magnus Herodes* and the *Conspiracio.* We find some, though not all, of these same devices in other cycles—Chester, Hegge (or "N. Town"), and York—but seldom are the devices worked out with the same degree of skill. And only here in the Towneley MS do we find that a few basic ideas organize the entire drama from Creation to Judgment.

And so it seems to me likely that the Wakefield Master may have played a far larger part in the composition of the Wakefield cycle than has generally been supposed. Even in pageants which show his characteristic stanza,

language, and humor, we find—as in the cycle as a whole—crude work alongside polished, early examples of pageant construction alongside late, and narrowly doctrinal material alongside imaginative elaborations of doctrinal points. What I suggest is that this single poet may have revised and reshaped the entire cycle in much the way we know he revised and reshaped an early Cain play, parts of which survive in *Mactacio Abel.*

None of this is to deny the standard opinion that the hodgepodge of forms and styles in the cycle as a whole, as well as in pageants assigned to one reviser, shows mystery cycle evolution to be, *in general,* a process of gradual accretion wherein, in a given town, new or longer pageants were created whenever new guilds joined the festival of *Corpus Christi* and needed something to stage. My theory simply argues that at a late stage of cycle evolution, one poet took the whole hodgepodge in hand and, by ingenious revision and some rewriting, shaped the collection into an artistic unity. Neither does my theory rule out the account brought down by the Towneley family, that the pageants were written or adapted by members of a cell of Augustinian or Black Canons at Widkirk (Woodkirk) near Wakefield. I argue only that however many poets helped to write the cycle, they worked according to one writer's plan.

Even when written or adapted by well-educated churchmen, mystery pageants were a folk art. Pageants developed or borrowed from somewhere else for the York cycle were modified and produced at nearby Wakefield very much as traditional ballads have been transported from place to place and sometimes significantly and artfully modified. To prove that a play "works" is not the same as proving it the creation of some individual genius. Both the famous Child version of "Little Musgrave and Lady Barnard" and John Jacob Niles's version of "Matty Groves" are coherent, though they do not use the same details or have, even, the same theme. The change of a few lines can make all the difference. Professor Vinaver has made clear [in *Modern Humanities Research,* 1966] the absurdity of arguing that a "well made" medieval work must be the product of individual composition and that a work which contains inconsistencies or self-contradiction must be assigned to traditional composition. By this standard, Faulkner's novels are all by several hands, and "Matty Groves" is an original poem composed by John Jacob Niles. What counts, then, is not that the Wakefield pageants are "well made" but that they are made by a limited set of aesthetic rules—rules not operative in other pageant cycles.

Sometimes the Wakefield-pageant reviser or revisers were satisfied with relatively minor changes, recasting and reinterpreting older material, perhaps borrowing heavily from cycles now lost; at other times these writers built from the ground up, as in the **Secunda Pastorum**. Pageants which preserve large chunks of some older work offer evidence that the reviser or revisers sometimes thought it sufficient merely to make dull texts more interesting; and often what the reviser did in such cases was not only to add the comic realism so obvious to modern readers, but also, and equally important, to increase the intellectual subtlety of the pageants and, at the same time, to increase dramatic intensity by cutting slow transitions in the action, breaking up dialogue, elaborating characterization, and introducing suspense and dramatic irony. Certain pageants which contain no trace of humor, such as the **Abraham** and the **Resurreccio Domini,** have this same intellectual subtlety, dramatic intensity, and irony.

The appearance of these characteristics pretty much throughout the Towneley manuscript suggests not only the work of some controlling intelligence but also that in the Wakefield cycle we are dealing with drama which has moved farther beyond the original conventions of the English mystery than has drama from, say, Chester or Hegge. It becomes worthwhile to ask again just what the mystery pageant was in its earlier, simpler form—or, more bluntly, why a thing so dull to us was so appealing to the people of its day, uneducated people, generally speaking, but presumably people not completely wanting in sense. It is useful to ask, too, what relationship, if any, the techniques found in the fully evolved pageants have to techniques in later drama.

Before we turn to these questions, it may be well to comment on certain once common objections to studying the "art" of the mystery pageants at all. Needless to say, the only solid proof that a pageant is worth analysis is the analysis itself: a literary critic makes his case not by arguing that the case can be made but by making it. Moreover, the important scholarly work which has been done on relationships between the mystery pageants and Christian typology, between the pageants and medieval church art, and so forth, may make any apology for close reading of the pageants seem unnecessary. But at least for some readers, objections to close reading of the pageants may need to be reviewed, not only because the objections have sometimes come from important scholars but also because they involve assumptions which may need to be reconsidered.

It is true, within limits, that in the mystery pageants we are dealing with what Hardin Craig has described [in *English Religious Drama of the Middle Ages,* 1955] as "a communal, anonymous, traditional drama the choice of whose subjects was predetermined. . .and whose end and aim was not dramatic but religious." (The limits, as Professor Hardison has shown, are in the implications of the contrastive words *dramatic* and *religious*.) The skeptic may feel, as does Professor Craig, that since the pageants were written or adapted anonymously for a mainly devotional purpose, and since the audience for whom they were performed was not Chaucer's aristocratic audience but the uneducated common man, close study of the pageants must be pointless.

On the communal and anonymous composition of the pageants hardly any comment should be necessary. *Beowulf* is anonymous; Shakespeare's *Hamlet* is partly a selection of old materials. As for what truly communal work could achieve in the Middle Ages, think of Chartres cathedral, or of that vastly elaborated literary leviathan of the twelfth and thirteenth centuries, the so-called Vulgate Cycle of Arthurian romances.

The argument that the mystery pageants are devotional and therefore not dramatic—not concerned with any "deliberate search for dramatic effects"—is almost as easily dismissed. Various critics have expressed their dissatisfaction with the older point of view by attempting to deny that the pageants are religious in the first place. John Spiers, most vocal of these dissenters, argues [in *Medieval English Poetry,* 1957] that the plays are rooted in pre-Christian ritual—a theory no one but Spiers any longer accepts. Professor Hardison, who grants the thorough Christianity of the plays, takes a more devastating line, a line I believe all sober judgment must accept. He calls attention again to the existence of an early and independent vernacular tradition—"consciously composed works, written for a theater that already possessed definite traditions of staging and acting, and conceived from the beginning as representation"—and he shows that the once common scholarly practice of tracing all the vernacular plays back to liturgy and to Latin tropes of the *Quem Quaeritis* type is not in accord with the evidence; that, in fact, there is no reason to believe that certain of the plays (e.g., **Adam** and **Cain**) were ever produced, in any form, inside a church. Hardison is surely right: the vernacular plays did not originate solely within the church. At the same time Hardison makes it impossible for serious scholars to deny that, whatever their origin, the mystery plays, both early and late, simple and complex, are emphatically, in Miss Prosser's words, [in *Drama and Religion in the English Mystery Plays,* 1961] "a community drama of worship and celebration." The pageants did not stop serving religion as they gained in popularity, though secondary motives for producing them must have gained in importance. In the mid-sixteenth century William Newhall says of one of the most doctrinal and undramatic cycles that these pageants were not only for "increase of the holy and catholic faith of our Savyour, Jhu' Crist, and to exort the mynds of the co'mon people to good devotion and holsome doctryne thereof, but also for the co'mon Welth and prosperitie of this Citie. . . ." If the solemn Chester cycle had economic value, we may be sure that the more "realistic" pageants of the great fifteenth-century trading centers York and Wakefield did too. The pageants were mounted by guilds, whose orientation was presumably more economic than pious. Religious orders did little more than the writing or revising.

Professor Craig explains the evolution of the pageants as follows: "New plays came into existence in response to the growth, very rapid in places like York, in the number of trading companies that wished to have a part in the great annual festival. Such new plays were usually the result of the expansion into a separate play of what had been a mere episode in some other play." The canon of events appropriate to the *Corpus Christi* redemption theme was more or less fixed. The obvious means of expanding scriptural subjects, that is, changing mere episodes into separate pageants, was to dilate scenes by the introduction of more fully developed characters and situations drawn from contemporary life—the activities of shepherds, the legalistic prattle of stupid judges. Both at York and at Wakefield, and frequently elsewhere, these forms of improvisation are evident.

As realistic modern scenes expanded, actual social and psychological problems of medieval men naturally drew the playwrights' increasing attention, particularly if the playwright was a close observer of life; but such concerns cannot be set down at once as secular—they are by no means uncommon in medieval sermons, homiletic poems, and the like. Humor for its own sake was at times introduced, whether by the performer who found he had a talent for making people laugh or by the writer who wished to capitalize on the natural popularity of funny scenes. Perhaps it is true, as Miss Prosser thinks, that this tended now and then to subvert the original motive of the pageants. But against the tendency to introduce humor for its own sake there were important checks. The church, or at all events certain churchmen, disapproved of such debasing of the pageants; the tradition of the pageants was devotional, in fact largely parallel in form to the Mass as allegorized by Amalarius and others; and even at their most realistic the pageants remained, at least in theory, a religious exercise. Considering these checks, it is not surprising to find that as a rule humorous elaboration of scriptural subjects introduces not only comic relief but also serious exploration, from a religious point of view, of contemporary problems. Sometimes this exploration is both literal and allegorical, employing the more obvious emblems used in popular sermons of the day.

The fact that a pageant is religious does not in fact rule out artistic consciousness. Whereas straight dramatization of God's plan for man's redemption was a doctrinal and public matter, social criticism and commentary on the actual behavior of medieval husbands and wives were to a certain extent matters of personal observa-

tion. At the same time, even with respect to characterization and the development of conflicts between characters, we must be cautious about calling the playwright's impulse secular. His selection of characters and attitudes to be held up for comic ridicule bears a striking resemblance to the selection made by the medieval preacher, the writer of books on virtues and vices, or the homiletic poet. The medieval preacher does not make much use of humor, admittedly, but humor is a common device in less formal religious writing, especially in poetry. . . .

Finally, it is not the case that the devotional impulse rules out any "deliberate search for dramatic effects"—unless we take the word dramatic in an extremely limited sense. Playwrights, like preachers, seek to move and persuade, not simply instruct, and each man moves his audience by the means at his command. In one of the sermons from the British Museum MS. Royal 18 B, xxiii, a collection some of the sermons in which seem to have been composed as preachers' models, we find a short quotation from St. Bernard concerning the Last Judgment, followed by what must be a recommendation to preachers for dramatic—that is, emotionally forceful—expansion of the subject: "And þat þis is dredefull, narrate þe xv signis"—a reference to the well known fifteen signs of approaching Doom. Instances of this sort of thing might be enumerated at length, but no such labor should be necessary for the present point. It was one of the preacher's jobs to make Christian doctrine persuasive, and he did his job by piling up stories, by dramatizing for his congregation the torments of hell and the joys of heaven—in other words, by hunting for "effect." The writers of personal meditations do the same. As for religious poets, think of the conscious dramatic effects in *Pearl, Purity, Patience,* and *Sir Gawain,* or think of the *Debate of Body and Soul.* It may be true that the kinds of effects found in the mystery pageants are not the kinds found in Marlowe or Shakespeare; but to insist that the mysteries contain no dramatic effects unless by accident is to misread the pageants.

The once common assumption that nothing intellectually complex will be found in pageants composed for simple and uneducated medieval people is equally mistaken. True, the English middle class of the fourteenth through sixteenth centuries was, in our terms, uneducated. But these people were not as simple as we have sometimes imagined. Though their congregations could not read, medieval preachers could safely allude to a host of biblical stories; artists could employ typology (Isaac carrying faggots in the shape of a cross), and lyric writers could assume an intelligent and fairly subtle audience.

So the question arises: if the audience was not in fact simple-minded, and if playwrights, like preachers, were capable of certain kinds of subtlety when they chose to use them, how are we to account for the manifest dullness and simplicity of so many of the pageants? Why were they so well attended throughout England? One part of the answer is that when the pageants were originally performed the texts themselves—all that has come down to us except for a few songs—were the least important element. Professor Swart has pointed out [in *Neophilologus* 41, 1952] that the traditional notion of the pageant stages, drawn from the Chester *Breviarye* (wrongly attributed to Archdeacon Rogers but in fact written by his son after 1609), must be replaced by a view of the pageant stages as complex structures equipped with traps, hoists, and even cloud machines; and he adds the observation that the English plays give hints that such complex stages were used there. Like the masques of the time, the plays may have been quasi-magical spectacles very impressive indeed. (Language reflects the magical side of medieval theater. The *tragetour* in Old French was a juggler or montebank; the OED in listings from 1300 to 1340 gives the word the denotation of a man having godlike or witchlike powers. By 1380 the *tragetour* is grouped with tumblers, jesters, and japers—he is now an actor, not a priest of the occult. Yet the actor-entertainers in Chaucer's *House of Fame,* written not long before 1380, are sorcerers, witches, magicians.) Though actors in the mystery pageants were not professionals, as a rule, but were citizens selected by a board of some kind, they were probably influenced by the professionals of the time; otherwise why the explicit rules, at York for instance, against the hiring of professionals? In courtly masques from Chaucer's day to after Ben Johnson's, levitation, ingenious machines of one sort or another, and clever disappearances were a standard part of the entertainment. It is true that simplified and symbolic props were usual in medieval courtly masques (as in mystery pageants or, later, the tragedies of Shakespeare), a single branch signifying a forest, a single soldier signifying an army, a few chairs signifying an assembly hall; but it is also true that within the same masque there might appear convincing and elaborately constructed buildings or pavilions, boats, even illusory forests. In other words, stylized representations in courtly medieval theater were chosen for aesthetic reasons, not because the company worked with a minimal budget; and the same may have been true in popular pageants. We see this aesthetic simplification wherever we look in medieval art—for instance, in the illustrations which accompany poems, wherein one figure represents a crew of sailors and two waves represent a storm at sea. We find analogous effects in medieval music.

What was true of the aristocratic masques may also have been true of popular drama—the mystery and morality plays, especially those of the fifteenth century. The guilds which selected actors and provided stage props appropriate to each guild's particular line of work (the "Golde Smythis," for example, outfitted the Magi

of the York cycle) must have provided lavishly for the pageants, vying with one another for the spectator's admiration and money. This fits with what we know of the pageant cars created for the Dutch middle class in the sixteenth century. The machinery of a fixed stage, like the stages admired in France, may have been even more spectacular.

If the chief interest of the mystery pageants in their earlier form was visual, then it need not surprise us that, on one hand, the pageants were enormously popular and that, on the other hand, when we look at the texts we discover that, as A. P. Rossiter says [in *English Drama From Early Times to the Elizabethans*, 1950], "from the literary point of view the workmanship is never far from crude and, in the older strata, insipid." One might, after all, say the same of the courtly masques. We need not expect "drama" in a masque which requires costumes for fourteen female figures, fourteen bearded men, fourteen angels, fourteen characters with headdresses topped by upside-down legs complete with shoes, fourteen figures with mountainlike heads possibly having rabbits running in and out of tunnels, fourteen dragons, fourteen peacocks, and fourteen swans. Neither is drama inevitable in a Noah pageant put together (as was the one at York) by "Fysshers and Marynars," an Expulsion from Eden pageant put together by "þe Crafte of Armourers," or an Angelic Visitation produced by chandlers. On the other hand, when drama does come into the pageants, we may safely guess that spectacle does not drop out.

With regard to the dullness of the early texts I will simply register here a second point. . . . O. B. Hardison has provided a new principle for judging these texts, that of fidelity to source when the source is biblical or biblical or traditionally devotional. It is no accident that in the brilliant Towneley **Extraccio** and **Judicium** pageants the character of Christ remains unchanged, while the roles of devils and villains are richly improvised.

Whereas earlier pageant writers threaded rhymes through engaging spectacles, seeking in their verse only the simplest devotional effects—solemn speeches for Deus, appropriately devout speeches for Noah and Abraham—more ingenious playwrights emerged in some localities, pressing beyond "theater" to characterization and profluence through conflict. The York Metrist and the Wakefield Master explored the possibility of creating greater immediacy for their dramatized Bible stories by establishing convincing characters, by introducing suspense, and by appealing to men's feeling for poetic style. Such was the evolution of the mystery from spectacle to art. The most important innovation of such poets was their use within the popular drama of an extremely subtle form of the allegorical method which was used, less subtly, in popular sermons of the day, had been used quite openly in earlier mysteries, especially in France and Germany, and was used with the greatest ingenuity by such poets as Dante and Chaucer. Whereas earlier mystery pageants made a point of introducing the traditional exegetical notion that Noah, Isaac, and other Old Testament figures are types or prefigurations of Christ, and explicitly allegorized the literal action for the audience (sometimes, as in the Chester Abraham pageant, by means of an Expositor), later playwrights craftily buried their allegory in the realistic behavior and punning speech of a medievalized Noah or Isaac, and were thus able to express the character's typic identification and at the same time to dramatize every man's involvement in the fundamental mysteries of Christian doctrine. Building on the traditional patristic contrast between the Old Jerusalem—a figure of this world—and the New, they developed a satirical comedy which focused on the pretensions of this world to rivalry with the next. The method of these playwrights is not the one we find characteristic of later drama, which is no doubt why it so long escaped attention; but it is indeed a method—it was still used in Elizabethan times and later—and it was one capable of fine effects. The fully evolved mystery cycle is not a stage in the development of drama as we find it in later ages but a closed evolutionary line, a culmination. Except as such playwrights as Marlowe borrow mystery-play devices (whether by accident or through influence), the individual mystery pageant can no more lead to Renaissance drama than, say, the fully evolved woodcut can lead to painting in oils. The *Corpus Christi* play as a whole is no more closely related to Renaissance drama than the *Iliad* is to the plays of Aeschylus.

In fact, the method of individual mystery pageants at their best is in fundamental conflict with most modern dramatic practice. The basically Aristotelian idea of conflict resulting in a causally related series of events which, taken together, make up a complete action—Aristotle's *energia* (the actualization of the potential which exists in character and situation)—can have no place in drama based not on a theory of reality as process but on a theory of reality as stasis. If reality is the unchanging Supreme Good, if Nature is God's revelation of Himself in emblematic form, and if the proper response to this mutable world is the search within it for the *vestigia* or traces of God's hand, the immutable principle, then a concern with action is not only unwarranted but perverse, a failure of right reason. Man's whole study should be the implicit unchangeable, the contrast between the physical Israel and the spiritual Israel, Babylon and the City of God. Of course work based on contrast rather than conflict is not really something we need to adjust ourselves to (*pace* D. W. Robertson, Jr., and others). It is the mode of satire from *The Alchemist* to *Pogo,* to speak only of things modern. What satire and Christian drama have in common is an absolute base: as satire depends for its effect on the unquestioned social and ethical values of the audi-

ence, Christian drama depends for its effect on unquestionable dogma. In the Wakefield cycle, each individual pageant works in this way; in the Wakefield *Corpus Christi* play as a whole, another, in some ways more modern kind of action, is developed.

I have emphasized the fact that the plays are religious—in subject, in purpose, even in their choice of method. That emphasis is perhaps misleading. I should have said they are "serious," and in medieval England serious thought is, inescapably, religious. To the medieval poet speaking to the middle class, the only terms available for describing human psychology, or for commenting on social problems, or for ridiculing human foibles—are Christian. The real purpose of my commentary on the Towneley ms plays is to demonstrate that if the pageants are religious they are also magnificent theater. Anyone who has looked closely at medieval sermons knows that they are often interesting, often extremely vivid; but the logic of the sermon, however entertaining the sermon may be, is linear—the logic of argument. The logic of the mystery pageants—even the textually dull ones—is poetic: meaning is not merely stated but is released by the juxtaposition of part against part. To speak of the pageants as dramatized sermons is to blur the age-old distinction between discourse and poetry. The distinction is not always clear in the plays themselves, needless to say: art and theology interpenetrate. This is merely to say that sermon content, when transferred to another form, remains itself while becoming something new. Reading the plays as though they were merely primitive plays, not dramas of doctrine, can lead to misapprehension; but studies of, say, the typology in the plays can be equally misleading. Miss Woolf's analysis [in *The English Mystery Plays,* 1972], several years ago, of the exegetical tradition reflected in the Abraham-Isaac plays revealed the way in which the most casual phrases can call up a rich scriptural association; but her evaluation of the York and Towneley plays was nevertheless wrong, because it ignored important poetic and dramatic effects within the Abraham play and ignored the construction of the Wakefield cycle as a whole. It is true that all Abraham-Isaac plays (or all mystery plays on any other subject) must deal with the same doctrinal matter; but it is not true that all playwrights set out to do exactly the same thing or that they succeed or fail in the same terms. A historical approach to the pageant subjects provides us with the playwright's point of departure, not his play. Some playwrights, of course, never got beyond their point of departure. Others wrote works of art which cannot be appreciated or understood until we have discovered by the techniques of literary criticism the exact reason why everything is as it is and not otherwise. . . .

Josie P. Campbell (essay date 1975)

SOURCE: "The Idea of Order in the Wakefield *Noah*,"

in *The Chaucer Review*, Vol. 10, No. 1, Summer, 1975, pp. 76-86.

[Here, Campbell suggests that the theme of Noah *is love and that the dramatic struggle in the play stems from the mistaken notion about mastery in marriage held by Noah and his wife.]*

On the surface, the Wakefield *Noah* seems to be simply a working out of its biblical counterpart. Noah's opening prayer states that the world suffers from a malaise. The prayer is a recapitulation of the history of mankind, beginning with the creation, moving to his lifetime, and looking toward doomsday; and Noah's story is that of a second creation following the destruction by flood of a sinful world. Yet the dramatization of what appears to be some of the traditional themes of the Noah story has misled some critics into confused, if not erroneous, readings of the drama. They fail to see that the theme of *Noah* is love and that the dramatic tension, very comically worked out in the family arena of domesticity, revolves around man's mistaken notion of "mastre."

Nearly all criticism of *Noah* begins with the premise that God created an ordered world that has since fallen into decay and disorder because of disobedience. If obedience could be restored, then the world would be saved. Noah is called on as a man of destiny because he is obedient to God, he is His trusted servant. Unfortunately, when Noah tries to exact obedience from his wife according to his understanding of what befits the "hierarchy" of things, he discovers how difficult it is to maintain order in his own home. Once Noah reasserts his "rightful" authority over his wife, however, the stars move into place, the flood recedes, and the microcosm harmoniously reflects the macrocosm once more. This critical view, generally accepted, although more eruditely stated, is marvelous romance, but it is a world apart from the Wakefield Master's play. The critics seem to have accepted at face value the conventions the dramatist included in the play, instead of realizing that he may have been attempting to explore their significance.

John Gardner is correct when he points out [in *Papers on Language and Literature* 4, (Winter, 1968)] that Noah has only half the story when he emphasizes God's power and man's debt of obedience in his opening prayer: "Whereas Noah's emphasis has been on the creature's debt to power, God's emphasis is on the creature's debt to divine love. Accord is thus not simply obedience, a negative quality, but also the positive quality, love." Gardner seems to suggest that the playwright is examining the very definition of obedience as a principle of accord. Yet Gardner fails to pursue this idea far enough to realize that, within the context of the play, Noah has to come to an understanding of the meaning of obedience, too. Noah sorely fears God's

power of vengeance over a world that has fallen into moral decay:

> Bot now before his sight / euery liffyng leyde,
> Most party day and nyght / syn in word and
>   dede ffull bold;
> Som in pride, Ire, and enuy,
> Som in Couet[yse] & glotyny,
> Som in sloth and lechery,
>   And other wise many fold.
>
>   (III. 48-54)

He sees the world deteriorating morally, a condition that is mirrored in his own physical deterioration:

> And now I wax old,
> seke, sory, and cold,
> As muk apon mold
>   I widder away. . . .
>
>   (III. 60-63)

His human response to his condition is twofold: a cry for mercy for himself and his family to be saved, both physically and morally. The prayer is from Noah, the "seruant," to his "lord" for protection; that is, it is a prayer to power in the name of obedience.

If God's soliloquy, however, stresses obedience in the name of His power, the strength of that power rests in love, an energizing force that permeates the universe:

> Me thoght I shewed man luf / when I made
>   hym to be
> All angels abuf / like to the trynyte. . . .
>
>   (III. 82-83)

Love is what ought to bind man to God: "Man must luf me paramoure" (80), but love has been forgotten. As a result, sin pervades the earth, and therefore God will work "thaym wo, / That will not repent." Only Noah, the "seruand," and his family will be saved. Implicit in the fact that God repeatedly calls Noah His servant and that He refers to Himself as Noah's "freend" is the bond of love that underlies the type of obedience that can save the world. And it is this idea that Noah must come to terms with on the human level if the world is to be created anew. He may not intellectualize this idea, but, more importantly, he enacts it.

When God speaks to Noah, He not only gives him the blueprints for the ark, but He suggests how to build the relationships between man and God, man and community, man and family, and man and nature that are essential to perpetuate the life of the earth. God's opening speech to Noah quite clearly establishes the first relationship:

> Noe, my freend, I thee commaund / from
>   cares the to keyle,

A ship that thou ordand / of nayle and bord
    ful wele.
Thou was alway well wirkand / to me trew as
    stele,
To my bydyng obediand / frendship shal thou
    fele
    To mede. . . .

                    (III. 118-22)

There are two conditions of this relationship that need to be noted, as well as the order in which they are stated. First of all, Noah is His friend, and that explains why the command is given to him. The idea of friendship is explicitly stated again in line 120, where Noah is referred to as "trew as stele." Moreover, God will return the friendship as a result of Noah's service. The order of service (or obedience, if one likes) and friendship is reversed in line 121 from that of line 117. They appear to be interchangeable; at least friendship and service go together.

After God gives Noah the instructions for building the ark, He proceeds to develop a guide for man's relationship with his community and with his family:

With the shal no man fyght / nor do the no
    kyn wrake.
When all is doyne thus right / thi wife, that is
    thi make,
  Take in to the;
Thi sonnes of good fame,
Sem, Iaphet, and Came,
Take in also hame,
  Thare wifis also thre.

                    (III. 138-44)

The emphasis is on accord, explicitly in the first two lines, and implicitly in the last lines. In addition, God implies that Noah should take care of his family; an essential part of man's relationship with his family, then, is the commitment to care for them. It is an important enough point for God specifically to include Noah's wife, his sons, and their wives. And Noah's relationship with nature also carries a commitment to care for the beasts brought on board the ark:

Of beestis, foull, and catayll / ffor thaym haue
    thou in thoght,
ffor thaym is my counsayll / that som socour
    be soght,
  In hast. . . .

                    (III. 156-58)

Out of some forty-three lines of instructions to Noah on building the ark, at least twenty are devoted to man and his personal relationship with his God and the world.

The strength of that relationship rests on commitment,

on whether or not man cares enough beyond himself. Undergirding the concept of commitment is love, God's love for man, which, if returned, vitalizes the earth. Noah instinctively recognizes the power of this kind of love when he says:

I thank the, lord, so dere / that wold vowch
    sayf
Thus low to appere / to a symple knafe;
Blis vs, lord, here / for charite I hit crafe,
The better may we stere / the ship that we
    shall hafe,
Certayn.

                    (III. 172-76)

It is this power of love that Noah will eventually take with him on that fragile ark so that they "shall wax and multiply, / And fill the erth agane. . . ."

The key to the play of **Noah,** then, is not merely obedience, in the sense of submission to control, but love and its resulting commitment to act upon that love. The whole middle section of the play dealing with Noah's relationship with his family works out this theme through the plot and its action. Just as there is a danger in ignoring the medieval cultural and social milieu and looking at the drama through twentieth-century eyes, there is equally a danger of imposing a cultural construction on the drama and ignoring its text. In some respects this has occurred in the criticism of *Noah,* and as a result the criticism fails to account for what actually takes place in the dialogue and action in the play.

The medieval belief in a hierarchical order in the world, beginning with God and moving down in a chain to angels, man, woman, child, and beast, has obscured most of the criticism of *Noah.* When this conception is applied to the play, it produces a conflation that has little to do with the Wakefield Master's dramatic effort. For example, V. A. Kolve is misled [in *The Play Called Corpus Christi,* 1966] into superimposing a definition of "mastre" on the Wakefield **Noah** that is contrary to the meaning of the play. Kolve's definition has to do with the assertion of "rightful" authority over what properly should be subject. Thus, only when Noah asserts his dominance over Uxor will the world be righted, the ark sail, and God be pleased.

But there is no evidence in the play that Noah ever succeeds in dominating Uxor by getting, so to speak, the upper hand. It is obvious, however, that she needs some sort of control, but it does not necessarily follow that Noah imposes it. Uxor herself is an interesting character, testy, quick to anger (in itself comic, since she is elected to be the mother of the new world). Noah recognizes that she is "full tethee," and she does not disappoint him or us when we first meet her. Her initial greeting to Noah is surely reminiscent of some wives the world over, not just medieval wives: she wants to know where he has been and why he stayed so long. Uxor is a materialist, although we are not quite sure how valid her complaint is that Noah is a poor provider:

> To dede may we dryfe / or lif for the,
>   ffor want.
> When we swete or swynk,
> thou dos what thou thynk,
> Yit of mete and of drynk
>   haue we veray skant.
>
> (III. 193-98)

There is, at least, some indication that her complaint is well-founded, since Noah replies, "Wife, we ar hard sted / with tythyngis new." The implication is that their old problems may have included poverty, but now they face additional trouble in the form of flood.

Uxor is very much like the Wife of Bath, who must have had her in mind when she said:

> Wommen desiren to have sovereynetee
> As wel over hir housbond as hir love,
> And for to been in maistrie hym above.

Like the Wife of Bath, Uxor delights in asserting herself over Noah "with gam & with gyle," to "smyte and smyle." In her opinion, she simply gives Noah what he deserves—and a little more: "Thou shal thre for two / I swere bi godis pyne." To her, Noah is a rather doddering old fool, easily fearful, and certainly not the best husband in the world. Uxor, like her sister, the Wife of Bath, is interested in material comfort, and Noah's tale of an ark is bothersome if it means she has to leave what she knows for what is unknown.

And in his domestic life, Noah could hardly be held up as a paragon of virtue. While it is true that we may sympathize with him because he has an overbearing wife, he is too quick to respond to Uxor's dare to strike her. He immediately forgets his commitment to build the ark and becomes embroiled in a battle with his wife. We do not think either Noah or Uxor malicious in their knockabout fight, but they are frivolous at a time when they can ill afford it. What stops their first fight is Noah's sudden remembrance of his task, triggered by his involuntary near-repetition of almost the same words God used in speaking to him: He would "fordo / All this medill-erd," a phrase that echoes in Noah's words to Uxor, "In fayth I hold none slyke / In all medill-erd." It is as if he is suddenly reminded of the doom hovering over "medill-erd" and realizes he should get to what is important. "Bot I will kepe charyte / ffor I haue at do." There is an almost unconscious acknowledgment that "charyte" is the binding force that will "kepe" the world. The first battle between Noah and Uxor simply dissipates with no one the

winner because of what appears to be an innate recognition in man that the rivalry for domination (or "mastre" in this sense of the word) is hardly worth the winning.

When Noah explains to Uxor that God intends to destroy the world, her fear is real enough to make her forget her querulousness:

> I wote neuer whedir,
> I dase and I dedir
> ffor ferd of that tayll.
>
> (III. 313-15)

And Noah spontaneously and immediately comforts her, "Be not aferd," and urges haste in getting their goods on the ark. Their three sons respond generously with their service, but Uxor's moment of fear is forgotten as she attempts to assert her role in the family and her parental authority: "Yit for drede of a skelp / help well thi dam" (323-24). The order she would like established is based on obedience, the sort of obedience which rests on the fear of physical retaliation. It is a wrong-headed notion of "mastre," and her sons presumably ignore her as they continue their work.

The final battle between Uxor and Noah occurs because of her stubborn refusal to leave her old home, what she is most familiar with, for a new. Even Noah's weather report of macrocosmic disorder, "And the planettis seuen / left has thare stall," fails to move her. Uxor's daughters-in-law also fail in their attempt to reason with her because her obstinate assertion of self can see no other logic than her own. It is only the reality of getting wet that forces her to board the ark; materialist that she is, seeing, or in this case, soaking, is believing. Again, it is not so much maliciousness on Uxor's part that prompts her obduracy as frivolity, a denial of commitment at a time when she should most care. There is no denying the danger she puts her family in, although she is seemingly unaware of it. She reveals more about herself than she realizes when she says: "In fath I can not fynd / which is before, which is behynd. . ." (330-31). Although she is speaking of the ark, it applies to her confusion of character as well. It is, of course, her very lack of faith, her lack of caring, that prevents her from entering the ship.

The crisis of the play occurs when Uxor rejects Noah's plea to act on his "frenship":

> Wheder I lose or I wyn / In fayth, thi
>   felowship,
> set I not at a pyn. . . .
>
> (III. 363-64)

The reversal comes about only through the final battle between husband and wife, a battle in which neither is the loser, and both are the winners. Kolve is right in the sense that "mastre" is the key to the brawling; it shapes the farce that contains the dramatic action between Noah and his wife. But "mastre" does not mean that Noah restores (or gains) domination over Uxor, despite what may be the "standard" medieval idea that a wife owes submission to her husband, analogous to the Church's submission to her Head. What does occur in the play as a result of the final battle is the disappearance of this notion of "mastre"; it simply drops out of the play as an irrelevancy as a new spirit of accord takes over.

In the final battle, Noah vainly attempts to assert masculine authority over Uxor, to beat her into submission until she cries "mercy." Uxor is just as determined not to submit, and they fight to a draw:

> *Vxor.* Out, alas, I am gone! / oute apon the,
>   mans wonder!
> *Noe.* Se how she can grone / and I lig vnder;
>   Bot, wife,
> In this hast let vs ho,
> ffor my bak is nere in two.
> *Vxor.* And I am bet so blo
>   That I may not thryfe.
>
> (III. 408-14)

Neither loses to the other in this fight; it is the absolute physical exhaustion of both that forces them to relinquish the battle for authority. Both husband and wife are chastised, and order is restored through a physical experience that makes them consider looking at their relationship in a different light.

It is their three sons who articulate the norm of the marital state, which has nothing in it of the tone of "mastre" or male sovereignty. Their words are to "ffader and moder both," and their advice is to learn to live together in a new spirit. Of course, it is really not a *new* spirit after all, if one recalls the words of God in *The Creation,* when He fashioned Eve from Adam's rib:

> therof shall be maide thi make,
>   And be to thi helpyng.
> Ye *both to gouerne* that here is, [my italics]
> and euer more to be in blis,
>   ye wax in my blissyng.
>
> (I. 187-91)

God's blessing emphasizes that true family order is based on accord, and "mastre" is irrelevant.

Noah, father and "head" of his household, accepts the advice from his sons; he suggests a different sort of relationship by saying, "we will do as ye bid vs / we will no more be wroth." Both Noah and Uxor turn to the task ahead of them with similar prayers to God for His help. Husband and wife now work together, and

neither could be considered master of the other. Uxor freely tends the helm, while Noah takes soundings of the depths of water. Noah asks his wife for counsel when the birds are released to find land, and when she makes a mistake and suggests the raven, Noah merely substitutes the dove. It can be argued that the raven is an appropriate choice for Uxor to make; it suits her sensual character. But the point the dramatist intends is finally that it does not matter. If the audience laughs, thinking this is one more bit of evidence that Uxor lacks reason, the joke recoils on them, because of its unimportance. Although Uxor erroneously suggested the raven be released, she does, nevertheless, correctly interpret the meaning of the dove—"A trew tokyn ist / we shall be sauyd all."

The comic structure of *Noah* follows a pattern that Shakespeare was to use later in many of his comedies. It involves a movement from an old order to a new, and frequently the voice of the new order belongs to youth. In the play of *Noah,* the old order is corrupt and rotten because man has ceased to care. He is no longer committed enough to "luf" God "paramoure." As a result, man sins, thoughtlessly and carelessly, "in word and dede / ffull bold," and this leads to the chaos that must be purged with the flood. Noah and his wife show how dangerous noncommitment can be. Yet, Noah is selected to bring to the new world the best out of the old; before he can do that, however, he and his wife need to learn what makes for true order. After the ark is completed, Noah grasps intuitively something of the force that preserves life:

> This will euer endure / therof am I paide;
>   ffor why?
> It is better wroght
> Then I coude haif thoght;
> hym that maide all of noght
>   I thank oonly.
>
> (III. 283-88)

But it takes several very human skirmishes for Noah and his wife to see concretely in their own domestic life what comes from caring enough. None of the above discussion is intended to suggest that the Wakefield Master was an ardent supporter of women's liberation or that he suddenly ripped asunder the hierarchical order of the medieval world. Order is maintained, but the bond of order is love, not "mastre" in the sense of authoritative domination.

God has "luf" for man, and so speaks to a "symple knafe," who out of love responds willingly. Noah seeks God's blessing out of "charite," and in turn, at least once, spontaneously, keeps charity at home with Uxor. But Noah and Uxor have their failings: they are all too human in forgetting that as they should care for the beasts on the ark, they should also give some care out of "felowship" for each other. Unfortunately, it is also perhaps too human that they must beat each other to a standstill in order to realize, from the quiet voices of their children, that in losing their individual struggle for domination, they literally win a battle for mankind.

Clifford Davidson (essay date 1982)

SOURCE: "Jest and Earnest: Comedy in the Work of the Wakefield Master," in *Annuale Mediaevale*, Vol. 22, 1982, pp. 65-83.

[*In the essay below, Davidson discusses the use of visual comedy in the Wakefield plays, focusing on* Second Shepherd's Play, Coliphizacio, Magnus Herodes, *and* Judicium. *He stresses that the combination of humor and high didactic seriousness in the rhetorical style of the plays "provides a surprisingly strong presentation."*]

The contribution of the Wakefield Master to the Towneley Manuscript has been carefully studied, and on the whole his work has received the highest praise from those who focus on theatrical skill rather than moral purpose or theological intent. He has been called a "genius," a writer with "remarkable gifts," one of the "best writers of [the] age," a master of "humour." It is, however, the supreme sense of the comic which marks the work of this dramatist, whose practice of comedy remains controversial among those who, like Eleanor Prosser, stress the importance of the didactic in medieval religious drama. But many of the difficulties perceived in the work of the Wakefield Master by antagonistic critics will be seen to disappear when careful attention is given to the context of the comedy, particularly when it is examined from a larger perspective than merely the *text* as set forth in the Towneley Manuscript. Careful attention to the *visual* side of the performance of the drama is, therefore, crucial for a proper understanding of the plays. This latter task can, of course, be made possible only through carefully chosen comparisons with the visual arts, for iconographic principles were often involved in the presentation of what we otherwise might see merely as the most lively literary horseplay.

It may also be useful to assert at the start that the intent of the Wakefield Master's plays is assuredly sacred, and also that an important clue to their use of the comic in the working out of action and spectacle may be found in the medieval understanding of *jest and earnest* as discussed in an important chapter in Ernst Curtius' *European Literature and the Latin Middle Ages*. In particular, the principle of *ridendo dicere verum*, which Curtius derives from later classical practice and which he identifies as a characteristic of the preaching of the later Middle Ages, describes with great precision what happens in the religious drama which includes the comic. Rhetorically, the mixed style which

brings together the high *seriousness* of devotional writing (joined, of course, to visual display in the acting out of the drama) with *jest* provides a surprisingly strong presentation.

I

In the work of the Wakefield Master as in medieval drama and literature generally, the category of the *comic* is, of course, much broader than *comedy* regarded merely as a genre. Thus, this genre in Middle English has only a single fully developed example—the Wakefield Master's ***Second Shepherds' Play***—in spite of the large amount elsewhere of the comic included within the extant religious and moral plays. Only in this one play is there the kind of plot structure that Northrop Frye characterizes as comedy—i.e., a ternary form that turns on rebelliousness and its triumph, followed by a very satisfactory conclusion that restores order. Parts I and II of this familiar play introduce the trickster Mak and show him in his triumph of deception, which is then spoiled by the comic action of the shepherds Coll, Gib, and Daw who feel impelled to present a gift to "the child"; Part III, following the mock punishment of Mak, dramatizes the triumphant theme of the Incarnation, followed by the shepherds in this instance giving symbolic gifts to the Child. In the end, however, the comic has been shown to have been purposeful. The stable where the Child is adored is the center of the world, the focus for all order; Mak's house, on the other hand, had been the opposite, an unfocused location that gave emphasis not only to the comedy-as-comedy but also to the absurdity of rebellion. Jest has its culmination in the sacred tableau of the Nativity and the epiphany scene in which divinity is first revealed to man through the humble shepherds.

But normally in the work of the Wakefield Master, the comic exists within other kinds of structures and in contexts that are distinct from what today is labelled *comic form*. In these other plays, therefore, the idea of *jest mixed with earnest*, utilizing the principle especially of *ridendo dicere verum*, remains very important indeed. Hence, for example, the very funny but also terrifying counting out of the sheaves by Cain in the Wakefield Master's ***Mactacio Abel*** serves to dramatize the exercise of essential stinginess at a most inappropriate time. The counting, surely highlighted by gestures and the manner of the actor's speech, reminds the audience of their own natural selfishness, but this is carefully done within a framework which establishes Cain's actions as absurd. Attempting to proclaim himself an autonomous man, Cain's mistreatment of those under him or equal with him and also his rebellion against the God who is over him separate him from the sympathy of those watching the play. However, if the religious framework were taken away, the comedy indeed would fail here in large measure.

Philosophically and theologically, the Middle Ages tended to expect earthly things and earthly acts to be imperfect reflections of the almost geometrical order of perfect divinity. Beauty in the arts therefore somehow reflects that perfection, though indeed in its effort to make us recall or remember the idea it may function in two ways: either through direct representation of the vision of harmony, or through distortion—the introduction of the absurd—in order to shock viewers and listeners into an understanding that is more perfect. The ugly and grotesque provide impetus toward the harmonious and heavenly. As Hugh of St. Victor wrote, "The ugliness of base objects does not allow us to linger quietly over them, but drives us away to seek other objects which are true and beautiful" [from Edgar de Bruyne, *Études d'ésthétique médiévale*]. Hence in the comic, imperfect shapes provide the important source of a "double vision" which has been identified as characteristic.

In the **Second Shepherds' Play,** therefore, language and action which have often been thought to be indicative only of the motive of *fun*—i.e., play and recreation which have their end in the activity itself—suggest instead the rather ordinary lives of men in need of grace. These biblical shepherds, who appear in the play in the guise of inhabitants of Yorkshire, are in spite of their lowly origin men who are among the favored of the earth, since it was to them that the Incarnation was first revealed. Here, as in the illustrations showing them in the visual arts, they are at once very much contemporary rustics and also musicians who can, at least haltingly, imitate the heavenly music. In visual examples, shepherds are commonly associated, of course, with music, and are often shown with musical instruments, especially bagpipes and other rural instruments. By the late Middle Ages, the shepherds to whom the angel Gabriel announces the birth of Christ seem also to have merged thoroughly with representatives of a pastoral tradition still alive from antiquity; hence a miniature in Bibliothèque Nationale MS. lat. 9471 shows a cluttered rural scene with musical and other rustic activity seemingly taking place almost oblivious of the announcement being made by the angels above. So too does the opening portion of the **Second Shepherds' Play** seem oblivious of what is to come later after the shepherds hear the angel's announcement, which not only transforms their lives but also marks the entry of the transcendent into history.

Quite appropriately, the element of the grotesque as introduced into the play is focused about the distorted figure of Mak, the imposter who announces his false character to the audience through his affectation of Southern speech—i.e., a speech that would have been identified as not only "foreign" but also associated with hated Southern officialdom. The contempt for the "South" is still strong in Yorkshire, where southern England, especially including London and Westminster, is even today considered effete and decadent. At the same time, Mak's foreign nature is also indicated through his name, which is indicative of an origin not in Yorkshire but of a region yet further north—i.e., Scotland. Scots border raids as far south as Yorkshire were known as late as the fourteenth century. Phenomenologically, Mak is therefore an outsider, and one who does not belong among the shepherds to whom the revelation of the Incarnation will be made. His knowledge of charms furthermore links him with occult folk arts passed down from pre-Christian times. Through this character, therefore, the stage is set for an outrageous parodying of the Christian story in advance of its happening. But of course the recounting of the story of the Annunciation to the Shepherds in the Towneley plays is not to be confused with the historical event itself, for it is only a way of remembering and *re*-creating the events which have already taken place in sacred history. The audience thus only looks on as the actors present scenes which show events not as they actually happened, but *as if* they were happening before the people's eyes. In such a re-creation as this, Mak is not to be seen as a real biblical character, though through his association with a principle of perversity that is entirely biblical he represents something that has indeed always been present among post-lapsarian human beings.

The foreigner Mak thus is the antithesis of the Good Shepherd who looks for the lost sheep in the well-known parable; instead he causes a sheep to be lost, whereupon he and his shrewish wife place it in a cradle and pretend that she has brought a new infant into the world. The sheep is the mock *Agnus Dei*—a desacralized version of the Child and also of the Eucharist which extends Christ's presence as the Lamb of God into the contemporary world. In particular the parodying of the Eucharist is a very important element, for Mak's references to eating "this chylde / That lygys in this credyll" (11.537-38) identify the meaning of the animal in relation to the structure of the Nativity story. Outrageous in its application of the comic even to the point of blasphemy, the visual presentation is *absurd* in the sense that it reflects as if in a mirror the nature of the divine event, for in a mirror right becomes left and left becomes right. Things are precisely turned around, and this is done in such a way as to call into play the audience's sense of comedy's "double vision" and its release into laughter at the impossibility of *things seen*. The *things seen* are precisely opposed to the *things done*—i.e., the ritual effects, especially within the structure of the Mass in which the Incarnation is made present for the participation of the congregation.

But a comparison may also be made with the tendency in the visual arts to parody sacred events in order to achieve grotesque scenes and absurd representations. The mimicking of that which cannot be successfully mimicked is known, of course, through the Fall of Lucifer, the imposter in the Towneley **Creation** who sits on God's seat and apparently assumes that *by appearance* he has as much right to sit there "as god hymself, if he were here" (1.125). But mimesis has its limits, and Lucifer discovers upon his arrival in hell that his previous posturing had been absurd, comic, and disastrous with regard to all his ambitions. This parodying of divine power is precisely set forth in the miniature on fol. 2 of the *Holkham Bible Picture Book*. Here God is shown in the center with his compasses in his right hand—symbolic of his role as Creator—while directly above him is Lucifer, usurping God's seat and pointing with his *left* hand toward himself. The good angels on Lucifer's *right* turn away in horror, while those on his *left* are giving him encouragement (one is offering him a crown). The joke is, of course, that at the bottom of the miniature is the mouth of hell, flamming and ready for those who will be transformed from angels into fiends. The transformation, shown in progress in a panel of painted glass in St. Michael, Spurriergate, York, and also in another example in the Great East Window in York Minster, is frightening enough in art, but in drama with its livelier form of presentation the effect must have been even more shocking. Furthermore, in both picture and play the event involved matters which imply an implicit comparison between *seeming* and *reality,* for the demons are those who were impossibily perverse romantics in their humorless striving for the empty fruits of ambition.

Another useful example from the visual arts which may be noted here as a parodying of sacred events is the "monkey funeral" in the painted glass in one of the nave windows of York Minster. It has recently been pointed out that this scene would appear to parody rather precisely the iconography of the Funeral of the Virgin. At the front of the procession is a monkey ringing handbells, followed by a monkey crucifer; thereupon come the pall bearers with the bier, which is being apparently attacked by another monkey in the same manner that the Jew named "Fergus" in the York plays would seem to have assaulted the bier of the Blessed Virgin—an assault that had precipitated laughter and sport during the production of the York play. If the scene is not recognized as parody of a sacred scene, it would seem perhaps no more daring than such representations as those showing a fox preaching from a pupit, as on misericords at Lincoln, Ripon, Beverley Minster, and elsewhere—a scene echoed in the Wakefield Master's *Mactacio Abel* ("let furth youre geyse; the fox will preche," 1. 84). But when specific parody of the sacred events is recognized, the effect of the *absurd* is much stronger, with the intent surely being to exploit the comic in a manner which does not point back upon itself but which directs the attention of the audience toward the divine realities. Jest and earnest are mixed in such a way as to emphasize the essential distortion of reality which may evoke laughter that in turn directs the mind back to the harmonious and beautiful and eternal. The effect more immediately is the release in recreative laughter, we should imagine; such release exorcises the evil without harm to the viewer. It is hence no accident that the **Second Shepherds' Play** therefore merely punishes Mak by having him tossed in a blanket—a punishment that, because of its traditional association with childbirth, ought to be linked to creativity. Ultimately Mak's malice, theft, and deception are paradoxically turned to creative use as the shepherds now are prepared to encounter the divine principle of creativity itself at Bethlehem.

II

As the discussion above has suggested, examples of the absurd in the visual arts may serve as important glosses on comic scenes and comic lines in those medieval religious plays which utilize the comic as a dramatic strategy. In the drama there is present, as Kolve insisted [in *The Play Called Corpus Christi,* 1966], a sense of *play* or *game*. These two terms are almost interchangeable for designating the drama presented on stage for the delight and participation of audiences, and they thus would appear to be regarded as synonymous in *A Tretise of Miraclis Pleyinge*. Kolve's important analysis of the **Coliphizacio** emphasizes the way in which the grim humor of the torturers indeed draws heavily on the actual medieval game, Hot Cockles, which is illustrated in three miniatures in the margins of Bodleian MS. 264, fols. 52, 97, 132ᵛ. That the **Coliphizacio** is not unique in thus visualizing the Buffeting is proved by other examples in the visual arts, including the alabaster published by W.L. Hildburgh in which Christ, who has been blindfolded and placed on a seat, is being taunted and hit on the head by his torturers in the way described as appropriate for Hot Cockles. The object of the game is to *"rede him that smote him,"* but Christ refuses to *play* and hence retains a dignity that emphasizes his patient suffering in the manner prescribed by late medieval accounts of his Passion.

The torturers are very human, with minds enclosed within their own selves and unable to see the cosmic absurdity of their actions. "They know not what they do," the words from the cross tell us. Their focus on themselves—a focus shared with Lucifer in the miniature in the *Holkham Bible Picture Book* which shows him pointing to himself—shows the lack of that charity that according to St. Augustine ought to radiate outward and to include others instead of the self alone. But no one is free from this turning inward of the will to love, particularly in moments of discomfort of either a physical or psychological sort. It is something very clear in the sculpture illustrating a man with a toothache at Wells, where the sufferer's gesture also has a deliberate absurdity. The same is true also of the much earlier "naughty" scenes of sexual desire in the borders of the Bayeaux Tapestry, completed in 1077, or in the later examples of bestial passion such as that represented in the sheep having intercourse in Merton College MS. 0.1.3, fol. 111ᵛ. And even nudity itself, considered comic during the Middle Ages, could be the source of an uncomfortable humor, as in the illustrations in the visual arts of the Expulsion from Eden which show Adam and Eve in extreme discomfort going forth into the world. Dramatic records show that nudity in the Creation plays was simulated by leather suits prepared for Adam and Eve, the unselfconscious nudity of man's unfallen parents could only therefore be recovered in play, while their self-conscious awareness of their naked bodies after the Fall is presumably through gestures and tableaux made to reflect the absurdity of all wrongheaded human behavior. To be engaged in the comic to the point of laughter therefore releases the spectator from his own tendency to shut out all but his own perverse vision with its self-love and paranoia.

These individual characteristics seem nowhere more prominent in secular iconography than in representation of husband-wife squabbles, obviously precipitated by shrewish wives. Examples are legion, expecially in woodcarvings and other minor arts. At Fairford, for example, a misericord shows a wife beating her husband with a scoop while she holds him by the hair. In a fifteenth-century misericord at Holy Trinity Church, Stratford-upon-Avon, a woman is beating a man with a pan and is pulling his beard. At Beverley Minster, a third misericord shows a woman being wheeled in a wheelbarrow by a man, whose hair is being pulled by her. Examples of this kind could be multiplied *ad infinitum*, of course, and it is also clear that we are dealing with the stuff of farce—e.g., as in John Heywood's *Johan Johan the Husbande, Tib his Wife, and Sir Johan the Preest*. Such commentary, often anti-feminist in nature, on domestic troubles provides a comic release from burdens which potentially threaten all of us, whether men or women.

Noah's wife as presented by the Wakefield Master is thus also more than merely an anti-feminist portrait, for she is the overly aggressive wife who willingly violates the personhood of her husband and shows her limited quality of mind in words and deeds. Additionally, she has no sense of humor. If the ancient tradition that the devil used her to attempt to prevent the floating of the ark finds its reflection here, she also as the second mother of the race illustrates the kind of perversity that characterizes human behavior even when the individuals involved are not among the reprobates to be grouped at the left hand of God at the Last Day. She threatens her husband, Noah, with a terrible beating when she says that he is "worthi [to] cled in Stafford blew" (l. 200), and to the wives in the audience she promises that she "shall smyte and smyle, / And qwite hym his mede" (l. 215-16). Noah insultingly orders her to "hold thi tong, ram-skyt, or I shall the still" (l. 217). Blows are exchanged, surely with the

effect of stirring laughter in the contemporary audience. Clearly neither character possesses the sense, perspective, or insight that would allow the settlement of grievances. When their spat is over, however, they return to their occupations: she spins, as we would expect of a daughter of Eve, and he goes about building the ark, which will be the means by which the race will be saved from the Flood. The ark, as an emblem representing the Christian Church, however, signifies a different perspective, and after her reluctance to join the company on the boat, the wife then not only comes aboard but, once she is there, her attitude is eventually transformed, though this does not happen before more comic squabbling between the husband, who threatens to beat her until she breaks wind (l. 382), and the wife. A panel in the East Window in York Minster shows her on the ark and still clearly showing her bad temper, but essentially the Flood must be seen as forcing her to put strife aside in favor of a more serious attitude toward the situation and toward her husband.

Informed as it is by comic iconography, the scenes which show Noah and his wife at strife again illustrate the absurdity of human behavior which closes in upon itself and which loses sight of the divine perspective. It therefore is most important to see that the play presents *spectacle* here and not merely a text, and it is the visual tableau as it shifts itself through the scene that communicates the principal meanings. These meanings normally are not something occult and hidden—i.e., meanings which can be uncovered only in the twentieth century by the subtleties of literary criticism. The strife of Noah and his wife is comic for a reason, and that reason appears to be quite simply the display of an absurdity which has the phenomenological function of freeing the members of the audience from a humorless (and therefore joyless) existence.

III

In the Towneley cycle, the principal exemplar of the humorless mind, which William F. Lynch has called [in *Christ and Apollo*, 1960] the "univocal mind," is surely the tyrant Herod, who extends the malice of Cain into an entire social order for which he as king ought to be responsible. Iconographically, this figure is not necessarily comic at all. At Fairford, he appears in the painted glass in the nave clerestory with a child impaled on his weapon. He is the very unfunny killer responsible for the death of the Innocents in an insane attempt to destroy the Christ Child—an attempt that even takes away the life of his own son, if we are to believe apocryphal tradition. The Wakefield Master's *Magnus Herodes,* however, makes the king an indecorous tyrant who shouts out in his anger and insists upon enforcing his unorthodox beliefs upon his subjects. He nearly explodes in his anger and, though he does not die at the end of the play (he merely breaks off with the exclamation "I can no more Franch" [l.

513] and leaves the stage—surely to the accompaniment of uneasy laughter), he nevertheless illustrates the same *deadly* singleness of mental attitude that severs itself from the principle of *life* because it fails to recognize a larger truth in things.

In the visual arts in the late Middle Ages, Herod is portrayed in various ways, usually emphasizing his demonic character but also depicting him as a king. His legs are frequently crossed in the regal posture, though the sense of balance usually present in the portrayal of a rightful king seems somehow missing. He may have a black face, indicating his extreme malice and anger, and a crown which is awry or grotesque, indicating that his pretension to kingly power and glory is based illegitimately in demonic power. At the same time, if there is a comic element in the appearance of Herod, the comedy completely escapes the tyrant himself. His sense of humor is necessarily entirely missing. The true nature of this kind of character is perhaps best expressed in an example in a panel of painted glass from St. Michael Spurriergate, York, where in spite of misguided restoration recently (as Solomon, made up from various pieces of glass!) the figure seems to be Herod wearing a grotesque demon crown—a head gear, therefore, that is entirely appropriate in its perversity.

The reception of Herod on stage in the Towneley play is quite certainly indicated in the text of the drama, for Herod's opening lines are indicative of unrestrained malice and of hostility toward everyone present, including the audience watching the play. His line "Stynt, brodels, youre dyn—yei, euerychon!" (l. 82) is directed not only at actors on stage, but also at the spectators, who seem to have responded jeeringly upon the appearance of the tyrant. Furthermore, his rhetoric is calculated to stress the absurdity of his logic, which is the logic of a man whose authority is undermined by elements that are beyond his understanding. Like Lucifer, his conception of his power involves mere control over events in his kingdom; without the reciprocal functioning of rightful rule, he cannot be a creative ruler. Hence he will become destructive, striking blindly and ineffectively in the Massacre of the Innocents. The violence of his words when he discovers the possibility that a young king and savior may have been born in his kingdom are ironically indicative of his own terrible fate—a fate which, however, is not dramatized in the Towneley play.

> My guttys will outt thryng
> Bot I this lad hyng;
> Withoutt I haue a vengyng,
> I may lyf no langer.
>
> (ll. 240-43)

Here, then, is the "univocal" mentality of which Father Lynch speaks, for Herod epitomizes supreme disrespect for "reality"—and indeed he does everything in his *power* to destroy that reality. Furthermore, while attempting to appear to be the "man of decision," Herod is indeed "the very reverse." It is not he who thinks of the plan to kill the Innocents, therefore, but rather the idea comes from his advisors. Herod, of course, greets the plan with glee—"my hart is rysand now in a glope!" (l. 264)—and proceeds to make insincere promises— e.g., "to make the[e] a pope" (l. 263).

Nevertheless, as Father Lynch points out, the "univocal man" is hardly free to act:

> He is rigid, unbending, fixed. One can understand the fixity of the ideas of logic and essences, but *his* fixed ideas are born of a fixity of all the forces in his personality and a refusal to remain open to existence. He is simply not free.

Comedy thus destroys the pretensions to super-human power of Herod, and shows him to be a ridiculous figure after all in spite of his terrible display of malice in ordering the Massacre of the Innocents. Indeed, even the Massacre itself is a demonstration that by attempting to act like an autonomous man, he is least able to achieve human dignity and freedom. Instead, he is an example of the grotesque and the source of derision as well as the cause of uneasy laughter. The audience thus has *not* identified itself with the character through any bond of empathy, but instead has made Herod *the Great* the butt of its scornful laughter.

Herod is therefore the kind of character Northrop Frye identifies as the *alazon,* the impostor, whose inverted values specify a relationship to the *topos* of "the world upside down." Completely lacking in the kingly virtue of magnificence, Herod turns the world order upside down in an amazing display of outrageous child-murder. The absurdity of such a world-upside-down is as much in evidence in the Wakefield Master's play as it is in extant examples of the humorous *topos* in the visual arts—e.g., a misericord in which the cart is before the horse at Beverley. The conclusion of the ***Magnus Herodes*** therefore appropriately shows Herod speaking directly to the audience and expressing his pleasure about the horrible deeds he has done. He has no guilt, for in his psychopathic way he has found murder to be the way to uphold his crown. The lawless king now is deceived into believing that he is free, while the members of the audience know that the opposite is indeed the case. His hollow bragging, which obviously was designed to elicit response from the audience, ends with threatening but not wholly coherent ranting—ranting which itself concludes with the advice "Bese not to[o] cruell" and a swift "Bot adew!—to the deuyll!" (ll. 511-12). To the devil he will indeed go with the malediction of the audience, if we are to accept the usual account of his final sickness and death, which are graphically depicted on the roof bosses at Norwich Cathedral.

IV

In the Towneley *Judicium,* which is incomplete in the manuscript, the Wakefield Master's additions to a previously extant play (borrowed from the York cycle) are very obviously intended to enliven a solemn play with comic elements. In particular, the Wakefield Master in his revision of the play introduces the grotesquerie of demons, whose role in the late medieval drama had been much expanded. We know that the costume of the late medieval devil was at once both frightening and comic since it displayed both evil and the absurd so supremely well, with grotesque masks and other features calculated to evoke uneasy laughter. In the dramtic records, hairy suits and cloth clubs are also assigned to stage demons, while from other sources we know that the sounds, including distorted music, associated with them were scatological and unharmonious. Can we assume that the singing of the demons in the Wakefield *Judicium* (ll. 536-37) would have been other than cacophonous and obscene? The acts of demons are, we know, of a piece with Cain's presumably indecent gestures to his brother in the *Mactacio Abel* when he tells him to "grese thi shepe vnder the toute" (l. 64) or to "kys the dwill right in the ars" (l. 287). An example of such an inappropriate act is illustrated in the well-known miniature by Jean Fouquet showing the martyrdom of St. Apollonia in which a reprobate is exposing his buttocks indecently to the saint, who is being tortured behind him.

Like Cain, demons attempt to dominate reality instead of participating in it. Thus, of course, they must repeat the Luciferian pattern. In the end, they are required to represent a principle of sadistic fixity which will inflict itself on that portion of mankind that does not choose release from the univocal mentality. In one sense these demons as they are present at the Last Day of history may seem not at all comic, for they represent the justified fears of the race concerning potential consignment to everlasting punishment "in pyk and tar euer dwelland" (l. 598). The devils have come to claim their own now, and there is no guarantee for anyone that he or she will not be among those enchained and dragged off to hell as illustrated, for example, in the restored wall painting over the chancel arch of the Church of St. Thomas of Canterbury at Salisbury. In spite of the "double vision" of the comic through which the release of laughter might be achieved, the vision nevertheless might be not at all funny under its surface. Again, appeal will need to be to the medieval rhetorical practice of mixing the serious and the absurd— *ludicra seriis miscere*—in order to move the mind toward a true understanding of reality. The comic thus serves here to impress serious things upon the mind of the spectator. Demonic rebellion is, of course, shown to be utterly futile in the end, and it proves the correctness of Hugh of St. Victor's insistence upon the usefulness of the comic in turning the mind from the gro-

tesque toward the more perfect and harmonious forms. Though demons and hellmouth seem more lively, the mind and soul cannot rest there; instead, it seems to be more spiritually healthy to turn away to the contemplation of the suffering of another, whose pain is emblemized in the Wakefield *Judicium* through the display of the wounds of the Savior (ll. 402-24). These wounds are *things seen* by those actors representing both good souls and bad, but for the good they are also truly *things done* in order that man may have salvation. But such salvation may not be achieved otherwise than by participation in the reality of the scene, and participation indeed cannot itself begin at the last moment of history, for then the time for participation will have ceased. Instead, the good souls must within their lifetimes have taken up actions identified by the Church as the Seven Corporal Acts of Mercy, which are remembered at the Last Day when the way is opened up for entrance into the harmonious bliss of heaven.

When the world of the demons is examined, it makes us realize quite forcibly that we are here among shadows and illusions. In this place the impostors of the race who are Cain's kin will have their fixed and final places, and the false pretensions of all will finally be unmasked. Proud pope or proud woman alike will be subjected to the cruel laughter of the demonic choristers whose sense of the comic excludes all sense of fun except at others' expense. Yet to see them is to exorcise them. The Wakefield Master did not repress the fears that all felt then concerning their potential for personal eschatological disaster; rather, to present the nightmare on stage meant that the fears could be ventilated and reduced through the human laughter which takes away tension from the mind and gives health to the soul.

Thus it is that the presence of such a popular demon as Tutivillus in the Towneley *Judicium* functions to place the events being depicted in the dramatic spectacle into perspective both emotionally and intellectually. He happens to be the devil assigned to collect the words skipped and mumbled in Mass and also the words uttered by "kyrkchaterars"—words which he writes down on a roll and stuffs into his bag—in addition to some other added duties in this play. In English medieval art he is shown on a benchend at Charlton Mackrell, where he is busily entering words on a fully extended roll with his right hand while he holds another, which is rolled up, with the claws of his left. Here he is, of course, a typically ugly little devil, with a tail and a repulsive little mask peering out from the area of his genitals. At Roskilde Cathedral in Denmark, Tutivillus appears in a wall painting dated 1511 in the Chapel of St. Bridget of Sweden; in this instance, he appears seated with legs crossed (he has one foot with claws and another with a hoof) and is writing on a piece of parchment, while an ink pot stands beside him. An inscription on a scroll proclaims "I write the names of those who are late or waste time in idle talk." The Wakefield Master also, on the basis of tradition, gives Tutivillus a horn, making him a musician demon of the type illustrated in the wall painting of hell mouth in the Guild Chapel at Stratford-upon-Avon. But his music, like his acts in writing down the verbal slips and indiscretions in church, could not have been very admirable ultimately, for the one must have shown his incompetence and the other his malice from a comic perspective. None of this, however, argues for understanding the Wakefield Master's additions to the Judgment play as mere "tampering" with the sacred story.

Comic response as a healthy reaction to Tutivillus' acts is indeed recorded in a medieval account that is included in Robert Mannyng of Brunne's *Handlyng Synne,* which thus provides us with an important explanation with regard to the medieval way of seeing this devil as he performs his tasks during a church service. As a holy man (sometimes elsewhere identified as St. Martin) was saying Mass, the deacon while he was reading the Gospel broke into "a grete laghter." After the conclusion of the Mass, the priest questioned the deacon about his laughter, and the latter responded as follows:

> "As y redde þat ychë tyde,
> Twey wymmen langled þere besyde;
> Betwyx hem to, y say a fende
> with penne and parchëmen yn honde,
> And, wrote alle þat euer þey spake,
> Pryuyly be-hynde here bake.
>   whan hys rolle was wryte all ful,
> To drawe hyt oute he gan to pul;
> with hys teþe he gan to drawe,
> And hardë for to tugge and gnawe,
> Þat hys rolle to-braste and rofe;
> And hys hede ayens þe walle drofe
> So hard, and so ferly sore,
> Whan hys parchemen was no more."
>
>   (ll. 9277-90)

When the deacon saw what was happening, he burst into laughter which in turn had its effect on the demon:

> ". . .when he parceyued þat y wyste,
> He al to-drofe hyt [his writing] with hys fyste,
> And went a-way, alle for shame;
> Þarfore y logh and hadde gode game."
>
>   (ll. 9295-98)

It is, however, in another account of this episode, Caxton's *Book of the Knight of the Tower,* that conveniently provides the explanation that is most relevant to the discussion of the comic in the Towneley *Judicium.* Here the deacon is identified as St. Brice, whose words explaining what he has seen which has inspired

his laughter actually prove something most significant to the priest: "And whan seint Martin herde hym, he knewe that seint Brice was an holy man." So too did medieval audiences know that the laughter they directed at such devils was not merely hostile or subversive.

Laughter in the Towneley *Judicium* and elsewhere in the work of the Wakefield Master was therefore an accepted part of the response of audiences to the late medieval vernacular religious drama, and in no sense can the comic which elicited such laughter be consigned merely to the category of "evidence of increasing secularization" or pointless "comic relief." Because of the deliberate rhetorical practice of mixing jest with earnest, the playwright's work which includes the comic was designed to serve a definite psychological and intellectual function in the service of the devotional intent of the plays. Through their spectacle, furthermore, the dramas extend the comic beyond the region of mere literature; when presented on stage, they illustrate not only the absurdities of human existence but also the standard against which those absurdities will need to be tested.

Martin Stevens (essay date 1987)

SOURCE: "The Wakefield Cycle: The Playwright as Poet," in *Four Middle English Mystery Cycles: Textual, Contextual, and Critical Interpretations*, Princeton University Press, 1987, pp. 88-180.

[*Stevens argues that a single individual, the Wakefield Master, was the compiler of the Wakefield cycle, marshalling historical, metrical, and "circumstantial" evidence to support his claim.*]

. . .[The] York cycle developed over the years as a corporate enterprise. As civic pageantry it apparently started in improvisational performance, gradually became recorded in a series of texts by the performing guilds, and eventually was compiled by the city fathers into a register, or a permanent, unified text that functioned both as official source and archival record. The whole play, in process and product, was a municipal enterprise of self-examination and self-celebration, and the York cycle as a whole was the first true "city play" in the history of the English drama.

The Wakefield cycle (if that is, indeed, the proper name for the collection of plays that survive in the Towneley volume of mystery plays now held by the Huntington Library MS HM 1) presents a very different case. Here we have a cycle that was quite clearly written and compiled for a much smaller community, which through commercial growth had at a certain point in its history become sufficiently prosperous to sponsor a Corpus Christi play. It was consequently built from scratch. The text, if it did not precede the performance, was at least coeval with it. In the Wakefield cycle then, we preserve more nearly a product than the record of a process, and the product we retain seems to have been the work of a single, guiding intelligence from the very beginning. While it has been customary to regard the well-known "Wakefield Master" in the same light as the "York Realist," or whatever name we wish to bestow upon that particular contributor to the York cycle, a strong case can be made for the Wakefield Master to have been the principal compiler and the guiding intelligence of the Wakefield cycle.

My argument is admittedly circumstantial. It is based on a reinterpretation of the Wakefield stanza, and it depends fundamentally on how authorship—that is, the invention and even the disposition and elocution of a narrative—functioned as creative acts in the Middle Ages. If I am right that in the plays of the Towneley manuscript we have a fully evolved text rather than the gradual compilation of a performance (that is to say, a text like that of York for which the expectation of growth was a built-in condition of its very existence), then the so-called Wakefield cycle is a model of mystery cycles quite different from that of York. While this second generation of English cycles was not exactly cut out of whole cloth—it was more nearly a patchwork of many fabrics—it was, from the beginning, the work of a compiler, and to the extent that he worked with a design of his own choice, the cycle is primarily a literary original and not an anthology edited for a reasonably uniform style and conceptual design. I am convinced that the Wakefield Master wrote his Shepherds play twice precisely because he was a poet, who, like Langland, needed to explore alternative possibilities, not because they were already there (in acting versions) but because they were provocative options. Any text that gives such a choice is, by its very nature, literary. It is addressed to a reader (who might, of course, be a theatrical director), and it invites that reader to choose one play over the other, or, at very least, to allow the one to resonate against the other. (The *Second Shepherds' Play* is entitled simply *alia eorundum*, "another of the same.") But whatever the choice, the very fact that there are two shepherds' plays creates a redundancy rich in potential reader response. I believe that of the other extant cycles, N-Town is very much like the plays of the Towneley manuscript, while Chester. . .is a mixture: It is at once a consciously wrought literary product and the consummation of a developing performance. In the four extant cycles, we have then what may well be perceived in overview as three different models of text and performance.

Without, for the time, differentiating between York and Wakefield as "city drama" and "town" or "manorial drama" respectively, I do want to linger for a moment on the contrast between the two collections as early examples of process and product-directed texts. The point I have made about the performance orientation of York against the literary orientation of Wakefield is nowhere better supported than in their two manuscripts. The York manuscript (British Library MS Additional 35290) is unmistakably a register. It has running titles naming the sponsoring guild throughout the volume at the top of each leaf. The purpose of these titles, as Beadle and Meredith have observed in their excellent facsimile volume [Richard Beadle and Peter Meredith, *The York Play: A Facsimile of British Library MS Additional 35290,* 1983], was to allow "any user of the manuscript. . .to find his way quickly and easily around a large compilation of short units." The York manuscript is clearly a collection, and it has an official stamp about it. Most important, . . .it leaves numerous blank pages at the end of pageants, indicating the compiler's intent to leave space for changes or additions. The York manuscript is truly put together as an open-ended compendium that could serve the city as an ongoing, adaptable record of changes in performance. The numerous marginalia, especially those by John Clerke, give indisputable evidence that in fact changes of performance, while not always integrated with the existing text, were carefully noted. They will indicate, for example, "here wantes a pece newly mayd for saynt John Baptiste" (f. 92v) or "this matter is newly mayd & devysed wherof we haue no coppy regystred" (f. 94) or, more generally, "nota quia non concordat / novo addicio facto" (f. 114). The many notes, in fact, make clear that the copy we have of the York plays, while still a register was unable to keep up with the performance changes that took place in the play.

The Towneley manuscript, in contrast, is a finished book. It contains no running titles, and except for one puzzling blank page (f. 20), its text runs continuously from beginning to end. Plays follow in close succession, one upon the other, so that often handsome titles conjoin explicits and incipits on the same page. The ornamentation of the manuscript, moreover, is more lavish than that of any other extant cycle. The handsome strap-work initials are clearly decorative, they are designed for the admiration of readers and viewers, not surely for the eyes of the practical-minded town clerk whose interest in the manuscript is solely to check it against the performance of the plays. I do not mean to suggest that the Towneley manuscript is a luxury volume; it is too uneven and unimpressive for that designation. But it is also not simply a book designed for ordinary record keeping and maintenance. It contains, above all, a continuous text. There is no apparent hesitation in its execution. It was meant to bring us a finite text, one that moved in steady progression from Creation to Doomsday with very little marginal comment and virtually no recognition that it had any connection with an ongoing, annual performance. Interestingly, the marginalia, unlike that of the York manuscript, is chiefly concerned with regulation or official examination of the text. Most of it must come from the period when the mystery cycles were under scrutiny by the archbishop of York, who had jurisdiction over Wakefield. We find several anti-Marian notations, as in the *Second Shepherds'* play where "lady" is crossed out and "lord" written above in the phrase "oure lady hym saue" (134/553) or the passage in which Joseph describes how the Son was to have descended from the heavens "in a madyn for to light" (183/59) with the remark "no maters ben as sade [said]" cryptically noted in the margin. There are also obvious passages of censorship, such as the stanza describing the seven sacraments in the play of *Johannes Baptista* crossed out in red (200-201/193-200) and marked "corected and not playd." But nowhere in the entire manuscript do we find the kind of notations about discrepancies of performance and text that John Clerke and other commentators left in the York volume. All this would suggest that the Towneley manuscript was probably not intended to be a register, as is usually surmised, but rather something like a presentation copy of the play for the safekeeping of the lord of the manor or some other eminent person. All signs are that the compiler set out to produce a book of literary value rather than an official municipal register.

Although I am persuaded that the plays of the Towneley manuscript were performed at Wakefield, that conclusion is not universally accepted. It was, in fact, recently challenged by several commentators at a scholarly symposium. The principal reasons for the challenge are apparently the absence of external records that link the plays with Wakefield and the fact that, although the name Wakefield occurs twice in the titles of the manuscript, there is no absolute and unmistakable attribution of the manuscript to the West Riding city. . . .

I have on several occasions referred to the Wakefield cycle as "second generation." That term is, I believe, an accurate representation of the process by which the mystery plays came to the West Riding in the course of the fifteenth century. My argument will be that the Wakefield cycle is, in effect, built upon already existing plays, borrowed from nearby communities, especially the city of York, when economic and demographic conditions in the western county permitted the development of a cycle and its attendant festivities. It is known, of course, that at least five plays in the Wakefield cycle are nearly identical in content and even phrasing with five in the extant York cycle. All the evidence—internal and external—shows that Wakefield borrowed those plays from York, and not vice versa. External to the plays are the records showing that York clearly did support a cycle performance (even if not yet recorded in a text) as early as the latter quarter of the fourteenth century, which was the time of York's greatest prosperity in the Middle Ages. Wakefield in contrast developed, as I shall show, into a commercial hub, especially in the wool trade after the mid-fifteenth century. Before that time, it could not have supported a cycle of mystery plays. As for

the internal evidence, it would be difficult to argue that the more polished, expanded versions of at least some of the Wakefield plays were the earlier of the two. Of special significance is the fact that the Wakefield *Judgment* play, which is one of the five, was expanded significantly and brilliantly by the Wakefield Master in his characteristic style and meter. If the borrowing had been in the other direction, one would have to explain the anomaly of the play's losing its best parts, including the role of Tutivillus, in the process.

The argument that the Wakefield plays are second generation is at odds with most explanations thus far offered about the development of the cycle. It was fashionable, from the very first, to assume that the Wakefield plays grew much in the same manner and time frame as the plays at York. This argument was, of course, simply inferential, since no records survive from a period earlier than mid-sixteenth century to ascertain the existence, much less the growth, of the Wakefield cycle. It was based partly on analogy, built no doubt on the unvoiced assumption that at a certain time in literary history all major towns or cities in England set out to create cycles. Though details of this putative history have been widely challenged, little has been written to refute the notion that cycles in one form or another arose simultaneously as part of the evolution of the vernacular religious drama. Even such an enlightened scholar as Woolf [in *The English Mystery Plays,* 1972] speaks of the northern dramatists as if they were indistinguishable:

> If there were London plays from about the middle of the fourteenth century onwards, the northern cycles could not have escaped their influence. Because the plays have been lost this influence cannot be investigated; but it is reasonable to suppose that the northern dramatists did not slavishly imitate the drama of the metropolis, that they were aware of the complex traditions that lay behind it, and that working within these traditions they designed their own form of cyclical play.

This view assumes an ineluctable historical progress: The basic germ of the drama was swept northward where so many undifferentiated dramatists allowed it to grow into an indigenous form (everywhere much the same) of what is, by inference, the ubiquitous play.

This view of a general growth of the drama has dominated historical scholarship from the beginning of the modern era. It is true that dates have been slightly adjusted to conform more nearly with the facts; we are now more ready to locate the birth of the cycles as we have them in the fifteenth rather than the fourteenth century. But the notion that cycles grew in relatively similar stages over the years to match the growth and interest of the communities that sponsored them is still

very much an unwritten premise of our published scholarship. What is usually envisioned is a period of ges-
tation during which a primitive cycle gradually became complex through a series of comprehensive revisions. The first stage is represented as consisting mostly of couplets and quatrains, and the notorious tail-
rhyme stanza of the metrical romances. This stage was
marked by simplicity and plain-spoken devotion. It was
followed by a reviser who wrote in more complex structures, perhaps in rime couée or the Northern Septenar
stanza, and whose outlook was more worldly because
he was attentive to contemporary texts from which he
might borrow passages or techniques. The last stage
burst forth with unbridled realism, in the work of "real"
poets who were given names like the York Realist
(clearly a compliment!) or the Wakefield Master. This
is the scheme essentially proposed by A. W. Pollard in
his introduction to *The Towneley Plays:*

> I think we may fairly regard this Towneley cycle as
> built up in at least three distinct stages. In the first
> of these we find the simple religious tone which we
> naturally assign to the beginning of the cyclical
> religious drama, the majority of them being written
> in one of the favourite metres of the fourteenth-
> century romances which were already going out of
> fashion in Chaucer's day. In the second stage we
> have the introduction by some playwright, who
> brought the knowledge of them from elsewhere, of
> at least five—possibly seven or eight—of the plays
> which were acted at York, and the composition of
> some others in the same style. In the third stage a
> writer of genuine dramatic power, whose humour
> was unchecked by any respect for conventionality,
> wrote, especially for this cycle, the plays in the 9-
> line stanza which form its backbone, and added here
> and there to others. Teken together, the three stages
> probably cover something like half a century, ending
> about 1410.

Remarkably this scheme looks almost exactly the same
as that posited by W. W. Greg for the York cycle.
Greg also conjures up three stages (he calls them "layers"—the other favorite word is "strata"), of which the
first was "a simple didactic cycle carefully composed
in elaborate stanzas and withal rather dull." The second introduced all the humor that we still find in the
cycle, and it is the work of "the only great metrist who
devoted his talents to the English religious drama as
we know it." The last and crowning stage was produced by "a very remarkable though uneven writer. .
.[who] is a real dramatist" and to whom we owe the
masterly portrait of Pilate. The date of this writer is
"hardly earlier than 1400"; a conclusion that would
make him a contemporary of Pollard's poet with "genuine dramatic power." These two sketches sound almost as if they were burlesque accounts of the Dar-
winian thesis that O. B. Hardison so effectively exposed. They are, unhappily, dead serious, and they show
that the conception of literary history that ruled the

early scholarship on the cycles was every bit as flawed
by the evolutionary analogy as was the treatment addressed by Hardison of the liturgical drama. Even the
notion that the cycles were essentially one model,
undifferentiated in time and purpose, is similar to the
conception that controlled the early historical accounts
of the church drama. The whole matter would not be
of great relevance to the present day were it not for the
fact that the Pollard/Greg perspective still inspires criticism. Here, for example, are the opening sentences of
a very recent book, otherwise a valuable study, about
the work of the Wakefield Master:

> The outstanding playwright of the Middle Ages
> probably began his work at Wakefield as a play-
> doctor. His was the last of at least three different
> hands that composed the cycle.

The passage is, of course, footnoted to Pollard.

The history of Wakefield makes clear that this three-
stage concept is manifestly unacceptable. The Pollard/
Greg models assume that cycles grew over time in performance and that periodically they were put back in
the shop, so to speak, for an overhaul by a reviser who
would improve the text for the next run of twenty or
thirty years. At York the process did not exactly work
that way, though it probably came closer to Greg's layers
than Towneley could have to Pollard's stages. To understand why the model could not have worked in
Wakefield, we need to look at some demographics. M.
G. Frampton has shown [in *PMLA* 50, 1935] that
Wakefield in the fourteenth century was simply too
poor and too sparsely populated to support a major
cycle, even in stage one. For example, the poll-tax
records for 1379 indicate that the adult population of
the town of Wakefield numbered a mere 315 (as compared with Beverley, for example, which seemingly
did support a cycle, with a figure of 2,663). All signs
indicate to Frampton that we must look to the reign of
Henry VI (between the years 1422 and 1460) for the
beginning of the cycle and the work of the Wakefield
Master. Other studies confirm Frampton's conclusion,
and if anything, prompt the positing of an even later
date. It is, for example, a fact that York reached the
depth of its economic depression in the fifteenth century in the decade between 1457 and 1467, due mainly
to the disastrous failure of the port of Hull as an export
center, and that the distribution of cloth passed "out of
the hands of York merchants. . .[to] that of the merchants and clothiers of Wakefield and Halifax" who
transported their wool overland (perhaps on the Watling
Street mentioned in the *Iudicium*?) directly to London
for export. By the 1470s, two-thirds of all the cloth
made in Yorkshire came from the Aire and Calder
valleys (the districts of Leeds and Wakefield respectively), and it was probably not until the turn of the
sixteenth century that the new-found prosperity occasioned by the enormous rise in the manufacture and

trade of wool manifested itself in Wakefield. It was probably then the latter third of the century during which the town would have had sufficient resources and people as well as occasion for civic pride to begin a Corpus Christi cycle.

The other reason for assigning a late date to the Wakefield cycle has to do with the manuscript. Most scholars are agreed that the Towneley manuscript seems to have been copied with remarkable fidelity and that its "copyist was faithfully reproducing the peculiarities of independent source manuscripts. The general sequence of recording independent pageant manuscripts into a book seems to have been the process at work at York as well. And if that is the right scenario for Wakefield, then there could have been only one reviser / compiler, and that person would have given shape to the material that was copied into the extant Towneley manuscript. If, in fact, there was no intervening manuscript between the individual pageant copies and the scribe's exemplar, then the reviser / compiler (who must have been the Wakefield Master since he clearly added material to already existing plays, as witness the transformation of the York Judgment play to the Wakefield *Iudicium*) must have done his writing, revising, rewriting, and compiling on the copies that ultimately went to the scribe. This step clearly rules out the Pollard scenario, and it allows us to think of the Wakefield Master as the Wakefield Author.

Given this process of composition, the date of the manuscript becomes a point of some importance, since it records what is the first true compilation of the Wakefield cycle. It serves at the very least as the logical *ad quem* date for the cycle. Recent paleographic research has shown that the initials of plays 1 and 2 are almost identical with capitals in printed books dated 1499 and 1506, while the strap-work initials of other plays suggest a date not earlier than 1500. It should be observed that at least some of the strap-work initials were made prior to the copying of the text. . . . It is therefore fair to conclude that the Wakefield cycle came into being some time in the last third of the fifteenth century, and if the process involved the compiling of pageants from other sources, as I believe to have been the case, the likelihood is that the cycle was not compiled until very shortly before it was "fair-written" into the extant manuscript—in other words, very nearly at the turn of the century.

There is, as already noted, no documentary evidence to tell how the Wakefield cycle came into being. Many have speculated on the point but none has ventured as credible a scenario as Arnold Williams, whose book on the characterization of Pilate in the Wakefield plays [*The Characterization of Pilate in the Towneley Plays*, 1950] still ranks among the most persuasive critical studies done on any of the English cycles to date. Williams argues that the Towneley cycle presents a uniquely conceived and consistently executed "evil" Pilate, one who is an overwhelming presence in the cycle and who meets every requirement of a complexly drawn dramatic character. In this consistency and complexity, he is quite unlike any other Pilate in the English medieval drama, including the York Pilate, who appears in one clearly borrowed pageant, that of the Resurrection, where, however, his role is used by the Wakefield playwright to reinforce his overall interpretation. The unmistakable dramatic continuity of the evil Pilate in Towneley raises inevitably the fundamental question with which we have been grappling: How is it possible for what appears to be a patchwork cycle, with so many apparent strata, to be so unified? Williams shows in detail that the character of Pilate appears in virtually every major metrical form within the cycle: quatrains, octaves, the Wakefield nine-liners, Northern Septenars, seven-line and thirteen-line stanzas, and even rime couée (though in the latter only briefly and in that stanza form Pilate is uncharacteristically tame). He concludes, "The structure of the passion group, the consistency of characterization, the numerous anticipations and motivations—all point to a single author working according to a definite plan." Here is Williams's speculation of how that sort of authorship occurred:

> About 1420 the city authorities of Wakefield, which was rapidly becoming a commercial center of importance, decided to inaugurate a cycle of plays. Everything we know about the authorship of medieval drama indicates that a cycle so initiated would be a patchwork, based on some existing cycle or cycles of plays, which would then be more or less edited and interpolated to form a new cycle. This individual, struck with the dramatic validity of one or more plays containing a villainous Pilate, decides that the character of Pilate in the cycle which he is putting together shall be that of a villain. He therefore chooses only plays or parts of plays which present Pilate in this light. Perhaps he removes sections suggesting a kindlier Pilate, revises and edits all into reasonable conformity to his dominating conception.

The date in Williams's speculation is, of course, too early, but the scenario he describes is in all respects quite possible. The single compiler or the group he conjectures might, of course, first have gathered the plays—perhaps each craft guild did its own searching among its counterparts in other cities—and after all potential performing groups and all dramatic subjects had been found, either the newly collected patchwork cycle was performed or it was handed to a "literary man," one would think a monk or perhaps another kind of cleric like a chantry priest, who then composed the book. If that was the scenario, we cannot of course know what influence the book ever had on the performance. All indications, as I have shown, are that the book was not used as an acting text or script, and that, in fact, the marginalia occurred only to show what was being censored after the 1550s, when the cycle was carefully scrutinized by the diocese. I suspect that the performance, however it was done, was guided by the scripts that the compiler used to develop his composite volume, though even if that did happen, we can of course not be sure that what was actually performed was the text that we retain.

The source of a very large part of the Wakefield play must have been individual pageants from the York cycle. However this borrowing took place, we can be certain that it was not from the York Register directly. Internal textual evidence supports that conclusion. One passage, for example, from the Towneley **Extraccio Animarum** reads as follows:

> SATHAN. Goddys son! nay, then myght thou be
> glad,
> For no catell *thurt the crave;*
> Bot thou has lyffyd ay lyke a lad,
> In sorrow, and as a sympill *knaue.*
> (301/255-258; italics added)

The York Register renders these lines:

> SATTAN. God sonne? þanne schulde þou be ful
> gladde,
> Aftir no catel *þus þe I telle!*
> But þou has leued ay like a ladde,
> And in sorowe a symple *braide.*
> (339/241-245; italics added)

Here, quite apart from the fact that the Towneley version is better metrically, more accurate in rhyme, and more meaningful in sense, the York text, in the hand of John Clerke strikes out the italicized words and replaces them, curiously, with the Towneley readings: i.e. *þus þe I telle* is replaced by "neyd thowe crave" (242), and the last line is corrected with interlining to "And in sorrowe *as* a symple *knave*" (245). It is clear that in this instance Towneley could not have copied from the York Register. The likelihood is that it copied the correct version from the York Saddlers' original copy and that John Clerke, who found the York meaning incomprehensible, corrected it from the same source or from a performance of the play based on that source. It follows, therefore, that the extant versions of the five nearly identical York and Towneley plays are not directly related, a point that should be borne in mind in any cross-analytical study. This fact may also help to explain differences in pairs of plays from the two cycles that are not so close in their verbal and narrative correspondences, as for example the Wakefield **Oblacio Magorum** and its York counterpart, the Magi play of the Goldsmiths. Here clearly the Towneley version must have originally been taken from the York pageant and then been revised (as the Goldsmiths' regynall itself might have been). The parallels in various portions of the two plays are too close, especially in phraseology, to allow another explanation. Here, for example, is the Angel's speech to the Kings in side-by-side juxtaposition from the two cycles:

Wakefield	York
Syr curtes kyngys, to me to take tent,	Nowe curtayse kynges, me take tent,
And turne by tyme or ye be tenyd;	And turne betyme or ye be tenyd,
From God his self thus am I sent	Fro God hymselfe þus am I sent
To warne you, as youre faythfull freynd,	To warne yow als youre faithfull frende.
How Herode kyng has mamallyce ment,	Herowde the king has malise ment
And shapys with shame you for to sheynd;	And shappis with shame yow for to shende,
And so that ye no harmes hent,	And for þat ye non harmes shulde hent
By othere ways God wyll ye ye weynd	Be othir waies God will ye wende
Into youre awne cuntre;	Euen to youre awne contré.
And if ye ask hym boyn,	And yf ye aske hym bone,
For this dede that ye haue done,	Youre beelde ay will he be,
Youre beyld ay wyll he be (159/595-606)	For þis þat ye haue (148/369-380)

What this isolated parallel passage shows, and there are many more from this pageant as well as from others, is that the Wakefield compilation probably borrowed the bulk of its plays from the already thriving mystery cycle at York. In her close study of the parallel passages of the two cycles [*The Original Identity of the York and Towneley Plays,* 1919], Marie C. Lyle showed that only nine of the thirty-two plays in the Towneley manuscript contained no instances of significant parallel phraseology, and of these nine, one was the late **Suspencio Iude,** an apparent intruder in the cycle, and another the **Processus Talentorum** of which an early York play did seem to exist though it was abandoned before the register was copied. The other seven plays may well have been borrowed from other relatively nearby cycles (e.g. Beverley, Hull, King's Lynn, New-castle upon Tyne, or Norwich), or they were changed so radically in revision that they no longer bore any clear traces of their York origin.

As I proceed now to examine the role of the Wakefield Master as contributor and likely the only important reviser and compiler of the Wakefield cycle, it is necessary to remember the nature of authorship in the Middle Ages. I shall argue that the Wakefield Master was, in fact, the author of the Wakefield cycle. For reasons not entirely clear to me, revisers and redactors have persistently been spoken of in the development of the vernacular religious drama, but never authors. This may be the result of the fact that we know none of the playwrights by name. Yet in all respects they were authors, writers, playwrights, or whatever designation properly gives them credit for their creative and, in medieval terms, original work. No one would suggest that Chaucer was a reviser or a redactor because he took works by Boccaccio, Petrarch, Jacobus de Varagine, Dante, Machaut, Froissart, and countless other sources and revised and adapted them to his own purposes. In fact, his literary performance depended on his wide frame of reference in the world of letters, and in *The Canterbury Tales* he undertook as a major purpose to test what he had garnered from books against the experience of "modern" life in the late fourteenth century. Robert B. Burlin has written about this Chaucerian process:

> Authoritatively, he may cite a proverb or scriptural text, or he may reproduce an entire book—in translation (*Melibeus*), adaptation (*Troilus*), or in summary abstract (the *Somnium* in the *Parliament of Fowls*). But the material comes from the written page and usually from the remote past; it constitutes a vicarious acquaintance with another man's conscious reshaping of his own apprehension of reality, as, for example, when Chanticleer's men of "auctoritee" are defined as transmitters of what they "han wel founden by experience". . . . All of Chaucer's major works depend structurally on this opposition: of what the speaker has read against what he experiences in a dream; of the old books that he scrupulously follows against the experience of the narrator in reproducing them.

> [*Chaucerian Fiction*, 1977]

In *The Canterbury Tales,* for example, Chaucer directly tests the *auctoritee* of the romance of antiquity by translating and adapting Boccaccio's *Teseide* as a vehicle for the Knight's storytelling performance against the *experience* of common folk who lived in contemporary Oxford (contrived as that wonderful story may be). The point is that he allows romance to be read in the framework of contemporary fabliau. I suggest that the Wakefield author does much the same type of thing. He, too, adapts and reshapes his sources—be they the York plays, or *The Northern Passion* from which in large part the York plays derived their Passion narrative, or even ultimately the Old and New Testaments. He was as much an author as Chaucer or Shakespeare or Dryden or Anouilh in reshaping a literary text into the sphere of his own experience and consciousness. The Wakefield Master is not a mere redactor, he is a playwright-poet of extraordinary genius.

How then did he reshape his auctoritee to his experience? He made a city play into one that fits the setting and the nuances of the manor. It must be remembered that Wakefield was not York, and what the Wakefield Master did was to make his cycle indigenous to his setting and responsive to his image of the people who inhabited that setting. Economically, Wakefield was a manorial seat and the chief town in the riding during the time that the plays were collected and performed. But even as a commercial hub it was always under seigneurial control, and its government in no way resembled the trade oligarchy of York with its mayor, aldermen, and common council. The manor court, whose rolls are still intact, was the chief juridical body, presided over by the steward and empowered to hear every kind of civil and criminal case that touched upon the manor.

> No detail of agricultural life was too insignificant to come before the court and be presented to the jurors, such as the keeping of unringed swine, their escape into the lord's woods or into other men's fields, or into the streets of the town, the neglect to scour ditches, or breaches of the pinfold laws.

> [Walker, *Wakefield History*]

True, the town also had a burgess court, but that was a body restricted to suits brought by freemen. Wakefield was very much a county seat, run by landed gentry. W. G. Rimmer sums up the differences with York as follows:

> The town did not trail behind York and Beverley on the same path; it took a different course. Whereas the production and marketing of cloth took place mainly *within* York, the spinners and weavers of the Calder lived in rural hamlets and homesteads. Indeed, the argument that steep tolls repelled traders from Wakefield, thereby sending them to nearby small free-trade towns, is bereft of meaning *unless* most of the cloth sold at Wakefield was made in outlying villages.

> ["Evolution of Leeds"]

While Rimmer argues that the tolls were not the cause of Wakefield's commercial downfall in the late sixteenth and early seventeenth centuries, there is no doubt that the lord of the manor set burdensome market tolls that impoverished trade by driving away foreigners and merchants from other parts of Yorkshire. All this helps to set the stage for the Wakefield plays.

The Wakefield author was not particularly interested in the commerce of the region, but he did make his cycle a mirror of the mean-spiritedness of both lords and vassals. If any tone dominates in the cycle, and especially in the plays that have traditionally been ascribed to the Wakefield Master, it is one of discordance, of the poor crying out about injustices, of farmers bewailing their poverty, of courts tyranizing one and all. Life, as the Wakefield author sees it, is miserable and mean in Yorkshire. If any place needs the return of Jesus, it is that bereft countryside and its churlish, crabbed, lying, and thieving inhabitants. He is as hard on lords (especially in their roles as rulers and judges) as he is on vassals, male and female. The evil Pilate is indigenous to this landscape. While, of course, the playwright is not oblivious to goodness in his "natural men" (the strength of Noah, the generosity of the Shepherds, the compassion of Joseph), mostly that quality is obscured until the force of God directly invigorates it (the Shepherds, Joseph, Noah's wife are basically distrustful people at the start). The vision is not exactly Bosch-like—it is not quite grotesque enough for that—but the distortions that the Wakefield author sees are not unrelated in mood and tone to what Bosch sees in the quasi-human figures that are so prominent in his world view. . . .

If a single play can capture the perspective of the Wakefield cycle, it is probably the *Mactacio Abel*. It is in this play, after the more or less traditional opening of the now fragmentary Creation play that establishes the "authority" of the Biblical vision, that the Wakefield playwright sets his stage as dictated by his perception of the Wakefield "experience." If as audience we are to perceive the real meaning of the coming of Christ, then we can do no better, in the playwright's view, than to visualize it and understand it in the midst of that stark manorial setting. We are in the field. A loud, cantankerous, foul-mouthed servant, the Garcio named Pikeharnes (the name means thief), comes forward preparing for the entrance of his master, a "good" yeoman but ominously one to avoid engaging in dispute. Yet the audience need not be told all this for, as Garcio says, "Som of you ar his men" (10/20). This broad burlesque entrance of the truly powerful—the conventional swaggering tyrant who comes in with a rant clearing a path for himself—does two things: It establishes that servants are in tone interchangeable with their masters, and it identifies at least a part of the audience with the brotherhood of Cain. The play, as Helterman has pointed out [in *Symbolic Action*], focuses from the first "on the criminal rather than the victim." It gives us from the start a "field of blood" on which the Crucifixion is the ultimate painful, though necessary, salvific event. Because life is so brutal and mean, the event of the Resurrection will be that much more glorious and inspiring.

I am, of course, suggesting that the *Mactatio Abel* must be read as a typological forecast, a kind of map for the full dramatic action to unfold before us. While I will save for [another discussion] a more systematic analysis of the function of typology as a dramatic form, we do need that important perspective as a way of understanding the Wakefield author's blueprint for the cycle. The play, after all, is called the *Mactacio Abel,* not as in York the *Sacrificium Cayme et Abell.* The emphasis is on murder. Abel is the quintessential good shepherd, who is, of course, both a figural and a social presence. He reminds Wakefielders of the importance of their agrarian and commercial economy, and he is,

in his social role, a precursor of the other Shepherds of the Wakefield plays, with a foreboding of all the hardships that we hear recited in their litanies within the opening passages of the two Shepherds' plays. Yet the play also focuses on another socioeconomic situation of moment in late-fifteenth-century Yorkshire: the festering rivalry between the tenant farmer and the sheep raiser. The anger of Cain reflects a social dislocation: The plowman had become in many ways a symbol of agrarian poverty, and therefore the Wakefield Cain, when he vents his ire at Abel, is surely speaking with an economic resentment that his "men" in the audience shared:

> Go grese thi shepe vnder the toute,
> For that is the moste lefe.

Or,

> How that I tend, rek the neuer a deill,
> Bot tend thi skabbid shepe wele;
> For if thou to my teynd tent take,
> It bese the wars for thi sake.

Cain tells Abel, If I prosper in my sacrifice, it is all the worse for you—and so it is in the fierce agricultural economy of Wakefield.

Not that Cain should be regarded as a sympathetic figure for his deprivation. To the contrary. He functions almost as an icon of the dispossessed man who fails to share his worldly goods and who lacks charity. He is the archetypal "bad" Plowman, the opposite figure to Langland's Piers or to the Parson's brother in *The Canterbury Tales*. He and his Garcio remind us of the two plowmen in the famous picture from the Luttrell Psalter, except that those two at least work together and Cain is not left to "both hold and drife". The discord in Cain's world is everywhere; even the plow team is disobedient. There is no charity there, and everything is reduced to its lowest and meanest significance, even to the point of Cain's search for a sheaf too small for God to "wipe his ars withall". That sort of scatological profanity occurs only in this play, but it defines for the audience just how much mankind as seen in its localized setting needs salvation.

The Wakefield author depicts mortal sin in the world of his own habitat, in "Gudeboure at the quarell hede" and later, Horbury and Watling Street, extending from the heart of town to the surrounding villages. His characters speak "Yorkshire"; they project an indigenous, homely proverbial wisdom, usually concerned with food and work: "ther is a podyng in the pot"; "cold rost is at my masteres hame"; "ill-spon weft ay comes foule out". This is no place for the outsider, the intruder who speaks with a "Sothren tothe"; it is a down-home drama that insistently asks the audience to bring Jesus into its midst. . . .

. . . . .

It is precisely for the brilliance and originality of its poetic vision that the Wakefield cycle has been singled out as the most "literary" of all the medieval Corpus Christi plays. As a step toward bringing that literary quality into perspective, I propose now to examine one of its significant thematic strands: its self-conscious interest in literary art as a medium, or to put it in other terms, its concern with the uses and abuses of language. I believe that we owe this focus to the Wakefield author as reviser and compiler of the cycle. We can find this theme not only in all the five full plays traditionally assigned to him, the *Procesus Noe cum filii* (Play 2), the *Prima Pastorum* (Play 12), the *Secunda Pastorum* (Play 13), the *Magnus Herodes* (Play 16), and the *Coliphizacio* (Play 21), but also in all the plays that bear evidence of his familiar scansion, whether put into the traditional stanza associated with him or others that resemble them in poetic form and substance. . . . In all, he clearly had a demonstrable role in editing or revising the following additional plays in the cycle: the *Mactacio Abel* (Play 2), the *Conspiracio [et Capcio]* (Play 20), the *Flagellacio* (Play 22), the *Processus Crucis* (Play 23), the *Processus Talentorum* (Play 24), the *Peregrini* (Play 27), the *Ascencio Domini* (Play 29), the *Iudicium* (Play 30), and the *Lazarus* (Play 31). And since he clearly reworked the plays borrowed from York—witness his major alteration of the York Judgment play to which he added 378 of his characteristic lines out of a total (in the Wakefield version) of 664—I think we can safely assume that he had a hand in compiling if not adapting all the plays in this category. Indeed, one must conclude that, if he was the principal compiler of the cycle, his editorial hand must be present everywhere, even if merely in what was retained and what was rejected in the final version.

The Wakefield author is pervasively concerned with "vayn carpyng," as Abel accusingly calls it, or to put it more fundamentally, with the abuse of language, especially by those who oppose God. The demonstration of that abuse is, ironically, a central feature of the cycle's rich verbal complexity and depth of meaning. We have already seen that the Wakefield author's most immediate interests are centered on humankind—on "natural man" in the terminology of V. A. Kolve [*The Play Called Corpus Christi*, 1966]—rather than on God, Christ, the angels, and the saintly. In the five plays ascribed to the Wakefield author, God makes but one speech, in the Noah play, and it is straightforward and distinctly colloquial: God begins by reproving man for his wickedness, announces that he will bring forth a Flood, and appears before Noah to give very practical instructions for building the ark and storing provisions. The Wakefield author is even more sparing in the lines that he gives to Jesus—four in all—and these lines in themselves, as I shall show later, are a ringing testament to the eloquence of silence. What interests the Wakefield author is the common man—such types as

tyrants, soldiers, shepherds, shrewish wives—the humble and the unregenerate in all their guises. He prefers to focus on middle earth, straying only once into the world of the demonic when he presents Tutivillus and his cohorts in the *Iudicium*. But even these characters are seen in worldly shape as if they were tax collectors or summoners rather than gatherers of the damned. As a reviser in his own peculiar format and language, he carefully chooses only those subjects which emphasize his interests, as in his characterization of Pilate in the *Processus Talentorum* or the Torturers in the *Flagellacio*. His contributions do not appear in the more solemn and sacred settings in the cycle, such as the *Annunciacio* or the play about John the Baptist. If indeed he was overall reviser of the cycle, as I argue here, he let such passages stand in their original language. His direct contributions, then, stand in marked contrast to the rest of the cycle; indeed, it is largely from the "counter-language" he provides for his natural man that the rest of the cycle, and particularly the lyrical passages in couplets and rimes couées, take on their eloquence.

The essential premise of the Towneley cycle as a whole about language is that simplicity and artlessness mark the speech of the virtuous. There is a homely eloquence about God's opening in the Creation play:

> Ego sum alpha et o,
> I am the first, the last also,
> Oone god in mageste;
> Meruelus, of myght most,
> ffader, & son, & holy goost,
> On god in trinyte.
>
>   (1/1-6)

One is tempted to take literally the opening line in the play from the Apocalypse (1:8). For God and his votaries speak everywhere with alphabetic clarity and concision. Their speeches are made largely in the simplest of stanzaic forms—couplets, quatrains, octaves, and rimes couées—and their diction is plain, direct, and uncomplicated. The rhythm of their language is even and free of the harsh alliterative dissonances that characterize the speech of errant men. E. Catherine Dunn has pointed out [in *American Benedictine Review* 20, No. 4, December, 1969] that there is a basic lyric voice in the Towneley cycle that she calls "the voice of the Church" ("la voix de l'église"), a voice that is highly subjective and that speaks or even chants characteristically in patterned sound structures. This is the voice of which I speak here, though I would expand its scope to extend far beyond its occurrence in the *Processus Prophetarum* play from which she takes her paradigm illustrations. It is, of course, first and foremost a prophetic voice—even God's speech at the outset is prophetic, drawing for its basic text on the Apocalypse and Isaiah (see especially 41:4 and 48:12)—and its lyricism is often expressed directly in hymns and chants, the only occasions except for straightforward prophecy when the playwright veers from the vernacular approvingly. Music (as part of the quadrivium) was, of course, one of the four highest subjects of learning, and in the form of *musica ecclesiastica,* it was the essential expression, among the arts, of cosmic harmony. The frequent appearance of hymns in the Towneley cycle, therefore, is by no means an unimportant thematic consideration in its own right, particularly when a pointed contrast is made several times between *musica ecclesiastica* and *musica vulgaris.* Even more dramatic is the contrast between the composite voice of the church, as expressed in various harmonic forms throughout the cycle, and the cacophony of demonic voices that rings forth from devils and the unregenerate. At its most extreme, this contrast is expressed throughout the medieval popular religious drama on the one hand by divine music, the language of the spirit, and on the other by obscenity (with emphasis on the excremental), or body language. The Devil who comes on stage "cracking wind," as in *The Castle of Perseverance,* is thus the perfect antithesis to the angelic choir. The Wakefield plays, while virtually confining their scatological references to one play, the **Mactacio Abel,** nevertheless make the contrast of music and noise a crucial consideration.

Before looking more specifically into the Wakefield author's concern with language as theme, I want to make a brief observation about stanzaic forms in general as used in the Wakefield cycle. While a good deal of attention was given by the early critics to the various metrical forms as strata within the cycle, little was done, then or later, to discover the function of the various metrical forms in the cycle. It is interesting to note, for example, that the Wakefield Creation play contains what is manifestly a patterned use of stanza forms. Thus, God speaks only in a six-line rime couée stanza, and Lucifer, who parodies God's speech, declaims to the multitude in five- and seven-line corruptions of that stanza demonstrating in the very form of his speech his incapacity to imitate God. Couplets, which may in the context be regarded as the lowest poetic form, are spoken regularly by the Fallen Angels and by man. While I do not wish to claim that this pattern holds in all the plays that follow, it does seem to suggest that stanza forms are not used indiscriminately by the Towneley playwright(s). The Wakefield stanza has its own tonality—one that is best suited to the speech of common men, a quality that comes through even in its most devout and solemn usages, such as God's speech in the passage already noted within the Noah play (Caw. 16-18/73-81) and the "hay-ll"-lyrics that Dunn so admires in the **Secunda Pastorum** (Caw. 62/710-736). . . . [The] Wakefield stanza is [flexible] in its potential for rhythmic variation, for end-stopping and for enjambment. It clearly is a vehicle to reduce the patterned tempo of the more conventional stanzas in the cycle, and the effect it achieves,

therefore, is to represent in its rhythm the characteristic tempo of spoken discourse. The remarkable achievement of the Wakefield author is the dual effect that he allows his stanza to create: It simultaneously communicates the disordered and unstructured and reminds the listener or reader to heed its disciplined form.

The Wakefield author's interest in language asserts itself everywhere, as much in the style as in the subject matter of his plays. Given his worldly perspective, he is, of course, responsible for much that is crude and ignoble and profane in the dramatic action of the cycle. But there is also something grandly paradoxical about his work. For it is in the very excess of language—the racy humor, the crackling alliterations, the earthy proverbs, the shrill tyrants' rants, the trumpet-tongued catalogs, the salty and resourceful dialectalisms—that the Wakefield plays are most dazzling and most engaging to the reader. It seems that the Wakefield author willfully provided a caution against the very fiber of his own art, as if to warn that the voice of poetry in the context of the highest verities can beguile its auditors. There is, in the Wakefield plays, a strong, implicit argument against the enchantment of art, and an equally strong affirmation of the artless. In yielding its most memorable scenes and its most flamboyant verbal art to rustics, scoundrels, miscreants, and demons, the Wakefield cycle is in a class with such works as *Henry IV, Part 1* and *Paradise Lost.* Many great artists have endowed their least hallowed characters with their own versatility and their own highest verbal gifts. It is in this sense that Mak and Herod and Tutivillus are precursors of Falstaff, Satan, Mr. Micawber, and even Humbert Humbert.

The extent to which language occupies a central place in the drama of the Wakefield author can quickly be established by an overview of his work. He is, of course, the foremost linguist among the contributors to the cycle. Two recently completed computer concordances show the extent of the Wakefield author's vocabulary. All told, there are over a thousand words that appear as single citations in the Wakefield stanzas, or slightly fewer than a third of all such words in the Towneley cycle. Moreover, the Wakefield author is not only the most persistent and colorful user of dialectalisms and local references, but he also makes conscious allusion to dialect as a tool of deception when he has Mak address the Shepherds in his "Sothren tothe," which is, after all, the dialect of the ruling class. The same can be said of his use of Latin and French—languages that appear consistently in the rants of tyrants for the purpose of intimidating their listeners. In fact, it is almost exclusively in the Wakefield stanzas that macaronic verse in Latin and English occurs in the Wakefield cycle; for example, the long opening rant in the **Processus Talentorum** (279-280/1-46) and the Latin proverbs spoken by Caiaphas and Annas in the **Flagellacio** (Caw. 82/143-144; Caw. 83/

214-215). When the Wakefield Herod, perhaps the most torrential ranter in the cycle, ends his play with a winded "I can no more Franch" (Caw. 77/513), the Wakefield author in characteristic fashion looks to the language of the upper class to identify for Yorkshiremen the bombast and fustian of tyrants. The Wakefield author is an adept linguist, but finally he distrusts all foreign languages and dialects. Yorkshire speech in itself may not often serve as a vehicle for the highest truths, but it is at least an authentic medium for the homespun wisdom of the earthy characters who make up the play and, we presume, the audience.

The Wakefield author more than any other writer in the medieval drama is aware of literary terms and traditions. He refers directly to "Vyrgyll" and "Homere," makes allusion, as already mentioned, to the learned languages of *Franch* (Caw. 77/513) and *Laton* (Caw. 39/391), knows technical musical language (see especially 384/537-540), and uses a wide variety of literary terms such as *pystyls* (Caw. 69/205), *verse* (Caw. 34/386), *legende* (Caw. 64/203), *poetré* (Caw. 39/386) *poecé-tayllys* (Caw. 69/204), *glose* (Caw. 54/413), *gendere* (372/161), *gospell* (376/302), *grales* (i.e. graduals; Caw. 69/205), and *gramere* (Caw. 39/387, Caw. 242/242; 375/253). In addition, he directs his scorn especially against the misusers of language. One of his favorite devices, the catalog of agent nouns, names, among other offenders, the following: *wryers, bollars, hullars, extorcyonars, carpers, slanderars, kyrkchaterars, swerars, iurars, writars, bakbyttars, quest-dytars, indytars, flytars, lyars, flyars, cryars, byllhagers, bragers, wragers, quest-mangers, bewshers, runkers,* and *rowners.* Like Dante, he regards fraud—at base a verbal offense—as among the most heinous of crimes. His attack on the misuse of language, his strong preference for the vernacular and especially the local, and his open slurs on such masters of verbal manipulation as friars (see Caw. 37/286, Caw. 39/389) suggest that he may have been a parish priest and possibly even a Wycliffite. Most important the Wakefield author chooses to end the cycle by introducing in the ***Iudicium,*** which was borrowed in its basic form from York, the devil Tutivillus, whose whole concern was to collect those offenders who had spoken out of turn in church. What emerges from this summary is a playwright who in his subject matter and his very language demonstrated an overriding concern with the falsity of man's word as contrasted with the Word. It is this contrast that constitutes a major theme and an artistic focus for the Wakefield cycle.

Let us now look somewhat more closely at a few of the crucial passages of the Wakefield author's work that concern themselves with this theme. I shall begin with an examination of the ***Iudicium*** because it serves as dramatic summary to the cycle and highlights the doom of those who abuse language (the "kyrkchaterars" of their time), among whom, ironically, we also

find their oppressors, the devils. Because the abuse of language centrally involves the law (with "parlement" and "debate" as its vehicle), the rantings of tyrants, and the contrast of cacophony and music, I shall move on to a consideration of these topics in the plays of the Doctors in the Temple, Noah, the Buffeting, and the two versions of the Shepherds, all of which are essential for an understanding of this theme in the cycle.

First, then, the Judgment play. Its principal character is the demon Tutivillus. From several allusions to his short stature, one would deduce that he was conceived as a sprite, and it would seem logical that he was played by a boy actor (see the references in 374/232 and 375/245, and his self-representation as one who sits atop the shoulder pads of dandies, 376/290). He is, therefore, not the usual devil figure of the mystery plays, and he certainly does not partake of the scatological humor so characteristic of the type. From the very outset, he announces his interest in language:

> Mi name is tutiuillus,
> my horne is blawen;
> ffragmina verborum / tutiullus colligit horum,
> Belzabub algorum / belial belium doliorum.
>   (375/249-252)

The Latin here is barely coherent, but it does tell us that Tutivillus collects "fragments of words" in contrast to Beelzebub who seemingly collects "the cold" (?) and Belial "the sorrows of war." I suspect that the Latin passage serves as something of a diabolic litany here, reflecting Tutivillus's verbal agility without calling for any particular literal sense (there is an oral gamesmanship in conjoining "belial" with "belium," and that may be the only justification for the line besides the rhyme on -*orum*). There is even a possibility that the Latin words were chanted, as is commonly the case with lines that are not part of the rhyme scheme. All this comes, of course, in response to the First Demon's saying "with wordes will thou fill vs," a perfectly calibrated rhyme with Tutivillus. Ironically, this loquacious devil is the very agent who traditionally gathers up in sacks the words mumbled or dropped by clergymen and those spoken idly by parishioners during church service ("kyrkchaterars"; 376/296). To the extent that Tutivillus at once practices the abuse that he is designed to guard against—that is, the incoherent and excessive utterance of words—he is a most interesting reflection of the Wakefield author himself.

The two most basic sins against which the energies of Tutivillus and the demons seem to be directed are excessive adornment (especially in apparel) and the frauds practiced by men of the law. Tutivillus reserves some of his best verbal showmanship in cataloging the latest excesses of fashion. With a chorus of approval from the demons who take delight in his "gramory" (learning; 253), Tutivillus describes the extravagant dress of the dandies and the women of fashion, obviously ready subjects for damnation, with a zest matched only by the extravagance of his own words. Indeed, there seems to be, in the mind of the playwright, a correspondence between sartorial and linguistic extravagance. With all the emphasis in the play on misusers of language—from "kyrkchaterars" (296) to "runkers" and "rowners" (298), and with the identification of excessive adornment with pride, the deadliest of sins (305-313), one cannot but recognize in passages like the following a lack of restraint in language, with the flamboyant alliterations, the double rhymes, and the eccentric diction, which resembles the very offense it describes:

> His luddokkys thai lowke / like walk-mylne
>   cloggys,
> his hede is like a stowke / hurlyd as hoggys,
> a woll blawen bowke / thise fryggys as
>   froggys,
> This Ielian Iowke / dryfys he no doggys
>   To felter;
> Bot with youre yolow lokkys,
> ffor all youre many mokkys
> ye shall clym on hell crokkys
>   With a halpeny heltere.
>
> (377/314-322)

Shortly thereafter, Tutivillus describes the drunkards who sit all night imbibing "with hawvell and Iawvell, syngyng of lawvell" (378/337-338: with wailing and jabbering and singing of lowbell, i.e. of drinking songs; *MED,* s.v. "lavel") until the bells of the church deafen them in the morning (378/341-345). It is so also with the demons who, in the tour de force language of the Wakefield Master, create their own "hawvell and Iawvell" to be chastened by the straightforward and direct words of Christ (in the version of the source play from York). The point to be remembered is that sinners and demons alike will be climbing "on hell crokkys." The demons betray their lust for power, much like earthly tyrants, in their language. The severest ironies in the play finally lie in linguistic self-condemnations.

Just as important as the issue of excessive adornment is the interest of the Wakefield playwright in the law as metaphor at the Last Judgment. The whole play, as indeed the cycle also, is structured to contrast the true law against the false—which is to say, the true word against the false. The very trumpet of the Judgment, which at the outset of the play gives such a "sturdy. . .showte" (370/91), is parodied by Tutivillus at his entrance ("my horne is blawen," 375/250). To the extent that the clarion call is to gather sinners from everywhere, it calls as much for the demons as it does for their prey. But the demons do not recognize the true significance of God's call despite the fact that it releases them from the bonds of Hell (370/89-116). While Christ is waiting to render the great Last Judgment, they still

use the idiom of the manorial economy:

> Bot fast take oure rentals / hy, let vs go
>   hence!
> ffor as this fals / the great sentence.
>
> (371/134-135)

They set out to go to "this dome / vp Watlyn strete" (126), but for them it undoubtedly meant the Roman road that actually crossed the parish of Wakefield, rather than the Milky Way, as, in the context, it must have been known to others (*OED,* s.v. "Watling Street," ¶2). The confusion here as elsewhere is between the civil and divine law. And the spokesmen of the civil law, who are ironically demons, invariably expatiate at length about the evil in the world, which they will expose and punish. Thus, the Second Demon reminds his compeers:

> It sittys you to tente / in this mater to mell,
> As a pere in a parlamente / what case so
>   befell.
>
> (371/118-119)

The fact is that the demons never cease to talk; they continue their "parlement" all the while that they are on stage. Their frantic catalogs and their extended, colorful descriptions of mostly venial rather than mortal sins are the only aspects of their scene that provide movement, for physically nothing happens through the major portions of the Judgment play. In contrast to the Devil's "parlement" is Christ's straightforward speech. The demons themselves tell us, "ffor wysely / he spekys on trete" (371/129-130). In perfect balance, he addresses the good souls and the bad souls, delivering his judgment fairly and succinctly. When his speech is all over, the good souls go to the right, the bad souls to the left, and the demons remain the only speakers on stage. The Highest Judge has spoken, and the petty civil judges make their way to their eternal doom, leading the whole company of sinners to the tune of their unceasing chatter:

> Hyte hyder warde, ho / harry ruskyne!
>   War oute!
> The meyn shall ye nebyll,
> And I shall syng the trebill
> A revant the devill
>   Till all this hole rowte.
>
> (384/535-540)

The judges are finally judged, and they all "go. . .sam" (386/610) to their eternal damnation while the good souls sing the Te Deum Laudamus. At the very last, the divine law triumphs ringingly over the false civil law, and silence triumphs over loquacity and chatter. In the *Iudicium,* which we know to be a borrowed play from York, we can observe to greatest advantage the skill of the Wakefield author as reviser. He adds those passages which emphasize the abuse of language in his characteristic stanza, diction, and meter. The rest he lets stand as a way of highlighting the contrast between the excess of language in substance and style and the quiet dignity of simple locution.

A word should be said about the frequently cited thematic contrast between the Old Law and the New in the Wakefield cycle. It is, of course, true that a major concern of the cycle as a whole is to show how the retributive justice of the Old Testament gives way to the mercy of the New Testament. This issue is brought into direct enactment in the Doctors' pageant, another of the plays that depend almost entirely for their dramatic interest on debate. The Doctors continuously refer to what they characterize as "oure lawes" (the word in its various forms appears seven times in the pageant) and what specifically at one point the Tercius Magister calls "Moyses lay." But interestingly, when challenged by the Doctors, Christ brings forth a perfect recitation of the Ten Commandments, the kernel of their own law, as living evidence that he has come to fulfill and not to destroy the Old Testament. The body of the divine law itself, whether Old or New, is thus not ever a matter of controversy in the Wakefield cycle, only the way that the laws are carried out. The Doctors are haughty and self-serving men who, in sending Jesus away, fail to honor their God and their neighbor, the very laws they say they espouse:

> yei, lett hym furth on his wayes,
> for if he dwell, withoutten drede
> The pepyll will ful soyn hym prayse
> well more then vs, for all oure dede.
>
> (192/185-188)

Jesus, who is the real Magister of the sequence, is, however, the embodiment of his own teaching—mild and generous to all men—and by his example he brings out the best even in the Doctors as he parts from them (see 194/261-268). While the play is, by the canon generally accepted, not the work of the Wakefield author, it does present the background on which he built his major thematic concentration. (And it is of course one of the York plays on which he made major revisions elsewhere.) The divine law, Old and New, is never out of harmony. It is only the faulty perception of its interpreters (and of impostors) that brings with it the resonance of chaos.

The real conflict, then, is between the divine law and the civil, a conflict central to the Wakefield author's dramatic vision. This contrast stands at the core of the dramatic action throughout the cycle; it exists literally from the beginning, with Lucifer proclaiming to all Creation "master ye shall me call" (4/98), to the very end when Jesus calmly presides at the highest doom. The civil law is constantly exposed for its abuses, and

primary among these is the tyranny of temporal rulers, the characteristic ranters of the cycle drama in whom the Wakefield author took a special interest. It is usually the arrogant, self-aggrandizing, and loquacious tyrant figure who disturbs God's stillness with his ear-piercing harangues. In a sense, the Noah pageant, which by conventional standards is the first of the Wakefield author's full-length plays in the cycle, is a microdrama in which the central issue of the Wakefield cycle is given a humorous first airing. The reason for the Flood is familiar to all; God complains

> I repente full sore that euer maide I man;
> Bi me he settys no store, and I am his
>   soferan.
>
> (Caw. 16/91-92)

The divine law is therefore entrusted to Noah, who in the familiar form of the *figura* becomes a type of Christ on stage. Opposed to him, at least in the process of his building the ark (or, as familiarly interpreted, the church) is his *uxor,* who thus becomes the first, if unlikely, tyrant figure in the Towneley cycle. She has all the attributes: She challenges right order (by opposing her "syre"; Caw. 24/396); she boasts and rants (sometimes addressing the audience directly, as in Caw. 19/208-209); and she freely uses her cudgel in the form of a distaff (see Cawley note to 200). For a time at least she holds sway, much as Herod will later even as the Christ Child is born. What is particularly noteworthy about Noah's wife is her garrulousness. Her husband entreats her over and over again to hold her tongue, and much of his humor is in his characterization of her as a shrew. He describes her perfectly when he tells first her and then the audience:

> Thou can both byte and whyne
> With a rerd;
> For all if she stryke,
> Yit fast will she skryke.
>
> (Caw. 20/229-232)

And, at one point, he admonishes men who have wives "whyls thay ar yong" to "chastice thare tong" (Caw. 24/397-398). The whole of the action in the pageant is to bring harmony out of discord, a process for which the silencing of Noah's *uxor* is the central dramatic metaphor. In effect, Noah tells us as much when, in the beginning of their conflict, he says to her: "We! hold thi tong, ram-skyt, or I shall the still" (Caw. 19/217), or again later, "I shall make þe still as stone" (Caw. 24/406). And of course, he succeeds entirely in stilling her and thus reestablishing order and harmony in the human family. Most significantly, at the very end, even the ark is brought to calmness: "As still as a stone oure ship is stold" (Caw. 28/525). Thus physical and verbal storms abate, and if we bear in mind the figural interpretation of Noah and the ark, then the stillness and stability at the end of the play tell us something about the role of the church in a world too much obsessed with the discord of words.

Stillness, as was observed in the York cycle as well, characterizes the stability of God. The silence of Jesus dominates the Wakefield author's play of the Buffeting. Here as elsewhere in the cycle, notably the Herod pageant, tyrants by contrast virtually expire from their overuse of words. Where in other cycles, such as the N-Town, the tyrants are generally brought to violent deaths, in the Wakefield author's pageants they simply fade out; they seemingly suspire. Herod boasts himself to oblivion with his "I can no more Franch." Caiaphas, Annas, and Pilate, after their virtuoso performances as speechmakers and ranters, disappear from sight in the onset of calmness and harmony. The central issue of the Buffeting is once more the law. Jesus is accused by one of the Torturers, ironically, for teaching the people "a new law" (Caw. 80/66), and Caiaphas and Annas are implored, in turn, to "defende all oure law" (Caw. 81/115). The civil law is thus made the instrument by which the divine law—the whole spirit of the New Testament—is to be measured and judged. All through the accusation scene, Jesus stands in glorious silence while his temporal, ecclesiastical judges, Caiaphas and Annas, let go a stream of oaths and imprecations to make him "speke on oone word" (Caw. 82/145). Never has flamboyant and biting language been undercut more eloquently by silence than the point in the Buffeting at which Caiaphas ends his long tirade literally crying and shouting in frustration for Jesus to speak one syllable "be it hole worde or brokyn" (Caw. 82/174). The more subdued and cunning Annas recognizes that the force of Jesus' stillness is infinitely more potent than all the words he can summon. He asks, almost plaintively, "Why standys thou so styll when men thus accuse the?" (Caw. 84/246). In the end, neither the verbal nor the physical assaults on Jesus break his silence or discredit his law. The play with its emphasis on "vayn carpyng"—a fault for which, ironically, Jesus is directly accused as he proceeds on the Via Crucis in the *Flagellacio* (243/346)—is a brilliant poetic attack on the limits of rhetoric.

Much as the law is one topic of great thematic concern to the Wakefield author, so music is another. Both serve him to make implicit statements about the uses and misuses of language, and, even more narrowly, about the function of poetry. I have already shown how *musica ecclesiastica,* usually in the form of hymns, inheres in all those parts of the Wakefield cycle which give direct expression to the voice of God. I now wish to suggest that it is the contrast of *musica vulgaris* and *musica ecclesiastica,* and even more pointedly the eventual merging of the two, that becomes the most significant feature in the Wakefield author's revision from the First to the Second Shepherds' plays. I will maintain that, in the view of the Wakefield author, the solemn angelic song, the Gloria in Excelsis Deo, is the

highest expression that common man can perceive and emulate. The shift from discord to harmony, both in speech and music, can be seen as the fundamental concern of the Wakefield author's masterpiece—the *Second Shepherds' play*—which in its Adoration scene is the yardstick for the eloquence of simple reverence. (Although the applications differ, it is worth noting the common concern of both York and Towneley with stillness as a state in which the presence of God is manifest.)

The nucleus of all the Shepherds' plays, including the two in the Wakefield cycle, is clearly the appearance of the Angel announcing the Nativity and the angelic choir singing the Gloria in Excelsis Deo. The contrast of the divine messenger and the earthly listeners is the frequent subject of parodic humor, as note the response to the angelic singing in the Chester cycle by the three Shepherds:

PRIMUS PASTOR.	Fellowes in feare, may yee not here this mutinge on highe?
SECUNDUS PASTOR:	In 'glore' and in 'glere'? Yett noe man was nere within our sight.
TERTIUS PASTOR.	Naye, yt was a 'glorye.' Nowe am I sorye bowt more songe. (141/358-366)

The point here, as also in *The Holkham Bible Picture Book,* is to bring the sacred into the context of the profane and thus to universalize the significance of the Nativity. But whereas the musical burlesque is simply a humorous excursion in the Chester plays, the whole subject of *musica vulgaris,* in its varying forms, becomes a matter of thematic importance in the Wakefield Shepherds' plays and of central significance in the *Secunda Pastorum.*

To make this point clear, I must make some observations about the essential differences in subject matter between the two Shepherds' pageants in the Wakefield cycle and about the apparent process of revision to which the Wakefield author subjected the first version. It is, of course, well known that the two plays share many situations. In both, we have three Shepherds who come on stage remarking about the hardships of life; in both a fourth character (Iak Garcio and Mak) joins the Shepherds; in both, there is festive singing first among the Shepherds themselves, then by the angelic choir; in both, the Shepherds depart singing. There is, as well, a hint that the Wakefield author already had at least one of the main ingredients of the Mak plot in mind when he has Iak Garcio respond to the Shepherds' concern over gathering up the imaginary contents of an empty sack with the following remark:

Sagh I neuer none so fare bot the foles of
   Gotham.
Wo is hir that yow bare! Youre syre and youre
   dam,
Had she broght furth an hare, a shepe, or a
   lam,
Had bene well.
                    (Caw. 34/180-183; and cf. 101/182n)

The similarities of plot in the two Shepherds' plays are perhaps less noticeable than the differences. First among the latter is certainly the inclusion of the Mak episode in the **Secunda Pastorum**. On quick glance one is, in fact, tempted to say that the Wakefield author simply revised the first play by including this plot and making otherwise minor revisions. But closer examination will not sustain this view and will lead to the conclusion that the revision from the first to the second version was a major one in subject matter as well as theme and approach. The first play is, to begin with, much less obviously unified. The Wakefield author makes no attempt here to link the first half of the play focusing on the discussion and merrymaking of the Shepherds with the second part involving the Nativity. Implicitly, of course, one can view the physical hardships of the world cited in the soliloquies of the First and Second Shepherds as preparation for the advent of Christ and the spiritual balm offered at the end of the pageant. There is even some direct pleading with God that he come to bring "a better way" for the souls of sinners, that he "send theym good mendyng / with a short endyng" (Caw. 31/79-79). In this sense, one can perceive the games of the first part—all concerned with the imaginary—as a statement about the inconsequential nature of the material in contrast with the centrality of the spiritual. It is not the physical presence of sheep but the idea of sheep that causes the territorial dispute between shepherds One and Two. It is not a full sack of meal but rather an empty one, and not a real feast but an imaginary one, which provides the sustenance of the Shepherds and the substance of their games. The emphasis throughout this early scene seems to be deliberately on the unseeable, perhaps to prepare emotionally for the Incarnation that occurs at the end. The play thus deals with a set of intellectual reversals: In the first part substance becomes shadow in a farcical setting, while in the second spirit becomes flesh in a profoundly serious setting. But it must be emphasized that whatever is here as a unifying thought must be supplied by the insight of the reader or performer; the Wakefield author provides neither direct explanation nor an easily discernable coherence.

It is quite different in the Second Shepherds' play. First, as is well known, there is an obvious situational and even verbal coherence between the parodic and the serious nativities. It takes little effort to connect the "credyll" in Mak's cottage (see 334, 432, 538, 600) with the "cryb" of the Holy Family (see 645, 689) or

to recognize that both the sheep and the Christ Child are referred to as that "lytyll day-starne" (577, 727). In contrast, the words "cryb" and "mangere" as well as "mangyng" are used in the First Shepherds' play only in the farcical first part and always with reference to "eating" (see 201, 232), thus implying a much subtler unity that may well be meant to suggest the concept of the Eucharist by linking the feast of Part One with the celebration of the Christ Child in Part Two. The revision, therefore, is very much in the direction of the more explicit. This tendency is especially noticeable in what the two plays have to say about the function of music. The Wakefield author seems to make no special effort to integrate the Gloria with what has preceded in the First Shepherds' play. It is true that the Shepherds engage in a singing contest to see who gets the first drink (Caw. 36/265-266). But even though this event occurs shortly before the outburst of angelic song, with which it no doubt contrasted sharply, the Wakefield author fails to draw attention to this interesting juxtaposition. While song is clearly of great significance to the remainder of the play—thus establishing a tone of reverence and peace—no special mention is made of its place in the overall scheme of the play.

In the Second Shepherds' play, the role of music is much more prominent; indeed, the contrast between noise and music (or cacophony and harmony) is of central thematic importance to the outcome of the play. R. W. Ingram has already pointed out [in "The Use of Music in English Miracle Plays," *Anglia* 75, 1957] that there is a special significance to the uses of music in the play:

> The music as a whole not only acquires more meaning in the context of the play but is neatly varied and patterned: The cheerful song of the shepherds leads to the creaking voice of Mak's wife, to the sweet singing of the angel and so back again to the shepherds' singing on their way to the manger.

I would like to propose that there is much more here than random patterning and variation. In the first place, the Second Shepherds' play does much from the outset to associate unrest and noise with the profane, and peace and harmony with the sacred. In this respect, it shares of course with the rest of the Wakefield cycle an interest in volatile and often shrill language as an instrument for the portrayal of the lewd and the secular. It also presents the Wakefield author with the rare opportunity of using his stanza, which so characteristically fits the rhythms of the colloquial, to dramatize the solemn, if simple, dignity of the Nativity scene. It is in the Second Shepherds' play where the versatility of his stanza is most fully realized and where he seems most pointedly concerned with its artistic range. In the second place, the play seems to present a deliberate progression from discord to harmony, suggesting that in their imitation of the Angels's song, the Shepherds learn a new tranquillity of discourse with which to address the sacred. The most profound of the Wakefield pageants always are concerned with bringing awareness of the sacred to the profane. In the larger perspective, such common people as the Shepherds or old Joseph or even Noah's *uxor*, drawn anachronistically to Yorkshire specifications, become representatives of the audience. Consequently, whatever they learn stands empathetically for what the Corpus Christi spectator must also learn in the course of the dramatic performance. It is thus that the concept of the sacred is made most directly meaningful by the playwright.

The Second Shepherds' play opens, both in its language and its subject matter, on a note of discord that is sustained and even intensified until the Angel makes his appearance some six hundred lines later. At the very outset the First Shepherd speaks of "stormes and tempest" from which no one has rest (Caw. 43/6-9), while the Second Shepherd complains of the woe caused to wedmen by cackling wives who do nothing but "crok" and "groyne" and "clok" (Caw. 45/69-70). Mak enters upon the scene after the three Shepherds have broken out into a song of mirth, which they discuss with some apparent knowledge of the technical parts that constituted polyphonic singing:

1. PASTOR: Lett me syng the tenory.
2. PASTOR: And I the tryble so hye.
3. PASTOR: Then the meyne fallys to me.
                                (Caw. 48/186-188)

Thereupon Mak interrupts their song with an incantation to God and the exclamation that he is "all vneuen" (Caw. 48/192), and the First Shepherd greets him with the question "Who is that pypys so poore?" (Caw. 48/195). This, from the very first, the language of Mak is associated with bad singing. He is consistently characterized as a noisemaker, one who "makys sich dyn" (Caw. 51/297) or "sich a bere" (i.e. noise; Caw. 54/405) or who "commys with a lote" (another word for "noise"; Caw. 54/409). In turn, he makes the Shepherds break out in "a fowll noyse" and causes them to "cry out apon" him when they discover the loss of their sheep (Caw. 54/429-430). On their arrival at the cottage, they are greeted by Mak singing a "lullay" while Gyll groans and cries "outt by the wall on Mary and Iohn" (Caw. 55/442-443), to which the Shepherds respond as follows:

3. PASTOR: Will ye here how they hak? Oure
              syre lyst croyne.
1. PASTOR: Hard I neuer none crak so clear out
              of toyne.
                                (Caw. 56/476-477)

There can be little doubt that the farcical plot of the Second Shepherds' play was deliberately meant to emphasize the dissonances of everyday life. The Wake-field author clearly revised the first version of his play to stress disharmony, as is attested alone by the much more diversified onomatopoetic vocabulary for noise. Thus the limited list of such words in the first play (*blast, brall, brayde, crak, rafys,* and *yelp*) is expanded to include the following: *cry, crok, croyne, grone, mone, bark, blast, blawes, blete, crak, crakyd, ianglyng, kakyls, knakt, pypys, raue, skawde, stamerd,* and *whystyll,* and some of these words are used more than once. Likewise the vocabulary for music is also much expanded in the second play. Where in the first we encounter only such rather common words as *syng, song, sang, tonyd,* and *voce,* in the second we find a much richer mix: *syng, lullay, note, song, stevyn, pypys, tenory, tryble, meyne, chauntt, brefes, long* (note), and *whystyll.* It is evident that the Wakefield author chose in his second version to emphasize the contrastive languages of noise and music.

With the appearance of the Angel and the singing of the Gloria in Excelsis Deo, a new peaceful tone suggesting solemnity and harmony is struck. The First Shepherd is immediately awed by the beauty of the song: "This was a qwant stevyn that euer yit I hard" (Caw. 60/647). In fact, as JoAnna Dutka has already pointed out [in *Music in the English Mystery Plays,* Early Drama, Art and Music (EDAM) Reference Series, no. 2, 1980], the Shepherds of the ***Secunda Pastorum,*** unlike those of the ***Prima Pastorum,*** are impressed especially by the musical complexity of the angelic song; they comment specifically on the division of long notes into notes of smaller value when they observe how the Angel "crakyt it, / Thre brefes to a long" (Caw. 60/656-657), a technical description of a perfect relation between *longa* and *brevis.* As I have already observed, the Shepherds in the ***Secunda Pastorum*** are themselves musicians capable of rendering polyphonic song. It is thus very much in character for them to try to imitate the Angel and to sing a song likewise "of myrth. . .withoutt noyse" (Caw. 61/667-669). That they ultimately fail—they can only "bark at the mone" (Caw. 61/662)—is of course simply acknowledgement of their human limitation. But in their act of imitation, they raise to a simple dignity and beauty their own language. The highest secular expression comes at the very end of the play when each of the three Shepherds recites (perhaps even chants) a perfect "hayll"-lyric (710-736). Manfred F. Bukozer reminds us in his chapter, "Popular and Secular Music in England," that there were such things as "popular" sacred compositions [in *Ars Nova and the Renaissance, 1300-1540,* 1960]. If any verse ever so qualified, it was surely the "hayll"-lyrics of the ***Secunda Pastorum.*** What has happened then in the overall progress of the Second Shepherds' play is a wholesale elevation of tone. The most dissonant voices of the secular world have been stilled, and the singers of popular song have been inspired by angelic example to raise their voices in sacred harmony to celebrate the birth of Christ. For the Wakefield author the ultimate interest in the Second Shepherds' play is to elevate the language of his rustics in order that they might find the right tone in which to hail God.

I have attempted to show in this analysis that, largely because of the special slant provided by the Wakefield author as reviser, the Wakefield plays make an important statement about the limits of art. Ironically, when viewed from this angle, the contributions of the Wakefield author must be accepted as deliberately flawed: The very virtuosity of language that gives his stanzas their special flair and distinction hinders communication on the highest level of intercourse. In a sense, the Wakefield stanza is to the simple couplet and quatrain what the Devil is to God: It is at once adversary and servant to the total design. It constantly brings static into the harmony of the cosmos; it cannot refrain from injecting dissonances into the most solemn of occasions. Its liveliness is also its greatest peril. The artist at his best has always been a rival of God; the Wakefield author knows that fact and fights to suppress his awesome challenge. His greatest moment of achievement is to make his stanza subservient to God at the end of the Second Shepherds' play. And yet he comes back again and again in his more accustomed dissident voice, until finally, in the play of the Great Doom he empirically passes judgement upon himself and leaves us to ponder the resonances of eternal salvation and damnation.

Peter Meredith (essay date 1994)

SOURCE: "The Towneley Cycle," in *The Cambridge Companion to Medieval English Theatre*, edited by Richard Beadle, Cambridge University Press, 1994, pp. 134-62.

[*In the following excerpt, Meredith discusses the general background of the Towneley plays, the style of the Wakefield Master, and the plays as part of a dramatic cycle.*]

Almost certainly the most anthologised of all medieval English dramatic pieces is the so-called **Second Shepherds' Play,** containing the double story of Mak the sheep-stealer and the visit of the shepherds to Bethlehem. Through this public exposure, not only the play but the 'name' of the author also has become familiar— 'The Wakefield Master'. Not everyone who knows of the **Second Shepherds',** however, will automatically connect it with the thirty-two short plays (better called 'pageants') that together make up the Towneley cycle, or realise that it is not so much the 'second' as an alternative Shepherds' pageant: *Alia eorundem* (another of the same). Even knowing the relationship between the pageant, the Wakefield Master and the Towneley cycle does not, however, take you very far; why, for example *Wakefield* Master, but *Towneley* cycle?

'Wakefield' refers to the smallish industrial town in what used to be the West Riding of Yorkshire, once the centre of the extensive medieval manor of Wakefield. Since early in this century it has been claimed, with varying degrees of certainty, as the original home and place of performance of this cycle of pageants. As the York play was to York, so, it was said, the Towneley cycle was to Wakefield. The name 'Wakefield Master' was hence created as a convenient reference name for the anonymous author of a strikingly original group of pageants within the cycle. His pageants contain a number of references to places in and around Wakefield and it is not, therefore, an inappropriate name. He is not, however, certainly known to be a Wakefield man. The name 'Towneley' comes from the family of Towneley in whose possession the manuscript of the pageants was when it came to public notice in the early nineteenth century. The name was established as that of the cycle by the publication of *The Towneley Mysteries* in 1836 by the Surtees Society—the first of the complete cycles to be published. The family were Catholics and their main seat was Towneley Hall near Burnley in Lancashire. The manuscript formed part of the library of Christopher Towneley, a seventeenth-century antiquary and collector, but how it came into his possession or where it came from is not known. As a Catholic, Towneley may have picked up and preserved the manuscript as a sample of a time when his faith was the acknowledged faith of the whole of the country.

The first problem with the cycle is, then, one of names and origins. A second, in some ways related, problem is the kind of performance that is appropriate to it, related because knowledge of the place of performance can provide knowledge of the type of staging. With no town records to serve as a context for the cycle we are thrown back on the manuscript and the text itself. Unfortunately, unlike those in N-Town, the stage directions do not give 'staging' information. That is, they do not talk in terms of scaffolds or 'place' or curtains unclosing but in the narrative terms of the story. The staging information in the stage directions tends to be details of movement, gesture and action, not broad indications of stages and sets. Furthermore, the association with Wakefield, even if it were certain, would provide no more information about the physical theatrical setting of the cycle, since the burgess court records refer only to text and responsibility.

A more basic problem even than those of provenance and staging is the nature of the cycle itself. Comparison with York again reveals how our certainty about the York cycle derives from a combination of text with civic information. The relationship of pageants to crafts, the responsibilities for performance, the type of performance, the date and to some extent the development of the cycle are all matters of certainty or relative certainty because of this combined evidence. Because of the absence of related records for Towneley, the smallest details of the writing, layout and make-up of the manuscript, and its later treatment, become of crucial importance in trying to understand the cycle. There are any number of questions for which answers might be sought in the manuscript but three related ones stand out: What kind of manuscript is it? What function did it serve? and What is its date?

Its most likely function was that of register, or official copy of a play cycle, but this is difficult to prove. Only one register exists, that for the York play, so the evidence for the nature of a register derives from one example only. The York Register is a complete text of all the pageants (except for a number never entered but for which spaces were left). By its very existence it demonstrates a civic concern with the play, and this is borne out by the marginal annotations, which show the city authorities attempting to keep an eye on the extent to which the text as performed was differing from the text as recorded in the Register. Further civic concern is with the responsibility of individual crafts for specific pageants. Craft names, not titles, are used as running headings in the manuscript.

Even a glance at the Towneley manuscript will reveal how little these features are present. There are no running headings. The pageants are titled and the only craft attributions are later additions at the beginnings of four pageants, with one craft ('Lysters pagon') repeated, vertically, in the margin of the last (unfinished) pageant, *Judas*. It would certainly not serve as a check on craft responsibility. The annotations are few. There are two deletions relating to what can only be Protestant censorship one being annotated: 'correctyd and not playd'. There is a small scattering of notes written vertically and horizontally in the margin (e.g. fol. 31, 'note this very. . .'; fol. 61, 'no materes ben as sade') and a few alterations to the text. These include the addition of a missing line (fol. 81V), the correction (again for Protestant purposes) of a line relating to the Mass (fol. 67), and minor alterations of words ('lady' to 'lord', fol. 44; 'a pope' erased, fol. 57V). In no way are these comparable to the York annotations. The Towneley manuscript looks like a register primarily because it has what looks like a complete cycle of pageants. There are gaps (no *Trial before Herod,* for example) and there are pageants out of order (**Pharaoh, Lazarus** and **Judas**) but it remains a cycle.

What the annotations do, it seems to me, is to suggest that this was a manuscript related (however distantly) to performance. This makes sense of noting that a passage was 'not playd'. That there are few annotations does not matter. We do not know whether the York Register was typical, or even whether there is such a thing as a typical register. Furthermore, if Towneley was from Wakefield the social set-up was of quite a different kind: a small town, the centre of a large manor and under the control of the lord of the manor and his bailiff, not, like York, a largely autonomous city. There is also no real reason why the craft names should appear in the same way in both play manuscripts. The craft guilds in York were directly responsible to the city authorities. We do not know what the relationship of the crafts to the Towneley cycle was. If we again use the Wakefield records, then it is clear that crafts were involved there and that they were subject to fines by the burgess court; but the records are of 1556. Could it be that the later additions of craft names in Towneley relate to a later development in Wakefield? There is at the moment no way of telling.

This raises the question of date. The manuscript used to be thought of as of the mid-fifteenth century, but the most recent study, the facsimile edition, puts it either very late in the fifteenth century or, perhaps more likely, into the sixteenth. The date of the manuscript is not, of course, the date of the cycle, but a late date for the one does allow a late date for the other, if there is no other reason for restricting it. It is also important to remember that the date of the cycle means the date of the compilation, the putting together of this group of pageants, and not the date of individual pageants. The nature of the compilation is somewhat complex but to take it at its simplest level there are three elements: pageants known to be from York, Wakefield Master pageants and pageants from another source or sources. Setting aside dubious cases, the Wakefield Master has added to or revised two of the York pageants, and also added (though only once substantially) to four pageants from other sources. No one has obviously revised or tampered with any of the complete Wakefield Master pageants and it would therefore seem a not unreasonable conclusion that his was the last revision of the cycle. 'Revision' sounds like a formal review of the whole work, but it would be wrong to think of it in those terms. These are plays, not acts of parliament, and no doubt the reviser added, altered and deleted only where he was specifically directed or where he saw an opportunity to improve. Certainly the Wakefield Master seems to have indulged his natural skill in extending the range of humour and grandeur of the ranting tyrants. The period of the whole compilation may well, therefore, be the period when the Wakefield Master was making his alterations. Unfortunately that does not provide a firm date. The most helpful internal evidence comes from the satirical costume references in the additions to the *Judgement,* but even that is open to question. Long hair and padded shoulders for men and low collars for women do suggest the late fifteenth century, but other references could as easily be earlier or not suggest any particular date. Hoods, which are referred to, apparently went out of fashion in the mid century; horned headdresses are usually taken to refer to the extravagances of the early part of the century, but could also refer to later fashions. The costume references cannot provide a firm date, but they certainly do not exclude the latter part of the century. . . .

Though there have been dissenting voices, the Wakefield Master's work has usually been highly praised. His skills are readily appreciated in the study, and criticism, often at a loss as to how to deal with the plays, has tended to concentrate on his work to the exclusion of the rest of the cycle. Two concurrent lines of investigation, apparently very diverse, have brought renewed attention to the whole cycle. One is the study of manuscripts. There the concern with understanding the nature of the manuscript, and in particular of explicating the relationship between play and performance, has brought attention back to the interrelationship of all pageants and, surprisingly, encouraged an interest in cycles in performance. The other is the renewed interest in the plays as theatrical experiences: day-long, popular, open-air (often street), celebratory performances, not extracts made to fit into twentieth-century prosceniumarch theatres or single pageants forced into the one-act play format. This welcome revival of interest in the cycles—as opposed to individual pageants—as theatrical pieces is a necessary step before criticism looks, as it has still not done properly, at the Towneley cycle as a whole. . . .

. . . . .

A. C. Cawley in his edition of *The Wakefield Pageants in the Towneley Cycle* puts forward three main pieces of evidence for the existence of the writer usually referred to as the 'Wakefield Master': the regular use of a particular nine-line stanza in five pageants (**Noah,** the two **Shepherds, Herod the Great** and the **Buffeting**), that the pageants written in this stanza are distinguished by a highly original use of colloquial idiom and that verbal parallels, as well as a number of other similarities of style and content, exist between the pageants. This may seem somewhat flimsy evidence upon which to base the existence of a writer, and yet anyone reading the five pageants will almost certainly be struck by their similarities of tone and style. To these pageants Cawley adds the **Killing of Abel,** which, though it has only one pure Wakefield Master stanza (and one with one line missing) (in 76, lines 450-62 and 463-70), seems to him and to most scholars to bear all the signs of Wakefield Master work. Cawley also draws attention to the existence of other uses of this characteristic stanza, equally in the same style, and concludes that the Wakefield Master had a hand in re-shaping or adding to the **Conspiracy** (stanzas 2-5), the **Scourging** (stanzas 5-27), the **Crucifixion** (stanza 57), the **Dicing** (stanzas 1-5 and 56-9), the **Pilgrims** (stanza 4), the **Ascension** (stanzas 57-8) and the **Judgement** (stanzas 16-48 and 68-76) (76, p. xviii). Apart from one or two minor uncertainties, this seems to be a convinc-

ing minimum view of the extent of his work.

I want to look at the Wakefield Master's work first through his revision of the York **Judgement,** where some of his talents and propensities are displayed in an extreme form. Most noticeable of all is his verbal extravagance. His characteristic stanza form may in part have commended itself to him because it demanded a high degree of verbal ingenuity, and then allowed a display of the results of that ingenuity in its series of rhymes. There is no doubt at all of his love of words. He reaches out for them in all directions: the language of fashion, of the streets, the law courts, the cloister. Where he cannot find a word he invents it (*tristur,* 'post, job', line 208; *pransawte,* 'prancing', line 561), or perhaps trawls through the lower levels of the language to turn it up (*fryggys?* 'fidget, jerk about', line 316; *skawte,* 'blow', line 559). There are constant reminders of his virtuosity:

With hawvell and Iawvell	*babbling; jabbering*
syngyng of lawvell	*?drinking songs*
	(lines 337-8)

his luddokkys thai lowke like walk-mylne cloggys,	*buttocks; look; fulling-mill blocks*
his hede is like a stowke, hurlyd as hoggys	*stook; bristly*
A woll blawen bowke—thise fryggys as froggys,	*puffed-out belly; jerk about*
This Ielian Iowke, dryfys he no doggys To felter.	*?hunt*
	(lines 314-18)

The **Judgement** also reveals his enjoyment of lists of words. One stanza indeed is to all intents and purposes simply a list:

Ye lurdans and lyars, mychers and thefes,	*rogues; pilferers*
Flytars and flyars, that all men reprefes,	*scolds; fugitives; reprove*
Spolars, extorcyonars, welcom, my lefes. . .	*spoilers; comrades*
	(lines 359-61)

He clearly delights in problems; series of rhymes on a Latin word, for example: 'thus/*eius,* tax/wax/*mendax/*' (lines 282-6); 'is/mys/*fecistis*' (lines 301-3); 'com/*eternum,* day/may/*mala*' (lines 381-5).

Sometimes he creates comically contrived rhymes: 'roll of ragman [a list of accusations] / breffes in my bag, man, / vnethes [scarcely] may I wag, man, / whils I set my stag [young horse], man.' (lines 224-7) or 'fill vs / till vs / Tutiuillus' (lines 246-8). He is only drawn once into identical rhymes in this pageant: 'hoket/hoket' (lines 233-4) or twice into nearly alike in: 'wedlake/ lake' (lines 586-7) and 'hande/nere-hande' (lines 189/ 891), but these are small failures amongst the eighty-six four-rhyme and forty-three three-rhyme series that are required.

Two things in particular, I think, undermine this bravura display. The first is that the words are not borne up by a sufficiently varied syntax. Though there are variations, the syntactical and rhythmic pattern is predominantly one of mid-line break and end-stopping. There is a considerable element of subjectivity here, but on my count the ratio of clear breaks (mid-line and end-line) to run-on lines is a little under two to one. Secondly, the thought and action of the additions are largely uncontrolled. The devils ramble and the lost souls (if we may consider their speeches also part of the Wakefield Master's revision) extend the laments by more than double. It is not that what they say is uninteresting, but that the impact of the Judgement is lost. The contrast is excellent between the ordered, rather old-fashioned, patterned statements of Jesus and the disordered verbal extravagances of the devils, but the delay in the action is too great between 'The tyme is commen I will make ende' (line 81) and the making of that end over three hundred lines later. What might have sustained the action would have been a continuous sense of the frightened compulsion to go to the Judgement occasionally apparent in the devils, but this is impossible to create out of the odd reference amidst an indulgent parading of sins. In addition the satirical descriptions do not grow into an absorbing of the audience into the dread of Doomsday. They become instead an entertaining display, as they are for the devils.

I have spent this long on the Wakefield Master's section of the *Judgement* because it demonstrates clearly some of the major strengths and weaknesses that reveal themselves, usually in a smaller way, in the rest of his work. His major strength, his command of a wide and varied vocabulary, provides the external appeal of many of his pageants and additions to pageants: an obvious example is the bravura Latin opening of the *Dicing*. It comes out clearly in the mock feast of the first of the *Shepherds* pageants, where the most exotic words of aristocratic cookery are laid side by side with mock French and comic English: 'oure mangyng' (eating, from French *manger*) where we 'foder/Oure mompyns' (feed our faces) with 'sawsed' and 'powderd' meat, 'chekyns endorde' (gilded), 'calf lyuer skorde with the veryose' (sliced and served with verjuice, lines 232, 209-10, 215, 216, 234, 236). It flourishes in the hypochondriac rages of Herod (though less exotically than in the vaunts of Pilate): 'losels, lyars, lurdans, tratoures, knafys' (lines 163-4), 'ditizance doutance' (Fr. 'say without doubt', line 171), 'Fy, dottypols' (crackpots', line 231), and in his list of literary sources: 'Vyrgyll, Homere, legende, poece tayllys, pystyls, grales, mes, matyns' (lines 202-7). It is

apparent too in the minor uses of Latin, not only the prophecies recorded by Herod's doctors and the shepherds, where it might be expected (though adding Virgil to the shepherds' catalogue, even if it is drawn from the well-known Pseudo-Augustinian sermon, gives it something of a virtuoso performance), but in night spells (*Shepherds* I, lines 290-4; *Shepherds* II lines 266-7) and to accompany the stretching and yawning awakening of one of the shepherds: *Resurrex a mortuus! . . . Judas carnas dominus!* (*Shepherds* II, lines 350-1). It exists too in his use of proverbs and proverb-like utterances and of traditional stories and incidents. Not only does he use them as a typical part of human language, but he uses them naturally; they are character-creating, not merely decorative, as with the proverb-capping meeting of the two shepherds:

2 SHEP.:	Poore men ar in the dyke and oft tyme mars,	*come to grief*
	The warld is slyke, also helpars	*like that*
	Is none here.	
1 SHEP.:	It is sayde full ryfe,	*commonly*
	'A man may not wyfe	*marry*
	And also thryfe,	*prosper*
	And all in a yere'.	
2 SHEP.:	Fyrst must vs crepe and sythen go.	*We must crawl before we can walk*

(*Shepherds* I, lines 93-100)

This verbal abundance creates characters at all levels, not just that of the shepherds. The vaunts of Pilate and the rages of Herod are more entertaining because of the words they use, but the words also individualise the characters. Words also create situation. The idea of the mock feast is good fun, the audience sees bread and ale (or maybe water) while it hears the words of medieval *haute cuisine,* but it is only the choice of those words that can give a reality to the artistocratic meal or create the kind of image that will make it parallel to the poverty of the stable embodying the royalty of the King of Kings.

The abundance of words and the images they carry with them might be expected to produce a sense of God's plenty, but instead they seem to me to convey man's plenty. This seems to be true in almost all the Wakefield Masters' pageants and adaptations. His major skill is an ability to create the variety of the world. Noah and his wife are a squabbling married couple. He is also a patriarch and the chosen of God, but first he is a hen-pecked husband. He is not a figure or type of Christ in this pageant because the playwright makes no attempt to present him as such. The ark is not the Church, his wife is not the saved Christian, the Flood is not the Last Judgement. This is another well-told story. Maybe the fights go on a bit too long, maybe two is too many, but the comedy and the humanity are what make the story effective. It is the fun of 'ram-skyt' (ram-shit); of the fearful husband knowing what's coming—'And I am agast that we get som fray / Betwixt vs both' (lines 184-5); of the knockabout fights; of the presentation of the typical human situation, not the type-antitype situation, that govern the pageant.

The Wakefield Master's work is not open throughout to typological explanation, because he tends to draw attention to it when its use is appropriate. One of his skills lies in his ability to touch a stable reference point in the spiritual world beyond this one when he wants to. Little touches like 'This is boyte of oure bayll' (**Shepherds** I, line 147) in relation to a bottle of ale (or water imagined as ale) rather than Christ, are intellectual/spiritual fun because they hint at this other world, but like the anachronistic curses and asseverations they do not draw that world to the fore. It is at most the sudden shock of the strangeness, not a complex presentation of time, that is involved. Hints of the fall of man do not turn the widow's farmyard of the Nun's Priest's Tale into the Garden of Eden, they intellectually enliven the story Chaucer is telling by hinting at and suggesting unexpected associations. The oaths and refences are there primarily because they are what people say. They are part of a localised contemporary humanity. Only secondarily do they give a glimpse of a world beyond.

Individualised humanity lies at the root of almost all the Wakefield Master's techniques. He deliberately eschews the 'shepherds are pastors', *Pilatus id est diabolus* kind of equation. His shepherds and Pilates are individuals, made so by what they say and how they say it. This is why suggestions that all the tyrants are merely clones of Satan or Antichrist is so unsatisfactory. It is not their likeness that makes them interesting but their individuality. Pilate lives through the details he reveals of himself—each time different from or an extension of the last.

The second of the **Shepherds** pageants is remarkable because it is in this pageant alone that the individualised humanity and the presence of the spiritual world are integrated in a broader way. The shepherds are created separate: one moans of the inequalities of the social order, the second of the conflicts of marriage, the third of those of employer and employed. The structure of their speeches, however, links them together. Each complains first of the elemental disorder of the world (the weather—they are after all English shepherds) before going on to the specific complaint. Each complaint is contained within six stanzas. The first and second shepherds have six stanzas each of soliloquy, the third, for variation, has three stanzas, then one of dialogue, and then another two to himself. They also have a less obvious similarity in the movement from complaint to resolution. The first having made his complaint, shrugs it off, 'It dos me good. . .Of this warld for to talk in maner of mone' (lines 46-7); the second

rounds his off with a comic caricature of his own wife which allows any seriousness that the complaint might have had to dissolve in laughter. For the third shepherd the audience witnesses the complaint acted out, since he is the servant and the other two the masters. As the complaint is enacted, so is its resolution, in the singing of the three-part song. The naming of the parts—'tenory', 'tryble' and 'meyne'—is not mere verbal gusto on the part of the Wakefield Master, but a deliberate indication that the song is in three parts and that they harmonise. The less obvious similarity in the **Shepherds'** opening, then, is one of movement in the case of each shepherd from discontent with one's state and with one's fellow human beings to content and harmony. Society may be grossly unjust, especially to the poor, marriage may be hell, especially if you're married (and a man), it may be no fun being a servant, especially with masters like these two, but it does not stop good fellowship and good humour from re-establishing contentment. The first part of the pageant is, then, a cleverly varied pre-echo of what most people now see as the main theme of the whole pageant, the movement from conflict to reconciliation, from a world at odds with God to one reconciled to him through the birth of Christ.

In the major part of the pageant this conflict must be felt, hence the value of the Wakefield Master's skill in establishing a sense of a real situation: natural suspicion of the known thief, natural animosity between masters and men, natural (if typical) conflict between husband and wife. But as with all else he does, the sense of 'natural' is primarily a product of his verbal vitality, especially apparent in Mak: his southern tooth, his night spell, his 'magic', his (and Gill's) ingenious excuses for the state of their 'baby'. The reconciliation of this conflict is equally natural. It is turned into a very ordinary game; but this is also the way in which lyric, carol and sermon writers described the birth of Christ and the end of man's separation from God. The two halves of the pageant thus stand as unequal but matching sides of a figural diptych: birth and birth, reconciliation and reconciliation. There is no need to read this into the pageant: it is there. Not so obvious as to be unexciting, but with sufficient indications as to be inevitable.

But what of the shepherds? The pre-echo of reconciliation that acted as a kind of prologue to the pageant is not merely another part of the matching diptych; it is also the first step in a demonstration that the shepherds are indeed the men to whom the angel's message should be addressed. Their coming to terms with their complaints in one way or another is a first sign of this. The second is the entirely natural (and heart-warming) reaction of the third shepherd and the others to their failure of common humanity in not giving Mak and Gill's newborn child a gift. The third is their common agreement to turn the punishment of Mak into a game.

Thus the Wakefield Master's elaborate creation of three believable human beings is part and parcel of the spiritual meaning of the pageant. The audience does not just understand that the angelic message was to men of goodwill, it feels what goodwill is by being moved by the common humanity, common humaneness, of the three shepherds.

The **Shepherds** pageant is also a demonstration that the Wakefield Master's knowledge is not just of words. It is apparent that the description of the song of the three shepherds is not merely a demonstration of the writer's technical competence but is to draw attention to the abstract idea of harmony. The Wakefield Master repeats this use of music in the course of the pageant thereby creating a kind of choric comment on the action. The discordant singing of Mak (accompanied perhaps by Gill's groans) is the other side of humanity's music. The angel's song (and it is important to remember that there is only one angel) is the perfect music of heaven. Again the Wakefield Master uses technical terms for a spiritual purpose: 'There brefes to a long' ('Three short notes to one long') is, according to the theorists, perfect time. It is also perfect audibly; the 'harmonies' are so true as to be indistinguishable from a single line. The shepherds then try to imitate it and fail comically. But the comic failure is a further sign of humanity. Laughter becomes in this pageant a sign of man's goodwill, a parallel to the game that is Mak's punishment.

The Wakefield Master is, then, as capable of controlled. structured writing as he is of boisterous exuberance. He is quite able to handle a complex parallel presentation of the spiritual and human world, but even here humanity dominates. His achievement in this pageant is to make his proven skill in the depiction of humanity subserve a spiritual aim (and to interweave with it) without losing any of its natural life.

Martin Stevens has recently suggested [in *Four Middle English Mystery Plays*, 1987] that the Wakefield Master was the 'guiding intelligence' for the whole cycle. This is impossible to prove or disprove but it does usefully raise the question of the extent to which his hand can be traced. The normal way of recognising his work is through the use of the characteristic nine-line stanza. Yet it is unlikely that such a skilful and ebullient writer would allow himself to be confined in such a way, and the fairly general agreement amongst scholars about his authorship or at least his participation in the writing of the **Killing of Abel** shows a willingness to accept this. But looking for his work outside the nine-line stanza can only be based on his work done in it, and judging only from that we may be getting a false impression of his complete range. In particular we know very little about what might be called his 'solemn' style. Almost everything that survives is for shepherds, devils, hen-pecked patriarchs, tyrants and the like. We have very little for God (ten stanzas, many of them directions for building the ark), for Mary (two stanzas), Jesus (four lines), for angels (two stanzas). Outside the five pageants there is a tiny sample for the apostles: Luke, one stanza in the *Pilgrims;* Matthew, one in the *Ascension*. Neither of these, though competent, is anything out of the ordinary, and anyway they are too brief to give a fair sample. It may, therefore, be that in our assessment of his work we are missing an important side of his output. The *Thomas of India* pageant should perhaps be looked at closely. It has what looks like a series of Wakefield Master rhymes in one of Peter's speeches:

> Bot euer alas! what was I wode! myght no
>   man be abarstir;
> I saide if he nede be-stode to hym shuld none
>   be trastir;
> And for a woman that there stode, that spake
>   to me of frastir,
> I saide I knew not that good creature my
>   master.
> (lines 73-5, with the missing line, 74a,
>   supplied from the manuscript)

The invention and adaptation that has gone into producing the rhymes 'abarstir/trastir/of frastir' (more ashamed/more trusty/?questioningly) are typical of those found elsewhere. Besides this, the argument between Thomas and the other apostles is handled with considerable ingenuity and naturalness. The fact that it goes on too long may also seem characteristic of some of his work. It is difficult to speculate about what the 'solemn' side of his writing would be like but at least this might be a starting-point for investigation.

. . . . .

It has been suggested that the pageants of the Towneley cycle do not combine well together. Rosemary Woolf expresses it most clearly:

> The only cycle in which the different styles and stages of revision have not grown together into an organic whole is the Towneley cycle. . .

This apparent lack of unity is up to a point a scholarly and literary problem rather than a theatrical one. The fact that we know that the York pageants in Towneley are from York gives them a separateness that they would not have if their different origin was unknown. Besides which the briefness of pageants like the **Salutation** or the **Flight into Egypt** that we can see in reading them is not nearly so noticeable in performance, where they have their own individuality and physical space. Equally the rather simple language of pageants like the **Creation, Isaac** or **Jacob** is less obvious when the pageant is seen as well as heard. Only the Wakefield Master's work, perhaps, because his pageants are so much more developed, literary and structured, stands out. There is a danger that they hold up the flow of the narrative. In performance again this seems not to be so. Pageant performance involves the isolation of incidents and episodes while at the same time allowing them to be part of the same story. Their temporal and spatial relation to the whole is therefore not the same as scenes in a continuous action. Pageant performance can absorb very different styles of writing as well as of playing—as it must if the responsibility for the playing is divided amongst a number of individual craft guilds, with, as far as we know, no overall control.

There are some odd gaps in the cycle, apart from those caused by the losses in the manuscript. There is no temptation of Christ, no institution of the sacrament at the Last Supper, no trial before Herod (though it is referred to). There are also unexpected additions: the *Isaac* and *Jacob* pageants, *Caesar Augustus,* the *Dicing*. But these do not prevent the cycle from being a whole. David Mills has suggested [in *Leeds Studies in English,* 1986] that the pageants exist within a known story and that there is therefore no need to perform every part of the story. This is surely right. How many people in seeing the cycle are aware that there is no Nativity or are worried by the fact that there has been no trial before Herod, even though the first torturer says that that is where they are coming from? As for the additions, *Isaac* and *Jacob* form part of an integrated family group with *Abraham,* and the *Dicing* provides yet another interesting sidelight on Pilate (and, for those who know the story, a lead into his later life) as well as providing an entertaining break between the horrors of the crucifixion and the joys of the harrowing and resurrection. *Caesar Augustus* is more difficult to justify. Trivial in language and oversimple as verse, it lacks any interest of plot and seems merely a tame preparation for Herod.

There is also a more positive unifying element, a sense of a concentration on human nature which gives the cycle a certain homogeneity. All the cycles translate biblical into human. It is good teaching practice—a way of making the Bible live; it is an obvious way of expanding what are often the bare hints of a story; and it is, in the fourteenth and fifteenth centuries, the normal approach to Christ's life. To say, therefore, that a cycle is characterised by its humanity would seem to be stating the inevitable. In Towneley, however, there seems to be far more particularising of human language, character and action than elsewhere. It is especially noticeable, of course, in the Wakefield Master and it may well be that the dominance of his presence in the cycle draws the reader's attention to this element in the other pageants. Even before the scatological humanity of Cain, however, there is a Lucifer who even before he falls doesn't care a 'leke' (*Creation,* line 129) and a Cherub who leads Adam into Paradise by the hand, giving him and Eve distinctly elder-broth-

er/sisterly advice (lines 210-25). What gives a strong sense of humanity to the cycle is the number of particularising words or phrases, or individualising emotions, actions or idea. The image of Cain's debased humanity is largely created by his individualised language. We may be used to God's 'back parts' (*posteriora mea,* Exodus 33.23) but 'his ars' (*Abel,* line 238) still seems the most incredible blasphemy. Cain's language not only particularises his humanity but attempts to re-create others, including God, in his image. In the main action of *Abraham* the human element almost of necessity predominates, but from the beginning that element is there. In his first speech Abraham recalls the past. Partly this links him into the story; but he does not do it impersonally, instead he sees it through a veil of pity for the sadness of it all. Remembering brings no comfort, only a longing for death (lines 33-6). Later, as Abraham pictures the return home without Isaac, he very sharply particularises Sarah's reactions and words.

> What shal I to his moder say?
> For 'Where is he?' tyte will she spyr;
>   *at once ask*
> If I tell hir 'Ron away',
> Hir answere bese belife—'Nay, sir!'
>   *will immediately be*
>   (lines 225-8)

Even some of the small additions to *Pharaoh* are in the direction of additional individuality of speech (e.g. lines 219, 225, 230, 232). The biblical account is altered at the end of *Jacob* in order to give greater weight to the reconciliation of Jacob and Esau and to the reuniting of the family in Esau's last words. In Genesis the reconciliation is rather a cold one and there is no invitation from Esau that they should together go to see their parents. Apparent anachronism can also be an individualising device, as it is most frequently in the oaths and asseverations of shepherds, torturers and others, but also in the tithes of Cain (lines 104-5 in particular) and Jacob (lines 55-8).

David Mills has seen a unifying element in memory in the cycle (209). I am sure he is right but I would prefer the term 'recollection'. In York, also, it is not uncommon for a character to run through earlier history at the opening of a pageant, but in Towneley this recalling occurs elsewhere as well and is far more personal to the character. It has already been suggested that Abraham's first speech is an individualising one, but its subject is the recalling of the past. *Noah* opens not with God recalling the past but with Noah, and what starts as an address to God in his majesty and might turns into a contemplation of sin and a fear of God's vengeance. Again the recalling has a personal and emotional basis. The same is true of other acts of recalling. The precise recollections of Christ's miracles are by the torturers, angrily condemning his failure to conform to the law (*Scourging,* lines 152-87), or, less individualised and more conventional, by Annas and Caiaphas trying to convince Pilate of the need for action (**Conspiracy,** lines 92-133). The lyric added to the **Resurrection** acts as a recalling of the crucifixion in the middle of the triumph of the resurrection. The disciples in the **Pilgrims** and in **Thomas of India** recall the same events in grief, and in disbelief of the fulfilment of remembered promises. The other element of recalling is prophecy, which, except for the **Prophets,** almost always appears as recollection. Like the moments of recalling, the prophecies are usually part of some human reaction to events: the kings' excited realisation that the star they are following is the fulfilment of Balaam's prophecy (**Magi,** lines 205-28), Simeon's pondering on the fate of his predecessors and gratitude for the prophecies that have been sent (**Purification,** lines 9-24), the doctors' faith that the prophecies will be fulfilled but their doubt about when (**Doctors** lines 1-48), the souls in hell recalling at the moment of fulfilment the prophecies of Christ's coming (**Deliverance,** lines 25-88). There are also the formal researchings into the past by Herod's doctors/councillors. Not all of these recall events present in the cycle. Some function instead within the Christian consciousness of history, but whether they are inside or outside the cycle they create an interweaving pattern of past and present.

Though recollection is important in the cycle, typology is not. There is one striking moment of poise between past and future when God at the beginning of the **Annunciation** balances past and future acts:

> For reson wyll that ther be thre,
> A man, a madyn, and a tre:
> Man for man, tre for tre,
> Madyn for madyn; thus shal it be.
>
> (lines 31-4)

It is the nearest that the cycle comes to explicit typological interpretation. Typology has for some time now been a way of approaching the structure and meaning of cycle plays. Not all critics have found it a satisfying approach, but the charismatic force of such works as Kolve's *Play called Corpus Christi* coupled with the scholarship of such writers as Rosemary Woolf has carried it into an almost automatic acceptance. I have said it is an approach to structure and meaning; I mean that it has been used to give order and coherence to what may have seemed haphazard and ill-constructed, and to give depth to what may have seemed shallow and superficial. Much good has come of it in the right hands, but there has also come a danger of feeling the typology and forgetting about the context. Typology needs exposition, or verbal reference or visual reference to make it effective, or it needs the structure of cycle or pageant to create an appropriate framework; in Towneley as a whole none of these seems to me to be present. Humanity and recollection, and the human-

ity of recollection, create a web of interrelation in the cycle which holds it together. It is a cycle of human beings, humble and natural, gross and inflated, but all human, not types and figures.

FURTHER READING

Cantelupe, Eugene B., and Richard Griffith. "The Gifts of the Shepherds in the Wakefield *Secunda Pastorum*: An Iconographical Interpretation." *Medieval Studies* XXVIII, (1966): 328-35.

> Explores the symbolism of the shepherds and their gifts to the Christ child in the *First* and *Second Shepherd's Play*. The critics conclude that the second play is the more unified work: "Every element in its triadic structure—number of shepherds, their salutations, their gifts—reinforces the doctrine of the Trinity, and the relationship between donor and present is organic."

Carey, Millicent. *The Wakefield Group in the Towneley Cycle: A Study to Determine the Conventional and Original Elements in Four Plays Commonly Ascribed to the Wakefield Author.* Baltimore: The Johns Hopkins Press, 1930, 251 p.

> Presents textual evidence to support the theory that "the Towneley Plays may belong not to Wakefield but to some place in Lancashire, possibly Whalley Abbey."

Carpenter, Nan Cooke. "Music in the *Secunda Pastorum*." *Speculum* XXVI, No. 4 (October 1951): 696-700.

> Comments on the structural, stylistic, and thematic use of music in the *Second Shepherd's Play*.

Cawley, A. C. "I. The Staging of Medieval Drama: 6. Presentation of the Wakefield Plays." In *The "Revels" History of Drama in English, Volume I: Medieval Drama,* by A. C. Cawley, Marion Jones, Peter F. McDonald, and David Mills, pp. 50-66. London and New York: Methuen, 1983.

> Discusses several issues pertaining to the organization and staging of the Wakefield plays.

Coletti, Theresa. "Theology and Politics in the Towneley *Play of the Talents*." In *Medievalia et Humanistica: Studies in Medieval & Renaissance Culture,* n.s., 9 (1979): 111-26.

> Argues that "the *Play of the Talents* is at once thematically appropriate to its position in the Towneley cycle and integrally related to the religious and dramatic significance of the Corpus Christi play."

Craig, Hardin. "York-Wakefield Plays." In *English Religious Drama of the Middle Ages,* pp. 199-238. Oxford at the Clarendon Press, 1955.

> Controversial reading of the plays that ties their development to the proliferation of medieval guilds.

Davidson, Clifford. "An Interpretation of the *Wakefield*

Judicium." *Annuale Mediaevale*, Vol. 10, 1969, pp. 104-19.

> Close analysis of the *Judicium.* Davidson maintains that the play is the culmination of the Wakefield cycle because it "shows the end of man's folly and also the re-union of the whole fellowship of the holy church."

―――. "From *Tristia* to *Gaudium*: Iconography and the York-Towneley *Harrowing of Hell*." *American Benedictine Review*, Vol. 28, No. 3, September, 1977, pp. 260-75.

> Examines the use of imagery and symbolism in the *Harrowing of Hell*, tracing their role in the play's tradition-al movement from sorrow to jubilation.

Earl, James W. "The Shape of Old Testament History in the Towneley Plays." *Studies in Philology* LXIX, No. 4 (October 1972): 434-52.

> Discusses "what theological, liturgical, and dramatic forces were at work in the shaping of [the] perverse recounting of OT history" in the Towneley plays.

Helterman, Jeffrey. "The Wakefield Master: Symbolism and Realism." In *Symbolic Action in the Plays of the Wakefield Master,* pp. 3-25. The University of Georgia Press, 1981.

> Discusses the use of typology and symbolism in the plays, noting that "one of the Wakefield Master's innovations. . .is the way he changes the look of typology so that it has the appearance of realism."

Kinneavy, Gerald Byron. *A Concordance to The Towneley Plays.* New York: Garland Publishing, 1990, 705 p.

> Based on George England's 1897 text, provides the verse and line for each word in the plays, along with one line of context.

Kolve, V. A. *The Play Called Corpus Christi.* Stanford: Stanford University Press, 1966, 337 p.

> Contains many passing references to the Towneley plays. Kolve also provides historical and social context for the plays and discusses their relation to the ver-nacular literature of the time.

Lyle, Marie C. *The Original Identity of the York and Towneley Cycles.* Research Publications of the University of Minnesota Vol. VIII, No. 3, June, 1919. Minneapolis: University of Minnesota, 1919, 113 p.

> Explores the relationship betweeen the York and Towneley cycles and concludes that they were the same.

Manly, William M. "Shepherds and Prophets: Religious Unity in the Towneley *Secunda Pastorum*." *PMLA* LXXVIII, No. 3 (June 1963): 151-55.

> Concludes that in this play, "as in no other mystery play, the cyclical, ritualistic nature of the play form is reinforced from within by a strong sense of ritual and prophetic movement in the language and structure, while not losing its delightful sense of secular vitality."

Munson, William F. "Typology in the Towneley *Isaac*." In *Research Opportunities in Renaissance Drama: The Report of the Modern Language Association Conference, IX, 1968,* edited by S. Schoenbaum, pp. 129-39. Evanston: Northwestern University Press, 1968.

> Discusses how the Towneley Isaac differs from the biblical type of Isaac.

Nelson, Alan H. "'Sacred' and 'Secular' Currents in *The Towneley Play of Noah*." *Drama Survey* 3, No. 3 (February 1964): 393-401.

> Attempts to resolve the conflict between sacred and farcical aspects in *Noah* by stressing that the meaning of the play lies in its figural significance as a foretelling of man's salvation.

―――. "Wakefield." In *The Medieval English Stage: Corpus Christi Pageants and Plays*, pp. 82-87. Chicago: The University of Chicago press, 1974.

> Brief overview of themes and staging.

Robinson, J. W. *Studies in Fifteenth-Century Stagecraft.* Kalamazoo: 1991, 246 p.

> Detailed study of the authorship, content, and staging of the Towneley plays, as well as related plays and issues.

Roney, Lois. "The Wakefield *First* and *Second Shepherds Plays* as Compliments in Psychology and Parody." *Speculum* 58, No. 3 (July 1983): 696-723.

> Explores the relationship between the two plays and demonstrates that they are "remarkably similar" since "each characterizes its people according to the damage done to their particular kind of human nature by the Fall, and each depends for its comedy on a surprisingly bold parody of the outward actions and inward expectations of one of the two great Corpus Christi mysteries."

Schell, Edgar. "The Limits of Typology and the Wakefield Master's *Processus Noe*." *Comparative Drama* 25, No. 2 (Summer 1991): 168-87.

> Argues that modern readers misrepresent the text of the *Noah* play "when they sacrifice the concrete details of the story for what they take to be its symbolic meaning."

Stevens, Martin. "The Missing Parts of the Towneley Cycle." *Speculum* XLV, No. 2 (April 1970): 254-65.

> Discusses several gaps in the Towneley manuscript and proposes reasons for the most important of these missing parts.

―――. "The Manuscript of the *Towneley Plays*: Its History and Editions." *The Papers of the Bibliographical Society of America* 67 (Third Quarter 1973): 231-44.

> A history of the text.

―――. "Language as Theme in the Wakefield Plays." *Speculum* LII, No. 1 (January 1977): 100-17.

Explores the Wakefield Master's particular interest in language, evident in his contributions to the cycle, and speculates about related thematic implications.

Tyson, Cynthia Haldenby. "Noah's Flood, the River Jordan, the Red Sea: Staging in the Towneley Cycle." *Comparative Drama* 8, No. 1 (Spring 1974): 101-11.

Asserts that real water, not just representations of it, was used in the staging of the Towneley plays.

Vinter, Donna Smith. "Didactic Characterization: The Towneley Abraham." *Comparative Drama* 14, No. 2 (Summer 1980): 117-36.

Concludes that it is "a fixed conception of character as pre-determined by his subsequent actions combined with a lively awareness of the kinesis of the moral life of an individual, and audience-oriented dramaturgy which calls upon the character to be also partly the narrator of his own actions and emotions, and an attention focused on the significant outline of attitude and action...that enables the playwrights of the cycle plays to create speaking pictures in which didacticism and drama are indistinguishable."

Williams, Arnold. "The Towneley *Pilate*: Dramatic Structure and Literary Achievement," and "The Towneley *Pilate* and Social Satire." In *Characterizations of Pilate in the Towneley Plays*, pp. 16-35, 37-51. Michigan State College, 1950.

Explores the various ways in which the author of the Towneley plays used the figure of Pilate to create dramatic structure and satire in the plays.

Additional coverage of the Towneley plays is contained in the following source published by Gale Research: *Dictionary of Literary Biography, Vol. 146: Old and Middle English Literature.*

York Plays

INTRODUCTION

A series of fifty or so plays eminently designed to be seen in performance, the York cycle was in every dimension a communal effort when it was presented annually from around 1375 to 1569. Originally the plays were staged as part of the city's day-long celebration of the Feast of Corpus Christi. The content of the cycle reflects its religious purpose: each play dramatizes a moment from the Bible, such as Adam and Eve's fall or the crucifixion of Jesus. Taken overall, they present the history of humanity's fall and ultimate salvation. Over the years, the pageants grew so popular and attracted so many spectators that in 1476 authorities decided it was no longer possible to combine the liturgical observance with play performances; from that time on, the ecclesiastical celebration took place the day after the theatrical pageant.

In the opinion of most modern scholars, the York cycle is a "true processional": the plays, staged on pageant wagons at street level, were presented in narrative sequence at a series of stations along a route laid out through the city. Each play was assigned to one or two of York's many craft guilds—from tailors to shipwrights, from plasterers to goldsmiths—who were responsible for mounting the production each year and for maintaining the pageant wagon, the stage properties, and costumes. Performances began at dawn, and scholars conjecture that it is unlikely that the full staging of the cycle at a dozen or more stations could have been completed before midnight. The wealthiest trade guilds produced lavish spectacles, and the annual performance provided an opportunity for groups of craftsmen to enhance their prestige—and for the City of York to celebrate its stature as one of England's most prosperous cities.

From 1375 until the cycle was suppressed nearly two hundred years later, individual plays were constantly revised. The composition of the cycle varied as pageants were added, withdrawn, or joined together. The texts of the plays, originally the work of several playwrights, were reworked by many authors. The Reformation movement led to the suspension of the cycle from time to time during the 1560s; in 1561 the plays devoted to Jesus' mother, Mary, were forbidden altogether on doctrinal grounds. When ecclesiastical authorities took control of the text of the cycle in the 1570s—and refused to return it despite pleas from civic leaders—the York plays vanished from public view.

Plot and Major Characters

The narrative range of the York cycle begins with the Creation of the universe and the Fall of Lucifer and ends with a Judgment Day pageant. It features Old Testament episodes from the books of Genesis and Exodus, New Testament accounts from the Annunciation to the Resurrection, and material from biblical legends and apocrypha. Figures and events from the Old Testament include Adam and Eve in the Garden of Eden and their expulsion, the story of Cain and Abel, one play on the building of Noah's Ark and another on the Flood, a pageant of Abraham and Isaac, and a dramatization of the Israelites in Egypt. New Testament plays—which comprise the majority of the cycle—principally focus on Christ's Nativity and Passion, although there are also some that enact his teachings and miracles. Apocryphal books and legends provided the basis for plays treating the Harrowing of Hell, the doubt of St. Thomas, and the post-Crucifixion life and death of the Virgin Mary.

Many scholars have pointed out that Old Testament characters in the cycle—Lucifer, Adam and Eve, Cain and Abel, Noah and his wife, Abraham and Isaac—are conscious "types" or foreshadowings of characters in the New Testament plays. For example, Abraham's resolve to take the life of his son Isaac prefigures God's willingness to sacrifice His son to redeem mankind. New Testament personages prominently featured in the York plays include Joseph, Judas, Herod, and Pilate; Caiaphas, Annas, and Pilate's wife Procula also have noteworthy roles in the drama. Some of the most vivid characters in the York cycle are the nameless ones representing Common Man. Most remarkable in this regard are the four men who carry out the Crucifixion; they are carefully individualized, and their struggles to stretch and nail Christ's body onto the cross and then move it to a nearby hill are forcefully—and gruesomely—presented. Although characterization is important to the plays, it is not consistent from one play to another: each pageant treats its central figures in its own particular fashion. For example, Pilate is arrogant and overbearing in the play depicting Jesus's first trial, while during the second trial Pilate seems at times to be a reasonable administrator of justice.

Textual History

The surviving text of the York cycle, known generally as the York Register, was apparently compiled from actors' prompt copies or individual play books maintained by the craft guilds. Modern scholars believe it was assembled between 1463 and 1477 and thus reflects the form of the plays during that period. They point out that the composition of the cycle was fluid over the 200-year period when it was part of the York Corpus Christi celebration. There is evidence that many of the individual plays were reworked or substantially rewritten during the fifteenth and sixteenth centuries.

The York text is the oldest and best preserved of the English mystery cycles. It was compiled under the auspices of the Common Clerk of York as a means of checking the authenticity of the dialogue being spoken by the actors in the pageants. Many of the notes in the Register are in the handwriting of a single individual, John Clerke. These notes include annotations; indications of additions, revisions, and conflations of plays; organizational details about the guilds that presented the pageants; and some remarks about stage business. The text contains dialogue for more than 300 speaking parts. It was kept by city officials until the 1570s, when ecclesiastical authorities acquired it for the ostensible purpose of reviewing it. Sometime during the next century it passed into private hands. Its ownership can be traced from 1695 to 1899, when it was acquired by the British Museum. The text, designated British Library MS Additional 35290, is also known as the Ashburnham manuscript, after the last private owner. Scholars and critics most frequently refer to it as the Register.

In addition to the Register, a wealth of contemporary documents from civic and ecclesiastical records continues to provide scholars with further evidence of the evolution of the York cycle and its actual performance. The *Ordo Paginorum* (Order of the Pageants), compiled by the town clerk Roger Burton in 1415, comprises a list of the guilds involved in the plays at that time, together with a brief description of the subject matter of their pageants. Burton compiled a second list a few years later, and discrepancies between these two records clearly show changes in the components of the cycle. The Mercers' guild inventory of 1433—describing at length their pageant wagon, properties, and costumes—is among the most notable of evidentiary documents. This inventory has proven to be a rich source of information, and the basis for much speculation about how the plays in the York cycle were staged. Other records include lists of stations, or "stopping places," along the processional route through the streets of York, correspondence betwen civil and church authorities about the pageant, and minutes from city council meetings that demonstrate how significant the annual performance was to the people of medieval York.

Major Themes

The overarching theme of the York cycle is the Fall and Redemption of mankind from the perspective of traditional Christian theology. Because of the sins that originated in the Garden of Eden, humanity must repent to win salvation. The dramatization of events in the York cycle had a didactic purpose: to instruct the audience in the principles of Christian teachings and show them, by example, how to conduct their lives in a way that would lead to salvation. As commentators have noted, the theme of sin and redemption in the York plays directly connects events in the past—the rebellion of Satan, Adam and Eve's fall from grace, the torture and killing of Jesus—to the immediate present of the spectators, who must experience an enactment of these events to fully appreciate their relevance not only to conduct here on earth, but to the future, in terms of eternal life. Consequently, the plays may have made very immediate the Biblical message that each Christian must choose to accept or reject the possibility of redemption represented by Christ's sacrifice. And everyone must recognize the moral implications and spiritual significance of their everyday actions.

Critical Reception

Serious critical evaluation of the York cycle of plays did not begin until the second half of the twentieth century. All the English mystery plays suffered a poor reputation from the late sixteenth century to modern times: commentators patronized the genre as crude folk literature and judged that popular audiences had become tired of them by the Elizabethan era. Lucy Toulmin Smith's edition of the York plays, published in 1885, brought them to the attention of other scholars, but for the next seventy-five years critical attention focused on textual and historial issues rather than aesthetic values. A recreation of the pageants at York in 1951 initated an appreciation of the plays' unusual stagecraft among enthusiastic audiences and scholars. Twelve years later Eleanor Prosser called for a "new approach to the religious drama of medieval England," and from that point the plays began to be regarded as the products of conscious artistry, deserving thoughtful consideration as dramatic literature.

In 1963 J. W. Robinson expanded the notion, first put forth by Charles Mills Gayley around the turn of the century, that a single author composed a core of plays in the York Passion sequence. In Robinson's estimation, the "York Realist"—as Gayley called him—had made a noteworthy contribution to English drama through creative use of detail, interest in the subtleties of characterization, and faithfulness to the essential significance of the Passion narrative. Other commentators began to give serious consideration to the language, versification, and dramatic technique of the cycle. Richard J. Collier identified the effectiveness of different styles throughout the York plays and pointed out the appropriateness of using vernacular language in "a drama which is the most popular and communal we know." For the past twenty years, critical interest in the relation between the York plays and their audience has remained high, with commentators emphasizing the unique way the street pageants involved the spectators in the dramatic action to a degree not possible in a traditional theater. Investigation and explanation of the methods of processional staging in York continue to be a central focus of late-twentieth-century scholars such as Meg Twycross, Richard Beadle, Martin Stevens, and Christine Richardson. A clearer understanding of the plays in performance has been aided by productions of the plays every three years in York, and on occasion at other sites in Britain and North America. Recent scholarship also fosters a deeper appreciation of the plays through study of the many surviving documents that shed light on the social, economic, and political conditions that helped determine the form, content, and fate of the York cycle.

THE PLAYS

i. The Creation, Fall of Lucifer
ii. The Creation to the Fifth Day
iii. God Creates Adam and Eve
iv. Adam and Eve in the Garden of Eden
v. Man's Disobedience and Fall
vi. Adam and Eve Driven from Eden
vii. Sacrificium Cayme et Abell
viii. Building of the Ark
ix. Noah and the Flood
x. Abraham's Sacrifice
xi. The Israelites in Egypt, the ten Plagues, and Passage of the Red Sea
xii. Annunciation, and Visit of Elizabeth to Mary
xiii. Joseph's Trouble with Mary
xiv. Journey to Bethlehem: Birth of Jesus
xv. The Angels and the Shepherds
xvi. Coming of the Three Kings to Herod
xvii. Coming of the Three Kings, the Adoration
xviii. Flight into Egypt
xix. Massacre of the Innocents
xx. Christ with the Doctors in the Temple
xxi. Baptism of Jesus
xxii. Temptation of Jesus
xxiii. The Transfiguration
xxiv. Woman Taken in Adultery, Raising of Lazarus
xxv. Entry into Jerusalem
xxvi. Conspiracy to Take Jesus
xxvii. The Last Supper
xxviii. The Agony and Betrayal
xxix. Peter Denies Jesus: Jesus Examined by Caiaphas
xxx. Dream of Pilate's Wife: Jesus before Pilate
xxxi. Trial before Herod
xxxii. Second Accusation before Pilate: Remorse of Judas: Purchase of Field of Blood
xxxiii. Second Trial Continued: Judgment on Jesus

xxxiv. Christ Led up to Calvary
xxxv. Crucifixio Christi
xxxvi. Mortificacio Christi
xxxvii. Harrowing of Hell
xxviii. Resurrection: Fright of the Jews
xxxix. Jesus Appears to Mary Magdalen after the Resurrection
xl. Travellers to Emmaus
xli. Purification of Mary: Simeon and Anna Prophesy
xlii. Incredulity of Thomas
xliii. The Ascension
xliv. Descent of the Holy Spirit
xlv. Death of Mary
xlvi. Appearance of Our Lady to Thomas
xlvii. Assumption and Coronation of the Virgin
xlviii. The Judgment Day
xlix. Coronation of Our Lady (fragment)

PRINCIPAL EDITIONS

The York Plays (edited by Lucy Toulmin Smith) 1885
Records of Early English Drama: York (edited by A. F. Johnston and Margaret Rogerson) 1979
York Plays (edited by R. A. Beadle) 1982
A Facsimile of British Library MS Additional 35290 together with a Facsimile of the "Ordo Paginorum" Section of the A/Y Memorandum Book (edited by Richard Beadle and Peter Meredith) 1983
York Mystery Plays: A Selection in Modern Spelling (edited by Richard Beadle and Pamela M. King) 1984

CRITICISM

Lucy Toulmin Smith (essay date 1885)

SOURCE: An introduction to *York Plays*, 1885. Reprint by Russell & Russell, 1963, pp. xlv-lx.

[*An authority on medieval English literature, Smith was the first modern editor of the York plays (1885). In the following excerpt from her introduction to that edition, she remarks on the skillfulness of the unknown author of the york plays and alludes to the influence of these and other religious cycles on later English dramatic literature. Smith calls attention to the deft use of alliterative verse, keen understanding of human nature, and thorough knowledge of the Bible and the legends associated with it.*]

Although the date of composition of the York Plays is not known, it may, I believe, safely be set as far back as 1340 or 1350. . . . The references to them. . .in 1378 and 1394. . .lead to this conclusion, no less than the style of language and the metre in which they are written. The unknown author, whoever he was, possessed much skill in versification at that period when the old alliteration of the English, altered though it were from its earlier forms, was still popular, yet when the poet had found the charms of rime, and the delights of French verse allured him to take on new shackles while casting off the old. That he belonged to one of the religious houses of the North in the Yorkshire district may well be hazarded, on account of the knowledge of the scriptures, and especially the careful concordance of the narrative from the gospels shown in the plays. . . .

Well-read in the bible, especially in the New Testament, and in the dependent legends allowed in those times, the imagination of this author had considerable play within his prescribed limits; a facile versifier (albeit aided by the conventional rules for his craft handed down from old time), he displayed not a little dramatic power in the arrangement of scenes with the means at his command (see especially Play XXV). Observant of human nature and sympathetic, his calls on the domestic affections are well worth notice, in the womanly weakness of Mary and the trustfulness of Joseph in the **Flight into Egypt,** outraged motherly affection in the **Massacre of the Innocents,** parental distress between love and duty in **Abraham's Sacrifice,** in the dutiful relationship of children shown by Isaac, and the sons of Noah and Pilate. The figures of Mary and Jesus stand out with simplicity and dignity, in no way grotesque. These finer touches stand in relief to the brutality of the scenes connected with the Passion which were deemed necessary to heighten the effect of the Saviour's sufferings.

Like a true artist, the dramatist called up mirth over incidents harmless enough; he allowed Noah's wife to flout her husband, the Shepherd to sing with a cracked throat, and Judas to be covered with ridicule and abuse by the Porter. The Porter or Beadle, in fact, plays an important part in several plays (XXV, XXX, &c.). The people must have fun and show, noise and light. The principal personage in a play, whether he is wanted at the beginning or not, generally comes on the stage first, with a long speech, in the case of Noah, Abraham, Deus, and Jesus, with befitting gravity and seriousness; in the case of Satan, Pharaoh, Herod, Pilate, and Caiaphas it is daring, pompous, and blustering, in that of Pilate tempered by a sense of benevolence and justice which runs through his actions. (This writer was surprisingly lenient to Pilate, and cannot have been tained by the old legend of his gruesome fate.) We can picture the people expectant, listening with eyes and ears for the entry and the rant of the hero of the piece. Nor were the effects of music and light neglected; the Shepherds must have both heard singing and sung themselves; the music itself is actually written for Play XLVI, and in several places we have stage directions for singing. The Transfiguration was accompanied by a cloud and a 'noys herde so hydously,' possibly for

thunder. Besides the star of Bethlehem bright lights were used at the Birth, Transfiguration, and Betrayal of Jesus, and in the Vision of Mary to Thomas.

Touches of current life and usage here and there stand out amid the ancient story; the carpenters' tools and measurement used by Noah, as well as those employed at the Crucifixion; the bitter cold weather at the Nativity, telling of a truly northern Christmas; the quaint offerings of the shepherds; the ruin of the poor by murrain in the account of the Ten Plagues; the drinking between Pilate and his wife; the sleeping of Herod; and the excellent representation of a heavy manual job by a set of rough workmen in the Crucifixion. Illustrative too of English custom and forms of justice are the borrowing of the town beast; Judas offering himself as bond-man in his remorse; the mortgage of a property (raising money by wed-set); and the trial scenes in Plays XXIX, XXX, XXXII, and XXXIII, in which Pilate 'in Parlament playne' vindicates the course of law, and puts down the eager malice of the accuser Caiaphas and the sharp pursuer Annas. Even Herod makes proclamation for the accusers to appear, and sympathizes with the oppressed,

> Sen þat he is dome [dumb], for to deme hym,
> Ware þis a goode lawe for a lorde?

Note too the sturdy common morality that will not tell a lie and that scorns a traitor's baseness.

Opportunity is improved in Play VII to enforce the necessity of tithes, and in XXI to inculcate the virtue of baptism, repeated in XLIII, stanza 17.

The value of the religious plays and players in leading up to what is called 'the regular drama' has not yet perhaps been fully recognized. Many allusions to them in old writers, Robert of Brunne, Chaucer, Langland, Heywood, &c. have been noticed. If Chaucer and Shakespeare caught at Herod, Erasmus or his translator Udall remembered Pilate's voice, 'when he heard a certain oratour speaking out of measure loude and high, and altogether in Pilate's voice,' and Sackville, in his Induction to the 'Mirror for Magistrates' describes the gloominess of Hell mouth. Reforming preachers very early began the crusade against them. Wiclif deprecates those 'þat kan best pleie a pagyn of the deuyl' at Christmas ["English Works," *Early English Text Society*] and an interesting witness to their effect and popularity is the treatise or sermon against miracle plays, written in the fourteenth century, showing how men and women wept at the sights before them, and gave credence to many lies as well as truths by their means. Shakespeare, in his good humoured way, laughs at the alliteration, the craftsmen players, and the stage bombast all grown conventional and out of date, as he does at the Vice of the moralities, but he too was not ashamed to borrow one of their prominent characters. The study of the Janitor or Porter who appears twice, needs must with a great deal of knocking, always with a voluble tongue, in several plays of this series, will, I think, add conviction to Prof. Hales' suggestion ["On the Porter in Macbeth," *New Shakspere Society Transactions*] that the idea of the Porter, and his action in Macbeth, Act II. Sc. 3, was an adaptation of an old familiar friend, although it happens that he does not appear here in the Harrowing of Hell. . . . The Janitor in Play XXV is an important person, but not Shakespeare's model; it is in the Porters of XXVI. . .and XXX that we may seek the likeness of their much discussed successor, with the knocking that accompanied him.

Charles Mills Gayley (essay date 1904)

SOURCE: "The York Schools of Humour and Realism," in *Plays of Our Forefathers,* 1904. Reprint by Duffield and Company, 1907, pp. 153-60.

[*In the following excerpt, Gayley identifies a core of six plays that, he suggests, are probably the work of a single author—to whom he refers as "the York realist." Gayley discusses the versification, style, and dramatic techniques of these plays, and postulates three distinct composition periods for the cycle.*]

The York cycle affords very few situations ministering to the humour of the incidental. Such as are of that character must be assigned to more than one period of composition; none, however, is to be found in the plays which, according to philological tests, belong to the formative stage of the cycle. This is but usual, for while the pageants were illustrating only the more important events of the church calendar, and were still reminiscent of their ecclesiastical origin, opportunity for ludicrous situations was limited: we find a touch of nature here and there perhaps; but not more.

All approaches to the comic in the plays of York—the abusive behaviour of Cain, the quarrel between Noah and his wife, the attempt of the shepherds to mimic the angelic choir, the beadle's intrusion upon the loves of Pilate and Percula, the effort of Herod and his sons "to have gaudis full goode and games or we go" with the prisoner brought to trial, and the failure of their bluster, threats, and shouting, to "gete one worde" out of him—may be safely attributed to schools, or periods, of composition which we shall style the middle and the later. A comparative study of the versification, phraseology, and occasion of these passages leads me, moreover, to the conclusion that the original comic parts of the *Sacrificium of Cayme and Abell,* of the *Noe and His Wife,* and of the *Shepherds,* are of a humorous master of what we may call the middle period.

The Beadle and Herod episodes are of the later school and are realistic. They occur in the *Dream of Pilate's Wife* and the *Trial before Herod*—plays which themselves form the core of a group of six that in literary style, conversational method, dramatic action and technique, might very well be the work of one individual. These six are XXVI, *The Conspiracy to Take Jesus;* XXVIII, *The Agony and Betrayal;* XXIX, *Peter's Denial; Jesus before Caiaphas;* XXX, *Pilate's Wife,* etc; XXXI, *Herod;* XXXIII, *Second Trial before Pilate Continued,* and probably XXXII, *Purchase of the Field of Blood.* The subjects are such as might reasonably have been used for an expansion of the cycle to accommodate the increasing number of guilds in York, at a time after the more important and obvious religious events had been dramatised. The materials are practically the same for these six plays, and are subjected in each case to the same free handling. The somewhat alliterative, experimental tendency of versification marks them all. Not only are the experimental or transitional stanzaic forms of this group of plays, the excessive alliteration, the substitution of anapæstic ease and rapidity for the regular beat and stiffer movement, indications of a later date, but the style itself is that of a different author, or school, retaining the facile idiom of the earlier days, but substituting for the old-fashioned humour an attempt at realistic portrayal of life, and for the homespun wit a bombast and abuse which, though idiomatic, are sometimes wearisome. The bombast is chiefly from the mouths of Pilate and Herod. The realism and other such advance in dramatic technique leap to the eye in the conduct of Caiaphas and Annas, their cunning, their virulence, their knowledge of the shady side of contract law; in the careful portraiture of Judas, who "wolde make a merchaundyse with the high priests their myscheffe to marre"; of his shifts for gain, his remorse when the triumph gutters; in the grim humour of the Janitor (the precursor of Shakespeare's Porter of hell-gate),—his reply to the arch-conspirator applying for admission, "Thy glyfftyng is so grimly thou gars my harte growe," . . . "thou lokist like a lurdane his liffelod hadde lost," and his description of him to the "Dukes":

> A hyne helte-full of ire, for hasty he is. . .
> I kenne hym noght, but he is cladde in a cope
> He cares with a kene face uncomely to kys;—

in the common sense of the beadle in the **Dream** who, knowing literally the laws, would send the lady home, ere "the day waxe ought dymme,"

> For scho may stakir in the strete,
> But scho stalworthely stande;
> Late hir take hir leve while that light is;

in the curtain side of Pilate and his lady; in the discriminate drawing of women from Percula and her maid down to the Mulier who detects Peter and taunts him with falsehood:

Itt were grete skorne that he schulde skape, . . .
Wayte nowe, he lokis like a brokke,
Were he in a bande for to bayte;
Or ellis like a nowele in a stok,
Full prevaly his pray for to wayte,

and Peter's plea that her accusation be rejected,—

For women are crabbed, that comes them of
    kynde;

in the vivid brutality of the soldiers, the minute and
horrible detail of their conversation, the quick retort
and apt, the picturesque phrase, the elaborate dramatic
dialogue, sometimes long-winded, to be sure; in the
unconscious but skilful distinction between characters
somewhat similar, Caiaphas, Annas, Pilate, Herod, and
the control of supernumeraries; in the interplay of the
pathetic, the wonderful, and the fearful; in the accu-
mulation of scenes within the act, and the frequent use
of dramatic surprise. These and other features of the
kind characterise the York school of realism. So peculiar and at the same time uniform is the technique that
its interpolation may be detected in plays not characterised by the transitional and elaborate verse structure
of the group, but written in an earlier ecclesiastical
stanza; and even at times in plays marked by the typical twelve-line septenar stanza of the parent cycle.
Wherever the York realist has inserted, elaborated,
revised, or recast, he has left his unquestionable mark,
though side by side with passages just as undoubtedly
of earlier date.

But if these six or seven Pilate and Herod plays are to
be attributed to one author, then that author is more or
less responsible also for three other plays, XXXVI-
XXXVIII, the *Mortificacio,* the *Harrowing,* and the
Resurrection. For in two of the former group, *Pilate's
Wife* and the *Second Trial,* he has quoted from memory and adapted to the stanzaic form portions of a
northern middle English *Gospel of Nicodemus.* Other
passages from this metrical *Gospel* are in like fashion
incorporated in the *Mortificacio, Harrowing,* and *Resurrection.* No other plays in this or other cycles utilise
the metrical version of the *Nicodemus;* and the adaptations here are of such a kind as to preclude the possibility of their insertion by ordinary copyists from the
original text. The *Mortificacio* (XXXVI) with its elaborate and unique stanza is an original production substituted by our playwright for some older play. The
Harrowing and the *Resurrection* (XXXVII, XXXVIII)
are survivals, in earlier stanzaic form, which he has
remodelled. If we assume, and not without reason, that
he also retouched the *Christ Led up' to Calvary* (XXX-
IV) and the *Crucifixion* (XXXV), we may regard him
as the Passion Playwright of York. For only one play
of the series beginning with the *Conspiracy* (XXVI)
and ending with the *Resurrection* (XXXVIII) evidently lacks his influence; and that is the *Last Supper*

(XXVII),—one of the pageants of the original didactic
stage of the cycle.

The longer one studies these York plays, the more is
one persuaded that not only were there three York
periods or schools, but that there was at least one playwright in each of the latter two who distinctly contributed to the development of English drama. A playwright of the middle period, to which belong *Caym,
Noe and His Wife,* and *The Angels and Shepherds,* is
characterised by an unsophisticated humour; the distinctive playwright of the later or realistic period is
marked by his observation of life, his reproduction of
manners, his dialogue, and the plasticity of his technique: whether in presentation of the comic, or of the
tragic and horrible, aspect of his narrative.

That the later school or period was influenced by the
manner of its predecessor is further indicated by the
fact that of its two most efficient stanzaic forms, one,
namely, that used in the *Conspiracy,* is anticipated
(though in simpler iambic beat) by that of *Noe,* the
typical play of the middle period, the school of humours, while the other, the stanzaic form, of which
variants are found in *The Mortificacio* and *The Second Trial,* has its germ probably in *The Cayme* of that
same middle period.

The rhyme-scheme of the *Noe* is a b a b a b a b $b_4 c_3 d_3$
$c_4 c_4 c_4 d_3$ in iambs varied with anapæsts, thus:

Filius. Fadir, I have done nowe as ye
        comaunde,
            My modir comes to you this daye.
Noe. Scho is welcome, I wele warrande,
        This worlde sall sone be waste
            awaye.
Uxor. Where art thou, Noye.
Noe.   Loo! here at hande,
        Come hedir faste, dame, I thee praye.
Uxor. Trowes thou that I wol leve the harde
        lande
            And tourne up here on toure deraye?
        Nay, Noye, I am nought bowne
        To fonde nowe over there ffelis,
        Doo barnes, goo we and trusse to
            towne.
Noe. Nay, certis, sothly than mon ye drowne.
Uxor. In faythe, thou were als goode come
        downe,
            And go do som what ellis.

The rhyme-scheme of the *Conspiracy* of the Realistic
school is the same; but the octave is in septenars, and
the triplet c c c is in trimeters.

The rhyme-scheme of the other perfected stanza of the
realistic York school, as seen in the *Mortificacio,* a b
a b b c b $c_3 d_1$ e e $e_2 d_3$, is merely an expansion of that

of the **Caym** of the earlier school, which runs thus, in
iambics, a b a b b c₄ d₁ b c c₄ d₂:

Caym.	We! Whythir now in wilde waneand
	Trowes thou I thynke to trusse of
	towne?
	Goo, jape thee, robard jangillande,
	Me liste nought nowe to rouk nor
	rowne.
Abell.	A! dere brothir, late us be bowne
	Goddis biddyng blithe to fulfille,
	I tell thee.
Caym.	Ya, daunce in the devilway, dresse
	thee downe,
	For I wille wyrke even as I will.
	What mystris thee, in gode or ille,
	Of me to melle thee.

The Mortificacio makes a quatrain out of the first b c,
rhymes the triplet, and slides into anapæsts; and so
doing prepares not only the best stanzaic instrument of
the York realistic school, but at the same time the
prototype of the brightest, wittiest, and most effective
verse-form of the finest plays of the neighbouring town
of Wakefield.

With these two stanzaic forms the realistic school, so
far as we may conclude from the mutilated condition
of surviving plays, seems to experiment; and the second of them, that of the **Mortificacio,** may be regarded
as the final and distinctive outcome of York versification. To the leading playwrights of each of these
schools, the former the best humourist, the latter the
best realist of the York drama,—to these anonymous
composers of the most facile and vivid portions of the
York cycle, our comedy owes a still further debt; for
from them it would appear that a poet of undoubted
genius derived something of his inspiration and much
of his method and technique,—our first great comic
dramatist, the anonymous Player-Clerk of Wakefield.

E. Hamilton Moore (essay date 1907)

SOURCE: "The Great Cycle," in *English Miracle Plays
and Moralities,* 1907. Reprint by AMS Press, 1969,
pp. 31-48.

[*In the excerpt below, Moore discusses the connection
between the York pageant plays and the celebration of
the annual Feast of Corpus Christi. By 1426, Moore
notes, the festival was characterized by crowds and
boisterous revelry—inappropriate for the observance
of a sacramental feast—and in that year the religious
procession itself was formally separated from the staged
production of pageants.*]

The latter half of the fourteenth century saw the translation of the Bible into the English tongue, for those
who were fortunate enough to have learned to read; for
the many to whom this was an impossibility, the Bible
was already a familiar book, thanks to the nationalis-
ing of the Theatre—the only Theatre—which was the
religious one. The rapid growth of religious drama all
over the country was at this time phenomenal; old Latin
and French plays were put into the vernacular, new
plays were written in the English tongue in all its variety
of dialects. To us, looking back on the period as a
whole, there appears one stream of tendency, watered
by many springs, but those who lived and wrought
then, failed to perceive the fact. Reform from the first
separated itself from the Theatre, and Wiclif himself
was an early instance of the narrowness of the Non-
conformist Conscience. The plays came under his censure and those of his followers, and the playwrights
retorted with a jibe at Lollards. He consented, none the
less, in pleading for a free translation of the Scriptures,
to take a text from the Devil, and thus we get one of
our earliest references to the Mystery Plays of York.
Friars, said Wiclif, have taught in England the Paternoster in the English tongue, as men see in the play of
York and in many other countries: since the Paternoster, as clerks know, is a part of Matthew's Gospel,
why may not the other portions be taught in English
also?

This *Play of the Paternoster* has gone the way of another doctrinal drama, highly popular in York, the *Play
of the Credo,* long supported by a large and enthusiastic guild or fellowship among the citizens. Both are
but names and serve merely to indicate the vitality of
the interest aroused by even the most abstract teachings of Christianity when put into dramatic form.

But contemporary with Wiclif's reference there existed in York the institution of a great cycle of plays to
be performed at the feast of Corpus Christi, and of
which forty-eight have come down to us in a MS. of the
early fifteenth century (the Ashburnham MS.). To witness the performance of these plays Richard II. visited
York in 1397; for the Corpus Christi play was to
mediæval kings almost what the race-meeting and bull-
fight are to their modern successors, and then as now,
the presence of the monarch drew additional crowds to
the festival. At the time of Richard's visit, the plays
had long since passed out of the four walls of the
Church into the street, and were played in rotation, on
movable stages called Pageants, which succeeded one
another at various Stations in the town. The route to be
taken by the pageants appears to have been a matter of
much dispute, particularly about this time, when the
first Station was at the Gates of the Priory of Holy
Trinity, the monks of which house had then or later the
property of what is now known as the Ashburnham MS.
Various routes are mapped out from time to time in the
city annals, for the greater convenience not only of the
players, but of the crowd of strangers gathered to see
the play, easily confused in the narrow, winding streets

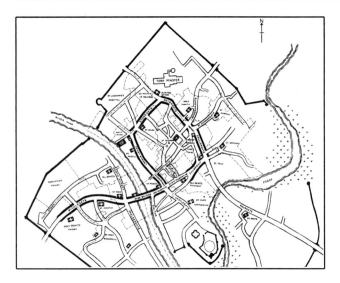

Map of the York pageant route, stops marked with crosses.

of the mediæval town. By 1417 the authorities seem to have despaired of a fixed route; probably as years went by, the character of districts altered and old landmarks were modified or removed, as in other towns; at any rate, in 1417, after a renewed attempt to direct proceedings, we find the suggestion that "those persons should be allowed to have the play before their houses who would pay the highest price for the privilege, but that no favour should be shown."

Twenty-nine years later it was found necessary to intervene again, owing to the boisterous character gradually acquired by the festival, and quite unsuiting to the original purpose of its institution, which was the honouring of the feast of Corpus Christi. Like many another custom, this was becoming "more honoured in the breach than in the observance," and it seemed advisable to separate the performance and the actual festival, to prevent any scandal from clinging to the latter. In addition to the plays, there was, it seems, a procession supported by a Guild of Corpus Christi, and no doubt similar in character to that described in Lydgate's poem. A Corpus Christi procession is, above all, a procession of the Sacraments, and such allegoric figures or tableaux as might be included in it, were meant to illustrate and typify the doctrine of the Eucharist. That those who had just beheld with reverence, the passing of such a procession, should turn at once to scramble for places for the play, was in itself, unseemly, and the overcrowding of the streets by the production of the plays on their movable scaffolds or stages, while the procession was passing from church to church, was highly dangerous. It was therefore resolved to separate the two, as follows:

> Whereas for a long course of time the artificers and tradesmen of the City of York have, at their own expence, acted plays, and particularly a certain sumptuous play exhibited in several pageants, wherein

the history of the Old and New Testaments, in divers places of the said city, in the feast of Corpus Christi, by a solemn procession, is represented . . . beginning first at the great gates of the *Priory of Holy Trinity* in York, and so going in procession to and into the *Cathedral Church* of the same, and afterwards to the *Hospital of St. Leonard* in York, leaving the aforesaid Sacrament in that place preceded by a vast number of lighted torches and a great multitude of priests in their proper habits, and followed by the Mayor and citizens with a prodigious crowd of the populace—

—A certain holy father, a Friar Minor, William Melton, observing that the play occasioned "revellings, drunkenness, shouts, songs and other insolences, little regarding the divine offices of the said day," whereby the indulgences granted by Pope Urban IV. (1264) for the good observance of Corpus Christi were in danger of forfeiture, advised, with the consent of the better part of the people, that the *play* should be performed on the *vigil* of the feast, and the *procession of the Sacraments* on the *day* of Corpus Christi, that all who came to see the play might have leisure to attend Mass and Vespers for their souls' health. This was done by decree of the Mayor and citizens on the 10th of June, 1426, Peter Buckley being Mayor of the city.

The last performance of the cycle in York was in 1584, two years before the author of the *Arcadia* fell at Zutphen, four years before Shakespeare wrote *Love's Labour's Lost*. Elizabeth, but not Protestantism, viewed such plays with favour. In 1568, it had been already agreed by the City Council of York, that the book of the plays must be perused and amended before the performance, and there is little doubt that this was a concession to Archbishop Grindal of reforming tendencies. The manuscript actually bears traces of erasure and amendment to meet the approval of the new days and the new thought, while it is to this time that we have to ascribe the loss of the *Play of the Credo*. Submitted, by his request to Archbishop Grindal, the manuscript disappeared, and repeated requests for its return fell as vainly on episcopal as to-day they might on managerial ears.

From the nature of their verse and of their dialect, it seems improbable that the York Plays were translated from French or Latin. They are too intimately native and local for the supposition, and we can safely presume them to have been of English authorship from the beginning. The verse, infinitely more varied in metre than is usual in old French Mysteries, is closely related to the alliterative lines of early English poetry, and would in itself preclude the possibility of translation or adaptation. There are touches, too, of rude nature poetry here and there, quite unlike the nature poetry of the imported romances, wild, free, intimate, as the touches in our oldest lyrics. It is only in the York play that Herod, the braggart, praises his power and his person in terms of pure poetry: the clear clouds trailing one behind the other above his realm rejoice him, the thunder is his to throw, he can "rapely ride the rack of the red sky"; and speaking of his beauty, he does not say in the conventional phrase of the Towneley Herod—"cleanly shapen, hide and hair, withouten lack"—but, with a soaring simile that paints a picture of wide, wheeling, sunlit wings, *I am fairer than glorious gulls, that are gayer than gold.*

Such touches, it must be confessed, are rare in the collection, but it should be remembered, that although written in one manuscript, in their present form, the plays are not likely to be the work either of one thought or of one period. . . .

Hardin Craig (essay date 1955)

SOURCE: "York-Wakefield Plays," in *English Religious Drama of the Middle Ages,* Oxford at the Clarendon Press, 1955, pp. 199-238.

[In the excerpt below, Craig contends that the York and Wakefield cycles were once identical. In his estimation, the York plays were earlier and provided the initial molds for Wakefield.]

There is only one theory that accounts completely for the likenesses and differences of the two cycles. Many alterations and developments had occurred during the fourteenth century and, as Burton's list of 1415 shows, the York plays had become a great and extensive cycle. At some time, probably before the year 1390, the York cycle was borrowed outright and set up at Wakefield, a city not far from York in the West Riding of Yorkshire. We know nothing of the circumstances, but one would think that such a thing must have been with the consent of the city council of York. After the Wakefield cycle was established, the dramatic contacts must have been, so far as we can see, only casual. Each cycle went its own way and underwent many changes not reflected in the other. The final results are embodied in the two great manuscripts described above. The case for an original identity, when considered from the point of view of circumstantial evidence and the argument from sign, is very clear. Indeed, it is inescapable that the two cycles were once, up to a certain point of development and a certain date, one and the same. One reasonably supposes that the cycle until the time of division had been developed at York, since York was a great ecclesiastical, educational, and commercial centre. No records throw light on the actual transaction or on the growth and development of the York cycle up to that time, and this is unfortunate, but one has a right to argue for truth on the basis of detail best explained by fitting and careful hypotheses or incapable of explanation on any basis except the terms of the hypothesis chosen and framed. One can thus by means of the

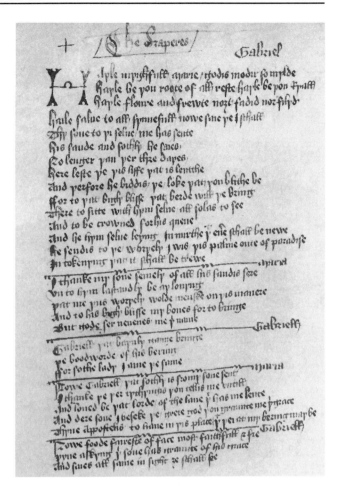

Manuscript page from the register of the York plays.

completest possible knowledge, great caution, and full attention to differing views arrive at high degrees of probability, and there need be nothing over-speculative about such a procedure if it is logically carried through and the work is sincerely done. We have two cycles of plays exactly alike in their origins and in the sources of their earliest forms. This is checked by evidence that, up to a fairly advanced stage of growth and development, these cycles underwent similar treatments in matters of revisions. The likenesses are too many and too detailed, both structurally and as regards contents and sources of revisions, to be accounted for in casual ways.

It has been thought that the resemblances between the York and the Towneley cycles came about through the borrowing on the one side or the other of individual plays, or through literary influences and imitations, or by the use of common liturgical sources, and these conjectures are not necessarily entirely wrong. They might, most of them, be better described as partial truths. There is no reason to deny *in toto* the facts and judgements advanced by O. Herttrich [*Studien zu den*

York Plays, 1886], Joseph Hall [article in *Englische Studien* IX, 1886], A. R. Hohlfeld, Charles Davidson [*Studies in the English Mystery Plays,* 1892], C. M. Gayley [*Plays of our Forefathers,* 1907], Frank W. Cady [article in *PMLA* XXIV, 1909], A. W. Pollard [*The Towneley Plays,* 1897], or by any of the more recent students of the subject. This is a simpler and more inclusive theory than those hitherto advanced. There are perhaps cases of inter-influence, special borrowing, and imitation, but the hypothesis that Towneley was taken over from York at a certain rather late stage of cyclic development explains the general situation and avoids most minor difficulties. . . .

Eleanor Prosser (essay date 1961)

SOURCE: "Joseph," in *Drama and Religion in the English Mystery Plays,* Stanford University Press, 1961, pp. 89-92.

[*In the excerpt below, Prosser examines York XIII, Joseph's Trouble about Mary, finding in it an innovative and vigorous portrayal of Joseph's doubts about his wife's virtue. Whereas the Chester treatment of this episode is sketchy, Prosser points out, the York play includes extended dialogues between the couple in which Joseph passionately scorns Mary and expresses his personal shame.*]

The best Joseph plays [in the English mysteries]. . . are those which most effectively fuse dramatic structure and doctrine. . . . [The] doctrine of repentance became the playwrights' most useful tool despite the fact that repentance does not figure in the gospel accounts and medieval sources. In the gospel version (Matt. 1:19-24), Joseph learned of Mary's pregnancy and, "being a just man and not willing publicly to expose her, was minded to put her away privily." When an angel appeared to him in a dream and told him of Mary's conception by the Holy Ghost, he merely "took unto him his wife."

From this brief hint, the Middle Ages developed an expanded tradition about "Joseph's trouble with Mary." Of course the old man must have been stunned at the news; of course he must have doubted the virtue of his virgin wife. The many vernacular versions deal sympathetically with his understandable suspicions, and as a result playwrights found in their sources no indication that Joseph should be judged for his lack of faith. There is no hint of repentance in the *Cursor Mundi,* the *Stanzaic Life of Christ,* or even the expanded legend of the *Protevangelium,* an apocryphal gospel. Indeed, in Nicholas Love's *Mirrour of the Blessed Lyf of Jesu Christ,* there is nothing to repent. In his silence, Joseph is seen as a model of virtuous patience. Thus it seems possible that Joseph's repentance is a dramatic invention to serve a specific purpose.

The Chester version, in play VI, *The Nativity,* is skeletal. Elizabeth brings Mary to Joseph after a three-month separation; he sees that his virgin wife is pregnant and laments her condition. An old man, he knows he is not the father, yet he is loath to harm her. What shall he do? A useful dramatic question has been posed, but immediately, with almost no internal conflict, the question is resolved: he will not publish her sin, but will secretly leave her so that no man will know. To this point the version is traditional. A short "Old Man's Lament" is added, a seed that is to grow in later versions:

> god let never an old man
> take him a yonge woman,
> ne set his hart her upon,
> lest he beguiled be!

(ll. 145-48)

Heavy with sorrow, he lies down to sleep, praying that God will have mercy on Mary. After he hears the angel's announcement, he expresses brief joy merely at knowing the truth—"A! now I wot, lord, it is soe" (l. 169)—and praises God. There is almost no sorrow for his doubt, merely relief at coming to knowledge.

The scene is a brief insertion (fifty-three lines) in the *Nativity* and has the sole purpose of presenting facts. There is no dialogue at all between Mary and Joseph. His lament is directed to the audience, and the scene closes with his praise of God. That is, there is no meeting of the two characters, no conflict, and no reconciliation. The little scene is independent, having no structural link with what precedes or follows, but it can scarcely be called drama. It is a brief interlude, really a "dramatic monologue."

York XIII, *Joseph's Trouble About Mary,* is over three hundred lines . . . , and what it gains in conflict it loses in prolixity. The play opens with a long soliloquy by Joseph, who is wandering in the wilderness. He already knows of Mary's pregnancy and, mourning his age and shame, repents of that "bad barganne" he made in the temple, an introduction to his recounting the apocryphal legend of the betrothal. There is no concern for Mary, no prayer that God be merciful to her, as in the Chester play. He is worried lest the paternity of the child be challenged. If he lies and claims he is the father, the law will punish him; but he cannot defame his wife. In either case he cannot escape shame, and thus he has resolved to leave her.

The rising action has all been handled by means of narration: structurally, the next incident should be the appearance of the angel, but the play reverts to the point of attack. Joseph returns home, the only reason being that he wants to know the father's name. But when he arrives, he sees, apparently for the first time, that Mary's "wombe is waxen grete" (l. 95). He asks her whose child she is carrying. Mary answers, "God-dis and youres" (l. 103), and he is, understandably, upset at the equivocal answer. (Interestingly, in the *Protevangelium* Mary forgets how she has conceived.) A long inquisition ensues, almost three times the length of the entire Chester play. He chides her handmaidens, who insist that no one but an angel has been with Mary in his absence. He derides Mary's protest that God's message is seen in her. "Goddis sande! yha Marie!" (l. 218). Such wild words, he knows, are all pretense. He is almost mad with shame.

> Rekkeles I raffe, reste is my rede,
> I dare loke no man in the face,
> Derfely for dole why ne were I dede.
>   Me lathis my liff!
>
>   (ll. 146-49)

Finally he leaves to go on an "errand" (a common lame motivation for exits) and returns to the wilderness. Now we pick up the original plot line as Joseph prays for God's guidance and the angel Gabriel tells him the truth. Here we find a significant addition to the traditional story. The playwright realized that after the extended portrayal of Joseph's doubts—after his scorn of Mary, his derision of what the audience knows to be the truth (though in this play Joseph is not specifically told the truth: that is, that the child will be Jesus, God's son)—he must be reconciled with Mary. And he must be made fit to be the temporal father of Jesus. The solution is sketchy apology and forgiveness on the secular level.

Joseph's reaction to Gabriel's announcement is solely one of relief and joy. There is no sorrow for his earlier anger, though the author pointedly added Gabriel's chastisement for his cruelty to Mary. In happiness he returns home and briefly asks forgiveness. As a humble, sweet housewife, Mary gently chides him that there is nothing to forgive. Yes, he insists,

>   I am to blame,
> For wordis land are I to the spak.
> But gadir same now all oure gere.
>   (ll. 299-301)

and the scene turns to preparations for the trip to Bethlehem.

There is an attempt here to realize the dramatic potential, but the play fails on two counts. First, the reconciliation has a rushed, perfunctory quality. When Joseph asks forgiveness, Mary sweetly dismisses the entire incident as unimportant and Joseph changes the subject. Although it is accompanied by touches of human tenderness, the reconciliation is not strong enough to counterbalance the violence of the old man's scorn.

Second, owing to redactions the play is redundant both in plot structure and in dialogue. Apparently the extended inquisition scene was grafted onto an old narrative monologue much like the Chester play. As a result, the action reverts twice to the original complication (when Joseph returns home he seems to discover Mary's pregnancy for the first time), and twice rises to the crisis (his resolution to leave her). Moreover, the inserted inquisition itself is very poor. Five times he asks the same question. Five times she sticks to the original answer: the child is his. There is little if any progression; the play is static and dull, despite the vigor of some of Joseph's lines.

Rosemary Woolf (essay date 1972)

SOURCE: "The Passion," in *The English Mystery Plays,* University of California Press, 1972, pp. 238-68.

[*In the excerpt below, Woolf remarks on the characterization of Judas and Pilate in the York plays. Judas's dialogue with the porter is a rare and effective dramatic device, she notes, while the role of Pilate is unusually elaborate and—by modern standards—inconsistent.*]

The characterisation of Judas in the [English mystery] plays is exceptional: though so pre-eminently a collaborator with the devil in his betrayal of Christ, and placed by Dante in the mouth of Satan himself in the deepest circle of hell, yet in the plays he is not modelled upon the devil, and is unique amongst the villains in being neither arrogantly boastful nor coarse-tongued. All the other villains are conceived as reflections of the devil, and therefore, though often lively, they are always stereotyped figures of evil; but Judas is shown as a human being moving along the path to damnation, and does once writ large, what everyone else does often in miniature, and the treatment of him is for this reason deliberately designed not to distance him from the audience. People can relax with the comfortable feeling that they are not Cain or Herod, but they cannot be so certain that they are not Judas, and therefore he is portrayed in such a way that his fate, unlike, for instance, that of Herod, arouses a mixture of horror and compassion.

Within the compass of this generalisation the treatment of Judas varies from cycle to cycle. The York author begins in an especially subtle and unusual way with Judas's arrival at Pilate's hall where he encounters a porter. His summons to be given leave to enter by stylistic parody inverts Christ's summons to enter hell, based on Psalm xxiv: 'Do open, porter þe porte of þis prowde place, / That I may passe to youre princes.' The porter replies in the grumbling, abusive style fitting to the porter of hell-gate, but lurking in his ready-tongued insults are terms pregnant with prophetic meaning: to him Judas is an 'onhanged harlott' with a face 'uncomely to kys'. Even the striking line, 'For Mars he hath morteysed his mark', in which the astrological ornament most immediately catches the eye, perhaps contains also a farther meaning in the figurative use of the verb *morteyse,* since the corresponding noun was so regularly used in the mystery plays of the socket into which Christ's Cross was fixed. Combined with these hints is the skilful characterisation of Judas through the eyes of the porter: Judas's speeches are mild and rather colourless, contrasting therefore the more strongly with the porter's horrified apprehension of him as an evil man and one already lost. This method is the more effective for being so rarely used.

This first scene, which seems to have no analogue, provides a sure foundation for the briefer reappearances of Judas, and in particular for his greeting of Christ at Gethsemane. For the falsity of Judas's kiss the dramatist of course followed the gospels, but Judas's hypocritical words of affection have a chilling effect against the background of the earlier scene. It is rare in the cycles for a character to say one thing and mean another.

In the scene of Judas's remorse the York author follows the tradition that Judas, grieving for his sin, attempted to persuade Pilate and the Jews to take back the money and set Christ free. After Judas's initial and moving monologue of repentance, there follows a powerful scene in which his pleas for Christ's release are rejected with cold rationality:

> Thyne is þe wronge, þou wroughte it,
> Þou hight us full trewlye to take hym,
> And oures is þe bargayne, we boughte it.

In these lines the unusual feminine rhymes drive home the iron simplicity of the situation as Caiaphas sees it. Equally striking is the passage in which Judas attempts to bribe the Jews to set Christ free by offering to make himself their bondsman, assuring them of faithful service, an offer rejected by Pilate with the exclamation, 'For by mahoundes bloode, þou wolde selle us all'. This scene has an unusual complexity in that Judas's touching speeches of self-reproach arouse in us a perhaps sentimental readiness to believe in his repentance, whilst the long-standing tradition of remembering Judas as the arch-traitor, compels us to accept that it is Pilate's cold-blooded assessment of the situation that is right. Judas's suicide is fittingly omitted (it had been represented in an earlier stage of the cycle): he leaves the stage with a short despairing monologue and with Pilate's last words of abuse resounding in our minds, 'þe devill mot þe hange'. . . .

Pilate's part in York is exceptionally elaborate and not by modern standards consistent. Scattered through Pilate's many speeches are the stylistic devices which had previously signalled a devilish affiliation. Nearly all of his appearances are heralded by a bombastic monologue in which Pilate asserts his pre-eminence and savagely threatens anyone who thwarts him. One of these, in which Pilate—strangely for a ruler—arrogantly rejoices in his own beauty, is particularly reminiscent of Satan:

> For I ame þe luffeliest lappid and laide,
> With feetour full faire in my face,
> My forhed both brente is and brade,
> And myne eyne þei glittir like þe gleme in þe glasse.
> And þe hore þat hillis my heed
> Is even like to þe golde wyre,
> My chekis are bothe ruddy and reede,
> And my coloure as cristall is cleere.

Consistent with these monologues are the many occasions on which Pilate swears by the devil, Lucifer and Mahoune, his abusive references to Christ, his happy acceptance of Judas's treachery, his own undisguised robbery when he defrauds the Squire of his land, and his fury in the apocryphal incident of the standard-bearers. Nevertheless intertwined with this presentation of Pilate as an agent of the devil is the theme of Pilate as a just ruler, since he is by no means acquiescent in the vindictiveness of Annas and Caiaphas and often insists upon a fair trial. The dramatist seems to have hit upon a fairly straightforward distinction, namely that Pilate is reasonable, even sympathetic, whenever Christ is represented only as a threat to the Jews, but raging and furious when his own power seems to be threatened. It is difficult to know what further conclusions should be drawn. Obviously Pilate's delaying tactics are essential to the length of the sequence, and if the author wished to give weight to this part by making a different ratio between narrative length and importance of subject-matter, this would be a sufficient explanation. This relationship between cause and effect could, however, be reversed, and one could maintain that this sequence was long at least partly for the reason that the dramatist was interested in making a study of Pilate as a vacillating character. The latter view, however, seems unlikely. The depiction of a ruler who administers justice composedly when personally unaffected by the issues, but flies into a fury when his own position is at stake, does not reveal any unusual insight into human vagary; it would seem to be a conception satisfactory enough if it serves some farther purpose, but poor if there is no literary justification for it save its own interest. Furthermore the interpretation of Pilate as a vacillating character is a misreading of the text. Admittedly the dramatist shows Pilate proceeding four times from an indifferent benevolence to anger against Christ, but these psychological movements should not be understood cumulatively: each play stands as a separate unit. If this were not so, the dramatist would have shown at least once, if not more often, what it was that appeased Pilate after his fit of anger. But, whilst he shows quite carefully why Pilate moves from friendliness to rage, he never shows the reversal of this: that Pilate is once more benevolent has to be accepted at the beginning of each play. . . .

The only Herod to be given elaborate treatment [in the English mysteries] is that of York, where the dramatist has distinguished him from Pilate by making him grotesquely savage and sadistic. His opening monologue establishes his ferocity: he is a subduer of giants and dragons, and those who oppose him will have their brains bashed in, their bones broken, or be clapped into chains. Like most monologues of its type, this creates a mood rather than a psychological foundation for what is to follow, though the threatening tone continues in Herod's recurrent swearing by the devil and in the abusive language applied to Christ, the latter being echoed in the speeches of Herod's two sons. This play confirms one's earlier impression that Middle English was especially rich in terms of contempt and that the unit of the alliterative phrase was very adaptable to insult. Especially striking in this play is the use of the insulting diminutive, such as *myting* (Christ is a *mummeland myghtyng* when he will not speak), and *sauterell,* which appears to mean a tiny saint. Striking too are some of the ironies which emerge from the mockery of Christ. Herod, for instance, at one point says to his son: 'No sone, þe rebalde seis us so richely arayed, / He wenys we be aungelis evere ilkone.' It is quite possible that there was a common joke that rich clothes led the naïve to believe their wearers to be angelic or divine: its most famous literary expression is the mistake of the youthful Parsifal. The dramatist's inventiveness in applying this jest to Christ is a superb example of literary audacity. It is this kind of pattern that is most satisfying in the play rather than sustained characterisation; and, whilst the author has rightly been praised for a new kind of realism (as, for instance, in the servant's invitation to Pilate to wash his hands whilst the water is still warm), his skilful elaborations of the more traditional style deserve equal attention.

Richard J. Collier (essay date 1977)

SOURCE: "The Poetry of the Play," in *Poetry and Drama in the York Corpus Christi Play,* Archon Books, 1978, pp. 38-61.

[*In the following excerpt, first published in 1977, Collier analyzes the language and versification of the York plays, emphasizing the flexibility, effectiveness, and appropriateness of both. More than twenty different stanzaic forms appear in the York cycle, he points out, with different forms used for different kinds of episodes, characters, and dramatic action. Collier discerns three levels of style or language in these plays—ornate, formulaic, and colloquial. The use of vernac-* *ular language and the prevalence of the formulaic style are wholly in keeping, he remarks, with "a drama which is the most popular and communal we know."*]

The Verse Form

At the time the Corpus Christi plays were written, one entrenched authoritarian attitude was that verse was to be condemned and avoided as a way of communicating God's word. It was "theatrical and unspiritual," a "deadly snare for the fashionable preachers who sought to seduce the ear rather than to convert the soul" [G.R. Owst, *Preaching in Medieval England,* 1926]. Yet the plays are in every case written throughout in verse, many of them in elaborate stanzaic verse. Why? One reason no doubt was that verse *was* theatrical, that it *was* a way of seducing the ear—for the audience had to be persuaded to stay through many hours of the drama. The appeal of rhyme and rhythm, the variety of textures and moods that could come from varied verse forms, these possibilities no doubt recommended verse. There would be other considerations—practical ones (verse was easier to memorize and to recite), and circumstantial (most of the works the dramatists turned to as sources would have been in verse), and perhaps the general aesthetic consideration that only verse would fit the sublimity of the drama's action. If there ever was any debate about verse or prose as the medium for the drama, it was probably inevitable that verse would be chosen.

But it was *not* inevitable that the dramatists in England should choose to work in stanzaic verse. Many of the narrative analogues to the drama were in couplets, like the *Cursor Mundi* or *Northern Passion,* as are some of the early dramatic fragments translated from the Anglo-Norman. And in France, the writers of the *mystères* adopted the couplet as the basic verse form, keeping stanzaic verse for special effects. On the other hand, there were substantial precedents for the use of stanzaic verse in drama. Rhymed, stanzaic verse found a natural place in the liturgical plays which were, of course, sung and chanted—though even here stanzaic verse tends to be reserved for emotionally heightened moments of lamentation or praise. For sustained use of stanzaic verse in drama we must look to the vernacular tradition. Both plays in which Latin and the vernacular were combined, such as the St.-Martial *Sponsus,* and the fully vernacular plays like the *Mystèrs d'Adam,* are marked by their metrical complexity. This coincidence suggests that the use of stanzaic verse, with many forms being taken over from secular tradition, was prompted like the use of the vernacular itself by the wish to extend the appeal of the drama. It also suggests that the heightened aural effects of rhyming metrical verse might have been felt to compensate for the loss of richness resulting from the substitution of the vernacular for the liturgical Latin. These suggestions are not— as they might seem—contradictory. As David Jeffrey has recently explained, in the religious and aesthetic program of the Franciscans, the goals sit comfortably together: "The Franciscans carried with them a passionate determination to harness popular culture as medium, and to elevate it as value" ["Franciscan Spirituality and the Rise of Early English Drama," *Mosaic,* 1975].

It may well prove that the influence of the Franciscans was the determining factor in the adoption of stanzaic verse as the medium for the popular religious drama. Certainly in England, the Franciscans had already produced a body of religious lyric verse marked by its metrical variety. In part this variety is a result of the many different modes in which the lyric poets worked—narrative, celebratory, devotional, didactic—modes which are freely mixed in the drama as they are not, for instance, in the predominantly narrative poems of the fourteenth century. But in part, too, the sense of pleasure in poetic experimentation that prompts such variety can be seen as a manifestation of the lyric poets' sense of themselves as poets. St. Francis saw himself and his followers as the minstrels of God, *joculatores Dei.* For them, song and poetry were a primary means of reaching the heterogeneous audiences they addressed and of encouraging them to participate in the sublime joy and grief of the Christian story. These goals encouraged the kind of poetic experimentation we more readily associate with secular troubadour verse: God called for the finest a poet could offer, and religious poetry had to be attractive to win men away from their enjoyment of worldly songs and bring them to an enjoyment of God's beauty. We have been made suspicious of verse in drama that seems merely ornamental—T. S. Eliot argued, for example, that poetry "should justify itself dramatically, and not merely be fine poetry shaped into dramatic form" ["Poetry and Drama," *On Poetry and Poets,* 1957]. But we can imagine that for the religious playwrights the very attractiveness of the ornament, the value of verse as embellishment and entertainment, represented a valuable resource. More precisely, we can approach the verse forms of the Corpus Christi plays with an awareness of the potential of verse for appealing to the ears of the audience and at the same time intimating the splendor and import of the action of God for men in which the audience is encouraged to participate.

Even given such justifications for stanzaic verse, however, the range of verse forms in the plays, and the complexity of many of them, are still remarkable. Especially so in the York plays. More than twenty different forms are used, ranging from a simple quatrain with alternative rhyme (Play III), to the fourteen-line stanza used in the play of the **Flood** (Play IX) and the play of the **Conspiracy to take Jesus** (Play XXVI), or the exceptionally complicated twelve-line stanza of the **Flight into Egypt** play (Play XVIII). This variety received much attention from early commentators on the York plays, for when the historical circumstances of

the cycle were being investigated, the verse forms were considered to hold clues to the growth of the cycle and its relationship with other cycles. We need to question some of the assumptions behind the traditional historical analyses of verse forms (simple forms are not *necessarily* a sign of early composition or of lack of artistic deliberateness, one writer need not use just a single verse form), yet there is little doubt that the variety in the York plays is to some extent the result of different writers having worked on the plays at different times. However, at Chester, a series of writers and revisers kept to the same stanza forms—can we find any other possible explanations for the variety of the York plays?

One possible explanation, all too rarely considered, is that the writers were alert to the particular appropriateness of a given stanza form, appropriateness to a character, or an incident, or the predominant mode of a play. The most idiosyncratic writer to work on the York plays is often identified by the distinctive, and demanding, verse form he used as "the York Alliterative Poet": his hand has been seen in the plays which organize heavily alliterated lines into stanzas of varying length and complexity. In many of the plays, notably the plays dealing with Christ's Trials, his vigorous alliterative verse borders on the prosaic in its rhythms. The long, often fragmented stanzas blur together, no matter how intricate the rhyme schemes that define them. It is ebullient, noisy verse, perfect for the excessive display of the court, the pretensions of the Princes, the cruelty of the henchmen, and so on, but little suited to the lyrical tones of lament or the rhythms of intimacy. For these effects, more concentrated stanza forms serve, most noticeably in the moving soliloquy of Judas, where the interruption of the established verse form poignantly captures the intrusion of conscience into a world of cruel obduracy (XXXII, 127 ff.). Whether the poet left an earlier version of this scene intact when he was revising or composed the whole scene himself, he shows himself alert to ways in which different verse forms can achieve different effects. That alertness is further evidenced by the possibility that some of the plays in the cycle that show the greatest sensitivity in the handling of complicated stanza forms—the **Creation play** (Play I) or the **Death of Christ play** (Play XXXVI)—were also composed by the "Alliterative Poet," though even if these plays were not the work of the same writer they still testify to the skill with which the alliterative verse can produce a wide range of effects in different stanzaic patterns.

Other plays in the cycle not written in alliterative verse show a similar use of different verse forms to reflect the changing tones of the dramatic action. The editor of the York plays noted that in Play XIII, for example, "the metre of this play changes, like a piece of music": [Lucy Toulmin Smith, *York Plays,* 1885] we can be more precise—one verse form is used for the lyrical moments of the play (for the exchanges between Joseph and Mary), another for the more public moments (Joseph's interrogation of Mary's servants, the appearance of the Angel to Joseph). The late play of the Purification of Mary uses many different forms to create a variety of often contrasting tones. Sober quatrains serve for the rehearsal of the Old Law at the start of the play, and for old Simeon's complaints; broken into two-line units, quatrains also serve throughout the play when functional dialogue is called for. There is a complicated nine-line stanza ($abab_4c_3ddd_4c_3$) which appears most consistently when intimate personal feelings are being voiced, as in the quiet exchange between Mary and Joseph. The play builds to a climax in the public celebrations of the Prisbeter, Anna, and finally the regenerated Simeon, whose hymns are cast in an ornately decorated four-line stanza (aaa_4b_2) patterned, appropriately, after the form of the liturgical sequence. Throughout the play, various patterns of rhyme shape the stanzas into larger groupings to add to the aural richness of this highly lyrical play. The play perhaps shows signs of the metrical excess that overwhelms much late fifteenth-century verse; E. K. Chambers does in fact find "metrical chaos" in the play [*English Literature at the Close of The Middle Ages,* 1945]. But to hear the play is to appreciate how finely modulated the verse is and how surely it defines and enhances the movements of the play's action.

Unlike the **Purification play,** most of the York plays—and, unlike the French plays, most of the English plays—do not use different verse forms within a single play. What variety of effects is created comes from the careful handling of a single form. To the extent that such effects are a matter of details, I will be pointing to them in subsequent chapters. But an initial indication that the verse is more deftly handled to dramatic effect than is usually granted can be given by looking at the variety of effects achieved within one stanza form in the York plays. Twelve of the plays make use of the "Northern septenar" stanza—a twelve-line stanza of simple structure and rhyme scheme ($abababab_4cdcd_3$). Sometimes enhanced by alliteration or stanza-linking, it is adapted to create effects as different as the plaintive dialogue between Abraham and Isaac (Play X); the horror of the Egyptians as they report the plagues visited upon them by God (Play XI); the ornate liturgical hymns of the Magi at the Adoration (Play XVII); Christ's expository rehearsal of the Ten Commandments before the Docotors in the temple (Play XX); the laments of Mary and Martha over the death of Lazarus (Play XXIV); the noisy commentary of the Soldiers as they crucify Christ (Play XXXV); and, with Latin verses neatly incorporated into the form, the wonder of the Apostles as they receive the gift of tongues at Pentecost (Play XLIV). It has been suggested that the widespread use of this form in the York plays is the result of a single reviser's using the *Gospel of Nichodemus,* where a similar form is used, as the basis of his revisions. It seems just

as likely that a dramatist, or even a number of dramatists, chose this stanza form to work with because it is such a flexible form.

For most of the stanza forms used in the York plays, as for the septenar form, there are precedents in contemporary nondramatic verse. The so-called "Burns' stanza," for instance, a six-line stanza ($aaa_4b_3a_4b_3$) found in four of the plays, is common in lyric and narrative verse in Middle English where it is probably an imitation of an earlier French stanza form. Perhaps there was a common stock of forms from which the dramatists drew. But what has determined the choice of one form over another? Is it, as has usually been implied, mere historical circumstance—or are we justified in thinking that an appreciation for a given form's flexibility or appropriateness determined the selection? Most of the evidence, I have been suggesting, points to aesthetic deliberateness. Such deliberateness is, at least, the only explanation I can find for the three stanza forms in the York plays for which there is no precedent in contemporary verse. They are among the most complicated of the forms in the cycle: one is the twelve-line stanza of the **Flight into Egypt play** ($ababcc_4dde_2fef_3$); the second is the eleven-line stanza of Play V, the play of the **Disobedience and Fall of Man** ($abab_4c_2bc_4dcdc_3$); the third is the form in the play of the **Appearance of Mary to Thomas** (Play XLVI), a thirteen-line stanza ($ababbcbc_4deee_2d_3$) which, like the music in the play, seems to have been composed especially for this play. All three forms combine complexity with flexibility. They are composite stanza forms, and so can serve as wholes for sustained speeches of lamentation, celebration, or explanation, or can readily be broken up into their constituent parts to allow for dialogue. It seems unlikely that dramatists would invent such complicated forms to work with unless they felt they added to the play and unless they were sure of their ability to handle them.

Whatever considerations lie behind the use of particular verse forms in the Corpus Christi plays, the use of stanzaic verse clearly determines the kinds of speeches the dramatists can provide for their characters. Many critics have felt it determines them adversely: "Clearly the writers are fettered by the various rimes and measures in which the dialogue is cast" [Allardyce Nicoll, *British Drama,* 5th ed., 1962]. To a great extent, such judgments seem to be based on anachronistic or inflexible requirements. There are few sustained attempts to create naturalistic speech in these plays; even dialogue—exchanges in which characters interact with each other in their speech—is only one kind of speech the plays call for. To a far greater extent than later drama, the Corpus Christi plays depend upon an alternation of "dynamic" and "static" speech, the latter kind furthering the rhetorical aims of the drama by allowing for lyrical concentration of the action, or for clear explanation of it. Since the York playwrights do for the most part maintain a single form throughout a play, one criterion of their skill in handling the verse forms should be the ease with which they adapt the form to the different demands made of it. There are remarkably few moments of awkwardness or obtrusiveness. One play where we can hear the flexibility very clearly is the play of Christ's being led to Calvary, Play XXXIV. The stanza form is an unusual and difficult one—a ten-line stanza, $aa_4b_3aa_4b_3cbcb_3$,—but it is surely handled. Broken up, it allows the unruly Soldiers to make their preparations for the Crucifixion at the start of the play and to taunt Christ as they strip Him at the end. Kept whole, it allows the extended laments of the three Marys and John and the bitter speech in which Christ reproaches the city of Jerusalem. At the heart of the play is the scene where Christ wipes His face, a scene that shockingly brings together the contrasting moods of the play through clever handling of the stanza:

iii Maria: Allas! þis is a cursed cas,
             He þat alle hele in hande has
             Shall here be sakles slayne.
             A lorde! be leve lete clense thy
                face.
             Behalde howe he hath schewed his
                grace,
             Howe he is moste of mayne.
             This signe schalle bere witnesse
             Unto all pepull playne,
             Howe goddes sone here gilteles
             Is putte to pereles payne.
i Miles: Saie, wherto bide ye here aboute?
             Thare quenys, with þer skymeryng
                and þer schoute
             Wille noght þer stevenis steere.
ii Miles: Go home, casbalde with þi clowte,
             Or be þat lorde we love and lowte
             Þou schall a-bye full dere.
iii Miria: This signe schall vengeaunce calle
             On yowe holly in fere.
iii Miles: Go, hye þe hense with alle
             Or ille hayle come þou here.
                       (XXXIV, 181-200)

A very similar form ($aa_4b_3cc_4b_3dbdb_3$) is used in the play in which God places Adam and Eve in the Garden of Eden (Play IV). The play as a whole is, fittingly, more formal and ordered than the Calvary play (as yet there is no cause for violence or lamentation), but the stanza is used to image both the harmonious rejoicings of Adam and Eve and, more ominously, the warnings given by God. Here the final quatrain serves in every one of the stanzas spoken by God to focus His warning.

Even in their handling of normal dialogue, the York playwrights take great care to avoid undue regularity. O. B. Hardison has shown how the early attempt in the twelfth-century *La Seinte Resureccion* to represent "the dialectic quality of dramatic speech" produces a highly symmetrical mode of speech in which the "speeches tend to fall into paired units" [*Christian Rite and Christian Drama in the Middle Ages,* 1965]. There are few traces of this uncertain approach to writing dialogue in the York plays. Patterned exchanges are usually used for deliberate effects, as in the Soldiers' torturings of Christ where the ritualistic quality of the ordered sequence of speakers controls their brutality. Instead of symmetry, regularity, and awkwardness—what we have been led to expect by most commentators—we find subtle variation. The lengthy exchange between Abraham and Isaac, for example, is conducted in twelve-line stanzas which could become ponderous were it not that the units of dialogue are never allowed to settle into a fixed pattern. Lines 137-272 (stanzas 12-22) are broken up in the following way between Abraham and Isaac: A:4, I:2, A:6; I:2, A:2, I:4, A:4, I:2, A:18, I:6, A:2, I:2, I:1, A:1, I:6; A:4, I:22, A:28; I:12; A:8, I:4 (Play X). The speeches are still often lengthy ones, as befits the sober mood of the play, but in the variations played with the units of the stanza form we can recognize a careful attempt to fuse formality and naturalness—a fusion which is the mark of the cycle as a whole.

Though there is no call for it in the Abraham and Isaac play, lively and realistic dialogue is well within the reach of the York dramatists. The York Realist shows himself capable of imitating naturalistic exchanges, but they can be found in less immediately striking plays as well. Thus, for example, a bewildered and apprehensive Mary and Joseph prepare to escape to Egypt with the newborn Christ:

Mary: Allas! Joseph, for grevaunce
              grete,
             Whan shall my sorowe slake?
             For I wote noght whedir to fare.
Joseph: To Egipte talde I þe lange are!
Mary: Whare standis itt?
             Fayne wolde I witt.
Joseph: What wate I?
             I wote not where it standis.
Mary: Joseph, I aske mersy—
             Helpe me oute of þis lande.
                      (XVIII, 173-182)

The metrical features of the stanza are hardly noticeable in this exchange—the rhythms and tones of a crabby old man and his helpless wife are brilliantly caught. But in the York plays—as in all medieval religious drama—such naturalistic effects are never an end in themselves. This image of a human family is offered only for a moment, long enough for us to recognize in the historical event a timeless resonance. Then Joseph takes the Christ child from Mary, and as he does, is filled with cheerful confidence:

Joseph: Are was I wayke, nowe am I wight,

My lymes to welde ay at my wille.
I love my maker most of myght,
That such grace has graunte me tille.
Nowe schall no hatyll do us harme
I have oure helpe here in myn arme.
He will us fende
Wherso we lende,
  Fro tene and tray.
Late us goo with goode chere!
Fare wele and have gud day!
God blisse us all in fere.
Mary: Amen, as he beste may.

(XVIII, 219-231)

Here the same stanza form supports the sustained expression of joy and hope. It is as if the verse has been healed along with Joseph's spirits, and now Mary's prayer complements Joseph's to resolve the stanza, and the scene, in an image of harmony. Their confidence, we can expect, is shared by the audience which knows that they will be protected from Herod's angry determination to frustrate God's will. In short space we have been taken from the confused and helpless world of men into the harmonious and stable world of God, a movement accomplished in the verse which images both.

This brief sequence from a little-noted play can serve as a paradigm of what I would claim is the most significant potential of the dramatists' use of stanzaic forms in the York plays. Even at its most prosaic and chaotic—in the screaming and cursing of Hell in the Creation play, or the wild shouting of the Trial scenes—the stanza forms imbue the verse with an immanent order which can and always will be restored.

The Language

"A principal consequence of writing drama in verse," it has been claimed, "is that it opens the same resources of language to the dramatist as to the lyric poet. . . . Imagery of all kinds, ambivalences of meaning and suggestion, words made uniquely potent by the circumstances of the context, figures of speech, in particular metaphors—all of these become available to the dramatist to be used as his artistic needs require" [Moody E Prior, *The Language of Tragedy,* 1947]. We are likely to be disappointed if we approach the Corpus Christi drama with these expectations. The claim is made in connection with the plays of Shakespeare; the expectations it embodies arise from the experience of Shakespearean drama and of traditions of poetic expression alien to the medieval poet. Metaphor, for instance, is clearly an appropriate poetic device where the dramatic aim involves "a pushing of the bounds of apprehension. . .into areas where literal certainty and systematic knowledge do not provide the appropriate answers" [Prior]. But it is not such an appropriate device when the dramatic aim is to reaffirm doctrinal truths and paradigmatic experiences—when, to exag-

gerate the distinction, systematic knowledge does provide the appropriate answers. By and large, the Corpus Christi drama is of this second kind. Its basic language, consequently, like that of the lyric poets of its time, tends to be public and formulaic rather than idiosyncratic.

This distinction, however, does not mean that the language of the Corpus Christi plays is necessarily crude, or dull, or undisciplined. It means only that it is of a certain kind, perhaps unfamiliar, and that it has its own kinds of poetic and dramatic force which may not be those we have become used to. The point needs stressing at the outset, for comments about the "halting, tedious, undeveloped speech" [Katherine Lee Bates, *The English Religious Drama,* 1921] of the plays all too frequently spring from anachronistic demands. D. S. Brewer has made a similar point: "No poet could stand up in his pulpit before the audience as medieval poets did if he was not prepared to use a poetic language with which his audience was reasonably familiar, and which it could be expected to understand and even to like. Such concepts of a recognizable, indeed conventional style, appropriate to both subject matter and audience, consciously chosen with the desire to communicate interest and pleasure, are remote from most modern theories of poetry. They are the concepts of medieval rhetoric" ["The Relationship of Chaucer to the English and European Traditions," in *Chaucer and Chaucerians,* 1966]. Brewer is writing about Chaucer, a poet whose imaginative independence, subject matter, and audience allowed him to manipulate the conventional bases of his language and the expectations of his audience to often startling new ends. But with the Corpus Christi dramatists we are not dealing with poets with Chaucer's freedom. Nor are we dealing with a drama like Shakespeare's which, though similarly addressed to a heterogeneous and unsophisticated audience, was the expression of a radically sophisticated vision. We are dealing with writers who remain anonymous and with a drama which is the most popular and communal we know.

These qualities of the drama help to explain, first of all, the fact that they are written in the vernacular. Scholars and critics used to believe that the use of the vernacular was the result of a gradual process of secularization of medieval religious drama, a process that urged the drama out of the church and into the marketplace, out of its somber, ritualistic beginnings into its use of farce, out of the liturgical Latin into the various European vernaculars. Such a view, we now can see, was an inaccurate convenience. Fresh examination of the extant texts and their history has established an extensive tradition of vernacular drama developing independently of the liturgical drama from the early twelfth century. Some of the most accomplished of the early plays come from this tradition, notably the twelfth-century *Mystère d'Adam.* In this light, the use of the vernacular seems more deliberate than we have been led to believe. No doubt it was prompted most immediately by a desire to bring the teachings of the Church to wider audiences—as Richard Axton has recently pointed out, the vernacular plays intended for popular audiences are more overtly didactic than the Latin plays. [*European Drama of the Middle Ages,* 1974]. But the use of the vernacular also coincides with (and perhaps helped to promote) a basic change in medieval spirituality:

> The use of liturgical Latin removed the personae and events of sacred history both from their actual context and from the everyday life of the medieval laity, insisting on the irrelevance of 'personal' motives and dissolving the chronological links between events. Gregorian chant, ecclesiastical costume, setting and ceremonial action carried the process of abstraction still further. When homilists, poets and playwrights adopted the vernaculars for the purposes of explaining sacred history to lay audiences, the nature of the everyday language as well as the purpose in hand encouraged a different focus on the divine events as human happenings in the contemporary world.

Besides the practical advantages to using the language of the audience, then, there was a spiritual appropriateness—the Christian story is one that most immediately concerns the people in the audience—and that appropriateness encourages an aesthetic sensitivity to the vernacular. It can be seen in those plays where the vernacular is used to express human emotions in the context of the divine events recounted in Latin verses. It can best be seen in the *Mystère d'Adam,* where the inventive and supple handling of the vernacular works to locate the eternal truths of man's fall and salvation firmly within the world most familiar to the audience.

Records from England are so sparse that it is hard to determine how substantial the tradition of drama written in English was prior to the compilation of the Corpus Christi cycles. From the late thirteenth and early fourteenth centuries there are cryptic fragments translated from Anglo-Norman, lines from "boasting prologues" of a kind later used in the cycle plays but here probably from miracle plays. Other miracle plays are known to have existed from the mid-thirteenth century. A collection of Latin sermons from around 1325 preserves a few lines of English verse constituting a speech in which the devil tempts Eve; the fragment testifies to an early interest in dramatizing biblical stories in English (though it is hardly enough to posit, as Rosemary Woolf [in *English Mystery Plays,* 1972] has done, "the existence of an English cycle beginning with the Fall round about the year 1340"). The fullest piece in English antedating the cycle plays is a morality play, *The Pride of Life,* an isolated experiment that draws exclusively from popular rather than ecclesiastical modes of presentation.

If such incomplete evidence is any reflection of the state of vernacular drama in England in the fourteenth century, it suggests that while there may have been a concept of drama sufficient to give the Corpus Christi playwrights a sense of generic possibilities, the cycle plays were nonetheless a dramatic undertaking unprecedented in scope and size. To a great extent, the dramatists were dependent upon non-dramatic material that they could shape into their plays. By the end of the fourteenth century there was available to them a varied and impressive tradition of poetry written in English, and the York plays, making use of a wide range of styles, draw variously from this tradition. Yet there are few traces in the plays of the idiosyncratic uses of language we find in Langland or Chaucer. Only the York Realist, in fact, shows any self-conscious concern for language—and even the poetry of his plays builds from styles used elsewhere in the cycle. For the most part, the language that constitutes the norm of the plays is the traditional language of the homiletic, narrative, and lyric traditions of popular poetry in England. It foregoes strikingness in favor of clarity, privateness in favor of an inclusive generalness. Whatever color it has comes from proverbial and popular similes. Joseph's heart is as heavy as lead (XIII, 15); Noah's cares are as keen as a knife (IX, 7). Simeon, as he receives Christ, is made as light as a leaf on a tree (XLI, 444); the cripple healed by Christ at the Entry into Jerusalem throws away his crutches "als lyght as birde on bowe" (XXV, 388). But that such language is the norm in the plays is thoroughly appropriate to the aims and nature of the drama. It allows the playwrights ready access to their audience as a community, and allows them to tell a story that concerns each and every one of the people in the audience. The language is everyday language—but even God uses it, in all its dialectal familiarity.

I am suggesting that in the past judgments based on taste have tended to determine reactions to the poetry of the Corpus Christi plays, and that if we consider the poetry—specifically here its language—in terms of its appropriateness to the audience and the subject matter of the plays, then we must hesitate before dismissing it as limited or crude. We can test this claim, and our expectations, against one predominant feature of the language, its highly formulaic quality. This quality—found in the use of doublets, repeated words and phrases, general rather than specific terms—is what has earned the poetry such a bad name. It is also a quality that the language shares with all other forms of contemporary vernacular poetry. Recent criticism has allowed us to see the aesthetic possibilities of this formulaic poetic style, and to recognize that while it can be a crude crutch to help a lesser poet struggle along, in the hands of a careful poet it can become—as it does for the Gawain-poet or Chaucer—a creative resource.

Though the writers of the York plays rarely try for the

kind of subtle irony that Chaucer is capable of in his handling of formulaic language, their use of formulae is often more careful than might seem. Take, for example, the following stanza from the second play of the York cycle in which God proceeds with the Creation to the fifth day:

> Moo sutyll werkys asse-say I sall,
>   for to be set in service sere:
> Alle ye wateris grete and smalle
>   þat undir hevyne er ordande here,
> Gose togedir and holde yow all,
>   and be a flode festynde in fere,
> So þat the erthe, bothe downe and dale,
>   in drynesch playnly may a-pere;
> þe drynes 'lande' sall be
>   namyd, bothe ferre and nere;
> And þen I name þe 'se,'
>   geddryng of wateris clere.
>
> (II, 27-32)

There is nothing startling in the language here to accompany God's cosmic act; in fact, the stanza could stand as illustrative of the basic language of the plays in its lack of imagery, its denotativeness, its blandness and abstractness. Read on the page, the doublets "grete and smalle," "downe and dale," and "ferre and nere" seem particularly obtrusive as line fillers. But they are not obtrusive when the stanza is recited, and they are not redundant when the passage is set in context. This particular play is full of such doublets, one for about every three lines: these three all occur in one other place (11. 53, 52, 19 respectively), others include "firth and fell" (1.63), "more and myn" (1.65) "se and sande" (1.73), and "more and lesse" (1.82). Cumulatively, these phrases work to express a sense of the vastness of God's creation and His bounty—"Begynnyng mydes and ende / I with my worde hase wrothe," God confirms at the end of the play (1. 80)—something which the limited stage cannot suggest. Similarly in the last play of the cycle, doublets like these will again be used to imply the inclusiveness of the action as God prepares for judgment: "ferre or ner" God finds no sinless man, and so He summons "leerid and lewde, both man and wiffe," and "grete" and "small" (XLVII, 57-72).

A second example, involving more than mere verbal doublets, comes from Simeon's speech as he presents himself in the Purification play:

> A! blyssed God, thowe be my beylde,
> And beat my baill both nyght and day,
> In hevynes my hart is hylde,
> Unto my self, loo, thus I say.
> For I ame wayke and all unwelde,
> My wealth ay wayns and passet away;
> Where so I fayre in fyrth or feylde
> I fall ay downe for febyll, in fay;

> In fay I fall where so I fayre,
> In hayre and hewe and hyde, I say,
> Owte of this worlde I wolde I were!
> Thus wax I warr and warr alway,
> And my myscheyf growes in all that may.
>
> (XLI, 87-99)

There is no attempt to offer a vivid insight into a distinctive personality as there might be in a later drama. The characterization is broad: Simeon's prayers to God locate him as a servant of God, his complaint establishes him as an old man. He is a patriarch, a "senyour / that is so semely in Godes syght" as the prophetess Anna has just described him (78-79). And that is all Simeon has to be, for he serves in the play primarily as an exemplar of how Christ's presence will regenerate those who faithfully await him. He is a type, not an individual; depth of characterization is not as important as recognizability. Whatever dramatic detail there is—the stumbling repetition of lines 93-95, made more awkward by the alliteration, suggests an old man trying "in hevynes" to collect his thoughts—is meant to bring us closer to the figure in preparation for his transformation at Christ's appearance.

These effects are given further point by the verbal formulae of these lines which, as well as generalizing the characterization, work to associate Simeon with other characters and situations in the plays. The phrase "wayke and all unwelde" has been used twice before, once by Noah, praising God for the strength he has received to enable him to build the ark in which he and his family will be saved (VIII, 93), once by Joseph as he mourned his feebleness and old age (XIII, 6). The phrase is part of a larger formula, the lament of the old man, and their use sets up analogies which are an essential part of the characterization. Like Noah, Joseph has been regenerated in physical strength and spirit by the presence of God; so too will Simeon be restored—he will later rejoice "Nowe am I light as leyf on tree, / My age is went, I feyll no fray" (XLI, 346-347). Moreover, this internal dramatic pattern is extended outwards to give point to the emotional recognition sought of the audience by the typical quality of the characterization. For like Simeon, all men will be restored when they accept Christ, this Simeon intimates when he prays to see the child born "mans myrth to mell" and this he confirms when he celebrates the child ordained to be "The helth for all men that be levand / here for ay" (XLI, 106, 417-418).

There are, to be sure, inactive tags and empty formulaic phrases in a series of plays of this length. Like the contemporary romances, the plays betray their popular and public nature most clearly in their language. But if we grant the plays the universal scope and significance of their action and their aim of bringing this significance home to a largely uneducated lay audience, we can recognize in the formulaic language both a rhetorical and a dramatic usefulness which have usually been denied it. The same can be said for the verbal repetition which is perhaps the most consistent verbal device used in the plays. "Obey," "bliss," "light," "will," "grace"—abstract nouns like these provide the staple vocabulary of the plays. But however obvious their repetition might be as an expository device to keep before the audience the premises of the action, their use serves also to inform the variety of the plays with cohesive patterns and to reflect the universal scope of the action they express. And like the formulaic language of the plays, this abstract language can be precise in its effects. We have seen how the **Creation** play of the York cycle establishes the "bliss" of heaven as the reward of the obedient—the word is used sixteen times in the play as a simple way of underlining the importance of the idea to the action. In the immediately following plays it remains a crucial term: God creates Adam and Eve to fulfill the bliss marred by Lucifer, and sets them in the bliss of Paradise with the warning that if they eat of the tree of good and ill they will be "brought owte of blysse" (IV, 59). So firmly has the idea been established that by the time Satan comes to tempt Adam and Eve, the word "bliss" is available for ironic use: "Byte on boldly," Satan urges Eve as he points to the apple, "And bere to Adam to amende his mode / And eke his blisse" (V, 80-82). The irony is obvious—for Adam the play ends not in bliss but in "sorowe and care" (V, 175). Thereafter throughout the cycle the word "bliss" will be repeated to express the promise that God makes to men, until God's "blissing" is restored in the very last word of the cycle. Effects such as these, derived from the verbal repetition that marks the style of the plays, may be obvious, but they are also essential in a drama of this kind. Shakespeare has trained us to expect a poetic language that keeps on extending the limits of a literally circumscribed action. The language of the York plays has to do different things: it has to circumscribe, interpret, make accessible the most comprehensive and mysterious action of all.

By concentrating thus far on the basic language of the York plays, I may have fostered the impression that the plays are uniformly formulaic, abstract, ordinary in their language. They are not. The action of the plays is varied and inclusive, and the playwrights respond with a range of styles that images this variety even as it organizes it and expresses its unchanging premises. The opening play defines the stylistic range of the language—it includes the elevated, ornate language of the Good Angels' hymns of praise, the noisy colloquialisms of the devils in hell, the sober style of God's expository speeches at the end of the play. These styles alternate throughout the cycle, with the dramatists showing not just a remarkable proficiency in creating them but also a sure alertness to their dramatic and rhetorical effects.

The most ornate language of the York plays comes at emotionally heightened moments of lyrical celebration or lamentation. The following stanzas provide a good example—they are from the hymn that Simeon sings as he receives Christ in the **Purification play:**

> Haill! floscampy, and flower vyrgynall,
> The odour of thy goodnes reflars to us all.
> Haill! moost happy to great and to small
>   for our weyll.
> Haill! ryall roose, moost ruddy of hewe.
> Haill! flower unfadyng, both freshe ay and
>   newe,
> Haill! the kyndest in comforth that ever man
>   knewe
>   for grete heyll.
>
>   (XLI, 366-373)

Verbal elaboration characterizes this style. As here, rhetorical figures such as *anaphora, exclamatio, repetitio,* along with heavy alliteration, create often brilliant aural effects. Its colorful imagery comes for the most part from the liturgy—though it is borrowed from the vernacular lyric. Richness and splendor, or, in the laments, intensity and power—these are the effects it aims at. There is often a precision to the profusion, however. In the stanzas above, the flower imagery helps to express the feeling of health and freshness which Christ's presence brings (most clearly to Simeon who sings these lines); it also expresses the sense of paradox that informs this play—the paradox that this child is the "redemptour omnium" the paradox that Simeon reflects in his very act of offering these verses fit for a king to a baby. But such precision is not necessary: the style aims at an emotional appeal through which the audience might be brought closer to the action of the drama.

This ornate style is used sparingly in the York plays. That it is so, however, may be an accident of history. Frequent marginal notes in the Register indicate that some speeches and whole plays have been "made anew" but not copied, and a fragment inserted at the end of the Register in a late hand gives us some indication of what such revision might have been like. In the fragment, the prologue to a play on the Coronation of the Virgin, Christ addresses the Father:

> Hayle! fulgent Phebus and fader eternall,
> Parfite plasmator and god omnipotent,
> Be whos will and power perpetuall
> All things hath influence and beyng verament. . .
> O! sapor suavitatis, O! succour and solace,
> O! life eternall and luffer of chastite. . .

And God replies in kind:

> O lampe of light! O lumen eternall!
> O coequale sonne! O verrey sapience!
> O mediatour and meen, and lyfe perpetuall
> In whome of derk clowedes may have none

accidence.

(pp. 514-515, 11. 1-4, 9-10, 40-43)

Sheer weight of language counts. The classical periphrasis for God, the Latinate diction, the scholastic theological terms—they are self-consciously decorative. Eloquence has become an end in itself, impressiveness has taken over from accessibility as the sign of divinity.

The York Realist frequently affects this kind of verbal extravagance, but in his hands it is justified and controlled by the dramatic context he establishes for it. Here, for instance, one of Pilate's servants warns Pilate's that night is coming:

My seniour, will ye see nowe þe sonne in
  youre sight,
For his stately strengh he stemmys in his
  stremys;
Behalde ovir youre hede how he holdis fro
  hight
And glydis to þe grounde with his glitterand
  glemys!
To þe grounde he gois with his bemys,
And þe nyght is neghand anone.

(XXX, 73-78)

Deliberate, and deliberately ludicrous, this verbal redundancy is part of the image of social display and worldly indulgence that provides the setting for Christ's trials by Pilate and Herod. As such, it has a telling appropriateness: just as the sun loses its brightness, even, perhaps, as the speech itself sinks into banality, so will this court be exposed and the Princes who try so ostentatiously to dominate it be brought low—brought low by a "sonne" who, though bound and silent and soon to be put to death, will rise again to glory.

At times, not insignificantly, the pseudo-high style of the speeches given to the enemies of Christ becomes virtually indistinguishable from the lowest of the styles found in the York plays. The noisy assertions of power readily degenerate into abusive cursing when that power is threatened. "Kyng! in þe devyl way, dogges, fy!" shouts Herod when he learns the mission of the three Kings, and "þe develes of helle you droune!" when he later learns that his plan to kill the Christ child has been frustrated (XVII, 121; XIX, 269). Pharaoh similarly curses Moses—"A dogg, þe devyll þe drowne!" (XI, 240)—with precise ironic anticipations of his own fate. However reluctant Pilate may be to condemn Christ, he too falls to cursing when he hears that Christ claims to be a King:

Kyng! in þe devyllis name, we! fye on him,
  dastard!
What! wenys þat woode warlowe overe-wyn
  us þus lightly?

A beggar of Bedlem, borne as a bastarde?
Now, by Lucifer, lath I þat ladde—I leve hym
  not lightly.

(XXXII, 104-106)

"By Lucifer" is right— . . . this kind of language serves dramatically to judge Pilate by aligning him with Satan. The plays are full of vivid, even vicious, expletives: "A! ffalse stodmere and stynkand stroye"—this is one of the Jews accusing the woman taken in adultery (XXIV, 13); "Go home, casbalde with þi clowte"—one of the soldiers screaming at Mary, who has just shown him the Veronica (XXXIV, 194). The York playwrights show themselves just as proficient with abusive epithets as with liturgical.

Between these two extremes lies the basic style of the plays, the norm against which the high and low styles gain their effectiveness. All three levels of style create contact with the audience in their different ways, and rhetorical effectiveness is one criterion we should be aware of in evaluating their use. But there is also a general dramatic appropriateness to the mixture of styles in the plays. As in the Canterbury Tales, the mixture of styles has as one of its effects the imaging of a variety which seems to be the variety of the world in which the people in the audience, sooner or later, come to see themselves reflected. At the same time, however, this variety can also be recognized as the manifestation of God who comes into the world. Responding to a similar variety in the *Mystere d'Adam*, Erich Auerbach has suggested that in all medieval religious drama, "all the heights and depths of stylistic expression find their morally or aesthetically established right to exist; and hence there is no basis for a separation of the sublime from the low and the everyday, for they are indissolubly connected in Christ's very life and suffering" [*Mimesis*, 1953]. We still can hear this sensitivity to style in the York plays, whatever other considerations have come to affect the handling of the poetry. It allows God to speak in the plainest of language; it sanctions scenes like that of the Flood where the crucial event of salvation history becomes a family squabble. It also produces some of the most beautiful moments in the plays—such as that at the heart of the **Nativity play** where Mary's prayer fuses the liturgical style and the familiar style in a perfect analogue of the event she celebrates:

Hayle my lord God! hayle prince of pees!
Hayle my fadir, and hayle my sone!
Hayle sovereyne sege all synnes to sesse!
Hayle God and man in erth to wonne!
    Hayle thurgh whos myht
All þis worlde was first be-gonne,
    merknes and light!
Sone, as I am sympill sugett of thyne,
Vowchesaffe, swete sone I pray þe,
That I myght þe take in þes armys of myne

And in þis poure wede to arraie þe.
   Graunte me þi blisse
As I am thy modir chosen to be
   in sothfastnesse.

(XIV, 57-70)

Perhaps—to use the effect of these stanzas to extend Auerbach's suggestion—we are to find a similar appropriateness in the art of poetry in the York plays as a whole. Through the use of the vernacular, the mysteries of God's will are brought to the audience in all their immediate relevance, yet through the use of verse, the drama reaches constantly for the beauty and harmony of God. T. S. Eliot was thinking of medieval religious drama as well as his own experiments when he wrote: "What poetry should do in the theatre is a kind of humble shadow or analogy of the Incarnation, whereby the human is taken up into the divine."

Meg Twycross (essay date 1981)

SOURCE: "Playing the Resurrection," in *Medieval Studies for J. A. W. Bennett,* edited by P. L. Heyworth, Oxford at the Clarendon Press, 1981, pp. 273-96.

[*In the following excerpt, Twycross describes the reconstruction of the production of the* Resurrection of Christ, *focusing on "what happens to the play in performance." Emphasizing the active involvement of the audience in the performance and the physical closeness of audience and actors, Twycross maintains that the* Resurrection *playwright made his audience aware of the part they played in the drama, engaging them directly in the emotional dynamics of the pageant.*]

This essay is about the performance of a medieval English mystery play, and what it showed me, the producer, about the way in which these plays seem to work dramatically. The play was the York Carpenters' pageant of *The Resurrection of Christ,* performed in March 1977 in the Nuffield Theatre Studio of the University of Lancaster. Here I attempted to re-create the effect of a pageant-waggon staging in a street-shaped space, with a standing and potentially mobile audience. I have documented the details, and the historical evidence for my reconstruction, elsewhere. [*Medieval English Theatre*, vol. 2, nos. 1 and 2]. I want here to concentrate on what happens to the play in performance: how the physical circumstances of production seem to me to have been exploited by the playwright, and especially how the audience is implicated in the play.

Let us start with the most obvious feature. With this kind of staging, actors and audience are very close to each other. There are of course no footlights. There is not even a respectful gulf of open space marking the divide between them: even in the widest urban street,

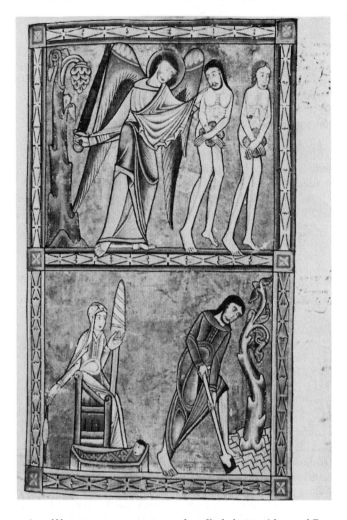

A twelfth-century manuscript page from York depicts Adam and Eve expelled from Eden (above) and laboring to survive.

there is no room for one. The actors may even have to walk into the crowd. Entrances and exits are of course made through the audience, but from the script of *The Resurrection* it is clear that several speeches, in certain cases even whole scenes, are played at some remove from the waggon. The Centurion, for example, begins to speak out of earshot of Pilate:

   [To] oure princes and prestes bedene
      Of this affray,
  I woll go *weten,* withouten wene
      What thei can saye.

(45-8)

The Maries see the Angel from a distance:

   Sisteris! a yonge child, *as we goo*
      Makand mornyng,
  I see it sitte wher we wende to,
      In white clothyng . . .

(225-8)

so they presumably play their whole scene of lamentation in the street. In our production, even on the nights when the audience tried to keep their distance, they were never more than three feet away from the actors.

This physical closeness made the audience very much an active factor in the performance, and to us an unpredictable one. We did not know until they were actually there on the first night how we, as well as they, were going to react in these unfamiliar 'medieval' circumstances. It was not just that we did not know where they were going to stand, or whether they would move out of the way at the right time, or whether the action we had rehearsed at street-level would be at all visible: they presented an active physical presence which had to be reckoned with. They might be responsive, or they might be inert, but they were *there*. In an open-air, close-up form of theatre like this, it is impossible, no, fatal, to pretend they are not. You cannot sustain the familiar darkened-auditorium illusion, that the audience are eavesdropping on a private conversation. The actors can solicit their attention, or they may pointedly ignore them, but they must acknowledge their presence.

Because we approach these plays from the other side of the three hundred years of the proscenium arch, we find it difficult to get this relationship in perspective. Critics tend to feel that the medieval theatre must have been either extremely naive, or extremely radical. In fact it is neither. The deliberate audience-involvement that we notice is not approached in the embarrassingly self-conscious way of some modern theatre. It is just accepted that the audience is there, and that the characters can talk to them. There is a certain self-confidence in the handling that precludes embarrassment.

This does not mean that the characters become 'part of' the audience, or that they are 'the same as' them. It is difficult, of course, to tell how far the fact that our characters were wearing fifteenth-century clothing marked them out as peculiarly separate; but the effect would have been the same in the original productions, because it is not primarily a matter of costuming, but that the actors belong to a different world, and that they are in charge of the action. Meeting the Magdalen face to face in the crowd was rather like seeing the Queen 'as near as I see you' in a Jubilee celebration—if one can imagine seeing the Queen in tears.

Despite the lack of physical separation, the actors are still inhabitants of the world of the play, the audience still onlookers. The illusion is not 'broken'. But the playwright uses this physical closeness to extend as it were the terms of the contract between them. The characters (not merely the actors) are made to acknowledge the audience's presence, and to make use of it.

This operates within strict limits. The audience have no independent hand in the action. They cannot control the course of events, nor is it ever suggested that they might. (Sometimes it is suggested that they *might have,* but that is a different kind of game.) They may occasionally be given the role of 'crowd', say as spectators at the *Via Dolorosa,* but this is not extended to full participation in the action; they are used as spectators because they *are* spectators, no more. Most of the time, if they have a role, it is the role of audience: a willing ear, sympathetic to lamentation, attentive to instruction, cheerfully submissive to bullying. But they have consented to be an audience more actively implicated than we are used to. The characters seem to be saying, 'We know you're there, and we intend to use you.' The audience respond, 'We're willing to be used, and we'll answer to any role you like to cast us in, friend or enemy. But we are still both aware that we're playing a game.'

This relationship is thus as much part of the dramatic illusion as the more obvious forms of stagecraft. The interesting thing is that this appears to be recognized openly. This is part and parcel of what seems to be in medieval theatre a heightened consciousness of the whole fact of dramatic illusion. This is partly due, no doubt, to the use of distinctly non-naturalistic stage props, like the Chester *Noah* animals on boards, and, for example, the use of masks. Far from trying to pretend that these things are real, the playwrights underline the lack of naturalism, as when Noah remarks on how smoothly his Ark-building is going. It is also partly due to the medieval sense, particularly in religious matters, of the 'figural view of reality', which produces a drama where it is quite natural for one character to hand another a symbol to commemorate a real but many-layered event: 'This beest, John, thou bere with the. . .John, it is the lamb of me'. The effect it seems to have in our present context is that the audience are invited into a kind of complicity with the players, in which they behave as if they were taking the illusion for reality, while at the same time reserving the right to remember that it is only illusion. But there would be no point in this game if it were not also accepted that the illusion represents a historical and spiritual reality which is vitally important to both actors and audience.

The play does not always, of course, operate on this intimate level of audience-recognition. There may not be a natural 'footlights' line of demarcation, but there is always the opportunity of withdrawing from acknowledged contact with the audience. When the actor climbs up on the stage, the height, and the fact that he has entered a frame, give him a certain distance which he can choose to use or ignore. Pilate can look down on the audience and hector them, or he can enter into a 'private' conversation with Annas and Caiaphas (though even this illusion of privacy can be manipulated by the playwright, as we shall see).

The extreme of distancing comes when the 'framing effect' of the waggon posts and fascia is exploited so that the playwright, in the midst of events, suddenly resolves the action into a familiar picture—the Annunciation, the Crucifixion, Pentecost. The contrast between action and image, the sudden shift of focus, can be emotionally extremely powerful; at one moment the characters are talking to the audience, at the next they are part of a venerable icon. This suddenness of contrast seems also to be part of the playing with illusion: 'Now you see it, now you don't' in reverse. But even on a less striking level, the playwrights seem conscious of their ability to exploit the contrasts between different distances, different depths of focus.

The writer of the York **Resurrection** is particularly good at these shifts. He is also particularly adept at manipulating the actor-audience relationship which we have been looking at. In part this is due to the theme of the play itself. I should like now to analyse his use of this relationship, starting off with some of the simpler and more familiar instances of audience-involvement, and gradually complicating things.

The comic effects are probably the most recognizable exploitation of the relationship, rather like circus or music-hall; the Soldiers threaten the audience with their swords, the audience shriek, knowing that the Soldiers are not really going to attack them, but thinking that those swords are sharp and dangerously close, all the same. Here we are only a step away from the circus clown with his hosepipe or bag of flour. We had planned for this in rehearsal; what we had not reckoned on was the way in which the playing to the audience would extend itself. What had in rehearsal been private conversations became public boasts or threats: 'And sone we schall crake his croune Whoso comes here' (185-6) became 'Don't any of *you* try anything on while we're asleep'. Audience-involving 'business' blossomed: the First Soldier, coming round after a stolen nap, found himself moved to exchange a luxurious stretch and self-satisfied smile with the audience before realizing, with a mighty double-take, that the body had gone.

This did not only happen with comedy, however. We found the whole balance of what we had read on the page and prepared in rehearsal as private deliberation, voice-over on which the audience were to be permitted to eavesdrop, shifting in performance. Suddenly there was no such thing as a private soliloquy. The Centurion's opening speech, 'A! blissid lorde Adonay!' (37) is ostensibly addressed either to himself or to God, but he found himself sharing what had read like private bewilderment with the audience among whom he was standing—'What may thes mervayles signifie?' (38), and thus calling on them to sympathize with his perplexity. But here something else is happening. The audience *know* what the marvels signify. They cannot tell him, because he is a character in the story, and they are not;

but they want him to realize what has happened, and then they want him to convince Pilate and the Bishops.

Because the audience are not coming to the play cold (indeed, in some ways they are already better informed than the characters), the playwright can use their superior knowledge to engage them emotionally. A 'good' character who doubts, or is mystified, or who gets things unwittingly wrong, and 'soliloquizes' about it, is in this kind of staging actively calling on the audience for help. (This technique is particularly striking in plays about 'Joseph's Doubts'.) The audience respond with a feeling of active support, and if, as here, the situation leads into a debate with agents of the 'other side', a feeling of definite partisanship. What they do not realize is that in drawing out this support, the playwright is making them give emotional consent to their own convictions—'strengthening their faith'.

In the debate with Pilate, in fact, the Centurion talks to persuade; his speech is as much an emotional appeal as a factual one. Taking up the 'all creation wept' theme found in the commentaries, he gives the inanimate world emotions:

> All elementis, both *olde and ying,*
> *In ther maneres thai made mornyng*
>   In ilke a stede,
> And *knewe be countenaunce* that *ther kyng*
>   Was done to dede.
>
> The sonne *for woo he waxed all wanne;*
> The mone and sterres of schynyng blanne;
> The erthe *tremeled,* and *also manne*
>   *Began to speke. . .*
>
>   (86-94)

Against this, the logical replies of Pilate and Caiaphas

> Ye wote oure clerkis the clipsis thei call
>   Such sodayne sight:
> Both sonne and mone that sesonne schall
>   Lak of ther light
>
>   (99-102)

sound like rationalizations. The Centurion has to use this kind of language because he is talking about something outside nature; the audience accept it, because they know that something outside nature has happened, and because by this time they want the unbelievers to realize it too.

It is characteristic of debates in medieval drama that they are there for the audience rather than for the characters. It does not matter if the Centurion fails to persuade Pilate, though of course we would like him to, provided he has persuaded us. It is a form of didacticism, but a more subtle one than straightforward assertion. The debate's function is to lay out both sides of the case for the audience to consider. To quote from a completely different context:

> If you put a superior thing side by side with an inferior, for the sake of comparison, that is, in this case, the virtue over against the vice, you will get a firm understanding of their important and distinctive qualities. For when you compare the qualities of contrary things, you should be immediately and clearly able to assess which are the better ones. So when you have surveyed these roots, branches, and fruits of ours, it will be up to you to choose which one you want [Pseudo-Hugh of St. Victor, *De fructibus carnis et spiritus*].

There is never any doubt about the eventual outcome; of the green tree and the dry, which would you choose? but the demonstration, against suitably strong, if suitably venal, opposition, is necessary, in order to confirm with you that your choice is the right one. The playwright manoeuvres you into partisanship with the right side to make quite sure that you give your emotional as well as your intellectual consent to it.

We have been concentrating on the evidence of the play in performance. The most striking example in the *Resurrection* of the use of the audience is almost invisible in the script, and yet it comes over very powerfully in performance to reinforce the theme of the play. It plays with the two worlds of involvement and illusion by first acknowledging the presence of the audience, and then pretending that in fact they aren't there, that there really is a private stage-world in which the characters can't be overheard. Then, in a final sleight of hand, this too is shown up to be an illusion.

Let me elucidate. The *Resurrection* is an extended *Quem Quaeritis;* it goes to some trouble to make this quite clear. It is not particularly concerned with expressing the cosmic, triumphal aspects of the Resurrection; this has been done already, in the preceding pageant of the *Harrowing of Hell*. Like the *Quem Quaeritis,* which takes its essential character from an earlier age, it concentrates on the theme of bearing witness to the event, true witness and false witness. The evidence is scrupulously displayed, both by the Maries and the Soldiers: the empty tomb; the sudary; the angelic message; the portents that surround the actual moment of Christ's rising. At the end, the epigraph could be

Credendum est magis soli Mariae veraci quam Judaeorum turbae fallaci.

But it goes beyond the *Ludus Paschalis* in giving the actual ocular proof: dressing up an actor as Christ, and making him emerge from the tomb in the sight of all. The audience are also made witnesses.

The end of the play thus rests on an immense dramatic irony. It seems to show Pilate and the Jews successful:

they have bribed the Soldiers to lie, the scandal has been swept under the carpet. But they have not succeeded, because the audience know the truth: they have seen it with their own eyes. Once the audience is there, the argument is no longer about fooling some hypothetical 'people' of first-century Jews and Romans: *they* are 'the people'. They were swept into the role in this play when Annas said

> *The pepull,* sirs, *in this same steede*
> Before you saide with a hole hede
> That he was worthy to be dede
>
> (19-21)

At the end of the play, Pilate and the Bishops are plotting to keep from them the truth of an event they have just witnessed with their own eyes. Caiaphas says, 'We nolde, for thyng that myght befall That no man wiste' (405-6); the reaction is, 'Well, that's a bit late, because *we* know'. The playwright plays off the fiction that Pilate, Annas, and Caiaphas are having a private conversation (which is reinforced visually if they draw together inside the 'walls' of their waggon while the Soldiers remain outside) against the real-life fact that the audience can hear everything they are saying.

This would not work if the play had not consistently implicated the audience and made them conscious of their own role in the drama. As it is, they are again in the familiar position of being one jump ahead of the characters (not only have they seen Christ, they have been privy to the Soldiers' desperate fabrication of a story). The playwright then points this up by making the characters openly despise the audience. Pilate sums up:

> And *to the pepull* schall we saie
> It is gretely agaynste oure lay
>   To trowe such thing.
> *So schall thei deme,* both nyght and day,
>   All is lesyng.
>
> (444-8)

'The people' can be easily fooled. The audience are probably made more aware of their own separateness because the characters have antagonized them: there would be no reason to feel that way if they were in agreement.

We then get a curious two-layer effect. Pilate ends the play with a piece of 'confession' moralizing, half-stepping out of character:

> Thus schall the sothe be bought and solde,
> And treasoune schall for trewthe be tolde
>
> (449-50)

and an ambiguous remark, addressed ostensibly to

Annas and Caiaphas,

> Therfore ay in youre hartis ye holde
> This counsaile clene
>
> (451-2)

To the Jews, this would seem to mean 'Keep quiet about this'; to the audience 'Remember what you have seen and think about it'. On one level, the cover-up conspiracy is going on here and now, aimed at the audience, who are, however, not fooled by it; thus, 'The Jowis and thair errour ar confoundit'. At the same time, we are watching a historical event, with the valid 'story-line' observation that 'this saying is commonly reported among the Jews to this day' (Matthew 28:15). This double time-focus, and its implications, is more usually commented on with reference to the 'anachronism' of, say, the Wakefield *Second Shepherds' Play;* but the presence and involvement of the audience make it an ongoing thing throughout the Cycles. The difference between this and ordinary anachronism is that, as here, one lens may show quite a different picture from the other, not the same one made contemporary.

To move to what may seem a completely different part of the play, both in style and technique, it may come as a surprise to the reader to be told that the three Maries and their lamentation were engaged in the most intense form of audience-involvement in the play. On paper, they look remote from this. Their role is about as far from naturalistic drama as can be imagined. A modern audience, used to the convention that grief is inarticulate, and to whom the vocabulary of lament is unfamiliar, finds the whole concept of public, ritualized mourning alien, the thought that they might actually be touched by it unimaginable. In the type of production that invites the audience to observe the Maries at a distance, as private persons undergoing an emotional crisis, they become tedious; we listen to them out of good manners, or because we feel we ought. Set them down in the audience, on their level, 'as we goo Makand mornyng' (225-6), and their role suddenly becomes quite different. They are almost agitators, inciters to emotion.

They are down among the audience partly because of the dictates of staging (they have a journey to go before they can see the Angel), partly because the audience seem to be rather more emotionally vulnerable to figures in their midst. (For some of them, perhaps, it is the shock of finding themselves close to the source of the magic.) There seems to be a certain intentional correlation of 'togetherness' with the characters who start off down in the street (the Maries, the Centurion, the Soldiers), and of distance, though not necessarily hostile, with those who put themselves up at a height, on stage (Pilate and his boasting, Christ and the Resurrection).

So far we have been looking at emotion as the unac-

knowledged handmaid of argument. We now see emotion almost as a goal in itself: 'Who cannot wepe, come lerne at me'. The writer's aim is that of popular affective piety: the techniques he uses are borrowed from the vernacular lyrics and meditations. But the drama does part of the job of imagination for us. Typically, in the meditations we stir up our own sorrow at the death of Christ by focusing it on the figure of one of those near to him; but here we do not have to imagine their sorrow, as we can see it before us. As the Christ from the York *Crucifixion* is a devotional image come to life, so the Maries are the figures from the meditations made visible, embodiments of mourning.

We are not, however, to stop at contemplating them. They share the techniques of affective piety in that they are there to engage us in activity; we are to use them as channels through which to direct our emotions. They describe their suffering, drawing the audience to share in it, because they are not asking for sympathy for themselves, but for the sufferings of Christ.

They are not even lamenting over a present scene, but a remembered one; Magdalen, in the meditative tradition, visualizes the crucified Christ: 'Allas! *that I schulde se* his pyne!' (193); Mary Jacobi suggests a meditation on the Five Wounds, 'Allas! who schall my balis bete *Whanne I thynke on* his woundes wete?' (199-200) A literature which was devised to help the late medieval reader imagine the emotions of being at the Crucifixion is being used to provide the techniques for representing those emotions in characters who are supposed to have just come from the Crucifixion. If the audience was at all familiar with this kind of aid to meditation, and it seems likely that they were, they would presumably recognize their own role in it, and the end to which it was working.

Because the Maries are used as conductors for this emotion, we are not particularly interested in the individuality of their feeling. The stress in the script on '*my* sorowe', '*my* balis', '*my* mone' makes it look as if their lamentations are personal and private: but when you hear them, the very fact that they echo each other makes them already part of a group emotion. Their laments are formal in shape, almost operatic; the three voices chime in one after the other, weaving variations on the same pattern, three in one. (It also ensures that though they are down among the audience, and so not visible to all of them and therefore harder to hear, nothing of the content of their lament is really lost, as it is repeated three times.) From the point of view of the story, this shows their unity of love and purpose. As in the liturgical drama, from which the over-all shape though not the detail of the scene seems to come, this is emphasized by their shared verbal patterns. But they are also urging the audience to join in their feeling. These shared patterns are also the familiar rhetorical patterns of language traditionally used to stir emotion in the hearers: repetition: 'Allas! . . . Allas! . . . Allas!', 'is dede. . .is dede. . . . '; concatenation: 'Withouten skill . . . Withowten skil . . . ', 'Sen he is dede . . .Sen he is dede. . .'; and audience-involving exclamations and rhetorical questions: 'Allas! to ded I wolde be dight!' (187), 'To whome nowe schall I make my mone?' (209).

It is a familiar observation that the 'I' of affective piety is meant to be the 'I' both of the (imagined) speaker and of the reader. Affective meditation calls on the individual to respond, but with those emotions which he shares with everyone. When he is set down in a crowd, and then spoken to in the same way, he is responding as an individual still, but he will find himself doing it at the same time and to the same stimuli as everyone else; and to a certain extent, he will surrender his individuality to the movement of the group.

Audiences are, it should be remembered, vulnerable to each other's emotion. Standing in an open-air crowd, you cannot isolate yourelf and your reactions from those of your neighbour. If you feel moved to weep (and some members of our audience did, mostly old women and small girls), you cannot hide it in the protective darkness of your cinema seat. I also got the impression that by joining such an audience, you had consented to share in the group emotion, as you would nowadays with a crowd watching a sporting event. Emotions, both grief and laughter, become catching.

This works in an interesting way to neutralize any disadvantages there might have been in setting scenes in the street. When the actors are on the waggons, they are perfectly visible even from the thick of the crowd. This is not so when they are on the ground. Then only a few people can see the actors perfectly, but they can all hear, and oddly enough, seem to *feel* the reactions of the people closest to the actors. Laughter or sensations run like a ripple through the crowd to the outside edge. The actual joke or appeal may have been indistinct, may even have been a visual one, and so lost, one would think, to any but the people standing next to the actor, but the mood manages to transmit itself through the crowd. Thus not only does the audience never lose concentration, but there is very much the sense of taking part in an occasion, rather than 'merely' being spectators to a play.

It is noticeable how quickly an audience like this can be shifted *en bloc* from one emotion to another, and how adept the playwrights are at such sudden contrastive shifts. It seems characteristic of the plays in performance that they turn out, many of them, to have been constructed in blocks, each with one ruling emotion or mood, which is then played almost to the limits of its capacity, but with a very sure sense of just how much the audience can take before the mood has to be switched.

In a way, particularly with comedy and lamentation, this exploitation of one particular mood is part of the awareness of artifice of which I have been talking. A scene of lamentation will not just show characters displaying a normal (certainly not a restrained) amount of distress, it will show distress itself, formalized and orchestrated to operatic heights. Comedy will wring the last ounce of laughter out of the audience. Both can thus be placed without incongruity alongside presentations of cosmic or symbolic acts, because they seem themselves to be aware that they too are representative. This does not mean that they are stylized to the point of being remote or unnatural. They are still true to life, in the sense that each emotion is perfectly recognizable, and evokes its proper response; it is just pushed as far as it can properly go.

I am not saying that every scene is so intense, or that there are no gradual movements from one emotion to another. But quite often one is aware that there has just been a complete switch of mood, precisely when one was ready for it. This often seems to operate more on instinct than on any logical basis. It can even run directly counter to narrative probability. In the ***Resurrection,*** the Magdalen's second lamentation seems completely illogical. Why, having just accepted the news of the Resurrection with delight, should she suddenly turn back to weeping? But it is emotionally and thematically necessary, as I shall hope to show, and at the time, nobody questions it.

This switch is most effective where it seems most daring, in the way in which the most serious episodes in the plays are often juxtaposed with scenes of high comedy. A riotously comic scene, which exhausts the audience with laughter, will be replaced—it is as distinct as that—by an act of immense seriousness, which grows out of the silence following the dying away of that laughter. In the ***Resurrection,*** the laughter that accompanies the setting of the watch fades as the Soldiers fall asleep, to be replaced by the earthquake, the plainsong, and the Resurrection itself. The new seriousness neither discredits the laughter nor is discredited by it; the laughter wipes away all potential restlessness, and enhances the seriousness of what follows.

This change of mood is often accompanied by a change of mode, a shift of verbal and dramatic style. This has been noticed in such plays as the York ***Crucifixion.*** Here Christ speaks only twice, and each time the stage picture has suddenly been resolved into a familiar devotional icon: the 'Christ seated on the Cross', and the Crucifix itself. Each time what he says, and how he says it, comes from a completely different tradition than the noisy jibing of the Soldiers. He is a living version of the devotional images illustrated by [Rosemary] Woolf [in *The English Religious Lyrics in the Middle Ages*] and [Douglas] Gray [in *Themes and*

Images in the Medieval English Religious Lyric], his words belong to the kind of lyric that accompanies them in the manuscripts. We would probably consider this a non-dramatic tradition, but the playwright has no qualms about using it, and is completely justified by the results.

The plays use a much wider variety of literary and dramatic traditions than is perhaps recognized: the overall pattern of the verse-forms tends to obscure this fact. This may partly be due to the kind of eclecticism that has never heard of the unities. We cannot know how much it is a matter of deliberate choice, and how much a matter of taking what was there. But in competent hands the effect is unmistakable. As the playwright moves from one tradition to another, he produces this sense of shifting focus, in time, and in nearness and distancing, that we have noticed.

The **Resurrection** is a particularly rich example of this. The subject itself has a complex literary and dramatic history. It was the earliest piece of liturgical drama and the playwright seems to realize its antiquity. Besides this, partly because of what the Bible leaves unsaid, and partly because of changes of emphasis in what was felt to be important about it, it has acquired more of apocryphal embroidery and of commentary than most other episodes. Our play attempts to give the fullest possible account of the event, and as a result each episode and each batch of characters belongs to a different tradition: the Soldiers, Annas, Caiaphas, Pilate, and the Centurion to the narrative apocryphal writings like the *Northern Passion* and the vernacular *Gospel of Nicodemus;* the Maries, and especially the Magdalen, from the tradition of popular affective meditation and romantic hagiography; the Resurrection itself, and the *Quem Quaeritis,* to religious iconography and liturgical drama. Each of these has its own style and preoccupations, which the playwright mirrors. In effect, the theme of the Resurrection is played over four times—as itself, by the Maries and in the *Quem Quaeritis,* by the Magdalen, and lastly by the Soldiers. Each time we are given a different reaction to the event (the 'witness' theme), and each time we see it in a different focus, so that by the end of the play we have experienced it through a fairly complex variety of emotions.

Let us trace these through, starting with the Resurrection itself. Seen soberly, it is an outrageous thing to have to present on stage, especially an open-air stage with no possibility of dimming the lights, or doing any of the other things which, in a modern theatre, denote the supernatural. This word has been devalued; it is an event so cosmic and mysterious that in fact none of the liturgical plays actually attempt to enact it. Instead they represent it, either by some variant on the Easter Sepulchre ceremony, in which the Cross or the Host stands for Christ, or by having the Angels sing a Resurrection anthem. But the York playwright is committed to im-

personation. He solves the problem by drawing on the audience's experiences of the sacred; he presents them with an icon of the Resurrection, and he uses singing to remind them of the Liturgy. Apart from this, the whole scene takes place in silence.

Because in the script the whole scene is limited to the laconic stage direction *Tunc Iesu resurgente,* it is possible for the reader to underestimate its dramatic effect. In practice, it took some three minutes of extreme tension to play through, heralded by the thundering of the earthquake, and acted in silence, while the Angel chanted its Easter Sepulchre anthem *Christus resurgens.* The pictorial effect was stunning. Within the frame of the waggon, the red of Christ's cloak seemed to fill the stage; the banner extended his height, which was enhanced by the fact that everyone else on stage, except for the young Angel, was either sitting or lying. He really seemed to be bursting the bonds of something confining. How much more powerful this must have seemed to an audience who were actually familiar with the traditional image.

For a modern audience, too, the singing of *Christus resurgens* was merely an appropriately unearthly accompaniment. In the fifteenth century, anyone who went conscientiously to his parish church on Easter Sunday at dawn must have been strongly reminded of his emotional response to the Easter Sepulchre ceremony. At the same time, being referred so strongly to a *ceremony* is a way of reminding the audience that this too is representational, that what they are seeing is only a shadow of something real. The actual emergence of a Christ-figure from the tomb must at first have seemed like the ritual come to life. Where there is usually a cross or a wooden figure, now there is a human being, with the wounds painted on him. The actual physicality of the actor playing Christ is almost shocking, especially since the audience has to watch the whole process of resurrection, not just contemplate, safely, a posed, two-dimensional, triumphal moment. Yet no one for a moment believes that this is really Christ: he is a representation of Christ.

The first sense of shock was succeeded by silence, awe, and amazement. The mood was so powerful that the only thing one could do, it seemed, was to break into it in some way. The playwright does this with the unexpected cry of anguish from Mary Magdalen. The focus is changed; there follows the canon of lamentation from the Maries, a complete shift of mood, tone, and distance. We are now to get the first of the replays; we are going to see the Resurrection through their eyes.

As far as the story is concerned, of course, they do not know what has happened. The audience do, and they might be expected to have some sort of 'superior knowledge' attitude towards the lamentation. In fact the lamentation is so intense the audience are swept into it. It is psychologically necessary for them that they should be. They have been stunned by the Resurrection: they now have to start realizing it. The Maries' ignorance of what has just happened enables the playwright to go back in time, to a situation when Christ is still dead. The Maries then talk the audience through the whole experience of Easter, starting with loss and lamentation, ending with realization and joy.

We have seen already how they engage the audience in their grief. They then have to engage them in their joy. This transition is very difficult to handle; it was in fact the most difficult part of the play to work out in rehearsal, because it was in no way naturalistic. The Maries do not react like the Soldiers. They have to witness in a different way, a formal, liturgical way: they are given the angelic message, are shown and display the evidence, the empty tomb, the sudary; they believe, they rejoice, they go off to obey the command *Ite nunciate*. In terms of naturalistic psychology, this scene does not work. It is too sudden. They have no time to get over the shock, to reassemble the picture. The Soldiers' reaction is much more plausible: they merely have to cope with the fact that the body has gone, and immediately they fasten on the one small part of it that seems to affect them, 'Witte sir Pilate of this affraye We mon be slone' (309-10). They then talk themselves into accepting the situation. The Maries are not even allowed to talk: they must react in silence.

It is in fact too big a thing to take in naturalistically. Tradition demands that they should accept it without question. (The Gospels are more naturalistic, and the 'Appearances' plays deal with the problem of acceptance at more length.) Two things operate to make the audience accept the Maries' acceptance. One is the fact of their own superior knowledge. They have actually seen Christ rise. (They also accept the way in which the Soldiers, reporting to Pilate, describe things which, if they were 'slepande whanne he yede' (318), they cannot possibly have seen.) The other is the very stylization of the acceptance, which refers them again to the ancient patterns of liturgical drama, and the familiar icon.

Again, the change of mode is accompanied by a physical distancing. The Maries have been lamenting in the street: Magdalen sees the Angel from a distance and they go up to him—'Nere will we wende' (232)—on the waggon. They thus enter the frame and complete the picture, the 'Holy Women at the Sepulchre', and the Angel engages them in the ancient dialogue.

This is so deliberate a translation of a *Quem Quaeritis* that it comes as a shock to find that no direct source has yet been discovered. It echoes the liturgical drama so strongly that it calls for a completely different style of acting. We found that the only way to make it work was to make it an accurate copy of the stylized ges-

tures of the early *Quem Quaeritis:*

> Quo viso, deponant turribula quae gestaverunt in eodem sepulchro, sumantque linteum et extendant contra clerum. . .veluti ostendentes quod surrexerit dominus, etiam non sit involutus. . . [K. Young, *The Drama of the Medieval Church*]

The displaying of the *sudarium* is an important feature of the *Ludus Paschalis* from its beginnings. Here, they display it while the Angel is saying 'He is resen and wente his way' (245), thus combining the angelic witness with the visible evidence: *Angelicos testes, Sudarium et vestes.* Here we get a curious historical reversal. In the early *Quem Quaeritis,* the displaying of the cloth was the high point of audience involvement. Instead of being spectators to a ritual which was being enacted for but not by them, the congregation were suddenly caught up into it, the evidence was being shown to *them.* Here, the showing had quite a different quality: it was being shown as part of a ritual. It remained curiously distant, high and dry on an ancient historical beach-head of drama.

The Maries then rejoice, embrace, and go off, still in unison and silence, until the Magdalen breaks abruptly into the mood with the declaration that she intends to stay behind. As soon as they go, she starts to lament again.

This new section seems, as I have said, illogical. Why, having heard of the Resurrection, and accepted it with joy, should she suddenly start to weep? Why should the audience be made to weep with her? It does not really help to be told that here the author was faced with an uncomfortable hiatus in his sources, which were trying to reconcile the Gospel according to St. Mark, which provided the *Quem Quaeritis,* with the Gospel according to St. John, which provided the *Hortulanus,* the next pageant. True, he has to provide a bridge to the next play. But it is not until we look at the actual content of her lament that the main reason for it becomes clear. In naturalistic terms this is bewildering, as she goes back to the Crucifixion again:

> Allas! what schall nowe worthe on me?
> Mi kaytiffe herte will breke in three
> Whenne I thynke on that body free
>   How it was spilte.
> Both feete and handes nayled tille a tre,
>   Withouten gilte.
>
>   (270-5)

The words 'Whenne I thynke on that body free' shows us where we are. The shift of mood is also a shift from the liturgical mode, which seems to be proper for the presentation of great events, back to the meditative, affective, personal mode. The audience have seen the Resurrection, they have been called on to live through the appropriate cycle of emotions, now they are to pause and consider what it means to them personally. It is reminiscent of the structure of those meditative works where each narrative section is followed by a prayer which brings the historical events to the here-and-now of the reader.

She stands before the audience as the Mary Magdalen of tradition, the beautiful, the rich, the emotional, the ex-courtesan, the great sinner, the penitent, whose 'sins, which are many, are forgiven, for she loved much' (Luke 7:47). Though on paper she seems to speak in first-person terms,

> The woundes he suffered many one
> > Was for my misse;
> It was my dede he was for slayne,
> > And nothyng his
>
> > (278-81)

every member of the audience is meant to take them personally. She is speaking for Every Sinner. She leads the audience through the stages of affective meditation—compassion, tears (the audience may be stirred to weep in sympathy), love; even her exit lines, which have a purely narrative linking function, express the devout longing of the soul for God:

> Ther is no thing to that we mete
> > May make me blithe.
>
> > (286-7)

Her lamentation dies away, and we wake up to the ordinary, short-sighted world of the Soldiers. I hesitate to mention the words 'comic relief', but this is how it seems to work; it provides a sudden release of tension from high serious emotional involvement into laughter, but also directs the laughter away through another set of people, with a different set of values, a new change of focus.

A young member of the audience said, when consulted, that she thought the Soldiers were there 'to restore our faith in human nature', and one can see what she meant. The high emotion of the centre part of the play has to be anchored to the everyday world: we cannot stay on the mountain peak. To a certain extent the audience are laughing at themselves, as they might have behaved in a situation that is just too big for them: even when the Soldiers confess the truth to Pilate, it becomes 'I was a-ferde, I durst not loke' (393). They even laugh in recognition when the Soldiers accept the bribe with such unbecoming alacrity: 'That's how things are', 'Thus schall the sothe be bought and solde' (449).

Yet somehow it is not reductive laughter. This is possibly because the Soldiers lack malice (and at the end, even Pilate dissociates himself from his role, and turns into an actor commenting on it); possibly because they

have in fact borne witness to the event by accepting it in front of the audience even though in the story they are too cowardly to stand up for their acceptance; possibly also because their betrayal does not actually make any difference to the outcome, for the audience are by now secure in their own knowledge. But the laughter is something more positive and simpler than these explanations might suggest. I have been talking about a play in performance, where the sense of mood often seems to override logic, and also where the effects are often simpler than literary criticism might like them to be. Here what came over most strongly was that the Soldiers were eventually 'on our side' because they were funny. We weren't even aware of anything complicated about accepting the shortcomings of human nature; rather it was as if the playwright had sensed that the play should end with laughter; the Resurrection is a joyful thing, and on the everyday level to which we had returned, comedy is the appropriate expression of this. *Haec dies quam fecit Dominus: exultemus et laetamur in ea.* 'This is the day which the Lord hath made: we will rejoice and be glad in it.'

Clifford Davidson (essay date 1984)

SOURCE: "After the Fall," in *From Creation to Doom: The York Cycle of Mystery Plays,* AMS Press, 1984, pp. 39-59.

[*In the following essay, Davidson calls attention to the traditional dialectical pattern of hope and despair in the York plays that are based on episodes from the Old Testament. He also traces this pattern in medieval English pictorial art, including windows in York Minster and other churches, ecclesiastical sculpture, and illuminated manuscripts.*]

A comparative method involving study of the York plays and analogous representations of subjects in the visual arts may suggest some new ways of approaching the vexed question of the selection of episodes in the portion of the cycle based on the Old Testament. Agreement seems fairly general that all theories which purport to explain the choice of episodes as determined by liturgical readings, by typology, or by the medieval understanding of the seven ages of man can never provide adequate explanations of the principles of selection. Let us for the time being put aside any attempt to identify the mechanism or principle which allowed certain plays to "evolve" within a certain pattern. Instead, if we are willing to consider the phenomenology of the plays in the Old Testament series, they suddenly make very good sense.

No argument defending a tightly-knit "organic unity" of the plays in the York cycle between the Fall and the Annunciation is either possible or desirable, but throughout these plays there is observable a more or less consistent treatment of the issue which rightly ought to be most prominent in any representation of the early history of the race according to the Christian myths. This issue involves the marked alteration in the human condition following the fall from the idyllic state experienced in the Garden of Eden. Choice obviously has entered into human life, but it is not so simple a matter as the Dominican Thomas Aquinas apparently believed when he expressed confidence that the intellect through the imparting of rational knowledge would produce a desire in the will to perform virtue and eschew vice. Through the Fall, demonic forces have made their way into the very spiritual and psychological make-up of man. Men can become wilfully blind: they can sever their relationships with their kinsmen and their Creator. Or they can, through openness and sensitivity to the divine realities, overcome the effects of the Fall. The tendency of the one kind is toward vice, the other is toward virtue.

The presentation of scenes from the early history of the race is, of course, the province of much medieval English and continental art, and here too the examination of meaning and structure must lead to the conclusion that no merely interesting images are being presented for their own sake. The visual arts illustrated the important events of the sacred story not scientifically and dispassionately, but with a view to understanding their true significance. The approach of the painter or sculptor was hence very much like the dramatist or actor who attempted to present in livelier fashion the same images and the same events.

I

For the history of mankind as interpreted by the York plays, the crucial moment is the fall of man. As portrayed in the Coopers' *Fall of Man,* the age of innocence in the Garden is very brief for Adam and Eve, who are created in the morning and are fallen already at noon. After the Fall, in the Armorers' *Expulsion from the Garden,* Adam laments:

> Allas, in blisse kouthe we noyt bee,
> For putte we were to grete plenté
>   At prime of þe day;
> Be tyme of none alle lost had wee,
>   Sa welawaye.

(VI.88-92)

Irreparable loss is the result of allowing themselves to be deceived by the "tales vntrewe" of the hypocrite Satan (V. 123). Thus in this play the audience is taken back to the time when the race was founded—a time marked by a touch of bliss against which all later sorrow may be judged.

In contrast to any strictly typological interpretation of Play V, our understanding of the dramatic handling of

the Fall ought to conclude that, like representations in the pictorial arts of the late Middle Ages in England, this work focuses most upon the moral and physical disaster brought upon mankind. The "gamys" and "glee" enjoyed by our innocent parents in the morning of sacred history are gone (VI.86-87), and they are overcome by shame at their naked state. Adam expresses his severe anxiety about his nudity—"Oure shappe for doole me defes" (V.I29)—and Eve suggests that they take up "fygge-leves" (V.I3I). Their discomfort is proof that they have something to hide. "Full wondyr fayne I wolde hyde me, / Fro my lordis sight," Adam exclaims (V.I35-36). As in the series of panels painted by John Thornton in the Great East Window of York Minster, the transgression is immediately followed by divine intervention. In Play V, God orders Adam and Eve out into the "erthe" where they will "swete and swynke, / And trauayle for [their] foode" (V.I6I-62) and calls upon his "Cherubyn" to "dryve these twoo" out of the Garden (V.I66-67). The angel is not present as the agent of expulsion in the scriptural account in *Genesis,* which only notes that after "the Lord God. . .drove out the man," he stationed "at the east of the garden of Eden cherubims, and a flaming sword which turned every way, to keep the way of the tree of life" (3.23-24). But in Thornton's Great East Window and in the York plays, the angel acts to expel man's first parents, who are still nude. Thornton's painted glass shows the angel placing one hand on Adam's shoulder—a very common gesture that probably was repeated in the Armorers' play, where the divine messenger also tells Eve that she shall as punishment bring forth her children in pain and woe (VI.69-72).

It is extremely unlikely that the medieval audience of Plays V and VI in the York cycle would naturally have been led to think about the typological significance of the Fall, which in the *Biblia Pauperum* and elsewhere points to the Temptation of Christ by Satan. This is not to say that medieval men failed to think of Christ as the second Adam and of the Blessed Virgin Mary as the second Eve who miraculously brought forth her Son without travail; however, the focus of the plays, even while preparing the way dramatically for the life of Christ which will follow later, is upon the human condition as encountered in a post-lapsarian world.

Primarily we note an Adam and Eve totally discomfited and desiring to hide from the reality represented by God. Having fallen from obedience, they expect punishment—and they receive stern treatment indeed. After they are expelled from Eden, they argue and fall into despair. "On grounde mon I never gladde gange, / Withowten glee," Adam complains (VI.I6I-62). Normally in the visual arts the next scene would be the scene in which "Adam delved and Eve span," as in the *Speculum Humanae Salvationis,* the fifteenth-century painted glass at Great Malvern or the fourteenth-century illumination in the *Bohun Psalter* now in the

Bodleian Library, but this is not represented in the York cycle or in Thornton's Great East Window. Yet in the plays the idea that Adam will be condemned to joyless labor is directly conveyed in a manner that must have made a deep impression on fifteenth- and sixteenth-century audiences.

The pattern established by the fall of man hence is essentially different from the fall of the rebel angels. When Lucifer and his cohorts fell, they first impressed audiences with their arrogance and pride—factors which separated them from the spectators and made them the objects of hatred at the same time that their absurd hopes made them the butt of laughter. In falling into a sado-masochistic hell, they appeared to receive what they deserve. Thereafter, they become simultaneously sinister and comic—angles of darkness who are at once foolish and malicious. On the other hand, Eve and Adam are deceived by Satan who, to be sure, appeals to their pride. But they eat almost reluctantly, and when then they voice their regret it is with a terrible sense of despair that is in no way funny. The relationship established with the deity has been broken, and in their alienation man's first parents lose all the joy which they formerly possessed. They are repentant—a sign that their despair actively is working for good within their souls. Hence when Christ, the second Adam, comes after the Crucifixion to rescue Adam and Eve during the Harrowing of Hell, he will be able to offer them salvation (XXXVII.385-88). But in the meantime the primordial couple has established a pattern which will resound through history.

This pattern as set forth in the story of Adam and Eve involves an essential conflict between *hope* (nourished by obedience and overcoming despair to re-establish communication with God) and a *despair* which brings together all the negative aspects of the sin of Adam and Eve as observed in Plays V and VI in the York cycle. The immediate effects of the Fall are to bring unhappiness, sin, and death into human life, as in the sixteenth-century Rouen glass panels recently inserted in one of the windows of York Minster. In this expulsion scene, the nude Adam and Eve with their hands bound have in attendance the allegorical figures of Poverty, Toil, Sorrow, and Credulity as well as the Seven Deadly Sins. Once the machinery of the allegory is stripped away, the image in the Rouen glass, like the York plays, presents us with the condition of natural man as a precarious and fragile state in which he must struggle to extend his existence in an environment that has become hostile. The natural condition for man in such an existence seems to be joyless despair, yet the memory of paradise lost breeds a desire to return to felicity and a hope that through renewed obedience communication with the deity might bring about this happy end.

II

Hope and despair hence become the essential elements in the dialectic of the play which follows the Armorers' *Expulsion from the Garden*. This play is the Glovers' *Sacrificium Cayme et Abell*, which. . .is not extant in complete form in the Register and which also contains an interpolation in a sixteenth-century hand. However, in spite of the fragmentary nature of the text, enough is present to document the manner in which the images communicated by the scenes are designed to illustrate the binary pattern of hope and despair. Thus Abel in his first speech announces his sincere obedience and devotion: "I worshippe þe with worthynes" (VII.36). He is a good steward, recognizing that it is only proper for God to have his share in sacrifice "sen [he] it sent" (VII.42). As the first shepherd and a worthy keeper of sheep, he likewise looks forward typologically to the divine Shepherd (i.e., Christ). While hence Abel on several levels represents hope, Cain from the very first epitomizes its opposite, which is despair. He makes fun of Abel's piety, and responds to his brother's plea that he too is required to fulfil "Goddis biddyng blithe" (VII.49-50) with the following inappropriate words:

> Ya, daunce in þe devil way, dresse þe downe,
> For I wille wyrke euen as I will.
>
> (VII. 52-53)

He substitutes his own *will* for the divine will, and hence becomes an emblem of disobedience to divine authority.

Cain's despair is a logical extension of his wilful isolation and alienation. He is unable to "set [his] hope high, to the good of all goods" [St. Augustine]. So he serves himself, placing narrow self-interest above service to the Maker of all things. As the first son of Eve born after the Fall, Cain clearly represents the lapsarian principle in mankind. Medieval theology popularly regarded him as a child of sin. He offends against kinship, and in him all human ties are dissolved. In the Towneley cycle, Cain's acts are regarded as foreshadowing all later deeds of ingratitude and malice, as when Judas betrays Christ. The Towneley Pilate, speaking to the Jews who maliciously attempt to destroy Jesus, calls them "kamys kyn" (*Conspiracy*, l. 639). And in the fragmentary Towneley *Suspencio Iude*, Judas calls himself a member of "that Cursyd Clott of Camys kyn" (l. 17). For the medieval Church, Judas is, of course, the prime exemplar of despair, for his hopelessness in the end leads to his utterly horrifying suicide—an act early represented in art as opposed precisely to the death of Christ in the Crucifixion, which ultimately is the source of hope for all Christians. Hence as early as the fifth century the artist responsible for an ivory now in the British Museum placed the betrayer Judas, hanging by his neck and utterly alone, on the left, while on the right Jesus on the cross is attended by the Virgin and St. John at the moment when Longinus (with a spear now lost) opens the side of the Savior. Judas' attitude toward self-interest and profit and his act of malice in betraying his Master to death are both already present in Cain, whose name, according to St. Ambrose, means "getting" in keeping with his refusal to tithe or sacrifice sincerely—and who, as everyone knows, killed his own brother. Cain is also linked with Christ's betrayer in the frieze on the West front of Lincoln Cathedral, where he curiously holds a bag or purse—an emblem which he shares with Judas. Indeed, Cain's followers—those who are destroyed at the Flood, tyrants such as Pharaoh and Herod, Judas, the Jews who oppose Christ and his religion—are set in permanent opposition to obedient Abel, Noah, Abraham, and the Apostles and other Christians who are Christ's followers before and after the Resurrection. Through these two sets of characters, the York plays establish a dialectic of despair and hope.

The York *Sacrificium Cayme et Abell* hence builds on the understanding of Cain set forth long ago in St. Ambrose's *Cain and Abel*. Ambrose wrote:

> I am inclined to hold that. . .we have reference to two classes of peoples. In disposing for the Church's use the faith of His devoted flock, God has made ineffective the perfidy of the people who fell away from Him. The very words of God seem to establish this meaning: 'Two nations are in your womb; two peoples stem from your body.' These two brothers, Cain and Abel, have furnished us with the prototype of the Synagogue and the Church. In Cain we perceive the parricidal people of the Jews, who were stained with blood of their Lord, their Creator, and, as a result of the Child-bearing of the Virgin Mary, their Brother, also. By Abel we understand the Christian who cleaves to God, as David says: 'It is good for me to adhere to my God,' that is, to attach oneself to heavenly things and to shun the earthly.

The idea of "two nations" is familiar from St. Augustine, who named them Babylon and Jerusalem. However, in the visual arts the usual equivalents of Ambrose's "two classes" are the Synagogue and the Church. A window in the east wall of the vestibule of the Chapter House at York contains late thirteenth-century painted glass showing Synagogue and Church, which also find representation at Lincoln and elsewhere. In Bodleian Library MS. Auct. D. 3. 5 (fol. 1), an illuminated initial typically depicts the Synagogue as a maiden blindfolded, holding a broken banner with her right hand, and dropping the tables of the law from the other hand. In the York glass, she has a crown which is falling, while the Church, above, is crowned and is holding a cross and a small model of a church. The Church triumphs ultimately, just as ultimately the descendants of Abel will inherit bliss. Cain's kin, on the other hand, lack such hope and, failing to grasp the vision shared by those who are obedient and pious,

can only despair.

It should be noted, of course, that the analogy of Cain and the Synagogue and of Abel and the Church may not be pressed too far in any discussion of the *Sacrificium Cayme et Abell*. This colorful imagery is not directly present in the York play, though its presence as background can hardly be denied. When the play takes up the biblical narrative, however, it focuses instead on pictorial details more closely related to the events being dramatized. The tendency of biblical interpretation, especially under the influence of the friars, was now more toward literalism and away from the more intellectualized figural schema preferred by earlier exegetes. Yet, from the standpoint of the entire cycle, the role of Cain and Abel remains immensely significant, for it confirms the pattern of the Fall which will resonate through the entire series of plays until finally the "two classes" of people will be separated on the Last Day of history. Cain in particular demonstrates how the negative aspects of the Fall attach themselves to men of the blind "nation" which devotes itself to self-interest and which hence is unable to recollect the bliss lost by the race when their parents ate of the forbidden fruit. In sharp contrast are those who, like Abel, devote themselves to obedience to a higher Good.

Cain's refusal to sacrifice is thus crucial. This act actually provides the first scene of the York play, though the Register breaks off at line 70, where two leaves are missing, before his refusal can culminate in his impious and hence unsatisfactory rendering of sheaves to his Creator. This scene is implied in the panel in the Great East Window of the Minster, which shows grain and sheep, the offerings tendered by Cain and Abel. More complete is the Cain and Abel story in the *Holkham Bible Picture Book*, which illustrates in graphic detail the rebellious Cain and obedient Abel. Here (fol. 5), as in the Towneley *Mactacio Abel*, the two sacrifices are shown: in contrast to the clean-burning sacrifice of Abel, Cain's offering smokes vilely and stinks "like the dwill in hell" (l. 283)—and the smoke mingles with the smoke of hell-mouth immediately below the altar. Between the two brothers stands God, approving the one on his right and condemning the faulty sacrifice on his left. Thus too at the Last Day will the Judge give his approval to those arrayed on his right and his curses to those on his left.

The next miniature in the *Holkham Bible Picture Book* (fol. 5ᵛ) illustrates the murder with the jawbone of an ass, . . .and also Cain's reaction after the murder. At the bottom left of the illumination, Cain, with a sour and unrepentant look on his face, appears to be saying to the dead Abel, as in the Towneley play, "lig down ther and take thi rest; / Thus shall shrewes be chastysed best" (ll. 326-27). On the right he impudently looks up at God, who personally speaks to him as in the biblical account. Appropriately in the Towneley play his arrogant disdain alternates with fear. Like Adam immediately after the Fall, he expresses a desire to hide himself: "Into som hole fayn wold I crepe" (l. 337). God, however, very soon calls to the quacking Cain, whose saucy rebelliousness quickly returns. In the York play, God is replaced by an angel, whose role is parallel to the angel of the Expulsion, for he sends the sinner into the field to till the soil.

There is, however, a terribly important difference between Adam sent forth to labor in the soil in Play VI and Cain's treatment in the *Sacrificium Cayme et Abell.* The angel does not tell Cain that he will earn his bread with the sweat of his brow, but that his labor henceforth will be fruitless:

> Þou shall be curssed vppon þe grounde,
>   God has geffyn þe his malisonne;
> Yff þou wolde tyll þe erthe so rounde
>   No frute to þe þer shalle be fonne.
>
> (VII. 106-10)

In the *Holkham Bible Picture Book* (fol. 6), as in the Towneley *Mactacio Abel*, Cain is actually seen plowing. The illumination pictures him with a medieval plow pulled by a team which includes an ass and two oxen— an impressive technological advance, certainly, over the spade which weary Adam typically uses to turn over ground. The plow appears to be traditionally linked to Cain, the tiller of the ground, and as a symbolic attribute it underlines the hopelessness of his occupation. Cain in the Chester plays laments that he will "never thryve" (II. 702).

Cain thus is cursed to till the fruitless ground, which will not bring forth any produce as a result of his labor. What is presented here is a traditional picture of despair. Medieval theologians, following Augustine and Gregory, described despair in terms of sterility and lack of growth. God's grace, made available through hope and faith, is like water necessary to make the soil fruitful, according to Gregory. Cain has successfully severed himself from the sources of life. Until Lamech will end his life with a misdirected arrow—a scene commonly represented in the visual arts but dramatized in the English cycles only in the N-town Plays where it forms an episode in the play of Noah (ll. 142-97)—Cain will suffer the pangs of those who are "dampned without grace" (*Chester* II.666). Early in the **Sacrificium Cayme et Abell,** Cain seems driven by anger—a sign of the irascible passions which, according to Aquinas, are associated with despair.

At the end, Cain is overcome with fear, the emotion more typically identified with despair. Completely out of touch with any remembrance of bliss past, he moans that his "synne it passis al mercie" (VII. 119). Like Judas later, he feels he has committed a sin so unfor-

givable that repentance is impossible. All he now can do is to live out his cursed life without any hope whatever.

III

At the opening of the **Building of Noah's Ark,** Deus comments that men have already become so wicked that "they make me to repente / My werke I wroght so wele and trewe" (VIII. 17-18). These men also, like Cain, have inherited all the negative qualities inherent in the Fall, and, for their inability to live lives based on hope, God will work their destruction. The world will be made "Al newe" through the Flood, which will "[de] stroye medilerthe" (VIII. 25-28). God's instrument of renewal will be one single obedient man, Noah, who is addressed by the deity as "my seruand"—the terminology reminiscent of the precise service wrought by Abel, the exemplar of good stewardship.

God's speech to Noah also opens a series of panels on the Flood in painted glass at the Great Malvern Priory Church. God is seen at the upper left "out of white clouds and a glory of gold rays." Below on the right, an aged Noah responds to the divine presence by kneeling and raising up his hands. The text below refers to the Vulgate (*Genesis* 6.13) and indicates that this is the moment when God appeared to Noah and spoke to him. Noah's response underlines his faith and obedience, both of which sustain him steadfastly during the long period when he secretly is building the vessel of salvation. His only worries in the play concern his age ("I am full olde and oute of qwarte," VIII.50) and his lack of skill ("of shippe-craft can I right noght," VIII.67), but God helps him to overcome all obstacles. He gives the builder strength and specific advice as he works on the ark.

It is no accident that this play at York was given to the Shipwrights, who must have produced a pre-fabricated ark that could be assembled in minutes, though surely it must have taken longer than the time apparently allowed by one modern critic, who would have the entire play performed in nine minutes [Margaret Dorrell (Rogerson), "Two Studies of the York Corpus Christi Plays," *Leeds Studies in English,* n.s.6, 1972]. And perhaps this ship, once it had been assembled, may have been used as well for the following play of **Noah's Ark during the Flood.** In contrast to some symbolic arks in the visual arts, the Shipwrights' vessel must have resembled an actual ship such as would normally sail out of the port of York by way of the Ouse River. As in a miniature in Bodleian MS. Barlow 53, dated 1420-30, Noah, working alone, takes up his carpenter's tools and hews a board, whereupon he joins and sets the pieces together. He drives "nayles" and inserts "a revette," then takes his "rewe" (rule). The hull of the ark now appears already to be assembled. The result would appear to be a substantial vessel at least able to hold eight actors, though it surely was less elaborate than the ark utilized in the Plough Day pageant at Hull.

Completion of the ark in the York Shipwrights' play apparently did not involve rigging, which prominently figures in the original glass in the panel representing the Flood in Thornton's Great East Window in York Minster. Similar attention to rigging had been present in the accounts relating to the Plough Ship at Hull. However, once the hull of the ark is finished, Noah in the York play is merely commanded to set up "dyuerse stawllys and stagis" to accommodate the animals and birds he is to take aboard (VIII.124-31). These are obviously set up very quickly, and may be simply some rooms atop the hull as in a thirteenth-century illumination in Bodleian MS. Lat. th. b. l. Nothing so complex as the usual three-tiered ark (e.g., on a nave boss in Norwich Cathedral) could be so rapidly assembled. Yet it is likely that this superstructure would involve *three* "stawllys" or compartments, since the ark was held to have a potent symbolic meaning as a representation of the Church—and in medieval number symbolism, the number for the Church is three. The Church is, of course, the institution that should provide the means of hope against the realities of individual death and the destruction by fire that eventually will overtake the world. Gregory the Great hence explained that the ark had three levels arranged in the shape of a pyramid, with reptiles and beasts below and birds and man above: thus is the ark like the Church, which contains a greater number of carnal men, along with a smaller number of spiritual men and with one man, Christ, who is without sin, at the highest level. The arrangement suggested above for the York ark would thus provide a practical solution to the demand that the ark have a tripartite structure, since the reptiles, animals, and birds could easily be shifted to the two enclosures on each end, while the central area could be reserved for Noah and his family.

At the beginning of the play of **Noah's Ark during the Flood,** produced by the Fishers and Mariners, Noah's promise to fill "With beestys and fewlys my shippe" (VIII.149) must already be realized, for, unlike a panel in the Noah series in the pained glass at Great Malvern and the Chester play of *The Deluge,* there appears to be at York no procession of animals and birds entering the ark. After a long monologue in which Noah laments the disaster coming to the world and recollects that it is a disaster predicted by his father Lamech, his children arrive at the ark and announce: "Fader we are all redy heere, / Youre biddyng baynly to fulfille" (IX.47-48).

At this point is inserted the lively episode of Noah's shrewish wife, who refuses to do as she is bid—i.e., she will not obediently follow orders from her lawful husband. This story has its source in Eastern legend, and has been observed in English art as early as the

illustration in Caedmonian MS. Junius XI (p. 66), which has been described by Sir Israel Gollancz as follows: "On the right hand, one of the women, whom we may assume to be Noah's wife, seems to be unwilling to mount the ladder, and is expostulating with one of the three sons [quoted by Katherine Garvin, "A Note on Noah's Wife," *Modern Language Notes* 49, 1934]. Similar reluctance has been observed in painted glass at the Great Malvern Priory Church, and in *Queen Mary's Psalter* the episode appears along with further remnants of the ancient tale, which posits the devil's plan to use Noah's wife as an instrument whereby the floating of the ark might be prevented. In this manner she is made to appear as a second Eve with all her negative qualities—an interpretation of her character that would have seemed quite logical to the medieval mind, which would have remembered that Noah's wife, like Eve, is also a mother of the entire race. The York play, however, has stripped away everything associated with the legend except Uxor's recalcitrance and unwillingness to enter the ark. (Instead of coming into the ark, she wants to go "to towne," IX.81, and then she wishes to return home for her goods and, later, for her "commodrys" and "cosynes," IX.143.)

As a person with no respect for God's will as revealed to her husband Noah, Uxor is perhaps allegorically representative of "the recalcitrant sinner. . .who refuses to repent and enter the church" symbolized here by the ark [Rosemary Woolf, *The English Mystery Plays,* 1972]. Her blindness at first toward the great spiritual and existential realities is as marked as Cain's, but the difference is also underlined in the play: her mood mends after she has entered the symbolic ark. Between line 55, when the son first announces himself to his mother as Noah's messenger, and lines 151-52, when she laments that her friends "Are ouere flowen with floode," the drama presents a very lively and much admired farce. It is farce characterized by all the precision of detail that is associated with the meticulous artistry and attention to detail of the glass painter John Thornton. But the frace is calculated to set off the absurdity which marks the behavior of those who, self-deceived, fail to understand the desperation inherent in the fallen condition of man. Such wilful blindness obviously needs to be taken in hand—i.e., the negative and self-destructive side of the post-lapsarian personality requires coercion when it interferes with the divine command. As a warning, the farce takes on a more serious meaning too in the light of the typological explanation of the Flood at the end of the play: the world has been ravaged now by water and, in spite of God's promise through the image of the rainbow that it will not happen again, this event looks forward to the time when "it sall ones be waste with fyre, / And never worþe to worlde agayne" (IX.301-02).

The survival of Noah through obedience, faith, and hope may be regarded as a remedy for despair. Even if in dramatic production the specific allegory of the Ark=Church is lost, the phenomenological lesson is clear: he who keeps the lines of communication open with the deity and obeys the divine commands will be given hope of salvation on the Last Day when the deluge shall be fire instead of water.

IV

In the Parchmentmakers' and Bookbinders' *Abraham and Isaac,* the lesson of obedience is continued in a drama which is more overtly based on typology than any of the other Old Testament plays in the York cycle. Figurally, Abraham represents the Father willing to sacrifice his only Son, and Isaac is a type of Christ. Isaac, as a sermon in Mirk's widely-known *Festial* explains, "was fygur of Crystys passyon long or he wer borne. . . ." The liturgy of the Feast of Corpus Christi, through the sequence *Lauda Sion* written by Thomas Aquinas, contains an explicit reference to the sacrifice of Isaac as a figure foreshadowing Christ. A similar reference is found in the Canon of the Mass, which compares the ritual act to "the sacrifice of our forefather Abraham." The entire matter is described by the Chester Expositor:

> By Abraham I may understand
> the Father of heaven that cann fonde
> with his Sonnes blood to breake that bonde
> that the dyvell had brought us to.
> By Isaack understande I maye
> Jesus that was obedyent aye,
> his Fathers will to worke alwaye
> and death for to confounde.
>
> (*Chester* IV.468-75)

Hence in the York play the Father-Son relationship is arranged to stress parallels between the Old Testament event and the Passion and Crucifixion.

It is, of course, in the character of Isaac that the typology presented in the York play is concerned. Following Peter Comestor, Isaac is not the child normally expected, but is a man approximately as old as Christ at his Crucifixion. His father notes that his son "is of eelde to reken right / Thyrty yere and more sumdele" (X.81-82). An Isaac of similar age appears on a misericord at Worcester Cathedral and formerly in the wall paintings, now lost, in the choir at Peterborough—in both instances carrying the faggots of wood for the sacrifice in two bundles shaped like the cross over his shoulders. In other representations of Isaac in the visual arts which show him younger than in the York play, he nevertheless carries the wood for his sacrifice. The York version of the story sees the journey which will lead to the sacrifice on the mount start, as required by the biblical account, with an ass led by servants and carrying the wood (X.109-10). When they approach the mount, Abraham and his son leave the ass and

servants in order to go up together. The father now orders Isaac to carry the wood: "þis wode behoues þe bere / Till þou come high vppon yone hill" (X.151-52).

When Isaac in the York play is told that he will be the sacrifice, he accepts his role at once since it is God's will. On one level, however, he cannot restrain his dread: his natural fear and anxiety threaten to overcome him. At one point he expresses his fear, as Rosemary Woolf has noted [in *The English Mystery Plays*], in terms of a paraphrase of the Office for the Dead: "dere fadir, lyff is full swete, / The drede of dede dose all my dere" (X.279-80). Such a reaction, however, does not disqualify him as a type of Christ. Indeed, the Franciscan *Meditations on the Life of Christ,* which so deeply influence the plays on New Testament topics, strongly stress Christ's fear and apprehension when looking forward to the anguish which he should suffer. This fear is especially important, for it underlines the point so significant for the *Meditations* (and for the York plays): Jesus must die as a human being, and his perfect humanity must atone for the imperfect humanity shared by all other men since Adam's disobedience in the Garden. Isaac's fear, like Christ's, is not a sign of sin.

As everyone knows, Isaac will not in fact be sacrificed: the deity will send an angel to stay the hand of execution and will provide a sheep for the offering. The sheep is also, of course, a type of the Lamb of God who will actually be slain for men's sin. It reinforces the appropriateness of Abel's offering and looks forward to the Lamb which is a standard attribute in the visual arts of John the Baptist, whose role is to announce: "Behold the Lamb of God, which taketh away the sin of the world" (*John* 1.22, *AV*).

But all of the typology evident in the York *Abraham and Isaac* only enriches and gives additional meaning to the basic pattern established by the Fall: through obedience and a will attuned to the divine commands, an individual may banish despair. Abraham's obedience hence is at the center of the York play as it is also the central lesson of the biblical story. In the visual arts, Abraham, pictured alone, was early associated with obedience, as in the *Bamberg Apocalypse* (c.1000). This interpretation is especially made clear in the twelfth-century *York Psalter,* in which in separate illuminations the sword held by the angel of the Expulsion and the sword raised by Abraham (plates 3-4) are not only identical in appearance but are held at the same angle in approximately the same space within the outline of the miniature. In the Expulsion, the sword threatens Adam and Eve for their disobedience; in the sacrifice of Isaac, an angel stays the sword with his hand as a response to Abraham's obedience. The York play opens with a monologue in which Abraham proclaims that the lines of communication between himself and his

Maker (who "alle þis world has wrought," X.1) are open. Because he has been able to establish "frenshippe" with God (X.12), Abraham, an old man, "þus fro barenhede has [been] broghte" (X.5). His son Isaac is a reward for obedience and is a sign of divine favor and hope. As despair is traditionally associated with sterility, so Abraham is given a hope which historically will be expressed through his fertile progeny. God has told him that his "seede shulde be multyplyed / Lyke to þe gravell of þe see, / And als þe sternes wer strewed wyde" (X.15-17).

The divine testing which Abraham endures when the angel commands the sacrifice of Isaac hence demonstrates that the patriarch does not merely do lip service to a loving God because he has been well treated. Abraham will not allow communication with the deity to break down, but will remain perfectly obedient in his heart in spite of the horrible task that is laid upon him. But unlike God the Father, he will not actually need to surrender his only son in sacrifice, and God will see that Abraham is rewarded for his steadfastness, which is precisely opposed to the attitude expressed by Cain in the *Sacrificium Cayme et Abell.* Because he puts his possessions and himself above things of higher value, Cain is led toward the quintessence of despair. On the other hand, because Abraham puts obedience and trust in God above everything else, he is given his son a second time when he is told to substitute the lamb as an offering. The typology contained in the plays looks forward to a more permanent solution to the problem presented by the fallen condition of man, while the presentation of Abraham as an exemplar of obedience points toward the immediate cementing of divine-human relations in a manner that delineates the structure of hope.

Abraham and Isaac are founders of a chosen people, just as at a later time Christ will establish a new people whose lives are characterized by hope. These people of hope are precisely set off against the people of despair (Cain, Pharaoh, Herod, Judas, the Jews unchanged by the message of Jesus) and against those whose blindness, permanent or temporary, prevents them from seeing the absurdity of their acts.

v

The final play, **Pharaoh with Moses,** of the Old Testament series in the York cycle tells the Exodus story (Miss Smith's title is *The departure of the Israelites from Egypt, the ten plagues, and the passage of the Red Sea),* for which the Hosiers were responsible. Here we see Cain's kin set in opposition to the chosen people, the descendants of Abraham who are now the followers of Moses, an apostle of hope, in a unique drama which is poetically and theatrically superior. Pharaoh brags:

All Egippe is myne awne
To lede aftir my lawe,
I will my myght be knawen
And honnoured as it awe.

(XI. 9-12)

The tyrant's will is placed above respect for divine and human relationships that are essential in the post-lapsarian world. Like Cain, he stresses *possession*—in Pharaoh's case, not merely of some sheaves of grain but of an entire kingdom. Such selfish rule is fated to break down the fabric of the society and eventually to lead to a national and personal disaster for the sovereign. Paradoxically, the very "pees" (peace) that he proclaims at lines 13-14 becomes the occasion for dissension, because the condition upon which he insists is obedience that will dissolve the Jews' ties to their Creator. Since they will not sever their ties with God voluntarily, Pharaoh brags that he will thrust them down into bondage.

The author of this play deliberately provided a sharp contrast between the bragging, abusive Pharaoh and Moses, who is introduced alone at line 85. Moses (who surely was presented as the horned man of tradition, as in the figure sculpture from St. Mary's Abbey, York, now in the Yorkshire Museum) immediately speaks of the "Grete God" whose power is passing all creatures and who "governes euere in gud degree" (XI. 85-86). Here is a man who, as leader of the chosen people, does not share any blind illusion about human power arising within any individual human being. Hence as God's instrument he will oppose Pharaoh. This is the man to whom God himself will appear in the burning bush near Mount "Synay" (XI. 92ff). It is a scene originally represented in the glass at Great Malvern where apparently, as in the *Biblia Pauperum,* Moses was seated and taking off his boots in the presence of God.

Deus, directly communicating with Moses through speech, reminds him of his previous special relationship with Abraham, Isaac, and Jacob (whose story is missing from the cycle but who is a popular figure in the visual arts); these men had been promised that they should be blessed with a great progeny—a fact that has already been commented upon by Pharaoh, who has marvelled that the Jewish population in Egypt has increased from only 70 to 300,000 "Withowten wiffe and childe, / And herdes" in only four hundred years (XI. 51-58). God will send the obedient and trusting Moses to Pharaoh, representative of "folke of wykkyd will" (XI. 142). The Egyptian leader will be warned that he must let the Israelites go—even though in his malice he wishes to see them stay in his country in slavery.

Rosemary Woolf has pointed out that the confrontation between Moses and Pharaoh contains foreshadowing of the Harrowing of Hell, when Satan, using even a similar vocabulary and the same "jeering tone," refuses at first to believe the claims of Christ, who has at last come to rescue his people and to give them salvation. The York author would appear to be building on the typology set forth in the *Speculum Humanae Salvationis,* which insists upon the escape from Egypt by the Israelites as a figural foreshadowing of the release of the Patriarchs from hell at the Harrowing. But what the York *Pharaoh with Moses* really presents is a dramatic version of a confrontation between the forces of evil, of selfishness and the power of the creative principle which controls the cosmos. Hence Pharaoh's exercise of false sovereignty and wilful disobedience provokes the expected response. After Moses lifts up his miraculous rod or "wande" without changing Pharaoh's attitude toward the Israelites, he prays that "God sende sum vengeaunce sone" (XI. 251). God does precisely this: messengers come in quickly to report the well-known plagues of Egypt, which are presented in a rather lively telescoped fashion.

Pharaoh, like Cain, has acted out of envy as well as pride against one who represents a standard of obedience that allows him to have a religious and spiritual hope. In particular, Pharaoh is angered when he hears that the Israelites have left and are commencing their wandering in the wilderness—a wandering that, like the journey undertaken by the individual Christian, will terminate in the promised land. He wrathfully announces that he will follow them:

> Horse harneys tyte, þat þei be tane,
>   Þis ryott radly sall þam rewe.
> We sall not sese or they be slone,
>   For to þe se we sall þam sew.
> Do charge oure charyottis swithe
>   And frekly folowes me.
>
> (XI. 389-94)

Like the infidel that he is, Pharaoh impiously advises the Egyptians to "Hefe vppe youre hartis ay to Mahownde," who, he believes, "will be nere vs in oure nede" (XI. 401-02). (In spite of the anachronism, Mahound or Mohammed is the appropriate god for him to call upon, since from the time of the crusades the prophet of Islam had appeared universally as a symbol of infidelity.) How the pursuit is effected and how the Red Sea is represented are unclear: not enough is known to reconstruct the staging with absolute certainty. Moses and the other Israelites, who by now have already crossed the sea, have had the advantage of the sea, controlled by Moses' "wande," standing "On aythir syde . . . / Tille [they] be wente, right as a wall" (XI. 377-80). Lacking the realism which would be afforded by a ditch such as may have been used in stationary production, the Hosiers probably merely arranged for some red cloth—a stage property which the guild itself ought to have been qualified to produce—which could

be held up to illustrate the sea wall and then dropped upon the Egyptian army to simulate drowning. It seems highly unlikely that anything other than pursuing foot soldiers would have been represented, in spite of Pharaoh's call for a horse and chariot. Yet the visual arts provide some spectacular illustrations of the drowning in which a cart in the midst of the sea is a central detail, as on a striking boss in the nave of Norwich Cathedral.

At the conclusion of the play, the wicked Pharaoh and his followers have died for their deeds—i.e., they have received the death promised as a reward for disobedience in the Fullers' play (IV. 66-69). The negative aspects of post-lapsarian nature are swallowed up in the waters of the Red Sea. Not surprisingly, this event was also regarded as typologically foreshadowing the baptism of Christ and hence the sacrament of baptism generally. Salvation from despair and danger is thus celebrated by the Israelite boy who cries out at the end of the York Play:

> Nowe ar we wonne fra waa
>   And saued oute of þe see,
> *Cantemus domino,*
>   To God a sange synge wee.
>
> (XI. 405-08)

Singing here, like the singing of Noah's family in the ark upon the receding of the Flood (IX. 260 and late marginal note at 266: "*Tunc cantent Noe et filii sui, etc.*"), affirms the kinship of obedient human beings with their Creator, who has rescued them from deluge and death. Through their song, they are able to attune themselves to the heavenly harmony or standard of angelic singing which has been observed in the *Creation of Heaven and Earth* and which again will be displayed in the *Offering of the Shepherds* at the time of the Nativity.

The Israelites who have been rescued from the sea have no reason to hide from the wrath of an angry God since they are among the people who in St. Ambrose's classification are associated with salvation through their obedience and their determination to act upon the commands of God. For them the lines of communication are kept open, and the deity protects them from an act of destruction that looks forward to the great catastrophe at the end of time. But even that catastrophe, frightening though it may seem to all who have tender consciences, will not finally affect the blessed, who will then be invited to enter the gates of bliss. For them, on the Last Day the negative aspects of the post-lapsarian condition will be forever cancelled. However, for the second class of people, including Pharaoh and all other wilful or blind followers of Cain, the Last Day will bring the ultimate vengeance upon those who have been responsible for breaking the ties of kinship which ought to link them in hope to their Maker.

Richard Beadle (essay date 1984)

SOURCE: An introduction to *York Mystery Plays: A Selection in Modern Spelling,* edited by Richard Beadle and Pamela M. King, Oxford at the Clarendon Press, 1984, pp. ix-xxx.

[In the excerpt that follows, Beadle provides an outline of the narrative scope of the plays and an overview of several issues connected with the York plays: the historical context of the Corpus Christi festival; the evidence of the manuscript, the Register, and other relevant documents; the role of the York craft guilds; the processional presentation of the plays; and stagecraft and dramatic technique in the cycle.]

The York cycle of Mystery Plays is one of the great literary and theatrical monuments of the later Middle Ages in England, though to describe the cycle as solely a medieval phenomenon is in some ways misleading. Though it came into being in the later fourteenth century, when Chaucer's *Canterbury Tales* and Langland's *Piers Plowman* were being composed, it enjoyed a generally continuous run of annual performances until the late 1560s, and Shakespeare's lifetime. The cycle was an immense undertaking for the city, both financially and in terms of the manpower required to mount it: the text as it has come down to us calls for over 300 speaking parts alone. Its spiritual purpose was the glorification of God, and its didactic intention to instruct the unlettered in the historical basis of their faith, but there is no doubt that the cycle was also intended to reflect the wealth and prestige of the city, particularly the economic pride and self-confidence of the merchants and master-craftsmen who financed the performances annually. The cycle seems to have come into being with the great flowering of York's prosperity in the second half of the fourteenth century, after the Black Death of 1349, when the city stood second only to London in national importance and wealth. Its decline after the middle of the sixteenth century parallels the economic decline of York itself during that period, whilst the rapid rise and spread of the extremer forms of Protestantism began to render the plays a doctrinally suspect relic of the old faith.

York's is the oldest and best preserved of the surviving English cycles. One similar in scope and nature has come down to us from Chester, and there are also comparable collections of plays in the 'Towneley' and 'N-Town' manuscripts. The Towneley manuscript contains plays connected with Wakefield, together with several pieces partially or wholly borrowed from York, which may well represent the Wakefield cycle. The 'N-Town' plays, judging by their dialect, originated in East Anglia, but are not known to have been connected with any particular town or with craft-guilds, as the northern cycles were. The antiquarian misnomer by which they were long known (*Ludus Coventriae*) is not now used, but fragments of the genuine Coventry cycle have survived, as have single plays from the lost cycles of Norwich and Newcastle. Many other towns and cities in the British Isles are known to have once had play-cycles, but now only fleeting documentary references to them remain, buried in old civic muniments. Such cycles in their own day were often known—at least in the north—by the generic title 'Corpus Christi plays'. Such was the case at York, where the surviving medieval muniments of the city tend to refer to the entire cycle in the singular: Corpus Christi play. It is a pity that this authentic expression has been replaced by the late antiquarian invention 'mystery plays.' 'Corpus Christi' preserves reference to the festival day on which the cycle was performed annually, and 'play' embodies the recognition that the cycle was intended to be seen as a coherent and unified work of art, a spiritual statement of a communal belief in God's relationship to man. The cycles at York and elsewhere were evidently the work of several dramatists from the start, and they were undoubtedly revised by others over the years but. . .the artistic and spiritual object of the whole and the subtle interrelatedness of the parts remain. An appropriate comparison to the cycles in this respect might be the Gothic cathedrals of northern Europe, such as York Minster, built and decorated in a succession of styles by generations of craftsmen but unified by a single spiritual aim.

Corpus Christi day was a movable feast, the first Thursday after Trinity Sunday, which might fall on any date between 23 May and 24 June. It became widely observed in England in the second decade of the fourteenth century, and was proclaimed in York in 1325. Theologically speaking, the feast of Corpus Christi celebrated the Real Presence of the Body of Christ in the Host at Mass. Arguments have been put forward in an attempt to link the content and structure of the cycles with the spiritual significance of the feast, but none is particularly convincing. The link between the feast and the cycle may equally have been a practical matter. When Corpus Christi was instituted it became in effect the Church's midsummer festival, coinciding with the obvious and traditional period for outdoor celebrations and observances of any kind, whether religious or secular or, of course, pre-Christian. It is interesting to note that one of the official requirements of Corpus Christi was an outdoor procession in which the laity and clergy followed a vessel carrying the Sacred Host around the streets of the town. As is explained in detail below, the York cycle was presented in the form of a procession, and the pageant-wagons on which the individual plays were performed at first followed the liturgical procession along a traditional ceremonial route through the city. No documentary evidence, however, has survived to show precisely why it was decided to stage the cycle processionally, or how the performance came to be attached to Corpus Christi. Perhaps the attraction of a great summer festival, which included an outdoor symbolic procession, was sufficient to stimulate the imagination of dramatists who had already brooded upon an established cycle of interrelated biblical and aprocryphal subjects, common in medieval art and narrative long before the Corpus Christi cycles came into being.

The York cycle and its congeners were dramas of the Fall and Redemption of man, cast as a historical narrative, drawing on the Bible and its apocryphal accretions for the subject-matter. The medieval audiences of the plays felt themselves to be deeply implicated in this presentation of sacred history. The essential episodes were the Creation of the world and of man, man's deception by the Devil, resulting in the Fall and the expulsion from Pareadise, and his Redemption through the Incarnation, Passion, and Resurrection of Christ. In addition, all the extant cycles proceeded beyond Christ's work of Redemption on earth and also treated an event of the future: Christ's second coming at the Last Judgement. One of the principal effects of the cycle as a whole in performance was to place the audience in a position of God-like omniscience as regards the continuing history and nature of their spiritual predicament on earth. Out of this arose a need for them to examine their consciences and to decide where their allegiance lay in the conflict between good and evil for possession of the souls of the human race—the need for such a decision being finally borne in upon them personally and urgently by the stark choice presented in the Last Judgement play. All the other biblical and legendary events dramatized in the cycles were in one way or another expansions or elaborations of these moments of central importance in the spiritual history of mankind. For example, the Creation and Fall were extended by dramatizing a series of Old Testament events sufficient to show the predicament of fallen man and his need for redemption, and to prefigure the coming of the Redeemer and his earthly existence. One of the chief organizing principles underlying the construction of the cycles was typology, whereby the persons and incidents of the Old Testament plays were held to foreshadow things to come later in the sequence. For instance, Noah and Moses were included as 'types' of Christ, with the Flood adumbrating the Last Judgement and the salvation of the righteous, whilst the Exodus looked forward to the Harrowing of Hell. This principle was also extended to the wicked characters of the drama, such as Pharaoh and the two Herods, whose words and actions were made to reflect those of the Devil in his various appearances in the story. The contemporary vogue for Gospel harmonies and contemplative treatments of the life of Christ led the playwrights to emphasize the events surrounding the Nativity and the Passion, at the expense of his ministry on earth. At York, the dramatization of the Passion came to occupy about half the cycle, and was much revised over the years.

At the earliest stage in the history of the York cycle a decision must have been taken to divide the long sequence of events stretching from the Creation to the Last Judgement into manageable units for the purposes of processional performance. Each of these units became a separate play, or, as it was then often known, 'pageant', and each was assigned to a particular craft-guild of the city. The craft-guilds therefore became responsible for furnishing the pageant-wagon on which the play was to be performed, and for finding suitable actors, properties, costumes, and so forth. It is also possible that the guilds commissioned scripts for their plays locally, but the names of the playwrights have not survived. Those sufficiently learned in sacred history are likely to have been clerics, such as parish priests, guild chaplains, and chantry priests, or perhaps members of the monastic or mendicant orders, who were strongly present in York. . . .

The manuscript containing the text of the cycle is a large volume, measuring about 11 inches by 8 inches, consisting of 268 parchment leaves, bound in oak boards covered with leather. It is nearly all in the handwriting of a single unidentified scribe, who probably executed the work at some time between 1463 and 1477. Known as the 'Register' of the Corpus Christi play, this manuscript constituted the city's official record of the content of the cycle, and was the property of the corporation. In the sixteenth century there are records of the fact that it was used by a city official to check what the actors were actually saying in the course of the annual performance. Many pages have later annotations deriving from this activity, showing where plays had been revised, or had even been completely rewritten since the compilation of the manuscript. Contrary to a widely held belief, these sixteenth-century annotations in the manuscript were not the work of reforming ecclesiastical censors, though we do know from other sources that the plays near the end of the cycle on the later life of the Virgin Mary were suppressed in 1548. During the eighteenth and nineteenth centuries the Register passed through the hands of several antiquarians and collectors, before coming to its final resting-place in the British Museum in 1899.

The Register was compiled from copies of the individual plays held by the craft-guilds for the purposes of rehearsal and performance. A sixteenth-century example of one of these prompt-copies, or 'originals' as they were known, has survived (the Scriveners' *Incredulity of Thomas*) but the rest are lost. For something of the history of the cycle prior to the compilation of the Register one must turn to documentary materials in the civic archives at York. Among them is the volume known as the 'A/Y Memorandum Book', which contains records of many of the most important decisions of the governing body of the city in the Middle Ages, the ordinances and constitutions of numerous craft-guilds, and an interesting document called the 'Ordo Paginarum', 'The Order of the Pageants'. This consists of a list of the guilds, . . .with a note of the content of their respective plays. It was compiled by the Town Clerk in 1415, and was probably used to check the ordering and content of the cycle in the period before the Register was compiled. The 'Ordo Paginarum', though itself much altered and revised, reveals that the cycle had by 1415 assumed the shape and scope it was to have for the rest of its career. Comparison with the text in the Register reveals that a number of plays were revised during the fifteenth century, and that some were reassigned to other guilds. The Passion section, in particular, was extensively reworked by an outstandingly able dramatist, known as the York Realist. However, the general aspect and scope of the cycle remained the same, as it was to do until its decline and eventual abandonment in the latter half of the sixteenth century.

The origins and progress of the cycle up to 1415 are much more difficult to trace because of the paucity of documentary evidence, but a reference in a document dated 1376, referring to the storage of three Corpus Christi pageant-wagons, is sometimes taken to imply that the entire cycle was already in existence at that date. A more certain construction may be placed on a petition, dated 1399, sent by the commons of the city to its governing body, pointing out that the Corpus Christi play was a great financial burden on the craft-guilds, and that it was tending to overrun its allotted day of performance. This petition also sets out for the first time the processional route through the city taken by the pageant-wagons, and the 'stations' where they stopped to perform before the audiences which had gathered.

The craft-guilds of medieval York were the principal units of social and economic organization in medieval English towns in general, being made up of master-craftsmen in the various trades and callings, who had gained the franchise of the city either through satisfactory apprenticeship or inheritance. As well as establishing standards of workmanship, administering the system of apprenticeship, and laying down the lines of demarcation between trades, the guilds also had important social characteristics and functions. The members of a guild, their families, and apprentices lived their lives partially in common, often occupying the same area of the city, as some of the surviving street-names of York show (Spurriergate, Tanner Row). They tended to worship together at the same church, and dined together on the feast of their patron saint or other liturgical occasion. A number had their own halls; those of the Merchant Adventures and Merchant Tailors are still to be seen in York. The craft-guilds were occasionally referred to as 'mysteries', and from the association of the crafts with the pageants of the Corpus Christi play arose the modern expression 'mystery plays'. 'Mystery' should not, therefore, be understood to connote anything as to the content of the cycle. The expenses of the annual performance of each play in the cycle were defrayed by a levy on the guild to which

that play was assigned. Little is known as to precisely how the guilds came to have responsibility for their particular plays, owing to lack of evidence from the earliest period of the cycle's history. The appropriateness of some of the assignments to the occupations of the guilds is obvious: the Shipwrights' ***Building of the Ark,*** the Vintners' ***Marriage at Cana*** (where Christ turned the water into wine), the Bakers ***Last Supper.*** These 'appropriate' assignments probably had much to do with the idea of the sanctity of a craft's daily labour, its part in the divine eternal scheme of things and the history of man's salvation, rather than the crude modern notion that the guilds used the plays to 'advertise' their products.

The performance of the cycle as a whole was organized and regulated by the governing body of the city, which was elected by and from the members of the craft-guilds. It appears that the ecclesiastical authorities had no part in it at this official level, though the parish clergy and members of religious orders were undoubtedly involved in helping to bring forth individual pageants, sometimes as 'directors'. The events leading up to the annual performance were set in motion early in Lent, when the civic authorities met and sent out formal instruction to each participating guild to bring forth its play on Corpus Christi day, three months or so hence. The guilds then held meetings to make detailed arrangements for their own productions. These were at first principally financial. Each guild elected officers known as 'pageant-masters', in effect the producers of the play, whose first task it was to collect the money paid by the craftsmen towards their play, their 'pageant silver'. As well as collecting annually from their members, the guilds also operated a system of fines for poor workmanship and various technical infringements of guild regulations, the proceeds of which also went towards the play. The pageant-masters laid out their money in a variety of ways. The storage and maintenance of the pageant-wagon and the purchase or refurbishment of properties and costumes were the main material expenses. In addition, a 'director' (though no such word then existed) and suitable actors had to be found, and their refreshments provided at rehearsal and on the day of performance. Evidence surviving in the records of the Mercers' and Bakers' guilds suggests that money was given to an individual, sometimes a cleric, who had responsibility for directing their play. It was evidently his task to hire, rehearse, and pay the actors, which suggests a degree of 'professionalism' in the presentation of the cycle. Finally, the pageant-masters gave a dinner shortly after Corpus Christi, at which the officers of the guild reviewed their financial position.

Before entering into greater detail about arrangements for the day of performance, it is necessary to enlarge upon what has already been said about the processional presentation of the plays. Each of the plays which make up the cycle was staged on a wagon. The wagons are thought to have processed in the appropriate order around the city, taking a traditionally established route, and halting at a series of 'stations' at which audiences had assembled, a performance of each play being given at each station. The number of stations along the route was usually twelve, and (though scholars differ about this) it appears that each pageant could have been given twelve times in the course of Corpus Christi day. The performance is known to have begun at 4.30 a.m., when the first pageant proceeded to the first station, and modern calculations suggest that it would not have been until after midnight when the last play ended at the twelfth station. It is not known how York arrived at this remarkable mode of presentation for its cycle, but in an age with little or no concept of a purpose-built theatre, processional production was an ingenious solution to the problem of how to show a large urban audience a cycle of plays running to over 14,000 lines.

Corpus Christi day was of course a public holiday and a day of popular festivity as well as a liturgical feast. Final arrangements for the presentation of the plays included the assignment of stations at which performances were to be given. At these stations along the processional route banners bearing the city's coat of arms were set up and a scaffold for the accommodation of the audience was built. Stations were let by the city to the highest bidder, who was then presumably in a position to charge the audience for seating and refreshments during the long performance. Many of the audience, however, must have stood in the street to see the plays, and have wandered from station to station in the course of the day.

The route along which the stations were distributed never varied, though the positions of some of the stations could change slightly from year to year. . . . The pageant-masters, actors, and others concerned with mounting the performance marshalled the pageant-wagons initially on an open space in the south-west angle of the city wall known as Pageant Green (or Toft Green). From there they moved into and along Micklegate, over Ouse Bridge, and then via Coney Street and Stonegate, past the Minster Gates, then through Low Petergate and Colliergate to the Pavement. It appears that the stations were on the left-hand side of this route, with the audiences facing them on the right. The positions of some of the stations never varied. No. 1 was at the gates of the Priory of the Holy Trinity not far from Micklegate Bar. It was here that a civic official sat with the manuscript Register and checked the first performance of each play annually. The eighth station was close to the Guildhall, and here members of the city's governing body saw the plays free. No. 10, at Minster Gates, was favoured by the cathedral clergy, and the last station, on the Pavement, brought the plays to the commercial centre of the city, the site

A medieval painted-glass rendition of Corpus Christi, originally from St. John's Church in York.

of markets, fairs, proclamations, and executions. Given the great length of the cycle and the number of times each play was performed, the swift and unhindered passage of the pageant-wagons from station to station was of the utmost importance. The civic authorities had the power to fine any guild whose play hindered the presentation of an orderly sequence. At the end of the Woolpackers' and Woolbrokers' play of the *Supper at Emmaus* one of the characters actually says to the audience that they must now hasten to the next station:

Here may we not mell more at this tide,
For process of plays that presses in plight.

('That is all we can say at this time, because of the procession of pageants which is queuing up [behind us]').

To have established broadly how the cycle was designed for presentation is not to visualize what it would have looked like. It is clear, both from guild records and from internal evidence in the plays, that a pageant-wagon was neither simply a stage on wheels, nor a commercial vehicle, like the modern pageant 'float', converted for the day. The wagons used in the production of the York cycle were custom-built for each guild, to suit its play, and, what is more, were manhandled around the route, not drawn by animals. At that point, however, it becomes more difficult to be specific. York is not short of material in its civic records relating to pageant-wagons, but since everyone evidently knew what such vehicles looked like, they are never described from first principles. What comes down to the modern investigator, by and large, is a collection of cryptic accounts using unfamiliar or ambiguous terminology.

There are some references to the Bakers' pageant-wagon in the records, which supply clues to its construction, but the picture would still be highly speculative, were it not for the survival of some important materials relating to the Mercers' *Last Judgement* wagon over a period of years. The first of these is an indenture of 1433 which provides the nearest thing to a description of a wagon we are likely to find. It includes an inventory of parts for what the Mercers later call their 'great pageant'. It is a 'pageant with four wheels', but clearly not a flat cart, for it has a complicated superstructure including a 'heaven of iron'. It also appears to have incorporated integral winching gear by means of which God descended from, and ascended to, the said heaven. When the 'hell-mouth', also described as part of the structure, is added, a picture of a complicated multi-level structure begins to emerge. This is in keeping with a later account from Norwich in which the Grocers' pageant-wagon is defined as, 'a house of wainscot. . .on a cart with four wheels'.

Apart from the mechanical details concerning the transportation of God from one level to another, other items in the Mercers' indenture also give an indication of how the pageant-wagon was decorated. The mention of a backcloth, or 'coster', of red damask instantly demonstrates that the performance area had a back and a front, ruling out the possibility that the audience was grouped around the vehicle on all sides. Other cloths are also listed which would have concealed the wheels and the unsightly underside of the vehicle once it was *in situ* at a station. God had his own special backdrop, also a 'brandreth of iron', possibly like a modern fire-basket, with four ropes at the corners, in which he came and went from heaven. Heaven itself was arrayed with red and blue clouds, gold stars, sunbeams, and a wooden rainbow. In addition there was a series of model angels, nine of which were operated mechanically by a 'long small cord', which caused them to 'run about in the heaven', as the final stage direction in the play indicates.

Even with all the above information available in what is indeed an exceptional case, there has still been room for interpretation to have produced at least three careful and scholarly reconstructions which diverge in certain major respects. Crucially, none of the dimensions of the various parts is mentioned. It is also clear from further documents associated with the guild that the Mercers, in times of particular affluence, were given to improving their equipage. In 1463 the guild added what appears to have been a completely separate entity, a 'new pageant that was made for the souls to rise out of'. About this 'pageant' there is much less information; it is not even clear that it had wheels, although this is probable, as the guild had had some small wheels made in the recent past. What is more, in 1501, the Mercers scrapped the 'great pageant' of the 1433 indenture and commissioned one built 'new substantially in everything thereunto belonging'. It is not until 1526 that there is anything approaching a description of the new vehicle, and then an inventory simply lists hell-door, windows, angels, an iron seat, several pulleys, and a cloud. Reconstruction on the basis of this meagre information is not really practicable.

What then is to be learned from the history of the Mercers' pageant-wagon over a period of nearly a hundred years? Perhaps most significantly it brings home the fact that a pageant-wagon was a very specific construction, intended solely for the production of a single episode in the cycle. In a sense, therefore, the Mercers' indenture tells us only about the manner in which the *Last Judgement* was staged. It may serve as a rough guide to what the other guilds' wagons were like, but it is important here to remember that the Mercers were an extremely wealthy guild throughout the period in question; wagons belonging to less affluent bodies may not have been so elaborate. Also there are plays in the cycle to which an enclosed playing space would not have been appropriate, for example *The Crucifixion,* which could well have been performed on a flat cart.

The Mercers' records contribute to a growing sense of the cycle as an essentially fluid event. In the same way that plays changed hands and were reworked, so too the visual aspect of the cycle must have changed over the years. As a guild's fortune increased it might have its play elaborated and rewritten, or have its pageant-wagon modified or replaced. One decision could lead to another, but the evidence for each change taking place survives, if it survives at all, in a variety of different sources. Similarly, declining fortunes would perhaps lead to guilds being unable to maintain their wagons and their plays at all, which in turn might lead to amalgamations with other small guilds, or transference of the play to different ownership.

The pageant-wagon itself was an item of considerable value and prestige. From the point of view of the quality of workmanship involved, the records of the Mercers' 1501 wagon, about which there is less detail, impart one important piece of information: for the construction of the wagon the Mercers engaged a famous carver, Thomas Drawswerd. Fortunately an example of Drawswerd's work survies in the beautiful rood screen in the church of St Mary Magdalen, Newark, Nottinghamshire. A cursory examination of the quality of carving involved serves to dispel any residual connection between the pageant-wagon and the farm cart, although the chassis and wheels were, in all probability, derived from the latter. It has indeed been suggested that the superstructure of the wagon was demountable for storage purposes, since storage of a multi-level vehicle, perhaps as much as 20 feet (6 metres) high, would pose considerable problems. Many guilds had their own 'pageant-houses' or garages for their wagons. Many of these were close to Pageant Green (from where the cycle set out), often on land rented on an annual basis from the city authority. There is some evidence also of guilds sub-letting pageant-houses to one another.

Although it is possible to tell from the records that the pageant-houses were large and stoutly constructed buildings, the actual dimensions of the York pageant-wagon cannot be ascertained with any degree of accuracy. The length and breadth must, however, have been limited, if a vehicle made of heavy materials was to be manhandled around the narrower corners in the city. Even allowing for a generous estimate of surface area, the playing space afforded was very limited, making it difficult to visualize the staging of multi-location plays, such as the Hosiers' *Moses and Pharaoh*. The Mercers' records make it clear that auxiliary pageants might be used, and the Masons' and Goldsmiths' composite play shows two wagons being used in tandem, but in the absence of further evidence these must be treated as exceptions. No true picture of the staging of a play

can be reached without due consideration of the evidence in the plays themselves for the use of the whole space available, not only on the pageant-wagon but also in the street around. It is in this respect that wagon performance diverges markedly from performance on the proscenium stage.

The York cycle's stage directions are few and far between, particularly when it comes to indicating movement from place to place, or the relative locations of different 'scenes' within the play. It is apparent in most of the longer plays that all of the action could not possibly have been accommodated on the deck of the wagon itself. In one of the surviving plays from the Coventry cycle there is the direction, 'Here Herod rages in the pageant and in the street also'. This has been eagerly seized upon as evidence that the arrangement suggested by the texts of many cycle plays was indeed correct. In twelfth- and thirteenth-century liturgical drama the action was divided between that which took place processionally, moving through the church, and that which was located in a symbolic area, such as around the Easter Sepulchre, an altar designed for the ritual representation of the Resurrection. It is possible to see the individual play within the cycle in the same way, except that the area on the pageant-wagon serves for all the specific playing spaces (*loci*) and the street as the area in which unlocalized action took place (*platea*). Hence, in *The Conspiracy,* the *locus* is Pilate's court, the wagon being decorated to represent that, which means that the dialogue between Judas and the Porter would be conducted outside the court, in the street. Similarly in *Joseph's Trouble,* the wagon is evidently Mary's house, and all of Joseph's long complaint, in which he solicits the sympathy of men in the audience, would have been delivered at their level. Obviously, there are still unexplained problems of staging when a play appears to involve more than one locus, but in broad terms the division of the action between street and wagon is the important one, particularly when the relationship between audience and players at a given moment is considered.

If the physical presentation of the York cycle can be reconstructed only in part, the manner in which it was acted is a matter of much greater speculation. As far as contemporary records are concerned, the necessary qualifications were cryptically described, but were apparently quite basic. After the 1415 'Ordo Paginarum' in the 'A/Y Memorandum Book' appears the Proclamation of the plays, which was made on the vigil of Corpus Christi, and also when the banners were set up in the designated positions for the stations, about a week before Corpus Christi. This specifies the manner in which the plays should be conducted, with an allusion to the players which simply requires that they be 'well arrayed and openly speaking'. An ordinance of 1476 shows that there was some means of auditioning the players: four of the 'most cunning [skilful], discreet and able players' were called before the mayor to examine the plays, and to dispense with the services of any player found to be wanting in 'cunning, voice or person'. These records merely confirm that the greatest offence a player can commit in an outdoor performance is to be inaudible.

In whatever way we choose to interpret this material, however, it is clear that, given a performance in which the same character was played by many different actors consecutively, there was no opportunity for anything like method acting. Indeed, a greater unity would best have been achieved by the use of a formal, demonstrative style, matching spoken word to gesture. This style was particularly appropriate to outdoor performance, which was often restricted to the confined area of the pageant-wagon, but had to be clearly understood by an audience crowding in the street. The demonstrative style was also appropriate to a drama which sought to convey eternal truths on a mythic scale. It is possible that medieval acting style in this respect owed something to the techniques advocated by the ancient rhetoricians. Echoes of Cicero's *De oratore* have been heard in the dramatist's instructions to the actors in the twelfth-century Anglo-Norman play the *Mystère d'Adam,* which exhort the players to 'speak coherently', and to 'make gestures agreeing with the thing they are speaking of'. When one considers the metrical intricacy of some of the York plays, it seems unlikely that naturalistic acting had a large part in their presentation.

There is one group of characters about which more can be said, as chance allusions to their manner of presentation have survived, namely Herod, Pilate, and—by extension—the other major figures of evil in the cycle. Chaucer's Miller in the General Prologue to the *Canterbury Tales* has a mouth like a furnace, and cries in 'Pilate's voice', whilst in the Paston Letters of the fifteenth century, the Duke of Suffolk, when in a rage, is compared to a play-Herod. Everyone is familiar with Hamlet's injunction to his players to avoid the style of over-acting that 'out-Herods Herod'. It is easy to imagine the alliterative lines of the trial plays in the York Passion sequence assisting some actors to an exaggeratedly bombastic performance.

Not all the characters in the York cycle lend themselves to stylized means of presentation, however. It seems most likely that a mixed style was employed, in keeping with the mixed physical levels of playing, introducing at certain points a more naturalistic aspect to the performance where it was desirable to achieve proximity to the audience, bringing sacred history to them as something immediate which encompassed them. It is, for instance, difficult to conceive of a demonstrative rendering of the dialogue between Judas and the Porter, alluded to above, or in the scenes of disarray amongst the soldiers in **The Resurrection,** when they discover that Christ has escaped. The plays are liber-

ally peppered with ordinary people and there was didactic capital to be made out of presenting them as such.

In this context it is necessary to consider how the plays were costumed. Clearly, in an age which had no sophisticated perspective on chronology, there was little attempt at historical costume, the cut of clothes being whatever was contemporary, with exotic touches added to denote race or rank. Much of the evidence we have for costume is construed from surviving inventories and contemporary pictures and stained glass. Most Jews, for instance, would have worn the strange pointed hats which mark them out in contemporary iconography; the Magi, dressed by the Goldsmiths, would have appeared as royalty should, as would Herod, although he may have had something about his person to associate him with the infidel. Biblical soldiers, peasants, and tradesmen must have looked very much like fifteenth-century Yorkshiremen of the same rank, and, as is clearly the case with the Shipwrights' Noah, carried the genuine tools of their trade.

Difficulties arise in clothing those whose rank is beyond anything present in any society: the extremes of good and evil, particularly the inhabitants of heaven and hell. The main way of dealing with these characters was to conceal the players behind masks. For evidence of this we return again to the Mercers' indenture of 1433 which contains an extensive list of 'visors' or 'faces', including six devils' faces, visors and wigs for evil souls and good souls, visors and diadems for the Apostles, and a gilded visor for God. It seems that masking was relatively common in the cycle plays, from full heads to faces made up in some unnatural manner, often by gilding. Long wigs and beards were also called for to make the fashionably clean-shaven fifteenth-century man, with his pudding-basin haircut, look like a patriarch or an apostle. From the strictly practical point of view, men who had to play the part of women, which was commonly if not absolutely the rule, certainly needed wigs, if not masks as well. The use of the full-face mask, or even, in the case of devils, the whole head, is most interesting because of the effect it must have created in performance, of completely depersonalizing the wearer, dissociating the actor from normal society, and, because of the limited expression it allowed, imparting a degree of inscrutability appropriate particularly to the Godhead. Thus, the audience was called upon to identify with certain characters, such as Joseph and the shepherds, while at the same time, by means of demonstrative acting style and facial masks, it was distanced from God, Satan, and the angels. The emotional impact of much of the action was thus achieved by bringing into close proximity the natural with the supernatural, an effect nowhere more concentrated than in the events surrounding the Nativity. Increasingly, the performance of a cycle of mystery plays emerges not as the theatre of total illusion, but of selected illusory effects to a didactic end.

To bring together all the details of production methods is to discover a theatre in which audience and performers are related in a way that is entirely different from that of the theatre of the recent past. The proximity of players and audience meant that although the latter could not influence the course of events, they were none the less implicated to bear witness. Despite the apparently fragmented nature of the cycle, the message which bore down upon that audience was strongly unified iconographically. Throughout the play texts, there are strong and basic images, which transcend the cycle's episodic nature: intellectually it is drawn together by means of typology, as the events of the Old Testament are clearly framed for the manner in which they anticipate the New. The images of light and darkness, for good and evil, recur constantly. Clothing too, which takes on a specific significance in the *Trial before Herod,* must have been visually arresting throughout. Costumes, props, masks, and language were designed in these plays to serve a function more specific than mere embellishment: they were, as Meg Twycross has convincingly demonstrated on numerous occasions, semantically expressive in themselves. Illusion was not illusion so much as a figural refinement of reality: characters and events were arranged to carry a specific didactic significance as they do in the religious art of the period. In the same way that a painting or a stained-glass window has its meaning, the cycle was a series of such pictures presented kaleidoscopically as the elements formed first one picture and were then rearranged in preparation for the appearance of another picture, framed within the space on the pageant-wagon. Considered from this point of view, it is easy to understand how mystery plays came to be defended from attacks by the Lollards against their supposed idolatry, as a 'living book'.

Finally, in reconstructing the nature of the original performance of the York cycle, it is necessary to consider the role played by music, since it too had its figural reverberations. Music played a large part in the presentation of the cycle, and many of the stage directions in the manuscript are in fact cues for music. They are invariably cues for vocal music, and, where the piece is specified, it can nearly always be traced to liturgical origins. It follows that some at least of the actors must also have been competent singers. There was apparently little or no use made of instrumental music in most of the cycle, there being only one place in the present selection where it would certainly have been heard in performance: in the *Last Judgement,* when the angels blow their trumpets, a moment perhaps the more striking if instrumental music had not been employed in the preceding plays. The vocal music was often introduced to express human thanksgiving for divine mercy, especially at or near the ends of plays, such as the *Flood, Moses and Pharaoh,* and the *Harrowing of Hell.* The unspecified singing called for in

the *Entry into Jerusalem* is likely to have consisted of appropriate pieces from the liturgy of Palm Sunday. On occasion, singing could also have a practical function, 'covering' action on stage for which there was no dialogue. Examples are the use of the Whitsun hymn 'Veni creator spiritus' to occupy the time taken by Christ to reach the pinnacle of the temple in the *Temptation,* or the presence of angelic singing to cover Christ's assumption of the judgement seat in the *Last Judgement.* In the *Resurrection,* Christ rises from the tomb and exits without speaking, while angels sing the Easter anthem 'Christus resurgens', and here the music not only covers the action but also comments on, or rather, in a different way, expresses its nature. It is often remarked that music in the drama of this period tends to be used for representational rather than for affective purposes. This is the case in the *Resurrection,* where the singing signifies Christ's reappearance in divine form, but it is music's most marked function in scenes where God appears, or where he intervenes in human affairs. The presence of music was essential to the depiction of heaven in the *Creation* and the *Last Judgement,* where it represented the harmony of the divinely ordained and divinely sustained universe. . . .

G. R. Owst refers to a fifteenth-century Monk's complaint regarding the rowdiness that accompanied the York pageants:

Coming to the city of York, in the year 1426, at the time of the Corpus Christi pageants, [Father William Melton] "in several sermons recommended the aforesaid play to the people, affirming that it was good in itself and very laudable". It is again worth noting that, in the case of these York performances, even so sympathetic a preacher has to complain "that the citizens of the said city, and other foreigners coming to the said Feast, had greatly disgraced the play by revellings, drunkenness, shouts, songs and other insolences, in no wise attending to the divine offices of the said day".

Drake's "Eboracum" quoted by G. R. Owst,
Literature and Pulpit in Medieval England,
Basil Blackwell, 1961.

Martin Stevens (essay date 1987)

SOURCE: "The York Cycle: City as Stage," in *Four Middle English Mystery Cycles,* Princeton University Press, 1987, pp. 17-87.

[*In the excerpt below, Stevens contends that the unity of the York cycle is based on the medieval view of the plays as a mirror image of the city of York and its inhabitants. He argues that the processional staging of the cycles—especially in the pageant depicting Jesus' entry into Jerusalem—reflects York's use of the Cor-*

*pus Christi festival as an opportunity for self-celebra-
tion that particularly emphasizes the tradition of royal
entries into the city.*]

The York plays present a special problem for those
who find thematic or structural unity in the medieval
Corpus Christi cycles. The difficulty is that the play in
York, perhaps because it was staged from the outset in
what was then a large regional city, was more nearly
a communal enterprise than any other extant English
cycle. One senses in reading the manuscript of the
plays and the copious municipal records from York
that the cycle itself is a corporate work, and not so
markedly as the other cycles the work of an individual
consciousness. In part one gets that feeling because
the documents themselves are testimony to the civic
enterprise of nurturing and preserving the play. In York
it was not enough to have a Corpus Christi play; it was
necessary in addition to have a civic record of that
play. The existence of a trove of municipal documents
in addition to an official copy of the Corpus Christi
play is not simply an accident of history; it is a reflection of the York civic temperament that placed a premium on the preservation of the city's institutions and
insisted on the recognition of its longstanding and
honored corporate identity. The Corpus Christi play
there was no mere popular entertainment, no ordinary
annual festive occasion; it was the city's proud and
solemn celebration of itself.

Medieval city drama, both in its manner of production
and its dramatic content, presented to its spectators a
mirror of their lives and their environment. The York
cycle derives its unity from its multifaceted view of
the city and its inhabitants. Thus, for example, the trade
symbolism in the York plays is no mere comic byprod-
uct of the dramatic presentation but a vital part of its
motivation and meaning. Modern sophistication often
makes fun of the quaintness and artlessness of medieval playcraft: the Bakers' making the Last Supper,
the Shipwrights' building Noah's Ark, the Couchers'
preparing Procula's bed, the Saucemakers' displaying
Judas's entrails. The fact is that the trade or the craft
was defined by what it did, and the demonstration of
its ware or its skill as part of the anachronism of playcraft linked the performer with the play and created a
larger meaning for the performance. The linkage helped
to incorporate the city's ordinary purpose—its daily
ritual of work and human intercourse—into the play
action and thus into the grand design of salvation history. There can be little doubt that the Armourers chose
(or were assigned) the play of the Expulsion because
the Archangel Michael is its principal character, and
traditionally he was depicted in medieval art as wearing
armor while wielding a huge sword to bar Adam and
Eve from Paradise. The Angel in the parallel Chester
scene describes his function in words (as the York
Angel does not): "Our swordes of fyer shall bee there
bonne" (31/422). Here then is an instance of positive

association between the handicraft and God's dominion. The play not only endowed the craft of the Armourers with an elevated mythology but it also brought
the Creation into the familiar setting of the City of
York. Some have argued that such trade symbolism
simply serves the practical purpose of providing the
guild with a showcase in which to display its product
or its skill. While, of course, it does that, and thus adds
to the immediate interest of the spectators for whom
the association would serve as what Brecht called an
"alienation device" by making the playcraft a self-conscious allusion, that would not have been its primary
purpose or function. It is worth noting that often the
trade symbolism does not elevate. Take, for example,
the Pinners, makers of pins, fishhooks, mousetraps, and
other small metallic objects, who put on the Crucifixion play. Clearly, they were associated in some way
with the nailing process itself and perhaps also with
the boring of holes into the Cross, an action that provides a gruesome tug-of-war game by the torturers to
pull Jesus' hands and feet in preparation for the nailing. Obviously, the Pinners are not elevated by this
association. But the action itself is brought into the
present; the Pinners of York demonstrate their human
culpability in the death of Christ, which, by extension
belongs to all persons. Guilds are part of the York
power structure; they also reflect all human enterprise
and government. By allowing them to be incorporated
into salvation history, York, the city, becomes a *the-
atrum mundi.* . . .

Almost literally at the center of the York cycle, both
physically and dramatically, is the Skinners' pageant of
Jesus' Entry into Jerusalem. It is the twenty-fifth play
in a collection of forty-eight, and it marks the end of the
Ministry and the beginning of the Passion. By all odds
it is the most developed Entry into Jerusalem play in the
medieval drama, and, more than any other pageant, it
puts in the foreground York's obsession with civic ceremony and self-celebration, for nowhere else is the issue of any play so directly the processional pageant, the
very mode of performance that the York cycle enacts
for its audience, than in this pivotal dramatic episode.
Indirectly, the play imitates a civic procession resembling the annual civic liturgical procession of Corpus
Christi, in which the city officials as well as the parish
clergy "entered" the city with the Host, the Body of
Christ. This event was, of course, the core of the civic
celebration of Corpus Christi, and it is thought by many
(myself included) to have been the germ of the Corpus
Christi play itself. Directly, it imitated the royal entry
ceremony, which came to be a highly developed genre
of civic procession in York. In both frames of reference,
the Skinners' play served the ultimate function of highlighting the corporate community of York. It focused
attention on the cycle itself and on the occasion of its
performance and thus caused the city to become identified with the dramatic subject being enacted. In short,
it transformed the city into the stage of the cycle. And

in the broadest terms, it mirrored the soul of its creation—the civic processional—which, in the words of
one critic, "affirmed corporate entity [and] manifested
the complexity and ideal stability of urban society."
[David Mills, "Religious Drama and Civic Ceremonial," in *The Revels History of Drama in England*]. The
Skinners' pageant of the Entry into Jerusalem is thus
the ultimate York play.

When Jesus enters Jerusalem, he also enters York.
He comes, of course, in a dramatized procession that
itself is an imitation of the event that, at the time
when the play was written, was the central festivity
of the Corpus Christi feast—the carrying of the Host
through the streets of York. The drama reminds us
of the historical reality of Jesus, and it gives us a
present-day setting within which to understand what
the York play calls his "rawnsom" (205/9, compare
219/525). It is, then, in the Skinners' play that we
find the core significance of the York cycle, the
dramatization of the meaning of the feast of Corpus
Christi. In it religious and dramatic processions
merge, and the city is led to a reenactment and commemoration of the Passion in the spirit that was
prescribed by the bull of Urban IV that established
the feast: "We rejoice with pious weeping and weep
with devout jubilation, happy in our lament and sad
in our joy" ("gaudemus pie lacrimantes et lacrima-
mus devote gaudentes, letas habendo lacrimas et leti-
tiam lacrimantem"). As V. A. Kolve has shown [in
The Play Called Corpus Christi], the joyful celebration of the Holy Sacrament was the object of the
Corpus Christi Feast; the day was set aside not only
to reflect upon the sorrow of the Cross but also upon
the joy of the Resurrection. Both, of course, are
contained in the meaning of the Host.

At the same time that the procession of the **Entry
into Jerusalem** imitates the civic liturgical procession, it also mirrors another kind of procession, the
royal entry. York throughout the Middle Ages was
noted for its splendid civic shows with which it greeted
visiting royalty. The prescribed route of the royal entry
processional was, interestingly, very much the same
as that of the Corpus Christi play, and when, therefore, Jesus is greeted in the course of the Skinners'
pageant with the accustomed royal entry ceremony as
the King of Kings in the streets of York, the spectators saw him take possession of their city much as
they had secular kings and queens. There was no more
powerful a link to be found between present-day York
and historic Jerusalem than this dramatic setting provided. Indeed, the setting of the Skinners' play puts
a whole new focus on everything that has transpired
and everything that will yet transpire in the cycle.
The Passion is taking place here and now. The characters are Yorkshire people. The place is York. And
yet the spectators in the streets gradually recognize
that they are really in Jerusalem.

To understand just how close the parallels are between
the agenda of the royal entry ceremony and the action
of the play, let us take a closer look at both. The royal
entry ceremony had a long history in medieval England at the time that the York plays were written.
Extending back to the thirteenth century, it developed
over the years not only to celebrate visits of royalty,
but also coronations, births, marriages, political events
(like the restoration of rights by Richard III to the
citizens of London in 1392), and victorious returns
from war, which eventually became expanded into
"triumphs." Customarily, royal entries involved the
greeting of the royal personage outside of town by a
carefully prescribed delegation of town officials, the
subsequent ceremonial ride into the city proper, welcoming speeches by persons enacting legendary heroes
of the city spoken at set points along the itinerary and
usually given on elaborate pageants, the giving of gifts
to the visitor, and the ending of the ceremonial ride
before a palace or a cathedral. By the second quarter of
the fifteenth century, descriptive or celebratory verses
came to be written for or about these triumphs, as for
example on the occasion of the return of Henry VI
from Paris in 1432 and the 1445 royal entry of Margaret of Anjou into London. Although we have no
precisely contemporary analogue of such a "show" from
York, two vivid accounts survive of Henry VII's entry
into the city in 1486. It would be instructive to examine
that entry in the context of the Skinners' play.

The triumph of Henry VII was a way for the City of
York to embrace the new monarch, who was not a
welcome replacement for Richard III in the eyes of York
citizens. Richard was a true patron of the city, and its
leading citizens were fiercely loyal to him. Under the
circumstances, the official city needed to do all in its
power to mask its former loyalties and to greet the new
king with a strong show of tribute. In consequence, the
city spent sixty-six pounds, a very princely sum, to greet
Henry VII; "along his route was presented a series of
pageants and speeches, all stressing his virtues and his
hereditary right, and culminating in a representation of
Our Lady, promising her son's aid for the King"[D. M.
Palliser, *Tudor York*]. The two surviving documents
describing this memorable occasion are first, an official
account of the processional greeting and a text of the
"speeches" in the York House Book; and second, an
independent account, apparently by an eyewitness, of
the event together with a transcript of the "speeches,"
in Cotton MS Julius B.xii (ff. 8b-21b). From a composite reading of these accounts, we learn that Henry VII,
dressed in a gown of gold cloth furred with ermine, was
met by the city's two sheriffs at Tadcaster, some ten
miles away from York and the outermost extremity of
the "franchise." The sheriffs brought twenty horses to
help conduct the king into the city. At Bilburgh Cross,
about five miles from the city, the king was met by the
common council, the city clerk, the chamberlains, and
many of the inhabitants of the city (apparently all

dressed in red livery). Then, either two or three miles from the city (depending on the account), the mayor, the aldermen, and still more citizens, probably the most privileged, all on horseback, waited to meet the king and his entourage. Finally, a half-mile outside the city gate, the king was greeted by all the orders of friars, the prior, and the brothers of Saint Trinity's, the abbot of Saint Mary's with his convent, the canons of Saint Leonard's, and "the general procession of al the parisshe churches of the saide citie" together with a great number of ordinary citizens on foot—men, women, and children—who lined the road, shouting "King Henry, King Henry." The ceremony of greeting along the road was clearly done in rank order, as York was accustomed to do in its civic processions.

At the city gate, apparently Micklegate (which also was traditionally the place from which civic processions and the Corpus Christi play itself began), the king was met by the first of the ceremonial pageants, a scene representing Heaven, the angels, and a world full of trees and flowers. This might have been the pageant of the Tanners for the Creation play in the York cycle; provision is made for its storage throughout the York records. . . . In the midst of this world, a rich red rose was contrived to pop up when Henry looked upon the scene, followed by a white rose, and all the other flowers were then made to bow to the roses. Thereafter, a crown descended from a cloud and covered the roses. Then (in some manner not specified) a city with citizens appeared and from its midst the founder of York, King Ebrauk, stepped forward to hand the keys of the city to the king and to read or recite a speech, the gist of which is that York greets him, submits to his royal power, and begs for his favor.

The entourage then proceeded along Micklegate, which was bedecked with cloths that hung from houses on both sides of the street so that no gaps showed between them, and a device was rigged up to spew forth rose water that fell, if the weather was fair, before the lords, but—in cautious restraint—not before the king. The procession moved forward to the foot of Ouse Bridge, where it was met by another pageant "garnysshede with shippes, and botes in every side". One is tempted to equate this pageant with that of the Shipwrights' play of Noah. If that is so, the order of pageants is reflective of the Corpus Christi cycle itself, and the association of the two civic shows becomes a matter for common recognition. The significance of the ships, we are told, was to recall the king's landing in England at Milford Haven.

The next stop for the procession was the middle of Ouse Bridge where it encountered a pageant (probably borrowed from the Goldsmiths who did Herod and the Magi in the Corpus Christi cycle), featuring a royal throne. Six kings, the previous Henrys, thereupon appeared, and as Henry VII watched, they handed a scepter to yet another king, Solomon, who in turn passed the scepter, signifying wisdom and justice, to Henry VII while reciting a speech of welcome and petition. After crossing the bridge, the procession moved on to the corner of Ousegate and Coneygate (the route is still identical with that of the Corpus Christi play and procession), where a hailstorm of sweetmeats, made by the craft of "cumfettes," showered the lords (but, again, not the king). Next, as the procession turned into Coneygate, and moved up to the Common Hall, it was met by a pageant in the form of a castle (perhaps the Pilate pageant of the Tapiters). In front of it appeared King David handing King Henry a sword of victory, and in the company of citizens dressed in white and green, signifying truth and heartfelt affection, David gave his speech of welcome and submission. The last processional station was the pageant of "Our Lady," standing at the end of Stonegate near the Minster, to which King Henry retired at the end of the civic festivities. She stood on what Cotton MS Julius B.xii identified as the "paiaunt of theassumptoun," which is manifestly the pageant of the Weavers from the Corpus Christi play. We are told that she ascended in this pageant up to Heaven, with angel song. . . , and she welcomed King Henry in behalf of her Son, because, as she put it, "this citie is a place of my pleasing."

With this summary in mind, we are now in a position to understand the full civic context of the Skinners' **Entry into Jerusalem**. But before we examine the play as entry ceremony, let us recall the Biblical passages upon which it draws. The principal ultimate source for the York Entry episode is the Gospel of Saint Matthew, though it also draws on Luke. The synoptic Gospels perceive the life of Christ as something of a pilgrimage, and his ministry is one that gains its strength from the grass roots from which it grew. In a very real sense, the whole of the ministry is seen by Saint Luke, for example, as an inevitable journey to Jerusalem (see Luke 13:23), the malevolent city that represents the epitome of the earthly, where moneylenders are in the Temple and Pharisees confuse God's power with Caesar's. The inevitability of the Passion being played out in Jerusalem is recognized by Jesus himself, who asserts shortly before his arrival, "it cannot be that a prophet perish outside Jerusalem" (Luke 13:33). The city then was conceived as the main site of corruption, and the Entry was portrayed at once as the end of the road for Jesus and the liberation of the citizens. The Biblical context is obviously different from the civic. The triumph in this instance is one of the spirit, not the corporate body, and thus the play reaches out for a higher meaning and a deeper truth than the civic ceremony. If in the royal entry the object was to impress King Henry with the splendor and good will of the city (for the purpose ultimately of seeking his support), the implicit purpose of the play is quite the opposite—to associate York with the old Jerusalem, a place of corruption and injustice, the city in which Jesus was to undergo the Passion. The Skinners' play of the Entry must put one in mind of a different York from that which furnishes the self-congratulatory festival. It must make known that York, like all earthly cities and like all civilization, is in need of renewal. The vicarious enactment of the death of Jesus within its corporate boundaries will perform that renewal. We must therefore apply to our comparison of play and civic ceremony an ironic perspective.

The entourage of Jesus and his Twelve Disciples is notable from the beginning by its contrast to the rich royal entry procession. Instead of being met by twenty white horses at the outermost point of greeting, Jesus will encounter his host riding an ass, and he himself has made the arrangement to obtain that lowly beast of burden. In the beginning of the play, he stands with Peter and Philip, instructing them to "vnbynde" the ass with her foal and to bring them to him, so that he can ride into the city as the prophecy of Isaiah has declared (compare Isaiah 62:11 and Matthew 21:5). The setting is just outside Jerusalem/York, in Bethpage (207/88), which in the constricted geography of the play corresponds to Tadcaster. He instructs the two disciples to go "vnto yone castell þat is you agayne," (205/15), that is, that is plainly visible from where they stand, and the ride itself will be brief, a mere "space" (206/23); or more precisely, "a mile," as we learn later (210/196).

In this entry, Jesus obviously plans his own triumph. When Peter and Philip enter the town, they make straight for the common pasture, and they decide that since the beasts that graze there belong to the city (Philip says, "the beestis are comen"; 207/57), they need not ask permission to fetch the ass. However, they are surprised by the Porter, who challenges them because he does not recognize them as townsmen (they appear "withoute leverie"; 207/65). The Porter is one of several splendid minor characterizations in the York cycle (compare the Beadle in the Pilate pageants), who as ordinary man lives the life of a true Christian. He is, indeed, the bedrock citizen of York, drawn by the playwright on the model of those in the audience to whom the play is meant to appeal. He allows them to borrow the animal (the contrast with the twenty white horses becomes all the more compelling as this scene is played out), and he arranges as well, after hearing for whom the ass is intended—"Jesus, of Jewes kyng" (207/80)—to go

> To the chiffe of þe Jewes, þat þei may sone
> Assemble same to his metyng.
>
> (208/94-95)

The chief of the Jews are, of course, the York Aldermen, who are also called "the citezens. . .of þis cyté," and who, he is sure, will want to come and "mete þat free" (208/103-105). The Aldermen are characterized as sympathetic to Jesus and eager for his new laws,

even at the expense of their own (here the Skinners may be flattering their oligarchs!):

> In oure tempill if he prechid
> Agaynste þe pepull that leued wrong,
> And also new lawes if he teched
> Agaynste oure lawis we vsed so lang,
> And saide pleynlye
> The olde schall waste, þe new schall gang,
> þat we schall see.
>
> (209/141-147)

They resolve to meet him as their king and to "honnoure [him] as we wele awe / worthely tyll oure citee" (210/184-185). Clearly they have in mind the royal entry in a manner similar to that which greeted English kings as they came to York. Since Jesus is "Kyng of Juuys" (211/223), they discuss his "genolagye," consisting of Jesse, David, and Solomon, as well as "his modir kynne" (211/240-242), a list suggesting a row of pageants that an audience familiar with York triumphs can easily picture. Thereupon we see the Aldermen assemble to form the greeting party:

> Go we þan with processioun
> To mete þat comely as vs awe,
> With braunches, floures and vnysoune.
> With myghtfull songes her on a rawe
> Our childir schall
> Go synge before, þat men may knawe.
>
> (212/260-266)

We must bear in mind that the Skinners' play was enacted in the streets of York. The procession of Aldermen thus looks very like the real thing, as it advances in the opposite direction of the play proper, toward Micklegate and implicitly out on the road to Tadcaster.

Meanwhile the ass is delivered to Jesus, and a cloth is spread for him on the animal's back, in keeping with Saint Matthew: "And they brought the ass and the colt, laid their cloaks on them, and made him sit thereon" (21:7; compare 212/275). This is the scene in which the Skinners associate their craft with the play, for they are makers of furred garments, and they are particularly associated with the making of civic ceremonial costumes. The trade symbolism is, therefore, a prominent feature in the play. We can assume that the actors playing the Aldermen were splendidly bedecked for their procession. It is also likely that, as in the Gospels, the Skinners strewed the way for Jesus with furred gowns. The Skinners, in any case, obtrude prominently upon their own performance.

As Jesus and his party now advance "vnto yone cyté ye se so nere" (212/283), the dramatic moment of meeting is highlighted with the two processions advancing toward each other. At this point the play creates its own audience, the spectators who stand to cheer the entry of the king. In its midst (this is no doubt the *real* audience of the play) stand four characters: the Pauper, the Blind Man (Cecus), the Cripple (Claudus), and the Man Stunted from Birth (Zaccheus). Amid the cheering, Jesus is drawn to them, and he performs his miracles, bringing sight to the Blind Man and straightening the legs of the Cripple. He also speaks with the rich publican Zaccheus, who has found a sycamore tree to climb from which to see Jesus amid the throng and to catch his attention. In these characters, the playwright manages to personalize the waiting crowd, and to associate the stage audience ("oure pepill same thurgh strete and gatte"; 216/402) with the street audience of the Corpus Christi play. The privileged spectators are thus the lame, the halt, the blind, and the poor, whom Jesus has, true to his role, brought forward from the York crowd with compassion.

The moment of the meeting is at hand. As Jesus and his entourage move with the stream of the Corpus Christi play, they suddenly stop, and Jesus exclaims:

Petir, take þis asse me fro
And lede it where þou are it toke.
I murne, I sigh, I wepe also
Jerusalem on þe to loke.
And so may þou rewe
þat euere þou þi kyng forsuke
And was vntrewe.

(217/468-474)

With this foreboding (echoing Luke 19:41-44) of what his entry into Jerusalem will mean, we somberly look forward to the Passion amid the street celebration simulated by the play. The counterpoint of voices is unmistakable, and York itself, so closely associated with this dramatic entry, must have shuddered at the prospect. Now the moment of climax is here: The two groups meet amid cheering from the crowd, and each of the Aldermen comes forward to give formal greeting in a string of stanzas in which every sentence begins with "Hayll."

When the Skinners' pageant is thus read in the context of the ceremonial procession that it mirrors, it becomes a central scene in the cycle. . . . [The] entry ceremony itself mirrors the Corpus Christi cycle in its clear progression from the Creation setting of the first pageant to the Assumption scene of the last. With that correspondence as background, and further with the processional and counterprocessional movements within the play as a point of parallelism to the street drama that contains them, the Skinners' pageant becomes a microcosm of not only the ceremonial triumphs of the city but also of the Corpus Christi procession and cycle proper. It links the City of York profoundly with the subject of the Passion, and it allows the spectators to assess the meaning of civic ceremonial in its most timeless sense. It is in the Skinners' play that the City of

York emerges as the focus of the Corpus Christi cycle.

Christine Richardson (essay date 1991)

SOURCE: "York *Crucifixion* Play," in *Medieval Drama*, edited by Christine Richardson and Jackie Johnston, St. Martin's Press, 1991, pp. 61-78.

[*In the following excerpt, Richardson examines the staging of the York* Crucifixion *play—in her judgment, "the central climactic point of the Mystery Cycle"— and demonstrates how it draws the spectators into the responsibility for Christ's suffering and death. She maintains that the vivid portrayal of Christ's sacrifice leads the audience, first, to understand its personal relevance and, second, to acknowledge it as the route to redemption for humanity.*]

A wealth of details in civic documents, guild accounts and church records survives for the organisation and performance of the York Mystery Cycle and the text survives complete in one manuscript which clearly indicates its provenance from York. Although this material gives many indications as to the method of staging the plays and to the status the cycle had in the life of the city, it does offer certain contradictions and is still far from providing a clear, full picture of the presentation of the cycle. The role of the trade guilds is quite clear and both civic records and the manuscript show the assignation of the individual plays to particular guilds.

The York material also records the method of financing the plays through 'pageant silver' collected from each member of the guild and augmented by contributions from fines for shoddy work or breaking guild rules. Each guild appointed a 'pageant master' who was responsible each year for the preparation of the play and who organised repairs to the pageant wagon, costumes, the purchase of items necessary for the performance, selection of actors and holding of rehearsals. A document surviving from the accounts of the York Mercers' guild, which produced the spectacular **Last Judgement Play,** shows that wagons could be highly decorated and contain machinery for an actor playing God, or an icon of God, to be raised and lowered from the floor of the wagon playing space. Maintenance of and responsibility for the wagon was therefore a demanding job for the pageant master.

All the details in the York records point to a 'true processional' manner of performance whereby the individual pageant wagons of each craft guild on which the plays were performed gathered at the Gates of Holy Trinity Church, Micklegate, at 4.30 a.m. on Corpus Christi Day and were then drawn to a number of sites, or 'stations', in the city where they stopped and performed their play, ending up outside the Church of All

Saints, Pavement. . . . Despite these details some critics have felt that such a method of staging is not practically possible, for the time required to perform sequentially the 52 pageants of the York Cycle at the ten to sixteen stations which are indicated in various years would far exceed a dawn-to-midnight playing period on Corpus Christi Day. Others have felt that even if this were the case for York, there is no reason to assume that this was the method of staging the cycle plays in other cities. Until we discover a full eye-witness account of the Corpus Christi plays in performance, clearly dated and referring to a named city, this kind of debate can never firmly be closed, but for York at least it seems reasonable to respect the records we do have and accept the 'true-processional' mode of staging for the York Cycle.

A record relating to the **Crucifixion Play** gives support to the theory that all the plays were performed at all the stations. In 1422 representatives of the Guild of the Painters and Stainers and the Guild of the Pinners and Latteners (workers with brass or similar metals) went before the Mayor and Council to propose an amalgamation of their two pageants as 'the play on the day of Corpus Christi. . .is impeded more than usual because of the multitude of pageants. . .knowing that the matter of both pageants could be shown together in one pageant for the shortening of the play rather profitably. . .'. It was decided that the Painters' and Stainers' pageant 'should be. . .removed' and that the Pinners' and Latteners' pageant be maintained with the addition of 'the speeches which were previously performed. . .in the pageant of the Painters and Stainers'. Both guilds were to be responsible for the financing of the new combined play. The stretching and nailing of Christ on the Cross, which had previously been the responsibility of the Painters and Stainers, was added to the raising up of the Crucified [Christ] on the Mount, which had been the responsibility of the Pinners' and Latteners' Guild, to produce the play which has survived in the manuscript of the York Cycle as No. XXXV or *Crucifixio Christi,* The Crucifixion.

The Crucifixion or **Passion Play** represents the central climactic point of the Mystery Cycle to which all the preceding action and all that follows is directly connected. After the Old Testament plays have demonstrated the Fall of Man and the foreshadowing of his Salvation through Christ, the Nativity plays have shown the birth of the Saviour and the plays of the Life of Christ have demonstrated His divine nature, in the Passion Play Christ is killed by those who do not recognise His true nature and refuse the offer of Salvation He represents. Following the Crucifixion, the plays of the Harrowing of Hell show the first effects of Salvation in redeeming the patriarchs from their captivity in Hell and the breaking of Satan's dominion over the dead, the Resurrection shows Christ affirmed in His divinity and the final Day of Judgement illustrates the consequences of the choices now possible through Christ's sacrifice. The Passion Play is also the illustration of the Corpus Christi feast. The physical body of Christ is sacrificed on the Cross so that mankind can be redeemed for the sins originated in the Garden of Eden which the Mass celebrates in the consecration of the host, the symbolic body of Christ, in the Communion ritual. In previous centuries the emphasis in the church year had been on the Resurrection, as indeed the earliest liturgical dramas seem to have been those created around the discovery of Christ's resurrection by the three Maries, but by the time of the Mystery Cycles focus had passed to the Crucifixion as the sequence most worthy of attention and celebration in both personal piety and art. The liturgical drama had not represented the Crucifixion but had celebrated the Resurrection for its focus was celebratory rather than participatory and didactic. Within the liturgical *Quem quaeritis* pieces the 'actors' and 'audience' are already participants within a sacred ritual, the Mass, and are already aware, through their very presence, of what they should do in order to live as God would have them live and thereby attain salvation. The liturgical drama is perhaps a more complacent drama in that it concentrates on what has already happened with no attempt to relate this to the actual lives of those present. In contrast, the Mystery Cycle plays focus on the present, showing the past of the biblical events to be integrally connected both to the present of the audience and actors and also to their future in terms of salvation or damnation. The cycle plays work within 'God's time' which is universal and contemporaneous, fixing the individual within the flow of Christian history. They are an active, didactic drama.

In order to appreciate the importance of Christ's sacrifice, which occurred in a past specific time and place, to appreciate the possibility of salvation which it offered to Christians of all times and places and to apprehend its relevance, late medieval theology and practical religion recommended the intense concentration on and contemplation of the Passion of Christ. Franciscan theology in particular exhorted the consideration of the practical details of the Crucifixion and Christ's suffering as a means of understanding the immense gift which the Sacrifice offered to mankind. The preaching of the Franciscan friars, who travelled extensively throughout the country giving sermons in churches or wherever a crowd might be gathered, was an important means of spreading this idea to all levels of the general populace. Works written for the private consumption of the more highly educated and pious such as the various versions of the *Meditationes Vitae Christi,* translated into English by Nicholas Love as the *Mirrour of the Blessyd Lyf of Jesu Christ* (1410), explicitly recommended the contemplation of the minute details of the Crucifixion as a meditation aid to understanding the nature of Christ's sacrifice and to appreciate the potential of Salvation which it represented:

who soo desyreth with thappostle Poule to be Joyeful in the crosse of oure lorde ihesu crist / and in the blessid passion / he must with hely meditacion theryn for the grete mysteryes & al the processe therof yf they were inwardly consyderyd with alle the inward mynde and beholdyng of mannes soule / as I fully trowe they shold brynge that beholder in to a newe state of grace. For to hym that wold serche the passion of oure lorde with all his herte and all his inward affection there sholde come many deuoute felynges and sterynges that he neuer supposed before.

To a certain extent this interest in consideration of details was part of the general intellectual climate in the fourteenth and fifteenth centuries. The nominalist philosophers at Oxford in the early fourteenth century had introduced the idea of the importance of details in defining the individuality of things and of experience of these details as being the key to reality. Something could be understood through direct personal experience of it. The same focus on and exploration of details can be seen in the visual arts of the fifteenth century as attention moved from the earlier exclusive concentration on the symbolic, iconographical element or action which is characteristic of Romanesque art. In fifteenth century art, and in the drama, the symbolic action does not disappear, but is surrounded by a greater display of contextualising place; it no longer takes place in an abstract, symbolic environment, but in perceptually visible and identifiable surroundings. Detail is not added merely for decorative effect, but in order to relate the event it portrays to the life of those who look at the picture. In the same way, the cycle plays illustrate the events of Christian history with the details of character, dialogue, humour, pomp and cruelty which can relate them more immediately to the lives of the spectators. The portrayal is more immediate for drama enables the enactment of sequences of events, showing cause and effect and progression, which pictorial representation cannot achieve so effectively. The involvement of the individual spectators is more intense and effective as the characters speak directly to them.

The Passion Play is the moment of the cycle which most directly affects the audience and which doctrinally most requires audience-involvement. The spectators must experience the sacrifice of Christ to understand its relevance but they must also be made aware of how they too are involved in the killing of Christ as representatives of Fallen Man whom He died to save. This twofold experience and recognition is achieved in the Mystery Cycle **Passion Plays** through extensive use of brutal physical detail and the use of executioners, torturers or simple soldiers who are ordered to carry out the Crucifixion by their leaders. In the York **Crucifixion Play** the religious and political authorities are entirely absent and the only characters are Christ and four soldiers who go about the practical business of performing the Crucifixion. The use of these four 'rude mechanicals' achieves both the doctrinal points of the

play: the details of their work stress the suffering of Christ and their interest in their work, their banter and their blatant unawareness of any kind of moral responsibility for what they are doing establishes the implication and guilt of Common Man in the Crucifixion.

The four soldiers go about the Crucifixion purely in terms of a job that has to be done. They are unnamed, like almost all of the non-biblical characters in the cycle plays, standing as representatives of Common Man who follows his orders and does his job without worrying about any higher moral responsibility or indeed the moral consequences of what he is doing. For them, crucifying Christ is merely a problem of stretching and nailing which they affront with hammers, nails and ropes and any unwillingness to perform it or doubts that they might have stem exclusively from the amount of effort involved or the fact that the equipment they have to work with has been badly prepared. Their concerns are all physical and practical, with no spiritual or moral overtones and this is already an indication of their status in the moral framework of the Mystery plays. Like Cain, they perceive the physical rather than the spiritual import of what they do; like Fallen Man, they cannot recognise the spiritual universe represented by the possibility of grace. When they attempt to fix Christ's hands to the cross they discover that the nail-holes are badly placed and too widely spaced to accommodate His arms. The same problem occurs when they attempt to fix His feet, for the hole has been made too low down on the Cross (ll. 107-12, 126-7). 4 soldier remarks that the 'work is all unmeet', but he is referring only to the bad workmanship they are being confronted with and must attempt to adapt in order to perform an efficient crucifixion, not to any moral qualms about the justice or cruelty of the Crucifixion of Christ. It is left to the spectators, the potentially saved, to grasp the extra, spiritual, meaning to his words.

When the soldiers have managed to nail Christ to the Cross, having overcome the practical problems of the wrongly-spaced holes by the cunning use of ropes to stretch His limbs longer to meet the holes (ll. 113-14, 129-40) they next have to confront the task of raising the Cross, with the crucified Christ on it, so that it stands on 'yon hill' as they have been instructed. They are less than enthusiastic at the prospect of such heavy work and once they have begun (l. 186), they begin to make loud complainst at how much they are suffering under the weight:

> For-great harm have I hent:
> My shoulder is asunder. . . .
> This cross and I in two must twin,
> Else breaks my back asunder soon.
>
> (ll. 189-94)

There is no concern expressed for the suffering of Christ which is obviously many times greater, the soldiers are interested only in the pain that they feel, in the physical effects of their work, not in the spiritual implications of what they are doing. Of course, to the members of the audience watching the play the contrast in suffering is very apparent, and the attention given by the soldiers to their petty suffering underlines all the more the enormity of Christ's physical suffering as well as the spiritual implications of this which are evident to the privileged point of view of the audience. Once again the soldiers can only perceive how their work affects them materially, while the audience can appreciate the effects that this 'job' will have on the spiritual destiny not only of the four soldiers but of all mankind. When the soldiers complain of aching backs the audience can identify on a personal level, remembering that in performing similar tasks of lifting or stretching they too have suffered such aches or pains, or would suffer them and no doubt similarly voice their pain. In this way, Christ's silence is all the more dramatic and revealing. He who suffers infinitely more is silent while those who cause him the pain make loud moans and groans. Christ's silence is a motif which appears in all the plays of the Passion sequence, from the Arrest in the Garden of Gethsemane through the Trials and Buffetings, and is indeed attested to in the scriptural narrative. Christ makes no answer to his accusers either to deny their claims or to attempt to save Himself. The contrast here between the response to pain of the four soldiers and Christ, particularly with respect to the amount of pain and proportional response, is perhaps the most moving and effective dramatic use of this silence.

Throughout their work, the soldiers treat Christ merely as another piece of their equipment, as an object rather than a person and certainly not as a God. Once the job is done and the Cross finally fixed securely with wedges so that it remains upright without wobbling (ll. 229-48), the soldiers can relax a little and turn to Christ to ask Him, mockingly, what He thinks of their handiwork. Once again the irony is there for the more informed and perceptive spectator who can understand the larger meaning of the 'work' they have 'wrought' and it is to the audience, rather than to the soldiers, that Christ replies. His answer is concerned with the wider issues of their 'work' and calls on 'All men that walk by way or street' to contemplate the soldiers' handiwork and to think about it carefully, just as the friars and the writers of the *Meditationes Vitae Christi* invited the pious to feel experientially the details of the Crucifixion and the pain that Christ must have experienced.

> All men that walk by way or street,
> Take tent ye shall no travail tine;
> Behold my head, my hands, my feet,
> And fully feel now, ere ye fine,
> If any mourning may be meet,
> Or mischief measured unto mine.
>
> (ll. 253-8)

In the context of the staging of the pageants, of course, the men that walk by the way or street are the spectators themselves, gathered around the pageant wagon in the streets of York. Christ then asks for forgiveness, in the play time for the soldiers who have nailed Him to the Cross, but in God's time for all mankind, including the audience, and for salvation:

> Therefore, my Father, I crave,
> Let never their sins be sought,
> But see their souls to save.
>
> (ll. 262-4)

The involvement of the audience now passes from direct identification with the soldiers to a sequence of suspense and hope engendered and inevitably denied by foreknowledge of the story. The soldiers remain unaware of what they are caught up in even after Christ's speech, and their response demonstrates yet again their lack of recognition both of who Christ is and what He represents. The audience is necessarily struck by this refusal to appreciate what is happening, for from their privileged position in God's time they understand the implication. The soldiers begin to associate Christ with rumours they have heard of someone who claimed to be God's son and said he would destroy the Temple (l. 273). This offers a tantalising hope to the audience that recognition is imminent, but once again the soldiers are capable of perceiving only the physical and not the spiritual, for they reject such claims stating that Christ had neither enough physical strength nor sufficient followers to knock the Temple down and build it up again. It is the audience who understands the metaphorical, spiritual meaning. The soldiers' last words on the matter are that they have done as Pilate ordered them to do, a final refusal to accept any kind of responsibility for what they have done.

Like the Shepherds as ordinary representatives of Common Man to whom the possibility of salvation is first offered, the soldiers or torturers are representatives of ordinary working men who refuse to recognise and accept this possibility. They can be seen as the negative image of the Shepherds and are just as important to the doctrinal technique of the cycle plays. Each individual Christian is responsible for his or her own destiny in making the decision whether or not to accept the possibility of salvation which Christ's sacrifice represents. The Shepherds accept, the soldiers do not. The Shepherds recognised the Christ-child as the Son of God and worshipped Him, the soldiers refuse to consider His God-head and nail Him to the Cross. These are in essence the two choices available to individual Christians and the cycle plays offer portrayals of these two groups of characters which will ease the identification of the audience with them and thus help them to see that the choice is relevant to their lives too.

The dramatic expression of the Crucifixion as a job of

work and the practical exponents of it as ordinary working men assure audience identification. The medieval trade and craftsmen watching the play could apply details of the work and problems of adapting awkward materials to their own life and work. Many in the medieval audience and indeed today could recognise the concern only with the present moment of their work and the refusal to think about what would happen to their work, or the stage in a long piece of work for which they were responsible, once it left their hands. Responsibility is often deferred to those higher in the labour hierarchy whose task it is to plan, judge and consider consequences. The four York soldiers are quite clear about the requirements of their job and their position in the order of authority. When 1 Soldier begins to get authoritarian and tell the others what to do they are quick to resent such a presumption: 'Yea, thou commandest lightly as a lord; / Come help to hale him, with ill hail!' (ll. 115-16).

Although the soldiers are not given individual names they are by no means types or abstractions. Their dialogue is recognisably realistic and personalities can be seen through their responses. 1 Soldier appears to be the foreman of the gang, or at least takes on this role. He orders the work to start, tells the others what to do, asks how they are getting on and suggests solutions to the technical problems they encounter. He also noticeably does less hard work than the others, choosing the head of the Cross to hold (ll. 87-8) and later preferring to order rather than help haul (ll. 117-18). 4 Soldier is the most conscientious and it is he who notices the defects in their equipment and who then wishes to report the job done to their superiors as soon as they have attached Christ to the Cross (ll. 151-2).

Staging requirements seem to have influenced the number of soldiers in the York play. There are four soldiers in the play rather than the standard grouping of three used in both scriptural narrative and other plays presumably because a minimum of four men were required to raise the Cross, one at the head, one at the foot and one each side. The actors in the play lift the Cross upright from the ground where it lies as they attach Christ to it to slot it into a mortice which holds if firmly for all to see. The mechanics of this elevation must have been carefully worked out and its execution represented a testimony to the skill of the actors and their guild just as much as it did within the play time to the four soldiers carrying out their commission from Pilate. The play itself has no stage directions and the sequence of actions and techniques involved must be drawn out from the dialogue. No list of props or details of the wagon used survive in the records of the Pinners' and Painters' Guild, but from the text the minimum properties appear to be a wooden cross, hammers, nails, a mortice, wedges, ropes and for the final section of the play where the soldiers squabble over Christ's clothes, a coat.

The soldiers refer several times to a hill on which they are supposed to mount the Cross and the 1415 description of the play in the general plays list refers to the raising of the Cross 'upon the mount of Calvary'. The stretching and nailing section of the play must surely have taken place on the wagon itself so that it would be clearly visible to the spectators, rather than on the ground in front of the wagon. The elevation of the Cross could also be played here and the slipping of it into a mortice fixed onto the wagon floor. Unless the Pinners and Painters had two wagons, one of which was smaller, like the Mercers' second Hell-mouth wagon, and represented Mount Calvary, it is difficult to imagine how the hill references in the dialogue could be realised in practical staging terms. It is unlikely that all the dialogue with reference to carrying the Cross to 'yon hill' and the lengthy complaints about how heavy it is would be inappropriate to the action. Because of this it seems likely that the sequence from lines 211 to 218 could cover carrying the Cross either onto the wagon from the ground or down from the wagon and onto a secondary wagon representing the mount. Lines 219 to 225 could then represent the final upright elevation of the Cross and the sliding of it into 'this mortice here' (l. 220). The iconographical importance of Christ on the Cross seems to require that this final image be well visible, on an elevated place, to the whole audience.

The fixing of Christ to the Cross on the ground, or 'supine Crucifixion' was already a common iconographical and narrative feature and many visual representations of the Passion also show ropes being used to stretch Christ's limbs and the holes in the cross being obviously too widely spaced. The technique is also featured in the Cornish Cycle Passion Play and it is interesting to note that the Chester Passion Play was performed by the Guild of the Ironmongers and Ropers. It is difficult to say whether drama drew its inspiration here from the narrative or visual tradition or vice versa, but the use of ropes was certainly necessary in the cycle plays in order to attach the actor playing Christ firmly to the Cross. The stretching motif may have been introduced in order to give a motivation for the necessary introduction of these ropes. Although the actor playing Christ no doubt did suffer physical discomfort, it is clear that actual nails were not used to fix his body to the Cross in performance. The image of the Crucifixion was extremely diffuse in fourteenth- and fifteenth-century religious art, yet the physical demonstration of the fixing, elevation and hanging of a live actor representing Christ must have been a much more effective and emotionally striking portrayal than that offered in the visual arts. The associated immediacy for the audience of witnessing the Crucifixion in the familiar surroundings of their own town, played out by people they knew socially or commercially is not to be underestimated in the creation of strong religious feeling and as exhortation to repentance and God-fearing life.

The use of realistic details in order to evoke emotional apprehension is used in all the plays of the York Passion sequence and indeed in many other of the Mystery Cycle plays, but only in the **Crucifixion Play** is it used primarily to create identification between the members of the audience and the physical perpetrators of the killing of Christ. In the other plays of the York sequence the details are not so clearly physical but rather psychological and this has led critics to identify them as the work of one author, now generally known as the York Realist. This playwright was careful to add details which motivated or explained decisions or actions and followed through 'processes of behaviour' so that the events became comprehensible to the audience in terms of individual characters doing certain things for reasons stemming from their lives and situations rather than merely because they were part of a preordained symbolic sequence. **The Crucifixion** Play is not generally considered to form part of the canon of the York Realist, . . . and in this play the realistic details are physical rather than psychological and are used both to heighten the emotional effect of the Crucifixion and to force an awareness of direct identification with the soldiers and thereby an implicit involvement in the responsibility for Christ's sacrifice.

Mankind's responsibility for the Crucifixion comes about because the Fallen world to which we belong is the result of Adam and Eve's original sin. In this sense the Crucifixion is a necessary corollary to the Fall of Man and as mankind sinned once in the Garden of Eden, so mankind will sin again in killing the Redeemer. The significant difference this time is that there will now be a possible happy outcome for those who choose to recognise Christ's sacrifice. Following the Fall, even the good souls were trapped in Hell from whence Christ liberates them after the Crucifixion in the Harrowing of Hell. Paradoxically, if Christ had not been crucified then mankind could not have been saved, but the Crucifixion was a result of mankind's choice, not of God's predetermination, a choice was made not to recognise good but to follow evil just as Adam had the choice not to follow the evil of the serpent's offer of the apple and disobedience in Eden. In Christ's first speech in the **Crucifixion Play,** he points to the inevitable link between His sacrifice and Adam's sin (ll. 49-60). He does not plead to be spared the pain of the Crucifixion but for His suffering to gain defence for mankind from evil:

> That they for me may favour find;
> And from the fiend them fend,
> So that their souls be safe
> In wealth withouten end.

(ll. 56-9)

The York **Passion sequence** clearly demonstrates that the responsibility for the Crucifixion is mankind's and not Satan's, though the Chester sequence suggests that Satan was principally to blame. The Dream of Pilate's Wife incident which is included in Play XXX, *Christ before Pilate I,* in the York sequence exculpates Satan by showing how he tries to stop the Crucifixion by sending a warning dream to Pilate's wife, not from any good will to mankind, but because he realises that once Christ is killed mankind will no longer be under his dominion.

The chattering of the soldiers and their interest in their work not only enables the members of the audience to see themselves in them and so establish their own role in the Christian story, but it also serves as a means of demonstrating the divinity of Christ. The soldiers are noisy and brutal, their physical violence towards Christ is matched by a violence of language in their swearing by Mahomet (ll. 61, 129), their jeering and their quarrelling. They are full of energy and as they bustle around attempting to finish their job they represent Common Man at his most vital yet least refined. They are fixed on the physical level and cannot comprehend moral responsibility or spiritual meaning. The overwhelming contrast between their noise and energy and Christ's silence and passivity is striking even in a reading of the play and in performance it would have been even greater. Christ does not talk to the soldiers even when they directly address Him but talks only to God and to mankind in general as represented by the audience. He is cooperative, yet passive; He lies down on the Cross when ordered to do so and makes no complaint as the soldiers stretch His limbs with the ropes, nail His hands and feet and then jar Him violently as the Cross is dropped into the mortice: 'This falling was more fell / Than all the harms he had;' (ll. 225-6). Christ is not what the soldiers are, Fallen Man in unbridled, ungoverned state, His dignity and silence before their rowdy brutality establishes this, yet He is Man, He has chosen to be born as a Man and to be killed for mankind's sake. The delight the soldiers seem to take in detailing the pain they are causing Him underlines Christ's physical nature. His sinews can snap when stretched, and do, His veins can burst as no doubt a sachet of paint provided by the Painters was burst to demonstrate at line 147, yet He makes no complaint. The soldiers, able to perceive only at the physical level, interpret this as a demonstration of His lack of God-head, for surely a divinity would be immune from such pain (ll. 187-8), yet, as is apparent to the audience, this is in fact a proof of His divinity and the payment He has agreed to make for Adam and Fallen Man's sins.

Richard Beadle (essay date 1994)

SOURCE: "The York Cycle," in *The Cambridge Companion to Medieval English Theatre,* edited by Richard Beadle, Cambridge University Press, 1994, pp. 100-08.

[*In the excerpt below, Beadle evaluates the variety of alliterative verse in the York cycle. Focusing in particular on the* Crucifixion *pageant and the second* Christ Before Pilate *play, he remarks on the verbal subtleties and structural details that are carefully woven into the twelve-line stanza throughout the play.*]

Most of the York cycle still awaits detailed study along lines that move towards an integration of the textual, documentary and theatrical evidence, complex and resistant to consensual interpretation though some of it is. Recent illuminating accounts of the *Nativity* (Play 14) and the *Resurrection* (Play 18) show what can be done. An extended commentary on the cycle as a whole, along the lines of that provided by [R. M.] Lumiansky and [David] Mills for Chester or [Stephen] Spector for N-Town is a major desideratum, and, where appropriate, attention must be paid to the presence of music in the plays, and the possibility of iconographic influences. The close attention devoted to the Passion sequence by J. W. Robinson has been well placed, though scrutiny of the textual, documentary and literary evidence for the existence of a dramatist whom he dubs the 'York Realist' is long overdue. In the space available here it is only possible to gesture towards [some] critical and interpretative implications. . . , and the Passion sequence—in particular the texture of its dramatic poetry—may be allowed to serve as an initial touchstone. Two plays from the York Passion sequence, seen in the context of the *Ordo Paginarum,* provide a point of entry into discussion of the styles of dramatic writing being practised in York in the 1420s. Play 35, the celebrated York Pinners' pageant of the *Crucifixion,* may be set alongside the Tilemakers' *Christ before Pilate 2: The Judgement* (33), a play regularly attributed to the 'York Realist'.

There is good reason to think that the *Crucifixion* as we now have it probably came into being in 1422. The situation prior to that date, from 1415 at least, is preserved unaltered in the brief pageant list that accompanies the *Ordo Paginarum* proper, which shows that the nailing of Christ on the cross and the rearing of the cross on Calvary were originally played as separate episodes by different guilds:

Payntours	Expansio & clauacio christi
latoners	leuacio christi super montem
(Painters	The stretching out and nailing of Christ
Latteners	The raising of Christ on the Mount)

[Alexandra F. Johston and Margaret Rogerson, eds., Records of Early English Drama]

Another document of 1422 in the Memorandum Book, however, makes clear that a decision had been made to amalgamate the two episodes into one pageant, under the control of the Pinners and Latteners. The intention was to simplify the organisation of the cycle, which because of the profusion of short pageants was proving cumbersome in performance. Careful examination of the relevant entry in the main *Ordo* list shows that erasures and substitutions. . .were made by Roger Burton, no doubt in or soon after 1422, in order to reflect the new circumstances. In the absence of evidence to the contrary it seems very likely that our extant text of the Pinners' pageant (copied 1463-77), which covers both the corresponding episodes, was originally composed in response to a practical need to shorten the cycle.

The York *Crucifixion* has never lacked high praise as a work of dramatic art, not least for the quality of the 'realism' that has gone into the portrayal of the executioners' work. The tools of their trade—hammers, nails, ropes, wedges, timber—are all studiedly displayed to the audience and constant reference made to them in the dialogue, largely to enhance the realistic impact of the presentation, but also because some of these objects later become the 'Instruments of the Passion' displayed by the angels at the Last Judgement (mentioned as properties in the Mercers' inventory . . .). The dialogue is expertly managed, and in such a way as to make the blocking of the play reasonably clear to any director, since it is possible at all important points to infer where each speaker is and what he is doing. The vivid realisation of the gruesome actions involved in stretching out and nailing Jesus to the cross owes much to the late medieval tradition of affective meditation on every minute physical detail of the Passion. This when it becomes embodied in dramatic form, compels the audience's absorption in the work (a key word in the play) of the executioners, so that when the cross is reared and Christ utters his lyrical appeal to 'Al men þat walkis by waye or strete', an onlooker's silent complicity in what has gone before precipitates a guilty sense of implication in the Crucifixion. Some idea of the dramatist's range of style and technique may be gained by considering this climactic moment in the play and the cycle as a whole. 'Where are oure hameres laide / þat we schulde wirke withall?' asks the third soldier:

IV MILES	We haue þem here euen atte oure hande.
II MILES	Gyffe me þis wegge, I schall it in dryue.
IV MILES	Here is anodir yitt ordande [*prepared*].
III MILES	Do take it me hidir belyue [*quickly*].
I MILES	Laye on þanne faste.
III MILES	yis, I warrande.
	I thryng þame same, so motte I thryve.
	Nowe will þis crosse full stabely stande,
	All-yf he raue þei will nought ryve.

In 1992 a theatre company played the York cycle on the streets of York; here, they raise the cross in a scene from Crucifixion.

I MILES	Say sir, howe likis you nowe,
	Þis werke þat we haue wrought?
IV MILES	We praye youe sais vs howe
	Ye fele, or faynte ye ought
	[*whether you faint*].
JESUS	Al men þat walkis by waye or strete,
	Takes tente ye schalle no trauayle tyne.
	Byholdes myn heede, myn handis, and my feete,
	And fully feele nowe, or ye fyne [*pass*],
	Yf any mournyng may be meete [*equal*],
	Or myscheue mesured vnto myne.
	My fadir, þat alle bales may bete,
	Forgiffis þes men þat dois me pyne [*cause me pain*].
	What þei wirke wotte þai noght;

Therfore, my fadir, I craue,
Latte neuere þer synnys be sought,
But see þer saules to saue.

(Play 35, lines 24I-64)

(246 I'll thrust them in together, so may I prosper 248 Even if he writhes about they will not split 254 Be sure that you miss none of my suffering 258 Or suffering compared. . .259. . .who may relieve all torments 26I 'They know not what they do' 263. . . visited upon them)

In this dramatist's hands the twelve-line stanza, abababab₄cdcd₃, is assimilated equally well to the very different dramatic requirements of Jesus's serene address, and the demotic hammerblows of the executioners' stichomythia. 'All men þat walkis. . .' describes not only the actual posture of much of the audience, but also calls forth emotional associations of the medieval liturgy, quoting 'O vos omnes qui transitis per viam' (Lamentations I.12) from the Good Friday *Improperia* or 'reproaches'. The strong deictic element in the language of the soldiers ('*oure* hameres', '*þis* wegge', '*þis* crosse' and so on) emphasises the nascent symbolic nature of the objects they are handling, and at the same time 'covers' the difficult and undoubtedly dangerous stage actions that the actors are called upon to perform. . . . The play's verbal and thematic emphasis on *work*, . . .converges on a kind of pun arising out of the third soldier's question in lines 249-50, followed by Jesus's oblique, delayed answer in line 26I, via 'trauayle' in line 254: the ignorant, physical, painful work of man in the cause of sin and death is transfigured into the sublime, spiritual work of redemption in the cause of life everlasting.

Whether the work of the York **Crucifixion** playwright occurs elsewhere in the cycle is largely a matter for speculation. A natural starting point is the metrical evidence, though one would not want to suggest either that this writer possessed a monopoly of the twelve-line stanza, or that he did not compose in other metres. Nevertheless, the same stanza, with more or less ornamental alliteration according to subject matter, occurs in a substantial number of other plays. It was adopted, for example, in the Doctor's long prefatory speech rehearsing the Old Testament prophecies of the birth of Christ, which was grafted on to an earlier **Annunciation and Visitation** (Play 12). Roger Burton recorded this as an addition to the cycle in an alteration to the *Ordo Paginarum,* and it evidently dates from much the same period as the revision that produced the **Crucifixion** of 1422. Unlike the latter play, however, the Doctor's speech is a significant enlargement of the cycle (144 lines), aimed at articulating more clearly the previously abrupt transition from the Old to the New Testament story. The twelve-line stanza of the **Crucifixion** is also the metre of parts or all of ten other plays:

the Parchmentmakers' and Bookbinders' *Abraham and Issac* (10), the Hosiers' *Moses and Pharaoh* (10), parts of the Chandlers' *Shepherds* (15), most of the Masons'/Goldsmiths' *Herod / Magi* (16), most of the Spurriers' and Lorimers' *Christ and the Doctors* (20), the Curriers' *Transfiguration* (23), the Cappers' *Woman Taken in Adultery / Raising of Lazarus* (24), the Bakers' *Last Supper* (27), the Saddlers' *Harrowing of Hell* (37) and the Potters' *Pentecost* (43). At least one of the plays in this group, the *Woman Taken in Adultery / Raising of Lazarus,* seems in its present form to be, like the *Crucifixion,* the result of an amalgamation of two episodes that feature earlier as discrete plays in the *Ordo Paginarum* lists, and could well be another part of the same campaign to reduce the number of separate components in the cycle. Other plays in the group have interesting compositional and stylistic links which have recently come to light. The *Abraham and Isaac* and the *Moses and Pharaoh* both rely to differing extents on a specific source, a northern vernacular narrative poem of around 1400 (which also happens to be in the same twelve-line stanza), now known as the *Middle English Metrical Paraphrase of the Old Testament.* The *Moses and Pharaoh* is in turn linked to its closest figural relative in the cycle, the *Harrowing of Hell,* by specific structural and verbal echoes, particularly in the respective treatments of Pharaoh and Satan.

Turning to the other play in the Passion sequence under consideration here, the Tilemakers' *Christ before Pilate 2: The Judgement,* it is also possible, with the help of recent research in the documents, to date the period of the writer's work fairly specifically. It appears that from at least the time of the original *Ordo Paginarum* until 1422, the events portrayed in the extant play, together with others that have not survived, were separate pageants brought forth by different guilds. Between 1422-3 and 1432 a series of documents in the Memorandum Book records the progressive acquisition of responsibility for the episode as a whole by the Tilemakers, during which time it appears that the new play came into being, perhaps developing through more than one phase. The end product, the extant text *Christ before Pilate 2* recorded in the Register a generation or so later, is thus very likely to date from the decade between 1422 and 1432. It could, therefore, be exactly contemporary with the revision of the *Crucifixion,* and though the documents do not say so explicitly, it seems likewise to have been written as a result of a prevailing desire to simplify the organisation of the cycle.

The Tilemakers' pageant is devoted to the events between Jesus's return from Herod's court and Pilate's decision to hand him over to the Jewish authorities for execution. It includes an apocryphal episode, elaborately developed from a brief allusion in the contemporary narrative poem the *Northern Passion,* to the legend that the banners held by the soldiers at Pilate's court bowed down, and that Pilate and the High Priests in-

voluntarily sprang to their feet when Jesus was brought in. The script was one of the longest in the cycle, running to over 500 lines when complete (a leaf now missing from the manuscript has carried away some fifty), and in the play as we have it only one short speech of eight lines is given to Jesus. Most of it is devoted to the ceremoniously wordy manoeuvrings of the High Priests and the evasions of Pilate, which break down suddenly into a prolonged scourging scene of ferocious violence:

PILATUS	Why suld I deme to dede þan withoute deseruyng in dede?
	But I haue herde al haly why in hertes ye hym hate.
	He is fautles, in faith, and so God mote me spede
	I graunte hym my gud will to gang on his gate.
CAIPHAS	Nought so ser, for wele ye it wate,
	To be kyng he claymeth, with croune,
	And whoso stoutely will steppe to þat state
	Ye suld deme ser, to be dong doune
	And dede.
PILATUS	Sir, trulye þat touched to treasoune,
	And or I remewe he rewe sall þat reasoune,
	And or I stalke or stirre fro þis stede.
	Sir knyghtis þat ar comly, take þis caystiff in keping,
	Skelpe hym with scourges and with skathes hym scorne.
	Wrayste and wrynge hym to, for wo to he be wepyng,
	And þan bryng hym beforc vs as he was beforne.
I MILES	He may banne þe tyme he was borne,
	Sone sall he be serued as ye saide vs.
ANNA	Do wappe of his wedis þat are worne.
II MILES	All redy ser, we haue arayde vs. Haue done,
	To þis broll late vs buske vs and brayde vs
	As ser Pilate has propirly prayde vs.
III MILES	We sall sette to hym sadly sone.

(Play 33, lines 324-47)

(*Pilate* Why should I condemn him to death, then, if he doesn't deserve it? But I have heard in full how you hate him in your hearts. So help me God, he is innocent, for certain. He has my ready permission to be on his way. *Caiaphas* By no means, sir, for as you know well, he claims to be a crowned king, and whosoever will boldly lay claim to that dignity, you should judge, sir, to be struck down and put to death. *Pilate* Sir, that indeed appertains to treason, and before I go he will repent that claim—before I move or stir from this place. You noble knights, take charge of this offender, lash him with whips and hurt him with blows. Twist him and wrench him, too, until he cries with pain, and then bring him again before us. *1st Soldier* he will curse the day he was born—soon he shall be treated as you command. *Annas* Rip off his tattered clothes. *2nd Soldier* Sir, we are already well prepared. Enough—let us hasten and apply ourselves to this wretch, as Sir Pilate has personally commanded us. *3rd Soldier* Soon we shall deal with him diligently.)

The metre is distinctive: the line consists, when fully extended, of a four-stress long alliterative line, all four stressed syllables being commonly reinforced by alliteration, aa / aa, rather than the 'classical' aa / ax pattern favoured by most fourteenth-century writers of alliterative poetry, such as Langland and the *Gawain* poet. Unstressed syllables tend to be numerous and irregularly distributed. It is not really appropriate to speak of the metre in terms of syllabic scansion, but the unstressed syllables are commonly paired before an alliterating stave ('hym my *gud* will to *gang* on his *gate*'), lending the dialogue an anapaestic drive, and probably making it easier for the actors to memorise. In its own time it was dubbed 'tumbling' verse in remarks attributed to the poet-king James I of Scotland, and a taste for the long alliterative line combined with complicated stanza forms seems to have been prevalent in Scotland and northern England during the fifteenth century. The analysis of the stanza form here is $abab_4bcbc_3d_1ccd_3$, and to provide over 500 lines of alliterative dialogue in this shape must have been no small challenge to the dramatist. But in spite of the artificiality of the mode, the natural, demotic tone of the exchanges is very marked. The use of spare lines or half-lines to pad out the verses or achieve the stanzas is avoided, the phatic expressions, on the contrary, being assimilated to everyday speech rhythms, and sometimes carrying a resonance beyond themselves. Lines and phrases like 'He is fautles, *in faith,* and *so God mote me spede*' and 'Sir knyghtis þat ar comly. . .' carry an ironic weight in this context.

More arresting, however, is the authentic sense of psychological movement captured in the texture of the verse. Pilate's genuine or affected exasperation with the continuous importunities of the High Priests is most effectively communicated in his turning of a real question into a rhetorical one, not waiting for an answer:

Why suld I deme to dede þan withoute

deseruyng in dede?
But I haue herde al haly why in hertes ye
hym hate.

Such evasions are called to a halt by Caiaphas, the senior and more calculating of the two High Priests, and the observant actor will notice the carefully placed 'ser's (lines 328, 331), which are minor features in the extended apparatus of deadly *politesse* Caiaphas employs throughout the play, converging here upon the unanswerable point, that Jesus, in claiming to be king, has challenged the Roman governor's own authority. In contrast with Caiaphas, Annas's taste for physical violence is instantly unveiled, for as soon as the order for the scourging has been given, he calls (true mark of the sadist in office) to see the naked flesh (line 343). After the scourging comes the now-famous moment in the play when, returning to the biblical narrative, Pilate is presented with the bowl wherein to wash his hands, an act whose symbolic significance is unconsciously embellished with a quotidian proverbial gloss in the obsequiousness to the servant who brings it:

Here is all, ser, þat ye for sende.
Wille ye wasshe whill þe watir is hote?
                            (Play 33, lines 442-3)

Like the ***Crucifixion*** play of 1422, the script provided for the Tilemakers at much the same time depends for its effect on an audience's fine attunement to the minutiae of a distinctive style of dramatic poetry. Other plays in the Passion sequence written in the long alliterative line (though the stanza forms vary widely) are the Cutlers' ***Conspiracy*** (26), the Cordwainers' ***Agony in the Garden and the Betrayal*** (28), the Bowers' and Fletchers' ***Christ before Annas and Caiaphas*** (29), the Tapiters' and Couchers' ***Christ before Pilate 1: The Dream of Pilate's Wife*** (30), the Litsters' ***Christ before Herod*** (31) and the Cooks' and Waterleaders' ***Remorse of Judas*** (32), any of which will repay the kind of close attention focused upon the episode from the Tilemakers' script above. Attractive though it is to attribute this group to one writer, it should be borne in mind that several other plays, whose subject matter did not perhaps lend itself to similar treatment, are nevertheless written in a comparable metrical form.

A variation on the alliterative mode within the **Passion sequence** is found in the Butchers' ***Death of Christ*** (Play 36), one of the most impressive plays in the cycle, where the number of alliterating staves to the line, in a characteristically complex stanza, is reduced from the usual four to three in the *frons*, $ababbcbc_3d_1eeee_2d_3$:

On roode am I ragged and rente,   *cross;*
                                     torn;
                                     gashed

Þou synfull sawle, for thy sake;
(Play 36, lines 120-1)

Though commonly assumed to be by the same dramatist as the alliterative Passion plays listed above, the *Death of Christ* actually differs from them considerably in both dramatic technique and the handling of the verse. A series of devotional icons familiar to the audience from the visual arts of the period—the Man of Sorrows, the lamenting Virgin, the Deposition and so on—are caused to melt into one another through a metrical medium that is best described as lyrical, the sublimity of the subject finding its most eloquent expression, then as in later ages, in image and music.

We may end with the beginning of the cycle. The superb Barkers' pageant of the *Creation and Fall of the Angels* (Play 1, and cf. Plays 40 and 44 for the same metre) is composed in yet another variety of the alliterative medium, a kind of rhetorical and expository 'high style', with no less attention to verbal nuance and structural detail than in the Passion plays. Here, the basic formal units are the stanzas taken as a whole, which are apportioned to the speakers on a numerological basis according to their roles, and in harmony with the symbolic development of the action. Since all the characters were supernatural, the actors would have worn masks, and the otherworldliness of the visual impact is reinforced by the stylisation of the language. God and the loyal angels in heaven speak throughout in complete stanzas, whilst the rebellious angels divide the stanza amongst them as they fall into hell. The effect is to absorb the audience's attention to dramatic language in a way quite different from the alliterative Passion plays, but no less imaginatively inventive.

God the Father opens this first pageant and the cycle as a whole, bringing together. . .the dawn of creation and time with the annual dawning of Corpus Christi Day in the city of York:

Ego sum Alpha et O: vita, via, veritas primus et novissimus.

The opening line, pregnant with allusion, stands as a kind of epigraph to the cycle as a whole: 'I am the way, and the truth, and the life: (no one cometh unto the Father, but by me', John 14.6), from Christ's parting words to the disciples after the Last Supper, is conflated with 'I am the Alpha and the Omega (the first and the last, the beginning and the end'), the closing words of the Apocalypse (22.13). The audience is invited to contemplate from this first, but effectively extra-temporal, moment the two events which at the same time form the structural cruxes of the cycle about to be played, and constitute the central facts of their spiritual lives—the episodes where Christ, having come from instituting the Eucharist (literally, Corpus Christi), embarks upon the work of redemption in the Passion—and then his general judgement of all mankind at the end of time on Doomsday.

FURTHER RERADING

Beadle, Richard. Introduction to *The York Plays*, edited by Richard Beadle, pp. 10-45. London: Edward Arnold, 1982.

A survey of important textual, historical, and performance issues. Beadle provides a thorough evaluation of the Ashburnam manuscript; the origins, early history, and mode of performing the York cycle; and a bibliographic guide to principal developments in the critical history of these plays.

———. "Poetry, Theology and Drama in the York *Creation and Fall of Lucifer*." In *Religion in the Poetry and Drama of the Late Middle Ages in England*, edited by Piero Boitani and Anna Torti, pp. 213-27. Cambridge: D. S. Brewer, 1990.

Focuses on the York Tanners' pageant depicting the creation of the universe and the fall of the insubordinate angels from heaven. Beadle discusses the play's construction, stanzaic form, and thematic concerns, noting that the York treatment of Lucifer is unique in representing him as guilty of intellectual pride.

Craig, Hardin. "York-Wakefield Plays." In *English Religious Drama of the Middle Ages*, pp. 199-238. Oxford: Clarendon Press, 1955.

A frequently-cited essay on the similarities and differences between the York and Towneley Corpus Christi cycles. Craig suggests that the York cycle underwent many revisions and that the thirteen alliterative plays in the cycle are most likely the work of a single author.

Davidson, Clifford. "The Realism of the York Realist and the York Passion." *Speculum* 50, No. 2 (April, 1975): 270-83.

Evaluates traditional elements of medieval iconography in the work of the dramatist known as the York Realist. Davidson maintains that the playwright combined the symbolism of earlier periods with his own innovative use of vivid, realistic detail to create an "emotionally charged drama" with wide popular appeal.

Dorrell, Margaret. "Two Studies of the York Corpus Christi Play." *Leeds Studies in English*, edited by A. C. Cawley and Stanley Ellis, n.s. VI (1972): 67-115.

Argues that the York Corpus Christ cycle was performed serially at several stations throughout the city in the course of a single day. Dorrell examines a host of civic documents to substantiate her theory. The article contains copious extracts from these records.

Gardiner, Harold G. "The Decline of the Religious Stage in England under Elizabeth, 1558-1603." In *Mysteries' End*, pp. 65-93. New Haven: Yale University Press, 1946.

> Asserts that the Protestant Reformation—not a flagging of popular interest—was responsible for the demise of the Corpus Christi plays. Gardiner surveys the political and religious controversies prevalent in late sixteenth-century England.

Holding, Peter. "Stagecraft in the York Cycle." *Theatre Notebook* XXXIV, No. 2 (1980): 51-60.

> Speculates that the York cycle of plays employed a broad range of symbolic and realistic staging. This sophisticated dramatic technique, Holding suggests, was complemented by an audience-play relationship based on the willing suspension of disbelief.

Jack, R. D. S. "Laughter and Wit in the Miracle Cycles." In *Patterns of Divine Comedy*, pp. 66-128. Cambridge: D. S. Brewer, 1989.

> Focuses, in a section subtitled "Les Cent Details Divers," on the York Realist. Jack proposes that the use of such devices as naturalistic details, irony, and dark humor is directly related to the author's didactic intent.

Johnston, Alexandra F., and Margaret Dorrell. "The Doomsday Pageant of the York Mercers, 1433." *Leeds Studies in English*, edited by A. C. Cawley and Stanley Ellis, n.s. V (1971): 29-34.

> Draws some tentative conclusions about the stage of the Mercers' Doomsday Pageant on the basis of a legal document detailing the stage properties owned by the guild.

Justice, Alan D. "Trade Symbolism in the York Cycle." *Theatre Journal* 31, No. 1 (March, 1979): 47-58.

> Discerns a direct connection between specific craft guilds and the pageants assigned to them in a majority of the York plays.

Kolve, V. A. "The Passion and Resurrection in Play and Game." In *The Play Called Corpus Christi*, pp. 175-205. Stanford: Stanford University Press, 1966.

> A comparative study of the ways in which the English mystery plays translate Christ's suffering, death, and resurrection into "game." Kolve maintains that the pathos of the crucifixion was successfully controlled through individual characterization of Christ's tormentors and careful structuring of successive stages of the Passion.

Nelson, Alan H. "Principles of Processional Staging: York Cycle." *Modern Philology* 67, No. 1 (1970): 303-20.

> Speculates about several ways it might have been possible to stage the York cycle serially at a number of locations in the course of a single day—and rejects them all. Nelson concludes that "true-processional" staging, where every audience sees all the plays in order, would be impractical, even impossible, in the case of the York cycle.

Robinson, J. W. "The Art of the York Realist." In *Medieval English Drama: Essays Critical and Contextual,* edited by Jerome Taylor and Alan H. Nelson, pp. 230-44. Chicago: University of Chicago Press, 1972.

> Comments on traditional and conventional themes and dramatic techniques in the plays and distinguishes the York Realist's contributions to medieval English drama.

————."A Commentary on the York Play of the Birth of Jesus." *Journal of English and Germanic Philology* 70, No. 2 (April 1971): 241-54.

> Emphasizes the dignity, economy, and skillfulness of the York Nativity pageant, pronouncing it the finest English mystery play on the subject. Robinson highlights the play's movement from misery and uncertainty to a sense of relief and harmony at the close; he also claims that St. Birgitta's legendary account of the Nativity was a significant influence on the York play.

Stevens, Martin. "The York Cycle: From Procession to Play." *Leeds Studies in English*, edited by A. C. Cawley and Stanley Ellis, n.s. VI (1972): 37-61.

> Conjectures an evolutionary development of the York cycle. Stevens believes that the pageants were expanded from a series of pantomimes, directly linked to the observance of Corpus Christi, into plays presented in a single, continuous, stationary performance separate from the religious observance.

Willis, Paul. "The Weight of Sin in the York *Crucifixion*," *Leeds Studies in English*, edited by A. C. Cawley and Stanley Ellis, n.s. XV (1984): 109-16.

> Views the cross-carrying episode in the York Crucifixion drama as a dramatic metaphor of Christ's atonement. Willis maintains that the executioners struggling under their burden reflect both the notion of sin as a dead weight for the sinner and the concept that Christ took on the responsibility of sin by dying on the cross.

> **Additional coverage of the York plays is contained in the following source published by Gale Research:** *Dictionary of Literary Biography, Vol 146: Old and Middle English Literature.*

Literature Criticism from 1400 to 1800

Cumulative Indexes

How to Use This Index

The main references

Calvino, Italo
1923-1985.....CLC 5, 8, 11, 22, 33, 39,
73; SSC 3

list all author entries in the following Gale Literary Criticism series:

BLC = *Black Literature Criticism*
CLC = *Contemporary Literary Criticism*
CLR = *Children's Literature Review*
CMLC = *Classical and Medieval Literature Criticism*
DA = *DISCovering Authors*
DC = *Drama Criticism*
HLC = *Hispanic Literature Criticism*
LC = *Literature Criticism from 1400 to 1800*
NCLC = *Nineteenth-Century Literature Criticism*
PC = *Poetry Criticism*
SSC = *Short Story Criticism*
TCLC = *Twentieth-Century Literary Criticism*
WLC = *World Literature Criticism, 1500 to the Present*

The cross-references

See also CANR 23; CA 85-88;
obituary CA 116

list all author entries in the following Gale biographical and literary sources:

AAYA = *Authors & Artists for Young Adults*
AITN = *Authors in the News*
BEST = *Bestsellers*
BW = *Black Writers*
CA = *Contemporary Authors*
CAAS = *Contemporary Authors Autobiography Series*
CABS = *Contemporary Authors Bibliographical Series*
CANR = *Contemporary Authors New Revision Series*
CAP = *Contemporary Authors Permanent Series*
CDALB = *Concise Dictionary of American Literary Biography*
CDBLB = *Concise Dictionary of British Literary Biography*
DLB = *Dictionary of Literary Biography*
DLBD = *Dictionary of Literary Biography Documentary Series*
DLBY = *Dictionary of Literary Biography Yearbook*
HW = *Hispanic Writers*
JRDA = *Junior DISCovering Authors*
MAICYA = *Major Authors and Illustrators for Children and Young Adults*
MTCW = *Major 20th-Century Writers*
NNAL = *Native North American Literature*
SAAS = *Something about the Author Autobiography Series*
SATA = *Something about the Author*
YABC = *Yesterday's Authors of Books for Children*

Literary Criticism Series
Cumulative Author Index

A. E. . . . . TCLC 3, 10
See also Russell, George William

Abasiyanik, Sait Faik   1906-1954
See Sait Faik
See also CA 123

Abbey, Edward   1927-1989 . . . . . . CLC 36, 59
See also CA 45-48; 128; CANR 2, 41

Abbott, Lee K(ittredge)   1947- . . . . . . CLC 48
See also CA 124; CANR 51; DLB 130

Abe, Kobo   1924-1993 . . . . . CLC 8, 22, 53, 81
See also CA 65-68; 140; CANR 24;
DAM NOV; MTCW

Abelard, Peter   c. 1079-c. 1142 . . . CMLC 11
See also DLB 115

Abell, Kjeld   1901-1961 . . . . CLC 15
See also CA 111

Abish, Walter   1931- . . . . CLC 22
See also CA 101; CANR 37; DLB 130

Abrahams, Peter (Henry)   1919- . . . . . CLC 4
See also BW 1; CA 57-60; CANR 26;
DLB 117; MTCW

Abrams, M(eyer) H(oward)   1912- . . . CLC 24
See also CA 57-60; CANR 13, 33; DLB 67

Abse, Dannie   1923- . . . . . . CLC 7, 29; DAB
See also CA 53-56; CAAS 1; CANR 4, 46;
DAM POET; DLB 27

Achebe, (Albert) Chinua(lumogu)
1930- . . . . . CLC 1, 3, 5, 7, 11, 26, 51, 75;
BLC; DA; DAB; DAC; WLC
See also AAYA 15; BW 2; CA 1-4R;
CANR 6, 26, 47; CLR 20; DAM MST,
MULT, NOV; DLB 117; MAICYA;
MTCW; SATA 40; SATA-Brief 38

Acker, Kathy   1948- . . . . CLC 45
See also CA 117; 122

Ackroyd, Peter   1949- . . . . CLC 34, 52
See also CA 123; 127; CANR 51; DLB 155;
INT 127

Acorn, Milton   1923- . . . . CLC 15; DAC
See also CA 103; DLB 53; INT 103

Adamov, Arthur   1908-1970 . . . . . . CLC 4, 25
See also CA 17-18; 25-28R; CAP 2;
DAM DRAM; MTCW

Adams, Alice (Boyd)   1926- . . . CLC 6, 13, 46
See also CA 81-84; CANR 26, 53;
DLBY 86; INT CANR-26; MTCW

Adams, Andy   1859-1935 . . . . TCLC 56
See also YABC 1

Adams, Douglas (Noel)   1952- . . . CLC 27, 60
See also AAYA 4; BEST 89:3; CA 106;
CANR 34; DAM POP; DLBY 83; JRDA

Adams, Francis   1862-1893 . . . . NCLC 33

Adams, Henry (Brooks)
1838-1918 . . . . . . TCLC 4, 52; DA; DAB;
DAC
See also CA 104; 133; DAM MST; DLB 12,
47

Adams, Richard (George)
1920- . . . . CLC 4, 5, 18
See also AAYA 16; AITN 1, 2; CA 49-52;
CANR 3, 35; CLR 20; DAM NOV;
JRDA; MAICYA; MTCW; SATA 7, 69

Adamson, Joy(-Friederike Victoria)
1910-1980 . . . . CLC 17
See also CA 69-72; 93-96; CANR 22;
MTCW; SATA 11; SATA-Obit 22

Adcock, Fleur   1934- . . . . CLC 41
See also CA 25-28R; CAAS 23; CANR 11,
34; DLB 40

Addams, Charles (Samuel)
1912-1988 . . . . CLC 30
See also CA 61-64; 126; CANR 12

Addison, Joseph   1672-1719 . . . . LC 18
See also CDBLB 1660-1789; DLB 101

Adler, Alfred (F.)   1870-1937 . . . . . . TCLC 61
See also CA 119

Adler, C(arole) S(chwerdtfeger)
1932- . . . . CLC 35
See also AAYA 4; CA 89-92; CANR 19,
40; JRDA; MAICYA; SAAS 15;
SATA 26, 63

Adler, Renata   1938- . . . . CLC 8, 31
See also CA 49-52; CANR 5, 22, 52;
MTCW

Ady, Endre   1877-1919 . . . . TCLC 11
See also CA 107

Aeschylus
525B.C.-456B.C. . . . . CMLC 11; DA;
DAB; DAC
See also DAM DRAM, MST

Afton, Effie
See Harper, Frances Ellen Watkins

Agapida, Fray Antonio
See Irving, Washington

Agee, James (Rufus)
1909-1955 . . . . TCLC 1, 19
See also AITN 1; CA 108; 148;
CDALB 1941-1968; DAM NOV; DLB 2,
26, 152

Aghill, Gordon
See Silverberg, Robert

Agnon, S(hmuel) Y(osef Halevi)
1888-1970 . . . . CLC 4, 8, 14
See also CA 17-18; 25-28R; CAP 2; MTCW

Agrippa von Nettesheim, Henry Cornelius
1486-1535 . . . . LC 27

Aherne, Owen
See Cassill, R(onald) V(erlin)

Ai   1947- . . . . CLC 4, 14, 69
See also CA 85-88; CAAS 13; DLB 120

Aickman, Robert (Fordyce)
1914-1981 . . . . CLC 57
See also CA 5-8R; CANR 3

Aiken, Conrad (Potter)
1889-1973 . . . CLC 1, 3, 5, 10, 52; SSC 9
See also CA 5-8R; 45-48; CANR 4;
CDALB 1929-1941; DAM NOV, POET;
DLB 9, 45, 102; MTCW; SATA 3, 30

Aiken, Joan (Delano)   1924- . . . . CLC 35
See also AAYA 1; CA 9-12R; CANR 4, 23,
34; CLR 1, 19; DLB 161; JRDA;
MAICYA; MTCW; SAAS 1; SATA 2,
30, 73

Ainsworth, William Harrison
1805-1882 . . . . NCLC 13
See also DLB 21; SATA 24

Aitmatov, Chingiz (Torekulovich)
1928- . . . . CLC 71
See also CA 103; CANR 38; MTCW;
SATA 56

Akers, Floyd
See Baum, L(yman) Frank

Akhmadulina, Bella Akhatovna
1937- . . . . CLC 53
See also CA 65-68; DAM POET

Akhmatova, Anna
1888-1966 . . . . CLC 11, 25, 64; PC 2
See also CA 19-20; 25-28R; CANR 35;
CAP 1; DAM POET; MTCW

Aksakov, Sergei Timofeyvich
1791-1859 . . . . NCLC 2

Aksenov, Vassily
See Aksyonov, Vassily (Pavlovich)

Aksyonov, Vassily (Pavlovich)
1932- . . . . CLC 22, 37
See also CA 53-56; CANR 12, 48

Akutagawa Ryunosuke
1892-1927 . . . . TCLC 16
See also CA 117

Alain   1868-1951 . . . . TCLC 41

Alain-Fournier . . . . TCLC 6
See also Fournier, Henri Alban
See also DLB 65

Alarcon, Pedro Antonio de
1833-1891 . . . . NCLC 1

Alas (y Urena), Leopoldo (Enrique Garcia)
1852-1901 . . . . TCLC 29
See also CA 113; 131; HW

Albee, Edward (Franklin III)
1928- . . . . . . CLC 1, 2, 3, 5, 9, 11, 13, 25,
53, 86; DA; DAB; DAC; WLC
See also AITN 1; CA 5-8R; CABS 3;
CANR 8; CDALB 1941-1968;
DAM DRAM, MST; DLB 7;
INT CANR-8; MTCW

Alberti, Rafael   1902- . . . . CLC 7
See also CA 85-88; DLB 108

Albert the Great   1200(?)-1280 . . . . CMLC 16
See also DLB 115

Alcala-Galiano, Juan Valera y
See Valera y Alcala-Galiano, Juan

Andrade, Mario de 1893-1945..... **TCLC 43**

Andreae, Johann V(alentin)
      1586-1654 .... **LC 32**
   See also DLB 164

Andreas-Salome, Lou 1861-1937... **TCLC 56**
   See also DLB 66

Andrewes, Lancelot 1555-1626 .... **LC 5**
   See also DLB 151

Andrews, Cicily Fairfield
   See West, Rebecca

Andrews, Elton V.
   See Pohl, Frederik

Andreyev, Leonid (Nikolaevich)
      1871-1919 .... **TCLC 3**
   See also CA 104

Andric, Ivo 1892-1975 .... **CLC 8**
   See also CA 81-84; 57-60; CANR 43;
      DLB 147; MTCW

Angelique, Pierre
   See Bataille, Georges

Angell, Roger 1920- .... **CLC 26**
   See also CA 57-60; CANR 13, 44

Angelou, Maya
      1928- .... **CLC 12, 35, 64, 77; BLC; DA;**
                                DAB; DAC
   See also AAYA 7; BW 2; CA 65-68;
      CANR 19, 42; DAM MST, MULT,
      POET, POP; DLB 38; MTCW; SATA 49

Annensky, Innokenty Fyodorovich
      1856-1909 .... **TCLC 14**
   See also CA 110

Anon, Charles Robert
   See Pessoa, Fernando (Antonio Nogueira)

Anouilh, Jean (Marie Lucien Pierre)
      1910-1987 ...... **CLC 1, 3, 8, 13, 40, 50**
   See also CA 17-20R; 123; CANR 32;
      DAM DRAM; MTCW

Anthony, Florence
   See Ai

Anthony, John
   See Ciardi, John (Anthony)

Anthony, Peter
   See Shaffer, Anthony (Joshua); Shaffer,
      Peter (Levin)

Anthony, Piers 1934-.............. **CLC 35**
   See also AAYA 11; CA 21-24R; CANR 28;
      DAM POP; DLB 8; MTCW; SAAS 22;
      SATA 84

Antoine, Marc
   See Proust, (Valentin-Louis-George-Eugene-)
      Marcel

Antoninus, Brother
   See Everson, William (Oliver)

Antonioni, Michelangelo 1912- ..... **CLC 20**
   See also CA 73-76; CANR 45

Antschel, Paul 1920-1970
   See Celan, Paul
   See also CA 85-88; CANR 33; MTCW

Anwar, Chairil 1922-1949 .... **TCLC 22**
   See also CA 121

Apollinaire, Guillaume .. **TCLC 3, 8, 51; PC 7**
   See also Kostrowitzki, Wilhelm Apollinaris
      de
   See also DAM POET

Appelfeld, Aharon 1932- .... **CLC 23, 47**
   See also CA 112; 133

Apple, Max (Isaac) 1941-........ **CLC 9, 33**
   See also CA 81-84; CANR 19; DLB 130

Appleman, Philip (Dean) 1926- ..... **CLC 51**
   See also CA 13-16R; CAAS 18; CANR 6,
      29

Appleton, Lawrence
   See Lovecraft, H(oward) P(hillips)

Apteryx
   See Eliot, T(homas) S(tearns)

Apuleius, (Lucius Madaurensis)
      125(?)-175(?) .... **CMLC 1**

Aquin, Hubert 1929-1977......... **CLC 15**
   See also CA 105; DLB 53

Aragon, Louis 1897-1982 .... **CLC 3, 22**
   See also CA 69-72; 108; CANR 28;
      DAM NOV, POET; DLB 72; MTCW

Arany, Janos 1817-1882........ **NCLC 34**

Arbuthnot, John 1667-1735 .... **LC 1**
   See also DLB 101

Archer, Herbert Winslow
   See Mencken, H(enry) L(ouis)

Archer, Jeffrey (Howard) 1940- .... **CLC 28**
   See also AAYA 16; BEST 89:3; CA 77-80;
      CANR 22, 52; DAM POP;
      INT CANR-22

Archer, Jules 1915- .... **CLC 12**
   See also CA 9-12R; CANR 6; SAAS 5;
      SATA 4, 85

Archer, Lee
   See Ellison, Harlan (Jay)

Arden, John 1930- .... **CLC 6, 13, 15**
   See also CA 13-16R; CAAS 4; CANR 31;
      DAM DRAM; DLB 13; MTCW

Arenas, Reinaldo
      1943-1990 .... **CLC 41; HLC**
   See also CA 124; 128; 133; DAM MULT;
      DLB 145; HW

Arendt, Hannah 1906-1975 .... **CLC 66**
   See also CA 17-20R; 61-64; CANR 26;
      MTCW

Aretino, Pietro 1492-1556 .... **LC 12**

Arghezi, Tudor.................... **CLC 80**
   See also Theodorescu, Ion N.

Arguedas, Jose Maria
      1911-1969 .... **CLC 10, 18**
   See also CA 89-92; DLB 113; HW

Argueta, Manlio 1936-............ **CLC 31**
   See also CA 131; DLB 145; HW

Ariosto, Ludovico 1474-1533........ **LC 6**

Aristides
   See Epstein, Joseph

Aristophanes
      450B.C.-385B.C. .... **CMLC 4; DA;**
                            DAB; DAC; DC 2
   See also DAM DRAM, MST

Arlt, Roberto (Godofredo Christophersen)
      1900-1942 .... **TCLC 29; HLC**
   See also CA 123; 131; DAM MULT; HW

Armah, Ayi Kwei 1939-.... **CLC 5, 33; BLC**
   See also BW 1; CA 61-64; CANR 21;
      DAM MULT, POET; DLB 117; MTCW

Armatrading, Joan 1950-.......... **CLC 17**
   See also CA 114

Arnette, Robert
   See Silverberg, Robert

**Arnim, Achim von (Ludwig Joachim von
      Arnim)** 1781-1831 .... **NCLC 5**
   See also DLB 90

Arnim, Bettina von 1785-1859.... **NCLC 38**
   See also DLB 90

Arnold, Matthew
      1822-1888 ..... **NCLC 6, 29; DA; DAB;**
                            DAC; PC 5; WLC
   See also CDBLB 1832-1890; DAM MST,
      POET; DLB 32, 57

Arnold, Thomas 1795-1842 ...... **NCLC 18**
   See also DLB 55

Arnow, Harriette (Louisa) Simpson
      1908-1986 .... **CLC 2, 7, 18**
   See also CA 9-12R; 118; CANR 14; DLB 6;
      MTCW; SATA 42; SATA-Obit 47

Arp, Hans
   See Arp, Jean

Arp, Jean 1887-1966............... **CLC 5**
   See also CA 81-84; 25-28R; CANR 42

Arrabal
   See Arrabal, Fernando

Arrabal, Fernando 1932- ... **CLC 2, 9, 18, 58**
   See also CA 9-12R; CANR 15

Arrick, Fran.................... **CLC 30**
   See also Gaberman, Judie Angell

Artaud, Antonin (Marie Joseph)
      1896-1948 .... **TCLC 3, 36**
   See also CA 104; 149; DAM DRAM

Arthur, Ruth M(abel) 1905-1979.... **CLC 12**
   See also CA 9-12R; 85-88; CANR 4;
      SATA 7, 26

Artsybashev, Mikhail (Petrovich)
      1878-1927 .... **TCLC 31**

Arundel, Honor (Morfydd)
      1919-1973 .... **CLC 17**
   See also CA 21-22; 41-44R; CAP 2;
      CLR 35; SATA 4; SATA-Obit 24

Asch, Sholem 1880-1957 .... **TCLC 3**
   See also CA 105

Ash, Shalom
   See Asch, Sholem

Ashbery, John (Lawrence)
      1927-...... **CLC 2, 3, 4, 6, 9, 13, 15, 25,**
                                41, 77
   See also CA 5-8R; CANR 9, 37;
      DAM POET; DLB 5, 165; DLBY 81;
      INT CANR-9; MTCW

Ashdown, Clifford
   See Freeman, R(ichard) Austin

Ashe, Gordon
   See Creasey, John

Ashton-Warner, Sylvia (Constance)
      1908-1984 .... **CLC 19**
   See also CA 69-72; 112; CANR 29; MTCW

Asimov, Isaac
1920-1992 ... **CLC 1, 3, 9, 19, 26, 76, 92**
See also AAYA 13; BEST 90:2; CA 1-4R;
137; CANR 2, 19, 36; CLR 12;
DAM POP; DLB 8; DLBY 92;
INT CANR-19; JRDA; MAICYA;
MTCW; SATA 1, 26, 74

Astley, Thea (Beatrice May)
1925- .... **CLC 41**
See also CA 65-68; CANR 11, 43

Aston, James
See White, T(erence) H(anbury)

Asturias, Miguel Angel
1899-1974 .... **CLC 3, 8, 13; HLC**
See also CA 25-28; 49-52; CANR 32;
CAP 2; DAM MULT, NOV; DLB 113;
HW; MTCW

Atares, Carlos Saura
See Saura (Atares), Carlos

Atheling, William
See Pound, Ezra (Weston Loomis)

Atheling, William, Jr.
See Blish, James (Benjamin)

Atherton, Gertrude (Franklin Horn)
1857-1948 ....**TCLC 2**
See also CA 104; DLB 9, 78

Atherton, Lucius
See Masters, Edgar Lee

Atkins, Jack
See Harris, Mark

Attaway, William (Alexander)
1911-1986 .... **CLC 92; BLC**
See also BW 2; CA 143; DAM MULT;
DLB 76

Atticus
See Fleming, Ian (Lancaster)

Atwood, Margaret (Eleanor)
1939- ..... **CLC 2, 3, 4, 8, 13, 15, 25, 44,
84; DA; DAB; DAC; PC 8; SSC 2; WLC**
See also AAYA 12; BEST 89:2; CA 49-52;
CANR 3, 24, 33; DAM MST, NOV,
POET; DLB 53; INT CANR-24; MTCW;
SATA 50

Aubigny, Pierre d'
See Mencken, H(enry) L(ouis)

Aubin, Penelope 1685-1731(?)........ **LC 9**
See also DLB 39

Auchincloss, Louis (Stanton)
1917- ...... **CLC 4, 6, 9, 18, 45; SSC 22**
See also CA 1-4R; CANR 6, 29;
DAM NOV; DLB 2; DLBY 80;
INT CANR-29; MTCW

Auden, W(ystan) H(ugh)
1907-1973 ...... **CLC 1, 2, 3, 4, 6, 9, 11,
14, 43; DA; DAB; DAC; PC 1; WLC**
See also AAYA 18; CA 9-12R; 45-48;
CANR 5; CDBLB 1914-1945;
DAM DRAM, MST, POET; DLB 10, 20;
MTCW

Audiberti, Jacques 1900-1965 ...... **CLC 38**
See also CA 25-28R; DAM DRAM

Audubon, John James
1785-1851 .... **NCLC 47**

Auel, Jean M(arie) 1936-.......... **CLC 31**
See also AAYA 7; BEST 90:4; CA 103;
CANR 21; DAM POP; INT CANR-21

Auerbach, Erich 1892-1957 ...... **TCLC 43**
See also CA 118

Augier, Emile 1820-1889 .... **NCLC 31**

August, John
See De Voto, Bernard (Augustine)

Augustine, St. 354-430 ..... **CMLC 6; DAB**

Aurelius
See Bourne, Randolph S(illiman)

Aurobindo, Sri 1872-1950 .... **TCLC 63**

Austen, Jane
1775-1817 ..... **NCLC 1, 13, 19, 33, 51;
DA; DAB; DAC; WLC**
See also CDBLB 1789-1832; DAM MST,
NOV; DLB 116

Auster, Paul 1947- .... **CLC 47**
See also CA 69-72; CANR 23, 52

Austin, Frank
See Faust, Frederick (Schiller)

Austin, Mary (Hunter)
1868-1934 .... **TCLC 25**
See also CA 109; DLB 9, 78

Autran Dourado, Waldomiro
See Dourado, (Waldomiro Freitas) Autran

Averroes 1126-1198 .... **CMLC 7**
See also DLB 115

Avicenna 980-1037 .... **CMLC 16**
See also DLB 115

Avison, Margaret 1918-.... **CLC 2, 4; DAC**
See also CA 17-20R; DAM POET; DLB 53;
MTCW

Axton, David
See Koontz, Dean R(ay)

Ayckbourn, Alan
1939- .... **CLC 5, 8, 18, 33, 74; DAB**
See also CA 21-24R; CANR 31;
DAM DRAM; DLB 13; MTCW

Aydy, Catherine
See Tennant, Emma (Christina)

Ayme, Marcel (Andre) 1902-1967... **CLC 11**
See also CA 89-92; CLR 25; DLB 72

Ayrton, Michael 1921-1975......... **CLC 7**
See also CA 5-8R; 61-64; CANR 9, 21

Azorin........................... **CLC 11**
See also Martinez Ruiz, Jose

Azuela, Mariano
1873-1952 .... **TCLC 3; HLC**
See also CA 104; 131; DAM MULT; HW;
MTCW

Baastad, Babbis Friis
See Friis-Baastad, Babbis Ellinor

Bab
See Gilbert, W(illiam) S(chwenck)

Babbis, Eleanor
See Friis-Baastad, Babbis Ellinor

Babel, Isaak (Emmanuilovich)
1894-1941(?) ...... **TCLC 2, 13; SSC 16**
See also CA 104

Babits, Mihaly 1883-1941 .... **TCLC 14**
See also CA 114

Babur 1483-1530.................. **LC 18**

Bacchelli, Riccardo 1891-1985 ..... **CLC 19**
See also CA 29-32R; 117

Bach, Richard (David) 1936-........ **CLC 14**
See also AITN 1; BEST 89:2; CA 9-12R;
CANR 18; DAM NOV, POP; MTCW;
SATA 13

Bachman, Richard
See King, Stephen (Edwin)

Bachmann, Ingeborg 1926-1973..... **CLC 69**
See also CA 93-96; 45-48; DLB 85

Bacon, Francis 1561-1626 .... **LC 18, 32**
See also CDBLB Before 1660; DLB 151

Bacon, Roger 1214(?)-1292 ...... **CMLC 14**
See also DLB 115

Bacovia, George................. **TCLC 24**
See also Vasiliu, Gheorghe

Badanes, Jerome 1937-........... **CLC 59**

Bagehot, Walter 1826-1877 ...... **NCLC 10**
See also DLB 55

Bagnold, Enid 1889-1981.......... **CLC 25**
See also CA 5-8R; 103; CANR 5, 40;
DAM DRAM; DLB 13, 160; MAICYA;
SATA 1, 25

Bagritsky, Eduard 1895-1934 ..... **TCLC 60**

Bagrjana, Elisaveta
See Belcheva, Elisaveta

Bagryana, Elisaveta............. **CLC 10**
See also Belcheva, Elisaveta
See also DLB 147

Bailey, Paul 1937- .... **CLC 45**
See also CA 21-24R; CANR 16; DLB 14

Baillie, Joanna 1762-1851 .... **NCLC 2**
See also DLB 93

Bainbridge, Beryl (Margaret)
1933- .... **CLC 4, 5, 8, 10, 14, 18, 22, 62**
See also CA 21-24R; CANR 24;
DAM NOV; DLB 14; MTCW

Baker, Elliott 1922- .... **CLC 8**
See also CA 45-48; CANR 2

Baker, Nicholson 1957-........... **CLC 61**
See also CA 135; DAM POP

Baker, Ray Stannard 1870-1946 ... **TCLC 47**
See also CA 118

Baker, Russell (Wayne) 1925-...... **CLC 31**
See also BEST 89:4; CA 57-60; CANR 11,
41; MTCW

Bakhtin, M.
See Bakhtin, Mikhail Mikhailovich

Bakhtin, M. M.
See Bakhtin, Mikhail Mikhailovich

Bakhtin, Mikhail
See Bakhtin, Mikhail Mikhailovich

Bakhtin, Mikhail Mikhailovich
1895-1975 .... **CLC 83**
See also CA 128; 113

Bakshi, Ralph 1938(?)-............ **CLC 26**
See also CA 112; 138

Bakunin, Mikhail (Alexandrovich)
1814-1876 .... **NCLC 25**

Baldwin, James (Arthur)
1924-1987 ...... CLC 1, 2, 3, 4, 5, 8, 13,
15, 17, 42, 50, 67, 90; BLC; DA; DAB;
DAC; DC 1; SSC 10; WLC
See also AAYA 4; BW 1; CA 1-4R; 124;
CABS 1; CANR 3, 24;
CDALB 1941-1968; DAM MST, MULT,
NOV, POP; DLB 2, 7, 33; DLBY 87;
MTCW; SATA 9; SATA-Obit 54

Ballard, J(ames) G(raham)
1930- .... CLC 3, 6, 14, 36; SSC 1
See also AAYA 3; CA 5-8R; CANR 15, 39;
DAM NOV, POP; DLB 14; MTCW

Balmont, Konstantin (Dmitriyevich)
1867-1943 .... TCLC 11
See also CA 109

Balzac, Honore de
1799-1850 .... NCLC 5, 35, 53; DA;
DAB; DAC; SSC 5; WLC
See also DAM MST, NOV; DLB 119

Bambara, Toni Cade
1939-1995 ...... CLC 19, 88; BLC; DA;
DAC
See also AAYA 5; BW 2; CA 29-32R; 150;
CANR 24, 49; DAM MST, MULT;
DLB 38; MTCW

Bamdad, A.
See Shamlu, Ahmad

Banat, D. R.
See Bradbury, Ray (Douglas)

Bancroft, Laura
See Baum, L(yman) Frank

Banim, John 1798-1842 .... NCLC 13
See also DLB 116, 158, 159

Banim, Michael 1796-1874 ...... NCLC 13
See also DLB 158, 159

Banks, Iain
See Banks, Iain M(enzies)

Banks, Iain M(enzies) 1954- .... CLC 34
See also CA 123; 128; INT 128

Banks, Lynne Reid .... CLC 23
See also Reid Banks, Lynne
See also AAYA 6

Banks, Russell 1940- .... CLC 37, 72
See also CA 65-68; CAAS 15; CANR 19,
52; DLB 130

Banville, John 1945- .... CLC 46
See also CA 117; 128; DLB 14; INT 128

Banville, Theodore (Faullain) de
1832-1891 .... NCLC 9

Baraka, Amiri
1934- .... CLC 1, 2, 3, 5, 10, 14, 33;
BLC; DA; DAC; DC 6; PC 4
See also Jones, LeRoi
See also BW 2; CA 21-24R; CABS 3;
CANR 27, 38; CDALB 1941-1968;
DAM MST, MULT, POET, POP;
DLB 5, 7, 16, 38; DLBD 8; MTCW

Barbauld, Anna Laetitia
1743-1825 .... NCLC 50
See also DLB 107, 109, 142, 158

Barbellion, W. N. P. .... TCLC 24
See also Cummings, Bruce F(rederick)

Barbera, Jack (Vincent) 1945- ...... CLC 44
See also CA 110; CANR 45

Barbey d'Aurevilly, Jules Amedee
1808-1889 .... NCLC 1; SSC 17
See also DLB 119

Barbusse, Henri 1873-1935 .... TCLC 5
See also CA 105; DLB 65

Barclay, Bill
See Moorcock, Michael (John)

Barclay, William Ewert
See Moorcock, Michael (John)

Barea, Arturo 1897-1957 .... TCLC 14
See also CA 111

Barfoot, Joan 1946- .... CLC 18
See also CA 105

Baring, Maurice 1874-1945 .... TCLC 8
See also CA 105; DLB 34

Barker, Clive 1952- .... CLC 52
See also AAYA 10; BEST 90:3; CA 121;
129; DAM POP; INT 129; MTCW

Barker, George Granville
1913-1991 .... CLC 8, 48
See also CA 9-12R; 135; CANR 7, 38;
DAM POET; DLB 20; MTCW

Barker, Harley Granville
See Granville-Barker, Harley
See also DLB 10

Barker, Howard 1946- .... CLC 37
See also CA 102; DLB 13

Barker, Pat(ricia) 1943- .... CLC 32, 94
See also CA 117; 122; CANR 50; INT 122

Barlow, Joel 1754-1812 .... NCLC 23
See also DLB 37

Barnard, Mary (Ethel) 1909- ...... CLC 48
See also CA 21-22; CAP 2

Barnes, Djuna
1892-1982 ... CLC 3, 4, 8, 11, 29; SSC 3
See also CA 9-12R; 107; CANR 16; DLB 4,
9, 45; MTCW

Barnes, Julian 1946- .... CLC 42; DAB
See also CA 102; CANR 19; DLBY 93

Barnes, Peter 1931- .... CLC 5, 56
See also CA 65-68; CAAS 12; CANR 33,
34; DLB 13; MTCW

Baroja (y Nessi), Pio
1872-1956 .... TCLC 8; HLC
See also CA 104

Baron, David
See Pinter, Harold

Baron Corvo
See Rolfe, Frederick (William Serafino
Austin Lewis Mary)

Barondess, Sue K(aufman)
1926-1977 .... CLC 8
See also Kaufman, Sue
See also CA 1-4R; 69-72; CANR 1

Baron de Teive
See Pessoa, Fernando (Antonio Nogueira)

Barres, Maurice 1862-1923 ...... TCLC 47
See also DLB 123

Barreto, Afonso Henrique de Lima
See Lima Barreto, Afonso Henrique de

Barrett, (Roger) Syd 1946- .... CLC 35

Barrett, William (Christopher)
1913-1992 .... CLC 27
See also CA 13-16R; 139; CANR 11;
INT CANR-11

Barrie, J(ames) M(atthew)
1860-1937 .... TCLC 2; DAB
See also CA 104; 136; CDBLB 1890-1914;
CLR 16; DAM DRAM; DLB 10, 141,
156; MAICYA; YABC 1

Barrington, Michael
See Moorcock, Michael (John)

Barrol, Grady
See Bograd, Larry

Barry, Mike
See Malzberg, Barry N(athaniel)

Barry, Philip 1896-1949 .... TCLC 11
See also CA 109; DLB 7

Bart, Andre Schwarz
See Schwarz-Bart, Andre

Barth, John (Simmons)
1930- ...... CLC 1, 2, 3, 5, 7, 9, 10, 14,
27, 51, 89; SSC 10
See also AITN 1, 2; CA 1-4R; CABS 1;
CANR 5, 23, 49; DAM NOV; DLB 2;
MTCW

Barthelme, Donald
1931-1989 ...... CLC 1, 2, 3, 5, 6, 8, 13,
23, 46, 59; SSC 2
See also CA 21-24R; 129; CANR 20;
DAM NOV; DLB 2; DLBY 80, 89;
MTCW; SATA 7; SATA-Obit 62

Barthelme, Frederick 1943- .... CLC 36
See also CA 114; 122; DLBY 85; INT 122

Barthes, Roland (Gerard)
1915-1980 .... CLC 24, 83
See also CA 130; 97-100; MTCW

Barzun, Jacques (Martin) 1907- .... CLC 51
See also CA 61-64; CANR 22

Bashevis, Isaac
See Singer, Isaac Bashevis

Bashkirtseff, Marie 1859-1884 ... NCLC 27

Basho
See Matsuo Basho

Bass, Kingsley B., Jr.
See Bullins, Ed

Bass, Rick 1958- .... CLC 79
See also CA 126; CANR 53

Bassani, Giorgio 1916- .... CLC 9
See also CA 65-68; CANR 33; DLB 128;
MTCW

Bastos, Augusto (Antonio) Roa
See Roa Bastos, Augusto (Antonio)

Bataille, Georges 1897-1962 .... CLC 29
See also CA 101; 89-92

Bates, H(erbert) E(rnest)
1905-1974 ...... CLC 46; DAB; SSC 10
See also CA 93-96; 45-48; CANR 34;
DAM POP; DLB 162; MTCW

Bauchart
See Camus, Albert

Baudelaire, Charles
1821-1867 .... NCLC 6, 29, 55; DA;
DAB; DAC; PC 1; SSC 18; WLC
See also DAM MST, POET

Baudrillard, Jean 1929- .... CLC 60

Baum, L(yman) Frank   1856-1919 . . . TCLC 7
See also CA 108; 133; CLR 15; DLB 22;
JRDA; MAICYA; MTCW; SATA 18

Baum, Louis F.
See Baum, L(yman) Frank

Baumbach, Jonathan   1933- . . . . . . CLC 6, 23
See also CA 13-16R; CAAS 5; CANR 12;
DLBY 80; INT CANR-12; MTCW

Bausch, Richard (Carl)   1945- . . . . . . CLC 51
See also CA 101; CAAS 14; CANR 43;
DLB 130

Baxter, Charles   1947- . . . . CLC 45, 78
See also CA 57-60; CANR 40; DAM POP;
DLB 130

Baxter, George Owen
See Faust, Frederick (Schiller)

Baxter, James K(eir)   1926-1972 . . . . CLC 14
See also CA 77-80

Baxter, John
See Hunt, E(verette) Howard, (Jr.)

Bayer, Sylvia
See Glassco, John

Baynton, Barbara   1857-1929 . . . . . . TCLC 57

Beagle, Peter S(oyer)   1939- . . . . CLC 7
See also CA 9-12R; CANR 4, 51;
DLBY 80; INT CANR-4; SATA 60

Bean, Normal
See Burroughs, Edgar Rice

Beard, Charles A(ustin)
1874-1948 . . . . TCLC 15
See also CA 115; DLB 17; SATA 18

Beardsley, Aubrey   1872-1898 . . . . . NCLC 6

Beattie, Ann
1947- . . . . CLC 8, 13, 18, 40, 63; SSC 11
See also BEST 90:2; CA 81-84; CANR 53;
DAM NOV, POP; DLBY 82; MTCW

Beattie, James   1735-1803 . . . . NCLC 25
See also DLB 109

Beauchamp, Kathleen Mansfield   1888-1923
See Mansfield, Katherine
See also CA 104; 134; DA; DAC;
DAM MST

Beaumarchais, Pierre-Augustin Caron de
1732-1799 . . . . DC 4
See also DAM DRAM

Beaumont, Francis
1584(?)-1616 . . . . LC 33; DC 6
See also CDBLB Before 1660; DLB 58, 121

Beauvoir, Simone (Lucie Ernestine Marie
Bertrand) de
1908-1986 . . . . CLC 1, 2, 4, 8, 14, 31, 44,
50, 71; DA; DAB; DAC; WLC
See also CA 9-12R; 118; CANR 28;
DAM MST, NOV; DLB 72; DLBY 86;
MTCW

Becker, Carl   1873-1945 . . . . TCLC 63:
See also DLB 17

Becker, Jurek   1937- . . . . CLC 7, 19
See also CA 85-88; DLB 75

Becker, Walter   1950- . . . . CLC 26

Beckett, Samuel (Barclay)
1906-1989 . . . . . . CLC 1, 2, 3, 4, 6, 9, 10,
11, 14, 18, 29, 57, 59, 83; DA; DAB;
DAC; SSC 16; WLC
See also CA 5-8R; 130; CANR 33;
CDBLB 1945-1960; DAM DRAM, MST,
NOV; DLB 13, 15; DLBY 90; MTCW

Beckford, William   1760-1844 . . . . NCLC 16
See also DLB 39

Beckman, Gunnel   1910- . . . . CLC 26
See also CA 33-36R; CANR 15; CLR 25;
MAICYA; SAAS 9; SATA 6

Becque, Henri   1837-1899 . . . . NCLC 3

Beddoes, Thomas Lovell
1803-1849 . . . . NCLC 3
See also DLB 96

Bedford, Donald F.
See Fearing, Kenneth (Flexner)

Beecher, Catharine Esther
1800-1878 . . . . NCLC 30
See also DLB 1

Beecher, John   1904-1980 . . . . CLC 6
See also AITN 1; CA 5-8R; 105; CANR 8

Beer, Johann   1655-1700 . . . . LC 5

Beer, Patricia   1924- . . . . CLC 58
See also CA 61-64; CANR 13, 46; DLB 40

Beerbohm, Henry Maximilian
1872-1956 . . . . TCLC 1, 24
See also CA 104; DLB 34, 100

Beerbohm, Max
See Beerbohm, Henry Maximilian

Beer-Hofmann, Richard
1866-1945 . . . . TCLC 60
See also DLB 81

Begiebing, Robert J(ohn)   1946- . . . . . CLC 70
See also CA 122; CANR 40

Behan, Brendan
1923-1964 . . . . CLC 1, 8, 11, 15, 79
See also CA 73-76; CANR 33;
CDBLB 1945-1960; DAM DRAM;
DLB 13; MTCW

Behn, Aphra
1640(?)-1689 . . . . . . LC 1, 30; DA; DAB;
DAC; DC 4; PC 13; WLC
See also DAM DRAM, MST, NOV, POET;
DLB 39, 80, 131

Behrman, S(amuel) N(athaniel)
1893-1973 . . . . CLC 40
See also CA 13-16; 45-48; CAP 1; DLB 7,
44

Belasco, David   1853-1931 . . . . TCLC 3
See also CA 104; DLB 7

Belcheva, Elisaveta   1893- . . . . CLC 10
See also Bagryana, Elisaveta

Beldone, Phil "Cheech"
See Ellison, Harlan (Jay)

Beleno
See Azuela, Mariano

Belinski, Vissarion Grigoryevich
1811-1848 . . . . NCLC 5

Belitt, Ben   1911- . . . . CLC 22
See also CA 13-16R; CAAS 4; CANR 7;
DLB 5

Bell, James Madison
1826-1902 . . . . TCLC 43; BLC
See also BW 1; CA 122; 124; DAM MULT;
DLB 50

Bell, Madison (Smartt)   1957- . . . . . . CLC 41
See also CA 111; CANR 28

Bell, Marvin (Hartley)   1937- . . . . . CLC 8, 31
See also CA 21-24R; CAAS 14;
DAM POET; DLB 5; MTCW

Bell, W. L. D.
See Mencken, H(enry) L(ouis)

Bellamy, Atwood C.
See Mencken, H(enry) L(ouis)

Bellamy, Edward   1850-1898 . . . . . . NCLC 4
See also DLB 12

Bellin, Edward J.
See Kuttner, Henry

Belloc, (Joseph) Hilaire (Pierre)
1870-1953 . . . . TCLC 7, 18
See also CA 106; DAM POET; DLB 19,
100, 141; YABC 1

Belloc, Joseph Peter Rene Hilaire
See Belloc, (Joseph) Hilaire (Pierre)

Belloc, Joseph Pierre Hilaire
See Belloc, (Joseph) Hilaire (Pierre)

Belloc, M. A.
See Lowndes, Marie Adelaide (Belloc)

Bellow, Saul
1915- . . . . . . CLC 1, 2, 3, 6, 8, 10, 13, 15,
25, 33, 34, 63, 79; DA; DAB; DAC;
SSC 14; WLC
See also AITN 2; BEST 89:3; CA 5-8R;
CABS 1; CANR 29, 53;
CDALB 1941-1968; DAM MST, NOV,
POP; DLB 2, 28; DLBD 3; DLBY 82;
MTCW

Belser, Reimond Karel Maria de   1929-
See Ruyslinck, Ward
See also CA 152

Bely, Andrey . . . . TCLC 7; PC 11
See also Bugayev, Boris Nikolayevich

Benary, Margot
See Benary-Isbert, Margot

Benary-Isbert, Margot   1889-1979 . . . CLC 12
See also CA 5-8R; 89-92; CANR 4;
CLR 12; MAICYA; SATA 2;
SATA-Obit 21

Benavente (y Martinez), Jacinto
1866-1954 . . . . TCLC 3
See also CA 106; 131; DAM DRAM,
MULT; HW; MTCW

Benchley, Peter (Bradford)
1940- . . . . CLC 4, 8
See also AAYA 14; AITN 2; CA 17-20R;
CANR 12, 35; DAM NOV, POP;
MTCW; SATA 3

Benchley, Robert (Charles)
1889-1945 . . . . TCLC 1, 55
See also CA 105; DLB 11

Benda, Julien   1867-1956 . . . . TCLC 60
See also CA 120

Benedict, Ruth   1887-1948 . . . . TCLC 60

Benedikt, Michael   1935- . . . . CLC 4, 14
See also CA 13-16R; CANR 7; DLB 5

Benet, Juan 1927-............... **CLC 28**
See also CA 143

Benet, Stephen Vincent
1898-1943 .... **TCLC 7; SSC 10**
See also CA 104; DAM POET; DLB 4, 48, 102; YABC 1

Benet, William Rose 1886-1950 ... **TCLC 28**
See also CA 118; DAM POET; DLB 45

Benford, Gregory (Albert) 1941-.... **CLC 52**
See also CA 69-72; CANR 12, 24, 49; DLBY 82

Bengtsson, Frans (Gunnar)
1894-1954 .... **TCLC 48**

Benjamin, David
See Slavitt, David R(ytman)

Benjamin, Lois
See Gould, Lois

Benjamin, Walter 1892-1940 ..... **TCLC 39**

Benn, Gottfried 1886-1956........ **TCLC 3**
See also CA 106; DLB 56

Bennett, Alan 1934-..... **CLC 45, 77; DAB**
See also CA 103; CANR 35; DAM MST; MTCW

Bennett, (Enoch) Arnold
1867-1931 .... **TCLC 5, 20**
See also CA 106; CDBLB 1890-1914; DLB 10, 34, 98, 135

Bennett, Elizabeth
See Mitchell, Margaret (Munnerlyn)

Bennett, George Harold 1930-
See Bennett, Hal
See also BW 1; CA 97-100

Bennett, Hal .... **CLC 5**
See also Bennett, George Harold
See also DLB 33

Bennett, Jay 1912-............... **CLC 35**
See also AAYA 10; CA 69-72; CANR 11, 42; JRDA; SAAS 4; SATA 41, 87; SATA-Brief 27

Bennett, Louise (Simone)
1919- .... **CLC 28; BLC**
See also BW 2; CA 151; DAM MULT; DLB 117

Benson, E(dward) F(rederic)
1867-1940 .... **TCLC 27**
See also CA 114; DLB 135, 153

Benson, Jackson J. 1930-......... **CLC 34**
See also CA 25-28R; DLB 111

Benson, Sally 1900-1972 .... **CLC 17**
See also CA 19-20; 37-40R; CAP 1; SATA 1, 35; SATA-Obit 27

Benson, Stella 1892-1933........ **TCLC 17**
See also CA 117; DLB 36, 162

Bentham, Jeremy 1748-1832 ..... **NCLC 38**
See also DLB 107, 158

Bentley, E(dmund) C(lerihew)
1875-1956 .... **TCLC 12**
See also CA 108; DLB 70

Bentley, Eric (Russell) 1916-....... **CLC 24**
See also CA 5-8R; CANR 6; INT CANR-6

Beranger, Pierre Jean de
1780-1857 .... **NCLC 34**

Berendt, John (Lawrence) 1939-.... **CLC 86**
See also CA 146

Berger, Colonel
See Malraux, (Georges-)Andre

Berger, John (Peter) 1926- ...... **CLC 2, 19**
See also CA 81-84; CANR 51; DLB 14

Berger, Melvin H. 1927-.......... **CLC 12**
See also CA 5-8R; CANR 4; CLR 32; SAAS 2; SATA 5, 88

Berger, Thomas (Louis)
1924- .... **CLC 3, 5, 8, 11, 18, 38**
See also CA 1-4R; CANR 5, 28, 51; DAM NOV; DLB 2; DLBY 80; INT CANR-28; MTCW

Bergman, (Ernst) Ingmar
1918- .... **CLC 16, 72**
See also CA 81-84; CANR 33

Bergson, Henri 1859-1941........ **TCLC 32**

Bergstein, Eleanor 1938-.......... **CLC 4**
See also CA 53-56; CANR 5

Berkoff, Steven 1937-............ **CLC 56**
See also CA 104

Bermant, Chaim (Icyk) 1929- ...... **CLC 40**
See also CA 57-60; CANR 6, 31

Bern, Victoria
See Fisher, M(ary) F(rances) K(ennedy)

Bernanos, (Paul Louis) Georges
1888-1948 .... **TCLC 3**
See also CA 104; 130; DLB 72

Bernard, April 1956- .... **CLC 59**
See also CA 131

Berne, Victoria
See Fisher, M(ary) F(rances) K(ennedy)

Bernhard, Thomas
1931-1989 .... **CLC 3, 32, 61**
See also CA 85-88; 127; CANR 32; DLB 85, 124; MTCW

Berriault, Gina 1926-............ **CLC 54**
See also CA 116; 129; DLB 130

Berrigan, Daniel 1921-............ **CLC 4**
See also CA 33-36R; CAAS 1; CANR 11, 43; DLB 5

Berrigan, Edmund Joseph Michael, Jr.
1934-1983
See Berrigan, Ted
See also CA 61-64; 110; CANR 14

Berrigan, Ted..................... **CLC 37**
See also Berrigan, Edmund Joseph Michael, Jr.
See also DLB 5

Berry, Charles Edward Anderson 1931-
See Berry, Chuck
See also CA 115

Berry, Chuck..................... **CLC 17**
See also Berry, Charles Edward Anderson

Berry, Jonas
See Ashbery, John (Lawrence)

Berry, Wendell (Erdman)
1934- .... **CLC 4, 6, 8, 27, 46**
See also AITN 1; CA 73-76; CANR 50; DAM POET; DLB 5, 6

Berryman, John
1914-1972 ...... **CLC 1, 2, 3, 4, 6, 8, 10, 13, 25, 62**
See also CA 13-16; 33-36R; CABS 2; CANR 35; CAP 1; CDALB 1941-1968; DAM POET; DLB 48; MTCW

Bertolucci, Bernardo 1940-........ **CLC 16**
See also CA 106

Bertrand, Aloysius 1807-1841 .... **NCLC 31**

Bertran de Born c. 1140-1215 ..... **CMLC 5**

Besant, Annie (Wood) 1847-1933 ... **TCLC 9**
See also CA 105

Bessie, Alvah 1904-1985.......... **CLC 23**
See also CA 5-8R; 116; CANR 2; DLB 26

Bethlen, T. D.
See Silverberg, Robert

Beti, Mongo.................. **CLC 27; BLC**
See also Biyidi, Alexandre
See also DAM MULT

Betjeman, John
1906-1984 ... **CLC 2, 6, 10, 34, 43; DAB**
See also CA 9-12R; 112; CANR 33; CDBLB 1945-1960; DAM MST, POET; DLB 20; DLBY 84; MTCW

Bettelheim, Bruno 1903-1990 ...... **CLC 79**
See also CA 81-84; 131; CANR 23; MTCW

Betti, Ugo 1892-1953 .... **TCLC 5**
See also CA 104

Betts, Doris (Waugh) 1932-.... **CLC 3, 6, 28**
See also CA 13-16R; CANR 9; DLBY 82; INT CANR-9

Bevan, Alistair
See Roberts, Keith (John Kingston)

Bialik, Chaim Nachman
1873-1934 .... **TCLC 25**

Bickerstaff, Isaac
See Swift, Jonathan

Bidart, Frank 1939-............... **CLC 33**
See also CA 140

Bienek, Horst 1930-............. **CLC 7, 11**
See also CA 73-76; DLB 75

Bierce, Ambrose (Gwinett)
1842-1914(?) .... **TCLC 1, 7, 44; DA; DAC; SSC 9; WLC**
See also CA 104; 139; CDALB 1865-1917; DAM MST; DLB 11, 12, 23, 71, 74

Biggers, Earl Derr 1884-1933 ..... **TCLC 65**
See also CA 108

Billings, Josh
See Shaw, Henry Wheeler

Billington, (Lady) Rachel (Mary)
1942- .... **CLC 43**
See also AITN 2; CA 33-36R; CANR 44

Binyon, T(imothy) J(ohn) 1936-.... **CLC 34**
See also CA 111; CANR 28

Bioy Casares, Adolfo
1914- .... **CLC 4, 8, 13, 88; HLC; SSC 17**
See also CA 29-32R; CANR 19, 43; DAM MULT; DLB 113; HW; MTCW

Bird, Cordwainer
See Ellison, Harlan (Jay)

Bird, Robert Montgomery
1806-1854 .... **NCLC 1**

Birney, (Alfred) Earle
1904- .... **CLC 1, 4, 6, 11; DAC**
See also CA 1-4R; CANR 5, 20; DAM MST, POET; DLB 88; MTCW

Booth, Philip 1925-. . . . . **CLC 23**
See also CA 5-8R; CANR 5; DLBY 82

Booth, Wayne C(layson) 1921- . . . . . **CLC 24**
See also CA 1-4R; CAAS 5; CANR 3, 43;
DLB 67

Borchert, Wolfgang 1921-1947 . . . . . **TCLC 5**
See also CA 104; DLB 69, 124

Borel, Petrus 1809-1859. . . . . **NCLC 41**

Borges, Jorge Luis
1899-1986 . . . **CLC 1, 2, 3, 4, 6, 8, 9, 10,
13, 19, 44, 48, 83; DA; DAB; DAC;
HLC; SSC 4; WLC**
See also CA 21-24R; CANR 19, 33;
DAM MST, MULT; DLB 113; DLBY 86;
HW; MTCW

Borowski, Tadeusz 1922-1951 . . . . . . **TCLC 9**
See also CA 106

Borrow, George (Henry)
1803-1881 . . . . **NCLC 9**
See also DLB 21, 55, 166

Bosman, Herman Charles
1905-1951 . . . . **TCLC 49**

Bosschere, Jean de 1878(?)-1953. . . **TCLC 19**
See also CA 115

Boswell, James
1740-1795 . . . . . . **LC 4; DA; DAB; DAC;
WLC**
See also CDBLB 1660-1789; DAM MST;
DLB 104, 142

Bottoms, David 1949-. . . . . **CLC 53**
See also CA 105; CANR 22; DLB 120;
DLBY 83

Boucicault, Dion 1820-1890. . . . . . **NCLC 41**

Boucolon, Maryse 1937(?)-
See Conde, Maryse
See also CA 110; CANR 30, 53

Bourget, Paul (Charles Joseph)
1852-1935 . . . . **TCLC 12**
See also CA 107; DLB 123

Bourjaily, Vance (Nye) 1922- . . . . **CLC 8, 62**
See also CA 1-4R; CAAS 1; CANR 2;
DLB 2, 143

Bourne, Randolph S(illiman)
1886-1918 . . . . **TCLC 16**
See also CA 117; DLB 63

Bova, Ben(jamin William) 1932-. . . . **CLC 45**
See also AAYA 16; CA 5-8R; CAAS 18;
CANR 11; CLR 3; DLBY 81;
INT CANR-11; MAICYA; MTCW;
SATA 6, 68

Bowen, Elizabeth (Dorothea Cole)
1899-1973 . . . . . . **CLC 1, 3, 6, 11, 15, 22;
SSC 3**
See also CA 17-18; 41-44R; CANR 35;
CAP 2; CDBLB 1945-1960; DAM NOV;
DLB 15, 162; MTCW

Bowering, George 1935-. . . . . **CLC 15, 47**
See also CA 21-24R; CAAS 16; CANR 10;
DLB 53

Bowering, Marilyn R(uthe) 1949-. . . **CLC 32**
See also CA 101; CANR 49

Bowers, Edgar 1924- . . . . **CLC 9**
See also CA 5-8R; CANR 24; DLB 5

Bowie, David . . . . **CLC 17**
See also Jones, David Robert

Bowles, Jane (Sydney)
1917-1973 . . . . **CLC 3, 68**
See also CA 19-20; 41-44R; CAP 2

Bowles, Paul (Frederick)
1910- . . . . **CLC 1, 2, 19, 53; SSC 3**
See also CA 1-4R; CAAS 1; CANR 1, 19,
50; DLB 5, 6; MTCW

Box, Edgar
See Vidal, Gore

Boyd, Nancy
See Millay, Edna St. Vincent

Boyd, William 1952-. . . . . . . **CLC 28, 53, 70**
See also CA 114; 120; CANR 51

Boyle, Kay
1902-1992 . . . . . **CLC 1, 5, 19, 58; SSC 5**
See also CA 13-16R; 140; CAAS 1;
CANR 29; DLB 4, 9, 48, 86; DLBY 93;
MTCW

Boyle, Mark
See Kienzle, William X(avier)

Boyle, Patrick 1905-1982. . . . . **CLC 19**
See also CA 127

Boyle, T. C. 1948-
See Boyle, T(homas) Coraghessan

Boyle, T(homas) Coraghessan
1948- . . . . **CLC 36, 55, 90; SSC 16**
See also BEST 90:4; CA 120; CANR 44;
DAM POP; DLBY 86

Boz
See Dickens, Charles (John Huffam)

Brackenridge, Hugh Henry
1748-1816 . . . . **NCLC 7**
See also DLB 11, 37

Bradbury, Edward P.
See Moorcock, Michael (John)

Bradbury, Malcolm (Stanley)
1932- . . . . **CLC 32, 61**
See also CA 1-4R; CANR 1, 33;
DAM NOV; DLB 14; MTCW

Bradbury, Ray (Douglas)
1920- . . . . **CLC 1, 3, 10, 15, 42; DA;
DAB; DAC; WLC**
See also AAYA 15; AITN 1, 2; CA 1-4R;
CANR 2, 30; CDALB 1968-1988;
DAM MST, NOV, POP; DLB 2, 8;
INT CANR-30; MTCW; SATA 11, 64

Bradford, Gamaliel 1863-1932. . . . . **TCLC 36**
See also DLB 17

Bradley, David (Henry, Jr.)
1950- . . . . **CLC 23; BLC**
See also BW 1; CA 104; CANR 26;
DAM MULT; DLB 33

Bradley, John Ed(mund, Jr.)
1958- . . . . **CLC 55**
See also CA 139

Bradley, Marion Zimmer 1930-. . . . . **CLC 30**
See also AAYA 9; CA 57-60; CAAS 10;
CANR 7, 31, 51; DAM POP; DLB 8;
MTCW

Bradstreet, Anne
1612(?)-1672 . . . . . . **LC 4, 30; DA; DAC;
PC 10**
See also CDALB 1640-1865; DAM MST,
POET; DLB 24

Brady, Joan 1939- . . . . **CLC 86**
See also CA 141

Bragg, Melvyn 1939- . . . . **CLC 10**
See also BEST 89:3; CA 57-60; CANR 10,
48; DLB 14

Braine, John (Gerard)
1922-1986 . . . . **CLC 1, 3, 41**
See also CA 1-4R; 120; CANR 1, 33;
CDBLB 1945-1960; DLB 15; DLBY 86;
MTCW

Brammer, William 1930(?)-1978 . . . . **CLC 31**
See also CA 77-80

Brancati, Vitaliano 1907-1954. . . . . **TCLC 12**
See also CA 109

Brancato, Robin F(idler) 1936-. . . . . **CLC 35**
See also AAYA 9; CA 69-72; CANR 11,
45; CLR 32; JRDA; SAAS 9; SATA 23

Brand, Max
See Faust, Frederick (Schiller)

Brand, Millen 1906-1980. . . . . **CLC 7**
See also CA 21-24R; 97-100

Branden, Barbara . . . . **CLC 44**
See also CA 148

Brandes, Georg (Morris Cohen)
1842-1927 . . . . **TCLC 10**
See also CA 105

Brandys, Kazimierz 1916- . . . . **CLC 62**

Branley, Franklyn M(ansfield)
1915- . . . . **CLC 21**
See also CA 33-36R; CANR 14, 39;
CLR 13; MAICYA; SAAS 16; SATA 4,
68

Brathwaite, Edward Kamau 1930-. . . **CLC 11**
See also BW 2; CA 25-28R; CANR 11, 26,
47; DAM POET; DLB 125

Brautigan, Richard (Gary)
1935-1984 . . . . **CLC 1, 3, 5, 9, 12, 34, 42**
See also CA 53-56; 113; CANR 34;
DAM NOV; DLB 2, 5; DLBY 80, 84;
MTCW; SATA 56

Brave Bird, Mary 1953-
See Crow Dog, Mary
See also NNAL

Braverman, Kate 1950- . . . . **CLC 67**
See also CA 89-92

Brecht, Bertolt
1898-1956 . . . . . . **TCLC 1, 6, 13, 35; DA;
DAB; DAC; DC 3; WLC**
See also CA 104; 133; DAM DRAM, MST;
DLB 56, 124; MTCW

Brecht, Eugen Berthold Friedrich
See Brecht, Bertolt

Bremer, Fredrika 1801-1865 . . . . . **NCLC 11**

Brennan, Christopher John
1870-1932 . . . . **TCLC 17**
See also CA 117

Brennan, Maeve 1917-. . . . . **CLC 5**
See also CA 81-84

Brentano, Clemens (Maria)
1778-1842 . . . . **NCLC 1**
See also DLB 90

Brent of Bin Bin
See Franklin, (Stella Maraia Sarah) Miles

Brenton, Howard 1942-. . . . . **CLC 31**
See also CA 69-72; CANR 33; DLB 13;
MTCW

Breslin, James   1930-
See Breslin, Jimmy
See also CA 73-76; CANR 31; DAM NOV;
MTCW

Breslin, Jimmy . . . . CLC 4, 43
See also Breslin, James
See also AITN 1

Bresson, Robert   1901- . . . . CLC 16
See also CA 110; CANR 49

Breton, Andre
1896-1966 . . . . . CLC 2, 9, 15, 54; PC 15
See also CA 19-20; 25-28R; CANR 40;
CAP 2; DLB 65; MTCW

Breytenbach, Breyten   1939(?)- . . CLC 23, 37
See also CA 113; 129; DAM POET

Bridgers, Sue Ellen   1942- . . . . CLC 26
See also AAYA 8; CA 65-68; CANR 11,
36; CLR 18; DLB 52; JRDA; MAICYA;
SAAS 1; SATA 22

Bridges, Robert (Seymour)
1844-1930 . . . . TCLC 1
See also CA 104; CDBLB 1890-1914;
DAM POET; DLB 19, 98

Bridie, James . . . . TCLC 3
See also Mavor, Osborne Henry
See also DLB 10

Brin, David   1950- . . . . CLC 34
See also CA 102; CANR 24;
INT CANR-24; SATA 65

Brink, Andre (Philippus)
1935- . . . . CLC 18, 36
See also CA 104; CANR 39; INT 103;
MTCW

Brinsmead, H(esba) F(ay)   1922- . . . . CLC 21
See also CA 21-24R; CANR 10; MAICYA;
SAAS 5; SATA 18, 78

Brittain, Vera (Mary)
1893(?)-1970 . . . . CLC 23
See also CA 13-16; 25-28R; CAP 1; MTCW

Broch, Hermann   1886-1951 . . . . TCLC 20
See also CA 117; DLB 85, 124

Brock, Rose
See Hansen, Joseph

Brodkey, Harold (Roy)   1930-1996 . . CLC 56
See also CA 111; 151; DLB 130

Brodsky, Iosif Alexandrovich   1940-1996
See Brodsky, Joseph
See also AITN 1; CA 41-44R; 151;
CANR 37; DAM POET; MTCW

Brodsky, Joseph . . CLC 4, 6, 13, 36, 50; PC 9
See also Brodsky, Iosif Alexandrovich

Brodsky, Michael Mark   1948- . . . . . CLC 19
See also CA 102; CANR 18, 41

Bromell, Henry   1947- . . . . CLC 5
See also CA 53-56; CANR 9

Bromfield, Louis (Brucker)
1896-1956 . . . . TCLC 11
See also CA 107; DLB 4, 9, 86

Broner, E(sther) M(asserman)
1930- . . . . CLC 19
See also CA 17-20R; CANR 8, 25; DLB 28

Bronk, William   1918- . . . . CLC 10
See also CA 89-92; CANR 23; DLB 165

Bronstein, Lev Davidovich
See Trotsky, Leon

Bronte, Anne   1820-1849 . . . . NCLC 4
See also DLB 21

Bronte, Charlotte
1816-1855 . . . . NCLC 3, 8, 33; DA;
DAB; DAC; WLC
See also AAYA 17; CDBLB 1832-1890;
DAM MST, NOV; DLB 21, 159

Bronte, Emily (Jane)
1818-1848 . . . . NCLC 16, 35; DA; DAB;
DAC; PC 8; WLC
See also AAYA 17; CDBLB 1832-1890;
DAM MST, NOV, POET; DLB 21, 32

Brooke, Frances   1724-1789 . . . . LC 6
See also DLB 39, 99

Brooke, Henry   1703(?)-1783 . . . . LC 1
See also DLB 39

Brooke, Rupert (Chawner)
1887-1915 . . . . TCLC 2, 7; DA; DAB;
DAC; WLC
See also CA 104; 132; CDBLB 1914-1945;
DAM MST, POET; DLB 19; MTCW

Brooke-Haven, P.
See Wodehouse, P(elham) G(renville)

Brooke-Rose, Christine   1926- . . . . . . CLC 40
See also CA 13-16R; DLB 14

Brookner, Anita
1928- . . . . CLC 32, 34, 51; DAB
See also CA 114; 120; CANR 37;
DAM POP; DLBY 87; MTCW

Brooks, Cleanth   1906-1994 . . . . . CLC 24, 86
See also CA 17-20R; 145; CANR 33, 35;
DLB 63; DLBY 94; INT CANR-35;
MTCW

Brooks, George
See Baum, L(yman) Frank

Brooks, Gwendolyn
1917- . . . . . . CLC 1, 2, 4, 5, 15, 49; BLC;
DA; DAC; PC 7; WLC
See also AITN 1; BW 2; CA 1-4R;
CANR 1, 27, 52; CDALB 1941-1968;
CLR 27; DAM MST, MULT, POET;
DLB 5, 76, 165; MTCW; SATA 6

Brooks, Mel . . . . CLC 12
See also Kaminsky, Melvin
See also AAYA 13; DLB 26

Brooks, Peter   1938- . . . . CLC 34
See also CA 45-48; CANR 1

Brooks, Van Wyck   1886-1963 . . . . . . CLC 29
See also CA 1-4R; CANR 6; DLB 45, 63,
103

Brophy, Brigid (Antonia)
1929-1995 . . . . CLC 6, 11, 29
See also CA 5-8R; 149; CAAS 4; CANR 25,
53; DLB 14; MTCW

Brosman, Catharine Savage   1934- . . . . CLC 9
See also CA 61-64; CANR 21, 46

Brother Antoninus
See Everson, William (Oliver)

Broughton, T(homas) Alan   1936- . . . CLC 19
See also CA 45-48; CANR 2, 23, 48

Broumas, Olga   1949- . . . . CLC 10, 73
See also CA 85-88; CANR 20

Brown, Charles Brockden
1771-1810 . . . . NCLC 22
See also CDALB 1640-1865; DLB 37, 59,
73

Brown, Christy   1932-1981 . . . . CLC 63
See also CA 105; 104; DLB 14

Brown, Claude   1937- . . . . CLC 30; BLC
See also AAYA 7; BW 1; CA 73-76;
DAM MULT

Brown, Dee (Alexander)   1908- . . CLC 18, 47
See also CA 13-16R; CAAS 6; CANR 11,
45; DAM POP; DLBY 80; MTCW;
SATA 5

Brown, George
See Wertmueller, Lina

Brown, George Douglas
1869-1902 . . . . TCLC 28

Brown, George Mackay
1921-1996 . . . . CLC 5, 48
See also CA 21-24R; 151; CAAS 6;
CANR 12, 37; DLB 14, 27, 139; MTCW;
SATA 35

Brown, (William) Larry   1951- . . . . . . CLC 73
See also CA 130; 134; INT 133

Brown, Moses
See Barrett, William (Christopher)

Brown, Rita Mae   1944- . . . . . CLC 18, 43, 79
See also CA 45-48; CANR 2, 11, 35;
DAM NOV, POP; INT CANR-11;
MTCW

Brown, Roderick (Langmere) Haig-
See Haig-Brown, Roderick (Langmere)

Brown, Rosellen   1939- . . . . CLC 32
See also CA 77-80; CAAS 10; CANR 14, 44

Brown, Sterling Allen
1901-1989 . . . . CLC 1, 23, 59; BLC
See also BW 1; CA 85-88; 127; CANR 26;
DAM MULT, POET; DLB 48, 51, 63;
MTCW

Brown, Will
See Ainsworth, William Harrison

Brown, William Wells
1813-1884 . . . . NCLC 2; BLC; DC 1
See also DAM MULT; DLB 3, 50

Browne, (Clyde) Jackson   1948(?)- . . . CLC 21
See also CA 120

Browning, Elizabeth Barrett
1806-1861 . . . . . NCLC 1, 16; DA; DAB;
DAC; PC 6; WLC
See also CDBLB 1832-1890; DAM MST,
POET; DLB 32

Browning, Robert
1812-1889 . . . . NCLC 19; DA; DAB;
DAC; PC 2
See also CDBLB 1832-1890; DAM MST,
POET; DLB 32, 163; YABC 1

Browning, Tod   1882-1962 . . . . CLC 16
See also CA 141; 117

Brownson, Orestes (Augustus)
1803-1876 . . . . NCLC 50

Bruccoli, Matthew J(oseph)   1931- . . CLC 34
See also CA 9-12R; CANR 7; DLB 103

Bruce, Lenny . . . . CLC 21
See also Schneider, Leonard Alfred

Bruin, John
See Brutus, Dennis

Brulard, Henri
See Stendhal

Brulls, Christian
See Simenon, Georges (Jacques Christian)

Brunner, John (Kilian Houston)
1934-1995 . . . . **CLC 8, 10**
See also CA 1-4R; 149; CAAS 8; CANR 2, 37; DAM POP; MTCW

Bruno, Giordano 1548-1600 . . . . **LC 27**

Brutus, Dennis 1924- . . . . **CLC 43; BLC**
See also BW 2; CA 49-52; CAAS 14; CANR 2, 27, 42; DAM MULT, POET; DLB 117

Bryan, C(ourtlandt) D(ixon) B(arnes)
1936- . . . . **CLC 29**
See also CA 73-76; CANR 13; INT CANR-13

Bryan, Michael
See Moore, Brian

Bryant, William Cullen
1794-1878 . . . . . **NCLC 6, 46; DA; DAB; DAC**
See also CDALB 1640-1865; DAM MST, POET; DLB 3, 43, 59

Bryusov, Valery Yakovlevich
1873-1924 . . . . **TCLC 10**
See also CA 107

Buchan, John 1875-1940 . . . **TCLC 41; DAB**
See also CA 108; 145; DAM POP; DLB 34, 70, 156; YABC 2

Buchanan, George 1506-1582 . . . . **LC 4**

Buchheim, Lothar-Guenther 1918- . . . **CLC 6**
See also CA 85-88

Buchner, (Karl) Georg
1813-1837 . . . . **NCLC 26**

Buchwald, Art(hur) 1925- . . . . **CLC 33**
See also AITN 1; CA 5-8R; CANR 21; MTCW; SATA 10

Buck, Pearl S(ydenstricker)
1892-1973 . . . . **CLC 7, 11, 18; DA; DAB; DAC**
See also AITN 1; CA 1-4R; 41-44R; CANR 1, 34; DAM MST, NOV; DLB 9, 102; MTCW; SATA 1, 25

Buckler, Ernest 1908-1984 . . . . **CLC 13; DAC**
See also CA 11-12; 114; CAP 1; DAM MST; DLB 68; SATA 47

Buckley, Vincent (Thomas)
1925-1988 . . . . **CLC 57**
See also CA 101

Buckley, William F(rank), Jr.
1925- . . . . **CLC 7, 18, 37**
See also AITN 1; CA 1-4R; CANR 1, 24, 53; DAM POP; DLB 137; DLBY 80; INT CANR-24; MTCW

Buechner, (Carl) Frederick
1926- . . . . **CLC 2, 4, 6, 9**
See also CA 13-16R; CANR 11, 39; DAM NOV; DLBY 80; INT CANR-11; MTCW

Buell, John (Edward) 1927- . . . . **CLC 10**
See also CA 1-4R; DLB 53

Buero Vallejo, Antonio 1916- . . . **CLC 15, 46**
See also CA 106; CANR 24, 49; HW; MTCW

Bufalino, Gesualdo 1920(?)- . . . . **CLC 74**

Bugayev, Boris Nikolayevich 1880-1934
See Bely, Andrey
See also CA 104

Bukowski, Charles
1920-1994 . . . . **CLC 2, 5, 9, 41, 82**
See also CA 17-20R; 144; CANR 40; DAM NOV, POET; DLB 5, 130; MTCW

Bulgakov, Mikhail (Afanas'evich)
1891-1940 . . . . **TCLC 2, 16; SSC 18**
See also CA 105; DAM DRAM, NOV

Bulgya, Alexander Alexandrovich
1901-1956 . . . . **TCLC 53**
See also Fadeyev, Alexander
See also CA 117

Bullins, Ed 1935- . . **CLC 1, 5, 7; BLC; DC 6**
See also BW 2; CA 49-52; CAAS 16; CANR 24, 46; DAM DRAM, MULT; DLB 7, 38; MTCW

Bulwer-Lytton, Edward (George Earle Lytton)
1803-1873 . . . . **NCLC 1, 45**
See also DLB 21

Bunin, Ivan Alexeyevich
1870-1953 . . . . **TCLC 6; SSC 5**
See also CA 104

Bunting, Basil 1900-1985 . . . . **CLC 10, 39, 47**
See also CA 53-56; 115; CANR 7; DAM POET; DLB 20

Bunuel, Luis 1900-1983 . . **CLC 16, 80; HLC**
See also CA 101; 110; CANR 32; DAM MULT; HW

Bunyan, John
1628-1688 . . . . . . **LC 4; DA; DAB; DAC; WLC**
See also CDBLB 1660-1789; DAM MST; DLB 39

Burckhardt, Jacob (Christoph)
1818-1897 . . . . **NCLC 49**

Burford, Eleanor
See Hibbert, Eleanor Alice Burford

Burgess, Anthony
CLC 1, 2, 4, 5, 8, 10, 13, 15, 22, 40, 62, 81, 94; DAB
See also Wilson, John (Anthony) Burgess
See also AITN 1; CDBLB 1960 to Present; DLB 14

Burke, Edmund
1729(?)-1797 . . . . **LC 7; DA; DAB; DAC; WLC**
See also DAM MST; DLB 104

Burke, Kenneth (Duva)
1897-1993 . . . . **CLC 2, 24**
See also CA 5-8R; 143; CANR 39; DLB 45, 63; MTCW

Burke, Leda
See Garnett, David

Burke, Ralph
See Silverberg, Robert

Burke, Thomas 1886-1945 . . . . **TCLC 63**
See also CA 113

Burney, Fanny 1752-1840 . . . . **NCLC 12, 54**
See also DLB 39

Burns, Robert 1759-1796 . . . . **PC 6**
See also CDBLB 1789-1832; DA; DAB; DAC; DAM MST, POET; DLB 109; WLC

Burns, Tex
See L'Amour, Louis (Dearborn)

Burnshaw, Stanley 1906- . . . . . **CLC 3, 13, 44**
See also CA 9-12R; DLB 48

Burr, Anne 1937- . . . . **CLC 6**
See also CA 25-28R

Burroughs, Edgar Rice
1875-1950 . . . . **TCLC 2, 32**
See also AAYA 11; CA 104; 132; DAM NOV; DLB 8; MTCW; SATA 41

Burroughs, William S(eward)
1914- . . . . **CLC 1, 2, 5, 15, 22, 42, 75; DA; DAB; DAC; WLC**
See also AITN 2; CA 9-12R; CANR 20, 52; DAM MST, NOV, POP; DLB 2, 8, 16, 152; DLBY 81; MTCW

Burton, Richard F. 1821-1890 . . . . **NCLC 42**
See also DLB 55

Busch, Frederick 1941- . . . **CLC 7, 10, 18, 47**
See also CA 33-36R; CAAS 1; CANR 45; DLB 6

Bush, Ronald 1946- . . . . **CLC 34**
See also CA 136

Bustos, F(rancisco)
See Borges, Jorge Luis

Bustos Domecq, H(onorio)
See Bioy Casares, Adolfo; Borges, Jorge Luis

Butler, Octavia E(stelle) 1947- . . . . . **CLC 38**
See also AAYA 18; BW 2; CA 73-76; CANR 12, 24, 38; DAM MULT, POP; DLB 33; MTCW; SATA 84

Butler, Robert Olen (Jr.) 1945- . . . . . **CLC 81**
See also CA 112; DAM POP; INT 112

Butler, Samuel 1612-1680 . . . . **LC 16**
See also DLB 101, 126

Butler, Samuel
1835-1902 . . . . . . **TCLC 1, 33; DA; DAB; DAC; WLC**
See also CA 143; CDBLB 1890-1914; DAM MST, NOV; DLB 18, 57

Butler, Walter C.
See Faust, Frederick (Schiller)

Butor, Michel (Marie Francois)
1926- . . . . **CLC 1, 3, 8, 11, 15**
See also CA 9-12R; CANR 33; DLB 83; MTCW

Buzo, Alexander (John) 1944- . . . . . . **CLC 61**
See also CA 97-100; CANR 17, 39

Buzzati, Dino 1906-1972 . . . . **CLC 36**
See also CA 33-36R

Byars, Betsy (Cromer) 1928- . . . . **CLC 35**
See also CA 33-36R; CANR 18, 36; CLR 1, 16; DLB 52; INT CANR-18; JRDA; MAICYA; MTCW; SAAS 1; SATA 4, 46, 80

Byatt, A(ntonia) S(usan Drabble)
1936- . . . . **CLC 19, 65**
See also CA 13-16R; CANR 13, 33, 50; DAM NOV, POP; DLB 14; MTCW

Byrne, David 1952- . . . . **CLC 26**
See also CA 127

Byrne, John Keyes 1926-
See Leonard, Hugh
See also CA 102; INT 102

Byron, George Gordon (Noel)
  1788-1824 ..... **NCLC 2, 12; DA; DAB;**
                              DAC; PC 16; WLC
  See also CDBLB 1789-1832; DAM MST,
  POET; DLB 96, 110

C. 3. 3.
  See Wilde, Oscar (Fingal O'Flahertie Wills)

Caballero, Fernan 1796-1877..... **NCLC 10**

Cabell, James Branch 1879-1958 ... **TCLC 6**
  See also CA 105; DLB 9, 78

Cable, George Washington
  1844-1925 .... **TCLC 4; SSC 4**
  See also CA 104; DLB 12, 74; DLBD 13

Cabral de Melo Neto, Joao 1920-... **CLC 76**
  See also CA 151; DAM MULT

Cabrera Infante, G(uillermo)
  1929- .... **CLC 5, 25, 45; HLC**
  See also CA 85-88; CANR 29;
  DAM MULT; DLB 113; HW; MTCW

Cade, Toni
  See Bambara, Toni Cade

Cadmus and Harmonia
  See Buchan, John

Caedmon fl. 658-680............. **CMLC 7**
  See also DLB 146

Caeiro, Alberto
  See Pessoa, Fernando (Antonio Nogueira)

Cage, John (Milton, Jr.) 1912- ..... **CLC 41**
  See also CA 13-16R; CANR 9;
  INT CANR-9

Cain, G.
  See Cabrera Infante, G(uillermo)

Cain, Guillermo
  See Cabrera Infante, G(uillermo)

Cain, James M(allahan)
  1892-1977 .... **CLC 3, 11, 28**
  See also AITN 1; CA 17-20R; 73-76;
  CANR 8, 34; MTCW

Caine, Mark
  See Raphael, Frederic (Michael)

Calasso, Roberto 1941- .... **CLC 81**
  See also CA 143

Calderon de la Barca, Pedro
  1600-1681 .... **LC 23; DC 3**

Caldwell, Erskine (Preston)
  1903-1987 .... **CLC 1, 8, 14, 50, 60;**
                                        SSC 19
  See also AITN 1; CA 1-4R; 121; CAAS 1;
  CANR 2, 33; DAM NOV; DLB 9, 86;
  MTCW

Caldwell, (Janet Miriam) Taylor (Holland)
  1900-1985 .... **CLC 2, 28, 39**
  See also CA 5-8R; 116; CANR 5;
  DAM NOV, POP

Calhoun, John Caldwell
  1782-1850 .... **NCLC 15**
  See also DLB 3

Calisher, Hortense
  1911- .... **CLC 2, 4, 8, 38; SSC 15**
  See also CA 1-4R; CANR 1, 22;
  DAM NOV; DLB 2; INT CANR-22;
  MTCW

Callaghan, Morley Edward
  1903-1990 ..... **CLC 3, 14, 41, 65; DAC**
  See also CA 9-12R; 132; CANR 33;
  DAM MST; DLB 68; MTCW

Callimachus
  c. 305B.C.-c. 240B.C........ **CMLC 18**

Calvino, Italo
  1923-1985 ..... **CLC 5, 8, 11, 22, 33, 39,**
                                     73; SSC 3
  See also CA 85-88; 116; CANR 23;
  DAM NOV; MTCW

Cameron, Carey 1952- .... **CLC 59**
  See also CA 135

Cameron, Peter 1959-............ **CLC 44**
  See also CA 125; CANR 50

Campana, Dino 1885-1932....... **TCLC 20**
  See also CA 117; DLB 114

Campanella, Tommaso 1568-1639 .... **LC 32**

Campbell, John W(ood, Jr.)
  1910-1971 .... **CLC 32**
  See also CA 21-22; 29-32R; CANR 34;
  CAP 2; DLB 8; MTCW

Campbell, Joseph 1904-1987 .... **CLC 69**
  See also AAYA 3; BEST 89:2; CA 1-4R;
  124; CANR 3, 28; MTCW

Campbell, Maria 1940-...... **CLC 85; DAC**
  See also CA 102; NNAL

Campbell, (John) Ramsey
  1946- .... **CLC 42; SSC 19**
  See also CA 57-60; CANR 7; INT CANR-7

Campbell, (Ignatius) Roy (Dunnachie)
  1901-1957 .... **TCLC 5**
  See also CA 104; DLB 20

Campbell, Thomas 1777-1844 .... **NCLC 19**
  See also DLB 93; 144

Campbell, Wilfred................. **TCLC 9**
  See also Campbell, William

Campbell, William 1858(?)-1918
  See Campbell, Wilfred
  See also CA 106; DLB 92

Campion, Jane.................... **CLC 95**
  See also CA 138

Campos, Alvaro de
  See Pessoa, Fernando (Antonio Nogueira)

Camus, Albert
  1913-1960 .... **CLC 1, 2, 4, 9, 11, 14, 32,**
        63, 69; DA; DAB; DAC; DC 2; SSC 9;
                                             WLC
  See also CA 89-92; DAM DRAM, MST,
  NOV; DLB 72; MTCW

Canby, Vincent 1924-............ **CLC 13**
  See also CA 81-84

Cancale
  See Desnos, Robert

Canetti, Elias
  1905-1994 .... **CLC 3, 14, 25, 75, 86**
  See also CA 21-24R; 146; CANR 23;
  DLB 85, 124; MTCW

Canin, Ethan 1960-.............. **CLC 55**
  See also CA 131; 135

Cannon, Curt
  See Hunter, Evan

Cape, Judith
  See Page, P(atricia) K(athleen)

Capek, Karel
  1890-1938 ...... **TCLC 6, 37; DA; DAB;**
                              DAC; DC 1; WLC
  See also CA 104; 140; DAM DRAM, MST,
  NOV

Capote, Truman
  1924-1984 ...... **CLC 1, 3, 8, 13, 19, 34,**
        38, 58; DA; DAB; DAC; SSC 2; WLC
  See also CA 5-8R; 113; CANR 18;
  CDALB 1941-1968; DAM MST, NOV,
  POP; DLB 2; DLBY 80, 84; MTCW

Capra, Frank 1897-1991.......... **CLC 16**
  See also CA 61-64; 135

Caputo, Philip 1941-............. **CLC 32**
  See also CA 73-76; CANR 40

Card, Orson Scott 1951- .... **CLC 44, 47, 50**
  See also AAYA 11; CA 102; CANR 27, 47;
  DAM POP; INT CANR-27; MTCW;
  SATA 83

Cardenal, Ernesto 1925-..... **CLC 31; HLC**
  See also CA 49-52; CANR 2, 32;
  DAM MULT, POET; HW; MTCW

Cardozo, Benjamin N(athan)
  1870-1938 .... **TCLC 65**
  See also CA 117

Carducci, Giosue 1835-1907...... **TCLC 32**

Carew, Thomas 1595(?)-1640........ **LC 13**
  See also DLB 126

Carey, Ernestine Gilbreth 1908-.... **CLC 17**
  See also CA 5-8R; SATA 2

Carey, Peter 1943-............ **CLC 40, 55**
  See also CA 123; 127; CANR 53; INT 127;
  MTCW

Carleton, William 1794-1869...... **NCLC 3**
  See also DLB 159

Carlisle, Henry (Coffin) 1926-...... **CLC 33**
  See also CA 13-16R; CANR 15

Carlsen, Chris
  See Holdstock, Robert P.

Carlson, Ron(ald F.) 1947-........ **CLC 54**
  See also CA 105; CANR 27

Carlyle, Thomas
  1795-1881 .. **NCLC 22; DA; DAB; DAC**
  See also CDBLB 1789-1832; DAM MST;
  DLB 55; 144

Carman, (William) Bliss
  1861-1929 .... **TCLC 7; DAC**
  See also CA 104; DLB 92

Carnegie, Dale 1888-1955 .... **TCLC 53**

Carossa, Hans 1878-1956........ **TCLC 48**
  See also DLB 66

Carpenter, Don(ald Richard)
  1931-1995 .... **CLC 41**
  See also CA 45-48; 149; CANR 1

Carpentier (y Valmont), Alejo
  1904-1980 .... **CLC 8, 11, 38; HLC**
  See also CA 65-68; 97-100; CANR 11;
  DAM MULT; DLB 113; HW

Carr, Caleb 1955(?)-.............. **CLC 86**
  See also CA 147

Carr, Emily 1871-1945........... **TCLC 32**
  See also DLB 68

Carr, John Dickson 1906-1977 ...... **CLC 3**
  See also CA 49-52; 69-72; CANR 3, 33;
  MTCW

Carr, Philippa
See Hibbert, Eleanor Alice Burford

Carr, Virginia Spencer 1929- .... **CLC 34**
See also CA 61-64; DLB 111

Carrere, Emmanuel 1957- .... **CLC 89**

Carrier, Roch 1937- ..... **CLC 13, 78; DAC**
See also CA 130; DAM MST; DLB 53

Carroll, James P. 1943(?)- .... **CLC 38**
See also CA 81-84

Carroll, Jim 1951- .... **CLC 35**
See also AAYA 17; CA 45-48; CANR 42

Carroll, Lewis .... **NCLC 2, 53; WLC**
See also Dodgson, Charles Lutwidge
See also CDBLB 1832-1890; CLR 2, 18;
DLB 18, 163; JRDA

Carroll, Paul Vincent 1900-1968.... **CLC 10**
See also CA 9-12R; 25-28R; DLB 10

Carruth, Hayden
1921- ...... **CLC 4, 7, 10, 18, 84; PC 10**
See also CA 9-12R; CANR 4, 38; DLB 5,
165; INT CANR-4; MTCW; SATA 47

Carson, Rachel Louise 1907-1964... **CLC 71**
See also CA 77-80; CANR 35; DAM POP;
MTCW; SATA 23

Carter, Angela (Olive)
1940-1992 ...... **CLC 5, 41, 76; SSC 13**
See also CA 53-56; 136; CANR 12, 36;
DLB 14; MTCW; SATA 66;
SATA-Obit 70

Carter, Nick
See Smith, Martin Cruz

Carver, Raymond
1938-1988 ... **CLC 22, 36, 53, 55; SSC 8**
See also CA 33-36R; 126; CANR 17, 34;
DAM NOV; DLB 130; DLBY 84, 88;
MTCW

Cary, Elizabeth, Lady Falkland
1585-1639 .... **LC 30**

Cary, (Arthur) Joyce (Lunel)
1888-1957 .... **TCLC 1, 29**
See also CA 104; CDBLB 1914-1945;
DLB 15, 100

Casanova de Seingalt, Giovanni Jacopo
1725-1798 .... **LC 13**

Casares, Adolfo Bioy
See Bioy Casares, Adolfo

Casely-Hayford, J(oseph) E(phraim)
1866-1930 .... **TCLC 24; BLC**
See also BW 2; CA 123; DAM MULT

Casey, John (Dudley) 1939-........ **CLC 59**
See also BEST 90:2; CA 69-72; CANR 23

Casey, Michael 1947-.............. **CLC 2**
See also CA 65-68; DLB 5

Casey, Patrick
See Thurman, Wallace (Henry)

Casey, Warren (Peter) 1935-1988... **CLC 12**
See also CA 101; 127; INT 101

Casona, Alejandro................. **CLC 49**
See also Alvarez, Alejandro Rodriguez

Cassavetes, John 1929-1989........ **CLC 20**
See also CA 85-88; 127

Cassill, R(onald) V(erlin) 1919-... **CLC 4, 23**
See also CA 9-12R; CAAS 1; CANR 7, 45;
DLB 6

Cassirer, Ernst 1874-1945 .... **TCLC 61**

Cassity, (Allen) Turner 1929- .... **CLC 6, 42**
See also CA 17-20R; CAAS 8; CANR 11;
DLB 105

Castaneda, Carlos 1931(?)-......... **CLC 12**
See also CA 25-28R; CANR 32; HW;
MTCW

Castedo, Elena 1937- .... **CLC 65**
See also CA 132

Castedo-Ellerman, Elena
See Castedo, Elena

Castellanos, Rosario
1925-1974 .... **CLC 66; HLC**
See also CA 131; 53-56; DAM MULT;
DLB 113; HW

Castelvetro, Lodovico 1505-1571..... **LC 12**

Castiglione, Baldassare 1478-1529 ... **LC 12**

Castle, Robert
See Hamilton, Edmond

Castro, Guillen de 1569-1631........ **LC 19**

Castro, Rosalia de 1837-1885 ..... **NCLC 3**
See also DAM MULT

Cather, Willa
See Cather, Willa Sibert

Cather, Willa Sibert
1873-1947 .... **TCLC 1, 11, 31; DA;
DAB; DAC; SSC 2; WLC**
See also CA 104; 128; CDALB 1865-1917;
DAM MST, NOV; DLB 9, 54, 78;
DLBD 1; MTCW; SATA 30

Catton, (Charles) Bruce
1899-1978 .... **CLC 35**
See also AITN 1; CA 5-8R; 81-84;
CANR 7; DLB 17; SATA 2;
SATA-Obit 24

Catullus c. 84B.C.-c. 54B.C. ..... **CMLC 18**

Cauldwell, Frank
See King, Francis (Henry)

Caunitz, William J. 1933- .... **CLC 34**
See also BEST 89:3; CA 125; 130; INT 130

Causley, Charles (Stanley) 1917-..... **CLC 7**
See also CA 9-12R; CANR 5, 35; CLR 30;
DLB 27; MTCW; SATA 3, 66

Caute, David 1936-............... **CLC 29**
See also CA 1-4R; CAAS 4; CANR 1, 33;
DAM NOV; DLB 14

Cavafy, C(onstantine) P(eter)
1863-1933 .... **TCLC 2, 7**
See also Kavafis, Konstantinos Petrou
See also CA 148; DAM POET

Cavallo, Evelyn
See Spark, Muriel (Sarah)

Cavanna, Betty .... **CLC 12**
See also Harrison, Elizabeth Cavanna
See also JRDA; MAICYA; SAAS 4;
SATA 1, 30

Cavendish, Margaret Lucas
1623-1673 .... **LC 30**
See also DLB 131

Caxton, William 1421(?)-1491(?)..... **LC 17**

Cayrol, Jean 1911-............... **CLC 11**
See also CA 89-92; DLB 83

Cela, Camilo Jose
1916- .... **CLC 4, 13, 59; HLC**
See also BEST 90:2; CA 21-24R; CAAS 10;
CANR 21, 32; DAM MULT; DLBY 89;
HW; MTCW

Celan, Paul ...... **CLC 10, 19, 53, 82; PC 10**
See also Antschel, Paul
See also DLB 69

Celine, Louis-Ferdinand
.... **CLC 1, 3, 4, 7, 9, 15, 47**
See also Destouches, Louis-Ferdinand
See also DLB 72

Cellini, Benvenuto 1500-1571 .... **LC 7**

Cendrars, Blaise .... **CLC 18**
See also Sauser-Hall, Frederic

Cernuda (y Bidon), Luis
1902-1963 .... **CLC 54**
See also CA 131; 89-92; DAM POET;
DLB 134; HW

Cervantes (Saavedra), Miguel de
1547-1616 .... **LC 6, 23; DA; DAB;
DAC; SSC 12; WLC**
See also DAM MST, NOV

Cesaire, Aime (Fernand)
1913- .... **CLC 19, 32; BLC**
See also BW 2; CA 65-68; CANR 24, 43;
DAM MULT, POET; MTCW

Chabon, Michael 1965(?)- .... **CLC 55**
See also CA 139

Chabrol, Claude 1930-............. **CLC 16**
See also CA 110

Challans, Mary 1905-1983
See Renault, Mary
See also CA 81-84; 111; SATA 23;
SATA-Obit 36

Challis, George
See Faust, Frederick (Schiller)

Chambers, Aidan 1934-........... **CLC 35**
See also CA 25-28R; CANR 12, 31; JRDA;
MAICYA; SAAS 12; SATA 1, 69

Chambers, James 1948-
See Cliff, Jimmy
See also CA 124

Chambers, Jessie
See Lawrence, D(avid) H(erbert Richards)

Chambers, Robert W. 1865-1933... **TCLC 41**

Chandler, Raymond (Thornton)
1888-1959 .... **TCLC 1, 7; SSC 23**
See also CA 104; 129; CDALB 1929-1941;
DLBD 6; MTCW

Chang, Jung 1952-............... **CLC 71**
See also CA 142

Channing, William Ellery
1780-1842 .... **NCLC 17**
See also DLB 1, 59

Chaplin, Charles Spencer
1889-1977 .... **CLC 16**
See also Chaplin, Charlie
See also CA 81-84; 73-76

Chaplin, Charlie
See Chaplin, Charles Spencer
See also DLB 44

Chapman, George 1559(?)-1634...... **LC 22**
See also DAM DRAM; DLB 62, 121

Chapman, Graham 1941-1989 ..... **CLC 21**
See also Monty Python
See also CA 116; 129; CANR 35

Chapman, John Jay 1862-1933 ..... **TCLC 7**
See also CA 104

Chapman, Lee
See Bradley, Marion Zimmer

Chapman, Walker
See Silverberg, Robert

Chappell, Fred (Davis) 1936-.... **CLC 40, 78**
See also CA 5-8R; CAAS 4; CANR 8, 33;
DLB 6, 105

Char, Rene(-Emile)
1907-1988 .... **CLC 9, 11, 14, 55**
See also CA 13-16R; 124; CANR 32;
DAM POET; MTCW

Charby, Jay
See Ellison, Harlan (Jay)

Chardin, Pierre Teilhard de
See Teilhard de Chardin, (Marie Joseph)
Pierre

Charles I 1600-1649 .... **LC 13**

Charyn, Jerome 1937- .... **CLC 5, 8, 18**
See also CA 5-8R; CAAS 1; CANR 7;
DLBY 83; MTCW

Chase, Mary (Coyle) 1907-1981 ...... **DC 1**
See also CA 77-80; 105; SATA 17;
SATA-Obit 29

Chase, Mary Ellen 1887-1973 .... **CLC 2**
See also CA 13-16; 41-44R; CAP 1;
SATA 10

Chase, Nicholas
See Hyde, Anthony

Chateaubriand, Francois Rene de
1768-1848 .... **NCLC 3**
See also DLB 119

Chatterje, Sarat Chandra 1876-1936(?)
See Chatterji, Saratchandra
See also CA 109

Chatterji, Bankim Chandra
1838-1894 .... **NCLC 19**

Chatterji, Saratchandra .... **TCLC 13**
See also Chatterje, Sarat Chandra

Chatterton, Thomas 1752-1770 .... **LC 3**
See also DAM POET; DLB 109

Chatwin, (Charles) Bruce
1940-1989 .... **CLC 28, 57, 59**
See also AAYA 4; BEST 90:1; CA 85-88;
127; DAM POP

Chaucer, Daniel
See Ford, Ford Madox

Chaucer, Geoffrey
1340(?)-1400 ... **LC 17; DA; DAB; DAC**
See also CDBLB Before 1660; DAM MST,
POET; DLB 146

Chaviaras, Strates 1935-
See Haviaras, Stratis
See also CA 105

Chayefsky, Paddy .... **CLC 23**
See also Chayefsky, Sidney
See also DLB 7, 44; DLBY 81

Chayefsky, Sidney 1923-1981
See Chayefsky, Paddy
See also CA 9-12R; 104; CANR 18;
DAM DRAM

Chedid, Andree 1920-............ **CLC 47**
See also CA 145

Cheever, John
1912-1982 ..... **CLC 3, 7, 8, 11, 15, 25,**
64; DA; DAB; DAC; SSC 1; WLC
See also CA 5-8R; 106; CABS 1; CANR 5,
27; CDALB 1941-1968; DAM MST,
NOV, POP; DLB 2, 102; DLBY 80, 82;
INT CANR-5; MTCW

Cheever, Susan 1943-.......... **CLC 18, 48**
See also CA 103; CANR 27, 51; DLBY 82;
INT CANR-27

Chekhonte, Antosha
See Chekhov, Anton (Pavlovich)

Chekhov, Anton (Pavlovich)
1860-1904 ..... **TCLC 3, 10, 31, 55; DA;**
DAB; DAC; SSC 2; WLC
See also CA 104; 124; DAM DRAM, MST

Chernyshevsky, Nikolay Gavrilovich
1828-1889 .... **NCLC 1**

Cherry, Carolyn Janice 1942-
See Cherryh, C. J.
See also CA 65-68; CANR 10

Cherryh, C. J. .... **CLC 35**
See also Cherry, Carolyn Janice
See also DLBY 80

Chesnutt, Charles W(addell)
1858-1932 .... **TCLC 5, 39; BLC; SSC 7**
See also BW 1; CA 106; 125; DAM MULT;
DLB 12, 50, 78; MTCW

Chester, Alfred 1929(?)-1971....... **CLC 49**
See also CA 33-36R; DLB 130

Chesterton, G(ilbert) K(eith)
1874-1936 .... **TCLC 1, 6, 64; SSC 1**
See also CA 104; 132; CDBLB 1914-1945;
DAM NOV, POET; DLB 10, 19, 34, 70,
98, 149; MTCW; SATA 27

Chiang Pin-chin 1904-1986
See Ding Ling
See also CA 118

Ch'ien Chung-shu 1910-........... **CLC 22**
See also CA 130; MTCW

Child, L. Maria
See Child, Lydia Maria

Child, Lydia Maria 1802-1880 .... **NCLC 6**
See also DLB 1, 74; SATA 67

Child, Mrs.
See Child, Lydia Maria

Child, Philip 1898-1978 .... **CLC 19, 68**
See also CA 13-14; CAP 1; SATA 47

Childers, (Robert) Erskine
1870-1922 .... **TCLC 65**
See also CA 113; DLB 70

Childress, Alice
1920-1994 .. **CLC 12, 15, 86; BLC; DC 4**
See also AAYA 8; BW 2; CA 45-48; 146;
CANR 3, 27, 50; CLR 14; DAM DRAM,
MULT, NOV; DLB 7, 38; JRDA;
MAICYA; MTCW; SATA 7, 48, 81

Chislett, (Margaret) Anne 1943-.... **CLC 34**
See also CA 151

Chitty, Thomas Willes 1926-....... **CLC 11**
See also Hinde, Thomas
See also CA 5-8R

Chivers, Thomas Holley
1809-1858 .... **NCLC 49**
See also DLB 3

Chomette, Rene Lucien 1898-1981
See Clair, Rene
See also CA 103

Chopin, Kate
.... **TCLC 5, 14; DA; DAB; SSC 8**
See also Chopin, Katherine
See also CDALB 1865-1917; DLB 12, 78

Chopin, Katherine 1851-1904
See Chopin, Kate
See also CA 104; 122; DAC; DAM MST,
NOV

Chretien de Troyes
c. 12th cent. - .... **CMLC 10**

Christie
See Ichikawa, Kon

Christie, Agatha (Mary Clarissa)
1890-1976 ...... **CLC 1, 6, 8, 12, 39, 48;**
DAB; DAC
See also AAYA 9; AITN 1, 2; CA 17-20R;
61-64; CANR 10, 37; CDBLB 1914-1945;
DAM NOV; DLB 13, 77; MTCW;
SATA 36

Christie, (Ann) Philippa
See Pearce, Philippa
See also CA 5-8R; CANR 4

Christine de Pizan 1365(?)-1431(?) .... **LC 9**

Chubb, Elmer
See Masters, Edgar Lee

Chulkov, Mikhail Dmitrievich
1743-1792 .... **LC 2**
See also DLB 150

Churchill, Caryl 1938-... **CLC 31, 55; DC 5**
See also CA 102; CANR 22, 46; DLB 13;
MTCW

Churchill, Charles 1731-1764........ **LC 3**
See also DLB 109

Chute, Carolyn 1947-............. **CLC 39**
See also CA 123

Ciardi, John (Anthony)
1916-1986 .... **CLC 10, 40, 44**
See also CA 5-8R; 118; CAAS 2; CANR 5,
33; CLR 19; DAM POET; DLB 5;
DLBY 86; INT CANR-5; MAICYA;
MTCW; SATA 1, 65; SATA-Obit 46

Cicero, Marcus Tullius
106B.C.-43B.C............... **CMLC 3**

Cimino, Michael 1943-............ **CLC 16**
See also CA 105

Cioran, E(mil) M. 1911-1995....... **CLC 64**
See also CA 25-28R; 149

Cisneros, Sandra 1954-..... **CLC 69; HLC**
See also AAYA 9; CA 131; DAM MULT;
DLB 122, 152; HW

Cixous, Helene 1937-............. **CLC 92**
See also CA 126; DLB 83; MTCW

Clair, Rene..................... **CLC 20**
See also Chomette, Rene Lucien

Clampitt, Amy 1920-1994 .... **CLC 32**
See also CA 110; 146; CANR 29; DLB 105

Clancy, Thomas L., Jr. 1947-
See Clancy, Tom
See also CA 125; 131; INT 131; MTCW

Clancy, Tom. CLC 45
See also Clancy, Thomas L., Jr.
See also AAYA 9; BEST 89:1, 90:1;
DAM NOV, POP

Clare, John 1793-1864. . . . . . NCLC 9; DAB
See also DAM POET; DLB 55, 96

Clarin
See Alas (y Urena), Leopoldo (Enrique
Garcia)

Clark, Al C.
See Goines, Donald

Clark, (Robert) Brian 1932-. . . . . . . CLC 29
See also CA 41-44R

Clark, Curt
See Westlake, Donald E(dwin)

Clark, Eleanor 1913-1996 . . . . CLC 5, 19
See also CA 9-12R; 151; CANR 41; DLB 6

Clark, J. P.
See Clark, John Pepper
See also DLB 117

Clark, John Pepper
1935- . . . . CLC 38; BLC; DC 5
See also Clark, J. P.
See also BW 1; CA 65-68; CANR 16;
DAM DRAM, MULT

Clark, M. R.
See Clark, Mavis Thorpe

Clark, Mavis Thorpe 1909- . . . . CLC 12
See also CA 57-60; CANR 8, 37; CLR 30;
MAICYA; SAAS 5; SATA 8, 74

Clark, Walter Van Tilburg
1909-1971 . . . . CLC 28
See also CA 9-12R; 33-36R; DLB 9;
SATA 8

Clarke, Arthur C(harles)
1917- . . . . . . CLC 1, 4, 13, 18, 35; SSC 3
See also AAYA 4; CA 1-4R; CANR 2, 28;
DAM POP; JRDA; MAICYA; MTCW;
SATA 13, 70

Clarke, Austin 1896-1974. . . . . CLC 6, 9
See also CA 29-32; 49-52; CAP 2;
DAM POET; DLB 10, 20

Clarke, Austin C(hesterfield)
1934- . . . . CLC 8, 53; BLC; DAC
See also BW 1; CA 25-28R; CAAS 16;
CANR 14, 32; DAM MULT; DLB 53,
125

Clarke, Gillian 1937- . . . . CLC 61
See also CA 106; DLB 40

Clarke, Marcus (Andrew Hislop)
1846-1881 . . . . NCLC 19

Clarke, Shirley 1925-. . . . . CLC 16

Clash, The
See Headon, (Nicky) Topper; Jones, Mick;
Simonon, Paul; Strummer, Joe

Claudel, Paul (Louis Charles Marie)
1868-1955 . . . . TCLC 2, 10
See also CA 104

Clavell, James (duMaresq)
1925-1994 . . . . CLC 6, 25, 87
See also CA 25-28R; 146; CANR 26, 48;
DAM NOV, POP; MTCW

Cleaver, (Leroy) Eldridge
1935- . . . . CLC 30; BLC
See also BW 1; CA 21-24R; CANR 16;
DAM MULT

Cleese, John (Marwood) 1939- . . . . . CLC 21
See also Monty Python
See also CA 112; 116; CANR 35; MTCW

Cleishbotham, Jebediah
See Scott, Walter

Cleland, John 1710-1789 . . . . LC 2
See also DLB 39

Clemens, Samuel Langhorne 1835-1910
See Twain, Mark
See also CA 104; 135; CDALB 1865-1917;
DA; DAB; DAC; DAM MST, NOV;
DLB 11, 12, 23, 64, 74; JRDA;
MAICYA; YABC 2

Cleophil
See Congreve, William

Clerihew, E.
See Bentley, E(dmund) C(lerihew)

Clerk, N. W.
See Lewis, C(live) S(taples)

Cliff, Jimmy. CLC 21
See also Chambers, James

Clifton, (Thelma) Lucille
1936- . . . . CLC 19, 66; BLC
See also BW 2; CA 49-52; CANR 2, 24, 42;
CLR 5; DAM MULT, POET; DLB 5, 41;
MAICYA; MTCW; SATA 20, 69

Clinton, Dirk
See Silverberg, Robert

Clough, Arthur Hugh 1819-1861. . NCLC 27
See also DLB 32

Clutha, Janet Paterson Frame 1924-
See Frame, Janet
See also CA 1-4R; CANR 2, 36; MTCW

Clyne, Terence
See Blatty, William Peter

Cobalt, Martin
See Mayne, William (James Carter)

Cobbett, William 1763-1835 . . . . . NCLC 49
See also DLB 43, 107, 158

Coburn, D(onald) L(ee) 1938- . . . . . . CLC 10
See also CA 89-92

Cocteau, Jean (Maurice Eugene Clement)
1889-1963 . . . . CLC 1, 8, 15, 16, 43; DA;
DAB; DAC; WLC
See also CA 25-28; CANR 40; CAP 2;
DAM DRAM, MST, NOV; DLB 65;
MTCW

Codrescu, Andrei 1946- . . . . CLC 46
See also CA 33-36R; CAAS 19; CANR 13,
34, 53; DAM POET

Coe, Max
See Bourne, Randolph S(illiman)

Coe, Tucker
See Westlake, Donald E(dwin)

Coetzee, J(ohn) M(ichael)
1940- . . . . CLC 23, 33, 66
See also CA 77-80; CANR 41; DAM NOV;
MTCW

Coffey, Brian
See Koontz, Dean R(ay)

Cohan, George M. 1878-1942 . . . . . TCLC 60

Cohen, Arthur A(llen)
1928-1986 . . . . CLC 7, 31
See also CA 1-4R; 120; CANR 1, 17, 42;
DLB 28

Cohen, Leonard (Norman)
1934- . . . . CLC 3, 38; DAC
See also CA 21-24R; CANR 14;
DAM MST; DLB 53; MTCW

Cohen, Matt 1942-. . . . . CLC 19; DAC
See also CA 61-64; CAAS 18; CANR 40;
DLB 53

Cohen-Solal, Annie 19(?)- . . . . CLC 50

Colegate, Isabel 1931- . . . . CLC 36
See also CA 17-20R; CANR 8, 22; DLB 14;
INT CANR-22; MTCW

Coleman, Emmett
See Reed, Ishmael

Coleridge, Samuel Taylor
1772-1834 . . . . . NCLC 9, 54; DA; DAB;
DAC; PC 11; WLC
See also CDBLB 1789-1832; DAM MST,
POET; DLB 93, 107

Coleridge, Sara 1802-1852. . . . . . NCLC 31

Coles, Don 1928- . . . . CLC 46
See also CA 115; CANR 38

Colette, (Sidonie-Gabrielle)
1873-1954 . . . . . . TCLC 1, 5, 16; SSC 10
See also CA 104; 131; DAM NOV; DLB 65;
MTCW

Collett, (Jacobine) Camilla (Wergeland)
1813-1895 . . . . NCLC 22

Collier, Christopher 1930-. . . . . CLC 30
See also AAYA 13; CA 33-36R; CANR 13,
33; JRDA; MAICYA; SATA 16, 70

Collier, James L(incoln) 1928- . . . . . CLC 30
See also AAYA 13; CA 9-12R; CANR 4,
33; CLR 3; DAM POP; JRDA;
MAICYA; SAAS 21; SATA 8, 70

Collier, Jeremy 1650-1726. . . . . LC 6

Collier, John 1901-1980. . . . . SSC 19
See also CA 65-68; 97-100; CANR 10;
DLB 77

Collins, Hunt
See Hunter, Evan

Collins, Linda 1931-. . . . . CLC 44
See also CA 125

Collins, (William) Wilkie
1824-1889 . . . . NCLC 1, 18
See also CDBLB 1832-1890; DLB 18, 70,
159

Collins, William 1721-1759 . . . . LC 4
See also DAM POET; DLB 109

Collodi, Carlo 1826-1890. . . . . . . NCLC 54
See also Lorenzini, Carlo
See also CLR 5

Colman, George
See Glassco, John

Colt, Winchester Remington
See Hubbard, L(afayette) Ron(ald)

Colter, Cyrus 1910- . . . . CLC 58
See also BW 1; CA 65-68; CANR 10;
DLB 33

Colton, James
See Hansen, Joseph

Cox, William Trevor 1928- ... **CLC 9, 14, 71**
See also Trevor, William
See also CA 9-12R; CANR 4, 37;
DAM NOV; DLB 14; INT CANR-37;
MTCW

Coyne, P. J.
See Masters, Hilary

Cozzens, James Gould
1903-1978 .... **CLC 1, 4, 11, 92**
See also CA 9-12R; 81-84; CANR 19;
CDALB 1941-1968; DLB 9; DLBD 2;
DLBY 84; MTCW

Crabbe, George 1754-1832...... **NCLC 26**
See also DLB 93

Craddock, Charles Egbert
See Murfree, Mary Noailles

Craig, A. A.
See Anderson, Poul (William)

Craik, Dinah Maria (Mulock)
1826-1887 .... **NCLC 38**
See also DLB 35, 163; MAICYA; SATA 34

Cram, Ralph Adams 1863-1942.... **TCLC 45**

Crane, (Harold) Hart
1899-1932 .... **TCLC 2, 5; DA; DAB;
DAC; PC 3; WLC**
See also CA 104; 127; CDALB 1917-1929;
DAM MST, POET; DLB 4, 48; MTCW

Crane, R(onald) S(almon)
1886-1967 .... **CLC 27**
See also CA 85-88; DLB 63

Crane, Stephen (Townley)
1871-1900 .... **TCLC 11, 17, 32; DA;
DAB; DAC; SSC 7; WLC**
See also CA 109; 140; CDALB 1865-1917;
DAM MST, NOV, POET; DLB 12, 54,
78; YABC 2

Crase, Douglas 1944- .... **CLC 58**
See also CA 106

Crashaw, Richard 1612(?)-1649...... **LC 24**
See also DLB 126

Craven, Margaret
1901-1980 .... **CLC 17; DAC**
See also CA 103

Crawford, F(rancis) Marion
1854-1909 .... **TCLC 10**
See also CA 107; DLB 71

Crawford, Isabella Valancy
1850-1887 .... **NCLC 12**
See also DLB 92

Crayon, Geoffrey
See Irving, Washington

Creasey, John 1908-1973......... **CLC 11**
See also CA 5-8R; 41-44R; CANR 8;
DLB 77; MTCW

Crebillon, Claude Prosper Jolyot de (fils)
1707-1777 .... **LC 28**

Credo
See Creasey, John

Creeley, Robert (White)
1926-..... **CLC 1, 2, 4, 8, 11, 15, 36, 78**
See also CA 1-4R; CAAS 10; CANR 23, 43;
DAM POET; DLB 5, 16; MTCW

Crews, Harry (Eugene)
1935-................. **CLC 6, 23, 49**
See also AITN 1; CA 25-28R; CANR 20;
DLB 6, 143; MTCW

Crichton, (John) Michael
1942-................. **CLC 2, 6, 54, 90**
See also AAYA 10; AITN 2; CA 25-28R;
CANR 13, 40; DAM NOV, POP;
DLBY 81; INT CANR-13; JRDA;
MTCW; SATA 9, 88

Crispin, Edmund .... **CLC 22**
See also Montgomery, (Robert) Bruce
See also DLB 87

Cristofer, Michael 1945(?)- .... **CLC 28**
See also CA 110; DAM DRAM; DLB 7

Croce, Benedetto 1866-1952 ...... **TCLC 37**
See also CA 120

Crockett, David 1786-1836 .... **NCLC 8**
See also DLB 3, 11

Crockett, Davy
See Crockett, David

Crofts, Freeman Wills
1879-1957 .... **TCLC 55**
See also CA 115; DLB 77

Croker, John Wilson 1780-1857 .. **NCLC 10**
See also DLB 110

Crommelynck, Fernand 1885-1970 .. **CLC 75**
See also CA 89-92

Cronin, A(rchibald) J(oseph)
1896-1981 .... **CLC 32**
See also CA 1-4R; 102; CANR 5; SATA 47;
SATA-Obit 25

Cross, Amanda
See Heilbrun, Carolyn G(old)

Crothers, Rachel 1878(?)-1958..... **TCLC 19**
See also CA 113; DLB 7

Croves, Hal
See Traven, B.

Crow Dog, Mary................. **CLC 93**
See also Brave Bird, Mary

Crowfield, Christopher
See Stowe, Harriet (Elizabeth) Beecher

Crowley, Aleister................. **TCLC 7**
See also Crowley, Edward Alexander

Crowley, Edward Alexander 1875-1947
See Crowley, Aleister
See also CA 104

Crowley, John 1942-............. **CLC 57**
See also CA 61-64; CANR 43; DLBY 82;
SATA 65

Crud
See Crumb, R(obert)

Crumarums
See Crumb, R(obert)

Crumb, R(obert) 1943-........... **CLC 17**
See also CA 106

Crumbum
See Crumb, R(obert)

Crumski
See Crumb, R(obert)

Crum the Bum
See Crumb, R(obert)

Crunk
See Crumb, R(obert)

Crustt
See Crumb, R(obert)

Cryer, Gretchen (Kiger) 1935-...... **CLC 21**
See also CA 114; 123

Csath, Geza 1887-1919.......... **TCLC 13**
See also CA 111

Cudlip, David 1933-............. **CLC 34**

Cullen, Countee
1903-1946 ...... **TCLC 4, 37; BLC; DA;
DAC**
See also BW 1; CA 108; 124;
CDALB 1917-1929; DAM MST, MULT,
POET; DLB 4, 48, 51; MTCW; SATA 18

Cum, R.
See Crumb, R(obert)

Cummings, Bruce F(rederick) 1889-1919
See Barbellion, W. N. P.
See also CA 123

Cummings, E(dward) E(stlin)
1894-1962 ...... **CLC 1, 3, 8, 12, 15, 68;
DA; DAB; DAC; PC 5; WLC 2**
See also CA 73-76; CANR 31;
CDALB 1929-1941; DAM MST, POET;
DLB 4, 48; MTCW

Cunha, Euclides (Rodrigues Pimenta) da
1866-1909 .... **TCLC 24**
See also CA 123

Cunningham, E. V.
See Fast, Howard (Melvin)

Cunningham, J(ames) V(incent)
1911-1985 .... **CLC 3, 31**
See also CA 1-4R; 115; CANR 1; DLB 5

Cunningham, Julia (Woolfolk)
1916- .... **CLC 12**
See also CA 9-12R; CANR 4, 19, 36;
JRDA; MAICYA; SAAS 2; SATA 1, 26

Cunningham, Michael 1952- .... **CLC 34**
See also CA 136

Cunninghame Graham, R(obert) B(ontine)
1852-1936 .... **TCLC 19**
See also Graham, R(obert) B(ontine)
Cunninghame
See also CA 119; DLB 98

Currie, Ellen 19(?)-.............. **CLC 44**

Curtin, Philip
See Lowndes, Marie Adelaide (Belloc)

Curtis, Price
See Ellison, Harlan (Jay)

Cutrate, Joe
See Spiegelman, Art

Czaczkes, Shmuel Yosef
See Agnon, S(hmuel) Y(osef Halevi)

Dabrowska, Maria (Szumska)
1889-1965 .... **CLC 15**
See also CA 106

Dabydeen, David 1955- .... **CLC 34**
See also BW 1; CA 125

Dacey, Philip 1939- .... **CLC 51**
See also CA 37-40R; CAAS 17; CANR 14,
32; DLB 105

Dagerman, Stig (Halvard)
1923-1954 .... **TCLC 17**
See also CA 117

Dahl, Roald
    1916-1990 . . . . . **CLC 1, 6, 18, 79; DAB;**
                                                        DAC
    See also AAYA 15; CA 1-4R; 133;
    CANR 6, 32, 37; CLR 1, 7, 41;
    DAM MST, NOV, POP; DLB 139;
    JRDA; MAICYA; MTCW; SATA 1, 26,
    73; SATA-Obit 65

Dahlberg, Edward 1900-1977. . . **CLC 1, 7, 14**
    See also CA 9-12R; 69-72; CANR 31;
    DLB 48; MTCW

Dale, Colin. **TCLC 18**
    See also Lawrence, T(homas) E(dward)

Dale, George E.
    See Asimov, Isaac

Daly, Elizabeth 1878-1967. . . . . **CLC 52**
    See also CA 23-24; 25-28R; CAP 2

Daly, Maureen 1921- . . . . **CLC 17**
    See also AAYA 5; CANR 37; JRDA;
    MAICYA; SAAS 1; SATA 2

Damas, Leon-Gontran 1912-1978 . . . **CLC 84**
    See also BW 1; CA 125; 73-76

Dana, Richard Henry Sr.
    1787-1879 . . . . **NCLC 53**

Daniel, Samuel 1562(?)-1619 . . . . **LC 24**
    See also DLB 62

Daniels, Brett
    See Adler, Renata

Dannay, Frederic 1905-1982 . . . . **CLC 11**
    See also Queen, Ellery
    See also CA 1-4R; 107; CANR 1, 39;
    DAM POP; DLB 137; MTCW

D'Annunzio, Gabriele
    1863-1938 . . . . **TCLC 6, 40**
    See also CA 104

Danois, N. le
    See Gourmont, Remy (-Marie-Charles) de

d'Antibes, Germain
    See Simenon, Georges (Jacques Christian)

Danticat, Edwidge 1969- . . . . **CLC 94**
    See also CA 152

Danvers, Dennis 1947- . . . . **CLC 70**

Danziger, Paula 1944- . . . . **CLC 21**
    See also AAYA 4; CA 112; 115; CANR 37;
    CLR 20; JRDA; MAICYA; SATA 36,
    63; SATA-Brief 30

Da Ponte, Lorenzo 1749-1838 . . . . **NCLC 50**

Dario, Ruben
    1867-1916 . . . . **TCLC 4; HLC; PC 15**
    See also CA 131; DAM MULT; HW;
    MTCW

Darley, George 1795-1846 . . . . **NCLC 2**
    See also DLB 96

Darwin, Charles 1809-1882 . . . . . . **NCLC 57**
    See also DLB 57, 166

Daryush, Elizabeth 1887-1977. . . . **CLC 6, 19**
    See also CA 49-52; CANR 3; DLB 20

Dashwood, Edmee Elizabeth Monica de la
        Pasture 1890-1943
    See Delafield, E. M.
    See also CA 119

Daudet, (Louis Marie) Alphonse
    1840-1897 . . . . **NCLC 1**
    See also DLB 123

Daumal, Rene 1908-1944 . . . . **TCLC 14**
    See also CA 114

Davenport, Guy (Mattison, Jr.)
    1927- . . . . **CLC 6, 14, 38; SSC 16**
    See also CA 33-36R; CANR 23; DLB 130

Davidson, Avram 1923-
    See Queen, Ellery
    See also CA 101; CANR 26; DLB 8

Davidson, Donald (Grady)
    1893-1968 . . . . **CLC 2, 13, 19**
    See also CA 5-8R; 25-28R; CANR 4;
    DLB 45

Davidson, Hugh
    See Hamilton, Edmond

Davidson, John 1857-1909 . . . . **TCLC 24**
    See also CA 118; DLB 19

Davidson, Sara 1943- . . . . **CLC 9**
    See also CA 81-84; CANR 44

Davie, Donald (Alfred)
    1922-1995 . . . . **CLC 5, 8, 10, 31**
    See also CA 1-4R; 149; CAAS 3; CANR 1,
    44; DLB 27; MTCW

Davies, Ray(mond Douglas) 1944- . . **CLC 21**
    See also CA 116; 146

Davies, Rhys 1903-1978. . . . . **CLC 23**
    See also CA 9-12R; 81-84; CANR 4;
    DLB 139

Davies, (William) Robertson
    1913-1995 . . . . . **CLC 2, 7, 13, 25, 42, 75,**
                            91; DA; DAB; DAC; WLC
    See also BEST 89:2; CA 33-36R; 150;
    CANR 17, 42; DAM MST, NOV, POP;
    DLB 68; INT CANR-17; MTCW

Davies, W(illiam) H(enry)
    1871-1940 . . . . **TCLC 5**
    See also CA 104; DLB 19

Davies, Walter C.
    See Kornbluth, C(yril) M.

Davis, Angela (Yvonne) 1944- . . . . . . **CLC 77**
    See also BW 2; CA 57-60; CANR 10;
    DAM MULT

Davis, B. Lynch
    See Bioy Casares, Adolfo; Borges, Jorge
    Luis

Davis, Gordon
    See Hunt, E(verette) Howard, (Jr.)

Davis, Harold Lenoir 1896-1960. . . . **CLC 49**
    See also CA 89-92; DLB 9

Davis, Rebecca (Blaine) Harding
    1831-1910 . . . . **TCLC 6**
    See also CA 104; DLB 74

Davis, Richard Harding
    1864-1916 . . . . **TCLC 24**
    See also CA 114; DLB 12, 23, 78, 79;
    DLBD 13

Davison, Frank Dalby 1893-1970 . . . **CLC 15**
    See also CA 116

Davison, Lawrence H.
    See Lawrence, D(avid) H(erbert Richards)

Davison, Peter (Hubert) 1928- . . . . . **CLC 28**
    See also CA 9-12R; CAAS 4; CANR 3, 43;
    DLB 5

Davys, Mary 1674-1732 . . . . **LC 1**
    See also DLB 39

Dawson, Fielding 1930- . . . . **CLC 6**
    See also CA 85-88; DLB 130

Dawson, Peter
    See Faust, Frederick (Schiller)

Day, Clarence (Shepard, Jr.)
    1874-1935 . . . . **TCLC 25**
    See also CA 108; DLB 11

Day, Thomas 1748-1789 . . . . **LC 1**
    See also DLB 39; YABC 1

Day Lewis, C(ecil)
    1904-1972 . . . . **CLC 1, 6, 10; PC 11**
    See also Blake, Nicholas
    See also CA 13-16; 33-36R; CANR 34;
    CAP 1; DAM POET; DLB 15, 20;
    MTCW

Dazai, Osamu . . . . **TCLC 11**
    See also Tsushima, Shuji

de Andrade, Carlos Drummond
    See Drummond de Andrade, Carlos

Deane, Norman
    See Creasey, John

de Beauvoir, Simone (Lucie Ernestine Marie
        Bertrand)
    See Beauvoir, Simone (Lucie Ernestine
    Marie Bertrand) de

de Brissac, Malcolm
    See Dickinson, Peter (Malcolm)

de Chardin, Pierre Teilhard
    See Teilhard de Chardin, (Marie Joseph)
    Pierre

Dee, John 1527-1608 . . . . **LC 20**

Deer, Sandra 1940- . . . . **CLC 45**

De Ferrari, Gabriella 1941- . . . . **CLC 65**
    See also CA 146

Defoe, Daniel
    1660(?)-1731 . . . . **LC 1; DA; DAB; DAC;**
                                                    WLC
    See also CDBLB 1660-1789; DAM MST,
    NOV; DLB 39, 95, 101; JRDA;
    MAICYA; SATA 22

de Gourmont, Remy(-Marie-Charles)
    See Gourmont, Remy (-Marie-Charles) de

de Hartog, Jan 1914- . . . . **CLC 19**
    See also CA 1-4R; CANR 1

de Hostos, E. M.
    See Hostos (y Bonilla), Eugenio Maria de

de Hostos, Eugenio M.
    See Hostos (y Bonilla), Eugenio Maria de

Deighton, Len . . . . **CLC 4, 7, 22, 46**
    See also Deighton, Leonard Cyril
    See also AAYA 6; BEST 89:2;
    CDBLB 1960 to Present; DLB 87

Deighton, Leonard Cyril 1929-
    See Deighton, Len
    See also CA 9-12R; CANR 19, 33;
    DAM NOV, POP; MTCW

Dekker, Thomas 1572(?)-1632 . . . . . . **LC 22**
    See also CDBLB Before 1660;
    DAM DRAM; DLB 62

Delafield, E. M. 1890-1943 . . . . **TCLC 61**
    See also Dashwood, Edmee Elizabeth
    Monica de la Pasture
    See also DLB 34

de la Mare, Walter (John)
    1873-1956 .... **TCLC 4, 53; DAB; DAC;**
                            SSC 14; WLC
    See also CDBLB 1914-1945; CLR 23;
    DAM MST, POET; DLB 162; SATA 16

Delaney, Franey
    See O'Hara, John (Henry)

Delaney, Shelagh 1939- .... **CLC 29**
    See also CA 17-20R; CANR 30;
    CDBLB 1960 to Present; DAM DRAM;
    DLB 13; MTCW

Delany, Mary (Granville Pendarves)
    1700-1788 .... **LC 12**

Delany, Samuel R(ay, Jr.)
    1942- .... **CLC 8, 14, 38; BLC**
    See also BW 2; CA 81-84; CANR 27, 43;
    DAM MULT; DLB 8, 33; MTCW

De La Ramee, (Marie) Louise 1839-1908
    See Ouida
    See also SATA 20

de la Roche, Mazo 1879-1961 ...... **CLC 14**
    See also CA 85-88; CANR 30; DLB 68;
    SATA 64

Delbanco, Nicholas (Franklin)
    1942- .... **CLC 6, 13**
    See also CA 17-20R; CAAS 2; CANR 29;
    DLB 6

del Castillo, Michel 1933- .... **CLC 38**
    See also CA 109

Deledda, Grazia (Cosima)
    1875(?)-1936 .... **TCLC 23**
    See also CA 123

Delibes, Miguel .... **CLC 8, 18**
    See also Delibes Setien, Miguel

Delibes Setien, Miguel 1920-
    See Delibes, Miguel
    See also CA 45-48; CANR 1, 32; HW;
    MTCW

DeLillo, Don
    1936- ..... **CLC 8, 10, 13, 27, 39, 54, 76**
    See also BEST 89:1; CA 81-84; CANR 21;
    DAM NOV, POP; DLB 6; MTCW

de Lisser, H. G.
    See De Lisser, Herbert George
    See also DLB 117

De Lisser, Herbert George
    1878-1944 .... **TCLC 12**
    See also de Lisser, H. G.
    See also BW 2; CA 109

Deloria, Vine (Victor), Jr. 1933-.... **CLC 21**
    See also CA 53-56; CANR 5, 20, 48;
    DAM MULT; MTCW; NNAL; SATA 21

Del Vecchio, John M(ichael)
    1947- .... **CLC 29**
    See also CA 110; DLBD 9

de Man, Paul (Adolph Michel)
    1919-1983 .... **CLC 55**
    See also CA 128; 111; DLB 67; MTCW

De Marinis, Rick 1934-........... **CLC 54**
    See also CA 57-60; CAAS 24; CANR 9, 25,
    50

Dembry, R. Emmet
    See Murfree, Mary Noailles

Demby, William 1922-....... **CLC 53; BLC**
    See also BW 1; CA 81-84; DAM MULT;
    DLB 33

Demijohn, Thom
    See Disch, Thomas M(ichael)

de Montherlant, Henry (Milon)
    See Montherlant, Henry (Milon) de

Demosthenes 384B.C.-322B.C. ... **CMLC 13**

de Natale, Francine
    See Malzberg, Barry N(athaniel)

Denby, Edwin (Orr) 1903-1983 ..... **CLC 48**
    See also CA 138; 110

Denis, Julio
    See Cortazar, Julio

Denmark, Harrison
    See Zelazny, Roger (Joseph)

Dennis, John 1658-1734............ **LC 11**
    See also DLB 101

Dennis, Nigel (Forbes) 1912-1989.... **CLC 8**
    See also CA 25-28R; 129; DLB 13, 15;
    MTCW

De Palma, Brian (Russell) 1940-.... **CLC 20**
    See also CA 109

De Quincey, Thomas 1785-1859 ... **NCLC 4**
    See also CDBLB 1789-1832; DLB 110; 144

Deren, Eleanora 1908(?)-1961
    See Deren, Maya
    See also CA 111

Deren, Maya .... **CLC 16**
    See also Deren, Eleanora

Derleth, August (William)
    1909-1971 .... **CLC 31**
    See also CA 1-4R; 29-32R; CANR 4;
    DLB 9; SATA 5

Der Nister 1884-1950........... **TCLC 56**

de Routisie, Albert
    See Aragon, Louis

Derrida, Jacques 1930-........ **CLC 24, 87**
    See also CA 124; 127

Derry Down Derry
    See Lear, Edward

Dersonnes, Jacques
    See Simenon, Georges (Jacques Christian)

Desai, Anita 1937- ...... **CLC 19, 37; DAB**
    See also CA 81-84; CANR 33, 53;
    DAM NOV; MTCW; SATA 63

de Saint-Luc, Jean
    See Glassco, John

de Saint Roman, Arnaud
    See Aragon, Louis

Descartes, Rene 1596-1650 .... **LC 20**

De Sica, Vittorio 1901(?)-1974 ..... **CLC 20**
    See also CA 117

Desnos, Robert 1900-1945....... **TCLC 22**
    See also CA 121; 151

Destouches, Louis-Ferdinand
    1894-1961 .... **CLC 9, 15**
    See also Celine, Louis-Ferdinand
    See also CA 85-88; CANR 28; MTCW

Deutsch, Babette 1895-1982 .... **CLC 18**
    See also CA 1-4R; 108; CANR 4; DLB 45;
    SATA 1; SATA-Obit 33

Devenant, William 1606-1649 ...... **LC 13**

Devkota, Laxmiprasad
    1909-1959 .... **TCLC 23**
    See also CA 123

De Voto, Bernard (Augustine)
    1897-1955 .... **TCLC 29**
    See also CA 113; DLB 9

De Vries, Peter
    1910-1993 .... **CLC 1, 2, 3, 7, 10, 28, 46**
    See also CA 17-20R; 142; CANR 41;
    DAM NOV; DLB 6; DLBY 82; MTCW

Dexter, John
    See Bradley, Marion Zimmer

Dexter, Martin
    See Faust, Frederick (Schiller)

Dexter, Pete 1943-............ **CLC 34, 55**
    See also BEST 89:2; CA 127; 131;
    DAM POP; INT 131; MTCW

Diamano, Silmang
    See Senghor, Leopold Sedar

Diamond, Neil 1941- .... **CLC 30**
    See also CA 108

Diaz del Castillo, Bernal 1496-1584 .. **LC 31**

di Bassetto, Corno
    See Shaw, George Bernard

Dick, Philip K(indred)
    1928-1982 .... **CLC 10, 30, 72**
    See also CA 49-52; 106; CANR 2, 16;
    DAM NOV, POP; DLB 8; MTCW

Dickens, Charles (John Huffam)
    1812-1870 ...... **NCLC 3, 8, 18, 26, 37,**
            50; DA; DAB; DAC; SSC 17; WLC
    See also CDBLB 1832-1890; DAM MST,
    NOV; DLB 21, 55, 70, 159, 166; JRDA;
    MAICYA; SATA 15

Dickey, James (Lafayette)
    1923- .... **CLC 1, 2, 4, 7, 10, 15, 47**
    See also AITN 1, 2; CA 9-12R; CABS 2;
    CANR 10, 48; CDALB 1968-1988;
    DAM NOV, POET, POP; DLB 5;
    DLBD 7; DLBY 82, 93; INT CANR-10;
    MTCW

Dickey, William 1928-1994 ...... **CLC 3, 28**
    See also CA 9-12R; 145; CANR 24; DLB 5

Dickinson, Charles 1951-.......... **CLC 49**
    See also CA 128

Dickinson, Emily (Elizabeth)
    1830-1886 .... **NCLC 21; DA; DAB;**
                            DAC; PC 1; WLC
    See also CDALB 1865-1917; DAM MST,
    POET; DLB 1; SATA 29

Dickinson, Peter (Malcolm)
    1927- .... **CLC 12, 35**
    See also AAYA 9; CA 41-44R; CANR 31;
    CLR 29; DLB 87, 161; JRDA; MAICYA;
    SATA 5, 62

Dickson, Carr
    See Carr, John Dickson

Dickson, Carter
    See Carr, John Dickson

Diderot, Denis 1713-1784 .... **LC 26**

Didion, Joan 1934-..... **CLC 1, 3, 8, 14, 32**
    See also AITN 1; CA 5-8R; CANR 14, 52;
    CDALB 1968-1988; DAM NOV; DLB 2;
    DLBY 81, 86; MTCW

Dietrich, Robert
    See Hunt, E(verette) Howard, (Jr.)

Author Index

Elytis, Odysseus 1911-1996..... **CLC 15, 49**
See also CA 102; 151; DAM POET; MTCW

Emecheta, (Florence Onye) Buchi
1944- .... **CLC 14, 48; BLC**
See also BW 2; CA 81-84; CANR 27;
DAM MULT; DLB 117; MTCW;
SATA 66

Emerson, Ralph Waldo
1803-1882 ..... **NCLC 1, 38; DA; DAB;**
                                          DAC; WLC
See also CDALB 1640-1865; DAM MST,
POET; DLB 1, 59, 73

Eminescu, Mihail 1850-1889 ..... **NCLC 33**

Empson, William
1906-1984 .... **CLC 3, 8, 19, 33, 34**
See also CA 17-20R; 112; CANR 31;
DLB 20; MTCW

Enchi Fumiko (Ueda) 1905-1986.... **CLC 31**
See also CA 129; 121

Ende, Michael (Andreas Helmuth)
1929-1995 .... **CLC 31**
See also CA 118; 124; 149; CANR 36;
CLR 14; DLB 75; MAICYA; SATA 61;
SATA-Brief 42; SATA-Obit 86

Endo, Shusaku 1923- ..... **CLC 7, 14, 19, 54**
See also CA 29-32R; CANR 21;
DAM NOV; MTCW

Engel, Marian 1933-1985......... **CLC 36**
See also CA 25-28R; CANR 12; DLB 53;
INT CANR-12

Engelhardt, Frederick
See Hubbard, L(afayette) Ron(ald)

Enright, D(ennis) J(oseph)
1920- .... **CLC 4, 8, 31**
See also CA 1-4R; CANR 1, 42; DLB 27;
SATA 25

Enzensberger, Hans Magnus
1929- .... **CLC 43**
See also CA 116; 119

Ephron, Nora 1941- .... **CLC 17, 31**
See also AITN 2; CA 65-68; CANR 12, 39

Epsilon
See Betjeman, John

Epstein, Daniel Mark 1948- .... **CLC 7**
See also CA 49-52; CANR 2, 53

Epstein, Jacob 1956- .... **CLC 19**
See also CA 114

Epstein, Joseph 1937-............. **CLC 39**
See also CA 112; 119; CANR 50

Epstein, Leslie 1938- .... **CLC 27**
See also CA 73-76; CAAS 12; CANR 23

Equiano, Olaudah
1745(?)-1797 .... **LC 16; BLC**
See also DAM MULT; DLB 37, 50

Erasmus, Desiderius 1469(?)-1536.... **LC 16**

Erdman, Paul E(mil) 1932- .... **CLC 25**
See also AITN 1; CA 61-64; CANR 13, 43

Erdrich, Louise 1954-......... **CLC 39, 54**
See also AAYA 10; BEST 89:1; CA 114;
CANR 41; DAM MULT, NOV, POP;
DLB 152; MTCW; NNAL

Erenburg, Ilya (Grigoryevich)
See Ehrenburg, Ilya (Grigoryevich)

Erickson, Stephen Michael 1950-
See Erickson, Steve
See also CA 129

Erickson, Steve .... **CLC 64**
See also Erickson, Stephen Michael

Ericson, Walter
See Fast, Howard (Melvin)

Eriksson, Buntel
See Bergman, (Ernst) Ingmar

Ernaux, Annie 1940- .... **CLC 88**
See also CA 147

Eschenbach, Wolfram von
See Wolfram von Eschenbach

Eseki, Bruno
See Mphahlele, Ezekiel

Esenin, Sergei (Alexandrovich)
1895-1925 .... **TCLC 4**
See also CA 104

Eshleman, Clayton 1935-........... **CLC 7**
See also CA 33-36R; CAAS 6; DLB 5

Espriella, Don Manuel Alvarez
See Southey, Robert

Espriu, Salvador 1913-1985........ **CLC 9**
See also CA 115; DLB 134

Espronceda, Jose de 1808-1842... **NCLC 39**

Esse, James
See Stephens, James

Esterbrook, Tom
See Hubbard, L(afayette) Ron(ald)

Estleman, Loren D. 1952- .... **CLC 48**
See also CA 85-88; CANR 27; DAM NOV,
POP; INT CANR-27; MTCW

Eugenides, Jeffrey 1960(?)- .... **CLC 81**
See also CA 144

Euripides c. 485B.C.-406B.C. .... **DC 4**
See also DA; DAB; DAC; DAM DRAM,
MST

Evan, Evin
See Faust, Frederick (Schiller)

Evans, Evan
See Faust, Frederick (Schiller)

Evans, Marian
See Eliot, George

Evans, Mary Ann
See Eliot, George

Evarts, Esther
See Benson, Sally

Everett, Percival L. 1956- .... **CLC 57**
See also BW 2; CA 129

Everson, R(onald) G(ilmour)
1903- .... **CLC 27**
See also CA 17-20R; DLB 88

Everson, William (Oliver)
1912-1994 .... **CLC 1, 5, 14**
See also CA 9-12R; 145; CANR 20; DLB 5,
16; MTCW

Evtushenko, Evgenii Aleksandrovich
See Yevtushenko, Yevgeny (Alexandrovich)

Ewart, Gavin (Buchanan)
1916-1995 .... **CLC 13, 46**
See also CA 89-92; 150; CANR 17, 46;
DLB 40; MTCW

Ewers, Hanns Heinz 1871-1943 ... **TCLC 12**
See also CA 109; 149

Ewing, Frederick R.
See Sturgeon, Theodore (Hamilton)

Exley, Frederick (Earl)
1929-1992 .... **CLC 6, 11**
See also AITN 2; CA 81-84; 138; DLB 143;
DLBY 81

Eynhardt, Guillermo
See Quiroga, Horacio (Sylvestre)

Ezekiel, Nissim 1924-............. **CLC 61**
See also CA 61-64

Ezekiel, Tish O'Dowd 1943- .... **CLC 34**
See also CA 129

Fadeyev, A.
See Bulgya, Alexander Alexandrovich

Fadeyev, Alexander.............. **TCLC 53**
See also Bulgya, Alexander Alexandrovich

Fagen, Donald 1948-.............. **CLC 26**

Fainzilberg, Ilya Arnoldovich 1897-1937
See Ilf, Ilya
See also CA 120

Fair, Ronald L. 1932-............. **CLC 18**
See also BW 1; CA 69-72; CANR 25;
DLB 33

Fairbairns, Zoe (Ann) 1948- .... **CLC 32**
See also CA 103; CANR 21

Falco, Gian
See Papini, Giovanni

Falconer, James
See Kirkup, James

Falconer, Kenneth
See Kornbluth, C(yril) M.

Falkland, Samuel
See Heijermans, Herman

Fallaci, Oriana 1930-............. **CLC 11**
See also CA 77-80; CANR 15; MTCW

Faludy, George 1913-............. **CLC 42**
See also CA 21-24R

Faludy, Gyoergy
See Faludy, George

Fanon, Frantz 1925-1961 ..... **CLC 74; BLC**
See also BW 1; CA 116; 89-92;
DAM MULT

Fanshawe, Ann 1625-1680......... **LC 11**

Fante, John (Thomas) 1911-1983 ... **CLC 60**
See also CA 69-72; 109; CANR 23;
DLB 130; DLBY 83

Farah, Nuruddin 1945-....... **CLC 53; BLC**
See also BW 2; CA 106; DAM MULT;
DLB 125

Fargue, Leon-Paul 1876(?)-1947... **TCLC 11**
See also CA 109

Farigoule, Louis
See Romains, Jules

Farina, Richard 1936(?)-1966 .... **CLC 9**
See also CA 81-84; 25-28R

Farley, Walter (Lorimer)
1915-1989 .... **CLC 17**
See also CA 17-20R; CANR 8, 29; DLB 22;
JRDA; MAICYA; SATA 2, 43

Farmer, Philip Jose 1918- .... **CLC 1, 19**
See also CA 1-4R; CANR 4, 35; DLB 8;
MTCW

Farquhar, George 1677-1707 .... **LC 21**
See also DAM DRAM; DLB 84

Farrell, J(ames) G(ordon)
1935-1979 .... **CLC 6**
See also CA 73-76; 89-92; CANR 36;
DLB 14; MTCW

Farrell, James T(homas)
1904-1979 .... **CLC 1, 4, 8, 11, 66**
See also CA 5-8R; 89-92; CANR 9; DLB 4,
9, 86; DLBD 2; MTCW

Farren, Richard J.
See Betjeman, John

Farren, Richard M.
See Betjeman, John

Fassbinder, Rainer Werner
1946-1982 .... **CLC 20**
See also CA 93-96; 106; CANR 31

Fast, Howard (Melvin) 1914- ...... **CLC 23**
See also AAYA 16; CA 1-4R; CAAS 18;
CANR 1, 33; DAM NOV; DLB 9;
INT CANR-33; SATA 7

Faulcon, Robert
See Holdstock, Robert P.

Faulkner, William (Cuthbert)
1897-1962 ..... **CLC 1, 3, 6, 8, 9, 11, 14,
18, 28, 52, 68; DA; DAB; DAC; SSC 1;
WLC**
See also AAYA 7; CA 81-84; CANR 33;
CDALB 1929-1941; DAM MST, NOV;
DLB 9, 11, 44, 102; DLBD 2; DLBY 86;
MTCW

Fauset, Jessie Redmon
1884(?)-1961 .... **CLC 19, 54; BLC**
See also BW 1; CA 109; DAM MULT;
DLB 51

Faust, Frederick (Schiller)
1892-1944(?) .... **TCLC 49**
See also CA 108; DAM POP

Faust, Irvin 1924- .... **CLC 8**
See also CA 33-36R; CANR 28; DLB 2, 28;
DLBY 80

Fawkes, Guy
See Benchley, Robert (Charles)

Fearing, Kenneth (Flexner)
1902-1961 .... **CLC 51**
See also CA 93-96; DLB 9

Fecamps, Elise
See Creasey, John

Federman, Raymond 1928- ...... **CLC 6, 47**
See also CA 17-20R; CAAS 8; CANR 10,
43; DLBY 80

Federspiel, J(uerg) F. 1931- .... **CLC 42**
See also CA 146

Feiffer, Jules (Ralph) 1929- .... **CLC 2, 8, 64**
See also AAYA 3; CA 17-20R; CANR 30;
DAM DRAM; DLB 7, 44;
INT CANR-30; MTCW; SATA 8, 61

Feige, Hermann Albert Otto Maximilian
See Traven, B.

Feinberg, David B. 1956-1994 ...... **CLC 59**
See also CA 135; 147

Feinstein, Elaine 1930- .... **CLC 36**
See also CA 69-72; CAAS 1; CANR 31;
DLB 14, 40; MTCW

Feldman, Irving (Mordecai) 1928- .... **CLC 7**
See also CA 1-4R; CANR 1

Fellini, Federico 1920-1993 ..... **CLC 16, 85**
See also CA 65-68; 143; CANR 33

Felsen, Henry Gregor 1916- .... **CLC 17**
See also CA 1-4R; CANR 1; SAAS 2;
SATA 1

Fenton, James Martin 1949- .... **CLC 32**
See also CA 102; DLB 40

Ferber, Edna 1887-1968 .... **CLC 18, 93**
See also AITN 1; CA 5-8R; 25-28R; DLB 9,
28, 86; MTCW; SATA 7

Ferguson, Helen
See Kavan, Anna

Ferguson, Samuel 1810-1886 ..... **NCLC 33**
See also DLB 32

Fergusson, Robert 1750-1774 ...... **LC 29**
See also DLB 109

Ferling, Lawrence
See Ferlinghetti, Lawrence (Monsanto)

Ferlinghetti, Lawrence (Monsanto)
1919(?)- .... **CLC 2, 6, 10, 27; PC 1**
See also CA 5-8R; CANR 3, 41;
CDALB 1941-1968; DAM POET; DLB 5,
16; MTCW

Fernandez, Vicente Garcia Huidobro
See Huidobro Fernandez, Vicente Garcia

Ferrer, Gabriel (Francisco Victor) Miro
See Miro (Ferrer), Gabriel (Francisco
Victor)

Ferrier, Susan (Edmonstone)
1782-1854 .... **NCLC 8**
See also DLB 116

Ferrigno, Robert 1948(?)- .... **CLC 65**
See also CA 140

Ferron, Jacques 1921-1985 ... **CLC 94; DAC**
See also CA 117; 129; DLB 60

Feuchtwanger, Lion 1884-1958 ..... **TCLC 3**
See also CA 104; DLB 66

Feuillet, Octave 1821-1890 ...... **NCLC 45**

Feydeau, Georges (Leon Jules Marie)
1862-1921 .... **TCLC 22**
See also CA 113; DAM DRAM

Ficino, Marsilio 1433-1499 .... **LC 12**

Fiedeler, Hans
See Doeblin, Alfred

Fiedler, Leslie A(aron)
1917- .... **CLC 4, 13, 24**
See also CA 9-12R; CANR 7; DLB 28, 67;
MTCW

Field, Andrew 1938- .... **CLC 44**
See also CA 97-100; CANR 25

Field, Eugene 1850-1895 .... **NCLC 3**
See also DLB 23, 42, 140; DLBD 13;
MAICYA; SATA 16

Field, Gans T.
See Wellman, Manly Wade

Field, Michael .... **TCLC 43**

Field, Peter
See Hobson, Laura Z(ametkin)

Fielding, Henry
1707-1754 ...... **LC 1; DA; DAB; DAC;
WLC**
See also CDBLB 1660-1789; DAM DRAM,
MST, NOV; DLB 39, 84, 101

Fielding, Sarah 1710-1768 .... **LC 1**
See also DLB 39

Fierstein, Harvey (Forbes) 1954- ... **CLC 33**
See also CA 123; 129; DAM DRAM, POP

Figes, Eva 1932- .... **CLC 31**
See also CA 53-56; CANR 4, 44; DLB 14

Finch, Robert (Duer Claydon)
1900- .... **CLC 18**
See also CA 57-60; CANR 9, 24, 49;
DLB 88

Findley, Timothy 1930- ...... **CLC 27; DAC**
See also CA 25-28R; CANR 12, 42;
DAM MST; DLB 53

Fink, William
See Mencken, H(enry) L(ouis)

Firbank, Louis 1942-
See Reed, Lou
See also CA 117

Firbank, (Arthur Annesley) Ronald
1886-1926 .... **TCLC 1**
See also CA 104; DLB 36

Fisher, M(ary) F(rances) K(ennedy)
1908-1992 .... **CLC 76, 87**
See also CA 77-80; 138; CANR 44

Fisher, Roy 1930- .... **CLC 25**
See also CA 81-84; CAAS 10; CANR 16;
DLB 40

Fisher, Rudolph
1897-1934 .... **TCLC 11; BLC**
See also BW 1; CA 107; 124; DAM MULT;
DLB 51, 102

Fisher, Vardis (Alvero) 1895-1968.... **CLC 7**
See also CA 5-8R; 25-28R; DLB 9

Fiske, Tarleton
See Bloch, Robert (Albert)

Fitch, Clarke
See Sinclair, Upton (Beall)

Fitch, John IV
See Cormier, Robert (Edmund)

Fitzgerald, Captain Hugh
See Baum, L(yman) Frank

FitzGerald, Edward 1809-1883 .... **NCLC 9**
See also DLB 32

Fitzgerald, F(rancis) Scott (Key)
1896-1940 .... **TCLC 1, 6, 14, 28, 55;
DA; DAB; DAC; SSC 6; WLC**
See also AITN 1; CA 110; 123;
CDALB 1917-1929; DAM MST, NOV;
DLB 4, 9, 86; DLBD 1; DLBY 81;
MTCW

Fitzgerald, Penelope 1916-... **CLC 19, 51, 61**
See also CA 85-88; CAAS 10; DLB 14

Fitzgerald, Robert (Stuart)
1910-1985 .... **CLC 39**
See also CA 1-4R; 114; CANR 1; DLBY 80

FitzGerald, Robert D(avid)
1902-1987 .... **CLC 19**
See also CA 17-20R

Fitzgerald, Zelda (Sayre)
1900-1948 . . . . **TCLC 52**
See also CA 117; 126; DLBY 84

Flanagan, Thomas (James Bonner)
1923- . . . . **CLC 25, 52**
See also CA 108; DLBY 80; INT 108;
MTCW

Flaubert, Gustave
1821-1880 . . . . **NCLC 2, 10, 19; DA;
DAB; DAC; SSC 11; WLC**
See also DAM MST, NOV; DLB 119

Flecker, Herman Elroy
See Flecker, (Herman) James Elroy

Flecker, (Herman) James Elroy
1884-1915 . . . . **TCLC 43**
See also CA 109; 150; DLB 10, 19

Fleming, Ian (Lancaster)
1908-1964 . . . . **CLC 3, 30**
See also CA 5-8R; CDBLB 1945-1960;
DAM POP; DLB 87; MTCW; SATA 9

Fleming, Thomas (James) 1927- . . . . **CLC 37**
See also CA 5-8R; CANR 10;
INT CANR-10; SATA 8

Fletcher, John 1579-1625 . . . . . **LC 33; DC 6**
See also CDBLB Before 1660; DLB 58

Fletcher, John Gould 1886-1950 . . . **TCLC 35**
See also CA 107; DLB 4, 45

Fleur, Paul
See Pohl, Frederik

Flooglebuckle, Al
See Spiegelman, Art

Flying Officer X
See Bates, H(erbert) E(rnest)

Fo, Dario 1926- . . . . **CLC 32**
See also CA 116; 128; DAM DRAM;
MTCW

Fogarty, Jonathan Titulescu Esq.
See Farrell, James T(homas)

Folke, Will
See Bloch, Robert (Albert)

Follett, Ken(neth Martin) 1949- . . . . **CLC 18**
See also AAYA 6; BEST 89:4; CA 81-84;
CANR 13, 33; DAM NOV, POP;
DLB 87; DLBY 81; INT CANR-33;
MTCW

Fontane, Theodor 1819-1898 . . . . . **NCLC 26**
See also DLB 129

Foote, Horton 1916- . . . . **CLC 51, 91**
See also CA 73-76; CANR 34, 51;
DAM DRAM; DLB 26; INT CANR-34

Foote, Shelby 1916- . . . . **CLC 75**
See also CA 5-8R; CANR 3, 45;
DAM NOV, POP; DLB 2, 17

Forbes, Esther 1891-1967 . . . . **CLC 12**
See also AAYA 17; CA 13-14; 25-28R;
CAP 1; CLR 27; DLB 22; JRDA;
MAICYA; SATA 2

Forche, Carolyn (Louise)
1950- . . . . **CLC 25, 83, 86; PC 10**
See also CA 109; 117; CANR 50;
DAM POET; DLB 5; INT 117

Ford, Elbur
See Hibbert, Eleanor Alice Burford

Ford, Ford Madox
1873-1939 . . . . **TCLC 1, 15, 39, 57**
See also CA 104; 132; CDBLB 1914-1945;
DAM NOV; DLB 162; MTCW

Ford, John 1895-1973 . . . . **CLC 16**
See also CA 45-48

Ford, Richard 1944- . . . . **CLC 46**
See also CA 69-72; CANR 11, 47

Ford, Webster
See Masters, Edgar Lee

Foreman, Richard 1937- . . . . **CLC 50**
See also CA 65-68; CANR 32

Forester, C(ecil) S(cott)
1899-1966 . . . . **CLC 35**
See also CA 73-76; 25-28R; SATA 13

Forez
See Mauriac, Francois (Charles)

Forman, James Douglas 1932- . . . . . . **CLC 21**
See also AAYA 17; CA 9-12R; CANR 4,
19, 42; JRDA; MAICYA; SATA 8, 70

Fornes, Maria Irene 1930- . . . . . . **CLC 39, 61**
See also CA 25-28R; CANR 28; DLB 7;
HW; INT CANR-28; MTCW

Forrest, Leon 1937- . . . . **CLC 4**
See also BW 2; CA 89-92; CAAS 7;
CANR 25, 52; DLB 33

Forster, E(dward) M(organ)
1879-1970 . . . . . **CLC 1, 2, 3, 4, 9, 10, 13,
15, 22, 45, 77; DA; DAB; DAC; WLC**
See also AAYA 2; CA 13-14; 25-28R;
CANR 45; CAP 1; CDBLB 1914-1945;
DAM MST, NOV; DLB 34, 98, 162;
DLBD 10; MTCW; SATA 57

Forster, John 1812-1876 . . . . **NCLC 11**
See also DLB 144

Forsyth, Frederick 1938- . . . . . . **CLC 2, 5, 36**
See also BEST 89:4; CA 85-88; CANR 38;
DAM NOV, POP; DLB 87; MTCW

Forten, Charlotte L. . . . . **TCLC 16; BLC**
See also Grimke, Charlotte L(ottie) Forten
See also DLB 50

Foscolo, Ugo 1778-1827 . . . . **NCLC 8**

Fosse, Bob . . . . **CLC 20**
See also Fosse, Robert Louis

Fosse, Robert Louis 1927-1987
See Fosse, Bob
See also CA 110; 123

Foster, Stephen Collins
1826-1864 . . . . **NCLC 26**

Foucault, Michel
1926-1984 . . . . **CLC 31, 34, 69**
See also CA 105; 113; CANR 34; MTCW

Fouque, Friedrich (Heinrich Karl) de la Motte
1777-1843 . . . . **NCLC 2**
See also DLB 90

Fourier, Charles 1772-1837 . . . . . . **NCLC 51**

Fournier, Henri Alban 1886-1914
See Alain-Fournier
See also CA 104

Fournier, Pierre 1916- . . . . **CLC 11**
See also Gascar, Pierre
See also CA 89-92; CANR 16, 40

Fowles, John
1926- . . . . . . **CLC 1, 2, 3, 4, 6, 9, 10, 15,
33, 87; DAB; DAC**
See also CA 5-8R; CANR 25; CDBLB 1960
to Present; DAM MST; DLB 14, 139;
MTCW; SATA 22

Fox, Paula 1923- . . . . **CLC 2, 8**
See also AAYA 3; CA 73-76; CANR 20,
36; CLR 1; DLB 52; JRDA; MAICYA;
MTCW; SATA 17, 60

Fox, William Price (Jr.) 1926- . . . . . **CLC 22**
See also CA 17-20R; CAAS 19; CANR 11;
DLB 2; DLBY 81

Foxe, John 1516(?)-1587 . . . . **LC 14**

Frame, Janet . . . . **CLC 2, 3, 6, 22, 66**
See also Clutha, Janet Paterson Frame

France, Anatole . . . . **TCLC 9**
See also Thibault, Jacques Anatole Francois
See also DLB 123

Francis, Claude 19(?)- . . . . **CLC 50**

Francis, Dick 1920- . . . . **CLC 2, 22, 42**
See also AAYA 5; BEST 89:3; CA 5-8R;
CANR 9, 42; CDBLB 1960 to Present;
DAM POP; DLB 87; INT CANR-9;
MTCW

Francis, Robert (Churchill)
1901-1987 . . . . **CLC 15**
See also CA 1-4R; 123; CANR 1

Frank, Anne(lies Marie)
1929-1945 . . . . **TCLC 17; DA; DAB;
DAC; WLC**
See also AAYA 12; CA 113; 133;
DAM MST; MTCW; SATA 87;
SATA-Brief 42

Frank, Elizabeth 1945- . . . . **CLC 39**
See also CA 121; 126; INT 126

Frankl, Viktor E(mil) 1905- . . . . **CLC 93**
See also CA 65-68

Franklin, Benjamin
See Hasek, Jaroslav (Matej Frantisek)

Franklin, Benjamin
1706-1790 . . . . . **LC 25; DA; DAB; DAC**
See also CDALB 1640-1865; DAM MST;
DLB 24, 43, 73

Franklin, (Stella Maraia Sarah) Miles
1879-1954 . . . . **TCLC 7**
See also CA 104

Fraser, (Lady) Antonia (Pakenham)
1932- . . . . **CLC 32**
See also CA 85-88; CANR 44; MTCW;
SATA-Brief 32

Fraser, George MacDonald 1925- . . . . **CLC 7**
See also CA 45-48; CANR 2, 48

Fraser, Sylvia 1935- . . . . **CLC 64**
See also CA 45-48; CANR 1, 16

Frayn, Michael 1933- . . . . . . **CLC 3, 7, 31, 47**
See also CA 5-8R; CANR 30;
DAM DRAM, NOV; DLB 13, 14;
MTCW

Fraze, Candida (Merrill) 1945- . . . . . **CLC 50**
See also CA 126

Frazer, J(ames) G(eorge)
1854-1941 . . . . **TCLC 32**
See also CA 118

Frazer, Robert Caine
See Creasey, John

Frazer, Sir James George
See Frazer, J(ames) G(eorge)

Frazier, Ian 1951-................ CLC **46**
See also CA 130

Frederic, Harold 1856-1898...... NCLC **10**
See also DLB 12, 23; DLBD 13

Frederick, John
See Faust, Frederick (Schiller)

Frederick the Great 1712-1786...... LC **14**

Fredro, Aleksander 1793-1876..... NCLC **8**

Freeling, Nicolas 1927-........... CLC **38**
See also CA 49-52; CAAS 12; CANR 1, 17, 50; DLB 87

Freeman, Douglas Southall
1886-1953 .... TCLC **11**
See also CA 109; DLB 17

Freeman, Judith 1946-........... CLC **55**
See also CA 148

Freeman, Mary Eleanor Wilkins
1852-1930 .... TCLC **9**; SSC **1**
See also CA 106; DLB 12, 78

Freeman, R(ichard) Austin
1862-1943 .... TCLC **21**
See also CA 113; DLB 70

French, Albert 1943-............. CLC **86**

French, Marilyn 1929-...... CLC **10, 18, 60**
See also CA 69-72; CANR 3, 31; DAM DRAM, NOV, POP; INT CANR-31; MTCW

French, Paul
See Asimov, Isaac

Freneau, Philip Morin 1752-1832.. NCLC **1**
See also DLB 37, 43

Freud, Sigmund 1856-1939 .... TCLC **52**
See also CA 115; 133; MTCW

Friedan, Betty (Naomi) 1921-...... CLC **74**
See also CA 65-68; CANR 18, 45; MTCW

Friedlander, Saul 1932-........... CLC **90**
See also CA 117; 130

Friedman, B(ernard) H(arper)
1926-....................... CLC **7**
See also CA 1-4R; CANR 3, 48

Friedman, Bruce Jay 1930-.... CLC **3, 5, 56**
See also CA 9-12R; CANR 25, 52; DLB 2, 28; INT CANR-25

Friel, Brian 1929-........... CLC **5, 42, 59**
See also CA 21-24R; CANR 33; DLB 13; MTCW

Friis-Baastad, Babbis Ellinor
1921-1970 .... CLC **12**
See also CA 17-20R; 134; SATA 7

Frisch, Max (Rudolf)
1911-1991 ..... CLC **3, 9, 14, 18, 32, 44**
See also CA 85-88; 134; CANR 32; DAM DRAM, NOV; DLB 69, 124; MTCW

Fromentin, Eugene (Samuel Auguste)
1820-1876 .... NCLC **10**
See also DLB 123

Frost, Frederick
See Faust, Frederick (Schiller)

Frost, Robert (Lee)
1874-1963 .... CLC **1, 3, 4, 9, 10, 13, 15, 26, 34, 44**; DA; DAB; DAC; PC **1**; WLC
See also CA 89-92; CANR 33; CDALB 1917-1929; DAM MST, POET; DLB 54; DLBD 7; MTCW; SATA 14

Froude, James Anthony
1818-1894 .... NCLC **43**
See also DLB 18, 57, 144

Froy, Herald
See Waterhouse, Keith (Spencer)

Fry, Christopher 1907-....... CLC **2, 10, 14**
See also CA 17-20R; CAAS 23; CANR 9, 30; DAM DRAM; DLB 13; MTCW; SATA 66

Frye, (Herman) Northrop
1912-1991 .... CLC **24, 70**
See also CA 5-8R; 133; CANR 8, 37; DLB 67, 68; MTCW

Fuchs, Daniel 1909-1993 .... CLC **8, 22**
See also CA 81-84; 142; CAAS 5; CANR 40; DLB 9, 26, 28; DLBY 93

Fuchs, Daniel 1934-.............. CLC **34**
See also CA 37-40R; CANR 14, 48

Fuentes, Carlos
1928-...... CLC **3, 8, 10, 13, 22, 41, 60**; DA; DAB; DAC; HLC; WLC
See also AAYA 4; AITN 2; CA 69-72; CANR 10, 32; DAM MST, MULT, NOV; DLB 113; HW; MTCW

Fuentes, Gregorio Lopez y
See Lopez y Fuentes, Gregorio

Fugard, (Harold) Athol
1932-.... CLC **5, 9, 14, 25, 40, 80**; DC **3**
See also AAYA 17; CA 85-88; CANR 32; DAM DRAM; MTCW

Fugard, Sheila 1932-............. CLC **48**
See also CA 125

Fuller, Charles (H., Jr.)
1939-........ CLC **25**; BLC; DC **1**
See also BW 2; CA 108; 112; DAM DRAM, MULT; DLB 38; INT 112; MTCW

Fuller, John (Leopold) 1937-....... CLC **62**
See also CA 21-24R; CANR 9, 44; DLB 40

Fuller, Margaret .... NCLC **5, 50**
See also Ossoli, Sarah Margaret (Fuller marchesa d')

Fuller, Roy (Broadbent)
1912-1991 .... CLC **4, 28**
See also CA 5-8R; 135; CAAS 10; CANR 53; DLB 15, 20; SATA 87

Fulton, Alice 1952-.............. CLC **52**
See also CA 116

Furphy, Joseph 1843-1912....... TCLC **25**

Fussell, Paul 1924-.............. CLC **74**
See also BEST 90:1; CA 17-20R; CANR 8, 21, 35; INT CANR-21; MTCW

Futabatei, Shimei 1864-1909 ...... TCLC **44**

Futrelle, Jacques 1875-1912 ...... TCLC **19**
See also CA 113

Gaboriau, Emile 1835-1873 ...... NCLC **14**

Gadda, Carlo Emilio 1893-1973 .... CLC **11**
See also CA 89-92

Gaddis, William
1922-..... CLC **1, 3, 6, 8, 10, 19, 43, 86**
See also CA 17-20R; CANR 21, 48; DLB 2; MTCW

Gaines, Ernest J(ames)
1933-......... CLC **3, 11, 18, 86**; BLC
See also AAYA 18; AITN 1; BW 2; CA 9-12R; CANR 6, 24, 42; CDALB 1968-1988; DAM MULT; DLB 2, 33, 152; DLBY 80; MTCW; SATA 86

Gaitskill, Mary 1954-............. CLC **69**
See also CA 128

Galdos, Benito Perez
See Perez Galdos, Benito

Gale, Zona 1874-1938 .... TCLC **7**
See also CA 105; DAM DRAM; DLB 9, 78

Galeano, Eduardo (Hughes) 1940-... CLC **72**
See also CA 29-32R; CANR 13, 32; HW

Galiano, Juan Valera y Alcala
See Valera y Alcala-Galiano, Juan

Gallagher, Tess 1943-.... CLC **18, 63**; PC **9**
See also CA 106; DAM POET; DLB 120

Gallant, Mavis
1922-...... CLC **7, 18, 38**; DAC; SSC **5**
See also CA 69-72; CANR 29; DAM MST; DLB 53; MTCW

Gallant, Roy A(rthur) 1924-....... CLC **17**
See also CA 5-8R; CANR 4, 29; CLR 30; MAICYA; SATA 4, 68

Gallico, Paul (William) 1897-1976 ... CLC **2**
See also AITN 1; CA 5-8R; 69-72; CANR 23; DLB 9; MAICYA; SATA 13

Gallo, Max Louis 1932-........... CLC **95**
See also CA 85-88

Gallois, Lucien
See Desnos, Robert

Gallup, Ralph
See Whitemore, Hugh (John)

Galsworthy, John
1867-1933 ...... TCLC **1, 45**; DA; DAB; DAC; SSC **22**; WLC **2**
See also CA 104; 141; CDBLB 1890-1914; DAM DRAM, MST, NOV; DLB 10, 34, 98, 162

Galt, John 1779-1839........... NCLC **1**
See also DLB 99, 116, 159

Galvin, James 1951-.............. CLC **38**
See also CA 108; CANR 26

Gamboa, Federico 1864-1939...... TCLC **36**

Gandhi, M. K.
See Gandhi, Mohandas Karamchand

Gandhi, Mahatma
See Gandhi, Mohandas Karamchand

Gandhi, Mohandas Karamchand
1869-1948 .... TCLC **59**
See also CA 121; 132; DAM MULT; MTCW

Gann, Ernest Kellogg 1910-1991.... CLC **23**
See also AITN 1; CA 1-4R; 136; CANR 1

Garcia, Cristina 1958-............. CLC **76**
See also CA 141

Gilbreth, Frank B., Jr. 1911- . . . . . . CLC 17
See also CA 9-12R; SATA 2

Gilchrist, Ellen 1935- . . CLC 34, 48; SSC 14
See also CA 113; 116; CANR 41;
DAM POP; DLB 130; MTCW

Giles, Molly 1942- . . . . CLC 39
See also CA 126

Gill, Patrick
See Creasey, John

Gilliam, Terry (Vance) 1940- . . . . . . CLC 21
See also Monty Python
See also CA 108; 113; CANR 35; INT 113

Gillian, Jerry
See Gilliam, Terry (Vance)

Gilliatt, Penelope (Ann Douglass)
1932-1993 . . . . CLC 2, 10, 13, 53
See also AITN 2; CA 13-16R; 141;
CANR 49; DLB 14

Gilman, Charlotte (Anna) Perkins (Stetson)
1860-1935 . . . . TCLC 9, 37; SSC 13
See also CA 106; 150

Gilmour, David 1949- . . . . CLC 35
See also CA 138, 147

Gilpin, William 1724-1804 . . . . NCLC 30

Gilray, J. D.
See Mencken, H(enry) L(ouis)

Gilroy, Frank D(aniel) 1925- . . . . CLC 2
See also CA 81-84; CANR 32; DLB 7

Ginsberg, Allen
1926- . . . . . . CLC 1, 2, 3, 4, 6, 13, 36, 69;
DA; DAB; DAC; PC 4; WLC 3
See also AITN 1; CA 1-4R; CANR 2, 41;
CDALB 1941-1968; DAM MST, POET;
DLB 5, 16; MTCW

Ginzburg, Natalia
1916-1991 . . . . CLC 5, 11, 54, 70
See also CA 85-88; 135; CANR 33; MTCW

Giono, Jean 1895-1970 . . . . CLC 4, 11
See also CA 45-48; 29-32R; CANR 2, 35;
DLB 72; MTCW

Giovanni, Nikki
1943- . . . . . . CLC 2, 4, 19, 64; BLC; DA;
DAB; DAC
See also AITN 1; BW 2; CA 29-32R;
CAAS 6; CANR 18, 41; CLR 6;
DAM MST, MULT, POET; DLB 5, 41;
INT CANR-18; MAICYA; MTCW;
SATA 24

Giovene, Andrea 1904- . . . . CLC 7
See also CA 85-88

Gippius, Zinaida (Nikolayevna) 1869-1945
See Hippius, Zinaida
See also CA 106

Giraudoux, (Hippolyte) Jean
1882-1944 . . . . TCLC 2, 7
See also CA 104; DAM DRAM; DLB 65

Gironella, Jose Maria 1917- . . . . CLC 11
See also CA 101

Gissing, George (Robert)
1857-1903 . . . . TCLC 3, 24, 47
See also CA 105; DLB 18, 135

Giurlani, Aldo
See Palazzeschi, Aldo

Gladkov, Fyodor (Vasilyevich)
1883-1958 . . . . TCLC 27

Glanville, Brian (Lester) 1931- . . . . . . CLC 6
See also CA 5-8R; CAAS 9; CANR 3;
DLB 15, 139; SATA 42

Glasgow, Ellen (Anderson Gholson)
1873(?)-1945 . . . . TCLC 2, 7
See also CA 104; DLB 9, 12

Glaspell, Susan (Keating)
1882(?)-1948 . . . . TCLC 55
See also CA 110; DLB 7, 9, 78; YABC 2

Glassco, John 1909-1981 . . . . CLC 9
See also CA 13-16R; 102; CANR 15;
DLB 68

Glasscock, Amnesia
See Steinbeck, John (Ernst)

Glasser, Ronald J. 1940(?)- . . . . CLC 37

Glassman, Joyce
See Johnson, Joyce

Glendinning, Victoria 1937- . . . . CLC 50
See also CA 120; 127; DLB 155

Glissant, Edouard 1928- . . . . CLC 10, 68
See also DAM MULT

Gloag, Julian 1930- . . . . CLC 40
See also AITN 1; CA 65-68; CANR 10

Glowacki, Aleksander
See Prus, Boleslaw

Gluck, Louise (Elisabeth)
1943- . . . . CLC 7, 22, 44, 81; PC 16
See also CA 33-36R; CANR 40;
DAM POET; DLB 5

Gobineau, Joseph Arthur (Comte) de
1816-1882 . . . . NCLC 17
See also DLB 123

Godard, Jean-Luc 1930- . . . . CLC 20
See also CA 93-96

Godden, (Margaret) Rumer 1907- . . . CLC 53
See also AAYA 6; CA 5-8R; CANR 4, 27,
36; CLR 20; DLB 161; MAICYA;
SAAS 12; SATA 3, 36

Godoy Alcayaga, Lucila 1889-1957
See Mistral, Gabriela
See also BW 2; CA 104; 131; DAM MULT;
HW; MTCW

Godwin, Gail (Kathleen)
1937- . . . . CLC 5, 8, 22, 31, 69
See also CA 29-32R; CANR 15, 43;
DAM POP; DLB 6; INT CANR-15;
MTCW

Godwin, William 1756-1836 . . . . . . NCLC 14
See also CDBLB 1789-1832; DLB 39, 104,
142, 158, 163

Goethe, Johann Wolfgang von
1749-1832 . . . . NCLC 4, 22, 34; DA;
DAB; DAC; PC 5; WLC 3
See also DAM DRAM, MST, POET;
DLB 94

Gogarty, Oliver St. John
1878-1957 . . . . TCLC 15
See also CA 109; 150; DLB 15, 19

Gogol, Nikolai (Vasilyevich)
1809-1852 . . . . NCLC 5, 15, 31; DA;
DAB; DAC; DC 1; SSC 4; WLC
See also DAM DRAM, MST

Goines, Donald
1937(?)-1974 . . . . CLC 80; BLC
See also AITN 1; BW 1; CA 124; 114;
DAM MULT, POP; DLB 33

Gold, Herbert 1924- . . . . CLC 4, 7, 14, 42
See also CA 9-12R; CANR 17, 45; DLB 2;
DLBY 81

Goldbarth, Albert 1948- . . . . CLC 5, 38
See also CA 53-56; CANR 6, 40; DLB 120

Goldberg, Anatol 1910-1982 . . . . CLC 34
See also CA 131; 117

Goldemberg, Isaac 1945- . . . . CLC 52
See also CA 69-72; CAAS 12; CANR 11,
32; HW

Golding, William (Gerald)
1911-1993 . . . . CLC 1, 2, 3, 8, 10, 17, 27,
58, 81; DA; DAB; DAC; WLC
See also AAYA 5; CA 5-8R; 141;
CANR 13, 33; CDBLB 1945-1960;
DAM MST, NOV; DLB 15, 100; MTCW

Goldman, Emma 1869-1940 . . . . TCLC 13
See also CA 110; 150

Goldman, Francisco 1955- . . . . CLC 76

Goldman, William (W.) 1931- . . . . CLC 1, 48
See also CA 9-12R; CANR 29; DLB 44

Goldmann, Lucien 1913-1970 . . . . . . CLC 24
See also CA 25-28; CAP 2

Goldoni, Carlo 1707-1793 . . . . LC 4
See also DAM DRAM

Goldsberry, Steven 1949- . . . . CLC 34
See also CA 131

Goldsmith, Oliver
1728-1774 . . . . . . LC 2; DA; DAB; DAC;
WLC
See also CDBLB 1660-1789; DAM DRAM,
MST, NOV, POET; DLB 39, 89, 104,
109, 142; SATA 26

Goldsmith, Peter
See Priestley, J(ohn) B(oynton)

Gombrowicz, Witold
1904-1969 . . . . CLC 4, 7, 11, 49
See also CA 19-20; 25-28R; CAP 2;
DAM DRAM

Gomez de la Serna, Ramon
1888-1963 . . . . CLC 9
See also CA 116; HW

Goncharov, Ivan Alexandrovich
1812-1891 . . . . NCLC 1

Goncourt, Edmond (Louis Antoine Huot) de
1822-1896 . . . . NCLC 7
See also DLB 123

Goncourt, Jules (Alfred Huot) de
1830-1870 . . . . NCLC 7
See also DLB 123

Gontier, Fernande 19(?)- . . . . CLC 50

Goodman, Paul 1911-1972 . . . . CLC 1, 2, 4, 7
See also CA 19-20; 37-40R; CANR 34;
CAP 2; DLB 130; MTCW

Gordimer, Nadine
1923- . . . . CLC 3, 5, 7, 10, 18, 33, 51, 70;
DA; DAB; DAC; SSC 17
See also CA 5-8R; CANR 3, 28;
DAM MST, NOV; INT CANR-28;
MTCW

Gordon, Adam Lindsay
1833-1870 . . . . **NCLC 21**

Gordon, Caroline
1895-1981 . . . **CLC 6, 13, 29, 83; SSC 15**
See also CA 11-12; 103; CANR 36; CAP 1;
DLB 4, 9, 102; DLBY 81; MTCW

Gordon, Charles William 1860-1937
See Connor, Ralph
See also CA 109

Gordon, Mary (Catherine)
1949- . . . . **CLC 13, 22**
See also CA 102; CANR 44; DLB 6;
DLBY 81; INT 102; MTCW

Gordon, Sol 1923- . . . . **CLC 26**
See also CA 53-56; CANR 4; SATA 11

Gordone, Charles 1925-1995 . . . . . **CLC 1, 4**
See also BW 1; CA 93-96; 150;
DAM DRAM; DLB 7; INT 93-96;
MTCW

Gorenko, Anna Andreevna
See Akhmatova, Anna

Gorky, Maxim . . . . **TCLC 8; DAB; WLC**
See also Peshkov, Alexei Maximovich

Goryan, Sirak
See Saroyan, William

Gosse, Edmund (William)
1849-1928 . . . . **TCLC 28**
See also CA 117; DLB 57, 144

Gotlieb, Phyllis Fay (Bloom)
1926- . . . . **CLC 18**
See also CA 13-16R; CANR 7; DLB 88

Gottesman, S. D.
See Kornbluth, C(yril) M.; Pohl, Frederik

Gottfried von Strassburg
fl. c. 1210- . . . . **CMLC 10**
See also DLB 138

Gould, Lois . . . . **CLC 4, 10**
See also CA 77-80; CANR 29; MTCW

Gourmont, Remy (-Marie-Charles) de
1858-1915 . . . . **TCLC 17**
See also CA 109; 150

Govier, Katherine 1948- . . . . **CLC 51**
See also CA 101; CANR 18, 40

Goyen, (Charles) William
1915-1983 . . . . **CLC 5, 8, 14, 40**
See also AITN 2; CA 5-8R; 110; CANR 6;
DLB 2; DLBY 83; INT CANR-6

Goytisolo, Juan
1931- . . . . **CLC 5, 10, 23; HLC**
See also CA 85-88; CANR 32;
DAM MULT; HW; MTCW

Gozzano, Guido 1883-1916 . . . . **PC 10**
See also DLB 114

Gozzi, (Conte) Carlo 1720-1806 . . **NCLC 23**

Grabbe, Christian Dietrich
1801-1836 . . . . **NCLC 2**
See also DLB 133

Grace, Patricia 1937- . . . . **CLC 56**

Gracian y Morales, Baltasar
1601-1658 . . . . **LC 15**

Gracq, Julien . . . . **CLC 11, 48**
See also Poirier, Louis
See also DLB 83

Grade, Chaim 1910-1982 . . . . **CLC 10**
See also CA 93-96; 107

Graduate of Oxford, A
See Ruskin, John

Graham, John
See Phillips, David Graham

Graham, Jorie 1951- . . . . **CLC 48**
See also CA 111; DLB 120

Graham, R(obert) B(ontine) Cunninghame
See Cunninghame Graham, R(obert)
B(ontine)
See also DLB 98, 135

Graham, Robert
See Haldeman, Joe (William)

Graham, Tom
See Lewis, (Harry) Sinclair

Graham, W(illiam) S(ydney)
1918-1986 . . . . **CLC 29**
See also CA 73-76; 118; DLB 20

Graham, Winston (Mawdsley)
1910- . . . . **CLC 23**
See also CA 49-52; CANR 2, 22, 45;
DLB 77

Grahame, Kenneth
1859-1932 . . . . **TCLC 64; DAB**
See also CA 108; 136; CLR 5; DLB 34, 141;
MAICYA; YABC 1

Grant, Skeeter
See Spiegelman, Art

Granville-Barker, Harley
1877-1946 . . . . **TCLC 2**
See also Barker, Harley Granville
See also CA 104; DAM DRAM

Grass, Guenter (Wilhelm)
1927- . . . . . **CLC 1, 2, 4, 6, 11, 15, 22, 32,
49, 88; DA; DAB; DAC; WLC**
See also CA 13-16R; CANR 20;
DAM MST, NOV; DLB 75, 124; MTCW

Gratton, Thomas
See Hulme, T(homas) E(rnest)

Grau, Shirley Ann
1929- . . . . **CLC 4, 9; SSC 15**
See also CA 89-92; CANR 22; DLB 2;
INT CANR-22; MTCW

Gravel, Fern
See Hall, James Norman

Graver, Elizabeth 1964- . . . . **CLC 70**
See also CA 135

Graves, Richard Perceval 1945- . . . . **CLC 44**
See also CA 65-68; CANR 9, 26, 51

Graves, Robert (von Ranke)
1895-1985 . . . . . . **CLC 1, 2, 6, 11, 39, 44,
45; DAB; DAC; PC 6**
See also CA 5-8R; 117; CANR 5, 36;
CDBLB 1914-1945; DAM MST, POET;
DLB 20, 100; DLBY 85; MTCW;
SATA 45

Graves, Valerie
See Bradley, Marion Zimmer

Gray, Alasdair (James) 1934- . . . . . . **CLC 41**
See also CA 126; CANR 47; INT 126;
MTCW

Gray, Amlin 1946- . . . . **CLC 29**
See also CA 138

Gray, Francine du Plessix 1930- . . . . **CLC 22**
See also BEST 90:3; CA 61-64; CAAS 2;
CANR 11, 33; DAM NOV;
INT CANR-11; MTCW

Gray, John (Henry) 1866-1934 . . . . **TCLC 19**
See also CA 119

Gray, Simon (James Holliday)
1936- . . . . **CLC 9, 14, 36**
See also AITN 1; CA 21-24R; CAAS 3;
CANR 32; DLB 13; MTCW

Gray, Spalding 1941- . . . . **CLC 49**
See also CA 128; DAM POP

Gray, Thomas
1716-1771 . . . . . . **LC 4; DA; DAB; DAC;
PC 2; WLC**
See also CDBLB 1660-1789; DAM MST;
DLB 109

Grayson, David
See Baker, Ray Stannard

Grayson, Richard (A.) 1951- . . . . **CLC 38**
See also CA 85-88; CANR 14, 31

Greeley, Andrew M(oran) 1928- . . . . **CLC 28**
See also CA 5-8R; CAAS 7; CANR 7, 43;
DAM POP; MTCW

Green, Anna Katharine
1846-1935 . . . . **TCLC 63**
See also CA 112

Green, Brian
See Card, Orson Scott

Green, Hannah
See Greenberg, Joanne (Goldenberg)

Green, Hannah . . . . **CLC 3**
See also CA 73-76

Green, Henry . . . . **CLC 2, 13**
See also Yorke, Henry Vincent
See also DLB 15

Green, Julian (Hartridge) 1900-
See Green, Julien
See also CA 21-24R; CANR 33; DLB 4, 72;
MTCW

Green, Julien . . . . **CLC 3, 11, 77**
See also Green, Julian (Hartridge)

Green, Paul (Eliot) 1894-1981 . . . . . . **CLC 25**
See also AITN 1; CA 5-8R; 103; CANR 3;
DAM DRAM; DLB 7, 9; DLBY 81

Greenberg, Ivan 1908-1973
See Rahv, Philip
See also CA 85-88

Greenberg, Joanne (Goldenberg)
1932- . . . . **CLC 7, 30**
See also AAYA 12; CA 5-8R; CANR 14,
32; SATA 25

Greenberg, Richard 1959(?)- . . . . **CLC 57**
See also CA 138

Greene, Bette 1934- . . . . **CLC 30**
See also AAYA 7; CA 53-56; CANR 4;
CLR 2; JRDA; MAICYA; SAAS 16;
SATA 8

Greene, Gael . . . . **CLC 8**
See also CA 13-16R; CANR 10

Greene, Graham
    1904-1991 .... **CLC 1, 3, 6, 9, 14, 18, 27,
        37, 70, 72; DA; DAB; DAC; WLC**
    See also AITN 2; CA 13-16R; 133;
        CANR 35; CDBLB 1945-1960;
        DAM MST, NOV; DLB 13, 15, 77, 100,
        162; DLBY 91; MTCW; SATA 20

Greer, Richard
    See Silverberg, Robert

Gregor, Arthur   1923- .... **CLC 9**
    See also CA 25-28R; CAAS 10; CANR 11;
        SATA 36

Gregor, Lee
    See Pohl, Frederik

Gregory, Isabella Augusta (Persse)
    1852-1932 .... **TCLC 1**
    See also CA 104; DLB 10

Gregory, J. Dennis
    See Williams, John A(lfred)

Grendon, Stephen
    See Derleth, August (William)

Grenville, Kate   1950- .... **CLC 61**
    See also CA 118; CANR 53

Grenville, Pelham
    See Wodehouse, P(elham) G(renville)

Greve, Felix Paul (Berthold Friedrich)
    1879-1948
    See Grove, Frederick Philip
    See also CA 104; 141; DAC; DAM MST

Grey, Zane   1872-1939 .... **TCLC 6**
    See also CA 104; 132; DAM POP; DLB 9;
        MTCW

Grieg, (Johan) Nordahl (Brun)
    1902-1943 .... **TCLC 10**
    See also CA 107

Grieve, C(hristopher) M(urray)
    1892-1978 .... **CLC 11, 19**
    See also MacDiarmid, Hugh; Pteleon
    See also CA 5-8R; 85-88; CANR 33;
        DAM POET; MTCW

Griffin, Gerald   1803-1840 .... **NCLC 7**
    See also DLB 159

Griffin, John Howard   1920-1980.... **CLC 68**
    See also AITN 1; CA 1-4R; 101; CANR 2

Griffin, Peter   1942- .... **CLC 39**
    See also CA 136

Griffiths, Trevor   1935-........ **CLC 13, 52**
    See also CA 97-100; CANR 45; DLB 13

Grigson, Geoffrey (Edward Harvey)
    1905-1985 .... **CLC 7, 39**
    See also CA 25-28R; 118; CANR 20, 33;
        DLB 27; MTCW

Grillparzer, Franz   1791-1872..... **NCLC 1**
    See also DLB 133

Grimble, Reverend Charles James
    See Eliot, T(homas) S(tearns)

Grimke, Charlotte L(ottie) Forten
    1837(?)-1914
    See Forten, Charlotte L.
    See also BW 1; CA 117; 124; DAM MULT,
        POET

Grimm, Jacob Ludwig Karl
    1785-1863 .... **NCLC 3**
    See also DLB 90; MAICYA; SATA 22

Grimm, Wilhelm Karl   1786-1859 .. **NCLC 3**
    See also DLB 90; MAICYA; SATA 22

Grimmelshausen, Johann Jakob Christoffel
    von   1621-1676 .... **LC 6**

Grindel, Eugene   1895-1952
    See Eluard, Paul
    See also CA 104

Grisham, John   1955- .... **CLC 84**
    See also AAYA 14; CA 138; CANR 47;
        DAM POP

Grossman, David   1954- .... **CLC 67**
    See also CA 138

Grossman, Vasily (Semenovich)
    1905-1964 .... **CLC 41**
    See also CA 124; 130; MTCW

Grove, Frederick Philip .... **TCLC 4**
    See also Greve, Felix Paul (Berthold
        Friedrich)
    See also DLB 92

Grubb
    See Crumb, R(obert)

Grumbach, Doris (Isaac)
    1918- .... **CLC 13, 22, 64**
    See also CA 5-8R; CAAS 2; CANR 9, 42;
        INT CANR-9

Grundtvig, Nicolai Frederik Severin
    1783-1872 .... **NCLC 1**

Grunge
    See Crumb, R(obert)

Grunwald, Lisa   1959- .... **CLC 44**
    See also CA 120

Guare, John   1938- .... **CLC 8, 14, 29, 67**
    See also CA 73-76; CANR 21;
        DAM DRAM; DLB 7; MTCW

Gudjonsson, Halldor Kiljan   1902-
    See Laxness, Halldor
    See also CA 103

Guenter, Erich
    See Eich, Guenter

Guest, Barbara   1920- .... **CLC 34**
    See also CA 25-28R; CANR 11, 44; DLB 5

Guest, Judith (Ann)   1936- .... **CLC 8, 30**
    See also AAYA 7; CA 77-80; CANR 15;
        DAM NOV, POP; INT CANR-15;
        MTCW

Guevara, Che .... **CLC 87; HLC**
    See also Guevara (Serna), Ernesto

Guevara (Serna), Ernesto   1928-1967
    See Guevara, Che
    See also CA 127; 111; DAM MULT; HW

Guild, Nicholas M.   1944-......... **CLC 33**
    See also CA 93-96

Guillemin, Jacques
    See Sartre, Jean-Paul

Guillen, Jorge   1893-1984......... **CLC 11**
    See also CA 89-92; 112; DAM MULT,
        POET; DLB 108; HW

Guillen, Nicolas (Cristobal)
    1902-1989 ..... **CLC 48, 79; BLC; HLC**
    See also BW 2; CA 116; 125; 129;
        DAM MST, MULT, POET; HW

Guillevic, (Eugene)   1907-......... **CLC 33**
    See also CA 93-96

Guillois
    See Desnos, Robert

Guillois, Valentin
    See Desnos, Robert

Guiney, Louise Imogen
    1861-1920 .... **TCLC 41**
    See also DLB 54

Guiraldes, Ricardo (Guillermo)
    1886-1927 .... **TCLC 39**
    See also CA 131; HW; MTCW

Gumilev, Nikolai Stephanovich
    1886-1921 .... **TCLC 60**

Gunesekera, Romesh............... **CLC 91**

Gunn, Bill .... **CLC 5**
    See also Gunn, William Harrison
    See also DLB 38

Gunn, Thom(son William)
    1929- .... **CLC 3, 6, 18, 32, 81**
    See also CA 17-20R; CANR 9, 33;
        CDBLB 1960 to Present; DAM POET;
        DLB 27; INT CANR-33; MTCW

Gunn, William Harrison   1934(?)-1989
    See Gunn, Bill
    See also AITN 1; BW 1; CA 13-16R; 128;
        CANR 12, 25

Gunnars, Kristjana   1948-......... **CLC 69**
    See also CA 113; DLB 60

Gurganus, Allan   1947-............ **CLC 70**
    See also BEST 90:1; CA 135; DAM POP

Gurney, A(lbert) R(amsdell), Jr.
    1930- .... **CLC 32, 50, 54**
    See also CA 77-80; CANR 32;
        DAM DRAM

Gurney, Ivor (Bertie)   1890-1937 ... **TCLC 33**

Gurney, Peter
    See Gurney, A(lbert) R(amsdell), Jr.

Guro, Elena   1877-1913.......... **TCLC 56**

Gustafson, Ralph (Barker)   1909-.... **CLC 36**
    See also CA 21-24R; CANR 8, 45; DLB 88

Gut, Gom
    See Simenon, Georges (Jacques Christian)

Guterson, David   1956-............ **CLC 91**
    See also CA 132

Guthrie, A(lfred) B(ertram), Jr.
    1901-1991 .... **CLC 23**
    See also CA 57-60; 134; CANR 24; DLB 6;
        SATA 62; SATA-Obit 67

Guthrie, Isobel
    See Grieve, C(hristopher) M(urray)

Guthrie, Woodrow Wilson   1912-1967
    See Guthrie, Woody
    See also CA 113; 93-96

Guthrie, Woody.................. **CLC 35**
    See also Guthrie, Woodrow Wilson

Guy, Rosa (Cuthbert)   1928-........ **CLC 26**
    See also AAYA 4; BW 2; CA 17-20R;
        CANR 14, 34; CLR 13; DLB 33; JRDA;
        MAICYA; SATA 14, 62

Gwendolyn
    See Bennett, (Enoch) Arnold

H. D. .... **CLC 3, 8, 14, 31, 34, 73; PC 5**
    See also Doolittle, Hilda

H. de V.
    See Buchan, John

Haavikko, Paavo Juhani
    1931- . . . . **CLC 18, 34**
    See also CA 106

Habbema, Koos
    See Heijermans, Herman

Hacker, Marilyn
    1942- . . . . **CLC 5, 9, 23, 72, 91**
    See also CA 77-80; DAM POET; DLB 120

Haggard, H(enry) Rider
    1856-1925 . . . . **TCLC 11**
    See also CA 108; 148; DLB 70, 156;
    SATA 16

Hagiwara Sakutaro   1886-1942 . . . . **TCLC 60**

Haig, Fenil
    See Ford, Ford Madox

Haig-Brown, Roderick (Langmere)
    1908-1976 . . . . **CLC 21**
    See also CA 5-8R; 69-72; CANR 4, 38;
    CLR 31; DLB 88; MAICYA; SATA 12

Hailey, Arthur   1920- . . . . **CLC 5**
    See also AITN 2; BEST 90:3; CA 1-4R;
    CANR 2, 36; DAM NOV, POP; DLB 88;
    DLBY 82; MTCW

Hailey, Elizabeth Forsythe   1938- . . . **CLC 40**
    See also CA 93-96; CAAS 1; CANR 15, 48;
    INT CANR-15

Haines, John (Meade)   1924- . . . . **CLC 58**
    See also CA 17-20R; CANR 13, 34; DLB 5

Hakluyt, Richard   1552-1616 . . . . **LC 31**

Haldeman, Joe (William)   1943- . . . . . **CLC 61**
    See also CA 53-56; CANR 6; DLB 8;
    INT CANR-6

Haley, Alex(ander Murray Palmer)
    1921-1992 . . . . **CLC 8, 12, 76; BLC; DA;**
                                        DAB; DAC
    See also BW 2; CA 77-80; 136; DAM MST,
    MULT, POP; DLB 38; MTCW

Haliburton, Thomas Chandler
    1796-1865 . . . . **NCLC 15**
    See also DLB 11, 99

Hall, Donald (Andrew, Jr.)
    1928- . . . . **CLC 1, 13, 37, 59**
    See also CA 5-8R; CAAS 7; CANR 2, 44;
    DAM POET; DLB 5; SATA 23

Hall, Frederic Sauser
    See Sauser-Hall, Frederic

Hall, James
    See Kuttner, Henry

Hall, James Norman   1887-1951 . . . **TCLC 23**
    See also CA 123; SATA 21

Hall, (Marguerite) Radclyffe
    1886-1943 . . . . **TCLC 12**
    See also CA 110; 150

Hall, Rodney   1935- . . . . **CLC 51**
    See also CA 109

Halleck, Fitz-Greene   1790-1867 . . **NCLC 47**
    See also DLB 3

Halliday, Michael
    See Creasey, John

Halpern, Daniel   1945- . . . . **CLC 14**
    See also CA 33-36R

Hamburger, Michael (Peter Leopold)
    1924- . . . . **CLC 5, 14**
    See also CA 5-8R; CAAS 4; CANR 2, 47;
    DLB 27

Hamill, Pete   1935- . . . . **CLC 10**
    See also CA 25-28R; CANR 18

Hamilton, Alexander
    1755(?)-1804 . . . . **NCLC 49**
    See also DLB 37

Hamilton, Clive
    See Lewis, C(live) S(taples)

Hamilton, Edmond   1904-1977 . . . . **CLC 1**
    See also CA 1-4R; CANR 3; DLB 8

Hamilton, Eugene (Jacob) Lee
    See Lee-Hamilton, Eugene (Jacob)

Hamilton, Franklin
    See Silverberg, Robert

Hamilton, Gail
    See Corcoran, Barbara

Hamilton, Mollie
    See Kaye, M(ary) M(argaret)

Hamilton, (Anthony Walter) Patrick
    1904-1962 . . . . **CLC 51**
    See also CA 113; DLB 10

Hamilton, Virginia   1936- . . . . **CLC 26**
    See also AAYA 2; BW 2; CA 25-28R;
    CANR 20, 37; CLR 1, 11, 40;
    DAM MULT; DLB 33, 52;
    INT CANR-20; JRDA; MAICYA;
    MTCW; SATA 4, 56, 79

Hammett, (Samuel) Dashiell
    1894-1961 . . . . **CLC 3, 5, 10, 19, 47;**
                                              SSC 17
    See also AITN 1; CA 81-84; CANR 42;
    CDALB 1929-1941; DLBD 6; MTCW

Hammon, Jupiter
    1711(?)-1800(?) . . . **NCLC 5; BLC; PC 16**
    See also DAM MULT, POET; DLB 31, 50

Hammond, Keith
    See Kuttner, Henry

Hamner, Earl (Henry), Jr.   1923- . . . **CLC 12**
    See also AITN 2; CA 73-76; DLB 6

Hampton, Christopher (James)
    1946- . . . . **CLC 4**
    See also CA 25-28R; DLB 13; MTCW

Hamsun, Knut . . . . **TCLC 2, 14, 49**
    See also Pedersen, Knut

Handke, Peter   1942- . . **CLC 5, 8, 10, 15, 38**
    See also CA 77-80; CANR 33;
    DAM DRAM, NOV; DLB 85, 124;
    MTCW

Hanley, James   1901-1985 . . . **CLC 3, 5, 8, 13**
    See also CA 73-76; 117; CANR 36; MTCW

Hannah, Barry   1942- . . . . **CLC 23, 38, 90**
    See also CA 108; 110; CANR 43; DLB 6;
    INT 110; MTCW

Hannon, Ezra
    See Hunter, Evan

Hansberry, Lorraine (Vivian)
    1930-1965 . . . . . . **CLC 17, 62; BLC; DA;**
                                        DAB; DAC; DC 2
    See also BW 1; CA 109; 25-28R; CABS 3;
    CDALB 1941-1968; DAM DRAM, MST,
    MULT; DLB 7, 38; MTCW

Hansen, Joseph   1923- . . . . **CLC 38**
    See also CA 29-32R; CAAS 17; CANR 16,
    44; INT CANR-16

Hansen, Martin A.   1909-1955 . . . . . **TCLC 32**

Hanson, Kenneth O(stlin)   1922- . . . . **CLC 13**
    See also CA 53-56; CANR 7

Hardwick, Elizabeth   1916- . . . . **CLC 13**
    See also CA 5-8R; CANR 3, 32;
    DAM NOV; DLB 6; MTCW

Hardy, Thomas
    1840-1928 . . . . . . **TCLC 4, 10, 18, 32, 48,**
        53; DA; DAB; DAC; PC 8; SSC 2; WLC
    See also CA 104; 123; CDBLB 1890-1914;
    DAM MST, NOV, POET; DLB 18, 19,
    135; MTCW

Hare, David   1947- . . . . **CLC 29, 58**
    See also CA 97-100; CANR 39; DLB 13;
    MTCW

Harford, Henry
    See Hudson, W(illiam) H(enry)

Hargrave, Leonie
    See Disch, Thomas M(ichael)

Harjo, Joy   1951- . . . . **CLC 83**
    See also CA 114; CANR 35; DAM MULT;
    DLB 120; NNAL

Harlan, Louis R(udolph)   1922- . . . . . **CLC 34**
    See also CA 21-24R; CANR 25

Harling, Robert   1951(?)- . . . . **CLC 53**
    See also CA 147

Harmon, William (Ruth)   1938- . . . . . **CLC 38**
    See also CA 33-36R; CANR 14, 32, 35;
    SATA 65

Harper, F. E. W.
    See Harper, Frances Ellen Watkins

Harper, Frances E. W.
    See Harper, Frances Ellen Watkins

Harper, Frances E. Watkins
    See Harper, Frances Ellen Watkins

Harper, Frances Ellen
    See Harper, Frances Ellen Watkins

Harper, Frances Ellen Watkins
    1825-1911 . . . . **TCLC 14; BLC**
    See also BW 1; CA 111; 125; DAM MULT,
    POET; DLB 50

Harper, Michael S(teven)   1938- . . **CLC 7, 22**
    See also BW 1; CA 33-36R; CANR 24;
    DLB 41

Harper, Mrs. F. E. W.
    See Harper, Frances Ellen Watkins

Harris, Christie (Lucy) Irwin
    1907- . . . . **CLC 12**
    See also CA 5-8R; CANR 6; DLB 88;
    JRDA; MAICYA; SAAS 10; SATA 6, 74

Harris, Frank   1856-1931 . . . . **TCLC 24**
    See also CA 109; 150; DLB 156

Harris, George Washington
    1814-1869 . . . . **NCLC 23**
    See also DLB 3, 11

Harris, Joel Chandler
    1848-1908 . . . . **TCLC 2; SSC 19**
    See also CA 104; 137; DLB 11, 23, 42, 78,
    91; MAICYA; YABC 1

Harris, John (Wyndham Parkes Lucas)
    Beynon 1903-1969
    See Wyndham, John
    See also CA 102; 89-92

Harris, MacDonald . . . . **CLC 9**
    See also Heiney, Donald (William)

Harris, Mark 1922- . . . . CLC 19
See also CA 5-8R; CAAS 3; CANR 2;
DLB 2; DLBY 80

Harris, (Theodore) Wilson 1921-. . . . CLC 25
See also BW 2; CA 65-68; CAAS 16;
CANR 11, 27; DLB 117; MTCW

Harrison, Elizabeth Cavanna 1909-
See Cavanna, Betty
See also CA 9-12R; CANR 6, 27

Harrison, Harry (Max) 1925- . . . . . . CLC 42
See also CA 1-4R; CANR 5, 21; DLB 8;
SATA 4

Harrison, James (Thomas)
1937- . . . . . . CLC 6, 14, 33, 66; SSC 19
See also CA 13-16R; CANR 8, 51;
DLBY 82; INT CANR-8

Harrison, Jim
See Harrison, James (Thomas)

Harrison, Kathryn 1961- . . . . CLC 70
See also CA 144

Harrison, Tony 1937-. . . . . CLC 43
See also CA 65-68; CANR 44; DLB 40;
MTCW

Harriss, Will(ard Irvin) 1922-. . . . . . CLC 34
See also CA 111

Harson, Sley
See Ellison, Harlan (Jay)

Hart, Ellis
See Ellison, Harlan (Jay)

Hart, Josephine 1942(?)- . . . . CLC 70
See also CA 138; DAM POP

Hart, Moss 1904-1961 . . . . CLC 66
See also CA 109; 89-92; DAM DRAM;
DLB 7

Harte, (Francis) Bret(t)
1836(?)-1902 . . . . TCLC 1, 25; DA; DAC;
SSC 8; WLC
See also CA 104; 140; CDALB 1865-1917;
DAM MST; DLB 12, 64, 74, 79;
SATA 26

Hartley, L(eslie) P(oles)
1895-1972 . . . . CLC 2, 22
See also CA 45-48; 37-40R; CANR 33;
DLB 15, 139; MTCW

Hartman, Geoffrey H. 1929-. . . . . . . CLC 27
See also CA 117; 125; DLB 67

Hartmann von Aue
c. 1160-c. 1205 . . . . CMLC 15
See also DLB 138

Hartmann von Aue 1170-1210. . . . CMLC 15

Haruf, Kent 1943- . . . . CLC 34
See also CA 149

Harwood, Ronald 1934-. . . . . CLC 32
See also CA 1-4R; CANR 4; DAM DRAM,
MST; DLB 13

Hasek, Jaroslav (Matej Frantisek)
1883-1923 . . . . TCLC 4
See also CA 104; 129; MTCW

Hass, Robert 1941-. . . . . CLC 18, 39; PC 16
See also CA 111; CANR 30, 50; DLB 105

Hastings, Hudson
See Kuttner, Henry

Hastings, Selina. . . . . CLC 44

Hatteras, Amelia
See Mencken, H(enry) L(ouis)

Hatteras, Owen . . . . TCLC 18
See also Mencken, H(enry) L(ouis); Nathan,
George Jean

Hauptmann, Gerhart (Johann Robert)
1862-1946 . . . . TCLC 4
See also CA 104; DAM DRAM; DLB 66,
118

Havel, Vaclav
1936- . . . . CLC 25, 58, 65; DC 6
See also CA 104; CANR 36; DAM DRAM;
MTCW

Haviaras, Stratis . . . . CLC 33
See also Chaviaras, Strates

Hawes, Stephen 1475(?)-1523(?) . . . . . LC 17

Hawkes, John (Clendennin Burne, Jr.)
1925- . . . . . . CLC 1, 2, 3, 4, 7, 9, 14, 15,
27, 49
See also CA 1-4R; CANR 2, 47; DLB 2, 7;
DLBY 80; MTCW

Hawking, S. W.
See Hawking, Stephen W(illiam)

Hawking, Stephen W(illiam)
1942- . . . . CLC 63
See also AAYA 13; BEST 89:1; CA 126;
129; CANR 48

Hawthorne, Julian 1846-1934 . . . . . TCLC 25

Hawthorne, Nathaniel
1804-1864 . . . . NCLC 39; DA; DAB;
DAC; SSC 3; WLC
See also AAYA 18; CDALB 1640-1865;
DAM MST, NOV; DLB 1, 74; YABC 2

Haxton, Josephine Ayres 1921-
See Douglas, Ellen
See also CA 115; CANR 41

Hayaseca y Eizaguirre, Jorge
See Echegaray (y Eizaguirre), Jose (Maria
Waldo)

Hayashi Fumiko 1904-1951. . . . . . . TCLC 27

Haycraft, Anna
See Ellis, Alice Thomas
See also CA 122

Hayden, Robert E(arl)
1913-1980 . . . . . . CLC 5, 9, 14, 37; BLC;
DA; DAC; PC 6
See also BW 1; CA 69-72; 97-100; CABS 2;
CANR 24; CDALB 1941-1968;
DAM MST, MULT, POET; DLB 5, 76;
MTCW; SATA 19; SATA-Obit 26

Hayford, J(oseph) E(phraim) Casely
See Casely-Hayford, J(oseph) E(phraim)

Hayman, Ronald 1932-. . . . . CLC 44
See also CA 25-28R; CANR 18, 50;
DLB 155

Haywood, Eliza (Fowler)
1693(?)-1756 . . . . LC 1

Hazlitt, William 1778-1830 . . . . . . NCLC 29
See also DLB 110, 158

Hazzard, Shirley 1931- . . . . CLC 18
See also CA 9-12R; CANR 4; DLBY 82;
MTCW

Head, Bessie 1937-1986. . . CLC 25, 67; BLC
See also BW 2; CA 29-32R; 119; CANR 25;
DAM MULT; DLB 117; MTCW

Headon, (Nicky) Topper 1956(?)- . . . CLC 30

Heaney, Seamus (Justin)
1939- . . . . . . CLC 5, 7, 14, 25, 37, 74, 91;
DAB
See also CA 85-88; CANR 25, 48;
CDBLB 1960 to Present; DAM POET;
DLB 40; DLBY 95; MTCW

Hearn, (Patricio) Lafcadio (Tessima Carlos)
1850-1904 . . . . TCLC 9
See also CA 105; DLB 12, 78

Hearne, Vicki 1946-. . . . . CLC 56
See also CA 139

Hearon, Shelby 1931-. . . . . CLC 63
See also AITN 2; CA 25-28R; CANR 18,
48

Heat-Moon, William Least. . . . . CLC 29
See also Trogdon, William (Lewis)
See also AAYA 9

Hebbel, Friedrich 1813-1863 . . . . . NCLC 43
See also DAM DRAM; DLB 129

Hebert, Anne 1916- . . . CLC 4, 13, 29; DAC
See also CA 85-88; DAM MST, POET;
DLB 68; MTCW

Hecht, Anthony (Evan)
1923- . . . . CLC 8, 13, 19
See also CA 9-12R; CANR 6; DAM POET;
DLB 5

Hecht, Ben 1894-1964 . . . . CLC 8
See also CA 85-88; DLB 7, 9, 25, 26, 28, 86

Hedayat, Sadeq 1903-1951. . . . . . . TCLC 21
See also CA 120

Hegel, Georg Wilhelm Friedrich
1770-1831 . . . . NCLC 46
See also DLB 90

Heidegger, Martin 1889-1976 . . . . . . CLC 24
See also CA 81-84; 65-68; CANR 34;
MTCW

Heidenstam, (Carl Gustaf) Verner von
1859-1940 . . . . TCLC 5
See also CA 104

Heifner, Jack 1946-. . . . . CLC 11
See also CA 105; CANR 47

Heijermans, Herman 1864-1924 . . . TCLC 24
See also CA 123

Heilbrun, Carolyn G(old) 1926-. . . . . CLC 25
See also CA 45-48; CANR 1, 28

Heine, Heinrich 1797-1856 . . . . NCLC 4, 54
See also DLB 90

Heinemann, Larry (Curtiss) 1944- . . CLC 50
See also CA 110; CAAS 21; CANR 31;
DLBD 9; INT CANR-31

Heiney, Donald (William) 1921-1993
See Harris, MacDonald
See also CA 1-4R; 142; CANR 3

Heinlein, Robert A(nson)
1907-1988 . . . . . . CLC 1, 3, 8, 14, 26, 55
See also AAYA 17; CA 1-4R; 125;
CANR 1, 20, 53; DAM POP; DLB 8;
JRDA; MAICYA; MTCW; SATA 9, 69;
SATA-Obit 56

Helforth, John
See Doolittle, Hilda

Hellenhofferu, Vojtech Kapristian z
See Hasek, Jaroslav (Matej Frantisek)

Heller, Joseph
      1923- .... **CLC 1, 3, 5, 8, 11, 36, 63; DA;**
            DAB; DAC; WLC
      See also AITN 1; CA 5-8R; CABS 1;
      CANR 8, 42; DAM MST, NOV, POP;
      DLB 2, 28; DLBY 80; INT CANR-8;
      MTCW

Hellman, Lillian (Florence)
      1906-1984 ...... **CLC 2, 4, 8, 14, 18, 34,**
            44, 52; DC 1
      See also AITN 1, 2; CA 13-16R; 112;
      CANR 33; DAM DRAM; DLB 7;
      DLBY 84; MTCW

Helprin, Mark 1947- ..... **CLC 7, 10, 22, 32**
      See also CA 81-84; CANR 47; DAM NOV,
      POP; DLBY 85; MTCW

Helvetius, Claude-Adrien
      1715-1771 .... **LC 26**

Helyar, Jane Penelope Josephine 1933-
      See Poole, Josephine
      See also CA 21-24R; CANR 10, 26;
      SATA 82

Hemans, Felicia 1793-1835 ...... **NCLC 29**
      See also DLB 96

Hemingway, Ernest (Miller)
      1899-1961 .... **CLC 1, 3, 6, 8, 10, 13, 19,**
            30, 34, 39, 41, 44, 50, 61, 80; DA; DAB;
            DAC; SSC 1; WLC
      See also CA 77-80; CANR 34;
      CDALB 1917-1929; DAM MST, NOV;
      DLB 4, 9, 102; DLBD 1; DLBY 81, 87;
      MTCW

Hempel, Amy 1951- .... **CLC 39**
      See also CA 118; 137

Henderson, F. C.
      See Mencken, H(enry) L(ouis)

Henderson, Sylvia
      See Ashton-Warner, Sylvia (Constance)

Henley, Beth .... **CLC 23; DC 6**
      See also Henley, Elizabeth Becker
      See also CABS 3; DLBY 86

Henley, Elizabeth Becker 1952-
      See Henley, Beth
      See also CA 107; CANR 32; DAM DRAM,
      MST; MTCW

Henley, William Ernest
      1849-1903 .... **TCLC 8**
      See also CA 105; DLB 19

Hennissart, Martha
      See Lathen, Emma
      See also CA 85-88

Henry, O. .... **TCLC 1, 19; SSC 5; WLC**
      See also Porter, William Sydney

Henry, Patrick 1736-1799 .... **LC 25**

Henryson, Robert 1430(?)-1506(?).... **LC 20**
      See also DLB 146

Henry VIII 1491-1547 .... **LC 10**

Henschke, Alfred
      See Klabund

Hentoff, Nat(han Irving) 1925- ..... **CLC 26**
      See also AAYA 4; CA 1-4R; CAAS 6;
      CANR 5, 25; CLR 1; INT CANR-25;
      JRDA; MAICYA; SATA 42, 69;
      SATA-Brief 27

Heppenstall, (John) Rayner
      1911-1981 .... **CLC 10**
      See also CA 1-4R; 103; CANR 29

Herbert, Frank (Patrick)
      1920-1986 ..... **CLC 12, 23, 35, 44, 85**
      See also CA 53-56; 118; CANR 5, 43;
      DAM POP; DLB 8; INT CANR-5;
      MTCW; SATA 9, 37; SATA-Obit 47

Herbert, George
      1593-1633 .... **LC 24; DAB; PC 4**
      See also CDBLB Before 1660; DAM POET;
      DLB 126

Herbert, Zbigniew 1924- .... **CLC 9, 43**
      See also CA 89-92; CANR 36;
      DAM POET; MTCW

Herbst, Josephine (Frey)
      1897-1969 .... **CLC 34**
      See also CA 5-8R; 25-28R; DLB 9

Hergesheimer, Joseph
      1880-1954 .... **TCLC 11**
      See also CA 109; DLB 102, 9

Herlihy, James Leo 1927-1993 ...... **CLC 6**
      See also CA 1-4R; 143; CANR 2

Hermogenes fl. c. 175- .... **CMLC 6**

Hernandez, Jose 1834-1886...... **NCLC 17**

Herodotus c. 484B.C.-429B.C..... **CMLC 17**

Herrick, Robert
      1591-1674 ..... **LC 13; DA; DAB; DAC;**
            PC 9
      See also DAM MST, POP; DLB 126

Herring, Guilles
      See Somerville, Edith

Herriot, James 1916-1995 .... **CLC 12**
      See also Wight, James Alfred
      See also AAYA 1; CA 148; CANR 40;
      DAM POP; SATA 86

Herrmann, Dorothy 1941- .... **CLC 44**
      See also CA 107

Herrmann, Taffy
      See Herrmann, Dorothy

Hersey, John (Richard)
      1914-1993 .... **CLC 1, 2, 7, 9, 40, 81**
      See also CA 17-20R; 140; CANR 33;
      DAM POP; DLB 6; MTCW; SATA 25;
      SATA-Obit 76

Herzen, Aleksandr Ivanovich
      1812-1870 .... **NCLC 10**

Herzl, Theodor 1860-1904........ **TCLC 36**

Herzog, Werner 1942- .... **CLC 16**
      See also CA 89-92

Hesiod c. 8th cent. B.C.- .... **CMLC 5**

Hesse, Hermann
      1877-1962 .... **CLC 1, 2, 3, 6, 11, 17, 25,**
            69; DA; DAB; DAC; SSC 9; WLC
      See also CA 17-18; CAP 2; DAM MST,
      NOV; DLB 66; MTCW; SATA 50

Hewes, Cady
      See De Voto, Bernard (Augustine)

Heyen, William 1940- .... **CLC 13, 18**
      See also CA 33-36R; CAAS 9; DLB 5

Heyerdahl, Thor 1914-............ **CLC 26**
      See also CA 5-8R; CANR 5, 22; MTCW;
      SATA 2, 52

Heym, Georg (Theodor Franz Arthur)
      1887-1912 .... **TCLC 9**
      See also CA 106

Heym, Stefan 1913-.............. **CLC 41**
      See also CA 9-12R; CANR 4; DLB 69

Heyse, Paul (Johann Ludwig von)
      1830-1914 .... **TCLC 8**
      See also CA 104; DLB 129

Heyward, (Edwin) DuBose
      1885-1940 .... **TCLC 59**
      See also CA 108; DLB 7, 9, 45; SATA 21

Hibbert, Eleanor Alice Burford
      1906-1993 .... **CLC 7**
      See also BEST 90:4; CA 17-20R; 140;
      CANR 9, 28; DAM POP; SATA 2;
      SATA-Obit 74

Hichens, Robert S. 1864-1950..... **TCLC 64**
      See also DLB 153

Higgins, George V(incent)
      1939-............... **CLC 4, 7, 10, 18**
      See also CA 77-80; CAAS 5; CANR 17, 51;
      DLB 2; DLBY 81; INT CANR-17;
      MTCW

Higginson, Thomas Wentworth
      1823-1911 .... **TCLC 36**
      See also DLB 1, 64

Highet, Helen
      See MacInnes, Helen (Clark)

Highsmith, (Mary) Patricia
      1921-1995 .... **CLC 2, 4, 14, 42**
      See also CA 1-4R; 147; CANR 1, 20, 48;
      DAM NOV, POP; MTCW

Highwater, Jamake (Mamake)
      1942(?)- .... **CLC 12**
      See also AAYA 7; CA 65-68; CAAS 7;
      CANR 10, 34; CLR 17; DLB 52;
      DLBY 85; JRDA; MAICYA; SATA 32,
      69; SATA-Brief 30

Highway, Tomson 1951-...... **CLC 92; DAC**
      See also CA 151; DAM MULT; NNAL

Higuchi, Ichiyo 1872-1896....... **NCLC 49**

Hijuelos, Oscar 1951- ...... **CLC 65; HLC**
      See also BEST 90:1; CA 123; CANR 50;
      DAM MULT, POP; DLB 145; HW

Hikmet, Nazim 1902(?)-1963....... **CLC 40**
      See also CA 141; 93-96

Hildesheimer, Wolfgang
      1916-1991 .... **CLC 49**
      See also CA 101; 135; DLB 69, 124

Hill, Geoffrey (William)
      1932-................ **CLC 5, 8, 18, 45**
      See also CA 81-84; CANR 21;
      CDBLB 1960 to Present; DAM POET;
      DLB 40; MTCW

Hill, George Roy 1921- .... **CLC 26**
      See also CA 110; 122

Hill, John
      See Koontz, Dean R(ay)

Hill, Susan (Elizabeth)
      1942-................... **CLC 4; DAB**
      See also CA 33-36R; CANR 29;
      DAM MST, NOV; DLB 14, 139; MTCW

Hillerman, Tony 1925-........... **CLC 62**
      See also AAYA 6; BEST 89:1; CA 29-32R;
      CANR 21, 42; DAM POP; SATA 6

Hillesum, Etty 1914-1943 .... **TCLC 49**
See also CA 137

Hilliard, Noel (Harvey) 1929- ...... **CLC 15**
See also CA 9-12R; CANR 7

Hillis, Rick 1956- .... **CLC 66**
See also CA 134

Hilton, James 1900-1954 .... **TCLC 21**
See also CA 108; DLB 34, 77; SATA 34

Himes, Chester (Bomar)
1909-1984 .... **CLC 2, 4, 7, 18, 58; BLC**
See also BW 2; CA 25-28R; 114; CANR 22;
DAM MULT; DLB 2, 76, 143; MTCW

Hinde, Thomas .... **CLC 6, 11**
See also Chitty, Thomas Willes

Hindin, Nathan
See Bloch, Robert (Albert)

Hine, (William) Daryl 1936- .... **CLC 15**
See also CA 1-4R; CAAS 15; CANR 1, 20;
DLB 60

Hinkson, Katharine Tynan
See Tynan, Katharine

Hinton, S(usan) E(loise)
1950- .... **CLC 30; DA; DAB; DAC**
See also AAYA 2; CA 81-84; CANR 32;
CLR 3, 23; DAM MST, NOV; JRDA;
MAICYA; MTCW; SATA 19, 58

Hippius, Zinaida .... **TCLC 9**
See also Gippius, Zinaida (Nikolayevna)

Hiraoka, Kimitake 1925-1970
See Mishima, Yukio
See also CA 97-100; 29-32R; DAM DRAM;
MTCW

Hirsch, E(ric) D(onald), Jr. 1928- ... **CLC 79**
See also CA 25-28R; CANR 27, 51;
DLB 67; INT CANR-27; MTCW

Hirsch, Edward 1950- .... **CLC 31, 50**
See also CA 104; CANR 20, 42; DLB 120

Hitchcock, Alfred (Joseph)
1899-1980 .... **CLC 16**
See also CA 97-100; SATA 27;
SATA-Obit 24

Hitler, Adolf 1889-1945 .... **TCLC 53**
See also CA 117; 147

Hoagland, Edward 1932- .... **CLC 28**
See also CA 1-4R; CANR 2, 31; DLB 6;
SATA 51

Hoban, Russell (Conwell) 1925- .. **CLC 7, 25**
See also CA 5-8R; CANR 23, 37; CLR 3;
DAM NOV; DLB 52; MAICYA;
MTCW; SATA 1, 40, 78

Hobbs, Perry
See Blackmur, R(ichard) P(almer)

Hobson, Laura Z(ametkin)
1900-1986 .... **CLC 7, 25**
See also CA 17-20R; 118; DLB 28;
SATA 52

Hochhuth, Rolf 1931- .... **CLC 4, 11, 18**
See also CA 5-8R; CANR 33;
DAM DRAM; DLB 124; MTCW

Hochman, Sandra 1936- .... **CLC 3, 8**
See also CA 5-8R; DLB 5

Hochwaelder, Fritz 1911-1986...... **CLC 36**
See also CA 29-32R; 120; CANR 42;
DAM DRAM; MTCW

Hochwalder, Fritz
See Hochwaelder, Fritz

Hocking, Mary (Eunice) 1921- ..... **CLC 13**
See also CA 101; CANR 18, 40

Hodgins, Jack 1938- .... **CLC 23**
See also CA 93-96; DLB 60

Hodgson, William Hope
1877(?)-1918 .... **TCLC 13**
See also CA 111; DLB 70, 153, 156

Hoeg, Peter 1957- .... **CLC 95**
See also CA 151

Hoffman, Alice 1952- .... **CLC 51**
See also CA 77-80; CANR 34; DAM NOV;
MTCW

Hoffman, Daniel (Gerard)
1923- .... **CLC 6, 13, 23**
See also CA 1-4R; CANR 4; DLB 5

Hoffman, Stanley 1944- .... **CLC 5**
See also CA 77-80

Hoffman, William M(oses) 1939- ... **CLC 40**
See also CA 57-60; CANR 11

Hoffmann, E(rnst) T(heodor) A(madeus)
1776-1822 .... **NCLC 2; SSC 13**
See also DLB 90; SATA 27

Hofmann, Gert 1931- .... **CLC 54**
See also CA 128

Hofmannsthal, Hugo von
1874-1929 .... **TCLC 11; DC 4**
See also CA 106; DAM DRAM; DLB 81,
118

Hogan, Linda 1947- .... **CLC 73**
See also CA 120; CANR 45; DAM MULT;
NNAL

Hogarth, Charles
See Creasey, John

Hogarth, Emmett
See Polonsky, Abraham (Lincoln)

Hogg, James 1770-1835 .... **NCLC 4**
See also DLB 93, 116, 159

Holbach, Paul Henri Thiry Baron
1723-1789 .... **LC 14**

Holberg, Ludvig 1684-1754 .... **LC 6**

Holden, Ursula 1921- .... **CLC 18**
See also CA 101; CAAS 8; CANR 22

Holderlin, (Johann Christian) Friedrich
1770-1843 .... **NCLC 16; PC 4**

Holdstock, Robert
See Holdstock, Robert P.

Holdstock, Robert P. 1948- .... **CLC 39**
See also CA 131

Holland, Isabelle 1920- .... **CLC 21**
See also AAYA 11; CA 21-24R; CANR 10,
25, 47; JRDA; MAICYA; SATA 8, 70

Holland, Marcus
See Caldwell, (Janet Miriam) Taylor
(Holland)

Hollander, John 1929- ...... **CLC 2, 5, 8, 14**
See also CA 1-4R; CANR 1, 52; DLB 5;
SATA 13

Hollander, Paul
See Silverberg, Robert

Holleran, Andrew 1943(?)- .... **CLC 38**
See also CA 144

Hollinghurst, Alan 1954- .... **CLC 55, 91**
See also CA 114

Hollis, Jim
See Summers, Hollis (Spurgeon, Jr.)

Holly, Buddy 1936-1959 .... **TCLC 65**

Holmes, John
See Souster, (Holmes) Raymond

Holmes, John Clellon 1926-1988.... **CLC 56**
See also CA 9-12R; 125; CANR 4; DLB 16

Holmes, Oliver Wendell
1809-1894 .... **NCLC 14**
See also CDALB 1640-1865; DLB 1;
SATA 34

Holmes, Raymond
See Souster, (Holmes) Raymond

Holt, Victoria
See Hibbert, Eleanor Alice Burford

Holub, Miroslav 1923- .... **CLC 4**
See also CA 21-24R; CANR 10

Homer
c. 8th cent. B.C.- ..... **CMLC 1, 16; DA;**
DAB; DAC
See also DAM MST, POET

Honig, Edwin 1919- .... **CLC 33**
See also CA 5-8R; CAAS 8; CANR 4, 45;
DLB 5

Hood, Hugh (John Blagdon)
1928- .... **CLC 15, 28**
See also CA 49-52; CAAS 17; CANR 1, 33;
DLB 53

Hood, Thomas 1799-1845........ **NCLC 16**
See also DLB 96

Hooker, (Peter) Jeremy 1941- ...... **CLC 43**
See also CA 77-80; CANR 22; DLB 40

hooks, bell .... **CLC 94**
See also Watkins, Gloria

Hope, A(lec) D(erwent) 1907- .... **CLC 3, 51**
See also CA 21-24R; CANR 33; MTCW

Hope, Brian
See Creasey, John

Hope, Christopher (David Tully)
1944- .... **CLC 52**
See also CA 106; CANR 47; SATA 62

Hopkins, Gerard Manley
1844-1889 .... **NCLC 17; DA; DAB;**
DAC; PC 15; WLC
See also CDBLB 1890-1914; DAM MST,
POET; DLB 35, 57

Hopkins, John (Richard) 1931- ...... **CLC 4**
See also CA 85-88

Hopkins, Pauline Elizabeth
1859-1930 .... **TCLC 28; BLC**
See also BW 2; CA 141; DAM MULT;
DLB 50

Hopkinson, Francis 1737-1791 ...... **LC 25**
See also DLB 31

Hopley-Woolrich, Cornell George 1903-1968
See Woolrich, Cornell
See also CA 13-14; CAP 1

Horatio
See Proust, (Valentin-Louis-George-Eugene-)
Marcel

Hunter, Mollie   1922- . . . . **CLC 21**
  See also McIlwraith, Maureen Mollie
    Hunter
  See also AAYA 13; CANR 37; CLR 25;
    DLB 161; JRDA; MAICYA; SAAS 7;
    SATA 54

Hunter, Robert   (?)-1734 . . . . **LC 7**

Hurston, Zora Neale
    1903-1960 . . . . **CLC 7, 30, 61; BLC; DA;
                                DAC; SSC 4**
  See also AAYA 15; BW 1; CA 85-88;
    DAM MST, MULT, NOV; DLB 51, 86;
    MTCW

Huston, John (Marcellus)
    1906-1987 . . . . **CLC 20**
  See also CA 73-76; 123; CANR 34; DLB 26

Hustvedt, Siri   1955- . . . . **CLC 76**
  See also CA 137

Hutten, Ulrich von   1488-1523 . . . . **LC 16**

Huxley, Aldous (Leonard)
    1894-1963 . . . . . **CLC 1, 3, 4, 5, 8, 11, 18,
                       35, 79; DA; DAB; DAC; WLC**
  See also AAYA 11; CA 85-88; CANR 44;
    CDBLB 1914-1945; DAM MST, NOV;
    DLB 36, 100, 162; MTCW; SATA 63

Huysmans, Charles Marie Georges
    1848-1907
  See Huysmans, Joris-Karl
  See also CA 104

Huysmans, Joris-Karl . . . . **TCLC 7**
  See also Huysmans, Charles Marie Georges
  See also DLB 123

Hwang, David Henry
    1957- . . . . **CLC 55; DC 4**
  See also CA 127; 132; DAM DRAM;
    INT 132

Hyde, Anthony   1946- . . . . **CLC 42**
  See also CA 136

Hyde, Margaret O(ldroyd)   1917- . . . **CLC 21**
  See also CA 1-4R; CANR 1, 36; CLR 23;
    JRDA; MAICYA; SAAS 8; SATA 1, 42,
    76

Hynes, James   1956(?)- . . . . **CLC 65**

Ian, Janis   1951- . . . . **CLC 21**
  See also CA 105

Ibanez, Vicente Blasco
  See Blasco Ibanez, Vicente

Ibarguengoitia, Jorge   1928-1983 . . . . **CLC 37**
  See also CA 124; 113; HW

Ibsen, Henrik (Johan)
    1828-1906 . . . . **TCLC 2, 8, 16, 37, 52;
                        DA; DAB; DAC; DC 2; WLC**
  See also CA 104; 141; DAM DRAM, MST

Ibuse Masuji   1898-1993 . . . . **CLC 22**
  See also CA 127; 141

Ichikawa, Kon   1915- . . . . **CLC 20**
  See also CA 121

Idle, Eric   1943- . . . . **CLC 21**
  See also Monty Python
  See also CA 116; CANR 35

Ignatow, David   1914- . . . . . . **CLC 4, 7, 14, 40**
  See also CA 9-12R; CAAS 3; CANR 31;
    DLB 5

Ihimaera, Witi   1944- . . . . **CLC 46**
  See also CA 77-80

Ilf, Ilya . . . . **TCLC 21**
  See also Fainzilberg, Ilya Arnoldovich

Illyes, Gyula   1902-1983 . . . . **PC 16**
  See also CA 114; 109

Immermann, Karl (Lebrecht)
    1796-1840 . . . . **NCLC 4, 49**
  See also DLB 133

Inclan, Ramon (Maria) del Valle
  See Valle-Inclan, Ramon (Maria) del

Infante, G(uillermo) Cabrera
  See Cabrera Infante, G(uillermo)

Ingalls, Rachel (Holmes)   1940- . . . . . **CLC 42**
  See also CA 123; 127

Ingamells, Rex   1913-1955 . . . . **TCLC 35**

Inge, William Motter
    1913-1973 . . . . **CLC 1, 8, 19**
  See also CA 9-12R; CDALB 1941-1968;
    DAM DRAM; DLB 7; MTCW

Ingelow, Jean   1820-1897 . . . . **NCLC 39**
  See also DLB 35, 163; SATA 33

Ingram, Willis J.
  See Harris, Mark

Innaurato, Albert (F.)   1948(?)- . . **CLC 21, 60**
  See also CA 115; 122; INT 122

Innes, Michael
  See Stewart, J(ohn) I(nnes) M(ackintosh)

Ionesco, Eugene
    1909-1994 . . . . **CLC 1, 4, 6, 9, 11, 15, 41,
                            86; DA; DAB; DAC; WLC**
  See also CA 9-12R; 144; DAM DRAM,
    MST; MTCW; SATA 7; SATA-Obit 79

Iqbal, Muhammad   1873-1938 . . . . . **TCLC 28**

Ireland, Patrick
  See O'Doherty, Brian

Iron, Ralph
  See Schreiner, Olive (Emilie Albertina)

Irving, John (Winslow)
    1942- . . . . **CLC 13, 23, 38**
  See also AAYA 8; BEST 89:3; CA 25-28R;
    CANR 28; DAM NOV, POP; DLB 6;
    DLBY 82; MTCW

Irving, Washington
    1783-1859 . . . . . **NCLC 2, 19; DA; DAB;
                                SSC 2; WLC**
  See also CDALB 1640-1865; DAM MST;
    DLB 3, 11, 30, 59, 73, 74; YABC 2

Irwin, P. K.
  See Page, P(atricia) K(athleen)

Isaacs, Susan   1943- . . . . **CLC 32**
  See also BEST 89:1; CA 89-92; CANR 20,
    41; DAM POP; INT CANR-20; MTCW

Isherwood, Christopher (William Bradshaw)
    1904-1986 . . . . **CLC 1, 9, 11, 14, 44**
  See also CA 13-16R; 117; CANR 35;
    DAM DRAM, NOV; DLB 15; DLBY 86;
    MTCW

Ishiguro, Kazuo   1954- . . . . . . **CLC 27, 56, 59**
  See also BEST 90:2; CA 120; CANR 49;
    DAM NOV; MTCW

Ishikawa, Takuboku
    1886(?)-1912 . . . . **TCLC 15; PC 10**
  See also CA 113; DAM POET

Iskander, Fazil   1929- . . . . **CLC 47**
  See also CA 102

Isler, Alan . . . . **CLC 91**

Ivan IV   1530-1584 . . . . **LC 17**

Ivanov, Vyacheslav Ivanovich
    1866-1949 . . . . **TCLC 33**
  See also CA 122

Ivask, Ivar Vidrik   1927-1992 . . . . . . **CLC 14**
  See also CA 37-40R; 139; CANR 24

Ives, Morgan
  See Bradley, Marion Zimmer

J. R. S.
  See Gogarty, Oliver St. John

Jabran, Kahlil
  See Gibran, Kahlil

Jabran, Khalil
  See Gibran, Kahlil

Jackson, Daniel
  See Wingrove, David (John)

Jackson, Jesse   1908-1983 . . . . **CLC 12**
  See also BW 1; CA 25-28R; 109; CANR 27;
    CLR 28; MAICYA; SATA 2, 29;
    SATA-Obit 48

Jackson, Laura (Riding)   1901-1991
  See Riding, Laura
  See also CA 65-68; 135; CANR 28; DLB 48

Jackson, Sam
  See Trumbo, Dalton

Jackson, Sara
  See Wingrove, David (John)

Jackson, Shirley
    1919-1965 . . . . **CLC 11, 60, 87; DA;
                                DAC; SSC 9; WLC**
  See also AAYA 9; CA 1-4R; 25-28R;
    CANR 4, 52; CDALB 1941-1968;
    DAM MST; DLB 6; SATA 2

Jacob, (Cyprien-)Max   1876-1944 . . . **TCLC 6**
  See also CA 104

Jacobs, Jim   1942- . . . . **CLC 12**
  See also CA 97-100; INT 97-100

Jacobs, W(illiam) W(ymark)
    1863-1943 . . . . **TCLC 22**
  See also CA 121; DLB 135

Jacobsen, Jens Peter   1847-1885 . . **NCLC 34**

Jacobsen, Josephine   1908- . . . . **CLC 48**
  See also CA 33-36R; CAAS 18; CANR 23,
    48

Jacobson, Dan   1929- . . . . **CLC 4, 14**
  See also CA 1-4R; CANR 2, 25; DLB 14;
    MTCW

Jacqueline
  See Carpentier (y Valmont), Alejo

Jagger, Mick   1944- . . . . **CLC 17**

Jakes, John (William)   1932- . . . . **CLC 29**
  See also BEST 89:4; CA 57-60; CANR 10,
    43; DAM NOV, POP; DLBY 83;
    INT CANR-10; MTCW; SATA 62

James, Andrew
  See Kirkup, James

James, C(yril) L(ionel) R(obert)
    1901-1989 . . . . **CLC 33**
  See also BW 2; CA 117; 125; 128; DLB 125;
    MTCW

James, Daniel (Lewis)   1911-1988
  See Santiago, Danny
  See also CA 125

James, Dynely
See Mayne, William (James Carter)

James, Henry Sr. 1811-1882..... NCLC **53**

James, Henry
1843-1916 ...... TCLC **2, 11, 24, 40, 47,
64; DA; DAB; DAC; SSC 8; WLC**
See also CA 104; 132; CDALB 1865-1917;
DAM MST, NOV; DLB 12, 71, 74;
DLBD 13; MTCW

James, M. R.
See James, Montague (Rhodes)
See also DLB 156

James, Montague (Rhodes)
1862-1936 .... TCLC **6; SSC 16**
See also CA 104

James, P. D. .... CLC **18, 46**
See also White, Phyllis Dorothy James
See also BEST 90:2; CDBLB 1960 to
Present; DLB 87

James, Philip
See Moorcock, Michael (John)

James, William 1842-1910..... TCLC **15, 32**
See also CA 109

James I 1394-1437 .... LC **20**

Jameson, Anna 1794-1860 ...... NCLC **43**
See also DLB 99, 166

Jami, Nur al-Din 'Abd al-Rahman
1414-1492 .... LC **9**

Jandl, Ernst 1925- .... CLC **34**

Janowitz, Tama 1957- .... CLC **43**
See also CA 106; CANR 52; DAM POP

Japrisot, Sebastien 1931-.......... CLC **90**

Jarrell, Randall
1914-1965 .... CLC **1, 2, 6, 9, 13, 49**
See also CA 5-8R; 25-28R; CABS 2;
CANR 6, 34; CDALB 1941-1968; CLR 6;
DAM POET; DLB 48, 52; MAICYA;
MTCW; SATA 7

Jarry, Alfred
1873-1907 .... TCLC **2, 14; SSC 20**
See also CA 104; DAM DRAM

Jarvis, E. K.
See Bloch, Robert (Albert); Ellison, Harlan
(Jay); Silverberg, Robert

Jeake, Samuel, Jr.
See Aiken, Conrad (Potter)

Jean Paul 1763-1825 .... NCLC **7**

Jefferies, (John) Richard
1848-1887 .... NCLC **47**
See also DLB 98, 141; SATA 16

Jeffers, (John) Robinson
1887-1962 .... CLC **2, 3, 11, 15, 54; DA;
DAC; WLC**
See also CA 85-88; CANR 35;
CDALB 1917-1929; DAM MST, POET;
DLB 45; MTCW

Jefferson, Janet
See Mencken, H(enry) L(ouis)

Jefferson, Thomas 1743-1826 .... NCLC **11**
See also CDALB 1640-1865; DLB 31

Jeffrey, Francis 1773-1850....... NCLC **33**
See also DLB 107

Jelakowitch, Ivan
See Heijermans, Herman

Jellicoe, (Patricia) Ann 1927- ...... CLC **27**
See also CA 85-88; DLB 13

Jen, Gish .... CLC **70**
See also Jen, Lillian

Jen, Lillian 1956(?)-
See Jen, Gish
See also CA 135

Jenkins, (John) Robin 1912- .... CLC **52**
See also CA 1-4R; CANR 1; DLB 14

Jennings, Elizabeth (Joan)
1926- .... CLC **5, 14**
See also CA 61-64; CAAS 5; CANR 8, 39;
DLB 27; MTCW; SATA 66

Jennings, Waylon 1937-.......... CLC **21**

Jensen, Johannes V. 1873-1950.... TCLC **41**

Jensen, Laura (Linnea) 1948- ...... CLC **37**
See also CA 103

Jerome, Jerome K(lapka)
1859-1927 .... TCLC **23**
See also CA 119; DLB 10, 34, 135

Jerrold, Douglas William
1803-1857 .... NCLC **2**
See also DLB 158, 159

Jewett, (Theodora) Sarah Orne
1849-1909 .... TCLC **1, 22; SSC 6**
See also CA 108; 127; DLB 12, 74;
SATA 15

Jewsbury, Geraldine (Endsor)
1812-1880 .... NCLC **22**
See also DLB 21

Jhabvala, Ruth Prawer
1927- .... CLC **4, 8, 29, 94; DAB**
See also CA 1-4R; CANR 2, 29, 51;
DAM NOV; DLB 139; INT CANR-29;
MTCW

Jibran, Kahlil
See Gibran, Kahlil

Jibran, Khalil
See Gibran, Kahlil

Jiles, Paulette 1943-........... CLC **13, 58**
See also CA 101

Jimenez (Mantecon), Juan Ramon
1881-1958 .... TCLC **4; HLC; PC 7**
See also CA 104; 131; DAM MULT,
POET; DLB 134; HW; MTCW

Jimenez, Ramon
See Jimenez (Mantecon), Juan Ramon

Jimenez Mantecon, Juan
See Jimenez (Mantecon), Juan Ramon

Joel, Billy .... CLC **26**
See also Joel, William Martin

Joel, William Martin 1949-
See Joel, Billy
See also CA 108

John of the Cross, St. 1542-1591 .... LC **18**

Johnson, B(ryan) S(tanley William)
1933-1973 .... CLC **6, 9**
See also CA 9-12R; 53-56; CANR 9;
DLB 14, 40

Johnson, Benj. F. of Boo
See Riley, James Whitcomb

Johnson, Benjamin F. of Boo
See Riley, James Whitcomb

Johnson, Charles (Richard)
1948- .... CLC **7, 51, 65; BLC**
See also BW 2; CA 116; CAAS 18;
CANR 42; DAM MULT; DLB 33

Johnson, Denis 1949-............. CLC **52**
See also CA 117; 121; DLB 120

Johnson, Diane 1934-........ CLC **5, 13, 48**
See also CA 41-44R; CANR 17, 40;
DLBY 80; INT CANR-17; MTCW

Johnson, Eyvind (Olof Verner)
1900-1976 .... CLC **14**
See also CA 73-76; 69-72; CANR 34

Johnson, J. R.
See James, C(yril) L(ionel) R(obert)

Johnson, James Weldon
1871-1938 .... TCLC **3, 19; BLC**
See also BW 1; CA 104; 125;
CDALB 1917-1929; CLR 32;
DAM MULT, POET; DLB 51; MTCW;
SATA 31

Johnson, Joyce 1935-............ CLC **58**
See also CA 125; 129

Johnson, Lionel (Pigot)
1867-1902 .... TCLC **19**
See also CA 117; DLB 19

Johnson, Mel
See Malzberg, Barry N(athaniel)

Johnson, Pamela Hansford
1912-1981 .... CLC **1, 7, 27**
See also CA 1-4R; 104; CANR 2, 28;
DLB 15; MTCW

Johnson, Samuel
1709-1784 ..... LC **15; DA; DAB; DAC;
WLC**
See also CDBLB 1660-1789; DAM MST;
DLB 39, 95, 104, 142

Johnson, Uwe
1934-1984 .... CLC **5, 10, 15, 40**
See also CA 1-4R; 112; CANR 1, 39;
DLB 75; MTCW

Johnston, George (Benson) 1913- ... CLC **51**
See also CA 1-4R; CANR 5, 20; DLB 88

Johnston, Jennifer 1930-.......... CLC **7**
See also CA 85-88; DLB 14

Jolley, (Monica) Elizabeth
1923- .... CLC **46; SSC 19**
See also CA 127; CAAS 13

Jones, Arthur Llewellyn 1863-1947
See Machen, Arthur
See also CA 104

Jones, D(ouglas) G(ordon) 1929-.... CLC **10**
See also CA 29-32R; CANR 13; DLB 53

Jones, David (Michael)
1895-1974 .... CLC **2, 4, 7, 13, 42**
See also CA 9-12R; 53-56; CANR 28;
CDBLB 1945-1960; DLB 20, 100; MTCW

Jones, David Robert 1947-
See Bowie, David
See also CA 103

Jones, Diana Wynne 1934- .... CLC **26**
See also AAYA 12; CA 49-52; CANR 4,
26; CLR 23; DLB 161; JRDA; MAICYA;
SAAS 7; SATA 9, 70

Jones, Edward P. 1950-........... CLC **76**
See also BW 2; CA 142

Kazan, Elia 1909-. . . . . CLC **6, 16, 63**
See also CA 21-24R; CANR 32

Kazantzakis, Nikos
1883(?)-1957 . . . . TCLC **2, 5, 33**
See also CA 105; 132; MTCW

Kazin, Alfred 1915- . . . . CLC **34, 38**
See also CA 1-4R; CAAS 7; CANR 1, 45;
DLB 67

Keane, Mary Nesta (Skrine) 1904-1996
See Keane, Molly
See also CA 108; 114; 151

Keane, Molly. . . . . CLC **31**
See also Keane, Mary Nesta (Skrine)
See also INT 114

Keates, Jonathan 19(?)-. . . . . CLC **34**

Keaton, Buster 1895-1966 . . . . CLC **20**

Keats, John
1795-1821 . . . . NCLC **8**; DA; DAB;
DAC; PC **1**; WLC
See also CDBLB 1789-1832; DAM MST,
POET; DLB 96, 110

Keene, Donald 1922- . . . . CLC **34**
See also CA 1-4R; CANR 5

Keillor, Garrison. . . . . CLC **40**
See also Keillor, Gary (Edward)
See also AAYA 2; BEST 89:3; DLBY 87;
SATA 58

Keillor, Gary (Edward) 1942-
See Keillor, Garrison
See also CA 111; 117; CANR 36;
DAM POP; MTCW

Keith, Michael
See Hubbard, L(afayette) Ron(ald)

Keller, Gottfried 1819-1890. . . . . . . NCLC **2**
See also DLB 129

Kellerman, Jonathan 1949- . . . . CLC **44**
See also BEST 90:1; CA 106; CANR 29, 51;
DAM POP; INT CANR-29

Kelley, William Melvin 1937-. . . . . . CLC **22**
See also BW 1; CA 77-80; CANR 27;
DLB 33

Kellogg, Marjorie 1922-. . . . . CLC **2**
See also CA 81-84

Kellow, Kathleen
See Hibbert, Eleanor Alice Burford

Kelly, M(ilton) T(erry) 1947-. . . . . . CLC **55**
See also CA 97-100; CAAS 22; CANR 19,
43

Kelman, James 1946-. . . . . CLC **58, 86**
See also CA 148

Kemal, Yashar 1923- . . . . CLC **14, 29**
See also CA 89-92; CANR 44

Kemble, Fanny 1809-1893 . . . . NCLC **18**
See also DLB 32

Kemelman, Harry 1908-. . . . . CLC **2**
See also AITN 1; CA 9-12R; CANR 6;
DLB 28

Kempe, Margery 1373(?)-1440(?) . . . . . LC **6**
See also DLB 146

Kempis, Thomas a 1380-1471 . . . . . . LC **11**

Kendall, Henry 1839-1882 . . . . NCLC **12**

Keneally, Thomas (Michael)
1935- . . . . . . CLC **5, 8, 10, 14, 19, 27, 43**
See also CA 85-88; CANR 10, 50;
DAM NOV; MTCW

Kennedy, Adrienne (Lita)
1931- . . . . CLC **66**; BLC; DC **5**
See also BW 2; CA 103; CAAS 20; CABS 3;
CANR 26, 53; DAM MULT; DLB 38

Kennedy, John Pendleton
1795-1870 . . . . NCLC **2**
See also DLB 3

Kennedy, Joseph Charles 1929-
See Kennedy, X. J.
See also CA 1-4R; CANR 4, 30, 40;
SATA 14, 86

Kennedy, William 1928-. . . CLC **6, 28, 34, 53**
See also AAYA 1; CA 85-88; CANR 14,
31; DAM NOV; DLB 143; DLBY 85;
INT CANR-31; MTCW; SATA 57

Kennedy, X. J.. . . . . CLC **8, 42**
See also Kennedy, Joseph Charles
See also CAAS 9; CLR 27; DLB 5;
SAAS 22

Kenny, Maurice (Francis) 1929- . . . . CLC **87**
See also CA 144; CAAS 22; DAM MULT;
NNAL

Kent, Kelvin
See Kuttner, Henry

Kenton, Maxwell
See Southern, Terry

Kenyon, Robert O.
See Kuttner, Henry

Kerouac, Jack . . . . . CLC **1, 2, 3, 5, 14, 29, 61**
See also Kerouac, Jean-Louis Lebris de
See also CDALB 1941-1968; DLB 2, 16;
DLBD 3; DLBY 95

Kerouac, Jean-Louis Lebris de 1922-1969
See Kerouac, Jack
See also AITN 1; CA 5-8R; 25-28R;
CANR 26; DA; DAB; DAC; DAM MST,
NOV, POET, POP; MTCW; WLC

Kerr, Jean 1923-. . . . . CLC **22**
See also CA 5-8R; CANR 7; INT CANR-7

Kerr, M. E.. . . . . CLC **12, 35**
See also Meaker, Marijane (Agnes)
See also AAYA 2; CLR 29; SAAS 1

Kerr, Robert . . . . CLC **55**

Kerrigan, (Thomas) Anthony
1918-. CLC **4, 6**
See also CA 49-52; CAAS 11; CANR 4

Kerry, Lois
See Duncan, Lois

Kesey, Ken (Elton)
1935- . . . . . . CLC **1, 3, 6, 11, 46, 64**; DA;
DAB; DAC; WLC
See also CA 1-4R; CANR 22, 38;
CDALB 1968-1988; DAM MST, NOV,
POP; DLB 2, 16; MTCW; SATA 66

Kesselring, Joseph (Otto)
1902-1967 . . . . CLC **45**
See also CA 150; DAM DRAM, MST

Kessler, Jascha (Frederick) 1929-. . . . CLC **4**
See also CA 17-20R; CANR 8, 48

Kettelkamp, Larry (Dale) 1933- . . . . CLC **12**
See also CA 29-32R; CANR 16; SAAS 3;
SATA 2

Key, Ellen 1849-1926. . . . . TCLC **65**

Keyber, Conny
See Fielding, Henry

Keyes, Daniel 1927-. . . . CLC **80**; DA; DAC
See also CA 17-20R; CANR 10, 26;
DAM MST, NOV; SATA 37

Keynes, John Maynard
1883-1946 . . . . TCLC **64**
See also CA 114; DLBD 10

Khanshendel, Chiron
See Rose, Wendy

Khayyam, Omar
1048-1131 . . . . CMLC **11**; PC **8**
See also DAM POET

Kherdian, David 1931-. . . . . CLC **6, 9**
See also CA 21-24R; CAAS 2; CANR 39;
CLR 24; JRDA; MAICYA; SATA 16, 74

Khlebnikov, Velimir . . . . TCLC **20**
See also Khlebnikov, Viktor Vladimirovich

Khlebnikov, Viktor Vladimirovich 1885-1922
See Khlebnikov, Velimir
See also CA 117

Khodasevich, Vladislav (Felitsianovich)
1886-1939 . . . . TCLC **15**
See also CA 115

Kielland, Alexander Lange
1849-1906 . . . . TCLC **5**
See also CA 104

Kiely, Benedict 1919-. . . . . CLC **23, 43**
See also CA 1-4R; CANR 2; DLB 15

Kienzle, William X(avier) 1928- . . . . CLC **25**
See also CA 93-96; CAAS 1; CANR 9, 31;
DAM POP; INT CANR-31; MTCW

Kierkegaard, Soren 1813-1855. . . . NCLC **34**

Killens, John Oliver 1916-1987. . . . . CLC **10**
See also BW 2; CA 77-80; 123; CAAS 2;
CANR 26; DLB 33

Killigrew, Anne 1660-1685. . . . . LC **4**
See also DLB 131

Kim
See Simenon, Georges (Jacques Christian)

Kincaid, Jamaica 1949- . . . CLC **43, 68**; BLC
See also AAYA 13; BW 2; CA 125;
CANR 47; DAM MULT, NOV;
DLB 157

King, Francis (Henry) 1923- . . . . . CLC **8, 53**
See also CA 1-4R; CANR 1, 33;
DAM NOV; DLB 15, 139; MTCW

King, Martin Luther, Jr.
1929-1968 . . . . CLC **83**; BLC; DA; DAB;
DAC
See also BW 2; CA 25-28; CANR 27, 44;
CAP 2; DAM MST, MULT; MTCW;
SATA 14

King, Stephen (Edwin)
1947- . . . . . . CLC **12, 26, 37, 61**; SSC **17**
See also AAYA 1, 17; BEST 90:1;
CA 61-64; CANR 1, 30, 52; DAM NOV,
POP; DLB 143; DLBY 80; JRDA;
MTCW; SATA 9, 55

King, Steve
See King, Stephen (Edwin)

King, Thomas 1943-. . . . . CLC **89**; DAC
See also CA 144; DAM MULT; NNAL

Kingman, Lee . . . . CLC 17
See also Natti, (Mary) Lee
See also SAAS 3; SATA 1, 67

Kingsley, Charles 1819-1875 . . . . . NCLC 35
See also DLB 21, 32, 163; YABC 2

Kingsley, Sidney 1906-1995 . . . . CLC 44
See also CA 85-88; 147; DLB 7

Kingsolver, Barbara 1955- . . . . . . CLC 55, 81
See also AAYA 15; CA 129; 134;
DAM POP; INT 134

Kingston, Maxine (Ting Ting) Hong
1940- . . . . CLC 12, 19, 58
See also AAYA 8; CA 69-72; CANR 13,
38; DAM MULT, NOV; DLBY 80;
INT CANR-13; MTCW; SATA 53

Kinnell, Galway
1927- . . . . CLC 1, 2, 3, 5, 13, 29
See also CA 9-12R; CANR 10, 34; DLB 5;
DLBY 87; INT CANR-34; MTCW

Kinsella, Thomas 1928- . . . . CLC 4, 19
See also CA 17-20R; CANR 15; DLB 27;
MTCW

Kinsella, W(illiam) P(atrick)
1935- . . . . CLC 27, 43; DAC
See also AAYA 7; CA 97-100; CAAS 7;
CANR 21, 35; DAM NOV, POP;
INT CANR-21; MTCW

Kipling, (Joseph) Rudyard
1865-1936 . . . . . . TCLC 8, 17; DA; DAB;
DAC; PC 3; SSC 5; WLC
See also CA 105; 120; CANR 33;
CDBLB 1890-1914; CLR 39; DAM MST,
POET; DLB 19, 34, 141, 156; MAICYA;
MTCW; YABC 2

Kirkup, James 1918- . . . . CLC 1
See also CA 1-4R; CAAS 4; CANR 2;
DLB 27; SATA 12

Kirkwood, James 1930(?)-1989 . . . . . . CLC 9
See also AITN 2; CA 1-4R; 128; CANR 6,
40

Kirshner, Sidney
See Kingsley, Sidney

Kis, Danilo 1935-1989 . . . . CLC 57
See also CA 109; 118; 129; MTCW

Kivi, Aleksis 1834-1872 . . . . NCLC 30

Kizer, Carolyn (Ashley)
1925- . . . . CLC 15, 39, 80
See also CA 65-68; CAAS 5; CANR 24;
DAM POET; DLB 5

Klabund 1890-1928 . . . . TCLC 44
See also DLB 66

Klappert, Peter 1942- . . . . CLC 57
See also CA 33-36R; DLB 5

Klein, A(braham) M(oses)
1909-1972 . . . . CLC 19; DAB; DAC
See also CA 101; 37-40R; DAM MST;
DLB 68

Klein, Norma 1938-1989 . . . . CLC 30
See also AAYA 2; CA 41-44R; 128;
CANR 15, 37; CLR 2, 19;
INT CANR-15; JRDA; MAICYA;
SAAS 1; SATA 7, 57

Klein, T(heodore) E(ibon) D(onald)
1947- . . . . CLC 34
See also CA 119; CANR 44

Kleist, Heinrich von
1777-1811 . . . . NCLC 2, 37; SSC 22
See also DAM DRAM; DLB 90

Klima, Ivan 1931- . . . . CLC 56
See also CA 25-28R; CANR 17, 50;
DAM NOV

Klimentov, Andrei Platonovich 1899-1951
See Platonov, Andrei
See also CA 108

Klinger, Friedrich Maximilian von
1752-1831 . . . . NCLC 1
See also DLB 94

Klopstock, Friedrich Gottlieb
1724-1803 . . . . NCLC 11
See also DLB 97

Knebel, Fletcher 1911-1993 . . . . CLC 14
See also AITN 1; CA 1-4R; 140; CAAS 3;
CANR 1, 36; SATA 36; SATA-Obit 75

Knickerbocker, Diedrich
See Irving, Washington

Knight, Etheridge
1931-1991 . . . . CLC 40; BLC; PC 14
See also BW 1; CA 21-24R; 133; CANR 23;
DAM POET; DLB 41

Knight, Sarah Kemble 1666-1727 . . . . . LC 7
See also DLB 24

Knister, Raymond 1899-1932 . . . . . . TCLC 56
See also DLB 68

Knowles, John
1926- . . . . . . CLC 1, 4, 10, 26; DA; DAC
See also AAYA 10; CA 17-20R; CANR 40;
CDALB 1968-1988; DAM MST, NOV;
DLB 6; MTCW; SATA 8

Knox, Calvin M.
See Silverberg, Robert

Knye, Cassandra
See Disch, Thomas M(ichael)

Koch, C(hristopher) J(ohn) 1932- . . . CLC 42
See also CA 127

Koch, Christopher
See Koch, C(hristopher) J(ohn)

Koch, Kenneth 1925- . . . . CLC 5, 8, 44
See also CA 1-4R; CANR 6, 36;
DAM POET; DLB 5; INT CANR-36;
SATA 65

Kochanowski, Jan 1530-1584 . . . . LC 10

Kock, Charles Paul de
1794-1871 . . . . NCLC 16

Koda Shigeyuki 1867-1947
See Rohan, Koda
See also CA 121

Koestler, Arthur
1905-1983 . . . . CLC 1, 3, 6, 8, 15, 33
See also CA 1-4R; 109; CANR 1, 33;
CDBLB 1945-1960; DLBY 83; MTCW

Kogawa, Joy Nozomi 1935- . . . CLC 78; DAC
See also CA 101; CANR 19; DAM MST,
MULT

Kohout, Pavel 1928- . . . . CLC 13
See also CA 45-48; CANR 3

Koizumi, Yakumo
See Hearn, (Patricio) Lafcadio (Tessima
Carlos)

Kolmar, Gertrud 1894-1943 . . . . . . TCLC 40

Komunyakaa, Yusef 1947- . . . . . . CLC 86, 94
See also CA 147; DLB 120

Konrad, George
See Konrad, Gyoergy

Konrad, Gyoergy 1933- . . . . . . CLC 4, 10, 73
See also CA 85-88

Konwicki, Tadeusz 1926- . . . . . CLC 8, 28, 54
See also CA 101; CAAS 9; CANR 39;
MTCW

Koontz, Dean R(ay) 1945- . . . . CLC 78
See also AAYA 9; BEST 89:3, 90:2;
CA 108; CANR 19, 36, 52; DAM NOV,
POP; MTCW

Kopit, Arthur (Lee) 1937- . . . . CLC 1, 18, 33
See also AITN 1; CA 81-84; CABS 3;
DAM DRAM; DLB 7; MTCW

Kops, Bernard 1926- . . . . CLC 4
See also CA 5-8R; DLB 13

Kornbluth, C(yril) M. 1923-1958 . . . . TCLC 8
See also CA 105; DLB 8

Korolenko, V. G.
See Korolenko, Vladimir Galaktionovich

Korolenko, Vladimir
See Korolenko, Vladimir Galaktionovich

Korolenko, Vladimir G.
See Korolenko, Vladimir Galaktionovich

Korolenko, Vladimir Galaktionovich
1853-1921 . . . . TCLC 22
See also CA 121

Korzybski, Alfred (Habdank Skarbek)
1879-1950 . . . . TCLC 61
See also CA 123

Kosinski, Jerzy (Nikodem)
1933-1991 . . . . CLC 1, 2, 3, 6, 10, 15, 53,
70
See also CA 17-20R; 134; CANR 9, 46;
DAM NOV; DLB 2; DLBY 82; MTCW

Kostelanetz, Richard (Cory) 1940- . . CLC 28
See also CA 13-16R; CAAS 8; CANR 38

Kostrowitzki, Wilhelm Apollinaris de
1880-1918
See Apollinaire, Guillaume
See also CA 104

Kotlowitz, Robert 1924- . . . . CLC 4
See also CA 33-36R; CANR 36

Kotzebue, August (Friedrich Ferdinand) von
1761-1819 . . . . NCLC 25
See also DLB 94

Kotzwinkle, William 1938- . . . CLC 5, 14, 35
See also CA 45-48; CANR 3, 44; CLR 6;
MAICYA; SATA 24, 70

Kozol, Jonathan 1936- . . . . CLC 17
See also CA 61-64; CANR 16, 45

Kozoll, Michael 1940(?)- . . . . CLC 35

Kramer, Kathryn 19(?)- . . . . CLC 34

Kramer, Larry 1935- . . . . CLC 42
See also CA 124; 126; DAM POP

Krasicki, Ignacy 1735-1801 . . . . NCLC 8

Krasinski, Zygmunt 1812-1859 . . . . NCLC 4

Kraus, Karl 1874-1936 . . . . TCLC 5
See also CA 104; DLB 118

Kreve (Mickevicius), Vincas
1882-1954 . . . . TCLC 27

Kristeva, Julia 1941- .... CLC 77

Kristofferson, Kris 1936- .... CLC 26
See also CA 104

Krizanc, John 1956- .... CLC 57

Krleza, Miroslav 1893-1981........ CLC 8
See also CA 97-100; 105; CANR 50;
DLB 147

Kroetsch, Robert
1927- .... CLC 5, 23, 57; DAC
See also CA 17-20R; CANR 8, 38;
DAM POET; DLB 53; MTCW

Kroetz, Franz
See Kroetz, Franz Xaver

Kroetz, Franz Xaver 1946- .... CLC 41
See also CA 130

Kroker, Arthur 1945- .... CLC 77

Kropotkin, Peter (Aleksieevich)
1842-1921 .... TCLC 36
See also CA 119

Krotkov, Yuri 1917- .... CLC 19
See also CA 102

Krumb
See Crumb, R(obert)

Krumgold, Joseph (Quincy)
1908-1980 .... CLC 12
See also CA 9-12R; 101; CANR 7;
MAICYA; SATA 1, 48; SATA-Obit 23

Krumwitz
See Crumb, R(obert)

Krutch, Joseph Wood 1893-1970.... CLC 24
See also CA 1-4R; 25-28R; CANR 4;
DLB 63

Krutzch, Gus
See Eliot, T(homas) S(tearns)

Krylov, Ivan Andreevich
1768(?)-1844 .... NCLC 1
See also DLB 150

Kubin, Alfred (Leopold Isidor)
1877-1959 .... TCLC 23
See also CA 112; 149; DLB 81

Kubrick, Stanley 1928-........... CLC 16
See also CA 81-84; CANR 33; DLB 26

Kumin, Maxine (Winokur)
1925- .... CLC 5, 13, 28; PC 15
See also AITN 2; CA 1-4R; CAAS 8;
CANR 1, 21; DAM POET; DLB 5;
MTCW; SATA 12

Kundera, Milan
1929- .... CLC 4, 9, 19, 32, 68
See also AAYA 2; CA 85-88; CANR 19,
52; DAM NOV; MTCW

Kunene, Mazisi (Raymond) 1930-... CLC 85
See also BW 1; CA 125; DLB 117

Kunitz, Stanley (Jasspon)
1905- .... CLC 6, 11, 14
See also CA 41-44R; CANR 26; DLB 48;
INT CANR-26; MTCW

Kunze, Reiner 1933-.............. CLC 10
See also CA 93-96; DLB 75

Kuprin, Aleksandr Ivanovich
1870-1938 .... TCLC 5
See also CA 104

Kureishi, Hanif 1954(?)-........... CLC 64
See also CA 139

Kurosawa, Akira 1910-........... CLC 16
See also AAYA 11; CA 101; CANR 46;
DAM MULT

Kushner, Tony 1957(?)- .... CLC 81
See also CA 144; DAM DRAM

Kuttner, Henry 1915-1958........ TCLC 10
See also CA 107; DLB 8

Kuzma, Greg 1944-............... CLC 7
See also CA 33-36R

Kuzmin, Mikhail 1872(?)-1936 .... TCLC 40

Kyd, Thomas 1558-1594...... LC 22; DC 3
See also DAM DRAM; DLB 62

Kyprianos, Iossif
See Samarakis, Antonis

La Bruyere, Jean de 1645-1696...... LC 17

Lacan, Jacques (Marie Emile)
1901-1981 .... CLC 75
See also CA 121; 104

Laclos, Pierre Ambroise Francois Choderlos
de 1741-1803 .... NCLC 4

Lacolere, Francois
See Aragon, Louis

La Colere, Francois
See Aragon, Louis

La Deshabilleuse
See Simenon, Georges (Jacques Christian)

Lady Gregory
See Gregory, Isabella Augusta (Persse)

Lady of Quality, A
See Bagnold, Enid

La Fayette, Marie (Madelaine Pioche de la
Vergne Comtes 1634-1693....... LC 2

Lafayette, Rene
See Hubbard, L(afayette) Ron(ald)

Laforgue, Jules
1860-1887 .... NCLC 5, 53; PC 14;
SSC 20

Lagerkvist, Paer (Fabian)
1891-1974 .... CLC 7, 10, 13, 54
See also Lagerkvist, Par
See also CA 85-88; 49-52; DAM DRAM,
NOV; MTCW

Lagerkvist, Par .... SSC 12
See also Lagerkvist, Paer (Fabian)

Lagerloef, Selma (Ottiliana Lovisa)
1858-1940 .... TCLC 4, 36
See also Lagerlof, Selma (Ottiliana Lovisa)
See also CA 108; SATA 15

Lagerlof, Selma (Ottiliana Lovisa)
See Lagerloef, Selma (Ottiliana Lovisa)
See also CLR 7; SATA 15

La Guma, (Justin) Alex(ander)
1925-1985 .... CLC 19
See also BW 1; CA 49-52; 118; CANR 25;
DAM NOV; DLB 117; MTCW

Laidlaw, A. K.
See Grieve, C(hristopher) M(urray)

Lainez, Manuel Mujica
See Mujica Lainez, Manuel
See also HW

Laing, R(onald) D(avid)
1927-1989 .... CLC 95
See also CA 107; 129; CANR 34; MTCW

Lamartine, Alphonse (Marie Louis Prat) de
1790-1869 .... NCLC 11; PC 16
See also DAM POET

Lamb, Charles
1775-1834 .... NCLC 10; DA; DAB;
DAC; WLC
See also CDBLB 1789-1832; DAM MST;
DLB 93, 107, 163; SATA 17

Lamb, Lady Caroline 1785-1828.. NCLC 38
See also DLB 116

Lamming, George (William)
1927- .... CLC 2, 4, 66; BLC
See also BW 2; CA 85-88; CANR 26;
DAM MULT; DLB 125; MTCW

L'Amour, Louis (Dearborn)
1908-1988 .... CLC 25, 55
See also AAYA 16; AITN 2; BEST 89:2;
CA 1-4R; 125; CANR 3, 25, 40;
DAM NOV, POP; DLBY 80; MTCW

Lampedusa, Giuseppe (Tomasi) di ... TCLC 13
See also Tomasi di Lampedusa, Giuseppe

Lampman, Archibald 1861-1899 .. NCLC 25
See also DLB 92

Lancaster, Bruce 1896-1963........ CLC 36
See also CA 9-10; CAP 1; SATA 9

Landau, Mark Alexandrovich
See Aldanov, Mark (Alexandrovich)

Landau-Aldanov, Mark Alexandrovich
See Aldanov, Mark (Alexandrovich)

Landis, John 1950-.............. CLC 26
See also CA 112; 122

Landolfi, Tommaso 1908-1979... CLC 11, 49
See also CA 127; 117

Landon, Letitia Elizabeth
1802-1838 .... NCLC 15
See also DLB 96

Landor, Walter Savage
1775-1864 .... NCLC 14
See also DLB 93, 107

Landwirth, Heinz 1927-
See Lind, Jakov
See also CA 9-12R; CANR 7

Lane, Patrick 1939- .... CLC 25
See also CA 97-100; DAM POET; DLB 53;
INT 97-100

Lang, Andrew 1844-1912......... TCLC 16
See also CA 114; 137; DLB 98, 141;
MAICYA; SATA 16

Lang, Fritz 1890-1976 .... CLC 20
See also CA 77-80; 69-72; CANR 30

Lange, John
See Crichton, (John) Michael

Langer, Elinor 1939- .... CLC 34
See also CA 121

Langland, William
1330(?)-1400(?) ...... LC 19; DA; DAB;
DAC
See also DAM MST, POET; DLB 146

Langstaff, Launcelot
See Irving, Washington

Lanier, Sidney 1842-1881 .... NCLC 6
See also DAM POET; DLB 64; DLBD 13;
MAICYA; SATA 18

Lanyer, Aemilia 1569-1645 ...... LC 10, 30
See also DLB 121

Lao Tzu . . . . CMLC 7

Lapine, James (Elliot) 1949- . . . . CLC 39
See also CA 123; 130; INT 130

Larbaud, Valery (Nicolas)
1881-1957 . . . . TCLC 9
See also CA 106; 152

Lardner, Ring
See Lardner, Ring(gold) W(ilmer)

Lardner, Ring W., Jr.
See Lardner, Ring(gold) W(ilmer)

Lardner, Ring(gold) W(ilmer)
1885-1933 . . . . TCLC 2, 14
See also CA 104; 131; CDALB 1917-1929;
DLB 11, 25, 86; MTCW

Laredo, Betty
See Codrescu, Andrei

Larkin, Maia
See Wojciechowska, Maia (Teresa)

Larkin, Philip (Arthur)
1922-1985 . . . . CLC 3, 5, 8, 9, 13, 18, 33,
39, 64; DAB
See also CA 5-8R; 117; CANR 24;
CDBLB 1960 to Present; DAM MST,
POET; DLB 27; MTCW

Larra (y Sanchez de Castro), Mariano Jose de
1809-1837 . . . . NCLC 17

Larsen, Eric 1941- . . . . CLC 55
See also CA 132

Larsen, Nella 1891-1964 . . . . . CLC 37; BLC
See also BW 1; CA 125; DAM MULT;
DLB 51

Larson, Charles R(aymond) 1938- . . . CLC 31
See also CA 53-56; CANR 4

Las Casas, Bartolome de 1474-1566 . . LC 31

Lasker-Schueler, Else 1869-1945 . . TCLC 57
See also DLB 66, 124

Latham, Jean Lee 1902- . . . . CLC 12
See also AITN 1; CA 5-8R; CANR 7;
MAICYA; SATA 2, 68

Latham, Mavis
See Clark, Mavis Thorpe

Lathen, Emma . . . . CLC 2
See also Hennissart, Martha; Latsis, Mary
J(ane)

Lathrop, Francis
See Leiber, Fritz (Reuter, Jr.)

Latsis, Mary J(ane)
See Lathen, Emma
See also CA 85-88

Lattimore, Richmond (Alexander)
1906-1984 . . . . CLC 3
See also CA 1-4R; 112; CANR 1

Laughlin, James 1914- . . . . CLC 49
See also CA 21-24R; CAAS 22; CANR 9,
47; DLB 48

Laurence, (Jean) Margaret (Wemyss)
1926-1987 . . . . CLC 3, 6, 13, 50, 62;
DAC; SSC 7
See also CA 5-8R; 121; CANR 33;
DAM MST; DLB 53; MTCW;
SATA-Obit 50

Laurent, Antoine 1952- . . . . CLC 50

Lauscher, Hermann
See Hesse, Hermann

Lautreamont, Comte de
1846-1870 . . . . NCLC 12; SSC 14

Laverty, Donald
See Blish, James (Benjamin)

Lavin, Mary 1912-1996 . . CLC 4, 18; SSC 4
See also CA 9-12R; 151; CANR 33;
DLB 15; MTCW

Lavond, Paul Dennis
See Kornbluth, C(yril) M.; Pohl, Frederik

Lawler, Raymond Evenor 1922- . . . . CLC 58
See also CA 103

Lawrence, D(avid) H(erbert Richards)
1885-1930 . . . . TCLC 2, 9, 16, 33, 48, 61;
DA; DAB; DAC; SSC 4, 19; WLC
See also CA 104; 121; CDBLB 1914-1945;
DAM MST, NOV, POET; DLB 10, 19,
36, 98, 162; MTCW

Lawrence, T(homas) E(dward)
1888-1935 . . . . TCLC 18
See also Dale, Colin
See also CA 115

Lawrence of Arabia
See Lawrence, T(homas) E(dward)

Lawson, Henry (Archibald Hertzberg)
1867-1922 . . . . TCLC 27; SSC 18
See also CA 120

Lawton, Dennis
See Faust, Frederick (Schiller)

Laxness, Halldor . . . . CLC 25
See also Gudjonsson, Halldor Kiljan

Layamon fl. c. 1200- . . . . CMLC 10
See also DLB 146

Laye, Camara 1928-1980 . . . CLC 4, 38; BLC
See also BW 1; CA 85-88; 97-100;
CANR 25; DAM MULT; MTCW

Layton, Irving (Peter)
1912- . . . . CLC 2, 15; DAC
See also CA 1-4R; CANR 2, 33, 43;
DAM MST, POET; DLB 88; MTCW

Lazarus, Emma 1849-1887 . . . . NCLC 8

Lazarus, Felix
See Cable, George Washington

Lazarus, Henry
See Slavitt, David R(ytman)

Lea, Joan
See Neufeld, John (Arthur)

Leacock, Stephen (Butler)
1869-1944 . . . . TCLC 2; DAC
See also CA 104; 141; DAM MST; DLB 92

Lear, Edward 1812-1888 . . . . NCLC 3
See also CLR 1; DLB 32, 163, 166;
MAICYA; SATA 18

Lear, Norman (Milton) 1922- . . . . . . CLC 12
See also CA 73-76

Leavis, F(rank) R(aymond)
1895-1978 . . . . CLC 24
See also CA 21-24R; 77-80; CANR 44;
MTCW

Leavitt, David 1961- . . . . CLC 34
See also CA 116; 122; CANR 50;
DAM POP; DLB 130; INT 122

Leblanc, Maurice (Marie Emile)
1864-1941 . . . . TCLC 49
See also CA 110

Lebowitz, Fran(ces Ann)
1951(?)- . . . . CLC 11, 36
See also CA 81-84; CANR 14;
INT CANR-14; MTCW

Lebrecht, Peter
See Tieck, (Johann) Ludwig

le Carre, John . . . . CLC 3, 5, 9, 15, 28
See also Cornwell, David (John Moore)
See also BEST 89:4; CDBLB 1960 to
Present; DLB 87

Le Clezio, J(ean) M(arie) G(ustave)
1940- . . . . CLC 31
See also CA 116; 128; DLB 83

Leconte de Lisle, Charles-Marie-Rene
1818-1894 . . . . NCLC 29

Le Coq, Monsieur
See Simenon, Georges (Jacques Christian)

Leduc, Violette 1907-1972 . . . . CLC 22
See also CA 13-14; 33-36R; CAP 1

Ledwidge, Francis 1887(?)-1917 . . . TCLC 23
See also CA 123; DLB 20

Lee, Andrea 1953- . . . . CLC 36; BLC
See also BW 1; CA 125; DAM MULT

Lee, Andrew
See Auchincloss, Louis (Stanton)

Lee, Chang-rae 1965- . . . . CLC 91
See also CA 148

Lee, Don L. . . . . CLC 2
See also Madhubuti, Haki R.

Lee, George W(ashington)
1894-1976 . . . . CLC 52; BLC
See also BW 1; CA 125; DAM MULT;
DLB 51

Lee, (Nelle) Harper
1926- . . . . CLC 12, 60; DA; DAB; DAC;
WLC
See also AAYA 13; CA 13-16R; CANR 51;
CDALB 1941-1968; DAM MST, NOV;
DLB 6; MTCW; SATA 11

Lee, Helen Elaine 1959(?)- . . . . CLC 86
See also CA 148

Lee, Julian
See Latham, Jean Lee

Lee, Larry
See Lee, Lawrence

Lee, Laurie 1914- . . . . CLC 90; DAB
See also CA 77-80; CANR 33; DAM POP;
DLB 27; MTCW

Lee, Lawrence 1941-1990 . . . . CLC 34
See also CA 131; CANR 43

Lee, Manfred B(ennington)
1905-1971 . . . . CLC 11
See also Queen, Ellery
See also CA 1-4R; 29-32R; CANR 2;
DLB 137

Lee, Stan 1922- . . . . CLC 17
See also AAYA 5; CA 108; 111; INT 111

Lee, Tanith 1947- . . . . CLC 46
See also AAYA 15; CA 37-40R; CANR 53;
SATA 8, 88

Lee, Vernon . . . . TCLC 5
See also Paget, Violet
See also DLB 57, 153, 156

Lee, William
See Burroughs, William S(eward)

Lee, Willy
    See Burroughs, William S(eward)

Lee-Hamilton, Eugene (Jacob)
    1845-1907 . . . . **TCLC 22**
    See also CA 117

Leet, Judith 1935- . . . . **CLC 11**

Le Fanu, Joseph Sheridan
    1814-1873 . . . . **NCLC 9; SSC 14**
    See also DAM POP; DLB 21, 70, 159

Leffland, Ella 1931- . . . . **CLC 19**
    See also CA 29-32R; CANR 35; DLBY 84;
    INT CANR-35; SATA 65

Leger, Alexis
    See Leger, (Marie-Rene Auguste) Alexis
    Saint-Leger

Leger, (Marie-Rene Auguste) Alexis
    Saint-Leger 1887-1975 . . . . **CLC 11**
    See also Perse, St.-John
    See also CA 13-16R; 61-64; CANR 43;
    DAM POET; MTCW

Leger, Saintleger
    See Leger, (Marie-Rene Auguste) Alexis
    Saint-Leger

Le Guin, Ursula K(roeber)
    1929- . . . . . . **CLC 8, 13, 22, 45, 71; DAB;**
                                            DAC; SSC 12
    See also AAYA 9; AITN 1; CA 21-24R;
    CANR 9, 32, 52; CDALB 1968-1988;
    CLR 3, 28; DAM MST, POP; DLB 8, 52;
    INT CANR-32; JRDA; MAICYA;
    MTCW; SATA 4, 52

Lehmann, Rosamond (Nina)
    1901-1990 . . . . **CLC 5**
    See also CA 77-80; 131; CANR 8; DLB 15

Leiber, Fritz (Reuter, Jr.)
    1910-1992 . . . . **CLC 25**
    See also CA 45-48; 139; CANR 2, 40;
    DLB 8; MTCW; SATA 45;
    SATA-Obit 73

Leimbach, Martha 1963-
    See Leimbach, Marti
    See also CA 130

Leimbach, Marti . . . . **CLC 65**
    See also Leimbach, Martha

Leino, Eino . . . . **TCLC 24**
    See also Loennbohm, Armas Eino Leopold

Leiris, Michel (Julien) 1901-1990 . . . **CLC 61**
    See also CA 119; 128; 132

Leithauser, Brad 1953- . . . . **CLC 27**
    See also CA 107; CANR 27; DLB 120

Lelchuk, Alan 1938- . . . . **CLC 5**
    See also CA 45-48; CAAS 20; CANR 1

Lem, Stanislaw 1921- . . . . **CLC 8, 15, 40**
    See also CA 105; CAAS 1; CANR 32;
    MTCW

Lemann, Nancy 1956- . . . . **CLC 39**
    See also CA 118; 136

Lemonnier, (Antoine Louis) Camille
    1844-1913 . . . . **TCLC 22**
    See also CA 121

Lenau, Nikolaus 1802-1850 . . . . . . **NCLC 16**

L'Engle, Madeleine (Camp Franklin)
    1918- . . . . **CLC 12**
    See also AAYA 1; AITN 2; CA 1-4R;
    CANR 3, 21, 39; CLR 1, 14; DAM POP;
    DLB 52; JRDA; MAICYA; MTCW;
    SAAS 15; SATA 1, 27, 75

Lengyel, Jozsef 1896-1975 . . . . **CLC 7**
    See also CA 85-88; 57-60

Lennon, John (Ono)
    1940-1980 . . . . **CLC 12, 35**
    See also CA 102

Lennox, Charlotte Ramsay
    1729(?)-1804 . . . . **NCLC 23**
    See also DLB 39

Lentricchia, Frank (Jr.) 1940- . . . . . . **CLC 34**
    See also CA 25-28R; CANR 19

Lenz, Siegfried 1926- . . . . **CLC 27**
    See also CA 89-92; DLB 75

Leonard, Elmore (John, Jr.)
    1925- . . . . **CLC 28, 34, 71**
    See also AITN 1; BEST 89:1, 90:4;
    CA 81-84; CANR 12, 28, 53; DAM POP;
    INT CANR-28; MTCW

Leonard, Hugh . . . . **CLC 19**
    See also Byrne, John Keyes
    See also DLB 13

Leonov, Leonid (Maximovich)
    1899-1994 . . . . **CLC 92**
    See also CA 129; DAM NOV; MTCW

Leopardi, (Conte) Giacomo
    1798-1837 . . . . **NCLC 22**

Le Reveler
    See Artaud, Antonin (Marie Joseph)

Lerman, Eleanor 1952- . . . . **CLC 9**
    See also CA 85-88

Lerman, Rhoda 1936- . . . . **CLC 56**
    See also CA 49-52

Lermontov, Mikhail Yuryevich
    1814-1841 . . . . **NCLC 47**

Leroux, Gaston 1868-1927 . . . . **TCLC 25**
    See also CA 108; 136; SATA 65

Lesage, Alain-Rene 1668-1747 . . . . . . **LC 28**

Leskov, Nikolai (Semyonovich)
    1831-1895 . . . . **NCLC 25**

Lessing, Doris (May)
    1919- . . . . . **CLC 1, 2, 3, 6, 10, 15, 22, 40,**
                                  94; DA; DAB; DAC; SSC 6
    See also CA 9-12R; CAAS 14; CANR 33;
    CDBLB 1960 to Present; DAM MST,
    NOV; DLB 15, 139; DLBY 85; MTCW

Lessing, Gotthold Ephraim
    1729-1781 . . . . **LC 8**
    See also DLB 97

Lester, Richard 1932- . . . . **CLC 20**

Lever, Charles (James)
    1806-1872 . . . . **NCLC 23**
    See also DLB 21

Leverson, Ada 1865(?)-1936(?) . . . . **TCLC 18**
    See also Elaine
    See also CA 117; DLB 153

Levertov, Denise
    1923- . . . . . . **CLC 1, 2, 3, 5, 8, 15, 28, 66;**
                                                            PC 11
    See also CA 1-4R; CAAS 19; CANR 3, 29,
    50; DAM POET; DLB 5, 165;
    INT CANR-29; MTCW

Levi, Jonathan . . . . **CLC 76**

Levi, Peter (Chad Tigar) 1931- . . . . . **CLC 41**
    See also CA 5-8R; CANR 34; DLB 40

Levi, Primo
    1919-1987 . . . . **CLC 37, 50; SSC 12**
    See also CA 13-16R; 122; CANR 12, 33;
    MTCW

Levin, Ira 1929- . . . . **CLC 3, 6**
    See also CA 21-24R; CANR 17, 44;
    DAM POP; MTCW; SATA 66

Levin, Meyer 1905-1981 . . . . **CLC 7**
    See also AITN 1; CA 9-12R; 104;
    CANR 15; DAM POP; DLB 9, 28;
    DLBY 81; SATA 21; SATA-Obit 27

Levine, Norman 1924- . . . . **CLC 54**
    See also CA 73-76; CAAS 23; CANR 14;
    DLB 88

Levine, Philip 1928- . . . **CLC 2, 4, 5, 9, 14, 33**
    See also CA 9-12R; CANR 9, 37, 52;
    DAM POET; DLB 5

Levinson, Deirdre 1931- . . . . **CLC 49**
    See also CA 73-76

Levi-Strauss, Claude 1908- . . . . **CLC 38**
    See also CA 1-4R; CANR 6, 32; MTCW

Levitin, Sonia (Wolff) 1934- . . . . **CLC 17**
    See also AAYA 13; CA 29-32R; CANR 14,
    32; JRDA; MAICYA; SAAS 2; SATA 4,
    68

Levon, O. U.
    See Kesey, Ken (Elton)

Lewes, George Henry
    1817-1878 . . . . **NCLC 25**
    See also DLB 55, 144

Lewis, Alun 1915-1944 . . . . **TCLC 3**
    See also CA 104; DLB 20, 162

Lewis, C. Day
    See Day Lewis, C(ecil)

Lewis, C(live) S(taples)
    1898-1963 . . . . . **CLC 1, 3, 6, 14, 27; DA;**
                                                    DAB; DAC; WLC
    See also AAYA 3; CA 81-84; CANR 33;
    CDBLB 1945-1960; CLR 3, 27;
    DAM MST, NOV, POP; DLB 15, 100,
    160; JRDA; MAICYA; MTCW;
    SATA 13

Lewis, Janet 1899- . . . . **CLC 41**
    See also Winters, Janet Lewis
    See also CA 9-12R; CANR 29; CAP 1;
    DLBY 87

Lewis, Matthew Gregory
    1775-1818 . . . . **NCLC 11**
    See also DLB 39, 158

Lewis, (Harry) Sinclair
    1885-1951 . . . . . **TCLC 4, 13, 23, 39; DA;**
                                                    DAB; DAC; WLC
    See also CA 104; 133; CDALB 1917-1929;
    DAM MST, NOV; DLB 9, 102; DLBD 1;
    MTCW

Lewis, (Percy) Wyndham
1884(?)-1957 . . . . TCLC 2, 9
See also CA 104; DLB 15

Lewisohn, Ludwig 1883-1955. . . . . . TCLC 19
See also CA 107; DLB 4, 9, 28, 102

Leyner, Mark 1956- . . . . CLC 92
See also CA 110; CANR 28, 53

Lezama Lima, Jose 1910-1976 . . . CLC 4, 10
See also CA 77-80; DAM MULT;
DLB 113; HW

L'Heureux, John (Clarke) 1934- . . . . CLC 52
See also CA 13-16R; CANR 23, 45

Liddell, C. H.
See Kuttner, Henry

Lie, Jonas (Lauritz Idemil)
1833-1908(?) . . . . TCLC 5
See also CA 115

Lieber, Joel 1937-1971. . . . . CLC 6
See also CA 73-76; 29-32R

Lieber, Stanley Martin
See Lee, Stan

Lieberman, Laurence (James)
1935- . . . . CLC 4, 36
See also CA 17-20R; CANR 8, 36

Lieksman, Anders
See Haavikko, Paavo Juhani

Li Fei-kan 1904-
See Pa Chin
See also CA 105

Lifton, Robert Jay 1926- . . . . CLC 67
See also CA 17-20R; CANR 27;
INT CANR-27; SATA 66

Lightfoot, Gordon 1938- . . . . CLC 26
See also CA 109

Lightman, Alan P. 1948- . . . . CLC 81
See also CA 141

Ligotti, Thomas (Robert)
1953- . . . . CLC 44; SSC 16
See also CA 123; CANR 49

Li Ho 791-817. . . . . PC 13

Liliencron, (Friedrich Adolf Axel) Detlev von
1844-1909 . . . . TCLC 18
See also CA 117

Lilly, William 1602-1681 . . . . LC 27

Lima, Jose Lezama
See Lezama Lima, Jose

Lima Barreto, Afonso Henrique de
1881-1922 . . . . TCLC 23
See also CA 117

Limonov, Edward 1944- . . . . CLC 67
See also CA 137

Lin, Frank
See Atherton, Gertrude (Franklin Horn)

Lincoln, Abraham 1809-1865 . . . . . NCLC 18

Lind, Jakov . . . . CLC 1, 2, 4, 27, 82
See also Landwirth, Heinz
See also CAAS 4

Lindbergh, Anne (Spencer) Morrow
1906- . . . . CLC 82
See also CA 17-20R; CANR 16;
DAM NOV; MTCW; SATA 33

Lindsay, David 1878-1945 . . . . TCLC 15
See also CA 113

Lindsay, (Nicholas) Vachel
1879-1931 . . . TCLC 17; DA; DAC; WLC
See also CA 114; 135; CDALB 1865-1917;
DAM MST, POET; DLB 54; SATA 40

Linke-Poot
See Doeblin, Alfred

Linney, Romulus 1930- . . . . CLC 51
See also CA 1-4R; CANR 40, 44

Linton, Eliza Lynn 1822-1898. . . . NCLC 41
See also DLB 18

Li Po 701-763 . . . . CMLC 2

Lipsius, Justus 1547-1606 . . . . LC 16

Lipsyte, Robert (Michael)
1938- . . . . CLC 21; DA; DAC
See also AAYA 7; CA 17-20R; CANR 8;
CLR 23; DAM MST, NOV; JRDA;
MAICYA; SATA 5, 68

Lish, Gordon (Jay) 1934- . . CLC 45; SSC 18
See also CA 113; 117; DLB 130; INT 117

Lispector, Clarice 1925-1977 . . . . . . CLC 43
See also CA 139; 116; DLB 113

Littell, Robert 1935(?)- . . . . CLC 42
See also CA 109; 112

Little, Malcolm 1925-1965
See Malcolm X
See also BW 1; CA 125; 111; DA; DAB;
DAC; DAM MST, MULT; MTCW

Littlewit, Humphrey Gent.
See Lovecraft, H(oward) P(hillips)

Litwos
See Sienkiewicz, Henryk (Adam Alexander
Pius)

Liu E 1857-1909 . . . . TCLC 15
See also CA 115

Lively, Penelope (Margaret)
1933- . . . . CLC 32, 50
See also CA 41-44R; CANR 29; CLR 7;
DAM NOV; DLB 14, 161; JRDA;
MAICYA; MTCW; SATA 7, 60

Livesay, Dorothy (Kathleen)
1909- . . . . CLC 4, 15, 79; DAC
See also AITN 2; CA 25-28R; CAAS 8;
CANR 36; DAM MST, POET; DLB 68;
MTCW

Livy c. 59B.C.-c. 17 . . . . CMLC 11

Lizardi, Jose Joaquin Fernandez de
1776-1827 . . . . NCLC 30

Llewellyn, Richard
See Llewellyn Lloyd, Richard Dafydd
Vivian
See also DLB 15

Llewellyn Lloyd, Richard Dafydd Vivian
1906-1983 . . . . CLC 7, 80
See also Llewellyn, Richard
See also CA 53-56; 111; CANR 7;
SATA 11; SATA-Obit 37

Llosa, (Jorge) Mario (Pedro) Vargas
See Vargas Llosa, (Jorge) Mario (Pedro)

Lloyd Webber, Andrew 1948-
See Webber, Andrew Lloyd
See also AAYA 1; CA 116; 149;
DAM DRAM; SATA 56

Llull, Ramon c. 1235-c. 1316 . . . . . CMLC 12

Locke, Alain (Le Roy)
1886-1954 . . . . TCLC 43
See also BW 1; CA 106; 124; DLB 51

Locke, John 1632-1704 . . . . LC 7
See also DLB 101

Locke-Elliott, Sumner
See Elliott, Sumner Locke

Lockhart, John Gibson
1794-1854 . . . . NCLC 6
See also DLB 110, 116, 144

Lodge, David (John) 1935- . . . . CLC 36
See also BEST 90:1; CA 17-20R; CANR 19,
53; DAM POP; DLB 14; INT CANR-19;
MTCW

Loennbohm, Armas Eino Leopold 1878-1926
See Leino, Eino
See also CA 123

Loewinsohn, Ron(ald William)
1937- . . . . CLC 52
See also CA 25-28R

Logan, Jake
See Smith, Martin Cruz

Logan, John (Burton) 1923-1987 . . . . . CLC 5
See also CA 77-80; 124; CANR 45; DLB 5

Lo Kuan-chung 1330(?)-1400(?) . . . . . . LC 12

Lombard, Nap
See Johnson, Pamela Hansford

London, Jack . . TCLC 9, 15, 39; SSC 4; WLC
See also London, John Griffith
See also AAYA 13; AITN 2;
CDALB 1865-1917; DLB 8, 12, 78;
SATA 18

London, John Griffith 1876-1916
See London, Jack
See also CA 110; 119; DA; DAB; DAC;
DAM MST, NOV; JRDA; MAICYA;
MTCW

Long, Emmett
See Leonard, Elmore (John, Jr.)

Longbaugh, Harry
See Goldman, William (W.)

Longfellow, Henry Wadsworth
1807-1882 . . . . . NCLC 2, 45; DA; DAB;
DAC
See also CDALB 1640-1865; DAM MST,
POET; DLB 1, 59; SATA 19

Longley, Michael 1939- . . . . CLC 29
See also CA 102; DLB 40

Longus fl. c. 2nd cent. - . . . . CMLC 7

Longway, A. Hugh
See Lang, Andrew

Lonnrot, Elias 1802-1884. . . . . . . NCLC 53

Lopate, Phillip 1943- . . . . CLC 29
See also CA 97-100; DLBY 80; INT 97-100

Lopez Portillo (y Pacheco), Jose
1920- . . . . CLC 46
See also CA 129; HW

Lopez y Fuentes, Gregorio
1897(?)-1966 . . . . CLC 32
See also CA 131; HW

Lorca, Federico Garcia
See Garcia Lorca, Federico

Machiavelli, Niccolo
1469-1527 . . . . . . **LC 8; DA; DAB; DAC**
See also DAM MST

MacInnes, Colin 1914-1976 . . . . . . **CLC 4, 23**
See also CA 69-72; 65-68; CANR 21;
DLB 14; MTCW

MacInnes, Helen (Clark)
1907-1985 . . . . **CLC 27, 39**
See also CA 1-4R; 117; CANR 1, 28;
DAM POP; DLB 87; MTCW; SATA 22;
SATA-Obit 44

Mackay, Mary 1855-1924
See Corelli, Marie
See also CA 118

Mackenzie, Compton (Edward Montague)
1883-1972 . . . . **CLC 18**
See also CA 21-22; 37-40R; CAP 2;
DLB 34, 100

Mackenzie, Henry 1745-1831 . . . . **NCLC 41**
See also DLB 39

Mackintosh, Elizabeth 1896(?)-1952
See Tey, Josephine
See also CA 110

MacLaren, James
See Grieve, C(hristopher) M(urray)

Mac Laverty, Bernard 1942- . . . . **CLC 31**
See also CA 116; 118; CANR 43; INT 118

MacLean, Alistair (Stuart)
1922-1987 . . . . **CLC 3, 13, 50, 63**
See also CA 57-60; 121; CANR 28;
DAM POP; MTCW; SATA 23;
SATA-Obit 50

Maclean, Norman (Fitzroy)
1902-1990 . . . . **CLC 78; SSC 13**
See also CA 102; 132; CANR 49;
DAM POP

MacLeish, Archibald
1892-1982 . . . . **CLC 3, 8, 14, 68**
See also CA 9-12R; 106; CANR 33;
DAM POET; DLB 4, 7, 45; DLBY 82;
MTCW

MacLennan, (John) Hugh
1907-1990 . . . . **CLC 2, 14, 92; DAC**
See also CA 5-8R; 142; CANR 33;
DAM MST; DLB 68; MTCW

MacLeod, Alistair 1936- . . . . . **CLC 56; DAC**
See also CA 123; DAM MST; DLB 60

MacNeice, (Frederick) Louis
1907-1963 . . . . . . **CLC 1, 4, 10, 53; DAB**
See also CA 85-88; DAM POET; DLB 10,
20; MTCW

MacNeill, Dand
See Fraser, George MacDonald

Macpherson, James 1736-1796 . . . . . . **LC 29**
See also DLB 109

Macpherson, (Jean) Jay 1931- . . . . . . **CLC 14**
See also CA 5-8R; DLB 53

MacShane, Frank 1927- . . . . **CLC 39**
See also CA 9-12R; CANR 3, 33; DLB 111

Macumber, Mari
See Sandoz, Mari(e Susette)

Madach, Imre 1823-1864 . . . . **NCLC 19**

Madden, (Jerry) David 1933- . . . . **CLC 5, 15**
See also CA 1-4R; CAAS 3; CANR 4, 45;
DLB 6; MTCW

Maddern, Al(an)
See Ellison, Harlan (Jay)

Madhubuti, Haki R.
1942- . . . . **CLC 6, 73; BLC; PC 5**
See also Lee, Don L.
See also BW 2; CA 73-76; CANR 24, 51;
DAM MULT, POET; DLB 5, 41;
DLBD 8

Maepenn, Hugh
See Kuttner, Henry

Maepenn, K. H.
See Kuttner, Henry

Maeterlinck, Maurice 1862-1949 . . . **TCLC 3**
See also CA 104; 136; DAM DRAM;
SATA 66

Maginn, William 1794-1842 . . . . . . **NCLC 8**
See also DLB 110, 159

Mahapatra, Jayanta 1928- . . . . **CLC 33**
See also CA 73-76; CAAS 9; CANR 15, 33;
DAM MULT

Mahfouz, Naguib (Abdel Aziz Al-Sabilgi)
1911(?)-
See Mahfuz, Najib
See also BEST 89:2; CA 128; DAM NOV;
MTCW

Mahfuz, Najib . . . . **CLC 52, 55**
See also Mahfouz, Naguib (Abdel Aziz
Al-Sabilgi)
See also DLBY 88

Mahon, Derek 1941- . . . . **CLC 27**
See also CA 113; 128; DLB 40

Mailer, Norman
1923- . . . . . . **CLC 1, 2, 3, 4, 5, 8, 11, 14,
28, 39, 74; DA; DAB; DAC**
See also AITN 2; CA 9-12R; CABS 1;
CANR 28; CDALB 1968-1988;
DAM MST, NOV, POP; DLB 2, 16, 28;
DLBD 3; DLBY 80, 83; MTCW

Maillet, Antonine 1929- . . . . . **CLC 54; DAC**
See also CA 115; 120; CANR 46; DLB 60;
INT 120

Mais, Roger 1905-1955 . . . . **TCLC 8**
See also BW 1; CA 105; 124; DLB 125;
MTCW

Maistre, Joseph de 1753-1821 . . . . **NCLC 37**

Maitland, Frederic 1850-1906 . . . . . **TCLC 65**

Maitland, Sara (Louise) 1950- . . . . . . **CLC 49**
See also CA 69-72; CANR 13

Major, Clarence
1936- . . . . **CLC 3, 19, 48; BLC**
See also BW 2; CA 21-24R; CAAS 6;
CANR 13, 25, 53; DAM MULT; DLB 33

Major, Kevin (Gerald)
1949- . . . . **CLC 26; DAC**
See also AAYA 16; CA 97-100; CANR 21,
38; CLR 11; DLB 60; INT CANR-21;
JRDA; MAICYA; SATA 32, 82

Maki, James
See Ozu, Yasujiro

Malabaila, Damiano
See Levi, Primo

Malamud, Bernard
1914-1986 . . . . . . **CLC 1, 2, 3, 5, 8, 9, 11,
18, 27, 44, 78, 85; DA; DAB; DAC;
SSC 15; WLC**
See also AAYA 16; CA 5-8R; 118; CABS 1;
CANR 28; CDALB 1941-1968;
DAM MST, NOV, POP; DLB 2, 28, 152;
DLBY 80, 86; MTCW

Malaparte, Curzio 1898-1957 . . . . . **TCLC 52**

Malcolm, Dan
See Silverberg, Robert

Malcolm X . . . . **CLC 82; BLC**
See also Little, Malcolm

Malherbe, Francois de 1555-1628 . . . . . **LC 5**

Mallarme, Stephane
1842-1898 . . . . **NCLC 4, 41; PC 4**
See also DAM POET

Mallet-Joris, Francoise 1930- . . . . . . **CLC 11**
See also CA 65-68; CANR 17; DLB 83

Malley, Ern
See McAuley, James Phillip

Mallowan, Agatha Christie
See Christie, Agatha (Mary Clarissa)

Maloff, Saul 1922- . . . . **CLC 5**
See also CA 33-36R

Malone, Louis
See MacNeice, (Frederick) Louis

Malone, Michael (Christopher)
1942- . . . . **CLC 43**
See also CA 77-80; CANR 14, 32

Malory, (Sir) Thomas
1410(?)-1471(?) . . . . . . **LC 11; DA; DAB;
DAC**
See also CDBLB Before 1660; DAM MST;
DLB 146; SATA 59; SATA-Brief 33

Malouf, (George Joseph) David
1934- . . . . **CLC 28, 86**
See also CA 124; CANR 50

Malraux, (Georges-)Andre
1901-1976 . . . . . . **CLC 1, 4, 9, 13, 15, 57**
See also CA 21-22; 69-72; CANR 34;
CAP 2; DAM NOV; DLB 72; MTCW

Malzberg, Barry N(athaniel) 1939- . . . **CLC 7**
See also CA 61-64; CAAS 4; CANR 16;
DLB 8

Mamet, David (Alan)
1947- . . . . . . **CLC 9, 15, 34, 46, 91; DC 4**
See also AAYA 3; CA 81-84; CABS 3;
CANR 15, 41; DAM DRAM; DLB 7;
MTCW

Mamoulian, Rouben (Zachary)
1897-1987 . . . . **CLC 16**
See also CA 25-28R; 124

Mandelstam, Osip (Emilievich)
1891(?)-1938(?) . . . . . . **TCLC 2, 6; PC 14**
See also CA 104; 150

Mander, (Mary) Jane 1877-1949 . . . **TCLC 31**

Mandiargues, Andre Pieyre de . . . . . . **CLC 41**
See also Pieyre de Mandiargues, Andre
See also DLB 83

Mandrake, Ethel Belle
See Thurman, Wallace (Henry)

Mangan, James Clarence
1803-1849 . . . . **NCLC 27**

Maniere, J.-E.
  See Giraudoux, (Hippolyte) Jean

Manley, (Mary) Delariviere
  1672(?)-1724 . . . . LC 1
  See also DLB 39, 80

Mann, Abel
  See Creasey, John

Mann, (Luiz) Heinrich 1871-1950. . . TCLC 9
  See also CA 106; DLB 66

Mann, (Paul) Thomas
  1875-1955 . . . . TCLC 2, 8, 14, 21, 35, 44,
  60; DA; DAB; DAC; SSC 5; WLC
  See also CA 104; 128; DAM MST, NOV;
  DLB 66; MTCW

Mannheim, Karl 1893-1947 . . . . . . TCLC 65

Manning, David
  See Faust, Frederick (Schiller)

Manning, Frederic 1887(?)-1935 . . . TCLC 25
  See also CA 124

Manning, Olivia 1915-1980 . . . . . . CLC 5, 19
  See also CA 5-8R; 101; CANR 29; MTCW

Mano, D. Keith 1942- . . . . CLC 2, 10
  See also CA 25-28R; CAAS 6; CANR 26;
  DLB 6

Mansfield, Katherine
  . . TCLC 2, 8, 39; DAB; SSC 9, 23; WLC
  See also Beauchamp, Kathleen Mansfield
  See also DLB 162

Manso, Peter 1940- . . . . CLC 39
  See also CA 29-32R; CANR 44

Mantecon, Juan Jimenez
  See Jimenez (Mantecon), Juan Ramon

Manton, Peter
  See Creasey, John

Man Without a Spleen, A
  See Chekhov, Anton (Pavlovich)

Manzoni, Alessandro 1785-1873 . . NCLC 29

Mapu, Abraham (ben Jekutiel)
  1808-1867 . . . . NCLC 18

Mara, Sally
  See Queneau, Raymond

Marat, Jean Paul 1743-1793 . . . . LC 10

Marcel, Gabriel Honore
  1889-1973 . . . . CLC 15
  See also CA 102; 45-48; MTCW

Marchbanks, Samuel
  See Davies, (William) Robertson

Marchi, Giacomo
  See Bassani, Giorgio

Margulies, Donald . . . . CLC 76

Marie de France c. 12th cent. - . . . . CMLC 8

Marie de l'Incarnation 1599-1672 . . . . LC 10

Mariner, Scott
  See Pohl, Frederik

Marinetti, Filippo Tommaso
  1876-1944 . . . . TCLC 10
  See also CA 107; DLB 114

Marivaux, Pierre Carlet de Chamblain de
  1688-1763 . . . . LC 4

Markandaya, Kamala . . . . CLC 8, 38
  See also Taylor, Kamala (Purnaiya)

Markfield, Wallace 1926- . . . . CLC 8
  See also CA 69-72; CAAS 3; DLB 2, 28

Markham, Edwin 1852-1940 . . . . . TCLC 47
  See also DLB 54

Markham, Robert
  See Amis, Kingsley (William)

Marks, J
  See Highwater, Jamake (Mamake)

Marks-Highwater, J
  See Highwater, Jamake (Mamake)

Markson, David M(errill) 1927- . . . . CLC 67
  See also CA 49-52; CANR 1

Marley, Bob . . . . CLC 17
  See also Marley, Robert Nesta

Marley, Robert Nesta 1945-1981
  See Marley, Bob
  See also CA 107; 103

Marlowe, Christopher
  1564-1593 . . . . . LC 22; DA; DAB; DAC;
  DC 1; WLC
  See also CDBLB Before 1660;
  DAM DRAM, MST; DLB 62

Marmontel, Jean-Francois
  1723-1799 . . . . LC 2

Marquand, John P(hillips)
  1893-1960 . . . . CLC 2, 10
  See also CA 85-88; DLB 9, 102

Marquez, Gabriel (Jose) Garcia
  See Garcia Marquez, Gabriel (Jose)

Marquis, Don(ald Robert Perry)
  1878-1937 . . . . TCLC 7
  See also CA 104; DLB 11, 25

Marric, J. J.
  See Creasey, John

Marrow, Bernard
  See Moore, Brian

Marryat, Frederick 1792-1848 . . . . NCLC 3
  See also DLB 21, 163

Marsden, James
  See Creasey, John

Marsh, (Edith) Ngaio
  1899-1982 . . . . CLC 7, 53
  See also CA 9-12R; CANR 6; DAM POP;
  DLB 77; MTCW

Marshall, Garry 1934- . . . . CLC 17
  See also AAYA 3; CA 111; SATA 60

Marshall, Paule
  1929- . . . . CLC 27, 72; BLC; SSC 3
  See also BW 2; CA 77-80; CANR 25;
  DAM MULT; DLB 157; MTCW

Marsten, Richard
  See Hunter, Evan

Marston, John 1576-1634 . . . . LC 33
  See also DAM DRAM; DLB 58

Martha, Henry
  See Harris, Mark

Martial c. 40-c. 104 . . . . PC 10

Martin, Ken
  See Hubbard, L(afayette) Ron(ald)

Martin, Richard
  See Creasey, John

Martin, Steve 1945- . . . . CLC 30
  See also CA 97-100; CANR 30; MTCW

Martin, Valerie 1948- . . . . CLC 89
  See also BEST 90:2; CA 85-88; CANR 49

Martin, Violet Florence
  1862-1915 . . . . TCLC 51

Martin, Webber
  See Silverberg, Robert

Martindale, Patrick Victor
  See White, Patrick (Victor Martindale)

Martin du Gard, Roger
  1881-1958 . . . . TCLC 24
  See also CA 118; DLB 65

Martineau, Harriet 1802-1876 . . . . NCLC 26
  See also DLB 21, 55, 159, 163, 166;
  YABC 2

Martines, Julia
  See O'Faolain, Julia

Martinez, Jacinto Benavente y
  See Benavente (y Martinez), Jacinto

Martinez Ruiz, Jose 1873-1967
  See Azorin; Ruiz, Jose Martinez
  See also CA 93-96; HW

Martinez Sierra, Gregorio
  1881-1947 . . . . TCLC 6
  See also CA 115

Martinez Sierra, Maria (de la O'LeJarraga)
  1874-1974 . . . . TCLC 6
  See also CA 115

Martinsen, Martin
  See Follett, Ken(neth Martin)

Martinson, Harry (Edmund)
  1904-1978 . . . . CLC 14
  See also CA 77-80; CANR 34

Marut, Ret
  See Traven, B.

Marut, Robert
  See Traven, B.

Marvell, Andrew
  1621-1678 . . . . . . LC 4; DA; DAB; DAC;
  PC 10; WLC
  See also CDBLB 1660-1789; DAM MST,
  POET; DLB 131

Marx, Karl (Heinrich)
  1818-1883 . . . . NCLC 17
  See also DLB 129

Masaoka Shiki . . . . TCLC 18
  See also Masaoka Tsunenori

Masaoka Tsunenori 1867-1902
  See Masaoka Shiki
  See also CA 117

Masefield, John (Edward)
  1878-1967 . . . . CLC 11, 47
  See also CA 19-20; 25-28R; CANR 33;
  CAP 2; CDBLB 1890-1914; DAM POET;
  DLB 10, 19, 153, 160; MTCW; SATA 19

Maso, Carole 19(?)- . . . . CLC 44

Mason, Bobbie Ann
  1940- . . . . CLC 28, 43, 82; SSC 4
  See also AAYA 5; CA 53-56; CANR 11,
  31; DLBY 87; INT CANR-31; MTCW

Mason, Ernst
  See Pohl, Frederik

Mason, Lee W.
  See Malzberg, Barry N(athaniel)

Mason, Nick 1945- . . . . CLC 35

Mason, Tally
  See Derleth, August (William)

Mass, William
See Gibson, William

Masters, Edgar Lee
1868-1950 . . . . . . **TCLC 2, 25; DA; DAC;**
PC 1
See also CA 104; 133; CDALB 1865-1917;
DAM MST, POET; DLB 54; MTCW

Masters, Hilary 1928- . . . . **CLC 48**
See also CA 25-28R; CANR 13, 47

Mastrosimone, William 19(?)- . . . . . . **CLC 36**

Mathe, Albert
See Camus, Albert

Matheson, Richard Burton 1926- . . . **CLC 37**
See also CA 97-100; DLB 8, 44; INT 97-100

Mathews, Harry 1930- . . . . **CLC 6, 52**
See also CA 21-24R; CAAS 6; CANR 18,
40

Mathews, John Joseph 1894-1979 . . . **CLC 84**
See also CA 19-20; 142; CANR 45; CAP 2;
DAM MULT; NNAL

Mathias, Roland (Glyn) 1915- . . . . . . **CLC 45**
See also CA 97-100; CANR 19, 41; DLB 27

Matsuo Basho 1644-1694 . . . . **PC 3**
See also DAM POET

Mattheson, Rodney
See Creasey, John

Matthews, Greg 1949- . . . . **CLC 45**
See also CA 135

Matthews, William 1942- . . . . **CLC 40**
See also CA 29-32R; CAAS 18; CANR 12;
DLB 5

Matthias, John (Edward) 1941- . . . . . . **CLC 9**
See also CA 33-36R

Matthiessen, Peter
1927- . . . . **CLC 5, 7, 11, 32, 64**
See also AAYA 6; BEST 90:4; CA 9-12R;
CANR 21, 50; DAM NOV; DLB 6;
MTCW; SATA 27

Maturin, Charles Robert
1780(?)-1824 . . . . **NCLC 6**

Matute (Ausejo), Ana Maria
1925- . . . . **CLC 11**
See also CA 89-92; MTCW

Maugham, W. S.
See Maugham, W(illiam) Somerset

Maugham, W(illiam) Somerset
1874-1965 . . . . **CLC 1, 11, 15, 67, 93;**
DA; DAB; DAC; SSC 8; WLC
See also CA 5-8R; 25-28R; CANR 40;
CDBLB 1914-1945; DAM DRAM, MST,
NOV; DLB 10, 36, 77, 100, 162; MTCW;
SATA 54

Maugham, William Somerset
See Maugham, W(illiam) Somerset

Maupassant, (Henri Rene Albert) Guy de
1850-1893 . . . . . **NCLC 1, 42; DA; DAB;**
DAC; SSC 1; WLC
See also DAM MST; DLB 123

Maupin, Armistead 1944- . . . . **CLC 95**
See also CA 125; 130; DAM POP; INT 130

Maurhut, Richard
See Traven, B.

Mauriac, Claude 1914- . . . . **CLC 9**
See also CA 89-92; DLB 83

Mauriac, Francois (Charles)
1885-1970 . . . . **CLC 4, 9, 56**
See also CA 25-28; CAP 2; DLB 65;
MTCW

Mavor, Osborne Henry 1888-1951
See Bridie, James
See also CA 104

Maxwell, William (Keepers, Jr.)
1908- . . . . **CLC 19**
See also CA 93-96; DLBY 80; INT 93-96

May, Elaine 1932- . . . . **CLC 16**
See also CA 124; 142; DLB 44

Mayakovski, Vladimir (Vladimirovich)
1893-1930 . . . . **TCLC 4, 18**
See also CA 104

Mayhew, Henry 1812-1887 . . . . . . **NCLC 31**
See also DLB 18, 55

Mayle, Peter 1939(?)- . . . . **CLC 89**
See also CA 139

Maynard, Joyce 1953- . . . . **CLC 23**
See also CA 111; 129

Mayne, William (James Carter)
1928- . . . . **CLC 12**
See also CA 9-12R; CANR 37; CLR 25;
JRDA; MAICYA; SAAS 11; SATA 6, 68

Mayo, Jim
See L'Amour, Louis (Dearborn)

Maysles, Albert 1926- . . . . **CLC 16**
See also CA 29-32R

Maysles, David 1932- . . . . **CLC 16**

Mazer, Norma Fox 1931- . . . . **CLC 26**
See also AAYA 5; CA 69-72; CANR 12,
32; CLR 23; JRDA; MAICYA; SAAS 1;
SATA 24, 67

Mazzini, Guiseppe 1805-1872 . . . . **NCLC 34**

McAuley, James Phillip
1917-1976 . . . . **CLC 45**
See also CA 97-100

McBain, Ed
See Hunter, Evan

McBrien, William Augustine
1930- . . . . **CLC 44**
See also CA 107

McCaffrey, Anne (Inez) 1926- . . . . . . **CLC 17**
See also AAYA 6; AITN 2; BEST 89:2;
CA 25-28R; CANR 15, 35; DAM NOV,
POP; DLB 8; JRDA; MAICYA; MTCW;
SAAS 11; SATA 8, 70

McCall, Nathan 1955(?)- . . . . **CLC 86**
See also CA 146

McCann, Arthur
See Campbell, John W(ood, Jr.)

McCann, Edson
See Pohl, Frederik

McCarthy, Charles, Jr. 1933-
See McCarthy, Cormac
See also CANR 42; DAM POP

McCarthy, Cormac 1933- . . . . . **CLC 4, 57, 59**
See also McCarthy, Charles, Jr.
See also DLB 6, 143

McCarthy, Mary (Therese)
1912-1989 . . . **CLC 1, 3, 5, 14, 24, 39, 59**
See also CA 5-8R; 129; CANR 16, 50;
DLB 2; DLBY 81; INT CANR-16;
MTCW

McCartney, (James) Paul
1942- . . . . **CLC 12, 35**
See also CA 146

McCauley, Stephen (D.) 1955- . . . . . **CLC 50**
See also CA 141

McClure, Michael (Thomas)
1932- . . . . **CLC 6, 10**
See also CA 21-24R; CANR 17, 46;
DLB 16

McCorkle, Jill (Collins) 1958- . . . . . . **CLC 51**
See also CA 121; DLBY 87

McCourt, James 1941- . . . . **CLC 5**
See also CA 57-60

McCoy, Horace (Stanley)
1897-1955 . . . . **TCLC 28**
See also CA 108; DLB 9

McCrae, John 1872-1918 . . . . **TCLC 12**
See also CA 109; DLB 92

McCreigh, James
See Pohl, Frederik

McCullers, (Lula) Carson (Smith)
1917-1967 . . . . **CLC 1, 4, 10, 12, 48; DA;**
DAB; DAC; SSC 9; WLC
See also CA 5-8R; 25-28R; CABS 1, 3;
CANR 18; CDALB 1941-1968;
DAM MST, NOV; DLB 2, 7; MTCW;
SATA 27

McCulloch, John Tyler
See Burroughs, Edgar Rice

McCullough, Colleen 1938(?)- . . . . . . **CLC 27**
See also CA 81-84; CANR 17, 46;
DAM NOV, POP; MTCW

McDermott, Alice 1953- . . . . **CLC 90**
See also CA 109; CANR 40

McElroy, Joseph 1930- . . . . **CLC 5, 47**
See also CA 17-20R

McEwan, Ian (Russell) 1948- . . . **CLC 13, 66**
See also BEST 90:4; CA 61-64; CANR 14,
41; DAM NOV; DLB 14; MTCW

McFadden, David 1940- . . . . **CLC 48**
See also CA 104; DLB 60; INT 104

McFarland, Dennis 1950- . . . . **CLC 65**

McGahern, John
1934- . . . . **CLC 5, 9, 48; SSC 17**
See also CA 17-20R; CANR 29; DLB 14;
MTCW

McGinley, Patrick (Anthony)
1937- . . . . **CLC 41**
See also CA 120; 127; INT 127

McGinley, Phyllis 1905-1978 . . . . . . **CLC 14**
See also CA 9-12R; 77-80; CANR 19;
DLB 11, 48; SATA 2, 44; SATA-Obit 24

McGinniss, Joe 1942- . . . . **CLC 32**
See also AITN 2; BEST 89:2; CA 25-28R;
CANR 26; INT CANR-26

McGivern, Maureen Daly
See Daly, Maureen

McGrath, Patrick 1950- . . . . **CLC 55**
See also CA 136

McGrath, Thomas (Matthew)
1916-1990 . . . . **CLC 28, 59**
See also CA 9-12R; 132; CANR 6, 33;
DAM POET; MTCW; SATA 41;
SATA-Obit 66

McGuane, Thomas (Francis III)
1939- . . . . **CLC 3, 7, 18, 45**
See also AITN 2; CA 49-52; CANR 5, 24,
49; DLB 2; DLBY 80; INT CANR-24;
MTCW

McGuckian, Medbh 1950- . . . . **CLC 48**
See also CA 143; DAM POET; DLB 40

McHale, Tom 1942(?)-1982 . . . . **CLC 3, 5**
See also AITN 1; CA 77-80; 106

McIlvanney, William 1936- . . . . **CLC 42**
See also CA 25-28R; DLB 14

McIlwraith, Maureen Mollie Hunter
See Hunter, Mollie
See also SATA 2

McInerney, Jay 1955- . . . . **CLC 34**
See also AAYA 18; CA 116; 123;
CANR 45; DAM POP; INT 123

McIntyre, Vonda N(eel) 1948- . . . . . **CLC 18**
See also CA 81-84; CANR 17, 34; MTCW

McKay, Claude
. . . . **TCLC 7, 41; BLC; DAB; PC 2**
See also McKay, Festus Claudius
See also DLB 4, 45, 51, 117

McKay, Festus Claudius 1889-1948
See McKay, Claude
See also BW 1; CA 104; 124; DA; DAC;
DAM MST, MULT, NOV, POET;
MTCW; WLC

McKuen, Rod 1933- . . . . **CLC 1, 3**
See also AITN 1; CA 41-44R; CANR 40

McLoughlin, R. B.
See Mencken, H(enry) L(ouis)

McLuhan, (Herbert) Marshall
1911-1980 . . . . **CLC 37, 83**
See also CA 9-12R; 102; CANR 12, 34;
DLB 88; INT CANR-12; MTCW

McMillan, Terry (L.) 1951- . . . . . **CLC 50, 61**
See also BW 2; CA 140; DAM MULT,
NOV, POP

McMurtry, Larry (Jeff)
1936- . . . . **CLC 2, 3, 7, 11, 27, 44**
See also AAYA 15; AITN 2; BEST 89:2;
CA 5-8R; CANR 19, 43;
CDALB 1968-1988; DAM NOV, POP;
DLB 2, 143; DLBY 80, 87; MTCW

McNally, T. M. 1961- . . . . **CLC 82**

McNally, Terrence 1939- . . . **CLC 4, 7, 41, 91**
See also CA 45-48; CANR 2;
DAM DRAM; DLB 7

McNamer, Deirdre 1950- . . . . **CLC 70**

McNeile, Herman Cyril 1888-1937
See Sapper
See also DLB 77

McNickle, (William) D'Arcy
1904-1977 . . . . **CLC 89**
See also CA 9-12R; 85-88; CANR 5, 45;
DAM MULT; NNAL; SATA-Obit 22

McPhee, John (Angus) 1931- . . . . . . **CLC 36**
See also BEST 90:1; CA 65-68; CANR 20,
46; MTCW

McPherson, James Alan
1943- . . . . **CLC 19, 77**
See also BW 1; CA 25-28R; CAAS 17;
CANR 24; DLB 38; MTCW

McPherson, William (Alexander)
1933- . . . . **CLC 34**
See also CA 69-72; CANR 28;
INT CANR-28

Mead, Margaret 1901-1978 . . . . **CLC 37**
See also AITN 1; CA 1-4R; 81-84;
CANR 4; MTCW; SATA-Obit 20

Meaker, Marijane (Agnes) 1927-
See Kerr, M. E.
See also CA 107; CANR 37; INT 107;
JRDA; MAICYA; MTCW; SATA 20, 61

Medoff, Mark (Howard) 1940- . . . **CLC 6, 23**
See also AITN 1; CA 53-56; CANR 5;
DAM DRAM; DLB 7; INT CANR-5

Medvedev, P. N.
See Bakhtin, Mikhail Mikhailovich

Meged, Aharon
See Megged, Aharon

Meged, Aron
See Megged, Aharon

Megged, Aharon 1920- . . . . **CLC 9**
See also CA 49-52; CAAS 13; CANR 1

Mehta, Ved (Parkash) 1934- . . . . **CLC 37**
See also CA 1-4R; CANR 2, 23; MTCW

Melanter
See Blackmore, R(ichard) D(oddridge)

Melikow, Loris
See Hofmannsthal, Hugo von

Melmoth, Sebastian
See Wilde, Oscar (Fingal O'Flahertie Wills)

Meltzer, Milton 1915- . . . . **CLC 26**
See also AAYA 8; CA 13-16R; CANR 38;
CLR 13; DLB 61; JRDA; MAICYA;
SAAS 1; SATA 1, 50, 80

Melville, Herman
1819-1891 . . . . . **NCLC 3, 12, 29, 45, 49;
DA; DAB; DAC; SSC 1, 17; WLC**
See also CDALB 1640-1865; DAM MST,
NOV; DLB 3, 74; SATA 59

Menander
c. 342B.C.-c. 292B.C. . . . . **CMLC 9; DC 3**
See also DAM DRAM

Mencken, H(enry) L(ouis)
1880-1956 . . . . **TCLC 13**
See also CA 105; 125; CDALB 1917-1929;
DLB 11, 29, 63, 137; MTCW

Mercer, David 1928-1980 . . . . **CLC 5**
See also CA 9-12R; 102; CANR 23;
DAM DRAM; DLB 13; MTCW

Merchant, Paul
See Ellison, Harlan (Jay)

Meredith, George 1828-1909 . . . **TCLC 17, 43**
See also CA 117; CDBLB 1832-1890;
DAM POET; DLB 18, 35, 57, 159

Meredith, William (Morris)
1919- . . . . **CLC 4, 13, 22, 55**
See also CA 9-12R; CAAS 14; CANR 6, 40;
DAM POET; DLB 5

Merezhkovsky, Dmitry Sergeyevich
1865-1941 . . . . **TCLC 29**

Merimee, Prosper
1803-1870 . . . . **NCLC 6; SSC 7**
See also DLB 119

Merkin, Daphne 1954- . . . . **CLC 44**
See also CA 123

Merlin, Arthur
See Blish, James (Benjamin)

Merrill, James (Ingram)
1926-1995 . . . . **CLC 2, 3, 6, 8, 13, 18, 34,
91**
See also CA 13-16R; 147; CANR 10, 49;
DAM POET; DLB 5, 165; DLBY 85;
INT CANR-10; MTCW

Merriman, Alex
See Silverberg, Robert

Merritt, E. B.
See Waddington, Miriam

Merton, Thomas
1915-1968 . . **CLC 1, 3, 11, 34, 83; PC 10**
See also CA 5-8R; 25-28R; CANR 22, 53;
DLB 48; DLBY 81; MTCW

Merwin, W(illiam) S(tanley)
1927- . . . **CLC 1, 2, 3, 5, 8, 13, 18, 45, 88**
See also CA 13-16R; CANR 15, 51;
DAM POET; DLB 5; INT CANR-15;
MTCW

Metcalf, John 1938- . . . . **CLC 37**
See also CA 113; DLB 60

Metcalf, Suzanne
See Baum, L(yman) Frank

Mew, Charlotte (Mary)
1870-1928 . . . . **TCLC 8**
See also CA 105; DLB 19, 135

Mewshaw, Michael 1943- . . . . **CLC 9**
See also CA 53-56; CANR 7, 47; DLBY 80

Meyer, June
See Jordan, June

Meyer, Lynn
See Slavitt, David R(ytman)

Meyer-Meyrink, Gustav 1868-1932
See Meyrink, Gustav
See also CA 117

Meyers, Jeffrey 1939- . . . . **CLC 39**
See also CA 73-76; DLB 111

Meynell, Alice (Christina Gertrude Thompson)
1847-1922 . . . . **TCLC 6**
See also CA 104; DLB 19, 98

Meyrink, Gustav . . . . **TCLC 21**
See also Meyer-Meyrink, Gustav
See also DLB 81

Michaels, Leonard
1933- . . . . **CLC 6, 25; SSC 16**
See also CA 61-64; CANR 21; DLB 130;
MTCW

Michaux, Henri 1899-1984 . . . . . . **CLC 8, 19**
See also CA 85-88; 114

Michelangelo 1475-1564 . . . . **LC 12**

Michelet, Jules 1798-1874 . . . . **NCLC 31**

Michener, James A(lbert)
1907(?)- . . . . **CLC 1, 5, 11, 29, 60**
See also AITN 1; BEST 90:1; CA 5-8R;
CANR 21, 45; DAM NOV, POP; DLB 6;
MTCW

Mickiewicz, Adam 1798-1855 . . . . . **NCLC 3**

Middleton, Christopher 1926- . . . . . . **CLC 13**
See also CA 13-16R; CANR 29; DLB 40

Middleton, Richard (Barham)
1882-1911 . . . . **TCLC 56**
See also DLB 156

Montgomery, Marion H., Jr. 1925- . . CLC 7
See also AITN 1; CA 1-4R; CANR 3, 48;
DLB 6

Montgomery, Max
See Davenport, Guy (Mattison, Jr.)

Montherlant, Henry (Milon) de
1896-1972 . . . . CLC 8, 19
See also CA 85-88; 37-40R; DAM DRAM;
DLB 72; MTCW

Monty Python
See Chapman, Graham; Cleese, John
(Marwood); Gilliam, Terry (Vance); Idle,
Eric; Jones, Terence Graham Parry; Palin,
Michael (Edward)
See also AAYA 7

Moodie, Susanna (Strickland)
1803-1885 . . . . NCLC 14
See also DLB 99

Mooney, Edward 1951-
See Mooney, Ted
See also CA 130

Mooney, Ted . . . . CLC 25
See also Mooney, Edward

Moorcock, Michael (John)
1939- . . . . CLC 5, 27, 58
See also CA 45-48; CAAS 5; CANR 2, 17,
38; DLB 14; MTCW

Moore, Brian
1921- . . . . . . CLC 1, 3, 5, 7, 8, 19, 32, 90;
DAB; DAC
See also CA 1-4R; CANR 1, 25, 42;
DAM MST; MTCW

Moore, Edward
See Muir, Edwin

Moore, George Augustus
1852-1933 . . . . TCLC 7; SSC 19
See also CA 104; DLB 10, 18, 57, 135

Moore, Lorrie . . . . CLC 39, 45, 68
See also Moore, Marie Lorena

Moore, Marianne (Craig)
1887-1972 . . . . CLC 1, 2, 4, 8, 10, 13, 19,
47; DA; DAB; DAC; PC 4
See also CA 1-4R; 33-36R; CANR 3;
CDALB 1929-1941; DAM MST, POET;
DLB 45; DLBD 7; MTCW; SATA 20

Moore, Marie Lorena 1957-
See Moore, Lorrie
See also CA 116; CANR 39

Moore, Thomas 1779-1852 . . . . NCLC 6
See also DLB 96, 144

Morand, Paul 1888-1976 . . CLC 41; SSC 22
See also CA 69-72; DLB 65

Morante, Elsa 1918-1985 . . . . CLC 8, 47
See also CA 85-88; 117; CANR 35; MTCW

Moravia, Alberto . . . . . . CLC 2, 7, 11, 27, 46
See also Pincherle, Alberto

More, Hannah 1745-1833 . . . . NCLC 27
See also DLB 107, 109, 116, 158

More, Henry 1614-1687 . . . . LC 9
See also DLB 126

More, Sir Thomas 1478-1535 . . . . LC 10, 32

Moreas, Jean . . . . TCLC 18
See also Papadiamantopoulos, Johannes

Morgan, Berry 1919- . . . . CLC 6
See also CA 49-52; DLB 6

Morgan, Claire
See Highsmith, (Mary) Patricia

Morgan, Edwin (George) 1920- . . . . . CLC 31
See also CA 5-8R; CANR 3, 43; DLB 27

Morgan, (George) Frederick
1922- . . . . CLC 23
See also CA 17-20R; CANR 21

Morgan, Harriet
See Mencken, H(enry) L(ouis)

Morgan, Jane
See Cooper, James Fenimore

Morgan, Janet 1945- . . . . CLC 39
See also CA 65-68

Morgan, Lady 1776(?)-1859 . . . . . . NCLC 29
See also DLB 116, 158

Morgan, Robin 1941- . . . . CLC 2
See also CA 69-72; CANR 29; MTCW;
SATA 80

Morgan, Scott
See Kuttner, Henry

Morgan, Seth 1949(?)-1990 . . . . CLC 65
See also CA 132

Morgenstern, Christian
1871-1914 . . . . TCLC 8
See also CA 105

Morgenstern, S.
See Goldman, William (W.)

Moricz, Zsigmond 1879-1942 . . . . . TCLC 33

Morike, Eduard (Friedrich)
1804-1875 . . . . NCLC 10
See also DLB 133

Mori Ogai . . . . TCLC 14
See also Mori Rintaro

Mori Rintaro 1862-1922
See Mori Ogai
See also CA 110

Moritz, Karl Philipp 1756-1793 . . . . . . LC 2
See also DLB 94

Morland, Peter Henry
See Faust, Frederick (Schiller)

Morren, Theophil
See Hofmannsthal, Hugo von

Morris, Bill 1952- . . . . CLC 76

Morris, Julian
See West, Morris L(anglo)

Morris, Steveland Judkins 1950(?)-
See Wonder, Stevie
See also CA 111

Morris, William 1834-1896 . . . . . . NCLC 4
See also CDBLB 1832-1890; DLB 18, 35,
57, 156

Morris, Wright 1910- . . . CLC 1, 3, 7, 18, 37
See also CA 9-12R; CANR 21; DLB 2;
DLBY 81; MTCW

Morrison, Chloe Anthony Wofford
See Morrison, Toni

Morrison, James Douglas 1943-1971
See Morrison, Jim
See also CA 73-76; CANR 40

Morrison, Jim . . . . CLC 17
See also Morrison, James Douglas

Morrison, Toni
1931- . . . . CLC 4, 10, 22, 55, 81, 87;
BLC; DA; DAB; DAC
See also AAYA 1; BW 2; CA 29-32R;
CANR 27, 42; CDALB 1968-1988;
DAM MST, MULT, NOV, POP; DLB 6,
33, 143; DLBY 81; MTCW; SATA 57

Morrison, Van 1945- . . . . CLC 21
See also CA 116

Mortimer, John (Clifford)
1923- . . . . CLC 28, 43
See also CA 13-16R; CANR 21;
CDBLB 1960 to Present; DAM DRAM,
POP; DLB 13; INT CANR-21; MTCW

Mortimer, Penelope (Ruth) 1918- . . . . CLC 5
See also CA 57-60; CANR 45

Morton, Anthony
See Creasey, John

Mosher, Howard Frank 1943- . . . . . . CLC 62
See also CA 139

Mosley, Nicholas 1923- . . . . CLC 43, 70
See also CA 69-72; CANR 41; DLB 14

Moss, Howard
1922-1987 . . . . CLC 7, 14, 45, 50
See also CA 1-4R; 123; CANR 1, 44;
DAM POET; DLB 5

Mossgiel, Rab
See Burns, Robert

Motion, Andrew (Peter) 1952- . . . . . . CLC 47
See also CA 146; DLB 40

Motley, Willard (Francis)
1909-1965 . . . . CLC 18
See also BW 1; CA 117; 106; DLB 76, 143

Motoori, Norinaga 1730-1801 . . . . NCLC 45

Mott, Michael (Charles Alston)
1930- . . . . CLC 15, 34
See also CA 5-8R; CAAS 7; CANR 7, 29

Mountain Wolf Woman
1884-1960 . . . . CLC 92
See also CA 144; NNAL

Moure, Erin 1955- . . . . CLC 88
See also CA 113; DLB 60

Mowat, Farley (McGill)
1921- . . . . CLC 26; DAC
See also AAYA 1; CA 1-4R; CANR 4, 24,
42; CLR 20; DAM MST; DLB 68;
INT CANAR-24; JRDA; MAICYA;
MTCW; SATA 3, 55

Moyers, Bill 1934- . . . . CLC 74
See also AITN 2; CA 61-64; CANR 31, 52

Mphahlele, Es'kia
See Mphahlele, Ezekiel
See also DLB 125

Mphahlele, Ezekiel 1919- . . . . . CLC 25; BLC
See also Mphahlele, Es'kia
See also BW 2; CA 81-84; CANR 26;
DAM MULT

Mqhayi, S(amuel) E(dward) K(rune Loliwe)
1875-1945 . . . . TCLC 25; BLC
See also DAM MULT

Mrozek, Slawomir 1930- . . . . CLC 3, 13
See also CA 13-16R; CAAS 10; CANR 29;
MTCW

Mrs. Belloc-Lowndes
See Lowndes, Marie Adelaide (Belloc)

Mtwa, Percy (?)-................ **CLC 47**

Mueller, Lisel 1924-.......... **CLC 13, 51**
See also CA 93-96; DLB 105

Muir, Edwin 1887-1959 .... **TCLC 2**
See also CA 104; DLB 20, 100

Muir, John 1838-1914 .... **TCLC 28**

Mujica Lainez, Manuel
1910-1984 .... **CLC 31**
See also Lainez, Manuel Mujica
See also CA 81-84; 112; CANR 32; HW

Mukherjee, Bharati 1940-......... **CLC 53**
See also BEST 89:2; CA 107; CANR 45;
DAM NOV; DLB 60; MTCW

Muldoon, Paul 1951-.......... **CLC 32, 72**
See also CA 113; 129; CANR 52;
DAM POET; DLB 40; INT 129

Mulisch, Harry 1927-............ **CLC 42**
See also CA 9-12R; CANR 6, 26

Mull, Martin 1943-.............. **CLC 17**
See also CA 105

Mulock, Dinah Maria
See Craik, Dinah Maria (Mulock)

Munford, Robert 1737(?)-1783 .... **LC 5**
See also DLB 31

Mungo, Raymond 1946-.......... **CLC 72**
See also CA 49-52; CANR 2

Munro, Alice
1931-...... **CLC 6, 10, 19, 50, 95; DAC;**
SSC 3
See also AITN 2; CA 33-36R; CANR 33,
53; DAM MST, NOV; DLB 53; MTCW;
SATA 29

Munro, H(ector) H(ugh) 1870-1916
See Saki
See also CA 104; 130; CDBLB 1890-1914;
DA; DAB; DAC; DAM MST, NOV;
DLB 34, 162; MTCW; WLC

Murasaki, Lady................. **CMLC 1**

Murdoch, (Jean) Iris
1919-...... **CLC 1, 2, 3, 4, 6, 8, 11, 15,**
22, 31, 51; DAB; DAC
See also CA 13-16R; CANR 8, 43;
CDBLB 1960 to Present; DAM MST,
NOV; DLB 14; INT CANR-8; MTCW

Murfree, Mary Noailles
1850-1922 .... **SSC 22**
See also CA 122; DLB 12, 74

Murnau, Friedrich Wilhelm
See Plumpe, Friedrich Wilhelm

Murphy, Richard 1927-.......... **CLC 41**
See also CA 29-32R; DLB 40

Murphy, Sylvia 1937-............ **CLC 34**
See also CA 121

Murphy, Thomas (Bernard) 1935-... **CLC 51**
See also CA 101

Murray, Albert L. 1916- .... **CLC 73**
See also BW 2; CA 49-52; CANR 26, 52;
DLB 38

Murray, Les(lie) A(llan) 1938- ..... **CLC 40**
See also CA 21-24R; CANR 11, 27;
DAM POET

Murry, J. Middleton
See Murry, John Middleton

Murry, John Middleton
1889-1957 .... **TCLC 16**
See also CA 118; DLB 149

Musgrave, Susan 1951- .... **CLC 13, 54**
See also CA 69-72; CANR 45

Musil, Robert (Edler von)
1880-1942 .... **TCLC 12; SSC 18**
See also CA 109; DLB 81, 124

Muske, Carol 1945- .... **CLC 90**
See also Muske-Dukes, Carol (Anne)

Muske-Dukes, Carol (Anne) 1945-
See Muske, Carol
See also CA 65-68; CANR 32

Musset, (Louis Charles) Alfred de
1810-1857 .... **NCLC 7**

My Brother's Brother
See Chekhov, Anton (Pavlovich)

Myers, L. H. 1881-1944.......... **TCLC 59**
See also DLB 15

Myers, Walter Dean 1937- ... **CLC 35; BLC**
See also AAYA 4; BW 2; CA 33-36R;
CANR 20, 42; CLR 4, 16, 35;
DAM MULT, NOV; DLB 33;
INT CANR-20; JRDA; MAICYA;
SAAS 2; SATA 41, 71; SATA-Brief 27

Myers, Walter M.
See Myers, Walter Dean

Myles, Symon
See Follett, Ken(neth Martin)

Nabokov, Vladimir (Vladimirovich)
1899-1977 ..... **CLC 1, 2, 3, 6, 8, 11, 15,**
23, 44, 46, 64; DA; DAB; DAC; SSC 11;
WLC
See also CA 5-8R; 69-72; CANR 20;
CDALB 1941-1968; DAM MST, NOV;
DLB 2; DLBD 3; DLBY 80, 91; MTCW

Nagai Kafu................... **TCLC 51**
See also Nagai Sokichi

Nagai Sokichi 1879-1959
See Nagai Kafu
See also CA 117

Nagy, Laszlo 1925-1978........... **CLC 7**
See also CA 129; 112

Naipaul, Shiva(dhar Srinivasa)
1945-1985 .... **CLC 32, 39**
See also CA 110; 112; 116; CANR 33;
DAM NOV; DLB 157; DLBY 85;
MTCW

Naipaul, V(idiadhar) S(urajprasad)
1932- .... **CLC 4, 7, 9, 13, 18, 37; DAB;**
DAC
See also CA 1-4R; CANR 1, 33, 51;
CDBLB 1960 to Present; DAM MST,
NOV; DLB 125; DLBY 85; MTCW

Nakos, Lilika 1899(?)-............ **CLC 29**

Narayan, R(asipuram) K(rishnaswami)
1906-................. **CLC 7, 28, 47**
See also CA 81-84; CANR 33; DAM NOV;
MTCW; SATA 62

Nash, (Fredric) Ogden 1902-1971 .. **CLC 23**
See also CA 13-14; 29-32R; CANR 34;
CAP 1; DAM POET; DLB 11;
MAICYA; MTCW; SATA 2, 46

Nathan, Daniel
See Dannay, Frederic

Nathan, George Jean 1882-1958 ... **TCLC 18**
See also Hatteras, Owen
See also CA 114; DLB 137

Natsume, Kinnosuke 1867-1916
See Natsume, Soseki
See also CA 104

Natsume, Soseki .... **TCLC 2, 10**
See also Natsume, Kinnosuke

Natti, (Mary) Lee 1919-
See Kingman, Lee
See also CA 5-8R; CANR 2

Naylor, Gloria
1950- ..... **CLC 28, 52; BLC; DA; DAC**
See also AAYA 6; BW 2; CA 107;
CANR 27, 51; DAM MST, MULT,
NOV, POP; MTCW

Neihardt, John Gneisenau
1881-1973 .... **CLC 32**
See also CA 13-14; CAP 1; DLB 9, 54

Nekrasov, Nikolai Alekseevich
1821-1878 .... **NCLC 11**

Nelligan, Emile 1879-1941....... **TCLC 14**
See also CA 114; DLB 92

Nelson, Willie 1933-.............. **CLC 17**
See also CA 107

Nemerov, Howard (Stanley)
1920-1991 .... **CLC 2, 6, 9, 36**
See also CA 1-4R; 134; CABS 2; CANR 1,
27, 53; DAM POET; DLB 5, 6;
DLBY 83; INT CANR-27; MTCW

Neruda, Pablo
1904-1973 ..... **CLC 1, 2, 5, 7, 9, 28, 62;**
DA; DAB; DAC; HLC; PC 4; WLC
See also CA 19-20; 45-48; CAP 2;
DAM MST, MULT, POET; HW; MTCW

Nerval, Gerard de
1808-1855 ..... **NCLC 1; PC 13; SSC 18**

Nervo, (Jose) Amado (Ruiz de)
1870-1919 .... **TCLC 11**
See also CA 109; 131; HW

Nessi, Pio Baroja y
See Baroja (y Nessi), Pio

Nestroy, Johann 1801-1862...... **NCLC 42**
See also DLB 133

Neufeld, John (Arthur) 1938- ...... **CLC 17**
See also AAYA 11; CA 25-28R; CANR 11,
37; MAICYA; SAAS 3; SATA 6, 81

Neville, Emily Cheney 1919-....... **CLC 12**
See also CA 5-8R; CANR 3, 37; JRDA;
MAICYA; SAAS 2; SATA 1

Newbound, Bernard Slade 1930-
See Slade, Bernard
See also CA 81-84; CANR 49;
DAM DRAM

Newby, P(ercy) H(oward)
1918-.................. **CLC 2, 13**
See also CA 5-8R; CANR 32; DAM NOV;
DLB 15; MTCW

Newlove, Donald 1928- .... **CLC 6**
See also CA 29-32R; CANR 25

Newlove, John (Herbert) 1938-..... **CLC 14**
See also CA 21-24R; CANR 9, 25

Newman, Charles 1938-.......... **CLC 2, 8**
See also CA 21-24R

Newman, Edwin (Harold) 1919- .... **CLC 14**
See also AITN 1; CA 69-72; CANR 5

Newman, John Henry
1801-1890 .... **NCLC 38**
See also DLB 18, 32, 55

Newton, Suzanne 1936- .... **CLC 35**
See also CA 41-44R; CANR 14; JRDA;
SATA 5, 77

Nexo, Martin Andersen
1869-1954 .... **TCLC 43**

Nezval, Vitezslav 1900-1958 ...... **TCLC 44**
See also CA 123

Ng, Fae Myenne 1957(?)-.......... **CLC 81**
See also CA 146

Ngema, Mbongeni 1955- .... **CLC 57**
See also BW 2; CA 143

Ngugi, James T(hiong'o)........ **CLC 3, 7, 13**
See also Ngugi wa Thiong'o

Ngugi wa Thiong'o 1938-..... **CLC 36; BLC**
See also Ngugi, James T(hiong'o)
See also BW 2; CA 81-84; CANR 27;
DAM MULT, NOV; DLB 125; MTCW

Nichol, B(arrie) P(hillip)
1944-1988 .... **CLC 18**
See also CA 53-56; DLB 53; SATA 66

Nichols, John (Treadwell) 1940-.... **CLC 38**
See also CA 9-12R; CAAS 2; CANR 6;
DLBY 82

Nichols, Leigh
See Koontz, Dean R(ay)

Nichols, Peter (Richard)
1927- .... **CLC 5, 36, 65**
See also CA 104; CANR 33; DLB 13;
MTCW

Nicolas, F. R. E.
See Freeling, Nicolas

Niedecker, Lorine 1903-1970.... **CLC 10, 42**
See also CA 25-28; CAP 2; DAM POET;
DLB 48

Nietzsche, Friedrich (Wilhelm)
1844-1900 .... **TCLC 10, 18, 55**
See also CA 107; 121; DLB 129

Nievo, Ippolito 1831-1861 .... **NCLC 22**

Nightingale, Anne Redmon 1943-
See Redmon, Anne
See also CA 103

Nik. T. O.
See Annensky, Innokenty Fyodorovich

Nin, Anais
1903-1977 ...... **CLC 1, 4, 8, 11, 14, 60;**
SSC 10
See also AITN 2; CA 13-16R; 69-72;
CANR 22, 53; DAM NOV, POP; DLB 2,
4, 152; MTCW

Nishiwaki, Junzaburo 1894-1982 .... **PC 15**
See also CA 107

Nissenson, Hugh 1933-........... **CLC 4, 9**
See also CA 17-20R; CANR 27; DLB 28

Niven, Larry .... **CLC 8**
See also Niven, Laurence Van Cott
See also DLB 8

Niven, Laurence Van Cott 1938-
See Niven, Larry
See also CA 21-24R; CAAS 12; CANR 14,
44; DAM POP; MTCW

Nixon, Agnes Eckhardt 1927-...... **CLC 21**
See also CA 110

Nizan, Paul 1905-1940........... **TCLC 40**
See also DLB 72

Nkosi, Lewis 1936-.......... **CLC 45; BLC**
See also BW 1; CA 65-68; CANR 27;
DAM MULT; DLB 157

Nodier, (Jean) Charles (Emmanuel)
1780-1844 .... **NCLC 19**
See also DLB 119

Nolan, Christopher 1965-.......... **CLC 58**
See also CA 111

Noon, Jeff 1957-................. **CLC 91**
See also CA 148

Norden, Charles
See Durrell, Lawrence (George)

Nordhoff, Charles (Bernard)
1887-1947 .... **TCLC 23**
See also CA 108; DLB 9; SATA 23

Norfolk, Lawrence 1963-.......... **CLC 76**
See also CA 144

Norman, Marsha 1947- .... **CLC 28**
See also CA 105; CABS 3; CANR 41;
DAM DRAM; DLBY 84

Norris, Benjamin Franklin, Jr.
1870-1902 .... **TCLC 24**
See also Norris, Frank
See also CA 110

Norris, Frank
See Norris, Benjamin Franklin, Jr.
See also CDALB 1865-1917; DLB 12, 71

Norris, Leslie 1921-.............. **CLC 14**
See also CA 11-12; CANR 14; CAP 1;
DLB 27

North, Andrew
See Norton, Andre

North, Anthony
See Koontz, Dean R(ay)

North, Captain George
See Stevenson, Robert Louis (Balfour)

North, Milou
See Erdrich, Louise

Northrup, B. A.
See Hubbard, L(afayette) Ron(ald)

North Staffs
See Hulme, T(homas) E(rnest)

Norton, Alice Mary
See Norton, Andre
See also MAICYA; SATA 1, 43

Norton, Andre 1912- .... **CLC 12**
See also Norton, Alice Mary
See also AAYA 14; CA 1-4R; CANR 2, 31;
DLB 8, 52; JRDA; MTCW

Norton, Caroline 1808-1877...... **NCLC 47**
See also DLB 21, 159

Norway, Nevil Shute 1899-1960
See Shute, Nevil
See also CA 102; 93-96

Norwid, Cyprian Kamil
1821-1883 .... **NCLC 17**

Nosille, Nabrah
See Ellison, Harlan (Jay)

Nossack, Hans Erich 1901-1978 ..... **CLC 6**
See also CA 93-96; 85-88; DLB 69

Nostradamus 1503-1566............ **LC 27**

Nosu, Chuji
See Ozu, Yasujiro

Notenburg, Eleanora (Genrikhovna) von
See Guro, Elena

Nova, Craig 1945-.............. **CLC 7, 31**
See also CA 45-48; CANR 2, 53

Novak, Joseph
See Kosinski, Jerzy (Nikodem)

Novalis 1772-1801 .... **NCLC 13**
See also DLB 90

Nowlan, Alden (Albert)
1933-1983 .... **CLC 15; DAC**
See also CA 9-12R; CANR 5; DAM MST;
DLB 53

Noyes, Alfred 1880-1958 .... **TCLC 7**
See also CA 104; DLB 20

Nunn, Kem 19(?)-................ **CLC 34**

Nye, Robert 1939- .... **CLC 13, 42**
See also CA 33-36R; CANR 29;
DAM NOV; DLB 14; MTCW; SATA 6

Nyro, Laura 1947- .... **CLC 17**

Oates, Joyce Carol
1938-...... **CLC 1, 2, 3, 6, 9, 11, 15, 19,**
33, 52; DA; DAB; DAC; SSC 6; WLC
See also AAYA 15; AITN 1; BEST 89:2;
CA 5-8R; CANR 25, 45;
CDALB 1968-1988; DAM MST, NOV,
POP; DLB 2, 5, 130; DLBY 81;
INT CANR-25; MTCW

O'Brien, Darcy 1939-............. **CLC 11**
See also CA 21-24R; CANR 8

O'Brien, E. G.
See Clarke, Arthur C(harles)

O'Brien, Edna
1936- ... **CLC 3, 5, 8, 13, 36, 65; SSC 10**
See also CA 1-4R; CANR 6, 41;
CDBLB 1960 to Present; DAM NOV;
DLB 14; MTCW

O'Brien, Fitz-James 1828-1862... **NCLC 21**
See also DLB 74

O'Brien, Flann........ **CLC 1, 4, 5, 7, 10, 47**
See also O Nuallain, Brian

O'Brien, Richard 1942-........... **CLC 17**
See also CA 124

O'Brien, Tim 1946-.......... **CLC 7, 19, 40**
See also AAYA 16; CA 85-88; CANR 40;
DAM POP; DLB 152; DLBD 9;
DLBY 80

Obstfelder, Sigbjoern 1866-1900... **TCLC 23**
See also CA 123

O'Casey, Sean
1880-1964 ...... **CLC 1, 5, 9, 11, 15, 88;**
DAB; DAC
See also CA 89-92; CDBLB 1914-1945;
DAM DRAM, MST; DLB 10; MTCW

O'Cathasaigh, Sean
See O'Casey, Sean

Ochs, Phil 1940-1976............. **CLC 17**
See also CA 65-68

O'Connor, Edwin (Greene)
1918-1968 .... **CLC 14**
See also CA 93-96; 25-28R

O'Connor, (Mary) Flannery
    1925-1964 .... CLC 1, 2, 3, 6, 10, 13, 15,
    21, 66; DA; DAB; DAC; SSC 1, 23; WLC
    See also AAYA 7; CA 1-4R; CANR 3, 41;
    CDALB 1941-1968; DAM MST, NOV;
    DLB 2, 152; DLBD 12; DLBY 80;
    MTCW

O'Connor, Frank .... CLC 23; SSC 5
    See also O'Donovan, Michael John
    See also DLB 162

O'Dell, Scott 1898-1989 .... CLC 30
    See also AAYA 3; CA 61-64; 129;
    CANR 12, 30; CLR 1, 16; DLB 52;
    JRDA; MAICYA; SATA 12, 60

Odets, Clifford
    1906-1963 .... CLC 2, 28; DC 6
    See also CA 85-88; DAM DRAM; DLB 7,
    26; MTCW

O'Doherty, Brian 1934- .... CLC 76
    See also CA 105

O'Donnell, K. M.
    See Malzberg, Barry N(athaniel)

O'Donnell, Lawrence
    See Kuttner, Henry

O'Donovan, Michael John
    1903-1966 .... CLC 14
    See also O'Connor, Frank
    See also CA 93-96

Oe, Kenzaburo
    1935- .... CLC 10, 36, 86; SSC 20
    See also CA 97-100; CANR 36, 50;
    DAM NOV; DLBY 94; MTCW

O'Faolain, Julia 1932- .... CLC 6, 19, 47
    See also CA 81-84; CAAS 2; CANR 12;
    DLB 14; MTCW

O'Faolain, Sean
    1900-1991 .... CLC 1, 7, 14, 32, 70;
                                    SSC 13
    See also CA 61-64; 134; CANR 12;
    DLB 15, 162; MTCW

O'Flaherty, Liam
    1896-1984 .... CLC 5, 34; SSC 6
    See also CA 101; 113; CANR 35; DLB 36,
    162; DLBY 84; MTCW

Ogilvy, Gavin
    See Barrie, J(ames) M(atthew)

O'Grady, Standish James
    1846-1928 .... TCLC 5
    See also CA 104

O'Grady, Timothy 1951- .... CLC 59
    See also CA 138

O'Hara, Frank
    1926-1966 .... CLC 2, 5, 13, 78
    See also CA 9-12R; 25-28R; CANR 33;
    DAM POET; DLB 5, 16; MTCW

O'Hara, John (Henry)
    1905-1970 .... CLC 1, 2, 3, 6, 11, 42;
                                    SSC 15
    See also CA 5-8R; 25-28R; CANR 31;
    CDALB 1929-1941; DAM NOV; DLB 9,
    86; DLBD 2; MTCW

O Hehir, Diana 1922- .... CLC 41
    See also CA 93-96

Okigbo, Christopher (Ifenayichukwu)
    1932-1967 ..... CLC 25, 84; BLC; PC 7
    See also BW 1; CA 77-80; DAM MULT,
    POET; DLB 125; MTCW

Okri, Ben 1959- .... CLC 87
    See also BW 2; CA 130; 138; DLB 157;
    INT 138

Olds, Sharon 1942- .... CLC 32, 39, 85
    See also CA 101; CANR 18, 41;
    DAM POET; DLB 120

Oldstyle, Jonathan
    See Irving, Washington

Olesha, Yuri (Karlovich)
    1899-1960 .... CLC 8
    See also CA 85-88

Oliphant, Laurence
    1829(?)-1888 .... NCLC 47
    See also DLB 18, 166

Oliphant, Margaret (Oliphant Wilson)
    1828-1897 .... NCLC 11
    See also DLB 18, 159

Oliver, Mary 1935- .... CLC 19, 34
    See also CA 21-24R; CANR 9, 43; DLB 5

Olivier, Laurence (Kerr)
    1907-1989 .... CLC 20
    See also CA 111; 150; 129

Olsen, Tillie
    1913- ..... CLC 4, 13; DA; DAB; DAC;
                                    SSC 11
    See also CA 1-4R; CANR 1, 43;
    DAM MST; DLB 28; DLBY 80; MTCW

Olson, Charles (John)
    1910-1970 ..... CLC 1, 2, 5, 6, 9, 11, 29
    See also CA 13-16; 25-28R; CABS 2;
    CANR 35; CAP 1; DAM POET; DLB 5,
    16; MTCW

Olson, Toby 1937- .... CLC 28
    See also CA 65-68; CANR 9, 31

Olyesha, Yuri
    See Olesha, Yuri (Karlovich)

Ondaatje, (Philip) Michael
    1943- ... CLC 14, 29, 51, 76; DAB; DAC
    See also CA 77-80; CANR 42; DAM MST;
    DLB 60

Oneal, Elizabeth 1934-
    See Oneal, Zibby
    See also CA 106; CANR 28; MAICYA;
    SATA 30, 82

Oneal, Zibby .... CLC 30
    See also Oneal, Elizabeth
    See also AAYA 5; CLR 13; JRDA

O'Neill, Eugene (Gladstone)
    1888-1953 ...... TCLC 1, 6, 27, 49; DA;
                                    DAB; DAC; WLC
    See also AITN 1; CA 110; 132;
    CDALB 1929-1941; DAM DRAM, MST;
    DLB 7; MTCW

Onetti, Juan Carlos
    1909-1994 .... CLC 7, 10; SSC 23
    See also CA 85-88; 145; CANR 32;
    DAM MULT, NOV; DLB 113; HW;
    MTCW

O Nuallain, Brian 1911-1966
    See O'Brien, Flann
    See also CA 21-22; 25-28R; CAP 2

Oppen, George 1908-1984 .... CLC 7, 13, 34
    See also CA 13-16R; 113; CANR 8; DLB 5,
    165

Oppenheim, E(dward) Phillips
    1866-1946 .... TCLC 45
    See also CA 111; DLB 70

Orlovitz, Gil 1918-1973 .... CLC 22
    See also CA 77-80; 45-48; DLB 2, 5

Orris
    See Ingelow, Jean

Ortega y Gasset, Jose
    1883-1955 .... TCLC 9; HLC
    See also CA 106; 130; DAM MULT; HW;
    MTCW

Ortese, Anna Maria 1914- .... CLC 89

Ortiz, Simon J(oseph) 1941- .... CLC 45
    See also CA 134; DAM MULT, POET;
    DLB 120; NNAL

Orton, Joe .... CLC 4, 13, 43; DC 3
    See also Orton, John Kingsley
    See also CDBLB 1960 to Present; DLB 13

Orton, John Kingsley 1933-1967
    See Orton, Joe
    See also CA 85-88; CANR 35;
    DAM DRAM; MTCW

Orwell, George
    .... TCLC 2, 6, 15, 31, 51; DAB; WLC
    See also Blair, Eric (Arthur)
    See also CDBLB 1945-1960; DLB 15, 98

Osborne, David
    See Silverberg, Robert

Osborne, George
    See Silverberg, Robert

Osborne, John (James)
    1929-1994 ..... CLC 1, 2, 5, 11, 45; DA;
                                    DAB; DAC; WLC
    See also CA 13-16R; 147; CANR 21;
    CDBLB 1945-1960; DAM DRAM, MST;
    DLB 13; MTCW

Osborne, Lawrence 1958- .... CLC 50

Oshima, Nagisa 1932- .... CLC 20
    See also CA 116; 121

Oskison, John Milton
    1874-1947 .... TCLC 35
    See also CA 144; DAM MULT; NNAL

Ossoli, Sarah Margaret (Fuller marchesa d')
    1810-1850
    See Fuller, Margaret
    See also SATA 25

Ostrovsky, Alexander
    1823-1886 .... NCLC 30, 57

Otero, Blas de 1916-1979 .... CLC 11
    See also CA 89-92; DLB 134

Otto, Whitney 1955- .... CLC 70
    See also CA 140

Ouida .... TCLC 43
    See also De La Ramee, (Marie) Louise
    See also DLB 18, 156

Ousmane, Sembene 1923- .... CLC 66; BLC
    See also BW 1; CA 117; 125; MTCW

Ovid 43B.C.-18(?) .... CMLC 7; PC 2
    See also DAM POET

Owen, Hugh
    See Faust, Frederick (Schiller)

Owen, Wilfred (Edward Salter)
　　1893-1918 . . . . . . **TCLC 5, 27; DA; DAB;**
　　　　　　　　　　　　　　DAC; WLC
　　See also CA 104; 141; CDBLB 1914-1945;
　　DAM MST, POET; DLB 20

Owens, Rochelle　1936- . . . . **CLC 8**
　　See also CA 17-20R; CAAS 2; CANR 39

Oz, Amos　1939- . . . **CLC 5, 8, 11, 27, 33, 54**
　　See also CA 53-56; CANR 27, 47;
　　DAM NOV; MTCW

Ozick, Cynthia
　　1928- . . . . **CLC 3, 7, 28, 62; SSC 15**
　　See also BEST 90:1; CA 17-20R; CANR 23;
　　DAM NOV, POP; DLB 28, 152;
　　DLBY 82; INT CANR-23; MTCW

Ozu, Yasujiro　1903-1963 . . . . **CLC 16**
　　See also CA 112

Pacheco, C.
　　See Pessoa, Fernando (Antonio Nogueira)

Pa Chin . . . . **CLC 18**
　　See also Li Fei-kan

Pack, Robert　1929- . . . . **CLC 13**
　　See also CA 1-4R; CANR 3, 44; DLB 5

Padgett, Lewis
　　See Kuttner, Henry

Padilla (Lorenzo), Heberto　1932- . . . **CLC 38**
　　See also AITN 1; CA 123; 131; HW

Page, Jimmy　1944- . . . . **CLC 12**

Page, Louise　1955- . . . . **CLC 40**
　　See also CA 140

Page, P(atricia) K(athleen)
　　1916- . . . . **CLC 7, 18; DAC; PC 12**
　　See also CA 53-56; CANR 4, 22;
　　DAM MST; DLB 68; MTCW

Page, Thomas Nelson　1853-1922. . . . **SSC 23**
　　See also CA 118; DLB 12, 78; DLBD 13

Paget, Violet　1856-1935
　　See Lee, Vernon
　　See also CA 104

Paget-Lowe, Henry
　　See Lovecraft, H(oward) P(hillips)

Paglia, Camille (Anna)　1947- . . . . . . **CLC 68**
　　See also CA 140

Paige, Richard
　　See Koontz, Dean R(ay)

Pakenham, Antonia
　　See Fraser, (Lady) Antonia (Pakenham)

Palamas, Kostes　1859-1943 . . . . **TCLC 5**
　　See also CA 105

Palazzeschi, Aldo　1885-1974 . . . . **CLC 11**
　　See also CA 89-92; 53-56; DLB 114

Paley, Grace　1922- . . . . **CLC 4, 6, 37; SSC 8**
　　See also CA 25-28R; CANR 13, 46;
　　DAM POP; DLB 28; INT CANR-13;
　　MTCW

Palin, Michael (Edward)　1943- . . . . . **CLC 21**
　　See also Monty Python
　　See also CA 107; CANR 35; SATA 67

Palliser, Charles　1947- . . . . **CLC 65**
　　See also CA 136

Palma, Ricardo　1833-1919 . . . . **TCLC 29**

Pancake, Breece Dexter　1952-1979
　　See Pancake, Breece D'J
　　See also CA 123; 109

Pancake, Breece D'J . . . . **CLC 29**
　　See also Pancake, Breece Dexter
　　See also DLB 130

Panko, Rudy
　　See Gogol, Nikolai (Vasilyevich)

Papadiamantis, Alexandros
　　1851-1911 . . . . **TCLC 29**

Papadiamantopoulos, Johannes　1856-1910
　　See Moreas, Jean
　　See also CA 117

Papini, Giovanni　1881-1956 . . . . . . **TCLC 22**
　　See also CA 121

Paracelsus　1493-1541 . . . . **LC 14**

Parasol, Peter
　　See Stevens, Wallace

Parfenie, Maria
　　See Codrescu, Andrei

Parini, Jay (Lee)　1948- . . . . **CLC 54**
　　See also CA 97-100; CAAS 16; CANR 32

Park, Jordan
　　See Kornbluth, C(yril) M.; Pohl, Frederik

Parker, Bert
　　See Ellison, Harlan (Jay)

Parker, Dorothy (Rothschild)
　　1893-1967 . . . . **CLC 15, 68; SSC 2**
　　See also CA 19-20; 25-28R; CAP 2;
　　DAM POET; DLB 11, 45, 86; MTCW

Parker, Robert B(rown)　1932- . . . . . . **CLC 27**
　　See also BEST 89:4; CA 49-52; CANR 1,
　　26, 52; DAM NOV, POP;
　　INT CANR-26; MTCW

Parkin, Frank　1940- . . . . **CLC 43**
　　See also CA 147

Parkman, Francis, Jr.
　　1823-1893 . . . . **NCLC 12**
　　See also DLB 1, 30

Parks, Gordon (Alexander Buchanan)
　　1912- . . . . **CLC 1, 16; BLC**
　　See also AITN 2; BW 2; CA 41-44R;
　　CANR 26; DAM MULT; DLB 33;
　　SATA 8

Parnell, Thomas　1679-1718 . . . . **LC 3**
　　See also DLB 94

Parra, Nicanor　1914- . . . . **CLC 2; HLC**
　　See also CA 85-88; CANR 32;
　　DAM MULT; HW; MTCW

Parrish, Mary Frances
　　See Fisher, M(ary) F(rances) K(ennedy)

Parson
　　See Coleridge, Samuel Taylor

Parson Lot
　　See Kingsley, Charles

Partridge, Anthony
　　See Oppenheim, E(dward) Phillips

Pascoli, Giovanni　1855-1912 . . . . . . **TCLC 45**

Pasolini, Pier Paolo
　　1922-1975 . . . . **CLC 20, 37**
　　See also CA 93-96; 61-64; DLB 128;
　　MTCW

Pasquini
　　See Silone, Ignazio

Pastan, Linda (Olenik)　1932- . . . . . . **CLC 27**
　　See also CA 61-64; CANR 18, 40;
　　DAM POET; DLB 5

Pasternak, Boris (Leonidovich)
　　1890-1960 . . . . . . **CLC 7, 10, 18, 63; DA;**
　　　　　　　　　　　　　DAB; DAC; PC 6; WLC
　　See also CA 127; 116; DAM MST, NOV,
　　POET; MTCW

Patchen, Kenneth　1911-1972 . . . **CLC 1, 2, 18**
　　See also CA 1-4R; 33-36R; CANR 3, 35;
　　DAM POET; DLB 16, 48; MTCW

Pater, Walter (Horatio)
　　1839-1894 . . . . **NCLC 7**
　　See also CDBLB 1832-1890; DLB 57, 156

Paterson, A(ndrew) B(arton)
　　1864-1941 . . . . **TCLC 32**

Paterson, Katherine (Womeldorf)
　　1932- . . . . **CLC 12, 30**
　　See also AAYA 1; CA 21-24R; CANR 28;
　　CLR 7; DLB 52; JRDA; MAICYA;
　　MTCW; SATA 13, 53

Patmore, Coventry Kersey Dighton
　　1823-1896 . . . . **NCLC 9**
　　See also DLB 35, 98

Paton, Alan (Stewart)
　　1903-1988 . . . . . . **CLC 4, 10, 25, 55; DA;**
　　　　　　　　　　　　　　　　　DAB; DAC; WLC
　　See also CA 13-16; 125; CANR 22; CAP 1;
　　DAM MST, NOV; MTCW; SATA 11;
　　SATA-Obit 56

Paton Walsh, Gillian　1937-
　　See Walsh, Jill Paton
　　See also CANR 38; JRDA; MAICYA;
　　SAAS 3; SATA 4, 72

Paulding, James Kirke　1778-1860. . **NCLC 2**
　　See also DLB 3, 59, 74

Paulin, Thomas Neilson　1949-
　　See Paulin, Tom
　　See also CA 123; 128

Paulin, Tom . . . . **CLC 37**
　　See also Paulin, Thomas Neilson
　　See also DLB 40

Paustovsky, Konstantin (Georgievich)
　　1892-1968 . . . . **CLC 40**
　　See also CA 93-96; 25-28R

Pavese, Cesare
　　1908-1950 . . . . . **TCLC 3; PC 13; SSC 19**
　　See also CA 104; DLB 128

Pavic, Milorad　1929- . . . . **CLC 60**
　　See also CA 136

Payne, Alan
　　See Jakes, John (William)

Paz, Gil
　　See Lugones, Leopoldo

Paz, Octavio
　　1914- . . . . **CLC 3, 4, 6, 10, 19, 51, 65;**
　　　　　　　　　　DA; DAB; DAC; HLC; PC 1; WLC
　　See also CA 73-76; CANR 32; DAM MST,
　　MULT, POET; DLBY 90; HW; MTCW

Peacock, Molly　1947- . . . . **CLC 60**
　　See also CA 103; CAAS 21; CANR 52;
　　DLB 120

Peacock, Thomas Love
　　1785-1866 . . . . **NCLC 22**
　　See also DLB 96, 116

Peake, Mervyn　1911-1968 . . . . **CLC 7, 54**
　　See also CA 5-8R; 25-28R; CANR 3;
　　DLB 15, 160; MTCW; SATA 23

Pearce, Philippa . . . . **CLC 21**
See also Christie, (Ann) Philippa
See also CLR 9; DLB 161; MAICYA;
SATA 1, 67

Pearl, Eric
See Elman, Richard

Pearson, T(homas) R(eid) 1956- . . . . **CLC 39**
See also CA 120; 130; INT 130

Peck, Dale 1967- . . . . **CLC 81**
See also CA 146

Peck, John 1941- . . . . **CLC 3**
See also CA 49-52; CANR 3

Peck, Richard (Wayne) 1934- . . . . . . **CLC 21**
See also AAYA 1; CA 85-88; CANR 19,
38; CLR 15; INT CANR-19; JRDA;
MAICYA; SAAS 2; SATA 18, 55

Peck, Robert Newton
1928- . . . . **CLC 17; DA; DAC**
See also AAYA 3; CA 81-84; CANR 31;
DAM MST; JRDA; MAICYA; SAAS 1;
SATA 21, 62

Peckinpah, (David) Sam(uel)
1925-1984 . . . . **CLC 20**
See also CA 109; 114

Pedersen, Knut 1859-1952
See Hamsun, Knut
See also CA 104; 119; MTCW

Peeslake, Gaffer
See Durrell, Lawrence (George)

Peguy, Charles Pierre
1873-1914 . . . . **TCLC 10**
See also CA 107

Pena, Ramon del Valle y
See Valle-Inclan, Ramon (Maria) del

Pendennis, Arthur Esquir
See Thackeray, William Makepeace

Penn, William 1644-1718 . . . . **LC 25**
See also DLB 24

Pepys, Samuel
1633-1703 . . . . . **LC 11; DA; DAB; DAC;**
WLC
See also CDBLB 1660-1789; DAM MST;
DLB 101

Percy, Walker
1916-1990 . . . . **CLC 2, 3, 6, 8, 14, 18, 47,**
65
See also CA 1-4R; 131; CANR 1, 23;
DAM NOV, POP; DLB 2; DLBY 80, 90;
MTCW

Perec, Georges 1936-1982 . . . . **CLC 56**
See also CA 141; DLB 83

Pereda (y Sanchez de Porrua), Jose Maria de
1833-1906 . . . . **TCLC 16**
See also CA 117

Pereda y Porrua, Jose Maria de
See Pereda (y Sanchez de Porrua), Jose
Maria de

Peregoy, George Weems
See Mencken, H(enry) L(ouis)

Perelman, S(idney) J(oseph)
1904-1979 . . . **CLC 3, 5, 9, 15, 23, 44, 49**
See also AITN 1, 2; CA 73-76; 89-92;
CANR 18; DAM DRAM; DLB 11, 44;
MTCW

Peret, Benjamin 1899-1959 . . . . . . **TCLC 20**
See also CA 117

Peretz, Isaac Loeb 1851(?)-1915 . . . **TCLC 16**
See also CA 109

Peretz, Yitzkhok Leibush
See Peretz, Isaac Loeb

Perez Galdos, Benito 1843-1920 . . . **TCLC 27**
See also CA 125; HW

Perrault, Charles 1628-1703 . . . . **LC 2**
See also MAICYA; SATA 25

Perry, Brighton
See Sherwood, Robert E(mmet)

Perse, St.-John . . . . **CLC 4, 11, 46**
See also Leger, (Marie-Rene Auguste) Alexis
Saint-Leger

Perutz, Leo 1882-1957 . . . . **TCLC 60**
See also DLB 81

Peseenz, Tulio F.
See Lopez y Fuentes, Gregorio

Pesetsky, Bette 1932- . . . . **CLC 28**
See also CA 133; DLB 130

Peshkov, Alexei Maximovich 1868-1936
See Gorky, Maxim
See also CA 105; 141; DA; DAC;
DAM DRAM, MST, NOV

Pessoa, Fernando (Antonio Nogueira)
1888-1935 . . . . **TCLC 27; HLC**
See also CA 125

Peterkin, Julia Mood 1880-1961 . . . . **CLC 31**
See also CA 102; DLB 9

Peters, Joan K. 1945- . . . . **CLC 39**

Peters, Robert L(ouis) 1924- . . . . **CLC 7**
See also CA 13-16R; CAAS 8; DLB 105

Petofi, Sandor 1823-1849 . . . . **NCLC 21**

Petrakis, Harry Mark 1923- . . . . **CLC 3**
See also CA 9-12R; CANR 4, 30

Petrarch 1304-1374 . . . . **PC 8**
See also DAM POET

Petrov, Evgeny . . . . **TCLC 21**
See also Kataev, Evgeny Petrovich

Petry, Ann (Lane) 1908- . . . . . **CLC 1, 7, 18**
See also BW 1; CA 5-8R; CAAS 6;
CANR 4, 46; CLR 12; DLB 76; JRDA;
MAICYA; MTCW; SATA 5

Petursson, Halligrimur 1614-1674 . . . . **LC 8**

Philips, Katherine 1632-1664 . . . . **LC 30**
See also DLB 131

Philipson, Morris H. 1926- . . . . **CLC 53**
See also CA 1-4R; CANR 4

Phillips, David Graham
1867-1911 . . . . **TCLC 44**
See also CA 108; DLB 9, 12

Phillips, Jack
See Sandburg, Carl (August)

Phillips, Jayne Anne
1952- . . . . **CLC 15, 33; SSC 16**
See also CA 101; CANR 24, 50; DLBY 80;
INT CANR-24; MTCW

Phillips, Richard
See Dick, Philip K(indred)

Phillips, Robert (Schaeffer) 1938- . . . **CLC 28**
See also CA 17-20R; CAAS 13; CANR 8;
DLB 105

Phillips, Ward
See Lovecraft, H(oward) P(hillips)

Piccolo, Lucio 1901-1969 . . . . **CLC 13**
See also CA 97-100; DLB 114

Pickthall, Marjorie L(owry) C(hristie)
1883-1922 . . . . **TCLC 21**
See also CA 107; DLB 92

Pico della Mirandola, Giovanni
1463-1494 . . . . **LC 15**

Piercy, Marge
1936- . . . . **CLC 3, 6, 14, 18, 27, 62**
See also CA 21-24R; CAAS 1; CANR 13,
43; DLB 120; MTCW

Piers, Robert
See Anthony, Piers

Pieyre de Mandiargues, Andre 1909-1991
See Mandiargues, Andre Pieyre de
See also CA 103; 136; CANR 22

Pilnyak, Boris . . . . **TCLC 23**
See also Vogau, Boris Andreyevich

Pincherle, Alberto 1907-1990 . . . **CLC 11, 18**
See also Moravia, Alberto
See also CA 25-28R; 132; CANR 33;
DAM NOV; MTCW

Pinckney, Darryl 1953- . . . . **CLC 76**
See also BW 2; CA 143

Pindar 518B.C.-446B.C. . . . . **CMLC 12**

Pineda, Cecile 1942- . . . . **CLC 39**
See also CA 118

Pinero, Arthur Wing 1855-1934 . . . **TCLC 32**
See also CA 110; DAM DRAM; DLB 10

Pinero, Miguel (Antonio Gomez)
1946-1988 . . . . **CLC 4, 55**
See also CA 61-64; 125; CANR 29; HW

Pinget, Robert 1919- . . . . **CLC 7, 13, 37**
See also CA 85-88; DLB 83

Pink Floyd
See Barrett, (Roger) Syd; Gilmour, David;
Mason, Nick; Waters, Roger; Wright,
Rick

Pinkney, Edward 1802-1828 . . . . . **NCLC 31**

Pinkwater, Daniel Manus 1941- . . . . **CLC 35**
See also Pinkwater, Manus
See also AAYA 1; CA 29-32R; CANR 12,
38; CLR 4; JRDA; MAICYA; SAAS 3;
SATA 46, 76

Pinkwater, Manus
See Pinkwater, Daniel Manus
See also SATA 8

Pinsky, Robert 1940- . . . . . **CLC 9, 19, 38, 94**
See also CA 29-32R; CAAS 4;
DAM POET; DLBY 82

Pinta, Harold
See Pinter, Harold

Pinter, Harold
1930- . . . . . **CLC 1, 3, 6, 9, 11, 15, 27, 58,**
73; DA; DAB; DAC; WLC
See also CA 5-8R; CANR 33; CDBLB 1960
to Present; DAM DRAM, MST; DLB 13;
MTCW

Piozzi, Hester Lynch (Thrale)
1741-1821 . . . . **NCLC 57**
See also DLB 104, 142

Pirandello, Luigi
1867-1936 . . . . . . **TCLC 4, 29; DA; DAB;**
DAC; DC 5; SSC 22; WLC
See also CA 104; DAM DRAM, MST

Pirsig, Robert M(aynard)
1928- . . . . **CLC 4, 6, 73**
See also CA 53-56; CANR 42; DAM POP;
MTCW; SATA 39

Pisarev, Dmitry Ivanovich
1840-1868 . . . . **NCLC 25**

Pix, Mary (Griffith) 1666-1709 . . . . **LC 8**
See also DLB 80

Pixerecourt, Guilbert de
1773-1844 . . . . **NCLC 39**

Plaidy, Jean
See Hibbert, Eleanor Alice Burford

Planche, James Robinson
1796-1880 . . . . **NCLC 42**

Plant, Robert 1948- . . . . **CLC 12**

Plante, David (Robert)
1940- . . . . **CLC 7, 23, 38**
See also CA 37-40R; CANR 12, 36;
DAM NOV; DLBY 83; INT CANR-12;
MTCW

Plath, Sylvia
1932-1963 . . . . . **CLC 1, 2, 3, 5, 9, 11, 14,**
17, 50, 51, 62; DA; DAB; DAC; PC 1;
WLC
See also AAYA 13; CA 19-20; CANR 34;
CAP 2; CDALB 1941-1968; DAM MST,
POET; DLB 5, 6, 152; MTCW

Plato
428(?)B.C.-348(?)B.C. . . . . **CMLC 8; DA;**
DAB; DAC
See also DAM MST

Platonov, Andrei . . . . **TCLC 14**
See also Klimentov, Andrei Platonovich

Platt, Kin 1911- . . . . **CLC 26**
See also AAYA 11; CA 17-20R; CANR 11;
JRDA; SAAS 17; SATA 21, 86

Plautus c. 251B.C.-184B.C. . . . . **DC 6**

Plick et Plock
See Simenon, Georges (Jacques Christian)

Plimpton, George (Ames) 1927- . . . . . **CLC 36**
See also AITN 1; CA 21-24R; CANR 32;
MTCW; SATA 10

Plomer, William Charles Franklin
1903-1973 . . . . **CLC 4, 8**
See also CA 21-22; CANR 34; CAP 2;
DLB 20, 162; MTCW; SATA 24

Plowman, Piers
See Kavanagh, Patrick (Joseph)

Plum, J.
See Wodehouse, P(elham) G(renville)

Plumly, Stanley (Ross) 1939- . . . . . . **CLC 33**
See also CA 108; 110; DLB 5; INT 110

Plumpe, Friedrich Wilhelm
1888-1931 . . . . **TCLC 53**
See also CA 112

Poe, Edgar Allan
1809-1849 . . . . **NCLC 1, 16, 55; DA;**
DAB; DAC; PC 1; SSC 1, 22; WLC
See also AAYA 14; CDALB 1640-1865;
DAM MST, POET; DLB 3, 59, 73, 74;
SATA 23

Poet of Titchfield Street, The
See Pound, Ezra (Weston Loomis)

Pohl, Frederik 1919- . . . . **CLC 18**
See also CA 61-64; CAAS 1; CANR 11, 37;
DLB 8; INT CANR-11; MTCW;
SATA 24

Poirier, Louis 1910-
See Gracq, Julien
See also CA 122; 126

Poitier, Sidney 1927- . . . . **CLC 26**
See also BW 1; CA 117

Polanski, Roman 1933- . . . . **CLC 16**
See also CA 77-80

Poliakoff, Stephen 1952- . . . . **CLC 38**
See also CA 106; DLB 13

Police, The
See Copeland, Stewart (Armstrong);
Summers, Andrew James; Sumner,
Gordon Matthew

Polidori, John William
1795-1821 . . . . **NCLC 51**
See also DLB 116

Pollitt, Katha 1949- . . . . **CLC 28**
See also CA 120; 122; MTCW

Pollock, (Mary) Sharon
1936- . . . . **CLC 50; DAC**
See also CA 141; DAM DRAM, MST;
DLB 60

Polo, Marco 1254-1324 . . . . **CMLC 15**

Polonsky, Abraham (Lincoln)
1910- . . . . **CLC 92**
See also CA 104; DLB 26; INT 104

Polybius c. 200B.C.-c. 118B.C. . . . . **CMLC 17**

Pomerance, Bernard 1940- . . . . **CLC 13**
See also CA 101; CANR 49; DAM DRAM

Ponge, Francis (Jean Gaston Alfred)
1899-1988 . . . . **CLC 6, 18**
See also CA 85-88; 126; CANR 40;
DAM POET

Pontoppidan, Henrik 1857-1943 . . . **TCLC 29**

Poole, Josephine . . . . **CLC 17**
See also Helyar, Jane Penelope Josephine
See also SAAS 2; SATA 5

Popa, Vasko 1922-1991 . . . . **CLC 19**
See also CA 112; 148

Pope, Alexander
1688-1744 . . . . . . **LC 3; DA; DAB; DAC;**
WLC
See also CDBLB 1660-1789; DAM MST,
POET; DLB 95, 101

Porter, Connie (Rose) 1959(?)- . . . . . **CLC 70**
See also BW 2; CA 142; SATA 81

Porter, Gene(va Grace) Stratton
1863(?)-1924 . . . . **TCLC 21**
See also CA 112

Porter, Katherine Anne
1890-1980 . . . . . . **CLC 1, 3, 7, 10, 13, 15,**
27; DA; DAB; DAC; SSC 4
See also AITN 2; CA 1-4R; 101; CANR 1;
DAM MST, NOV; DLB 4, 9, 102;
DLBD 12; DLBY 80; MTCW; SATA 39;
SATA-Obit 23

Porter, Peter (Neville Frederick)
1929- . . . . **CLC 5, 13, 33**
See also CA 85-88; DLB 40

Porter, William Sydney 1862-1910
See Henry, O.
See also CA 104; 131; CDALB 1865-1917;
DA; DAB; DAC; DAM MST; DLB 12,
78, 79; MTCW; YABC 2

Portillo (y Pacheco), Jose Lopez
See Lopez Portillo (y Pacheco), Jose

Post, Melville Davisson
1869-1930 . . . . **TCLC 39**
See also CA 110

Potok, Chaim 1929- . . . . **CLC 2, 7, 14, 26**
See also AAYA 15; AITN 1, 2; CA 17-20R;
CANR 19, 35; DAM NOV; DLB 28, 152;
INT CANR-19; MTCW; SATA 33

Potter, Beatrice
See Webb, (Martha) Beatrice (Potter)
See also MAICYA

Potter, Dennis (Christopher George)
1935-1994 . . . . **CLC 58, 86**
See also CA 107; 145; CANR 33; MTCW

Pound, Ezra (Weston Loomis)
1885-1972 . . . . . . **CLC 1, 2, 3, 4, 5, 7, 10,**
13, 18, 34, 48, 50; DA; DAB; DAC; PC 4;
WLC
See also CA 5-8R; 37-40R; CANR 40;
CDALB 1917-1929; DAM MST, POET;
DLB 4, 45, 63; MTCW

Povod, Reinaldo 1959-1994 . . . . **CLC 44**
See also CA 136; 146

Powell, Adam Clayton, Jr.
1908-1972 . . . . **CLC 89; BLC**
See also BW 1; CA 102; 33-36R;
DAM MULT

Powell, Anthony (Dymoke)
1905- . . . . **CLC 1, 3, 7, 9, 10, 31**
See also CA 1-4R; CANR 1, 32;
CDBLB 1945-1960; DLB 15; MTCW

Powell, Dawn 1897-1965 . . . . **CLC 66**
See also CA 5-8R

Powell, Padgett 1952- . . . . **CLC 34**
See also CA 126

Power, Susan . . . . **CLC 91**

Powers, J(ames) F(arl)
1917- . . . . **CLC 1, 4, 8, 57; SSC 4**
See also CA 1-4R; CANR 2; DLB 130;
MTCW

Powers, John J(ames) 1945-
See Powers, John R.
See also CA 69-72

Powers, John R. . . . . **CLC 66**
See also Powers, John J(ames)

Powers, Richard (S.) 1957- . . . . **CLC 93**
See also CA 148

Pownall, David 1938- . . . . **CLC 10**
See also CA 89-92; CAAS 18; CANR 49;
DLB 14

Powys, John Cowper
1872-1963 . . . . **CLC 7, 9, 15, 46**
See also CA 85-88; DLB 15; MTCW

Powys, T(heodore) F(rancis)
1875-1953 . . . . **TCLC 9**
See also CA 106; DLB 36, 162

Prager, Emily 1952- . . . . **CLC 56**

Pratt, E(dwin) J(ohn)
1883(?)-1964 .... **CLC 19; DAC**
See also CA 141; 93-96; DAM POET;
DLB 92

Premchand .... **TCLC 21**
See also Srivastava, Dhanpat Rai

Preussler, Otfried 1923- .... **CLC 17**
See also CA 77-80; SATA 24

Prevert, Jacques (Henri Marie)
1900-1977 .... **CLC 15**
See also CA 77-80; 69-72; CANR 29;
MTCW; SATA-Obit 30

Prevost, Abbe (Antoine Francois)
1697-1763 .... **LC 1**

Price, (Edward) Reynolds
1933- .. **CLC 3, 6, 13, 43, 50, 63; SSC 22**
See also CA 1-4R; CANR 1, 37;
DAM NOV; DLB 2; INT CANR-37

Price, Richard 1949- .... **CLC 6, 12**
See also CA 49-52; CANR 3; DLBY 81

Prichard, Katharine Susannah
1883-1969 .... **CLC 46**
See also CA 11-12; CANR 33; CAP 1;
MTCW; SATA 66

Priestley, J(ohn) B(oynton)
1894-1984 .... **CLC 2, 5, 9, 34**
See also CA 9-12R; 113; CANR 33;
CDBLB 1914-1945; DAM DRAM, NOV;
DLB 10, 34, 77, 100, 139; DLBY 84;
MTCW

Prince 1958(?)- .... **CLC 35**

Prince, F(rank) T(empleton) 1912- .. **CLC 22**
See also CA 101; CANR 43; DLB 20

Prince Kropotkin
See Kropotkin, Peter (Aleksieevich)

Prior, Matthew 1664-1721 .... **LC 4**
See also DLB 95

Pritchard, William H(arrison)
1932- .... **CLC 34**
See also CA 65-68; CANR 23; DLB 111

Pritchett, V(ictor) S(awdon)
1900- .... **CLC 5, 13, 15, 41; SSC 14**
See also CA 61-64; CANR 31; DAM NOV;
DLB 15, 139; MTCW

Private 19022
See Manning, Frederic

Probst, Mark 1925- .... **CLC 59**
See also CA 130

Prokosch, Frederic 1908-1989 .... **CLC 4, 48**
See also CA 73-76; 128; DLB 48

Prophet, The
See Dreiser, Theodore (Herman Albert)

Prose, Francine 1947- .... **CLC 45**
See also CA 109; 112; CANR 46

Proudhon
See Cunha, Euclides (Rodrigues Pimenta) da

Proulx, E. Annie 1935- .... **CLC 81**

Proust, (Valentin-Louis-George-Eugene-)
Marcel
1871-1922 .... **TCLC 7, 13, 33; DA;**
DAB; DAC; WLC
See also CA 104; 120; DAM MST, NOV;
DLB 65; MTCW

Prowler, Harley
See Masters, Edgar Lee

Prus, Boleslaw 1845-1912 .... **TCLC 48**

Pryor, Richard (Franklin Lenox Thomas)
1940- .... **CLC 26**
See also CA 122

Przybyszewski, Stanislaw
1868-1927 .... **TCLC 36**
See also DLB 66

Pteleon
See Grieve, C(hristopher) M(urray)
See also DAM POET

Puckett, Lute
See Masters, Edgar Lee

Puig, Manuel
1932-1990 ... **CLC 3, 5, 10, 28, 65; HLC**
See also CA 45-48; CANR 2, 32;
DAM MULT; DLB 113; HW; MTCW

Purdy, Al(fred Wellington)
1918- .... **CLC 3, 6, 14, 50; DAC**
See also CA 81-84; CAAS 17; CANR 42;
DAM MST, POET; DLB 88

Purdy, James (Amos)
1923- .... **CLC 2, 4, 10, 28, 52**
See also CA 33-36R; CAAS 1; CANR 19,
51; DLB 2; INT CANR-19; MTCW

Pure, Simon
See Swinnerton, Frank Arthur

Pushkin, Alexander (Sergeyevich)
1799-1837 ..... **NCLC 3, 27; DA; DAB;**
DAC; PC 10; WLC
See also DAM DRAM, MST, POET;
SATA 61

P'u Sung-ling 1640-1715 .... **LC 3**

Putnam, Arthur Lee
See Alger, Horatio, Jr.

Puzo, Mario 1920- .... **CLC 1, 2, 6, 36**
See also CA 65-68; CANR 4, 42;
DAM NOV, POP; DLB 6; MTCW

Pym, Barbara (Mary Crampton)
1913-1980 .... **CLC 13, 19, 37**
See also CA 13-14; 97-100; CANR 13, 34;
CAP 1; DLB 14; DLBY 87; MTCW

Pynchon, Thomas (Ruggles, Jr.)
1937- ... **CLC 2, 3, 6, 9, 11, 18, 33, 62,**
72; DA; DAB; DAC; SSC 14; WLC
See also BEST 90:2; CA 17-20R; CANR 22,
46; DAM MST, NOV, POP; DLB 2;
MTCW

Qian Zhongshu
See Ch'ien Chung-shu

Qroll
See Dagerman, Stig (Halvard)

Quarrington, Paul (Lewis) 1953- .... **CLC 65**
See also CA 129

Quasimodo, Salvatore 1901-1968 ... **CLC 10**
See also CA 13-16; 25-28R; CAP 1;
DLB 114; MTCW

Quay, Stephen 1947- .... **CLC 95**

Quay, The Brothers
See Quay, Stephen; Quay, Timothy

Quay, Timothy 1947- .... **CLC 95**

Queen, Ellery .... **CLC 3, 11**
See also Dannay, Frederic; Davidson,
Avram; Lee, Manfred B(ennington);
Sturgeon, Theodore (Hamilton); Vance,
John Holbrook

Queen, Ellery, Jr.
See Dannay, Frederic; Lee, Manfred
B(ennington)

Queneau, Raymond
1903-1976 .... **CLC 2, 5, 10, 42**
See also CA 77-80; 69-72; CANR 32;
DLB 72; MTCW

Quevedo, Francisco de 1580-1645 .... **LC 23**

Quiller-Couch, Arthur Thomas
1863-1944 .... **TCLC 53**
See also CA 118; DLB 135, 153

Quin, Ann (Marie) 1936-1973 .... **CLC 6**
See also CA 9-12R; 45-48; DLB 14

Quinn, Martin
See Smith, Martin Cruz

Quinn, Peter 1947- .... **CLC 91**

Quinn, Simon
See Smith, Martin Cruz

Quiroga, Horacio (Sylvestre)
1878-1937 .... **TCLC 20; HLC**
See also CA 117; 131; DAM MULT; HW;
MTCW

Quoirez, Francoise 1935- .... **CLC 9**
See also Sagan, Francoise
See also CA 49-52; CANR 6, 39; MTCW

Raabe, Wilhelm 1831-1910 .... **TCLC 45**
See also DLB 129

Rabe, David (William) 1940- ... **CLC 4, 8, 33**
See also CA 85-88; CABS 3; DAM DRAM;
DLB 7

Rabelais, Francois
1483-1553 ...... **LC 5; DA; DAB; DAC;**
WLC
See also DAM MST

Rabinovitch, Sholem 1859-1916
See Aleichem, Sholom
See also CA 104

Racine, Jean 1639-1699 .... **LC 28; DAB**
See also DAM MST

Radcliffe, Ann (Ward)
1764-1823 .... **NCLC 6, 55**
See also DLB 39

Radiguet, Raymond 1903-1923 .... **TCLC 29**
See also DLB 65

Radnoti, Miklos 1909-1944 .... **TCLC 16**
See also CA 118

Rado, James 1939- .... **CLC 17**
See also CA 105

Radvanyi, Netty 1900-1983
See Seghers, Anna
See also CA 85-88; 110

Rae, Ben
See Griffiths, Trevor

Raeburn, John (Hay) 1941- .... **CLC 34**
See also CA 57-60

Ragni, Gerome 1942-1991 .... **CLC 17**
See also CA 105; 134

Rahv, Philip 1908-1973 .... **CLC 24**
See also Greenberg, Ivan
See also DLB 137

Raine, Craig 1944- .... **CLC 32**
See also CA 108; CANR 29, 51; DLB 40

Raine, Kathleen (Jessie) 1908- ... **CLC 7, 45**
See also CA 85-88; CANR 46; DLB 20;
MTCW

Rainis, Janis 1865-1929 .... **TCLC 29**

Rakosi, Carl .... **CLC 47**
See also Rawley, Callman
See also CAAS 5

Raleigh, Richard
See Lovecraft, H(oward) P(hillips)

Raleigh, Sir Walter 1554(?)-1618 .... **LC 31**
See also CDBLB Before 1660

Rallentando, H. P.
See Sayers, Dorothy L(eigh)

Ramal, Walter
See de la Mare, Walter (John)

Ramon, Juan
See Jimenez (Mantecon), Juan Ramon

Ramos, Graciliano 1892-1953 ..... **TCLC 32**

Rampersad, Arnold 1941- .... **CLC 44**
See also BW 2; CA 127; 133; DLB 111;
INT 133

Rampling, Anne
See Rice, Anne

Ramsay, Allan 1684(?)-1758 .... **LC 29**
See also DLB 95

Ramuz, Charles-Ferdinand
1878-1947 .... **TCLC 33**

Rand, Ayn
1905-1982 ...... **CLC 3, 30, 44, 79; DA;**
DAC; WLC
See also AAYA 10; CA 13-16R; 105;
CANR 27; DAM MST, NOV, POP;
MTCW

Randall, Dudley (Felker)
1914- .... **CLC 1; BLC**
See also BW 1; CA 25-28R; CANR 23;
DAM MULT; DLB 41

Randall, Robert
See Silverberg, Robert

Ranger, Ken
See Creasey, John

Ransom, John Crowe
1888-1974 .... **CLC 2, 4, 5, 11, 24**
See also CA 5-8R; 49-52; CANR 6, 34;
DAM POET; DLB 45, 63; MTCW

Rao, Raja 1909- .... **CLC 25, 56**
See also CA 73-76; CANR 51; DAM NOV;
MTCW

Raphael, Frederic (Michael)
1931- .... **CLC 2, 14**
See also CA 1-4R; CANR 1; DLB 14

Ratcliffe, James P.
See Mencken, H(enry) L(ouis)

Rathbone, Julian 1935- .... **CLC 41**
See also CA 101; CANR 34

Rattigan, Terence (Mervyn)
1911-1977 .... **CLC 7**
See also CA 85-88; 73-76;
CDBLB 1945-1960; DAM DRAM;
DLB 13; MTCW

Ratushinskaya, Irina 1954- .... **CLC 54**
See also CA 129

Raven, Simon (Arthur Noel)
1927- .... **CLC 14**
See also CA 81-84

Rawley, Callman 1903-
See Rakosi, Carl
See also CA 21-24R; CANR 12, 32

Rawlings, Marjorie Kinnan
1896-1953 .... **TCLC 4**
See also CA 104; 137; DLB 9, 22, 102;
JRDA; MAICYA; YABC 1

Ray, Satyajit 1921-1992 .... **CLC 16, 76**
See also CA 114; 137; DAM MULT

Read, Herbert Edward 1893-1968.... **CLC 4**
See also CA 85-88; 25-28R; DLB 20, 149

Read, Piers Paul 1941- ...... **CLC 4, 10, 25**
See also CA 21-24R; CANR 38; DLB 14;
SATA 21

Reade, Charles 1814-1884 .... **NCLC 2**
See also DLB 21

Reade, Hamish
See Gray, Simon (James Holliday)

Reading, Peter 1946- .... **CLC 47**
See also CA 103; CANR 46; DLB 40

Reaney, James 1926- .... **CLC 13; DAC**
See also CA 41-44R; CAAS 15; CANR 42;
DAM MST; DLB 68; SATA 43

Rebreanu, Liviu 1885-1944 .... **TCLC 28**

Rechy, John (Francisco)
1934- .... **CLC 1, 7, 14, 18; HLC**
See also CA 5-8R; CAAS 4; CANR 6, 32;
DAM MULT; DLB 122; DLBY 82; HW;
INT CANR-6

Redcam, Tom 1870-1933 .... **TCLC 25**

Reddin, Keith .... **CLC 67**

Redgrove, Peter (William)
1932- .... **CLC 6, 41**
See also CA 1-4R; CANR 3, 39; DLB 40

Redmon, Anne .... **CLC 22**
See also Nightingale, Anne Redmon
See also DLBY 86

Reed, Eliot
See Ambler, Eric

Reed, Ishmael
1938- ... **CLC 2, 3, 5, 6, 13, 32, 60; BLC**
See also BW 2; CA 21-24R; CANR 25, 48;
DAM MULT; DLB 2, 5, 33; DLBD 8;
MTCW

Reed, John (Silas) 1887-1920 ...... **TCLC 9**
See also CA 106

Reed, Lou .... **CLC 21**
See also Firbank, Louis

Reeve, Clara 1729-1807 .... **NCLC 19**
See also DLB 39

Reich, Wilhelm 1897-1957 .... **TCLC 57**

Reid, Christopher (John) 1949- ..... **CLC 33**
See also CA 140; DLB 40

Reid, Desmond
See Moorcock, Michael (John)

Reid Banks, Lynne 1929-
See Banks, Lynne Reid
See also CA 1-4R; CANR 6, 22, 38;
CLR 24; JRDA; MAICYA; SATA 22, 75

Reilly, William K.
See Creasey, John

Reiner, Max
See Caldwell, (Janet Miriam) Taylor
(Holland)

Reis, Ricardo
See Pessoa, Fernando (Antonio Nogueira)

Remarque, Erich Maria
1898-1970 .... **CLC 21; DA; DAB; DAC**
See also CA 77-80; 29-32R; DAM MST,
NOV; DLB 56; MTCW

Remizov, A.
See Remizov, Aleksei (Mikhailovich)

Remizov, A. M.
See Remizov, Aleksei (Mikhailovich)

Remizov, Aleksei (Mikhailovich)
1877-1957 .... **TCLC 27**
See also CA 125; 133

Renan, Joseph Ernest
1823-1892 .... **NCLC 26**

Renard, Jules 1864-1910 .... **TCLC 17**
See also CA 117

Renault, Mary .... **CLC 3, 11, 17**
See also Challans, Mary
See also DLBY 83

Rendell, Ruth (Barbara) 1930- .. **CLC 28, 48**
See also Vine, Barbara
See also CA 109; CANR 32, 52;
DAM POP; DLB 87; INT CANR-32;
MTCW

Renoir, Jean 1894-1979 .... **CLC 20**
See also CA 129; 85-88

Resnais, Alain 1922- .... **CLC 16**

Reverdy, Pierre 1889-1960 .... **CLC 53**
See also CA 97-100; 89-92

Rexroth, Kenneth
1905-1982 ...... **CLC 1, 2, 6, 11, 22, 49**
See also CA 5-8R; 107; CANR 14, 34;
CDALB 1941-1968; DAM POET;
DLB 16, 48, 165; DLBY 82;
INT CANR-14; MTCW

Reyes, Alfonso 1889-1959 .... **TCLC 33**
See also CA 131; HW

Reyes y Basoalto, Ricardo Eliecer Neftali
See Neruda, Pablo

Reymont, Wladyslaw (Stanislaw)
1868(?)-1925 .... **TCLC 5**
See also CA 104

Reynolds, Jonathan 1942- .... **CLC 6, 38**
See also CA 65-68; CANR 28

Reynolds, Joshua 1723-1792 .... **LC 15**
See also DLB 104

Reynolds, Michael Shane 1937- .... **CLC 44**
See also CA 65-68; CANR 9

Reznikoff, Charles 1894-1976 .... **CLC 9**
See also CA 33-36; 61-64; CAP 2; DLB 28,
45

Rezzori (d'Arezzo), Gregor von
1914- .... **CLC 25**
See also CA 122; 136

Rhine, Richard
See Silverstein, Alvin

Rhodes, Eugene Manlove
1869-1934 .... **TCLC 53**

R'hoone
See Balzac, Honore de

Rhys, Jean
1890(?)-1979 .... **CLC 2, 4, 6, 14, 19, 51;**
SSC 21
See also CA 25-28R; 85-88; CANR 35;
CDBLB 1945-1960; DAM NOV; DLB 36,
117, 162; MTCW

Ribeiro, Darcy 1922- .... **CLC 34**
See also CA 33-36R

Ribeiro, Joao Ubaldo (Osorio Pimentel)
1941- .... **CLC 10, 67**
See also CA 81-84

Ribman, Ronald (Burt) 1932- .... **CLC 7**
See also CA 21-24R; CANR 46

Ricci, Nino 1959- .... **CLC 70**
See also CA 137

Rice, Anne 1941- .... **CLC 41**
See also AAYA 9; BEST 89:2; CA 65-68;
CANR 12, 36, 53; DAM POP

Rice, Elmer (Leopold)
1892-1967 .... **CLC 7, 49**
See also CA 21-22; 25-28R; CAP 2;
DAM DRAM; DLB 4, 7; MTCW

Rice, Tim(othy Miles Bindon)
1944- .... **CLC 21**
See also CA 103; CANR 46

Rich, Adrienne (Cecile)
1929- .... **CLC 3, 6, 7, 11, 18, 36, 73, 76;**
PC 5
See also CA 9-12R; CANR 20, 53;
DAM POET; DLB 5, 67; MTCW

Rich, Barbara
See Graves, Robert (von Ranke)

Rich, Robert
See Trumbo, Dalton

Richard, Keith .... **CLC 17**
See also Richards, Keith

Richards, David Adams
1950- .... **CLC 59; DAC**
See also CA 93-96; DLB 53

Richards, I(vor) A(rmstrong)
1893-1979 .... **CLC 14, 24**
See also CA 41-44R; 89-92; CANR 34;
DLB 27

Richards, Keith 1943-
See Richard, Keith
See also CA 107

Richardson, Anne
See Roiphe, Anne (Richardson)

Richardson, Dorothy Miller
1873-1957 .... **TCLC 3**
See also CA 104; DLB 36

Richardson, Ethel Florence (Lindesay)
1870-1946
See Richardson, Henry Handel
See also CA 105

Richardson, Henry Handel .... **TCLC 4**
See also Richardson, Ethel Florence
(Lindesay)

Richardson, John
1796-1852 .... **NCLC 55; DAC**
See also DLB 99

Richardson, Samuel
1689-1761 ...... **LC 1; DA; DAB; DAC;**
WLC
See also CDBLB 1660-1789; DAM MST,
NOV; DLB 39

Richler, Mordecai
1931- .... **CLC 3, 5, 9, 13, 18, 46, 70;**
DAC
See also AITN 1; CA 65-68; CANR 31;
CLR 17; DAM MST, NOV; DLB 53;
MAICYA; MTCW; SATA 44;
SATA-Brief 27

Richter, Conrad (Michael)
1890-1968 .... **CLC 30**
See also CA 5-8R; 25-28R; CANR 23;
DLB 9; MTCW; SATA 3

Ricostranza, Tom
See Ellis, Trey

Riddell, J. H. 1832-1906 .... **TCLC 40**

Riding, Laura .... **CLC 3, 7**
See also Jackson, Laura (Riding)

Riefenstahl, Berta Helene Amalia 1902-
See Riefenstahl, Leni
See also CA 108

Riefenstahl, Leni .... **CLC 16**
See also Riefenstahl, Berta Helene Amalia

Riffe, Ernest
See Bergman, (Ernst) Ingmar

Riggs, (Rolla) Lynn 1899-1954 .... **TCLC 56**
See also CA 144; DAM MULT; NNAL

Riley, James Whitcomb
1849-1916 .... **TCLC 51**
See also CA 118; 137; DAM POET;
MAICYA; SATA 17

Riley, Tex
See Creasey, John

Rilke, Rainer Maria
1875-1926 .... **TCLC 1, 6, 19; PC 2**
See also CA 104; 132; DAM POET;
DLB 81; MTCW

Rimbaud, (Jean Nicolas) Arthur
1854-1891 ..... **NCLC 4, 35; DA; DAB;**
DAC; PC 3; WLC
See also DAM MST, POET

Rinehart, Mary Roberts
1876-1958 .... **TCLC 52**
See also CA 108

Ringmaster, The
See Mencken, H(enry) L(ouis)

Ringwood, Gwen(dolyn Margaret) Pharis
1910-1984 .... **CLC 48**
See also CA 148; 112; DLB 88

Rio, Michel 19(?)- .... **CLC 43**

Ritsos, Giannes
See Ritsos, Yannis

Ritsos, Yannis 1909-1990 ..... **CLC 6, 13, 31**
See also CA 77-80; 133; CANR 39; MTCW

Ritter, Erika 1948(?)- .... **CLC 52**

Rivera, Jose Eustasio 1889-1928... **TCLC 35**
See also HW

Rivers, Conrad Kent 1933-1968...... **CLC 1**
See also BW 1; CA 85-88; DLB 41

Rivers, Elfrida
See Bradley, Marion Zimmer

Riverside, John
See Heinlein, Robert A(nson)

Rizal, Jose 1861-1896.......... **NCLC 27**

Roa Bastos, Augusto (Antonio)
1917- .... **CLC 45; HLC**
See also CA 131; DAM MULT; DLB 113;
HW

Robbe-Grillet, Alain
1922- ...... **CLC 1, 2, 4, 6, 8, 10, 14, 43**
See also CA 9-12R; CANR 33; DLB 83;
MTCW

Robbins, Harold 1916-............ **CLC 5**
See also CA 73-76; CANR 26; DAM NOV;
MTCW

Robbins, Thomas Eugene 1936-
See Robbins, Tom
See also CA 81-84; CANR 29; DAM NOV,
POP; MTCW

Robbins, Tom............... **CLC 9, 32, 64**
See also Robbins, Thomas Eugene
See also BEST 90:3; DLBY 80

Robbins, Trina 1938- .... **CLC 21**
See also CA 128

Roberts, Charles G(eorge) D(ouglas)
1860-1943..............**TCLC 8**
See also CA 105; CLR 33; DLB 92;
SATA 88; SATA-Brief 29

Roberts, Kate 1891-1985 .... **CLC 15**
See also CA 107; 116

Roberts, Keith (John Kingston)
1935- .... **CLC 14**
See also CA 25-28R; CANR 46

Roberts, Kenneth (Lewis)
1885-1957 .... **TCLC 23**
See also CA 109; DLB 9

Roberts, Michele (B.) 1949-........ **CLC 48**
See also CA 115

Robertson, Ellis
See Ellison, Harlan (Jay); Silverberg, Robert

Robertson, Thomas William
1829-1871 .... **NCLC 35**
See also DAM DRAM

Robinson, Edwin Arlington
1869-1935 .... **TCLC 5; DA; DAC; PC 1**
See also CA 104; 133; CDALB 1865-1917;
DAM MST, POET; DLB 54; MTCW

Robinson, Henry Crabb
1775-1867 .... **NCLC 15**
See also DLB 107

Robinson, Jill 1936-............. **CLC 10**
See also CA 102; INT 102

Robinson, Kim Stanley 1952- ...... **CLC 34**
See also CA 126

Robinson, Lloyd
See Silverberg, Robert

Robinson, Marilynne 1944-........ **CLC 25**
See also CA 116

Robinson, Smokey................. **CLC 21**
See also Robinson, William, Jr.

Robinson, William, Jr. 1940-
See Robinson, Smokey
See also CA 116

Robison, Mary 1949-............. **CLC 42**
See also CA 113; 116; DLB 130; INT 116

Rod, Edouard 1857-1910 .... **TCLC 52**

Roddenberry, Eugene Wesley 1921-1991
See Roddenberry, Gene
See also CA 110; 135; CANR 37; SATA 45;
SATA-Obit 69

Roddenberry, Gene .... **CLC 17**
See also Roddenberry, Eugene Wesley
See also AAYA 5; SATA-Obit 69

Rodgers, Mary 1931- .... **CLC 12**
See also CA 49-52; CANR 8; CLR 20;
INT CANR-8; JRDA; MAICYA;
SATA 8

Rodgers, W(illiam) R(obert)
1909-1969 .... **CLC 7**
See also CA 85-88; DLB 20

Rodman, Eric
See Silverberg, Robert

Rodman, Howard 1920(?)-1985 ..... **CLC 65**
See also CA 118

Rodman, Maia
See Wojciechowska, Maia (Teresa)

Rodriguez, Claudio 1934- .... **CLC 10**
See also DLB 134

Roelvaag, O(le) E(dvart)
1876-1931 .... **TCLC 17**
See also CA 117; DLB 9

Roethke, Theodore (Huebner)
1908-1963 ...... **CLC 1, 3, 8, 11, 19, 46;**
PC 15
See also CA 81-84; CABS 2;
CDALB 1941-1968; DAM POET; DLB 5;
MTCW

Rogers, Thomas Hunton 1927- ..... **CLC 57**
See also CA 89-92; INT 89-92

Rogers, Will(iam Penn Adair)
1879-1935 .... **TCLC 8**
See also CA 105; 144; DAM MULT;
DLB 11; NNAL

Rogin, Gilbert 1929- .... **CLC 18**
See also CA 65-68; CANR 15

Rohan, Koda .... **TCLC 22**
See also Koda Shigeyuki

Rohmer, Eric .... **CLC 16**
See also Scherer, Jean-Marie Maurice

Rohmer, Sax .... **TCLC 28**
See also Ward, Arthur Henry Sarsfield
See also DLB 70

Roiphe, Anne (Richardson)
1935- .... **CLC 3, 9**
See also CA 89-92; CANR 45; DLBY 80;
INT 89-92

Rojas, Fernando de 1465-1541 ...... **LC 23**

Rolfe, Frederick (William Serafino Austin
Lewis Mary) 1860-1913 ..... **TCLC 12**
See also CA 107; DLB 34, 156

Rolland, Romain 1866-1944 .... **TCLC 23**
See also CA 118; DLB 65

Rolvaag, O(le) E(dvart)
See Roelvaag, O(le) E(dvart)

Romain Arnaud, Saint
See Aragon, Louis

Romains, Jules 1885-1972 .... **CLC 7**
See also CA 85-88; CANR 34; DLB 65;
MTCW

Romero, Jose Ruben 1890-1952 ... **TCLC 14**
See also CA 114; 131; HW

Ronsard, Pierre de
1524-1585 .... **LC 6; PC 11**

Rooke, Leon 1934- .... **CLC 25, 34**
See also CA 25-28R; CANR 23, 53;
DAM POP

Roper, William 1498-1578 .... **LC 10**

Roquelaure, A. N.
See Rice, Anne

Rosa, Joao Guimaraes 1908-1967 ... **CLC 23**
See also CA 89-92; DLB 113

Rose, Wendy 1948- .... **CLC 85; PC 13**
See also CA 53-56; CANR 5, 51;
DAM MULT; NNAL; SATA 12

Rosen, Richard (Dean) 1949- .... **CLC 39**
See also CA 77-80; INT CANR-30

Rosenberg, Isaac 1890-1918 ...... **TCLC 12**
See also CA 107; DLB 20

Rosenblatt, Joe .... **CLC 15**
See also Rosenblatt, Joseph

Rosenblatt, Joseph 1933-
See Rosenblatt, Joe
See also CA 89-92; INT 89-92

Rosenfeld, Samuel 1896-1963
See Tzara, Tristan
See also CA 89-92

Rosenthal, M(acha) L(ouis) 1917- ... **CLC 28**
See also CA 1-4R; CAAS 6; CANR 4, 51;
DLB 5; SATA 59

Ross, Barnaby
See Dannay, Frederic

Ross, Bernard L.
See Follett, Ken(neth Martin)

Ross, J. H.
See Lawrence, T(homas) E(dward)

Ross, Martin
See Martin, Violet Florence
See also DLB 135

Ross, (James) Sinclair
1908- .... **CLC 13; DAC**
See also CA 73-76; DAM MST; DLB 88

Rossetti, Christina (Georgina)
1830-1894 ..... **NCLC 2, 50; DA; DAB;**
DAC; PC 7; WLC
See also DAM MST, POET; DLB 35, 163;
MAICYA; SATA 20

Rossetti, Dante Gabriel
1828-1882 .... **NCLC 4; DA; DAB;**
DAC; WLC
See also CDBLB 1832-1890; DAM MST,
POET; DLB 35

Rossner, Judith (Perelman)
1935- .... **CLC 6, 9, 29**
See also AITN 2; BEST 90:3; CA 17-20R;
CANR 18, 51; DLB 6; INT CANR-18;
MTCW

Rostand, Edmond (Eugene Alexis)
1868-1918 ...... **TCLC 6, 37; DA; DAB;**
DAC
See also CA 104; 126; DAM DRAM, MST;
MTCW

Roth, Henry 1906-1995 .... **CLC 2, 6, 11**
See also CA 11-12; 149; CANR 38; CAP 1;
DLB 28; MTCW

Roth, Joseph 1894-1939 .... **TCLC 33**
See also DLB 85

Roth, Philip (Milton)
1933- ...... **CLC 1, 2, 3, 4, 6, 9, 15, 22,**
31, 47, 66, 86; DA; DAB; DAC; WLC
See also BEST 90:3; CA 1-4R; CANR 1, 22,
36; CDALB 1968-1988; DAM MST,
NOV, POP; DLB 2, 28; DLBY 82;
MTCW

Rothenberg, Jerome 1931- .... **CLC 6, 57**
See also CA 45-48; CANR 1; DLB 5

Roumain, Jacques (Jean Baptiste)
1907-1944 .... **TCLC 19; BLC**
See also BW 1; CA 117; 125; DAM MULT

Rourke, Constance (Mayfield)
1885-1941 .... **TCLC 12**
See also CA 107; YABC 1

Rousseau, Jean-Baptiste 1671-1741 ... **LC 9**

Rousseau, Jean-Jacques
1712-1778 ..... **LC 14; DA; DAB; DAC;**
WLC
See also DAM MST

Roussel, Raymond 1877-1933 ..... **TCLC 20**
See also CA 117

Rovit, Earl (Herbert) 1927- .... **CLC 7**
See also CA 5-8R; CANR 12

Rowe, Nicholas 1674-1718 .... **LC 8**
See also DLB 84

Rowley, Ames Dorrance
See Lovecraft, H(oward) P(hillips)

Rowson, Susanna Haswell
1762(?)-1824 .... **NCLC 5**
See also DLB 37

Roy, Gabrielle
1909-1983 ..... **CLC 10, 14; DAB; DAC**
See also CA 53-56; 110; CANR 5;
DAM MST; DLB 68; MTCW

Rozewicz, Tadeusz 1921- .... **CLC 9, 23**
See also CA 108; CANR 36; DAM POET;
MTCW

Ruark, Gibbons 1941- .... **CLC 3**
See also CA 33-36R; CAAS 23; CANR 14,
31; DLB 120

Rubens, Bernice (Ruth) 1923- ... **CLC 19, 31**
See also CA 25-28R; CANR 33; DLB 14;
MTCW

Rudkin, (James) David 1936- ...... **CLC 14**
See also CA 89-92; DLB 13

Rudnik, Raphael 1933- .... **CLC 7**
See also CA 29-32R

Ruffian, M.
See Hasek, Jaroslav (Matej Frantisek)

Ruiz, Jose Martinez .... **CLC 11**
See also Martinez Ruiz, Jose

Rukeyser, Muriel
1913-1980 .... **CLC 6, 10, 15, 27; PC 12**
See also CA 5-8R; 93-96; CANR 26;
DAM POET; DLB 48; MTCW;
SATA-Obit 22

Rule, Jane (Vance) 1931- .... **CLC 27**
See also CA 25-28R; CAAS 18; CANR 12;
DLB 60

Rulfo, Juan 1918-1986 .... **CLC 8, 80; HLC**
See also CA 85-88; 118; CANR 26;
DAM MULT; DLB 113; HW; MTCW

Runeberg, Johan 1804-1877 ...... **NCLC 41**

Santiago, Danny .... CLC 33
  See also James, Daniel (Lewis)
  See also DLB 122

Santmyer, Helen Hoover
  1895-1986 .... CLC 33
  See also CA 1-4R; 118; CANR 15, 33;
    DLBY 84; MTCW

Santos, Bienvenido N(uqui)
  1911-1996 .... CLC 22
  See also CA 101; 151; CANR 19, 46;
    DAM MULT

Sapper .... TCLC 44
  See also McNeile, Herman Cyril

Sappho fl. 6th cent. B.C.-.... CMLC 3; PC 5
  See also DAM POET

Sarduy, Severo 1937-1993 .... CLC 6
  See also CA 89-92; 142; DLB 113; HW

Sargeson, Frank 1903-1982 .... CLC 31
  See also CA 25-28R; 106; CANR 38

Sarmiento, Felix Ruben Garcia
  See Dario, Ruben

Saroyan, William
  1908-1981 ..... CLC 1, 8, 10, 29, 34, 56;
    DA; DAB; DAC; SSC 21; WLC
  See also CA 5-8R; 103; CANR 30;
    DAM DRAM, MST, NOV; DLB 7, 9, 86;
    DLBY 81; MTCW; SATA 23;
    SATA-Obit 24

Sarraute, Nathalie
  1900- .... CLC 1, 2, 4, 8, 10, 31, 80
  See also CA 9-12R; CANR 23; DLB 83;
    MTCW

Sarton, (Eleanor) May
  1912-1995 .... CLC 4, 14, 49, 91
  See also CA 1-4R; 149; CANR 1, 34;
    DAM POET; DLB 48; DLBY 81;
    INT CANR-34; MTCW; SATA 36;
    SATA-Obit 86

Sartre, Jean-Paul
  1905-1980 .... CLC 1, 4, 7, 9, 13, 18, 24,
    44, 50, 52; DA; DAB; DAC; DC 3; WLC
  See also CA 9-12R; 97-100; CANR 21;
    DAM DRAM, MST, NOV; DLB 72;
    MTCW

Sassoon, Siegfried (Lorraine)
  1886-1967 .... CLC 36; DAB; PC 12
  See also CA 104; 25-28R; CANR 36;
    DAM MST, NOV, POET; DLB 20;
    MTCW

Satterfield, Charles
  See Pohl, Frederik

Saul, John (W. III) 1942- .... CLC 46
  See also AAYA 10; BEST 90:4; CA 81-84;
    CANR 16, 40; DAM NOV, POP

Saunders, Caleb
  See Heinlein, Robert A(nson)

Saura (Atares), Carlos 1932-....... CLC 20
  See also CA 114; 131; HW

Sauser-Hall, Frederic 1887-1961.... CLC 18
  See also Cendrars, Blaise
  See also CA 102; 93-96; CANR 36; MTCW

Saussure, Ferdinand de
  1857-1913 .... TCLC 49

Savage, Catharine
  See Brosman, Catharine Savage

Savage, Thomas 1915- .... CLC 40
  See also CA 126; 132; CAAS 15; INT 132

Savan, Glenn 19(?)- .... CLC 50

Sayers, Dorothy L(eigh)
  1893-1957 .... TCLC 2, 15
  See also CA 104; 119; CDBLB 1914-1945;
    DAM POP; DLB 10, 36, 77, 100; MTCW

Sayers, Valerie 1952-............. CLC 50
  See also CA 134

Sayles, John (Thomas)
  1950- .... CLC 7, 10, 14
  See also CA 57-60; CANR 41; DLB 44

Scammell, Michael .... CLC 34

Scannell, Vernon 1922- .... CLC 49
  See also CA 5-8R; CANR 8, 24; DLB 27;
    SATA 59

Scarlett, Susan
  See Streatfeild, (Mary) Noel

Schaeffer, Susan Fromberg
  1941- .... CLC 6, 11, 22
  See also CA 49-52; CANR 18; DLB 28;
    MTCW; SATA 22

Schary, Jill
  See Robinson, Jill

Schell, Jonathan 1943-............ CLC 35
  See also CA 73-76; CANR 12

Schelling, Friedrich Wilhelm Joseph von
  1775-1854 .... NCLC 30
  See also DLB 90

Schendel, Arthur van 1874-1946 ... TCLC 56

Scherer, Jean-Marie Maurice 1920-
  See Rohmer, Eric
  See also CA 110

Schevill, James (Erwin) 1920-....... CLC 7
  See also CA 5-8R; CAAS 12

Schiller, Friedrich 1759-1805 .... NCLC 39
  See also DAM DRAM; DLB 94

Schisgal, Murray (Joseph) 1926-..... CLC 6
  See also CA 21-24R; CANR 48

Schlee, Ann 1934-................ CLC 35
  See also CA 101; CANR 29; SATA 44;
    SATA-Brief 36

Schlegel, August Wilhelm von
  1767-1845 .... NCLC 15
  See also DLB 94

Schlegel, Friedrich 1772-1829 .... NCLC 45
  See also DLB 90

Schlegel, Johann Elias (von)
  1719(?)-1749 .... LC 5

Schlesinger, Arthur M(eier), Jr.
  1917- .... CLC 84
  See also AITN 1; CA 1-4R; CANR 1, 28;
    DLB 17; INT CANR-28; MTCW;
    SATA 61

Schmidt, Arno (Otto) 1914-1979 .... CLC 56
  See also CA 128; 109; DLB 69

Schmitz, Aron Hector 1861-1928
  See Svevo, Italo
  See also CA 104; 122; MTCW

Schnackenberg, Gjertrud 1953-..... CLC 40
  See also CA 116; DLB 120

Schneider, Leonard Alfred 1925-1966
  See Bruce, Lenny
  See also CA 89-92

Schnitzler, Arthur
  1862-1931 .... TCLC 4; SSC 15
  See also CA 104; DLB 81, 118

Schopenhauer, Arthur
  1788-1860 .... NCLC 51
  See also DLB 90

Schor, Sandra (M.) 1932(?)-1990 ... CLC 65
  See also CA 132

Schorer, Mark 1908-1977 .... CLC 9
  See also CA 5-8R; 73-76; CANR 7;
    DLB 103

Schrader, Paul (Joseph) 1946-..... CLC 26
  See also CA 37-40R; CANR 41; DLB 44

Schreiner, Olive (Emilie Albertina)
  1855-1920 .... TCLC 9
  See also CA 105; DLB 18, 156

Schulberg, Budd (Wilson)
  1914- .... CLC 7, 48
  See also CA 25-28R; CANR 19; DLB 6, 26,
    28; DLBY 81

Schulz, Bruno
  1892-1942 .... TCLC 5, 51; SSC 13
  See also CA 115; 123

Schulz, Charles M(onroe) 1922-.... CLC 12
  See also CA 9-12R; CANR 6;
    INT CANR-6; SATA 10

Schumacher, E(rnst) F(riedrich)
  1911-1977 .... CLC 80
  See also CA 81-84; 73-76; CANR 34

Schuyler, James Marcus
  1923-1991 .... CLC 5, 23
  See also CA 101; 134; DAM POET; DLB 5;
    INT 101

Schwartz, Delmore (David)
  1913-1966 ... CLC 2, 4, 10, 45, 87; PC 8
  See also CA 17-18; 25-28R; CANR 35;
    CAP 2; DLB 28, 48; MTCW

Schwartz, Ernst
  See Ozu, Yasujiro

Schwartz, John Burnham 1965- .... CLC 59
  See also CA 132

Schwartz, Lynne Sharon 1939-..... CLC 31
  See also CA 103; CANR 44

Schwartz, Muriel A.
  See Eliot, T(homas) S(tearns)

Schwarz-Bart, Andre 1928-....... CLC 2, 4
  See also CA 89-92

Schwarz-Bart, Simone 1938-........ CLC 7
  See also BW 2; CA 97-100

Schwob, (Mayer Andre) Marcel
  1867-1905 .... TCLC 20
  See also CA 117; DLB 123

Sciascia, Leonardo
  1921-1989 .... CLC 8, 9, 41
  See also CA 85-88; 130; CANR 35; MTCW

Scoppettone, Sandra 1936-........ CLC 26
  See also AAYA 11; CA 5-8R; CANR 41;
    SATA 9

Scorsese, Martin 1942- .... CLC 20, 89
  See also CA 110; 114; CANR 46

Scotland, Jay
  See Jakes, John (William)

Scott, Duncan Campbell
  1862-1947 .... TCLC 6; DAC
  See also CA 104; DLB 92

Shaw, George Bernard
1856-1950 ... **TCLC 3, 9, 21; DA; DAB; DAC; WLC**
See also Shaw, Bernard
See also CA 104; 128; CDBLB 1914-1945;
DAM DRAM, MST; DLB 10, 57;
MTCW

Shaw, Henry Wheeler
1818-1885 .... **NCLC 15**
See also DLB 11

Shaw, Irwin 1913-1984...... **CLC 7, 23, 34**
See also AITN 1; CA 13-16R; 112;
CANR 21; CDALB 1941-1968;
DAM DRAM, POP; DLB 6, 102;
DLBY 84; MTCW

Shaw, Robert 1927-1978 .... **CLC 5**
See also AITN 1; CA 1-4R; 81-84;
CANR 4; DLB 13, 14

Shaw, T. E.
See Lawrence, T(homas) E(dward)

Shawn, Wallace 1943- .... **CLC 41**
See also CA 112

Shea, Lisa 1953-................ **CLC 86**
See also CA 147

Sheed, Wilfrid (John Joseph)
1930- .... **CLC 2, 4, 10, 53**
See also CA 65-68; CANR 30; DLB 6;
MTCW

Sheldon, Alice Hastings Bradley
1915(?)-1987
See Tiptree, James, Jr.
See also CA 108; 122; CANR 34; INT 108;
MTCW

Sheldon, John
See Bloch, Robert (Albert)

Shelley, Mary Wollstonecraft (Godwin)
1797-1851 .... **NCLC 14; DA; DAB; DAC; WLC**
See also CDBLB 1789-1832; DAM MST,
NOV; DLB 110, 116, 159; SATA 29

Shelley, Percy Bysshe
1792-1822 .... **NCLC 18; DA; DAB; DAC; PC 14; WLC**
See also CDBLB 1789-1832; DAM MST,
POET; DLB 96, 110, 158

Shepard, Jim 1956-.............. **CLC 36**
See also CA 137

Shepard, Lucius 1947- .... **CLC 34**
See also CA 128; 141

Shepard, Sam
1943- .... **CLC 4, 6, 17, 34, 41, 44; DC 5**
See also AAYA 1; CA 69-72; CABS 3;
CANR 22; DAM DRAM; DLB 7;
MTCW

Shepherd, Michael
See Ludlum, Robert

Sherburne, Zoa (Morin) 1912-...... **CLC 30**
See also AAYA 13; CA 1-4R; CANR 3, 37;
MAICYA; SAAS 18; SATA 3

Sheridan, Frances 1724-1766........ **LC 7**
See also DLB 39, 84

Sheridan, Richard Brinsley
1751-1816 .... **NCLC 5; DA; DAB; DAC; DC 1; WLC**
See also CDBLB 1660-1789; DAM DRAM,
MST; DLB 89

Sherman, Jonathan Marc.......... **CLC 55**

Sherman, Martin 1941(?)-......... **CLC 19**
See also CA 116; 123

Sherwin, Judith Johnson 1936-... **CLC 7, 15**
See also CA 25-28R; CANR 34

Sherwood, Frances 1940-......... **CLC 81**
See also CA 146

Sherwood, Robert E(mmet)
1896-1955 .... **TCLC 3**
See also CA 104; DAM DRAM; DLB 7, 26

Shestov, Lev 1866-1938 .... **TCLC 56**

Shevchenko, Taras 1814-1861 .... **NCLC 54**

Shiel, M(atthew) P(hipps)
1865-1947 .... **TCLC 8**
See also CA 106; DLB 153

Shields, Carol 1935-........ **CLC 91; DAC**
See also CA 81-84; CANR 51

Shiga, Naoya 1883-1971... **CLC 33; SSC 23**
See also CA 101; 33-36R

Shilts, Randy 1951-1994 .... **CLC 85**
See also CA 115; 127; 144; CANR 45;
INT 127

Shimazaki, Haruki 1872-1943
See Shimazaki Toson
See also CA 105; 134

Shimazaki Toson .... **TCLC 5**
See also Shimazaki, Haruki

Sholokhov, Mikhail (Aleksandrovich)
1905-1984 .... **CLC 7, 15**
See also CA 101; 112; MTCW;
SATA-Obit 36

Shone, Patric
See Hanley, James

Shreve, Susan Richards 1939-...... **CLC 23**
See also CA 49-52; CAAS 5; CANR 5, 38;
MAICYA; SATA 46; SATA-Brief 41

Shue, Larry 1946-1985........... **CLC 52**
See also CA 145; 117; DAM DRAM

Shu-Jen, Chou 1881-1936
See Lu Hsun
See also CA 104

Shulman, Alix Kates 1932-...... **CLC 2, 10**
See also CA 29-32R; CANR 43; SATA 7

Shuster, Joe 1914- .... **CLC 21**

Shute, Nevil.................... **CLC 30**
See also Norway, Nevil Shute

Shuttle, Penelope (Diane) 1947-..... **CLC 7**
See also CA 93-96; CANR 39; DLB 14, 40

Sidney, Mary 1561-1621 .... **LC 19**

Sidney, Sir Philip
1554-1586 ..... **LC 19; DA; DAB; DAC**
See also CDBLB Before 1660; DAM MST,
POET; DLB 167

Siegel, Jerome 1914-1996 .... **CLC 21**
See also CA 116; 151

Siegel, Jerry
See Siegel, Jerome

Sienkiewicz, Henryk (Adam Alexander Pius)
1846-1916 .... **TCLC 3**
See also CA 104; 134

Sierra, Gregorio Martinez
See Martinez Sierra, Gregorio

Sierra, Maria (de la O'LeJarraga) Martinez
See Martinez Sierra, Maria (de la
O'LeJarraga)

Sigal, Clancy 1926-............... **CLC 7**
See also CA 1-4R

Sigourney, Lydia Howard (Huntley)
1791-1865 .... **NCLC 21**
See also DLB 1, 42, 73

Siguenza y Gongora, Carlos de
1645-1700 .... **LC 8**

Sigurjonsson, Johann 1880-1919... **TCLC 27**

Sikelianos, Angelos 1884-1951 .... **TCLC 39**

Silkin, Jon 1930- .... **CLC 2, 6, 43**
See also CA 5-8R; CAAS 5; DLB 27

Silko, Leslie (Marmon)
1948-.......... **CLC 23, 74; DA; DAC**
See also AAYA 14; CA 115; 122;
CANR 45; DAM MST, MULT, POP;
DLB 143; NNAL

Sillanpaa, Frans Eemil 1888-1964... **CLC 19**
See also CA 129; 93-96; MTCW

Sillitoe, Alan
1928-.......... **CLC 1, 3, 6, 10, 19, 57**
See also AITN 1; CA 9-12R; CAAS 2;
CANR 8, 26; CDBLB 1960 to Present;
DLB 14, 139; MTCW; SATA 61

Silone, Ignazio 1900-1978 .... **CLC 4**
See also CA 25-28; 81-84; CANR 34;
CAP 2; MTCW

Silver, Joan Micklin 1935-....... **CLC 20**
See also CA 114; 121; INT 121

Silver, Nicholas
See Faust, Frederick (Schiller)

Silverberg, Robert 1935-........... **CLC 7**
See also CA 1-4R; CAAS 3; CANR 1, 20,
36; DAM POP; DLB 8; INT CANR-20;
MAICYA; MTCW; SATA 13

Silverstein, Alvin 1933-........... **CLC 17**
See also CA 49-52; CANR 2; CLR 25;
JRDA; MAICYA; SATA 8, 69

Silverstein, Virginia B(arbara Opshelor)
1937-...................... **CLC 17**
See also CA 49-52; CANR 2; CLR 25;
JRDA; MAICYA; SATA 8, 69

Sim, Georges
See Simenon, Georges (Jacques Christian)

Simak, Clifford D(onald)
1904-1988 .... **CLC 1, 55**
See also CA 1-4R; 125; CANR 1, 35;
DLB 8; MTCW; SATA-Obit 56

Simenon, Georges (Jacques Christian)
1903-1989 .... **CLC 1, 2, 3, 8, 18, 47**
See also CA 85-88; 129; CANR 35;
DAM POP; DLB 72; DLBY 89; MTCW

Simic, Charles 1938-... **CLC 6, 9, 22, 49, 68**
See also CA 29-32R; CAAS 4; CANR 12,
33, 52; DAM POET; DLB 105

Simmel, Georg 1858-1918 .... **TCLC 64**

Simmons, Charles (Paul) 1924-..... **CLC 57**
See also CA 89-92; INT 89-92

Simmons, Dan 1948-............. **CLC 44**
See also AAYA 16; CA 138; CANR 53;
DAM POP

Author Index

Stowe, Harriet (Elizabeth) Beecher
1811-1896 . . . . . **NCLC 3, 50; DA; DAB; DAC; WLC**
See also CDALB 1865-1917; DAM MST, NOV; DLB 1, 12, 42, 74; JRDA; MAICYA; YABC 1

Strachey, (Giles) Lytton
1880-1932 . . . . **TCLC 12**
See also CA 110; DLB 149; DLBD 10

Strand, Mark 1934- . . . . . . **CLC 6, 18, 41, 71**
See also CA 21-24R; CANR 40; DAM POET; DLB 5; SATA 41

Straub, Peter (Francis) 1943- . . . . . . **CLC 28**
See also BEST 89:1; CA 85-88; CANR 28; DAM POP; DLBY 84; MTCW

Strauss, Botho 1944- . . . . **CLC 22**
See also DLB 124

Streatfeild, (Mary) Noel
1895(?)-1986 . . . . **CLC 21**
See also CA 81-84; 120; CANR 31; CLR 17; DLB 160; MAICYA; SATA 20; SATA-Obit 48

Stribling, T(homas) S(igismund)
1881-1965 . . . . **CLC 23**
See also CA 107; DLB 9

Strindberg, (Johan) August
1849-1912 . . . . . . **TCLC 1, 8, 21, 47; DA; DAB; DAC; WLC**
See also CA 104; 135; DAM DRAM, MST

Stringer, Arthur 1874-1950 . . . . . . **TCLC 37**
See also DLB 92

Stringer, David
See Roberts, Keith (John Kingston)

Strugatskii, Arkadii (Natanovich)
1925-1991 . . . . **CLC 27**
See also CA 106; 135

Strugatskii, Boris (Natanovich)
1933- . . . . **CLC 27**
See also CA 106

Strummer, Joe 1953(?)- . . . . **CLC 30**

Stuart, Don A.
See Campbell, John W(ood, Jr.)

Stuart, Ian
See MacLean, Alistair (Stuart)

Stuart, Jesse (Hilton)
1906-1984 . . . . **CLC 1, 8, 11, 14, 34**
See also CA 5-8R; 112; CANR 31; DLB 9, 48, 102; DLBY 84; SATA 2; SATA-Obit 36

Sturgeon, Theodore (Hamilton)
1918-1985 . . . . **CLC 22, 39**
See also Queen, Ellery
See also CA 81-84; 116; CANR 32; DLB 8; DLBY 85; MTCW

Sturges, Preston 1898-1959 . . . . . . **TCLC 48**
See also CA 114; 149; DLB 26

Styron, William
1925- . . . . **CLC 1, 3, 5, 11, 15, 60**
See also BEST 90:4; CA 5-8R; CANR 6, 33; CDALB 1968-1988; DAM NOV, POP; DLB 2, 143; DLBY 80; INT CANR-6; MTCW

Suarez Lynch, B.
See Bioy Casares, Adolfo; Borges, Jorge Luis

Su Chien 1884-1918
See Su Man-shu
See also CA 123

Suckow, Ruth 1892-1960 . . . . **SSC 18**
See also CA 113; DLB 9, 102

Sudermann, Hermann 1857-1928 . . **TCLC 15**
See also CA 107; DLB 118

Sue, Eugene 1804-1857 . . . . **NCLC 1**
See also DLB 119

Sueskind, Patrick 1949- . . . . **CLC 44**
See also Suskind, Patrick

Sukenick, Ronald 1932- . . . . . **CLC 3, 4, 6, 48**
See also CA 25-28R; CAAS 8; CANR 32; DLBY 81

Suknaski, Andrew 1942- . . . . **CLC 19**
See also CA 101; DLB 53

Sullivan, Vernon
See Vian, Boris

Sully Prudhomme 1839-1907 . . . . . . **TCLC 31**

Su Man-shu . . . . **TCLC 24**
See also Su Chien

Summerforest, Ivy B.
See Kirkup, James

Summers, Andrew James 1942- . . . . . **CLC 26**

Summers, Andy
See Summers, Andrew James

Summers, Hollis (Spurgeon, Jr.)
1916- . . . . **CLC 10**
See also CA 5-8R; CANR 3; DLB 6

Summers, (Alphonsus Joseph-Mary Augustus)
Montague 1880-1948 . . . . **TCLC 16**
See also CA 118

Sumner, Gordon Matthew 1951- . . . . **CLC 26**

Surtees, Robert Smith
1803-1864 . . . . **NCLC 14**
See also DLB 21

Susann, Jacqueline 1921-1974 . . . . . . **CLC 3**
See also AITN 1; CA 65-68; 53-56; MTCW

Su Shih 1036-1101 . . . . **CMLC 15**

Suskind, Patrick
See Sueskind, Patrick
See also CA 145

Sutcliff, Rosemary
1920-1992 . . . . **CLC 26; DAB; DAC**
See also AAYA 10; CA 5-8R; 139; CANR 37; CLR 1, 37; DAM MST, POP; JRDA; MAICYA; SATA 6, 44, 78; SATA-Obit 73

Sutro, Alfred 1863-1933 . . . . **TCLC 6**
See also CA 105; DLB 10

Sutton, Henry
See Slavitt, David R(ytman)

Svevo, Italo . . . . **TCLC 2, 35**
See also Schmitz, Aron Hector

Swados, Elizabeth (A.) 1951- . . . . . . **CLC 12**
See also CA 97-100; CANR 49; INT 97-100

Swados, Harvey 1920-1972 . . . . **CLC 5**
See also CA 5-8R; 37-40R; CANR 6; DLB 2

Swan, Gladys 1934- . . . . **CLC 69**
See also CA 101; CANR 17, 39

Swarthout, Glendon (Fred)
1918-1992 . . . . **CLC 35**
See also CA 1-4R; 139; CANR 1, 47; SATA 26

Sweet, Sarah C.
See Jewett, (Theodora) Sarah Orne

Swenson, May
1919-1989 . . . . **CLC 4, 14, 61; DA; DAB; DAC; PC 14**
See also CA 5-8R; 130; CANR 36; DAM MST, POET; DLB 5; MTCW; SATA 15

Swift, Augustus
See Lovecraft, H(oward) P(hillips)

Swift, Graham (Colin) 1949- . . . . **CLC 41, 88**
See also CA 117; 122; CANR 46

Swift, Jonathan
1667-1745 . . . . . . **LC 1; DA; DAB; DAC; PC 9; WLC**
See also CDBLB 1660-1789; DAM MST, NOV, POET; DLB 39, 95, 101; SATA 19

Swinburne, Algernon Charles
1837-1909 . . . . . . **TCLC 8, 36; DA; DAB; DAC; WLC**
See also CA 105; 140; CDBLB 1832-1890; DAM MST, POET; DLB 35, 57

Swinfen, Ann . . . . **CLC 34**

Swinnerton, Frank Arthur
1884-1982 . . . . **CLC 31**
See also CA 108; DLB 34

Swithen, John
See King, Stephen (Edwin)

Sylvia
See Ashton-Warner, Sylvia (Constance)

Symmes, Robert Edward
See Duncan, Robert (Edward)

Symonds, John Addington
1840-1893 . . . . **NCLC 34**
See also DLB 57, 144

Symons, Arthur 1865-1945 . . . . **TCLC 11**
See also CA 107; DLB 19, 57, 149

Symons, Julian (Gustave)
1912-1994 . . . . **CLC 2, 14, 32**
See also CA 49-52; 147; CAAS 3; CANR 3, 33; DLB 87, 155; DLBY 92; MTCW

Synge, (Edmund) J(ohn) M(illington)
1871-1909 . . . . **TCLC 6, 37; DC 2**
See also CA 104; 141; CDBLB 1890-1914; DAM DRAM; DLB 10, 19

Syruc, J.
See Milosz, Czeslaw

Szirtes, George 1948- . . . . **CLC 46**
See also CA 109; CANR 27

Tabori, George 1914- . . . . **CLC 19**
See also CA 49-52; CANR 4

Tagore, Rabindranath
1861-1941 . . . . **TCLC 3, 53; PC 8**
See also CA 104; 120; DAM DRAM, POET; MTCW

Taine, Hippolyte Adolphe
1828-1893 . . . . **NCLC 15**

Talese, Gay 1932- . . . . **CLC 37**
See also AITN 1; CA 1-4R; CANR 9; INT CANR-9; MTCW

Author Index

Trogdon, William (Lewis) 1939-
See Heat-Moon, William Least
See also CA 115; 119; CANR 47; INT 119

Trollope, Anthony
1815-1882 ..... **NCLC 6, 33; DA; DAB;
DAC; WLC**
See also CDBLB 1832-1890; DAM MST,
NOV; DLB 21, 57, 159; SATA 22

Trollope, Frances 1779-1863 ..... **NCLC 30**
See also DLB 21, 166

Trotsky, Leon 1879-1940 .... **TCLC 22**
See also CA 118

Trotter (Cockburn), Catharine
1679-1749 .... **LC 8**
See also DLB 84

Trout, Kilgore
See Farmer, Philip Jose

Trow, George W. S. 1943- .... **CLC 52**
See also CA 126

Troyat, Henri 1911- .... **CLC 23**
See also CA 45-48; CANR 2, 33; MTCW

Trudeau, G(arretson) B(eekman) 1948-
See Trudeau, Garry B.
See also CA 81-84; CANR 31; SATA 35

Trudeau, Garry B. .... **CLC 12**
See also Trudeau, G(arretson) B(eekman)
See also AAYA 10; AITN 2

Truffaut, Francois 1932-1984 ...... **CLC 20**
See also CA 81-84; 113; CANR 34

Trumbo, Dalton 1905-1976 .... **CLC 19**
See also CA 21-24R; 69-72; CANR 10;
DLB 26

Trumbull, John 1750-1831 .... **NCLC 30**
See also DLB 31

Trundlett, Helen B.
See Eliot, T(homas) S(tearns)

Tryon, Thomas 1926-1991 .... **CLC 3, 11**
See also AITN 1; CA 29-32R; 135;
CANR 32; DAM POP; MTCW

Tryon, Tom
See Tryon, Thomas

Ts'ao Hsueh-ch'in 1715(?)-1763 .... **LC 1**

Tsushima, Shuji 1909-1948
See Dazai, Osamu
See also CA 107

Tsvetaeva (Efron), Marina (Ivanovna)
1892-1941 .... **TCLC 7, 35; PC 14**
See also CA 104; 128; MTCW

Tuck, Lily 1938- .... **CLC 70**
See also CA 139

Tu Fu 712-770 .... **PC 9**
See also DAM MULT

Tunis, John R(oberts) 1889-1975 ... **CLC 12**
See also CA 61-64; DLB 22; JRDA;
MAICYA; SATA 37; SATA-Brief 30

Tuohy, Frank .... **CLC 37**
See also Tuohy, John Francis
See also DLB 14, 139

Tuohy, John Francis 1925-
See Tuohy, Frank
See also CA 5-8R; CANR 3, 47

Turco, Lewis (Putnam) 1934- ... **CLC 11, 63**
See also CA 13-16R; CAAS 22; CANR 24,
51; DLBY 84

Turgenev, Ivan
1818-1883 .... **NCLC 21; DA; DAB;
DAC; SSC 7; WLC**
See also DAM MST, NOV

Turgot, Anne-Robert-Jacques
1727-1781 .... **LC 26**

Turner, Frederick 1943- .... **CLC 48**
See also CA 73-76; CAAS 10; CANR 12,
30; DLB 40

Tutu, Desmond M(pilo)
1931- .... **CLC 80; BLC**
See also BW 1; CA 125; DAM MULT

Tutuola, Amos 1920- ... **CLC 5, 14, 29; BLC**
See also BW 2; CA 9-12R; CANR 27;
DAM MULT; DLB 125; MTCW

Twain, Mark
..... **TCLC 6, 12, 19, 36, 48, 59; SSC 6;
WLC**
See also Clemens, Samuel Langhorne
See also DLB 11, 12, 23, 64, 74

Tyler, Anne
1941- .... **CLC 7, 11, 18, 28, 44, 59**
See also AAYA 18; BEST 89:1; CA 9-12R;
CANR 11, 33, 53; DAM NOV, POP;
DLB 6, 143; DLBY 82; MTCW; SATA 7

Tyler, Royall 1757-1826 .... **NCLC 3**
See also DLB 37

Tynan, Katharine 1861-1931 .... **TCLC 3**
See also CA 104; DLB 153

Tyutchev, Fyodor 1803-1873 ..... **NCLC 34**

Tzara, Tristan .... **CLC 47**
See also Rosenfeld, Samuel
See also DAM POET

Uhry, Alfred 1936- .... **CLC 55**
See also CA 127; 133; DAM DRAM, POP;
INT 133

Ulf, Haerved
See Strindberg, (Johan) August

Ulf, Harved
See Strindberg, (Johan) August

Ulibarri, Sabine R(eyes) 1919- ..... **CLC 83**
See also CA 131; DAM MULT; DLB 82;
HW

Unamuno (y Jugo), Miguel de
1864-1936 .... **TCLC 2, 9; HLC; SSC 11**
See also CA 104; 131; DAM MULT, NOV;
DLB 108; HW; MTCW

Undercliffe, Errol
See Campbell, (John) Ramsey

Underwood, Miles
See Glassco, John

Undset, Sigrid
1882-1949 .... **TCLC 3; DA; DAB;
DAC; WLC**
See also CA 104; 129; DAM MST, NOV;
MTCW

Ungaretti, Giuseppe
1888-1970 .... **CLC 7, 11, 15**
See also CA 19-20; 25-28R; CAP 2;
DLB 114

Unger, Douglas 1952- .... **CLC 34**
See also CA 130

Unsworth, Barry (Forster) 1930- .... **CLC 76**
See also CA 25-28R; CANR 30

Updike, John (Hoyer)
1932- ..... **CLC 1, 2, 3, 5, 7, 9, 13, 15,
23, 34, 43, 70; DA; DAB; DAC; SSC 13;
WLC**
See also CA 1-4R; CABS 1; CANR 4, 33,
51; CDALB 1968-1988; DAM MST,
NOV, POET, POP; DLB 2, 5, 143;
DLBD 3; DLBY 80, 82; MTCW

Upshaw, Margaret Mitchell
See Mitchell, Margaret (Munnerlyn)

Upton, Mark
See Sanders, Lawrence

Urdang, Constance (Henriette)
1922- .... **CLC 47**
See also CA 21-24R; CANR 9, 24

Uriel, Henry
See Faust, Frederick (Schiller)

Uris, Leon (Marcus) 1924- .... **CLC 7, 32**
See also AITN 1, 2; BEST 89:2; CA 1-4R;
CANR 1, 40; DAM NOV, POP; MTCW;
SATA 49

Urmuz
See Codrescu, Andrei

Urquhart, Jane 1949- .... **CLC 90; DAC**
See also CA 113; CANR 32

Ustinov, Peter (Alexander) 1921- .... **CLC 1**
See also AITN 1; CA 13-16R; CANR 25,
51; DLB 13

Vaculik, Ludvik 1926- .... **CLC 7**
See also CA 53-56

Valdez, Luis (Miguel)
1940- .... **CLC 84; HLC**
See also CA 101; CANR 32; DAM MULT;
DLB 122; HW

Valenzuela, Luisa 1938- ... **CLC 31; SSC 14**
See also CA 101; CANR 32; DAM MULT;
DLB 113; HW

Valera y Alcala-Galiano, Juan
1824-1905 .... **TCLC 10**
See also CA 106

Valery, (Ambroise) Paul (Toussaint Jules)
1871-1945 .... **TCLC 4, 15; PC 9**
See also CA 104; 122; DAM POET; MTCW

Valle-Inclan, Ramon (Maria) del
1866-1936 .... **TCLC 5; HLC**
See also CA 106; DAM MULT; DLB 134

Vallejo, Antonio Buero
See Buero Vallejo, Antonio

Vallejo, Cesar (Abraham)
1892-1938 .... **TCLC 3, 56; HLC**
See also CA 105; DAM MULT; HW

Valle Y Pena, Ramon del
See Valle-Inclan, Ramon (Maria) del

Van Ash, Cay 1918- .... **CLC 34**

Vanbrugh, Sir John 1664-1726 ...... **LC 21**
See also DAM DRAM; DLB 80

Van Campen, Karl
See Campbell, John W(ood, Jr.)

Vance, Gerald
See Silverberg, Robert

Vance, Jack .... **CLC 35**
See also Vance, John Holbrook
See also DLB 8

Vance, John Holbrook   1916-
See Queen, Ellery; Vance, Jack
See also CA 29-32R; CANR 17; MTCW

Van Den Bogarde, Derek Jules Gaspard Ulric
Niven   1921-
See Bogarde, Dirk
See also CA 77-80

Vandenburgh, Jane . . . . **CLC 59**

Vanderhaeghe, Guy   1951- . . . . **CLC 41**
See also CA 113

van der Post, Laurens (Jan)   1906- . . . **CLC 5**
See also CA 5-8R; CANR 35

van de Wetering, Janwillem   1931- . . **CLC 47**
See also CA 49-52; CANR 4

Van Dine, S. S. . . . . **TCLC 23**
See also Wright, Willard Huntington

Van Doren, Carl (Clinton)
1885-1950 . . . . **TCLC 18**
See also CA 111

Van Doren, Mark   1894-1972 . . . . . **CLC 6, 10**
See also CA 1-4R; 37-40R; CANR 3;
DLB 45; MTCW

Van Druten, John (William)
1901-1957 . . . . **TCLC 2**
See also CA 104; DLB 10

Van Duyn, Mona (Jane)
1921- . . . . **CLC 3, 7, 63**
See also CA 9-12R; CANR 7, 38;
DAM POET; DLB 5

Van Dyne, Edith
See Baum, L(yman) Frank

van Itallie, Jean-Claude   1936- . . . . **CLC 3**
See also CA 45-48; CAAS 2; CANR 1, 48;
DLB 7

van Ostaijen, Paul   1896-1928 . . . . . **TCLC 33**

Van Peebles, Melvin   1932- . . . . . . **CLC 2, 20**
See also BW 2; CA 85-88; CANR 27;
DAM MULT

Vansittart, Peter   1920- . . . . **CLC 42**
See also CA 1-4R; CANR 3, 49

Van Vechten, Carl   1880-1964 . . . . . . **CLC 33**
See also CA 89-92; DLB 4, 9, 51

Van Vogt, A(lfred) E(lton)   1912- . . . . . **CLC 1**
See also CA 21-24R; CANR 28; DLB 8;
SATA 14

Varda, Agnes   1928- . . . . **CLC 16**
See also CA 116; 122

Vargas Llosa, (Jorge) Mario (Pedro)
1936- . . . . **CLC 3, 6, 9, 10, 15, 31, 42, 85;
DA; DAB; DAC; HLC**
See also CA 73-76; CANR 18, 32, 42;
DAM MST, MULT, NOV; DLB 145;
HW; MTCW

Vasiliu, Gheorghe   1881-1957
See Bacovia, George
See also CA 123

Vassa, Gustavus
See Equiano, Olaudah

Vassilikos, Vassilis   1933- . . . . **CLC 4, 8**
See also CA 81-84

Vaughan, Henry   1621-1695 . . . . **LC 27**
See also DLB 131

Vaughn, Stephanie . . . . **CLC 62**

Vazov, Ivan (Minchov)
1850-1921 . . . . **TCLC 25**
See also CA 121; DLB 147

Veblen, Thorstein (Bunde)
1857-1929 . . . . **TCLC 31**
See also CA 115

Vega, Lope de   1562-1635 . . . . **LC 23**

Venison, Alfred
See Pound, Ezra (Weston Loomis)

Verdi, Marie de
See Mencken, H(enry) L(ouis)

Verdu, Matilde
See Cela, Camilo Jose

Verga, Giovanni (Carmelo)
1840-1922 . . . . **TCLC 3; SSC 21**
See also CA 104; 123

Vergil
70B.C.-19B.C. . . . . . **CMLC 9; DA; DAB;
DAC; PC 12**
See also DAM MST, POET

Verhaeren, Emile (Adolphe Gustave)
1855-1916 . . . . **TCLC 12**
See also CA 109

Verlaine, Paul (Marie)
1844-1896 . . . . **NCLC 2, 51; PC 2**
See also DAM POET

Verne, Jules (Gabriel)
1828-1905 . . . . **TCLC 6, 52**
See also AAYA 16; CA 110; 131; DLB 123;
JRDA; MAICYA; SATA 21

Very, Jones   1813-1880 . . . . **NCLC 9**
See also DLB 1

Vesaas, Tarjei   1897-1970 . . . . **CLC 48**
See also CA 29-32R

Vialis, Gaston
See Simenon, Georges (Jacques Christian)

Vian, Boris   1920-1959 . . . . **TCLC 9**
See also CA 106; DLB 72

Viaud, (Louis Marie) Julien   1850-1923
See Loti, Pierre
See also CA 107

Vicar, Henry
See Felsen, Henry Gregor

Vicker, Angus
See Felsen, Henry Gregor

Vidal, Gore
1925- . . . . . **CLC 2, 4, 6, 8, 10, 22, 33, 72**
See also AITN 1; BEST 90:2; CA 5-8R;
CANR 13, 45; DAM NOV, POP; DLB 6,
152; INT CANR-13; MTCW

Viereck, Peter (Robert Edwin)
1916- . . . . **CLC 4**
See also CA 1-4R; CANR 1, 47; DLB 5

Vigny, Alfred (Victor) de
1797-1863 . . . . **NCLC 7**
See also DAM POET; DLB 119

Vilakazi, Benedict Wallet
1906-1947 . . . . **TCLC 37**

Villiers de l'Isle Adam, Jean Marie Mathias
Philippe Auguste Comte
1838-1889 . . . . **NCLC 3; SSC 14**
See also DLB 123

Villon, Francois   1431-1463(?) . . . . . . **PC 13**

Vinci, Leonardo da   1452-1519 . . . . . . **LC 12**

Vine, Barbara . . . . **CLC 50**
See also Rendell, Ruth (Barbara)
See also BEST 90:4

Vinge, Joan D(ennison)   1948- . . . . . . **CLC 30**
See also CA 93-96; SATA 36

Violis, G.
See Simenon, Georges (Jacques Christian)

Visconti, Luchino   1906-1976 . . . . **CLC 16**
See also CA 81-84; 65-68; CANR 39

Vittorini, Elio   1908-1966 . . . . . . **CLC 6, 9, 14**
See also CA 133; 25-28R

Vizinczey, Stephen   1933- . . . . **CLC 40**
See also CA 128; INT 128

Vliet, R(ussell) G(ordon)
1929-1984 . . . . **CLC 22**
See also CA 37-40R; 112; CANR 18

Vogau, Boris Andreyevich   1894-1937(?)
See Pilnyak, Boris
See also CA 123

Vogel, Paula A(nne)   1951- . . . . **CLC 76**
See also CA 108

Voight, Ellen Bryant   1943- . . . . **CLC 54**
See also CA 69-72; CANR 11, 29; DLB 120

Voigt, Cynthia   1942- . . . . **CLC 30**
See also AAYA 3; CA 106; CANR 18, 37,
40; CLR 13; INT CANR-18; JRDA;
MAICYA; SATA 48, 79; SATA-Brief 33

Voinovich, Vladimir (Nikolaevich)
1932- . . . . **CLC 10, 49**
See also CA 81-84; CAAS 12; CANR 33;
MTCW

Vollmann, William T.   1959- . . . . **CLC 89**
See also CA 134; DAM NOV, POP

Voloshinov, V. N.
See Bakhtin, Mikhail Mikhailovich

Voltaire
1694-1778 . . . . . **LC 14; DA; DAB; DAC;
SSC 12; WLC**
See also DAM DRAM, MST

von Daeniken, Erich   1935- . . . . **CLC 30**
See also AITN 1; CA 37-40R; CANR 17,
44

von Daniken, Erich
See von Daeniken, Erich

von Heidenstam, (Carl Gustaf) Verner
See Heidenstam, (Carl Gustaf) Verner von

von Heyse, Paul (Johann Ludwig)
See Heyse, Paul (Johann Ludwig von)

von Hofmannsthal, Hugo
See Hofmannsthal, Hugo von

von Horvath, Odon
See Horvath, Oedoen von

von Horvath, Oedoen
See Horvath, Oedoen von

von Liliencron, (Friedrich Adolf Axel) Detlev
See Liliencron, (Friedrich Adolf Axel)
Detlev von

Vonnegut, Kurt, Jr.
1922- . . . . . . **CLC 1, 2, 3, 4, 5, 8, 12, 22,
40, 60; DA; DAB; DAC; SSC 8; WLC**
See also AAYA 6; AITN 1; BEST 90:4;
CA 1-4R; CANR 1, 25, 49;
CDALB 1968-1988; DAM MST, NOV,
POP; DLB 2, 8, 152; DLBD 3; DLBY 80;
MTCW

Wassermann, (Karl) Jakob
        1873-1934 . . . . **TCLC 6**
        See also CA 104; DLB 66

Wasserstein, Wendy
        1950- . . . . **CLC 32, 59, 90; DC 4**
        See also CA 121; 129; CABS 3; CANR 53;
        DAM DRAM; INT 129

Waterhouse, Keith (Spencer)
        1929- . . . . **CLC 47**
        See also CA 5-8R; CANR 38; DLB 13, 15;
        MTCW

Waters, Frank (Joseph)
        1902-1995 . . . . **CLC 88**
        See also CA 5-8R; 149; CAAS 13; CANR 3,
        18; DLBY 86

Waters, Roger 1944- . . . . **CLC 35**

Watkins, Frances Ellen
        See Harper, Frances Ellen Watkins

Watkins, Gerrold
        See Malzberg, Barry N(athaniel)

Watkins, Gloria 1955(?)-
        See hooks, bell
        See also BW 2; CA 143

Watkins, Paul 1964- . . . . **CLC 55**
        See also CA 132

Watkins, Vernon Phillips
        1906-1967 . . . . **CLC 43**
        See also CA 9-10; 25-28R; CAP 1; DLB 20

Watson, Irving S.
        See Mencken, H(enry) L(ouis)

Watson, John H.
        See Farmer, Philip Jose

Watson, Richard F.
        See Silverberg, Robert

Waugh, Auberon (Alexander) 1939- . . **CLC 7**
        See also CA 45-48; CANR 6, 22; DLB 14

Waugh, Evelyn (Arthur St. John)
        1903-1966 . . . . . . **CLC 1, 3, 8, 13, 19, 27,
                            44; DA; DAB; DAC; WLC**
        See also CA 85-88; 25-28R; CANR 22;
        CDBLB 1914-1945; DAM MST, NOV,
        POP; DLB 15, 162; MTCW

Waugh, Harriet 1944- . . . . **CLC 6**
        See also CA 85-88; CANR 22

Ways, C. R.
        See Blount, Roy (Alton), Jr.

Waystaff, Simon
        See Swift, Jonathan

Webb, (Martha) Beatrice (Potter)
        1858-1943 . . . . **TCLC 22**
        See also Potter, Beatrice
        See also CA 117

Webb, Charles (Richard) 1939- . . . . . . **CLC 7**
        See also CA 25-28R

Webb, James H(enry), Jr. 1946- . . . . **CLC 22**
        See also CA 81-84

Webb, Mary (Gladys Meredith)
        1881-1927 . . . . **TCLC 24**
        See also CA 123; DLB 34

Webb, Mrs. Sidney
        See Webb, (Martha) Beatrice (Potter)

Webb, Phyllis 1927- . . . . **CLC 18**
        See also CA 104; CANR 23; DLB 53

Webb, Sidney (James)
        1859-1947 . . . . **TCLC 22**
        See also CA 117

Webber, Andrew Lloyd . . . . **CLC 21**
        See also Lloyd Webber, Andrew

Weber, Lenora Mattingly
        1895-1971 . . . . **CLC 12**
        See also CA 19-20; 29-32R; CAP 1;
        SATA 2; SATA-Obit 26

Webster, John
        1579(?)-1634(?) . . . . . . **LC 33; DA; DAB;
                                   DAC; DC 2; WLC**
        See also CDBLB Before 1660;
        DAM DRAM, MST; DLB 58

Webster, Noah 1758-1843 . . . . **NCLC 30**

Wedekind, (Benjamin) Frank(lin)
        1864-1918 . . . . **TCLC 7**
        See also CA 104; DAM DRAM; DLB 118

Weidman, Jerome 1913- . . . . **CLC 7**
        See also AITN 2; CA 1-4R; CANR 1;
        DLB 28

Weil, Simone (Adolphine)
        1909-1943 . . . . **TCLC 23**
        See also CA 117

Weinstein, Nathan
        See West, Nathanael

Weinstein, Nathan von Wallenstein
        See West, Nathanael

Weir, Peter (Lindsay) 1944- . . . . **CLC 20**
        See also CA 113; 123

Weiss, Peter (Ulrich)
        1916-1982 . . . . **CLC 3, 15, 51**
        See also CA 45-48; 106; CANR 3;
        DAM DRAM; DLB 69, 124

Weiss, Theodore (Russell)
        1916- . . . . **CLC 3, 8, 14**
        See also CA 9-12R; CAAS 2; CANR 46;
        DLB 5

Welch, (Maurice) Denton
        1915-1948 . . . . **TCLC 22**
        See also CA 121; 148

Welch, James 1940- . . . . **CLC 6, 14, 52**
        See also CA 85-88; CANR 42;
        DAM MULT, POP; NNAL

Weldon, Fay
        1933- . . . . **CLC 6, 9, 11, 19, 36, 59**
        See also CA 21-24R; CANR 16, 46;
        CDBLB 1960 to Present; DAM POP;
        DLB 14; INT CANR-16; MTCW

Wellek, Rene 1903-1995 . . . . **CLC 28**
        See also CA 5-8R; 150; CAAS 7; CANR 8;
        DLB 63; INT CANR-8

Weller, Michael 1942- . . . . **CLC 10, 53**
        See also CA 85-88

Weller, Paul 1958- . . . . **CLC 26**

Wellershoff, Dieter 1925- . . . . **CLC 46**
        See also CA 89-92; CANR 16, 37

Welles, (George) Orson
        1915-1985 . . . . **CLC 20, 80**
        See also CA 93-96; 117

Wellman, Mac 1945- . . . . **CLC 65**

Wellman, Manly Wade 1903-1986 . . **CLC 49**
        See also CA 1-4R; 118; CANR 6, 16, 44;
        SATA 6; SATA-Obit 47

Wells, Carolyn 1869(?)-1942 . . . . . . **TCLC 35**
        See also CA 113; DLB 11

Wells, H(erbert) G(eorge)
        1866-1946 . . . . **TCLC 6, 12, 19; DA;
                              DAB; DAC; SSC 6; WLC**
        See also AAYA 18; CA 110; 121;
        CDBLB 1914-1945; DAM MST, NOV;
        DLB 34, 70, 156; MTCW; SATA 20

Wells, Rosemary 1943- . . . . **CLC 12**
        See also AAYA 13; CA 85-88; CANR 48;
        CLR 16; MAICYA; SAAS 1; SATA 18,
        69

Welty, Eudora
        1909- . . . . . . **CLC 1, 2, 5, 14, 22, 33; DA;
                        DAB; DAC; SSC 1; WLC**
        See also CA 9-12R; CABS 1; CANR 32;
        CDALB 1941-1968; DAM MST, NOV;
        DLB 2, 102, 143; DLBD 12; DLBY 87;
        MTCW

Wen I-to 1899-1946 . . . . **TCLC 28**

Wentworth, Robert
        See Hamilton, Edmond

Werfel, Franz (V.) 1890-1945 . . . . . . **TCLC 8**
        See also CA 104; DLB 81, 124

Wergeland, Henrik Arnold
        1808-1845 . . . . **NCLC 5**

Wersba, Barbara 1932- . . . . **CLC 30**
        See also AAYA 2; CA 29-32R; CANR 16,
        38; CLR 3; DLB 52; JRDA; MAICYA;
        SAAS 2; SATA 1, 58

Wertmueller, Lina 1928- . . . . **CLC 16**
        See also CA 97-100; CANR 39

Wescott, Glenway 1901-1987 . . . . **CLC 13**
        See also CA 13-16R; 121; CANR 23;
        DLB 4, 9, 102

Wesker, Arnold 1932- . . **CLC 3, 5, 42; DAB**
        See also CA 1-4R; CAAS 7; CANR 1, 33;
        CDBLB 1960 to Present; DAM DRAM;
        DLB 13; MTCW

Wesley, Richard (Errol) 1945- . . . . . . **CLC 7**
        See also BW 1; CA 57-60; CANR 27;
        DLB 38

Wessel, Johan Herman 1742-1785 . . . . **LC 7**

West, Anthony (Panther)
        1914-1987 . . . . **CLC 50**
        See also CA 45-48; 124; CANR 3, 19;
        DLB 15

West, C. P.
        See Wodehouse, P(elham) G(renville)

West, (Mary) Jessamyn
        1902-1984 . . . . **CLC 7, 17**
        See also CA 9-12R; 112; CANR 27; DLB 6;
        DLBY 84; MTCW; SATA-Obit 37

West, Morris L(anglo) 1916- . . . . . **CLC 6, 33**
        See also CA 5-8R; CANR 24, 49; MTCW

West, Nathanael
        1903-1940 . . . . . **TCLC 1, 14, 44; SSC 16**
        See also CA 104; 125; CDALB 1929-1941;
        DLB 4, 9, 28; MTCW

West, Owen
        See Koontz, Dean R(ay)

West, Paul 1930- . . . . **CLC 7, 14**
        See also CA 13-16R; CAAS 7; CANR 22,
        53; DLB 14; INT CANR-22

Williams, John A(lfred)
  1925- . . . . CLC 5, 13; BLC
  See also BW 2; CA 53-56; CAAS 3;
  CANR 6, 26, 51; DAM MULT; DLB 2,
  33; INT CANR-6

Williams, Jonathan (Chamberlain)
  1929- . . . . CLC 13
  See also CA 9-12R; CAAS 12; CANR 8;
  DLB 5

Williams, Joy 1944- . . . . CLC 31
  See also CA 41-44R; CANR 22, 48

Williams, Norman 1952- . . . . CLC 39
  See also CA 118

Williams, Sherley Anne
  1944- . . . . CLC 89; BLC
  See also BW 2; CA 73-76; CANR 25;
  DAM MULT, POET; DLB 41;
  INT CANR-25; SATA 78

Williams, Shirley
  See Williams, Sherley Anne

Williams, Tennessee
  1911-1983 . . . . . CLC 1, 2, 5, 7, 8, 11, 15,
    19, 30, 39, 45, 71; DA; DAB; DAC;
    DC 4; WLC
  See also AITN 1, 2; CA 5-8R; 108;
  CABS 3; CANR 31; CDALB 1941-1968;
  DAM DRAM, MST; DLB 7; DLBD 4;
  DLBY 83; MTCW

Williams, Thomas (Alonzo)
  1926-1990 . . . . CLC 14
  See also CA 1-4R; 132; CANR 2

Williams, William C.
  See Williams, William Carlos

Williams, William Carlos
  1883-1963 . . . . CLC 1, 2, 5, 9, 13, 22, 42,
    67; DA; DAB; DAC; PC 7
  See also CA 89-92; CANR 34;
  CDALB 1917-1929; DAM MST, POET;
  DLB 4, 16, 54, 86; MTCW

Williamson, David (Keith) 1942- . . . . CLC 56
  See also CA 103; CANR 41

Williamson, Ellen Douglas 1905-1984
  See Douglas, Ellen
  See also CA 17-20R; 114; CANR 39

Williamson, Jack. . . . . CLC 29
  See also Williamson, John Stewart
  See also CAAS 8; DLB 8

Williamson, John Stewart 1908-
  See Williamson, Jack
  See also CA 17-20R; CANR 23

Willie, Frederick
  See Lovecraft, H(oward) P(hillips)

Willingham, Calder (Baynard, Jr.)
  1922-1995 . . . . CLC 5, 51
  See also CA 5-8R; 147; CANR 3; DLB 2,
  44; MTCW

Willis, Charles
  See Clarke, Arthur C(harles)

Willy
  See Colette, (Sidonie-Gabrielle)

Willy, Colette
  See Colette, (Sidonie-Gabrielle)

Wilson, A(ndrew) N(orman) 1950- . . CLC 33
  See also CA 112; 122; DLB 14, 155

Wilson, Angus (Frank Johnstone)
  1913-1991 . . CLC 2, 3, 5, 25, 34; SSC 21
  See also CA 5-8R; 134; CANR 21; DLB 15,
  139, 155; MTCW

Wilson, August
  1945- . . . . CLC 39, 50, 63; BLC; DA;
    DAB; DAC; DC 2
  See also AAYA 16; BW 2; CA 115; 122;
  CANR 42; DAM DRAM, MST, MULT;
  MTCW

Wilson, Brian 1942- . . . . CLC 12

Wilson, Colin 1931- . . . . CLC 3, 14
  See also CA 1-4R; CAAS 5; CANR 1, 22,
  33; DLB 14; MTCW

Wilson, Dirk
  See Pohl, Frederik

Wilson, Edmund
  1895-1972 . . . . CLC 1, 2, 3, 8, 24
  See also CA 1-4R; 37-40R; CANR 1, 46;
  DLB 63; MTCW

Wilson, Ethel Davis (Bryant)
  1888(?)-1980 . . . . CLC 13; DAC
  See also CA 102; DAM POET; DLB 68;
  MTCW

Wilson, John 1785-1854. . . . . NCLC 5

Wilson, John (Anthony) Burgess 1917-1993
  See Burgess, Anthony
  See also CA 1-4R; 143; CANR 2, 46; DAC;
  DAM NOV; MTCW

Wilson, Lanford 1937- . . . . CLC 7, 14, 36
  See also CA 17-20R; CABS 3; CANR 45;
  DAM DRAM; DLB 7

Wilson, Robert M. 1944- . . . . CLC 7, 9
  See also CA 49-52; CANR 2, 41; MTCW

Wilson, Robert McLiam 1964- . . . . . CLC 59
  See also CA 132

Wilson, Sloan 1920- . . . . CLC 32
  See also CA 1-4R; CANR 1, 44

Wilson, Snoo 1948-. . . . . CLC 33
  See also CA 69-72

Wilson, William S(mith) 1932- . . . . . CLC 49
  See also CA 81-84

Winchilsea, Anne (Kingsmill) Finch Counte
  1661-1720 . . . . LC 3

Windham, Basil
  See Wodehouse, P(elham) G(renville)

Wingrove, David (John) 1954-. . . . . . CLC 68
  See also CA 133

Winters, Janet Lewis . . . . CLC 41
  See also Lewis, Janet
  See also DLBY 87

Winters, (Arthur) Yvor
  1900-1968 . . . . CLC 4, 8, 32
  See also CA 11-12; 25-28R; CAP 1;
  DLB 48; MTCW

Winterson, Jeanette 1959-. . . . . CLC 64
  See also CA 136; DAM POP

Winthrop, John 1588-1649. . . . . LC 31
  See also DLB 24, 30

Wiseman, Frederick 1930-. . . . . CLC 20

Wister, Owen 1860-1938 . . . . TCLC 21
  See also CA 108; DLB 9, 78; SATA 62

Witkacy
  See Witkiewicz, Stanislaw Ignacy

Witkiewicz, Stanislaw Ignacy
  1885-1939 . . . . TCLC 8
  See also CA 105

Wittgenstein, Ludwig (Josef Johann)
  1889-1951 . . . . TCLC 59
  See also CA 113

Wittig, Monique 1935(?)-. . . . . CLC 22
  See also CA 116; 135; DLB 83

Wittlin, Jozef 1896-1976 . . . . CLC 25
  See also CA 49-52; 65-68; CANR 3

Wodehouse, P(elham) G(renville)
  1881-1975 . . . CLC 1, 2, 5, 10, 22; DAB;
    DAC; SSC 2
  See also AITN 2; CA 45-48; 57-60;
  CANR 3, 33; CDBLB 1914-1945;
  DAM NOV; DLB 34, 162; MTCW;
  SATA 22

Woiwode, L.
  See Woiwode, Larry (Alfred)

Woiwode, Larry (Alfred) 1941-. . . CLC 6, 10
  See also CA 73-76; CANR 16; DLB 6;
  INT CANR-16

Wojciechowska, Maia (Teresa)
  1927- . . . . CLC 26
  See also AAYA 8; CA 9-12R; CANR 4, 41;
  CLR 1; JRDA; MAICYA; SAAS 1;
  SATA 1, 28, 83

Wolf, Christa 1929- . . . . CLC 14, 29, 58
  See also CA 85-88; CANR 45; DLB 75;
  MTCW

Wolfe, Gene (Rodman) 1931-. . . . . . . CLC 25
  See also CA 57-60; CAAS 9; CANR 6, 32;
  DAM POP; DLB 8

Wolfe, George C. 1954- . . . . CLC 49
  See also CA 149

Wolfe, Thomas (Clayton)
  1900-1938 . . . . . TCLC 4, 13, 29, 61; DA;
    DAB; DAC; WLC
  See also CA 104; 132; CDALB 1929-1941;
  DAM MST, NOV; DLB 9, 102; DLBD 2;
  DLBY 85; MTCW

Wolfe, Thomas Kennerly, Jr. 1931-
  See Wolfe, Tom
  See also CA 13-16R; CANR 9, 33;
  DAM POP; INT CANR-9; MTCW

Wolfe, Tom . . . . CLC 1, 2, 9, 15, 35, 51
  See also Wolfe, Thomas Kennerly, Jr.
  See also AAYA 8; AITN 2; BEST 89:1;
  DLB 152

Wolff, Geoffrey (Ansell) 1937- . . . . . CLC 41
  See also CA 29-32R; CANR 29, 43

Wolff, Sonia
  See Levitin, Sonia (Wolff)

Wolff, Tobias (Jonathan Ansell)
  1945- . . . . CLC 39, 64
  See also AAYA 16; BEST 90:2; CA 114;
  117; CAAS 22; DLB 130; INT 117

Wolfram von Eschenbach
  c. 1170-c. 1220 . . . . CMLC 5
  See also DLB 138

Wolitzer, Hilma 1930-. . . . . CLC 17
  See also CA 65-68; CANR 18, 40;
  INT CANR-18; SATA 31

Wollstonecraft, Mary 1759-1797. . . . . . LC 5
  See also CDBLB 1789-1832; DLB 39, 104,
  158

Zappa, Francis Vincent, Jr. 1940-1993
See Zappa, Frank
See also CA 108; 143

Zappa, Frank . . . . **CLC 17**
See also Zappa, Francis Vincent, Jr.

Zaturenska, Marya 1902-1982 . . . . **CLC 6, 11**
See also CA 13-16R; 105; CANR 22

Zelazny, Roger (Joseph)
1937-1995 . . . . **CLC 21**
See also AAYA 7; CA 21-24R; 148;
CANR 26; DLB 8; MTCW; SATA 57;
SATA-Brief 39

Zhdanov, Andrei A(lexandrovich)
1896-1948 . . . . **TCLC 18**
See also CA 117

Zhukovsky, Vasily 1783-1852 . . . . **NCLC 35**

Ziegenhagen, Eric . . . . **CLC 55**

Zimmer, Jill Schary
See Robinson, Jill

Zimmerman, Robert
See Dylan, Bob

Zindel, Paul
1936- . . . . . **CLC 6, 26; DA; DAB; DAC;**
DC 5
See also AAYA 2; CA 73-76; CANR 31;
CLR 3; DAM DRAM, MST, NOV;
DLB 7, 52; JRDA; MAICYA; MTCW;
SATA 16, 58

Zinov'Ev, A. A.
See Zinoviev, Alexander (Aleksandrovich)

Zinoviev, Alexander (Aleksandrovich)
1922- . . . . **CLC 19**
See also CA 116; 133; CAAS 10

Zoilus
See Lovecraft, H(oward) P(hillips)

Zola, Emile (Edouard Charles Antoine)
1840-1902 . . . . . . **TCLC 1, 6, 21, 41; DA;**
DAB; DAC; WLC
See also CA 104; 138; DAM MST, NOV;
DLB 123

Zoline, Pamela 1941- . . . . **CLC 62**

Zorrilla y Moral, Jose 1817-1893 . . **NCLC 6**

Zoshchenko, Mikhail (Mikhailovich)
1895-1958 . . . . **TCLC 15; SSC 15**
See also CA 115

Zuckmayer, Carl 1896-1977 . . . . **CLC 18**
See also CA 69-72; DLB 56, 124

Zuk, Georges
See Skelton, Robin

Zukofsky, Louis
1904-1978 . . . . **CLC 1, 2, 4, 7, 11, 18;**
PC 11
See also CA 9-12R; 77-80; CANR 39;
DAM POET; DLB 5, 165; MTCW

Zweig, Paul 1935-1984 . . . . **CLC 34, 42**
See also CA 85-88; 113

Zweig, Stefan 1881-1942 . . . . **TCLC 17**
See also CA 112; DLB 81, 118

Literary Criticism Series
Cumulative Topic Index

This index lists all topic entries in Gale's *Classical and Medieval Literature Criticism, Contemporary Literary Criticism, Literature Criticism from 1400 to 1800, Nineteenth-Century Literature Criticism,* and *Twentieth-Century Literary Criticism.*

Topic Index

Topic Index

Topic Index

LC Cumulative Nationality Index

AFGHAN
Babur **18**

AMERICAN
Bradstreet, Anne **4, 30**
Edwards, Jonathan **7**
Eliot, John **5**
Franklin, Benjamin **25**
Hopkinson, Francis **25**
Knight, Sarah Kemble **7**
Munford, Robert **5**
Penn, William **25**
Taylor, Edward **11**
Washington, George **25**
Wheatley (Peters), Phillis **3**
Winthrop, John **31**

BENINESE
Equiano, Olaudah **16**

CANADIAN
Marie de l'Incarnation **10**

CHINESE
Lo Kuan-chung **12**
P'u Sung-ling **3**
Ts'ao Hsueh-ch'in **1**
Wu Ch'eng-en **7**
Wu Ching-tzu **2**

DANISH
Holberg, Ludvig **6**
Wessel, Johan Herman **7**

DUTCH
Erasmus, Desiderius **16**
Lipsius, Justus **16**
Spinoza, Benedictus de **9**

ENGLISH
Addison, Joseph **18**
Andrewes, Lancelot **5**
Arbuthnot, John **1**
Aubin, Penelope **9**
Bacon, Francis **18, 32**
Beaumont, Francis **33**
Behn, Aphra **1, 30**
Boswell, James **4**
Bradstreet, Anne **4, 30**
Brooke, Frances **6**
Bunyan, John **4**
Burke, Edmund **7**
Butler, Samuel **16**
Carew, Thomas **13**
Cary, Elizabeth, Lady Falkland **30**
Cavendish, Margaret Lucas **30**
Caxton, William **17**
Chapman, George **22**
Charles I **13**
Chatterton, Thomas **3**
Chaucer, Geoffrey **17**
Churchill, Charles **3**
Cleland, John **2**
Collier, Jeremy **6**
Collins, William **4**
Congreve, William **5, 21**
Crashaw, Richard **24**
Daniel, Samuel **24**
Davys, Mary **1**
Day, Thomas **1**
Dee, John **20**
Defoe, Daniel **1**
Dekker, Thomas **22**
Delany, Mary (Granville Pendarves) **12**
Dennis, John **11**
Devenant, William **13**
Donne, John **10, 24**
Drayton, Michael **8**

Dryden, John **3, 21**
Elyot, Sir Thomas **11**
Equiano, Olaudah **16**
Fanshawe, Ann **11**
Farquhar, George **21**
Fielding, Henry **1**
Fielding, Sarah **1**
Fletcher, John **33**
Foxe, John **14**
Garrick, David **15**
Gray, Thomas **4**
Hakluyt, Richard **31**
Hawes, Stephen **17**
Haywood, Eliza (Fowler) **1**
Henry VIII **10**
Herbert, George **24**
Herrick, Robert **13**
Howell, James **13**
Hunter, Robert **7**
Johnson, Samuel **15**
Jonson, Ben(jamin) **6, 33**
Julian of Norwich **6**
Kempe, Margery **6**
Killigrew, Anne **4**
Kyd, Thomas **22**
Langland, William **19**
Lanyer, Aemilia **10, 30**
Lilly, William **27**
Locke, John **7**
Lovelace, Richard **24**
Lyttelton, George **10**
Malory, (Sir) Thomas **11**
Manley, (Mary) Delariviere **1**
Marlowe, Christopher **22**
Marston, John **33**
Marvell, Andrew **4**
Middleton, Thomas **33**
Milton, John **9**
Montagu, Mary (Pierrepont) Wortley **9**

LC Cumulative Title Index

Title Index

Title Index

Title Index

Title Index

Title Index

Title Index

Title Index

"Man in Glory" (Vaughan) **27**:312

The Man in the Moone (Drayton) **8**:14, 17, 27, 32, 34, 36-7

"Man Naturally God's Enemies" (Edwards) **7**:98

The Man of Discretion (Gracian y Morales)
See *El Discreto*

"Man of Lawe's Tale" (Chaucer)
See "Man of Law's Tale"

"Man of Law's Prologue" (Chaucer) **17**:214

"Man of Law's Tale" (Chaucer) **17**:60, 63, 83, 119, 176, 196, 205, 232, 237

"Man Was Made to Mourn" (Burns) **3**:48, 52, 67, 74, 87; **29**:28, 32-3, 64, 79

The Man with Forty Ecus (Voltaire)
See *L'homme aux quarante écus*

"Manciple's Tale" (Chaucer) **17**:173

Mandragola (Machiavelli)
See *Commedia di Callimaco: E di Lucretia*

The Mandrake (Grimmelshausen)
See *Das Galgen-Männlin*

Manductio ad Stoicam philosophiam (Lipsius)
See *Manductionis ad philosophiam stoicam libri tres*

Manductionis ad philosophiam stoicam libri tres (Lipsius) **16**:257-58

Manifest (Siguenza y Gongora)
See *Manifesto philosophico contra los cometas despojados del imperio que tenian sobre los timidos*

Manifesto philosophico contra los cometas despojados del imperio que tenian sobre los timidos (Siguenza y Gongora) **8**:341-42

"Manliness" (Donne) **10**:95

"Manne, Womanne, Syr Rogerre" (Collins) **4**:214, 229, 231, 237, 239-43

"The Manner of Writing History" (Racine) **28**:294

"A Man's a Man for a' That" (Burns) **1**:518; **29**:93

Man's Disobedience and Fall (York) **34**:343, 359

"Mans Fall and Recovery" (Vaughan) **27**:325, 327

"Man's Injustice toward Providence" (Finch) **3**:451

The Man's the Master (Davenant) **13**:186-87, 189

Manual of Metaphysics (More) **9**:297

Manual of the Christian Knight (Erasmus)
See *Enchiridion militis christiani*

The Manual Oracle and Art of Prudence (Gracian y Morales)
See *Oráculo manual y arte de prudencia*

Map of the Bay and the Rivers, with an Annexed Relation of the Countries and Nations That Inhabit Them (Smith)
See *A Map of Virginia. With a Description of the Countrey, the Commodities, People, Government, and Religion*

A Map of Virginia. With a Description of the Countrey, the Commodities, People, Government, and Religion (Smith) **9**:352, 355, 357, 359, 374, 380-81, 383

Marco Bruto (Quevedo)
See *La vida de Marco Bruto*

Marcus heroicum (Hutten) **16**:238, 241

Marescalco (Aretino) **12**:19, 26-7, 29-30, 35-7

Marfisa (Aretino) **12**:35

"Le mari sylphide" (Marmontel) **2**:212; **30**:

Maria (Wollstonecraft)
See *The Wrongs of Woman; or, Maria*

"Maria Wentworth" (Carew) **13**:48

Le mariage forcé (Moliere) **10**:283, 287, 311; **28**:229, 255

Les Mariages de Canada (Lesage) **28**:210-11

Mariam (Cary)
See *The Tragedie of Mariam, Faire Queene of Jewry*

Mariamne (Voltaire) **14**:397

Marian: A Comic Opera, in Two Acts (Brooke) **6**:107-09

El marido más firme (Vega) **23**:393

Marina regina di Scozia (Campanella) **32**:211

Marmor Norfolciense (Johnson) **15**:206

Marriage as Retribution (P'u Sung-ling)
See *Hsing-shih yin-yuan chuan*

Marriage at Cana (York) **34**:369

A Marriage Booklet for Simple Pastors (Luther) **9**:151

The Marriage Contract (Brooke) **1**:63

"Marriage that was no Marriage" (Erasmus) **16**:141, 193

Marriage-á-la-Mode (Dryden) **3**:208, 210, 214, 222, 230-33

"The Marrow Ballad" (Ramsay) **29**:362-3

Martin Mar-All (Dryden)
See *Sir Martin Mar-All; or, The Feign'd Innocence*

El mártir de Sacramento (Juana Ines de la Cruz) **5**:158

"Martyrdome" (Vaughan) **27**:370

"Mary Blaize" (Goldsmith) **2**:74

Mary: A Fiction (Wollstonecraft) **5**:426-28, 442-43, 453, 460-61

"Mary in Heaven" (Burns)
See "To Mary in Heaven"

Mary in the Temple (N-Town) **34**:174, 181-2, 184, 188-9, 192, 201-2

"Mary Morison" (Burns)
See "Ye Are Na Mary Morison"

"Mary Scot" (Ramsay) **29**:329

Mascarade (Holberg) **6**:259, 269, 277

Masculine Birth of Time (Bacon)
See *Temporis partus masculus*

Mask of Comus (Milton)
See *Comus: A Maske*

Mask of Semele (Congreve) **5**:72; **21**:44

Maskarade (Holberg)
See *Mascarade*

"Le masque de Laverne" (Rousseau) **9**:345

Masque of Beauty (Jonson) **6**:338; **33**:128

Masque of Blacknesse (Jonson) **6**:321, 337-38

The Masque of Queens (Jonson) **6**:315, 337, 339; **33**:172

Masques (Jonson) **6**:323

Massacre at Paris (Marlowe) **22**:336, 339, 348, 361, 364, 368

The Massacre is (Marlowe) **22**:368 **22**:368

Massacre of the Innocents (Towneley) **34**:288

Massacre of the Innocents (York) **34**:332

Le massere (Goldoni) **4**:264-66

The Master Critic (Gracian y Morales)
See *El Criticón*

"Master Glass" (Cervantes)
See "El licienciado vidriera"

"Master Herrick's Farewell unto Poetry" (Herrick)
See "Farewell to Poetry"

"The Match" (Marvell) **4**:403, 408

"The Match" (Vaughan) **27**:351

Match Me in London (Dekker) **22**:88, 95, 107-9, 111, 126-7, 132

Mathematical Bellerophon against the Astrological Chimera of Don Martin de la Torre, etc. (Siguenza y Gongora) **8**:341

"A Mathematician" (Butler) **16**:50

"Matilda the Faire" (Drayton) **8**:30, 33

The Matrimonial Trouble (2) (Cavendish) **30**:227

La Matrone d'Ephèse (Lesage) **28**:208

"Mattens" (Herbert) **24**:272, 274

"A Mauchline Wedding" (Burns) **6**:91; **29**:3-4, 13, 16, 63

Maundy II (N-Town) **34**:211

Maundy III (N-Town) **34**:208, 211

Maximes (Gracian y Morales) **15**:142

May Day (Chapman) **22**:6, 12, 15, 64

May Day (Garrick) **15**:121

El mayor encanto, amor (Calderon de la Barca) **23**:9, 64

El mayor monstruo del mundo (Calderon de la Barca) **23**:13, 64-5

The Mayor of Queenborough; or, Hengist of Kent (Middleton) **33**:264

The Mayor of Zalamea (Calderon de la Barca)
See *El alcade de Zalamea*

La mayor virtud de un rey (Vega) **23**:392-93

"The Maypole Is Up" (Herrick) **13**:331, 364

"Me Thinks I See Some Crooked Mimicke Jeere" (Drayton)
See "Sonnet 31"

The Medall. A Satire Against Sedition (Dryden) **3**:187, 199, 222, 234-35, 240; **21**:51, 57, 59, 65, 68, 86, 90

Medea (Buchanan)
See *Medea Euripidis poetae tragici Georgio Buchanano Scoto interprete*

Medea (Corneille)
See *Médée*

Medea Euripidis poetae tragici Georgio Buchanano Scoto interprete (Buchanan) **4**:134-35

Le médecin malgré lui (Moliere) **10**:278, 283, 291, 312, 327; **28**:236, 255-56, 266, 269

Le médecin volant (Moliere) **10**:281, 283, 309, 314, 327; **28**:258

Médée (Corneille) **28**:20, 23, 31, 38, 43, 47

Medicine for a Cursed Wife (Dekker) **22**:110

"A Medicine-Taker" (Butler) **16**:50

El médico de su honra (Calderon de la Barca) **23**:13-14, 39, 41, 54-5, 64, 70, 72, 74, 79

Medico olandese (Goldoni) **4**:259

"A Meditation at the setting of the Sun, or the souls Elevation to the true light" (Vaughan) **27**:323

"Meditation before the receiving of the holy Communion" (Vaughan) **27**:304

"Meditation Eight" (Taylor) **11**:351-52

"A Meditation for His Mistresse" (Herrick) **13**:364

"A Meditation on a Quart Mug" (Franklin) **25**:111

"Meditation One" (Taylor) **11**:349

"Meditation Six" (Taylor) **11**:356

"Meditation 7" (Taylor) **11**:360

"Meditation 19" (Taylor) **11**:360

"Meditation 30" (Taylor) **11**:360

"Meditation 77" (Taylor) **11**:359

Meditationes sobre el Cantar (Teresa de Jesus) **18**:400-05

Meditationis Sacrae (Bacon) **18**:149; **32**:187

Meditations (Taylor) **11**:344, 347-48, 355, 359, 365, 367-68, 373, 376-77, 382-84, 396

"Meditations Divine and Moral" (Bradstreet) **4**:96-7, 99-100, 114; **30**:114

"Meditations upon an Egg" (Bunyan) **4**:182

The Meeting of the Company; or, Baye's Art of Acting (Garrick) **15**:100, 102, 122

Title Index

Title Index

Title Index

Title Index

Title Index

Title Index

ISBN 0-8103-9976-8